k_s	Required return on common stock; cost of internally generated common equity
k_x	Expected rate of return on a common stock with constant growth
$\overline{K}_p$	Expected rate of return on a portfolio
L	Before-tax lease payment (in Chapter 22, it stands for lower control limit)
m	number of discounting or compounding periods in a year
M	Maturity (or par) value of a bond
MIRR	Modified internal rate of return
n	Number of periods
N	Number of rights to buy 1 additional share
N(d)	Cumulative normal probability density function
NPV	Net present value
O	Incremental operating costs
P	Market price per share of stock (or treasury bill)
P_i	Probability of state i occurring
P_{np}	Net proceeds from issuing common or preferred stock
P_o	Rights-on market price per share
P_s	Subscription price
P_x	Ex-rights market price per share
P/E	Price/earnings ratio
PMT	Constant annual cash flow stream
$PV_{k,n}$	Present value factor for a single amount
PV_0	Present value (in Chapter 1, it stands for initial investment)
$PVA_{k,n}$	Present value factor for an annuity
PVGO	Present value of growth opportunities
RV	Net resale value
S	Total market value of a firm's common stock (in Chapter 23, it stands for sales)
σ	Standard deviation
σ^2	Variance
$S_{2/1}$	Today's spot rate of exchange of country 2's currency to country 1's currency
SML	Security market line
t	Time
T	Firm's marginal tax rate
T_{ps}	Personal tax rate on stock income
T_{pb}	Personal tax rate on bond income
TS	Size of a transaction
τ	Tau; payback period
UCC	Undepreciated capital cost
V	Total market value of firm $(S + B)$
VC	Variable cash outflow
V_c	Call option value
V_L	Value of levered firm
V_p	Put option value
V_r	Value of a right
V_U	Value of unlevered firm
W	Weight, or proportion of the total
X	Exercise price
Z	Target cash balance

Some Useful Formulas

Number in parentheses indicates primary chapter(s) where each is introduced.

INTEREST RATES AND FOREIGN EXCHANGE (2)

Long-term *spot rate of interest* (*expectation theory*)

$$k_n = [(1 + k_1)(1 + f_2)(1 + f_3) \ldots (1 + f_n)]^{1/n} - 1$$

Implied *forward rate* over any single year

$$f_n = \frac{(1 + k_n)^n}{(1 + k_{n-1})^{n-1}} - 1$$

Expectations theory of exchange

$$\frac{F_{2/1}}{S_{2/1}} = \frac{E(S_{2/1})}{S_{2/1}}$$

Purchasing power parity

$$\frac{E(S_{2/1})}{S_{2/1}} = \frac{E(1 + i_2)}{E(1 + i_1)}$$

International Fisher effect

$$\frac{E(1 + i_2)}{E(1 + i_1)} = \frac{1 + k_{RF2}}{1 + k_{RF1}}$$

Interest rate parity

$$\frac{1 + k_{RF2}}{1 + k_{RF1}} = \frac{F_{2/1}}{S_{2/1}}$$

PRESENT AND FUTURE VALUE (3)

Present value of a single future amount

$$PV_0 = FV_n/(1 + k)^n$$

Future value of a current single amount

$$FV_n = PV_0(1 + k)^n$$

Present value of a *perpetuity*

$$PV_0 = PMT/k$$

Present value of an (*ordinary*) *annuity*

$$PV_0 = PMT \left[\frac{1 - [1/(1 + k)^n]}{k} \right]$$

Future value of an (*ordinary*) *annuity*

$$FV_n = PMT \left[\frac{(1 + k)^n - 1}{k} \right]$$

Net present value

$$NPV = \sum_{t=1}^{n} \frac{CF_t}{(1 + k)_t} - PV_0$$

Internal rate of return, IRR

$$\sum_{t=1}^{n} \frac{CF_t}{(1 + IRR)^t} = PV_0$$

Present value with more frequent than annual discounting

$$PV_0 = \frac{FV_n}{[1 + (k/m)]^{nm}}$$

Present value with continuous discounting

$$PV_0 = FV_n/e^{kn} = FV_n e^{-kn}$$

Effective annual (*compound*) *interest rate*

$$k_{\text{effective annual}} = \left[1 + \frac{k_{nominal}}{m} \right]^m - 1$$

Effective monthly interest rate for a mortgage

$$k_{EM} = \left[1 + \frac{k_{nominal}}{2} \right]^{1/6} - 1$$

(continued on back endpapers)

CANADIAN FINANCIAL MANAGEMENT

CANADIAN FINANCIAL MANAGEMENT

Third Edition

Alfred H. R. Davis
Queen's University

George E. Pinches
University of Missouri, Kansas City

 ADDISON-WESLEY PUBLISHERS LIMITED

Don Mills, Ontario • Reading, Massachusetts • Menlo Park, California
New York • Harlow, England • Sydney • Mexico City • Madrid • Amsterdam

Senior Editor: Brian Henderson
Project Editorial Manager: Melonie Salvati
Design Manager: John Callahan
Text Designer: Interactive Composition Corporation
Cover Designer: Kay Petronio
Cover Photo: ©PhotoDisc, Inc.
Art Studio: Interactive Composition Corporation
Electronic Production Manager: Su Levine
Senior Manufacturing Manager: Willie Lane
Electronic Page Makeup: Interactive Composition Corporation
Printer and Binder: R. R. Donnelley and Sons, Company
Cover Printer: The Lehigh Press, Inc.

Canadian Cataloguing in Publication Program

Davis, Alfred H. R., 1946–
    Canadian financial management

3rd ed.
Includes bibliographical references and index.
ISBN 0-673-99331-0

    1. Finance—Canada. 2. Corporations—Canada—Finance. 3. Small business—Canada—Finance. 4. International business enterprises—Finance.   I. Pinches, George E. II. Title.

HG4090.D38 1997   658.15'0971   C95–920868–2

ISBN 0-673-99331-0

12345678910—DOC—99989796

Brief Contents

Contents

Preface

*T*he world of business in the 1990s presents financial managers with tremendous challenges. The 1980s saw major changes in the field of financial management. Numerous mergers, acquisitions (friendly and hostile), bankruptcies, and recapitalizations occurred as firms devoted increased attention to devising strategies for maximizing shareholder value and providing managerial independence as many public firms privatized. The market for options and other synthetic securities matured and provided financial managers with new tools for managing risk. Global financial markets are now a fact of life, and the role of computers has fundamentally changed the way financial managers do their jobs. Given these changes, we felt that a fresh, new approach was needed to provide students with a basis for understanding financial management.

Accordingly, we undertook a major revision of *Canadian Financial Management*, focusing on (1) stressing seven key ideas that occur throughout finance, (2) expanding the amount of coverage of capital structure issues, and (3) dealing with the use of options and option pricing concepts in financial management, and the hedging of risk that arises from fluctuating interest rates or exchange rates. In addition, the practice and theory of financial management is constantly changing, especially internationally. All firms, whether purely domestic or international, are finding that change is the rule, rather than the exception. To stay at the forefront of this rapidly changing environment, we made numerous smaller changes; without them, it would have been impossible to provide an up-to-date financial management text. Our purpose in this revision is to make the third edition of *Canadian Financial Management* even more relevant and forward-looking—for today's students and tomorrow's managers.

DISTINGUISHING FEATURES

Students who use this book should realize that there is more to know about finance than what appears between these covers. It is our hope that you acquire an understanding of the core concepts of finance and an appreciation of the role of finance in all business activities. With this in mind, the third edition of *Canadian Financial Management* contains the following distinguishing features:

FUNDAMENTAL CONCEPTS

The text links financial decisions to seven fundamental concepts:

1. *Maximization of the market value of the firm.* By market value, we mean the price that someone is willing to pay for the firm. For publicly traded firms, this translates to the total market value of the firm's stock plus the total market value of its debt.

2. *Financial markets are efficient.* In efficient markets, the current prices reflect all publicly available information. Students can understand financial management and the implication of decisions only if they have an appreciation of the financial environment and markets and the way they operate.

3. *Agency theory.* Agency theory simply means that individuals act in their own self-interest. As a follow-up to financial market efficiency, agency theory is examined extensively so that students can appreciate the human issues involved in finance.

4. *Cash flows.* By emphasizing the incremental inflow and outflow of cash, we focus on the financial lifeblood of the firm. This would not be the case if we incorrectly focused our attention on the firm's accounting earnings.

5. *Time value of money and net present value.* Time value of money means that a dollar today is worth more than a dollar tomorrow. Net present value compares the economic benefits and costs of decisions. These two concepts form an organizing principle underlying financial management, which is stressed so that students accept it as a paradigm, rather than an equation to be memorized and applied.

6. *Risk and return.* We emphasize that in all financial decisions risk and return go hand-in-hand. In order to increase expected return, a firm or individual must incur more risk.

7. *Options and financial risk management.* Because options are used extensively by financial managers as a hedge against risk, more attention is paid to options than in many texts. The application and use of options as a tool for financial managers is examined in detail. Special tables make the calculation of option values easy, so the emphasis remains on the application of options, rather than the calculation of their value.

The emphasis on these basic concepts has three major advantages. First, it provides a logical and consistent structure that ties all of the firm's decisions together. Second, it provides students with a framework they can relate to; put simply, it enables students to see the forest and not get lost in the trees. Finally, this approach is theoretically correct; therefore, without any special effort, we help students develop an appreciation for the subject that can be applied to further study in finance.

A BALANCED, MODULAR APPROACH

The book contains balanced coverage of all of the facets of financial management. It includes three chapters on options in financial management, four chapters on short-term financial management, where coverage is sometimes skimpy, and coverage of small business finance.

The textbook has been designed to provide instructors with flexibility in course design, allowing them to include or exclude material as desired. The first 14 chapters provide excellent coverage of the essential elements of long-term financial management.

EXAMPLES

Step-by-step examples illustrate the calculations so that students will understand the tools used in the decision-making process and will not be left guessing how the calculations were made.

INTERNATIONAL TOPICS

Because of their growing importance, foreign exchange rates are introduced early in the book (in Chapter 2). International financial management issues are discussed in Chapter 17. In addition to the more traditional coverage, how firms hedge exchange rate exposure is also discussed in detail.

UP-TO-DATE COVERAGE

Numerous items have been added, such as expanded treatment of agency issues, option pricing concepts, capital structure issues, ethics in finance, annual percentage interest rates, convertible securities, and changes in electronic payment systems.

FLEXIBILITY IN THE CLASSROOM

This book is designed to be used flexibly. By selecting the appropriate topics, the instructor can use it for a two-course sequence or a single course. The book provides ample expository material that will serve as preparatory reading for lectures, or as background material and as a reference for analyzing cases. We have provided a complete review of the core theory of finance in Chapters 1 through 6. After reading these chapters, students should understand the standard financial knowledge: basic accounting concepts, financial theory, time value of money, valuation of stocks and bonds, returns from investing in financial assets, portfolio theory, the relationship between risk and return, and how much it costs firms to raise capital in financial markets. Then, additional topics can be covered in any sequence desired by the instructor.

Changes in the Third Edition

In many respects the third edition of *Canadian Financial Management* is almost a completely new text. Major changes incorporated in this new edition are (1) the continual focus on seven key ideas that underlie finance; (2) the systematic approach taken to substantially update and enliven the text based on the rapidly changing developments both in finance and in the world we live in; (3) the restructuring and reorganization of the book; and (4) the substantial increase in pedagogical features.

There are five major changes in the third edition.

1. Extended coverage of capital structure theory and practice: Chapter 12 focuses on taxes and capital structure, and Chapter 13 treats the capital structure decision in a dynamic context.
2. Extended and integrated coverage of option pricing theory: Chapter 18 provides in-depth coverage of what options are and how they are valued, Chapter 19 discusses option applications in financial management, and Chapter 20 covers warrants and convertibles.
3. Updates to all material, and substantial rewrites to many of the chapters as indicated below, with special emphasis on financial ethics, agency issues, and the occurrence and use of derivatives for hedging interest rate or foreign exchange risk.
4. Completely new (1) executive summaries at the beginning of each chapter, (2) concept review questions at the end of each part in a chapter, (3) concept review problems at the end of each chapter, with solutions at the end of the book, and (4) bulleted summaries at the end of each chapter of the key points in the chapter.
5. Fewer appendices.

As in the first two editions of *Canadian Financial Management*, we emphasize the role that cash inflows and outflows play in financial management. With the increased emphasis on seven key ideas in finance, this emphasis is reinforced throughout the text.

CHAPTER-BY-CHAPTER CHANGES

Chapter 1 starts by presenting a brief discussion of the various types of firms, then introduces the seven key ideas in finance that are used throughout the text. It introduces net present value (NPV) in simple form and includes a section on ethics and finance and a section on international finance.

Chapter 2 contains an in-depth discussion of foreign exchange rates, since their impact must be understood before dealing with international financial management issues.

Chapter 3 presents an extensively modified, rearranged, and streamlined discussion of present and future values. It introduces growing annuities and calculates their present value, and discusses how to make financial calculations. The opportunity cost of capital is introduced. In the discussion of determining interest rates, the chapter explains that finding an interest rate is a specific application of the internal rate of return (IRR), and discusses internal rates of return. Finally, Chapter 3 provides an extensive, completely up-to-date discussion on effective interest rates, including the reason that the annual percentage rate (APR) is not an effective interest rate.

Chapter 4 notes that the yield to maturity (YTM) on a bond is simply an internal rate of return. The discussion of bonds that pay interest semiannually has been clarified to highlight the fact that bonds with semiannual payments can be based on an effective annual rate or a nominal rate. Chapter 4 includes a completely new section showing how the concepts of net present value and internal rate of return apply to investing in common stock. Finally, the chapter has new sections on price/earning ratios, the present value of growth opportunities, and how accepting positive net present value projects leads to increases in the value of the firm.

Chapter 5 has been streamlined and clarified. A section on the use and misuse of historical data for estimating future returns has been added. The discussion of market efficiency has been updated and revised, reflecting the latest empirical developments.

Chapter 6 has been modified to stress that it is the firm's opportunity cost of capital that is being determined. It estimates the opportunity cost of capital for Loblaw, showing how the data and estimates are obtained. Finally, the discussion on determining the cost of capital for a division of a firm has been substantially rewritten to show how to unlever and relever a pure play firm's beta and what relationships exist between divisional costs of capital and the firm's overall opportunity cost of capital.

Chapter 7 now focuses solely on the techniques employed in making capital budgeting decisions. The topic of moral hazard is also discussed.

Chapter 8 provides a complete, integrated discussion of the impact of capital cost allowance (depreciation for tax purposes) and taxes on the firm's capital budgeting cash flows. The specification of the initial, operating, and ending cash flows for both expansion and replacement projects is presented clearly. Finally, a section on estimating hard-to-determine costs and benefits has been added.

Chapter 9 begins with a new section focused on the factors to consider when estimating risk in capital budgeting decisions. The material on breakeven points has been rewritten, with more emphasis on understanding the accounting breakeven point before discussing the correct financial breakeven point.

Chapter 10 includes a completely new section addressing the topic of financial ethics for investment dealers.

Chapter 11 has added discussions of extendible and retractable bonds, and term loans and amortization schedules. It has expanded coverage of junk (high-yield) bonds, and a new section has been added on hybrids, asset-backed securities, and other innovations. Finally, it provides a complete discussion of interest rate swaps.

Chapter 12 has been substantially rewritten and refocused. It now discusses in a detailed but more intuitive fashion than previous editions the basic Modigliani–Miller (MM) capital structure propositions, and the impact of taxes on a firm's capital structure. By examining the MM assumptions, we see what factors might make a difference when firms determine their capital structure. New sections have been added on non-debt tax shields, bond clienteles and marginal tax rates, and the maturity structure of debt. Finally, the need for financial slack when making capital structure decisions is emphasized.

Chapter 13 is a substantially new chapter that extends the capital structure discussion begun in Chapter 12 by focusing on issues (other than taxes) that affect a firm's capital structure decision and make it dynamic rather than static. Asset substitution, underinvestment problems, and how capital structure and capital investment decisions may be intertwined are among the topics discussed. Completely new sections have been added on financial distress and agency considerations, and other factors—such as growth options, economic conditions, and corporate control—which may also affect a firm's capital structure decision.

Chapter 14, rewritten and streamlined, contains a new section on the Modigliani–Miller dividend irrelevance argument, plus a section on why firms pay dividends, including a discussion of personal taxation of dividends.

Chapter 15 introduces the cancellation option and similar factors, showing why firms may choose to lease assets.

Chapter 16 material has been moved forward so that mergers and restructuring can be covered earlier in a course. Parts of the chapter have been rewritten and sections have been added on free cash flow, voluntary restructuring, and spinoffs.

Chapter 17 covers the topic of international financial management which has been moved forward and substantially expanded. New and expanded sections include those on evaluating acquisitions, investment strategy, capital structure, dividend policy, and leasing. Substantially expanded discussion has been incorporated on foreign exchange exposure, and how firms can deal with foreign exchange exposure through operating, investment, and financing approaches. Finally, the discussion on the use of futures for hedging has been expanded, and new sections have been added on parallel loans and currency swaps.

Chapter 18 has been expanded and rewritten to provide complete coverage of options, and how to value them in either a binomial or a Black–Scholes world. New sections have been added on why there are sellers of options, and the anticipated benefits from selling (or writing) options.

Chapter 19 focuses on the application of options in financial management. It includes a section on why common stock is just a call option, and how changes in risk affect the value of the firm's equity and debt. In the capital budgeting portion, a new section has been added on how to value the option to delay a capital investment. Completely new sections show how options are employed to manage interest rate risk and foreign exchange risk. Chapter 19 concludes with a discussion on the growth of the derivatives market.

Chapter 20 is almost completely new. It begins by examining the similarities and differences between the options on a firm's stock and the warrants issued by a firm. The material on warrants has been substantially expanded, and the entire coverage and discussion of convertible securities is new.

Chapter 21 provides more discussion on the managerial implications of the cash conversion cycle. The chapter differentiates between aggressive (action-oriented) and conservative (passive) asset or liability management policies and discusses financial slack, its tie to a firm's capital structure, and the role of liquidity.

Chapter 22 includes a new section on paper-based (e.g., cheque-driven) versus electronic payment systems, as well as electronic funds transfer (EFT), electronic data interchange (EDI), and how firms are changing their ordering and payment systems.

Chapter 23 contains a modified discussion of the relationship of the credit granting system and the firm's decision process for granting credit, and the material requirements planning (MRP) approach to inventory management is introduced.

Chapter 24 includes a section that emphasizes the importance of calculating effective rates in assessing the cost of alternative short-term financing and a completely new section that addresses the role of banks as monitors of a firm's activities and the impact that this role has on the cost of bank loans.

Chapter 25 provides a step-by-step example of the accounting statement of Loblaw, and the financial implications of the analysis of Loblaw.

Chapter 26 contains a discussion of the statement of changes in financial position, using Loblaw as an example. A discussion of the relationship between financial and strategic planning has been added to Chapter 26.

Chapter 27 has been updated and new sections on venture capital and on the taxation of small businesses have been added.

PEDAGOGICAL FEATURES

The third edition of *Canadian Financial Management* has been designed with the student in mind. To that end, there are substantially more pedagogical features than in previous editions. The primary pedagogical features are:

1. Complete step-by-step discussions and illustrations of how to proceed in making decisions and conducting the analysis. A hallmark of *Canadian Financial Management* has always been that, instead of downplaying the details, it provides complete step-by-step examples. This emphasis has been heightened in the third edition, which includes many more examples of where to obtain the necessary information, how to proceed with the analysis, and what conclusions can be drawn from the analysis.
2. The seven key ideas in finance are presented in Chapter 1. Thereafter, the underlying themes are continuously reinforced providing students with a means of focusing on the underlying concepts that are crucial throughout finance.
3. An executive summary is provided at the beginning of each chapter to highlight the important material covered, and the way it relates to other important financial decisions and concepts.
4. Concept review questions have been added at the end of each section in a chapter, to encourage focus on the key knowledge to be obtained from each section as it is covered.

5. Timelines representing cash inflows and cash outflows are used once again in the third edition of *Canadian Financial Management*.

6. In-depth examples of how to determine a firm's opportunity cost of capital and conduct a financial analysis, is provided in Chapters 6 and 25 for an actual firm, Loblaw. Other texts discuss the ideas but do not show how the actual process should be undertaken.

7. A summary is provided at the end of each chapter, listing the key elements of the chapter.

8. Completely new concept review problems are included at the end of each chapter.

9. Mini cases in each chapter provide comprehensive discussion questions and problems.

10. A reference list is provided for each chapter.

11. Step-by-step solutions to concept review problems are provided in Appendix A.

12. Answers to selected problems are provided in Appendix C.

13. An extensive end-of-book glossary has been provided.

14. The front and back endpapers contain an annotated listing of all relevant symbols and equations employed in the text.

A COMPLETE TEACHING SUPPORT PACKAGE

Canadian Financial Management, third edition, offers a complete support package designed to enhance the teaching of financial management and maximize student understanding and mastery of the subject. The entire teaching support package has been reviewed for accuracy. The following supplementary items are available.

Instructor's Manual. The *Instructor's Manual* has been personally prepared by Alfred H. R. Davis. It contains the answers to all of the chapter questions and complete step-by-step solutions to all of the problems in the text.

Test Bank. A separate *Test Bank*, prepared by John D'Amato and Alfred H. R. Davis, contains multiple-choice items as well as longer problem-type test items. The multiple-choice items are available in a computerized format as well as in a printed form.

Study Guide. An extensive *Study Guide*, prepared by Francis Boabang and Alfred H. R. Davis, is available to provide students with explanations and extensions of the material in the text. The *Study Guide* contains an outline for each chapter, summaries of key equations, and more than 200 problems with detailed worked-out solutions that illustrate the key concepts presented in each chapter.

USING FINANCIAL AND BUSINESS CALCULATORS

Free with every new copy of the text, a 36-page booklet, "Using Financial and Business Calculators" is available. It includes extensive coverage of how students can most effectively use any of three popular financial calculators: the HP 10B, the HP 12C, and the TI BAII+.

ACKNOWLEDGMENTS

Canadian Financial Management, third edition, has been extensively class-tested, and the comments, criticisms, and encouragement given freely and often vocally by students have contributed in no small way to the development and refinement of the text. We thank the individuals who reviewed and provided comments and suggestions on the first two editions:

Arshad Ahmad	Kenneth R. Hartviksen
Ben Amoako-Adu	P. Basil Healy
Angus Armour	Robert Kieschnick
Tom Barnes	Eric Kirzner
Robert Bell	R. Krishnan
J. Maxwell Brownlie	Rick Newburg
Dennis E. Connelly	Sharon Parker
Willard Ellis	Michael A. Perretta
Karen L. Farkas	Gordon S. Roberts
Eldon Gardner	Richard Stienke
Lawrence I. Gould	Jill Wanless

The reviewers for the third edition of *Canadian Financial Management* provided substantial guidance and many fine suggestions to enhance the clarity and user-friendliness of the text. They are:

Ben Amoako-Adu	John Humphrey
Wilfrid Laurier University	*University of Western Ontario*
Tom Barnes	Itzhak Krinsky
Brock University	*McMaster University*
Sylvie Béquet	Charles Priester
Bishop's University	*British Columbia Institute of Technology*
Francis Boabang	Brian Smith
St. Mary's University	*Wilfrid Laurier University*
Sean Hennessey	Hua Zhang
University of Prince Edward Island	*McGill University*
Art Hensel	
Lakehead University	

In addition, a number of other individuals made important contributions to the book. Doug Doll and Matthew Rivard provided research assistance in updating the examples, tables, and figures. Mark Dolfato helped with the preparation of the instructor's manual. Mridu Vashist worked long and hard on the calculator booklet that accompanies the book. Laurian C. Lytle provided comments on ethics in finance. David A. Volkman provided the new Concept Review Problems. A note of gratitude must also go to the staff of Addison-Wesley Publishers and Addison Wesley Longman, especially Joan Cannon, Brian Henderson, Melonie Salvati, and John Callahan for their cooperation and guidance. We would also like to thank Kate Forster for an outstanding copyediting job and her many constructive suggestions.

Finally, we acknowledge the continued love and support of our families. Without their understanding, neither the first two editions nor this revision could have been completed.

To the extent we have succeeded in writing a clear, up-to-date statement of the fundamental concepts, theoretical developments, and practical aspects of financial management, we owe a large debt of thanks to the people who have given us their help and criticism. We encourage all users to provide comments, suggestions, and criticisms. All are most welcome in our attempt to provide an ever-improving means of learning financial management.

Alfred H. R. Davis
George E. Pinches

The Financial Management Environment

*F*inancial management provides the rationale and tools for firms to make effective decisions. These decisions fall into three main categories: (1) the investments the firm makes in both long- and short-term assets, (2) how the firm is financed, and (3) how it makes its day-to-day operating decisions. Underlying all of these decisions is the primary objective of the firm, which is to maximize the long-run market value of its equity and debt. Think of the firm as a pie. The objective of maximizing the market value of the firm translates into making decisions that enlarge the size of the pie and avoiding decisions that reduce its size.

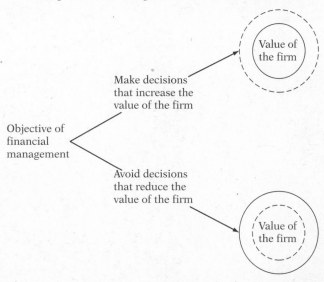

By making decisions which maximize its total market value, the firm benefits its providers of capital, its managers and employees, its customers and its suppliers. Only when decisions are made that maximize the value of the firm are the resources of individual firms being used in their most efficient manner. When the long-run market value of the firm is maximized, the resources of firms and, therefore, the resources of the entire economy are being used optimally. This underlying focus on the optimal use of resources is the focus of financial management and the foundation of any market-based economy.

Chapter 1 examines seven key ideas that underlie financial decision making. Chapter 2 examines the domestic financial system, interest rates and their importance, and how foreign exchange markets operate. These two chapters provide background for the rest of the book.

1 *Why Financial Management Matters*

EXECUTIVE SUMMARY

Financial management focuses on acquiring, managing, and financing a firm's resources by means of money, with due regard for prices in external economic markets. It is concerned with the efficient use of resources by firms and by the economy. The firm, however, does not operate in a vacuum; it is directly affected by its external environment in two primary ways. First, it has to pay the going market rates to obtain financing, purchase assets, and secure the services of employees and managers. Second, the ultimate success of the firm—which is measured by its total market value—is determined in the financial marketplace. The market value of the firm, which indicates the firm's economic worth, is the ultimate indicator of how effective the firm is. As firms maximize their value, the assets of firms and the entire economy are being employed in their most effective manner.

The seven key ideas you should understand, and remember, after reading this book are: (1) the goal of the firm is to maximize its market value; (2) financial markets in developed countries are efficient, and prices respond quickly to new information; (3) individuals act in their own self-interest, and the sometimes conflicting interests of the providers of capital, managers, employees, customers, and suppliers must be taken into account when firms make decisions; (4) in order to make value-maximizing decisions, firms focus on cash flows and their incremental effects; (5) the timing of the cash flows is important, so we use net present value to make investment decisions; (6) risk and return go hand-in-hand, so that higher returns cannot be achieved without higher risk; and (7) options, which provide the right, but not the obligation, to undertake some financial opportunity, are valuable.

By focusing on maximizing the long-run market value of the firm, and using these other ideas in the decision-making process, firms make decisions so that all assets—financial, real, and human—are used in their most effective manner. In addition, financial managers can no longer be concerned solely with domestic markets. Today, because nations of the world are economically linked as never before, financial managers must also be concerned with international markets for resources (both raw material and capital) and their finished products.

WHAT IS FINANCIAL MANAGEMENT?

Finance is the word used to describe both the money resources available to governments, firms, or individuals, and the management of those resources. Our focus is on the second aspect, management. For our purposes, **financial management** is the acquisition, management, and financing of resources for firms by means of money, with due regard for prices in external economic markets. Let us look at this definition, part by part.

First, our focus is on the *acquisition, management, and financing of resources needed by firms*. Resources are generally physical, such as cash, inventory, accounts receivable, equipment and machinery, or manufacturing and distribution facilities. But they also include people—the managers and employees of the firm. The money for these resources comes from a variety of sources, such as the internal cash flow generated by the firm's activities, borrowing, leasing, and new stock issues. The firm's goal is to provide and manage all of these resources as efficiently as possible—that is, to balance needs against the risks and the returns expected from the use of the firm's resources.

Second, firms keep track of resources in terms of *money*. They could use production runs, tons, boxcar loads, or any other unit, but it is far simpler if all firms use a single standard. That standard is money, and the unit in Canada is dollars. The results of almost any activity considered by firms can be expressed in dollars. For example, one firm might consider using its stock to purchase another firm. The value of the transaction can still be expressed in dollars, even though stock is used to finance the deal.

The third part of the definition enlarges our focus to include the firm's *external environment*. Our primary concern is the firm and its operations, but no firm exists in a vacuum. Performance is affected by a variety of external factors, such as the health of the economy, taxes, interest rates, international tensions, and the prevailing political and regulatory moods. In fact, the performance of the firm is ultimately judged by the external **financial markets**, where stocks and bonds are traded.

The ideas, tools, and techniques of financial management apply to all kinds of businesses and to individuals. However, although there are more unincorporated businesses (proprietorships plus partnerships) than incorporated businesses in Canada, corporations account for more than 90 percent of total sales. Consequently, because of their importance to our national economy, our focus in this book will be on corporations, rather than proprietorships or partnerships. A **proprietorship** is an unincorporated business owned by one individual. In a **partnership**, two or more individuals own the business. A proprietorship or partnership is easy to set up, but most successful ones are eventually converted into corporations. A **corporation** is an artificial person, created by law, with rights to contract in its own name. In addition to being a legal entity that can act as an individual, a corporation also has limited liability. **Limited liability** is a major advantage of the corporation over the unincorporated forms of business; it means that if the firm goes bankrupt, the owners can lose no more than the money they have invested in the firm.[1] Corporations can raise funds by issuing and selling shares of their **common stock**. In return for investing in the firm, the common shareholders become the owners of the firm. Corporations can also obtain funds by selling **bonds**, which are long-term debt instruments. Bonds are nothing more than IOUs that firms employ to obtain financing. The bondholders have a fixed, but limited, claim on the firm. In addition, firms obtain needed funds, and incur financial obligations, through bank loans and credit extended to the firm.

Concept Review Questions

- What are the three major elements in the definition of financial management?
- Describe the three major forms of ownership of a business.

KEY IDEAS YOU NEED TO UNDERSTAND

As we proceed, new terms, ideas, and relationships will be introduced. While they are all important in one way or another, certain key ideas underlie the theory and practice of financial management. The seven key ideas that guide our discussions are: (1) the goal of the firm is to maximize its market value; (2) financial markets are efficient; (3) individuals act in their own self-interest; (4) firms focus on cash flows and incremental effects; (5) a dollar today is worth more than a dollar tomorrow; (6) risk and return go hand-in-hand; and (7) options are valuable. Before beginning to use these ideas in making financial decisions, let us briefly explore them one by one.

KEY IDEA 1: THE GOAL OF THE FIRM IS TO MAXIMIZE ITS MARKET VALUE

To achieve the goal of acquiring, managing, and financing resources efficiently, the firm must have an objective—a purpose. The fundamental objective of the firm is to maximize its market value.[2] To understand this objective, or purpose, it is helpful to think of the firm as a pie, as shown in Figure 1.1. The ingredients that go into the pie include the basic factors that financial management stresses—the acquisition of resources for the firm, and the financing and management of these resources. How effectively these resources are used, however, is determined by *how much someone else is willing to pay for a claim on them.* Thus, if the resources can be used more efficiently by another firm or in another part of the economy, market forces will operate—the firm can sell the assets to someone else for more than they are worth to the firm. For

---

[1] The limited liability feature usually does not hold completely for small, riskier corporations because banks, their main source of financing, often require personal guarantees from the owners. The financing of small businesses is considered in Chapter 27.

[2] Value maximization is socially optimal as long as there are no externalities or monopoly power. Externalities arise when a party benefits and does not bear any costs. An example of an externality is air and water pollution without tax penalties on the parties causing the pollution or compensation to those affected.

Figure 1.1

The Firm as a Pie

Depending on how the investment community assesses a firm's decisions (via the financial markets), the size of the pie—the firm—can be enlarged or shrunk, often dramatically.

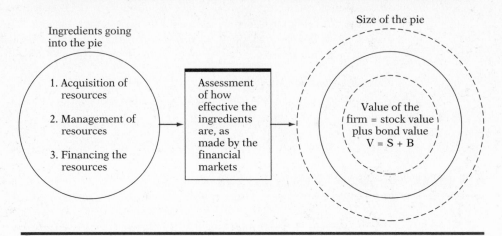

firms with publicly traded securities outstanding, the value of the firm is determined in the financial markets, where stocks and bonds trade.

Thus, the financial markets come into play. The value of any publicly owned firm is determined in the financial markets. As the firm makes decisions that maximize the usefulness of its assets, they create value for the firm. Alternatively, the firm will sell the assets if they are worth more to others. Firms that make value-maximizing decisions will be rewarded: The financial markets will recognize the value-maximizing decisions, and the market value of the firm will increase. Conversely, the financial markets will also notice if the firm does a poor job of making decisions, and the market value of the firm will decrease. The point to remember is this: Poor decisions within the firm will be recognized—you cannot fool the financial markets for very long.

We can express the value-maximization goal mathematically. The total value of the firm, V, or the size of the pie, is a function of the claims of both shareholders and bondholders on the firm,

$$\text{market value of firm, } V = S + B$$

where S is the market value of the stock and B is the market value of the firm's bonds (and other debt). The objective is to maximize the market value of the firm, V. For simplicity, we sometimes assume this can be accomplished by maximizing S—the market value of shareholder claims on the firm. This objective of **shareholder wealth maximization**, which typically assists in maximizing the total value of the firm, underlies most financial decisions. As you will see, however, management may not always adhere to the objective of maximizing the value of the firm, and sometimes this objective puts shareholders into conflict with the firm's bondholders and creditors, and with others who are interested in the firm.

The way to achieve the objective of maximizing the firm's market value is to maximize the value of shareholder and bondholder (or creditor) claims on the firm. An alternative way to think about these claims is to recognize the difference in the claims on the firm held by shareholders and bondholders. First, let us consider shareholders. The value of the shareholders' claim, ignoring bondholders for a minute, is a function of the total value of the firm. Thus, the potential payoff for shareholders can be depicted as follows:

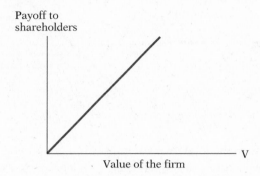

Next, consider the claims of bondholders (without considering the shareholders' claims). Suppose bondholders loan $100 to a firm, with the loan to be repaid in one year. Ignoring interest (for simplicity), we can depict this claim as follows:

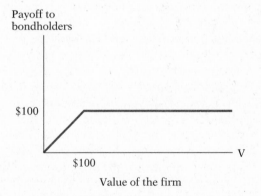

As long as the firm is healthy, and the total value of the firm exceeds the claims of the bondholders, then everything is fine. What happens, however, if the firm is not doing well? Shareholders, by law, have limited liability. Limited liability means that shareholders (with a few exceptions) are *not personally responsible* for seeing that the firm's debts are paid, if the value of the firm is not sufficient to pay the bondholders' claims.

If in one year the market value of the firm, V, is at least $100, the loan will be repaid, and the bondholders will get their $100. Even if the firm is worth a lot more than $100, the bondholders still receive only $100 (as depicted by the horizontal line above). As creditors, they have agreed to a fixed claim of $100, no matter how well the firm does.

If in one year the firm is not worth at least $100, the shareholders receive nothing, while the bondholders take over the firm. But, if the firm is worth more than $100, the bondholders receive their $100, and the shareholders claim the rest of the value of the firm. Putting both bondholder and shareholder claims together, we have:

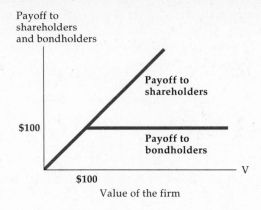

where the total claims are depicted as a function of the total firm value, V. Viewed in this context, the bondholders have a fixed, but limited, claim on the value of the firm. The shareholders may receive nothing, if the firm is worth less than $100 in one year; or they may receive a lot—everything beyond the $100 claimed by the bondholders. Whether viewed in this manner or in terms of a "pie," the goal of the firm remains the same: to maximize market value.

The objective of maximizing the market value does not mean that shareholders are an especially deserving group, or that other parties who have an interest in the firm (such as employees, customers, suppliers, or the community in which the firm is located) should be ignored. Rather, value maximization means that all corporate resources should be allocated to the point where marginal costs equal marginal benefits among all parties having an interest in the firm and its well-being. Value-maximizing decision making allocates resources to each important party to improve the terms on which they deal with the firm, to maintain and enhance the firm's reputation, and to reduce the threat of expensive (and restrictive) regulation on the firm.

One final point should be made in discussing market value and its maximization. Theoretically, maximizing the market value results in maximizing the value of the firm both in the short run and in the long run. If there ever is any conflict, it is the long-run market value in which we are interested.

KEY IDEA 2: FINANCIAL MARKETS ARE EFFICIENT

Another key idea is that in a developed country like Canada, the financial markets, where stocks and bonds trade, have been found to be "efficient." Let us see what is meant by a market being efficient. Think about what you already know about financial markets. Take a firm such as Bombardier, Canadian Tire, Cott, Mitel, or Seagram, and ask yourself these questions about it: Is the firm well known? Is there plenty of information available about the firm? Is new information made readily available (in newspapers, on television, and the like) to anyone who is interested in the firm? Is this new information made available quickly? Are there many investors who may quickly place buy or sell orders for common stock in these firms when they receive important new information about the firm or the economic setting the firm operates in? For the above-mentioned firms, the answer to all these questions is yes.

The preceding questions describe the characteristics of an efficient market. An **efficient market** is one in which market prices quickly reflect all available information about the firm. If the information about the economy, the firm, and the firm's prospects for the future are favourable, the price of the firm and its common stock will go up over time. Likewise, if the information about the firm indicates continued hard times, increased competition that is driving down profit margins, and the like, the market price of the firm and its common stock will also reflect that information. Hence, *in an efficient market, the best indication of what a firm is worth is what someone is willing to pay for a claim on the firm.*

This simple idea may seem a little strange at first, but apply it to yourself. Let us say you are going to buy a used car. What is that car worth? One way to attempt to determine its worth is to calculate how much the steel, plastic, aluminum, glass, and rubber that make up the car are worth. A second way is to see what the separate parts of the car—the tires, engine, transmission, and so forth—would sell for if you disman-tled the car. But neither of these ways of valuing the car is very direct, and both suffer from a variety of problems. What is the most direct way to determine the worth of the car? Simply determine what you are willing to pay and what someone else is willing to sell the car for. If you are willing to pay $5,000, but the seller wants $8,000, and neither of you will budge, we do not know what the car is worth. Either you are a tightwad or the seller has an overly optimistic view of the car's value. But if, after negotiation, you jointly arrive at a price of $6,700, then we know what the car is worth. It is worth the price that you, as a purchaser with other options (or cars) available, and the seller, with other individuals interested in the car, agree to.

When there is plenty of information, and many informed and active investors, markets tend to be efficient. The financial markets in developed countries have been found to be highly efficient. One of the key lessons we learn from knowing that markets are efficient is the following: *If the market is efficient, trust market prices.* That is, if you want to know what an asset is worth, and it trades in an efficient market where there are many informed buyers and sellers, then look to the market price—the price at which knowledgeable parties to the transaction (buyers and sellers) are "willing to deal." A second key lesson we learn from knowing markets are efficient is this: *Start from the market price, and then look for factors that, if changed, could make the asset worth more or less.* For example, if your firm decides to purchase another publicly traded firm, the market value of that firm's assets is already known—it is given by the market value of the firm. If you are going to pay a premium (an amount over and above its current market value) to purchase the firm, you should ask yourself, "Why are the assets worth more to me than their current market value?"

The idea of market efficiency is both simple and important and is very well supported by the facts. You will see it underlying many of the financial decisions we consider. At the same time, there are some financial markets that are not efficient. These are most likely to be in places where the government or other forces interfere with the markets, where information is not freely or readily available, where there are few informed buyers and sellers, or in third- and fourth-world countries. In such situations market values do not necessarily reflect the economic value of the assets.

KEY IDEA 3: INDIVIDUALS ACT IN THEIR OWN SELF-INTEREST

Underlying much of what you will study in this book is the idea that individuals usually act in their own self-interest. As a simple example, assume an individual chooses to go to the beach four days a week and lie in the sun. While you and I might question the decision, the individual is making what to him or her is a rational (and self-interest-based) decision. Say the individual's alternative is to spend those four days working for $150 per day (to keep things simple, let us ignore taxes). By going to the beach, the individual has implicitly placed a value on going to the beach of more than the $150 per day that could have been earned. We often speak of the **opportunity cost** associated with choosing one course of action instead of another. The opportunity cost associated with this action is the $150 per day bypassed by choosing to go to the beach.

The idea of self-interest comes up in many ways in finance, in the form of agency problems or agency relationships. Narrowly defined, an **agency relationship** is a contract in which one or more parties [the principal(s)] engages another (the agent) to perform a service and delegates some decision-making authority to the agent. In the context of firms, think of the owners (the principals) engaging the managers (as their agents) to operate the firm on their behalf. In a slightly broader perspective, agency relationships emphasize that managers, shareholders, bondholders, and other interested parties act in their own self-interest and that costly conflicts may arise due to these self-interests.

Think of a small business where you are owner and manager of the firm. You as the owner-manager will maximize your wealth by balancing the combination of wages, perquisites (or "perks") such as a company car, luxurious offices, and so on, and the market value of the firm's common shares. As long as a firm is owned and operated by a single owner-manager, no complication interferes with the objective of maximizing shareholder wealth. Because management and shareholders are the same person, actions taken in the shareholders' best interests also serve the self-interest of the manager.

However, if management owns less than 100 percent of the shares, there is a potential agency problem between management (the agent) and shareholders (the principals). For example, as sole owner the owner-manager obtains part of his or her wealth from perks and the market value of the firm's common stock. In this situation, the owner not only receives all of the benefits of these perks but also bears all of the costs. However, if the owner-manager sells part ownership of the firm to outsiders, while retaining the management capacity, he or she has an incentive to obtain more perks because part of the cost will be borne by the outside shareholders. Another example is seen when the management of a larger firm owns only a small percentage of the firm's outstanding common shares. In this case managers may be "satisfiers" rather than maximizers. That is, their goal may be performance that ensures their own career security and advancement, rather than the goal of maximizing the value of the firm, because only a small proportion of their wealth comes from changes in the value of the firm's common shares. This might cause them to bypass a risky but potentially beneficial new investment. Managers may prefer a safe project to a risky one which, if it fails, might cause them to lose their jobs.

In any agency relationship there are **agency costs**. These costs can be broken into three general classes:[3]

Financial contracting costs: the costs of structuring formal or informal contracts, opportunity costs that arise when firms make decisions or bypass opportunities that lower the value of the firm, and the costs of incentive plans designed to encourage the agent to act in the principal's best interests

Costs of monitoring: the expenses incurred to check the performance of the agent, such as auditing the firm's accounting statements and performance

Loss of wealth when agents pursue their own interests: costs such as excessive expense accounts or other perks

All organizations in which there are divergent interests suffer some loss in value due to agency costs. *Agency costs are borne by the principals*—in this case the shareholders. Recently, firms such as Eastman Kodak and Chrysler have put in place restrictions that require top managers to purchase an amount of stock equal to at least one year's salary. These firms believe this requirement is the simplest and most effective way to align the interests of managers and shareholders.

Firms raise funds from **creditors** as well as from common shareholders. Creditors are parties that hold fixed-type financial claims against the firm: long-term debt (bonds, mortgages, leases), short-term debt (bank loans or commercial paper), accounts payable, wages and salaries, pension liabilities, and so forth. The creditors' claims against the firm create a second example of agency costs, this time because of potential conflicts between shareholders and creditors. For example, consider a firm that, in order to undertake the acquisition of another firm, issues a large amount of new debt. If this new debt is perceived by the financial marketplace to have decreased the bankruptcy protection of existing bondholders (creditors), the market value of the existing bonds will fall. To protect against such expropriation, constraints are often written into debt instruments. If constraints are not present, new bondholders will attempt to protect themselves from expropriation by requiring higher than normal rates of return. Either way, the firm incurs additional agency costs because of the conflict between shareholders and creditors. Other forms of these agency costs relate to differences over which assets the firm should hold, sinking fund provisions, and restrictions on the payment of cash dividends.

Finally, in addition to shareholders, management, and creditors, the firm has to deal with other parties who are sometimes referred to as **stakeholders**. These include the firm's employees, customers, and suppliers, and the community at large. Because of the possibility of conflicts of interest between the goal of maximizing the value of the firm and the self-interest of other parties, constraints exist. These constraints are reflected in the form of agency costs (related to managers or creditors) and requirements imposed by the government (for employees and communities) if shareholders attempt to expropriate wealth from the firm's stakeholders.

Agency problems arise when not all parties have the same information—that is, when there is **asymmetric information**. Throughout the book, we will explore a

---

[3] The examples of agency costs relate to those between managers and owners.

number of agency problems that involve parties having differing amounts of information. The important point to remember is that the self-interests of various groups must be taken into account as financial decisions are made. Also, because of differing self-interests and amounts of information, virtually all organizations incur agency costs. Firms seek to minimize total agency costs as they make financial decisions.

KEY IDEA 4: FIRMS FOCUS ON CASH FLOWS AND INCREMENTAL EFFECTS

How do firms go about maximizing the value of the firm? Our interest is in maximizing the value of the firm *in the financial marketplace*, not in its **book value** (assets minus liabilities in an accounting sense) or some other figure such as replacement value. We, as managers or investors, are interested in the highest market value of the firm. How do we go about valuing a firm? Theoretically, *the value of the firm is determined by the magnitude of the future cash flows to be received, the timing of these cash flows, and the risks involved*. By **cash flows** we mean actual cash to be received or paid. This amount is not the same as earnings or net income in an accrual-based accounting sense. There is a fundamental difference between accounting and financial management: *The accountant looks at earnings; financial managers use cash flows*. Earnings are only a clue to the ability of the firm to generate cash flows. Earnings, in fact, are often misleading, because they are calculated by matching revenues and expenses in the proper time period based on historical costs. *The accounting system is not designed to report the inflow and outflow of cash*.

Accountants prepare the firm's statements in accordance with **generally accepted accounting principles (GAAP)**. Although some exceptions exist, accounting's primary focus is on recording what has happened in the past and matching income and expenses in the appropriate time period. In finance, our concern is with the future and with cash inflows and outflows.

While we are interested in cash flows, our primary focus is on the **incremental cash flows**—i.e., new minus existing cash flows. For example, if someone currently takes home $9,000 a year from a part-time job and, due to a promotion, will take home a total of $11,000 in the future, the incremental amount by which he or she is better off is $2,000. Financial management is always concerned with these incremental cash flows.

We have emphasized that cash flows are important, but we have not yet said why. They are important because *cash flow is theoretically correct, unambiguous, and essential to the well-being of the firm. Also, one cannot spend net income*. Financial theory has its roots in economics. Based on economic considerations, the value of the firm at any point in time is equal to the present value of the expected cash flows. Only by calculating cash flows will the firm and investors be able to determine if actions taken are consistent with the goal of maximizing the value of the firm.

Emphasizing cash flow gives us an unambiguous measure of the returns coming to the firm. This would not be true if we used net income as determined by generally accepted accounting principles. Under GAAP, different inventory, depreciation, or other generally accepted alternatives can result in differences in reported net income for two firms that are otherwise the same. Alternatively, two firms can report the same net income but have vast differences in actual cash flows for the period. Firms also employ different depreciation amounts for tax purposes (based on the Income Tax Act) than they incorporate in their GAAP accounting statements. The use of cash flow instead of net income removes all of these accounting-induced ambiguities.

Finally, the flow of cash is essential to the well-being of the firm. Firms may have high profits but inadequate cash flow, or low profits but high cash flow. To see how this can be the case, consider the example in Table 1.1. The **balance sheet** for a firm

---

Table 1.1

Difference Between Net Income and Cash Flow

Cash flow and net income are never the same. In some situations, cash flows far exceed net income; in others, they fall short. For this reason, the emphasis in financial management must be on cash flow.

Balance Sheet as of December 31

Assets		Liabilities and Shareholders' Equity	
Cash	$ 200	Short-term debt[a]	$ 200
Other assets	800	Long-term debt	300
Total	$1,000	Equity	500
		Total	$1,000

Projected Income Statement for three Months Ending March 31

Sales (50% cash)	$2,000
Cash expenses except interest	1,480
Depreciation	100
Earnings before interest and taxes (EBIT)	420
Interest	20
Earnings before tax (EBT)	400
Taxes (40%)	160
Earnings after tax (EAT) (or net income)	$ 240
Cash dividend to be paid in 2 months	$ 60

Cash Flows

For the next three-month period, the projected cash inflows and outflows are as follows:

Cash Inflows		Cash Outflows	
Sales for cash	$1,000	Cash expenses	$1,480
Cash on hand	200	Interest	20
Total	$1,200	Taxes	160
		Cash dividend	60
		Repay short-term debt	200
		Total	$1,920

Resulting cash shortage = $1,920 − $1,200 = $720

[a] Due in 2 months.

reports the accounting-based value of the firm's assets, and the claims against those assets in the form of liabilities (held by creditors) and owners' equity. In addition to the balance sheet, firms also provide **income statements**, which show sales, cash and noncash expenses, and other adjustments. Because interest on borrowing is important in financial management, **earnings before interest and taxes (EBIT)** can be determined. Then, when interest is deducted we arrive at **earnings before tax (EBT)**. Subtracting taxes, we are left with **earnings after tax (EAT)**, or net income.

Table 1.1 also shows that the firm is paying to its owners **cash dividends**, which are a direct cash outflow. For the next three months the firm is projecting its income and its cash needs. With net income of $240, the situation appears stable. However, looking closely, we realize that only half of the firm's sales of $2,000 will be for cash, and that $1,480 in cash expenses must be paid, along with $20 in interest, taxes of $160, a cash dividend of $60, and repayment of a $200 short-term loan. Even after drawing its cash account down to zero, the firm has projected cash outflows that exceed projected inflows by $720. Over time, as the credit sales are collected, the firm's cash flow problem will probably be corrected. But it will suffer from a shortage of cash during the next quarter.

One additional point needs to be emphasized. Even though cash flow is the proper focus for financial decision making, in practice many firms concentrate on growth in sales, market share, or earnings. Often, too much attention is given to these aspects and not enough to how they relate to cash flows. By focusing on cash flow, financial decision makers strive in the most direct manner possible to serve the interests of owners, creditors, managers, employees, customers, and suppliers of the firm. If cash flows are maximized, the accounting numbers (over time) will reflect this, and the value of the firm will be maximized. Inadequate cash flows will also be reflected in the firm's accounting statements and its market price. The firm pays a price if it ignores, or pays too little attention to, cash flows. That price is an opportunity cost equal to the attainable maximum market value of the firm minus the actual value of the firm.

KEY IDEA 5: A DOLLAR TODAY IS WORTH MORE THAN A DOLLAR TOMORROW

The next key idea in finance is easy. Simply put, a dollar today is worth more than a dollar tomorrow. That is, if we offer you $100 today, or the same $100 a year from now, you will be better off if you take the $100 today. In finance we formalize this idea when dealing with cash flows that occur at different points in time through the use of present value and future value techniques. But *your basic instincts are correct: When in doubt, take the cash sooner rather than later.*

When dealing with timing problems, finance employs a standardized methodology to determine whether the cash flows associated with making an investment are worthwhile or not. Say you are offered an investment that promises a return of $150 in one year if you invest $100 today. (Let us assume away risk for now, to keep things simple.) The question is, should you make the proposed investment? By investing $100 today you will receive $150 in one year. What should you do? If you are rational and act in your own self-interest, you would make the investment *unless* you had another opportunity that provided a better return. Let us say your next-best opportunity would provide a return of $120 in one year based on the $100 investment. Faced with these alternatives, you would make the investment that provides the return of $150 in one year. In financial management we deal with problems like this by determining the **net present value** of the proposed investment. The procedure is to discount the future cash inflows at a rate that reflects the opportunities bypassed and the risks involved, and then subtract the initial investment. Thus, the net present value of any proposed investment is:

$$\text{net present value} = \frac{\text{future cash inflows}}{1 + \text{discount rate based on forgone opportunities}} - \text{initial investment} \qquad (1.1)$$

In this case the discount rate (or forgone return) on the next-best investment is $120/$100 − 1 = 1.20 − 1 = 0.20. The net present value of the proposed investment is, then, $150/(1 + 0.20) − $100 = $125 − $100 = $25. Because the net present value of $25 is positive, you would make the investment. By doing so you are making a value-maximizing decision.

KEY IDEA 6: RISK AND RETURN GO HAND-IN-HAND

The next important idea is the relationship of risk and return. By **risk**, we mean the uncertainty of something happening, or the possibility of a less-than-desirable outcome. Other things being equal, rational individuals require a higher return for exposing themselves to higher risk. Thus, if you believe investment B has more risk than investment A, investment B would have to offer you a higher return potential before you would invest in it.

The other side of this idea is that in order to increase the return expected from any kind of investment, we must increase our exposure to risk. Putting it more directly, we could say "There is no free lunch!" The key ideas are captured in the following diagram,

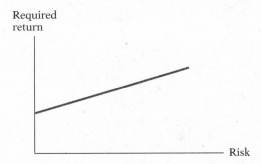

where, other things being equal, the **required return** demanded by investors increases as they expose themselves to more risk. If firms or individuals desire higher returns, then they must expose themselves to more risk. Likewise, if firms or individuals are exposed to more risk, they have two basic choices. *The first choice is to price the risk*—that is, to see that the expected returns are high enough to justify undertaking that much risk. *The second choice is to do something to eliminate part or all of the risk*—in financial terms, to hedge. In most of what follows we will discuss "pricing the risk" by demanding a high enough return to compensate for the risk involved. In Chapters 11 and 17 we examine how firms can hedge specific kinds of risk arising from fluctuations in interest rates and foreign exchange rates.

In a practical sense, if someone promises you a "guaranteed" 25 percent return with no risk, our advice is simple—be extremely sceptical! Firms and individuals have lost billions by not understanding that risk and return go hand-in-hand.

KEY IDEA 7: OPTIONS ARE VALUABLE

The final key idea relates to **options**, which provide the opportunity, but not the requirement, to undertake some financial opportunity. Let us go back to the example where you received $100 and had the opportunity to make an investment that would return $150. Let us assume the opportunity to make the investment was available to you, and you alone, for 10 days. During those 10 days *you hold an option to make the investment, but you are not required to make the investment.* If something better comes along during that time period, you can elect to bypass this investment. If that happens, you have decided not to "exercise the option." If at the end of the 10 days you make the $100 investment, you have exercised the option.

During the last 30 years we have found that options exist in many different and unusual ways in financial management. And we have also developed the ability to value both simple and very complex options. Any time a firm or individual has the opportunity, but not the requirement, to undertake some financial opportunity, an option exists. The flexibility provided by options—to either exercise them or let them expire—is what makes them so valuable. Options in financial management include the managerial flexibility associated with making capital investment decisions; they are present in various securities employed by firms; and they are part of any guarantee, loan, or insurance contract. Without the ability to incorporate and value options, we cannot properly evaluate the various courses of action available to firms and the costs or benefits associated with these alternatives. Financial management cannot be fully understood without understanding options.

Concept Review Questions
- What is the fundamental objective of any firm?
- Define an efficient market and describe how it affects the worth of a firm.
- What are the three general classes of agency costs?
- Define an agency relationship and describe how it affects financial decision making.
- How are risk and return related?

FINANCIAL MANAGEMENT AND THE FIRM

Financial management deals with the efficient allocation of resources—financial assets, such as stocks and bonds; real assets, such as plant and equipment; and human assets, the managers and employees. Figure 1.2 depicts the interaction of the main factors that affect financial decisions as firms attempt to maximize their market value. First in

Figure 1.2

Factors Affecting the Firm's Market Value

Firms cannot do much to affect the external environment, but their strategic and policy decisions have a direct impact on how the firm's resources are acquired, managed, and financed. These decisions, in turn, determine the magnitude, timing, and riskiness of the firm's expected cash flows. How the management of the firm's resources and its cash flows is assessed in the financial markets determines the market value of the firm.

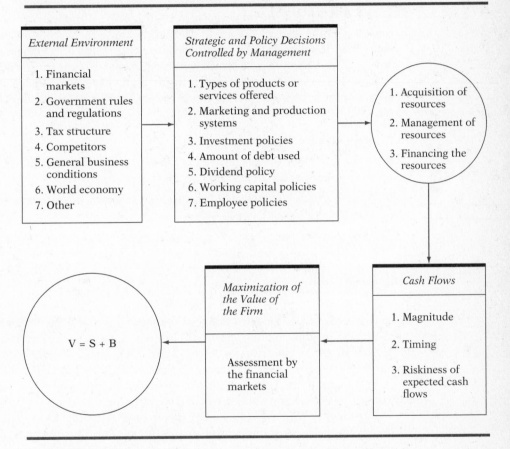

importance are *external factors* such as the financial markets (where firms raise funds), government regulations, the tax structure, competition, and the state of the economy. The firm has only indirect influence over these—through lobbying the government and market positioning, for instance. Next are the *strategic policy decisions* directly under management control. These include the choice of products or services offered; marketing and production systems; investment, financing, and dividend policies; and employee practices.

Many of these strategic factors may appear fixed in the short run. Over the long run, though, all can be changed by the firm as it acquires assets, manages the assets, and secures the financing needed to support the firm's resources. These policies directly determine the magnitude, timing, and riskiness of the firm's future cash flows. While all of these decisions are being made, the self-interests of the providers of capital, customers, managers, employees, and suppliers must be kept in mind. By doing so, and by focusing on increasing and maximizing the long-run market value of the firm, management can allocate all of the resources of the economy in the most efficient manner. At the same time, the needs of customers will be met, because if they are not met, the firm will wither away. Finally, the needs and desires of management and employees will be met; only if the firm prospers will the firm be in a position to reward individuals for their contributions to its success.

In practice, the objective of maximizing the value of the firm has three important messages. First, it is theoretically correct and leads to the most efficient use of all resources in the firm and economy. Second, because there are obviously some constraints on the objective, firms can maximize their value only subject to these constraints. Third, the objective provides a clear and precise frame of reference with which to make and judge decisions. In other words, it provides a standard of comparison and allows us to determine whether the decisions are the best ones under the circumstances.

Concept Review Questions

- As firms attempt to maximize their market value, what are the main factors that affect their financial decisions?
- What messages are implied when the stated objective of management is the maximization of the value of the firm?

THE FINANCIAL MANAGER

In this book we use the term **financial manager** to refer to anyone directly engaged in making or implementing financial decisions. Except in the smallest firms, many individuals are responsible for financial activities. In most large firms the person ultimately responsible is the financial vice-president, who is the **chief financial officer (CFO)** of the firm. The chief financial officer is deeply involved in financial policy making, as well as in corporate or strategic planning.

Typically, at least two individuals report directly to the CFO. The **treasurer** is usually the person responsible for seeing that the firm obtains funds as needed, for making sure cash is collected and invested, for maintaining relations with banks and other financial institutions, and for seeing that bills are paid on time. In some organizations, the treasurer also oversees capital budgeting decisions and credit management. The **controller** is responsible for preparing accounting statements, for cost accounting, for internal auditing, for budgeting, and for the firm's tax department.

Because of the importance of financial decisions to the long-run success of the firm, major decisions are often made by the board of directors or the executive committee. For example, major capital expenditures, proposed financing changes, and the firm's dividend policy are decided at the highest level of the firm. However, authority for less important decisions, such as small- or medium-sized investments, credit policies, and cash management changes, is often delegated to division managers or others at lower levels in the firm. Financial managers are all those individuals whose decision-making responsibility affects the financial health of the firm.

Concept Review Questions

- Who is a financial manager in a firm?
- What two individuals within a firm report directly to the chief financial officer?

FINANCE, BUSINESS, AND ETHICS

Since the 1980s the field of finance and business in general have witnessed a greater focus on ethics. The concern about ethical behaviour, some assert, is caused by the loss of values and jobs, and lack of caring for employees and other stakeholders of a firm due to the unleashing of market forces as firms and industries are deregulated or privatized. At the same time, we hear of the tremendous problems in South Africa due to apartheid, the lack of human rights in countries such as Myanmar and China, and the potential loss of jobs in Canada as firms take advantage of the North American Free Trade Agreement (NAFTA) and move production to the United States and Mexico or as they move production to other low-cost countries in the Far East or Eastern Europe.

In analyzing the issue of ethics, it is helpful to distinguish between two types of ethical concerns. The first involves firms taking action to prevent conduct that is either a violation of law or is sufficiently close to the line of illegality that the firm has instituted policies and procedures to prevent such occurrences. The second deals with much broader stakeholder and societal considerations, such as human rights, environmental concerns, and balancing the value-maximization interests of the shareholders against those of stakeholders in general.

Most would agree that, in general, larger firms in a free market society practise responsible ethical behaviour. Most firms do not violate the law, and they generally avoid questionable business practices. Although there may be short-run adverse financial consequences to ethical behaviour, in the long run only firms that act ethically will be in a position to maximize their value.

There is much less agreement, in terms of the firm's responsibilities and value-maximizing consequences, on whether firms should take a proactive stance towards dealing with the broader societal and stakeholder aspects of ethical behaviour. At one end of this issue is Levi Strauss & Co., the world's biggest supplier of brand-name apparel. What Levi's aspires to in the area of ethics includes the following:

New behaviours: Management must exemplify "directness, openness to influence, commitment to the success of others, and willingness to acknowledge our own contributions to problems."

Diversity: Levi's "values a diverse workforce (age, sex, ethnic group, etc.) at all levels of the organization . . . . Differing points of view will be sought; diversity will be valued and honesty rewarded, not suppressed."

Recognition: Levi's will "provide greater recognition—both financial and psychic—for individuals and teams that contribute to our success . . . those who create and innovate and those who continually support day-to-day business requirements."

Ethical management practices: Management should epitomize "the stated standards of ethical behaviour. We must provide clarity about our expectations and must enforce these standards throughout the corporation."

Communications: Management must be "clear about company, unit, and individual goals and performance. People must know what is expected of them and receive timely, honest feedback . . . ."

Empowerment: Management must "increase the authority and responsibility of those closest to our products and customers. By actively pushing that responsibility, trust, and recognition into the organization, we can harness and release the capabilities of all our people."[4]

Levi's commitment to an ethical business approach stems from the beliefs of its chairman and chief executive, Robert Haas, the great-great-grandnephew of founder Levi Strauss. It does not hurt that Levi Strauss is a private company, with almost all of the shares held by members of the Haas family. Levi Strauss believes that the interests of its employees, suppliers, and other stakeholders are directly related to financial success. Since Haas became CEO in 1984, Levi's has doubled its percentage of minority managers to 36 percent, and the percentage of women in the management ranks has climbed from 32 percent to 54 percent during the same period. Also, Levi eliminated suppliers in China because of human rights concerns, and it has inspectors monitor its roughly 700 contract factories throughout the world.[5] On the other hand, Levi Strauss is still a business, as decisions such as the one to close a plant in San Antonio, Texas—idling 1,110 workers—and move its operations to Costa Rica to take advantage of lower wages demonstrate. The company's reply when asked about this type of action is that guaranteed employment is not part of the Levi's value system.

Levi Strauss is at one end of the spectrum; most firms have a much more low-key approach to the issue of ethics in finance and business. Sometimes firms find themselves in unanticipated situations because of actions they have taken. For example, a few years ago Sears faced consumer indignation and legal sanctions due to reports of unnecessary, and expensive, auto repairs. The unnecessary repairs occurred not because Sears did not believe in an ethical approach to business, but because of a faulty compensation system that encouraged managers and employees in their auto service business to maximize sales at almost any cost. Thus, its faulty compensation system had a direct, and unanticipated, impact on Sears. One lesson from this example is that firms should spend a lot more of their time considering potential conflicts of interest among the firm's management, employees, customers, suppliers, creditors, communities, and shareholders than they typically do. By examining these conflicts, firms will—by necessity—adopt a broader view, and their actions will encourage and support broad-based ethical behaviour that is consistent with, and supportive of, value maximization.

Concept Review Questions

- What are the two types of ethical issues faced by firms?
- What are the key elements of Levi Strauss's approach to ethics? What, in part, enables the company to take this approach?
- Describe how conflicts of interest can lead to unanticipated consequences.

---

[4] "Managing by Values," *Business Week,* August 1, 1994, p. 47.

[5] "Levi Tries to Make Sure Contract Plants in Asia Treat Workers Well," *The Wall Street Journal,* July 28, 1994, pp. 1 and 6.

THE INTERNATIONALIZATION OF BUSINESS AND FINANCIAL MANAGEMENT

In recent years major changes have taken place in business all over the world. The Japanese, after making rapid industrial progress for the last four decades, have experienced an economic slowdown. To spur growth on our own continent, Canada, Mexico, and the United States on January 1, 1994, entered into the North American Free Trade Agreement (NAFTA), which removed tariffs on more than 50 percent of all goods flowing between these countries; in the future additional tariffs covered by NAFTA will also be reduced. One likely result will be increasing cross-border integration of the economies of Canada, Mexico, and the United States, linking states and provinces with an increased North–South flow of products. Other regional trade agreements exist, both in Europe and in the Pacific Rim. At the same time, the recent agreement among the 117 member nations of the General Agreement on Tariffs and Trade (GATT) removed or lowered many tariffs throughout the world.

As cross-border trade and investment flows reach new heights, global firms are making decisions with little regard for national boundaries. The trend towards stateless firms is unmistakable. Increasingly, European, Japanese, and North American firms, though not untethered from their home countries, are learning how to juggle multiple identities and loyalties. To combat the increasing emergence of regional trading blocs in Europe, North America, and the Pacific Rim, world firms are developing the ability to resemble insiders no matter where they operate. At the same time, they may move factories and labs around the world with little reference to national borders.

Some of these stateless firms include the following:

Percent of Sales Outside Home Country	Firm	Home Country
More than 90%	Nestle	Switzerland
	SKF	Sweden
	Philips	Netherlands
More than 75%	Smithkline Beecham	Britain
	Reuters	Britain
	Volvo	Sweden
	Michelin	France
	Hoechst	Germany
More than 50%	Canon	Japan
	Northern Telecom	Canada
	Sony	Japan
	Bayer	Germany
	Colgate	United States
	IBM	United States
	Dow Chemical	United States

These developments have profound implications for financial management. More than ever, we live and work in a world-wide economy. Business, and financial management, are increasingly conducted on a global basis. The fundamental ideas discussed in this chapter and the remainder of the book generally apply equally well in any country in the world. However, two important points of difference exist. First, some of the specifics assumed—such as efficient financial markets, details of the tax law, the primacy of shareholder wealth maximization, and so forth—often differ. Second, any time cash flows move between two countries, the impact of *exchange rates*—that is, how much one currency is worth in terms of another currency—must be taken into consideration. For example, the level of economic activity between Canada and our most important trading partner, the United States, is influenced by the exchange rate between the two currencies. When our dollar is low relative to the U.S. dollar, we export more to than we import from the United States. The exchange rate will also have an impact on the operating and pricing policies of Canadian firms. For instance, a Canadian firm with U.S. suppliers will want to pay for any purchases as quickly as possible if the Canadian dollar is expected to depreciate relative to the U.S. dollar, but slowly if an appreciation is expected. On the other hand, we would expect this firm's domestic prices to increase with a weak Canadian dollar and decrease with a strong one.

In today's global economy firms raise funds not only domestically but also throughout the world. Consequently, firms operating in Canada, whether independent Canadian firms, subsidiaries of foreign-based multinationals, or Canadian-based multinationals, must compete in international markets to raise funds. In essence Canadian firms must outbid firms from all over the world for the limited supply of available funds. The price that these firms have to pay for funds will depend, among other things, on world financial and political conditions, expected inflation, and the strength of the Canadian dollar relative to the other currency involved.

The ever-changing nature of world markets and relationships between countries makes the international aspects of financial management a complex and exciting area. Discussion of important aspects of international financial management is integrated as appropriate throughout the book, and Chapter 17 explores in detail financial management in an international context.

Concept Review Questions

■ What is the impact of NAFTA, other regional trade agreements, and GATT?

■ How are many firms dealing with the increasingly global economy?

■ Why are foreign exchange rates important?

KEY POINTS

- Financial management focuses on the acquisition, management, and financing of resources. The ideas are universal, but we focus on applying them to firms organized as corporations.
- Firms strive to maximize their long-run market value, as reflected by the market value of the owners' claims (through stock) and the creditors' claims.
- In developed countries, financial markets, where stocks and bonds trade, are

efficient. Thus, the best indication of value is what someone else is willing to pay for an asset. When valuing assets in efficient markets, look first to market prices.

- Individuals operate in their own self-interest. When differences in interests exist, agency costs are incurred in an attempt to ensure that joint interests are pursued. Differences in interests, and information, may exist between owners (shareholders) and management, between owners and creditors, and between any of them and other stakeholders such as employees, customers, and suppliers.
- Focus on cash flows and their incremental effects. Do not be misled by accounting-induced influences; you cannot spend net income.
- A dollar today is worth more than a dollar tomorrow.
- Risk and return go hand-in-hand. The only way for individuals or firms to increase their expected return is to increase their risk exposure.
- Options, which provide the right, but not the requirement, to do something, are valuable.
- By focusing on maximizing the long-run market value of the firm, financial management in a free enterprise economy leads to the most efficient allocation of all resources—financial, real, and human.
- Financial managers are all the individuals in a firm who make decisions that have financial consequences. The chief financial officer (CFO) is ultimately responsible for the financial operations of a firm.
- Ethical behaviour by managers enhances the prospects of maximizing firm value.
- Because of the globalization of product and financial markets, an understanding of the international aspects of financial management is important.

QUESTIONS

1.1   Explain what is meant by the statement "Financial management is the acquisition, management, and financing of resources for firms by means of money, with due regard for prices in external economic markets."

1.2   How can the firm be viewed as a pie? Make sure to distinguish between the ingredients that go into the pie and the factors that determine the ultimate size of the pie.

1.3   The fixed nature of the bondholders' claim and the limited liability associated with common share are important when considering the potential payoffs to bondholders and shareholders. Explain the potential payoffs as a function of the total value of the firm.

1.4   How do agency relationships and agency costs relate to the idea of constraints on the objective of maximizing the value of the firm?

1.5   There are agency costs related to both managers and creditors (among others). How do they differ from each other? What is their effect?

1.6   Explain why cash flow and net income are not, and cannot be, equal for firms.

1.7   Comment on the following statement made by Chris in the firm's executive suite: "I'm on the spot because I'm going to be judged by the common shareholders on the basis of market price, over which I have absolutely no control. In fact, I can't even control sales or earnings per share as well as I'd like, and they are the primary determinants of the market price."

1.8   Explain how cash flows, timing, and risk relate to the firm's objective of maximizing its market value.

1.9   Why are the international aspects of finance so important for Canadian financial managers?

1.10 What are the key ideas you should understand after reading this book?

CONCEPT REVIEW PROBLEMS

See Appendix A for solutions.

CR1.1   Prepare a projected income statement for Johnstons & Associates from the following information: sales, $700,000; cost of goods sold, $100,000; administrative expenses, $300,000; depreciation, $50,000; interest paid, $60,000; and a tax rate of 40 percent.

CR1.2   Assume Johnstons & Associates, from CR1.1, operates on a cash budget—that is, all revenue and expenses are on a cash basis. In addition, the firm will pay a dividend of $100,000 at the end of the year.

a.   What is Johnstons & Associates' net cash flow?

Now assume Johnstons & Associates offers trade credit to its customers and the firm will receive only 60 percent of the projected sales over the next year.

b.   How does the offering of trade credit affect the net cash flow for Johnstons & Associates?

CR1.3   Whiz Kids, Ltd., has the following balance sheet and projected income statement:

Accounting Balance Sheet as of December 31

Assets, Liabilities, and Shareholders' Equity

Cash	$ 500	Short-term debt	$ 1,500
Other assets	80,000	Long-term debt	59,000
Total	$80,500	Equity	20,000
		Total	$80,500

Projected Income Statement for Six Months Ending June 30

Sales (70% cash)	$30,000
Expenses	15,000
Depreciation	1,000
Earnings before interest and taxes (EBIT)	14,000
Interest	6,000
Earnings before tax (EBT)	8,000
Taxes (40%)	3,200
Earnings after tax (EAT) (or net income)	$ 4,800
Cash dividend to be paid in 5 months	$ 500

The following information also pertains to Whiz Kids:

a.   All of the short-term debt of $1,500 will become due within six months.

b.   Whiz Kids will receive $5,000 in cash from sales of the previous year.

c.   Eighty percent of the estimated expenses will be paid in the first six months of the following year. The remaining 20 percent will be paid in the second half of the year.

d.   Taxes will be paid in full during the first half of the year.

What are Whiz Kids' expected cash inflows and outflows for the next six months? Is there a cash shortage or a cash excess?

CR1.4   Tom Moyers is considering investing in a new firm. Tom estimates his $10,000 investment will be worth $11,000 in one year.

a. What is the projected return on the investment?

b. Tom is considering another investment of similar risk with a return of 15 percent. What is the net present value of the investment in the new firm?

CR1.5 Bill and Mary were discussing a problem assigned to them in their financial management course. They were to find the net cash flow for XYZ firm. The firm had sales of $80,000, expenses of $60,000, depreciation of $15,000, and interest expense of $10,000. The firm collected 80 percent of its sales in cash and paid 80 percent of its expenses in cash. In addition, the firm's marginal tax rate was 40 percent, and no dividends were paid. Bill and Mary calculated the firm had a negative net income of $5,000, but they were confused when they found net cash flow was positive $6,000.

Did Bill and Mary correctly calculate net income and net cash flow? Is it possible to have a negative net income and a positive net cash flow?

PROBLEMS

1.1 Mott's Transit has run into some cash flow problems due to rapid expansion. Kevin, the chief financial officer, is making plans for the next six months. Assume it is December 31. The balance sheet for the year just completed and the firm's projected income statement (for both accounting and tax purposes) for the first half of next year are as follows:

Balance Sheet as of December 31		Projected Income Statement for Next Six Months	
Assets	$300	Sales	$500
Liabilities and equity		Expenses	360
Current debt	$100	Depreciation	30
Long-term debt	50	EBIT	110
Equity	150	Interest	25
Total	$300	EBT	85
		Taxes (40%)	34
		Net income	$ 51

In addition, Kevin notes the following:

a. Eighty dollars of the $100 in current debt comes due in the first half of next year, and the bank has indicated it will not renew the loan.

b. A long-term debt issue of $50 is planned for the first half of next year.

c. Seventy percent of the sales projected for the first half of next year will be received in cash by June 30; the remainder will not be collected until the second half of next year.

d. Forty dollars in cash will be received during the first half of next year from sales in the last half of this year. (Thus, this is an account receivable that will be collected.)

e. Ninety percent of the estimated expenses for the first half of next year will be paid in cash during the period; the remainder can be paid in the second half of next year.

f. Taxes and interest must be paid in full during the first half of next year. Also, cash dividends of $16 are payable during the first half of next year.

g. The cash account cannot be reduced from its present level.

Prepare an estimate of Mott's expected cash inflows and outflows for the next six months. Do you foresee any problems? What actions might Kevin take to secure the additional cash needed?

1.2   Parkwest Hotel has the following income statement for reporting purposes:

Income Statement	
Revenues	$180,000
All operating expenses except depreciation	142,000
Depreciation	15,000
EBIT	23,000
Interest	11,000
EBT	12,000
Taxes (30%)	3,600
Net income	$ 8,400

Assume that all revenues and expenses (except depreciation) are for cash. The firm uses acceler-ated depreciation for tax purposes, so the actual depreciation charged is $20,000, not $15,000. Given the difference between GAAP financial statements and those prepared for tax purposes, what is Parkwest's actual cash flow from operations?

1.3   **Mini Case** Four weeks into the current term you go home for the first time. While there you are asked to explain what you have learned so far in your finance course.

a.   What is financial management? Why is the primary focus on corporations instead of propri-etorships or partnerships?

b.   What are the basic ideas in finance that should be understood? Explain why each is impor-tant.

c.   How, instead of using the "pie" concept, can we visualize the claims of bondholders and shareholders? What role does the fixed claim held by bondholders play? What is the role of limited liability for shareholders?

d.   What is an agency relationship? How does it influence the firm's goal?

e.   Why are incremental cash flows so important?

f.   During the conversation your uncle comes by. He does not understand balance sheets, income statements, and the difference between net income and cash flow. Using the following information, explain these three concepts to him. Calculate the projected cash flow for the next two months, and then explain why the focus has to be on cash flow.

Balance Sheet				
Assets			**Liabilities and Shareholders' Equity**	
Cash	$ 3,000		Short-term debt	$ 5,000[a]
Other	37,000		Long-term debt	15,000
Total	$40,000		Equity	20,000
			Total	$40,000

[a] $2,000 due this month.

Projected Income Statement for Next Two Months

Sales (90% cash)	$10,000
Cash expenses except interest	6,000
Depreciation	900
Earnings before interest and taxes (EBIT)	3,100
Interest	400
Earnings before tax (EBT)	2,700
Taxes (40%)	1,080
Earnings after tax (EAT) (or net income)	$ 1,620
Cash dividend to be paid next month	$ 200

---

g. During the conversation, an investment salesperson telephones and offers a "guaranteed" 20 percent return with no risk on a $5,000 investment. If banks, trust companies, and the like are paying 7 percent on current deposits, explain why individuals should be suspicious of a "guaranteed" 20 percent return with no risk.

REFERENCES

BARNEA, AMIR, ROBERT A. HAUGEN, AND LEMMA W. SENBET. *Agency Problems and Financial Contracting.* Englewood Cliffs, N.J.: Prentice-Hall, 1985.

BERNSTEIN, PETER L. "The Vindication of the Professors." *Institutional Investor* 24 (November 1990): 81–87.

BREALEY, RICHARD A., STEWART C. MYERS, GORDON SICK, AND RONALD GIAMMARINO. *Principles of Corporate Finance*, 2nd Canadian ed., Ch 36. Toronto: McGraw-Hill Ryerson, 1992.

JENSEN, MICHAEL C., AND WILLIAM H. MECKLING. "Theory of the Firm: Managerial Behavior, Agency Costs, and Ownership Structure." *Journal of Financial Economics* 2 (October 1976): 305–60.

RAPPAPORT, ALFRED. *Creating Shareholder Value: The New Standard for Performance.* New York: Free Press, 1986.

SMITH, CLIFFORD W., JR. "The Theory of Corporate Finance: A Historical Overview." In *The Modern Theory of Corporate Finance*, 2nd ed., edited by Clifford W. Smith, Jr., pp. 3–24. New York: McGraw-Hill, 1984.

STEWART, G. BENNETT, III. "Market Myths." In *The New Corporate Finance: Where Theory Meets Practice*, edited by Donald H. Chew, pp. 3-20. New York: McGraw-Hill, 1993.

WILLIGAM, GERALDINE E. "The Value-Adding CFO: An Interview with Disney's Gary Wilson." *Harvard Business Review* 68 (January–February 1990): 85–93.

2

The Financial System, Interest Rates, and Foreign Exchange

EXECUTIVE SUMMARY

The financial system provides the framework within which managers operate to maximize the value of the firm. In developed countries, sophisticated financial markets and institutions have developed over the years to provide an efficient and effective means of bringing together suppliers and demanders of capital. The entire financial system is influenced by many factors, including international developments, the economic climate in Canada, and monetary and fiscal policy. Effective managers must have some understanding of how these various forces affect the firm.

Interest rates reflect the cost of borrowed funds to demanders of capital or the return earned by suppliers. The sum of the real rate of return and a premium for expected inflation is called the risk-free rate, k_{RF}. An indication of the expected rates of inflation can be obtained by examining the yield curve, or term structure of interest rates, which shows the relationship between return (yield) and maturity for securities of equivalent risk. Observed differences in the shape and level of the term structure over time can be explained by the expectations, liquidity (maturity) preference, and market segmentation theories of term structure.

Other premiums relate to maturity, default, liquidity, and issue-specific factors; the sum of these premiums is called the risk premium. The return expected from owning a bond is equal to the risk-free rate plus a risk premium. Investors will demand a higher required return to invest in bonds of higher risk.

Finally, more than ever before, Canadian firms are accessing the international financial marketplace. A fundamental difference between activities in the domestic and world-wide financial marketplaces is the introduction of foreign exchange fluctuations. Many firms have significant foreign transactions; consequently, foreign exchange fluctuations add another element of risk for these firms. Therefore, some understanding of the difference between spot and forward rates is essential.

The expectations theory of forward exchange rates, purchasing power parity, the international Fisher effect, and interest rate parity establish the expected relationship between product prices, interest rates, and spot and forward exchange rates. In the short run these relationships do not always hold as expected; this is often due to government intervention, transactions costs, and other imperfections. In the longer run the relationships usually conform more closely to those predicted by the four parity conditions cited above.

THE CANADIAN FINANCIAL SYSTEM

The fundamental goal of our financial system is to help transform the savings (income minus consumption) of individuals, firms, and governments into investments (the purchase of assets to produce goods or services) by others. If an individual and Alcan Aluminium both have excess funds right now, the function of the financial system is to channel these funds to (1) governments; (2) individuals, who may use them for many things; and (3) firms. This transfer of funds almost always results in the creation of financial assets by the suppliers of funds and of financial liabilities by the demanders of funds. The purpose of the financial system is to provide an efficient means of bringing together suppliers (sellers) and demanders (buyers) of capital. The basic relationships are shown in Figure 2.1. Note, however, that not only are suppliers and demanders part of the system, so are financial institutions and the financial markets, which have evolved to increase the efficiency and smoothness of the system.

FINANCIAL INSTITUTIONS

Financial institutions, or **financial intermediaries**, as they are called, often come between suppliers and demanders of funds. Some financial intermediaries accept savings, and in return the suppliers of funds acquire claims against them. Then the intermediaries make loans or investments to the demanders of funds. As a reward for entrusting savings to a financial intermediary, the supplier expects some return in the form of interest or cash dividends. Other financial institutions act as intermediaries between financial markets and the demanders of funds. Among the advantages of handling money transfers through financial institutions are that they (1) provide flexibility and liquidity, (2) are convenient, (3) provide expertise, and (4) spread risk.

The major financial institutions in our financial system include the following:

1. Chartered banks, the traditional department stores of finance. They take deposits, issue personal and corporate loans, and invest in marketable securities.
2. Insurance companies and pension funds, including life insurance companies, property and casualty companies, and private and federal/provincial government pension plans.

Figure 2.1.

Relationship Among Suppliers and Demanders of Funds, Financial Institutions, and Financial Markets

Funds are supplied through the financial markets directly or by going through financial institutions. A well-developed network of financial institutions and financial markets is important for financial decision making.

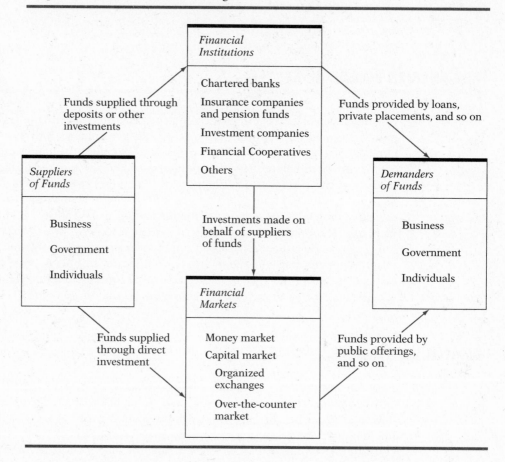

3. Investment companies, including various mutual funds in which investors pool their funds into a large fund managed by an investment advisor.[1]

4. Financial cooperatives, including credit unions and *caisses populaires.*

5. Other financial organizations, including finance companies, mortgage loan companies, and trust companies.

---

[1] Mutual funds are sometimes called "open-end" investment companies because they continually sell and redeem shares. A much smaller number of investment companies are "closed-end"; they do not redeem their shares.

In recent years financial institutions have undergone a profound restructuring. Integration of financial services through common ownership of financial institutions has resulted in financial conglomerates—commonly owned banks, trust and loan companies, insurance companies, and investment dealers—whose neighbourhood branch offices can provide a wide range of new and convenient services, with greater potential for one-stop shopping.

Financial institutions provide a substantial portion of the funds available to corporations and other demanders of funds. Chartered banks and near banks (e.g., trust companies, mortgage loan companies, and financial cooperatives) have been the largest suppliers of funds in recent years. Other financial institutions, such as insurance companies and pension funds, purchase stocks or bonds through the financial markets. Firms may also approach a financial institution to make a **private placement** of a new stock or bond issue. If Canadian Tire, for example, needs to raise additional funds, it might approach the Ontario Hydro pension fund directly concerning a private placement of a new issue of bonds. **Investment dealers**, such as ScotiaMcleod, Nesbitt Burns, RBC Dominion Securities, Wood Gundy, Richardson Greenshields, and Lévesque Beaubien Geoffrion, often provide assistance to firms needing funds. The investment dealer may purchase a new stock or bond issue from the firm and immediately resell it to investors—the suppliers of funds. Investment dealers assist in bringing suppliers and demanders together by providing expertise and marketing capabilities to the firm and by guaranteeing the firm a prenegotiated price on the issue. Without investment dealers, the world-wide financial system would not operate as smoothly as it does.[2]

Whether the financial institutions interact directly with the demanders of funds through loans or private placements or indirectly through the financial markets, the important point to remember is that these institutions play a major role in assuring the smooth flow of funds in our economy. In fact, a hallmark of most developed countries is an extensive set of financial institutions or some other mechanism (such as government agencies or trading groups of interrelated companies) for seeing that suppliers and demanders of funds are brought together.

FINANCIAL MARKETS

Financial markets exist whenever a financial transaction takes place. For our purposes, it is helpful to divide financial markets into two general types—the money market and the capital market. The **money market** is the market for new short-term (one year or less) debts. Included in the money market are securities such as (1) treasury bills issued by the federal and some provincial governments; (2) day-to-day (or day) loans, which are demand loans made by chartered banks to money market dealers, secured by short-term government securities; (3) certificates of deposit, which are negotiable short-term, interest-bearing deposits issued by banks; (4) commercial paper, which is short-term debt issued by businesses that have established a sound credit rating; (5) bankers' acceptances, which are negotiable bank-backed credit instruments typi-

---

[2] Investment dealers and the raising of long-term funds are discussed in Chapter 10.

cally used in international trade; and (6) purchase and resale agreements, which are transactions between a bank or government securities dealer and another party (typically a corporation, individual, or government) in which the party buys government securities and simultaneously agrees to sell them back to the bank or securities dealer within a specified time period. The money market also includes securities originally issued with maturities of more than one year but that now have a year or less until maturity. The tremendous growth of the money markets in recent years has created opportunities for both investors and firms. Investors have a wide variety of short-term investments to choose from, and firms (and other demanders such as the government) can secure short-term financing more easily than ever before.

In contrast to the short-term or money market is the **capital market,** which is the market for long-term bonds or stocks. Included in the capital markets are (1) long-term (municipal, provincial, and federal) government bonds; (2) various forms of debt issued by firms; and (3) common and **preferred stock**[3] issued by firms. The primary distinguishing feature of the securities that constitute the capital markets is their life—they all have an anticipated life of longer than one year. They may range from a five-year note issued by the government or some business to common stock that has no specified maturity date.

All securities, when they are originally offered—that is, with the proceeds of the sale going to the issuer of the securities—are issued in the **primary market**. (This applies to both money market and capital market securities.) By primary market, all we are saying is that the proceeds go to the principal, which is typically a corporation or some government unit. After the securities begin to trade between individuals and/or institutional investors, they become part of the **secondary market**. In the primary market, the firm and its lead investment dealer firm generally work together to set the price at which securities are issued. However, in the secondary market, the original issuer has no part in the transaction. This market exists to facilitate investor trading.

A well-developed secondary market is important for two reasons. First, by creating the mechanism for trading, it enables investors to add to or liquidate holdings easily. If an institution wishes to sell 10,000 common shares of Magna International, the transaction can be made quickly and efficiently because of the existence of a fully developed secondary market. The other reason secondary markets are important is that they make it easier for firms (or the government) to issue additional securities. Because investors know they can buy and sell securities easily, they will be more likely to purchase an additional new issue. The existence of a well-developed secondary market, therefore, has important implications for financial management. Without secondary markets, firms would have to use very different financing strategies because issuing both short- and long-term securities would be much more difficult. We might have only smaller firms that financed most of their capital needs with internally generated funds. Another alternative would be more direct government financing of firms, as occurs in countries that have less well-developed secondary markets.

Transactions in the secondary market occur on **organized security exchanges** or in the over-the-counter market. There are five organized security exchanges in

---

[3] Preferred stock represents ownership that has a prior but limited claim on assets and income before common stock. Cash dividends usually cannot be paid on common stock until after they have been paid on preferred stock.

Table 2.1

Stock Exchange Share and Dollar Volume, 1994

The approximately 1,500 issues traded on the Toronto Stock Exchange make it the largest organized securities market in Canada.

Exchange	Share Volume	%	Dollar Volume	%
Toronto	15,459,616,200	60.6	$182,202,048,508	81.8
Montreal	2,486,628,142	9.8	32,443,361,862	14.6
Vancouver	5,302,555,185	20.8	5,795,273,715	2.6
Alberta	2,236,073,914	8.8	2,226,772,381	1.0
Winnipeg	47,242	[a]	598,615	[a]
Total	25,484,920,683	100.0	$222,668,055,081	100.0

[a] Less than 0.1%.
Source: 1994 Official Trading Statistics, Toronto Stock Exchange.

Canada: Alberta, Montreal, Toronto, Vancouver, and Winnipeg. The Toronto Stock Exchange (TSE) is the largest and most prestigious of these exchanges. There are currently more than 1,100 companies[4] listed on the TSE. Table 2.1 shows that the TSE accounted for 60.6 percent of the share volume and 81.8 percent of the dollar value of shares traded in Canada during 1994. This volume of trading made the TSE the twelfth-largest secondary market in the world in terms of the market value of shares traded. Among organized exchanges, the New York Stock Exchange (NYSE) is the largest secondary market for stocks in the world (in total dollar volume). (A few years ago the market value of stocks listed on the Tokyo Stock Exchange surpassed the market value of stocks listed on the NYSE. However, with the substantial decline in the value of Japanese stocks, the NYSE is again the largest stock exchange.)

In practice, some large Canadian firms interlist on different Canadian exchanges (primarily Toronto and Montreal) as well as on different U.S. exchanges (primarily New York and American). That is to say, some Canadian-based companies trade not only in Canada but also in the United States. There are more than 160 Canadian-based firms currently listed on both the TSE and U.S. exchanges. Table 2.2 (p. 47) shows a sample of these firms. It indicates a wide range in the trading volume and value of these interlisted firms as well as a significant variation in the breakdown of the percentage of their traded value on markets in Canada and the United States. On average, more than 50 percent of the share value of Canadian-based interlisted firms traded on stock markets in the United States during the first eight months of 1995.

In Chapter 10 we discuss the requirements that firms must meet before they can list their stocks on the TSE. At this time, however, it is sufficient to say that only corporations that meet the listing requirements of an exchange can trade their stocks on it. If a firm is not listed (because it cannot meet, or refuses to comply with, all listing requirements), its stocks are traded in the unlisted or **over-the-counter (OTC) market**. In addition to unlisted corporate stocks, most bonds are traded in the OTC market. OTC is the term used to describe all buying and selling activity that does not

---

[4] Some companies list more than one type of stock; consequently, more than 1,500 issues are traded.

take place on an organized exchange. The OTC market is made up of security dealers and brokers who, using telecommunications, interact to create a market for various unlisted securities. Because, in practice, the OTC market is made by dealers who hold inventories of unlisted securities and are willing to trade in them, much of the trading in this market involves dealers trading on their own account and not as brokers or agents.

THE GOVERNMENT'S ROLE

The provincial and federal governments have a major impact on our financial system. Both levels of government share regulatory responsibilities, but only the federal government operates the Bank of Canada and formulates fiscal policy.

Regulation   The federal and provincial governments share in regulating financial activity. The federal government has exclusive jurisdiction over banking operations in Canada, and the provinces regulate the securities markets through provincial securities commissions, with an overlap occurring in the regulation of insurance, trust and mortgage companies, financial cooperatives, and other financial institutions. The Office of the Superintendent of Financial Institutions has complete regulatory responsibility for all federal financial institutions. Nevertheless, insurance agents and trust and mortgage loan companies need provincial licences to operate in each province; thus, although these companies are federally chartered, they are also subject to provincial regulatory authorities. Similarly, local credit unions and *caisses populaires* are chartered and regulated provincially; however, the Canadian Co-operative Credit Society, the national umbrella organization (outside of Quebec), is federally chartered and regulated by the Office of the Superintendent of Financial Institutions.

The Bank of Canada   The **Bank of Canada** is Canada's central bank. As the bank of our financial system, it has at its disposal an array of tools that can influence the operations of chartered banks and therefore our entire financial market system. Unlike the Federal Reserve System in the United States, the Bank of Canada cannot change the reserve requirements (the percentage of deposits that chartered banks must keep on reserve at the Bank of Canada). In Canada, the reserve requirements are laid out in the Bank Act and can be altered only through periodic revisions. However, one of the Bank of Canada's most useful tools is influencing the financial system by changing its pattern of open market operations. Through the purchase and sale of government securities, the open market operations of the Bank of Canada can shrink or expand the amount of money in the public's hands. Similarly, buying or selling of short-term government securities can be used by the Bank to influence the rate earned on treasury bills at their weekly (Tuesday) auction. For 15 years prior to February 22, 1996 the trend setting bank rate (i.e., the rate charged to chartered banks when they borrow from the Bank of Canada[5]) was set each Tuesday at 0.25 percent above the average interest rate paid

---

[5] The bank rate applies only to the first amount borrowed from the Bank of Canada by a chartered bank during any month; renewals or additional borrowing are at a higher rate.

for three-month treasury bills that day. This allowed the Bank of Canada to have only an indirect effect on the cost of funds throughout the economy. Currently the bank rate is based on a rate that is directly controlled by the Bank of Canada. It is set at the upper limit of the rate that the Bank of Canada charges financial institutions for overnight loans. Furthermore, it is no longer changed weekly. It is only changed when the Bank of Canada, responding to market conditions, believes that a change in other interest rates is warranted. Thus, through open market operations and the setting of the bank rate, the Bank of Canada can affect the availability and cost of funds provided through the financial system.

Fiscal Policy   In addition to its monetary policy, the fiscal policy followed by the federal government also has a great impact on the cost and availability of funds. In recent years, the operations of the federal government have resulted in large deficits. To finance these net cash requirements, the government has had to raise funds in the open market by selling bonds. This means that the government has been competing with private borrowers for the limited funds available. Consequently, to bid funds away from private borrowers, the government has had to offer higher interest rates on its bonds than private borrowers. This action has contributed to relatively higher interest rates.

Concept Review Questions

- How do financial institutions aid the transfer of funds between suppliers and demanders?
- How are primary and secondary markets different?
- What is the role of the Bank of Canada in the financial system?

INTEREST RATES, INFLATION, AND RISK

In a market economy, capital is allocated by means of the price system—that is, through the interaction of supply and demand. The cost of debt capital is reflected in the interest rate paid by the firm, whereas the cost of equity capital is a function of both cash dividends and capital gains (or losses). In this and the following section we seek to understand how interest rates, inflation, and risk interact.

INTEREST RATES

Interest rates are the prices paid when an individual, firm, or government unit borrows funds. **Interest** is the cost incurred by demanders of funds when they use debt financing. From the suppliers' standpoint, interest is what is earned when money is loaned to someone else. So interest is both a cost and a revenue—it simply depends on whether one is a demander or a supplier of funds. Interest is generally stated on a per year percentage basis. If you borrow $1,000 (the **principal**) and agree to repay $1,080 (principal plus interest) in one year, you are paying 8 percent interest for the

---

Figure 2.2

Supply of and Demand for Loanable Funds

In a perfect market the real rate of interest is an equilibrium rate resulting from the interaction of the supply of loanable funds (savings) and the demand for loanable funds (for investment purposes).

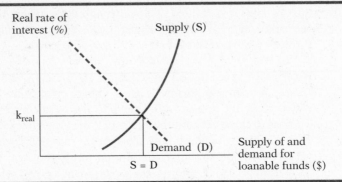

---

use of the funds. Even if you borrow or lend for periods longer or shorter than one year, the interest is almost always stated on an annual basis.[6]

Real Rate of Interest In a perfect world, with no expected inflation or risk premiums, the cost of funds (i.e., the **real rate of interest**) would be determined solely by the interaction of the supply of loanable funds from savings and the demand for loanable funds for investment. As shown in Figure 2.2, the real rate of interest, k_{real}, is an equilibrium rate that is a function of the aggregate supply of and demand for capital. This real rate of interest is not static but fluctuates over time as the actions by suppliers, the Bank of Canada, and others determine the amount of loanable funds available for investment. The demand for funds comes from firms, individuals, and the government. As the need for funds strengthens or weakens, the demand curve for loanable funds will shift. As the supply of funds decreases or the demand increases (and assuming no other changes), the real rate of interest will rise. Correspondingly, an increase in supply or a reduction in demand will result in lowering the real rate of interest. The real interest rate is thus a function of the actions of the government and the state of the economy, as both influence the supply of and demand for funds.

Expected Inflation **Inflation** refers to a change in purchasing power as reflected by changes in the general price level. Expected inflation has a direct impact on interest rates because suppliers of funds will demand a higher rate to make up for being paid back in dollars that are expected to have less purchasing power. The result is that interest rates rise when a high rate of inflation is expected and fall when the expected rate of inflation is low (i.e., **disinflation**).

---

[6] An exception occurs with consumer credit or bank charge cards. These often state interest as being, for example, 1.5 percent per month. Obviously, this translates into 18 percent per year, but it does not sound quite so bad when stated on a monthly basis.

The relationship between the expected rate of inflation and the observed (or nominal) rate of interest is called the **Fisher effect**: The **nominal risk-free interest rate** is equal to the real rate of interest, plus an **inflation premium,** so that

$$\begin{array}{c} \text{Nominal risk-free} \\ \text{rate of interest} \end{array} = \begin{array}{c} \text{real rate of} \\ \text{interest} \end{array} + \begin{array}{c} \text{expected rate} \\ \text{of inflation} \end{array} \qquad (2.1)$$

Canadian **treasury bills**, which are short-term borrowing by the government of Canada, are the best proxy we have for a default-free nominal rate of interest. This rate is called the **risk-free rate**, k_{RF}. We can rewrite Equation 2.1 as follows:

$$\text{Risk-free rate, } k_{RF} = \text{real rate of interest} + \text{inflation premium} \qquad (2.2)$$

The risk-free rate encompasses the real rate of return plus a premium for expected inflation.

The real rate of interest is thought to be around 2 to 3 percent. Thus, we would predict the risk-free rate, k_{RF}, to be 2 to 3 percent above the expected rate of inflation. To see if this is true, look at Figure 2.3, which compares the rate of interest on Canadian treasury bills with changes in inflation from 1960 to 1994. We see that the real rate of interest was actually negative during the mid-1970s and has exceeded 3 percent since 1980. The large gap between the risk-free rate and inflation in recent years can be directly attributed to the high interest rate policy used by the Bank of Canada to counteract inflation.

Figure 2.3

Relationship Between the Return on Treasury Bills and Changes in the Consumer Price Index

On average, the risk-free rate of return has exceeded inflation by 2 to 3 percent. However, in recent years the gap has been larger.

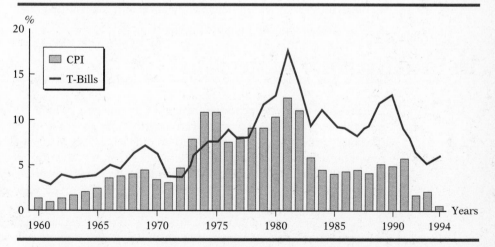

Source: Canadian Economic Observer, Statistics Canada: Catalogue No. 11-010, various issues.

However, the following data, which summarize the information in Figure 2.3, show that over the whole period the real rate of interest was within the anticipated range.

Time Period	Treasury Bills	Inflation
1960–1994	7.6%	5.1%
1970–1994	8.9	6.1
1980–1994	10.1	5.3

While investing in treasury bills has provided returns that have been greater than inflation (especially for the 1980–1994 period), these data support an important point: *On average, the return on short-term treasury bills compensates investors only slightly better than changes in the rate of inflation.*

Maturity Premium   So far we have considered the real rate of interest and the effect of expected inflation on the level of interest rates. The security examined, Canadian treasury bills, has an initial maturity of three months, six months, or occasionally, one year. Now we examine longer-term debt offerings of the Canadian government. As we discuss in Chapter 4, the market prices of long-term bonds change much more dramatically than do the market prices of short-term bonds whenever overall interest rates change. This difference gives rise to a **maturity premium** to compensate for the additional risk. The effect is to raise the rates on long-term bonds relative to those on short-term bonds. In recent years, the maturity premium on long-term government bonds has been about 1 percentage point.

Concept Review Questions

■ Why can interest rates be considered both a cost and a revenue?

■ What causes the real rate of interest to change?

■ What is the relationship between inflation and the risk-free rate?

■ Why does a maturity premium arise?

THE TERM STRUCTURE OF INTEREST RATES

Canadian government securities are free of any default risk (to be discussed subsequently) because there is a virtual certainty that the government will pay interest on the bonds and redeem them in full and on time when they mature. Thus, the nominal return on any government security is equal to the sum of the risk-free return, k_{RF}, and a maturity premium. The returns for Canadian government securities, as of June 1990 and July 1993, are plotted in Figure 2.4. The lines are called **yield curves**, and the graph depicts the **term structure** of interest rates for a given risk class of securities. The risk class we are examining is government securities; a similar but higher yield curve exists for various classes of corporate debt. A downward-sloping (inverted) yield curve, such as that existing in June 1990, indicates an expectation of lower rates of inflation in the future. An upward-sloping yield curve, like that existing in July 1993, indicates

Figure 2.4

The Term Structure as of June 1990 and July 1993

A downward-sloping yield curve occurs when inflation is expected to decrease. An upward-sloping yield curve occurs when inflation is expected to increase.

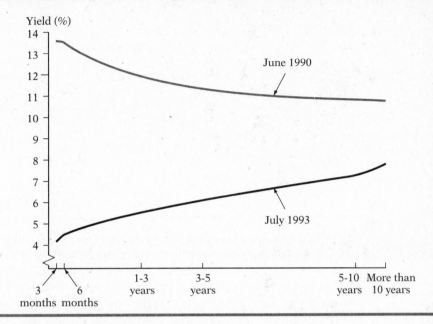

Source: Bank of Canada Review, various issues.

an expectation of higher inflation in the future. Some observations concerning yield curves are:

1. They fluctuate up and down, depending on the general supply of and demand for funds.
2. Their shape changes, from downward-sloping to flat to upward-sloping, depending on the future rate of inflation expected by investors.
3. Yield curves for firms will be above those of the government. The riskier the firm is perceived to be, the higher the yield curve.

The yield curves plotted in Figure 2.4 also embody the maturity premium, which increases with the length to maturity of any bond. The effect of maturity premiums is to raise interest rates on long-term bonds relative to those of short-term bonds. This effect can be seen in Figure 2.5, where the solid lines depict the nominal yield curves that encompass the expected inflation and maturity premiums along with the real rate of interest. The dashed curves, which lie below the yield curves, indicate what the yield curves would look like if no maturity premium existed.

TERM STRUCTURE THEORIES

The term structure of interest rates depicts the yield–maturity relationships for securities of equivalent risk. Figure 2.4 shows that at times the term structure is upward-

| Figure 2.5 |

Effect of the Maturity Premium on Yield Curves

Maturity premiums, which arise due to the heightened interest rate sensitivity of longer-term bonds, increase with the maturity of the bond.

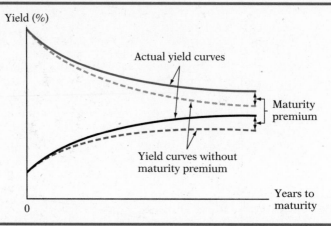

sloping, when long-term rates of interest are higher than short-term rates, while at other times the opposite holds, with short-term rates higher than long-term rates. Why do we observe these different shapes and levels in the term structure over time? A great deal of theoretical and empirical work has focused on this question. Three of the theories offered in explanation are the expectations theory, the liquidity (maturity) preference theory, and the market segmentation theory.

The Expectations Theory   The **expectations theory** argues that the shape of the term structure can be explained *solely* on the basis of investors' expectations about the course of future interest rates. If investors expect future rates to be higher than current rates, the term structure will be upward-sloping, and vice versa. Specifically, the theory leads to the conclusion that long-term rates are the geometric average of the current one-year rate and the one-year **forward interest rates** expected to occur between the current year and the maturity date of the long-term bonds.

To understand the expectations theory and the concept of forward rates, assume the current rate, often called the **spot interest rate**, on a two-year Government of Canada bond is 9 percent. In terms of the return to be received on this security, with annual compounding[7] we have

$$
\begin{array}{c}
0 \quad \text{Year 1} \quad 1 \quad \text{Year 2} \quad 2 \\
\vert\!\!\longleftarrow 9\% \longrightarrow\!\!\vert\!\!\longleftarrow 9\% \longrightarrow\!\!\vert
\end{array}
$$

The total return earned over the two years will be $(1 + 0.09)(1 + 0.09) = (1.09)^2$. Now consider a second Government of Canada bond, this time a one-year security with a return of 7 percent. Graphically, we can depict both securities as follows:

$$
\begin{array}{c}
0 \quad \text{Year 1} \quad 1 \quad \text{Year 2} \quad 2 \\
\vert\!\!\longleftarrow 7\% \longrightarrow\!\!\vert\!\!\longleftarrow ?\% \longrightarrow\!\!\vert \\
\vert\!\!\longleftarrow\!\!\longrightarrow 9\% \longrightarrow\!\!\longrightarrow\!\!\vert
\end{array}
$$

---

[7] Compound interest is discussed in detail in Chapter 3.

The expectations theory says that an individual investing in two consecutive one-year bonds will be exactly as well off at the end of year 2 as one investing in the two-year bond. The question then becomes this: What is the rate that would have to be earned in year 2 so that an investor originally investing in the one-year 7 percent bond is equally well off? More formally, we require that

$$(1 + k_2)^2 = (1 + k_1)(1 + f_2) \tag{2.3}$$

where k_2 = the current two-year spot rate of interest, k_1 = the current one-year spot rate of interest, and f_2 = the forward one-year rate of interest occurring one year from now.

For the expectations theory to hold, Equation 2.3 must be true. Rearranging Equation 2.3 to solve for the implied forward rate, f_2, we have

$$f_2 = \frac{(1 + k_2)^2}{1 + k_1} - 1 \tag{2.4}$$

$$= \frac{(1.09)^2}{1.07} - 1 = \frac{1.1881}{1.07} - 1$$

$$= 1.1104 - 1 = 0.1104 = 11.04\%$$

Thus, we can think of an investor in the two-year bond, who earns 9 percent compounded annually, as getting the one-year spot rate of 7 percent and locking in a return of 11.04 percent over the second year.

From this simple example, a general equation for the expectation theory can be developed. That is, the long-term spot rate of interest for an n-year bond, k_n, can be expressed as a series made up of the product of the current one-year spot rate, k_1, and $n - 1$ one-year forward rates of interest expected to occur between the current year and the maturity date of the long-term security:

$$(1 + k_n)^n = (1 + k_1)(1 + f_2)(1 + f_3) \cdots (1 + f_n) \tag{2.5}$$

The rate f_2 is the one-year forward rate for a bond bought at the end of year 1 and held until the end of year 2; f_3 is the one-year forward rate for a bond bought at the end of year 2 and held until the end of year 3, and so forth. By rearranging Equation 2.5, the return on a bond with n years to maturity is

$$k_n = [(1 + k_1)(1 + f_2)(1 + f_3) \cdots (1 + f_n)]^{1/n} - 1 \tag{2.6}$$

Likewise, the implied forward rate over any single year can be calculated by

$$f_n = \frac{(1 + k_n)^n}{(1 + k_{n-1})^{n-1}} - 1 \tag{2.7}$$

where f_n is the one-year implied forward rate over the nth year, k_n is the n-year spot rate, and k_{n-1} is the spot rate for $n - 1$ years.

To illustrate this idea, assume you pick up a newspaper and find the following current spot rates of interest for Government of Canada securities:

Years to Maturity	Current Spot Rate
1	6.0%
2	7.0
3	7.5
4	8.0

We can calculate the implied forward rates of interest for years 2, 3, and 4 by using Equation 2.7 as follows:

$$f_2 = \frac{(1 + k_2)^2}{(1 + k^1)} - 1 = \frac{(1.07)^2}{1.06} - 1 = 1.0801 - 1 = 8.01\%$$

$$f_3 = \frac{(1 + k_3)^3}{(1 + k_2)^2} - 1 = \frac{(1.075)^3}{(1.07)^2} - 1 = 1.0851 - 1 = 8.51\%$$

$$f_4 = \frac{(1 + k_4)^4}{(1 + k_3)^3} - 1 = \frac{(1.08)^4}{(1.075)^3} - 1 = 1.0951 - 1 = 9.51\%$$

This illustration tells us that investing in a four-year bond with a spot rate of return of 8 percent is exactly the same as investing in a one-year bond with a spot rate of 6 percent, followed by investing in a series of one-year forward rate securities with interest rates of 8.01 percent, 8.51 percent, and 9.51 percent, respectively. This is easy to see using Equation 2.6 as follows:

$$k_4 = [(1 + k_1)(1 + f_2)(1 + f_3)(1 + f_4)]^{1/4} - 1$$
$$= [(1.0600)(1.0801)(1.0851)(1.0951)]^{1/4} - 1$$
$$= (1.3605)^{1/4} - 1 = 1.0800 - 1 = 8.00\%$$

If the yield on the four-year bond were anything other than 8 percent, there would be an opportunity for wealth-maximizing investors to choose the security, or combination of securities, that maximizes their return over the four-year period. For example, if the yield on the four-year bond were only 7.75 percent, all investors would prefer to hold the combination of one-year bonds because it promises a higher return. Consequently, investors would sell the four-year bond, thereby driving down its price and driving up its yield. This process will continue until any difference in yields between the two investment strategies is eliminated.

The expectations theory says that in equilibrium the long-term rate must be a geometric average of the present and future short-term interest rates, as indicated by Equation 2.6. Accordingly, a long-term bond is a perfect substitute for a series of short-term bonds, and vice versa. A long-term investor can earn the same return by buying a long-term security that coincides with his or her investment period or by successive investments in short-term securities.

The Liquidity (Maturity) Preference Theory   The **liquidity preference theory** postulates that investors find short-term securities more desirable than long-term securities, and therefore long-term securities must offer a premium to attract investors. Consequently, *yields on long-term securities are greater than those indicated by the expectations theory.* It should be clear that the theory's name is somewhat misleading since it actually explains "maturity premiums," not "liquidity premiums."

The crux of this theory is that future interest rates are not certain, as implied by the expectations theory; rather, unexpected changes may occur. We will see in Chapter 4 that long-term bond prices fluctuate more as market interest rates change than do short-term bond prices. This results in greater risk being associated with long-term bonds than with short-term bonds. Consequently, since investors prefer less risk to more, they will prefer to invest in short-term bonds rather than long-term bonds with the same expected rate of return. On the other hand, to reduce the uncertainty of financing long-term projects, firms will prefer to borrow with long-term bonds. As a result, the maturity preferences of borrowers and lenders do not coincide. Therefore, for firms to raise long-term funds they must offer a (maturity) premium to investors to compensate for the greater potential price volatility of long-term bonds compared with short-term bonds. As shown in Figure 2.5, the actual yield curve will be above that obtained from the expectations theory. Therefore, to calculate the return on an n-year bond under the liquidity preference theory, we simply adjust Equation 2.6 by adding a maturity premium to the one-year spot rate and to each forward rate.

The Market Segmentation Theory   The **market segmentation theory** holds that the short-term and long-term markets are independent of one another, and rates of return (or yields) are determined by supply and demand in each market. It is argued that different groups of investors have different maturity needs, which lead them to restrict their security purchases to specific portions of the maturity spectrum. Similarly, borrowers are believed to tailor the maturity of their securities to the type of assets they wish to finance or the length of time over which they need funds. For example, banks, with primarily short-term liabilities, prefer short-term investments, whereas pension funds or insurance companies, with long-term liabilities, prefer long-term investments. On the other side of the market, firms that need funds to finance seasonal increases in current assets (such as inventories or accounts receivable) would borrow on a short-term basis, whereas firms that want to finance large long-term projects will prefer to borrow on a long-term basis.

If these borrowing and lending requirements are strictly adhered to, long-term and short-term securities would not be perfect substitutes for one another. Consequently, the rates of return in the short and long segments of the market would be determined solely by the interaction of supply and demand for funds in the particular segment. If the demand for funds is stronger than the supply of funds in the long-term market relative to the demand–supply relationship in the short-term market, long-term rates will be higher than short-term rates. In such a situation, not only will the term structure be upward-sloping, but it would also lie above those indicated by the expectations and/or liquidity preference theories.

Theory, Testing, and Volatility   Over time an impressive amount of research has examined various alternative term structure theories. Unfortunately, there is a lack of agreement about which, if any, of the three theories discussed is the most descriptive of the term structure of interest rates. In the last few years a number of new approaches have been suggested. One of the most important is the Cox, Ingersoll, and Ross equilibrium model. At the same time more attention is being given to the role that volatility may play in explaining the observed term structure of interest rates. Although all of the theories have both some logical elements and empirical support, we lean slightly towards the liquidity (maturity) premium argument.

THE RISK PREMIUM

So far we have examined two risk premiums for bonds, related to expected inflation and maturity. In practice, there are other sources of risk for corporate bonds. For example, the risk that a corporate borrower will not pay interest and principal on a bond is greater than the risk of the government of Canada not meeting its obligations. This additional risk is called default risk and is evidenced by the **default premium**, which makes corporate bond rates higher than government bond rates. The general level of interest rates from 1975 to 1994, as reflected by Government of Canada bonds and corporate bonds, is shown in Figure 2.6. In the absence of other risks, the difference between the yield on a government bond and the yield on a corporate bond of equal maturity is its default premium.

Two other risks arise from the liquidity of the bond and the nature and character- istics of the bond. The **liquidity premium** arises because investors in securities that are harder to sell, or less liquid, incur more transactions costs; they therefore demand additional compensation. A final type of risk relates to the basic nature and character- istics of the bond. This **issue-specific premium** arises because individual bonds may contain a variety of features (or provisions).[8] Some are more or less attractive to investors; hence, different features result in an issue-specific premium.

In finance the term **risk premium** is used to reflect the risks over and above the risk-free rate, k_{RF}. The risk premium is equal to

$$\text{Risk premium} = \frac{\text{maturity}}{\text{premium}} + \frac{\text{default}}{\text{premium}} + \frac{\text{liquity}}{\text{premium}} + \frac{\text{issue-specific}}{\text{premium}} \qquad (2.8)$$

The investor's required return, k, is equal to the sum of (1) the risk-free rate and (2) the risk premium. Thus,

$$\text{Required return, k} = k_{RF} + \text{risk premium} \qquad (2.9)$$

Short-term debt securities, such as those issued by Bell Canada, will have a very small risk premium (over the risk-free rate). On the other hand, if you hold the long-term debt of Joe's Bakery you have taken on substantially greater risk. Other things being equal, you will expect a higher rate of return from investing in Joe's Bakery than from investing in Bell Canada.

---

[8] Provisions of bonds are discussed in Chapter 11.

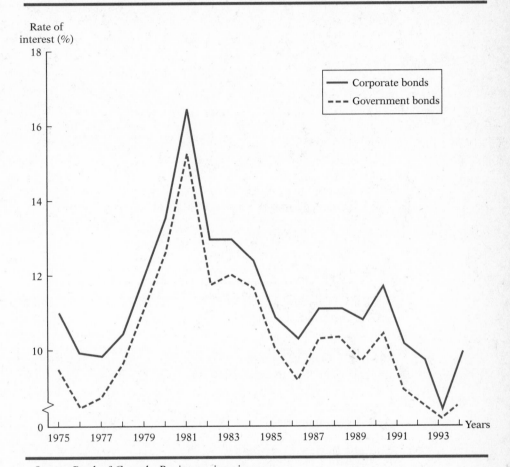

Figure 2.6

Average Yield on Long-Term Government of Canada and Corporate Bonds

The yields shown below are average yields as of December 31 of each year for bonds with at least 10 years to maturity. Although the yield on corporate bonds is always higher than on government bonds, the difference between them, the default premium, varies over time.

Source: Bank of Canada Review, various issues.

RETURNS AND RISK FOR SECURITIES

We will explore the topic of returns and risk in detail in Chapter 5; here, it is important to establish the fundamental relationship. The relationship between returns and risk is also the relationship between risk and cost to the issuer. Looking at it from the investor's viewpoint, if you expose yourself to more risk, you require a higher return. *Higher returns demanded by investors have to come from somewhere; they come from the higher costs of raising capital borne by the firm.*

As risk increases for different types of securities, so does the return demanded by investors, and therefore the cost to the issuer. This relationship is depicted in

Figure 2.7

Relationship Between Required Return (or Cost to the Issuer) and Risk

Canadian treasury bills provide a risk-free return. As risk increases (as evidenced by default, liquidity, or issue-specific premiums), the returns demanded by investors increase; so do the costs to the issuer.

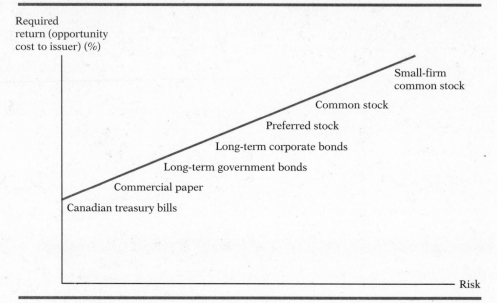

Figure 2.7. The relationship between return (or the cost to the firm) and risk is another of the fundamental ideas of finance; it will be pursued throughout the book. For now, all you need to remember is this: If a firm increases its risk exposure, it increases the return demanded by investors, and hence its costs. *There is no free lunch; increases in risk cause increases in costs.*

Concept Review Questions

- What makes a yield curve upward- or downward- sloping?
- What theories do we have to explain the different shapes and levels of the term structure?
- According to the expectations theory, what factor(s) explain the shape of the term structure? In equilibrium, how does this theory represent long-term interest rates?
- Why does a yield curve derived according to the liquidity preference theory lie above one derived according to the expectations theory?
- According to the market segmentation theory, why are short- and long-term rates not perfect substitutes for each other?
- What are the different risk premiums that compose the bond risk premium required by investors?
- What is the relationship between return and risk for securities?

INTERNATIONAL FINANCIAL MARKETS

In addition to domestic financial markets, firms now have access to the world-wide financial marketplace. Large Canadian firms routinely issue bonds or seek short-term financing overseas. Some firms, such as those in Table 2.2, have their stock listed on exchanges in the United States while others, such as Bell Canada, Northern Telecom, and Alcan Aluminium, even have their stock listed on the Tokyo exchange.

While many of the same forces are at work world-wide, there are two fundamental differences. First, the role of a single government, or a government unit such as the Bank of Canada, is diminished since funds tend to flow fairly freely between many countries. Second, exchange rates can and do change between various currencies. Understanding exchange rates is important for any financial manager who deals in international transactions but is of particular importance to managers of firms like SR Telecom and Husky Injection Molding Systems who have sales in more than 60 countries. In fact, competition is now global in nature for most major industries,

---

Table 2.2

Interlisted Stocks

This is a sample of the more than 160 Canadian-based firms that list on markets in both Canada and the United States.

	All Markets		Market as % of Traded Value	
Company Name	Volume	Value ($000)	Canadian	U.S.
Abitibi Price	13,439,246	322,221	74.6	25.4
Alcan Aluminium	30,276,433	1,405,723	56.4	43.6
B.C.E.	13,556,659	571,253	84.2	15.8
Canadian Pacific	24,300,289	572,387	63.0	37.0
Cineplex Odeon	3,588,644	9,825	26.8	73.2
Cominco	2,387,103	65,954	96.3	3.7
Domtar	6,009,259	82,660	88.4	11.6
Echo Bay	27,231,713	385,371	20.0	80.0
Gandalf Tech	58,879,808	623,538	17.0	83.0
Gulf Resources	8,156,772	51,844	59.3	40.7
Inco	23,992,006	1,144,024	60.8	39.2
MacMillan Bloedel	4,940,996	91,161	96.3	3.7
Magna International	5,103,821	315,087	43.0	57.0
Northern Telecom	10,292,644	508,348	39.5	60.5
Nova Corp.	29,625,313	327,579	88.1	11.9
Placer Dome	28,315,674	1,002,539	42.7	57.3
Quebecor	135,720	2,824	54.7	45.3
Seagram	20,002,303	983,551	33.2	66.8
Westcoast Energy	5,024,032	101,627	67.6	32.4

Source: TSE Review August 1995, Toronto Stock Exchange.

and almost all firms are affected one way or another by changing foreign exchange rates. Consider, for example, the experience of Eastman Kodak. During the early 1980s the economic performance of Eastman's photography sector was coming under increasing pressure from competitors. In particular, Fuji Photo of Japan had become a major world-wide competitor of Eastman Kodak. Fuji was benefiting from the quality of its product and from its marketing efforts. In addition, Fuji was benefiting from the yen/U.S. dollar exchange rate: With a weak yen, Fuji's largely yen-denominated cost of production was lower than Kodak's dollar-denominated cost of production. The effect was to make Kodak film less price-competitive with Fuji film both in Japan and in other parts of the world, and to make Fuji more price-competitive in Kodak's domestic market—the United States. The currency exposure, which arose from the denomination of Kodak's costs primarily in U.S. dollars and the denomination of Fuji's costs primarily in yen, was having a direct bearing on Kodak's sales and bottom line cash flows.

The global economy is a fundamental development affecting financial management. Consequently, the need to deal with more than one currency is an important feature of financial management. Therefore, we need to look at how foreign exchange markets operate and why exchange rates change.

Concept Review Question

- What are the fundamental differences between doing business domestically and abroad?

FOREIGN EXCHANGE RATES

A fundamental difference between domestic and international financial management is that international transactions are conducted in more than one currency. For example, the dollar is used in Canada, the franc in France, the rupee in India, the yen in Japan, the mark in Germany, and the peso in Mexico.

SPOT AND FORWARD RATES

Foreign exchange rates are the conversion rates between currencies. They depend on the relative supply of and demand for two currencies, inflation in the two countries, and other factors. Foreign exchange rates are important not only to multinationals but also to any firm that operates (has facilities) only in Canada and obtains some of its raw materials or sells its finished products abroad. **The spot rate of exchange** is the exchange rate between two currencies for immediate delivery today. The spot rate between the Canadian dollar and several other currencies for immediate delivery is shown in Table 2.3.

Until the early 1970s, the world was on a fixed exchange rate system. Since 1973, it has operated on a "managed" floating system. Major world currencies move—float—somewhat freely with market forces. Nevertheless, the central banks of countries intervene by buying or selling in the foreign exchange market to smooth out some of the fluctuations. Each central bank also attempts to keep its exchange rates

Table 2.3

Selected Foreign Exchange Rates Listed in the October 13, 1995, Issue of
The Globe and Mail

Exchange rates can be stated two different ways; however, conversion from one to the other is straightforward. Exchange rates may change daily as conditions change in either of the countries, or as events throughout the world influence the rates.

Country	Currency	Canadian Dollars Required to Buy One Unit (1)	Number of Units of Foreign Currency per Canadian Dollar[a] (2)
Austria	Schilling	0.1337	7.4775
Britain	Pound	2.1042	0.4752
France	Franc	0.2700	3.7037
Germany	Mark	0.9408	1.0629
Hong Kong	Dollar	0.1730	5.7803
India	Rupee	0.03957	25.2717
Japan	Yen	0.013340	74.9625
Saudi Arabia	Riyal	0.3566	2.8043
Venezuela	Bolivar	0.00789	126.7427
United States	Dollar	1.3373	0.7478

[a] Column 2 equals 1.0 divided by column 1.

within prescribed government limits to help the country's export or import situation. Floating exchange rates are a fact of life with which all managers must be prepared to cope.

In practice, foreign currencies are generally quoted as the number of units of the foreign currency per dollar. An exception to this is the pound sterling, which is generally quoted in dollars per pound sterling. We will begin by concentrating on understanding foreign exchange rates as units of foreign currency per dollar. Thus, if the current, or spot, rate of exchange between Germany and Canada is 1.200, that means M/$1 = 1.200, which indicates that 1.200 marks equal $1, or that the dollar price of a single mark is $0.833 (i.e., 1/1.200).

In addition to the spot rate of exchange, there are also **forward rates of exchange** that, quoted as of today, indicate the future rate of exchange for some period, such as the 30-day forward rate, the 60-day forward rate, and the 180-day forward rate. Thus, the current 180-day forward rate of exchange between the mark and the dollar may be 1.183. This simply says that the current rate of exchange for delivery 180 days from now is 1.183 M/$ (that is, 1.183 marks for every dollar).

SOME FUNDAMENTAL RELATIONSHIPS

Assuming away transactions costs, intervention by governments, and other imperfections, we can state some fundamental relationships that apply to produce prices, interest rates, and spot and forward exchange rates between two countries. To generalize, assume country 1 is the domestic country and country 2 is the foreign country.

Figure 2.8

The Relationship Between Spot Exchange Rates, Forward Exchange Rates, Inflation, and Interest

While imperfections, transactions costs, and government central bank intervention affect these relationships, over longer periods of time the relationships appear to hold.

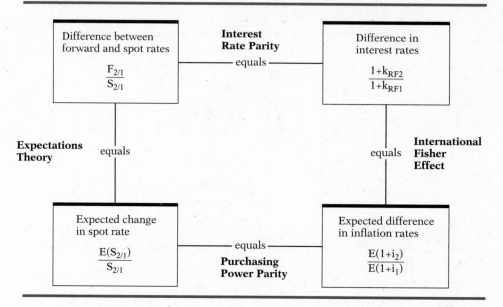

Let us define the following

where

$F_{2/1}$ = forward rate in units of country 2's currency to one unit of country 1's currency

$S_{2/1}$ = spot rate in units of country 2's currency to one unit of country 1's currency

k_{RF2} = risk-free interest rate in country 2 for the appropriate forward period

k_{RF1} = risk-free interest rate in country 1 for the appropriate forward period

i_2 = rate of inflation in country 2 for the appropriate forward period

i_1 = rate of inflation in country 1 for the appropriate forward period

The relationship between forward and spot exchange rates, inflation rates, and interest rates in this simple world is shown in Figure 2.8.

To understand these relationships, we will begin at the top left of Figure 2.8 and move counterclockwise. The first relationship, based on the **expectations theory of forward exchange rates,** says that the percentage difference between the forward rate and today's spot rate is equal to the expected change in the spot rate, or

$$\frac{F_{2/1}}{S_{2/1}} = \frac{E(S_{2/1})}{S_{2/1}} \tag{2.10}$$

where E signifies the expected future spot rate of exchange of country 2's currency relative to country 1's currency. Thus, in the absence of other interventions and occurrences, the expectations theory of foreign exchange rates say that the best estimation of the future spot rate is the current forward rate of exchange.[9]

The second link is between the expected change in the spot rate of exchange and the inflation rate differential between the two countries. **Purchasing power parity** explains that the relationship between today's spot rate of exchange and the spot rate of exchange in the future is determined by expected differential rates of inflation between the two countries, so

$$\frac{E(S_{2/1})}{S_{2/1}} = \frac{E(1 + i_2)}{E(1 + i_1)} \tag{2.11}$$

An alternative way to think about purchasing power parity is that it implies that a unit of the domestic currency should have the same purchasing power anywhere in the world. One example of purchasing power parity is provided in Table 2.4, which compares the price of a Big Mac in different countries. For example, in China it takes 9.00 yuan to buy as many Big Macs as with 2.32 U.S. dollars. The rate of exchange implied by Big Macs is 9.00 yuan = $2.32 U.S., or $1 U.S. = 3.88 yuan. The actual rate of exchange was 8.54 yuan per U.S. dollar. Thus, prices in China were more than twice as expensive as implied by purchasing power parity.

The third link is between expected differences in inflation rates and differences in interest rates. The **international Fisher effect**, which is based on the Fisher effect mentioned earlier in this chapter, says that countries with high rates of inflation should have higher interest rates than countries with lower rates of inflation, so that

$$\frac{E(1 + i_2)}{E(1 + i_1)} = \frac{1 + k_{RF2}}{1 + k_{RF1}} \tag{2.12}$$

Thus, in addition to the real rate of interest, which is assumed to be essentially the same in all countries, the international Fisher effect indicates that differences in expected rates of inflation will be reflected by differences in risk-free interest rates between two countries.

Finally, we can complete the loop specified in Figure 2.8 by examining the **interest rate parity** relationship. It says that differences in interest rates between two countries will affect the relationship between spot and forward rates of exchange, so that

$$\frac{1 + k_{RF2}}{1 + k_{RF1}} = \frac{F_{2/1}}{S_{2/1}} \tag{2.13}$$

Thus, interest rate differentials between two countries will have to be offset by differences in the forward rate of exchange and the spot rate of exchange between the countries.

---

[9] The notion of the expectations theory employed here is similar to that employed previously in this chapter when discussing the expectations theory of interest rates, except that now we are referring to exchange rates.

Table 2.4

Big Mac Prices in Different Countries

Although it is meant to be a little "tongue in cheek," the Big Mac index has been found to provide estimates that are strikingly similar to those provided by more sophisticated calculations.

	Price in Local Currency	Big Mac Exchange Rate	Actual Exchange Rate	Percent Local Currency Is Under (−) or Over (+) Valued %
United States	**$2.32**	—	—	—
Argentina	Peso 3.00	1.29	1.00	+29
Australia	A$2.45	1.06	1.35	−22
Austria	Sch 39.00	16.80	9.72	+73
Belgium	BFr 109	47.00	28.40	+66
Brazil	Real 2.42	1.04	0.90	+16
Britain	£1.74	1.33	1.61	+21
Canada	C$2.77	1.19	1.39	−14
Chile	Peso 950	409.00	395.00	+4
China	Yuan 9.00	3.88	8.54	−55
Czech Republic	CKr 50.00	21.6	26.2	−18
Denmark	DKr 26.75	11.50	5.43	+112
France	FFr 18.50	7.97	4.80	+66
Germany	M 4.80	2.07	1.38	+50
Holland	F 15.45	2.35	1.55	+52
Hong Kong	HK$9.50	4.09	7.73	−47
Hungary	Forint 191	82.30	121.00	−32
Indonesia	Rupiah 3,900	1,681.00	2,231.00	−25
Israel	Shekel 8.90	3.84	2.95	+30
Italy	Lira 4,500	1,940.00	1,702.00	+14
Japan	Y391	169.00	84.20	+100
Malaysia	M$3.76	1.62	2.49	−35
Mexico	Peso 10.90	4.70	6.37	−26
New Zealand	NZ$2.95	1.27	1.51	−16
Poland	Zloty 3.40	1.47	2.34	−37
Russia	Ruble 8,100	3,491.00	4,985.00	−30
Singapore	S$2.95	1.27	1.40	−9
S. Korea	Won 2,300	991.00	769.00	+29
Spain	Ptas 355	153.00	124.00	+23
Sweden	SKr 26.00	11.20	7.34	+53
Switzerland	SwFr 5.90	2.54	1.13	+124
Taiwan	NT$65.0	28.00	25.70	+9
Thailand	Baht 48.00	20.70	24.60	−16

Source: "Big Mac Currencies," *The Economist* (April 15, 1995): 74.

In practice, things are not quite so simple. Trade barriers exist between countries; government actions through their central banks impact inflation, interest rates, and foreign exchange rates; and other imperfections exist. Numerous empirical tests have been conducted on portions of the relationships discussed above. In general, over longer periods of time, the relationships tend to hold up fairly well. Although violations do occur, and may last for some time, the relationships provide a means of estimating the relationship between spot and future exchange rates, using data supplied by the financial markets.

INTEREST RATES, SPOT RATES, AND FORWARD RATES

Using the interest rate parity relationship, at any point in time the relationship between spot and forward rates of exchange of the number of units of country 2's currency per country 1's currency unit is given by

$$F_{2/1} = \frac{S_{2/1}(1 + k_{RF2})}{1 + k_{RF1}} \qquad (2.14)$$

Let us use an example to see this relationship. For the 180-day forward rate of German marks per Canadian dollar of 1.183 M/$, mentioned previously, we have

$$F_{M/\$} = \frac{S_{M/\$}(1 + k_{RFM})}{1 + k_{RF\$}}$$

where

$F_{M/\$}$ = the current 180-day forward exchange rate in marks per dollar
$S_{M/\$}$ = the current spot exchange rate in marks per dollar
k_{RFM} = risk-free interest rate on 180-day German securities, expressed in terms of a 180-day return
$k_{RF\$}$ = risk-free interest rate on 180-day Canadian securities, expressed in terms of a 180-day return

Assume that the risk-free rate in Germany is 4 percent and that the risk-free rate in Canada is 7 percent. Then, for simplicity, assuming a 360-day year, the 180-day rates are 2 percent and 3.5 percent, respectively. With a current spot rate of 1.200 M/$, the forward rate of exchange is

$$F_{M/\$} = \frac{1.200(1.02)}{1.035} = 1.183$$

If we enter into a contract today, in 180 days we would deliver (or receive, depending on the contract) 1.183 marks per dollar.

Let us summarize and clarify this by spelling out what the relationship means. If k_{RF2} is *greater than* k_{RF1}, then

1. The forward rate, $F_{2/1}$, is greater than the spot rate, $S_{2/1}$.
2. Country 2's currency is selling at a discount.
3. Country 2's currency is weakening relative to country 1's currency.

Alternatively, if k_{RF2} is *less than* k_{RF1}, then

1. The forward rate, $F_{2/1}$, is less than the spot rate, $S_{2/1}$.
2. Country 2's currency is selling at a premium.
3. Country 2's currency is strengthening relative to country 1's currency.

Assuming country 2 is Germany and country 1 is Canada, then

$$\text{if the M strengthens} \rightarrow \text{price of M} \uparrow \text{ so } \begin{cases} \text{M/\$}\downarrow, \text{ you get fewer M/\$} \\ \text{\$/M}\uparrow, \text{ it takes more \$ to buy a M} \end{cases}$$

This relationship also implies that future interest rates and inflation in Germany are expected to be *lower* than in Canada. Alternatively,

$$\text{if the M weakens} \rightarrow \text{price of M} \downarrow \text{ so } \begin{cases} \text{M/\$}\uparrow, \text{ you get more M/\$} \\ \text{\$/M}\downarrow, \text{ it takes fewer \$ to buy a M} \end{cases}$$

This relationship implies that future interest rates and inflation in Germany are expected to be *higher* than in Canada.

An example of the impact of changing exchange rates occurs every time a firm buys goods from abroad. Assume a domestic firm orders some new equipment from a Swiss toolmaker. The equipment will be shipped in six months, and the cost is 900,000 Swiss francs (Sf), due when the machinery is shipped. If the spot rate of exchange is 1.50 Sf per dollar, the outlay if paid today would be $900,000/1.50 = \$600,000$. What will it be if in six months the spot rate of exchange is only 1.25 Sf/\$? The outlay will be $900,000/1.25 = \$720,000$. Due to the change in exchange rates, the outlay will end up being \$120,000 more than if payment had occurred immediately or if exchange rates had not changed. Firms dealing with buying and selling in the global economy face such situations all the time. If the risk appears to be small, the firm may do nothing; on the other hand, many firms hedge some, but generally not all, of their foreign exchange risk.

How firms can hedge against foreign exchange fluctuations and handle other international aspects of their operations will be dealt with in our discussion of international financial management in Chapter 17.

Concept Review Questions

- What are the spot rate of exchange and the forward rate of exchange?
- Briefly describe the relationship between spot and forward rates of exchange based on the expectations theory of forward exchange rates, purchasing power parity, the international Fisher effect, and interest rate parity.

KEY POINTS

- The role of the financial system is to provide an effective and efficient way to bring together suppliers and demanders of capital.
- Secondary markets allow investors to buy and sell financial securities, such as bonds and stocks, after they have been issued.
- By facilitating the buying and selling of outstanding securities, an organized secondary market makes it easier for a firm to raise external debt or equity capital.
- The financial system changes rapidly, affording new opportunities for astute firms to use new sources or securities for raising capital.
- Both levels of government share regulatory responsibilities for financial institutions; however, the federal government operates the Bank of Canada and formulates fiscal policy.
- Interest is a cost incurred by a firm and a revenue to the investor.
- On average, risk-free Canadian treasury bills have provided returns slightly in excess of changes in inflation.
- Yield curves, or the term structure of interest rates, depict the relationship between return (yield) and maturity for securities of equivalent risk.
- If the term structure is downward-sloping, long-term debt is cheaper than short-term debt. This suggests that long-term debt may be a likely financing source.
- According to the expectations theory, the shape of the term structure can be explained exclusively by investors' expectations about the course of future interest rates, and leads to the conclusion that long-term rates are the geometric average of the current one-year spot rate and other one-year forward interest rates expected to occur between the current period and the maturity date of the long-term bonds.
- The liquidity preference theory postulates that investors prefer short-term securities to long-term securities; therefore, long-term securities must offer a premium to attract investors. Consequently, yields on long-term securities are greater than those indicated by the expectations theory.
- The market segmentation theory holds that the short-term and long-term markets are independent of one another, and that the rates of return in the short and long segments of the market are determined solely by the interaction of supply and demand for funds in the particular segment. Therefore, the resulting term structure will lie above those indicated by the expectations and/or liquidity preference theories.
- The return required, or demanded, by an investor is equal to the risk-free rate of interest plus a risk premium. For a bond the risk premium may include a maturity premium, a default premium, a liquidity premium, and an issue-specific premium.
- Returns and risk go hand-in-hand. To increase expected returns, it is necessary to increase the exposure to risk.
- The spot rate of exchange is for settlement today, whereas the forward rate of exchange is determined today but with settlement set for some specified time in the future.
- The expected relationship between product prices, interest rates, and spot and future exchange rates can be specified using the expectations theory of forward

exchange rates, purchasing power parity, the international Fisher effect, and interest rate parity. In practice, government intervention, transactions costs, and other imperfections cause these relationships to hold more in the long run than in the short run.

QUESTIONS

2.1   How do financial institutions and financial markets interact to bring suppliers and demanders of funds together? Why are financial institutions so important in this process?

2.2   Distinguish between primary and secondary markets. Why is a well-developed secondary market important even though the firm does not actively participate in it?

2.3   Explain how the federal government influences the domestic financial system.

2.4   How is a yield curve constructed? Can both Canadian government and corporate securities be used to determine a single-yield curve? How do expected inflation and the risk premium affect the yield curve?

2.5   Explain why the yield curve in the market segmentation theory lies above those implied by the expectations and liquidity preference theories.

2.6   Explain the concepts of risk premiums and required returns. What fundamental relationship exists between risk and required return?

2.7   Explain the difference between spot and forward exchange rates.

2.8   The average exchange rate (in terms of the number of units of the foreign currency per Canadian dollar) in year −1 and year 0 for three countries was

	Year −1	Year 0
Mexico (peso)	22.727	41.429
Singapore (dollar)	0.971	0.752
Belgium (franc)	1.678	2.032

What can you conclude about the worth of the Canadian dollar vis-à-vis the currencies of these other countries in year −1 and in year 0? What about the expected rate of inflation in these countries compared to the expected rate of inflation in Canada?

CONCEPT REVIEW PROBLEMS

See Appendix A for solutions.

CR2.1   Use Table 2.3 to answer the following questions:
a.   If a Honda Accord costs $20,000 in Canada, what will it cost in yen in Japan?
b.   If a BMW costs 47,356 marks in Germany, what will the BMW cost in dollars in Canada?
c.   If a British MG costs $15,000 in Canada, how many pounds will it cost in Britain?

CR2.2   Assume inflation *over the next 6 months* is expected to be 3 percent in Canada and 6 percent in France. Using Table 2.3, what is the six-month forward rate of exchange between the franc and the dollar?

PROBLEMS

2.1 The following data exist on Government of Canada securities at three different times.

Maturity	Four Years Ago	Two Years Ago	Today
3 months	6%	10%	17%
1 year	7	11	16
5 years	8	11	15
10 years	9	11	14
20 years	9	11	14

a. Plot the three yield curves on the same graph.
b. Describe the shape of each yield curve and then, assuming that the real rate of interest at each point in time was 3 percent, discuss what has happened to inflationary expectations over the last four years.

2.2 Current spot rates exist as follows:

Years to Maturity	Spot Rate
1	6.95%
2	7.86
3	8.43

a. Assume the expectations theory holds. What are the implied one-year forward interest rates for years 2 and 3?
b. Verify that your answers in (a) are correct by using the one-year spot rate and your two implied forward rates of interest to obtain the three-year spot rate of 8.43 percent.

2.3 The following series of spot interest rates exist:

Years to Maturity	Spot Rate
1	8.62%
2	7.78
3	7.49
4	7.40
5	7.38

a. Under the expectations theory, what are the implied one-year forward rates of interest?
b. Given your results from (a) and assuming that the real rate of interest is 3 percent, what do investors expect the rate of inflation to be in each year?

2.4 Assume the three-year spot rate of interest at time zero is 9 percent while the four-year spot rate at time zero is 10 percent.
a. What is the implied forward rate of interest for year 4?
b. What does the expectations theory of interest rates say about the forward rate of interest for year 4 and the one-year spot rate at year 3?

c. Over a long period of time, the term structure has been, on average, upward-sloping. Does this support the expectations theory?

d. Under the liquidity preference theory, what is the relationship between the implied forward rate for year 4 and the one-year spot rate of interest at year 3?

e. Assuming inflation is predictable, and you need to plan on meeting long-term liabilities, should you invest in long- or short-term bonds if you accept the liquidity preference theory? Why?

f. If the market segmentation theory holds, and the demand for funds is stronger than the supply of funds in the long-term market relative to the short-term market, what can we say about the term structure of interest rates?

2.5 Assume that the real rate of interest is 3 percent and that investors expect inflation to be 6 percent in year 1, 8 percent in year 2, and 9 percent in year 3 and thereafter. A maturity premium on Government of Canada securities exists as follows: zero in year 1, and then it will increase at 0.25 percent a year until the end of year 5; after that time it remains constant at the year 5 level.

a. Assuming that the expectations theory holds, determine the rate of return (yield) for 1-, 2-, 3-, 4-, 5-, 10-, 15-, and 20-year Government of Canada securities.

b. Assuming that, in addition to the expectations theory, the liquidity preference theory also holds, determine the rates of return (yield) for the same Government of Canada securities as in (a).

c. Plot the results from (b) to form a yield curve.

d. Suppose now that Canadian Pacific (very low risk) and Ann's Air Balloons (a very risky firm) are both attempting to estimate their yield curves. Plot each in relation to the treasury bill yield curve and explain how each is similar to or different from your original yield curve.

2.6 The following information exists for four securities:

	Treasury Bills	Long-Term Government Bonds	Listed Corporate Bonds	Risky OTC Common Stocks
Real rate of interest	2.5%	2.5%	2.5%	2.5%
Expected inflation	6.5	6.5	6.5	6.5
Maturity premium	—	1.0	1.0	—
Default premium	—	—	3.0	2.0
Liquidity premium	—	—	—	1.0
Issue-specific premium	—	—	—	5.0

a. Calculate the risk-free rate, k_{RF}, and then calculate the risk premiums and required returns for government bonds, corporate bonds, and risky common stocks.

b. If you were to plot the data, what general relationship would exist between risk and required return? Why?

2.7 If the British pound has a spot rate of 1.771 Canadian dollars per pound while the German mark has a spot rate of 0.544 dollars per German mark, what is the spot rate of exchange between the pound and the mark?

2.8 The current spot rate for the Israeli shekel is 1.817 shekels to the Canadian dollar, while it is 7.15 Chinese yuan to the Canadian dollar. What is the spot rate of exchange between the shekel and the yuan?

2.9 Assume that the current rate of exchange is 1,250 Italian lira per dollar. If the current yearly nominal risk-free interest rate in Italy is 14 percent per year and it is 6 percent in Canada, what is the implied six-month forward rate between the lira and the dollar? (*Note*: For simplicity, assume a 360-day year and 30-day months.)

2.10 Given a spot rate of 0.159 Swedish krona per dollar and expected rates of inflation of 9 percent in Sweden and 5 percent in Canada, what is the expected spot rate of exchange in one year, three years, and six years?

REFERENCES

ABUAF, NISO, AND PHILIPPE JORION. "Purchasing Power Parity in the Long Run." *Journal of Finance* 45 (March 1990): 157–74.

COX, JOHN C., JONATHAN E. INGERSOLL, JR., AND STEPHEN A. ROSS. "A Theory of the Term Structure of Interest Rates." *Econometrica* 53 (March 1985): 385–408.

FROOT, KENNETH A. "New Hope for the Expectations Hypothesis of the Term Structure of Interest Rates." *Journal of Finance* 44 (June 1989): 283–305.

HUANG, ROGER D. "Risk and Parity in Purchasing Power." *Journal of Money, Credit & Banking* 22 (August 1992): 338–56.

RICHARDSON, MATTHEW, PAUL RICHARDSON, AND TOM SMITH. "The Monotonicity of the Term Structure." *Journal of Financial Economics* 31 (February 1992): 97–105.

SHEARER, R. A., J. F. CHANT, AND D. E. BOND. *The Economics of the Canadian Financial System*, 2nd ed. Scarborough, Ont.: Prentice Hall, 1984.

SMITH, BRIAN F., AND ROBERT W. WHITE. "The Capital Market Impact of Recent Canadian Bank Failures." *Canadian Journal of Administrative Sciences* 7 (June 1990): 41–47.

PART II

Fundamental Concepts for Financial Management

*B*efore financial managers can achieve the goal of maximizing the long-term value of their firm, they must understand some fundamental concepts of finance. First, managers must know that a dollar today is worth more than a dollar tomorrow, and how this idea is applied in financial decision making. Second, since the firms value is equal to the market value of the firm's stock plus the market value of the firm's bonds, a basic understanding of stock and bond valuation is indispensable to the goal of maximizing firm value. Furthermore, many of the firm's investment and financing decisions are directly influenced by current and anticipated prices and returns for securities. Third, it is critical that managers realize that risk cannot be avoided in financial decision making. Along with cash flows and time value, risk affects the value of any asset. Therefore, financial managers must understand what causes risk and how it should be measured. Managers must recognize that risk and return go hand-in-hand and that without an understanding of risk they cannot make value-maximizing decisions. Finally, managers must understand how to calculate the cost of any funds that they raise to finance investments in real assets. Knowing the cost of capital enables successful firms to make capital investments that provide adequate returns. If too low a cost estimate is used, firms will make capital investments that provide inadequate returns, and the value of the firm will decrease because costs exceed the return.

Chapter 3 examines the importance of the timing of cash inflows and outflows and how firms create value. Chapter 4 discusses two primary vehicles employed by firms to raise funds—bonds and common stock. Risk and return are examined in detail in Chapter 5. Finally, in Chapter 6 we examine how firms determine firm-wide, divisional, and project-specific opportunity costs of capital. These chapters provide the foundation for making decisions that assist in maximizing the long-run market value of the firm.

3

Time Value of Money

EXECUTIVE SUMMARY

An understanding of present value and future value calculations is fundamental to financial decision making. We know from Chapter 1 that a dollar today is worth more than a dollar tomorrow. Thus, we may want to determine what tomorrow's dollars are worth today, by calculating their present value. At other times, it may be more suitable to determine what today's dollars will grow to over time, by calculating their future value. Therefore, calculating present and future values, both for single amounts (or lump sums) and for streams of cash flows, requires an understanding of the time value of money.

An important application of time value of money in financial management is in investment evaluation. In this case, we first calculate the present value of the future cash inflows generated by the project. Then we subtract the initial investment required to undertake the project from the present value of tomorrow's dollars. The result is the net present value (NPV) of the proposed investment. Any investment with a positive NPV will enhance the value of the firm and, therefore, should be undertaken. The discount rate employed is the opportunity cost of the return forgone by making the investment, i.e., the return that could have been earned by investing in some other equally risky alternative.

Although annual cash flows and discounting are often employed in this book, financial practitioners often use more-frequent-than-yearly cash flows and discounting. When this is the case, the decision maker should determine the effective annual interest rate to properly evaluate the cost or return of a proposal. The concept of effective annual interest rate is also important in determining monthly mortgage payments.

The messages from this chapter are clear: A dollar today is worth more than a dollar tomorrow; maximize net present value; and time value of money concepts are fundamental to financial management because of their numerous applications.

BASIC CONCEPTS

To maximize the size of our pie, or firm, it is essential to have the proper ingredients. Also, it is important to understand that how these ingredients are mixed together influences the size of the pie. In this part of the book we concentrate on four basic concepts: (1) the timing of when the cash flows (or ingredients) occur, (2) how to value bonds and stocks (or determine the size of the pie), (3) how risk (or the mix of ingredients) affects the size of the pie, and (4) how firms determine their opportunity cost of capital (required rates of return) to maximize the size of the pie. To maximize the size of the pie we must understand the impact of the magnitude, timing, and riskiness of the cash flows. Holding other things constant, we can visualize this as follows:

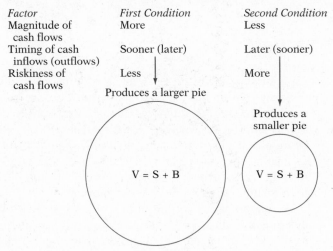

Factor	*First Condition*	*Second Condition*
Magnitude of cash flows	More	Less
Timing of cash inflows (outflows)	Sooner (later)	Later (sooner)
Riskiness of cash flows	Less	More
	Produces a larger pie	Produces a smaller pie
	$V = S + B$	$V = S + B$

It is to these topics we now turn our attention.

Calculating the **present value**, or **discounting**, involves finding the value today of an amount to be received in the future discounted at k percent per year. Finding the **future value**, or **compounding**, involves taking an amount today and determining what it will be worth sometime in the future if it earns a return of k percent per year. When discounting is used, k is the **discount rate**. When compounding is used, k is the **compound rate**. We begin by discussing both ideas, and then we will see how they are related.[1]

PRESENT VALUE

Let us begin with a situation where there are two dates—today and one period (or year) from now. For example, if you need $550 one year from now, how much would

---

[1]It is assumed all students have a basic calculator. However, many financial calculators are inexpensive, and they make financial calculations extremely simple. The footnotes in the rest of this chapter will assist you in using both basic and financial calculators.

you have to put aside today if you can earn 10 percent on the funds? We can use a timeline to show this graphically:[2]

Let us define the variables we will consider:

PV_0 = the present value today, at time $t = 0$, of the future amount
  k = the annual interest rate, which is 10 percent, or 0.10
 FV = the future, or ending, value of the amount, or $550
  t = the number of periods or years, which can vary from zero to infinity, but is a whole number, n

The present value of the amount desired in one year is found by discounting as follows:

$$\text{present value, } PV_0 = \frac{FV_1}{1 + k} \qquad (3.1)$$

Substituting, we find that the present value today of $550 to be received one year from now, discounted at 10 percent is

$$PV_0 = \frac{\$550}{(1.10)} = \$500$$

Next let us consider a case where there are cash flows at two dates, when these dates are not necessarily right next to each other. For example, the cash flows might occur today ($t = 0$) and three years from now ($t = 3$). Consider the following situation: What if you need $665.50 in three years? How much would you have to put aside today at a 10 percent annual compound interest rate to end up with the $665.50? Once again, we can use a timeline to show this graphically:

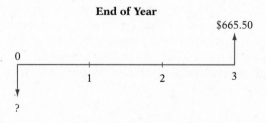

------

[2] By convention, the present value is usually shown as an outflow (with the arrow going down), and the future value is shown as an inflow (with the arrow going up).

Table 3.1

Present Value Factors for $1 Discounted at k Percent for n Periods:

$$PV_{k,n} = \frac{1}{(1 + k)^n}$$

PV factors for any period greater than zero are always less than 1. They decrease as the time period lengthens or the discount rate increases.

			Discount Rate, k				
Period, n	7%	8%	9%	10%	11%	12%	13%
1	0.935	0.926	0.917	0.909	0.901	0.893	0.885
2	0.873	0.857	0.842	0.826	0.812	0.797	0.783
3	0.816	0.794	0.772	0.751	0.731	0.712	0.693
4	0.763	0.735	0.708	0.683	0.659	0.636	0.613
5	0.713	0.681	0.650	0.621	0.593	0.567	0.543
6	0.666	0.630	0.596	0.564	0.535	0.507	0.480
7	0.623	0.583	0.547	0.513	0.482	0.452	0.425
8	0.582	0.540	0.502	0.467	0.434	0.404	0.376
9	0.544	0.500	0.460	0.424	0.391	0.361	0.333
10	0.508	0.463	0.422	0.386	0.352	0.322	0.295

To determine the amount to put aside today, the present value, we have[3]

$$PV_0 = \frac{FV_3}{(1 + k)^3} = \frac{\$665.50}{(1.10)(1.10)(1.10)} = \frac{\$665.50}{1.331} = \$500$$

The general equation for the present value of a single amount to be received n periods in the future, discounted at k percent, is

$$\text{present value, } PV_0 = \frac{FV_n}{(1 + k)^n} \tag{3.2}$$

The two cases just solved simply used Equation 3.2 with n = 1 and n = 3, respectively. Equation 3.2 may also be written as follows: $PV_0 = FV_n[1/(1 + k)^n]$. The term in brackets is called the **present value factor**, $PV_{k,n}$. Table 3.1 lists some of them; the more complete Table B.1 may be found at the end of the book. Using PV factors, the basic present value equation (Equation 3.2) is

$$PV_0 = FV_n(PV_{k,n}) \tag{3.3}$$

---

[3] Using a basic calculator, you divide $665.50 by $(1.10)^3$. With a financial calculator, you enter n = 3, i = k = 10, FV = 665.50, and then select PV to determine the answer of $500.

Thus,

$$PV_0 = FV_3(PV_{10\%,\,3yr}) = \$665.50(0.751) = \$499.79$$

Thus, with the exception of a rounding difference of 21 cents, Equations 3.2 and 3.3 provide the same result. We employ Equation 3.3 throughout the book.

FUTURE VALUE

So far, we have started with a future amount and then solved for a present value. Let us turn the situation around. Given a present value today at time $t = 0$, what is its future value at the end of time period $t = n$?

Finding the future value involves taking a cash flow today and determining what it will be worth sometime in the future if it earns a return of k percent per period. If you purchase a security worth $500 today that pays 10 percent interest compounded annually, how much will it be worth in one year? When compounding is employed, as is the case here, k is the compound rate. Graphically, this is

To answer this we take Equation 3.1 and solve for FV_1 to obtain

$$FV_1 = PV_0(1 + k) \qquad (3.4)$$

We can now use this relationship to find out how much your security is worth at the end of one year:

$$FV_1 = \$500(1 + 0.10) = \$500(1.10) = \$550$$

What about the value of your investment at the end of three years? Graphically this is

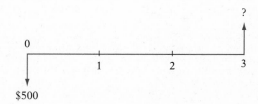

Table 3.2

Future Value Factors for $1 Compounded at k Percent for n Periods:

$$FV_{k,n} = (1 + k)^n$$

A more extensive table is presented as Table B.3 in the Appendix. Tables with four or five decimal places can be obtained if greater accuracy is needed.

				Compound Rate, k			
Period, n	7%	8%	9%	10%	11%	12%	13%
1	1.070	1.080	1.090	1.100	1.110	1.120	1.130
2	1.145	1.166	1.188	1.210	1.232	1.254	1.277
3	1.225	1.260	1.295	1.331	1.368	1.405	1.443
4	1.311	1.360	1.412	1.464	1.518	1.574	1.630
5	1.403	1.469	1.539	1.611	1.685	1.762	1.842
6	1.501	1.587	1.677	1.772	1.870	1.974	2.082
7	1.606	1.714	1.828	1.949	2.076	2.211	2.353
8	1.718	1.851	1.993	2.144	2.305	2.476	2.658
9	1.838	1.999	2.172	2.358	2.558	2.773	3.004
10	1.967	2.159	2.367	2.594	2.839	3.106	3.395

For a three-year period, we have

$$FV_3 = PV_0(1 + k)^3 = PV_0(1 + k)(1 + k)(1 + k)$$
$$= \$500(1.10)(1.10)(1.10) = \$500(1.331) = \$665.50$$

In general, the future value at the end of n periods is

$$\text{future value, } FV_n = PV_0(1 + k)^n \tag{3.5}$$

In the preceding examples we used Equation 3.5, first for n = 1, then for n = 3. With a calculator it is easy to compute the future value of any amount for any period of time.[4] However, tables are also available that provide **future value factors**, $FV_{k,n}$, for the quantity $(1 + k)^n$ in Equation 3.5. Table 3.2 is a portion of the more complete Table B.3, given at the end of the book. In terms of future value factors, Equation 3.5 can be rewritten as

$$FV_n = PV_0(FV_{k,n}) \tag{3.6}$$

---

[4] To solve for the value $(1.10)^3$ with a basic calculator, it is necessary to use the exponential function, y^x. In this problem, y = 1.10, n = x = 3, y^x = 1.331, and FV_3 = \$500(1.331) = \$665.50. If you have a financial calculator, simply enter n = 3, k = i = 10, and PV = 500, and then select FV to obtain the answer of \$665.50.

Using this equation, we find the future value is

$$FV_3 = PV_0(FV_{10\%,\,3yr}) = \$500(1.331) = \$665.50$$

Thus, the same future sum, $665.50, is obtained by using Equation 3.5 or Equation 3.6 and the FV table. We employ Equation 3.6 throughout the book.

COMPARING PRESENT VALUE AND FUTURE VALUE

Because a thorough understanding of present value versus future value is essential, let us pause for a moment and make sure we understand that these two concepts are simply the inverse of one another. If we start with the general equation of compounding, which is Equation 3.5,

$$FV_n = PV_0(1 + k)^n$$

we see that by dividing through by the quantity $(1 + k)^n$ and simplifying, we have the basic equation for present value, Equation 3.2: $PV_0 = FV_n/(1 + k)^n$.

In terms of future value versus present value factors, the $PV_{k,n}$ factor is the reciprocal of the $FV_{k,n}$ for the same discount rate and time period, so that

$$PV_{k,n} = \frac{1}{FV_{k,n}}$$

For example, the PV factor for 10 percent and three years of 0.751 is simply the comparable FV factor divided into 1, or

$$PV_{10\%,\,3yr} = \frac{1}{FV_{10\%,\,3yr}} = \frac{1}{1.331} = 0.751$$

This corresponds to the 10 percent three-year PV factor presented in Table 3.1.

These relationships hold for all comparable rates and time periods. So it should be easy to see that discounting to find present values and compounding to find future values are simply the inverse of one another. Present values are always less than the future value; as shown in Table 3.1, the PV factors are always less than 1 and decline with both time and the discount rate used. Similarly, when we are compounding, future values will always be higher than the initial amount; as shown in Table 3.2, FV factors are always greater than 1 and increase both with time and with the compounding rate. This relationship between PV factors, FV factors, interest rates, and time is shown in Figure 3.1. Note the effect that both time and the interest rates have on FV and PV factors.

Figure 3.1

Relationship Between $FV_{k,n}$ $PV_{k,n}$, Interest Rates, and Time

Because of compounding, $FV_{k,n}$ becomes steeper and steeper over time, indicating that the future values grow larger the longer the period and the higher the rate. Similarly, because of discounting, $PV_{k,n}$ becomes flatter and flatter over time.

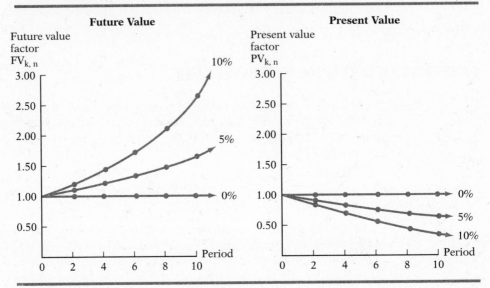

Concept Review Questions

- Explain how you would find the present and future values of a single cash flow.
- How do the $PV_{k,n}$ factor and the $FV_{k,n}$ factor relate to each other?

WHEN THERE ARE MULTIPLE CASH FLOWS

Up to now we have considered situations that involve only two cash flows and dates. It is also necessary to deal with a series of cash flows. Let us begin by discussing the present value of a *perpetuity*, which is simply a series of cash flows of the same amount that continues indefinitely. Then we will consider the special case of an *annuity*, where the constant cash flows continue for only a finite period of time. Finally, we will examine the case of an uneven series of cash flows.

PERPETUITIES

Instead of single cash flows, let us go to the other extreme and consider how to value a series of cash flows of a constant amount that goes on forever—a **perpetuity**. The present value of a perpetuity with the first payment starting one period from now is equal to the constant cash flow stream, often called PMT (for payment), divided by the discount rate k, as follows:[5]

$$\text{present value of a perpetuity, } PV_0 = \frac{\text{annual cash flow}}{\text{discount rate}} = \frac{PMT}{k} \qquad (3.7)$$

Thus, if you have a benefactor who will provide a perpetuity of $140 per year *beginning 1 period (or year) from now*, discounted at 7 percent, so that

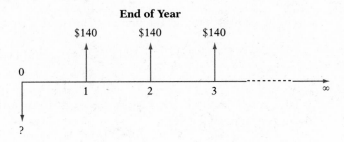

its present value is

$$PV_0 = \frac{PMT}{k} = \frac{\$140}{0.07} = \$2,000$$

Growing Perpetuities Suppose that instead of a constant amount per year, the size of the payment provided by your benefactor is growing at a constant (percentage) rate of 3 percent per year, so the cash flow stream is:

---

[5] We can verify Equation 3.7 by starting with the present value equation when there are many (an infinite number of) cash flows. Letting the individual future cash flows, the FVs, be PMT because they are the same amount in each future period,

$$PV_0 = \frac{PMT}{(1+k)} + \frac{PMT}{(1+k)^2} + \frac{PMT}{(1+k)^3} + \cdots$$

Let $PMT/(1+k) = a$ and $1/(1+k) = x$. Then

$$PV_0 = a(1 + x + x^2 + \cdots) \qquad (1)$$

Multiplying both sides by x produces

$$xPV_0 = a(x + x^2 + \cdots) \qquad (2)$$

Subtracting (2) from (1) gives

$$PV_0(1 - x) = a$$

Substituting in for a and x, and rearranging, gives

$$PV_0 = PMT/k$$

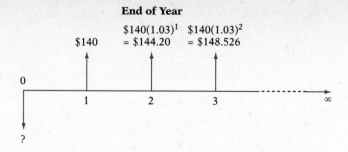

Given the **growth rate, g**, the present value of this stream of growing cash flows is

$$PV_0 = \frac{PMT}{(1 + k)^1} + \frac{PMT(1 + g)^1}{(1 + k)^2} + \frac{PMT(1 + g)^2}{(1 + k)^3} + \cdots$$

As long as the discount rate, k, is greater than the growth rate, g, this complicated-looking equation simplifies to[6]

$$\text{present value of a growing perpetuity, } PV_0 = \frac{PMT}{k - g} \quad\quad (3.8)$$

With the size of the cash flow increasing by 3 percent per year, the value of your growing perpetuity is

$$PV_0 = \frac{PMT}{0.07 - 0.03} = \frac{\$140}{0.04} = \$3,500$$

As common sense tells us, the value of a growing perpetuity must be substantially greater than the value of a level perpetuity.

PRESENT VALUE OF AN ORDINARY ANNUITY

Once we understand how to value perpetuities, it is easy to value an **annuity**, which is just a limited-life perpetuity. That is, an annuity is a series of cash flows of the same amount that continues for a limited period of time, say four years. Consider the case in which a promise is made to pay $600 at the *end* of each of four years as follows:

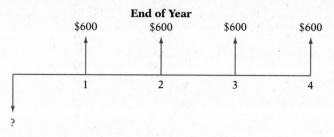

---

[6] As in footnote 5, we need to determine the sum of the infinite geometric series $PV_0 = a(1 + x + x^2 + \cdots)$ where a is PMT/1 + k) and x is now $(1 + g)/(1 + k)$. Substituting variables in and simplifying results in

$$PV_0 = PMT_1/(k - g)$$

Figure 3.2

The Present Value of an Annuity Equals the Difference in the Present Value of Two Perpetuities

An ordinary, or typical, perpetuity has constant cash flows that begin at time $t = 1$ and continue to infinity. A delayed perpetuity has constant cash flows that begin at time $n + 1$ and continue to infinity. By determining the present value at time $t = 0$ of the delayed perpetuity and subtracting it from the present value of the ordinary perpetuity, we determine the present value of an annuity that has constant cash flows from time $t = 1$ to time $t = n$.

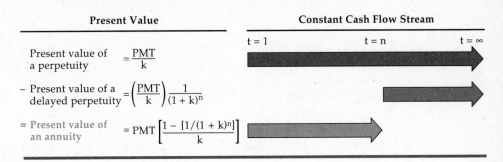

Present Value		Constant Cash Flow Stream

Present value of a perpetuity $= \dfrac{PMT}{k}$

$-$ Present value of a delayed perpetuity $= \left(\dfrac{PMT}{k}\right)\dfrac{1}{(1+k)^n}$

$=$ Present value of an annuity $= PMT\left[\dfrac{1 - [1/(1+k)^n]}{k}\right]$

(When the cash flows occur at the end of each period, this is an **ordinary annuity**.) If the discount rate is 10 percent, what is the present value of this annuity?

Figure 3.2 indicates that there is an easy way to determine the present value of an annuity. For an typical perpetuity with the first cash flow starting one year from now, its value (as given by Equation 3.7) is

$$PV_0 = \frac{PMT}{k}$$

Now consider a second perpetuity that does not begin its cash flows until time period $n + 1$. That is, the second perpetuity is a *delayed perpetuity* whose constant cash flows start $n + 1$ periods in the future. The present value of this delayed perpetuity *at time n* is PMT/k, so its present value *today* (at $t = 0$) is

$$\text{present value of delayed perpetuity, } PV_0 = \left(\frac{PMT}{k}\right)\frac{1}{(1+k)^n}$$

Both perpetuities provide payments from time period $n + 1$ onward. The first perpetuity also provides cash flows from period 1 to period n. Therefore, as shown in Figure 3.2, by taking the difference between the present value of the typical perpetuity and the present value of the delayed perpetuity we have the present value of an annuity of amount PMT for n periods, or years. This is

$$\text{present value of an (ordinary) annuity, } PV_0 = PMT\left[\frac{1}{k} - \frac{1}{k(1+k)^n}\right]$$

which can be simplified further to

$$\text{present value of an (ordinary) annuity, } PV_0 = PMT\left[\frac{1 - [1/(1 + k)^n]}{k}\right] \quad (3.9)$$

The present value of an annuity of $600 to be received at the end of each of the next four years discounted at 10 percent is

$$PV_0 = \$600\left[\frac{1 - [1/(1 + 0.10)^4]}{0.10}\right] = \$600(3.1698\ldots) \approx \$1,902$$

Tables are available for the bracketed portion in Equation 3.9; these are called **present value factors for an annuity, $PVA_{k,n}$.** Table 3.3 illustrates these; Table B.2 is more complete.

Using the table, the present value of this annuity is

$$PV_0 = PMT(PVA_{k,n})$$
$$PV_0 = \$600(PVA_{10\%,4yr}) = \$600(3.170) = \$1,902 \quad (3.10)$$

Table 3.3

Present Value Factors for an Annuity of $1 Discounted at k Percent for n Periods:

$$PVA_{k,n} = \frac{1 - [1/(1 + k)^n]}{k}$$

The PVA factor is always less than the number of years the annuity is received (or paid). Note that the PVA factor (3.170) used in our example to find the present value of a four-year annuity at 10 percent is less than 4.

Period, n	Discount Rate, k						
	7%	8%	9%	10%	11%	12%	13%
1	0.935	0.926	0.917	0.909	0.901	0.893	0.885
2	1.808	1.783	1.759	1.736	1.713	1.690	1.668
3	2.624	2.577	2.531	2.487	2.444	2.402	2.361
4	3.387	3.312	3.240	3.170	3.102	3.037	2.974
5	4.100	3.993	3.890	3.791	3.696	3.605	3.517
6	4.767	4.623	4.486	4.355	4.231	4.111	3.998
7	5.389	5.206	5.033	4.868	4.712	4.564	4.423
8	5.971	5.747	5.535	5.335	5.146	4.968	4.799
9	6.515	6.247	5.995	5.759	5.537	5.328	5.132
10	7.024	6.710	6.418	6.145	5.889	5.650	5.426

With the exception of a small rounding difference, Equations 3.9 and 3.10 produce the same result.[7] We employ Equation 3.10 throughout the book.

PRESENT VALUE OF AN ANNUITY DUE

Although our primary concern is with ordinary annuities, what if the four cash inflows in the example above had occurred at the *beginning* of each period, not the end? This is the case of an **annuity due**. Each of the payments is shifted back one period, or year, on the timeline, so they now occur at $t = 0$, $t = 1$, $t = 2$, and $t = 3$:

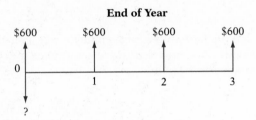

If we were to apply either of the equations for the present value of an annuity (Equation 3.9 or 3.10) directly, the resulting present value would actually be at time $t = -1$ and not at time $t = 0$, where we want it. This is true because the present value of a series of cash flows always represents the value one period before the initial flow occurs. Therefore, to calculate the present value of an annuity due, we multiply the present values determined before by the term $(1 + k)$. Equations 3.9 and 3.10 become

$$PV_0(\text{annuity due}) = PMT\left[\frac{1 - [1/(1 + k)^n]}{k}\right](1 + k) \qquad (3.9a)$$

and

$$PV_0(\text{annuity due}) = PMT(PVA_{k,n})(1 + k) \qquad (3.10a)$$

For our example, the present value in the case of an annuity due is[8]

$$PV_0(\text{annuity due}) = \$600(3.170)(1.10) = \$2,092$$

Since the payments are made in advance, the present value of an annuity due is more valuable than that of an ordinary annuity.

---

[7] Using a financial calculator, enter $n = 4$, $i = k = 10$, $PMT = 600$, and then select PV to produce the answer of $\$1,901.91 \approx \$1,902$.

[8] An alternative way to solve this problem is to (1) look up the $PVA_{k,n}$ for $n - 1$ periods, and (2) then add 1.0. The $PVA_{10\%, 3\,yr}$ is 2.487. Adding 1.0, we find that the PVA for a 10 percent four-year annuity due is 3.487. PV_0 (annuity due) = $\$600(3.487) = \$2,092.20$.

FUTURE VALUE OF AN ORDINARY ANNUITY

What if, instead of finding the present value of an annuity, we need to find its future value? If you receive $600 at the end of each year and immediately invest it at 10 percent, how much will you have at the end of the four years? Graphically this is

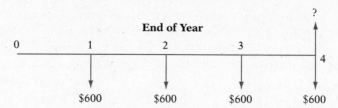

To find the future value of an annuity, we can make use of the knowledge developed previously. We know that the present value (at time t = 0) of an annuity, as given by Equation 3.9, is

$$PV_0 = PMT\left[\frac{1 - [1/(1 + k)^n]}{k}\right]$$

And we also know that we can move any single (or lump sum) present value to the future, using Equation 3.5 as follows:

$$FV_n = PV_0(1 + k)^n$$

Therefore, the future value of an annuity is equal to its present value at time t = 0 multiplied by the appropriate future value factor, so

$$FV_n = PMT\left[\frac{1 - [1/(1 + k)^n]}{k}\right](1 + k)^n$$

This simplifies to

$$\text{future value of an (ordinary) annuity, } FV_n = PMT\left[\frac{(1 + k)^n - 1}{k}\right] \qquad (3.11)$$

The future value of an annuity of $600 to be received at the end of each of the next four years at 10 percent is[9]

$$FV_4 = \$600\left[\frac{(1 + 0.10)^4 - 1}{0.10}\right] = \$2,784.60$$

Alternatively, **future value factors for an annuity, $FVA_{k,n}$,** have been calculated

---

[9] Using a financial calculator, enter n = 4, i = k = 10, PMT = 600, and then select FV to produce the same answer of $2,784.60.

Table 3.4

Future Value Factors for an Annuity of $1 Compounded at k Percent for n Periods:

$$FVA_{k,n} = \frac{(1 + k)^n - 1}{k}$$

The FVA factor is always greater than or equal to the number of years the annuity is received (or paid). In our example the annuity is received for four years at 10 percent. The corresponding FVA factor is 4.641, which is greater than 4.

Period, n	Compound Rate, k						
	7%	8%	9%	10%	11%	12%	13%
1	1.000	1.000	1.000	1.000	1.000	1.000	1.000
2	2.070	2.080	2.090	2.100	2.110	2.120	2.130
3	3.215	3.246	3.278	3.310	3.342	3.374	3.407
4	4.440	4.506	4.573	4.641	4.710	4.779	4.850
5	5.751	5.867	5.985	6.105	6.228	6.353	6.480
6	7.153	7.336	7.523	7.716	7.913	8.115	8.323
7	8.654	8.923	9.200	9.487	9.783	10.089	10.405
8	10.260	10.637	11.028	11.436	11.859	12.300	12.757
9	11.978	12.488	13.021	13.579	14.164	14.776	15.416
10	13.816	14.487	15.193	15.937	16.722	17.549	18.420

for the bracketed portion of Equation 3.11. These are presented in Table 3.4; a more complete table is Table B.4 at the end of the book.

In terms of the table values, the future value of an ordinary annuity is

$$FV_n = PMT(FVA_{k,n}) \tag{3.12}$$

$$FV_4 = \$600(FVA_{10\%, 4yr}) = \$600(4.641) = \$2{,}784.60$$

Either Equation 3.11 or 3.12 produces exactly the same value. We employ Equation 3.12 throughout the book.

FUTURE VALUE OF AN ANNUITY DUE

With the cash flows occurring at the beginning of the year, they must be compounded forward an extra year to determine the future value of an annuity due, so that

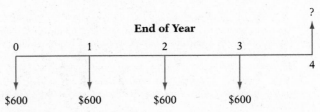

Because each cash flow is compounded for an extra year, Equations 3.11 and 3.12 are modified as follows:

$$FV_n(\text{annuity due}) = PMT\left[\frac{(1 + k)^n - 1}{k}\right](1 + k) \qquad (3.11a)$$

and

$$FV_n(\text{annuity due}) = PMT(FVA_{k,n})(1 + k) \qquad (3.12a)$$

Solving the earlier example as an annuity due, we have[10]

$$FV(\text{annuity due}) = \$600(4.641)(1.10) = \$3,063.06$$

The future value of an annuity due is larger than the future value of an ordinary annuity because of the extra year's compounding. Other things being equal, an annuity due is more valuable.

PRESENT VALUE OF AN UNEVEN CASH FLOW SERIES

It is also important to understand how to determine the present value when an uneven series of cash flows occurs. First, consider cash flows of $100 at year 1, $150 at year 2, $325 at year 3, and a discount rate of 12 percent. Graphically, this is

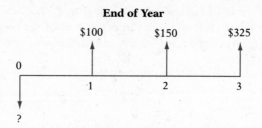

The general equation to find the present value of any series of cash flows is

$$\text{present value of any cash flow series, } PV_0 = \sum_{t=1}^{n} \frac{FV_t}{(1 + k)^t} = \sum_{t=1}^{n} FV_t(PV_{k,t}) \qquad (3.13)$$

Using Equation 3.13, we have:[11]

---

[10] An alternative way to solve this problem is to look up the $FVA_{k,n}$ for $n + 1$ periods and subtract 1.0. The $FVA_{10\%,5\,yr}$ is 6.105. Subtracting 1.0, the FVA for a 10 percent four-year annuity due is 5.105. Calculating the future value of the annuity due, we have FV_4 (annuity due) = $600(5.105) = $3,063.00, which is the same answer as before except for a rounding difference of six cents.

[11] With a financial calculator, you enter the three cash inflows, and $i = k = 12$. Selecting present value (typically called NPV, for net present value) produces the answer of $440.19. The six cent difference results from rounding.

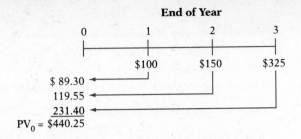

Year	Cash Flow	× PV$_{12\%,n}$ =	Present Value of Cash Flows
1	$100	0.893	$ 89.30
2	150	0.797	119.55
3	325	0.712	231.40
			PV$_0$ = $440.25

Now consider another example in which the cash flows are $100 at year 1, $150 at year 2, and then $325 for *each* of years 3 through 8, so that

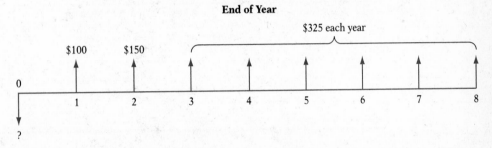

The discount rate remains 12 percent. This problem can be solved in eight separate steps using Equation 3.13, but time can be saved by using the techniques we have learned for annuities. To solve, proceed as follows:

STEP 1:   Determine the present value at t = 2 of the annuity of $325 to be received in years 3 through 8. Because this annuity is for 6 years (years 3, 4, 5, 6, 7, and 8), its present value at t = 2 is

$$PV_2 = \$325(PVA_{12\%,6\,yr}) = \$325\ (4.111) = \$1{,}336.08$$

STEP 2:   The lump sum of $1,336.08 is then discounted back to time t = 0, which is $1,064.86 [i.e., ($1,336.08)(PV$_{12\%,2\,yr}$) = ($1,336.08)(0.797)], as shown in Figure 3.3.[12]

---

[12] An alternative way to obtain the present value of the annuity portion is to multiply the annuity stream PMT by the difference in an 8-year PVA minus a 2-year PVA factor. Thus, $325[(PVA$_{12\%,8\,yr}$) − (PVA$_{12\%,2\,yr}$)] = $325(4.968 − 1.690) = $325 (3.278) = $1,065.35. Except for a rounding difference of 49 cents, this is the same result for the annuity portion of the example obtained from the procedure described in steps 1 and 2.

Figure 3.3

Present Value of an Eight-Year Uneven Series Incorporating an Annuity, Discounted at 12 Percent

Instead of six separate steps, it is easier and faster to use the PVA factor to value the annuity at time t = 2 and then discount it to time t = 0.

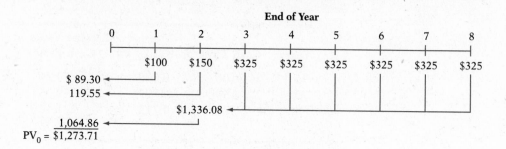

Year	Cash Flow × PV$_{12\%, n}$ =		Present Value of Cash Flow
1	$ 100	0.893	$ 89.30
2	150	0.797	119.55
3	1,336.08^a	0.797	1,064.86
			PV$_0$ = $1,273.71

^{a}Year	Cash Flow × PVA$_{12\%, 6yr}$ =		Present Value of Years 3-8 Cash Flows, at End of Year 2
3-8	$325	4.111	$1,336.08

STEP 3: Discount the $100 to be received at the end of year 1 and the $150 to be received at the end of year 2 back to time t = 0. The amounts are $89.30 and $119.55, respectively.

STEP 4: Sum the values from steps 2 and 3. Thus, $89.30 + $119.55 + $1,064.86 = $1,273.71. This is the present value of the entire cash flow series discounted at 12 percent.[13]

Concept Review Questions

- Explain how you would find the present and future values of multiple cash flows.
- What is the difference between an ordinary annuity and an annuity due?
- How do you modify the equations for the present value and future value of an ordinary annuity to determine the future and present value of an annuity due?

---

[13] Using a financial calculator, the present value is $1,274.08. The 37 cent difference results from rounding.

DETERMINING INTEREST RATES

In many cases both the present value (or cash outflow) at time t = 0 and the future cash flows and timing are known, but the interest or discount rate is not. We begin by examining individual cash flows, and then consider annuities and the case of a series of uneven cash flows.

INDIVIDUAL CASHFLOWS

Suppose you borrowed $1,000 today and agreed to pay the principal (of $1,000) and interest back in a lump sum in five years. The agreed payment at that time is $2,011. What compound annual rate of interest are you paying on the loan? To answer that question, we start with the present value formula given by Equation 3.3, $PV_0 = FV_n(PV_{k,n})$, and solve for the present value factor, which is

$$PV_{k,n} = \frac{PV_0}{FV_n} \qquad (3.14)$$

To determine the interest rate, we simply solve Equation 3.14 for the PV factor, and then look up the value of the PV factor in Table B.1 for the appropriate year. Thus

$$PV_{?\%,\, 5yr} = \frac{\$1,000}{\$2,011} = 0.497$$

Looking across the period (year) 5 row, we find the value of 0.497 in the 15 percent column.[14] The rate of interest on a $1,000 loan that will be paid back as a lump sum of $2,011 in five years is 15 percent.

Because present value and future value are mirror images of one another, this problem could be solved by using FV factors instead of PV factors. In this case, we would use Equation 3.6, $FV_n = PV_0(FV_{k,n})$, and solve for the future value factor. Therefore,

$$FV_{k,n} = \frac{FV_n}{PV_0} \qquad (3.14a)$$

In our example,

$$FV_{?\%,\, 5yr} = \frac{\$2,011}{\$1,000} = 2.011$$

---

[14] A financial calculator makes this an easy problem to solve. If you enter in n = 5, PV = 1,000, and FV = 2,011 and then select i = k, the answer is 14.995 percent. The same result can be obtained by using Equation 3.2 to solve for k, the unknown interest rate. This results in

$$k = \left(\frac{FV_n}{PV_0}\right)^{1/n} - 1 = \left(\frac{\$2,011}{\$1,000}\right)^{1/5} - 1 = 0.14995 \text{ or } 14.995 \text{ percent}$$

Looking across the period (year) 5 row in Table B.3, we find that the FV factor under the 15 percent column is 2.011, indicating once again that the unknown annual interest rate is 15 percent.

ANNUITIES

Precisely the same approach can be used when an (ordinary) annuity is being considered. Suppose you borrow $2,124.90 today and agree to repay $900 at the end of each of the next three years. What is the annual rate of interest you are paying on the loan? To determine this, we solve Equation 3.10, $PV_0 = PMT(PVA_{k,n})$, for the PVA factor, which is

$$PVA_{k,n} = \frac{PV_0}{PMT} \qquad (3.15)$$

$$PVA_{?\%, 3\,yr} = \frac{\$2,214.90}{\$900} = 2.361$$

Looking across the period (year) 3 row in Table B.2, we find the PVA of 2.361 under the 13 percent column. Thus, the interest rate on the loan is 13 percent.[15]

In both examples the interest rates turned out to be whole percents—15 percent in the first case, 13 percent in the second. In practice this rarely happens, and you are left with one of three alternatives: Determine the interest rate to the nearest percent, use a financial calculator, or estimate where it falls between two rates.

UNEVEN CASHFLOW SERIES

Unfortunately, determining the interest rate becomes more difficult if the series is uneven. Essentially you are left with two options—a trial-and-error approach or using a calculator that has an internal rate of return function. To illustrate the trial-and-error approach, suppose you invest $352.31 today, and the series of payments promised is $80 at t = 1, $125 at t = 2, and $225 at t = 3. What is your expected annual compound percentage return? With this approach, it is necessary to determine what set of PV factors associated with a specific interest rate causes *the present value of the cash inflows to equal exactly the initial present value*, PV_0. We want to determine what interest rate causes the present value of $80 at year 1, $125 at year 2, and $225 at year 3 to equal exactly the present value of $352.31. As shown in Table 3.5, at a 12 percent discount rate the present value of $331.26 is too low, so the discount rate must be lowered. If we use 8 percent, the present value of $359.85 is greater than the PV_0 of $352.31, so the discount rate must be increased. The actual interest rate that equates the present value of the expected cash inflows with $352.31 is 9 percent. Thus, the

---

[15] With a financial calculator, we enter in PV = 2,124.90, PMT = 900, and n = 3 and then select i = k to produce the exact interest rate of 13.004 percent.

Table 3.5

Solving for the Interest Rate in an Uneven Cash Flow Series with the Trial-and-Error Method

The trial-and-error method can be time-consuming. Two recommendations: First, make the first estimate some "reasonable" number, perhaps between 10 and 20 percent. Second, when adjusting interest rates for a new trial, jump as much as 5 to 10 percent the first time or two in order to bracket the actual rate. Once the rate is bracketed, you can estimate it and solve for the actual rate fairly quickly.

Decision Rule: Find the discount rate that equates the present value of the cash inflows with the present value, PV_0.

Step 1: Try 12 Percent

Year	Cash Inflow	×	$PV_{12\%, n}$	=	Present Value of Cash Inflow
1	$ 80		0.893		$ 71.44
2	125		0.797		99.62
3	225		0.712		160.20
					$331.26

Because the present value of the inflows of $331.26 is *less* than $352.31, the discount rate must be *lowered*.

Step 2: Try 8 Percent

Year	Cash Inflow	×	$PV_{8\%, n}$	=	Present Value of Cash Inflow
1	$ 80		0.926		$ 74.08
2	125		0.857		107.12
3	225		0.794		178.65
					$359.85

Because the present value of the inflows of $359.85 is *greater* than $352.31, the discount rate must be *increased*.

Step 3: Try 9 Percent

Year	Cash Inflow	×	$PV_{9\%, n}$	=	Present Value of Cash Inflow
1	$ 80		0.917		$ 73.36
2	125		0.842		105.25
3	225		0.772		173.70
					$352.31

Because the present value of the inflows of $352.31 *exactly equals* $352.31, the discount rate is 9 percent.

annual interest rate, or return on the investment, is 9 percent.[16] Normally with uneven cash flows, the interest rate does not come out exactly equal to some whole percent. In that case, estimating is required in conjunction with the trial-and-error approach.

Concept Review Questions

■ Explain how you would find the unknown interest rate when you are dealing with a present value and a single future lump sum amount.

■ How do you find the unknown interest rate for an uneven cash flow series?

APPLICATIONS IN FINANCIAL MANAGEMENT

The concept of the time value of money may still seem a bit abstract. In fact, it has numerous applications in financial management. Five are investment decision making, growth rates, future sums, effective interest rates, and mortgage calculations, but many other uses will appear throughout the book.

INVESTMENT DECISION MAKING

Firms invest in many different assets. These include tangible assets such as buildings and machinery as well as intangible assets such as patents, research and development programmes, and training for employees. Firms need a frame of reference, or a decision-making process, that allows them to ask the right questions at the right time to make effective decisions so that the firm prospers.

Suppose as a member of the management team of Ventura Ltd. it is your responsibility to evaluate new business ventures. An exciting new three-year venture has just been brought to you for evaluation. The total cash outflow required to undertake this project at t = 0 is $222,489, and it is expected to produce cash inflows of $75,000 at t = 1, $117,000 at t = 2, and $210,000 at t = 3. The decision you face is simple: Do you proceed with the venture?

Net Present Value and Internal Rate of Return   To answer that question we have to compare the present value of the future cash inflows with the $222,489 cash outflow to be made today. That comparison rests on understanding how to determine the

---

[16] If the trial-and-error approach is used, the question often asked is "What interest rate should I start with?" One approach is to calculate a "simulated" annuity by summing the inflows and then dividing by the number of periods. Thus, ($80 + $125 + $225)/3 = $430/3 = $143.33. Dividing the present value of $352.31 by the simulated annuity of $143.33 gives a PVA factor of 2.458, which indicates what the rate would be *if* the series were in fact an annuity. The period (year) 3 row of Table B.2 indicates that the simulated annuity discount rate is between 10 and 11 percent. *Then you have to proceed by trial-and-error, as in Table 3.5, starting at 10 percent* to determine the exact answer.

With a financial clauclator, enter in the present value, PV, of 352.31; the future returns of 80, 125, and 225; and then select IRR = k. The rate is 9.005 ≈ 9 percent.

present value of a set of future cash flows, or, alternatively, how to determine the rate of return you will earn on your investment. In order to enhance the value of the firm, the present value of all future cash inflows must exceed the initial cost of the investment. Another way to state this relationship is to determine the net present value of the investment, which is

net present value, NPV = present value of future cash inflows − initial investment

Or more formally

$$NPV = \sum_{t=1}^{n} \frac{CF_t}{(1 + k)^t} - PV_0 \qquad (3.16)$$

Where k, the discount rate, is the return demanded for accepting the delayed receipt of the cash inflows.

If we initially assume the new venture is a sure thing, then what kind of return, k, would you demand on the investment? A completely safe alternative is to invest in Government of Canada securities that mature in three years. Suppose that three-year government securities are yielding 8 percent. Then the appropriate discount rate for this venture is 8 percent and its NPV is

$$NPV = \$75,000(PV_{8\%, 1yr}) + \$117,000 (PV_{8\%, 2yr})$$
$$+ \$210,000(PV_{8\%, 3yr}) - \$222,489$$
$$= \$75,000(0.926) + \$117,000(0.857) + \$210,000(0.794) - \$222,489$$
$$= \$336,459 - \$222,489 = \$139,920$$

Should you make the investment? That is easy to answer: By making an investment of \$222,489, you are acquiring something that is worth (in present value terms) \$336,459. Thus, you should invest in the new venture because it makes a net contribution to value of \$139,920 after considering the timing of the expected cash flows and the alternative use of the funds.

Instead of calculating the net present value of the proposed new venture, we can make the same decision another way. This approach involves finding the *rate of return* on the project. To do this we employ the principles learned in the "Determining Interest Rates" section to find a rate of return that equates the present value of the cash inflows to the initial investment. More formally, the **internal rate of return (IRR)** is determined by solving for the unknown rate in the following equation:

$$\sum_{t=1}^{n} \frac{CF_t}{(1 + IRR)^t} = PV_0 \qquad (3.17)$$

The IRR for our new venture must be found by trial-and-error since the project provides an uneven series of future cash inflows. The final step of that process for an IRR of 30 percent is shown below:

Year	Cash Inflow	× PV$_{30\%,n}$	= Present Value of Cash Inflow
1	$ 75,000	0.769	$ 57,675
2	117,000	0.592	69,264
3	210,000	0.455	95,550
			$222,489

Because the present value of the inflows of $222,489 *exactly equals* the initial investment for the project at 30 percent, its IRR is 30 percent. Although this *internal rate of return* may initially seem strange to you, it is nothing more than a compound rate of interest.[17] Consequently, by investing in the project you achieve a return of 30 percent. Because this return is greater than the 8 percent you could earn by investing in an equally risky alternative, you would accept the project.

Thus, we have two ways to make the capital investment decision:[18]

1. NET PRESENT VALUE   Accept the proposed opportunity if the NPV is positive. The net present value is equal to the present value of the future cash inflows minus the initial investment required.
2. INTERNAL RATE OF RETURN   Accept the proposed opportunity if the return is greater than the discount rate, k. The return is the compound return earned based on the initial investment and the future cash inflows.

What About Risk?   Until now we have assumed the investment in the new venture was a sure thing. However, that assumption is unrealistic. In practice, not many investments (except short-term government securities) provide a risk-free return. You know the investment in the office complex is riskier than the investment in government securities. At the same time it is probably not as risky as investing in a professional soccer team or digging for gold. Let us say that based on your own knowledge and information you received from other members of the management team, you conclude the risk of the new venture is equal to that of the stock market. The firm's financial markets expert forecasts a 14 percent return from the stock market for the next three years. Now the discount rate, k, employed to make the decision becomes 14 percent and the net present value is

$$NPV = \$75,000(PV_{14\%,1yr}) + 117,000(PV_{14\%,2yr}) + \$210,000(PV_{14\%,3yr})$$
$$- \$222,489$$
$$= \$75,000(0.877) + \$117,000(0.769) + \$210,000(0.675) - \$222,489$$
$$= \$297,498 - \$222,489 = \$75,009$$

---

[17] Chapters 4 and 7 include detailed discussions of internal rate of return, both for determining the yield to maturity on a bond and for capital budgeting purposes.

[18] The two decision criteria may not always produce the same decision. This topic is explored in Chapter 7. At that time we will discuss why net present value provides a better basis for decision making than internal rate of return.

The investment is not as attractive now as it was before. However, you should still proceed, because the present value of the future cash inflows is greater than the initial cash outflow of $222,489. Using the internal rate of return, the comparison is now between a return of 30 percent and one of 14 percent from an equally risky alternative investment. Again, you would make the investment. Later in the book we have a lot to say about risk and how it should be dealt with in capital investment decisions. For the present, just remember that *risk is one of the major items* that has to be considered in every financial decision.

The Opportunity Cost of Capital   Before proceeding we need to explore another topic briefly: the rate k employed as the discount rate when calculating the net present value, or the rate that the internal rate of return is compared to. The terms discount rate, required return, **hurdle rate**, and **opportunity cost of capital** are used interchangeably. It is considered the *required rate of return* because it is what investors or firms seek as the reward for making an investment now and receiving payments (cash inflows) at some time in the future. It is a *hurdle rate* when it is employed as the standard against which the internal rate of return is compared. It is an *opportunity cost* because it is the return forgone by investing in a specific asset rather than investing in some equally risky investment, such as the stock market. In the above example, the required rate of return, hurdle rate, or opportunity cost of capital was 8 percent in the absence of risk; it was 14 percent once the risk of the new venture was considered. Appendix 3A demonstrates that firms create value by accepting positive net present value investments in real assets which return more than the firm's opportunity cost of capital. Determining the required rate of return, or opportunity cost of capital, is discussed in detail in Chapter 6. In general, dealing with uncertainty requires the use of higher discount rates for the opportunity cost of capital. Throughout our discussion of capital investment decision making in Chapters 7 through 9, and elsewhere in the book, we use the terms required rate of return, discount rate, hurdle rate, and opportunity cost of capital *assuming there is uncertainty.* Hence, a higher discount rate than the risk-free rate is appropriate.

GROWTH RATES

It is frequently useful to estimate growth rates from financial data. For example, suppose that Emery Brothers had sales of $15 million in 19X5 and estimates that by 19X9 its sales will be $35 million. What compound rate of growth is Emery predicting?

First, we need to determine the number of time periods by subtracting 19X5 from 19X9. There are four years *between* the two dates. (Not five! Be sure *not* to count both the first and last years.) Then we simply employ a modification of Equation 3.14 (for determining interest rates):

$$PV_{?\%,\,4yr} = \frac{\text{beginning value}}{\text{ending value}} = \frac{\$15 \text{ million}}{35 \text{ million}} = 0.429$$

Reading across the period (year) 4 row of Table B.1, we find that a PV factor of 0.429 lies between 23 percent and 24 percent.

Alternatively, we could have used Equation 3.14a:

$$FV_{?\%,\,4yr} = \frac{\text{ending value}}{\text{beginning value}} = \frac{\$35 \text{ million}}{\$15 \text{ milion}} = 2.333$$

Reading across the period (year) 4 row of Table B.3, we also find that an FV factor of 2.333 lies between 23 and 24 percent. The rate is a bit closer to 24 percent, so call it 23.6 percent.[19] Obviously, Emery Brothers expects rapid sales growth over the next four years.

FUTURE SUMS

Another application of time value is accumulating to a future sum. Consider Consolidated Electronics, which, as an inducement to retaining its president, has promised a bonus of $10 million on retirement, seven years hence. If Consolidated can earn 8 percent on its money and plans to start making annual payments one year from now to fund the retirement bonus, how much will each payment have to be?

The first step is to recognize that this is a future value of an annuity problem. We therefore employ Equation 3.12:

$$FV_n = PMT(FVA_{k,\,n})$$
$$\$10 \text{ million} = PMT(FVA_{8\%,\,7yr})$$
$$PMT = \$10 \text{ million}/8.923 = \$1,120,699.32$$

Thus, Consolidated Electronics will have to set aside more than $1.1 million every year to fund the retirement bonus.[20]

EFFECTIVE INTEREST RATES

Another application involves finding the effective annual interest rate. From the standpoint of the borrower, this is the effective before-tax percentage cost; from the standpoint of the lender, it is the effective before-tax percentage return. Before deter-

---

[19] With a financial calculator we enter in PV = 15, FV = 35, and n = 4, and then select i = k to determine the growth rate of 23.59 percent. Alternatively,

$$g = \left(\frac{\text{ending value}}{\text{beginning value}}\right)^{1/4} - 1$$
$$= \left(\frac{\$35 \text{ million}}{\$15 \text{ million}}\right)^{1/4} - 1 = 23.59 \text{ percent}$$

This approach must be used with caution because it assumes that the series does not behave in an erratic manner.

[20] Using a financial calculator, we find that the size of the annuity, PMT, required is $1,120,724.01 per year. The difference between this and the $1,120,699.32 determined previously is due to rounding.

mining the effective annual cost, we need to understand the impact of more frequent compounding intervals on the outcomes of the discounting and compounding processes. In the next section we see how these concepts are applied to mortgage payment calculations.

More Frequent Intervals So far we have assumed that the compounding and discounting is done annually. That is, the period (or interval) has been specified as "years." When compounding or discounting intervals of less than a year are employed, it is important to use the appropriate rate. The **nominal interest rate** is the quoted rate per year. The **effective interest rate** is the true rate *per time period*, and it depends on both the frequency of compounding and the nominal rate. Thus,

$$\text{effective rate per period} = \frac{\text{nominal interest rate, k}}{\text{number of compounding periods per year, m}} \quad (3.18)$$

For example, if the nominal rate of interest is 8 percent per year, the effective *semiannual* rate is 8%/2 = 4%, and the effective *monthly* rate is 8%/12 = 0.66667%.

Discounting and Compounding To illustrate more frequent periods, let us determine the present value of $10,000 to be received at the end of two years when the nominal interest rate is 8 percent and different discounting intervals are employed. Equation 3.2 becomes[21]

$$\text{present value with more frequent discounting, } PV_0 = \frac{FV_n}{[1 + (k/m)]^{nm}} \quad (3.19)$$

where

    k = the annual nominal rate
    m = the number of discounting intervals per year
  k/m = the effective rate per period
    n = the number of years

The present value, employing different discounting intervals, is

$$PV_0 \text{ (annual)} = \frac{\$10,000}{[1 + (0.08/1)]^{2(1)}} = \$8,573.39$$

$$PV_0 \text{ (semiannual)} = \frac{\$10,000}{[1 + (0.08/2)]^{2(2)}} = \$8,548.04$$

$$PV_0 \text{ (quarterly)} = \frac{\$10,000}{[1 + (0.08/4)]^{2(4)}} = \$8,534.90$$

$$PV_0 \text{ (monthly)} = \frac{\$10,000}{[1 + (0.08/12)]^{2(12)}} = \$8,525.96$$

---

[21] To use the PV table, we convert Equation 3.19 as follows:

$$PV_0 = FV_n(PV_{k/m, \, nm})$$

Although this equation works for simple cases (i.e., when the time period, nm, and the interest rate, k/m, correspond to a row and column in Table B.1), in general it is necessary to use a calculator with an exponential function, y^x, to solve more frequent than yearly compounding or discounting problems.

Likewise, when continuous discounting is employed, Equation 3.2 becomes[22]

present value with continuous discounting, $PV_0 = FV_n/e^{kn} = FV_n e^{-kn}$ (3.20)

where e is the value 2.71828. The present value of $10,000 to be received two years from now if the nominal discount rate is 8 percent, employing continuous discounting, is[23]

$$PV_0 = \$10,000e^{-0.08(2)} = \$8,521.44$$

To determine future values instead of present values, Equation 3.5 is modified to

future value with more frequent compounding, $FV_n = PV_0 \left(1 + \dfrac{k}{m}\right)^{nm}$ (3.21)

To illustrate, suppose we need to determine the future value in four years of $3,000 today, with a nominal interest rate of 9.5 percent, using daily compounding. It is

$$FV_4 = \$3,000\left(1 + \frac{0.095}{365}\right)^{4(365)} = \$4,386.64$$

Continuous compounding could be employed instead of daily compounding. In this case the future value equation (3.5) becomes[24]

future value with continuous compounding, $FV_n = PV_0 e^{kn}$ (3.22)

The future value at $t = 4$ of $3,000 today, when the nominal interest rate is 9.5 percent and continuous compounding is used, is[25]

$$FV_4 = \$3,000e^{0.095(4)} = \$4,386.85$$

Effective Annual Interest Rates   There is one other item to cover in this section—how to determine an **effective annual interest rate**. The effective annual interest rate is

effective annual interest rate, $k_{\text{effective annual}} = \left(1 + \dfrac{k_{\text{nominal}}}{m}\right)^m - 1$ (3.23)

Note that dividing k_{nominal} by m provides the effective rate per period as indicated by Equation 3.18. Then, Equation 3.23 converts this effective rate *per period* to an effective annual rate. For example, if the nominal rate is 12 percent per year, and the

---

[22] Note that dividing FV_n by e^{kn} is the same mathematically as multiplying FV_n by e^{-kn}. All the minus sign in the exponent to e does is indicate the inverse.

[23] Enter -0.16 [i.e., $(0.08)(2) = 0.16$] followed by the e^x key. Then multiply by $10,000 to get $8,521.4379 \approx \$8,521.44$.

[24] If continuous discounting or compounding must be used for annuities, then Equation 3.9 becomes $PV_0 = PMT\left[(1 - e^{-kn})/k\right]$ and Equation 3.11 becomes $FV_n = PMT\left[(e^{kn} - 1)/k\right]$

[25] Enter (0.09) $(4) = 0.38$ followed by the e^x key. Then multiply by 3,000 to get $4,386.85.

compounding period is quarterly, the effective annual rate is

$$k_{\text{effective annual}} = \left(1 + \frac{0.12}{4}\right)^4 - 1 = 0.1255 = 12.55 \text{ percent}$$

From a decision-making standpoint the effective annual rate should be used when evaluating costs and returns. Otherwise, important cost (yield) differences may be overlooked. As long as there is only one compounding interval per year (m = 1 in Equation 3.23), the effective annual rate is equal to the nominal rate. However, as the compounding interval decreases, the effective annual rate increases.[26]

Often the interest rates that banks and depository institutions quote on savings accounts are effective annual rates. However, for virtually all consumer loans, the Bank Act mandates that the lending institution advise customers of the **annual percentage rate (APR)** of the loan. The APR is determined by multiplying the periodic interest rate by the number of compounding periods in a year. Hence, *the APR is a nominal interest rate, not an effective annual rate*. For example, if the Frontenac National Bank is charging you $3\frac{1}{8}$ percent per quarter on a one-year $10,000 loan, it is obliged to quote you an APR of 12.5 percent (0.03125 × 4). However, employing Equation 3.23, we see that the effective annual rate (cost) of the loan is

$$k_{\text{effective annual}} = \left(1 + \frac{0.125}{4}\right)^4 - 1 = 0.1310$$

In this case your loan will cost you $60 [$10,000 (0.1310 − 0.1250)] more than you think. Although this does not seem like a large difference, it does illustrate that care must be exercised at all times to ensure that effective annual rates are used to evaluate loan alternatives.

Equation 3.23 can also be used by policy makers at financial institutions to calculate the nominal rate that must be charged in order to obtain a desired effective annual rate. For example, suppose a lender desires to earn an effective annual rate of 13 percent on a loan that features monthly compounding. What nominal rate or APR will it quote? To answer this question we use Equation 3.23 to solve for k_{nominal} as follows:

$$0.13 = \left(1 + \frac{k_{\text{nominal}}}{12}\right)^{12} - 1$$

$$(1.13)^{1/12} = \left(1 + \frac{k_{\text{nominal}}}{12}\right)$$

$$\frac{k_{\text{nominal}}}{12} = 0.0102368$$

$$k_{\text{nominal}} = 0.1228 = 12.28\%$$

---

[26] If we want to determine effective annual interest rates when continuous compounding is used, Equation 3.23 becomes:

$$k_{\text{effective annual}} = e^{k_{\text{normal}}} - 1$$

Thus the lending institution will quote a nominal rate or APR of 12.28 percent compounded quarterly in order to earn an effective annual rate of 13 percent.

MORTGAGE PAYMENT CALCULATIONS

The concepts of compounding periods and effective annual interest rates come into play in the calculation of monthly mortgage payments. There are some important differences, however. First, because mortgage payments are made monthly we need an effective *monthly* interest rate; and second, in calculating this effective monthly interest rate we must recognize that Canadian law requires standard (fixed-rate) mortgage interest to be compounded *semiannually* even though payments are made monthly.[27]

To accommodate these differences, Equation 3.23 is adjusted as follows:

$$\text{effective monthly interest rate, } k_{EM} = \left(1 + \frac{k_{nominal}}{m}\right)^{m/12} - 1 \qquad (3.23a)$$

However, because there are two compounding periods in a year (m = 2) the equation for the effective monthly interest rate may be rewritten as

$$k_{EM} = \left(1 + \frac{k_{nominal}}{2}\right)^{1/6} - 1 \qquad (3.24)$$

This value is then used in the present value of an annuity equation (Equation 3.9) adjusted to reflect 12 monthly payments:

$$PV_0 = PMT \left[\frac{1 - [1/(1 + k_{EM})^{12n}]}{k_{EM}}\right] \qquad (3.25)$$

To find the monthly mortgage payments, Equation 3.25 is solved for PMT, the annuity payment. (*Note:* n = the years of the mortgage.)

Although most mortgages are amortized over 25 or 30 years, the mortgage interest rate is fixed for a shorter subperiod, called a "term," which can commonly last from 6 months to 7 years. Thus the answer obtained from Equation 3.25 will apply only over the period of time for which the interest rate is fixed. After the term has expired, the mortgage holder has to negotiate a new interest rate and term with the lending institution. Once this is done, a new effective monthly rate must be calculated by using Equation 3.24. The new monthly mortgage payment is then obtained from Equation 3.25; however, the amortization period must be reduced by the term of the previous fixed-interest subperiod, and the amount of the mortgage (PV_0) must be reduced by the principal payments made over the subperiod.

To illustrate, suppose Frankie's Chicken is considering moving to new facilities. To purchase the new facilities Frankie's will have to obtain a $100,000 mortgage. Frankie's banks with the Royal Bank, and the bank manager has reported that the bank would be willing to grant the necessary mortgage, for 25 years, at an annual (nominal)

---

[27] This requirement is mandated in section 6 of the Interest Act.

rate of 8 percent fixed for a five-year term. Frankie's now wants to know what the monthly mortgage payments would be for the next five years if the bank's offer is accepted.

To solve this problem we must first calculate the effective monthly interest rate. Using Equation 3.24 we get

$$k_{EM} = \left(1 + \frac{0.08}{2}\right)^{1/6} - 1 = 0.0065582$$

Since Frankie's mortgage will be $100,000 for 25 years, from Equation 3.25 we have

$$\$100,000 = PMT\left[1 - \frac{[1/(1.0065582)^{12 \times 25}]}{0.0065582}\right]$$

$$\$100,000 = PMT(131.0248829)$$

$$PMT = \$763.21$$

Therefore, Frankie's monthly mortgage payment over the next fiive years will be $763.21. As with any loan amortization, in the early years of the mortgage the majority of this payment will go to pay the interest on the mortgage, and only a small portion of the payments will be used as a repayment of principal. For example, of the first payment, $655.82 ($100,000 × 0.0065582) will be for interest and only $107.39 ($763.21 − $655.82) for payment of principal.

It should be noted that because the interest on most mortgages in Canada is compounded semiannually, but payments are monthly, the payments required to retire a Canadian mortgage are slightly lower than they would be if interest were compounded monthly. For example, if Frankie's $100,000, 8 percent mortgage required the interest to be compounded monthly, the monthly payments could be calculated by using the following equation:

$$PV_0 = PMT\left[\frac{1 - \left[1/\left(1 + \frac{k_{nominal}}{m}\right)^{mn}\right]}{\frac{k_{nominal}}{m}}\right] \tag{3.26}$$

Equation 3.26 is simply the equation for an ordinary annuity (Equation 3.9) adjusted to reflect the number of compounding intervals, m, in a year, and it can be used *only* if the number of payments in a year are equal to the number of compounding intervals. Using monthly interest compounding for Frankie's mortgage, the monthly mortgage payment would be[28]

$$\$100,000 = PMT\ \frac{1 - \left[1 / \left(1 + \frac{0.08}{12}\right)^{12 \times 25}\right]}{\frac{0.08}{12}}$$

---

[28] Equations 3.23a and 3.25 could be used. From 3.23a, $k_{EM} = (1 + 0.08/12) - 1 = 0.0066667$, and substituting this value into Equation 3.25 will yield exactly the same result as Equation 3.26.

$$\$100,000 = PMT \left[\frac{1 - [1/(1.0066667)^{300}]}{0.0066667} \right]$$

$$PMT = \$771.82$$

Thus we see that Frankie's mortgage would cost $8.61 ($771.82 − $763.21) more per month if interest were compounded monthly, instead of semiannually as is the case with most Canadian mortgages. The only time that a mortgage's interest rate is compounded monthly is if it is a variable-rate mortgage, where the interest rate charged on the mortgage may change monthly to reflect changing market conditions (see Concept Review Problem 3.6).

Concept Review Questions

- Briefly describe the net present value (NPV) and internal rate of return (IRR) methods and their respective accept-or-reject criteria.
- Explain how the opportunity cost of capital affects the acceptance of an investment project.
- Explain why you can use either the PV or FV tables to calculate growth rates.
- What changes would you make to the future value and present value equations if the interest rate were compounded for less than a year?
- Explain how the calculations of monthly payments for fixed-rate mortgages differs from those for variable-rate mortgages.

KEY POINTS

- A dollar today is worth more than a dollar tomorrow.
- The present value of some future cash flow is $PV_0 = FV_n/(1 + k)^n = FV_n(PV_{k,n})$. The future value is $FV_n = PV_0(1 + k)^n = PV_0(FV_{k,n})$.
- The present value of a perpetuity is $PV_0 = PMT/k$. The present value of a perpetuity growing by a constant percentage rate per period is $PV_0 = PMT/(k - g)$.
- The present value of an annuity is

$$PV_0 = PMT \left[\frac{1 - [1/(1 + k)^n]}{k} \right] = PMT(PVA_{k,n})$$

while the future value of an annuity is

$$FV_n = PMT \left[\frac{(1 + k)^n - 1}{k} \right] = PMT(FVA_{k,n})$$

- The unknown interest rate can be calculated if the present and future values of the cash flow series are known.
- The net present value is the present value of the expected cash inflows (discounted at the opportunity cost of capital) minus the initial cash outflow on an investment. Value is enhanced when positive net present value projects are accepted.

- The opportunity cost of capital is the forgone return that could have been earned by investing in a comparably risky asset.
- Determining growth rates is an application of the concept of determining the unknown interest rate.
- With more-frequent-than-annual discounting, the present value is

$$PV_0 = \frac{FV_n}{[1 + (k/m)]^{nm}}$$

while with continuous discounting the present value is

$$PV_0 = FV_n/e^{kn} = FV_n e^{-kn}$$

- In order to determine the effective annual interest rate, the yearly nominal rate is converted to an effective per period interest rate and then annualized, so that

$$k_{\text{effective annual}} = \left(1 + \frac{k_{\text{nominal}}}{m}\right)^m - 1$$

- Interest on fixed-rate mortgages is compounded semiannually and payments are made monthly. As a result the effective monthly interest rate is calculated as

$$k_{EM} = \left(1 + \frac{k_{\text{nominal}}}{2}\right)^{1/6} - 1$$

and the monthly payment is found by solving the following equation for PMT

$$PV_0 = PMT\left[\frac{1 - [1/(1 + k_{EM})^{12n}]}{k_{EM}}\right]$$

QUESTIONS

3.1 Present value and future value are the inverse, or mirror images, of each other. Explain why this is true. Then demonstrate how present value and future value relate to each other.

3.2 The following series of cash flows exists:

Time Period	Amount
t = 1	$300
t = 2	200
t = 3	100
t = 4	100

Find the present value of this stream. Show at least four different ways you could set up the cash flow stream to solve for this present value.

3.3 A firm's earnings are expected to increase by 50 percent, from $200,000 at the end of $t = 3$ to $300,000 at the end of $t = 8$. Show why the compound (or annual) growth rate is less than 10 percent per year.

3.4 Explain the relationship between net present value and internal rate of return. Is it true that the net present value can be positive only if the internal rate of return is greater than the opportunity cost of capital?

3.5 What is meant by the term "opportunity cost of capital"? What opportunities are we talking about?

3.6 Explain why you are not indifferent to having your money invested in a bank that may, at its discretion, compound annually, semiannually, quarterly, monthly, daily, or continuously. (*Note*: Assume everything else stays the same.)

3.7 Explain how the number of compounding intervals in the year influences the effective annual interest rate.

CONCEPT REVIEW PROBLEMS

See Appendix A for Solutions.

CR3.1 You recently sold your Porsche for $25,000. With this nest egg you place your funds in a savings account paying 8 percent compounded annually for three years and then move it into another savings account paying 10 percent interest compounded semiannually. How large will your nest egg be at the end of seven years?

CR3.2 Susan is trying to save $5,000 for a vacation.
a. How much will she need to place in her account today if the rate of interest is 10 percent compounded monthly and she expects to make the trip in three years?
b What is the effective annual interest rate paid on her savings account?

CR3.3 You recently won $1,000,000 from a national magazine firm. Upon announcing the winner, the entry officials notified you that you will be receiving the $1 million in equal payments over the next 20 years.
a. If you receive the first payment after one year and all other payments at the end of subsequent years, and the appropriate discount rate is 8 percent, what is the present value of your winnings?
b. If you receive the first payment immediately and all other payments at the beginning of subsequent years, given the appropriate discount rate of 8 percent, what is the true present value of your winnings?

CR3.4 Applied Communications is considering an investment with the following cash flows:

Year	Cash Flow
0	−$500,000
1	140,000
2	200,000
3	250,000

a. If the firm's opportunity cost of capital is 12 percent, what is the project's net present value?
b. What is the project's internal rate of return?

CR3.5   Mary is considering purchasing a new car costing $20,000. The dealership is offering its customers one of two financing packages. Mary can either receive a $2,000 rebate or 2.9 percent financing with monthly payments for two years (24 payments). If she can obtain financing at her bank for 8 percent with monthly payments for two years, should she take the rebate or the 2.9 percent financing?

CR3.6   Frederick recently negotiated a $150,000 variable-rate mortgage to purchase a new home. The amortization period is 25 years, and monthly payments are adjusted each month to reflect the new interest rate.

a.   The nominal annual interest rate for the first month is $10\frac{3}{4}$ percent. Calculate the value of the first payment and the balance remaining at the end of the first month.

b.   The bank has set the nominal annual interest rate for the second month at $11\frac{1}{4}$ percent. Calculate the size of the payment Fred makes in the second month and the balance remaining in the principal at that point.

c.   For the payment in (b), compute the breakdown between interest and principal paid.

PROBLEMS

3.1   Determine the future value of each of the following amounts:

a.   An initial $325 compounded at 12 percent for four years.

b.   An initial $650 compounded at 6 percent for nine years.

c.   An annuity of $150 per year for each of six years compounded at 10 percent.

d.   An annuity of $480 per year for each of three years compounded at 17 percent.

3.2   Your firm has a retirement plan that matches all contributions on a one-to-two basis. That is, if you contribute $2,000 per year, the company will add $1,000 to make it $3,000. The firm guarantees an 8 percent return on the funds. Alternatively, you can "do it yourself," and you think you can earn 11 percent on your money by doing it this way. The first contribution will be made one year from today. At that time, and every year thereafter, you will put $2,000 into the retirement account. If you want to retire in 25 years, which way are you better off? (*Note*: Ignore any tax considerations.)

3.3   You plan to deposit $250 in a savings account for each of five years, starting one year from now. The interest rate is 9 percent compounded annually. What is the future value in each of the following cases?

a.   At the end of five years.

b.   At the end of six years if *no additional deposits* are made.

c.   At the end of five years, as in (a), if an *additional* $250 is deposited today (i.e., at t = 0), so there are six deposits of $250 each.

3.4   Art is planning for retirement. He plans to work for 25 more years. For the next 10 years, he can save $3,000 per year (with the first deposit being made one year from now), and at that time he wants to buy a weekend vacation home he estimates will cost $40,000. How much will he need to save in years 11 through 25 so that he has saved up exactly $300,000 when he retires? Assume he can earn 10 percent compounded annually for each of the next 25 years. (*Note*: Ignore any tax implications.)

3.5   Henderson is establishing a fund to pay off a $200,000 lump sum loan when it matures in 10 years. The funds will earn 8 percent interest per year. What is the size of the yearly payment in each case below?

a.   The payment is made at the end of the year.

b.   The payment is made at the beginning of the year.

3.6 Determine the present values of the following:
a.   A single cash flow of $1,142 at time t = 6 discounted at 8 percent.
b.   An annuity of $300 per year to be received for each of seven years discounted at 15 percent.
c.   An annuity of $400 per year to be received for each of five years, followed by a single cash flow of $1,000 at the end of year 6, discounted at 20 percent.
d.   An annuity of $200 for each of six years followed by an annuity of $800 for years 7 through 10, all discounted at 12 percent.

3.7 Olsen Electric has a line of small motors that no longer fits its corporate image. It is attempting to determine the minimum selling price for the small motors line. Olsen presently receives $250,000 per year after taxes in cash flows from the line. If its opportunity cost of capital is 16 percent, how much should Olsen ask if it thinks the life expectancy of the line is as follows?
a.   10 years.
b.   20 years.
c.   Infinity.

3.8   Find the interest rates or internal rates of return implied by the following:
a.   You lend $500 today and receive a promise for a repayment of $595.23 in three years.
b.   You invest $500 today and have a promise of receiving $197.55 for each of the next three years.
c.   You invest $1,400 today and will receive $2,592.59 back at the end of eight years.
d.   You lend $1,400 today and the repayments will be $281.80 for each of the next eight years.

3.9   Richards Enterprises has decided to automate to increase efficiency. By purchasing word processing equipment costing $6,627.60, it can save $1,800 per year for each of 10 years in labour costs. What is the internal rate of return on the word processing equipment?

3.10   You are a lucky winner in the Lotto-750. As a result, you have a choice between three alternative payment plans.

Plan A: A lifetime annuity of $60,425 annually, with the first payment one year from now.

Plan B: An annuity of $70,000 for 20 years, with the first payment one year from now.

Plan C: $800,000 today.

Your life expectancy is 45 more years. Ignoring any tax effects, determine the following:
a.   At what interest rate would you be indifferent between plans A and C?
b.   At what interest rate would you be indifferent between plans B and C?
c.   At what interest rate (to the nearest whole number) would you be indifferent between plans A and B? (*Note*: It is easier to solve this by trial-and-error than algebraically.)
d.   What if (c) is now changed so you know the interest rate for both plans A and B is 12 percent for the first 20 years? What rate would you have to earn on the remaining 25 years of the $60,425 annuity to be indifferent between plans A and B?

3.11   Suppose you pay $50,000 for an investment and it can be sold for $56,500 in one year.
a.   What is the internal rate of return on the investment?
b.   If the opportunity cost of capital is 11 percent, what is the present value of the investment? What is its net present value?

3.12   Suppose the market interest rate is 14 percent. An investment is available that will provide $125,000 *this* year in return for an investment of $150,000 *next* year. Should the investment be made?

3.13 You are contemplating an investment represented by the following series of cash flows:

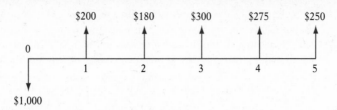

a. Determine the internal rate of return for the investment.
b. If your opportunity cost of capital is 8 percent, what can you say about the net present value of the investment? Should you make the investment?
c. What is the net present value of the investment if your opportunity cost of capital is 8 percent?

3.14 You can purchase the following cash flow series:

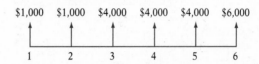

a. If you have an opportunity cost of capital of 14 percent, what is the maximum you would be willing to pay for this series?
b. If the purchase price is $10,000, what is the net present value of the investment? Explain why you should or should not make the investment.

3.15 Consider the following set of annual cash inflows: year 1 = $200, year 2 = $200, year 3 = $200, year 4 = $500, and year 5 = $500.
a. Find the present value of this series if the discount rate is 12 percent.
b. If you could acquire the right to receive this series of cash inflows by paying $1,000 today, what would the internal rate of return be on your investment?

3.16 After graduating from college you make it big—all because of your success in financial management. You decide to endow a scholarship for needy finance students that will provide $3,000 per year indefinitely, beginning *one year from now*. How much must be deposited *today* to fund the scholarship under the following conditions?
a. The interest rate is 10 percent.
b. The interest rate is 8 percent.
c. For both 10 and 8 percent, if everything stays the same except that the first disbursement will not be made until *three years from now*.

3.17 In each of the following cases, calculate the compound growth rate implied by the figures.
a. It is now t = 0, and LAD Ltd. has just paid a $1 cash dividend. Your financial advisor believes that the firm's dividend will be $3 at t = 7.
b. Susan bought a stock for $26 today and hopes to sell it at the end of four years for $100.
c. Canadian Paper Products Ltd. had net income of $262,000 at the end of t = 1 and expects to have net income of $1 million at the end of t = 7.

3.18 B.C. Winery needs $500,000 for expansion of its warehouse. The company plans to finance $100,000 with internally generated funds but wants to secure a loan for the remainder.

The contracting firm's finance subsidiary has offered to provide the loan based on six annual payments of $97,299.93 each. Alternatively, B.C. Winery's banker will lend the firm $400,000, to be repaid in six equal annual instalments. The bank has quoted B.C. an annual percentage rate of 12 percent with monthly compounding of interest. Finally, an insurance firm would also loan the money; it requires a lump sum payment of $747,663.55 at the end of six years.

a. Based on the respective annual percentage costs of the three loans, which one should B.C. select?

b. What other considerations might be important in addition to cost?

3.19 If $1,000 is invested today, how much will it be worth in (a) 5 years or (b) 10 years, if interest at a 12 percent nominal rate is compounded annually, semiannually, or quarterly?

3.20 How much would you have in the future in each of the following cases?

a. $2,500, invested today, if continuous compounding is employed, the nominal rate is 9 percent, and the period is two and a half years.

b. $4.80, invested today, if the nominal rate is 12.6 percent continuously compounded, and the period is 15 years.

c. $300, invested one year from now, another $300 invested at t = 2, and another $300 invested at t = 3; the continuously compounded nominal rate is 10 percent; and the time period is three years. (*Note*: You will require the information Footnote 24 in order to find the answer.)

d. If everything is the same as in (c), except (1) no more cash flows are received and (2) the time period is eight years.

e. If everything is the same as in (c), except there is $300 also invested at t = 0.

3.21 How much would you have at the end of 10 years if you invest $100 at the nominal rate of 14 percent compounded *annually*? Compounded *continuously*?

3.22 Find the present value of each of the following:

a. $1,500 to be received in eight years at a nominal rate of 6 percent discounted continuously.

b. $10 to be received in four years, and $50 to be received in five years, at a nominal rate of 15 percent discounted continuously.

c. An annuity of $200 per year for each of seven years, with the first payment starting one year from now, at a nominal rate of 12 percent discounted continuously. (*Note*: You will require the information in footnote 24 in order to find the answer.)

d. If everything is the same as in (c), and you also receive $200 today.

3.23 What is the effective annual interest rate if the nominal rate is 9 percent per year, a 365-day year is used, and the compounding period is (a) yearly, (b) quarterly, (c) daily, or (d) hourly?

3.24 What is the effective annual interest rate on an account paying a nominal rate of 7 percent compounded continuously? What if it is compounded quarterly? Yearly? (*Note*: You will require the information in footnote 26 in order to find the answer.)

3.25 Kathy has decided to buy a ski chalet in Jasper and is trying to decide between mortgage types. She wishes to borrow $60,000, and she would like to make monthly payments, with the final payment made at the end of 25 years.

a. One option open to Kathy, through her bank, is a fixed-rate mortgage carrying a nominal annual interest rate of $10\frac{1}{2}$ percent compounded semiannually. This mortgage will be for a six-month term, after which time she will have to renew it. Calculate the monthly payment and principal balance remaining at the end of month 6.

b. A second option would be a variable-rate mortgage with a six-month term and a current nominal annual interest rate of $10\frac{1}{2}$ percent. Normally, the interest rate would be adjusted each month based on market conditions, but Kathy feels the rate will not change over the six months. Calculate the principal balance that would remain at the end of six months, given Kathy's assumption. Why is this value different from the answer to (a)?

c. In considering the variable-rate mortgage described in (b), Kathy researched expected movements in interest rates over the next six months. Based on this information, she now expects the interest rate on the six-month term variable-rate mortgage to follow this pattern:

Month	1	2	3	4	5	6
Nominal Annual Rate	10%	$10\frac{1}{4}$%	$10\frac{1}{2}$%	$10\frac{3}{4}$%	11%	$10\frac{1}{2}$%

Use these nominal rates to calculate the mortgage payment and the breakdown between interest and principal paid each month. Also, compute the final principal balance at the end of the six-month term.

d. Briefly describe what factors one should consider when choosing between variable- and fixed-rate mortgages.

3.26 Mini Case Your best friend Ralph does not understand much about financial decision making and time value. He has heard the expression "a dollar today is worth more than a dollar tomorrow" and it makes sense to him. However, he does not understand how this concept works or how it can apply to his everyday life. He knows that you are taking a course in financial management, so he asks for your help. To help him, you have found the following questions from some old financial management books. However, you do not have any answers to determine whether his calculations are correct. Thus, you need to answer the following:

a. What is the future value of $300 at the end of four years if the interest rate is 9 percent compounded annually? What would be the future value at the end of six years if for the last two years the interest rate decreased from 9 percent to 7 percent?

b. What is the value today (at t = 0) of $600 to be received at t = 6 if the required rate of return is 8.6 percent per year?

c. An annuity of $300 per year for seven years exists. If the discount rate is 10 percent, what is the present value if it is an ordinary annuity? An annuity due? Explain the difference in values between the annuity and the annuity due.

d. You just won the Lotto. The payments are $350,000 for each of 13 years, with the first payment to be made at t = 2 and the last at t = 14. If you have an opportunity cost of capital of 12 percent, what is the present value of your winnings?

e. What is the present value of a perpetuity of $200 per year if the discount rate is 16 percent? What if the first payment on the perpetuity does not occur until t = 4?

f. A cash flow stream exists as follows:

Year	Cash Flows
1	$100
2	300
3	−200
4	500

1. What is the value at t = 4 if the interest rate is 11 percent?

2. What is the value at t = 6 if the interest rate remains 11 percent?

3. If this stream can be purchased for $500, when the opportunity cost of capital is 8 percent, what is the net present value of the stream? Is it a good buy? Why?

g. If an investment requires an outlay of $400 today, and promises to pay $50 at t = 1, $350 at t = 2, and $150 at t = 3, what internal rate of return would you earn if you made the investment? If your hurdle rate is 13 percent, should you make the investment?

h. What is the present value of $20,000 to be received four years from now if the discount rate is 10 percent and discounting is done:

1. annually?
2. quarterly?
3. monthly?
4. daily? (Assume all years have 365 days.)
5. continuously?

i. You can borrow from two banks as follows: Bank A will lend at an annual percentage rate of 11.75 percent with interest compounded monthly while bank B has quoted an annual percentage rate of 11.70 percent compounded daily. If all else is equal, which loan are you better off with?

REFERENCES

BHANDARI, SHYAM B. "Compounding/Discounting of Intrayear Cash Flows: Principles, Pedagogy and Practices." *Financial Practice and Education* 1 (Spring 1991): 87–89.

CISSELL, ROBERT, HELEN CISSELL, and DAVID C. FLASPOHLER. *Mathematics of Finance*, 8th ed. Boston: Houghton Mifflin, 1990.

WHITE, MARK A. "Financial Problem-Solving with an Electronic Calculator." *Financial Practice and Education* 1 (Fall/Winter 1991): 73–88.

APPENDIX

3A

Financial Markets, Consumption, and Investment

VALUE CREATION

Present value and the net present value of an investment sound like common sense. They are. But a greater understanding of current versus future decisions and the role played by the financial markets is needed; these ideas are key elements that underpin much of financial decision making.

Borrowing and Lending Opportunities

The problem of choosing between spending today versus spending in the future is illustrated in Figure 3A.1. Assume you have a cash inflow of A dollars today and C dollars one period, or year, from now. If there is no way to save and borrow, you are forced to consume the A dollars today and then, one year from now, consume the C

Figure 3A.1

Financial Market Effect

The interest rate line shows the cash flows from borrowing or lending. For example, by borrowing against future cash flow OC, an individual can consume an extra AB today.

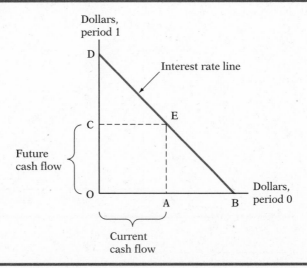

dollars. In some circumstances that may be fine. But what if you have a need for more consumption today (to purchase a car or house, for example) than provided for by the A dollars in cash flow? The answer is to go to financial markets and financial intermediaries, which enable you to transfer your cash flows across time.

A financial market is simply a market that provides the opportunity to trade between dollars (or cash flows) today and dollars in the future. The downward-sloping line DB in Figure 3A.1 is the **interest rate line** which indicates the rate of exchange, called interest, between dollars today and dollars in one year.[1] The slope of line DB is $(1 + k)$, where k is the one-year rate of interest. In Figure 3A.1 there is only one interest rate—you can borrow at the risk-free rate, k_{RF}, or you can lend (or invest in financial assets) at the same rate, k_{RF}.

Assume your cash inflow today is $50,000, your inflow in one year is $60,000, and the risk-free rate of interest is 8 percent. If you invest all $50,000 of today's cash inflow at 8 percent, in one year you will have a future value of $($50,000$)(1 + 0.08) =$ $54,000. This future value is composed of the original principal of $50,000 and the interest of $4,000. In one year you will also have another cash inflow of $60,000, for a *total* future value of $114,000. This total future value is shown on the vertical axis in Figure 3A.2. Likewise, you could borrow against the $60,000 you will receive one year from now. The present value of the $60,000 discounted at 8 percent is $60,000/$ $(1 + 0.08) = $55,556$. Adding this amount to the current $50,000 cash inflow from time zero provides a *total* present value of $105,556. This amount is shown on the

Figure 3A.2

Borrowing and Lending

If you consume $50,000 today and $60,000 in period 1, you neither borrow nor lend. But if you consume less than $50,000 today, you can lend; to consume more than $50,000 today, you must borrow.

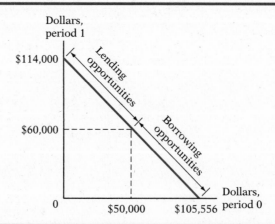

horizontal axis in Figure 3A.2. Because of the existence of financial markets, opportunities to borrow or lend exist, as indicated in Figure 3A.2.

Where on the interest rate line would you end up? It all depends on your needs and preferences for current consumption versus your desire and ability to save for the future. If you are a spendthrift, you will borrow against next year's cash inflows. On the other hand, if you are a tightwad, you will not spend all of this year's cash flows and will, instead, lend some of this year's cash flows. Even if you simply put your money in the bank, that is a lending decision. Assume you are a spendthrift and need $65,000 this year. You have $50,000 from current cash inflow and you will borrow $15,000 against next year's cash inflow. How much will be left for next year? Since you will have to repay principal and interest on the $15,000, it is simply the cash inflow next year of $60,000 − ($15,000)(1.08) = $43,800. The tradeoff of current versus future consumption for a spendthrift is illustrated in Figure 3A.3 (a).

What if you are a tightwad? Say you need only $40,000 of this year's cash inflow and will invest (or lend) the rest at the risk-free rate of 8 percent, for which you will receive principal and interest next year. Thus, the amount available for consumption one year from now will be $60,000 + ($10,000)(1.08) = $70,800. This is shown in Figure 3A.3 (b). By borrowing and lending in the financial markets, individuals can move anywhere they desire along the interest rate line. Thus, one of the crucial roles a well-developed financial market plays is to allow individuals the freedom to consume more or less than their current cash flow. Well-developed financial markets play a crucial role in financial decision making for both individuals and firms.

Figure 3A.3

Spendthrift and Tightwad

By borrowing or lending, both the spendthrift and the tightwad can satisfy their desires for current versus future consumption.

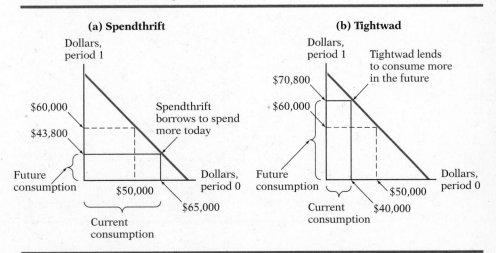

Investing in Real Assets

Not only can individuals invest in assets from the financial markets, they can also invest in real assets like buildings, machinery, and equipment. The return on the "best" real asset investments should be higher than the return on financial market investments; if it were otherwise, no one would invest in real assets. Therefore, the **investment opportunities line**, which shows all the investments in real assets ranked according to their returns, may at first have a steep slope, as shown in Figure 3A.4. In addition, unless an inexhaustible supply of "good" investments in real assets exists, the investment opportunities line is concave to the origin, indicating that the anticipated returns from subsequent investments decline. Thus, the best investment (shown at the far right in Figure 3A.4) produces the highest future cash flow, the next-best (moving from right to left) has the second-highest future cash flow, and so forth.

Now we need to consider what occurs when the opportunity for individuals to invest in both financial market assets and real (or capital) assets is available. This situation is shown in Figure 3A.5. The line DB is simply the interest rate line from Figure 3A.1; it indicates the opportunities available from investing or borrowing in the financial markets. The line FB is the investment opportunities line from Figure 3A.4, which shows all the investments in and associated returns from investing in real assets. For simplicity, let us assume you are initially at point B. What should you

---

Figure 3A.4

Real Asset Investment Opportunities

The investment opportunities line indicates the investment in and returns from investing in real assets. Due to diminishing returns, its slope becomes flatter with each additional project undertaken.

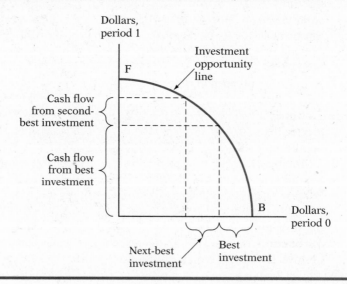

Figure 3A.5

Specific Real Asset Investment Opportunities

The first investment in real assets of $20,000 produces a return of $45,000; clearly it should be undertaken. The second investment of $25,000 produces a return of $30,000 and should also be made.

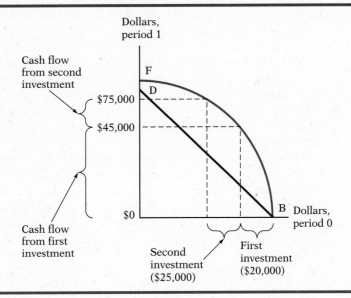

do in the way of investing? If you invest in the financial markets (with returns as shown along the interest rate line DB), you will earn a return of 8 percent. But if you make an investment in real assets with part of your wealth, you will earn a higher return, as shown by the curved investment opportunities line FB.

Suppose the first investment in real assets requires an investment, or cash outflow, of $20,000 and has cash inflows of $45,000 one year from now. Should you make the investment? If you invest in financial market assets, instead of real assets, you would earn 8 percent; the future value in one year would be ($20,000)(1.08) = $21,600. However, if you invest in real assets, the future value is $45,000. Clearly, $45,000 is greater than $21,600, so you would invest in real assets with the first $20,000. The opportunities, investments, and returns available are shown in Figure 3A.5.

An alternative way to make the same decision is to find the present value of the $45,000, discounted at 8 percent. The present value is $45,000/1.08 = $41,667. Because the present value of the inflow is greater than the initial investment of $20,000, the net present value of $41,667 − $20,000 = $21,667 is positive. Thus, the first investment in real assets should be made. Note what we accomplished by discounting at the opportunity cost of 8 percent. For the net present value to be positive, the project had to earn a return *greater* than the opportunity cost, or discount rate, of 8 percent. Hence, *discounting by the opportunity cost automatically compares the proposed investment in real assets to the next-best alternative use of the funds*, in this case, investing in financial market assets with an 8 percent return.[2]

What about the proposed second investment of $25,000 shown in Figure 3A.5? It promises to return $30,000 (i.e., $75,000 − $45,000, from Figure 3A.5) in one year. Should the investment be made? The net present value is ($30,000/1.08) − $25,000 = $2,778. By making the second investment you earn a return that is also greater than the opportunity rate of 8 percent available from investing in financial assets. Make the second investment.

Should any more investments be made? The answer is yes: *Invest in real assets as long as the net present value is positive.* Continue to invest in real assets as long as the return is greater than the opportunity cost, or opportunity rate of return. What happens when the net present value from making an investment in real assets becomes negative? The decision is clear cut: Do not invest; the incremental return earned on the investment in real assets is less than the incremental return of 8 percent from investing in financial assets.

Although we have not shown the net present value graphically, we can easily do so. Consider Figure 3A.6, where it is assumed that the two investments of $20,000 and $25,000 in real assets from Figure 3A.5 are optimal. That is, there are no other investments in real assets that have a positive net present value. We saw in Figure 3A.5 that the future value of the cash inflows from investing a total of $45,000 in real assets was $75,000. The present value from making the investments is $75,000/1.08 = $69,444, and the net present value is $69,444 − $45,000 = $24,444. Investing in real assets produces a net present value of $24,444, so the *total* present value has increased from the original $105,556 to $130,000. This increase is shown as BG in Figure 3A.6. Is the individual better off? Yes, wealth has increased by $24,444. This increase in wealth is due to accepting positive net present value investments in real assets, i.e., those that return more than the opportunity cost (or return) available from investing in financial market assets.

We reached this conclusion for one specific individual, but what about the spendthrift and the tightwad? Are they better off? Yes, because once the total present value has increased to $130,000 due to investing in real assets, individuals can move anywhere along the new interest rate line, HG, shown in Figure 3A.6. [Note that point H is ($130,000)(1.08) = $140,400.] This is accomplished by borrowing or lending through the financial markets, as we discussed previously. The important

---

[2] The internal rate of return could also be used to make this decision. We have:

$$\frac{\$45,000}{1 + IRR} = \$20,000$$

$$\$45,000 = \$20,000 + \$20,000 \, IRR$$

$$IRR = \frac{\$45,000 - \$20,000}{\$20,000} = 1.25 \text{ or } 125 \text{ percent.}$$

The return on financial assets is 8 percent; because the IRR is substantially greater than the opportunity cost, the decision to make the investment is the same as reached with net present value.

Figure 3A.6

New Interest Rate Line and Net Present Value

By investing in real assets, individuals can attain any position on the new interest rate line, HG. The net present value equals the present value of the inflows minus the initial investment, or $69,444 − $45,000 = $24,444.

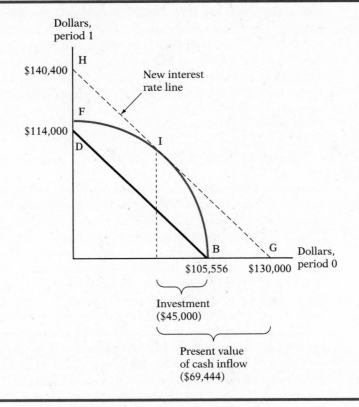

conclusion is that *no matter what the preferences of individuals, they are better off by accepting positive net present value investments.* Value creation through use of the net present value rule benefits all individuals, no matter what their preferences for consumption versus savings.

Note in Figure 3A.6 that by accepting all positive net present value projects, we have made investments up to the point where the investment opportunities line FB just touches and is tangent to the new interest rate line HG. (The new interest rate line has exactly the same slope as the original interest rate line, DB. This has to be true unless the risk-free rate of interest changes.) The slope of the investment opportunities line represents the *return on the marginal investment* in real assets. The slope of the investment opportunities line is the internal rate of return on the investment. By moving up the investment opportunities line from B to I, we are accepting projects whose internal rate of return is greater than the opportunity cost of capital. When do we stop investing in real assets? When the investment opportunities line is just tangent to the new interest rate line, at point I. Before the point of tangency at I, the net present value is positive *and* the internal rate of return is greater than the opportunity cost of capital. Beyond the point of tangency (from I to F), the net present value is negative and the internal rate of return is less than the opportunity cost of capital.

Finally, one other item must be understood. The *presence of financial markets plays a major role* in what we have discussed. Without well-developed financial markets, individuals would not easily be able to borrow and lend. The presence of well-functioning financial markets effectively "uncouples" the individual's investment and saving decisions. Thus, in parts of the world that do not possess well-functioning financial markets, much of the above discussion does not hold nearly as well. Hence, be forewarned: Before you take your new-found knowledge to a third- or fourth-world country, ask yourself whether that country has anything resembling a well-developed financial market.

Moving from Individuals to Firms

So far we have discussed the rationale for investing in real assets and the net present value rule from the standpoint of individuals. Moving from individuals to firms is straightforward. Think of a firm that is owned by 100 individuals, each holding 1 percent of the firm's stock. For simplicity, assume that none of the owners is directly involved in running the firm, so they hire a management team to do so. What kinds of investments should the firm make? Exactly the same rule applies for the firm as for individuals: Take all positive net present value investment projects. Doing so maximizes the value of the firm, no matter what the preferences of the owners for investment versus consumption. Taking positive net present value projects increases the value of the firm. All of the owners, as well as the firm's creditors, managers, and employees, benefit from the decision to make positive net present value investments.

This idea of making the same investment decisions in real assets no matter what the specific preferences of different individuals is called the Fisher **separation theorem**. In short, it says that the investment and financing decisions of the firm are separate. For the owners of the firm to maximize their value, the firm should take all positive net present value projects. How they are financed is a separate decision. We will discuss the separate investment and financing decisions in a number of later chapters. In Appendix 8A we will explore how to proceed when the investing and financing decisions are not separable. For now, remember four basic ideas of finance: A dollar today is worth more than a dollar tomorrow; well-developed financial markets are important; maximize the value of the firm by accepting positive net present value projects; and investment and financing decisions typically are separable.

Some Complications

One complication is that in Figures 3A.1 through 3A.6 we have employed the risk-free interest rate as the opportunity cost of capital. That is fine in a world of certainty, but once the cash inflows are *forecasts*—i.e., not a sure thing—we have to deal with uncertainty. In general, dealing with uncertainty requires the use of higher discount

rates for the opportunity cost of capital. Throughout our discussion of capital investment decision making in Chapters 7 through 9, and elsewhere in the book, we use the
terms required rate of return, discount rate, hurdle rate, and opportunity cost of
capital *assuming there is uncertainty*. Hence, a higher discount rate than the risk-free
rate is appropriate.

Another complication is that in the discussion up to now we have assumed the
interest rate for borrowing and for lending is the same. That is, any individual could
borrow or lend at the same interest rate. For borrowing and lending rates to be the
same, the following assumptions (implicitly or explicitly) are being made:

1. There is perfect competition; that is, no participants are large enough to have any
    material impact on prices.
2. There are no barriers to entry or frictions such as **transactions costs**. Transactions
    costs are the direct and indirect costs of issuing securities or carrying out a trans-
    action.
3. Information is freely available to all financial market participants. When informa-
    tion is known to some but not all of the participants, we have asymmetric informa-
    tion.
4. There are no **taxes**, or if there are any, all participants are taxed at the same rate
    so that no distortions exist. The presence of taxes, or unequal tax rates, also affects
    financial prices and decisions.

In effect, the assumption of identical borrowing and lending rates is that perfectly
competitive financial markets exist. Clearly this is not the case. Therefore, two questions arise: (1) How imperfect are the financial markets? and (2) what is the impact of
less-than-perfectly-competitive financial markets? There have been many studies of the
financial markets, the extent of frictions and other distortions, and the impact they
have on the functioning of financial markets and on individuals and firms. As we
proceed we will encounter situations in which transactions costs, asymmetric information, or taxes have important impacts on financial decisions.

The impact of less-than-perfectly-competitive financial markets means that individuals do not face the same borrowing and lending rates. This being the case,
spendthrifts and tightwads would not select the previously indicated points on the
investment opportunities line, because the slope of the interest rate line is different for
borrowers than for lenders. How far apart are they? Probably not too far. How much
impact do different borrowing and lending rates have on the decisions that individuals
and firms make? Probably very little *at the margin*. Thus, although in some situations
different borrowing and lending rates might change a decision, when considered *in
total* the impact of different borrowing and lending rates does not appear to invalidate
the major conclusions presented above.

The worst-case scenario is that the difference in borrowing and lending rates makes
some decisions a little less precise. Should that worry financial decision makers? We do
not think so, because finance is simply a way of structuring a common-sense approach
to making financial decisions. If the prescription is "correct" in its direction and
magnitude 98-plus percent of the time, why throw it out unless we have something
better to offer? And with each passing year we are learning still more about the theory,
empirical aspects, and common sense of finance.

PROBLEMS

3A.1   FiFi makes $80,000 this year and will make $95,000 next year. If the interest rate is 10 percent, what will FiFi's consumption be next year if:
a. $100,000 is desired this year?
b. $45,000 is desired this year?

3A.2   Answer based on the following figure:

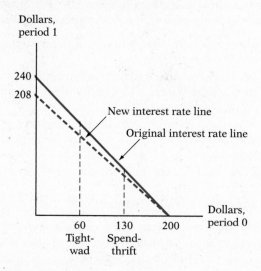

a.   What is the original interest rate?
b.   For the spendthrift, what is the future value of today's consumption? How much will be left for consumption tomorrow? What is the present value of tomorrow's consumption?
c.   For the tightwad, what is the future value of today's consumption? How much will be left for consumption tomorrow? What is the present value of tomorrow's consumption?

Now suppose that the interest rate falls and is now depicted by the line labelled "New interest rate line."
d.   What is the new interest rate?
e.   For the spendthrift at the new interest rate, what is the future value of today's consumption? How much will be left for consumption tomorrow? What is the present value of tomorrow's consumption?
f.   For the tightwad, what is the future value of today's consumption at the new interest rate? How much will be left for consumption tomorrow? What is the present value of tomorrow's consumption?

3A.3 Answer based on the following figure:

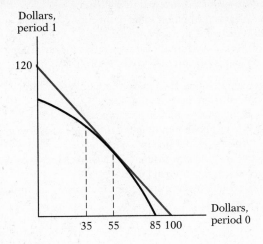

a. What is the interest rate?
b. How much should be invested in real assets?
c. What is the present value of the future cash flow generated by the investment in real assets?
d. What is the net present value of the investment?
e. What is the future cash flow received from making the investment in real assets?
f. What is the internal rate of return on the investment in real assets?
g. How much will the individual consume today? How much tomorrow?

Now suppose the investment opportunities line remains as drawn in the figure but the investment in real assets is only $15 and the present value of the future cash flow generated by the investment in real assets is $25.

h. What is the net present value?
i. What is the new total present value, or worth? What is the total future value?
j. If the individual continues to consume $35 today, how much can be consumed tomorrow?
k. What can we conclude about the real asset investment policy?

3A.4 Answer based on the following figures:

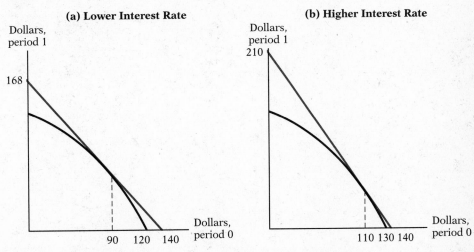

a. At the original interest rate given in (a) above, what is the interest rate?
b. How much is invested in real assets?
c. What is the present value of the future cash flow generated by the investment in real assets?
d. What is the net present value?
e. What is the future cash flow reeived from making the investment in real assets?
f. What is the internal rate of return?

Now suppose that the interest rate increases as shown in (b) above.
g. What is the new interest rate?
h. How much is now invested in real assets?
i. What is the present value of the future cash flow generated by the investment in real assets?
j. What is the net present value?
k. What is the new future cash flow received from making the investment in real assets?
l. What is the internal rate of return?
m. Explain why an increase in the interest rate results in a decline in the investment in real assets.

4

Valuation of Bonds and Stocks

EXECUTIVE SUMMARY

Understanding how financial assets, such as stocks and bonds, are valued is important for effective financial decision making. The required return for investing in financial assets equals the risk-free rate plus a risk premium.

Bonds are valued based on their expected interest payments and maturity values, discounted at the investor's required rate of return. A bond's yield to maturity is the compound rate of return that equates the present value of future interest payments plus the maturity value to the bond's current market value.

In principle, the market value of a common stock is determined in the same way as the market value of a bond. Thus, the market value of common stock is equal to the present value of all expected cash dividends, where the investor's required rate of return is employed as the discount rate. The magnitude and length of the expected growth in cash dividends has a major impact on stock prices.

The firm's stock price can be thought of as being composed of the capitalized value of the firm under a no-growth policy, plus the present value of growth opportunities. Firms create value, as shown by increases in their market value, by accepting positive net present value projects. Investing in zero net present value projects does not lead to value creation, while investing in negative net present value projects will result in a decrease in value.

Expected (*ex ante*) returns and realized (*ex post*) returns are generally not equal. On an *ex ante* basis, risk and return are positively related. Thus, the greater the risk, the greater the return required by investors. The relationship among financial management decisions, the market value of the firm, and its opportunity cost of capital is continuous and ongoing.

FINANCIAL ASSETS

As discussed in Chapter 2, the fundamental goal of the financial markets, and the purpose of the financial system that has developed to support the financial markets, is to allow individuals, firms, or governments to transform savings into investments in physical assets. An extensive financial system, such as that in developed countries, provides an effective means of bringing together suppliers and demanders of capital. The transfer of funds between parties leads to the creation of financial assets. For example, if a firm needs to raise funds to finance a project it may do so by borrowing or by selling part of the ownership of the firm. In either case, the suppliers of the capital receive a claim against the firm in the form of financial assets. Bonds and stocks are two of the major financial assets (instruments) that exist in a well-developed financial system. We need to understand how they are valued.

Thus, we first focus our attention on understanding how bonds and stocks are valued. Then, later in the chapter, we examine how firms create value by accepting positive net present value projects, how to calculate returns, and how returns impact on effective financial management.

Concept Review Question

■ What are the two major financial assets?

DETERMINING BOND VALUES AND YIELDS

A bond is simply a borrowing by a firm or government. Bonds carry a stated **par** (or **maturity**) **value**. This value is typically $1,000. Thus, the firm has borrowed $1,000 from investors with a promise to repay the principal of $1,000 in the future. The firm also pays interest on the borrowing as determined by the **coupon interest rate** stated in the bond.[1] On a borrowing of $1,000 and assuming a coupon interest rate of 9 percent, interest of ($1,000)(0.09) = $90 is paid by the firm to the owners of the bond each year. Although some bonds are relatively short-lived, most have an initial maturity of 10 to 30 years. At the maturity of the bond, the firm pays back the principal of $1,000.

The bond is initially sold in the primary market, with the proceeds going to the issuer. At the time bonds are initially sold, they are typically priced so that they sell close to their par value. *Outstanding bonds*, on the other hand, are all bonds that have previously been issued and are still held by investors. They may be bought or sold in the secondary market; their price may be close to or far from par value.

BOND VALUATION

The market price of a bond is equal to the present value of the series of interest payments to be received over the bond's life, plus the present value of the maturity value of $1,000, all discounted at the investor's required rate of return for the bond.

---

[1] Another type of bond, the zero-coupon bond, does not have a stated coupon interest rate. These bonds are discussed in Chapter 11.

Thus, a bond's price is equal to

$$\text{price, } B_0 = \sum_{t=1}^{n} \frac{I}{(1 + k_b)^t} + \frac{M}{(1 + k_b)^n} \tag{4.1}$$

$$= I(PVA_{k_b, n}) + M(PV_{k_b, n})$$

where

B_0 = the current market price of the bond
 I = the dollar amount of interest expected to be received each year (or par value $\times$ coupon interest rate)
 n = the number of years to **maturity** for the bond
k_b = the required rate of return for the bond
M = the par or maturity value of the bond

Consider a $1,000 par bond that has a 10 percent coupon rate and a 25-year maturity. If investors demand (or require) a return of 10 percent on this bond and it pays interest annually, its value is[2]

$$B_0 = \frac{\$100}{(1.10)^1} + \frac{\$100}{(1.10)^2} + \cdots + \frac{\$100}{(1.10)^{25}} + \frac{\$1,000}{(1.10)^{25}}$$

$$= \$100 \, (PVA_{10\%, \, 25\text{yr}}) + \$1,000 \, (PV_{10\%, \, 25\text{yr}})$$

$$= \$100(9.077) + \$1,000(0.092) = \$907.70 + \$92.00$$

$$= \$999.70 \approx \$1,000$$

In this example, the bond has a current market value of $1,000, which is exactly equal to its par value. Thus, if the required rate of return demanded by investors is equal to the bond's coupon rate, the current market value of a bond is equal to its par value.[3]

INTEREST RATES AND BOND PRICES

Bonds generally do not sell for their par value. Instead, a $1,000 bond would sell for more or less than $1,000, depending on current economic conditions. To see why, remember what we learned in Chapter 3. In the absence of risk, the interest or discount rate required to satisfy borrowers and lenders is the risk-free rate. As a rough approximation, we can think of the risk-free rate as compensating investors for changes in expected inflation.[4] The best proxy we have for the risk-free rate, k_{RF}, is short-term government borrowing called treasury bills that typically mature in 90 or 180 days. Treasury bills are safe, but investors will not get rich investing in them.

---

[2] By financial calculator, enter 0 at $t = 0$, 100 for $t = 1$ through $t = 24$, 1,100 for $t = 25$, and $i = k_b = 10$. Selecting net present value (NPV) produces a value of $1,000. The 30 cent difference results from rounding.

[3] Bonds actually sell at their current market price plus accrued interest. For a new issue there is typically little or no accrued interest. However, if the bond were purchased one-fourth of the way through the year, then its actual purchase cost would be $1,000 + $\frac{1}{4}$($100), or $1,025.

[4] In Chapter 2, Equation 2.1, the **Fisher effect**, named after Irving Fisher, says that the nominal, or observed, risk-free interest rate = the real rate of interest + expected inflation.

When the world is not certain, the return required on a bond, k_b, is equal to the risk-free rate plus a risk premium. So,

$$\text{required return on a bond, } k_b = k_{RF} + \text{risk premium}$$

As discussed in Chapter 2, we may think of the risk premium demanded by investors in bonds issued by firms as being composed of

$$\text{bond risk premium} = \begin{array}{c}\text{maturity}\\\text{premium}\end{array} + \begin{array}{c}\text{default}\\\text{premium}\end{array} + \begin{array}{c}\text{liquidity}\\\text{premium}\end{array} + \begin{array}{c}\text{issue-specific}\\\text{premium}\end{array}$$

It is worth reiterating what each of these premiums represents. The maturity premium arises because, as general interest rates change, longer-term bonds tend to fluctuate more in value than do shorter-term bonds. The default premium arises because bonds issued by firms are more risky than government bonds and because firms differ in terms of their financial condition and likelihood of failing. The liquidity premium arises because investors in securities that are harder to sell, or less liquid, incur more transactions costs; they therefore demand additional compensation. Finally, individual bonds may contain many issue-specific features. Some are more or less attractive to investors; hence, different features result in an issue-specific premium.[5]

Putting this all together, the return required by bond investors—which is the same as the cost to the bond issuers—is a function of the risk-free rate and premiums related to maturity, default, liquidity, and issue-specific characteristics of the bond.

BONDS ISSUED BY THE GOVERNMENT

For the moment, let us consider long-term bonds issued by the government. In this case we can ignore the last three types of premiums and say that

$$k_{\text{long-term government securities}} = k_{RF} + \text{maturity premium}$$

Let us consider the two primary determinants of the return demanded by investors from long-term government securities—expected inflation and the maturity premium.

Expected Inflation Assume the 25-year bond discussed above is a Government of Canada bond. At the time it is issued, investors hold expectations as to future inflation. Suppose that after the bond is issued, due to changes in either world-wide or domestic economic conditions, expected inflation suddenly and unexpectedly jumps by 4 percent. Other things being equal, this jump will cause the **market rate of interest** demanded by investors for new bonds of similar quality and maturity to increase from 10 to 14 percent. This change in market interest rates will also cause the required rate of return demanded by investors on *all outstanding bonds of similar quality and maturity* to increase—again, to 14 percent. This occurs because investors considering

---

[5] Other features of bonds are discussed in Chapter 11.

the 10 percent coupon rate bond will not be willing to settle for less than they can receive in newly issued securities of comparable quality but with a higher coupon rate. What would be the market value of these Government of Canada bonds? To determine this new market price, the interest payments and principal (or maturity value) are discounted at the new market rate of interest (or required rate of return) of 14 percent, so that[6]

$$B_0 = \$100(PVA_{14\%,\,25yr}) + \$1,000(PV_{14\%,\,25yr})$$
$$= \$100(6.873) + \$1,000(0.038) = \$687.30 + \$38.00 = \$725.30$$

An investor purchasing this 10 percent coupon rate bond for $725.30 and holding it for 25 years expects to receive a compound return of 14 percent.[7] This return is composed of two parts—the 10 percent coupon, which is expected to provide $100 per year, plus the expected capital appreciation of $274.70 (i.e., $1,000 − $725.30) that occurs over the life of the bond. The difference between the $1,000 par value and the current market price of $725.30 is called the **discount** on the bond.

Bonds may also sell at a **premium**. To continue our example, what if economic conditions suddenly change, causing general market interest rates to unexpectedly drop to 6 percent on bonds of comparable quality and maturity? The current market price of the 25-year, 10 percent coupon rate Government of Canada bond becomes[8]

$$B_0 = \$100(PVA_{6\%,\,25yr}) + \$1,000(PV_{6\%,\,25yr})$$
$$= \$100(12.783) + \$1,000(0.233) = \$1,278.30 + \$233.00 = \$1,511.30$$

Because the coupon rate of 10 percent is greater than the new market interest rate of 6 percent, investors pay a premium of $511.30 (i.e., $1,511.30 − $1,000) for the bond. The relationship between the current market yield and the market price is graphed in Figure 4.1. The fundamental point to remember is this: *The price of a bond and general market interest rates move inversely.* If the market interest rate is less than a bond's coupon rate, the bond will sell at a premium. If market interest rates are greater than the coupon rate on a bond, the bond will sell at a discount. A second point to remember, as discussed previously, is: *The primary determinant of market interest rates is expected inflation.*

Interest Rate Risk and the Maturity Premium Bond prices are influenced not only by market interest rates but also by the term (or length) to maturity of the bonds. To see this relationship, consider what happens to the current market price of the 10 percent

---

[6] By financial calculator, enter 0 at t = 0, 100 for t = 1 through t = 24, 1,100 for t = 25, and i = k_b = 14. Selecting net present value (NPV) produces a value of $725.08. The 22 cent difference results from rounding.

[7] This statement assumes the investor can reinvest the periodic interest payments at the promised return—14 percent in this case. If the interest received from this bond is reinvested at a rate lower than 14 percent, the actual return will be less than the promised return of 14 percent. This is the reinvestment rate risk discussed later.

[8] By financial calculator, enter 0 at t = 0, 100 for t = 1 through t = 24, 1,100 for t = 25, and i = k_b = 6. Selecting net present value (NPV) produces a value of $1,511.33. The 3 cent difference results from rounding.

Figure 4.1

Relationship Between a Bond's Market Price and the Current Market Rate of Interest

As market interest rates fall, the bond price rises. Similarly, a rise in the market interest rate causes bond prices to decline.

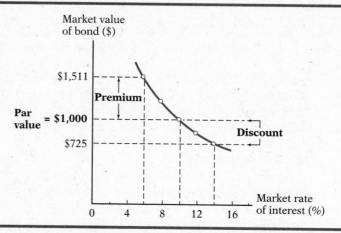

Government of Canada bonds if they have only 3 years left until maturity, instead of 25. As Figure 4.2 shows, the market prices of the 3-year bonds adjust substantially less to changes in market interest rates than do the prices of 25-year bonds. This tendency for prices on short-term bonds to fluctuate less in response to market interest rate changes is called **interest rate risk**. It is because of interest rate risk that, as we observed in our discussion of the liquidity (or maturity) preference theory of term structure in Chapter 2, the return on long-term bonds typically incorporates a maturity premium (or requires a higher interest rate) over comparable short-term bonds.

BONDS ISSUED BY FIRMS

Up to now, we have discussed the relationship between the prices on Government of Canada bonds, the returns required by investors, expected inflation, bond maturity, and bond prices. Corporate bonds are subject to additional risks arising from the possibility of default, liquidity, or issue-specific features. One impact of these other risks is to increase the whole term structure of interest rates for corporate bonds versus government bonds; investors demand a higher return to compensate them for the additional risks arising from investing in corporate bonds. Because investors demand more return, the cost to the firm for issuing bonds is higher than the cost to the government.

How might various factors affect the value of a firm's bonds? Consider what happens if Warehouse SuperStores has had substantial losses and files for protection under the federal bankruptcy laws. Because the risk of loss due to default is high, the required rate of return demanded by investors increases, leading to lower market prices for Warehouse SuperStores' outstanding bonds. The same effect occurs if the bond is

Figure 4.2

Relationship Among a Bond's Market Price, the Current Market Rate of Interest, and Bond Maturity

The market price of shorter-maturity bonds fluctuates substantially less than that for longer-maturity bonds as the market interest rates change.

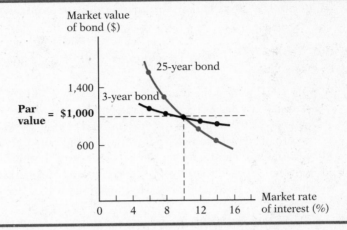

not very liquid (i.e., if there is a "thin market" with few potential buyers). Similarly, if the bond differs in terms of some of its features, it may be seen as either more risky or less desirable than other bonds of comparable maturity. The result is higher returns demanded by investors, which translates into higher costs when firms issue new bonds with these features.

Two other sources of risk exist. One is **reinvestment rate risk**, which is the risk that an investor's income may fall if there is a need to reinvest in another bond issue. Suppose you purchased a bond a few years ago that has a 13 percent coupon rate. Due to the changes in economic conditions, bonds of comparable maturity and risk now provide an 8 percent return. If your bond matures, or is called by the issuing firm, and you reinvest in a new 8 percent bond, you will now receive only $80 per year; in other words, you have lost $130 − $80 = $50 in interest per year.

Another source of risk is **event risk**, where a drastic change in circumstances turns a "safe" bond into a "risky" one. This type of risk can be illustrated by looking at the leveraged buyout of RJR Nabisco that occurred in 1989. Before the buyout, RJR Nabisco had about $5 billion in bonds outstanding. To fund the leveraged buyout, another $16 billion in borrowing took place. Overnight, the possibility of default went up, and investors demanded a higher return to compensate themselves for the increased risk. The market value of already-outstanding RJR Nabisco bonds dropped 20 percent almost overnight. This is an example of a completely new kind of risk that most bondholders are not protected against. It also involves *risk shifting*, where part of the potential value created by the leveraged buyout was, in fact, due to the shift in risk from owners to bondholders.

Many factors can affect bond prices. The key point to remember is that as risk increases, market price decreases, and vice versa. Higher risk leads to higher returns demanded by investors and higher costs to the firm.

DETERMINING THE YIELD TO MATURITY

Instead of being given the required rate of return on a bond, suppose you are told that a 15-year maturity, $1,000 par bond with a 7 percent coupon rate sells for $914.13. What is the compound rate of return, called the **yield to maturity (YTM)**, you would earn if you purchased the bond and held it for the entire 15 years? Answering this question involves finding the unknown discount rate, k_b, as follows:

$$B_0 = I(PVA_{k_b,n}) + M(PV_{k_b,n})$$
$$914.13 = \$70(PVA_{?\%,15yr}) + \$1,000(PV_{?\%,15yr})$$

Our job is to find the discount rate (or $PVA_{k_b,n}$ and $PV_{k_b,n}$ for the same time period or years) that makes the present value of the interest of $70 per year and the maturity value of $1,000 equal to the current market price of $914.13. Before starting, note two points: First, the yield to maturity is simply an internal rate of return, as discussed in Chapter 3. Hence, we already know how to determine the unknown rate, k_b, which is the bond's yield to maturity. Second, because the market price of $914.13 is *less* than the par value of $1,000, the yield to maturity will be *greater* than the coupon interest rate of 7 percent.

If we try 9 percent, the present value is

$$B_0 = \$70(8.061) + \$1,000(0.275) = \$564.27 + \$275 = \$839.27$$

which is too low. Lowering the discount rate to 8 percent, we get

$$B_0 = \$70(8.559) + \$1,000(0.315) = \$599.13 + \$315 = \$914.13$$

Thus, the yield to maturity, which represents the investor's expected compound return from buying the bond at $914.13 and holding it to maturity, is 8 percent.[9]

If the bonds can be called by the firm and retired prior to maturity, it is often helpful to compute the **yield to call (YTC)**, which is the unknown k_b such that

$$B_0 = I(PVA_{k_b,n}) + \text{call price } (PV_{k_b,n})$$

where n is the number of years until call. The call price is typically greater than (or occasionally equal to) the bond's par value.

BONDS WITH SEMIANNUAL INTEREST

Most bonds pay interest semiannually. Valuing bonds with semiannual interest payments is easy *if* we remember the discussion from Chapter 3 on discounting and compounding when it is done more frequently than yearly. Our basic bond valuation

---

[9] With a financial calculator, we solve for yield to maturity, using the internal rate of return (IRR) function, by entering 914.13 at t = 0, 70 for t = 1 through t = 14, and 1,070 for t = 15. Selecting IRR produces the yield to maturity, k_b, of 8.003 percent. The slight difference is due to rounding.

equation (Equation 4.1) is modified as follows:

$$\text{price with semiannual interest, } B_0 = \sum_{t=1}^{2n} \frac{I/2}{(1 + k/2)^t} + \frac{M}{(1 + k/2)^{2n}}$$

$$= \frac{I}{2} (PVA_{k/2, 2n}) + M(PV_{k/2, 2n}) \tag{4.2}$$

Note that the yearly interest, I, is divided by 2 in order to determine the semiannual interest payments. Also, the number of periods, n, is doubled to 2n. A potential stumbling block is the rate k in Equation 4.2. If k_b is a nominal annual rate as discussed in Chapter 3, then k in Equation 4.2 is

$$k(\text{if } k_b \text{ is a nominal annual rate}) = k_b/2$$

However, if k_b is intended to be an effective annual interest rate, then

$$k(\text{if } k_b \text{ is an effective annual rate}) = (1 + k_b)^{0.5} - 1$$

For example, if k_b is 10 percent, then assuming it is a nominal rate produces a rate, k, of $10/2 = 5$ percent; assuming it is an effective annual rate means that k is $(1.10)^{0.5} - 1 = 4.881$ percent. We follow convention and assume k_b is a nominal rate.

To illustrate bond valuation with semiannual interest payments, consider the earlier example of a 25-year, 10 percent coupon rate bond. With semiannual interest and a required rate of return of 14 percent per year or 7 percent per semiannual period, the value of the bond is[10]

$$B_0 = \$100/2 \ (PVA_{14\%/2, \, 2\times25\,yr}) + \$1,000 \ (PV_{14\%/2, \, 2\times25\,yr})$$
$$= \$50(PVA_{7\%, \, 50}) + \$1,000 \ (PV_{7\%, \, 50})$$
$$= \$50(13.801) + \$1,000(0.034) = \$690.05 + \$34.00 = \$724.05$$

What if we want to determine the yield to maturity when interest is paid semiannually? Assume the current market value of a bond, B_0, is $1,054.09, the coupon interest rate is 11 percent per year, interest is paid semiannually, and the bond has a maturity of 8 years. We divide the coupon interest rate in half, so it becomes 5.5 percent per 6 months, and double the maturity to 16 periods. The yield to maturity is found by solving for the unknown discount rate, where

$$\$1,054.09 = \$55(PVA_{?\%, \, 16 \, periods}) + \$1,000(PV_{?\%, \, 16 \, periods})$$

At 5 percent and 16 periods we have $55 (10.838) + $1,000 (0.458) = $1,054.09. The YTM on an annual basis is (5 percent)(2) = 10 percent. At a purchase price of

---

[10] By financial calculator, enter 0 at t = 0, 50 for t = 1 through t = 49, 1,100 for t = 50, and i = $k_b/2$ = 7. Selecting net present value (NPV) produces a value of $723.99. The 6 cent difference results from rounding.

$1,054.09 for the bond, with interest paid semiannually, the bond's expected yield to maturity is 10 percent per year.[11]

CONSOLS AND PREFERRED STOCK

A **consol** is a perpetual coupon rate bond. These bonds got their name from British consols, issued to help finance the Napoleonic wars in the early nineteenth century. In Chapter 3 we determined how to find the present value of a perpetuity. Using that same idea, the market price of a perpetual bond is

$$\text{price of perpetual bond, } B_0 = \frac{I}{k_b} \tag{4.3}$$

where I is the dollar amount of interest to be received at time $t = 1$ and every subsequent t, and k_b is the required return demanded by investors. If the return demanded by investors is 9 percent, and the coupon interest rate is 4 percent, then a $1,000 par value perpetual bond would be worth $40/0.09 = $444.44.

Preferred stock has a prior, but limited, claim on the firm. This claim takes precedence over the claim of the firm's common shareholders. The valuation of preferred stock that is not expected to be retired (at least not for a long time) is similar to that of consols. Therefore, the same approach can be employed using dividends, instead of interest, in Equation 4.3. If the preferred stock has an $80 par value,[12] and the dividend is 9 percent per year, the yearly dividend is ($80)(0.09) = $7.20. If the required rate of return is 12 percent, the price of the preferred stock is $7.20/0.12 = $60.

Bonds trade in the financial markets based on their discounted present value. Thus, for bonds their actual market price and yield to maturity are a direct function of the cash flow expected, the time value of money, and the returns demanded by investors.

BOND VALUATION AND FINANCIAL MANAGEMENT

In recent years bond yields (as shown in Figure 4.3) have fluctuated widely, primarily because of wide swings in actual and expected inflation. Because bond yields and prices are inversely related, bond prices have also been volatile. Understanding this relationship is important because debt is one of the firm's main sources of capital. Determining the firm's opportunity cost of capital (the topic of Chapter 6), and understanding capital structure decisions (Chapters 12 and 13) requires a thorough understanding of bonds—their valuation and pricing. Managers must also compare the costs and risks of financing with intermediate- or long-term sources such as term loans (Chapter 11) and leases (Chapter 15).

---

[11] By financial calculator, enter 1,054.090 at $t = 0$, 55 for $t = 1$ through $t = 15$, and 1,055 for $t = 16$. Selecting internal rate of return (IRR) produces a result of 5.0008 percent ≈ 5 percent per semiannual period or 10 percent annually.

[12] While most bonds have a par value of $1,000, the par value on preferred stock can be almost anything; often it is $100 or less.

Figure 4.3

Relationship Between Long-Term Corporate Bond Yields and Changes in the Consumer Price Index

Market interest rates and inflation move together. In recent years inflation declined much more rapidly than interest rates.

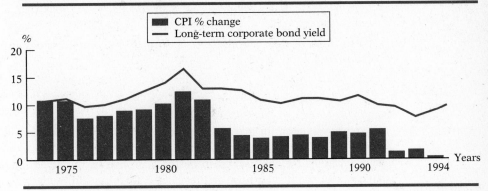

Source: Bank of Canada Review, various issues.

The term structure, investor expectations, and required rates of return become important when comparing the risks and costs of using short-term debt (discussed in Chapter 24) with those of long-term debt. Finally, managers must understand the interaction of risk, returns, and costs when examining whether to replace an outstanding bond issue with a new one; these refunding decisions are examined in Appendix 11A. Hence, we see that there are many instances in financial management when knowledge of the valuation and pricing of bonds is important.

Concept Review Questions

- What series of payments determines a bond's market price?
- Explain what happens to the price of a bond if (1) interest rates increase or (2) interest rates decrease.
- How are consols and perpetual preferred stocks priced?

DETERMINING COMMON STOCK VALUES

The valuation of common stock, although conceptually similar to bond valuation, has some additional complications because neither the cash dividends nor the ending values are constant (as the interest and maturity value are for bonds). Also, with bonds the interest and maturity value are a legal liability of the firm; they have to be paid or the firm can be forced into bankruptcy. With common stock, the cash dividends and any anticipated future price of the stock can be predicted only with a great deal of uncertainty. And there is no legal requirement that forces firms to pay cash dividends.

Common stock represents the primary ownership in firms. If financial markets are efficient, then the actual market price of a share of common stock is a direct function of the cash flow expected, the time value of money, the risks involved, and the returns required by investors. Like investors in bonds, the return demanded by common stock investors, k_s, is equal to the risk-free rate plus a risk premium, or

$$\text{required return on a stock, } k_s = k_{RF} + \text{risk premium}$$

We can think of the risk premium demanded by common stock investors as being composed of

$$\text{stock risk premium} = \frac{\text{default}}{\text{premium}} + \frac{\text{liquidity}}{\text{premium}} + \frac{\text{issue-specific}}{\text{premiums}}$$

The maturity premium that bond investors demand is not relevant when considering common stock because common stock has an infinite life. Common stock investors have a residual (or the last) claim on the firm; that is, the government and creditors have a prior claim that must be met before anything can be distributed to common shareholders. Therefore the size of the default premium demanded by common stock investors will be larger than that demanded by investors in the same firm's bonds. Similarly, common stock investors will demand a liquidity premium if it is hard to sell the stock or if, when they sell, the market price has a tendency to drop significantly because there is a small, or "thin," market for the stock. Finally, issue-specific characteristics of common stock may also affect their risk.[13]

Due to the risks involved, the risk premium on stocks is typically higher than the risk premium on bonds. With rare exceptions, the required return demanded for investing in stocks is higher than the required return demanded for investing in bonds.

DIVIDEND VALUATION

To start, think of common stock valuation as being exactly like bond valuation. The current market price of a share of common stock is theoretically equal to the present value of the expected cash dividends and future market price. Thus a stock's price is equal to

$$\text{price, } P_0 = \sum_{t=1}^{n} \frac{D_t}{(1 + k_s)^t} + \frac{P_n}{(1 + k_s)^n} \tag{4.4}$$

where

D_t = the amount of cash dividends per share expected to be received at the end of the tth period (or year). For example, D_0 = the current dividend *just* paid, and D_1 = the cash dividend expected one period from now (at t = 1).[14]

---

[13] Some other features, such as different classes of stock, are discussed in Chapter 10.

[14] In practice, most firms pay cash dividends on a quarterly basis (see Chapter 14). However, for simplicity we assume they are all paid at one time—the end of the year.

k_s = the rate of return required by investors on the stock

n = the number of time periods, or years

P_t = the expected market price of the stock at the end of period t *right after* the receipt of cash dividend D_t. For example, P_0 = the price today *right after* the receipt of the cash dividend, D_0, and P_1 = the expected price one period from now (at t = 1) *right after* receiving the dividend, D_1.

Thus the current market price of a stock that is expected to pay cash dividends of $1.00 at time t = 1, $1.50 at t = 2, and $2.00 at t = 3, and have an expected market value of $40.00 at t = 3 can be determined in a straightforward manner. If the return demanded by investors is 14 percent, the price of this stock is[15]

$$
\begin{aligned}
P_0 &= \frac{D_1}{(1 + k)^1} + \frac{D_2}{(1 + k)^2} + \frac{D_3}{(1 + k)^3} + \frac{P_3}{(1 + k)^3} \\[2mm]
&= \frac{\$1.00}{(1.14)^1} + \frac{\$1.50}{(1.14)^2} + \frac{\$2.00}{(1.14)^3} + \frac{\$40.00}{(1.14)^3} \\[2mm]
&= \$1.00(PV_{14\%,\,1yr}) + \$1.50(PV_{14\%,\,2yr}) + \$2.00(PV_{14\%,\,3yr}) + \$40.00(PV_{14\%,\,3yr}) \\[2mm]
&= \$1.00(0.877) + \$1.50(0.769) + \$2.00(0.675) + \$40.00(0.675) \\[2mm]
&= \$0.88 + \$1.15 + \$1.35 + \$27.00 = \$30.38
\end{aligned}
$$

If an investor pays $30.38 for the stock, and the stream of dividends and ending market price occurs as projected, the compound rate of return realized on the stock will be 14 percent.[16]

What if we keep adding more years of dividends to Equation 4.4, so that we can think of the cash dividends going on forever? In that case, we have a fundamental common stock model—the **dividend valuation model**—which states that the market price of a share of common stock is equal to the present value of all future dividends:

$$
\begin{aligned}
\text{price, } P_0 &= \frac{D_1}{(1 + k_s)^1} + \frac{D_2}{(1 + k_s)^2} + \cdots + \frac{D_\infty}{(1 + k_s)^\infty} \\[2mm]
&= \sum_{t=1}^{\infty} \frac{D_t}{(1 + k_s)^t}
\end{aligned}
\qquad (4.5)
$$

In Equation 4.4, the second term is $P_n/(1 + k_s)^n$, where P_n represents the market price at time t = n. But what determines the market price at time n? It is simply the present value of all cash dividends expected to be received *from period n + 1 to infinity*, discounted at the investor's required rate of return of k_s. Equation 4.4 is simply a special case of the more general Equation 4.5. This relationship will prove

---

[15] We could add together the $2 cash dividend at t = 3 and the market price of $40; however, for clarity they are kept separate. By financial calculator, enter 0 at t = 0, 1 at t = 1, 1.50 at t = 2, 42 at t = 3, and i = k_s = 14. Selecting net present value (NPV) produces the value of $30.38.

[16] This assumes, similar to the interest received on bonds, as noted in footnote 7, that the cash dividends received at time t = 1 and t = 2 can be reinvested for two years and one year, respectively, at 14 percent. By financial calculator, enter 30.38 at t = 0, 1 at t = 1, 1.50 at t = 2, and 42 at t = 3. Selecting internal rate of return (IRR) produces the value of 14 percent.

useful when we consider valuing stocks that are expected to have nonconstant growth in future cash dividends. However, before doing that, we want to consider the simpler cases of no growth in cash dividends and constant growth in cash dividends.

NO GROWTH IN CASH DIVIDENDS

In the special case of no future expected growth in cash dividends, assume that the stock will pay a constant dividend of, say, $2 per year from now until infinity. Although the no-growth model is obviously unrealistic, it often provides a convenient benchmark. In such a case, the dividend valuation equation (Equation 4.5) is simply a perpetuity. As with consol bonds and preferred stocks, we can use our knowledge from Chapter 3 on how to value a perpetuity to find the current market price of a common stock with a constant expected cash dividend from time $t = 1$ to infinity as follows:

$$\text{price with no growth, } P_0 = \frac{D}{k_s} \qquad (4.6)$$

If the stock of No-Gro Ltd. is expected to pay a cash dividend of $2 per year from time $t = 1$ until infinity, and the investor's required rate of return is 16 percent (or 0.16), then its current price, P_0, is $2/0.16 = $12.50. A rational investor would pay no more than $12.50 for a share of No-Gro's stock if his or her required rate of return is 16 percent.

CONSTANT GROWTH IN CASH DIVIDENDS

In another special case, consider what happens if cash dividends are expected to increase at a constant (percentage) rate each year. This situation is just a growing perpetuity, so we can use our knowledge from Chapter 3 (Equation 3.8) to value this stream of constantly growing dividends. The **constant-growth model** (also known as the **Gordon growth model**) is

$$\text{price with constant growth, } P_0 = \frac{D_1}{k_s - g} \qquad (4.7)$$

where g = the expected (compound) growth rate in the cash dividends. We also assume this is the rate of growth in the market price.

In valuing a stock with constantly growing cash dividends, we must use *the cash dividends expected one year hence*, or D_1. If the current cash dividend (at time $t = 0$) for the stock of Gro Ltd. is $2, the constant compound growth rate in dividends is 10 percent per year, and the return demanded by investors is 16 percent, the value of a share of Gro's stock is

$$P_0 = \frac{D_1}{k_s - g} = \frac{D_0(1 + g)}{k_s - g} = \frac{\$2(1.10)}{0.16 - 0.10} = \frac{\$2.20}{0.06} = \$36.67$$

Note that this price of $36.67 for Gro Ltd. is substantially higher than the $12.50 for No-Gro Ltd. when no growth in future cash dividends was assumed. This makes common sense because, other things being equal, an investor would value a growing cash flow stream at a higher rate than a nongrowing stream.

NONCONSTANT GROWTH IN CASH DIVIDENDS

The next situation we consider is when a firm grows at a fast rate for a few years and then reverts to a constant- or no-growth situation. This might occur because a firm made previous positive net present value investments that produced high cash flows and increases in value, but increasing competition is expected to reduce the future growth rate. For example, if the required rate of return demanded by investors remains at 16 percent, consider how we would value the stock of Rapid-Gro Ltd. when: (1) dividends at time t = 0 are $2; (2) followed by 10 percent growth in dividends for each of years 1, 2, and 3; (3) followed by 3 percent compound growth thereafter until infinity.

The following four-step procedure can be used to solve this problem:

STEP 1: Determine the cash dividends until the series reverts to either constant growth to infinity or no growth. Thus,

$$D_1 = \$2.00(FV_{10\%, 1yr}) = \$2.00(1.100) = \$2.20$$
$$D_2 = \$2.00(FV_{10\%, 2yr}) = \$2.00(1.210) = \$2.42$$
$$D_3 = \$2.00(FV_{10\%, 3yr}) = \$2.00(1.331) = \$2.66$$

STEP 2: Determine the first year's dividend *after* the growth rate changes to either constant growth to infinity or no growth.

$$D_4 = D_3(FV_{3\%, 1yr}) = \$2.66(1.030) = \$2.74$$

Because the growth rate changed to 3 percent (from 10 percent), the new growth rate of 3 percent must be used in this step.

STEP 3: Determine the market price of the stock as of time t = 3 for the constant- or no-growth period. Thus

$$P_3 = \frac{D_4}{k_s - g} = \frac{\$2.74}{0.16 - 0.03} = \frac{\$2.74}{0.13} = \$21.08$$

Note that (1) the growth rate used is the constant one expected from time t = 3 until infinity, and (2) the market price is as of time t = 3.

STEP 4: Using Equation 4.4 and the required rate of return of 16 percent, discount both the expected cash dividends from step 1 and the expected market price from step 3 back to the present. As shown in Figure 4.4, the present value of this stream of expected cash flows is $18.91. Thus, the current market price of the stock should be $18.91.

Figure 4.4

Time Line and Solution for Nonconstant Dividend Series

The dividend in year 4 equals $2.66 ($FV_{3\%, 1yr}$). The market price determined using D_4 is the price at time t = 3. This market price must be brought back to time t = 0, as are the cash dividends for years 1, 2, and 3, by discounting at 16 percent.

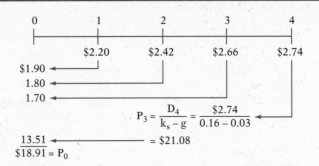

To see the relationship among the amount and rate of growth in expected cash dividends and the current market price of a stock, consider Table 4.1, which summarizes our calculations. In the case of no future growth, the market price is $12.50, whereas it is $36.67 at a 10 percent compound rate to infinity. Finally, growth at 10 percent for three years followed by low or no growth[17] thereafter produces market prices of $18.91 and $16.05, respectively. Clearly, *the rate and duration of expected growth opportunities leading to growth in cash dividends have a major impact on the market price of a common stock.* (Later in the chapter we will discuss the present value of growth opportunities, which is closely related to the present discussion.) Accurate estimation of growth opportunities and expected growth rates is the most important aspect of common stock valuation using the dividend valuation approach. It is also one of the most difficult.

TO INVEST OR NOT TO INVEST?

The valuation procedures discussed above can help us assess whether we should buy a security or not. One way to evaluate a potential investment in a security is to apply the concept of net present value (NPV) in conjunction with our valuation procedures. As we saw in Chapter 3, NPV = present value of future cash inflows − initial investment. According to Equation 4.5, P_0 represents the present value of all future dividends (or cash inflows) while the current market price represents the initial investment necessary to purchase the stock. Therefore, when we apply NPV to stocks it becomes NPV = P_0 − market price. For example, we placed a value of $36.67 on the stock of Gro Ltd.; if the actual market price of Gro is $40, then the NPV = $36.67 − $40 = −$3.33. Since we should invest only in positive NPV projects, under these circumstances we should not buy Gro, or we should sell if we own it, because we believe the

---

[17] If there was no growth in cash dividends expected after year 3, $P_3 = D_4/k_s = \$2.66/0.16 = \$16.625$. Discounting this back to time zero at 16 percent and adding it to the discounted value of the cash dividends to be received for periods 1, 2, and 3 produces a market price of $16.05.

Table 4.1

Relationship Between Expected Growth and Market Price

There is a direct relationship between the amount and length of expected growth in cash dividends and a stock's market price.

Condition[a]	Resulting Market Price (P_0)
No future growth in expected cash dividends	$12.50
10 percent compound growth in expected cash dividends for t = 1, t = 2, and t = 3, followed by no future growth[b]	16.05
10 percent compound growth in expected cash dividends for t = 1, t = 2, and t = 3, followed by 3 percent compound growth to infinity	18.91
10 percent compound growth in expected cash dividends to infinity	36.67

[a] D_0 = $2 and k_s = 16 percent for all conditions.
[b] From footnote 17.

market is overvaluing the shares of this firm. On the other hand, if the shares can be bought for $30, then we should buy because the NPV is positive: NPV = $36.67 − $30 = $6.67. This means that we believe that the market is undervaluing the shares and they are, therefore, a good buy. Finally, if the shares can be purchased at $36.67, then we would be indifferent because we believe the market value is correct and as a result NPV = $36.67 − $36.67 = 0. Thus, when we use one of the valuation equations to calculate a value that we would place on a stock and then compare this value to current market price, we are conceptually using the NPV criterion to evaluate the investment opportunity.

Alternatively, we can determine if a stock is a good buy or not by calculating the rate of return that we expect to earn from an investment in the stock and comparing it to our required rate of return of 16 percent. Suppose an investor pays $36.67 for a share of Gro's stock today when it is expected that the current dividend (D_0) of $2 will grow indefinitely at 10 percent per year. What rate of return can this investor expect to realize on the investment in this firm? Equation 4.7 provides us with a method to determine the rate of return that this investor can expect. The expected rate of return is obtained by simply solving Equation 4.7 for k_s. If we do this and replace k_s with k_x, to represent the expected rate of return, we have

$$\text{expected rate of return, } k_x = \frac{D_1}{P_0} + g \qquad (4.8)$$

Therefore, in our example we have k_x = $2.20/$36.67 + 0.10 = 0.16 or 16 percent.

Conceptually, the expected rate of return is the internal rate of return (IRR) that will be earned by investing in the stock. From Chapter 3, we know that the IRR of an investment opportunity must be greater than the investor's required rate of return for the investment to be worthwhile. Here the expected rate of return is equal to the investor's required rate of return of 16 percent. Therefore, the investor should be indifferent about buying this stock. However, if the shares can be purchased for $30, the expected rate of return would be $k_x = \$2.20/\$30 + 0.10 = 0.173$ or 17.3 percent. Since the expected rate of return is now greater than the investor's required rate of return the shares are a good buy. On the other hand, if the market price of the shares is $40 then the expected rate of return is only 15.5 percent ($2.20/40 + 0.10$) which is less than the required rate; therefore, the firm is not a good buy now.

Thus we see that NPV and IRR can help us to make investment decisions concerning financial assets as well as physical assets. Although we have used common stock to demonstrate how to evaluate investments in financial assets, the same procedure applies to bonds or preferred stock. In any case, for an investment in any security to enhance the investor's well-being, its NPV must be greater than zero, or its IRR must be greater than the investor's required rate of return.

NONDIVIDEND-PAYING STOCKS

We have discussed stock valuation when the firm pays cash dividends, but not all firms pay them. How should we value nondividend-paying stocks? There are three ways. The first is to estimate *when* the firm will start paying dividends, their size, growth rate, and so forth; then simply proceed as we have discussed. The second is a variation of the first, except you must estimate some future market price and then discount it back to the present, as we have done previously. The final approach employs earnings and multiplies (or capitalizes) them by some factor (based on perceived growth, risk, and/or estimates derived by looking at "similar" firms) to arrive at an estimated value.

VOLATILITY, LIQUIDITY, AND STOCK PRICES

Recently many empirical studies have examined the volatility of stock prices and returns. In doing so they have often focused on one or more of the three basic variables that can lead to stock price volatility. These are (1) shocks (or unexpected changes) in a firm's cash flows and, therefore, cash dividends; (2) changes in the discount rate (k_s) due to predictable changes in macro forces such as gross domestic product (GDP), industrial production, and investment, which are important determinants of the cash flows for firms; and (3) unexpected shocks (or changes) in the discount rate employed. At the same time, there is some evidence that investors demand additional compensation for investing in less-liquid stocks. Given the apparent acceleration in the research in these areas, it is safe to say that a lot more will be known in the future about the causes and impact of volatility and liquidity on stock prices.

Most investors, amateur or professional, do not employ the dividend valuation model exactly as we have described it. However, their decision making does have some characteristics in common with the model: They (1) focus on cash flows and dividends; (2) consider the returns needed to compensate them for the risks incurred (given their alternatives and economic conditions); and (3) look for growth opportunities. Thus the intuition behind the dividend valuation model underlies much of what drives the decisions made by investors.

Concept Review Questions

- What are the risk premiums that affect a stock's price?
- What are the cash flows that determine a stock's price?
- Describe how you would price a stock with nonconstant growth and cash dividends.
- What are the three basic variables that lead to stock price volatility?

THE PRESENT VALUE OF GROWTH OPPORTUNITIES

Based on what we have just learned, a number of important observations can be made about stocks and the creation of value for the firm. First, let us go back to determining the stock price when the firm and its cash dividends are expected to grow at a constant compound rate g until infinity. As given by Equation 4.7, the stock price is

$$P_0 = \frac{D_1}{k_s - g}$$

Assume you are looking at two firms, Growth and Nongrowth. For simplicity, assume both will pay dividends of $1 at time t = 1 and the required rate of return is (for illustration purposes) the same in each case—15 percent. What should their market prices be if g is 10 percent for Growth and 0 percent for Nongrowth? The prices are:

$$P_0(\text{Growth}) = \frac{\$1}{0.15 - 0.10} = \$20$$

$$P_0(\text{Nongrowth}) = \frac{\$1}{0.15 - 0} = \$6.67$$

Other things being equal, we see that the market price of a firm which is expected to grow is higher than the market price of a firm that is not expected to grow. Although firms do not grow at a constant percentage compound rate forever, and the return required by investors might not be the same for Growth and Nongrowth, the basic conclusion from this example holds: *Expected growth is valuable.*

PRICE/EARNINGS RATIOS

The term **price/earnings (P/E) ratio** is often heard when common stocks are analyzed. The price/earnings ratio is simply the market price per share of common stock divided by the **earnings per share (EPS)**, where earnings per share equal (total earnings available for common shareholders)/(number of shares of common stock outstanding). Likewise, the **dividend payout ratio** is simply (cash dividends paid per share of common stock)/(earnings per share of common stock). For example, if a firm has earnings of $5 per share and pays a cash dividend of $2 per share, the dividend payout ratio is $2/$5 = 40 percent. Let us go back to the constant-growth model given by Equation 4.7 and define the dividend next year, D_1, as being equal to the earnings per share next year, EPS_1, times the dividend payout ratio. Thus, $D_1 = (EPS_1)$ (dividend payout ratio). Therefore, Equation 4.7 becomes

$$P_0 = \frac{EPS_1(\text{dividend payout ratio})}{k_s - g} \qquad (4.9)$$

Rearranging Equation 4.9, we find the price/earnings ratio is

$$\frac{P_0}{EPS_1} = \frac{\text{dividend payout ratio}}{k_s - g}$$

Looked at in this manner, *the price/earnings ratio is a function of the firm's dividend payout ratio, the return demanded by investors, k_s, and the expected future growth, g, for the firm.*

Should a firm and investors be happy if a stock has a "high" price/earnings ratio? That depends. One way a firm can have a high P/E ratio is if it has little or no earnings. For example, if the market price for a stock is $15 and the firm had a very bad year and expects earnings per share will be only $0.20, its P/E ratio would be 75 (i.e., $15/$0.20 = 75). In this instance the high price/earnings ratio is due to the depressed level of earnings.

But another possibility that leads to high P/E ratios is for the expected growth, g, to be high. As we saw in the previous example of Growth and Nongrowth, other things being equal, higher expected growth and higher stock prices go hand-in-hand. Thus, a second and more favourable meaning of a high P/E ratio is that the expected growth for the firm is high. The message is simple and straightforward: High P/E ratios may be "good news" or "bad news." Do not automatically assume a high P/E ratio signals good news in the form of high expected growth.

GROWTH OPPORTUNITIES AND VALUE CREATION

Now let us consider growth opportunities and how firms create value. Assume Everyday Supply is not growing at all. The earnings per share are $100 per year and the required return demanded by Everyday's investors is 10 percent. Because the firm is not growing, the earnings can be distributed to the common shareholders; thus, the dividend payout ratio is 100 percent, or 1.0. The market value of Everyday, using Equation 4.9, is

$$P_0 = \frac{EPS_1(\text{dividend payout ratio})}{k_s - g} = \frac{\$100(1.00)}{0.10 - 0} = \$1,000$$

and the firm pays all of the earnings of $100 out in cash dividends each year.

What if Everyday has the opportunity to make a $100 investment next year (at time t = 1) in a project that promises to return $10 forever? In order to make the capital investment, Everyday will forgo paying cash dividends at time t = 1, but from t = 2 on the dividends will be $110. This project is as risky as the firm, so the required return on it is 10 percent. What is the net present value of the proposed project? With the returns going on forever, this investment is a perpetuity. The net present value is equal to the present value of the future cash flows minus the initial investment, so

$$\text{net present value}_1 = \frac{\$10}{0.10} - \$100 = 0$$

What about the market price of Everyday after it makes this investment? Earnings (i.e., dividends) will not be paid out to investors at time $t = 1$, but from time $t = 2$ until infinity they will be $110. What is the new market price of Everyday? Because the cash inflow stream is still a perpetuity, the price at $t = 1$ is EPS_2/k_s, so its price at $t = 0$ is

$$P_0 = \frac{P_1}{1 + k_s} = \frac{EPS_2/k_s}{1 + k_s} = \frac{\$110/0.10}{1.10} = \frac{\$1,100}{1.10} = \$1,000$$

This example illustrates a simple and important fact: *The value of a firm does not increase or decrease when it accepts zero net present value projects.*

What if there is another project to consider? Suppose this project requires Everyday to invest $100 at time $t = 1$, promises a return of $20 from $t = 2$ on, and the investor's required return remains 10 percent? The net present value at $t = 1$ is $100, where

$$\text{net present value}_1 = \frac{\$20}{0.10} - \$100 = \$100$$

and the new market price of Everyday at $t = 0$, after making this positive net present value investment, is $1,091, or

$$P_0 = \frac{\$120/0.10}{1 + 0.10} = \frac{\$1,200}{1.10} = \$1,091$$

By investing in a positive net present value project, Everyday has increased its market value.

What if Everyday could invest the $100 in another project that promised a return of $30 forever, or alternatively one that promised a return of only $5 forever? The figures for these alternative investments along with the two already considered are as follows:

Return from t = 2 on	Investment at t = 1	Net Present Value	Market Price
$30	$100	$200	$1,182
20	100	100	1,091
10	100	0	1,000
5	100	−50	955

The message from these figures is clear: *To increase the value of the firm, positive net present value projects—which promise to return above the required return—are necessary. Simply investing in projects that provide the return demanded by investors, which is also the firm's opportunity cost of capital, does not create value. Likewise, when firms accept projects that have a negative net present value, the firm and its investors suffer a loss in value.*

The above discussion can be summarized as follows: The stock price can be thought of as being composed of the capitalized value of the assets in place under a no-growth policy plus the **present value of growth opportunities (PVGO)**:

$$\text{stock price, } P_0 = \frac{EPS_1}{k_s} + PVGO$$

$$= \frac{\text{present value of}}{\text{assets in place}} + \frac{\text{present value of}}{\text{growth opportunities}} \tag{4.10}$$

For a firm to prosper, it must find and exploit investment opportunities that allow it to grow. *Investing in a project that provides an average rate of return is not growth!* Likewise, investing in projects that can be easily replicated by others invites immediate competition and price cutting and, therefore, limits the opportunity of the firm to increase its value. The message is simple and direct: The way for firms to create value is to find and exploit investment projects that have positive net present values. *Positive net present value projects and value creation are synonymous.* This finding is one of the central ideas of finance. We examine net present value, and how to make wealth-maximizing capital investment decisions, in Chapters 7 through 9.

Concept Review Questions

- Is it true that investors prefer a high P/E ratio stock? Explain.
- How does the growth rate affect a firm's value?
- How does the present value of growth opportunities affect a firm's market value?

RETURNS AND FINANCIAL MANAGEMENT

Before leaving this chapter, let us take a look at returns and risk. We will define how returns are measured, then consider actual versus expected returns, and finally discuss its relevance for effective financial management.

RETURNS

The **return** from investing in any financial asset comes from one of two sources: (1) income from interest, dividends, and so forth; and (2) capital gains or losses—that is, the difference between the asset's beginning and ending market values. For common stocks these returns are cash dividends received during the period, and capital appreciation or loss. For any period (e.g., a month, a year) we can define the return on a stock as

$$\text{return, } k = \frac{D_1 + (P_1 - P_0)}{P_0} \qquad (4.11)$$

If a firm expects to pay cash dividends of $3.50 per share at time $t = 1$, the market price today is $40, and the expected price at time $t = 1$ is $42, then the return is

$$k = \frac{\$3.50 + (\$42 - \$40)}{\$40} = \frac{\$5.50}{\$40} = 0.1375 = 13.75\%$$

In the example, this is an *ex ante* (expected) rate of return; it is what investors anticipate receiving *before* the fact. Their *ex post* (realized) rate of return over the period (calculated using Equation 4.11, but with historical data) may differ from the expected return if cash dividends are more or less than the expected $3.50, or if the ending market price is different from the $42 projected.

Returns from bonds or from any other financial asset can be computed in exactly the same way, using appropriately specified values in Equation 4.11. In practice, we can measure returns over any time period, but a year is typical. Also, note that we can calculate realized returns whether or not we actually sell the financial asset. To illustrate this, suppose an investor purchased a stock and plans to hold it for three years. If the actual cash dividend received at the end of the first year was $3.50 and the actual ending market price was $42, then the return over the first year was 13.75 percent— whether or not the investor actually sold the security. For the second year $42 represents the initial price; any capital gain or loss for the year is measured against the $42 figure. This process is repeated over and over again, and a series of realized, or *ex post*, returns exists as long as the stock is owned by the investor.

EXPECTED VERSUS REALIZED RETURNS

An investor's realized return may differ from his or her expected return. In theory, expected returns are always positive, because investors will not expose themselves to risk without the prospect of appropriate returns over and above the risk-free rate. But an examination of Figure 4.5 shows that realized common stock returns have not always been positive. While the dividend component is relatively stable, the capital (or price) appreciation or loss is not. Over the 1960–1994 period, 40 percent of the total return on common stocks came from dividend income; the remainder was due to changes in the market price of common stocks.

IMPORTANCE FOR FINANCIAL MANAGEMENT

Return, risk, bond prices, stock prices, and managerial decisions are closely related, as Figure 4.6 shows. Beginning at the top left, we start with financial management decisions. These affect the magnitude, timing, and riskiness of the firm's expected cash flow. Next, based on all the information coming to them about the firm, the economy,

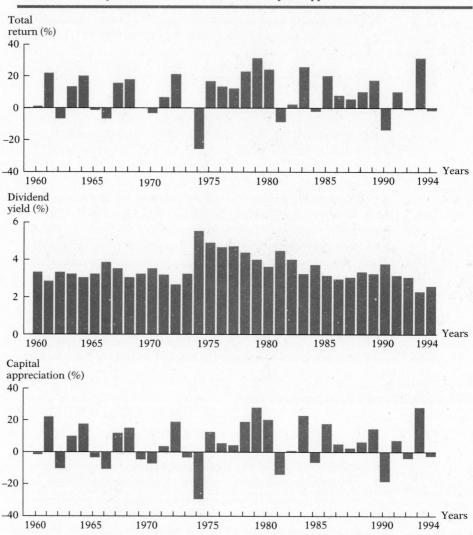

Figure 4.5

Total Returns, Dividend Income, and Capital Appreciation for Common Stocks, 1960–1994

These data, for the Toronto Stock Exchange 300 index, indicate that returns from dividends are much more dependable than those attributed to price appreciation or loss.

Source: Bank of Canada Review, various issues.

and so forth, investors assess the perceived risk for the firm—which directly affects the returns they demand. These actions determine the market value of the firm. Based on the performance of the firm's stock and bonds and the firm's opportunity cost of capital, additional financial management decisions are made: The relationship among financial management decisions, the market value of the firm, and its opportunity cost of capital is continuous and ongoing.

Figure 4.6

Relationship Between the Firm's Financial Management Decisions and Investors' Actions

Because of the interrelated and circular nature of the decision-making process, investors' actions, and the value of the firm, managers must understand the importance of financial markets and financial assets in the decision-making process.

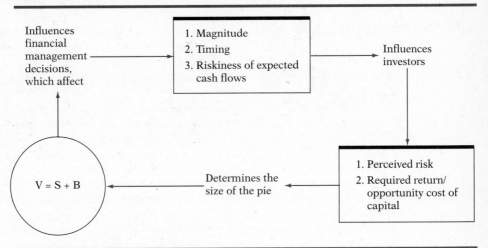

Concept Review Questions

■ Explain the difference between *ex ante* and *ex post* rates of return.

■ What is the relationship between return and risk for financial assets?

KEY POINTS

- Based on cash flows, the market price of any financial asset, such as a bond or stock, is equal to the expected cash flows coming from the asset, discounted at the investor's required rate of return.
- The return required, or demanded, by an investor is equal to the risk-free rate of interest plus a risk premium. For a stock the risk premium may include a default premium, a liquidity premium, and an issue-specific premium.
- As general market interest rates increase, the market price of a bond decreases. Alternatively, as general market interest rates decrease, the market price of a bond increases.
- The yield to maturity is the compound rate of return expected to be earned by purchasing a bond at the current market price and holding it to maturity.
- The rate and duration of the expected growth in cash dividends have a major impact on the market price of common stock. Other things being equal, higher expected growth and higher stock prices go hand-in-hand.
- The firm's stock price is composed of the present value of the assets in place plus

the present value of growth opportunities. The firm can create value, as shown by increases in the market price, only by accepting positive net present value projects.

- *Ex post* (or realized) returns will not necessarily equal *ex ante* (expected) returns.
- Higher returns demanded by investors lead to higher costs of debt and equity financing for the firm.

QUESTIONS

4.1 Using both stocks and bonds, explain why their current market price is equal to the present value of the future cash flows expected by investors, discounted at their required rate of return.

4.2 Why is it that bonds do not typically sell at face value? How do fluctuations in market interest rates and the length of time to maturity influence bond price fluctuations?

4.3 The rate of return you will receive on a bond if you buy it today and hold it until maturity is its yield to maturity (YTM). (*Note:* In answering these questions, ignore any reinvestment problem associated with the future interest to be received.)

a. What happens to the YTM as market interest rates change?
b. Will you receive any more, or any less, if interest rates change as long as you hold the bond to maturity? Why?
c. Will you receive any more, or any less, as interest rates change if you are forced to sell before maturity? Why?

4.4 Explain the difference in determining either the value of a bond or its yield to maturity, employing annual versus semiannual discounting. With semiannual discounting, why do we adjust for the number of periods not only for the coupon interest but also for the maturity value?

4.5 The following formula is used when dividends have been estimated for a few years, at which time the estimated future market price is then employed:

$$P_0 = \sum_{t=1}^{n} \frac{D_t}{(1 + k_s)^t} + \frac{P_n}{(1 + k_s)^n}$$

Explain where the term P_n comes from.

4.6 Carl is in the process of valuing a common stock under various circumstances, as follows:

Conditions	Estimated Stock Price
Required return = 15%; D_0 = $1.00; g = 0; period = ∞	$ 6.67
Required return = 15%; D_0 = $1.00; g = 10%; period = ∞	22.00
Required return = 15%; D_0 = $1.00; g = 10% for each of five years followed by 5% from there to infinity; period = ∞	10.00
Required return = 15%; D_0 = $1.00; g = 5%; period = ∞	10.50

Which one of his answers does not make sense? Why?

4.7 Does a high price/earnings ratio mean a firm is a "growth firm"? Explain.

4.8 Under what conditions does the P/E ratio equal $1/k_s$?

4.9   The market price of a firm can be thought of as:

$$P_0 = \frac{EPS_1}{k_s} + PVGO$$

Explain the ideas behind this formula. How does it relate to value creation and accepting positive, zero, or negative net present value projects?

CONCEPT REVIEW PROBLEMS

See Appendix A for solutions.

CR4.1   Ark Ltd. has a bond with a 10 percent coupon rate and a $1,000 face value. Interest is paid semiannually, and the bond has 15 years to maturity.
a.   If investors require an 8 percent yield, what is the bond's value?
b.   If the bond is expected to be called in five years at $1,100, what is the bond's value?

CR4.2   Tyco bonds are selling for $945. These 20-year $1,000 par value bonds pay 6 percent interest semiannually. If they are purchased at the market price, what is the yield to maturity?

CR4.3   You are thinking of buying 300 shares of B.C. Tel preferred stock which currently sells for $70 per share and pays annual dividends of $6.50 per share. If you require a 10 percent return, would you buy B.C. Tel's preferred stock?

CR4.4   Dwyer's common stock paid $1.65 in dividends last year and is expected to grow indefinitely at an annual rate of 6 percent. What is the value of the stock if you require a 14 percent return?

CR4.5   In CR4.4, what would the stock sell for today if the dividend is expected to grow at 20 percent for the next four years and grow at 6 percent per year thereafter? (*Note*: The required return remains the same.)

CR4.6   Homestake recently paid a dividend of $2.00 per share and is expected to have a growth rate of −15 percent infinitely. If you require a 20 percent return, what is the current value of Homestake?

CR4.7   The common stock of NBDC is selling for $35. The stock recently paid dividends of $2.50 per share and has a projected growth rate of 6 percent. If you purchase this stock at the market price and hold it for one year, what is your expected rate of return?

PROBLEMS

4.1   Yang Computer bonds pay $80 annual interest, mature in 10 years, and pay $1,000 at maturity. What will their price be if the market rate of interest is (**a**) 6 percent or (**b**) 10 percent, and interest is paid (**1**) annually or (**2**) semiannually?

4.2   Find the current market price of a 20-year, 9 percent coupon rate bond with a par value of $1,000, if interest is paid annually and if current market rates are (**a**) 11 percent or (**b**) 7 percent. What are the current market prices if everything is the same except the bond has only (**1**) 10 years to maturity or (**2**) 2 years to maturity? What can we say about the relative influence of changing market interest rates on the market prices of short-term versus long-term bonds? Can you speculate on why this is so?

4.3   Greenman Engineering has some 15-year, $1,000 par bonds outstanding, which have a coupon interest rate of 9 percent and pay interest annually. What is the yield to maturity on the bonds if their current market price is

a. $1,181.72?

b. $795.99?

c.   Would you be willing to pay $795.99 if your minimum required rate of return was 11 percent? Why or why not?

4.4   Zepher's has some 12-year, $1,000 par bonds outstanding. The bonds have a coupon interest rate of 10.4 percent and pay interest semiannually. What is the yield to maturity on the bonds if their current market price is

a. $960?

b. $1,125?

4.5   A $1,000 par value bond has a 12 percent coupon rate, pays interest annually, and has 15 years remaining until it matures.

a.   If $B_0 = \$1,151.72$, what is its yield to maturity (YTM)?

b.   If the bond can be called in six years at $1,030, what is the bond's yield to call (YTC)? Why is the YTC in this problem lower than the YTM? Would this always be true?

4.6   You are interested in buying 100 shares of a $60 par value preferred stock that has an $8\frac{1}{2}$ percent dividend rate.

a.   If your required return is 11 percent, how much would you be willing to pay to acquire the 100 shares?

b.   Assume no dividends will be paid until time t = 3. At the same required return, how much would you now be willing to pay?

4.7   Smith Supermarkets' common stock is selling at $54, the cash dividend expected next year (at time t = 1) is $3.78 per share, and the required rate of return is 15 percent. What is the implied compound growth rate (to infinity) in cash dividends?

4.8   A stock currently pays cash dividends of $4 per share ($D_0 = \$4$), and the required rate of return is 12 percent. What is its market price in the following cases?

a.   There is no future growth in dividends.

b.   Dividends grow at 8 percent per year to infinity.

c.   Dividends grow at 5 percent for each of two years, and there is no growth expected after D_2.

4.9   Siegel Mines' ore reserves are depleted. Hence, the expected future rate of growth in the firm's cash dividends is −5 percent. (That is, the cash dividends will decline 5 percent per year.) The cash dividend at time t = 0 is $4.40, and the required rate of return is 11 percent. What is the current market price of the stock if we assume dividends decline at 5 percent per year until infinity?

4.10   Steve is contemplating the purchase of a small, one-island service station. After-tax cash flows are presently $20,000 per year, and his required rate of return is 14 percent.

a.   What is the maximum price Steve should pay for the service station if he expects cash flows to grow at 4 percent per year to infinity?

b.   If Steve decides he needs a 15 percent return, and there will be no growth in after-tax cash flows for three years, followed by 10 percent per year for years 4 and 5, followed by 3 percent growth to infinity, what is the maximum amount he should pay?

4.11   Dubofsky Energy is a new enterprise that is not expected to pay any cash dividends for the next five years. Its first dividend (D_6) is expected to be $2, and the cash dividends are expected to grow for the next four years (through time t = 10) at 25 percent per year. After that, cash dividends are expected to grow at a more normal 5 percent per year to infinity. If $k_s = 18$ percent, what is P_0?

4.12   Jane is considering purchasing stock and holding it for three years. The projected dividends (at a 5 percent growth rate) and market price are: $D_1 = \$4.20$; $D_2 = \$4.41$; $D_3 = \$4.63$; and $P_3 = \$97.23$. Her required rate of return, given the risk involved, is 10 percent.

a.   What is the maximum price Jane should pay for the stock?

b.   If the dividends for years 1 and 2 remain at $4.20 and $4.41, respectively, and are expected to grow at 5 percent per year to infinity, what would the market price have to be at the end of the second year if Jane sold the stock but still demanded a 10 percent return?

c.   Based on the information given in (b), what is the maximum price Jane should pay for the stock if she plans to sell it after two years?

d.   Why are your answers the same for (a) and (c), aside from any rounding errors?

e.   Does the price of the stock today depend on how long Jane plans to hold it? That is, does its price today depend on whether Jane plans to hold the stock for two years, three years, or any other period of time?

4.13   Suppose you believe that Legler Products common stock will be worth $144 per share two years from now. What is the maximum you would be willing to pay per share if it pays no cash dividends and your required rate of return is 16 percent?

4.14   Nelson's Enterprises is a no-growth firm that pays cash dividends of $8 per year. Its current required rate of return is 12 percent.

a.   What is Nelson's current market price?

b.   Management is considering an investment that will convert the firm into a constant-growth firm, but it requires shareholders to forgo cash dividends for the next six years. When cash dividends are resumed in year 7, they will be $8.88; the expected constant growth is 11 percent from year 6 to infinity. If its new required return is 16 percent, will the shareholders be better off?

c.   What happens if everything is the same as in (b), except that the growth rate is only 10 percent?

4.15   Alfred's is able to generate an EPS of $4 on its existing assets. If the firm does not invest except to maintain the existing assets, its EPS is expected to remain at $4 per year. A new investment opportunity has come up which requires an investment of $4 per share at time $t = 1$. The return required by investors is 10 percent.

a.   What is the net present value of the project, and the market price of Alfred's, if:

1.   The project provides a return of $1 per year forever?

2.   The project provides a return of $1 per year for only 10 years (that is, for $t = 2$ through $t = 11$)?

b.   How much did the market price increase in each case in (a) from what the market price was before the investment?

4.16   Consider three firms with market prices, earnings per share, and returns required (or expected) by investors as follows:

Firm	Market Price, P_0	Earnings per Share (EPS)	Required Return, k_s
A	$40	$2.00	0.18
B	90	8.50	0.10
C	76	7.00	0.17

a.   Determine the price/earnings ratio, the implied present value of growth opportunities

(PVGO), and the ratio of PVGO to P_0 for each of the firms.

b. Does each of the firms look as if it is valued properly by investors?

4.17   Mini Case As a junior analyst for Walden and Sons, your boss just gave you the following group of securities to analyze:

Security	Today's Market Value
7% coupon rate, $1,000 par, 20-year bond, paying interest annually	$900
10 shares of $7\frac{1}{2}$ percent, $100 par, preferred stock	900
18 shares of a low-growth common stock	900
30 shares of a high-growth common stock	900
Total value	$3,600

a. What is the yield to maturity on the 20-year bond?

b. What is the required return on the preferred stock?

c. Your boss is afraid that due to world-wide economic and political problems, expected inflation will increase. If that happens, she predicts the required rates of return demanded for all securities will increase. Her specific projections for the securities are as follows:

Security	New Required Return
Bond	11.0%
Preferred stock	11.5
Low-growth common stock	17.0
High-growth common stock	20.0

The details for the two common stocks are as follows:

Low-growth D_0 = $4.00, growth at 6 percent per year for three years, followed by decline from 6 percent to 4 percent forever.

High-growth D_0 = $1.00, growth for the next four years at 40 percent per year, followed by a decline from 40 percent to 5 percent forever.

1. Do you agree that required rates of return would increase if expected inflation increases? Why or why not? Explain.
2. What would be the new market price for the bond, the preferred stock, and the two common stocks if your boss is correct?
3. What is the new total market value of the group of securities?
4. How much, in terms of percentage, does the value of the group of securities fall? Which security suffers the most loss in value? The least loss in value? Why does this occur?

d. Explain, in terms of the low-growth and high-growth stocks, the present value of growth opportunities. Other things being equal, does a high price/earnings ratio mean the stock is a high-growth stock and a low price/earnings ratio mean the stock is low-growth? Explain.

REFERENCES

BARTHOLDY, JAN. "Testing for a Price-Earnings Effect on the Toronto Stock Exchange." *Canadian Journal of Administrative Sciences* 10 (March 1993): 60–67.

CRABBE, LELAND. "Event Risk: An Analysis of Losses to Bondholders and 'Super Poison Put' Bond Covenants." *Journal of Finance* 46 (June 1991): 689–706.

GEHR, ADAM K., JR. "A Bias in Dividend Discount Models." *Financial Analysts Journal* 48 (January/February 1992): 75–80.

FAMA, EUGENE F. "Stock Returns, Expected Returns, and Real Activity." *Journal of Finance*, 45 (September 1990): 1089–1108.

HATCH, JAMES E., and ROBERT W. WHITE. *Canadian Stocks, Bonds, Bills and Inflation: 1950–1987.* Charlottesville, VA: Research Foundation of the Institute of Chartered Financial Analysts, 1988.

HAUGEN, ROBERT A., ELI TALMOR, and WALTER N. TOROUS. "The Effect of Volatility Changes on the Level of Stock Prices and Subsequent Expected Returns." *Journal of Finance* 46 (July 1991): 985–1007.

HICKMAN, KENT, and GLENN H. PETRY. "A Comparison of Stock Price Predictions Using Court Accepted Formulas, Dividend Discount, and P/E Models." *Financial Management* 19 (Summer 1990): 76–87.

JOHNSON, LEWIS D. "Dividends, Duration, and Price Volatility." *Canadian Journal of Administrative Sciences* 8 (March 1991): 43–46.

APPENDIX

4A   *Reading the Financial Press*

How to read the financial pages is one of the first things students of finance want to learn. This appendix presents a brief overview of stock and bond quotations. There are many sources of financial quotations, and local newspapers also provide varying coverage of the financial markets. But the most comprehensive daily listing is in *The Globe and Mail (G&M)*. *The G&M* provides information on all Canadian-listed stocks that are traded on any given day, plus a variety of other financial information on other stocks, bonds, money-market instruments, foreign-exchange rates, options, and the like.

Toronto Stock Exchange (TSE) quotation information from the *G&M* for one day follows for the common stock and $2.00 preferred stock of Alcan Aluminum Limited.

52-Week									Vol
High	Low	Stock	Sym	Div	High	Low	Close	Chg	(100s)
$49\frac{5}{8}$	$36\frac{3}{4}$	Alcan	AL	a0.60	45.50	44.50	45.50	+1.00	7734
27.75	$22\frac{1}{4}$	Alcan	AL.PR.E	1.79	25.50	25.40	25.40	−0.10	13
$23\frac{1}{4}$	$19\frac{1}{2}$	Alcan	AL.PR.F	1.34	22.95	22.75	22.85		221

The stock's name is preceded by two columns indicating the high and low stock prices for the last 52 weeks. The stock's name is followed by its trading symbol. The .PR on the trading symbol indicates a preferred stock and the final suffix, .E and .F in this case, identifies the specific issue or series of preferred stock. The Div column indicates the yearly cash dividend. The "a" before the common stock dividend indicates that it is paid in U.S. dollars. The next three columns indicate the high, low, and closing (or last) price for the day. The Chg column indicates the change (difference) in the quoted closing price and the closing price on the preceding day. In this case, Alcan's common stock closed up $1, whereas its E series preferred stock was down ten cents and its F series preferred stock was unchanged from the previous session. The Vol column indicates the number of shares traded on this day in hundreds. Thus the 7734 in the volume column for the common stock means that 773,400 shares were traded that day.

As you can see from the Alcan quotations, stock prices are quoted in decimals. This was not always the case. Prior to April 15, 1996, stocks with a value over $5 were quoted in increments of one-eighth of a dollar, or 12.5 cents, on all Canadian stock exchanges. However, on April 15, 1996, Canada's stock exchanges moved to decimal trading—quoting stock prices for stocks trading over $5 in increments of 5 cents. As was noted in Chapter 2, more than 50 percent of the dollar value of trades for Canadian-based firms that are interlisted on U.S. exchanges takes place in the United States, where stocks are still quoted in increments of 12.5 cents. The move to decimal trading is an attempt by Canadian Exchanges, particularly the TSE, to attract volume back to domestic exchanges by lowering the spread between buying and selling prices from 12.5 to 5 cents. As before, stocks that are trading at less than $5 are quoted in increments of 1 cent.

TSE stocks that do not trade on a given day are listed separately showing only bid and ask prices since there are no trading prices. Information for Suzy Shier that appeared in a separate section, "Toronto Bid/Asked," on the same day is as follows[1]:

Div	Stock	Sym	Bid	Ask
	Suzy Shi sv	SZS	5.75	6.20

The **bid price** represents the highest price that has been offered (or bid) to buy the stock and the **ask price** represents the lowest price demanded (or asked) by a seller. With this in mind it is easy to see why there were no trades for Suzy Shier on this day. No buyer was willing to pay the lowest price asked by a seller.

---

[1] The "sv" that follows the stock's name signifies that it is a "subordinate-voting" stock. The different classes of common stock are discussed in Chapter 10.

Some corporate bonds are also traded on the TSE. Those for Air Canada (Air Cda) and Cambridge Shopping Centres Ltd (Cam) for the same day are as follows:

| 52-Week | | | | | | | | Vol |
High	Low	Stock	Sym	High	Low	Close	Chg	(100s)
103	$93\frac{3}{4}$	Air Cda	AC.DB	100.00	99.70	100.00		2374
83	$73\frac{3}{4}$	Cam	CBG.DB.B	80.50	80.00	80.50	+0.50	3330

As with stocks, the first thing shown is the 52-week high and low prices. However, unlike those for stocks, the prices for bonds are quoted as a percentage of face (or maturity) value. The vast majority of corporate bonds have a face value of $1,000. Therefore, the 52-week high for Air Canada was 103 percent of $1,000, or $1,030, and the low was $937.50. Comparable figures for Cambridge were $830 and $737.50, respectively. Next are the company names followed by their trading symbol where the suffix .DB indicates that this security is a debenture or unsecured bond.[2] For Cambridge there is an additional .B on the symbol, indicating that it is the firm's series B debenture. Following are the high, low, and close prices for the day. Here we see that the Cambridge bond closed at $805 on this day and from the change column we see that this figure was $5 higher than the previous close. In the case of Air Canada there was no change from the previous day. The Vol column indicates that 237,400 bonds of Air Canada worth $237.4 million and 333,000 of Cambridge series B bonds worth $333 million changed hands on this day. These amounts, although quite large, are not unusual because bonds are usually bought and sold in large blocks by financial institutions.

Finally, let us consider unlisted or over-the-counter (OTC) stocks. Information on these stocks appears in the same manner as that for TSE stocks in a separate section called "CDN Unlisted." The vast majority of OTC stocks are "penny stocks," that is, they trade at less than $5 and are quoted in increments of 1 cent. For example, here is the information for Afton Food for the same day.

| 52-Week | | | | | | | | Vol |
High	Low	Stock	Sym	High	Low	Close	Chg	(100s)
0.70	0.60	Afton Food	AFTN	0.11	0.11	0.11	+0.02	400

---

[2] The different types of bonds are discussed in Chapter 11.

5

Risk and Return

EXECUTIVE SUMMARY

Investors are risk averse. To induce investors to buy the firm's securities—in other words, to raise capital—the firm must offer investors a rate of return that compensates them for the risk they bear. This brings us to two important tasks: first, to define and measure the risk of the firm's securities; and, second, to establish a quantifiable relationship between risk and the required rate of return.

An asset's total risk is measured by the standard deviation of its expected future returns. When an asset is held in isolation, or as part of a nondiversified portfolio, the standard deviation is a good measure of an asset's risk. In a diversified portfolio, however, risk can be divided into two components: diversifiable risk and nondiversifiable risk. Because diversifiable risk can be eliminated in a portfolio, the appropriate measure of the remaining nondiversifiable risk is beta, β_j.

The capital asset pricing model relates risk and the returns required by investors via the security market line, which says that the required rate of return on any asset in equilibrium is equal to the risk-free rate, plus a risk premium based on the asset's nondiversifiable risk. Increases in expected returns require an increase in nondiversifiable risk as measured by beta. Although assets are occasionally out of equilibrium, this is not generally the case; the expected rate of return and the required rate of return are typically equal.

Financial markets in developed countries are reasonably efficient. Due to the widespread availability of information that many potential buyers and sellers have access to, the current price of a financial asset reflects all available information about the asset, including its risk. The best estimate of the value of any widely traded asset is its market price.

MEASURING RISK

Whenever you are in a situation in which the outcome is unknown or at least not known with certainty, you are exposed to risk, or **uncertainty**. We use these terms interchangeably to mean that the outcome is subject to chance and not definitely known, or to describe a situation in which there is exposure to possible loss.[1] If you gamble in the casinos around the country, you bear risk. Investing in stocks, bonds, real estate, or gold bullion also exposes you to risk. Most of the decisions a business makes—to raise prices, to expand production, or to bring out a new product—expose the firm, its owners, its creditors, and other stakeholders to risk. Thus, although the firm's managers make the decision, it is the firm's securities holders, along with the firm's managers, employees, suppliers, and other stakeholders, who experience the risk. Risk arises from many different sources and has a number of different meanings in practice. The important point to remember is this: *As firms face risk, so do their owners, creditors, and other interested parties.* To understand risk we focus on it from an investor's standpoint. The ideas developed, however, enable us to understand the risks that financial managers must consider in order to make wealth-maximizing decisions.

To measure risk, we begin with individual assets and then move to **portfolios**, which are just groups of assets. To start, suppose we are interested in measuring the risk associated with two common stocks—Hudson International and Ace Chemical. Although we discuss common stock throughout this chapter, the concepts and ideas apply to all financial assets.

PROBABILITY DISTRIBUTIONS

The **probability** associated with an event is the chance the event will occur. Because we are interested in future events, we focus on *ex ante*, or expected, states of the economy and returns. In column 1 of Table 5.1 the possible states of the economy are given,[2] followed by the estimated probabilities associated with the various states in column 2. The probability of a boom during the next period is 0.30, the probability of a normal state of the economy is 0.40, and the probability of a recession is 0.30. Note that the probabilities must sum to 1.00.[3] Column 3 shows the estimated returns associated with the three states of the economy. One point should be stressed: *Finance has a future orientation; our interest is in the expected rate of return.* Because the future is uncertain, there is risk associated with owning either Hudson International or Ace Chemical common stock.

---

[1] In a purely statistical sense there is a difference between uncertainty (when there is no knowledge about the likelihood of a future outcome) and risk (when a probability distribution is known for a future outcome); however, in finance the two terms are commonly interchanged.

[2] In this example we deal with only three states of the economy—boom, normal, and recession—although more could be used if desired.

[3] More formally, the following three conditions hold: First, all outcomes must be accounted for. Second, each individual probability must be greater than or equal to zero. Third, the probabilities must sum to 1.00.

Table 5.1

Probability Distributions for Hudson International and Ace Chemical

The rates of return are those expected to occur under various states of the economy. These rates could be given in decimal form, but we employ percentages throughout.

State of the Economy (1)	Probability of State Occurring (2)	×	Associated Rate of Return (3)	=	Mean or Expected Rate of Return (4)
Hudson International					
Boom	0.30		60%		18.0%
Normal	0.40		20		8.0
Recession	0.30		−20		−6.0
	1.00		expected rate of return = $\bar{k}$ =		20.0%
Ace Chemical					
Boom	0.30		25%		7.5%
Normal	0.40		15		6.0
Recession	0.30		5		−1.5%
	1.00		expected rate of return = $\bar{k}$ =		15.0%

The probability distributions presented in Table 5.1 and graphed in Figure 5.1 are called *discrete* probability distributions. By discrete, we simply mean that the probabilities are assigned to specific outcomes. Another type of probability distribution is continuous. Except when dealing with options in Chapter 18 and elsewhere, we primarily emphasize discrete distributions.

THE MEAN OR EXPECTED RATE OF RETURN

Two measures are typically employed to summarize information contained in probability distributions. The first is the **mean** or **expected value**. For *ex ante*, or expected outcomes, this value is calculated by multiplying the probabilities of occurrence by their associated outcome values, so that

$$\text{expected value, } \bar{k} = \sum_{i=1}^{n} k_i P_i \qquad (5.1)$$

where

$\bar{k}$ = the expected value or expected return
n = the number of possible states
k_i = the rate of return associated with the ith possible state
P_i = the probability of the ith state occurring

Thus, the expected value (or expected return) is the weighted average of the possible outcomes (k_i values), with the weights being determined by the probability of occurrence (P_i values).

Figure 5.1

Discrete Probability Distributions for Hudson International and Ace Chemical

A discrete probability distribution means that a spike occurs at each specific outcome. A continuous probability distribution would show a smooth curve.

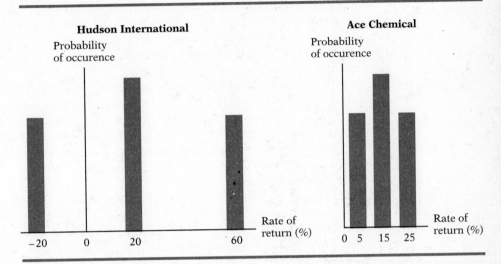

The expected returns for both firms are presented in Table 5.1. Hudson International's expected return is 20 percent; Ace Chemical's is 15 percent. As noted in Chapter 4, these expected (or *ex ante*) rates of return will generally not be equal to the actual (or *ex post*) rate of return. The actual rate of return depends on which specific state of the economy occurs.

STANDARD DEVIATION

The second summary measure arising from probability distributions is a measure of risk or variability in the possible outcomes. Risk is a difficult concept; one measure that is helpful is the **standard deviation**, σ, which is a measure of **total risk**. It measures how "tightly" the probability distribution is centred around the expected value. Looking back at Figure 5.1, we can easily see that Ace Chemical's possible rates of return are much more tightly bunched than Hudson International's. However, it is hard to say much else about the riskiness of the two stocks without some measure that allows us to determine the spread of the distribution. The standard deviation is such a measure. Using *ex ante* (or expected) outcomes, it is defined as

$$\text{standard deviation, } \sigma = \left[\sum_{i=1}^{n} (k_i - \bar{k})^2 P_i \right]^{0.5} \tag{5.2}$$

where

σ = sigma or the standard deviation (the bigger the spread of the distribution, the larger the standard deviation)

k_i = the outcome associated with the ith state
$\bar{k}$ = the expected value or expected return
P_i = the probability associated with the ith outcome

Note that the standard deviation is the square root of the variance, σ^2, of a distribution.

To calculate the standard deviation, we use the steps shown in Table 5.2.[4] We see that the standard deviation for Hudson International is 30.98 percent, and for Ace Chemical it is 7.75 percent. These results confirm our observation from looking at Figure 5.1. There is more total risk associated with Hudson International because it has a larger standard deviation.

Two additional points should be made concerning standard deviations. First, the scale of measurement for the standard deviation is exactly the same as the original data and the expected value. In our example, the original unit of measure was the percentage rate of return per unit of time. Both the expected value and the standard deviation are expressed in exactly the same unit of measure. Thus, we can summarize the information contained in a probability distribution simply by reporting its expected value and standard deviation.[5]

The second point is that as long as we are talking about single assets, the standard deviation, which measures total risk, *is* the appropriate measure of risk. If that asset is part of a nondiversified portfolio, then the standard deviation is still a valid measure of risk. (A nondiversified portfolio might contain two assets, with 95 percent represented by one asset, or security, and only 5 percent of the portfolio invested in the second asset.) However, *when we consider an asset in a diversified portfolio with a number of other assets, the standard deviation is not the most appropriate measure.* Before developing this idea further, let us focus on understanding portfolios and portfolio theory.

Concept Review Questions

- What two measures are typically employed to summarize information contained in probability distributions?
- What is a standard deviation?
- What type of risk does the standard deviation measure?
- Describe how to calculate a variance.

---

[4] Although our concern is primarily with the chance of a loss, indicating that only downside risk is important, the standard deviation measures risk on both sides of the expected value. Because standard deviations are relatively easy to calculate, and because of the development to follow, we use the standard deviation. If the distribution is skewed, with a long tail in one direction or the other, both the expected value and the standard deviation may be deficient. In those cases, some other measure is often needed. These complications are ignored.

Sometimes it is useful to calculate the **coefficient of variation (CV)**, which is the standard deviation divided by the mean. This is a measure of risk *relative* to the mean and is useful for examining the relative variability when two or more means are not the same.

[5] This statement assumes that the probability distributions are relatively normal. This assumption, although not strictly true for securities, allows considerable simplification. Also, for groups of securities in a portfolio, the portfolio returns tend to be approximately normal.

Table 5.2

Calculation of Variances and Standard Deviations for Hudson International and Ace Chemical

Calculating standard deviations based on discrete returns is easy following this procedure, as long as there are not too many possible outcomes.

$(k_i - \bar{k})$	$(k_i - \bar{k})^2$	$\times$	P_i	$=$	$(k_i - \bar{k})^2 P_i$
Hudson International					
(60 − 20)	16,00		0.30		480
(20 − 20)	0		0.40		0
(−20 − 20)	1,600		0.30		480
				variance $= \sigma^2 =$	960

standard deviation $= \sigma = (\sigma^2)^{0.5} = (960)^{0.5} = 30.98\%$

Ace Chemical					
(25 − 15)	100		0.30		30
(15 − 15)	0		0.40		0
(5 − 15)	100		0.30		30
				variance $= \sigma^2 =$	60

standard deviation $= \sigma = (\sigma^2)^{0.5} = (60)^{0.5} = 7.75\%$

PORTFOLIO RISK AND DIVERSIFICATION

Up to now we have been examining risk for single assets. However, most individuals do not hold just one asset; they hold a portfolio of assets. If you hold only one asset, you suffer a loss if the return turns out to be very low. If you hold two assets, the chance of suffering a loss is reduced; returns on both assets must be low for you to suffer a loss. By **diversifying**, or investing in multiple assets that do not move proportionally in the same direction at the same time, you reduce your risk. The important point to remember is this: *It is the total portfolio risk and return that is important. The risk and return of individual assets should not be analyzed in isolation; rather, they should be analyzed in terms of how they affect the risk and return of the portfolio in which they are included.* Much of what follows is based on the work of Harry Markowitz, a recent Nobel Laureate in economics for his pioneering work in portfolio theory.

PORTFOLIO RETURNS

Measures of risk and return for a portfolio are exactly the same as for individual assets—the expected return, or mean, and the total risk as measured by the standard deviation. The **expected return on a portfolio**, $\bar{K}_p$, is simply the average of the returns for the assets weighted by the proportion of the portfolio devoted to each asset. We can write this as

$$\text{expected return on a portfolio, } \overline{K}_p = W_A\overline{k}_A + W_B\overline{k}_B + \cdots + W_Z\overline{k}_Z \qquad (5.3)$$

where

$\overline{K}_p$ = the expected rate of return on a portfolio

$W_A \ldots W_Z$ = the proportion of the portfolio devoted to asset A through asset Z (the sum of the W's = 1.00, or 100%)

$\overline{k}_A \ldots \overline{k}_Z$ = the expected rates of return on assets A through Z

To illustrate, consider a portfolio of three stocks, A, B, and C, with expected returns of 16 percent, 12 percent, and 20 percent, respectively. The portfolio consists of 50 percent stock A, 25 percent stock B, and 25 percent stock C. The expected return on this portfolio is

$$\overline{K}_p = W_A\overline{k}_A + W_B\overline{k}_B + W_C\overline{k}_C$$
$$= 0.50(16\%) + 0.25(12\%) + 0.25(20\%) = 8\% + 3\% + 5\% = 16\%$$

PORTFOLIO RISK

Unlike the expected return, the portfolio risk, as measured by its standard deviation, is (with the exception of one special case) *not* a weighted average of the standard deviations of the assets making up the portfolio. To understand why, we must consider the concept of **correlation**. Correlation (Corr) measures the degree to which two variables, such as the returns on two assets, move together in a linear relationship. Corr

---

Figure 5.2

Correlation Coefficient Under Three Different Conditions

If the correlation were perfectly positive (+1.0), all the points in (a) would lie on a straight line with an upward (to the right) slant. Likewise, perfectly negative correlation (−1.0) would result in all points in (b) plotted on a straight line with a downward slant.

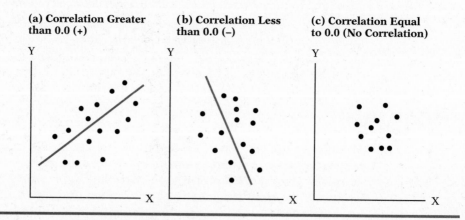

(a) Correlation Greater than 0.0 (+)

(b) Correlation Less than 0.0 (−)

(c) Correlation Equal to 0.0 (No Correlation)

takes on numerical values that range from +1.0 to −1.0. The sign (either + or −) indicates whether the returns move together or inversely. If the sign is positive, the returns on the two assets tend to move up and down together. If it is negative, the assets move inversely; that is, when the return on one asset (or stock, in our example) decreases, the return on the other increases.

The magnitude of the correlation coefficient indicates the strength (or degree) of relationship between the returns on the two assets. If the correlation is +1.0, the returns on the two assets move up and down together, meaning that the relative magnitude of the movements is exactly the same. If Corr is between 0.0 and +1.0, the returns usually move up and down together, but not all the time. The closer Corr is to 0.0, the less the two sets of returns move together. When the correlation is exactly 0.0, there is no relationship between the returns. Similarly, when Corr is negative, the closer it is to −1.0, the more the returns on the two assets tend to move *exactly opposite* to each other. These general relationships are shown in Figure 5.2.

TWO-SECURITY PORTFOLIOS

A portfolio's standard deviation depends not only on the risk of the individual securities, or assets, but also on the correlations between their returns. We calculate portfolio risk, σ_p, for a two-security portfolio as follows:

standard deviation (two-security portfolio),

$$\sigma_p = (W_A^2\sigma_A^2 + W_B^2\sigma_B^2 + 2W_AW_B\sigma_A\sigma_B Corr_{AB})^{0.5} \tag{5.4}$$

where

W_A, W_B	= the proportion of the total portfolio devoted to asset A and to asset B, respectively
σ_A^2, σ_B^2	= the variances for securities A and B, respectively
$Corr_{AB}$	= the degree of correlation between the returns on assets A and B
σ_A, σ_B	= the standard deviations for assets A and B, respectively
$\sigma_A\sigma_B Corr_{AB}$	= the covariance, or comovement, between assets A and B[6]

To see the impact of different degrees of correlation on portfolio standard deviation, consider a portfolio made up of 20 percent Hudson International and 80 percent Ace Chemical. Any portfolio's expected rate of return, no matter what the correlation is between the two assets, will always be determined by Equation 5.3. Recalling that Hudson International had an expected return of 20 percent and Ace Chemical had an expected return of 15 percent, our portfolio's expected would be

$$\overline{K}_p = W_{HI}\overline{k}_{HI} + W_{AC}\overline{k}_{AC}$$
$$= 0.20(20\%) + 0.80(15\%) = 4\% + 12\% = 16\%$$

---

[6] Calculation of covariances is discussed in Appendix 5A.

Let us assume for the moment that the correlation between the returns for the two stocks is perfectly positive, or +1.0 (i.e., $\text{Corr}_{\text{HI:AC}} = +1.0$). Also, recall that Hudson had a standard deviation, σ_{HI}, of 30.98 percent, while Ace's standard deviation, σ_{AC}, was 7.75 percent. With this information, we can now use Equation 5.4 to calculate the portfolio's standard deviation as follows:

$$\sigma_p = (W_{\text{HI}}^2 \sigma_{\text{HI}}^2 + W_{\text{AC}}^2 \sigma_{\text{AC}}^2 + 2W_{\text{HI}}W_{\text{AC}}\sigma_{\text{HI}}\sigma_{\text{AC}}\text{Corr}_{\text{HI:AC}})^{0.5}$$

$$= [(0.20)^2(30.98\%)^2 + (0.80)^2(7.75\%)^2$$

$$+ 2(0.20)(0.80)(30.98\%)(7.75\%)(1.00)]^{0.5}$$

$$= (38.39\% + 38.44\% + 76.83\%)^{0.5} = (153.6\,6\%)^{0.5} \approx 12.40\%$$

This same result can be obtained more directly by recognizing that when the returns on two assets are perfectly positively correlated, the portfolio standard deviation is simply the weighted average of the standard deviations of the two individual assets. Thus,

$$\sigma_p(\text{when Corr} = +1.0), = W_A\sigma_A + W_B\sigma_B$$

$$= 0.20(30.98\%) + 0.80(7.75\%) \qquad (5.5)$$

$$= 6.196\% + 6.200\% \approx 12.40\%$$

The important implication is that *when two assets' returns are perfectly positively correlated, there are no diversification benefits* to be achieved and consequently no reduction in the portfolio standard deviation. *This is the only situation in which forming portfolios does not provide risk reduction to an investor.*

Now consider the other extreme case—the returns on the two assets have a perfect negative correlation, $\text{Corr}_{\text{HI:AC}} = -1.0$. What happens to the portfolio standard deviation in this case? Using Equation 5.4, we find that the standard deviation in this example is now zero:

$$\sigma_p = [(0.20)^2 (30.98\%)^2 + (0.80)^2 (7.75\%)^2$$

$$+ 2 (0.20)(0.80)(30.98\%)(7.75\%)(-1.00)]^{0.5}$$

$$= (38.39\% + 38.44\% - 76.83\%)^{0.5} = 0.00\%$$

Because the returns for these two assets move exactly opposite to one another in both sign and magnitude, when one goes up the other goes down—with the result that the portfolio standard deviation is zero. Obviously, this is the best of all worlds: We have maintained our 16 percent portfolio expected return but eliminated the risk. Why? Because the correlation between the two assets was perfectly negative.(*Note that the total elimination of risk in this example is a direct result of how it was constructed.* More generally, when the returns on two assets are perfectly negatively correlated, the standard deviation is reduced, but not all the way to zero.)

What happens to the portfolio risk when we have positive, but less than perfectly positive, correlation between the returns? To answer this, let us calculate the portfolio standard deviation when the correlation between the returns for the two assets is +0.50. The portfolio standard deviation is

$$\sigma_p = [(0.20)^2 (30.98\%)^2 + (0.80)^2 (7.75\%)^2$$
$$+ 2(0.20)(0.80)(30.98\%)(7.75\%)(+0.50)]^{0.5}$$
$$= (38.39\% + 38.44\% + 38.42\%)^{0.5} = (115.25\%)^{0.5} \approx 10.74\%$$

Remember that when we had perfectly positive correlation, the portfolio standard deviation was 12.40 percent. We see that *with positive, but less than perfectly positive, correlation in the returns, some risk reduction has occurred. The primary finding is that, because the portfolio standard deviation is less than the weighted average of the individual asset standard deviations, portfolio diversification led to a reduction in total portfolio risk.* We conclude that part of the total risk can be eliminated, or diversified away. Table 5.3 presents the portfolio standard deviation for various correlations between the two stocks when 20 percent of the portfolio is invested in Hudson International and 80 percent is invested in Ace Chemical. We see that the portfolio standard deviation declines as the degree of correlation goes from +1.0 to −1.0.

In addition, it is important to recognize that in a two-security case with perfect negative correlation, *some* set of weights will cause the portfolio standard deviation to be zero. For our two stocks the weights are 20 percent and 80 percent, respectively. *However*, the weights that drive a portfolio's standard deviation to zero may be anything and depend on the specific standard deviation of returns for the two assets in question. Therefore, *do not* assume that a 20/80 weighting always results in a portfolio standard deviation of zero.

Table 5.3

Standard Deviation for a Two-Security Portfolio Made Up of 20 Percent Hudson International and 80 Percent Ace Chemical as the Degree of Correlation Changes

With perfect positive correlation, the portfolio standard deviation is a weighted average of the two assets' standard deviations. In all other cases, the portfolio standard deviation is less.

Data

Hudson International: $W_{HI} = 20\%$ $\bar{k}_{HI} = 20\%$ $\sigma_{HI} = 30.98\%$
Ace Chemical: $W_{AC} = 80\%$ $\bar{k}_{AC} = 15\%$ $\sigma_{AC} = 7.75\%$

$$\bar{K}_p = W_{HI}\bar{k}_{HI} + W_{AC}\bar{k}_{AC} = 0.20(20\%) + 0.80(15\%) = 16\%$$
$$\sigma_p = (W_{HI}^2\sigma_{HI}^2 + W_{AC}^2\sigma_{AC}^2 + 2W_{HI}W_{AC}\sigma_{HI}\sigma_{AC}Corr_{HI:AC})^{0.5}$$

$Corr_{HI:AC}$	Portfolio Return, $\bar{K}_p$	Portfolio Standard Deviation, σ_p
+1.00	16.00%	12.40%
+0.50	16.00	10.74
+0.00	16.00	8.77
−0.50	16.00	6.20
−1.00	16.00	0.00

Table 5.4

Portfolio Expected Returns and Standard Deviations for Various Correlations and Weights

With perfect positive correlation there is no benefit to diversification, because the portfolio standard deviation is a weighted average of the two assets' standard deviations. With perfect negative correlation there is one portfolio that has a standard deviation of zero. Most assets, or securities, are positively, but not perfectly positively, correlated; therefore, forming portfolios of these assets can reduce, but not eliminate, risk.

Weight		Portfolio Expected Return, $\overline{K}_p$	Portfolio Standard Deviation, σ_p Given Corr$_{HI:AC}$				
HI	AC		1.00	0.50	0.00	−0.50	−1.00
0.00	1.00	15.0%	7.75%	7.75%	7.75%	7.75%	7.75%
0.10	0.90	15.5	10.07	8.94	7.63	6.05	3.88
0.20	0.80	16.0	12.40	10.74	8.77	6.20	0.00
0.30	0.70	16.5	14.72	12.89	10.76	8.09	3.87
0.40	0.60	17.0	17.04	15.26	13.24	10.84	7.74
0.50	0.50	17.5	19.36	17.75	15.97	13.96	11.61
0.60	0.40	18.0	21.69	20.32	18.84	17.25	15.49
0.70	0.30	18.5	24.01	22.94	21.81	20.62	19.36
0.80	0.20	19.0	26.33	25.59	24.83	24.05	23.23
0.90	0.10	19.5	28.66	28.28	27.89	27.50	27.11
1.00	0.00	20.0	30.98	30.98	30.98	30.98	30.98

THE EFFICIENT FRONTIER

The foregoing shows that, given any particular pair of weights, the standard deviation of the portfolio's returns decreases as the correlation between the assets' returns decreases. An investor is not restricted, however, to investing only one fixed amount in each asset. Table 5.4 shows a sample of the many portfolios of Hudson International and Ace Chemical that can be formed, and their expected return and standard deviation for various correlations.

Figure 5.3 graphs the set of all possible portfolios that can be formed from these two stocks when the correlation between their returns is +1.0, 0.0, and −1.0, respectively. The set of all possible portfolios for a given correlation is called the **feasible set**, which for a two-security portfolio is either a straight line or a curve. For example, if the correlation is +1.0, the feasible set is a straight line from AC, where 100 percent of the portfolio is invested in Ace, to HI, where 100 percent is invested in Hudson. If the correlation is −1.0, the feasible set is made up of two straight line segments, and there is one portfolio in the set (in this case, portfolio E) for which the risk of the portfolio is zero. If the correlation is anything other than +1.0 or −1.0, we have a feasible set that is a curve. This situation is representative of most portfolios, because risk can be reduced but not eliminated.[7]

---

[7] For simplicity, we are assuming no short selling is allowed. Short selling involves the sale of a security that is not owned but, instead, has been borrowed. It can be shown that under certain conditions, risk reduction can be accomplished even when the correlation between the two sets of returns is +1.0.

Figure 5.3

The Feasible Sets of Portfolios That Can Be Formed From Hudson International and Ace Chemical If the Correlation Between Them Is −1.0, 0.0, or +1.0

The feasible set for a two-security portfolio is a straight or a curved line.

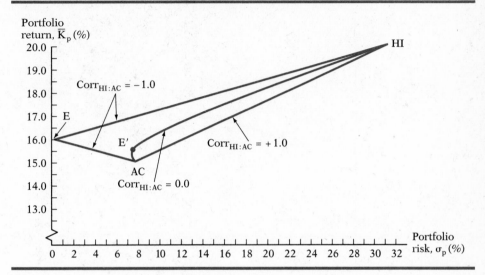

The objective behind forming portfolios is not simply to reduce risk but, rather, to select efficient portfolios. An **efficient portfolio** is one that provides the highest possible expected return for a given level of risk, and the lowest possible risk for a given level of expected return. Not all portions of the feasible sets in Figure 5.3 represent efficient portfolios. If the correlation between Hudson and Ace is −1.0, then the portion of the set from E to HI dominates the portion from AC to E because it offers a higher return for risk levels between zero and 7.75 percent. Thus, E to HI represents the **efficient frontier** of portfolios when the correlation is −1.0. Similarly, E′ to HI is the efficient frontier of portfolios when the correlation is zero. A rational investor will choose the portfolio from the efficient frontier that best suits his or her personal risk–return preferences.

Returns on most securities are positively (but not perfectly positively) correlated. This occurs because the returns on most assets tend to move, to a greater or lesser degree, with the general movements in the economy. For stocks the correlation tends to be between +0.40 and +0.75.

An Example: Diversifying Internationally   An efficient frontier can also be generated when the two individual assets are portfolios. Say you want to invest outside of Canada. One of the assets available to you is the Standard & Poor's 500 Index of U.S. stocks; another is Morgan Stanley's Europe, Australia, and Far East (EAFE) Index. For 10 recent years, the means of their yearly returns were 16.7 and 19.1 percent, respectively; their standard deviations were 12.4 and 28.2 percent, respectively. Security returns in different countries do not move exactly together; that is, the returns are

---

Figure 5.4

Efficient Frontier Attainable from Investing in U.S. and EAFE Securities

Due to the correlation of +0.50, there were substantial benefits from diversifying among U.S. and EAFE securities.

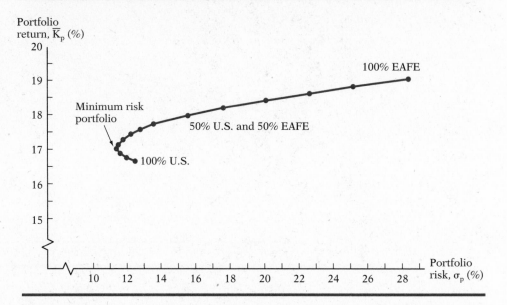

---

less than perfectly positively correlated. The correlation between these two indices (or markets) was +0.50 over the period. Graphically, the efficient frontier for these two sets of securities is shown in Figure 5.4. Both the returns and risks for EAFE stocks were higher than for U.S. stocks.

Thus, if you are interested in investing internationally, but want to increase your expected return above that available with U.S. stocks while taking advantage of the less than perfectly positive correlation between the returns in different countries, you can do so by adding some EAFE stocks to your portfolio. The minimum-risk portfolio should have had about 20 percent of its assets in EAFE stocks and the other 80 percent in United States stocks.

When There Are More Than Two Assets When we move beyond two assets, the same relationships discussed previously exist; however, the feasible set is no longer a line or a curve but a space, as represented by the shaded area in Figure 5.5. The two-security portfolio case can be generalized to the N-security case, and the feasible set is the infinite number of portfolios (and their respective risks and returns) into which the N securities can be formed. For example, points A, B, C, and D represent single-security portfolios where the investor would have 100 percent of his or her portfolio funds invested in security A, B, C, or D, respectively. On the other hand, all other points in the feasible set, including its boundary, represent portfolios of two or more securities combined in all possible proportions. Because the correlation between (among) most securities is positive, but not perfectly positive, the feasible set might look like the umbrella-shaped area in Figure 5.5. The curve EF is the efficient frontier. All portfo-

Figure 5.5

The Efficient Frontier for an N-Security Portfolio

The feasible set for a many-security portfolio is a space, not a straight or curved line. All portfolios to the left of the space are unattainable.

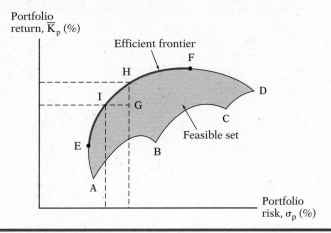

lios on this curve dominate the rest of the feasible set because they offer the highest expected return for a given level of risk, and the lowest risk for a given level of expected return. To see this, consider portfolio H on the efficient frontier and portfolio G in the feasible set. Although they both provide the same level of risk, H has the higher expected return; therefore, portfolio H dominates portfolio G. Other portfolios on the efficient frontier could be determined in the same manner or by minimizing the level of risk for a given return, as could be done between portfolios I and G. *Because portfolios on the efficient frontier dominate all others by providing a higher return for a given amount of risk, and a lower level of risk for a given expected return, they are preferred.*

DIVERSIFIABLE AND NONDIVERSIFIABLE RISK

Risk can be reduced by forming portfolios. But just how much risk reduction can we achieve? The answer has been provided by a number of studies, as shown in Figure 5.6. The total portfolio risk, measured by its standard deviation, declines as more stocks are added to the portfolio. Adding more stocks to the portfolio can eliminate some of the risk, but not all of it.

The total risk can thus be divided into two parts: diversifiable risk (sometimes called *company-specific* or *unsystematic* risk) and nondiversifiable (sometimes called *systematic* or *market*) risk, so that

$$\text{total risk} = \text{diversifiable risk} + \text{nondiversifiable risk} \qquad (5.6)$$

Diversifiable risk relates to events that affect individual companies, such as strikes, product development, new patents, and other activities unique to an individual firm.

Figure 5.6

The Impact of the Number of Securities on Portfolio Risk

By the time 20 to 30 securities are in a portfolio, most of the diversifiable risk has been eliminated, leaving only nondiversifiable (i.e., systematic or market) risk. The benefits of diversification arise from reducing the exposure to diversifiable risk.

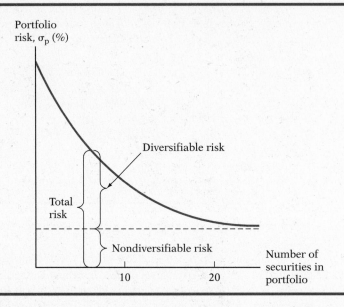

Because these events occur somewhat independently, they can be largely diversified away, so that negative events affecting one firm can be offset by positive events for other firms. The second type, **nondiversifiable risk**, includes general economic conditions, the impact of monetary and fiscal policies, inflation, and other events that affect all firms (to a greater or lesser extent) simultaneously. Because these risks remain, whether or not a portfolio is formed,

$$\text{relevant risk} = \text{nondiversifiable risk}$$

The only risk a well-diversified portfolio has is the nondiversifiable or systematic portion. Therefore, *the contribution of any one asset to the riskiness of a portfolio is its nondiversifiable or systematic risk.*

Concept Review Questions

- Describe how diversifying your assets will help lower the risk of your portfolio.
- If the expected return on a portfolio, $\overline{K}_p$, is simply the average of the returns for the assets, weighted by the proportion of the portfolio devoted to each asset, then is the portfolio's standard deviation, σ_p, simply a weighted average of the standard deviations of the assets making up the portfolio? Explain why or why not.
- Explain what an efficient portfolio is and how it is related to the efficient frontier.
- Describe the two types of risks that make up an individual stock's total risk.

RISKLESS BORROWING AND LENDING

So far, we have concentrated on the ideas of portfolio theory. Portfolio theory, as articulated by Harry Markowitz, deals with portfolios of risky assets. By "risky assets" we mean that in order to invest in an asset with an expected return greater than zero, some exposure to risk, as measured by a standard deviation of greater than zero, is required. William Sharpe, who also is a recent Nobel Laureate in economics, carried these ideas further by noting that individuals also have the ability to invest in (or, alternatively, to lend) a risk-free asset. By *adding the idea of risk-free borrowing and lending to portfolio theory*, Sharpe makes it possible to examine investment not only in a portfolio of risky assets but also in a risk-free asset (e.g., treasury bills). The inclusion of this risk-free asset alters the shape of the efficient frontier from that shown in Figure 5.5 for the N-security case.

Figure 5.7 shows the efficient frontier of risky assets, EF, from Figure 5.5, and also the risk-free asset, k_{RF}. Because a risk-free asset is defined as one that has a known return and a standard deviation of zero, its return plots on the vertical axis. Investors can now combine investing in this riskless asset with investing in portfolios on the efficient frontier of risky portfolios to obtain combinations of risk–return payoffs that did not exist before. For example, the line $k_{RF}N$ represents all possible portfolios formed by buying various combinations of the risk-free asset and the risky portfolio N. All portfolios along this line dominate the part of the efficient frontier below N (i.e., E to N) because all points on the line $k_{RF}N$ provide a higher return for a given level of risk.

The Efficient Frontier When Borrowing and Lending Are Allowed

The inclusion of borrowing and lending possibilities changes the efficient frontier from the curve (arc) EF to the straight line $k_{RF}ML$.

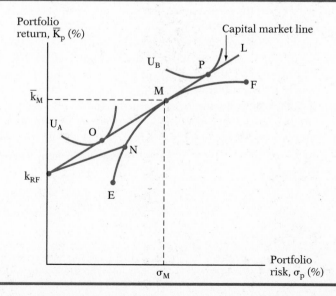

Portfolios can also be formed between the risk-free asset and risky portfolios that lie higher up on the efficient frontier. They would be represented by lines drawn from k_{RF} to successively higher points on the efficient frontier, each successively higher line dominating all previous lines. This process stops when the line drawn from k_{RF} is tangent to the efficient frontier. This occurs at point M in Figure 5.7. Thus, the new set of risk–return opportunities is given by the line $k_{RF}ML$ in Figure 5.7. All portfolios on the line segment between k_{RF} and M represent lending portfolios, because when an investor buys a treasury bill, he or she is lending to the government at the risk-free rate. Investors are also assumed to be able to borrow at the risk-free rate. Consequently, any investor who is willing to accept higher risk (than σ_M) to obtain a higher return (than $\bar{k}_M$) may borrow at k_{RF} and invest the borrowings plus their initial funds in the risky portfolio, M. These borrowing portfolios are represented by the line segment that extends from M to L in Figure 5.7.

As shown in Figure 5.7, all investors are better off holding portfolios that are linear combinations of the risk-free asset (either lending or borrowing) and one risky portfolio, M. They are better off because they can obtain a higher return (represented by the straight line $k_{RF}ML$) for the same amount of risk than at their original position (given by the efficient frontier represented by the curved line EF). The portfolio M is called the **market portfolio** and is a value-weighted portfolio of all risky assets. In equilibrium[8] it must contain all risky assets in proportion of their market value to the total value of the portfolio. Accordingly, if the market value of Bombardier represents 1 percent of the market value of all risky assets, then Bombardier would constitute 1 percent of the market portfolio.

Because investors can borrow and lend at the risk-free rate, they are able to attain portfolios that were previously unattainable. As shown in Figure 5.7, the *new* efficient frontier represents linear combinations of the risk-free asset and the market portfolio. As depicted by the line designated $k_{RF}ML$, this new efficient frontier represents the risk–return tradeoff for *efficient* portfolios. Once presented with this new efficient frontier, each investor chooses the point on the line that corresponds to his or her preferences. In Figure 5.7 this is shown by the tangency point between the individual's utility function and the new efficient frontier. Here we see that investor A prefers portfolio O and is a lender, implying that A is relatively risk averse, whereas investor B, who is less risk averse, prefers the borrowing portfolio P.

This new efficient frontier, the straight line $k_{RF}ML$ in Figure 5.7, is called the **capital market line (CML)**. This line has an intercept of k_{RF}, which represents the return on the risk-free asset. If investors are to invest in risky assets, they must receive a risk premium to compensate for the added risk. We see from Figure 5.7 that for an investor to invest in the market portfolio, he or she must receive a return of $\bar{k}_M$. The amount $(\bar{k}_M - k_{RF})$ represents the risk premium, or excess return over the risk-free rate, expected for incurring the risk, σ_M, associated with the market portfolio. Therefore

$$\text{slope of the CML} = \frac{\bar{k}_M - k_{RF}}{\sigma_M} \tag{5.7}$$

---

[8] The theory calls for the market portfolio to contain all risky financial assets (e.g., stocks, bonds, options) and all risky real assets (e.g., precious metals, jewellery, real estate, stamp collections). Such a market, however, is not observable. Therefore, in practice, a broad-based stock index is often used as a proxy for the market portfolio.

The slope of the CML is called the **market price of risk**. It can be thought of as the equilibrium expected reward per unit of risk. Because the capital market line shows the tradeoff between return and risk for efficient portfolios, the unit of risk must be the portfolio standard deviation. Therefore, the equation for the CML is written as

$$\text{capital market line,} \quad \overline{K}_P = k_{RF} + \left[\frac{\overline{k}_M - k_{RF}}{\sigma_M} \right] \sigma_P \qquad (5.8)$$

where

$\overline{K}_p$ = the required rate of return for any efficient portfolio on the CML

k_{RF} = the risk-free rate of return, which is generally measured by the return on treasury bills

$\overline{k}_M$ = the expected rate of return on the market portfolio

σ_M = the standard deviation of returns on the market portfolio

σ_p = the standard deviation of the returns on the efficient portfolio being considered

Because all efficient portfolios must lie on the capital market line, Equation 5.8 states that the required return on an efficient portfolio *in equilibrium* is equal to the risk-free rate plus the market price of risk multiplied by the amount of risk on the portfolio being considered. It is important to remember that *only efficient portfolios made up of various linear combinations of the risk-free asset and the market portfolio, M, lie on the CML.* Also, remember that the benefits of diversification, which allow us to diversify away part of the total risk, underlies our present discussion.

BETA AS THE MEASURE OF NONDIVERSIFIABLE, OR SYSTEMATIC, RISK

The capital market line applies to portfolios. We need to extend the analysis to individual assets. For assets held in a diversified portfolio, the contribution of any one asset to the riskiness of a particular portfolio is its nondiversifiable, or systematic, risk. Therefore, for assets in a diversified portfolio, risk can best be measured by how their returns move, or are correlated, with the returns of the portfolio as a whole. If the portfolio is reasonably well diversified, we can, for simplicity, talk about the returns for assets in general as measured by the market portfolio, not just for the portfolio in question.

This market portfolio is often measured by some broad-based stock index, such as the Toronto Stock Exchange (TSE) 300 Index. The important point is that *for individuals holding diversified portfolios of assets, the appropriate measure of risk is how the return on an individual asset moves relative to the returns for the market portfolio.* This nondiversifiable risk is measured by **beta, β_j,** where the subscript j refers to the jth asset. Thus, beta reflects the nondiversifiable risk remaining for asset j after a portion of its total risk has been diversified away by forming a portfolio. The beta coefficient, β_j, is the measure of the asset's volatility in relation to the riskiness of the market portfolio as a whole. In other words, it measures what the returns on the asset are expected to be, relative to the returns on the market.

Generally the stock market as a whole is our frame of reference; it has a beta of 1.0. The beta for an individual stock indicates the expected volatility of that stock in relation to the volatility of the market portfolio. Any stock whose returns fluctuate

Figure 5.8

Beta, Volatility, and Returns

High-beta stocks have much greater volatility in their returns relative to market portfolio returns than do low-beta stocks.

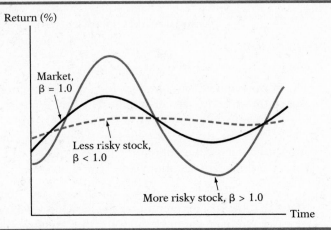

over time exactly as the market does has average systematic risk and thus a beta of 1.0. More risky stocks (see Figure 5.8), such as airlines and high-technology firms, whose returns tend to move up and down faster than the general market's returns, are more volatile and have betas greater than 1.0.

We can be even more specific: The returns on a stock with a beta of 1.40 will, on average, increase 40 percent faster than the market in up markets; likewise, they will decrease 40 percent faster in down markets. Lastly, as also shown in Figure 5.8, less risky (conservative) firms with very stable cash flows and returns, such as public utilities, fluctuate less than the market and therefore have betas of less than 1.0.

Betas for a select group of stocks are listed in Table 5.5. The range of beta values in the table, from 0.57 to 1.85, indicates the general range of betas in practice. Examining this table we see that Bank of Montreal, Alcan, and Toronto Dominion

Table 5.5

Beta Coefficients for Selected Firms

Beta is a measure of the volatility of the firm's returns versus the market's returns. It measures risk for individual stocks, or assets, in well-diversified portfolios.

Alcan	1.08	Inco	1.30
Bank of Montreal	0.90	Labatt	0.60
BCE Inc.	0.57	Maple Leaf Foods	0.59
Bombardier	1.59	Magna International	1.52
CAE Industries	1.35	Placer Dome	1.72
Dofasco	1.85	Rogers Communications	1.49
Domtar	0.77	Seagram	0.83
Gandalf Technologies	0.85	Toronto Dominion Bank	0.97

Source: Nesbitt Burns, *Nesbitt Burns Research: Red Book,* Second Quarter, 1995.

Bank had betas close to 1.00. Their returns were of average volatility. On the other hand, Dofasco, with a beta of 1.85, had very volatile returns, while returns for BCE Inc. (Bell Canada Enterprises) were very stable, as indicated by its beta of 0.57.

THE CAPITAL ASSET PRICING MODEL

We have seen that the capital market line, as depicted in Figure 5.7, represents the risk–return tradeoff for efficient portfolios and that the standard deviation of portfolio returns, σ_p, represents the total risk of a portfolio. We also have seen that the best measure of an asset's relevant or nondiversifiable risk is its beta and that betas are distributed around 1.0, the beta of the market. The final step is to formulate the risk–return relationship for an individual asset. This can be done by recognizing that *individual assets bear the same direct relationship between risk and return as portfolios do. The only fundamental difference is that the standard deviation of portfolio returns, σ_p, represents the risk of the portfolio, whereas the relevant measure of risk for individual assets is beta, β_j.* To obtain the return relationship for an individual asset, we reformulate the tradeoff of Figure 5.7, now using beta on the horizontal axis, as shown in Figure 5.9. This relationship is the **capital asset pricing model (CAPM)**.[9] This figure shows that if a higher return is desired, more risk must be incurred.[10] The line shown in Figure 5.9 is called the **security market line (SML)**. It shows the risk–return tradeoff for individual assets, securities, and portfolios.

The SML relationship depicted in Figure 5.9 is specified as

$$\text{security market line, } k_j = k_{RF} + \beta_j(k_M - k_{RF}) \tag{5.9}$$

where

k_j = the required (or expected) rate of return on any risky asset j held in a diversified portfolio

k_{RF} = the risk-free rate of return, which is generally measured by the return on treasury bills[11]

β_j = the beta coefficient for the asset

k_M = the expected rate of return on the market portfolio

$(k_M - k_{RF})$ = the market risk premium required to encourage investment in the market portfolio as opposed to investing in some risk-free asset

---

[9] The major assumptions of the CAPM are: (1) all investors are expected wealth maximizers who evaluate portfolios on the basis of means and standard deviations; (2) all investors can borrow or lend an unlimited amount at the risk-free rate, k_{RF}, and there is no restriction on short sales; (3) all investors have homogeneous expectations concerning expected returns and risks on securities; (4) the market is frictionless, and there are no taxes (or taxes do not affect investment decisions); and (5) all investors are price takers and cannot, based on their buying or selling, influence the market price. Even though these assumptions may appear to be very limiting, all of them can be relaxed without seriously affecting the basic conclusions derived from the model.

[10] This assumes that the beta is positive, as it is for the vast majority of assets. Only occasionally are there assets whose returns move counter to the returns on the market. An example of a negative beta stock might be a gold mining company.

[11] If the term structure of interest rates is essentially flat, then the use of treasury bills as the risk-free rate is justified. However, if the term structure is upward-sloping, so that the interest rate on intermediate- or long-term government bonds is substantially higher than the rate of treasury bills, then the intermediate- or long-term government bond rate is a better proxy for the risk-free rate.

Figure 5.9

The Security Market Line (SML)

The security market line is a graphic representation of the capital asset pricing model (CAPM).

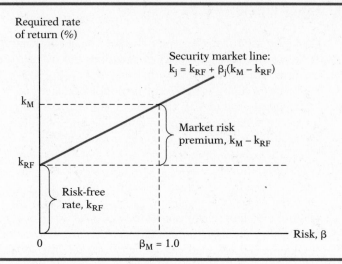

$$\beta_j(k_M - k_{RF}) =$$ the risk premium for the asset or security in question. This premium is greater than or less than the market risk premium depending on the size of β_j, which measures how the returns on asset j move in relation to the returns for the market portfolio.

The security market line, Equation 5.9, when graphed as in Figure 5.9, shows that the rate of return required, or demanded, by an investor is equal to the return on a risk-free asset, k_{RF}, plus a risk premium $\beta_j(k_M - k_{RF})$. In a risk-free world, only the risk-free rate would be relevant. Because the world is not risk-free, the risk premium is added to the risk-free rate to determine the required return an investor demands for investing in a risky asset.[12]

USING THE CAPITAL ASSET PRICING MODEL

In order to use the capital asset pricing model to estimate the rate of return required, or demanded, on an investment, it is necessary to have three elements: the expected risk-free rate, k_{RF}; the expected return on the market portfolio, k_M; and the asset's (in this instance, the stock's) beta, β_j. At any point in time, these might be estimated as follows:

1. RISK-FREE RATE, k_{RF} The risk-free rate is primarily a function of expected inflation and economic conditions. Typically the rate on treasury bills is employed

---

[12] In Chapter 2 (Equation 2.8) we defined the risk premium to be equal to a maturity premium, a default premium, a liquidity premium, and an issue-specific premium. The capital asset pricing model, as specified by Equation 5.9, is a formal model for specifying this risk premium. Further, Equation 2.9 was an intuitive statement of the CAPM.

as a proxy for k_{RF}. Assuming the term structure of interest rates is relatively flat, by looking at *The Globe and Mail*, or some other source of current financial market information, we can determine the return on one-year treasury bills. Let us assume it is 7 percent.

2. EXPECTED RETURN ON THE MARKET PORTFOLIO, k_M.   The expected return on the market portfolio can be estimated by relying on econometric forecasts, or by viewing the expected return on the market as a function of three items:

$$k_M = \frac{\text{expected}}{\text{inflation}} + \frac{\text{real growth in}}{\text{the economy}} + \frac{\text{risk premium of}}{\text{stocks over bonds}} \qquad (5.10)$$

Thus, if the expected (not historical) rate of inflation is 2.5 percent, real growth (in constant dollars) in gross domestic product (GDP) is expected to be 3.5 percent, and the risk premium (or return) of stocks over bonds is 4 percent, then we would estimate k_M = 10 percent.

3. BETA, β_j We could estimate a stock's riskiness by relying on betas published by *Value Line*, Richardson Greenshields, or other investment advisory services. Alternatively, employing the techniques discussed subsequently, we could estimate β_j based on historical returns for the asset and the market. Assume we estimate beta to be 1.40.

To find the required return on the asset, we use Equation 5.9 as follows:

$$k_j = k_{RF} + \beta_j(k_M - k_{RF})$$
$$= 7\% + 1.40(10\% - 7\%) = 7\% + 4.2\% = 11.2\%$$

This approach can be used to find the required rate of return for any asset, or a portfolio of assets.

Historical Risk Premiums   An alternative approach to estimating the returns on the market portfolio, k_M, is to use the market risk premium. The market risk premium is simply the difference between the returns on the market portfolio, k_M, and the risk-free rate, k_{RF}. Thus, this alternative way of estimating the return on the market portfolio is:

$$k_M(\text{based on market risk premium}) = k_{RF} + \text{market risk premium} \qquad (5.11)$$

Data for three different time periods, all ending with 1994, for historical returns on common stocks and treasury bills are as follows:[13]

	1960–1994	1970–1994	1980–1994
Common stock returns	10.5%	10.7%	11.0%
−Treasury bill returns	7.6	8.9	10.1
Market risk premium	2.9%	1.8%	0.9%

---

[13] *Bank of Canada Review*, various issues.

An examination of these figures indicates that historical market risk premiums have fluctuated depending on the specific time period employed. Hence, *the use of historical market risk premiums to estimate the expected return on the market portfolio using Equation 5.11 invites trouble.* Remember, the returns on the market portfolio when using the capital asset pricing model *must be the expected returns, not historical returns.*

The same problem of using historical data exists with the premium that common stocks have earned relative to long-term corporate bonds, as required in Equation 5.10. The historical risk premium of stocks over bonds for three different time periods, all ending in 1994, is:[14]

	1966–1994	1970–1994	1980–1994
Common stock returns	10.7%	10.7%	11.7%
−Corporate bond returns	10.2	10.9	11.8
Risk premium of stocks over bonds	0.5%	−0.2%	−0.8%

Just like the market risk premium, the risk premium of stocks over bonds has fluctuated over time. Also, on average, it has not been in the range that we expect. The message we get from looking at all of these historical returns is simple: No matter what method is used to estimate the expected return on the market portfolio, *it is the future returns in Equation 5.9 that are important.* Any past returns provide, at best, only a rough guideline to the expected returns in the future.

Calculating Beta   We also need to measure the nondiversifiable or systematic risk needed in the capital asset pricing model. To calculate beta directly, we might begin with the *ex post,* historical or realized, returns for the asset in question, k_j, and the market portfolio, k_M. Consider the returns presented in Table 5.6. To determine beta for asset j, we can begin by plotting the data as in Figure 5.10. Note that there is a relationship between the returns on the market and the returns on asset j, such that when the returns on the market are high, the returns on asset j tend to be high, and vice versa. This relationship can be expressed as a least-squares regression of the form $Y = \alpha + \beta X$, where α is the intercept on the vertical axis, and β is the slope of the fitted line. The fitted regression, which is called the **characteristic line**, is:[15]

$$\text{characteristic line, } k_j = \alpha + \beta k_M$$
$$= 1.44 + 1.40 k_M \qquad (5.12)$$

where

$\alpha = 1.44 = $ alpha, the intercept on the vertical axis

$\beta = 1.40 = $ beta, the sensitivity of the returns on asset j relative to the returns on the market portfolio

---

[14] *Bank of Canada Review,* various issues.

[15] Most financial calculators have a built-in regression function. Alternatively, the procedure for calculating a least-squares regression (or simple linear regression) is illustrated in Chapter 26.

Table 5.6

Historical Rates of Return on Stock j and the Market Portfolio

The returns encompass both cash dividends and any capital gain or loss for the year and were calculated using Equation 4.11.

Year	Stock j, k_j	Market, k_M
−4	22.51%	8.78%
−3	14.96	4.06
−2	−10.05	−3.99
−1	26.46	20.70
0	5.12	7.45
Mean	11.80%	7.40%
Standard deviation	14.68%	8.94%
Correlation$_{jM}$		0.85

Figure 5.10

Plot and Fitted Regression of the Returns on Stock j and the Market

The least-squares regression line is called the characteristic line. The slope coefficient from this regression is beta.

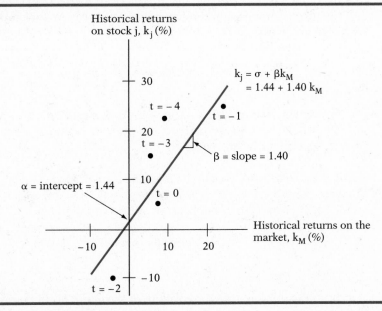

The beta for asset, or stock, j is 1.40, meaning that its nondiversifiable risk is 40 percent more than the average nondiversifiable risk. Therefore, asset j is more risky than the market.

Instead of fitting a least-squares regression, beta may also be determined using the standard deviation of the asset's returns, the standard deviation of the market's returns, and the correlation between the two returns. Employing this approach, we find that beta equals the covariance (or comovement) between the asset's and the market's returns divided by the variance of the market's returns, or

$$\text{beta, } \beta_j = \frac{\text{covariance}_{jM}}{\text{variance}_M} = \frac{\text{Cov}_{jM}}{\sigma_M^2} \tag{5.13}$$

The covariance of the returns between asset j and the market is equal to the standard deviation of asset j, σ_j, times the standard deviation of the market, σ_M, times the correlation between asset j and the market M, Corr_{jM}, so

$$\text{Cov}_{jM} = \sigma_j \sigma_M \text{Corr}_{jM} \tag{5.14}$$

Inserting Equation 5.14 into Equation 5.13 and simplifying, we have

$$\beta_j = \frac{\text{Cov}_{jM}}{\sigma_M^2} = \frac{\sigma_j \sigma_M \text{Corr}_{jM}}{\sigma_M^2} = \frac{\sigma_j \text{Corr}_{jM}}{\sigma_M} \tag{5.15}$$

Note that the standard deviation, σ_M, of the market returns appeared in the numerator of Equation 5.15 before simplifying, while the variance of the market returns, σ_M^2, appeared in the denominator. By dividing through, we are left with the result that beta is equal to the standard deviation of the asset's returns times the correlation between the returns on the asset and the market's returns, divided by the standard deviation of the market's returns. Returning to the data given in Table 5.6, beta could be calculated as follows:

$$\beta_j = \frac{\sigma_j \text{Corr}_{jM}}{\sigma_M} = \frac{(14.68)\,(0.85)}{8.94} = \frac{12.478}{8.94} \approx 1.40$$

Hence, employing either a linear regression approach or Equation 5.15, we calculate the beta to be 1.40. In practice, adjustments are made when deriving expected, as opposed to historical, betas.

Portfolio Betas   We have been discussing the capital asset pricing model and examining betas for individual assets. A *portfolio* of assets also has a beta. This **portfolio beta** is a weighted average of the betas of individual assets:

$$\text{portfolio beta, } \beta_P = \sum_{j=1}^{n} W_j \beta_j \tag{5.16}$$

where

β_p = the portfolio beta or volatility of the entire portfolio relative to the market n = the number of assets in the portfolio

W_j = the percent of the total value of the portfolio in asset j

β_j = the beta for asset j

Depending on the composition of the portfolio, the beta can be more than 1.0, equal to 1.0, or less than 1.0.

Suppose you have $10,000 invested in each of 10 stocks, so that your total investment is $100,000; the amount invested in each stock is 10 percent, or 0.10. If all the stocks have a beta of 1.20, then the portfolio beta is also 1.20. What happens if you sell one of the stocks and reinvest in another stock with a different beta? If the new stock has a beta of 0.60, then the new portfolio beta will be

$$\text{new portfolio beta} = \beta_P = \sum_{j=1}^{n} W_j \beta_j$$
$$= 0.90(1.20) + 0.10\,(0.60) = 1.14$$

Similarly, if the new stock has a beta of 2.00, then the portfolio's new beta will be 1.28 [i.e., 0.90 (1.20) + 0.10 (2.00)]. The required return on the portfolio of stocks can be estimated using the CAPM, based on the portfolio beta, and the expected returns on risk-free assets and on the market portfolio.

Concept Review Questions

■ Describe how the capital market line (CML) is formed and how it affects investors' portfolio decisions.

■ What type of risk does β measure?

■ Verbally describe the capital asset pricing model and how it is used to determine a stock's required rate of return.

■ What three elements are necessary to employ the capital asset pricing model when estimating an investment's required rate of return?

MORE ON THE CAPITAL ASSET PRICING MODEL

There are three other points related to the capital asset pricing model that we need to discuss. These relate to changes in risk and prices, the equilibrium nature of the capital asset pricing model, and some cautions about applying the CAPM.

CHANGES IN RISK AND PRICES

The CAPM can assist us to see what happens to the required rate of return, and to the market price of a firm's stock, as risk changes. To illustrate the price impact, let us suppose that a firm is expecting a constant growth in dividends of 8 percent per year, the current cash dividend (at time t = 0) is $3, and the required rate of return, which is the return demanded by investors, is 16 percent. Employing the constant-growth formula (Equation 4.7) for valuing stocks, we find that the current market price of the stock is

$$P_0 = \frac{D_0(1 + g)}{k_s - g} = \frac{\$3.00\,(1 + 0.08)}{0.16 - 0.08} = \frac{\$3.24}{0.08} = \$40.50$$

What happens if, because of changes in risk, the investor's required rate of return increases to 18 percent or if it decreases to 13 percent, while everything else remains unchanged? With an increase in risk and required return, the new market value falls to $P_0 = \$3.24/(0.18 - 0.08) = \$32.40$. On the other hand, a decrease in risk and required return results in an increase in market value to $P_0 = \$3.24/(0.13 - 0.08) = \$64.80$. Other things being equal, *increased risk lowers the market value of the firm's stock, and reduced risk increases its value.* This result shows that risk, as perceived by investors, has a major impact on the value of the firm. Managers must always be aware of the impact of their actions on the *perceived* riskiness of the firm, for this is how they influence the firm's market value.

THE EQUILIBRIUM NATURE OF THE CAPM

The capital asset pricing model specifies what the required rate of return on any asset should be. In **equilibrium**, the rate of return required, or demanded, as specified by the CAPM, equals its expected return, which is the best estimate of the return expected from making the investment. What happens if this is not the case? Consider Figure 5.11, which shows a security market line based on investor beliefs about the relationship between required rates of return and nondiversifiable risk. Suppose that,

Figure 5.11

Process When Securities Are Not in Equilibrium

Hudson International is underpriced and therefore is providing an excess (risk-adjusted) return; the opposite is true for Ace Chemical. The price of Hudson will increase and that of Ace Chemical will decrease until their expected and required returns are equal.

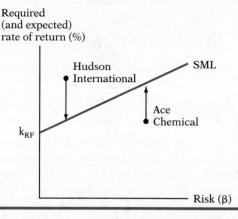

for some reason, the two stocks from earlier in the chapter, Hudson International and Ace Chemical, are improperly priced: Hudson is underpriced; Ace Chemical is over-priced. This mispricing occurs because Hudson International's expected rate of return is greater than its required rate of return (as specified by the SML); therefore the stock is **underpriced**. In contrast, Ace Chemical's expected rate of return is less than the required return; consequently, it is **overpriced**.

To solidify our understanding, let us use an example. Assume Hudson does not pay cash dividends; its current market price, P_0, is $20; and its expected market price, P_1, is $28. Using Equation 4.11 to calculate the expected return, we have

$$k = \frac{D_1 + (P_1 - P_0)}{P_0} = \frac{0 + (\$28 - \$20)}{\$20} = \frac{\$8}{\$20} = 0.40 = 40\%$$

If Hudson's required return, as given by the security market line (SML) is 25 percent, what will happen to the current market price? It will increase as investors see that Hudson is undervalued and begin to buy it. To what level will the price rise? We can determine that by setting k equal to 25 percent and solving for the new equilibrium price as follows:

$$k = \frac{P_1 - P_0}{P_0}$$

$$0.25 = \frac{\$28 - P_0}{P_0}$$

$$1.25\ (P_0) = \$28$$

$$P_0 = \$28/1.25 = \$22.40$$

We see that if the price increases from $20 to $22.40, the expected and required rates of return for Hudson will be equal, at 25 percent.

Exactly the opposite will happen to Ace Chemical. Because its expected return is below its required return, investors will sell Ace Chemical, driving the market price down. This will continue until the expected and required rates of return are equal; that is, until they are in equilibrium.

SOME WORDS OF CAUTION

The capital asset pricing model is simple and logical; its assumptions can be relaxed without invalidating the model; and it describes in a formal manner how non-diversifiable risk and return are related. Even so, caution needs to be employed when using it.

1. The model is based on *ex ante*, or expected, conditions; yet we have only *ex post*, or realized, data. To use historical data without adjustment for future expectations invites trouble. Future, not past, risk and return are the items of concern.
2. The capital asset pricing model explains, on average, only about 30 percent of the fluctuations in firms' returns as a function of the fluctuations in the returns on the

market portfolio. Thus, there are many other factors that affect the returns on common stocks.

3. Evidence exists that certain stocks provide *ex post* returns greater than could be expected based on the CAPM. Three of these "anomalies" relate to stocks of smaller firms, stocks with low price/earnings ratios, and certain seasonal effects. The seasonal, or January, effect relates to the fact that a large part of the total returns for stocks historically has occurred in January.

4. Recently, Fama and French (1992) argued that (1) the market value of equity (or size of the firm) and (2) the ratio of the book value of equity divided by the market value of equity "provide a simple and powerful characterization of the cross-section of average stock returns for the 1963–1990 period." In addition, they show that average stock returns are weakly, if at all, positively related to beta. (In effect, they are saying that beta does not matter.) Given the Fama and French results, we can confidently say that the next few years will produce much more empirical and theoretical work on risk and return.

The capital asset pricing model is the simplest model available at present that depicts the relationship between risk and return. Although other models are available (such as arbitrage pricing theory, discussed briefly later in the chapter, or option pricing models developed in Chapter 18), the CAPM is still the general frame of reference.

Concept Review Question

■ Describe what will happen to the security market line (SML) if investors become more risk averse and require higher market risk premiums.

THE EFFICIENT MARKET HYPOTHESIS

Extensive empirical evidence suggests that the prices of stocks and other financial assets in developed countries adjust rapidly to disequilibrium situations. Consequently, equilibrium ordinarily exists, and, in general, required and expected returns are equal. Stock prices certainly change, sometimes violently or rapidly, but these changes simply reflect changing economic or firm-specific conditions and expectations. Stock prices may also continue to react over longer periods of time to favourable or unfavourable information. This is to be expected because as new information becomes available, the market adjusts to the new information.

An efficient market, as discussed in Chapter 1, is one in which information is widely and cheaply available to all investors, and in which all relevant and ascertainable information is already reflected in security prices. The notion that financial markets are efficient has been around for about 25 years. The **efficient market hypothesis** states that market participants react quickly to events that convey useful information; therefore, prices of financial assets adjust quickly and unambiguously to new information. By unambiguously, we mean that although sometimes the price may overreact and other times it may underreact, on net the magnitude of the reaction will be "on target."

There are three main streams of research that have focused on the efficient market hypothesis.[16]

1. TESTS FOR RETURN PREDICTABILITY   This research is based on the past record of stock or bond prices and on other historical information such as dividend yields, earnings/price (the inverse of price/earnings) ratios, and interest rates. The results of these tests suggest that future returns are, to some extent, predictable from past returns, dividend yields, and various term-structure variables. With respect to returns on stocks, the research points to certain factors (i.e., size, earnings/price ratios, the amount of debt to equity employed, and book-to-market effects) that are not adequately explained by the capital asset pricing model. However, at the present time we have no better model that explains these anomalous results.

2. TESTS FOR RETURN MOVEMENT   This research takes all publicly available information as the information base. Thus, information about earnings, dividends, new products, mergers, and so forth, has been examined to see how prices react to the release of this information by firms. The results of a wide range of empirical studies indicate that, with respect to firm-specific events, stock prices react quickly; that is, the markets are efficient.

3. TESTS FOR PRIVATE INFORMATION   This research focuses on assessing whether there is an ability to earn excess returns (i.e., returns that are greater than expected based on the amount of risk incurred) from insider trading, security analysis, and professional portfolio management. The results of these studies suggest that informed investors do not appear to earn excess returns after taking account of transactions costs and the costs of generating the unique, or informed, information.

In recent years a number of studies have challenged the efficient market hypothesis. Although the upshot of this trend is not completely clear, it may be summarized as follows:

> Though evidence of market inefficiency has soared in recent years, that does not mean markets have become less efficient. More likely, it means academics have got better computers and bigger databases, and that there are more of them data-crunching. In fact, most economists believe financial markets are more efficient now than ever before, thanks not least to shrinking official intervention.[17]

There is a very important lesson we need to understand because of market efficiency: *You can trust market prices because they reflect available information about the value of a security.* For the average investor, this means there is no way to achieve *consistently* superior rates of return. To do so you have to have *more* information than is publicly available; you have to have access to (or generate) unique private information beyond that available to other investors. Does that mean you should despair? Not at all. *What is important in an efficient market is to determine the amount of risk you are willing to bear.* The most important decision is to determine how comfortable you are with a higher versus a lower risk exposure. If you cannot tolerate much risk, that

---

[16] Instead of the three categories of weak-form, semistrong-form, and strong-form efficiency used in finance for many years, we will use Fama's (1991) more recent descriptive titles.

[17] "Yes, It Can Be Done," *The Economist* (December 5, 1992): 21–23.

dictates the type of investments you will make, and the returns you can expect (or require).

The efficient market hypothesis also has a number of very important messages for managers:

1. Because markets are efficient, the best indication of the worth of the firm and the actions of managers is obtained by looking at market prices. Thus, the best estimate of the value of the firm is the market value of its stock and bonds.
2. When estimating value, start first with market prices, if they exist, and then consider what impact subsequent actions undertaken by the firm might have on the value.
3. In making investment decisions, the only way to increase the value of the firm is to find superior investments whose expected return is greater than the required return. Actions of the firm that have been anticipated by the financial markets are already incorporated in the prices of its financial assets.
4. In an efficient market you should expect to pay an equilibrium rate (or price) for the financing obtained, commensurate with the riskiness of the firm as perceived by investors.

Throughout this book we will make use of the findings and implications of the efficient market hypothesis when making wealth-maximizing financial management decisions.

Concept Review Questions

- Describe the three main streams of research that are focused on the efficient market hypothesis.
- Why is the efficient market hypothesis important to corporate managers?

ARBITRAGE PRICING THEORY

An alternative to the CAPM, the **arbitrage pricing theory (APT)**, has received considerable attention. The APT requires fewer assumptions than the CAPM; likewise, the market portfolio does not play a special role in the theory. The return for an individual asset, j, in the APT is assumed to be a linear function of a number of factors common to all assets

$$\text{return on asset under APT, } k_j = a_j + b_{j1}F_1 + b_{j2}F_2 + \cdots + b_{jN}F_N + e_j \qquad (5.17)$$

where

k_j = actual return on asset j
a_j = the expected return on asset j if unaffected by all factors
b_j's = the sensitivity of asset j to factors $1, \ldots, N$
F's = factors common to the returns of all assets being considered
e_j = unique effects on the return of asset j

Like the CAPM, the APT is interested only in nondiversifiable risk. The APT theorizes, however, that the risk premium associated with this nondiversifiable risk is a function of a number of factors rather than solely the expected returns on the market portfolio. This means that the risk premium is actually the sum of a set of risk premiums. Thus, the required rate of return on asset j is written as

$$k_j = k_{RF} + \sum_{n=1}^{N} b_{jn}(k_n - k_{RF}) \qquad (5.18)$$

where

$$k_n = \text{the required rate of return on the } n^{th} \text{ factor}$$
$$(k_n - k_{RF}) = \text{the market price of risk for the } n^{th} \text{ factor}$$
$$\sum_{n=1}^{N} b_{jn}(k_n - k_{RF}) = \text{the risk premium for asset j}$$

The APT is more general than the CAPM. One problem with the APT is that the underlying factors are not known *ex ante*. Some research on the APT includes factors for short-term inflation, long-term inflation, the spread of long- vs. short-term interest rates, default risk, and industrial activity. If only one factor affects an asset's return, and that factor is the market portfolio, then Equation 5.18 reduces to Equation 5.9, the SML equation of the CAPM. Empirical testing indicates that the return on the market portfolio appears to be the most important risk variable for the majority of firms. That being the case, the CAPM continues to be a useful model for representing the relationship between risk and required rates of return for large, actively traded firms.

Concept Review Question

■ How do the capital asset pricing model and the arbitrage pricing theory differ?

KEY POINTS

- Financial management deals with the future; hence, it is future returns and actions that are important.
- The mean, or expected value, and the standard deviation are used to capture the information contained in probability distributions.
- When the correlation between the returns on two or more assets is less than $+1.0$, there are benefits to be gained by diversifying in terms of lower risk, as shown by a lower portfolio standard deviation.
- Efficient portfolios provide the highest return for a given amount of risk, and the least risk for a given level of returns.
- Because part of the total risk can be diversified away, the relevant risk for assets in a diversified portfolio is the nondiversifiable, or systematic, risk measured by beta, β_j.
- The consideration of risk-free borrowing and lending, along with the essential results from portfolio theory, changes the efficient frontier to a straight line called the capital market line. All individuals are better off with the new efficient frontier

specified by the capital market line than they were without the addition of the risk-free asset.

- The capital asset pricing model, CAPM, describes the return required, or demanded, on an asset as a function of the return on a risk-free asset plus a risk premium that incorporates beta. Thus, increases in expected returns require increases in risk.
- In estimating the capital asset pricing model, it is the future risk-free rate, the future return on the market portfolio, and the future beta that are relevant.
- Other things being equal, increases in risk lead to decreases in the prices of financial assets.
- The expected return and required return for financial assets are generally equal; that is, they are in equilibrium.
- Financial markets in developed countries are reasonably efficient. Consequently, security prices react quickly and unambiguously to new information.
- Efficient financial markets mean that:
  a. The best estimate of the value of the firm is provided by the market prices of the firm's stock and bonds.
  b. When estimating the value of financial assets, look first to their current market value; then consider any incremental value that might be created.
  c. To increase its value, the firm has to make investment decisions that provide returns above those already incorporated in the prices of its financial assets.
  d. Expect to pay an equilibrium rate for any new financing provided from the financial markets.

QUESTIONS

5.1   In what situation is an asset's standard deviation an appropriate measure of risk? Why is this so?

5.2   Security A has a mean of 25 and a standard deviation of 15; security B has a mean of 40 and a standard deviation of 10.
a.   Which security is more risky? Why?
b.   What if the standard deviation on security B were 15? 20? (*Note:* In answering this part, you must consider whether it is absolute risk, as measured by the standard deviation, or relative risk, as measured by the coefficient of variation, that is important.)

5.3   Explain how forming a portfolio may result in a reduction in risk. What is the necessary condition for this risk reduction to occur?

5.4   Explain the ideas behind the efficient frontier concept. What does the efficient frontier look like if we are considering (a) only risky assets and (b) a risk-free asset and the market portfolio of risky assets?

5.5   The primary outcome of the capital asset pricing model (CAPM) is the security market line (SML), which is $k_j = k_{RF} + \beta_j(k_M - k_{RF})$. What do all these terms mean? How can they be estimated?

5.6   Why is it that most stocks have positive betas? What would be the required rate of return, relative to the risk-free rate, on a stock that had a negative beta?

5.7   Security j has a beta of 0.90, the risk-free rate is 8 percent, and the expected return on the market portfolio is 16 percent. What will happen to the required rate of return on security j under the following conditions (assuming each part is independent)?

a. Inflation is expected to increase by 3 percent over the next few years.
b. Due to stringent monetary and fiscal controls, the government is shrinking its deficits and encouraging additional optimism for industry, consumers, and investors.
c. The company just won an unexpected victory in a major lawsuit concerning patent infringement.
d. International competition is increasing rapidly in the firm's market areas, leading to increased risk.
e. The government has decided to place an excess profits tax, amounting to 50 percent, on all corporate profits.

5.8 The capital asset pricing model indicates the relationship between risk and the required return. However, occasionally securities get out of equilibrium, and their expected rates of return are greater or less than their required rates of return.
a. What process occurs to bring the expected rate of return back into equilibrium so that it equals the required rate of return?
b. How does the idea of market efficiency relate to this process?

5.9 Explain the efficient market hypotheses, being sure to distinguish between the three streams of research that have evolved in assessing market efficiency. What important implications does market efficiency have for investors and for managers?

5.10 Two securities exist as follows: Security A has an expected return of 10 percent and a standard deviation of 15 percent; security B has an expected return of 8 percent and a standard deviation of 20 percent. Explain in detail whether this information supports or refutes the notion that risk and return are related.

CONCEPT REVIEW PROBLEMS

See Appendix A for solutions.

CR5.1 Jay is considering investing in one of two stocks, IBM or Discount Computers (DC). Given the following probability distribution of returns, what is the expected rate of return for each stock? What is the expected rate of return for the market?

State	Probability	IBM	DC	Market
1	0.2	−15%	42%	−8%
2	0.6	10	12	10
3	0.2	35	−30	25

CR5.2 Given the probability distributions in CR5.1, what is the standard deviation for each of the investments? What is the coefficient of variation for each of the investments?

CR5.3 Assume that Jay is holding a well-diversified portfolio in which the expected returns on his portfolio resemble the expected market returns as in CR5.1. If Jay adds IBM to his investment portfolio, in which the new portfolio comprises 20 percent of IBM and 80 percent of the old portfolio, what is the new portfolio's expected return? If Jay added Discount Computers, instead of IBM, to his new portfolio in the same proportion, what would be the expected return on his new portfolio?

CR5.4 Cris has been asked by her employer to estimate the systematic risk of two different investment opportunities, Bram Inc. and Itel Labs. She estimates the standard deviation for Bram is 10.56 percent and its correlation coefficient with the market is +0.45. Itel has a standard deviation of 12.15 percent and a correlation coefficient with the market of +0.85. If the standard deviation of the market is 8.67 percent, what are the beta estimates for both Bram and Itel?

CR5.5   Cris obtained information about the risk-free rate of return and the market rate of return from a local brokerage firm. The brokerage firm estimates the expected risk-free rate of return is 6 percent and that investors require a return from the market of 11 percent. Using her beta estimates from CR5.4, what is the required rate of return for both Bram and Itel?

CR5.6   After estimating the required rate of return for both Bram and Itel Labs in CR 5.5, Cris was interested in what would happen to the required rates of return of both firms if inflation expectations increased the risk-free rate to 8 percent. What are the required returns? (*Note*: Other things being equal, does k_M stay at 11 percent, or change?)

CR5.7   Bram recently paid a dividend of $2.00 per share and is expected to grow at 3 percent indefinitely. Itel Labs just paid a dividend of $4.00 per share and has an anticipated growth rate of 6 percent.

a.   Using the required rates of return estimated in CR5.5, what is the stock price for each of the firms?

b.   Now assume that inflation increased by 2 percent as stated in CR5.6. What is the stock price for both Bram and Itel after the increase in inflation?

PROBLEMS

5.1   A firm is considering investing in one of two projects, which have the following returns and probabilities of occurrence:

Probability	Project A	Project B
0.10	40%	50%
0.20	20	20
0.40	10	5
0.20	0	−20
0.10	−20	−40

a.   Calculate the expected return for each project. Which is more profitable?
b.   Calculate the standard deviation for each project. Which is more risky?
c.   Which project is preferable?

5.2   Securities A, B, and C have rates of return and probabilities of occurrence as follows:

Probability	Security Return (%)		
	A	B	C
0.30	60	50	10
0.40	40	30	50
0.30	20	10	90

a. Calculate the probability distribution of expected rates of return for a portfolio composed of 50 percent security A and 50 percent security B. Now do the same for a portfolio composed of 50 percent security A and 50 percent security C.
b. Calculate the expected value (or mean) and standard deviation for portfolios AB and AC from (a).
c. Which portfolio has the highest expected return? The lowest risk? Which portfolio is preferable?
d. Assume that the standard deviation calculated for portfolio AC is 21 percent, but that everything else remains the same. Which portfolio would now be preferable? Why?

5.3   Securities D, E, and F have the following characteristics with respect to expected return, standard deviation, and correlation among them:

Security	Expected Return, $\bar{k}$	Standard Deviation, σ	Correlation
D	8%	2%	$Corr_{DE} = +0.40$
E	16	16	$Corr_{DF} = +0.60$
F	12	8	$Corr_{EF} = +0.80$

What are the expected return and standard deviation of a portfolio composed of 50 percent security D, 25 percent security E, and 25 percent security F? *Note*: For three securities, Equation 5.4 becomes:

$$\sigma_p = (W_D^2\sigma_D^2 + W_E^2\sigma_E^2 + W_F^2\sigma_F^2 + 2W_DW_E\sigma_D\sigma_E Corr_{DE}$$
$$+ 2W_DW_F\sigma_D\sigma_F Corr_{DF} + 2W_EW_F\sigma_E\sigma_F Corr_{EF})^{0.5}$$

5.4   Consider two stocks, A and B, with their expected returns and standard deviations, as follows:

	A	B
Expected return, $\bar{k}$	15%	10%
Standard deviation, σ	10	8

a. What is the expected return if the portfolio contains equal amounts (0.50) of each security?
b. What is the standard deviation for the equally weighted portfolio in (a) if the correlation between the security returns is (1) $Corr_{AB} = +1.00$, (2) $Corr_{AB} = +0.50$, and (3) $Corr_{AB} = -0.50$?
c. How does the decrease in the portfolio standard deviation (as the correlation between the security returns drops) relate to diversifiable and nondiversifiable risk?

5.5   Leonard has a portfolio made up of 75 percent stock A and 25 percent stock B. He is currently considering a single asset portfolio composed of 100 percent of either stock A or stock B. The data for the two stocks are as follows:

Stock	A	B
Expected return	0.10	0.15
Standard deviation	0.14	0.19
$Corr_{AB}$	0.40	

a. What is the expected return and standard deviation of his portfolio of stocks A and B?
b. Would Leonard be better or worse off by investing solely in stock A or in stock B as opposed to his portfolio of A and B?

5.6 You have estimated the following probability distribution of returns for two stocks:

Stock N		Stock O	
Probability	Return	Probability	Return
0.20	8%	0.20	26%
0.30	4	0.30	12
0.30	0	0.30	0
0.20	−4	0.20	−4

a. Calculate the expected rate of return and standard deviation for each stock.
b. If the correlation between the returns on the two stocks is −0.40, calculate the portfolio return and the standard deviation for portfolios containing 100 percent, 75 percent, 50 percent, 25 percent, and 0 percent of security N, respectively.
c. Plot the results from (b). Which portfolios lie on the efficient frontier?
d. If there is no risk-free asset, which portfolio would *you* prefer? Why? Would other individuals necessarily choose the same portfolio?

5.7 The following portfolios are available for selection:

Portfolio	Return, $\overline{K}_p$	Risk, σ_p
1	16%	16%
2	14	10
3	8	4
4	12	14
5	9	8
6	10	12
7	7	11
8	5	7
9	11	6
10	3	3

a. By plotting the data, determine which portfolios lie on the efficient frontier.
b. Which portfolio would *you* prefer? Why? Would other individuals necessarily choose the same portfolio?
c. Independent of (b), now assume a risk-free asset exists that returns 10 percent. What is the market portfolio of all risky assets? Which portfolio would *you* now prefer? Why?

5.8 The risk-free rate is 8 percent, and the expected return on the market portfolio is 14 percent. What are the required rates of return for the four stocks listed below?

Stock	R	S	T	U
Beta	2.0	0.6	1.0	−0.2

What can we say about the volatility of each stock relative to the market's volatility?

5.9 Returns for the next period for two stocks, A and B, and for the market, M, are given by the following probability distribution:

State of the Economy	Probability of State Occurring	Rate of Return		
		A	B	M
Boom	0.20	40%	50%	40%
Normal	0.50	0	5	15
Recession	0.30	−10	−5	−15

a. Calculate the expected rate of return for stocks A and B individually. Then calculate (**1**) the associated rates of return for a portfolio comprising 50 percent stock A and 50 percent stock B and (**2**) the expected rate of return for the portfolio AB.

b. Calculate the standard deviation for stock A, stock B, and the portfolio AB. (Carry to two decimal points.) Comparing the average of the individual stock's standard deviations with the portfolio's standard deviation, what can we say about the correlation between the two stocks?

c. Calculate the expected return on the market.

d. If the risk-free rate is 5 percent and the market is efficient so that the expected and required returns for portfolio AB are equal, what is the beta for portfolio AB?

5.10 Larry is attempting to estimate the required rate of return for Davidson Steel. The risk-free rate is 7 percent. Based on the analysis provided by a number of investment advisory firms, Larry estimates the expected return on the market portfolio is 15 percent and the beta for Davidson Steel is 1.25.

a. What is the required rate of return for Davidson Steel?

b. Larry decides to estimate the expected return on the market himself. He believes expected inflation is 6 percent, the real rate of growth in the economy is 3 percent, and the risk premium of stocks over bonds is 4 percent. The risk-free rate remains at 7 percent, and beta is still 1.25. What impact does this have on Larry's estimate of Davidson's required rate of return?

5.11 Haber Fund has a total investment in five stocks as follows:

Stock	Investment (Market Value)	Beta
1	$3.0 million	0.50
2	2.5 million	1.00
3	1.5 million	2.00
4	2.0 million	1.25
5	1.0 million	1.50

The risk-free rate, k_{RF}, is 7 percent, and the returns on the market portfolio are given by the following probability distribution:

Probability	k_M
0.10	8%
0.20	10
0.30	13
0.30	15
0.10	17

What is Haber Fund's required rate of return?

5.12 Suppose that two securities lie exactly on the security market line (SML), with the following characteristics:

Security	k_j	β_j
A	19.6%	2.25
B	16.8	1.75

What are k_{RF} and k_M? (*Note:* The solution involves solving simultaneous equations.) What does the graph of the SML look like?

5.13 The returns and probabilities for a stock and the market are as follows:

Probability of Occurrence	Stock Returns	Market Returns
0.20	45%	50%
0.30	0	20
0.30	−5	10
0.20	−15	−10

a. What is the expected rate of return for each?
b. What is the standard deviation of each?
c. If the correlation between the stock's and the market's returns is +0.95, what is the beta for the stock?

5.14 If a security's required rate of return is 18 percent, the return on the market portfolio is 15 percent, the risk-free rate is 9 percent, the correlation between the security's and the market's returns is +0.50, and the standard deviation of the security's return is 16 percent, what is the variance about the expected market return?

5.15 Assume that you hold the following two securities, A and B:

Security A		Security B	
Probability, P_i	Return, k_i	Probability, P_i	Return, k_i
0.40	40%	0.30	65%
0.40	10	0.40	15
0.20	−10	0.30	−15

The correlation between security A and the market, M, is +0.50.

a. Calculate the expected return and standard deviation for each security.
b. What must the value of $Corr_{BM}$ be to make the two securities equally risky in terms of their beta coefficients?

5.16 Year-end stock prices and dividends for J. C. Penney and the S&P 500 stock index for some recent years are as follows:

	J. C. Penney		
Year	Dividend	Ending Price	S&P 500 Ending Value
−8	—	$14.312	122.55
−7	$1.00	24.188	140.64
−6	1.08	28.312	164.93
−5	1.18	23.188	167.24
−4	1.18	27.750	211.28
−3	1.24	36.125	242.17
−2	1.48	43.375	247.08
−1	2.00	50.625	277.72
0	2.18	72.750	348.81

a. Using the formula, return = $(D_1 + P_1 - P_0)/P_0$, calculate the returns for each year for Penney and the S&P 500. (*Note*: Ignore dividends for the index.)
b. What is the beta for Penney? (Either use a calculator with a linear regression function, or see Chapter 26, which shows how to calculate a least-squares regression.)

5.17 Hoisington Investments has the following portfolio:

Stock	Investment	Stock's Beta
A	$20 million	0.90
B	40 million	1.40
C	10 million	2.00
D	30 million	1.20

a. What is the portfolio's beta coefficient?
b. If the risk-free rate is 8 percent and the return on the market portfolio is 15 percent: (1) What is the SML equation? (2) What is the (percentage) return Hoisington should be earning on the portfolio if its risk–return pattern puts it right on the SML?
c. Hoisington has just received $25 million in additional funds and is considering investing it in security E, which has a beta of 1.80 and an expected return of 19 percent. (1) Should stock E be purchased? (2) If not, at what rate of return would it be suitable for purchase (if its beta remains at 1.80)?

5.18 Brad has the following investments:

Stock	Required Return, k_j	Portfolio Weight, W_j	β_j
Calgary Power & Light	7.5%	0.40	0.60
Uptown	12.7	0.30	1.40
Summit Industries	10.3	0.30	1.10

a. What is the required return on the portfolio?

b. What is the portfolio beta?

c. Brad has decided to take on some more risk in order to increase his return. He sold some of the Calgary Power & Light stock and invested the proceeds into the other two stocks already held. If the new portfolio's required return is 11.06 percent, and the new portfolio beta is 1.165, how much is now invested in each of the three stocks? (*Note*: The solution involves solving simultaneous equations. Let X equal the proportion of the portfolio invested in Calgary Power & Light, and Y equal the proportion of the portfolio invested in Uptown. Because the sum of all three proportions equals 100 percent, or 1.0, then $1 - X - Y$ equals the proportion of the portfolio invested in Summit Industries.)

5.19 Trade-Marke Products has a current dividend of $2 per share, an expected growth rate of 9 percent per year to infinity, and a beta of 1.40, and the market risk premium is expected to be 5 percent. Trade-Marke is contemplating three different courses of action:

1. The divestiture of an unprofitable but stable revenue-producing division. The effect will be to increase the growth rate in cash dividends to 11 percent, and also increase beta to 1.60.

2. Merge with another firm that is a steady cash producer but is less risky. The effect would be to lower beta to 1.20 and reduce the growth rate in dividends to 8 percent.

3. A new, aggressive management could be brought in. Beta would go to 2.00, and the growth rate in dividends would be 13 percent.

Is Trade-Marke better off staying where it is, or moving to one of the three plans? If it is better off moving, which plan should the firm choose? Why is this the best plan?

5.20 You are considering buying 100 shares of Nu-Lite Electronics' common stock. The common stock is expected to pay a dividend of $3.15 next year; the growth rate is 5 percent; the covariance between Nu-lite's and the market's return is expected to be 0.003; the standard deviation of the market's return is expected to be 0.04472; $k_M = 15$ percent; and $k_{RF} = 7$ percent.

a. Should you buy the shares if the current market price of Nu-Lite's common stock is $27.50 per share?

b. Does your decision change if the combined actions of the federal government and the Bank of Canada cause the risk-free rate to drop to 5 percent? (*Note*: At every beta, the SML is 2 percent less than before.)

c. Would you buy the shares if, *in addition to the change in (b)*, risk aversion has decreased, so the return on the market is now 11 percent?

d. Finally, *in addition to the changes in (b) and (c)*, the firm closes some of its marginal operations. Beta decreases to 1.333, while D_1 is $3.12 and g decreases to 4 percent. What would you do now?

5.21 L & M Industries is in the process of evaluating the effect of different factors on its market value. L & M expects to pay dividends of $3 a year from now, and the growth rate in its dividends is 4 percent per year until infinity. L & M estimates the following: $k_{RF} = 6\%$, $k_M = 11\%$, $\sigma_j = 16\%$, $\sigma_M = 10\%$, and $Corr_{jM} = 0.50$.

a. What is the current market value of L & M's stock?

b. What is L & M's stock market value if everything stays the same, except that its correlation with the market increases to 0.75?

c. If all the conditions are as in (a) except that σ_j increases to 64 percent and σ_M increases to 20 percent, what is the market price for L & M?

d. If all the conditions are as in (a) except that σ_j decreases to 8 percent, what is the market price for L & M?

5.22   The risk-free rate is 5 percent, and the expected return on the market portfolio, k_M, is 10 percent. The expected returns and betas for four stocks are listed below:

Stock	Expected Return	Beta
Steelman Zinc	12.0%	1.3
Rose Paint	9.5	0.8
Ramakrishnan Automotive	10.5	1.1
Blythe Electronics	13.0	1.7

a. Which stocks are over- or undervalued?

b. In an efficient market, what occurs to bring expected and required rates of return back into equilibrium?

c. Which stocks are over- or undervalued if the risk-free rate increases to 7 percent and the expected return on the market portfolio goes to 11 percent?

5.23   The stock of M^2A^2 Hardware is currently selling for $25. You have evaluated the future prospects of both the firm and the market and have come up with the following estimates. M^2A^2 is expected to pay a dividend of $2.00 at the end of the year, and this dividend is expected to grow indefinitely at 6 percent a year. The standard deviation for M^2A^2's return is expected to be 10 percent while the variance of the market return is expected to be 39.0625 percent. The correlation between the returns for M^2A^2 and for the market is +0.80. If the return on the market is 14 percent and the risk-free rate is 8 percent, is M^2A^2 a good buy?

5.24   **Mini Case**   Answer the following questions that deal with portfolios and the capital asset pricing model.

a. Total risk for a stock is measured by its standard deviation. What do we mean by total risk?

b. Two stocks, Cyclical and Stable, exist with probability distributions and associated possible rates of return as follows:

State of the Economy	Probability of State Occurring	Rate of Return	
		Cyclical	Stable
Boom	0.30	50%	25%
Normal	0.50	15	10
Recession	0.20	−20	5

Calculate the mean, or expected value, for each stock, and its standard deviation.

c. The correlation between the returns on Cyclical and Stable is estimated to be $+0.20$. What are the expected portfolio return and standard deviation for a portfolio of these two securities if the following portfolio weights are employed?

Weight	
Cyclical	**Stable**
0.00	1.00
0.25	0.75
0.50	0.50
0.75	0.25
1.00	0.00

Plot the results. What does the efficient frontier tell us?

d. Do the same as in (c) except now assume the correlation between the returns on the two securities is -0.75. What happens to the efficient frontier compared with the efficient frontier determined in (c)? What would the efficient frontier be if the correlation between Cyclical and Stable were $+1.0$? If it were -1.0?

e. What is the primary lesson to be learned from portfolio theory?

f. Distinguish between diversifiable and nondiversifiable risk. Why is nondiversifiable risk, as measured by beta, the relevant measure of risk?

g. What are the differences between the capital market line and the security market line? The similarities?

h. Assume the two stocks in (b) have prices and betas as follows: $P_{Cyclical} = \$50$ while $\beta_{Cyclical} = 1.58$, and $P_{Stable} = \$25$ while $\beta_{Stable} = 0.75$. A portfolio with 20 percent invested in Cyclical and 80 percent invested in Stable has been formed. What is the beta of the portfolio? If the stock market as a whole increases by 30 percent, by approximately what percent should the value of the portfolio increase? What should be the new market price of the two stocks after the 30 percent increase in the stock market?

i. Independent of (h), assume the risk-free rate is 9 percent and the expected return on the market, $\overline{k}_M$, is 15 percent. What is the required return on the two stocks, Cyclical and Stable? What do we know about the two stocks?

j. Assume the risk-free rate increases to 10 percent while the expected return on the market portfolio increases to 18 percent. What are the new required returns for Cyclical and Stable?

REFERENCES

BOABANG, FRANCIS. "Stationarity of the Market Model: Joint Tests of Progress and Parameter Nonstationarity." *Canadian Journal of Administrative Sciences* 9 (September 1992): 192–204.

FAMA, EUGENE F. "Efficient Capital Markets: II." *Journal of Finance* 46 (December 1991): 1575–1617.

FAMA, EUGENE F., and KENNETH R. FRENCH. "The Cross-Section of Expected Stock Returns." *Journal of Finance* 47 (June 1992): 427–65.

GREEN, RICHARD C., and BURTON HOLLIfiELD. "When Will Mean-Variance Efficient Portfolios Be Well Diversified?" *Journal of Finance* 47 (December 1992): 1785–1809.

KRYZANOWSKI, LAWRENCE, SIMON LALANCETTE, and MINH CHAU TO. "Performance Attribution Using a Multivariate Intertemporal Asset Pricing Model with One State Variable." *Canadian Journal of Administrative Sciences* 11 (March 1994): 75–85.

MARKOWITZ, HARRY M. "Foundations of Portfolio Theory." *Journal of Finance* 46 (June 1991): 469–78.

MARKOWITZ, HARRY M. "Portfolio Selection." *Journal of Finance* 7 (March 1952): 77–91.

ROSS, STEPHEN A. "The Arbitrage Theory of Capital Asset Pricing." *Journal of Economic Theory* 13 (December 1976): 341–60.

SHARPE, WILLIAM F. "Capital Asset Prices: A Theory of Market Equilibrium under Conditions of Risk." *Journal of Finance* 19 (September 1964): 425–42.

SHARPE, WILLIAM F. "Capital Asset Prices With and Without Negative Holdings." *Journal of Finance* 46 (June 1991): 489–509.

APPENDIX

5A *Calculating Covariances and Correlations*

The covariance is

$$\text{covariance, } \text{Cov}_{AB} = \sigma_A \sigma_B \text{Corr}_{AB} \tag{5A.1}$$

where

σ_A, σ_B = the standard deviations for assets A and B, respectively
Corr_{AB} = the degree of correlation between the respective returns on assets A and B

Like the correlation coefficient, the covariance is a measure of the degree of linear relationship between two variables. However, the covariance may take on any value (positive or negative), whereas the correlation coefficient can take on values only from +1.0 through zero to −1.0.

USING *EX ANTE* (EXPECTED) RETURNS

The formula for calculating the covariance from expected returns is

$$\text{Cov}_{AB} = \sum_{t=1}^{n} (k_{Ai} - \bar{k}_A)(k_{Bi} - \bar{k}_B)P_i \tag{5A.2}$$

where

k_{Ai}, k_{Bi} = the outcome associated with the ith state for assets A and B, respectively
$\bar{k}_A$, $\bar{k}_B$ = the expected value for assets A and B, respectively
P_i = the probability associated with the ith state
n = the number of possible states

To illustrate the calculation of the covariance, let us continue with the two stocks from Figure 5.1, Hudson International and Ace Chemical. The mean, or expected rate of return, is 20 percent for Hudson International and 15 percent for Ace Chemical. To determine the covariance, we need to perform the following calculations:

State of the Economy (1)	Hudson International's Deviations from the Mean $(k_{HI} - \bar{k}_{HI})$ (2)	×	Ace Chemical's Deviations from the Mean $(k_{AC} - \bar{k}_{AC})$ (3)	×	Probability of State Occurring P_i (4)	=	Product of Probability × Deviations (5)
Boom	(60 − 20)		(25 − 15)		0.30		+120
Normal	(20 − 20)		(15 − 15)		0.40		0
Recession	(−20 − 20)		(5 − 15)		0.30		120
							$Cov_{HI:AC}$ = +240

Once we know the covariance is +240, we can calculate the correlation between Hudson International's and Ace Chemical's returns using Equation 5A.1. Because Hudson International's standard deviation is 30.98 percent, whereas Ace Chemical's is 7.75 percent, we have

$$Cov_{HI:AC} = \sigma_{HI}\sigma_{AC}Corr_{HI:AC}$$
$$+240 = (30.98)(7.75)Corr_{HI:AC}$$
$$Corr_{HI:AC} = \frac{+240}{(30.98)(7.75)} = \frac{+240}{240.95} \approx +1.00$$

Hence, the correlation between the expected returns on Hudson International and Ace Chemical is +1.00. As we should have expected by inspecting Figure 5.1, their returns tend to move together (even though those of Hudson International have wider fluctuations than those for Ace Chemical).

USING *EX POST* (HISTORICAL OR REALIZED) RETURNS

Instead of having discrete probabilities of occurrence, we might want to calculate the covariance between the returns for two assets using historical returns. The formula for calculating the covariance in that case is

$$\text{covariance, Cov}_{FG} = \frac{\sum_{t=1}^{n} (k_{Ft} - \bar{k}_F)(k_{Gt} - \bar{k}_G)}{n - 1} \tag{5A.3}$$

where

k_{Ft}, k_{Gt} = the outcome associated with the tth time period for assets F and G, respectively
$\bar{k}_F, \bar{k}_G$ = the expected value for assets F and G, respectively
n = the total number of time periods

To illustrate this, let us calculate the covariance between the historical returns for stocks F and G with the data below:

Year	Stock F k_{Ft}	Stock G k_{Gt}
−3	5%	25%
−2	30	15
−1	−10	0
0	15	40
Average return	10%	20%
Standard deviation	16.83%	16.83%

From these data we see that the average return for stock F is 10 percent, and its standard deviation is 16.83 percent.[1] Stock G's return is 20 percent, even though its

---

[1] To calculate the standard deviation when historical returns are available, the following formula is employed:

$$\sigma = \left[\frac{\sum_{t=1}^{n} (k_i - \bar{k})^2}{n - 1} \right]^{0.5}$$

For stock F we proceed as follows:

$$\bar{k} = \frac{\sum_{t=1}^{n} k_t}{n} = \frac{5 + 30 - 10 + 15}{4} = 10\%$$

$$\sigma = \left[\frac{(5 - 10)^2 + (30 - 10)^2 + (-10 - 10)^2 + (15 - 10)^2}{4 - 1} \right]^{0.5}$$

$$= \left[\frac{25 + 400 + 400 + 25}{3} \right]^{0.5} = \left[\frac{850}{3} \right]^{0.5} = [283.3333]^{0.5} = 16.8325 \approx 16.83\%$$

Note that we use 4, because there are 4 years in figuring the mean, but only 3 $(n - 1)$ in calculating the standard deviation.

standard deviation is also 16.83 percent. Given these data, the calculations necessary to determine the covariance are as follows:

Year	Stock F's Deviations from the Mean, $(k_{Ft} - \bar{k}_F)$ (1)	×	Stock G's Deviations from the Mean, $(k_{Gt} - \bar{k}_G)$ (2)	=	Product of the of the Deviations $(k_{Ft} - \bar{k}_F)(k_{Gt} - \bar{k}_G)$ (3)
−3	(5 − 10)		(25 − 20)		−25
−2	(30 − 10)		(15 − 20)		−100
−1	(−10 − 10)		(0 − 20)		400
0	(15 − 10)		(40 − 20)		100
			$\sum\limits_{t=1}^{n}(k_{Ft} - \bar{k}_F)(k_{Gt} - \bar{k}_G) = $		+375

From Equation 5A.3, the covariance is:

$$\text{Cov}_{FG} = \frac{+375}{4-1} = \frac{+375}{3} = +125$$

Knowing the covariance between the historical returns on stocks F and G, we can calculate the correlation between them using Equation 5A.1 as follows:

$$\text{Cov}_{FG} = \sigma_F \sigma_G \text{Corr}_{FG}$$

$$+125 = (16.83\%)(16.83\%)\text{Corr}_{FG}$$

$$\text{Corr}_{FG} = \frac{+125}{283.2489} \approx +0.44$$

PROBLEMS

5A.1 Two securities have probability distributions of returns as follows:

Security A		Security B	
Probability	Return	Probability	Return
0.10	40%	0.10	30%
0.40	25	0.40	60
0.40	10	0.40	20
0.10	0	0.10	−10

a. Calculate the mean and the standard deviation of the returns for both securities.
b. What are their covariance and their correlation?

5A.2   Hull Brothers and Tubbs Trucking have returns as follows:

Year	Hull Brothers	Tubbs Trucking
−4	3%	15%
−3	−8	10
−2	15	−3
−1	22	16
0	−2	7

a.   Calculate the mean and the standard deviation of the returns for both securities.
b.   What are their covariance and their correlation?

5A.3   Irene currently has 100 percent of her funds invested in stock A. She is contemplating forming a portfolio consisting of 75 percent stock A and 25 percent stock B. She asks for your advice in making her decision. You have been able to determine the following returns and probabilities for the two stocks:

Probability of Occurrence	Stock A Returns	Stock B Returns
0.20	60%	30%
0.30	10	20
0.30	−5	0
0.20	−15	−10

In doing your analysis, answer the following questions:
a.   What is the expected return for each stock?
b.   What is the standard deviation for each stock?
c.   What are the expected return and the standard deviation of returns on her proposed portfolio?
d.   Is Irene better or worse off by holding her proposed portfolio than by investing only in stock A, or is it impossible to say?

5A.4   Stocks A and B have the following historical cash dividend and price data:

	Stock A		Stock B	
Year	Cash Dividend, D_t	Year-End Price, P_t	Cash Dividend, D_t	Year-End Price, P_t
−4	$_____	$40.00	$_____	$15.00
−3	2.00	43.00	_____	22.00
−2	2.50	38.50	0.50	18.50
−1	2.50	48.00	0.50	14.00
0	3.00	44.00	0.50	28.50

a. Calculate the yearly returns for stock A, stock B, and a portfolio composed of 50 percent A and 50 percent B. (*Note*: Carry the calculations to four decimal places; then convert the returns to percentages with two decimal places for use in the rest of the problem.)

b. Calculate the means for stock A, stock B, and the portfolio AB. Do the same for the standard deviation.

c. Take the simple average of the two individual stocks' standard deviations and compare this with the portfolio standard deviation, AB. Based on the extent to which the portfolio has a lower risk than the average of the two stocks' standard deviations, what would you estimate the correlation to be between the returns on stock A and stock B? More specifically, if you were told the correlation was either +0.85 or −0.65, which one would you choose? Why?

6

The Opportunity Cost of Capital

EXECUTIVE SUMMARY

Calculating an appropriate opportunity cost, or required rate of return—whether it is a firm-wide, divisional, or project-specific rate—is an integral part of the investment decision process. As discussed previously, to maximize the market value of the firm, the firm uses the net present value decision criterion and accepts any project that returns more than it costs. The costs to the firm are captured by the discount rate, or opportunity cost of capital employed. Because financial markets are efficient, they provide reliable and up-to-date information about the returns demanded by investors, which are the costs to the firm.

In determining the opportunity cost of capital, debt is typically the cheapest source, and common equity is the most expensive. By using the costs of new financing and the market value proportions, a firm can calculate its opportunity cost of capital. This is the *minimum* market-determined required rate of return for new projects of average risk undertaken by the firm. By investing in these projects, a firm assists in maximizing its market value.

If a project's risk differs significantly from the average risk of projects undertaken, an opportunity cost that reflects that degree of risk must be employed as the discount rate. The most frequently used method is to calculate divisional opportunity costs, based on the assumption that risk is homogeneous within a division but differs between divisions. Project-specific opportunity costs can also be employed.

WHAT IS THE FIRM'S OPPORTUNITY COST OF CAPITAL?

The most important determinant of the value of the firm is its investment decisions. To maximize the market value of the firm, V, a thorough understanding of capital budgeting techniques is required. An important part of the decision involves the use of the proper opportunity cost as the discount rate for net present value decisions.

To keep things simple, we start with projects that can be viewed as being equal in risk to the firm as a whole. The proper rate to employ can be viewed in one of two ways:

1. THE OPPORTUNITY COST OF CAPITAL   When viewed as the opportunity cost of capital, the discount rate is what the funds could earn in an alternative investment of similar risk. If a firm has $1 million that could be invested externally to yield 15 percent, then an internal (i.e., capital investment) project with equal risk should return more than 15 percent. Otherwise, the value of the firm will not be maximized.

2. THE WEIGHTED AVERAGE COST OF CAPITAL (WACC)   The **weighted average cost of capital** is simply the average after-tax cost of new funds available for investment by the firm. For example, if the firm's average after-tax cost of the last dollar of new funds is 15 percent, then it must earn more than 15 percent (after taxes) on new investments in order to maximize the value of the firm.

When talking about the appropriate discount rate for average-risk projects, *we use the terms opportunity cost of capital, required rate of return, or weighted average cost of capital interchangeably.* Whatever it is called, it is the minimum rate the firm must earn to ensure that the value of the firm does not fall. In addition, it is important to recognize that the feasibility of a project depends on how much it will cost the firm to raise *new* funds. Therefore, the opportunity cost of capital represents the cost of *new funds* needed to finance the project and *not* the cost of funds raised in the past.

Accurate estimation of the firm's opportunity cost of capital (when dealing with projects whose risk is equal to the firm's risk) is important. We begin by determining how to calculate the firm's opportunity cost of capital—first for a hypothetical example and then for Loblaw Companies. Remember, if a project returns less than it costs, then the net present value (NPV), will be negative and the value of the firm will decrease if the project is accepted. So, *the opportunity cost of capital represents the minimum return a firm must earn.* Accepting projects whose expected returns are higher than their costs, as evidenced by positive NPVs, assists in maximizing the value of the firm. Later in the chapter we also consider how to proceed when the risk of proposed capital budgeting projects differs from the firm's average risk.

DEFINITIONS AND CALCULATIONS

Before calculating the firm's opportunity cost of capital, we begin by defining some terms we will use throughout:

opportunity cost of capital = the weighted average of the cost of the last dollar of capital expected to be raised by the firm from each source of financing.

k_b = the before-tax cost of new debt issued by the firm. Ignoring flotation costs, this is equal to the yield to maturity (YTM) expected by investors, as defined in Chapter 4.

$k_i = k_b(1 - T)$, the after-tax cost of new debt issued by the firm, where T equals the firm's effective marginal corporate tax rate.

k_{ps} = the after-tax cost of new preferred stock issued by the firm.

k_s = the after-tax cost of internally generated equity capital, which arises from retention of the excess of cash inflows over cash outflows. Some of these funds may be distributed to the firm's shareholders through cash dividends; the remainder can be retained and reinvested in the firm. This k_s is identical to the k_s defined in Chapter 4, where it was called the investor's required return on common stock.

k_e = the after-tax cost of issuing new common stock by the firm.

W_i = the weights that indicate the future financing proportions to be employed by the firm.

The firm's opportunity cost of capital is a weighted average of the various sources of new capital. Note that the costs are expressed on an after-tax basis. This is to ensure consistency for decision-making purposes with the cash flows that are also calculated on an after-tax basis. If a firm raises capital with debt, preferred stock, and internally generated common equity, the opportunity cost of capital would be

$$\text{opportunity cost of capital} = k_i W_{\text{debt}} + k_{ps} W_{\text{preferred stock}} + k_s W_{\text{common equity}} \qquad (6.1)$$

where the *W's indicate the proportions of future funding to be raised from each specific source.*

BASIC ASSUMPTIONS

In order to determine a firm's opportunity cost of capital, we begin by going back to the notion that financial markets in developed countries are efficient. As informed investors in efficient financial markets process all available information and make decisions to invest in various financial assets (such as stocks and bonds), their actions reflect all that is known about the firm, the economy, and the future. Hence, to determine what a financial asset is worth, we "look to market values." In addition, to determine how the firm is expected to finance itself in the future, we also "look to market values." Efficient financial markets play an important role in many of the firm's decisions; one of them is determining the firm's opportunity cost of capital. The returns demanded by the firm's investors, and the possible returns that could be earned on comparable risky investments, can best be determined by examining the firm's existing financial assets. As returns demanded by investors increase or decrease, the costs to the firm must also increase or decrease.

To use the firm-wide opportunity cost of capital for decision-making purposes, two basic conditions must be met. First, the risk of the project under examination must be approximately equal to the risk of all new projects being undertaken by the firm. Although, as we discuss in Chapter 9, the precise estimation of project risk is not easy, our concern is that the risk not be substantially above or below that of the other projects being undertaken. When risk differs significantly, a divisional or project-specific opportunity cost of capital (as discussed later in the chapter) should be employed. Second, it is important that the firm not materially change its financing policies as a result of the investments it undertakes. Because these proportions directly affect the opportunity cost, the cost of capital will change as the financing mix and the firm's **capital structure** (which reflects the mix of debt and equity employed) change.

At this point, we are assuming that the firm's **target capital structure** (or desired debt/market value of equity ratio) will be constant. The reason for making this assumption is that different capital structures may influence the firm's cost of capital.[1] Our concern here is with determining the opportunity cost of capital, assuming a firm is at the appropriate target capital structure. In Chapters 12 and 13 we examine the impact the firm's capital structure may have on the value of the firm.

Before proceeding, it is important to emphasize that *the opportunity cost of capital is a marginal cost*. What is meant by the term "marginal"? We are using "marginal" in the economic sense—as the cost of raising the last dollar of funds. For each of the components—debt, preferred stock, and common equity—we are interested in the cost of the last dollar of additional funds. If the cost of the last dollar of additional funds increases, so does the firm's required return. *Calculation of the firm's cost of capital has a future orientation.* The opportunity cost of capital is a weighted average of the after-tax costs of various future sources of capital; *any past or historical costs are irrelevant.* The only reason to consider historical costs when calculating an opportunity cost is to obtain some idea of the future-oriented estimates that must be made. But, in general, it is best to ignore them; considering historical costs or proportions often leads to incorrect conclusions.

Concept Review Questions

- What does a firm's opportunity cost of capital measure?
- What two basic conditions must be met to use the firm-wide opportunity cost of capital for decision-making purposes?
- What is meant by the term marginal cost of capital when describing the opportunity cost of capital?

CALCULATING COSTS AND FINANCING PROPORTIONS

First we will consider the explicit costs of three types of financing—debt, preferred stock, and common equity—and then the specific financing proportions.

---

[1] In addition, we are asssuming that risk does not change and that the firm's cash dividend policy is constant. If either of these changes, some of the costs might change, affecting the whole decision-making process.

COST OF DEBT

The cost of debt to be used for cost of capital purposes is the before-tax cost, k_b, adjusted for the tax "subsidy" provided by the government to profitable firms (because interest is a tax-deductible expense). The after-tax cost of debt, k_i, is

$$\text{after-tax cost of debt} = k_i = k_b(1 - T) \qquad (6.2)$$

where

k_b = the before-tax cost of debt
T = the firm's marginal corporate tax rate

To calculate the before-tax cost for long-term debt, we solve for the expected yield to maturity (YTM) with Equation 4.1, except that we substitute the net proceeds to be raised from the bond, B_{np}, for the bond's market value, B_0, used previously. The net proceeds to the firm, B_{np}, equals the selling price of the bond (or gross proceeds) minus any flotation costs.[2] Thus, the before-tax cost to the firm, k_b, is found by solving for the unknown discount rate:

$$
\begin{aligned}
B_{np} &= \sum_{t=1}^{n} \frac{I}{(1 + k_b)^t} + \frac{M}{(1 + k_b)^n} \\
&= I(PVA_{k_b,n}) + M(PV_{k_b,n}) \qquad (6.3) \\
&= I(PVA_{?\%,n}) + M(PV_{?\%,n})
\end{aligned}
$$

where

B_{np} = the net proceeds from the bond
I = dollar amount of interest paid on a bond each year
M = the par or maturity value of the bond (typically $1,000)
n = the number of years to maturity for the bond
k_b = the before-tax cost to the firm

Consider the example of Ambassador Corporation, which plans to issue a new 20-year bond that has a $1,000 par value, carries a 12.75 percent coupon rate, and pays interest annually. The firm expects to receive $980 after flotation costs. The before-tax cost to Ambassador is

$$
\begin{aligned}
\$980 &= \sum_{t=1}^{20} \frac{\$127.50}{(1 + k_b)^{20}} + \frac{\$1,000}{(1 + k_b)^{20}} \\
&= \$127.50(PVA_{?\%,\ 20yr}) + \$1,000(PV_{?\%,\ 20yr})
\end{aligned}
$$

so, $k_b = 0.13035 \approx 13\%$.[3]

---

[2] Flotation costs represent the amount the firm has to pay to an investment dealer for underwriting services pertaining to a new issue of securities. These costs will be discussed more fully in Chapter 10.

[3] With the PV and PVA tables, the percent value (at 13 percent) of the interest payments and principal is $982.69, which indicates k_b is slightly more than 13 percent. Using a financial calculator, k_b is 13.035 percent.

The before-tax cost is 13 percent.[4] The after-tax cost, calculated using Equation 6.2 and assuming a marginal tax rate of 40 percent, is

$$k_i = k_b(1 - T) = 13\%(1 - 0.40) = 7.8\%$$

The after-tax cost of debt is used because it is, in fact, the cost to the firm. Although the before-tax cost is 13 percent, as long as the firm is profitable, interest is a deductible expense for tax purposes. So, the after-tax cost with a 40 percent effective marginal tax rate is only 7.8 percent.[5]

Remember that we are interested in the cost of new debt financing. The coupon rate on existing debt is not relevant, nor are any costs connected with existing debt. The explicit cost of debt tends to be the *least expensive* of the three sources we consider, for two reasons: First, from the investor's standpoint, it is a fixed legal claim; bondholders have greater security than preferred or common shareholders. On a risk–return basis, we would expect bond investors to demand less return than shareholders—which they do. Second, the tax status of interest also makes debt cheaper than other sources, as long as the firm is profitable (and it does not use so much debt that it becomes as expensive as or more expensive than equity).[6]

Determining the cost of debt financing for a firm becomes more complicated in practice because most firms employ many different kinds of debt. Some of these include short-term debt, zero-coupon bonds, convertible securities, and leases. The cost of some of these alternative sources of debt financing may differ from the cost of debt financing given by Equation 6.3.

For short-term debt, the shape of the term structure of interest rates (as discussed in Chapter 2) will determine whether its before-tax cost is higher or lower than k_b from Equation 6.3. The before-tax cost of zero-coupon bonds can be determined using the approach discussed in Chapter 11. Convertible securities (Chapter 20) have a before-tax cost that is between that of debt and common equity (discussed shortly). Finally, as discussed in Chapter 15, the before-tax cost of lease financing is approximately equal to the cost of long-term debt financing given by Equation 6.3.

COST OF PREFERRED STOCK

The cost of preferred stock is calculated in much the same manner as the cost of debt, except for one basic difference. Because dividends on preferred stock are paid out of

---

[4] This before-tax cost can be approximated by
$$\text{Approximate before-tax cost of debt} = \frac{I + (M - B_{np})/n}{M + 0.6\,(B_{np} - M)}$$
The approximation is more accurate than the typical bond yield approximation used. (See the Hawawini and Vora article in the chapter references.) The 0.6 in the denominator is a constant and has nothing to do with any tax adjustment; the impact of taxes is treated by Equation 6.2. This approximation does not work well with deep discount or zero-coupon bonds.

[5] This calculation assumes that the flotation costs can be expensed in the year of issuance (t = 0). In reality, however, the flotation costs associated with bonds must be amortized over the life of the bond. In this case $20/20 = $1 per year. This rate results in an annual after-tax cost of $1(1 − T) = $1(0.60) = $0.60, or a tax saving of $0.40 per year. Technically, these tax savings should be considered; however, because of their size, ignoring them does not result in a significantly different answer since flotation costs on debt are usually no more than 2 percent of face value.

[6] If a firm is operating at a loss, its marginal tax rate is zero. For a firm that does not expect to pay taxes for a long time, there is no tax subsidy for using debt, and $k_i = k_b$.

after-tax earnings, no tax adjustment is required. Thus, the cost of preferred stock, k_{ps}, is[7]

$$\text{cost of preferred stock} = k_{ps} = \frac{D_{ps}}{P_{np}} \tag{6.4}$$

where

D_{ps} = the cash dividends paid on the preferred stock each year
P_{np} = the proceeds from the sale of the preferred stock

If Ambassador is planning to issue a $50 par preferred stock that pays $6 in dividends per year and the firm expects to realize $48 per share, the after-tax cost of the preferred stock is[8]

$$k_{ps} = \frac{D_{ps}}{P_{np}} = \frac{\$6}{\$48} = 0.125 = 12.5\%$$

Compared with the 7.8 percent cost of debt calculated above, the cost of preferred stock is higher. This occurs primarily because the dividends on preferred stock are not tax-deductible.

COST OF COMMON EQUITY

The final cost to be considered is that of common equity. Actually, there are two possible costs here—one if the firm uses internally generated funds, and the other if it expects to issue additional shares of common stock. **Internally generated funds** are those cash flows that arise as a result of the firm's ongoing activities and that can be reinvested in the business. Because internally generated funds typically supply most of the common equity, we begin with them.

Cost of Internally Generated Funds   Like the cost of debt and preferred stock, the cost of equity capital is also a function of the returns expected by investors. To estimate the cost of internally generated funds, k_s, it is necessary to estimate the returns demanded by investors. As with preferred stock, there is no need to adjust for taxes, because cash dividends on common stock are paid out of after-tax earnings. The difficulty in estimating the cost of equity capital arises because, unlike debt or preferred stock, there is no stated interest or dividend rate. In addition, due to the ability to share in both the good and bad fortunes of the firm, common stock may incur substantial price changes. Consequently, estimating the cost of equity capital is more difficult than estimating the cost of debt or preferred stock. We examine three approaches for

---

[7] Equation 6.4 assumes the preferred stock is a perpetuity. If it is expected to be called or retired in a specific number of years, the cost of preferred stock should be obtained by using Equation 6.3, after adjusting to reflect preferred stock instead of debt.

[8] Current tax law requires that the flotation costs on preferred stock be amortized over five years, or $2/5 = \$0.40$ per year. This results in a tax saving of $0.16 per year for five years, which should be considered; however, ignoring it does not significantly alter the result.

estimating the cost of internally generated funds—the dividend valuation approach, the capital asset pricing model (CAPM), and an ad hoc method using bond yield plus a risk premium.

The logic behind assigning a cost to internally generated funds involves the opportunity cost concept. Management faces a choice with the funds generated by the firm: It can distribute them to the firm's owners (its common shareholders) in the form of cash dividends, or it can reinvest them in the firm on behalf of the same common shareholders. The decision to reinvest funds instead of paying them out involves an opportunity cost. Shareholders could have taken the funds and reinvested them in something else. Therefore, the firm must earn a return on the reinvested funds equal to what common shareholders could have earned in alternative investments of comparable risk.

What return is this? It's simply k_s, which is the return investors require on investments with comparable risk. If the firm cannot earn a return of at least k_s on the reinvested internally generated funds, it should distribute the funds to investors so they can invest them in other assets that provide an expected return equal to k_s.

Dividend Valuation Approach   In Chapter 4, we saw that one way to determine the value of a share of stock was the dividend valuation model. This model states that the market value, P_0, is equal to the present value of the future dividends, $D_1, \ldots, D_\infty$, where the discount rate, k_s, is the investor's required rate of return. Thus,

$$P_0 = \frac{D_1}{(1 + k_s)} + \frac{D_2}{(1 + k_s)^2} + \cdots + \frac{D_\infty}{(1 + k_s)^\infty} \qquad (6.5)$$

If the growth rate in dividends, g, is expected to be constant and less than k_s, Equation 6.5 reduces to

$$P_0 = \frac{D_1}{k_s - g} \qquad (6.6)$$

where D_1 is the cash dividend expected one year from now, k_s is the investor's required rate of return, and g is the constant percentage growth rate in cash dividends. Solving Equation 6.6 for k_s, we have one way of estimating the investor's required rate of return (which is the firm's cost of internally generated funds). Thus,

$$\begin{array}{l}\text{dividend valuation approach} \\ \text{to the cost of internally} \\ \text{generated funds}\end{array} = k_s = \begin{array}{l}\text{expected} \\ \text{dividend} + \text{expected growth} \\ \text{yield}\end{array}$$

$$= \frac{D_1}{P_0} + g \qquad (6.7)$$

Investors expect to receive a **dividend yield**, D_1/P_0, plus growth of g, for a total return of k_s.

To illustrate, assume the present market price on Ambassador's common stock is $25, dividends to be paid in one year, D_1, are $1.75, and the expected growth in dividends is 9 percent per year. The dividend valuation approach[9] to estimating the cost of equity capital yields

$$k_s = \frac{D_1}{P_0} + g = \frac{\$1.75}{\$25} + 9\% = 0.07 + 9\% = 7\% + 9\% = 16\%$$

The estimation of the expected growth rate in cash dividends is the most difficult aspect of applying the dividend valuation approach. We could start by analyzing past growth rates. That information is generally supplemented, however, by projections made by the firm itself or by security analysts. And it is the future growth rate that is important.

Capital Asset Pricing Model Approach   The second approach to estimating the cost of common equity employs the capital asset pricing model (CAPM). As described in Chapter 5, the CAPM states that the investors' required rate of return is equal to the risk-free rate plus a risk premium, so that

$$\begin{array}{l} \text{CAPM approach to cost} \\ \text{of internally generated funds} \end{array} = k_s = \frac{\text{risk-free}}{\text{rate}} + \frac{\text{expected risk}}{\text{premium}} \qquad (6.8)$$

$$= k_{RF} + \beta_j(k_M - k_{RF})$$

where

k_{RF} = the risk-free rate of return
β_j = the beta of security j
k_M = the expected rate of return on the market portfolio

The risk-free rate is generally measured by the yield on Canadian treasury bills. Betas can be obtained by referring to *Value Line Investment Survey*, ScotiaMcLeod, or many other investment advisory services. Although the expected rate of return on the market cannot be measured directly, it can be approximated. One approach to estimating the expected return on the market, k_M, involves focusing on three components: (1) expected inflation, (2) expected real growth in the economy, and (3) an expected risk premium commanded by stocks relative to bonds.[10]

To illustrate the CAPM approach, assume Ambassador's beta is 0.95, the yield on treasury bills is 10 percent, expected growth in the economy (as measured by projected GDP growth in constant dollars) is 3 percent, and the expected risk premium of stocks over bonds is 5 percent. Adding the last three components together provides an estimate of the future returns on the market of 10 + 3 + 5 = 18 percent. The investor's required rate of return, which is the cost of internally generated funds, is

$$k_s = 11\% + 0.95(18\% - 11\%) = 11\% + 6.65\% = 17.65\%$$

---

[9] If the expected growth rate in cash dividends is not constant, the nonconstant growth valuation approach discussed in Chapter 4 will have to be employed. Also, be careful if the expected growth rate in cash dividends is "high." In such a case, blind usage of the constant dividend valuation approach often leads to a "high" estimate of the cost of equity capital.

[10] Another way would be to add the expected market-risk premium $(k_M - k_{RF})$ to the risk-free rate. Research indicates that risk premiums are not constant over time.

This second approach to estimating the cost of internally generated funds provides a figure of 17.65 percent versus the earlier figure of 16 percent estimated by the dividend valuation approach. The dividend valuation and CAPM approaches should provide approximately the same answer, unless some drastic differences in assumptions are made. Our difference is not too large and should give us some confidence in the reliability of the estimates.

Bond Yield Plus Expected Risk Premium Approach   The third approach to estimating the cost of internally generated funds is an ad hoc method that states the investor's required rate of return is equal to what he or she could get on the bonds of the firm plus a premium for risk, so that

$$\begin{matrix} \text{bond yield plus expected} \\ \text{risk premium approach to} \\ \text{the cost of internally} \\ \text{generated funds} \end{matrix} = k_s = \text{bond yield} + \begin{matrix} \text{expected risk premium} \\ \text{of common} \\ \text{stock over} \\ \text{corporate bonds} \end{matrix} \qquad (6.9)$$

This method is useful when the firm does not pay any cash dividends (so that the dividend valuation approach is not applicable) or when the common stock is not traded (so that neither the dividend valuation nor CAPM approaches can be employed). To continue our earlier example, the before-tax bond yield of Ambassador was 13 percent, and the risk premium of stocks over corporate bonds was expected to be 5 percent.[11] The required rate of return is then

$$k_s = \text{bond yield} + \text{expected risk premium} = 13\% + 5\% = 18\%$$

Putting It All Together   For Ambassador, we have three estimates of its cost of internally generated funds, as follows:

Approach	Estimated k_s
Dividend valuation	16.00%
CAPM	17.65
Bond yield plus expected risk premium	18.00

All differ slightly, but they are close. Taking everything into account, we would estimate Ambassador's cost of internally generated funds is between 16 and 18 percent. A simple average of these estimates is 17.22 percent [i.e., $(16\% + 17.65\% + 18\%)/3$]. We will round this to 17.25 percent for use below when calculating Ambassador's opportunity cost of capital.

Although the use of three different approaches may seem unduly complicated, it is very useful in practice. By using several alternative approaches to estimating the cost of internally generated funds, managers are forced to consider which estimates are

---

[11] This risk premium is firm-specific and may be more or less than the market risk premium employed in estimating k_M. For simplicity, we assume the two risk premiums are equal.

most useful. Estimating the cost of equity capital requires both judgment and an understanding of what the firm's common shareholders expect. Even though internal equity financing is more expensive than debt or preferred stock financing, firms routinely use it. They do so to retain ownership of the firm (especially for smaller firms), and balance the benefits of debt financing versus the increased risks that go along with it, as discussed in Chapters 12 and 13.

Cost of New Common Stock   Although the primary source of common equity for most firms is internally generated funds, firms sometimes sell additional shares of common stock to raise capital. The cost of newly issued common stock, k_e, is the same as that of internally generated common equity except for one adjustment—the flotation or issuance costs that are incurred when new common stock is sold. Using the dividend valuation approach, we find that the cost of new common stock is

$$\text{dividend valuation approach to cost of new common stock} = k_e = \frac{D_1}{P_{np}} + g \qquad (6.10)$$

where everything is the same as in Equation 6.7 except that the net proceeds, P_{np}, are used instead of the current market price, P_0.

To illustrate, assume that Ambassador has used up its internally generated common equity funds and has to issue new common stock. The dividends next year are still $1.75, but to sell the new shares flotation costs of $4 per share must be incurred. Thus the net proceeds are expected to be $25 - $4 = $21 per share. Also, the growth rate is still 9 percent. Using Equation 6.10 to estimate the cost of new common stock, we have[12]

$$k_e = \frac{D_1}{P_{np}} + g = \frac{\$1.75}{\$21} + 9\% = 8.3\% + 9\% = 17.3\%$$

Issuing new common stock is more expensive than raising equity capital through internally generated funds because of flotation costs and underpricing. For Ambassador, the dividend valuation approach indicates that the cost of new common stock is 17.3 percent, versus 16 percent for internally generated funds.

Although this flotation cost adjustment is straightforward for the dividend valuation approach, it is not so simple for either the CAPM or bond yield plus expected risk premium approaches. The reason is that the price of common stock does not appear directly in Equations 6.8 or 6.9. The best one can do by using Equation 6.8 or 6.9 is to make a slight subjective adjustment if new common stock is to be issued.

The cost of common equity is higher than the cost of debt or preferred stock. This occurs because, from the investor's standpoint, there is more risk with common stock than with debt or preferred stock. Investors therefore have a higher required rate of return for common stock. But because the investor's required rate of return is the firm's cost, we see that the cost of common equity is the *most expensive* form of financing to the firm.

---

[12] As with preferred stock, the current tax law requires flotation costs on common stock to be amortized over five years. Although the resulting tax savings are larger than for preferred stock, ignoring them will not have a significant impact on the results.

An Alternative Flotation Cost Adjustment   Some finance experts argue that the dollar amount of flotation costs should be incorporated as an additional cash outflow when estimating the initial investment for capital budgeting purposes. (Estimation of the initial investment is discussed in Chapter 8.) Conceptually, there are some points in favour of this argument, but the problem is that the firm is *estimating the cost of a pool of funds raised over time* and invested in numerous capital projects. Also, the standard approaches used to evaluate capital investments rest on the premise that the investment (or capital budgeting) decision and the financing (or fund-raising) decision are separate and distinct activities. Therefore, it is often impractical to ascribe specific flotation costs to specific projects, and it is also unnecessary (if we are to separate the investment and financing decisions). If flotation costs are small, our preference is to ignore them. If they are larger, we typically reduce the proceeds received from the specific financing employed. It can be shown that this latter treatment produces a biased low estimate of a project's NPV. We prefer that result, however, to trying to tie specific financing to specific projects, so that the investment and financing decisions are not kept separate. The interaction of investment and financing decisions is discussed in Appendix 8A.

THE FINANCING PROPORTIONS

Now that we know how to calculate the specific after-tax costs of debt, preferred stock, and common equity, we are almost ready to calculate the firm's after-tax opportunity cost of capital. Before doing that, however, we need to determine the financing proportions, or amount of **financial leverage**, to be employed by the firm. These proportions are a function of the firm's target capital structure, which is its desired mix of debt to total market value. The target capital structure should be the long-run desired mix of financing the firm intends to employ for meeting all of its financing needs, *measured in market value terms*. To calculate the financing mix, we again employ current market value information, assuming that financial markets are efficient and incorporate all that is known about the firm.

Thus, if the firm intends to finance with 50 percent debt and 50 percent equity, the target capital structure should reflect that mix. Although many things influence a firm's target capital structure, it can be approximated by determining the current market value of the firm's outstanding securities. *These current market values provide the best estimate of the firm's future financing mix*.[13] However, temporary deviations from the target capital structure should be taken into account if the firm knows its current market-value-based capital structure does not provide a valid indication of the future target capital structure. Proper estimation of the future financing proportions is essential when estimating the firm's opportunity cost of capital.

Concept Review Questions

- What are the three primary component costs used when estimating the opportunity cost of capital?

---

[13] An altertnative would be to employ a cash budget that provides an estimate of the expected sources of funds over the next three to five years.

- Is a tax adjustment required when estimating the cost of either preferred or common stock? Why?
- Describe three methods used to estimate the cost of common equity.

ESTIMATING THE OPPORTUNITY COST OF CAPITAL

Once we have the specific market costs and proportions, calculating the firm's opportunity cost of capital is straightforward. Let us return to the Ambassador example, and then we will briefly discuss what happens if Ambassador decides to increase its capital stubstantially. Finally, before proceeding to estimate Loblaw Companies' opportunity cost of capital, we will consider the question of how often firms should estimate their cost of capital.

THE OPPORTUNITY COST FOR AMBASSADOR

Earlier we calculated the specific costs of debt, preferred stock, and internally generated funds for Ambassador Corporation. In addition to these after-tax costs, let us assume the market value proportions of financing to be employed are 30 percent debt, 10 percent preferred stock, and 60 percent common equity. Given these market value costs and proportions, Ambassador's opportunity cost of capital is 13.94 percent, as shown below:

Component	After-Tax Cost ×	Market Value Weight =	Opportunity Cost of Capital
Debt	7.8%	0.30	2.34%
Preferred stock	12.5	0.10	1.25
Internally generated funds	17.25	0.60	10.35
		Opportunity cost of capital =	13.94%

By using this as the minimum discount rate for net present value calculations, Ambassador can make investment decisions for projects of average risk that assist in maximizing the long-run market value of the firm.[14]

WHAT IF THE AMOUNT OF FINANCING INCREASES?

So far we have considered a firm raising a given amount of financing at a specific period in time. What if one or a number of new investment opportunities come along that require additional financing? The general rule in such a case requires us to recognize that not only are there new investment opportunities, but also the total amount of

---

[14] We are assuming Ambassador is at its target capital structure.

capital to be raised has increased substantially. In such a case, the risks involved, and therefore the costs of each financing source, may increase substantially. If that happens, the firm's opportunity cost of capital should be recalculated, and the new higher discount rate should be used in making all investment decisions faced by the firm.

Suppose Ambassador now has the opportunity to invest in a number of previously unavailable projects. However, undertaking all of the projects currently available to the firm will require it to increase substantially the amount of capital raised. Furthermore, it will exhaust its internally generated funds. Consequently, Ambassador will not only have to issue more debt and preferred stock, it will also have to issue new common stock to fulfil the equity requirements of its capital structure. As Ambassador attempts to raise significantly more capital at a given time, the cost of the last dollar of all of its various sources of funds will increase.

Assume that the new after-tax costs and financing proportions of Ambassador are as follows:

Component	After-Tax Cost	×	Market Value Weight	=	Opportunity Cost of Capital
Debt	8.5%		0.30		2.34%
Preferred stock	14.0		0.10		1.25
Additional common equity	19.25		0.60		11.55
			Opportunity cost of capital =		15.50%

Figure 6.1 graphs Ambassador's opportunity cost of capital schedule. Note that as Ambassador increases the amount of financing required, its cost of capital increases. If Ambassador needed to raise even more capital at the same time, the costs of some or all of the sources would rise again. Conceptually, the cost of capital schedule could increase as a smoothed line if the firm raises small incremental amounts of capital. But because most firms raise capital in fairly large and discrete amounts, the acquisition process is lumpy. Firms are concerned about only one or possibly two costs of capital at any one time.

HOW OFTEN SHOULD THE COST OF CAPITAL BE CALCULATED?

How often does the firm's cost of capital need to be recalculated? There is no hard-and-fast rule—we know firms that do it yearly and others that estimated their opportunity cost five years ago and have not really looked at it since. The best guide is to reexamine it periodically, especially when the financing proportions have changed (or are expected to change) or when economic conditions, such as interest rates, have changed substantially. In these rapidly changing economic times, firms would be wise to review their cost of capital at least every year. Given the rapid rise in actual and expected inflation in the late 1970s and early 1980s, firms that did not reestimate their

Figure 6.1

Opportunity Cost of Capital (OCC) Schedule for Ambassador

As the cost of the last dollar of a specific capital source increases, so does the firm's opportunity cost of capital.

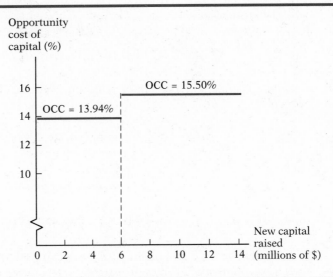

cost of capital ended up underestimating their real cost of funds. Likewise, when inflation decreased, as it did in the early 1990s, a downward revision was necessary.

Concept Review Questions

- What is the formula for a firm's opportunity cost of capital?
- Comment on why a firm should recalculate its opportunity cost of capital when considering a number of new investment opportunities requiring substantial amounts of financing.

ESTIMATING LOBLAW'S OPPORTUNITY COST OF CAPITAL

In practice, calculating a firm's opportunity cost of capital follows the same process we have described. We will use Loblaw Companies Limited, Canada's largest retail and wholesale food distributor with sales of $8.5 billion across Canada and $1.5 billion in the United States in 1994. *Our calculations are made as of March 1996.* This is an example of how to make the calculations, but obviously they would have to be reestimated to calculate today's opportunity cost of capital, or required return, for Loblaw. At the time of our calculations the firm's 1995 annual report was not available; consequently, we had to use data based on the 1994 annual report.

MARKET VALUE PROPORTIONS

The book value balance sheet for Loblaw as of January 1, 1995, in millions, was as follows:

Assets		Liabilities and Shareholders' Equity		
Current	$1,118.7	Payables and accruals		$1,062.3
Long-term	1,828.5	Deferred taxes		39.7
Total	$2,947.2	Interest-bearing debt and lease		
		obligations		723.3
		Shareholders' equity		
		Preferred shares		90.9
		Common equity		
		Common shares	$232.8	
		Retained earnings	798.2	1,031.0
		Total		$2,947.2

Note that we have grouped the liabilities in a somewhat different manner than is used by accountants. All accounts payable, accruals (for taxes, cash dividends, and so forth), and other liabilities are lumped together. These are typically ignored for cost of capital purposes. The reason is that for capital budgeting purposes, we will net out increases in current liabilities against increases in the current assets and will deal only with incremental net working capital needs. Because of this netting-out process (and assuming the firm pays these on time so their direct cost is zero), accounts payable and accruals are typically ignored. Deferred taxes are also excluded, because this is an accounting phenomenon that arises from using different depreciation methods for tax and accounting purposes. Short-term debt is typically included when firms calculate their cost of capital. However, at the time of our calculations, Loblaw did not have any short-term debt outstanding. Lease obligations are included, because they represent a form of long-term financing.

Loblaw's interest-bearing debt and lease obligations are listed in Table 6.1. The long-term debentures and notes are listed along with their market prices. The other long-term debt and lease obligations of $105.6 million were taken at their book value. Looking again at Table 6.1, we see that although the par value of Loblaw's debt is $723.3 million, its estimated market value as of March 1996 was $721.9 million.[15]

Looking further down Table 6.1 we see that the book values of Loblaw's preferred stock and common equity are $90.9 million and $1,031.0 million, respectively, whereas the respective market values of the firm's preferred and common stock are $92.8 million and $2,793.7 million. Although the book and market values of Loblaw's preferred stock are fairly close, as is often the case, those for the firm's

---

[15] As is fairly typical, the book value and market value of Loblaw's debt are close. This is especially true when current market interest rates are close to the coupon interest rates on the firm's debt. However, in this case it is due, in part, to the maturing of the firm's $40 million, 11 percent, debentures in 1995.

Table 6.1

Calculation of Market Value Weights for Loblaw, as of March 21, 1996

Where market prices are not available, judgment has to be employed to determine the estimated market value. For other debt and lease obligations, the par (or book) value was employed.

Interest-Bearing Debt and Lease Obligations	Par (or Book) Value (in millions)	Market Price	Market Value (in millions)
11% debentures due 1995	$ 40.0	—[a]	—
$9\frac{3}{4}$% debentures due 2001	75.0	$106\frac{3}{8}$[b]	$ 79.8
9% debentures due 2001	14.0	100	14.0
10% debentures due 2006	50.0	110	55.0
10% debentures due 2007	60.7	$108\frac{1}{8}$	65.6
11.4% notes due 2031	178.0	$120\frac{3}{4}$	214.9
$8\frac{3}{4}$% notes due 2033	200.0	$93\frac{1}{2}$	187.0
Other long-term debt and lease obligations	105.6	—	105.6
Total debt	$ 723.3		$ 721.9
Preferred stock	$ 90.9		$ 92.8[c]
Common equity			
Common shares	$ 232.8		
Retained earnings	798.2		
	$1,031.0		$2,793.7[d]

Market Value	Dollars	Proportions
Long-term debt and lease obligations	$ 721.9	0.200
Preferred stock	92.8	0.026
Common equity	2,793.7	0.774
Total	$3,608.4	1.000

[a] This issue was retired in 1995.
[b] Bond price as a percent of par.
[c] The firm has three different series of preferred stock outstanding.
First preferred shares:
    First series 437,952 shares × $38 5/8 = $16.9
    Second series 273,294 shares × $58   = $15.9
Second preferred shares:
    Fourth series 120 shares × $500,000 = $60.0
                                           ———
                                           $92.8
[d] 79,821,346 shares × $35 market value.

common stock are significantly different. Using these market-value proportions, we estimate that Loblaw will raise approximately 20 percent of its new financing with debt, 77 percent through common equity, and the remaining 3 percent through preferred stock. These are the proportions to use in calculating Loblaw's opportunity cost of capital. Obviously, Loblaw plans to rely on equity financing (its internal cash-generation capability and/or the issuance of new common stock) to finance about three-quarters of its financing needs.

COST OF DEBT

The before-tax cost of debt for Loblaw is the amount the firm has to pay to raise additional debt. Loblaw had a number of bonds and notes outstanding, and all had an A (High) rating according to the Dominion Bond Rating Service. We can assume that any new long-term debt will have a 10-year or longer maturity. What rate of return would the market require on a new issue with this risk? One approach is to calculate the yield to maturity on Loblaw's existing long-term debt. However, a more straight-forward approach is to determine what the market rate of return (or interest) was on comparable debt in March 1996. At that point in time, the yield to maturity on bonds rated A (High) was about 8.50 percent. In our judgment, if Loblaw had decided to issue new long-term debt in March 1996, the firm would have had to pay approximately 8.50 percent. This is their before-tax cost, k_b. Loblaw's effective tax rate for 1994 was 39.7 percent; therefore, our estimate of the after-tax cost of debt is

$$k_i = k_b(1 - T) = 8.50\%(1 - 0.397) = 5.13\%$$

Loblaw also had lease obligations in its capital structure. What should we do about them? As we discuss in Chapter 15, the cost of both debt and lease financing should be the same for the firm. We will use 8.50 percent for the before-tax cost of leasing for Loblaw.

COST OF PREFERRED STOCK

The cost of Loblaw's preferred stock is estimated by determining how the market values its present issues. On March 21, 1996, Loblaw's first preferred stock (second series) carried a $3.70 dividend and was trading at $58. We estimate that the flotation costs for Loblaw to issue new preferred stock would be 4 percent. Thus, if the firm were to issue preferred stock at $58 it would receive net proceeds of $55.68 [i.e., ($58)(0.96)]. Therefore we estimate the cost of preferred stock to be

$$k_{ps} = \frac{D_{ps}}{P_{np}} = \frac{\$3.70}{\$55.68} = 6.65\%$$

COST OF COMMON EQUITY

In recent years Loblaw has financed all its common equity needs through internally generated funds, so our approach is to ignore any possible sale of common stock. The first step is to estimate the growth rate in future dividends, as required by the dividend valuation approach. Although our calculations were made prior to the release of the firm's 1995 annual report, we were able to obtain the dividend and earnings figures

Table 6.2

Growth Rates of Earnings per Share and Dividends per Share for Loblaw

The historical growth rates are useful only as guides for the future. In this case there are some differences between historical and expected growth rates for both earnings and cash dividends.

Year	Dividends per Share	Earnings per Share
1985	$0.155	$0.85
1986	0.175	0.91
1987	0.195	0.87
1988	0.200	0.21
1989	0.200	0.80
1990	0.200	1.10
1991	0.230	1.17
1992	0.240	0.88
1993	0.240	1.07
1994	0.260	1.51
1995	0.360	1.81

	Dividends per Share	Earnings per Share
10-year growth rate	$= \dfrac{\$0.155}{\$0.36}$ $= 0.4306$ $= PV_{?\%,\,10yr}$ Closest PV is 9%	$= \dfrac{\$0.85}{\$1.81}$ $= 0.4696$ $= PV_{?\%,\,10yr}$ Closest PV is 8%
5-year growth rate	$= \dfrac{\$0.20}{\$0.36}$ $= 0.5556$ $= PV_{?\%,\,5yr}$ Closest PV is 13%	$= \dfrac{\$1.10}{\$1.81}$ $= 0.6077$ $= PV_{?\%,\,5yr}$ Closest PV is 10%

for 1995. As Table 6.2 shows, the 10-year and 5-year historical growth rates in dividends per share are 9 and 13 percent, respectively.[16] At the time of our calculations, analysts at Richardson Greenshields and Nesbitt Burns noted that Loblaw's 1994 earnings were up more than 40 percent over 1993 and that 1995 earnings were up about 20 percent over 1994. They attributed this to an aggressive capital expenditure programme embarked upon by the firm in 1993. As a result, the analysts felt that in the future Loblaw would reap the benefits of their larger and more efficient stores, the high acceptance of their private label products, and opportunities to export private label products and merchandising expertise to the United States. Based on this, Nesbitt Burns was estimating 1996 and 1997 earnings per share to be $2.10 and

---

[16] The 10-year historical growth rate in dividends can also be calculated as $(\$0.36/\$0.155)^{1/10} - 1 = 0.088 \approx 9$ percent. The 5-year historical growth rate is $(\$0.36/\$0.20)^{1/5} - 1 = 0.125 \approx 13$ percent. The growth rates in EPS can be calculated in a similar fashion.

Table 6.3

Calculation of Loblaw's Cost of Equity Capital, as of March 1994

These three estimates provide some measures of the "reasonableness" of the final k_s figure.

Assumptions

current market price, P_0 = \$35

expected growth rate in dividends, g = 12%

next year's cash dividends, D_1 = \$0.36(1.12) = \$0.40

risk-free rate[a], k_{RF} = 7.75%

market risk for Loblaw, β_j = 0.83

expected return on market portfolio, k_M = risk-free rate + expected real growth in economy + expected risk premium = 7.75% + 2.00% + 5.00% = 14.75%

expected bond yield = 8.5%

expected long-term risk premium of stocks over bonds = 5%

Dividend Valuation Approach

$$k_s = \frac{D_1}{P_0} + g = \frac{\$0.40}{\$35.00} + 12\% = 0.0114 + 12\% = 1.14\% + 12\% = 13.14\%$$

CAPM Approach

$$k_s = k_{RF} + \beta_j(k_M - k_{RF}) = 7.75\% + 0.83(14.75\% - 7.75\%)$$
$$= 7.75\% + 5.81\% = 13.56\%$$

Bond Yield Plus Expected Risk Premium

$$k_B = \text{bond yield plus expected risk premium} = 8.50\% + 5\% = 13.50\%$$

---

[a] As of March 1996 the term structure of interest rates was fairly steeply upward-sloping. The yield on 3-month Canadian treasury bills was about 5.25 percent, the yield on 6-month treasury bills was about 5.45 percent, the yield on 10-year Government of Canada bonds was about 7.75 percent, and the yield on 30-year Government of Canada bonds was about 8.30 percent. When the yield curve is upward-sloping, as it was then, we recommend employing the intermediate- or long-term Government of Canada bond rate for the risk-free rate when estimating the opportunity cost of capital.

\$2.55, respectively. This represents a forecasted growth rate in earnings of 16 percent and 21 percent, respectively, for 1996 and 1997. Therefore, based on these discussions and similar ones with analysts at ScotiaMcLeod and Wood Gundy, we believe that an estimate of 12 percent is a reasonable estimate of the expected compound growth rate in cash dividends as of March 1996.

All three approaches discussed earlier were employed to estimate the cost of equity capital for Loblaw. First, using the dividend valuation approach (shown in Table 6.3), the cost of equity capital is estimated to be 13.14 percent. Then, employing Loblaw's beta of 0.83 (provided by Nesbitt Burns), a risk-free rate of 7.75 percent,[17] and an

---

[17] As was noted in Table 6.3 the term structure of interest rates was fairly steeply upward-sloping in March 1996. The yield on 3-month treasury bills was about 5.25 percent, the yield on 6-month treasury bills was about 5.45 percent, the yield on 10-year Government of Canada bonds was about 7.75 percent and the yield on 30-year Government of Canada bonds was about 8.30 percent. In such a situation we recommend employing the intermediate-or-long-term bond rate instead of the short-term Canadian treasury bill rate. We employ the intermediate-term bond rate of 7.75 percent.

expected return on the market portfolio of 14.75 percent, the CAPM approach produces an estimated cost of common equity of 13.56 percent. Finally, the bond yield plus expected risk premium approach produces an estimated cost of 13.50 percent.

The three approaches produce similar estimates of Loblaw's cost of equity capital. For simplicity, we averaged the three estimates to provide an estimate of Loblaw's cost of equity capital of 13.40 percent [i.e., (13.14% + 13.56% + 13.50%)/3]. (If the three approaches had produced very divergent estimates of the cost of equity capital, we would have gone back and investigated the assumptions going into the various calculations in an attempt to reconcile any major differences in the estimates.)

LOBLAW'S OPPORTUNITY COST OF CAPITAL

Now that we have estimates of Loblaw's after-tax cost of long-term debt of 5.13 percent, cost of preferred stock of 6.65 percent, and an estimated cost of equity of 13.40 percent, we can calculate the opportunity cost of capital as of March 1996. As shown below, we estimate that Loblaw's opportunity cost of capital is 11.57 percent.

Component	After-Tax Cost	×	Market Value Weight	=	Opportunity Cost of Capital
Long-term debt	5.13%		0.200		1.03%
Preferred stock	6.65		0.026		0.17
Common equity	13.40		0.774		10.37
			Opportunity cost of capital =		11.57%

Given all the estimates that go into calculating an opportunity cost of capital, we would round this up to 12.0 percent. This is the minimum discount rate Loblaw should use as of March 1996 for projects of average risk; accepting projects with less than a 12.0 percent expected return is not consistent with the goal of maximizing the long-run market value of the firm.

This opportunity cost of capital can be used for making capital budgeting decisions (for projects of average risk) *as long as Loblaw does not attempt to increase its level of financing substantially.* If it seeks to secure a large increase in financing, then the cost of some or all of its capital sources would increase, and consequently Loblaw's opportunity cost of capital would also increase.

Concept Review Questions

■ When we estimated Loblaw's opportunity cost of capital, we excluded accounts payable, accruals, and deferred taxes. Why?

■ Describe the steps used to estimate Loblaw's opportunity cost of capital.

DIVISIONAL AND PROJECT-SPECIFIC OPPORTUNITY COSTS

Up to now we have determined how to calculate the firm's opportunity cost of capital, which can be employed if new projects have a risk approximately equal to the firm's overall risk. We know, however, that each project must stand on its own legs if the firm is going to maximize its value. Firms must expect to receive a return sufficient to compensate them for the risk involved—that is, what they could get by investing in an equally risky project outside the firm. To deal with differences in risk, many medium- and large-size firms employ an approach that calculates the divisional cost of capital.

DIVISIONAL OPPORTUNITY COSTS OF CAPITAL

The essence of this approach is shown in Figure 6.2, where different discount rates will be employed depending on the riskiness of the division. If a firm employs a firm-wide opportunity cost of capital when differences in risk exist, it makes the mistake of setting too high a required return for low-risk projects and too low a return for high-risk projects. The result is to underallocate capital to low-risk divisions and to overallocate funds to high-risk divisions.

The most widely used method in practice to implement risk adjustment is based on the assumption that project risks within divisions are somewhat similar but that risk between divisions differs. To estimate **divisional opportunity costs of capital**, we proceed as follows:

STEP 1: Determine the firm's after-tax cost of debt, k_i, and use this as the cost of debt for each division. (Slightly more precision can be obtained by using separate after-tax costs for each division, but our approach is simpler and generally provides approximately the same answer.)

Figure 6.2

Relating Risk to Divisional Opportunity Costs of Capital for Capital Budgeting Purposes

Use of a firm-wide opportunity cost of capital when risk differs results in underallocation of resources to low-risk divisions and overallocation to high-risk divisions.

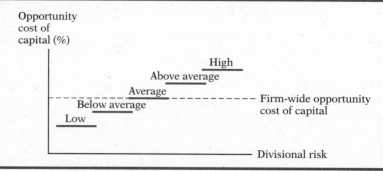

STEP 2:   Because we do not have any market-based estimate of the risk of the division and its cost of equity capital, identify one or more publicly traded firms that are similar in terms of product line to each separate division. These should be **pure-play firms**—publicly traded firms that are engaged solely in the same line of business as the division with the same operating risks. If the publicly traded firm has a different capital structure (or amount of financial risk) than the division, an adjustment will be required because this difference will affect beta. Also, the effective tax rate of the pure-play firm and the division are often different. One way to estimate an **asset** (or unlevered) **beta** is as follows:

$$\beta_{asset} = \beta_U = \frac{\beta_{levered\ firm}}{1 + (1 - T)(B/S)} \tag{6.11}$$

where

$\beta_{asset} = \beta_U =$ the beta for an unlevered firm or unlevered set of assets
$\beta_{levered\ firm} =$ the observed market beta for the publicly traded pure-play firm
$T =$ the pure-play firm's effective marginal tax rate
$B =$ the market value of the pure-play firm's debt (this includes bonds, loans from banks, leases, and short-term debt)
$S =$ the market value of the pure-play firm's equity

After calculating the unlevered asset beta, we can estimate the divisional beta by substituting in the β_{asset}, marginal tax rate for the division, T, and target capital structure proportions, S and B, and then solving for the levered β for the division.

STEP 3:   Employing the beta of the pure-play firm (with or without adjustment for differences in financial risk and taxes, as explained in step 2), calculate each division's cost of equity capital as if each were a separate firm. Thus, each division's estimated cost of common equity is

$$\text{divisional cost of equity} = k_{RF} + \beta_{division}(k_M - k_{RF}) \tag{6.12}$$

STEP 4:   Estimate the division's target or appropriate capital structure as if it were a freestanding firm. Due to differences in the basic risk and business conditions between divisions, some may be able to employ substantially more debt than others.

STEP 5:   Calculate the division's opportunity cost of capital using the costs and financing proportions estimated in steps 1, 3, and 4 above.

To illustrate step 2 above (how to calculate a division's appropriate beta), assume that we have identified a pure-play firm similar to the division in question.[18] Its beta (which is a levered beta because the pure-play firm uses debt), is 1.50; its ratio of debt to stock in market value terms, B/S, is 0.667; and its effective marginal tax rate, T, is 40 percent. For the division in question, its target ratio of debt to stock, B/S, is 0.40, and its effective marginal tax rate is 30 percent. To determine the appropriate beta for

---

[18] In practice, considerable work and a good deal of knowledge and judgment is required to identify appropriate pure-play firms. There is no substitute for a thorough understanding of possible pure-play firms.

the division, we first "unlever" the pure-play firm's beta using Equation 6.11 as follows:

$$\beta_U = \frac{\beta_{\text{levered firm}}}{1 + (1 - T)(B/S)} = \frac{1.50}{1 + (1 - 0.40)(0.667)} \approx 1.07$$

Now that we have an unlevered or asset beta, we can "relever" it to determine the division's systematic risk after adjusting for its effective marginal tax rate and capital structure. Rearranging Equation 6.11, we have:

$$\beta_{\text{levered division}} = \beta_U[1 + (1 - T)(B/S)]$$
$$= 1.07[1 + (1 - 0.30)(0.40)] \approx 1.37$$

Thus, based on using a pure-play firm, the appropriate beta for estimating the division's cost of equity capital is 1.37.

To illustrate the calculation of divisional opportunity costs of capital, consider the example of Wagner Industries. As shown in Table 6.4, with a beta of 1.25, k_{RF} of 10 percent, $k_M = 18$ percent, $k_i = 8$ percent, and using 40 percent debt and 60 percent common equity, we would estimate Wagner's firm-wide opportunity cost of capital to be 15.20 percent. This would be the appropriate rate for capital budgeting purposes if all of Wagner's divisions were equally risky.

However, what if Wagner has three very different divisions? The furniture division is in a very mature industry with low risk; the paper division has a risk that is close to the average risk of the firm; the data services division is very risky. Due to the differences in risk, the divisions have different betas, which range from 0.75 for furniture to 1.25 for paper and 2.0 for data services (as determined by examining

Table 6.4

Calculation of Opportunity Cost of Capital for Wagner Industries

This firm-wide opportunity cost is appropriate for divisions or projects whose risk is approximately equal to the average risk of new projects undertaken by the firm.

Assumptions
after-tax cost of debt, $k_i = 8\%$
market risk, $\beta_j = 1.25$
risk-free rate, $k_{RF} = 10\%$
expected return on the market portfolio, $k_M = 18\%$

Cost of Common Equity
$k_s = k_{RF} + \beta_j(k_M - k_{RF})$
  $= 10\% + 1.25(18\% - 10\%) = 10\% + 10\% = 20\%$

Opportunity Cost of Capital

Component	After-Tax Cost ×	Market Value Weight =	Opportunity Cost of Capital
Debt	8%	0.40	3.20%
Common equity	20%	0.60	12.00
		Opportunity cost of capital =	15.20%

publicly traded pure-play firms with similar product lines). The financing proportions also differ, with the more risky divisions being less able to employ as much debt financing. As shown in Table 6.5, these differences produce very different divisional opportunity costs of capital. The furniture division's opportunity cost is 12 percent, while 15.20 percent is appropriate for the paper division. The data services division's opportunity cost of capital is 22.40 percent, indicating that projects originating from that division must have a substantially higher expected return to compensate for the increased risk.[19]

Estimating divisional opportunity costs of capital in practice requires a thorough understanding of the firm's divisions and identification of appropriate publicly traded firms that are similar to the divisions, following the steps as given here. The most difficult part of the process is coming up with "good" pure-play firms.[20]

PROJECT-SPECIFIC OPPORTUNITY COSTS OF CAPITAL

The same basic steps used to determine divisional opportunity costs of capital can be applied to specific projects. That is, we estimate the risk of the project, estimate an appropriate cost of equity capital, determine the amount of debt financing (and hence the debt/market value of equity ratio) to be employed, and then calculate a project-specific opportunity cost, or required rate of return. If the project is really a major undertaking, we may be able to employ the pure-play approach involving some other publicly traded firm in the same line. For smaller projects, however, we will have to estimate the project's beta. It is often difficult to come up with a good means of estimating project betas. Finance theory does not help us much in terms of providing a simple procedure for estimating project-specific betas if the pure-play approach does not work. Even subjective estimates by knowledgeable managers, however, are far better than no adjustment for risk. Generally, their estimates will provide a good idea of the direction of the adjustment required, even if the magnitude of the adjustment is subject to some unknown amount of error.

Concept Review Questions

- Why is it important to use divisional opportunity costs of capital rather than a firm-wide opportunity cost of capital?
- Describe the steps used to estimate a divisional opportunity cost of capital.

---

[19] When calculating firm-wide and divisional opportunity costs of capital, certain relationships must hold. For example, the firm-wide equity beta must equal the average of the divisional betas. Thus, for a firm with two divisions,

$$\beta_{\text{firmwide}} = \beta_{\text{Division A}} W_{\text{Division A}} + \beta_{\text{Division B}} W_{\text{Division B}}$$

where the weights reflect the respective sizes of the two divisions. Likewise, when firm-wide and divisional opportunity costs of capital are calculated, the following relationship must hold:

$$\text{opportunity cost of capital}_{\text{firm-wide}} = \text{opportunity cost}_A W_{\text{Division A}} + \text{opportunity cost}_B W_{\text{Division B}}$$

Keeping these relationships in mind is important to ensure that the estimates for the divisions are compatible with what we know about the firm as a whole.

[20] Recently some modified approaches using industry data to estimate the "pure-play" firms have been suggested. See Harris, O'Brien, and Wakeman (1989) and Ehrardt and Bhagwat (1991).

Table 6.5

Calculation of Divisional Opportunity Costs of Capital for Wagner Industries

Using divisional opportunity costs improves resource allocation decisions if risk differs substantially among a firm's divisions.

Divisional Opportunity Cost of Capital

Component	After-Tax Cost ×	Division's Financing Proportions =	Opportunity of Capital
Furniture Division			

$\beta_{furniture} = 0.75$

$$k_{furniture} = k_{RF} + \beta_{furniture}(k_M - k_{RF})$$
$$= 10\% + 0.75(18\% - 10\%) = 10\% + 6\% = 16\%$$

Component	After-Tax Cost ×	Division's Financing Proportions =	Opportunity of Capital
Debt	8%	0.50	4.00%
Common equity	16	0.50	8.00
		Furniture Division's opportunity cost of capital =	12.00%

Paper Division

$\beta_{paper} = 1.25$

$$k_{paper} = 10\% + 1.25(18\% - 10\%) = 10\% + 10\% = 20\%$$

Component	After-Tax Cost ×	Division's Financing Proportions =	Opportunity of Capital
Debt	8%	0.40	3.20%
Common equity	20	0.60	12.00
		Paper Division's opportunity cost of capital =	15.20%

Data Services Division

$\beta_{data\ services} = 2.00$

$$k_{data\ services} = 10\% + 2.00(18\% - 10\%) = 10\% + 16\% = 26\%$$

Component	After-Tax Cost ×	Division's Financing Proportions =	Opportunity of Capital
Debt	8%	0.20	1.60%
Common equity	26	0.80	20.80
		Data Services Division's opportunity cost of capital =	22.40%

KEY POINTS

- The opportunity cost of capital is a future-oriented marginal cost which is used as the discount rate in net present value calculations when average-risk projects are being evaluated. It is the forgone return that could have been earned by investing in a similar-risk project.
- In order to determine the firm's opportunity cost of capital, we employ the knowledge that financial markets are efficient and, therefore, fully reflect the returns demanded by the firm's providers of capital and the risks faced by the firm.
- By accepting all investment projects with positive net present values, in which the returns are more than the costs involved, the firm is making wealth-maximizing decisions that assist in maximizing the long-run market value of the firm.
- Debt is typically the least expensive source of financing, whereas common equity capital is the most expensive. This is because of tax considerations and the risk and return requirements of investors.

- The opportunity cost of capital is a weighted average of the expected future costs of funds. The weights are given by the market-value proportions of the firm's capital structure.
- When risk differs substantially across various divisions of the firm, the use of a firm-wide opportunity cost of capital overallocates capital to safer divisions and projects and underallocates capital to more risky divisions and projects. The misallocation serves to reduce the value of the firm.
- The most difficult, and most important, part of estimating divisional costs of capital involves determining the division's cost of equity capital. Identifying publicly traded pure-play firms similar to the divisions is the most important, and most difficult, step in the process.

QUESTIONS

6.1   Explain the concept of a firm's opportunity cost of capital. In what two ways can we approach this return?

6.2   Why is the cost of debt typically the lowest, and the cost of common equity the highest, of the specific costs?

6.3   "Internally generated funds are costless. Accordingly, the cost of new common stock is the only relevant cost of common equity for cost of capital purposes." Evaluate this statement.

6.4   How do flotation costs affect the cost of various capital structure components?

6.5   Compare and contrast the dividend valuation, CAPM, and bond yield plus expected risk premium approaches to estimating the cost of common equity. Which do you believe is theoretically the best? Which is best in a practical sense?

6.6   Discuss the practical aspects of estimating a firm's opportunity cost of capital. Under what circumstances can you ignore payables and accruals? What about leases?

6.7   Under what circumstances will a firm's opportunity cost of capital increase?

6.8   Explain how you might use the dividend valuation or bond yield plus expected risk premium approach to estimate the cost of common equity when calculating a divisional opportunity cost of capital. Does either of these approaches have any advantages or disadvantages compared to the CAPM approach for estimating a division's cost of common equity?

6.9   How would each of the following affect the firm's after-tax cost of debt, k_i; cost of equity, k_s; and opportunity cost of capital? Use a plus sign ($+$) to indicate an increase, a minus sign ($-$) to indicate a decrease, and a zero to indicate either no effect or an indeterminate effect. (*Note*: Treat only the direct effect, not any secondary effects.)

	k_i	k_s	Opportunity Cost of Capital
a. The corporate tax rate is decreased.	_____	_____	_____
b. The firm begins to make substantial new investments in assets that are less risky than its present assets.	_____	_____	_____
c. The firm is selling more bonds. Because Dominion Bond Rating Service decides the firm is more risky, it lowers the bond rating.	_____	_____	_____
d. The firm decides to triple its financing.	_____	_____	_____
e. Investors become less risk averse.	_____	_____	_____

CONCEPT REVIEW PROBLEMS

See Appendix A for solutions.

CR6.1   Armstrong Inc. is planning to issue new debt. Armstrong can currently issue debt that has an annual coupon interest rate of 10 percent, pays interest semiannually, has 20 years to maturity, to net $1,198 per bond. If Armstrong's tax rate is 35 percent, what is the after-tax cost of debt?

CR6.2   In addition, Armstrong is planning on issuing $100 par value preferred stock with an $8.50 dividend payment. The firm expects to receive $93 per share. What is the cost of preferred stock?

CR6.3   Armstrong obtains all of its equity financing internally. The firm's stock is currently selling at $40 per share, has an expected EPS at t = 1 of $7.20, a dividend payout ratio of 50 percent, and an expected growth rate of 4 percent. *Value Line* has estimated Armstrong's beta at 1.5. If the risk-free rate of return is 6 percent, the return on the market is 12 percent, and the average return on corporate bonds is 8 percent, what is Armstrong's cost of equity? (*Note:* Use all three methods and then take an average of them.)

CR6.4   If Armstrong's target capital structure is 20 percent debt, 10 percent preferred stock, and 70 percent equity, what is Armstrong's opportunity cost of capital?

The following facts given for National Products are needed for CR6.5 through CR6.9.

National Products Company (in millions)

Assets		Liabilities and Shareholders' Equity	
Cash	$ 5	Accounts payable	$ 5
Accounts receivable	5	Short-term debt	10
Inventories	10	Long-term debt	30
Long-term assets	55	Preferred stock	10
		Common stock (2 million	
		shares outstanding)	5
Total assets	$75	Retained earnings	15
		Total liabilities and	
		shareholders' equity	$75

1. Short-term debt consists of bank loans that currently cost 6 percent.
2. Long-term debt consists of 20-year semiannual payment bonds with a coupon rate of 12 percent. Currently these bonds provide a yield to investors of 9 percent.
3. National Products' perpetual preferred stock has a $100 par value, pays a dividend of $12, and has a yield to investors of 10 percent.
4. The current stock price is $37.50. The firm expects to pay a dividend of $4.00 next year, the growth rate is 6 percent, beta is 1.2, the required return on the market is 15 percent, the marginal tax rate is 35 percent, and the risk-free rate is 6 percent.

CR6.5   What are the market value proportions of debt, preferred stock, and common equity for National Products? (*Note:* Carry to three decimal places.)

CR6.6   Assuming there are no flotation costs, what is the cost of short-term debt, long-term debt, preferred stock, and common equity for National Products? (*Note:* Calculate all three costs of common equity and then average them.)

CR6.7   What is National Products' opportunity cost of capital?

CR6.8   Now assume all equity financing for National Products will have to be obtained from external sources. If the only flotation cost involved is $3.50 per share of common stock, what is the firm's new opportunity cost of capital?

CR6.9   The CEO of National Products wants to expand. The new division is expected to be riskier than the firm as a whole. Therefore, the capital structure of the division will contain no short-term financing, no preferred stock financing, 20 percent long-term debt, and 80 percent common equity financing. Similar firms have an average beta of 1.5, a debt-to-equity ratio of 50 percent, and a tax rate of 40 percent. What is the opportunity cost of capital for the division?

PROBLEMS

6.1   Calculate the after-tax cost of debt under the following conditions if the maturity value of the debt is $1,000, interest is paid annually, and the corporate tax rate is 35 percent.
a.   Coupon interest rate is 8 percent, net proceeds are $900, and the life is 20 years.
b.   Bond pays $100 per year in interest, net proceeds are $960, and the life is 10 years.
c.   Coupon interest rate is 14 percent, net proceeds are $1,120, and the bond has a 30-year life.
d.   Net proceeds are $1,000, coupon interest rate is 12 percent, and the life is 5 years.

6.2   What is the after-tax cost of preferred stock under the following circumstances?
a.   Par is $80, dividend is $8 per year, and the net proceeds are $76.
b.   Net proceeds are $46, and dividends are $7.
c.   Par is $60, dividend is 9 percent (of par), and net proceeds are $55.
d.   Par is $40, dividend is 11 percent (of par), and net proceeds are $40.

6.3   Given the following information, calculate the cost of internally generated funds, k_s, or new common stock, k_e, under each of the following conditions.
a.   Cost of internally generated funds if $P_0 = $80, g = 8$ percent, and $D_1 = 5.
b.   It is now January 1, 19X7, and you are calculating the cost of new common stock. Cash dividends in 19X2 were $2.05; they were $3 in 19X6. $P_{np} = 47.
c.   Cost of new common stock if historical growth in dividends is 4 percent, expected growth is 7 percent, $D_0 = 4, P_0 is $84.80, and $P_{np} = 73.
d.   Cost of internally generated funds if $P_0 = 50, and the past dividends have been

Year	Dividends per Share
−5	$2.50
−4	2.80
−3	2.80
−2	3.10
−1	3.67
0	3.67

6.4   Calculate the cost of internally generated funds, k_s, under the following conditions:

a. Expected return on the market portfolio is 16 percent, risk-free rate is 6 percent, and beta is 1.50.

b. k_M = 18 percent, k_{RF} = 12 percent, σ_M (standard deviation of the market) = 14 percent, σ_s (standard deviation of stock s) = 35 percent, and $Corr_{sM}$ (correlation between returns on stock s and returns on the market) = + 0.80.

c. The current market interest rate on comparable long-term debt is 9 percent, and the expected risk premium differential of stocks over bonds is 4 percent.

d. The coupon rate on the firm's existing debt is 9 percent; current market yield on short-term debt is 10 percent; current market yield on long-term debt is 12 percent; and the expected risk premium differential of stocks over bonds is 5 percent.

6.5 Dale Development has called you in as a consultant to estimate its cost of common equity. After talking with its chief financial officer and consulting an econometric forecasting firm, you have come up with the following facts and estimates:

Estimates	Year	Dividends per Share
P_0 = $85	−5	$1.21
β_{Dale} = 1.50	−4	1.21
Canadian treasury bill rate = 10%	−3	1.30
market yield on comparable quality	−2	1.40
long-term debt = 13%	−1	1.71
expected return on the market portfolio = 16%	0	1.86
expected risk premium of stocks over bonds = 4%		
current earnings per share, EPS = $5.75		

Dale plans to use 30 percent debt and 70 percent equity for its incremental financing. Also, the firm's marginal tax rate is 33 percent.

a. What do you estimate the past growth rate in cash dividends per share has been? Employ this as your estimate of g (round to the nearest whole number).

b. What is the estimated cost of common equity employing the following approaches: (1) dividend valuation, (2) CAPM, and (3) bond yield plus expected risk premium?

c. Explain why one of the estimates from (b) is substantially lower than the other two.

d. Take an average of all three answers from (b) for your estimate of Dale's cost of common equity.

e. What is your estimate of Dale's opportunity cost of capital? How confident of it are you?

6.6 Schwendiman Tire plans to raise $20 million this year for expansion. The firm's current market value capital structure, shown below, is considered to be optimal.

Debt	$ 40,000,000
Common equity	60,000,000
	$100,000,000

New debt will have a market interest rate of 10 percent. Common stock is currently selling at $40 per share, expected growth in dividends is 7 percent, and D_1 = $3.60. If new common stock is sold, the net proceeds are expected to be $36 per share. Internally generated funds available for capital budgeting purposes are expected to be $6 million, and Schwendiman's marginal tax rate is 30 percent.

What is Schwendiman's opportunity cost of capital?

6.7   The chief financial officer of Edmonton Oil has given you the assignment of determining the firm's cost of capital. The present capital structure, which is considered optimal, is as follows:

	Book Value	Market Value
Debt	$50 million	$ 40 million
Preferred stock	10 million	5 million
Common equity	30 million	55 million
	$90 million	$100 million

The anticipated financing opportunities are these: Debt can be issued with a 15 percent before-tax cost. Preferred stock will be $100 par, carry a dividend of 13 percent, and can be sold to net the firm $96 per share. Common equity has a beta of 1.20, and the market risk premium is 5 percent.

a.   If the firm's tax rate is 40 percent, what is its opportunity cost of capital?

b.   What happens to its opportunity cost of capital if Edmonton's marginal tax rate is zero?

6.8   The management of King Hotel is considering further expansion. To evaluate the various alternatives, management needs to estimate King's cost of capital. Various financial data are given, as follows:

Balance Sheet (in $ millions)

Total assets	$500		
		Accounts payable and accruals	$ 50
		Short-term debt	100
		Bonds ($1,000 par)	100
		Common stock (50 million shares)	50
		Retained earnings	200
		Total liabilities and	
		shareholders' equity	$500

Estimates	Year	Dividends per Share
$P_0 = \$15.50$	−7	$1.00
expected return on the market portfolio = 12%	−6	1.00
risk-free rate (Canadian treasury bills) = 7%	−5	1.05
market interest rate on comparable bonds = 9%	−4	1.05
beta for King Hotel = 0.80	−3	1.10
	−2	1.10
	−1	1.18
	0	1.23

a. Estimate the cost of common equity using both the dividend valuation and CAPM approaches. Average the two estimates and then round to the nearest whole number.
b. Calculate King's after-tax cost of long-term debt if the firm's marginal tax rate is 35 percent.
c. The short-term debt will carry a different cost. Using the Canadian treasury bill rate and adding 1 percent to estimate King's before-tax cost of short-term debt, calculate the after-tax cost of King's short-term debt.
d. What is King's opportunity cost of capital, if all of the following hold simultaneously:
   1. Accounts payable and accruals are ignored.
   2. Short-term debt is taken at face value.
   3. The current market value of long-term debt is $125 million.
   4. Common equity is determined by multiplying the number of shares times the stock price.

6.9 Gourmet Grocery has asked for your help in estimating its cost of capital. Financial data for the firm are as follows:

Balance Sheet (in $ millions)

Total assets	$100	Accounts payable and accruals	$ 15
		Short-term debt	15
		Bonds ($1,000 par)	25
		Common stock (12 million shares)	20
		Retained earnings	25
		Total liabilities and shareholders' equity	$100

Estimates	Year	Dividends per Share
$P_0 = \$8.00$	−5	$0.25
expected return on the market portfolio = 17%	−4	0.25
risk-free rate (Canadian treasury bills) = 10%	−3	0.28
market interest rate on comparable bonds = 13%	−2	0.28
beta for Gourmet = 1.30	−1	0.36
marginal tax rate for Gourmet = 40%	0	0.40

The firm requests that you estimate the cost of equity capital using the dividend valuation, CAPM, and bond yield plus expected risk premium approaches. To do this you are asked to assume that the expected risk premium is 6 percent. Once you have the three estimates you are requested to take their average, rounding to the nearest whole number. The firm also informs you that you should estimate the before-tax cost of short-term debt as the Canadian treasury bill rate plus 1 percent. Finally the firm tells you to assume that all of the following hold simultaneously:

1. Accounts payable and accruals are ignored.
2. Short-term debt is taken at face value.
3. The long-term debt consists of one bond issue that has a 9 percent coupon rate (paid annually) and six years left to maturity. The total market value of the bonds should be rounded to the nearest million dollars.

What is Gourmet's opportunity cost of capital?

6.10   Humphrey Ltd. requires $15 million to fund its current year's capital projects. Humphrey will finance part of its needs with $9 million in internally generated funds. The firm's common stock market price is $120 per share. Dividends of $5 per share at time $t = 0$ are expected to grow at a rate of 11 percent per year for the foreseeable future. Another part will be funded with the proceeds (at $96 per share) from an issue of 9,375 shares of 12 percent $100 par preferred stock that will be privately placed. The remainder will be financed with debt. Five thousand 10-year $1,000 par bonds with a coupon rate of 15 percent will be issued to net the firm $1,050 each, *minus* 3 percent of the par value for flotation costs. Interest is paid annually on the bonds. The firm's tax rate is 30 percent.

a.   What is Humphrey's opportunity cost of capital?

b.   Humphrey has now decided to double its funding requirements. The financing proportions will remain as in (a). No additional internally generated funds are available. New common stock can be sold to net the firm $100 per share. Additional preferred stock and debt can be sold with all of the same conditions as in (a) *except* the dividend rate on preferred stock is 13.5 percent and the coupon interest rate on bonds will be 17 percent. What is Humphrey's opportunity cost of capital for this second increment of financing?

6.11   Honeycutt is calculating its opportunity cost of capital. The following has been determined:

Debt. $1,000 par value, 20-year, 9 percent coupon-rate bond can be sold at a discount of $30 per bond. Flotation costs will be an additional $20 per bond; interest is paid annually, and the marginal corporate tax rate is 40 percent.

Preferred Stock. $100 par value, 8.5 percent preferred stock can be sold at a discount of $7 per share; flotation costs are expected to be $2 per share.

Common Equity.   The present market price is $75 per share. The cash dividend next year is expected to be $5, and the growth rate is expected to be 7 percent for the foreseeable future.

Internally Generated Financing.   All the common equity needs will be funded by internally generated funds.

Honeycutt's current market value capital structure is as follows:

Debt	30%
Preferred stock	20
Common equity	50
	100%

a.   What is Honeycutt's opportunity cost of capital?

b.   Assume now that instead of (a), Honeycutt decides to increase its financing substantially. Everything is the same as in (a) except:

Debt.   Eleven percent coupon interest rate.
Preferred Stock.   Ten percent dividend rate.
Common Stock.   Underpricing is $12 per share.
Internally Generated Financing.   All used up, so none available.

What is Honeycutt's new opportunity cost of capital?

6.12 Khilnani Products has three different divisions—A, B, and C. In estimating divisional opportunity costs of capital, management has determined that $\beta_A = 1.20$, $\beta_B = 0.60$, and $\beta_C = 2.00$. Also, $k_{RF} = 8$ percent and $k_M = 13$ percent. If the after-tax cost of debt is 5 percent, and the appropriate capital structures for the divisions are given below, what are the three divisional opportunity costs of capital?

	Target Financing Proportions		
	Division A	Division B	Division C
Debt	0.50	0.20	0.60
Common equity	0.50	0.80	0.40

6.13 Gage Equipment has traditionally employed a firm-wide opportunity cost of capital for capital budgeting purposes. However, its two divisions—machinery and farm implements—have different degrees of risk. Data on the firm and the divisions are as follows:

	Gage Equipment	Machinery Division	Farm Implement Division
Beta	1.4	1.0	2.0
Appropriate percentage of debt	40%	50%	20%
Appropriate percentage of common equity	60	50	80

The following estimates have been made: $k_i = 7$ percent, $k_{RF} = 10$ percent, and $k_M = 15$ percent. The firm is considering the following independent capital expenditures:

	Proposed Capital Projects	Initial Investment (in millions)	IRR
Machinery	M-1	$1	15%
	M-2	3	12
	M-3	2	9
Farm implements	F-1	4	16
	F-2	6	20
	F-3	5	12

a. Based on a firm-wide opportunity cost of capital, which projects should Gage select? What is the size of the capital budget?

b. Based on the opportunity costs of capital for the two divisions, which projects should now be selected? What is the size of the resulting capital budget?

c. What happens if a firm uses a firm-wide opportunity cost for capital budgeting purposes when it should be using divisional opportunity costs?

6.14   In order to estimate the equity cost of capital for their electronics division, Li Industries has identified a pure-play firm. Data for the electronics division and the pure-play firm are:

	Electronics Division	Pure-Play Firm
Marginal tax rate, T	0.45	0.35
B/S	0.50	0.60

If the pure-play firm's levered β is 1.20, and the market risk premium is 9 percent, what is the electronics division's cost of equity capital?

6.15   Gene's Suprs has two divisions, wholesale and retail. Data are as follows:

marginal tax rate for Gene's, T = 0.40

after-tax cost of debt, k_i = 9%

B/S for the wholesale division = 0.65

B/S for the retail division = 0.50

risk-free rate, k_{RF} = 10%

expected return on the market, k_M = 18%

Two pure-play firms for each division and pertinent data for them include

	Firm	
Pure-Play for Wholesale Division	**A**	**B**
market risk, β_j	1.20	1.40
marginal tax rate, T	0.30	0.40
B/S	0.60	0.40

	Firm	
Pure-Play for Retail Division	**C**	**D**
market risk, β_j	1.50	1.40
marginal tax rate	0.35	0.40
B/S	0.45	0.50

a.   Calculate the asset beta for each of the four pure-play firms. Then take a simple average for each pair to determine an unlevered pure-play asset beta for each division.
b.   Determine the opportunity cost of capital for the wholesale division and for the retail division.

6.16   Mini Case   Alliance Consolidated's new CFO is undertaking a thorough review of how the firm makes its capital investment decisions. A major component of this review is to examine how the firm determines its opportunity cost of capital.

a. What is meant by "opportunity cost of capital"? What assumptions are employed in arriving at a firm's opportunity cost of capital? What role do efficient financial markets play?

b. What sources are the least expensive? The most expensive? Why? What role do corporate taxes play?

c. Debt can be issued at par and will carry a 13.5 percent coupon interest rate, and preferred stock can also be issued at par and will carry a 13 percent dividend. Information on common stock is as follows:

	Year	Dividends per Share
$P_0 = \$40$	-4	$2.00
$\beta = 1.25$	-3	2.00
$k_{RF} = 11\%$	-2	2.40
expected return on the market portfolio = 16%	-1	2.75
expected risk premium of stocks over bonds = 5%	0	2.93

The market value capital structure for Alliance is 40 percent debt, 50 percent common equity, and 10 percent preferred stock. The firm's marginal tax rate is 35 percent.

1. Determine the cost of common equity using the three different approaches. (*Note:* For the dividend valuation approach, round g to the nearest whole percent.) Take an average of the three estimates for Alliance's cost of equity.
2. What is Alliance's opportunity cost of capital?

d. What is the impact of flotation costs on the firm's cost of capital? On short-term debt financing?

e. After further investigation it is determined that Alliance's three divisions have vastly different risks. Hence, divisional opportunity costs of capital are required. What occurs if a firm-wide opportunity cost is employed when risk differs significantly among divisions?

f. Three pure-play firms have been identified as follows:

	Pure-Play Firms		
	A	B	C
Levered beta, β	1.83	1.35	0.70
Marginal tax rate, T	0.40	0.30	0.40
B/S	0.30	0.90	1.00

For Alliance Consolidated the appropriate B/S ratios for the three 9 divisions are: division A, 0.20; division B, 0.70; and division C, 1.10. What are the appropriate opportunity costs of capital for the three divisions if $k_{RF} = 11\%$, $k_M = 16\%$, and T = 0.35. (*Note:* Only debt and common equity need to be considered.)

REFERENCES

BOOTH, LAURENCE. "Estimating the Cost of Equity Capital of a Non-Traded Unique Canadian Entity." *Canadian Journal of Administrative Sciences* 10 (June 1993): 122–127.

EHRARDT, MICHAEL, and YATIN N. BHAGWAT. "A Full-Information Approach for Estimating Divisional Betas." *Financial Management* 21 (Summer 1991): 60–69.

FULLER, RUSSELL J., and KENT A. HICKMAN. "A Note on Estimating the Historical Risk Premium." *Financial Practice and Education* 1 (Fall/Winter 1991): 45–48.

HARRIS, ROBERT S., and FELICIA C. MARSTON. "Estimating Shareholder Risk Premia Using Analysts' Growth Forecasts." *Financial Management* 21 (Summer 1992): 63–70.

HARRIS, ROBERT S., THOMAS J. O'BRIEN, and DOUG WAKEMAN. "Divisional Cost-of-Capital Estimation for Multi-Industry Firms." *Financial Management* 18 (Summer 1989): 74–84.

HAWAWINI, GABRIEL A., and OSHOK VORA. "Yield Approximations: A Historical Perspective." *Journal of Finance* 37 (March 1982): 145–56.

PATTERSON, CLEVELAND S. "The Cost of Equity Capital of a Non-Traded Unique Entity: A Canadian Study." *Canadian Journal of Administrative Sciences* 10 (June 1993): 115–21.

PATTERSON, CLEVELAND S. "Estimating the Cost of Equity Capital of a Non-Traded Unique Canadian Entity: Reply." *Canadian Journal of Administrative Sciences* 10 (June 1993): 128–33.

PART

3

Long-Term Investment Decisions

*T*he primary objective of the firm is to maximize its long-run value. While many items contribute to maximizing the value of the firm, the most important single factor is its investment decisions. All firms, whether large or small, continually invest in new long-term, or capital, assets. The profitability of these investment decisions directly affects the value of the firm. Effective capital budgeting procedures for making long-term investment decisions are therefore a key ingredient for success. Successful firms, as evidenced by increases in market value, make good capital budgeting decisions.

If we think of the value of the firm as being a function of its investment decisions, its financing decisions, and its operating decisions (i.e., the day-to-day management), then

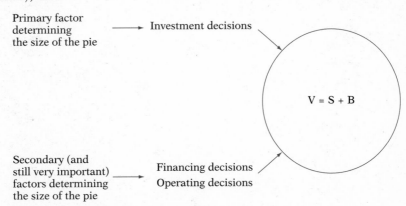

So, to maximize the long-run market value of the firm, $V = S + B$, the first and most important step is to make good investment decisions. In Chapter 7 we discuss capital budgeting techniques and show how these techniques must be altered to accommodate projects of unequal lives, interrelated projects, or capital rationing. Chapter 8 examines how tax considerations and other issues are taken into account when these techniques are applied. In Chapter 9 we consider how risk is handled in capital investment decision making.

7 *Capital Budgeting Techniques*

EXECUTIVE SUMMARY

The analysis of proposed capital expenditures is probably the most important topic in financial management. As discussed previously, net present value (NPV) is the decision criterion to employ in making investment decisions that assist in maximizing the long-run market value of the firm. In practice, the capital budgeting process has four phases: search and identification; estimation of the magnitude, timing, and riskiness of cash flows; selection or rejection; and control and postcompletion audit.

Although net present value is the preferred decision criterion, the internal rate of return is often employed in practice. In most circumstances the two techniques will lead to the same accept or reject decision. The two methods may rank mutually exclusive projects differently, however, because they implicitly assume different reinvestment rates. Because of the possibility of multiple internal rates of return and ranking problems, the net present value criterion is preferred; it always leads to wealth-maximizing decisions. Value-enhancing investment projects derive from the unique abilities of firms or projects. However, due to competitive markets, virtually all positive-NPV projects have limited lives. Special consideration must be given if the projects being evaluated are interrelated. In this case, all possible combinations of the projects must be considered before a proper decision can be made. In mutually exclusive situations where the assets will be replaced, unequal lives must also be considered in the analysis. Firms with capital rationing constraints are not able to accept all positive-NPV projects; this leads to suboptimal decisions because value maximization cannot be achieved.

Without an effective capital budgeting process it is difficult to consistently make decisions, and select the growth opportunities, that maximize the long-run market value of the firm.

CAPITAL BUDGETING AND THE VALUE OF THE FIRM

The primary goal of the firm is to maximize its long-run market value, or, in the analogy of Chapter 1, to maximize the size of the pie. Although many things contribute to maximizing the value of the firm, the most important single factor is the investments the firm makes. These investments determine the direction of the firm, because, over time, how the firm has positioned itself (in terms of its products or services, its position in its industry, and so forth) is a direct function of its past, present, and future investment decisions. Good investment decisions build on the firm's growth opportunities and take advantage of the unique advantages a firm has vis-à-vis its competitors.

Capital budgeting techniques are used to evaluate proposed investments in long-term assets. *Long-term* is taken to mean any investment for which returns are expected to extend beyond one year. An investment can be as small as the purchase of some office furniture or as large as a complete new plant. The **capital budget** contains estimates of cash flows for long-term projects. **Capital budgeting** is the process by which long-term investments are generated, analyzed, and placed in the capital budget.

PROJECT CLASSIFICATION

Capital budgeting projects can be placed in three broad categories: expansion, replacement, and regulatory. **Expansion projects** are those designed to improve the firm's ability to produce or market its products. If a firm decides to add a new line of machine tools, the plant necessary to produce the tools is an expansion project. A **replacement project** is one designed to take the place of existing assets that have become physically or economically obsolete. Finally, there are **regulatory projects**. These provide no direct cash benefits to the firm but must be completed for the firm's operations to continue. For example, the provincial Workers' Compensation Boards and Environment Canada can require firms to spend billions of dollars to improve health and safety in the workplace or to prevent harm to the environment.

Another method of classifying projects is as **mutually exclusive projects** or **independent projects**. When two projects are mutually exclusive, the acceptance of one precludes the acceptance of the other. A proposal to purchase one computer network system precludes a proposal to acquire another computer network system, if only one system is needed. The two proposals are mutually exclusive. However, a proposal to acquire a computer network system and another proposal to build a new warehouse are independent. The cash flows are unrelated, and the firm may choose one, both, or neither.

VALUE MAXIMIZATION

In capital budgeting, we calculate the net present value (NPV), which is equal to the present value of the expected after-tax cash flows, discounted at the opportunity cost of capital, or minimum required rate of return, minus the initial cash investment required. Accepting positive-NPV projects has a direct impact on the value of the firm. Consider an all-equity firm that has a current market value of $6 million. That amount includes $2 million in cash that can be invested in new long-term investment projects. You have to decide whether to invest the $2 million in a proposed new project or keep it in cash. The choice is as follows:

	Market Value (in millions)	
Asset	Reject New Project	Accept New Project
Cash	$2	$0
Other	4	4
New project	0	PV
	$6	$4 + PV

Clearly, the new project is worthwhile if its present value, PV, is greater than the $2 million required investment. This occurs only if the NPV is greater than zero; when the NPV is zero, the discounted cash inflows from the project would *just equal* the initial investment of $2 million.

What happens, for example, if the proposed project has a net present value of $3.5 million? The firm will receive back its $2 million investment plus an additional $1.5 million (both after discounting). What will happen to the value of the firm? It will increase by $1.5 million as investors recognize the impact of the capital investment decision. *Only by accepting positive NPV projects can a firm increase its long-run market value; accepting projects with negative NPVs leads to a decrease in the value of the firm.*

Concept Review Questions

- Describe three different types of capital budgeting projects.
- How is the long-run market value of a firm related to a project's net present value?

THE CAPITAL BUDGETING PROCESS

While the ideas behind capital budgeting using net present value are simple and straightforward, complications develop when we put our knowledge to work. To see why, it is important to understand that capital budgeting is a process involving a number of somewhat separate but interrelated activities. The **capital budgeting process** can be broken down into four steps:

1. Search for and identification of growth opportunities
2. Estimation of the magnitude, timing, and riskiness of cash flows
3. Selection or rejection
4. Control and postcompletion audit

The relationships among these steps are shown in Figure 7.1.

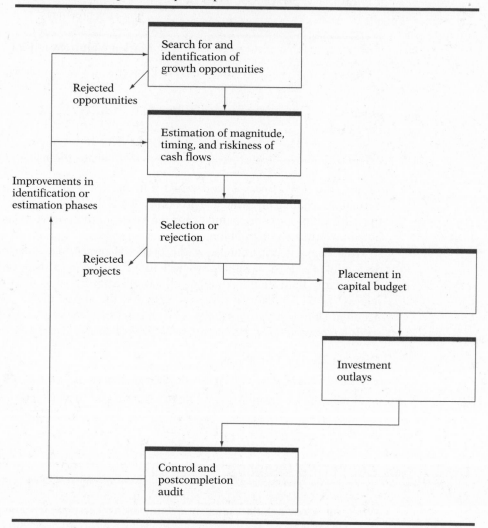

Figure 7.1

The Capital Budgeting Process

Capital budgeting is an ongoing process in which effective feedback should assist in improving decision making for subsequent capital investments.

SEARCH FOR AND IDENTIFICATION OF GROWTH OPPORTUNITIES

The search and identification stage involves actively searching for new growth opportunities within the firm's expertise *or* identifying problems that need attention. It is a triggering process: The thrust of this phase is not to analyze and solve well-defined problems, but to identify growth opportunities for possible capital investment.

In the broadest sense, there is a direct connection between the search and identification stage and the firm's overall strategic objectives. The relationship between long-term strategic objectives and the capital budgeting process must be fully integrated and consistent. Too often, this is not the case. The decision to grow by entering a new market or adopting a new production technology is often just the first in a long series of investment decisions. Then either additional investments are made because they "are necessary" given the previous decision, or the capital budgeting decision-making process is employed only *within* the previously defined strategic plan.

Either way, the firm has the cart before the horse. It should be the firm's capital budgeting techniques that determine the firm's long-run strategic decisions—not the other way around.

ESTIMATING THE MAGNITUDE, TIMING, AND RISKINESS OF CASH FLOWS

Once growth opportunities have been searched for and identified, the next step is to develop alternative courses of action and to estimate the magnitude, timing, and riskiness of the cash flows associated with each one. This is often the most difficult part of the entire process. It requires extensive knowledge, hard work, and an understanding of how possible competitor actions will affect cash flow projections. The estimation phase tends to become narrower in focus than the search and identification phase. The reason is that the desired outcome is detailed and specific: a set of alternative capital budgeting projects and associated cash flows, with risk estimates and specification of the key assumptions incorporated into the forecasts. This topic is examined in detail in Chapter 8.

SELECTION OR REJECTION

After the estimates have been made, the firm will select the most promising projects. The important points to remember about this phase are these:

1. The methods used to select or reject projects must be consistent with the objective of maximizing the value of the firm.
2. The key underlying assumptions (concerning the techniques employed and the data used) must be understood by the firm's capital budgeting experts as well as by senior management.
3. Alternative courses of action (including the possibility of delaying a project and the follow-on nature of many capital investment growth opportunities), changes in risk, and possible actions of competitors must be considered.

CONTROL AND POSTCOMPLETION AUDIT

The final phase is the control and postcompletion audit. Control can be thought of as the process by which the actual cash flows are compared with the projections. In addition, this phase should involve the subsequent reevaluation of the economic merits of ongoing projects, in order to determine whether to continue them. Evaluating the performance of ongoing capital investments is important for any complete capital budgeting process. A successful feedback programme suggests needed revisions in the identification procedure, provides information to improve future estimates of cash flows and risk, and indicates projects that should be abandoned. Effective control and postcompletion audits are vital to maximizing the long-run market value of the firm.

All four steps are important. In our study of financial management, we will focus on the second and third—estimation of the magnitude, timing, and riskiness of cash flows, and project selection. *Throughout this chapter and the next, we assume that all projects being considered are equally risky.* That is, their risk is equal to the firm's overall level of risk. Although this assumption is obviously unrealistic, it allows us to focus on the essential elements of the capital budgeting process. Assuming all projects are equally risky means we can use a single hurdle (or discount) rate throughout. This rate is the firm's opportunity cost of capital. In Chapter 9 we will consider situations in which the risk of the project is not equal to the firm's overall risk level.

Concept Review Questions

■ Describe the four steps of the capital budgeting process.

■ Why is estimating the magnitude, timing, and riskiness of cash flows important in capital budgeting decisions?

SELECTING CAPITAL BUDGETING PROJECTS

Firms use a variety of techniques to determine whether to accept proposed projects. The payback period is a simple but naive (unsophisticated) technique that does not employ discounting. The net present value (NPV) and internal rate of return (IRR) techniques both employ discounting to deal with the magnitude, timing, and riskiness of the cash flow stream.[1] The relevant cash flow stream, as discussed in Chapter 8, is the *incremental after-tax* cash flow stream related to the project. This stream is referred to as cash flow (CF).

PAYBACK PERIOD

The **payback period** is the number of years it takes for the firm to recover its initial investment in a project. Payback occurs when the cumulative net cash inflows minus the initial investment equals zero, or

$$\text{payback is the time, } \tau, \text{ such that } \sum_{t=1}^{\tau} CF_t = CF_0 \qquad (7.1)$$

---

[1] Two other techniques are the average (or accounting) rate of return and the profitability index. Given the deficiencies of accounting data for effective decision making, we should be wary of any attempt to make capital investment decisions with the average rate of return. The profitability index is discussed in footnote 12.

The decision rule for the payback period is as follows:

1. If τ is less than the maximum τ, accept.
2. If τ is greater than the maximum τ, reject.
3. If τ is equal to the maximum τ, you are indifferent.

Consider the two projects in Table 7.1. Project A has an initial investment of $442 and cash inflows of $200 for each of three years. Project B requires an initial investment of $718 followed by cash inflows of $250, $575, and $100, respectively, for the three years. For project A, which is an annuity, the payback period can be found simply by dividing the initial investment by the annual CF. Thus, $442 divided by $200 yields a payback period, τ, of 2.21 years. For project B, the payback is found by determining how many years are needed to recoup the initial investment of $718. In the first year, $250 is recovered; by the end of the second year, a total of $825 is recovered. So, the payback period is between one and two years. Table 7.1 shows that the payback period is about 1.8 years. Thus, project B has the shorter payback period. If a firm's maximum acceptable payback period is two years, it would accept project B and reject project A.

The payback period has some advantages. First, it is simple to calculate. Second, it is easy to understand and can be explained easily. Third, it provides a rough indicator of the riskiness of the project, because projects that pay back sooner are often viewed as being more liquid and hence less risky than those with longer payback periods.

At the same time, the payback period has three significant disadvantages. The first is that the maximum acceptable payback period is arbitrary; that is, it is set without any economic justification. Second, it does not take into account the timing of the cash

Table 7.1

Calculation of the Payback Period for Projects A and B

When the cash inflows are unequal, as in project B, interpolation can be employed to determine the exact payback period.

Cash Flow Streams

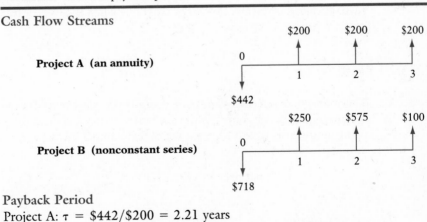

Payback Period

Project A: $\tau = \$442/\$200 = 2.21$ years

Project B: $\tau = 1 \text{ year} + \dfrac{\$718 - \$250}{\$825 - \$250} = 1 \text{ year} + \dfrac{\$468}{\$575} = 1.81$ years

flows, because discounting is not employed. Third, it does not deal with any cash flows that occur beyond the payback period. To illustrate, suppose that we had two projects with cash flows as follows:

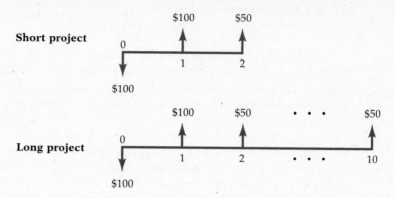

It is obvious that the longer project is better than the shorter one. However, both projects have the same payback of one year. Because of these disadvantages, the payback period is not normally considered an appropriate decision-making criterion.[2]

Although the payback period does not appear to be a viable decision criterion, it is widely employed in practice. Why might this be so? One possible explanation[3] involves agency-related issues between the firm's managers (the agents) and the firm's shareholders (the principals). **Moral hazard** is said to exist when the information available to the firm's managers is superior to that available to outside investors (a case of asymmetric information). In such a case the agent (or managers) can take unobserved self-interested actions that are detrimental to the principals. Risk averse managers can take self-interested actions in relation to (1) the amount of effort they expend, (2) the amount of risk (or total variability in firm value) they expose the firm to, and (3) the time horizon adopted for decision making (i.e., will they be with the firm for 6 months, 5 years, or 20 years?). Because of self-interest, managers may prefer shorter-payback capital investment projects, especially when the risk (or total possible variability) in a project's cash flows is high.

NET PRESENT VALUE

The appropriate selection technique is our familiar net present value, NPV. The NPV is determined by discounting the cash inflows back to the present (t = 0) at the opportunity cost, k, and then subtracting the initial investment, so that

$$\text{net present value, NPV} = \sum_{t=1}^{n} \frac{CF_t}{(1 + k)^t} - CF_0 \qquad (7.2)$$

---

[2] Some firms calculate a discounted payback period.
[3] See Chaney (1989) in the end-of-chapter references.

The decision rule for net present value is as follows:

1. If NPV is greater than zero, accept.
2. If NPV is less than zero, reject.
3. If NPV is equal to zero, you are indifferent.

When the NPV is greater than zero, the firm is generating funds above and beyond those necessary to (1) repay the initial investment and (2) provide it with a return of k percent on its investment. This incremental return represents the funds generated by the project that can be used for other purposes by the firm. The net present values for projects A and B, assuming an opportunity cost of 12 percent, are calculated in Table 7.2. Because both projects have positive NPVs, both should be accepted. Notice that the net present value criterion says project A is preferable (because it has

Table 7.2

Calculation of the Net Present Value for Projects A and B

The opportunity cost employed was 12 percent. Because both NPVs are positive, both projects assist in maximizing the value of the firm.

Cash Flow Streams

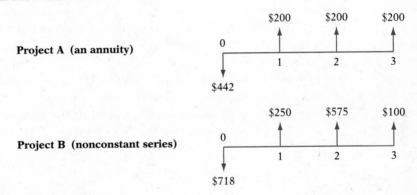

Net Present Value

Project A
Present value of inflows: $200(PVA_{12\%,\,3yr}) = \$200(2.402) = \$480.40$
Less: Initial investment   442.00
                                              NPV = $ 38.40

Project B
Present value of inflows: $250(PV_{12\%,\,1yr}) = \$250(0.893) = \$223.25$
                          $575(PV_{12\%,\,2yr}) = 575(0.797) = 458.28$
                          $100(PV_{12\%,\,3yr}) = 100(0.712) = 71.20$
Present value of inflows   752.73
Less: Initial investment   718.00
                                              NPV = $ 34.73

a larger NPV), whereas the payback criterion (from Table 7.1) indicates project B is preferred. If we were choosing between the two projects, the net present value would lead us to make the correct decision; the payback period would lead to an erroneous decision.

In addition to solving for a project's NPV, we can depict the capital budgeting decision graphically. When a variety of rates are used to discount a project's cash flows, a present value profile can be constructed. For project A, employing various discount rates results in the following net present values:

Discount Rate	Net Present Value
0%	$158
5	103
10	55
15	15
20	−21
25	−52

Plotting these values produces the present value profile shown in Figure 7.2. The present value profile provides a pictorial representation of the sensitivity of NPV to the discount rate employed. The steeper the slope of the present value profile, the more sensitive the NPV is to the opportunity cost of capital employed.

Figure 7.2

Present Value Profile for Project A

A present value profile shows what happens to the NPV as the discount rate changes. The internal rate of return is the point at which the present value profile line intersects the horizontal axis (or discount rate).

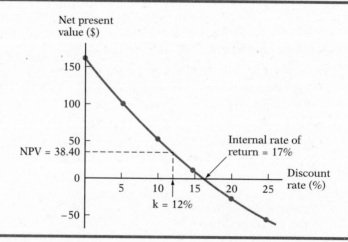

INTERNAL RATE OF RETURN

A third decision criterion is the internal rate of return (IRR); it is the discount rate that equates the present value of the cash inflows with the initial investment. Stated differently, the IRR is the rate that causes the net present value to equal zero. The internal rate of return is found by solving for the unknown IRR in Equation 7.3:

$$\sum_{t=1}^{n} \frac{CF_t}{(1 + IRR)^t} - CF_0 = 0, \text{ or } \sum_{t=1}^{n} \frac{CF_t}{(1 + IRR)^t} = CF_0 \qquad (7.3)$$

This internal rate of return for a project is then compared with the hurdle rate, k, which is the opportunity cost of capital. The internal rate of return decision rule is as follows:

1. If IRR is greater than k, accept.
2. If IRR is less than k, reject.
3. If IRR is equal to k, you are indifferent.

We discussed the steps for determining internal rate of return in Chapter 3. As shown in Table 7.3, the calculated IRR for project A is 17 percent,[4] whereas for project B it is 15 percent.[5] Because the hurdle rate is 12 percent, both projects would be accepted by this criterion.

Another way to think about the IRR can be seen by going back to the present value profile in Figure 7.2. The point where the present value profile intersects the horizontal axis is the internal rate of return on a project. As shown in Figure 7.2, the profile line intersects the horizontal axis at 17 percent.

WHY NPV IS PREFERRED

Surveys and discussions with firms indicate that the internal rate of return tends to be widely employed in practice, presumably because it is easier to understand than the NPV technique. For example, an NPV of $25 may not have the same intuitive appeal as an IRR of 18 percent. However, there are circumstances in which employing the internal rate of return may lead to incorrect decisions that do not maximize the value of the firm. For this reason, net present value is the preferred capital investment decision criterion. To understand why this is so, it is necessary to consider two additional topics—multiple internal rates of return and ranking problems.

---

[4] By financial calculator, enter 442 at t = 0 and 200 for t = 1 through t = 3. Selecting IRR results in 16.988 ≈ 17 percent.

[5] By financial calculator, enter 718 at t = 0, 250 at t = 1, 575 at t = 2, and 100 at t = 3. Selecting IRR results in 14.993 ≈ 15 percent.

Table 7.3

Calculation of the Internal Rate of Return for Projects A and B

Because both projects have internal rates of return that exceed the hurdle rate, or opportunity cost of capital, of 12 percent, both would be selected.

Cash Flow Streams

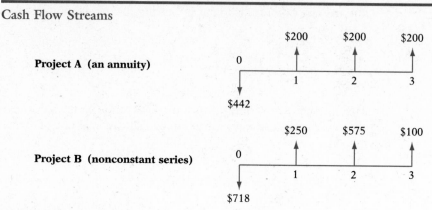

Project A (an annuity)

Project B (nonconstant series)

Internal Rate of Return

Project A

STEP 1: Divide the initial CF by the annual operating CF to determine a PVA: $442/$200 = 2.210.

STEP 2: Find the closest PVA from the row appropriate to the number of years from Table B.2. In the three-year row, the closest PVA is exactly 2.210 at 17 percent. Hence, the IRR is 17 percent.[a]

Project B

STEP 1: Calculate the average annual operating CF to get a "simulated" annuity.[b] ($250 + $575 + $100)/3 = $308.33 ≈ $310.

STEP 2: Divide the initial CF by the simulated annuity to determine a PVA: $718/$310 = 2.316.

STEP 3: Find the closest PVA from the row appropriate to the number of years from Table B.2. This is an "approximate" IRR, which provides a starting point for further analysis. The closest three-year PVA is 2.322 at 14 percent, so the IRR is approximately 14 percent.

STEP 4: Use the discount rate from step 3 as a starting point. The present value of the cash inflows is determined by using PV factors from Table B.1. If this present value is greater than CF_0, raise the discount rate; if it is less than CF_0, lower the rate.

Year	CF	PV at 14%	Present Value
1	$250	0.877	$219.25
2	575	0.769	442.18
3	100	0.675	67.50
			$728.93

Table 7.3 *continued*

Because the present value of the inflows at 14 percent is greater than the initial investment of $718, raise the discount rate to 15 percent.

Year	CF	PV at 15%	Present Value
1	$250	0.870	$217.50
2	575	0.756	434.70
3	100	0.658	65.80
			$718.00

Because this present value of the cash inflows exactly equals the initial investment, the IRR is 15 percent.

[a] If the value falls between two factors, estimation will be needed.
[b] This approach is unnecessary if you have a financial calculator. For those without such a calculator, the simulated annuity approach generally saves time by providing an approximate internal rate of return, which serves as a starting point for the final calculations.

Multiple Internal Rates of Return One problem that occasionally occurs when the IRR is calculated is that there may be more than one return. **Multiple internal rates of return** may occur when a nonsimple cash flow series occurs. A **simple cash flow** series is one in which there is an initial investment (which is negative) followed by a series of positive cash inflows:

Because there is only one change of sign, from negative to positive, there can be only one IRR.[6] A **nonsimple cash flow** series, however, has more than one change in the cash flow sign:

In this case, there are three changes in sign, and there may be three internal rates of return. *None is meaningful for decision making.* Graphically, a present value profile of this multiple-IRR problem with three sign changes might appear as follows:[7]

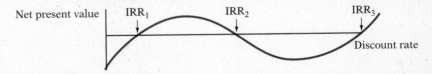

---

[6] Mathematically this is a result of Descartes' rule of signs, which implies that every time the sign of the cash flows change, there will be a maximum of one new real root.

[7] The present value profile could have other shapes and still be consistent with three sign changes. For example, the profile could be just the opposite and still have three intersections with the discount rate line. Alternatively, it could also be tangent to (just touch) the discount rate line and then go back up (or down). Finally, it could turn back up (or down) before reaching the discount rate line, in which case the roots are imaginary.

Under circumstances such as these, the IRR criterion is inappropriate for decision making, and the net present value should be used. Examples of projects producing nonsimple cash flows are strip mining or forest harvesting, where after a section of land has been mined or harvested, an after-tax cash outlay is required to return the land to its original condition.

Ranking Problems   The net present value and internal rate of return always make the same accept–reject decision for *independent* projects.[8] However, when two (or more) mutually exclusive projects are considered, the firm can select only one. That one should be the project that contributes most to the value of the firm. Unfortunately, IRR and NPV do not always rank projects in the same order in terms of their economic desirability. Consider two projects, F and G, with cash flows as follows:

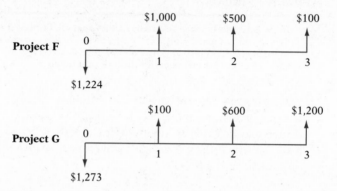

The net present values for these two projects at 11 percent are $156.10 for project F and $181.50 for project G. According to the NPV criterion, we should select project G. This is easy to see with NPV because if we select project F, we give up the opportunity to take project G. The opportunity cost associated with taking F instead of G is

$$\text{NPV}_{\text{F-G}} = \$156.10 - \$181.50 = -\$25.40$$

The internal rate of return for project F is 21 percent; for project G it is 17 percent. According to the IRR criterion, we should select project F. Obviously, a conflict exists.
   We can calculate the net present values at various discount rates, as follows:

Discount Rate	Project F	Project G
0%	$376.00	$627.00
5	267.90	403.20
10	173.10	214.70
15	89.80	57.20
20	13.90	−78.50
25	−52.80	−194.60

We now have the data necessary to plot the projects' present value profiles in Figure 7.3. As shown in the figure, up to the crossover discount rate of 12.67 percent,

---

[8] Excluding the possibility of multiple internal rates of return.

Figure 7.3

Conflicting Rankings Between Net Present Value and Internal Rate of Return

Using NPV, the firm would select project G; however, project F has a higher IRR.

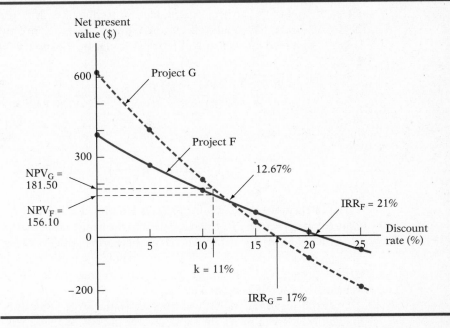

the net present value of project G will be higher than the NPV of project F. Above 12.67 percent, the net present value of project F is greater than that of project G.

Conflicting rankings can occur with mutually exclusive projects under two conditions: (1) when the *size of the initial investment* for one project is considerably different from the initial investment for the other, and (2) when the *timing of the two projects' cash inflows* differs significantly. Looking at the cash flow streams for projects F and G, we see that the timing of their cash inflows does differ significantly.

The ultimate factor that causes the difference in rankings is the implicit reinvestment rate assumptions incorporated into the NPV and IRR formulas. The NPV method assumes that intermediate cash flows (those from years 1 and 2 for projects F and G) are reinvested at a rate equal to the discount rate employed. In our example the implicit reinvestment rate for the NPV method is the opportunity cost of capital of 11 percent for both projects. The IRR method assumes that these same intermediate cash flows can be reinvested at the project's internal rate of return. Under the IRR method, the implicit reinvestment rate assumption is 21 percent for project F and 17 percent for project G.

Which reinvestment rate assumption is better—the opportunity cost of capital in the NPV approach or the project's IRR in the internal rate of return method? The opportunity cost of capital is, because (1) it is a market-based rate that is the same across all projects of similar risk; (2) any project that returns more than it costs is contributing to the maximization of the long-run market value of the firm; and (3) it allows us to maximize dollars, not percentages.

Modified Internal Rate of Return An attempt to "save" the internal rate of return has been proposed. This method computes an IRR with an *explicit* reinvestment rate assumption. It assumes that the intermediate cash inflows are reinvested at the opportunity cost of capital, k, not at the project's internal rate of return. This **modified internal rate of return (MIRR)** calls for the project's cash inflows to be compounded out to the end of the project's useful life at k to obtain their future value, FV_n. Then the discount rate that equates this future value to the initial investment is determined. Thus the modified internal rate of return is found by solving for the unknown MIRR in:

$$\frac{\sum_{t=1}^{n} CF_t(1 + k)^{n-t}}{(1 + MIRR)^n} - CF_0 = 0, \text{ or } \frac{FV_n}{(1 + MIRR)^n} = CF_0$$

which results in Equation 7.4

$$MIRR = \left(\frac{FV_n}{CF_0}\right)^{1/n} - 1 \tag{7.4}$$

The calculations of MIRR for projects F and G are shown in Table 7.4. With the required rate of return of 11 percent used as the explicit reinvestment rate, we see that project F has an MIRR of 15.52 percent whereas project G's is 16.04 percent. Because these projects are mutually exclusive, we would choose the project with the higher MIRR—project G. This choice is the same as that made when these projects are evaluated by the NPV criterion.

Does this mean the MIRR will *always* give the same result as NPV? The answer is no. The MIRR will select the same project as NPV *if* the initial investments are of equal size. In addition, MIRR also overcomes the problem of multiple rates of return.[9] If the initial investments differ significantly in size, however, MIRR may not rank the projects in the same order as NPV. For example, assume we are considering the following two mutually exclusive projects, D and E:

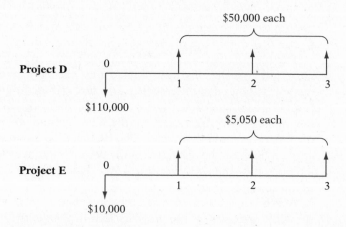

---

[9] This is accomplished because the MIRR approach allows any negative cash flow that occurs after t = 0 to retain its negative value when calculating the future value of the flows. If the sum of the individual future values is greater than zero, there will be only one MIRR for the project; however, if the future sum is less than zero, there is no real MIRR for the project.

Table 7.4

Calculation of the Modified Internal Rate of Return for Projects F and G

With an opportunity cost of 11 percent, project G is chosen. For these two projects, this is the same project that was selected using NPV.

Modified Internal Rate of Return

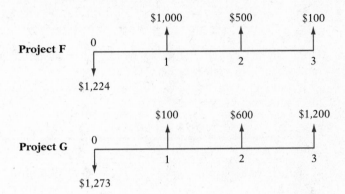

Project F

1. *Future value of inflows:*
$$
\begin{aligned}
\$1{,}000(\text{FV}_{11\%,\,2\text{yr}}) &= \$1{,}000(1.232) = \$1{,}232 \\
500(\text{FV}_{11\%,\,1\text{yr}}) &= 500(1.110) = 555 \\
100(\text{FV}_{11\%,\,0\text{yr}}) &= 100(1.000) = \underline{100} \\
&\hphantom{= 100(1.000) =} \$1{,}887
\end{aligned}
$$

2. *Calculation of MIRR:*

$$
\text{MIRR} = \left(\frac{\$1{,}887}{\$1{,}224}\right)^{1/3} - 1 = 15.52\%
$$

Project G

1. *Future value of inflows:*
$$
\begin{aligned}
\$\ 100(1.232) &= \$\ 123.20 \\
600(1.110) &= 666.00 \\
1{,}200(1.000) &= \underline{1{,}200.00} \\
\text{FV} &= \$1{,}989.20
\end{aligned}
$$

2. *Calculation of MIRR:*

$$
\text{MIRR} = \left(\frac{\$1{,}989.20}{\$1{,}273}\right)^{1/3} - 1 = 16.04\%
$$

If the minimum opportunity cost of capital, k, is 14 percent, then

	Project	
	D	E
NPV (at 14%)	$6,100.00	$1,726.10
IRR	17.27%	24.04%

Using the net present value, we would select project D; using the internal rate of return, we would select project E.

If a modified internal rate of return is calculated using 14 percent as the reinvestment rate, then we have:

	Project D	Project E
Future value at time t = 3	$172,000.00	$17,372
MIRR	16.07%	20.21%

Based on MIRR, project E is still preferred to project D—the same conclusion reached with the IRR criterion, and the opposite of that reached with the NPV criterion. Thus, incorporation of an explicit reinvestment rate assumption for the IRR criterion *does not overcome the ranking problem associated with significant size disparities between projects.* Hence, the MIRR criterion only partially solves the ranking problem and may not lead a firm to select those projects with the highest net present value. The message is clear: Attempts to "save" the internal rate of return by modifying it create more trouble than they are worth. Why not simply stick with net present value? It is easy to calculate and always provides the correct wealth-maximizing investment decision.

Reconciliation of IRR and NPV   From the previous examples we see that choosing the mutually exclusive project with the higher IRR or MIRR may lead to a choice that is inconsistent with the NPV criterion. We can show how the internal rate of return could be used correctly, if you had to use it, so that the selection from both criteria is the same.

The IRR method will rank mutually exclusive projects such as F and G in the same order as the NPV method if we apply the **incremental IRR approach**. This approach is used to make choices between two projects by carrying out the following steps:

STEP 1:   Calculate the IRR for both of the projects under consideration. For projects F and G, these are 21 percent and 17 percent, respectively.

STEP 2:   If both projects have IRRs that are lower than the opportunity cost of capital, reject both. If only one project has an IRR that is above the opportunity cost of capital, select it and reject the other project. If both projects have IRRs that are above the opportunity cost of capital, then the one with the higher IRR is set up as the "defender," the project presumed preferable for the time being. In our example, both projects have an IRR that is greater than the opportunity cost of capital; however, project F has the higher IRR at 21 percent. Therefore, F is our defender.

STEP 3:   Calculate the incremental cash flows for the "challenger," project G, minus those for the defender. The incremental cash flows in our example are

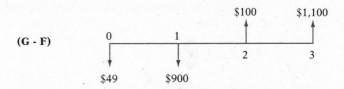

STEP 4:   Calculate the IRR for these incremental cash flows. In our example the IRR for (G − F) is 12.67 percent.[10]

STEP 5:   Compare the IRR for the incremental cash flows to the opportunity cost of capital, k. If it is less than k, the defender should be chosen; if it is greater than k, the challenger should be chosen. In our example, the IRR of 12.67 percent is greater than 11 percent; therefore, project G, the challenger, should be chosen. This is the same choice that the NPV criterion provides.

This five-step procedure has reconciled the IRR and NPV methodologies. It shows us how we can properly apply the IRR methodology to mutually exclusive projects. In effect, the procedure has broken project G into two parts. One is equivalent to project F and has an IRR of 21 percent, and the other is project (G − F) with an IRR of 12.67 percent. Thus, the firm has undertaken a package of projects, consisting of F and (G − F), that provides the highest total NPV of the two projects under consideration.

This procedure has been applied to projects with timing differences in their cash inflows; however, it can be applied equally well to projects that differ significantly in initial investment. In such a case, as long as both projects have IRRs that are above the opportunity cost of capital, then in step 2 the one with the smaller initial investment is set up as the defender. The other steps are followed as outlined. In either case this procedure can be applied to many mutually exclusive projects by considering them two at a time.

The procedure as outlined above using the incremental IRR may not solve the multiple rate of return problem. It will solve the problem *if* there is a size disparity in the initial investments and the cash flows are such that all of the incremental cash flows after t = 0 are positive. The same cannot be said for the time disparity problem with nonsimple cash flows, because a meaningful IRR cannot be calculated for the first step of the procedure. However, if you have a choice, why go to all this trouble? The net present value criterion always leads to the correct decision, without these complications.

---

[10] Note that the IRR for (G − F) of 12.67 percent is the same as the crossover rate of return in Figure 7.3. The reason is that the crossover rate of return, known as the Fisher rate, is the rate of return that makes the NPV of the two projects equal to each other. Thus, this must be the same rate of return that makes the NPV of the difference between the projects equal to zero.

ARE THERE REDEEMING QUALITIES OF INTERNAL RATE OF RETURN?

As indicated above, the internal rate of return is widely used. The primary redeeming quality of the internal rate of return is that the expected return on a project, such as a new plant, can be communicated to executives and the board of directors in percentage terms, such as "it provides an expected return of greater than 30 percent." In practice, firms often require that the initial investment be negative and that all subsequent inflows be positive. Therefore, any possibility of multiple internal rates of return is avoided. Hence, firms act as if they understand some of the problems with internal rate of return. Over time there appears to have been some movement away from internal rate of return in practice. Our best guess is that its demise will be slow but continual, as the problems with internal rate of return become more widely known. In the meantime, if you are required to use the IRR, you should use it properly and *be aware of its shortcomings.*

Concept Review Questions

■ What are some of the advantages and disadvantages of using the payback period?

■ Describe how you would use a project's internal rate of return when evaluating whether to accept or reject a project.

■ What are some problems with the internal rate of return?

■ Describe the steps performed when calculating the modified internal rate of return.

■ When do the net present value, the internal rate of return, and the modified internal rate of return all lead to the same accept/reject decision?

■ Describe how one would calculate the incremental internal rate of return.

SOME COMPLICATIONS

We have concluded that long-term investments having a positive net present value should be accepted. By accepting them, the firm is maximizing its value. As discussed in Chapter 4, the value of the firm is equal to the present value of the assets in place (that is, a nongrowing firm that is simply reinvesting enough to maintain its value) plus the present value of growth opportunities (PVGO). We have discussed some of the most important aspects of capital budgeting, but is that all of the story? The answer is that *a lot remains to be said.* A number of complications exist when making wealth-maximizing capital budgeting decisions. Four of these are (1) interrelated projects, (2) projects with unequal lives, (3) how to proceed when only cash outflows exist, and (4) capital rationing. However, before addressing these complications, let us start by considering the characteristics of projects with positive net present values.

WHAT LEADS TO POSITIVE NPVs?

If product and labour markets are completely efficient, competition will quickly bid prices down or costs up to a level at which the NPVs are equal to zero. That is, competitors will continue to enter the market until prices allow no more than the minimum acceptable return on capital, k. Hence, for a capital budgeting project to have a positive net present value, one of two situations must exist:

1. There are unique attributes of the firm or project.
2. We have estimated the data incorrectly—overstating the magnitude or timing of the cash inflows, understating the outflows, or employing too low a discount rate.

Let us examine these one by one. First, although we know that financial markets are reasonably efficient in developed countries, there is evidence that the labour and product markets are not as efficient. Less efficient labour and product markets may result from numerous causes—such as unique advantages in quality or cost (perhaps due in part to the special abilities of the firm's management and employees, or the use of nonunion employees), and legally imposed barriers to competition (such as patents). Other possible sources include consistent technological leadership, economies of scale that provide a continuing cost advantage, an established distribution and marketing system, or brand loyalty and trusted product warranties. All these barriers serve to accomplish one important goal: They delay the effective response of competitors and provide opportunities for firms to capture positive net present values before they erode away. But unless there are legal or other effective barriers to entry, others will become aware of the excess returns (evidenced by positive NPVs) and dedicate the resources necessary to become effective competitors. Hence, *effective capital budgeting procedures must recognize the limited life potential of virtually all projects for producing positive NPVs*, and they should include an analysis of market imperfections, unique capabilities of the firm, and barriers to entry that form the keystone of positive-NPV projects.

In less-developed countries, simply producing and selling goods may provide unique advantages and the ability to earn excess returns. Within the last few years one of the authors spent some time in India. While there, he visited with numerous executives about their capital budgeting decision-making process and the value-creating opportunities in India. A number of executives indicated that due to the tremendous demand for certain types of goods, simply having the goods available for sale, irrespective of their quality or price (within some limits), provided the opportunity to earn substantial returns. In an environment such as this, the combination of high demand and lack of effective competition means firms may enjoy the substantial returns that go along with positive-NPV projects. In fact, it is not even necessary to do a very sophisticated capital budgeting analysis; back-of-the-envelope calculations may be sufficient. Over time, however, as the country's economy develops and competition enters, the ability to earn excess returns will be eroded away, just as in any other competitive market.

The second possible reason for positive NPVs is estimation problems. Several studies, along with discussions with numerous managers, suggest that in practice capital investment plans tend to be overly optimistic in formulating cash flow and risk estimates. Depending on the approach taken, this tendency can be traced to many different factors—the inherent optimism of managers, statistical problems, peer pressure, or ineffective performance and measurement systems. Whatever the cause, the result is that the input data used in the capital budgeting process may be deficient. The old saying "garbage in, garbage out" clearly applies to the capital budgeting process.

No matter how sophisticated the selection technique, if the estimated cash flow or discount rate is specified incorrectly, the resulting net present value will also be incorrect.

Although there is no simple "cure" for measurement problems, there is one important ingredient of any successful capital investment program: a process and atmosphere which ensure that all assumptions are articulated and challenged, and that the unique strengths of the firm and project, and the potential reactions of competitors, are incorporated into the analysis. If you do not quiz the decision maker too hard or look at the assumptions very closely, he or she can make the numbers in almost any investment project look good. But that in no way ensures success for the project; poor analysis and making the numbers *look* good may be worse than seat-of-the-pants capital investment decision making by informed and demanding managers.

INTERRELATED PROJECTS

Up to this point we have classified projects as either mutually exclusive or independent. A more accurate picture would show a continuum of relationships among projects, as in Figure 7.4. At one end stand **complementary projects**. If one of several complementary projects is undertaken, the cash flows of all related projects also increase. An example is a combination self-service gasoline station and convenience store; combining both in one operation generally produces incremental business beyond the simple sum of what each would generate separately. In the extreme case, the cash flows and success or failure of the projects are so closely related that a decision has to be made to accept or reject a **system-wide project**. The entire system must be evaluated, because accepting only part of it produces nothing of value.

At the other end of the continuum are **substitute projects**. In this case acceptance of one project reduces the cash flows from another. If the effect is pronounced enough, the projects are said to be mutually exclusive; that is, accepting one precludes accepting others. A special case, lying between system-wide and mutually exclusive projects, is that of independent projects. In this case acceptance of one has no appreciable impact on the cash flows of other independent projects.

Finally, as shown in Figure 7.4, we have a broad spectrum of **interrelated projects**, where the acceptance of one project can partially affect—either positively or nega-

---

Figure 7.4

Degree of Dependence Among Capital Budgeting Projects

A continuum of projects exists, from those that are perfect complements to those that are perfect substitutes. Knowing the degree of dependence is necessary for effective decision making.

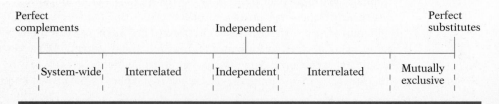

tively—the cash flows of other possible projects. *The joint cash flows for two (or more) interrelated projects must be analyzed together.* Suppose that Wilson Paint, which as part of its activities manufactures paint sprayers, is evaluating the desirability of producing two new models—the Quik Painter and the Quik Painter II. The firm has the choice of producing and selling either or both paint sprayers. The initial investment, cash inflows, and NPVs for both are as follows:

	Producing and Selling Only Quik Painter	Producing and Selling Only Quik Painter II	Producing and Selling Both
Initial investment	$200,000	$250,000	$400,000
After-tax cash flows for each of 10 years	50,000	60,000	70,000
Net present value at 13%	71,300	75,560	−20,180

At the opportunity cost of capital of 13 percent, both projects considered independently have positive net present values and should be selected.

But look what happens if Wilson decides to introduce both sprayers. Wilson's combined initial investment is slightly less than the sum of the two separate outlays, so there are some economies from producing both. The total after-tax cash flows, however, increase only slightly when both sprayers are introduced. Why? Because the two paint sprayers are really substitutes. A customer needs only one of the sprayers, and two different models provide very little in the way of incremental sales. The cash inflows are interrelated, so the total NPV from producing both paint sprayers is negative. Obviously, Wilson should not introduce both sprayers—and because the Quik Painter II has the higher NPV, it should be produced and sold.

This example suggests a basic procedure to be followed when interrelated projects exist:

STEP 1: Identify all possible combinations of interrelated projects. Assume three projects, A, B, and C, are interrelated. In addition to analyzing A, B, and C separately, the combinations of A and B, A and C, B and C, and A and B and C must also be evaluated.

STEP 2: Determine the initial investment and after-tax cash flow stream for each project and combination, along with the total NPV of each project and combination.

STEP 3: Choose the individual project or combination of projects that has the highest total NPV.

One could argue that all projects within a firm are somewhat related. If this is the case, then the analysis of any project is a tremendous chore, because all possible combinations have to be considered. However, many projects are mutually exclusive, independent, or system-wide. The key, then, is to make sure that proper analysis has been done to determine the appropriate relationship, if any, between proposed capital budgeting projects. When the analysis has been done correctly, the proper projects are considered, the proper cash flows are identified, and the proper decisions will result.

UNEQUAL LIVES

In addition to interrelated projects, firms must often make a decision between two or more mutually exclusive projects that have unequal lives. Consider the choice between purchasing two different sanding machines. Model A-3 is semiautomated, requires an initial investment of $320,000, and produces after-tax cash flows of $160,000 for each of three years, at which time it will have to be replaced. Model B-6 is an automated machine with a six-year life, requires an initial investment of $420,000, and produces annual after-tax cash flows of $120,000. As Table 7.5 shows, at a 10 percent discount rate, the net present value of the automated machine is greater. With an NPV of $102,600, it appears that model B-6 should be chosen.

But the net present value is a function of the life of the project. Although this does not matter when projects are independent, it does matter when they are mutually exclusive and future replacement is expected (i.e., it is *not* a one-shot investment). To make a valid comparison, it is necessary to equalize the lives of the two projects. There are a number of ways to do this. We will consider two—replacement chains and the equivalent annual NPV method.

Replacement Chains   If we choose Model A-3, we will have the opportunity in three more years to make another similar investment. However, if we choose Model B-6, we do not have the second investment opportunity. One way to make a valid comparison of the two models is to find the NPV of Model A-3 over six years and compare it with the NPV of Model B-6 over the same six years. This is the **replacement chain** approach to equalizing lives.

If we assume that the CFs and discount rate remain the same for Model A-3 when it is replaced in three years, its total NPV over six years is equal to the original NPV over the first three-year stage, plus the present value of the second-stage NPV of the investment to be made in three more years. The appropriate NPV is

$$
\begin{aligned}
\text{NPV for Model A-3 over 6 years} &= \text{original 3-year NPV} \\
&\quad + \text{second 3-year NPV } (PV_{10\%,\,3yr}) \\
&= \$77{,}920 + \$77{,}920(0.751) \\
&= \$136{,}437.92
\end{aligned}
$$

Comparing this six-year NPV for Model A-3 of $136,437.92 with the NPV of $102,600 for Model B-6, we see that the wealth-maximizing decision is to invest in Model A-3 and then reinvest in another Model A-3 in three more years. The replacement chain procedure works fine in this case, but what happens if the lives of the two projects are seven years and nine years? Then the analysis has to be taken out to 63 years, because that is the least common denominator of the lives of the two

Table 7.5	

Net Present Value for Two Mutually Exclusive Projects, Ignoring Their Unequal Lives

Other things being equal, model B-6 would be chosen because it has the higher NPV. However, because NPV is a function of the life of the project, it is necessary in mutually exclusive cases to adjust for differences in lives.

Cash Flow Streams

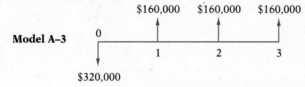

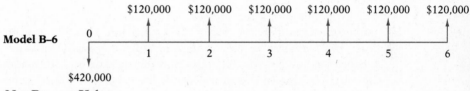

Net Present Value

$$\text{Model A-3 NPV} = \$160,000(\text{PVA}_{10\%,\,3\text{yr}}) - \$320,000$$
$$= \$160,000(2.487) - \$320,000$$
$$= \$397,920 - \$320,000$$
$$= \$77,920$$
$$\text{Model B-6 NPV} = \$120,000(\text{PVA}_{10\%,\,6\text{yr}}) - \$420,000$$
$$= \$120,000(4.355) - \$420,000$$
$$= \$522,600 - \$420,000$$
$$= \$102,600$$

projects. Due to potential problems of this type, we use the equivalent annual NPV method.[11]

Equivalent Annual NPV The **equivalent annual NPV** approach to the unequal-life problem converts the original NPVs to yearly net present value figures. The effect is to assume the existing projects will be replicated over and over, with the result that the NPV can be stated as a yearly figure. The equivalent annual NPV is:

$$\text{equivalent annual NPV} = \frac{\text{NPV}_n}{\text{PVA}_{k,\,n}} \qquad (7.5)$$

[11] There are other methods. One is the infinite replication approach, which converts both projects to perpetuities.

where

NPV_n = the project's net present value over its original life

$PVA_{k,n}$ = the present value factor for an annuity based on the opportunity cost of capital and original life of the project

The equivalent annual NPVs for the two models are

$$\text{Model A-3: } \frac{\$77{,}920}{PVA_{10\%,\,3\text{yr}}} = \frac{\$77{,}920}{2.487} = \$31{,}331$$

$$\text{Model B-6: } \frac{\$102{,}631}{PVA_{10\%,\,6\text{yr}}} = \frac{\$102{,}600}{4.355} = \$23{,}559$$

Because Model A-3 has the higher equivalent annual NPV, *it contributes more to the firm's goal of maximizing the value of the firm per year.* Therefore, Model A-3 is preferable.

Two points should be stressed. First, managers and students sometimes get the impression that different lives have to be taken into account for *all* projects. This is not true: *Unequal lives must be dealt with only for mutually exclusive projects.* For all independent projects, the NPV criterion already takes into account timing differences. By selecting independent projects with the largest NPV, we are making the correct decision without having to adjust for unequal lives. Second, the equivalent annual NPV approach does not allow for differing rates of inflation or other changes (such as new technology). The best way to handle complications such as these is to build the effects of expected inflation, new technology, and so forth, into the cash flow estimates. Then the replacement chain, but not the equivalent annual NPV, method should be used as before. Alternatively, the lives of the two projects can be equalized—perhaps by assuming some common termination point and considering the resale value at that point in time for each project. The NPVs for the two projects can then be calculated and compared.

WHEN ONLY CASH OUTFLOWS EXIST

Occasionally you will run into capital investment decisions in which only the cash outflows are relevant. This may occur when a firm argues that it has to have the machine (perhaps to stay in business) and the only issue is to choose the best machine from a number of mutually exclusive alternatives.

Three points should immediately be recognized in such a situation. First, are the inflows really irrelevant? As we discuss in Chapter 8, often firms do not consider the abandonment decision or ask the question, "Should we continue in this business?" Second, *with only cash outflows, the objective becomes that of minimizing the value of the discounted cash outflows.* Thus, you need to determine the **equivalent annual cost** of the alternatives. Third, the goal is to select the alternative with the *lowest* equivalent annual cost. The procedures are exactly the same as for NPV and equivalent annual NPV, but there are only cash outflows to consider.

CAPITAL RATIONING

Unfortunately, all acceptable projects cannot always be undertaken. This is the case of **capital rationing**: A limit is placed on the size of the capital budget. It generally arises because of *internally imposed constraints* on the amount of external funds a firm will raise or because of dollar limits imposed on the capital expenditures various divisions of firms can undertake. These can be thought of as **soft capital rationing** constraints; they are limits adopted by management. There exists another type of capital rationing—**hard capital rationing**, in which the firm cannot raise any more funds in the capital markets. Theoretically, hard capital rationing rarely, if ever, exists if the proposed project has a positive NPV, because additional funds should be available (at some cost) to finance the project.

To see the effect of capital rationing, consider the following information on four independent proposed projects:

Project	CF_0	NPV
L	$10	$5
M	20	5
N	30	8
P	30	4

Without any capital rationing constraint, the value-maximizing decision is to accept all four projects. The initial cash outlay is $90, and the total NPV is $22. But what occurs if a capital rationing constraint exists and only $30 is available? The objective is to maximize the total NPV *up to the constraint*. This can be accomplished by accepting projects L and M; the outlay is $30, and the total NPV is $10.

Capital rationing leads to suboptimal decisions because it does not allow the firm to attain its maximum value. It is another opportunity cost that reduces the value of the firm if positive NPV projects are bypassed. In the face of capital rationing, the goal is to *maximize the total net present value over all projects accepted*. If there are not too many projects, this can be accomplished by listing all feasible combinations (within the budget constraint) and then determining which combination has the largest total NPV.[12] If the number of projects becomes too large, and/or capital is expected to be rationed over a number of years, integer programming can be used.

---

[12] An alternative selection criterion, the **profitability index**, is often recommended when a one-period capital rationing constraint is considered. The profitability index is

$$\text{profitability index} = \frac{\displaystyle\sum_{t=1}^{n} \frac{CF_t}{(1 + k)^t}}{CF_0}$$

Because the discounted after-tax operating and ending cash flows are divided by the initial investment, CF_0, the profitability index is a *relative* measure of economic desirability. Projects are ranked from highest to lowest, and all those with PIs greater than 1.0 are selected up to the dollar limit. With a one-period capital rationing constraint, this approach selects the best set of projects *only if all the funds available for investment (up to the capital constraint) are expended*. Because the total NPV approach is not affected by this problem, it is a more appropriate selection criterion.

If capital rationing, especially soft capital rationing, is an opportunity cost and tends to reduce the value of the firm, why does it exist? One possibility is that in large firms the use of fixed (or relatively fixed) divisional allocations of capital is simply a means of imposing control on the activities of subordinates. One of the key ideas in finance is that individuals act in their own self-interest. Subordinates have a vested interest in proposing capital expenditure projects and having them accepted. Doing so makes employees look good, and being a self-starter who produces results is one of the keys to promotion and financial well-being in many firms. Imposing capital limits on divisions may simply be one means of dealing with the tendency of employees to be overly optimistic or aggressive in proposing capital projects for inclusion in the firm's capital budget.[13]

A second possibility is that soft capital rationing is simply a reflection of the fact that managers have large amounts of firm-specific human capital. That is, managers have both their reputation and their chances for advancement, as well as their financial livelihood, invested in the firm. With a great deal of their own wealth tied up in the firm, managers have incentives to manage the firm "conservatively" and, therefore, to reduce the firm's riskiness and any possibility of financial distress. Risk reduction can be accomplished by practising asset substitution—that is, by accepting projects that have less total risk (or variability in their cash flows) than might be desirable. Managers may also have incentives to retain more cash in the firm and to employ less debt than might be optimal. These actions are simply another form of agency costs which arise due to differential interests between the firm's managers and its owners. Whatever the reasons, capital rationing tends to be practised by many firms. As such, we need to be aware of possible reasons for and the consequences of capital rationing.

Thus far we have examined the basic procedures by which most medium and large firms make capital investment decisions. We have examined what selection technique to employ, and we have discussed why positive net present value projects exist. We have also considered unequal lives between mutually exclusive projects, and how capital rationing restricts firm value. However, capital budgeting is a complex subject. Other important issues are discussed in Chapters 8 and 9.

Concept Review Questions

- What are the two situations that may exist in order for a capital budgeting project to have a positive net present value?
- What are complementary projects and substitute projects?
- What are two methods used to evaluate capital budgeting projects with unequal lives?
- When using the equivalent annual NPV to compare projects of unequal lives, what assumptions are being made?
- How are accept/reject decisions applied to capital budgeting projects that have only cash outflows?
- Define the terms "soft capital rationing" and "hard capital rationing."
- Why does capital rationing exist?

---

[13] Further discussion of this point can be found in the publications listed in the end-of-chapter references.

KEY POINTS

- Only by accepting positive net present value investment projects can the firm maximize its long-run market value.
- Expansion projects result in the net addition of assets as the firm makes decisions that expand the scope of its activities; replacement decisions involve the consideration of retaining existing assets or replacing them with other assets.
- When projects are independent of one another, all positive NPV projects should be taken, in order to maximize the market value of the firm. However, when projects are mutually exclusive, accepting one automatically leads to the rejection of the other project(s).
- In practice, the capital budgeting process has four phases: search and identification of growth opportunities; estimation of the magnitude, timing, and riskiness of cash flows; selection or rejection; and control and postcompletion audit. All are important, but we focus on the second and third steps.
- Although the payback period is widely employed in practice, it is not economically justifiable, it does not take the timing of the cash flows into account, and it does not account for expected cash flows that occur beyond the payback period.
- Net present value (NPV) is the only decision criterion that always produces decisions consistent with the goal of maximizing the value of the firm. Despite its widespread use, the internal rate of return suffers from possible multiple internal rates of return and from ranking problems.
- The modified internal rate of return may provide an incorrect ranking of which mutually exclusive project to accept when projects require different initial investments.
- Positive NPV projects build on the unique strengths of the firm or project and have limited lives.
- When projects are interrelated, the net after-tax cash flow stream over the projects must be employed in order to make wealth-maximizing decisions.
- When the lives of mutually exclusive projects are unequal, they must be equalized. The easiest way to accomplish this is by employing equivalent annual NPVs.
- If only cash outflows exist, the objective becomes one of minimizing the discounted cash outflows.
- Under capital rationing, the firm should select the set of positive NPV projects that maximizes total NPV and stays within the budget constraint.

QUESTIONS

7.1 A firm is considering two construction projects. Project A is a new receiving dock for supply trucks. Project B is a rail car receiving dock that will accept supplies by rail. Are projects A and B mutually exclusive, independent, or interdependent? Why?

7.2 Trace the important relationships among the four phases of the capital budgeting process. Irrespective of Figure 7.1, indicate how all four phases could be related to one another.

7.3 Three decision criteria examined in this chapter were payback period, net present value, and internal rate of return. Why is the NPV an appropriate technique, whereas the payback period and IRR are not?

7.4 What does it mean when the NPV is zero? What decision should be made? What is the IRR when the NPV is zero?

7.5 What causes the internal rate of return occasionally to have multiple rates? Are any of these rates useful for decision making?

7.6   Under what conditions do the NPV and IRR methods provide different rankings? Explain the cause of the difference between the two.

7.7   Explain how the modified internal rate of return (MIRR) is similar to or different from both IRR and NPV. What problem does it overcome? What problem will it not overcome?

7.8   How are positive NPVs, the unique attributes of firms and projects, and good data related?

7.9   Explain the difference between complementary and substitute projects. How are they related to (a) system-wide projects, (b) interrelated projects, (c) independent projects, and (d) mutually exclusive projects?

7.10   Many firms calculate the equivalent annual NPV of mutually exclusive projects when making capital budgeting decisions. In what circumstances does this approach lead to sensible investment decisions? In what circumstances does it not?

7.11   Define capital rationing, and explain why it does not lead to the maximization of the value of the firm.

CONCEPT REVIEW PROBLEMS

See Appendix A for solutions.

CR7.1   United Railroad is considering purchasing one of two different types of locomotives. Both cost $500,000 and are expected to last for three years. Cash inflows from each of the locomotives are as follows:

Locomotive	CF_1	CF_2	CF_3
A	$350,000	$250,000	$80,000
B	0	0	800,000

What is the internal rate of return for each of the locomotives?

CR7.2   If United Railroad's opportunity cost of capital is 10 percent, what is the net present value of the two projects considered in CR7.1?

CR7.3   United Railroad is also considering a third project, project C, with the following cash flows:

CF_0	CF_1	CF_2	CF_3
-$500,000	$8,000,000	$8,000,000	-$20,000,000

What is the internal rate of return and the net present value of project C? Should the project be accepted?

CR7.4   Calculate the modified internal rate of return for A and B being considered by United Railroad in CR7.1.

CR7.5   Jed is planning to plant one of two types of alfalfa seed. The more expensive of the two will produce higher yields over a three-year period. The projects are mutually exclusive, and the opportunity cost of capital is 12 percent. He has calculated the following after-tax net cash flows:

Year	Select Seed	Cheap Seed
0	−$4,000	−$840
1	3,000	630
2	2,000	630
3	1,000	420

Calculate each project's net present value, internal rate of return, and modified internal rate of return. Which type of alfalfa seed should Jed plant?

CR7.6   Calculate the incremental internal rate of return of the two seed projects in CR7.5. Which seed should be planted?

CR7.7   ConCor is considering two mutually exclusive pieces of machinery. One piece of machinery, A, has a three-year life, and the other piece of machinery, B, has a nine-year life. The two alternatives provide the following after-tax cash flows:

Year	Machine A	Machine B
0	−$40,000	−$40,000
1	25,000	13,200
2	25,000	13,200
3	25,000	13,200
4		13,200
5		13,200
6		13,200
7		13,200
8		13,200
9		13,200

Using the replacement chain approach, which project should be accepted? Assume ConCor's opportunity cost of capital is 15 percent.

CR7.8   Using the equivalent annual net present value approach, evaluate both of the machines considered by ConCor in CR7.7.

CR7.9   Roper is considering six capital investment proposals, as follows:

Project	CF_0	CF_n	Years
A	$ 500	$175	4
B	1,000	350	4
C	200	50	6
D	150	40	7
E	200	100	3
F	150	42	6

Under a capital rationing constraint of $1,200, and assuming an opportunity cost of capital of 13 percent, in which projects should Roper invest?

PROBLEMS

7.1 Cash flow streams for two mutually exclusive projects are given below.

	After-Tax Cash Inflows	
Year	Project A	Project B
1	$300	$600
2	400	200
3	50	100
4	50	700

Project A requires an initial investment of $600, and project B requires an initial investment of $1,000.

a. Use the payback period to determine which project should be selected.

b. If the opportunity cost is 8 percent, determine the net present value for both projects.

c. Which project should be chosen? What are the drawbacks of the payback period method?

7.2 Trennepohl Production is contemplating the acquisition of a new multiperson word processing system for $90,000. The system is expected to produce after-tax cash inflows of $25,800 for each of five years.

a. What is the net present value of the system if the discount rate is 0, 5, 10, 15, or 20 percent?

b. Graph the project's present value profile. What is the project's approximate IRR?

7.3 The initial cash outlay for a machine is $300,000. The expected after-tax cash inflows from the machine are $90,000, $104,400, $88,800, $84,000 and $82,800 in years 1 through 5, respectively. The machine has no anticipated resale value in five years. What is the project's IRR?

7.4 Each of two mutually exclusive projects involves an investment of $120,000. The estimated CFs are as follows:

Year	X	Y
1	$70,000	$10,000
2	40,000	20,000
3	30,000	30,000
4	10,000	50,000
5	10,000	90,000

The opportunity cost is 11 percent. Calculate the NPV and IRR for both projects. Which project should be chosen? Why?

7.5 The projected cash flows from a project are as follows:

Year	After-Tax Cash Inflows
1	$1,000
2	1,300
3	2,000
4	2,500
5	1,400

a. If the opportunity cost is 16 percent, what is the maximum the firm can afford to invest in the project?
b. If the firm can actually implement the project by making an initial investment of $4,200, what is the project's internal rate of return?

7.6 Projects A and B both require a $20,000 initial investment and have projected cash inflows as follows:

	After-Tax Cash Inflows	
Year	Project A	Project B
1	$10,000	$7,000
2	8,000	7,000
3	6,000	7,000
4	4,000	7,000

a. Calculate each project's net present value if the opportunity cost is 12 percent.
b. Calculate the internal rate of return for each project.
c. Should either project be rejected if they are independent?
d. Which project should be selected if they are mutually exclusive?

7.7 A mining company can open a new strip mine for an initial investment of $24 million (at t = 0). In year 1, the mine produces a net cash inflow of $78 million. In year 2, the land must be returned to its original state, which requires an outflow of $60 million.
a. Find the net present values not calculated below.

Rate (%)	NPV (in millions)
0	$_____
25	_____
50	_____
75	0.980
100	0
125	$−1.185

b. Construct a present value profile with the data from (a).
c. Should the mine be built if the hurdle rate is 20 percent?

7.8 Richardson Products is analyzing two mutually exclusive projects. Both require an initial investment of $65,000 and provide cash inflows as follows:

	After-Tax Cash Inflows	
Year	Project C	Project D
1	$40,000	0
2	30,000	0
3	20,000	$104,200

a. If the opportunity cost is 10 percent, which project would Richardson choose if NPV is employed?

b. Calculate the internal rate of return for both projects. Which project should be selected according to IRR? Why does the difference in rankings occur?

7.9 Miles Equipment is considering two mutually exclusive projects, each with a five-year life. Project P requires an initial investment, CF_0, of $20,000 and has CFs of $6,540.22 for each of five years. Project Q has an initial investment of $100,000 and CFs of $29,832.94 for each of five years.

a. Calculate the IRR for each project, and select the preferred project.

b. Assuming the projects are of equal risk and the opportunity cost is 13 percent, which project is preferable? Defend your answer.

c. At what specific discount rate would the firm be indifferent between the two projects?

d. Calculate the MIRR for each project, and select the preferred project. Has the use of MIRR given the same choice as NPV? Explain.

7.10 Two mutually exclusive projects have after-tax cash flows as follows:

Time	Project X	Project Y
t = 0	−$50	−$30
t = 1	15	35
t = 2	85	15

a. If the discount rate is 10 percent, what are the NPVs for the two projects? What are their IRRs? Which project should be chosen?

b. Using the incremental IRR approach, determine which project should be chosen. Is this a value-maximizing decision? Explain.

7.11 West Coast Developers has designed an apartment building that will cost $7 million and produce after-tax cash inflows of $1.5 million for each year of its 10-year life. The firm also has plans for a recreation centre that would cost $3.2 million and produce after-tax cash flows of $600,000 per year for 10 years. The firm owns land near Vancouver and must decide which project to build. The land is large enough to accommodate both projects. West Coast Developers believes that if the two projects are built next to each other, the residents of the apartment building will use the recreation centre and increase its expected cash inflows to $700,000 per year. If the opportunity cost of capital is 14 percent, what should the company do?

7.12 Pisano Industries is considering two possible capital projects. Project I has the following CFs:

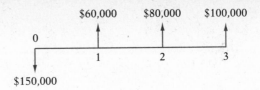

Project II can be undertaken only if the $150,000 initial investment for project I has been made. The *additional* CFs for project II are as follows:

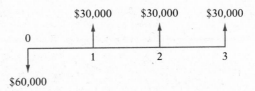

However, because projects I and II are partial substitutes, the CFs from project I will decrease by $10,000 in each of years 1, 2, and 3 if project II is also undertaken. If the discount rate is 14 percent, what should the company do?

7.13 Consider a firm in need of a stamping machine. It can buy a one-speed machine that requires an initial investment of $350 and produces after-tax cash inflows of $300 for each of two years, or it can purchase a three-speed machine that costs $1,200 and produces cash inflows of $500 for each of four years. Because of improved technology, a new one-speed machine is expected to cost only $275 in two years; however, because of increased competition, the after-tax cash flows are expected to be reduced to $250 for each of the next two years. Neither machine has a resale value, and the opportunity cost is 16 percent. Which machine should be purchased?

7.14 Either of two new moulding machines that makes drinking glasses requires an initial investment of $2,000. Model 3SR produces short glasses and has a five-year life. Model 3TR produces tall glasses and has a nine-year life. CFs expected from the purchase of Model 3SR and Model 3TR are $700 and $500 per year, respectively. If the opportunity cost is 13 percent and there is no resale value, which model should be purchased?

7.15 Constantia is contemplating replacing its existing boiler, which is worn out and has no resale value. One of two boilers will be chosen; both offer increased operating efficiency. The after-tax cash flows are as follows:

Year	Short-Life Boiler	Long-Life Boiler
Initial investment	$5,000	$8,000
1	2,500	2,750
2	2,500	2,750
3	2,500	2,750
4		2,750
5		2,750

a. Calculate the internal rate of return and net present value for both boilers over their original lives. The appropriate opportunity cost is 18 percent.

b. Which boiler should be chosen? Why?

7.16 Aqua-Products has the following independent investments under examination:

Project	Initial Investment	After-Tax Cash Flow per Year	Life of the Project (in years)
A	$100,000	$39,000	4
B	50,000	12,000	6
C	80,000	39,000	3
D	60,000	15,000	7
E	75,000	25,000	5
F	90,000	25,000	6

Aqua-Products' opportunity cost of capital is 14 percent.
a. In the absence of capital rationing, which projects should be selected? What is the size (in total dollars) of the capital budget? The total NPV of all of the projects selected?
b. Now suppose that a limit of $250,000 (maximum) is placed on new capital projects. Which projects should be selected?
c. What is the total NPV determined in (b)? What is the loss to Aqua-Products due to the capital rationing constraint?

7.17 Hindle Resources is a medium-sized, diversified company involved in both natural resource production and manufacturing. At the present time, capital is raised in a 6:3:1 ratio of common stock:debt:preferred stock. Hindle's dividend is expected to grow at a rate of 8 percent a year.

Hindle's common stock paid a dividend of $1.22 last year and is currently selling at $16. Preferred stock for similar companies is now selling at $23 per share and is expected to bear a dividend of $2.41. Common stock has a flotation cost of 8.6 percent; preferred stock has a flotation cost of 5.0 percent. Hindle is rated A (high) by a reputable bond-rating service, and so can expect to pay a coupon rate of 10 percent on newly issued debt. The company will be financing future projects with external funds, not with internally generated funds; also, Hindle faces a marginal tax rate of 40 percent.

Hindle now has the opportunity to invest in a project that has an initial cost of $70,000 but will generate CFs of $20,000 in each of the first three years of operation and $16,500 per year for each of the four years after that. Should Hindle invest in this project? (*Note*: Assume no capital rationing, and round your cost of capital to the nearest whole percent.)

7.18 Mini Case Gullett Manufacturing is expanding into producing see-through bottle caps. The relevant data has been estimated as follows: The initial cash outlay is $44,000, and the after-tax cash inflows are $14,800, $16,480, $14,660, $14,100 and $25,960 in years 1 through 5, respectively.
a. What is the purpose of capital budgeting? How does it relate to the firm's objective?
b. Assuming the opportunity cost of capital is 15 percent, calculate the payback period, net present value, and internal rate of return. Should the project be accepted?
c. Instead of the machine outlined above, a second machine that requires substantially less investment but has higher operating cash outflows could be employed to produce the see-through bottle caps. The estimated after-tax cash flows for the second machine are as follows: CF_0, $-$11,000; CF_1, $7,000; CF_{2-5}, $5,000 each. Calculate the payback period, net present value, and internal rate of return for this second alternative. Which machine—the first or second—should be selected? Does a ranking problem exist?

d. Why is the net present value the preferred decision criterion for making capital investment decisions while the internal rate of return is not?

e. If we did not know the net present values for the two machines, how could we use the incremental IRR to make the correct decision? What is the incremental IRR between these two machines?

f. One of the firm's managers has heard of the modified IRR criterion, but does not understand it completely. Explain it to the manager. Then calculate modified IRRs for the two alternatives. Does the modified IRR lead to the correct decision in this case? In all cases?

7.19 Mini Case You are working as a financial analyst for Kaw Resources. The firm is about to evaluate some projects that it considers to be of average risk. Your boss has assigned you the task, and informs you that the cash flows for two projects have already been estimated. However, he tells you that the firm needs an estimate of its opportunity cost of capital before the evaluation can be completed. To help you complete your task, he provides the following estimates of the expected returns on Kaw's common stock and the market portfolio:

State	Probability of State Occurring	Return	
		Kaw Resources	Market Portfolio
Boom	0.30	50%	35%
Average	0.50	20	15
Recession	0.20	−20	−10

The risk-free rate is 10 percent, Kaw's marginal tax rate is 40 percent, and the correlation between Kaw's returns and the market returns is +0.70.

He also provides the following information: (1) 1,833,333 common shares are outstanding. The next dividend is expected to be $2.25 and its growth rate is estimated to be 9.04 percent for the foreseeable future. New common stock can be issued to net Kaw $28.50. (2) There are 250,000 preferred shares, paying a $6.60 dividend, outstanding. Investors currently require an 11 percent return on similar preferred shares. New preferred shares with a $6.60 dividend will net the firm $57.39. (3) There are 31,134 bonds ($1,000 par), 11 percent coupon rate, outstanding with five years left to maturity. These bonds are currently selling to yield 12 percent. New 20-year, 12 percent, $1,000 par bonds can be sold to net the firm $1,000. (4) The firm's current market value capital structure is considered optimal and will be maintained when raising the needed funds.

a. What is the after-tax cost of each component of Kaw's capital structure (including internal and external equity funds)?

b. What is the opportunity cost of capital for Kaw Resources, if it obtains all of its equity financing internally? (*Note*: Round to the nearest whole number.)

c. The two investments that Kaw is considering have after-tax cash flows as follows:

Time Periods	Project A	Project B
0	−$20,000,000	−$20,000,000
1	−3,000,000	6,000,000
2	−1,000,000	6,000,000
3	2,000,000	6,000,000
4–10	5,000,000	2,700,000
11–15	10,000,000	

1. Calculate the internal rates of return for the projects. If the two projects are independent, what decision should be made?
2. What decision should be made if the two projects are mutually exclusive?

REFERENCES

BIERMAN, HAROLD, JR., and SEYMOUR SMIDT. *The Capital Budgeting Decision.* 7th ed. New York: Macmillan, 1988.

CHANEY, PAUL K. "Moral Hazard and Capital Budgeting." *Journal of Financial Research* 12 (Summer 1989): 113–128.

DORFMAN, ROBERT. "The Meaning of Internal Rates of Return." *Journal of Finance* 36 (December 1981): 1011–1021.

HIRSHLEIFER, DAVID. "Managerial Reputation and Corporate Investment Decisions." Financial Management 22 (Summer 1993): 145–160.

HOWE, KEITH M. "Perpetuity Rate of Return Analysis." *Engineering Economist* 36 (Spring 1991): 248–57.

JOG, VIJAY M., and ASHWANI K. SRIVASTAVA. "Corporate Financial Decision Making in Canada." Canadian Journal of Administrative Sciences 11 (June 1994): 156–176.

PINCHES, GEORGE E. "Myopia, Capital Budgeting and Decision Making." *Financial Management* 11 (Autumn 1982): 6–19.

PRUITT, STEPHEN W., and LAWRENCE J. GITMAN. "Capital Budgeting Forecast Biases: Evidence from the Fortune 500." *Financial Management* 16 (Spring 1987): 46–51.

SHULL, DAVID A. "Interpreting Rates of Return: A Modified Rate of Return Approach." *Financial Practice and Education* 3 (Fall 1993): 67–72.

TAGGART, ROBERT A., JR. "Allocating Capital Among a Firm's Divisions: Hurdle Rates vs. Budgets." *Journal of Financial Research* 10 (Fall 1987): 177–89.

WEAVER, SAMUEL C., DONALD PETERS, and JOE DALEIDEN. "Capital Budgeting." *Financial Management* 18 (Spring 1989): 10–17.

8

Application of Capital Budgeting Techniques

EXECUTIVE SUMMARY

Wealth-maximizing capital investment decisions require a well-designed capital budgeting process, knowledge of the proper selection techniques, a thorough understanding of the nature of the projects under consideration, and determination of the relevant cash flows. Understanding depreciation for tax purposes (or capital cost allowance) and other tax factors based on the Income Tax Act, not as recorded by accountants under generally accepted acounting principles (GAAP), is essential to determining the relevant cash flows. To calculate capital cost allowance (CCA), assets are pooled into designated asset classes (pools), each with a prescribed maximum CCA rate, which is usually applied on a declining balance. The Act mandates that when an asset is put-in-use during a year, only one-half of its capital cost can be added to the pool in that year, with the remaining one-half entering in the year after.

For all three parts of the cash flow stream—initial, operating, and ending—it is necessary to determine the incremental (new minus old) after-tax cash flows. Failure to do so results in an incomplete and faulty analysis. We must also recognize that the opportunity cost of capital already takes into account expected inflation. Failure to incorporate the effect of inflation in the cash flow stream therefore leads to biased figures, and possibly wrong decisions. Financing costs are not incorporated into the cash flow stream; the investment, or capital budgeting, decision and the financing decision are normally made separately. If that is impossible, then techniques discussed in Appendix 8A should be employed.

CORPORATE TAXES

Before we can evaluate expansion or replacement projects using net present value, we must understand how corporations treat depreciation and taxes under the Income Tax Act, and what impact this has on accurately estimating the relevant cash flows for an investment project. The first and most important point to remember is that what matters is the actual depreciation and tax provisions built into the Income Tax Act. Do not be led astray by what is used for GAAP purposes. Only what firms do as required by Revenue Canada is important—because it directly affects the taxes paid, and hence the cash flows of the firm.

CAPITAL COST ALLOWANCE

Depreciation for tax purposes is called **capital cost allowance (CCA)**. Under GAAP the purpose of depreciation is to match revenue and associated expenses in the same period. This is not the purpose of capital cost allowance. CCA represents that portion of the total cost of depreciable assets that Revenue Canada allows a business to subtract from its revenue in arriving at taxable income for a year, when filing its tax return.

Under the CCA method all depreciable assets are grouped into prescribed classes. The Income Tax Act mandates 44 different asset classes for grouping depreciable assets. Each class has a designated maximum **CCA rate** that is applied to the **undepreciated capital cost (UCC)** of the class at the end of each year. The UCC is analogous to "net fixed assets" in GAAP and is defined as the total cost of all assets in a class minus the accumulated CCA for that class. If, during a year, an asset is put-in-use, the regulations prescribe that only one-half of the capital cost of the asset is added to the UCC of the other assets, if any, in the same class. The remaining 50 percent is added to the pool (class) in the year after the asset is put-in-use. For most asset classes, the Income Tax Act permits only the declining balance method in calculating CCA. This is different from GAAP, under which firms may employ various depreciation methods and apply them on an individual asset basis. Another difference between capital cost allowance and GAAP accounting depreciation is that in accounting the firm often takes the original cost of the equipment and then subtracts the estimated salvage value before determining the per year depreciation. However, *under the Income Tax Act any estimated salvage value is irrelevant when determining CCA; the original value of any asset is not reduced by the estimated salvage value.* Table 8.1 shows some of the most common asset classes and their maximum CCA rates.

The following example will be used to show how CCA is calculated. Atlantic Region Trucking Company Ltd. is starting up business and has just purchased and put-in-use its first truck for $25,000. According to Table 8.1, this truck falls into class 10, with a CCA rate of 30 percent. The $25,000 represents the total or **capital cost** of the truck and includes such things as legal fees, delivery and setup costs, and so on. Table 8.2 shows the yearly CCA calculations for Atlantic.

Table 8.2 points out an important feature of the CCA method. That is, because it employs the declining balance method, an existing asset or class of assets cannot be

Table 8.1

Common Capital Cost Allowance Classes

The Income Tax Act mandates that all depreciable assets must be put into one of 44 asset classes. Each class also has a maximum CCA rate prescribed.

Class 3 (CCA rate 5%):	Most buildings acquired after 1987
Class 6 (CCA rate 10%):	Fences, most greenhouses, and frame buildings
Class 7 (CCA rate 15%):	Canoes, rowboats, and most other vessels
Class 8 (CCA rate 20%):	Assets not included in other classes
Class 9 (CCA rate 25%):	Aircraft
Class 10 (CCA rate 30%):	Vans, trucks, and tractors; personal computers
Class 12 (CCA rate 100%):	Chinaware, cutlery, or other tableware; computer software
Class 16 (CCA rate 40%):	Taxicabs and rental cars
Class 17 (CCA rate 8%):	Roads, etc.
Class 38 (CCA rate 30%):	Most power-operated movable equipment acquired after 1987 used for moving, excavating
Class 39 (CCA rate 25%):	Machinery and equipment acquired after 1987 that is used in Canada primarily to manufacture and process goods for sale or lease
Class 43 (CCA rate 30%):	Manufacturing and processing machinery and equipment acquired after February 25, 1992, described in class 39 above

Source: T2 Corporation Income Tax Guide, Revenue Canada.

fully written off. Thus, the CCA and UCC are shown extending to year n. Although Table 8.2 shows the maximum yearly CCA, Atlantic is not required to charge this entire amount if, for example, it is already in a loss position.

As long as there is only one asset in the pool, as there is here, the calculations for CCA and UCC in Table 8.2 can be written as the following equations:

$$UCC_n = \begin{cases} \dfrac{1}{2}C & \text{for } n = 1 \\[2ex] C\left(1 - \dfrac{d}{2}\right)(1-d)^{n-1} & \text{for } n \geq 2 \end{cases} \tag{8.1}$$

$$CCA_n = d(UCC_n) \tag{8.2}$$

where

UCC_n = UCC at the *beginning* of year n[1]
CCA_n = CCA for year n
C = Capital cost of asset
d = CCA rate

---

[1] UCC_n may also be interpreted as the UCC in year n just before the CCA for year n is calculated.

Table 8.2

CCA Calculations for Atlantic

Only one-half of the capital cost of an asset is added to the appropriate pool in the year it is put-in-use; the remaining half is added in the subsequent year. Because the CCA calculations must be done on the declining balance, an asset or pool of assets can never be fully written off.

Year 1

$\frac{1}{2}$ capital cost $12,500

$CCA_1 = \$12,500 \times 0.3$ (3,750)

UCC end of year 1   8,750

Year 2

Add: $\frac{1}{2}$ capital cost   12,500

UCC beginning of year 2   21,250

$CCA_2 = \$21,250 \times 0.3$ (6,375)

UCC end of year 2   14,875

Year 3

$CCA_3 = \$14,875 \times 0.3$ (4,463)

UCC end of year 3 $10,412

$\vdots$

Year n

$CCA_n = $ UCC end of $n - 1 \times 0.3$

UCC end of year $n = (UCC_{end\,of\,n-1} - CCA_n)$

There are two things you must recognize to use the preceding equations properly:

1. These equations apply only when there is one asset in the pool.
2. The ending UCC of one year is the beginning UCC of the next year. Thus, when you want to calculate UCC at the end of year 1, you calculate it for the beginning of year 2, using Equation 8.1.

With these two caveats in mind, we can use these equations to calculate the values in Table 8.2:

$$UCC_1 = \frac{1}{2}C = \frac{1}{2}(\$25,000) = \$12,500$$

$$CCA_1 = d(UCC_1) = 0.3 \times \$12,500 = \$3,750$$

$$UCC_2 = C\left(1 - \frac{d}{2}\right)(1 - d)^0 = \$25,000\left(1 - \frac{0.3}{2}\right) = \$21,250$$

$$CCA_2 = d(UCC_2) = 0.3(\$21,250) = \$6,375$$

Acquisition and Sale of Assets   If a single asset from a pool (asset class) is sold, the lesser of the net proceeds from the sale (sales price minus any costs) or the capital cost of the asset is deducted from the pool's presale UCC to arrive at the year-end UCC.

For example, suppose after one year of business Atlantic Ltd. is booming, so it decides to buy and put-in-service another truck for a total cost of $35,000 in year 2 and to sell its original truck in year 3 for $7,000. Remember that only one-half of the $35,000 cost of the new truck is used in calculating the CCA for the put-in-use year; and because the capital cost of the first truck was $25,000, the net proceeds from its sale ($7,000) must be deducted from the pool in year 3. Table 8.3 shows the relevant calculations.

If Atlantic had both bought and sold an asset from the same class in the same year (i.e., replaced an asset) it would have had to apply the **50% Rule**. This rule states that, in the replacement year, one-half of the **net acquisitions** (i.e., capital costs of the new asset minus the lesser of capital cost or net proceeds of sale from the old asset) is added to the beginning of the year UCC. The remaining 50 percent of the net acquisitions is added to the pool in the following year. Thus, if Atlantic had replaced the original truck with the new truck in year 2, the net acquisitions would have been $28,000 ($35,000 − $7,000), and the CCA for years 2 and 3 would be as shown in Table 8.4.

Note that the full amount of truck 1 must enter the pool; therefore, in year 2 the remaining 50 percent of truck 1 ($12,500) is added to the pool along with one-half

---

Table 8.3

CCA Calculations for Atlantic With New Acquisition and Sale of Assets

When an asset is sold, the lesser of its capital cost or net proceeds from its sale must be deducted from the pool in the year the asset is sold.

Year 1	
$\frac{1}{2}$ capital cost truck 1	$12,500
$CCA_1 = \$12,500 \times 0.3$	(3,750)
UCC end of year 1	8,750
Year 2	
Add: $\frac{1}{2}$ capital cost truck 1 +	
$\frac{1}{2}$ capital cost truck 2	
$= \$12,500 + \$17,500$	30,000
UCC beginning of year 2	38,750
$CCA_2 = \$38,750 \times 0.3$	(11,625)
UCC end of year 2	27,125
Year 3	
Add: $\frac{1}{2}$ capital cost truck 2	17,500
Deduct: Proceeds from sale truck 1	(7,000)
UCC beginning of year 3	37,625
$CCA_3 = \$37,625 \times 0.3$	(11,288)
UCC end of year 3	$26,337

Table 8.4	

CCA Calculations for Atlantic When the Original Truck Is Replaced in Year 2

When assets are replaced the 50% Rule must be used.

UCC end of year 1 (from Table 8.3)	$ 8,750
Year 2	
Add: $\frac{1}{2}$ capital cost truck 1 +	
$\frac{1}{2}$ net acquisition	
= $12,500 + $14,000	26,500
UCC beginning of year 2	35,250
CCA$_2$ = $35,250 × 0.3	(10,575)
UCC end of year 2	24,675
Year 3	
Add: $\frac{1}{2}$ net acquisition	14,000
UCC beginning of year 3	38,675
CCA$_3$ = $38,675 × 0.3	(11,602)
UCC end of year 3	$ 27,073

of the net acquisitions. If the firm were faced with a situation in which the lower of the cost or net proceeds of the replaced asset were greater than the purchase price of the new asset, the 50% Rule would not apply. In this case the difference between the lower of the cost or net proceeds and the purchase price would be subtracted from the beginning of the year UCC.

Table 8.5 shows the Revenue Canada schedule that must be used to calculate CCA. All of the calculations made in Tables 8.2, 8.3, and 8.4 would be made with this schedule. In an attempt to reduce errors in annual CCA calculations, column 11 of Table 8.5 actually represents the UCC at the beginning of the subsequent year. Thus, if you were using this schedule to recalculate the information in Table 8.2, the amount that would appear in this column would be $21,250—the amount that we show in Table 8.2, under year 2, as "UCC beginning of year 2." If you use the form, the second half of the capital cost or net acquisition cost of the asset(s) is automatically added to the pool and allows you to carry the figure from this column to column 2 of the schedule for the subsequent year, thus eliminating the possibility of not adding the second half of any transaction to the pool. You may find it beneficial to recalculate some of the numbers in Tables 8.2, 8.3, and 8.4 by using Table 8.5.

Terminating a Pool of Assets   When a firm sells off all of the assets in a pool (class) it has terminated that pool. In this case, the firm must subtract the lesser of the net proceeds or the total capital costs of *all assets in the pool* from the UCC of the class at the time of disposition. After this is done, the UCC balance for the pool may be positive even though there are no assets in the pool. In this case, the positive UCC is known as a **terminal loss**. It results because the firm has not taken enough CCA for the pool over

Table 8.5

Capital Cost Allowance Schedule

This table provides the Revenue Canada schedule that must be used by businesses to calculate the CCA deduction for a given year.

Revenue Canada　**Revenu Canada**
Taxation　　　　**Impôt**

Capital Cost Allowance (CCA)

For more information, see the section called "Capital Cost Allowance" in the *T2 Corporation Income Tax Guide*.

Name of corporation							Account number		Taxation year-end		
									Day　Month　Year		
1	**2**	**3**	**4**	**5**	**6**	**7**	**8**	**9**	**10**		**11**
Class number	Undepreciated capital cost at the beginning of the year (column 11 from last year's T2S(8))	Cost of acquisitions during the year (new property must be available for use Note 1	Adjustments (show negative amounts in brackets) Note 2	Proceeds of dispositions during the year (amount not to exceed the capital cost)	Undepreciated capital cost (column 2 plus column 3 plus or minus column 4 minus column 5)	50% rule (deduct 1/2 of the amount, if any, by which the net cost of acquisitions exceeds column 5) Note 3	Reduced undepreciated capital cost (column 6 minus column 7)	CCA rate %	Capital cost allowance (column 8 multiplied by column 9; or a lower amount) Note 4		Undepreciated capital cost at the end of the year (column 6 minus column 10)
									Total		

Note 1.　Include any property acquired in previous years that has now become available for use. This property would have been previously excluded from column 3.

Note 2.　In addition to the other adjustments, include as negative adjustments any GST input tax credits or rebates claimed in the year for property acquired, and include as positive adjustments any amounts repaid in the year for GST input tax credits previously deducted

Note 3.　The net cost of acquisitions is the cost of acquisitions from column 4, except for investment tax credits the corporation claimed in the previous taxation year.

Note 4.　If the taxation year is shorter than 365 days, prorate the CCA claim. See the T2 Guide for more information.

Source: Schedule T2S(8), Revenue Canada.

Table 8.6

Example of Asset Sales

Upon the sale of one or all assets in a pool, the lesser of its (their) capital cost or net proceeds must be deducted from the pool. A negative UCC results in CCA recapture and is taxed as regular income. If all assets are sold and the resulting UCC is positive, this represents a terminal loss and can be used as an expense to offset income in the year it is incurred. A capital gain occurs when one or more assets are sold for more than their original cost.

Scenario	1	2	3	4	5
UCC before	$82,500	$82,500	$82,500	$82,500	$82,500
Asset(s) sold:					
Capital cost	35,000	85,000	117,000	117,000	117,000
Proceeds	12,000	90,000	100,000	50,000	135,000
Capital gains	0	5,000	0	0	18,000
UCC after					
transaction	70,500	−2,500	−17,500	32,500	−34,500
Terminal loss	0	0	0	32,500	0
CCA recapture	0	2,500	17,500	0	34,500
Ending UCC	$70,500	0	0	0	0

the years. Consequently, the firm's taxable income was overstated and it paid too much in taxes. Therefore, the terminal loss is used as an expense to offset income in the tax year in which the termination of the pool takes place. On the other hand, if there is a negative UCC—that is, if the lesser of the proceeds from the sale or the total capital cost of all assets in the pool is greater than the prior UCC—we have what is called a **CCA recapture**. This means that the firm has taken too much CCA for the pool and, thus, underreported its taxable income and underpaid its taxes. Therefore the recaptured amount must be taken into regular income during the termination year.

If the firm sells all of the assets in the pool for more than their total capital cost, it incurs a **capital gain**.[2] In this case the total capital cost is subtracted from the pool, and the resulting negative UCC is closed off to a CCA recapture. In addition, the amount by which the net proceeds exceed the total capital cost is a capital gain and is taxed accordingly. It should be noted, however, that a CCA recapture may occur even if the pool is not terminated. This occurs when the lesser of the proceeds from the sale of some of the assets in the pool or their total original cost is greater than the beginning of the year UCC plus the amounts of any additions made during the year.

Table 8.6 represents an example that summarizes our disposition of assets discussion. Here a firm purchased a number of assets in a single class some time ago for $117,000, and at the beginning of the current year this pool of assets has a UCC of $82,500. Five different scenarios are presented.

Under scenario 1, the firm sells a single asset, whose original capital cost was $35,000, for $12,000. We must always subtract the lower of net proceeds or capital

---

[2] Capital gains and their taxation are discussed in the next section.

costs. So in this case we subtract the $12,000, leaving the UCC after the transaction at $70,500. In scenario 2, the firm sells some assets that had an original cost of $85,000 for $90,000. Here $85,000 is deducted from the pool, leaving a negative UCC after the transaction of $2,500. Here, although the pool is not terminated, there is a negative UCC after the transaction that must be closed off to a recapture and taxed as ordinary income. In addition, the difference between the net proceeds and the capital cost ($5,000) is recognized as a capital gain and taxed accordingly. In scenarios 3, 4, and 5, the asset pool is terminated. In scenario 3, all of the assets are sold for $100,000. Because the original capital cost of all assets in the pool was $117,000, we must subtract $100,000 from the beginning UCC. This leaves a negative UCC after the transaction of $17,500, which represents a CCA recapture and is taxed as regular income. In scenario 4, all of the assets are sold for $50,000; this results in a $32,500 ($82,500 − $50,000) positive UCC afterward. This represents a terminal loss and will be used as a tax-deductible expense during the termination year. Finally, in scenario 5, all of the assets are sold for $135,000. This results in a negative UCC afterward of $34,500 ($82,500 − $117,000), which is a recapture and is taxed as regular income. In addition, there is a capital gain of $18,000 ($135,000 − $117,000), which will be taxed accordingly.

OTHER IMPORTANT PROVISIONS OF THE INCOME TAX ACT

Corporate Tax Rates   Corporations pay taxes on taxable income to both the federal and provincial governments and are required to pay their income taxes in monthly instalments. Taxable income may be defined as

$$\text{Taxable income} = \text{revenue} - \text{expenses} - \text{CCA} \qquad (8.3)$$

The federal corporate tax rates applied to taxable income in 1995 are as follows:[3]

Basic corporations	28
Manufacturing and processing	21
Small basic corporations	12
Small manufacturing and processing	12

The provincial tax rates on corporate income range from 8.9 percent in Quebec to 17 percent in Manitoba, New Brunswick, and Saskatchewan, and are added to the total federal rate. For example, the maximum total (federal and provincial) corporate tax rate for 1995 is 45 percent (0.28 + 0.17).

The preceding tax rates show that there is a significant difference between the federal tax rate for large and small corporate incomes. Currently, the small-business tax rate is applicable to the first $200,000 of taxable income for *all* Canadian-controlled

---

[3] There are also a 4 percent Corporate Surtax and a 0.225 percent Large Corporation Tax, which we do not consider in our discussion.

private corporations. The total small-business tax rate is obtained by adding the provincial small-business tax rates, which vary from 5 to 10 percent, to the 12 percent federal small-business rate. Consequently, the maximum tax rate on the first $200,000 of taxable income for a Canadian-controlled private corporation is 22 percent $(0.12 + 0.10)$; on the remainder, it is 45 percent. Although this "small-business" tax rate actually applies to all Canadian-controlled private corporations, its impact on large corporations is relatively insignificant. Thus, the marginal tax rate, to be applied to taxable income, may be thought of as ranging from 36 to 45 percent for large corporations and from 17 to 22 percent for small corporations.

Dividends and Interest Earned or Paid   Aside from the revenue generated from normal operations, a firm may also receive income in the form of dividends, if it owns the stock of another firm, or interest, if it owns corporate or government bonds. In general, dividends and interest *earned* by a corporation are fully taxable. However, the dividends received from another taxable Canadian corporation are 100 percent tax-exempt; that is, corporations pay no taxes on dividends received from other taxable Canadian firms. On the other hand, interest *paid* on bonds and loans outstanding is considered an expense of doing business and is, therefore, fully deductible, as is any other operating expense, in arriving at taxable income. However, dividends *paid* on stock (both common and preferred) and interest paid on income bonds[4] do not serve as deductions.

Capital Gains   A capital gain occurs when a firm sells financial assets (such as stocks and bonds) or depreciable assets for more than it paid for them. On the other hand, a capital loss is incurred when the firm sells a financial asset for less than its purchase price; however, as we saw in our discussion of CCA, selling a depreciable asset for less than its purchase price does not result in a capital loss. In any given year, capital gains are reduced by capital losses to arrive at net capital gains. Currently, net capital gains are taxed at three-quarters of the firm's marginal rate.

Tax Loss Carryback and Carryforward   A firm incurs an **operating** or **noncapital loss** when its allowable expenses and deductions exceed its revenues. Noncapital losses incurred in a given year can be used (carried back) to reduce *all types* of income (including capital gains) for the three immediately previous years. If all of these losses cannot be applied to the three previous years, the remaining amount can be used (carried forward) to reduce *all types* of future income for seven years from the year of origin. Any noncapital loss that is not used at the end of the seventh year cannot be used at any future date.

   Capital gains and capital losses were discussed in a previous section. There we saw that the capital losses of a given year must be used to offset capital gains in the same year. This may result in a net capital loss, which may be carried back to offset *only* capital gains in the three immediately preceding years. Any unapplied capital losses can be carried forward indefinitely to offset future capital gains.

---

[4] An income bond is a bond that requires interest to be paid only if the firm has the funds to do so.

Concept Review Questions

- How much is added to the asset class in the year that an asset is put-in-use?
- What is deducted from the pool when an asset is sold?
- How is a terminal loss treated when a firm is filing its income tax return?
- What is the difference in the treatment of dividends paid and interest paid for tax purposes?
- How is a capital gain incurred?

HOW TO ESTIMATE THE RELEVANT CASH FLOWS

Three points should be mentioned in connection with estimating cash flows: First, we are interested in cash flows (both inflows and outflows) as stated on an *after-tax basis*. Because taxes are an important determinant of cash flows, we are interested in looking at cash flows after all taxes have been taken into account. These are called cash flows after tax (CF), to distinguish them from cash flows before tax (CFBT). Second, we must guard against carelessly counting costs or benefits that should not be considered. A classic example is the treatment by accountants of certain overhead costs. If these overhead costs are fixed and their total amount does not change as a result of implementing a project, they do not affect the cash flows and are irrelevant for decision-making purposes. Finally, it is helpful to divide the cash flow stream into three segments:

1. The initial investment is the net after-tax cash outflow that typically occurs at the start (i.e., at time t = 0) of the project under consideration.
2. The operating cash flows are the relevant net after-tax cash flows expected over the economic life of the project.
3. The ending cash flow is the net after-tax inflow or outflow that occurs when the project is completed.

First we will consider the cash flow stream for a simple decision in which a firm is expanding, not replacing, existing assets. Then we will consider the relevant incremental cash flows for replacement decisions.

THE INITIAL INVESTMENT

The **initial investment, CF_0,** is the net after-tax cash flow that occurs at time zero. For an expansion project, it is calculated as follows:

  Cost of equipment, facilities, and land purchased

+ All other costs related to the investment (transportation, installation, additional personnel, training expenses, and so forth)

+ Additional **net working capital** required[5]
+ Opportunity costs, net of taxes (e.g., land used for this project that could have been sold to net after-capital-gains tax revenue)

Althouth the initial investment in many complex projects is spread over a number of years, for simplicity we treat it as occurring at the present ($t = 0$). When after-tax cash outflows occur beyond time $t = 0$, they are treated like other CFs, except that the negative sign is retained.

OPERATING CASH FLOWS

The second part of the cash flow stream, **operating cash flows (CFs)**, are the net cash flows that occur while the asset is in operation. They begin in year 1 and continue throughout the project's useful or **economic life**.[6] These operating cash flows are typically positive, although there may be occasional years when the outflows are greater than the inflows. Operating cash flows are calculated by taking the difference in the cash inflows minus the cash outflows, to provide the cash flow before tax (CFBT) attributable to the proposed project. Capital cost allowance (CCA) then enters into the picture, because it is a deductible expense for tax purposes and serves to reduce taxes.

To illustrate the calculation of operating cash flows for an expansion project, consider Warner Manufacturing, a firm that is in the process of evaluating a new project. The firm estimates that the project's annual before-tax cash inflows and outflows will be $50 million and $38 million, respectively. Furthermore, assume that the firm will be able to claim $6 million in CCA each year of the project's life and that the firm's marginal tax rate is 40 percent. Consequently, the firm will incur $2.4 million [i.e., ($50 − $38 − $6)(0.40)] in taxes directly attributable to the project in each of the next three years. One method of calculating the annual after-tax operating cash flows for the project is

$$\text{operating CF}_t = (\text{cash inflows}_t - \text{cash outflows}_t) - \text{taxes}_t$$
$$= \text{CFBT}_t - \text{taxes}_t \tag{8.4}$$

where CFBT_t is the **cash flow before tax (CFBT)**. Applying this to Warner's project, we have

$$\text{operating CF}_t = (\$50 \text{ million} - \$38 \text{ million}) - \$2.4 \text{ million} = \$9.6 \text{ million}$$

---

[5] Net working capital is the difference between current assets and current liabilities such as accounts payable and accruals. Often a project requires an increase in accounts receivable or inventory, say by $300,000, while at the same time causing a spontaneous increase in accounts payable of, perhaps, $100,000. The additional net working capital attributable to the project would be $200,000. At the end of the project's life the additional net working capital is no longer needed, and current assets and current liabilities may return to normal levels.

[6] This assumes that the project is the only asset in its class and that the class is not being continued at the end of this project.

Another calculation that highlights the impact of taxes and the tax shield arising from CCA recognizes that

$$\text{taxes}_t = (\text{CFBT}_t - \text{CCA}_t)\text{T} \tag{8.5}$$

where T is the firm's marginal tax rate. Substituting Equation 8.5 into Equation 8.4, we get

$$
\begin{aligned}
\text{operating CF}_t &= \text{CFBT}_t - (\text{CFBT}_t - \text{CCA}_t)\text{T} \\
&= \text{CFBT}_t - \text{CFBT}_t(\text{T}) + \text{CCA}_t(\text{T}) \\
&= \text{CFBT}_t(1 - \text{T}) + \text{CCA}_t(\text{T})
\end{aligned} \tag{8.6}
$$

The second part of Equation 8.6—that is, $\text{CCA}_t(\text{T})$—is the CCA (depreciation) tax shield. Because CCA is a tax-deductible expense, even though no cash outflow occurs at the time of the CCA charge, the presence of CCA allows firms to reduce their income taxes. That is, they receive a "tax shield" due to CCA. Equation 8.6 can be employed directly to calculate the **cash flows after tax (CF)**. Applying it to Warner, we have

$$
\begin{aligned}
\text{operating CF}_t &= (\$50 \text{ million} - \$38 \text{ million})(1 - 0.40) + \$6 \text{ million}(0.40) \\
&= \$12 \text{ million}(0.60) + \$6 \text{ million}(0.40) \\
&= \$7.2 \text{ million} + \$2.4 \text{ million} = \$9.6 \text{ million}
\end{aligned}
$$

In calculating CCA, remember that land cannot be depreciated and sometimes there are opportunity costs that have to be considered as part of the operating cash flows.

Opportunity Costs   Opportunity costs also have to be taken into consideration. For example, suppose a firm is analyzing a project that would employ warehouse space currently being rented out for $4,800 a year. If the company decides to expand, it loses the benefit of $4,800 per year in rental income. If the firm has a marginal tax rate of 40 percent, the loss in after-tax cash inflows of $2,880 [i.e., $4,800(1 − 0.40)] is an opportunity cost and must be deducted from each year's operating cash flows. Similarly, if a car manufacturer decides to market a new model, sales of the firm's other models may decline. The decline in after-tax cash inflows due to reduced sales of the other models is an opportunity cost of the new model.

Sunk Costs   Equally important is the notion of **sunk costs**—that is, cash outflows that have already been incurred and therefore do not affect the decision. For example, suppose a firm spent $200,000 two years ago for a detailed feasibility study by some consultants about the possibility of doubling the size of their present physical plant. No action was taken then, but now the firm is reassessing the project. Should the $200,000 be included as a cash outflow of the project for capital budgeting purposes? The answer is no. Sunk costs should be ignored; they are not incremental cash flows that are relevant for decision making.

ENDING CASH FLOW

Ending cash flows are the net after-tax cash flows other than the operating cash flows that occur in the last year of the project's life. For an expansion project, they are calculated as

> Funds realized from the sale of the asset plus a tax benefit if it is expected to be sold at a loss, or minus a tax liability if it is expected to be sold at a gain[7]

+   Release of net working capital

−   Disposal costs (net of taxes)

The ending cash flow typically is positive, but it may be negative.

THOSE HARD-TO-ESTIMATE COSTS AND BENEFITS

Some costs and benefits are inherently more difficult to estimate than others. For example, how do you estimate the benefits (and the costs, for that matter) from implementing a total quality management (TQM) system? Or, if your firm is taking advantage of new developments in information technology, how do you estimate the costs and benefits likely to result from such an investment? If you introduce a new technology-driven information system, it will be thoroughly intertwined with the firm's operations. In addition to the direct costs associated with computers and software, the firm may need to consider its business strategy, faster product cycles, potential reorganization of operations and divisions, changes in the number and types of employees, improved job training, and many other factors.

Alternatively, there are other possible items such as potential legal costs and loss in value of the firm arising from product liability lawsuits, manufacturing pollution, and the impact of closing a plant on the welfare of its employees and the neighbourhood in which the plant is located. For firms operating multinationally, what are the costs associated with the mountains of toxic waste that burgeoning industrialization is creating in developing countries? Are these costs that firms need to consider directly in determining the relevant cash flows for capital budgeting, or should they ignore them until governments act and they are forced to pay for maintaining the environment?

None of these issues are easy to address. Because of the uncertainties involved, and the nonfirm-specific nature of some of the issues, the quantification of the costs and benefits increases in complexity, while confidence in the estimates decreases. In such cases, firms can consider two general approaches. First, they can ignore quantifying the costs and benefits and simply make seat-of-the-pants decisions. Second, they can quantify the costs and benefits—even if with a great deal of uncertainty—and then make sure that the decision makers are fully aware of the level of uncertainty in the

---

[7] Assuming the firm is profitable, a tax benefit will occur only if the asset is the sole asset in its class and the asset is going to be sold for an amount that will result in a terminal loss, whereas a tax liability will occur only if the project is the sole asset in its class and the asset is going to be sold for an amount that results in a CCA recapture and/or a capital gain.

estimates. We strongly recommend the second approach: Quantify what you can, communicate all of the assumptions and uncertainties to the decision makers, and then deal with the nonquantifiable factors. This way, the capital budgeting process can provide the best possible basis for making informed, value-maximizing decisions.

AN EXPANSION PROJECT EXAMPLE

Before we present detailed calculations to evaluate projects, recall that because the CCA deduction is calculated on a declining balance of a pool of assets, and not a single asset, a firm is able to receive CCA deductions and thus cash flows from a project *even after the project has been disposed of.* In fact, these cash flows will occur in perpetuity providing that there are other assets in the class subsequent to the disposition of the project and that it is disposed of for less than its UCC. We shall assume this to be the case in the examples that follow. If this were not the case, a terminal loss, CCA recapture, and/or capital gain would occur at the termination date of the project, and therefore no subsequent cash flows would be received.

To refine our understanding of the capital budgeting process, let us consider an expansion project. Ideal Industries is contemplating the purchase of a fleet of automobiles for $117,000. In addition, Ideal will have to pay a $3,000 delivery and handling fee to acquire the automobiles. The automobiles will be part of an already existing Class 10 pool of assets that has a CCA rate of 30 percent. This pool of assets is critical to the firm's existence and must be retained permanently.

The new automobiles are to be used by Ideal's sales force and are expected to increase efficiency. They are considered to have a useful life of three years with a net resale value of $15,000 at the end of that time. The cash inflows and outflows are $85,000 and $20,000 per year, respectively. The firm's marginal tax rate is 40 percent, and its opportunity cost of capital is 14 percent. Should Ideal buy the new automobiles? To answer this question we follow the steps outlined previously, by calculating the (1) initial investment, (2) operating cash flows, (3) ending cash flows, and (4) NPV of the project.

STEP 1: *Initial Investment.* There are no opportunity costs or increases in working capital required by this project; therefore the initial investment required is the sum of the cost of the fleet and its delivery fee. Consequently,

$$\text{Initial investment, } CF_0 = \$117,000 + \$3,000 = \$120,000$$

STEP 2: *Operating Cash Flows.* To calculate operating cash flows we must first calculate the annual CCA deductions and tax shields associated with the new fleet. Table 8.7 shows these calculations. The table also shows that the UCC at the end of the project's useful life (year 3) is $49,980. At that time the fleet will be sold to net the firm $15,000. Because the lower of the capital cost of the fleet ($120,000) or net proceeds ($15,000) must be deducted from the pool, the UCC at the beginning of year 4 is $34,980 ($49,980 − $15,000). Thus, even though the new fleet no longer exists, the declining balance method allows the firm to obtain CCA deductions and tax shields indefinitely into the future.

Table 8.7

Expansion Problem
: Annual CCA and Tax Shields

Because the new fleet is sold at the end of its useful life for less than its UCC, the firm is able to obtain CCA deductions and tax shields indefinitely.

Year	UCC	CCA = UCC × 0.30	Ending UCC = UCC − CCA	Tax Shields = T(CCA)
1	$ 60,000.00[a]	$18,000.00	$42,000.00	$ 7,200.00
2	102,000.00	30,600.00	71,400.00	12,240.00
3	71,400.00	21,420.00	49,980.00	8,568.00
4	34,980.00[b]	10,494.00	24,486.00	4,197.60
5	24,486.00	7,345.80	17,140.20	2,938.32
6	17,140.20	5,142.06	11,998.14	2,056.82
↓	↓	↓	↓	↓
∞	0	0	0	0

[a] Only one-half of the capital cost is added to the preacquisition UCC of the pool in year 1; the remainder is added in year 2.
[b] $49,980 − net proceeds = $49,980 − $15,000 = $34,980

Now we can use Equation 8.6 to calculate the annual operating cash flows, CF, which represent the relevant after-tax cash flows generated by the project. Table 8.8 shows these calculations. We see that the operating cash flow generated by the project extends indefinitely beyond the disposition of the new fleet. Therefore, when evaluating the attractiveness of a project, the entire operating cash flow

Table 8.8

Expansion Problem: Annual Operating Cash Flows

This approach emphasizes the operating cash flows as being equal to the CFBT(1 − T) + CCA(T). Because the CFs continue after the disposition of a project, the entire CF stream must enter the analysis, not simply those over the project's useful life.

Year	Cash Inflows	− Cash Outflows =	CFBT	CFBT × (1 − T)[a] +	CCA(T)[b] =	CF
1	$85,000	$20,000	$65,000	$39,000	$ 7,200.00	$46,200.00
2	85,000	20,000	65,000	39,000	12,240.00	51,240.00
3	85,000	20,000	65,000	39,000	8,568.00	47,568.00
4	—	—			4,197.00	4,197.60
5	—	—			2,938.00	2,938.32
6	—	—			2,056.82	2,056.82
↓					↓	↓
∞					0	0

[a] The tax rate is 40 percent.
[b] From Table 8.7.

stream must be considered, not only those cash flows occurring over the useful life of the project.

STEP 3:   *Ending Cash Flows.* Because the class 10 pool of assets will continue after the proposed fleet is disposed of, there are no tax benefits or liabilities to be considered. There is also no release of working capital to be considered, because undertaking this project did not require any increase in working capital. Therefore the ending cash flow (ECF) represents only the **net resale value** of $15,000 expected to be received by the firm at the end of year 3.

STEP 4:   *NPV of the Project.* NPV represents the present value (PV) of all cash inflows generated by the project minus its initial investment. Therefore, we can write the equation for NPV as

$$
\begin{aligned}
\text{NPV} = {}& \text{PV of after-tax cash operating income} \\
& + \text{PV of CCA tax shields} + \text{PV of ending cash flows} \qquad (8.7) \\
& - \text{initial investment}
\end{aligned}
$$

The only part of this equation to present a problem is the PV of the CCA tax shields, because these tax shields represent an infinite stream, as was seen in Table 8.7. However, the present value of this perpetual stream of CCA tax shields can be written as[8]

$$
\begin{array}{l}
\text{present value of} \\
\text{CCA tax shields}
\end{array}
=
\left[\frac{TdC_0}{k + d}\right]\left[\frac{1 + 0.5k}{1 + k}\right]
-
\left[\frac{1}{(1 + k)^n}\right]\left[\frac{Td(RV)}{k + d}\right]
\qquad (8.8)
$$

where

T = the firm's marginal tax rate

d = CCA rate

C_0 = capital cost of the asset. This represents the total cost of the project that can be added to the asset class in order to calculate CCA. It does not necessarily equal the initial investment—for example, if the project requires additions to working capital.

k = the opportunity cost of capital

RV = net resale value of the project at the end of its useful life. This may differ from ending cash flows if, for example, working capital is released by the project.

n = the useful life of the project

The first part of Equation 8.8 (i.e., to the left of the minus sign) represents the present value of all tax shields that would derive from the project if it were never

---

[8] There is a good deal of discussion about the appropriate discount rate to use when finding the present value of the CCA tax shield. Some argue that once the asset is purchased, there is no uncertainty about the CCA, and hence, the CCA tax shield is riskless. Accordingly, a risk-free discount rate should be employed. Two issues are important. First, firms are not always profitable and hence may not always be certain of receiving the benefits of the CCA tax shield. Second, Parliament can and does change the Income Tax Act and capital cost allowances from time to time. We treat all cash flows and tax shields as risky; accordingly we employ the opportunity cost of capital as the appropriate discount rate. The effect, compared to treating the CCA tax shield as risk-free, is a slightly lower net present value.

disposed of, given that only half of the capital cost of the project enters the asset class in the first year and the remaining half in the second year. The second part represents the tax shields that are lost subsequent to selling the project at the end of its useful life for its net resale value. With this equation for the present value of tax shields, we can now rewrite Equation 8.7 as

$$NPV = \sum_{t=1}^{n} \frac{CFBT_t(1-T)}{(1+k)^t} + \left\{ \left[\frac{TdC_0}{k+d} \right] \left[\frac{1+0.5k}{1+k} \right] \right.$$
$$\left. - \left[\frac{1}{(1+k)^n} \right] \left[\frac{Td(RV)}{k+d} \right] \right\} + \frac{ECF}{(1+k)^n} - CF_0 \qquad (8.9)$$

where the additional variables are

$CFBT_t$ = annual operating cash flows before tax (i.e., cash inflows$_t$ − cash outflows$_t$)

ECF = ending cash flows

CF_0 = initial investment or net after-tax cash outflow that occurs at time t = 0

Using information from the previous steps in Equation 8.9 we get

$$NPV = \sum_{t=1}^{n} \frac{\$39,000}{(1.14)^t} + \left\{ \left[\frac{(0.40)(0.30)(\$120,000)}{0.14+0.30} \right] \left[\frac{1.07}{1.14} \right] \right.$$
$$\left. - \left[\frac{1}{(1.14)^3} \right] \left[\frac{(0.40)(0.30)(\$15,000)}{0.14+0.30} \right] \right\} + \frac{\$15,000}{(1.14)^3} - \$120,000$$

$$= \$39,000(PVA_{14\%,\,3yr}) + \{\$30,717.70 - (PV_{14\%,\,3yr})(\$4,090.91)\}$$
$$+ (PV_{14\%,\,3yr})(\$15,000) - \$120,000$$

$$= \$39,000(2.322) + \{\$30,717.70 - (0.675)(\$4,090.91)\}$$
$$+ (0.675)(\$15,000) - \$120,000$$

$$= \$90,558 + \{\$30,717.70 - \$2,761.36\} + \$10,125$$
$$- \$120,000$$

$$= \$8,639.34$$

Because the NPV is positive, Ideal should proceed with the acquisition of the fleet of automobiles. By doing so, Ideal is contributing to an increase in its value. You can think of a firm as a portfolio of projects. The value of the firm is equal to the sum of the projects' NPVs. Acceptance of a positive-NPV project increases the value of the firm; hence, Ideal is contributing to the maximization of its value by accepting the project. (Note: *When using Equation 8.9 to calculate NPV, you do not have to construct tables like Tables 8.7 and 8.8. In order to use Equation 8.9, all you need from step 2 is the value for* $CFBT_t(1-T)$.)

Concept Review Questions

■ What three major segments should be considered when estimating a firm's cash flows?

- Briefly describe how to calculate a project's initial investment.
- How are "operating cash flows" calculated?
- Explain how opportunity costs and sunk costs affect a firm's cash flows.
- What impact do CCA calculations have on a project's operating cash flows?

REPLACEMENT DECISIONS

Replacing assets is often necessary. Determining the cash flows for a replacement project can be complicated. These are incremental cash flows—that is, the cash flows related to the new equipment less the cash flows for the old equipment. While the idea seems straightforward, it is fundamental to effective capital investment decision making.

INCREMENTAL CASH FLOWS

Consider Bits & Bytes, a computer software firm that produces a popular computer game called Spacelords. The firm estimated after-tax operating cash flows (CFS) over a three-year period as follows:

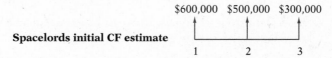

The estimated cash flows decline due to an anticipated increase in competition and the development of more complicated and challenging games. Bits & Bytes planned, therefore, to withdraw Spacelords from the market after three years.

Recently, Bits & Bytes came up with a new computer game called Rampagers. Although similar to Spacelords, Rampagers has many features that make it more challenging. The estimated initial investment and subsequent cash inflows were estimated as follows:

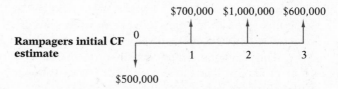

Given the favourable cash flow estimates, Bits & Bytes developed and is now marketing Rampagers. All indications are that the projected CFs appear accurate, but a strange thing is happening—Spacelords sales have fallen off dramatically. What did Bits & Bytes forget to consider when it developed the after-tax CF estimates for Rampagers?

The answer should not surprise you. The two games have overlapping markets, with the result that the products are viewed as being partial *substitutes* for each other.

Instead of buying Spacelords, many would-be purchasers are now acquiring Rampagers, so the cash flows from Spacelords have declined sharply. The newly revised cash flows for Spacelords are

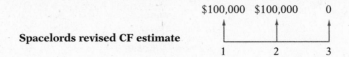

Spacelords revised CF estimate

The problem arose because in making the initial estimate of the CFs attributed to Rampagers, Bits & Bytes did not properly evaluate the incremental cash flows. *It is the incremental (denoted by a delta, Δ) cash flows that are important.* The relevant incremental operating cash flow stream, ΔCF, that Bits & Bytes should have considered before introducing Rampagers is calculated as follows;

	Year		
	1	**2**	**3**
Original CFs, Rampagers	$700,000	$1,000,000	$600,000
Less: Decrease in CFs, Spacelords	500,000	400,000	300,000
Incremental (Δ) operating CFs	$200,000	$ 600,000	$300,000

Based on this more complete analysis, the incremental cash flow stream for the new product should have been estimated as follows:

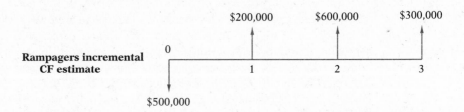

Rampagers incremental CF estimate

Even with this revised set of after-tax CFs, the NPV (at any reasonable discount rate) is positive, so Bits & Bytes should still come out ahead on its investment. But the message is clear: To make effective investment decisions, managers must focus on the incremental cash flow stream. This involves an analysis of the cash inflows and outflows related to the new investment, minus the anticipated inflows and outflows associated with an existing investment.

Often it is important to ask, "What will happen to the existing (or anticipated) cash flows if we do not make the investment?" In today's highly competitive and rapidly changing environment, managers cannot simply assume that existing cash flows will continue. Price cutting, product or marketing innovations, and the like can undermine a profitable investment. For this reason, managers need to know what to look for when calculating incremental cash flows.

ESTIMATING INCREMENTAL CASH FLOWS FOR REPLACEMENT DECISIONS

To calculate incremental after-tax cash flows, we proceed by breaking them into three parts—initial investment, operating cash flow, and ending cash flow. We make our capital budgeting decision by focusing on the difference between the new and the existing cash flows. Any other cash flow stream is erroneous and may lead to incorrect replacement decisions.

The Initial Investment   The incremental initial investment, ΔCF_0, is calculated as follows:[9]

Cost of new equipment, facilities, and land purchased

+   All other costs related to the investment (transportation, installation, additional personnel, and so forth, net of taxes)

+   Additional net working capital required

+   Opportunity costs, net of taxes

−   Funds realized from the sale of replaced assets plus tax benefit if assets are expected to be sold at a loss, or minus tax liability if they are expected to be sold at a gain[10]

As with expansion projects, we assume the initial investment occurs at time t = 0; in practice, however, it may be spread out over a number of time periods.

Operating Cash Flows   The incremental operating after-tax cash flow, ΔCF, must take into consideration the difference in the cash flows before tax, CFBT, for the new and the old projects, as well as the CCA on both the new and the old assets. To calculate the incremental operating cash flows, we have the following:

$$\text{incremental operating CF} = (CFBT_{tnew} - CFBT_{told})(1 - T)$$
$$+ (CCA_{tnew} - CCA_{told})(T) \qquad (8.10)$$
$$\Delta CF_t = \Delta CFBT_t(1 - T) + \Delta CCA(T)$$

The first term, $\Delta CFBT (1 - T)$, is the change in the cash flows expected, ignoring the tax shield due to CCA. The net effect on the tax shield is captured in the second term, $\Delta CCA(T)$. As we saw in the Bits & Bytes example, it is especially important to consider the exact nature of the cash flow before tax (CFBT) stream expected from the old (or existing) asset. Often a good deal of interchange between marketing, production, and the capital budgeting group will be required to arrive at reasonable estimates of both the new and the old CFBT streams. In addition, opportunity costs must also be taken into consideration.

---

[9] In calculating the initial, operating, and ending incremental cash flows, we assume that the firm is profitable and, therefore, taxes are relevant.

[10] The tax implications would arise if the replaced assets are in a different CCA class and that class is terminated for less (more) than its UCC and if the firm is profitable.

Ending Cash Flow   Finally, we need to estimate the incremental after-tax ending cash flow that occurs in the last year of the replacement project's life. The incremental ending after-tax cash flow, ΔECF, is calculated as follows:

> Funds realized from the sale of the new asset plus tax benefit if it is expected to be sold at a loss, or minus tax liability if it is expected to be sold at a profit (i.e., for more than its UCC)[11]

- $+$ Release of net working capital (assuming the project will be terminated at time period n)
- $-$ Disposal costs for new asset (less disposal costs on old asset, if any, net of taxes)
- $-$ Funds realized from the sale of the replaced asset plus tax benefit if it is expected to be sold at a loss, or minus tax liability if it is expected to be sold at a profit (i.e., for more than its UCC)[12]

A REPLACEMENT PROJECT EXAMPLE

Consider Lethbridge Industries, which is contemplating replacing an existing assembly line with a new, automated one. The existing assembly line was installed three years ago at a cost of $500,000; it belongs in CCA Class 8, with a CCA rate of 20 percent. The old equipment will last five more years, at which time its net resale value will be $15,000, but it could be sold now to net the firm $40,000.

The main benefit of the project would be to reduce yearly expenses from $510,000 on the existing line to $200,000 for the newer, automated line. However, the new line would require a $20,000 increase in inventory. The new line would cost $1 million and belong in Class 8. It has a useful life of five years,[13] and its net resale value at the end of this time will be $50,000. Lethbridge's tax rate is 40 percent, and the opportunity cost of capital for this project is 16 percent.

In solving this replacement problem we carry out the four steps shown for the expansion problem; however, now we use incremental values.

STEP 1:   *Incremental Initial Investment.* This amount is calculated as follows:

Cost of new asset	$1,000,000
Less: Net proceeds from sale of old asset	40,000
Incremental capital cost (ΔC_0)	960,000
Add: Increase in working capital (inventory)	20,000
Incremental initial investment (ΔCF_0)	$ 980,000

---

[11] Assuming that the firm is profitable and the asset class is terminated at the end of the project's useful life.

[12] Assuming that the firm is profitable and the replaced asset class is terminated.

[13] For simplicity, the lives of the old and new assembly lines are both five years. If the lives were unequal, the modified approach, discussed in Chapter 7 for projects of unequal lives, must be used.

Note that the incremental capital cost (or net acquisitions), the amount that must be added to the asset pool, is not the same as the incremental initial investment because of the additional net working capital (a nondepreciable item) required by the project.

STEP 2:   *Incremental Operating Cash Flows.* The old assembly line has cash outflows of $510,000 per year, whereas the new one has cash outflows of $200,000 per year. Therefore the yearly incremental before-tax savings, over the life of the project, are calculated as

Old cash outflows	$510,000
Less: New cash outflows	200,000
Incremental before-tax savings (ΔCFBT)	$310,000

Therefore, the incremental after-tax savings, ΔCFBT$(1 - 0.40)$, is $186,000. The construction of tables like Tables 8.7 and 8.8 is left as an exercise. In constructing these tables, remember that only one-half of the incremental cost of $960,000 is added to the pool in year 1, and the remainder is added in year 2. Also remember that the line is sold at the end of year 5. If the old asset were not replaced, the firm would have sold it at this time to net $15,000, but by replacing it with the new assembly line the firm will receive $50,000 as net resale value. Therefore, at the end of the fifth year the firm must deduct the incremental net resale value of $35,000 from the pool.

STEP 3:   *Incremental Ending Cash Flow.* As in the expansion example, the class of assets to which the assembly line belongs is not being terminated at the end of the project's useful life; neither is the replaced nor the new asset sold for more than its UCC. Therefore, there are no tax benefits or liabilities to be considered. Consequently, the incremental ending cash flow is calculated as

Net resale value new asset	$50,000
Less: Net resale value old asset	15,000
Incremental net resale value, ΔRV	35,000
Add: Release of net working capital	20,000
Incremental ending cash flow, ΔECF	$55,000

Thus the incremental net resale value, along with the release of the $20,000 of additional net working capital, is treated as ending cash flow.[14]

---

[14] This assumes that the assembly line is shut down at the end of year 5. In reality, net working capital often is an ongoing commitment and cannot be assumed to be released.

STEP 4: *Calculating NPV of the Project.* The NPV of this project can be calculated by adapting Equation 8.9 to recognize that incremental values must be used for replacement problems, as follows:

$$
\begin{aligned}
NPV = \sum_{t=1}^{n}\left[\frac{\Delta CFBT_t(1-T)}{(1+k)^t}\right] &+ \left\{\left[\frac{Td(\Delta C_0)}{k+d}\right]\left[\frac{1+0.5k}{1+k}\right]\right. \\
&\left.- \left[\frac{1}{(1+k)^n}\right]\left[\frac{Td(\Delta RV)}{k+d}\right]\right\} + \frac{\Delta ECF}{(1+k)^n} - \Delta CF_0
\end{aligned}
$$

(8.11)

Using the data calculated in the previous three steps, we get from Equation 8.11

$$
\begin{aligned}
NPV = \ &\$186,000(PVA_{16\%,\,5yr}) + \left[\frac{(0.40)(0.20)(\$960,000)}{0.16+0.20}\right]\left[\frac{1.08}{1.16}\right] \\
&- (PV_{16\%,\,5yr})\left[\frac{(0.40)(0.20)(\$35,000)}{0.16+0.20}\right] + (PV_{16\%,\,5yr})(\$55,000) \\
&- \$980,000 \\
= \ &\$186,000(3.274) + \{\$198,620.69 - (0.476)(\$7,777.78)\} \\
&+ (0.476)(\$55,000) - \$980,000 \\
= \ &\$608,964 + \{\$198,620.69 - \$3,702.22\} + \$26,180 - \$980,000 \\
= \ &-\$149,937.53
\end{aligned}
$$

Because the NPV is negative, the firm should reject the new line and continue to use the existing one in order to maximize the value of the firm.

Replacement decisions are an important part of the capital budgeting process. Following the steps outlined, and making sure we understand incremental cash flows, we can make the proper decisions to maintain the firm's competitive advantage and maximize its value.

Concept Review Questions

- What are the incremental cash flows in a replacement decision?
- What are the differences in the cash flows for an expansion project and a replacement project?

More on Cash Flow Estimation

So far in Chapters 7 and 8 we have focused on three primary topics—the capital budgeting process, gaining a fuller understanding of net present value and internal rate of return, and estimating the incremental cash flows. Now we need to consider inflation, why financing costs are excluded, and abandonment.

INFLATION

Often cash flows are estimated on the basis that they are not expected to change much over the life of the project. If inflation is low, they may not. But if inflation is high, or if it changes during the life of the project, then we have to consider specifically any impacts on the estimated cash flows. In only one special case do the effects of inflation cancel each other out and not affect the decision: when both the CFs and the opportunity cost of capital properly anticipate and adjust for the same percentage rate of inflation. *If this special case occurs, then inflation does not have to be considered as a separate issue.*

A more likely occurrence, however, is for the opportunity cost of capital to reflect expected inflation while the cash flows do not. Investors incorporate expectations of inflation into their required rates of return. Because this is the case, the firm's opportunity cost of capital also reflects expected inflation. But what about the estimated cash flows? If inflation is taken into account in the discount rate but not in the after-tax CFs, then the calculated NPV will be biased downward. Alternatively, if low expected inflation is reflected in the discount rate used but a higher inflation estimate is built into the CFs, then the NPV will be biased upward.

To see the importance of adjusting for inflation, consider Sullivan Paper. Table 8.9 shows that the firm calculated the net present value of a proposed capital expenditure

---

Table 8.9

Cash Flows and Net Present Value for Sullivan Paper Project, Without Adjusting for Inflation

For simplicity, the $21,000 investment (capital cost) is assumed to be depreciated on a straight line basis to zero over three years. Hence, the CCA is $7,000 per year.

Initial Investment
$21,000

Operating Cash Flows

Year	Cash Inflows	−	Cash Outflows	=	CFBT	CFBT $(1 - T)^a$	+	CCA$(T)^a$	=	CF
1	$20,000		$8,000		$12,000	$7,200		$2,800		$10,000
2	20,000		8,000		12,000	7,200		2,800		10,000
3	20,000		8,000		12,000	7,200		2,800		10,000

Ending Cash Flow
None

Cash Flow Stream

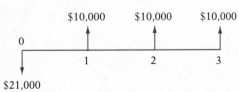

Net Present Value
NPV = $10,000(PVA$_{15\%,3\,yr}$) − $21,000 = 10,000(2.283) − 21,000 = $1,830

---

^{a} The tax rate is 40 percent.

Table 8.10

Cash Flows and Net Present Value for Sullivan Paper Project, Taking Account for Inflation

With the substantial increase in the estimated cash outflows once inflation is taken into account, the project should be rejected.

Initial Investment
$21,000

Operating Cash Flows

Year	Cash Inflows	−	Cash Outflows	=	CFBT	CFBT $(1 - T)^a$ + $CCA(T)^a$ =		CF
1	$20,000		$ 9,000		$11,000	$6,600	$2,800	$ 9,400
2	20,000		10,000		10,000	6,000	2,800	8,800
3	20,000		11,000		9,000	5,400	2,800	8,200

Ending Cash Flow
None

Cash Flow Stream

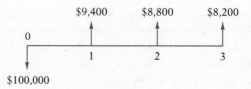

Net Present Value

$$\text{NPV} = \$9,400(PV_{15\%, 1yr}) + \$8,800(PV_{15\%, 2yr}) + \$8,200(PV_{15\%, 3yr}) - \$21,000$$
$$= \$9,400(0.870) + \$8,800(0.756) + \$8,200(0.658) - \$21,000$$
$$= -\$773.60$$

---

[a] The tax rate is 40 percent.

to be $1,830 at its opportunity cost of capital of 15 percent. The project should be selected, because its net present value is positive. But what happens if expected inflation was ignored in estimating the cash outflows in Table 8.9? Once inflation is taken into account, the cash outflows are projected to increase by $1,000 each year. As Table 8.10 shows, the project's NPV is now −$773.60, which changes Sullivan's decision. Now the firm should reject the project.

Anticipating inflation is not easy, but it is important if the proper capital budgeting decisions are to be made. Managers should remember the following:

1. Be consistent—make sure the inflation consequences are built into the cash flows, because they are already incorporated in the discount rate (unless a real instead of a nominal discount rate is employed).
2. Even if cash inflows and regular cash outflows change in line with the general rate of inflation, CFs generally do not change because of the tax structure. Taxes tend to increase more than proportionately as cash inflows rise. Also, inflation often

requires an increased working capital investment above and beyond that required with little or no inflation.

3. Inflation is not constant across different sections of the economy. Therefore, it may *not* be reasonable to use a general price index to incorporate the effects of changing rates of inflation on expected CFs for a project.

4. Differential price changes may occur due to supply and demand considerations. These effects, which are due to factors other than the rate of inflation, can also have a significant impact on the CFs and must be taken into account.

WHY ARE FINANCING COSTS EXCLUDED?

We have ignored one cash flow that a firm incurs when undertaking a capital budgeting project—the financing costs. Suppose that a firm is evaluating whether to build a new plant. If the firm decides to use debt financing, should we recognize the after-tax interest and principal repayments as ongoing cash outflows? Similarly, if equity is employed, should any costs related to it be treated as part of the ongoing cash outflow stream? *In both cases, the answer is no.* The investment, or capital budgeting, decision should be separated from the financing decision. The investment decision is based on the economic desirability of the project, irrespective of how it is financed; the financing costs are built into the opportunity cost of capital. If financing costs were to be deducted from the after-tax cash flows, they would be double-counted (once in the numerator of the NPV and again in the denominator, as part of the opportunity cost of capital, k) and the project's net present value would be underestimated. *However,* there are some decisions in which the investment and financing cash flows are interrelated. One example is when the financing of a plant is tied directly to the investment. For example, when considering a new plant in Mexico, very cheap debt financing may be provided by a government-sponsored agency, so it becomes a direct part of the proposed investment and cash flow analysis. In this case, the financing cash flows must be included in determining the relevant CFs. An evaluation method that accomplishes this is the adjusted present value (APV) method, which is discussed in detail in Appendix 8A.

HAS ABANDONMENT BEEN CONSIDERED?

One of the most difficult problems in estimating cash flows is to make sure all the options are examined. Consider a manufacturing firm reevaluating an ongoing machine line. Assume that the machine line has a three-year life, and the expected after-tax cash inflows are as follows:

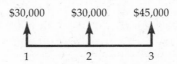

Looking at this cash flow stream, we might be tempted to conclude that the machine line has a positive NPV. But what happens if you discover that the machine line could be sold today to net the company $85,000? This $85,000 is an opportunity cost that must be considered. The choice now is between $85,000 today or the stream of expected after-tax cash flows, as follows:

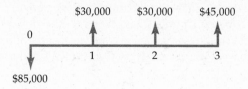

Assuming a discount rate of 14 percent, we find that the NPV is

$$NPV = \$30,000(PV_{14\%,\,1\,yr}) + \$30,000(PV_{14\%,\,2\,yr}) + \$45,000(PV_{14\%,\,3\,yr})$$
$$- \$85,000$$
$$= \$30,000(0.877) + \$30,000(0.769) + \$45,000(0.675) - \$85,000$$
$$= \$26,310 + \$23,070 + \$30,375 - \$85,000$$
$$= \$79,755 - \$85,000 = -\$5,245$$

The machine line now has a negative NPV.

In the absence of any further information, the proper decision would be to abandon the project.[15] This **abandonment decision** would maximize the value of the firm. However, let us assume that an option to modernize the machine line exists and the cash flows associated solely with the modernization are as follows:

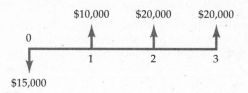

The relevant set of cash flows for decision making is the combination of the existing and the new cash flows. Assuming that the cash flows are additive (i.e., not complements or substitutes), the relevant cash flows for this abandon versus modernization decision are

	t = 0	t = 1	t = 2	t = 3
Existing machine line	−$ 85,000	$30,000	$30,000	$45,000
Plus: Modernization	− 15,000	10,000	20,000	20,000
Relevant CFs	−$ 100,000	$40,000	$50,000	$65,000

---

[15] The decision to keep or divest some divisions of a firm, as discussed in Chapter 16, is another example of an abandonment decision.

At a discount rate of 14 percent, the NPV is

$$NPV = \$40,000(0.877) + \$50,000(0.769) + \$65,000(0.675) - \$100,000$$
$$= \$35,080 + \$38,450 + \$43,875 - \$100,000 = \$17,405$$

Based on the relevant set of cash flows, the firm should keep and modernize the machine line. The second-best alternative is to abandon the present line. The worst path is to continue operating the machine line as it is. By doing so, the firm passes up the opportunity of modernizing or abandoning—both of which are preferable.

In any abandonment-type decision it is important to recognize that some assets are much easier to bail out of than others. It is typically easier to bail out of tangible assets when a good secondary market exists. For very specialized or unique tangible assets, and for many intangible assets, good secondary markets do not exist, and their abandonment value may be almost nonexistent.

Concept Review Questions

■ Why is it important to adjust a firm's cash flows for inflation?

■ Comment on the statement: "A firm's cash flows will be biased downward if financing costs are included."

■ Describe how the ability to abandon a project is of value in making capital budgeting decisions.

KEY POINTS

- An important consideration in capital budgeting decisions is depreciation for tax purposes, or capital cost allowance (CCA), which must be calculated as prescribed in the Income Tax Act.
- To calculate CCA, assets are pooled into designated asset classes, each with a prescribed maximum CCA rate. For an asset put-in-use during the year, only one-half of its capital cost can be added to the pool in that year, with the remaining one-half entering in the year after.
- For effective capital budgeting to occur, the relevant incremental after-tax cash flows must be determined. This determination requires an understanding of CCA.
- Opportunity costs are an important component of the costs; they must be considered. Sunk costs are just that; they should be ignored in determining the proper cash flows, which are the incremental (new minus old) CFs.
- The cash flows must be determined at three times: at the initiation of the project; over the expected economic life of the project, using the operating cash flows (including incremental CCA tax shields); and at the end of the project.
- Because capital cost allowance is calculated on a declining balance method, the operating cash flows of a project may extend indefinitely into the future.
- For replacement-type decisions, the focus is on the incremental cash flows.
- Proper decision making requires that inflation, but not financing costs, be considered in the after-tax cash flow stream.
- Abandonment, either now or in the future, is an option that should always be recognized and built into capital budgeting decision making.

QUESTIONS

8.1 Discuss the differences between capital cost allowance and depreciation.

8.2 Why is a CCA recapture taxed as regular income?

8.3 Why is the amount of a terminal loss used as an expense during the termination year?

8.4 Explain the differences between the initial investment, operating cash flows, and the ending cash flow.

8.5 Explain the idea of opportunity costs. How do they relate to the notion of the operating CF stream?

8.6 Which of the following should be considered when calculating the incremental CFs associated with a new warehouse? Assume the firm owns the land but that existing buildings would have to be demolished.
a. Demolition costs and site clearance.
b. The cost of an access road built a year ago.
c. New forklifts and conveyer equipment for the warehouse.
d. The market value of the land and existing buildings.
e. A portion of the firm's overhead.
f. Lost earnings on other products due to managerial time spent during the construction and stocking of the new warehouse.
g. Future CCA on the old buildings and equipment.
h. Landscaping for the warehouse.
i. Financing costs related to the bonds issued to build the new warehouse.
j. The effects of inflation on future labour costs.

8.7 By comparing the calculations necessary for determining ΔCFs of replacement decisions with the calculations for determining CFs for expansion decisions, identify the *specific* differences that exist for the initial, operating, and ending cash flows.

8.8 Explain why a firm may receive cash flows from a project even after the project has been disposed of by the firm.

8.9 How does inflation affect the capital budgeting process?

8.10 Differentiate between financing and investment decisions. Why are financing costs excluded when calculating the CFs necessary for capital investment decision making?

8.11 Evaluate the following statement: "For a firm to remain in business, it must keep and update its equipment and processes. Hence, abandonment decisions are not relevant in practice."

CONCEPT REVIEW PROBLEMS

See Appendix A for solutions.

CR8.1 In 1996, Myers Ltd. purchased some office furniture costing $200,000, with installation and shipping costs of $5,000. The furniture is a class 8 asset (CCA rate 30 percent).
a. Calculate the annual CCA deduction for 1996 to 1998.
b. Does it matter if the furniture was purchased in the first half of the year or the second half of the year?

CR8.2 Paymore Rent-a-Car purchased five new cars in 1996 with an average cost of $18,400 per car. The cars are in class 16, CCA rate 40 percent.

a. Calculate the value of the UCC for the pool at the end of 1998.

b. The firm plans to replace the cars after three years. If, at that time, the firm pays $87,000 for the replacement cars and sells the old cars for 50 percent of their purchase price, how much will Paymore add to its class 16 pool?

CR8.3   The Great Lakes Fishing charter service had transactions in two CCA classes this year. The first transaction, in class 7 (15 percent), was to purchase and put-in-use a cabin cruiser for $43,500 and sell a motorboat for $12,000 (the cost of the motorboat was $35,000). The second transaction, in class 9 (25 percent), was to put-in-use a small aircraft at a cost of $32,000 and sell a float plane that had cost $52,500 for $46,000. The beginning UCC for class 7 was $82,500; for class 9, $97,800. Calculate the CCA deduction for the year.

The following information is used in CR8.4 and CR8.5.

Chateau Plonk has spent $500,000 on research to develop low-fat imitation wine. The firm is planning to spend $200,000 on a machine to produce the new wine. Shipping and installation costs of the machine will be $100,000. The machine has an expected life of six years and a $10,000 estimated resale value, and it falls in class 43 (CCA rate 30 percent). Revenue from the low-fat wine is expected to be $650,000 per year, with costs of $400,000 per year. The firm has a tax rate of 35 percent and an opportunity cost of capital of 14 percent, and it expects net working capital to increase by $40,000.

CR8.4   What is the net present value of the project? Should Plonk expand into the low-fat wine market?

CR8.5   John, who is in charge of Plonk's premium wine division, estimates that the low-fat wine would lower premium wine CFBT by approximately $125,000 per year. Now what is the NPV?

CR8.6   Zio's Pizza specializes in ready-made frozen pizzas. Zio's is considering replacing its old refrigerators with new ones. The old refrigerators have a current resale value of $100,000 and are in class 8 with a CCA rate of 20 percent. It is estimated that if the refrigerators are held for four years, the old refrigerators will have a resale value of $20,000.

The new refrigerators will cost $335,000 and will also be in class 8. Sales using the old equipment were around 75,000 pizzas at time t = 0, with an average selling price of $10 per pizza. Sales have been growing at a rate of 1 percent per year. The selling price with the new refrigerators remains at $10 per pizza; the units sold at time t = 1 are 81,600 and are expected to grow at 2 percent per year.

Operating costs using the old refrigerators are 80 percent of total revenue, while operating costs using the new equipment are expected to be 75 percent of total revenue. Management estimates the new refrigerators will have a resale value of $50,000 in four years. The corporate tax rate is 40 percent, and the opportunity cost of capital is 12 percent. Should Zio's replace the refrigerators?

PROBLEMS

8.1   Laylo Leasing purchased a warehouse in 1996 for $110,000 and then spent $13,000 on renovations, which it capitalized (class 3, 5 percent). In addition, a new access road and parking lot were constructed for $11,000 (class 17, 8 percent). The total project was completed and put-in-use in 1996. Calculate the total CCA deduction for Laylo in 1999.

8.2   Sybel's Travel Agency purchased new personal computers (class 10, 30 percent) in 1995 for $8,000. In 1996 the fast pace of the PC industry had left the agency with outdated technology; in response, it sold the original computers for $5,000, and purchased larger and faster PCs for $12,500. Calculate the UCC for the pool at the end of 1995, 1996, and 1997.

8.3 In 1996, Andy's Cartage Company revamped operations and expanded into the car rental business. As a result, it sold off an extra parking garage (terminating class 3), sold a parking lot (terminating class 17), purchased three new cars and sold two used ones (class 16), and purchased two new moving vans while selling a truck (class 10). In addition, Andy's disposed of an old radio transmission system, replacing it with a newer but smaller model (class 9). In that year, Andy's had $350,000 of before-CCA taxable income. Calculate what Andy's tax payable will be for 1996.

Taxable income (before CCA) $350,000
Tax rate 46%

	Class 3 4%	Class 17 8%	Class 16 40%	Class 10 30%	Class 9 25%
Beginning UCC	$45,600	$15,000	$140,000	$27,000	$13,000
Purchases	—	—	33,000	32,000	2,500
Asset sold					
Cost	78,000	26,500	19,000	11,000	4,200
Proceeds	102,000	2,800	23,000	8,500	3,500

8.4 Hennessey Stores is considering opening a new store in Ottawa. Gross cash inflows are expected to be $1,000,000 per year, and cash outflows are predicted to be $800,000 per year. In addition, Hennessey's cost accounting department estimates that overhead costs of $75,000 per year should be charged to the new store. These costs include the store's share of the firm's management salaries, general administrative expenses, and so forth. Finally, the new store is expected to reduce CFBTs by $50,000 per year from one of the firm's existing stores. Hennessey's marginal tax rate is 40 percent. (*Note:* For simplicity, ignore any impact of CCA.)
a. If all the overhead consists of fixed costs that will be incurred whether or not the new store is opened, what is the relevant operating CF?
b. What if $50,000 of the overhead consists of variable costs related to the new store, and $25,000 consists of fixed overhead costs? What is the relevant operating CF now?

8.5 Evert Fashions is contemplating bringing out a new line of sweaters to add to its existing lines. The projected initial investment is $100,000, CF is expected to be $40,000 per year for each of five years, and the cost of capital is 15 percent.
a. Should the new line of sweaters be produced?
b. What happens if you discover that introducing the new line of sweaters will reduce CFs from existing sweater lines by $12,000 per year?
c. Why must the possibility of opportunity costs always be considered when the cash flow stream is being estimated?

8.6 New equipment that has a five-year life costs $40,000. Freight is $1,000, and site preparation costs are $5,000. Both the freight and site preparation costs occur at t = 0. The equipment will be added to the firm's class 9 assets, CCA rate 25 percent. After-tax cash inflows are $23,000 per year for each of five years, and cash outflows are $6,000 per year. At the end of five years the equipment can be sold for $10,000, less $2,000 in dismantling costs. The firm's tax rate is 46 percent, and its opportunity cost of capital is 15 percent. Should the equipment be acquired?

8.7   Norris is a manufacturer of electronic devices. Sales have recently been lost because of the inability to store sufficient finished goods inventory, even though Norris has the capability of increasing production. The solution under discussion is to increase production to create a larger finished goods inventory so that lost sales will not occur in the future. To increase the inventory, Norris estimates the following will be required:

1. The finished goods inventory needs to be expanded by $150,000.
2. Existing vacant warehouse space is available for storing the additional inventory. However, new equipment costing $80,000, with a five-year useful life is required. Straight-line CCA will be employed, and Norris's marginal tax rate is 40 percent. Additional wages will be $40,000 per year. (*Note:* Ignore the half-year convention when calculating CCA.)
3. The sales and production people estimate that the increased sales will result in a net cash inflow to the firm (after all production costs, but before considering the additional warehouse expense and taxes) of $100,000 per year.
4. In five years the equipment will have a resale value of zero. The $150,000 build-up in inventory is no longer required.

a. If the opportunity cost of capital is 13 percent, should the expansion take place?
b. What decision should be made if everything remains the same as in (a), except that the warehouse space is currently rented out for $50,000 (before taxes) per year?

8.8   Best Products has a proposed project for $200,000 of equipment that will be added to the firm's class 8 assets; the CCA rate is 20 percent. Additional net working capital of $40,000 will be required, and the estimated benefits (CFBT) are $70,000 per year for each of five years. The equipment has an estimated resale value of $50,000 in five years, the firm's tax rate is 43 percent, and Best estimates that a 20 percent return is required for this project. Should the new equipment be acquired?

8.9   Greenfield Park Packers (GPP) is considering an expansion project which calls for the firm to move into warehouse space that it does not use, but *currently* rents for $75,000 per year. No modifications to the warehouse will be necessary; however, GPP will purchase state of the art packing equipment that will cost $750,000 installed. The new equipment will be placed in CCA class 8 (CCA rate 20 percent) and has a useful life of six years and an expected resale value of $100,000. It will enable the firm to increase revenues by $500,000 per year, but at the same time it will increase expenses by $175,000 per year. If GPP has a marginal tax rate of 40 percent and an opportunity cost of capital of 15 percent, should the firm undertake the project?

8.10   Three and one-half years ago, Springfield Ltd. bought a $20,000 tractor (class 10, 30 percent). Now Springfield has decided to replace it with a new $28,000 tractor. What is the incremental CCA on a year-by-year basis for each of the next five years if the old tractor is sold for its UCC?

8.11   SafteFirst has moved into new quarters and wants to replace its office equipment (class 8, 20 percent). The existing equipment can be sold today for $40,000. In another five years it will have a resale value of zero. The new equipment costs $250,000, has a five-year life, and has a $47,000 resale value in five years. The tax rate is 45 percent, and the opportunity cost of capital is 12 percent. Due to increased worker productivity and morale, the estimated benefits before tax (ΔCFBT) are $65,000 per year.

a. Determine the incremental initial and ending cash flows.
b. Should the equipment be replaced?

8.12   Swift Trip Ltd. bought a $150,000 luxury cruiser (class 7, 15 percent) two years ago; its present UCC for the pool is $81,900. It can be sold today for $100,000 (before taxes). However, if kept, it will last five more years and is expected to produce cash flows before tax

(CFBTs) of $37,037 for each of years 1, 2, and 3, followed by $27,778 in each of years 4 and 5. A replacement vessel costs $180,000 and is expected to produce CFBTs of $70,370 for each of five years. Neither vessel has any resale value in five years. If the marginal tax rate is 46 percent, and the discount rate is 10 percent, should the old vessel be replaced?

8.13 Hi-Flying Aviation is contemplating the replacement of some equipment. The existing equipment was purchased two years ago for $80,000 and belongs in CCA class 9 (25 percent); right now, it can be sold for $60,000. Its resale value in five years will be $9,000. The new equipment will cost $120,000 and belongs in class 9 as well. The resale value of the new equipment in five years will be $15,000. Additional working capital of $5,000 is required, the tax rate is 43 percent, and Hi-Flying's opportunity cost of capital is 15 percent. Hi-Flying estimates that the new equipment will reduce cash outflows by $32,000 per year for five years but will incur an opportunity cost of $2,400 per year, as it will occupy additional hangar space that could have been rented out from year 2 through year 6. The rental income would be received in advance (i.e., at $t = 1, \ldots, t = 5$). Should Hi-Flying replace the old equipment?

8.14 YourToys is contemplating the replacement of one of its machines (class 39, 30 percent). The new machine costs $1,400,000, has a 10-year economic life, and is expected to save $250,000 (before taxes) in operating expenses each year over the next five years. The old machine had an original cost of $950,000 and has a 10-year economic life remaining. The incremental initial investment, ΔCF_0, is $998,000. At the end of 10 years, neither machine will have any resale value. The discount rate is 14 percent, and the marginal tax rate is 48 percent. Should the old machine be replaced?

8.15 A project has an initial investment of $30,000, CFBT of $16,000 for each of three years, and an opportunity cost of capital of 13 percent. Straight-line CCA will be employed, and the firm's marginal tax rate is 40 percent. (*Note:* Ignore the half-year convention when calculating CCA.)

a. What is the project's NPV? Should it be accepted?
b. Due to inflation, the CFBT in years 2 and 3 was overstated. It should be $14,000 in year 2 and $12,000 in year 3. Does this information cause you to change the decision made in (a)?

8.16 Noreiko Instruments sells a number of specialized product lines. Because of increasing competition, the CFs for its Gamma product line for $t = 1, \ldots, 4$ are estimated to be $350,000, $250,000, $150,000, and $100,000 respectively. A competitor has approached Noreiko and offered $650,000, after taxes, for the product line. If Noreiko Instruments' opportunity cost of capital for this line is 17 percent, what should it do?

8.17 Hill's Products is considering abandoning a product line. The line could be sold for $50,000 after taxes, or it could be kept and will produce after-tax cash flows of $17,500 for each of four years. In addition, the possibility of modernizing the line for $30,000 will produce after-tax cash flows in years 1 through 4, due solely to the modernization, of $15,000, $11,000, $7,000, and $3,000 respectively. Should Hill's abandon or modernize if the discount rate is 14 percent?

8.18 A machine belonging to Clifton Ltd. is worn out (class 8, 20 percent). It can be sold today for scrap for $300 (after taxes). Alternatively, it can be overhauled completely for $900 and will produce a CF of $500 a year for years 1 through 5. Finally, it can be replaced for $2,500. The economic life of the machine is five years if it is overhauled or replaced; the resale value at the end of five years is zero. If it is overhauled, the $900 will be expensed. If it is replaced, cash flows after tax over the life of the project will equal $500 + $\Delta CCA(T)$. If the marginal tax rate is 40 percent and the opportunity cost of capital is 15 percent, what should Clifton do?

8.19 Mini Case You are the chief financial analyst for Service Systems. Your boss wants to know what should be done with a piece of equipment that was purchased three years ago for $60,000, and is generating CFBT of $15,000 per year. The equipment is the only asset in class 8 (CCA rate 20 percent). The firm has been offered $21,000 for this piece of equipment; however, if kept until the end of its useful life, in five years, its estimated resale value is only $10,000. If the firm accepts the offer, it will terminate asset class 8. Alternatively, a new piece of equipment (also in class 8) can be purchased to replace the old one. The cost of this new piece is $75,000 plus installation-related costs of $8,000. The new equipment has a useful life of five years and is expected to generate CFBT of $30,000 per year. At the end of five years the new equipment's estimated resale value is $20,000. The marginal tax rate is 40 percent, and the opportunity cost of capital is 14 percent. You, as chief financial analyst for the firm, have been assigned the responsibility of deciding what action Service Systems should take.

a. Should the firm keep or abandon the existing equipment?

b. Should the firm replace the old piece of equipment with the new one? Given the results of (a) and (b), what is your recommendation?

c. In further conversation with your boss you mention that the two projects considered in (a) and (b) are mutually exclusive. What is meant by the term "mutually exclusive"? How would you have to proceed if the two projects were either partial complements or partial substitutes, not mutually exclusive?

d. Two other projects exist with after-tax cash flows as follows, where the required return is now 16 percent:

Year	Project A	Project B
0	−$20,000	−$30,000
1	5,000	18,000
2	7,000	15,000
3	9,000	13,000
4	9,000	10,000
5	9,000	
6	16,000	

1. Calculate the internal rate of return for each project.
2. If the projects are independent, what decision should be made? Why?
3. If the projects are mutually exclusive, what decision should be made? Why?
What assumptions are you making in answering (3)? How comfortable are you with the assumptions?

e. In estimating the CFs for the two projects in (d), you inadvertently ignored the effects of inflation on the operating cash flows. The net after-tax cash flows for project A will decline at 6 percent each year, and those for project B will decline at 8 percent each year. [*Note:* The cash flow for project A in year 1 will be $5,000 $(1 − 0.06)$. For year 2 it will be $7,000(1 − 0.06)^2$, etc.] If the projects are independent, does this new information change the decisions made in (2)?

f. Your boss is continually lamenting that many profitable capital budgeting projects have to be turned down because funds are not available. How would you make your boss understand that from a financial standpoint funds are not limited and can always be secured for good projects? What causes your boss, and many managers, to argue that funds are limited?

REFERENCES

DEO, PRAKASH S. "Practical Approach to Fixed-Asset Policy." *Financial Practice and Education* 2 (Spring/Summer 1992): 83–88.

HARRIS, ROBERT S., and JOHN J. PRINGLE. "Risk-Adjusted Discount Rates: Extensions from the Average Risk Case." *Journal of Financial Research* 8 (Fall 1985): 237–244.

HOWE, KEITH M. "Capital Budgeting Discount Rates Under Inflation: A Caveat." *Financial Practice and Education* 2 (Spring/Summer 1992): 31–35.

MCLAUGHLIN, ROBYN, and ROBERT A. TAGGART. "The Opportunity Cost of Using Excess Capacity." *Financial Management* 21 (Summer 1992): 12–23.

MILES, JAMES A., and JOHN R. EZZELL. "The Weighted Average Cost of Capital, Perfect Capital Markets, and Project Life: A Clarification." *Journal of Financial and Quantitative Analysis* 15 (September 1980): 719–730.

MYERS, STEWART C. "Interactions of Corporate Financing and Investment Decisions—Implications for Capital Budgeting." *Journal of Finance* 29 (March 1974): 1–25.

POHLMAN, RANDOLPH A., EMMANUEL S. SANTIAGO, and F. LYNN MARKEL. "Cash Flow Estimation Practices of Large Firms." *Financial Management* 17 (Summer 1988): 71–79.

RUMSEY, JOHN. "Testing for Tax Effects of Dividend Yields on Pre-Tax Returns." *Canadian Journal of Administrative Sciences* 9 (December 1992): 305–309.

THORNTON, DANIEL B. *Managerial Tax Planning.* Toronto: Wiley, 1993.

APPENDIX

Adjusted Present Value

In previous chapters we have discussed how firms determine their opportunity cost of capital, based on the firm's weighted average cost of capital, divisional costs of capital, or some project-specific cost of capital (Chapter 6), and how they make capital expenditure decisions (Chapters 7 and 8). The primary decision criterion we have employed has been net present value (NPV), with a weighted cost of capital used as the discount rate. Net present value—whether using the firm's weighted average cost of capital, some divisional cost of capital, or any other proportion of debt and equity costs as the discount rate—incorporates the benefits of the after-tax operating cash flows of the project along with the benefits of the financing employed for the project. As we know, *the financing costs and benefits are typically captured by the discount rate employed in net present value. That is why no financing costs or benefits (as discussed in Chapter 8) are incorporated in the cash flow stream when a project's net present value is determined.* Implicitly, two important assumptions are generally made when employing NPV. The first is that the firm is currently paying taxes (so it gets the benefit of the interest tax shield).[1] The second assumption is that the project's debt capacity is a constant proportion of the project's present value. By **project debt capacity** we mean the incremental contribution a project makes to the firm's ability to borrow. As a firm adds more projects, it increases the cash flows and consequently increases its ability to borrow. Similarly, as the project continues over time towards termination, the amount of debt the project and firm can support normally diminishes. In this appendix we examine an alternative to the NPV—the **adjusted present value (APV)**, proposed by Myers (1974).[2]

THE ADJUSTED PRESENT VALUE METHOD

The essence of the adjusted present value is to separate the effects of the investment (or capital budgeting) decision from the effects of the financing decision. This is accomplished by first estimating the project's base-case NPV *as if* the project were all-equity financed. The financing effects are then considered in a separate present value calculation. Thus,

$$\begin{matrix} \text{adjusted present} \\ \text{value, APV} \end{matrix} = \begin{matrix} \text{base-case NPV of} \\ \text{project's operating} \\ \text{cash flows} \end{matrix} + \begin{matrix} \text{present value of} \\ \text{financing benefits} \end{matrix} \qquad (8A.1)$$

To illustrate the adjusted present value approach, let us assume that we have a proposed capital budgeting project that has the following expected operating cash flows:

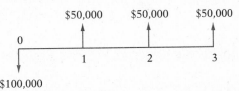

The risk-free rate, k_{RF}, is 10 percent; the expected return on the market portfolio, k_M, is 16 percent. The firm also uses financial leverage; that is, fixed-cost financing such as debt, in addition to equity financing. As a consequence the firm has a levered equity beta, β_s^L, of 0.8, and the firm has determined that its target market value ratio of total debt to total value (W_{debt}, or B) is 0.40, or 40 percent.

To calculate the base-case NPV of the project's operating CFs, the unlevered cost of equity capital (which signifies the operating risk of the project) must be used. However, as yet we have only the information to calculate its levered cost of equity capital, which is

$$k_s^L = k_{RF} + \beta_s^L(k_M - k_{RF})$$
$$= 10\% + 0.8(16\% - 10\%) - 14.80\% \qquad (8A.2)$$

---

[1] If the firm is not profitable for a period of time, the before- and after-tax costs of debt capital are the same. One way to handle different tax rates with net present value is to employ different opportunity costs (or discount rates) for different years.

[2] See the references at the end of Chapter 8.

To calculate the cost of equity *as if* the firm has no debt outstanding, that is, the unlevered cost of equity capital, k_s^U, we have to calculate the firm's unlevered beta[3]

$$\beta_s^U = \beta_s^L \left(\frac{S}{B + S} \right) \tag{8A.3}$$

where

β_s^U = the unlevered beta
S = market (or target) value of the firm's common stock
B = market (or target) value of the firm's bonds

Thus, the unobservable unlevered equity beta can be estimated to be

$$\beta_s^U = 0.80 \left(\frac{0.60}{0.40 + 0.60} \right) = 0.48$$

and the unlevered cost of equity capital is

$$k_s^U = k_{RF} + \beta_s^U (k_M - k_{RF}) = 10\% + 0.48(6\%) = 12.88\%$$

Now that we have the unlevered cost of equity capital, we can determine the base-case NPV of the project's operating cash flows, which is

$$\text{base-case NPV} = \frac{\$50,000}{(1 + k_s^U)^1} + \frac{\$50,000}{(1 + k_s^U)^2} + \frac{\$50,000}{(1 + k_s^U)^3} - \$100,000$$

$$= \frac{\$50,000}{(1.1288)^1} + \frac{\$50,000}{(1.1288)^2} + \frac{\$50,000}{(1.1288)^3} - \$100,000$$

$$= \$44,295 + \$39,241 + \$34,763 - \$100,000 = \$18,299$$

VALUE OF THE ADDITIONAL DEBT CAPACITY

The financing benefits, which are equal to the present value of the interest tax shield, must now be determined. To calculate them *we must specify the exact form of the financing to be used*. To see the effect of different financing methods, let us consider two different debt financing plans. The first is based on the assumption that we borrow 40 percent of the value of the project, or $40,000, and pay only interest on the loan until the end of the project at $t = 3$; the principal is repaid at the end of the loan. With a before-tax cost of debt of 10 percent and a marginal corporate tax rate of 35 percent, the present value of the interest tax shield (discounted at the unlevered equity rate of 12.88 percent because we do not want to capture any of the tax or financing benefits in the discount rate) is[4]

---

[3] In reality, $\beta_s^U = \beta_s^L \left(\frac{S}{B + S} \right) + \beta_{debt} \left(\frac{B}{B + S} \right)$, but we are assuming that the firm's debt is risk-free and, hence, $\beta_{debt} = 0$.

[4] There is some debate about what discount rate to use. Miles and Ezzell (1980; see the references at the end of Chapter 8) use the before-tax cost of debt for one period and then the unlevered cost of equity for the rest, whereas Harris and Pringle (1985) use the unlevered cost of equity throughout. The difference between Miles and Ezzell and Harris and Pringle is that the former consider the first interest tax shield to be known with certainty and all the rest to be uncertain, whereas Harris and Pringle assume all interest tax shields to be uncertain. For simplicity we follow Harris and Pringle.

Year	Borrowing (1)	Interest (1)(0.10) (2)	Interest Tax Shield (2)(0.35) (3)	Present Value of Interest Tax Shield at 12.88% (4)
1	$40,000	$4,000	$1,400	$1,240
2	40,000	4,000	1,400	1,099
3	40,000	4,000	1,400	973
				Total $3,312

With this particular form of debt financing, the adjusted present value of the project is

$$APV = \text{base-case NPV} + \text{present value of interest tax shield}$$
$$= \$18,299 + \$3,312 = \$21,611$$

Alternatively, what happens to the adjusted present value if the second debt financing plan is used where the borrowing is paid off in equal increments over time? In this case, less total interest is paid, so the present value of the financing benefits are less, as follows:

Year	Borrowing at the Start of the Year (1)	Interest (1)(0.10) (2)	Interest Tax Shield (2)(0.35) (3)	Present Value of Interest Tax Shield at 12.88% (4)
1	$40,000	$4,000	$1,400	$1,240
2	26,667	2,667	933	733
3	13,334	1,333	467	324
				Total $2,297

The APV with this lower level of financing over time, and hence lower interest tax shield, is

$$APV = \$18,299 + \$2,297 = \$20,596$$

as opposed to $21,611 when no principal payments are made until the end of the project's life. This example illustrates a very important point: *With adjusted present value, the specific form of financing directly affects the subsequent APV.*

FLOTATION COSTS

The proposed project is going to be financed based on the proportions specified by the firm's target capital structure, so 60 percent of the financing, or $60,000 in common equity, is needed. What if no internally generated common equity exists and the firm has to sell additional common stock to finance the equity portion of the project? Suppose the flotation costs (to underwriters, lawyers, and others) amounts to 5.5

percent of the gross proceeds of the issue. This means the firm has to issue $63,492 [i.e., $60,000/(1 − 0.055)] in stock to obtain the $60,000 in cash. The $3,492 difference (which occurs at time t = 0) is a direct cost of the financing. The flotation costs must now be subtracted, to arrive at the project's adjusted present value. Therefore, the APV, assuming the first debt case, in which the principal is not repaid until the end of the project, and new common stock is required, is

$$APV = \text{base-case NPV} + \begin{array}{c}\text{present value of}\\\text{financing benefits}\end{array} - \begin{array}{c}\text{present value of the}\\\text{cost of new equity financing}\end{array}$$

$$= \$18,299 + \$3,312 - \$3,492 = \$18,119$$

We see that once financing costs are considered, the adjusted present value of the proposed project declines. Although these financing costs relate to equity, financing costs related to debt financing could be treated in the same manner.

We see from the analysis that, to determine the adjusted present value, the present value of the financing benefits and any financing or flotation costs are calculated separately and then combined with the base-case NPV of the project's operating cash flows. Different financing amounts or arrangements will influence the present value of the financing benefits (or costs), and hence will affect the adjusted present value.

SUBSIDIZED LOANS

Consider now the situation in which the firm, because of an economic incentive, is able to receive subsidized financing on the loan. Say the subsidized interest rate is 4 percent, when the market interest rate is 10 percent. This subsidy results in the firm paying less interest over the life of the loan; accordingly, the discounted present value of the loan (which includes both its interest and principal) is less. *To determine the present value of the financing benefits, two separate calculations are now required.* The first is just the present value of the interest tax shield, calculated as before, but now using 4 percent interest. In effect, owing to the subsidy, the firm has a smaller interest tax shield than at the higher 10 percent market interest rate. The second calculation takes into account the fact that the firm will (in present value terms) actually pay back less with the subsidized loan than with the non-subsidized loan.

To illustrate the calculations needed, let us go back to the first debt financing plan for $40,000, in which no principal payments were made until the end of the project. At the subsidized interest rate of 4 percent, the present value of the interest tax shield (discounted at the firm's unlevered cost of equity capital of 12.88 percent) is less than it was before:

Year	Borrowing (1)	Interest (1)(0.04) (2)	Interest Tax Shield (2)(0.35) (3)	Present Value of Interest Tax Shield at 12.88% (4)
1	$40,000	$1,600	$560	$ 496
2	40,000	1,600	560	439
3	40,000	1,600	560	389
				Total $1,324

This is the first part of the benefit that the firm receives from the subsidized loan financing. The firm also benefits from having to pay back less (in present value terms) with the subsidized loan.

How much less? The cash outflows experienced by the firm with the subsidized loan—and its present value discounted at the after-tax borrowing rate[5] on the *un*subsidized loan of $(10\%)(1 - 0.35) = 6.5\%$—are

Year	Principal Repayment (1)	Interest ($40,000)(0.04) (2)	Interest Outflow (2)(1 − 0.35) (3)	Principal Plus After-Tax Interest (1) + (3) (4)	Value at 6.50% (5)
1	—	$1,600	$1,040	$1,040	$ 977
2	—	1,600	1,040	1,040	917
3	$40,000	1,600	1,040	41,040	$33,975
					Total $35,869

Because of the subsidized loan, the present value (which is the market value or worth) of the debt financing is only $35,869, instead of $40,000 with the unsubsidized borrowing; hence the firm saved $4,131 with the subsidized loan. The adjusted present value, ignoring any costs of new common stock, is

$$\text{APV} = \text{base-case NPV} + \frac{\text{present value of}}{\text{interest tax shield}} + \frac{\text{present value of savings}}{\text{due to subsidized financing}}$$

$$= \$18,299 + \$1,324 + \$4,131 = \$23,754$$

Comparing this with the APV of $21,611 for the unsubsidized loan, we see that the firm is better off by $2,143 (i.e., $23,754 − $21,611) in present value terms because of the cut-rate financing obtained. We will not illustrate it here, but exactly the same type of calculations could be carried out if the subsidized loan were paid off in equal (or any other) increments over time.

WHEN APV COMES IN HANDY

The adjusted present value method should be used in the following situations:

1. When the firm is in a temporary loss position and there are no benefits due to interest tax shields. The interest tax shield benefits can then be built into the APV, but not the NPV, approach, if and when they are expected to occur.

---

[5] The 6.50 percent rate is employed to discount these cash flows because that is the after-tax rate at which the firm could borrow without the benefits of subsidization.

2. When the project contains some type of specialized financing that cannot be readily incorporated into the discount rate determined with the weighted average cost of capital (or some other required rate of return).[6]

Otherwise the net present value approach—which is far easier to use—can and generally should be employed.

WHEN DO APV AND NPV GIVE THE SAME ANSWER?

Providing that exactly the same assumptions are employed, the APV and NPV methods will produce the same answer. The basic assumptions required are that

1. Market value proportions of debt and equity are used, and the project's debt capacity is determined by the present value of the project's operating and financing cash flows.
2. The tax system is symmetrical, so profits or losses are reflected immediately.

For the project described earlier we had operating cash flows as follows:

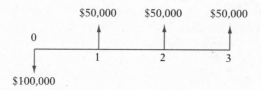

and the rest of the assumptions were

$\beta_s^L = 0.80$, so k_s^L = 14.80%
k_b(the before-tax cost of debt)   = 10%
$T = 0.35$, so k_i (the after-tax cost)   = 10%(1 − 0.35) = 6.50%
W_{debt}(or B, the proportion of debt)   = 0.40
$W_{common\ equity}$(or S, the proportion of equity) = 0.60

Using Equation 6.1 we find that the opportunity cost of capital is

$$\text{opportunity cost of capital} = k_s^L W_{common\ equity} + k_i W_{debt}$$
$$= 14.80\%(0.60) + 6.50\%(0.40)$$
$$= 8.88\% + 2.60\% = 11.48\%$$

---

[6] Note that the risk of the project does not have to equal the firm's average risk. Even though we did not calculate it in Chapter 6, there is no conceptual reason why a required return cannot be calculated for each project—and then used to determine the economic desirability of projects that are more or less risky than the firm as a whole and hence require a higher or lower required return than the firm's opportunity cost of capital.

The project's NPV at 11.48 percent is

$$NPV = \frac{\$50,000}{(1.1148)^1} + \frac{\$50,000}{(1.1148)^2} + \frac{\$50,000}{(1.1148)^3} - \$100,000$$
$$= \$44,851 + \$40,232 + \$36,089 - \$100,000 = \$21,172$$

To get the same figure from the adjusted present value method, we must make sure the loan implied by the NPV decision criterion is actually calculated and then employed in determining the project's adjusted present value. The base-case NPV at the unlevered equity discount rate of 12.88 percent is just what we determined earlier—that is, $18,299. Now *the exact loan implied by the NPV criterion must be determined.* This loan is equal to 40 percent of the present value of both the after-tax operating cash flows (CF) and the financing tax benefits provided by the project. Note that the value of the implied loan will decrease over time as the present (or economic) value of the remaining operating cash flows and financing benefits declines.

To calculate the implied loan incorporated in the net present value, we first discount the after-tax cash flows, employing the unlevered cost of equity capital, because we are examining the financing benefits as a separate part of the process. The implied loan is determined as follows:

$$PV_2 = \frac{\$50,000}{(1.1288)^1} = \$44,294.83$$

$$PV_1 = \frac{\$50,000}{(1.1288)^1} + \frac{\$50,000}{(1.1288)^2} = \$83,535.46$$

$$PV_0 = \frac{\$50,000}{(1.1288)^1} + \frac{\$50,000}{(1.1288)^2} + \frac{\$50,000}{(1.1288)^3} = \$118,298.60$$

These cash flows are summarized in row 2 of Table 8A.1. Then the borrowing of 40 percent of the present value of the cash flows is calculated in row 3, followed by the interest at 10 percent in row 4, the tax shield (at 35 percent) in row 5, and the present value of the interest tax shield in row 6. The present value (at time t = 0) of the interest tax benefits is $2,816.20. Thus, as discussed earlier, *there is a financing benefit to the project, in addition to its operating benefit* of $18,299 determined earlier.

Can we stop there? The answer is no, because the present value of a $2,816.20 financial benefit permits another layer of borrowing. This second layer of borrowing, and the present value of the final total interest tax shield of $2,873.20, is shown in Table 8A.2. When we add the present value of the interest tax shield of $2,873.20 to the base-case NPV of $18,299, we get an adjusted present value of

$$APV = \text{base-case NPV} + \text{present value of financing benefits}$$
$$= \$18,299 + \$2,873 = \$21,172$$

which is the same as we got by using the NPV approach.

Thus, when we specify the loan consistently (i.e., as implicitly assumed by NPV), the adjusted present value and NPV give exactly the same answer.

Table 8A.1

Loan Implied by the NPV Method: Tax Shield Benefit From the First Layer of Financing

To obtain the same value from adjusted present value as from the NPV method, the exact loan implied by the NPV must be calculated. This loan financing provides an interest tax shield that is incorporated in the adjusted present value calculation.

		Year		
	0	**1**	**2**	**3**
1. Operating cash flows (CF)		$50,000.00	$50,000.00	$50,000.00
2. Present value of the remaining cash flows (row 1 from following year + row 2 from following year)/(1.1288)	$118,298.60	83,535.46	44,294.83	
3. Borrow 40 percent of the value of the project: (row 2)(0.40)	47,319.44	33,414.18	17,717.93	
4. Interest at 10 percent (lagged 1 year)		4,731.94	3,341.42	1,771.79
5. Tax benefit of the interest: (row 4)(0.35)		1,656.18	1,169.50	620.13
6. Present value of the tax benefit [(row 5 from following year + row 6 from following year)/(1.1288)]	2,816.20	1,522.74	549.37	

The loan and principal repayments implied by NPV (calculated from line 4 in Table 8A.2) are as follows:[7]

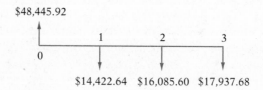

$48,445.92

0 — 1 — 2 — 3

$14,422.64 $16,085.60 $17,937.68

This loan must be calculated, and then the principal repayments must be paid off in exactly the manner determined, if we are to get the same figure from adjusted present value and NPV. Using any other borrowing pattern with APV will result in a figure different from that reached using adjusted discount rate NPV.

---

[7] Row 4 of Table 8A.2 shows the principal balance remaining in each year. In year 3 there is no balance remaining; therefore, the entire amount of $17,937.68 shown at the end of year 2 was repaid in year 3. The principal repayment in year 2 is $16,085.60 ($34,023.28 − $17,937.68) and in year 1 it is $14,442.64 ($48,445.92 − $34,032.28).

Table 8A.2

Loan Implied by the NPV Method: Tax Shield Benefit From the Second Layer of Financing

Due to the first layer of financing shown in Table 8A.1, the firm obtains an interest tax shield and therefore can obtain more financing. We could go on to a third layer of financing for greater accuracy.

		Year		
	0	1	2	3
1. Present value of the operating cash flows (row 2 from Table 8A.1) at 12.88 percent	$118,298.60	$83,535.46	$44,294.83	
2. Present value of the first layer of tax benefits (row 6 from Table 8A.1) at 12.88 percent	2,816.20	1,522.74	549.37	
3. Total present value of operating cash flows and the first layer of tax benefits: (row 1 + row 2)	121,114.80	85,058.20	44,844.20	
4. Borrow 40 percent of the value of the project: (row 3)(0.40)	48,445.92	34,023.28	17,937.68	
5. Interest at 10 percent (lagged 1 year)		4,844.59	3,402.33	1,793.77
6. Tax benefit of the interest: (row 5)(0.35)		1,695.61	1,190.81	627.82
7. Present value of the tax benefit [(row 6 from following year + row 7 from following year)/(1.1288)]	2,873.20	1,547.66	556.18	

PROBLEMS

8A.1 Manitoba Industries follows a policy of financing 55 percent with debt and 45 percent with equity. It plans to pay a cash dividend of $4.00 next year, and the expected growth rate in dividends is forecasted to be 6 percent per year. The firm's current stock price is $25, its marginal tax rate is 34 percent, the before-tax cost of debt capital is 11.50 percent, the risk-free rate is 8.50 percent, and the expected return on the market portfolio is 15.50 percent.

a. Determine the firm's opportunity (or weighted average) cost of capital.

b. What is the unlevered cost of equity capital for Manitoba?

c. What would you conclude about your answers to (a) and (b) if you now determined that Manitoba's investment dealer informed you that the firm's levered beta is 1.25?

8A.2 Johnson's Textiles has evaluated a proposed project that is all debt financed and has determined its adjusted present value is $69,688, of which the base-case NPV is $29,942 and the present value of the interest tax shield is $39,746. The project requires an initial outlay of $500,000 and is expected to produce after-tax operating cash inflows of $160,000 for each of four years. Johnson's marginal tax rate is 40 percent, the expected return on the market portfolio is 10 percent, and Johnson's typically finances with 40 percent equity and 60 percent debt.

a. What is Johnson's unlevered cost of equity?
b. Assume the firm's debt is no more risky than required by the risk-free rate. What is the before-tax cost of debt in percentage terms (which is also k_{RF})?
c. What is the firm's opportunity cost of capital and the NPV of the project? Why are the APV and NPV figures not equal?

8A.3 Jason's Technology is considering the development of a new plant in Indonesia. The initial after-tax cash outflow to fund the project (all cash flows in Canadian dollars) is $5,000,000, and Jason's expects the after-tax cash inflows to be $900,000 for each of the seven years of the project's expected life. Due to the nature of the project, Jason's expects to fund most of the project by issuing $4,000,000 of 10 percent, seven-year bonds that pay interest annually. Jason's unlevered equity cost of capital is 15 percent, and the firm is in the 40 percent tax bracket.

a. Determine the adjusted present value for the project. Should Jason's proceed?
b. Before the final decision was made, the government of Indonesia indicated it would provide $3,000,000 in a seven-year loan at 5 percent interest. Interest will be paid each year, but the principal will not be repaid until the end of the loan. The rest of the project (of $2,000,000) will be funded with a seven-year, 10 percent coupon rate bond issued by Jason's. What decision should Jason's make now?

8A.4 A project's after-tax operating cash flows are $175,000 per year for each of four years, and the initial investment is $500,000. The unlevered cost of equity capital is 15 percent.

a. What is the base-case NPV?
b. If the project is financed entirely with stock, the flotation costs are equal to 6 percent of the gross proceeds. What is the project's adjusted present value?
c. Independent of (b), assume that the project will be financed entirely with debt. The interest rate is 11 percent and the firm's marginal tax rate is 30 percent. What is the project's adjusted present value if the loan is
   1. Paid back in total at the end of four years?
   2. Paid back in equal principal amounts per year for each of the four years?
   3. Amortized so that the total before-tax payment is constant each year?

8A.5 The government of Nigeria has agreed to lend $10 million to a firm for four years at a fixed annual rate of 4 percent for a project. The market rate of interest on a similar loan is 13 percent. The principal will be repaid at the end of four years. The project will require an investment of $15 million, of which $5 million will be supplied from the firm's internally generated equity capital. The operating CFs on the project are estimated to be $5 million per year for each of four years.

a. If the firm's corporate tax rate is 30 percent and the unlevered cost of equity is 17 percent, what is the base-case NPV of the project?
b. What is the present value of the interest tax shield?
c. How much is the subsidized loan worth (without considering the present value of the interest tax shield)?
d. What is the project's adjusted present value?
e. How would your answer be affected if there were no subsidized loan?

8A.6 A project calls for an initial investment of $400,000 and is expected to generate after-tax cash inflows of $200,000, $250,000, and $300,000 in years 1, 2, and 3, respectively. Other facts are as follows:

$$k_{RF} = k_b = 9\%$$ $\quad\quad$ T $\quad\quad\quad\quad\quad\quad\quad = 0.40$

$$k_M = 15\%$$ $\quad\quad\quad$ $W_{common\ equity}(\text{or } S) = 0.50$

$$\beta_s^L = 1.5$$ $\quad\quad\quad\quad$ $W_{debt}(\text{or } B) \quad\quad\ = 0.50$

a. Calculate the net present value (NPV) by using the appropriate opportunity cost of capital.

b. Calculate the loan implied by the NPV method (carry through two layers of financing) and show that the adjusted present value provides approximately the same answer as the NPV method.

9 *Risk and Capital Budgeting*

EXECUTIVE SUMMARY

The effective treatment of risk is both difficult and important in capital budgeting decisions. Some firms have employed a strategic planning approach without fully understanding the use of present values in making wealth-maximizing capital budgeting decisions. Failure to do so is dysfunctional and can lead to a decline in the value of the firm.

First and foremost, the cash flows should reflect all possible sources of risk. For projects of average risk, a firm-wide opportunity cost of capital is appropriate. For other projects, a project-specific or divisional cost of capital should be employed to account for the above- or below-average risk. These approaches assume implicitly that risk is above or below the average risk of the project for its entire economic life. For projects for which risk differs over time, the use of sequential analysis is appropriate. Thus, later cash flows are not inappropriately penalized as they would be if a single discount rate were used.

Sensitivity analysis, in which one input variable is changed at a time, is often employed in analyzing capital budgeting projects. A specific case in point is the use of break-even analysis. It is inappropriate from a wealth-maximizing standpoint to conduct a break-even analysis based on GAAP net income. Simulation, in which all of the relevant variables are allowed to change, may also be employed in order to deal with risk when capital budgeting decisions are made.

RISK AND STRATEGIC DECISIONS

We know that risk and return are positively related. To improve expected return, investors must expose themselves to more risk. Exactly the same relationship holds for capital budgeting decisions: For a firm to increase its expected return, it must increase its exposure to risk. Yet many questions remain. We shall find that managers must still use judgment whenever there is risk.

STRATEGIC DECISIONS

All sources of risk are important for the capital budgeting process because of their effect on cash flows. However, cash flows are not the only source of uncertainty; managers must also consider the firm's strategic position in its segment of the industry and market. Unfortunately, when considering strategic and risky decisions, firms may find reasons to ignore the capital budgeting techniques described in Chapters 7 and 8. One reason is the inherent complexity of some projects—especially when future investments may be contingent on the success or failure of an initial investment. Another reason is the difficulty, both in practice and in theory, of effectively identifying and quantifying which of the risks should be considered in analyzing prospective capital budgeting projects. Taking risk into account is one of the most difficult tasks in the capital budgeting process, but it cannot be ignored. To do so is simply to invite further problems.

Risk Can Be Beneficial Risk can also be a positive factor in project selection. That idea may seem strange, but remember that higher expected returns are possible only as a result of exposure to additional risk. "If you know everything there is to know about a new product," said an executive of a major firm, "it's not going to be good business. There have to be some major uncertainties to be resolved. This is the only way to get a product with a major profit opportunity." This manager has learned an important lesson: If the firm is to prosper, it must find new product areas that have the potential to increase the value of the firm significantly. That is, it must find positive net present value projects from which the firm can earn excess returns due to its competitive advantages. To find these areas, the firm may expose itself to risks above and beyond the average risks it faces. Is that additional risk exposure bad? No—not unless the firm does a poor job of evaluating and considering the risks.Most significant, profitable investments and innovations have faced high risks. But higher expected returns accompanied those higher risks. Of course, not all high-risk capital investments pan out. But managers must foster an environment within the firm that does two things: (1) encourages the development and consideration of high risk–high expected return projects, and (2) provides a proper format for adequately considering and evaluating these projects. Otherwise, the environment either will not encourage risk taking or will lead to making high-risk, complex capital investment decisions based on seat-of-the-pants analysis. Either result can have serious—and perhaps fatal—long-run consequences for the firm.

A Common Mistake Many managers believe they must increase the opportunity cost of capital to account for the greater risk of the more distant cash flows. This is wrong. *The use of any discount rate (above the risk-free rate) automatically recognizes that more distant cash flows are proportionally more risky.* One way to think about the opportunity cost of capital for a project, or its required return, is to view it as a function of both the risk-free rate and a risk premium. That is,

$$\text{opportunity cost of capital (required return)} = \text{risk-free rate} + \text{risk premium based on project risk} \quad (9.1)$$

If the risk-free rate is 6 percent and the risk premium for the project is 8 percent, for a total of 14 percent, both the 6 percent and the 8 percent compound over time. The compounding of the 6 percent adjusts solely for differences in the timing of the cash flows—in the absence of risk. The compounding of the 8 percent risk premium recognizes that more distant cash flows for the project are more risky. Thus, if cash flow distributions become more risky over time (as shown in Figure 9.1), then discounting implicitly takes account of some or all of this increase.

The use of a discount rate that embodies a built-in risk premium compensates for the *risk borne per period*. The more distant the cash flows, the greater the number of periods and, hence, the greater the adjustment for risk. The only question is how much more risky the more distant cash flows are. If they are highly risky, then a higher discount rate, embodying a higher risk premium, may be needed. The point to remember is this: Some, and perhaps all, of the increase in riskiness of more distant cash flows is already accounted for simply by using the opportunity cost of capital.

FACTORS TO CONSIDER WHEN ESTIMATING RISK

Risk relates to variability in returns, particularly returns that are less than those expected. Although the assessment of the risk associated with capital budgeting decisions is not easy, executives make such judgments every day. Some of the things they need to take into consideration are fudge factors, cyclicality, operating leverage, and financial leverage.

Figure 9.1

Increasing Risk Over Time

As the dispersion increases, risk increases. Using any rate above the risk-free rate in the discounting process implicitly compensates for some increases in risk.

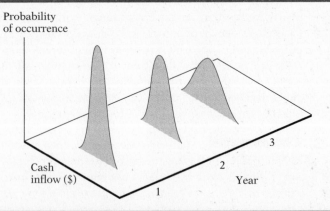

Fudge Factors, or Making the Adjustment in the Cash Flows   In working with firms, we have encountered situations in which the firm felt that some projects were more risky than the average risk of the firm. Their "solution" was to add a fudge factor to the opportunity cost of capital to compensate for the additional risk. Although that may be the correct procedure in some cases, too often the impact of potential bad outcomes is not fully reflected in the cash flow forecasts. Thus, mistakes in estimating cash flows are "compensated for" by adding a fudge factor to the discount rate.

Consider a project that requires a $5 million outflow and is expected to produce after-tax inflows of $2.25 million for each of three years. If the discount rate is 13 percent, the net present value of the project is

$$\text{NPV} = \$2,250,000 \ (\text{PVA}_{13\%, \, 3\text{yr}}) - \$5,000,000$$
$$= \$2,250,000(2.361) - \$5,000,000 = \$312,250$$

It looks as if the project should be accepted. However, upon investigation you find out that due to problems getting government clearance there is a strong possibility that no cash inflow will occur in the first year. If that happens, and assuming that $2.25 million in cash inflow will occur in each of years 2 through 4, the revised NPV is

$$\text{NPV}_{\text{revised}} = \$5,312,250 \ (\text{PV}_{13\%, \, 1\text{yr}}) - \$5,000,000$$
$$= \$5,312,250(0.885) - \$5,000,000 = -\$298,659$$

Clearly, this revised NPV is very different from the first NPV. In this case, there is *some* discount rate that, when applied to the original set of cash inflows of $2.25 million for years 1 through 3, will produce the revised NPV of −$298,659. That discount rate happens to be 20.52 percent; but how do you know beforehand to add a risk premium of $20.52 - 13.00 = 7.52$ percent to account for the probability that no cash flows will occur until year 2? The answer is that you generally do not have any idea. Hence, the preferable approach in *all* capital investment decisions is to spend a lot of time, ask a lot of questions, and make sure that all possible assumptions and contingencies have been built into the cash flows. *Many of the problems in dealing with risk can be solved by first and foremost focusing on the cash flows.*

Cyclicality   The revenues and cash flows of some firms and projects are tied very closely to the state of the economy. Thus, firms and projects in high-tech industries, automobile firms, and retailers tend to be affected by the stage of the business cycle much more than firms in utilities or foods are. Due to this greater risk, which typically cannot be diversified away, higher returns and discount rates are needed on investments whose performance is strongly tied to the stage of the business cycle.

Operating Leverage   The concept of **operating leverage** refers to the commitment of the firm to incur fixed cash outflows for production and administration, no matter what the level of sales. Other things being equal, firms that have more operating leverage (that is, relatively more fixed cash outflows for operations) will see their cash flows fluctuate much more in response to a change in sales.

Consider two firms as follows:

	Low-Fixed-Cost Firm	High-Fixed-Cost Firm
Sales	$1,000,000	$1,000,000
Variable operating costs	600,000	200,000
Fixed operating costs	100,000	500,000
EBIT	$ 300,000	$ 300,000

operating leverage can be determined by

$$\text{operating leverage} = \frac{(\text{sales} - \text{variable costs})}{\text{EBIT}} \tag{9.2}$$

where EBIT is the earnings before interest and taxes.[1] Using Equation 9.2, we find that the operating leverage for the low-fixed-cost firm is 1.33, while it is 2.67 for the high-fixed-cost firm. As sales fluctuate, the low-fixed-cost firm's EBIT will fluctuate 1.33 times as much. Thus, if sales go up by 20 percent, then due to the lower use of fixed operating costs, EBIT will go up by about 27 percent [i.e., (20 percent)(1.33) = 26.60 percent ≈ 27 percent]. For the high-fixed-cost firm, the higher operating leverage indicates that for a 20 percent increase in sales, EBIT will increase by about 53 percent [i.e., (20 percent)(2.67) = 53.40 ≈ 53 percent].

Firms or projects that have mostly high fixed operating costs have more operating leverage. Other things being equal, higher operating leverage means that the firm's or project's cash flows vary much more over the stage of the business cycle. These higher-risk projects require higher returns and discount rates.

Financial Leverage   Financial leverage refers to the presence or absence of high fixed costs of financing. It is a concept that is analogous to operating leverage, except that now the fixed costs relate to financing, not operations. Firms or projects that employ a lot of debt or other fixed-financing-costs sources of financing (such as leases or preferred stock) have more financial leverage. As EBIT fluctuates, high financial leverage means that more of the cash flows go to the fixed-cost providers of capital and less to the firm and its owners. The impact of financial leverage on the value of the firm is examined in detail in Chapters 12 and 13.

Since many factors affect the riskiness of projects, estimating the specific amount of risk is not an easy task. By first focusing on the cash flows, financial managers can avoid many of the problems related to adjusting the opportunity cost of capital to reflect the

---

[1] Operating leverage can also be measured by:

$$\text{Operating leverage} = \frac{\text{percentage change in EBIT}}{\text{percentage change in sales}}$$

Operating leverage, as given by Equation 9.2, is simply the linear approximation for the elasticity measured at a given level of output.

project's riskiness. Then, the key is to focus on the major uncertainties facing the economy and how they will affect the proposed project and to consider the action (and/or reaction) of competitors.

Concept Review Questions

- Why is consideration of a project's risk important for capital budgeting decisions?
- How can risk benefit the firm?
- Describe the factors that should be considered when estimating risk.
- What is the difference between operating leverage and financial leverage?

OPPORTUNITY COST OF CAPITAL FOR CAPITAL BUDGETING DECISIONS

Once we start considering risk adjustment, we need to distinguish between two different situations. The first is those for which *both initially and over time* the risks are above or below the average risk of the projects considered by the firm. The second involves projects for which *initially the risks are above the average risk of the firm, but after some initial period the risks decrease.* Because different approaches are needed to deal with these two cases, we examine them separately. In this section we first consider opportunity costs of capital for capital budgeting projects, then we examine possible portfolio effects, and, finally, we consider situations in which risk is expected to decrease after an initial start-up period.

FIRM, DIVISIONAL, AND PROJECT-SPECIFIC OPPORTUNITY COSTS

In Chapters 7 and 8 we assumed, for simplicity, that risk was the same for all projects faced by the firm. But we know this cannot be true. Some projects must be more risky, while others are probably very safe. In cases in which risk differs significantly from the firm's overall level of risk, the use of a firm-wide opportunity cost of capital results in the misallocation of resources.

Consider Figure 9.2, which depicts the effect of using a single firm-wide opportunity cost of capital when risk is not uniform across projects. If the firm is an all-equity firm and its firm-wide opportunity cost is employed, project A will be rejected and project B will be accepted. However, if project A is less risky than the average project faced by the firm, then a lower discount rate (as given by the sloped project-specific opportunity cost of capital line) should be employed. All projects whose expected return and risk fall on the solid line whose intercept is k_{RF} are zero net present value projects, since these projects are expected to earn only their risk-adjusted cost. Those above the line are positive NPV projects; those below the line are negative NPV projects. Because project A has an IRR greater than its appropriate (risk-adjusted) opportunity cost of capital, it should be accepted. Conversely, project B is more risky; accordingly, an opportunity cost higher than the firm's overall opportunity cost of capital should be employed. Because the anticipated return on project B is less than its project-specific opportunity cost, it should be rejected. It is easy to see the effect of

Figure 9.2

Firm-Wide and Project-Specific Opportunity Costs of Capital

Use of a firm-wide cost of capital will overallocate funds to risky projects (like project B) and underallocate them to safe projects (project A).

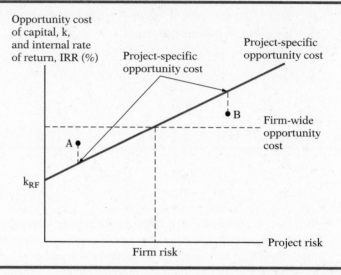

using a single rate for discounting all capital budgeting proposals: We overallocate resources to risky projects, while we underallocate resources to safer projects. The impact of such a mistake is to reduce the value of the firm.

As noted previously, the opportunity cost of capital appropriate for evaluating any capital budgeting project can be thought of as:

opportunity cost of capital = risk-free rate + risk premium based on project risk

There are, in fact, three different approaches (as discussed in Chapter 6) to specifying what this opportunity cost should be. The first, based on the firm's weighted average cost of capital, provides a single firm-wide opportunity cost of capital. This rate is appropriate for use when considering most replacement projects for a firm, or when the firm is homogeneous in terms of its projects and is not investing in any high- or low-risk projects.

The second approach is embodied in the form of divisional costs of capital. For example, an integrated oil company may have four divisions: domestic exploration, international exploration, refining, and marketing. Based on perceived risks in the different areas, the firm may establish divisional opportunity costs of capital as follows:

Domestic exploration	20%
International exploration	30
Refining	16
Marketing	12

These are the discount rates used in each division when calculating net present value. The use of divisional rates may be thought of as a way station between the use of a single firm-wide opportunity cost of capital and, alternatively, different opportunity costs of capital for each project. In practice many firms employ some type of divisional cost of capital for capital budgeting purposes.

Finally, a project-specific opportunity cost of capital can be used based on the risk associated with an individual project. Often the capital asset pricing model (CAPM) is employed to estimate these project-specific rates of return. Based on nondiversifiable risk, *for an all-equity-financed firm* a project's opportunity cost of capital using the CAPM would be

$$k_{project} = k_{RF} + \beta_{project}(k_M - k_{RF}) \tag{9.3}$$

where

$k_{project}$ = the project's opportunity cost of capital
$\quad k_{RF}$ = the risk-free rate of interest
$\beta_{project}$ = the project's nondiversifiable risk as measured by its beta coefficient
$\quad k_M$ = the expected rate of return on the market portfolio

Thus, if the firm is all equity financed, the project-specific discount rate based on the CAPM is given by the security market line (SML), introduced in Chapter 5. These three approaches to estimating the opportunity cost of capital are depicted in Figure 9.3.

Two points should be emphasized regarding the use of alternative opportunity costs of capital that consider the risk of capital budgeting projects. First is the **stand-alone principle**. This principle says that a proposed project should be accepted or

Figure 9.3

Alternative Opportunity Costs of Capital

Use of appropriate opportunity costs of capital, based on the risks and forgone opportunities, is essential for effective capital budgeting decision making.

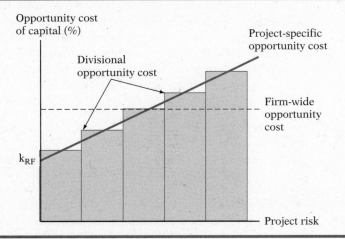

rejected by comparing it with the returns that could be secured based on investing in a similar-risk project. The forgone returns from the bypassed investment are captured by using the appropriate opportunity cost of the forgone alternative for the project. For example, if an equally risky investment involves investing in securities that would provide an expected return of 20 percent, then the proposed capital investment must return at least 20 percent. Otherwise the firm should reject the proposed capital project and invest in the securities. This stand-alone principle is important for all capital investment decisions made by the firm.

Second, estimation of the appropriate opportunity cost of capital in the face of risk is part science and part judgment. Although no method of dealing with risk is entirely precise, it is an important step that managers must take if they want to maximize the value of the firm. Failure to do so results in the same effect the ostrich achieves by burying its head in the ground: The world continues to spin and change while the ostrich (or firm) maintains its naive view that all is well.

WHAT ABOUT PORTFOLIO EFFECTS?

Should firms concern themselves about the possible interaction between the cash flows expected from a new project and those from existing projects? The answer to that question is generally no, but it is more complicated than that. *First and foremost*, if a new project is expected to have any positive or negative effect on cash flows associated with existing projects, then these must (as noted in Chapter 8) be treated as opportunity costs or benefits and incorporated into the cash flows estimated for the new project.

The bigger question is this: Are there risk-reducing benefits that arise when a firm undertakes a project whose returns are less than perfectly positively correlated with those of the firm? That is, should the firm consider itself a portfolio and attempt to accept projects that reduce the risk (or standard deviation) of the portfolio returns? If financial markets are efficient, the answer is no. The reason is that investors are able to diversify on their own; they do not receive any incremental benefits from having the firm diversify. In effect, the firm is performing a redundant service.

In countries where financial markets are not completely efficient, there may be some risk reduction (in terms of the volatility of the firm's cash flows, probability of bankruptcy, and so forth) that can be achieved. It is very hard, however, to measure this benefit, and very easy to overestimate its impact. For this reason, projects should be considered on their individual merits, without attempting to quantify any benefits from risk reduction. Then, if (and only if) they appear to be very important, possible portfolio effects can be introduced into the decision-making process.

WHEN A SINGLE DISCOUNT RATE CANNOT BE USED

Up to now we have considered how to deal with risk that is above or below the firm's risk over the entire economic life of the project. But what about the situation in which risk is high at first but then decreases? Consider the proposed development and marketing of Clean-Ez, a portable electric car washer. In making its capital budgeting decision, the firm estimated that the preliminary phase, involving a small pilot plant and test marketing, would require a $7 million initial investment at time t = 0. If the preliminary phase is successful, a $40 million cash investment will be required to build the plant at time t = 1; then for the next nine years (times t = 2 through t = 10), the after-tax cash inflows will be $12 million per year. Thus, the estimated cash flow stream is as follows:

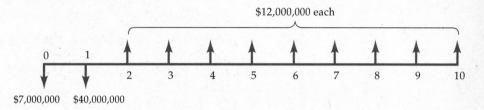

$12,000,000 each

$7,000,000 $40,000,000

Because of the high risk of the project, a 20 percent return (versus the firm's opportunity cost of capital of 12 percent) was used. Based on a 20 percent discount rate, the NPV was

$$\text{NPV} = \$12{,}000{,}000(\text{PVA}_{20\%,\,9\,\text{yr}})(\text{PV}_{20\%,\,1\,\text{yr}}) - \$40{,}000{,}000(\text{PV}_{20\%,\,1\,\text{yr}}) - \$7{,}000{,}000$$

$$= \$12{,}000{,}000(4.031)(0.833) - \$40{,}000{,}000(0.833) - \$7{,}000{,}000$$

$$= \$40{,}293{,}876 - \$33{,}320{,}000 - \$7{,}000{,}000 = -\$26{,}124$$

Because the NPV is negative, the initial decision was to reject Clean-Ez.

However, Kay, one of the finance staff, asked: "Have we accurately considered the riskiness of Clean-Ez? If risk decreases after the preliminary phase, then the use of a 20 percent discount rate over the entire life of Clean-Ez unnecessarily penalizes more distant cash flows." After some discussion, it was determined that there was only a 50–50 probability that the second investment (of $40 million) would be made at time t = 1. If the test marketing in the preliminary phase was below expectations, then the additional funds would not be spent. On the other hand, if the preliminary phase was a success, then Clean-Ez would be of average risk, and a 12 percent discount rate would be appropriate over its remaining life.

Based on this additional information, Kay proceeded to employ **sequential analysis** as follows. First, she pointed out that there are two separate parts to the proposed project. The $7 million for the preliminary phase will be spent regardless. Depending on the results of that phase, there is a 50 percent chance that a $40 million cash investment will be made in one year for a project of average risk. Likewise, there is a 50 percent chance that no additional investment will be made. So,

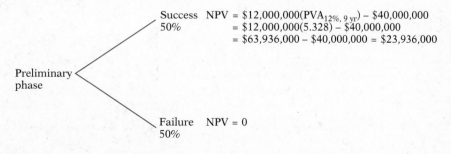

Success   NPV = $12,000,000(PVA$_{12\%,\,9\,\text{yr}}$) − $40,000,000
50%   = $12,000,000(5.328) − $40,000,000
                = $63,936,000 − $40,000,000 = $23,936,000

Preliminary
phase

Failure   NPV = 0
50%

The **expected NPV** in year 1 is simply $0.50(\$23,936,000) + 0.50(0) =$ $\$11,968,0000$. But this NPV is for a project starting at $t = 1$, and we have not considered the \$7 million initial investment. Looking at the NPV of the total project from its inception, it is

$$NPV = \$11,968,000(PV_{20\%, 1yr}) - \$7,000,000$$

$$= \$11,968,000(0.833) - \$7,000,000$$

$$= \$9,969,344 - 7,000,000 = \$2,969,344$$

Based on this analysis, Kay concluded (correctly) that the Clean-Ez project has a positive NPV and should be funded.[2]

One often hears executives or other critics of the present value approach say it unnecessarily penalizes long-term projects. As we have just seen, that does not have to be the case. By treating the decision as a sequential investment, we can handle the risk-adjustment question. However, if we simply use a high discount rate, we *will* be guilty of penalizing long-term projects unnecessarily if risk is not consistently at the higher level.

Concept Review Questions

- What are the effects of using the firm's opportunity cost of capital when evaluating projects with different risks?
- What are the three different approaches to estimating an opportunity cost of capital?
- Describe how to adjust a project's opportunity cost of capital if you anticipate a decrease of risk in future years.

INFORMATION ABOUT THE RISKINESS OF PROJECTS

Up to now we have discussed risk in general as it relates to capital budgeting projects, and then considered how differences in risk can be dealt with through the use of a firm-wide opportunity cost of capital, divisional opportunity costs, or project-specific opportunity costs of capital. Before making capital budgeting decisions, it is important to examine the critical variables and assumptions that are expected to affect the project's success or failure. To do so we can employ sensitivity analysis, break-even analysis, and simulation.

SENSITIVITY ANALYSIS

Sensitivity analysis does not formally attempt to quantify risk. Rather, it focuses on determining how sensitive the net present value is to changes in any of the input variables. To understand sensitivity analysis, let us consider the following example:

---

[2] An alternative approach to this problem involves the use of option concepts. The subsequent investment is an option that will be exercised only if the pilot plant and test marketing phase are successful. This topic is discussed further in Chapter 19.

Year	CF
0	−$55,000
1	20,000
2	20,000
3	20,000
4	20,000
5	20,000

At a discount rate of 13 percent, the base-case NPV is

$$NPV = \$20,000(PVA_{13\%,\,5yr}) - \$55,000$$
$$= \$20,000(3.517) - \$55,000$$
$$= \$70,340 - \$55,000 = \$15,340$$

To conduct a sensitivity analysis, we need to change one of the input variables to determine how sensitive the NPV is to changes in that particular variable. The input data can be changed by a certain percentage, or by a given dollar amount.

To see how sensitive the NPV is to changes in the initial investment and number of years, we changed them each by 20 percent.[3] This results in an NPV of $4,340 for a 20 percent increase or $26,340 for the same size decrease in the initial investment. Likewise, the NPV is $24,960 if the number of years increases by 20 percent (to six years) or $4,480 if it decreases by 20 percent (to four years). In Figure 9.4, this

Figure 9.4

Sensitivity Analysis of 20 Percent Change in Initial Investment and Years
The steeper the slope, the more sensitive the NPV is to a change in the input variable.

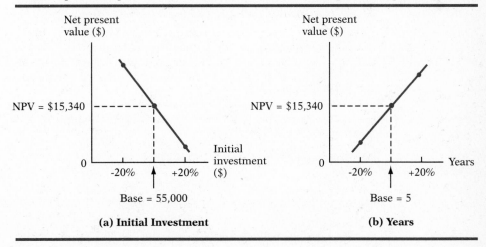

(a) Initial Investment   **(b) Years**

[3] For simplicity we assume the per year capital cost allowance remains constant, although the initial investment changes.

information is plotted against the base-case NPV. The steeper the slope, the more sensitive the project's NPV is to a change in the input variable. We see that this project's NPV is slightly more sensitive to a 20 percent change in the initial investment than to a 20 percent change in its life. Sensitivity analysis is widely employed in practice. This is especially true with the increasing use of spreadsheet programs and on-line capital budgeting computer systems.

BREAK-EVEN ANALYSIS

When undertaking a sensitivity analysis of a project, we are asking how serious it would be if some factor (i.e., cash inflows, life of the project, and so forth) turns out far worse than expected. Managers sometimes prefer to rephrase this question and ask how bad sales (and, therefore, cash inflows) could get before the project loses money. This approach is known as **break-even analysis**.

There are two approaches to conducting break-even analysis. The accounting approach focuses on accounting-based revenues and costs, whereas the financial approach focuses on the discounted cash inflows and cash outflows. We shall see that the accounting approach, based on accounting costs and revenues, provides a biased estimate of the actual break-even point; it is too low. Hence, when firms break even in an accounting sense they are losing money. The correct, financial-based break-even point occurs when the present value of the inflows equals the present value of the outflows, so that the net present value is zero.

To illustrate break-even analysis, assume that Whiz-Bang Motors is projecting net income and cash flows for its new product line as shown in Table 9.1. Under simplifying assumptions—where sales equal gross cash inflows, there are no accruals, and tax and GAAP depreciation are the same—Whiz-Bang estimates that when sales are $300,

| Table 9.1 | |

GAAP Net Income and Cash Flow for Whiz-Bang

For simplicity, we assume that the equipment costs $1,000 and is depreciated to zero over 10 years via straight line for both accounting and tax purposes. (The half-year convention built into straight line capital cost allowance is ignored in this example.) Also, we assume that there are no accruals, and that sales and costs are all collected (or incurred) so they are equal to cash inflows and outflows.

	GAAP Income	**Cash Flow**
Sales	$300	$300
Variable costs (20% of sales)	60	60
Fixed costs	50	50
Depreciation	100	
Earnings before tax (EBT)	90	
Taxes (40%)	36	36
Net income	$ 54	
Cash flow		$154

net income will be $54. To determine the accounting break-even point, we want to find the dollar level of sales at which the net income is equal to zero. (To estimate an answer, we know that at sales of $300, net income is $54, so we know that the accounting-based break-even level of sales is less than $300.) The accounting-based break-even point is determined as follows:

$$\text{zero sales} = \text{revenues} - \text{costs}$$
$$0 = \text{sales}(1 - \text{variable costs}) - \text{fixed costs} - \text{depreciation} - \text{taxes}$$
$$0 = [\text{sales}(1 - \text{variable costs}) - \text{fixed costs} - \text{depreciation}](1 - \text{tax rate})$$
$$0 = [\text{sales}(1 - 0.20) - \$50 - \$100](1 - 0.40)$$
$$0 = (0.80\text{sales} - \$150)(0.60)$$
$$0 = 0.48\text{sales} - \$90$$
$$0.48\text{sales} = \$90$$
$$\text{sales} = \$90/0.48 = \$187.50$$

Thus, the accounting-based break-even level of sales occurs at $187.50. In Figure 9.5 we have plotted this relationship. The accounting-based break-even point indicates that the firm loses money up to a sales level of $187.50 and that it makes money (i.e., has revenue greater than costs) above a sales level of $187.50.

There are three differences between the accounting-based and the finance-based approaches to determining the break-even point. First, in finance we focus on cash

Figure 9.5

Break-Even Chart Based on GAAP Net Income

By ignoring the opportunity costs associated with capital investments, net-income-based break-even analysis seriously understates the financial break-even point.

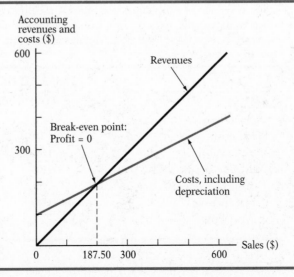

flow, not on accounting-based revenues and costs. Second, we take account of the time value of money by discounting. Finally, in finance we consider the opportunity cost of the investment. Let us see the differences when the correct finance-based approach is employed. Going back to the sales level of $300 as discussed in Table 9.1, we see that based on an initial cash investment of $1,000, a 10-year life, and a discount rate of 15 percent, the per year cash flows after tax, CF_t, are $154. With cash flows of $154 per year for 10 years, the net present value of the proposed project for Whiz-Bang is:

$$NPV = \$154(PVA_{15\%, 10yr}) - \$1,000$$
$$= \$154(5.019) - \$1,000 = \$772.93 - \$1,000 = -\$227.07$$

At sales of $300 the accounting-based revenues and costs (from Table 9.1) indicate a profit of $54; but we have just determined that the project has a negative net present value. Being financial experts by now, we know that if we accept negative-NPV projects we are lowering the value of the firm. How can the accounting-based analysis produce a profit, when we have just concluded that accepting the project will cause the value of the firm to decline? The crux of the problem is the accountants' lack of discounting and their treatment of the $1,000 initial investment, as we will see.

To continue our example, taking the financial approach, what happens if (with all of the same assumptions) sales are zero or, alternatively, if they are $600? As shown in Table 9.2, when sales are zero the after-tax cash flows are $10 each year; with sales of $600 the after-tax cash flows are $298 each year. The net present value at zero sales[4]

Table 9.2

GAAP Net Income and Cash Flow for Whiz-Bang With Sales of Zero and $600

Using the same assumptions as in Table 9.1, we see that cash flows differ significantly for these two levels of sales. When sales are zero the project incurs a loss of $150, which can be used to reduce the taxes paid on income generated by the firm's other projects. Consequently, at zero sales the project produces a tax saving of $60 (150 × 0.40)—the tax cash outflow is negative.

	GAAP Income		Cash Flow	
Sales	$ 0	$600	$ 0	$600
Variable costs (20% of sales)	0	120	0	120
Fixed costs	50	50	50	50
Depreciation	100	100		
Earnings before tax (EBT)	−150	330		
Taxes (40%)	−60	132	−60	132
Net income	$ −90	$198		
Cash flow			$ 10	$298

---

[4] When sales equal zero the NPV is $10(5.019) − $1,000 = $50.19 − $1,000 = −$949.81, whereas at sales of $600 the NPV is $298(5.019) − $1,000 = $1,495.66 − $1,000 = $495.66.

is −$949.81, whereas the NPV when sales are $600 per year is $495.66. To summarize, the accounting net income, cash flow, and net present value for the three levels of sales of zero, $300, and $600 are:

	Sales of $0 per Year	Sales of $300 per Year	Sales of $600 per Year
Net income	−$ 90	$ 54	$198
Cash flow per year, CF$_t$	10	154	298
NPV	−949.81	−227.07	495.66

We see that the NPV is highly negative when sales are zero, moderately negative when sales equal $300, and positive when sales equal $600 per year. Clearly, the zero-NPV point occurs between $300 and $600 in sales.

To solve for the zero-NPV level we proceed as follows:

$$\text{zero NPV} = \text{PV of inflows} - \text{PV of outflows} = 0$$
$$CF_t\,(PVA_{15\%,\,10\,\text{yr}}) - \$1{,}000 = 0$$
$$CF_t\,(5.019) = \$1{,}000$$
$$CF_t = \$1{,}000/5.019 = \$199.25$$

The sales volume (before variable costs, fixed costs, and taxes) needed to generate after-tax cash inflows of $199.25 for each of 10 years is obtained as follows:

$$\text{sales} - (\text{variable} + \text{fixed costs}) - \text{taxes} = \$199.25$$
$$\text{sales} - (0.20\text{sales} + \$50) - (\text{sales} - 0.20\text{sales} - \$50 - \$100)(0.40) = \$199.25$$
$$\text{sales} - 0.20\text{sales} - \$50 - 0.40\text{sales} + 0.08\text{sales} + \$20 + \$40 = \$199.25$$
$$0.48\text{sales} + \$10 = \$199.25$$
$$\text{sales} = \$189.25/0.48$$
$$= \$394.27$$

This relationship is plotted in Figure 9.6. The present value of the cash inflows and the present value of the cash outflows cross at sales of $394.27. This is the point where the project has a zero NPV. As long as sales are greater than $394.27 per year, the project has a positive NPV.

What is the difference between the accounting and the financial approach to break-even analysis? First, the accounting approach, as shown in Figure 9.5, indicates Whiz-Bang breaks even at sales of $187.50. On the other hand, the financial approach (in Figure 9.6) indicates that Whiz-Bang does not break even until sales are $394.27—a sales level more than double that indicated by the accounting approach. What causes this vast difference? The difference in the two approaches hinges on the depreciation of $100 per year that is deducted for GAAP purposes and the required rate of return of 15 percent for the project. *By treating break-even analysis in an accounting manner, managers are ignoring the opportunity cost of the $1,000 investment.* We must allow for

Figure 9.6

Break-Even Chart Based on Total Present Values

This is a form of sensitivity analysis, allowing sales (or the present value of the cash inflows) to change.

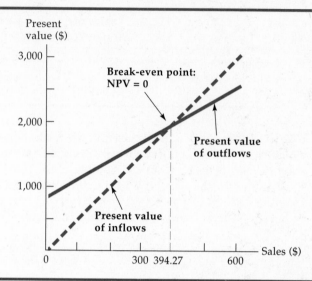

the fact that the $1,000 could have been invested elsewhere to earn a return of 15 percent. Depreciation thus understates the true cost by ignoring the forgone opportunity to earn a return on the $1,000 initial investment. Companies that break even on an accounting basis are actually losing money—*they are losing the opportunity cost of their investment.* Whiz-Bang should not introduce the project unless sales are expected to be at least $394.27 per year. To do so will lower the value of the firm.

SIMULATION

Sensitivity analysis allows you to consider the effect of changing one variable at a time. A more refined approach, **scenario analysis**, is based on changing a limited number of possible combinations. A further refinement is **simulation**, which is a technique for considering the effect of changing *all* of the relevant variables in an analysis. Simulation used to require relatively sophisticated computer programming, but recent developments in computer software make it easy to use within a **spreadsheet program** like Enable or Lotus 1-2-3®.

The first step in a computer simulation is to specify the relevant variables and the probability distributions associated with each variable. In our Whiz-Bang example, the relevant variables (at a minimum) are sales, the relationship of variable costs to sales, the initial investment, and the economic life of the project. In fact, as any manager will testify, this is a very short list of relevant variables. To illustrate simulation, suppose that the probabilities of Whiz-Bang's sales associated with this new project have been estimated as follows:

Sales (1)	Probability (2)	Associated Random Number (3)
$ 0	0.05	0–4
150	0.25	5–29
300	0.40	30–69
450	0.25	70–94
600	0.05	95–99

The sales may be between $0 and $600, with the probabilities as indicated in column 2. Also, the associated random variables, as shown in column 3, are recorded.[5] Once this probability distribution of possible outcomes is estimated for sales, we then proceed to estimate probability distributions for all of the other relevant variables that are likely to change. Specifying the variables and their probabilities is not easy, but it is often easier than the next step.

The second step involves specifying the interdependencies between variables and across time. Specifying the interdependencies is the hardest, and also the most important, part of a simulation. If all of the components of a project's cash flows are unrelated, then the simulation is easy.

Once the variables, probabilities, and interdependencies have been specified, the simulation proceeds as follows:

STEP 1:   Computers, through random number generations, will select a possible outcome for each variable. For sales, let us assume the random number 73 comes up.

STEP 2:   For each variable, the random number selected determines the value to be employed for that variable. The 73 associated with sales means that the appropriate sales level for the first run of the simulation is $450. Values for all of the other variables are set in a similar manner.

STEP 3:   Once a value has been established for each of the variables, the computer generates an NPV for the first run of the simulation.

STEP 4:   This NPV is then stored, and the computer runs the second analysis. Here a different set of random numbers, and therefore a different set of values for the variables, is selected. The NPV is then computed and stored. This procedure goes on for 250 to 500 (or more) runs.

STEP 5:   Once the 250 or 500 runs are completed, the frequency distribution of NPVs, the expected value, and the standard deviation are all printed out. Often a graph is presented, much like that shown in Figure 9.7.

Simulation, though complicated, has the obvious merit of compelling managers to face up to uncertainty and interdependency. Once the model is constructed, it is simple to analyze what would happen if the probability distribution changed for any one variable, or if the degree of interdependency increased or decreased from that

---

[5] For simplicity, we assume sales are a discrete variable that takes on only five values. This is solely for illustrative purposes; computer simulations routinely deal with continuous distributions.

Figure 9.7

Probability Distribution of NPVs

Calculating the probability of success gives us information about the advisability of accepting a project that has the potential to increase the value of the firm.

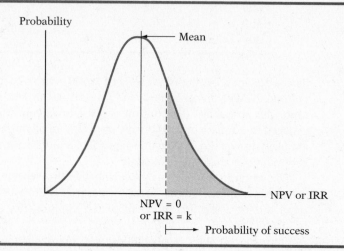

specified. Thus, simulation has the potential to enable us to ascertain many facets of the risk associated with proposed capital budgeting projects. Before we jump on the bandwagon, however, and conclude that simulation solves all of our ills, we need to consider a few of the problems with simulation.

The main problems are as follows:

1. COST AND TIME. Until recently it was very difficult to do realistic computer simulations on PCs. Although new computer software is changing that, it must be recognized that big, complex projects still require significant amounts of time to set up and run. Equally important, unless the decision makers have been instrumental in setting up the simulation, they may not have confidence in the results and/or the specific assumptions underlying the simulation.

2. INTERDEPENDENCIES. As indicated previously, specifying the interdependencies between variables, and over time, is the most difficult part of any simulation. Here, it is crucial for managers to pool their resources and knowledge and to come up with reasonable educated guesses as to interdependencies. Then these assumptions should be tested in the simulation, and communicated to the final decision makers.

3. INTERPRETATION. In capital budgeting techniques considered up to now, the outcome has been a single NPV. This simplifies the analysis and decision making, even though it may be unrealistic. But simulation may go to the other extreme: It provides a whole distribution of possible outcomes that can be converted into the probability of success. This **probability of success**, as shown in Figure 9.7, indicates what the chances are that the project will have a positive NPV. Not all managers are comfortable, however, with this additional information. They may have too much information or too little guidance as to what are acceptable probabilities of success or risk levels.

4. PROBLEMS RELATED TO NPV.   Finally, there are some peculiar problems related to probability distributions of NPVs. If the NPV approach is employed, then the appropriate discount rate may not be the project's opportunity cost of capital. Rather, all of the risk may be captured by specifying the probability distributions of the relevant variables. If all the risk is incorporated into the probability distribution, the NPV is calculated by *discounting at the risk-free rate*, k_{RF}. Once this step is taken, however, the resulting probability distribution of NPVs is very different from what is typically encountered. This is because we normally discount at the opportunity cost of capital, not at the risk-free rate. Hence, calculating NPVs in a simulation may lead to as many problems as it solves.

Where do we stand on using simulation for dealing with risk in capital budgeting decisions? Although many theoretical and empirical advances have been made in using probability distribution approaches to make capital budgeting decisions, their use by firms has been very limited until recently. The availability of more powerful PCs and good simulation software is, however, refocusing attention on using simulation to help get a better handle on risk. Used wisely, with a knowledge of both its strengths and its limitations, simulation can aid effective decision making. While no panacea, it has progressed to the point where it can help decision makers gain a better understanding of the importance different variables, assumptions, and interactions have for capital budgeting decisions. As such, we view it as a reasonable addition to a good capital budgeting programme.

In this chapter we have identified a number of different ways of handling risk. Because risk comes from many sources, it is difficult to generalize about it. One thing is certain, however: Effective managers make a determined effort to probe for possible risks associated with capital budgeting projects. By proceeding in the manner described in this chapter, *they are ensuring that the right questions about risk are asked at the right time and that reasonable methods of dealing with it are being employed.*

Concept Review Questions

■ What is the purpose of employing sensitivity analysis, break-even analysis, and simulation?

■ What is wrong with using accounting revenues and costs to determine a break-even point? What factors does the financial approach to determining the break-even point consider that the accounting approach ignores?

■ What are some of the advantages and disadvantages of using simulation to evaluate a capital budgeting project?

KEY POINTS

- Risk may be beneficial; only by searching out their competitive advantages and accepting risks can firms expect to earn above-average returns.
- First and foremost, build all risk impacts into a project's cash flows if possible.
- Using any discount rate above the risk-free rate assumes implicitly that risk increases over time. The only questions are these: Is too much (too little) risk adjustment built into the

discount rate employed? Does risk change over time more (or less) than accounted for by the discount rate employed?

- "High" cyclicality, operating leverage, and financial leverage can all lead to greater risk.
- Project-specific or divisional opportunity costs of capital should be employed for more- or less-risky projects.
- The stand-alone principle is important: A project should be accepted or rejected based on a comparison with the returns that could be secured by investing in a similar-risk project.
- Sequential analysis can be employed when risk changes over the economic life of a project. Sensitivity analysis is also widely used. Break-even analysis should be conducted based on discounted cash flows, not GAAP accounting numbers. Firms that break even on the basis of GAAP accounting numbers are losing money—they are losing the opportunity cost of their investment.
- Simulation can provide a great deal of information to decision makers by allowing all of the input variables to change simultaneously. At the same time, it has some peculiar quirks that must be recognized when using it in capital budgeting decision making.

QUESTIONS

9.1 Mike, the CEO of Larson Enterprises, believes that the risk of a proposed capital budgeting project increases over time. As a result, a project-specific or divisional opportunity cost of capital must be chosen. As Larson's chief financial officer, explain to Mike when this strategy may not be appropriate.

9.2 The divisional opportunity cost of capital approach to capital budgeting, employing categories of projects with different risks, might be graphed as follows:

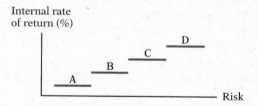

Explain how divisional opportunity costs capture many of the risk and return ideas of the capital asset pricing model. In what significant ways do the two differ?

9.3 Explain the importance of the stand-alone principle. Why are opportunity costs (or the forgone returns from bypassed investments) so important in making wealth-maximizing capital budgeting decisions?

9.4 Adam believes that sensitivity analysis is a viable way to deal with risk. Do you agree with him? Why or why not?

CONCEPT REVIEW PROBLEMS

See Appendix A for solutions.

CR9.1 Volkman Inc. is considering purchasing a coal mine in Nova Scotia. Cost of the coal mine is $8 million, and the opportunity cost of capital is 15 percent. Volkman's engineers believe (with 50 percent probability) that there is enough coal to produce $2 million in after-tax cash flows for the next five years. On the other hand, there may be (with 50 percent probability) enough coal to produce $2 million in after-tax cash flows for 10 years. What is the expected net present value of the project?

CR9.2 Mary, owner of Flowers Forever, is considering expanding into the silk flower market. She estimates that the expansion will cost $60,000 and that she will sell approximately 600 different silk floral arrangements per year over the next four years, at an average price of $100 per arrangement. Her operating costs are estimated to be approximately 50 percent of revenue.

a. If Flowers Forever's tax rate is 28 percent and the opportunity cost of capital is 10 percent, what is the net present value of this project? (For simplicity, assume no capital cost allowance will be taken on the $60,000 expenditure.)

b. Mary is concerned about the risk of the silk floral arrangement project. She is concerned that sales may not be 600 floral arrangements per year. Perform a sensitivity analysis on the number of silk floral arrangements sold per year in which the floral arrangements drop by 10 percent, 20 percent, or 30 percent or increase by 10 percent, 20 percent, or 30 percent.

CR9.3 Using the information for Flowers Forever given in CR9.2, what is the break-even for the number of units of floral arrangements sold per year?

CR9.4 Mary is concerned about the effects of a fluctuating economy on the profitability of the silk flower expansion in CR9.2. If a downturn in the economy occurs, she will be able to sell only 500 units at $80 per unit. However, if the economy is better than anticipated, she will be able to sell 700 units at $120 per unit. (*Note:* Costs remain 50 percent of revenue.)

a. If the probabilities are 30 percent for a downturn in the economy, 40 percent for the base-case economy with 600 units sold at $100 per unit, and 30 percent for an improved economy, what is the expected net present value of the three scenarios?

b. What is the standard deviation about the expected net present value?

PROBLEMS

9.1 Priester Industries employs the capital asset pricing model to estimate project-specific costs of capital for capital budgeting decisions. The risk-free rate is 7 percent, the expected return on the market portfolio is 15 percent, and the project's beta is 1.50. The cash flow stream is as follows:

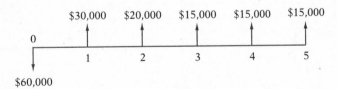

a. Should Priester undertake the proposed project?

b. Can you see any problems associated with using the capital asset pricing model to estimate project-specific costs of capital for capital budgeting decision making?

9.2 Hexter is considering investing in some new equipment. The equipment costs $175,000 and will generate after-tax cash flows of $55,000 a year for five years. The CAPM approach will be used to estimate the appropriate project-specific opportunity cost of capital; $k_{RF} = 7$ percent, $\sigma_{project}$(standard deviation of the project's returns) $= 32.20$ percent, $Corr_{project, M} = +0.60$, and the distribution of the market's return is:

Probability, P_i	Market Return, k_M
0.20	30%
0.20	20
0.30	15
0.30	−5

Should Hexter purchase the equipment?

9.3   Your firm is considering two mutually exclusive projects with the following CFs:

	Project A		Project B	
Initial investment	$120,000		$150,000	
CFs and probabilities	0.30	$35,000	0.30	$60,000
of occurrence	0.40	30,000	0.40	40,000
for *each of 6 years*	0.30	20,000	0.30	30,000

The following equation is employed to estimate the project-specific opportunity cost of capital:

$$\text{opportunity cost of capital} = \text{risk-free rate} + 10\% \text{ (coefficient of variation)}$$
$$= 11\% + 10\% \text{ CV}_{project}$$

a.   Which project is riskier, based on its coefficient of variation? (*Note:* The coefficient of variation is standard deviation/mean.)
b.   Which, if either, of the projects should be selected? (*Note:* Round the opportunity cost of capital to the nearest whole percent.)

9.4   GED Enterprises is evaluating whether to build an exclusive resort on the island of St. Vincent in the Caribbean. The CFs are estimated to be $23 million for each of 15 years, the initial after-tax investment is $150 million, and the appropriate discount rate is 10 percent.
a.   Should GED proceed with the project?
b.   Upon further investigation, it is decided that the CFs could be better characterized by the following probability distribution:

Condition	Probability	CFs per Year
Economy great	0.2	$30 million
Economy average	0.7	23 million
Hurricane: resort demolished	0.1	0

Does this new information affect the decision?

9.5   Berry Foods has developed chocolate marbles. The product will be test marketed in western Canada for two years, requires an initial investment of $2 million, and because of heavy promotional expenses is not expected to generate any positive CFs during the first two years. There is a 60 percent chance that demand for the chocolate marbles will be satisfactory; if that is so, an $8 million after-tax cash investment will be incurred at t = 2 to market the chocolate marbles nation-wide. Subsequent CFs are as follows:

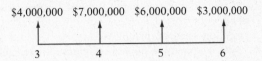

If the test-market results are unfavourable (a 40 percent chance), then the chocolate marbles will be withdrawn from the market. Once consumer preferences are known, Berry Foods considers chocolate marbles an average-risk project requiring a 14 percent return. During the test-marketing phase a 25 percent return is required. What decision should Berry make?

9.6   Greentree Products is considering investing in a capital budgeting project with the following CFs:

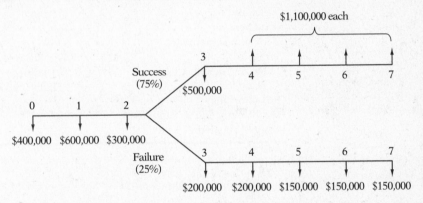

For the first three years, the appropriate opportunity cost of capital is 30 percent; after that, it drops to 10 percent. What decision should Greentree make?

9.7   Rainbow Painters would like to purchase a mixing machine for an initial investment of $11,000. It would last five years and produce after-tax operating cash flows of $3,900 per year. The discount rate is 16 percent.

a.   Decide whether the company should purchase the mixer under each of the following independent conditions. To which variable is the accept–reject decision most sensitive?
1.   The estimates are correct.
2.   The machine lasts only four years.
3.   After-tax operating cash flows, which are constant over time, decrease by 10 percent for years 1 through 5.
4.   The discount rate is 3 percent too low.

b.   Should the company invest in the mixer if all of the following conditions exist simultaneously?
1.   Machine cost = $13,000.
2.   Discount rate = 15 percent.
3.   Marginal tax rate = 33 percent.
4.   Ending resale value (before tax) = $2,000.
5.   Machine will last 10 years.
6.   After-tax operating cash flows, which are constant over time, increase by 25 percent for years 1 through 10.

9.8 The board of directors of Peninsula Industries has just received a proposal that requires an initial investment of $1 million and is expected to produce cash flows before tax (CFBT) of $300,000 for each year of its life. As presented, the project has a seven-year economic life, but because of a special tax ruling Peninsula is being allowed to use straight-line CCA over five years. The discount rate is 15 percent, and the firm's tax rate is 35 percent. (*Note:* Ignore the half-year convention when calculating CCA.)

a. Should Peninsula's board recommend acceptance of the project?

b. After discussing the project, certain members of the board feel the economic life will be only **(1)** five years or **(2)** six years, not seven. Does this new information change the previous decision?

9.9 A proposed project has the following characteristics:

Units sold per year	110,000
Price per unit	$600
Variable cost per unit	$460
Fixed cost	$4 million per year
Initial investment, CF_0	$21 million
CCA	straight-line over 7 years
Economic life	7 years
Opportunity cost of capital, k	0.20
Marginal tax rate, T	0.35

a. What is the NPV for the proposed project? (*Note:* Ignore the half-year convention when calculating CCA.)

b. A second alternative calls for increasing the initial investment to $28 million. As a result variable costs will be cut to $420 per unit and fixed costs will be cut to $3 million per year. What is the financial break-even number of units between this and the original alternative?

9.10 McManus Systems has developed a whole new concept for distributing "gee-whizzes." Excluding land costs, the new outlets require an initial investment of $4 million per location. The following conditions apply:

1. Depreciation for both GAAP accounting and for tax purposes will be to a value of zero over 10 years using straight-line. (*Note:* Ignore the half-year convention when calculating depreciation.)
2. Variable costs are 50 percent of sales.
3. Fixed costs are $300,000 per year.
4. The firm's marginal tax rate is 30 percent, and the discount rate is 18 percent.

Excluding land costs, what is the accounting break-even point per year? What is the financial break-even point (also excluding land costs)? Why does the accounting break-even point underestimate the volume of sales necessary to produce a zero-NPV project?

9.11 Costs have decreased, and P.E.I. National is considering replacing some of its existing equipment. To help in negotiating the final purchase price, it has hired you as a consultant. The relevant facts are:

Existing Equipment

Only asset in asset class.

Purchased 5 years ago for $800,000.

Being depreciated to zero employing straight-line CCA over 10 years. (*Note*: Five years have already elapsed; ignore the half-year convention when calculating CCA.)

Will last 10 more years if retained.

Resale value if sold today is $150,000; resale value in 10 more years is $20,000.

Asset class will be terminated now if the new equipment is purchased, or in 10 years if the new equipment is not purchased.

New Equipment

Will be in a different asset class than the old equipment, and will be the only asset in the new class.

Will be depreciated to zero employing straight-line CCA over 10 years. (*Note*: Ignore the half-year convention when calculating CCA.)

Will last 10 years.

Resale value in 10 years is $50,000.

Benefits are a before-tax reduction in operating cash outflows of $75,000 per year.

The new asset class will be terminated at the end of the new equipments useful life in 10 years.

a. If the tax rate is 35 percent and the opportunity cost of capital is 15 percent, what is the initial purchase price on the new equipment so that the NPV equals zero? (*Note*: Assume the firm is profitable, so it receives the tax benefit from selling the existing system at a loss.)

b. Explain why the information calculated in (a) is important for effective decision making.

9.12 Mini Case   You were recently hired by Hensel Products to head its capital and strategic decisions group. Hensel has three major divisions as follows: a farm implements division that continues to experience intense competition and weak demand, a high-tech metal and materials division, and a financial services division. The financial services division originally provided financing only to dealers and farmers, but over the last 15 years it has undergone tremendous changes. Now it provides many different financial services to firms world-wide. At present Hensel employs a firm-wide opportunity cost of capital of 15 percent and does little to consider risk when making capital expenditure decisions.

a. One of your first jobs is to educate the board of directors and upper management on the basic ideas concerning the importance of risk-taking when making capital budgeting decisions, and the negative impact that the reliance on a firm-wide opportunity cost of capital may have on project selection. What should the firm be doing in terms of the opportunity costs of capital employed? How would you respond when one of the top executives challenges you by saying, "As long as we are discounting future cash flows we are considering risk, because future cash flows are treated as being inherently risky."

b. The metals and materials division is evaluating a new project. The division's projections for the after-tax cash flows associated with the proposed project are as follows:

Year	CF
0	−$2,500,000
1	−3,000,000
2	−4,000,000
3	5,000,000
4	6,000,000
5	6,000,000
6	3,000,000

1. At the firm's opportunity cost of capital, what decision should be made?
2. After listening to your presentation in (a), the board adopts a new divisional cost of capital. The new discount rate for the metals and materials division is 20 percent. Does this change the decision?
3. After talking with individuals in the metals and materials division, you find that the proposed project is actually more complicated. Specifically, you find out that there are two phases to the proposed project. The preliminary phase requires the investments at times t = 0, t = 1, and t = 2. Depending on the outcome of the preliminary phase the following might happen:

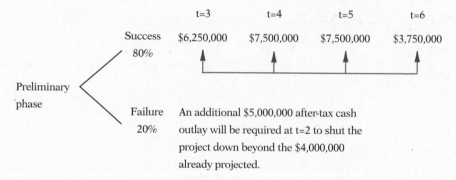

The preliminary phase is viewed as being very risky; a 40 percent discount rate is appropriate. After the preliminary phase, the 20 percent discount rate is viable. Does this new information affect the decision to accept or reject the project?

c. Now the financial services division comes to you with a project that has cash flows as follows:

Year	Cash Inflow	Cash Outflow
0	$ 0	$80,000
1	30,000	5,000
2	30,000	5,000
3	50,000	10,000
4	50,000	10,000
5	50,000	10,000
6	40,000	25,000
7	40,000	25,000
8	40,000	25,000

Capital cost allowance will be straight-line over five years, the appropriate tax rate is 30 percent, and the discount rate is 15 percent.

1. What is the base-case NPV? (*Note:* Ignore the half-year convention when calculating CCA.)
2. What is the NPV if each of the following occurs? (*Note:* Each part is separate and distinct from the other parts.) To which variable is the NPV most sensitive?
   a. Cash inflows decrease by 20 percent each year.
   b. Cash outflows in times t = 1 through t = 8 increase by 20 percent each year.
   c. The tax rate increases by 20 percent.
   d. The initial investment increases by 20 percent. (*Note:* This also changes the per year CCA.)
   e. The discount rate increases by 20 percent.
   f. The life of the project decreases to six years.
3. How is break-even analysis just another form of sensitivity analysis?

d. The farm implements division has been considering using simulation to assess the riskiness of its projects. What are the strengths and weaknesses of simulation?

REFERENCES

BUTLER, J. S., and BARRY SCHACHTER. "The Investment Decision: Estimation Risk and Risk Adjusted Discount Rates." *Financial Management* 18 (Winter 1989): 13–22.

DAY, GEORGE S., and LIAM FAHEY. "Putting Strategy into Shareholder Value Analysis," *Harvard Business Review* 68 (March–April 1990): 156–62.

GIACCOTTO, CARMELO. "A Simplified Approach to Risk Analysis in Capital Budgeting with Serially Correlated Cash Flows." *Engineering Economist* 29 (Summer 1984): 273–86

HODDER, JAMES E., and HENRY E. RIGGS. "Pitfalls in Evaluating Risky Projects." *Harvard Business Review* 63 (January–February 1985): 128–35.

LEVARY, REUVEN R., and NEIL E. SEITZ. *Quantitative Methods for Capital Budgeting*. Cincinnati: South-Western Publishers, 1990.

PART IV

Long-Term Financing Decisions

*F*irms have two primary sources of funds. They can generate funds internally from continuing operations or they can secure them externally from creditors or investors. Financing in the form of internally generated cash flows provides the vast majority of the average firm's needs, and short-term (one year or less) external financing provides another source. The remainder comes from net external long-term sources. Our attention will be focused on what securities can be used to raise these external long-term funds, and whether the composition of the different securities used has an impact on firm value. The primary way in which a firm maximizes its value is through the investment, or capital budgeting, decisions it makes. However, other decisions may also have an impact on the value of the firm. Two areas that have received a tremendous amount of attention, both in theory and in practice, are the firm's capital structure decision and its dividend policy. Strong cases have been made for each of these areas having, or not having, an impact on the market value of the firm.

Our attention in Chapters 10 and 11 will be primarily on the two main vehicles used by firms to raise external long-term capital—common stocks and bonds. In Chapters 12 and 13 we explore the impact of the firm's debt/equity, or capital structure, decision on the value of the firm. Finally, in Chapter 14 the implications of dividend policy are considered. As we will see, maximizing the long-run value of the firm in the marketplace requires an understanding of how these activities may affect the value of the firm.

10

Raising Long-Term Funds

EXECUTIVE SUMMARY

Firms acquire the majority of their financing from internally generated funds. Bonds are the most important source of long-term *external* financing. Public offerings involve either cash offerings or, to a far lesser extent, rights offerings. Bond and stock issues can be underwritten by investment dealers either on a firm commitment basis or through a best efforts offering. Underwriting transfers the risk from the issuing firm to the underwriting syndicate formed to sell the issue.

An alternative to the public offering is private placement. The major advantages of private placements are the speed with which they may be effected and elimination of the registration procedure. In addition, terms can be tailored to meet the needs of both issuer and investor. The Prompt Offering Prospectus (POP) system, adopted in 1982, allows large firms to lower their issuing costs by using a short-form prospectus; it also increases the speed and flexibility of the issuing process. The POP system has also led to the increased use of bought deals, where usually only one underwriter, instead of a syndicate, aids in bring an issue to market.

Common shareholders are the residual owners of the firm; as such, they have last claim on earnings in the form of cash dividends and assets in case of liquidation. Empirical evidence indicates that the value of the firm's stock falls as common stock is publicly issued. The sum of cash expenses and the fall in the price of stock accompanying a new issue of common stock are substantial; they range from 15 to 30 percent of the total financing. If preemptive rights exist, they allow current shareholders to purchase additional shares before the shares are offered to outsiders.

RAISING EXTERNAL LONG-TERM FUNDS

Firms can raise long-term funds in two ways: internally, by generating funds within the firm, and externally, by selling stock or debt. Table 10.1 indicates the funds raised by nonfinancial Canadian firms between 1984 and 1994 both internally and externally. The data indicate that over this period firms raised, on average, 57 percent of the funds they needed from internally generated sources. Thus, *the primary source of financing is the retention of cash flows generated by the firm*. The data also show that during this period the majority of external financing took the form of debt. This is due to the lower cost of debt in comparison to the cost of equity. One other important point illustrated in Table 10.1 is the cyclical nature of new debt and equity financing.

MEANS OF RAISING EXTERNAL FUNDS

Firms have a number of means of securing financing. These are shown in Figure 10.1. Once the firm decides it has to raise funds externally,[1] it has four basic alternatives. First, it can use a **public offering**. The two main types available are (1) a cash offering, which is made to investors at large, or (2) a rights offering (or privileged subscription),

---

Table 10.1

Internal and External Financing for Nonfinancial Canadian Firms, 1984–1994

In recent years firms have raised, on average, 57 percent of their funds from internally generated sources.

| | Financing in Dollars (millions) | | | | | Financing in Percentages | | | |
| | | External | | | | | External | | |
Year	Internal	Net Equity	Net Debt	Total	Total Financing	Internal	Net Equity	Net Debt	Total
1984	$38,627	$ 8,796	$11,745	$20,541	$ 59,168	65%	15%	20%	35%
1985	45,064	10,839	11,068	21,907	66,971	67	16	17	33
1986	41,609	13,042	18,494	31,536	73,145	57	18	25	43
1987	48,787	10,619	23,412	34,031	82,818	59	13	28	41
1988	54,427	4,236	35,552	39,788	94,215	58	4	38	42
1989	50,177	10,465	44,120	54,585	104,762	48	10	42	52
1990	43,464	6,530	33,008	39,538	83,002	52	8	40	48
1991	42,406	7,784	21,449	29,223	71,639	59	11	30	41
1992	42,232	8,122	18,255	26,377	68,609	62	12	26	38
1993	46,262	15,083	38,097	53,180	99,442	47	15	38	53
1994	57,878	16,964	40,106	57,070	114,948	50	15	35	50

Source: Statistics Canada, *Financial Flow Accounts, Catalogue no. 13–014.*

---

[1] This determination is made based on cash budgets or pro forma statements, as discussed in Chapter 26.

Figure 10.1

Methods of Securing Financing

Since its introduction, the short-form prospectus method has become important for most large firms.

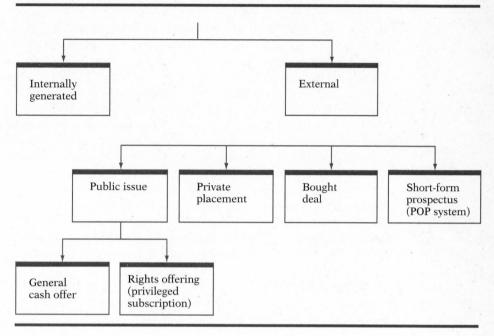

which is available only to the firm's current shareholders. Second, if the securities are not offered to the general public, then a private placement is made. The securities are sold to one or more institutional investors such as insurance companies, banks, or pension funds. Third, a firm can issue securities through a method that differs from the traditional public offering and private placement in a number of ways, called a **bought deal**. Here an investment dealer, usually acting alone, lines up potential buyers of the securities and then approaches the issuing firm. Finally, large, creditworthy firms can take advantage of the **short-form prospectus** method of financing. The use of a short-form prospectus usually results in a private placement or a bought deal, but this is not always the case. We will look at the basic features of all four methods and at the role played by investment dealer firms.

CASH OFFERINGS

Firms can issue common stock, preferred stock, or long-term debt through a **cash offering**. However, the majority of funds raised in cash offerings involve long-term debt. This is not surprising, because firms can generate substantial equity capital internally but can secure debt financing only by going to the public markets or through private placements.

The Role of Investment Dealers   Most firms making a cash offering of securities use the services of an investment dealer, which does the actual selling. As noted in Chapter 2, investment dealers serve as an intermediary between the financial markets and firms needing capital. Firms generally prefer to have the new issue **underwritten**. This is generally called a **firm commitment offering**: The investment dealer purchases the issue from the firm *at a fixed price* and then resells it. When an issue is underwritten, the risk of its not selling is borne by the investment dealer—that is, the selling firm is guaranteed a fixed dollar amount. Another approach is for the investment dealer to take the issue on a **best efforts** basis, under which the securities are sold for a fixed commission but any unsold securities are the responsibility of the selling firm, not the investment dealer. This method is often used by large, well-known firms which feel the issue will sell easily or by very small firms when the risks and costs are too great for underwriting. Finally, some firms sell securities via **direct placement** (generally a rights offering to their shareholders) without using the services of investment bankers.

Investment dealers, through the underwriting syndicate, provide marketing services, risk bearing, and monitoring of the firm's managers and its affairs. Marketing services include searching the primary market for buyers and compensating participants for their costs of providing funds. Risk bearing involves the underwriters taking the risk of the issue not selling. Finally, by engaging the services of well-known investment dealers, the issuing firm is seeking additional monitoring in the hope of adding value to the offering and firm.[2]

The Underwriting Process   To understand the investment banking process, it is helpful to trace the steps required. Our focus is on the negotiated underwriting process and the role played by the lead investment dealer or dealers.

Preunderwriting Conference.   Members of the issuing firm and the investment dealer hold preunderwriting conferences in which they discuss how much capital to raise, the type (or types) of security to employ, and the terms of the agreement. The investment dealer then begins the underwriting investigation. In addition to its own investigation of the issuing firm, the investment dealer calls in a chartered accounting firm to audit the firm's financial condition and to assist in preparing the registration statement submitted to the provincial securities commission of the provinces where the securities are to be sold.[3] Lawyers are also required to rule on the legal aspects of the proposed issue.

After the investigation is completed, an underwriting agreement is drawn up. This agreement, which may be changed by subsequent approval of the parties, contains all the details of the issue except its price. For firms that already have securities outstanding similar to those being issued, the underwriting agreement may also have an **out clause**, which would cause the contract to be voided if the security's market price falls below a predetermined level.

---

[2] For more on the role played by investment banking firms see, for example Carter and Manaster (1990), and Hansen and Torregrosa (1992).

[3] In Canada the issuance of securities to the public is regulated at the provincial level through provincial Securities Acts.

Registration and Pricing.   The **registration statement**, or **prospectus**, is then filed with the securities commissions of the various provinces. This statement presents all the pertinent facts concerning the firm and the proposed issue. During a waiting period (about three to five weeks), the factual adequacy of the information is judged. The securities commissions assess only the accuracy of the information; *they do not judge the investment quality of the security*. During this period, the firm cannot engage in any unusual activity that might affect the sale.

The registration system in the provinces of Alberta, Saskatchewan, Manitoba, and Ontario requires a two-step process in which the firm, through its underwriter, first files a preliminary prospectus, or **red herring**, and then the final prospectus.[4] The preliminary prospectus is called a red herring because of the statement that must be printed on its front page, in red print, that the securities have not been approved or disapproved by the securities commission of the province where the securities are to be issued. Although the underwriters are not allowed to enter into purchase and sales agreements before the final prospectus has been approved, the red herring can be distributed in order to gauge public interest in the new issue.

Once the issue has cleared registration and an offering price has been determined, a "tombstone" advertisement listing the names of the underwriting firms from whom the prospectus may be obtained is often made. Figure 10.2 shows an example of a tombstone for an Alliance Forest Products common stock issue that involved 10 underwriters.

Underwriting Syndication and Selling.   The primary investment dealer that the issuing firm has dealt with does not typically handle the purchase and distribution of an issue by itself. Instead, a **syndicate** or **banking group** is formed for the purpose of underwriting (buying and then reselling) the issue. Syndicates often have between 10 and 60 underwriters in addition to the managing investment dealer. The primary reasons for underwriting syndicates are to spread the risk and to ensure national or international marketing capability. Consequently, for large issues the principal underwriter and manager of the syndicate will form a **selling group** to assist in selling the issue. The dealers who make up the selling group never take title of any of the issue and thus bear no risk; rather, they act as agents (brokers), providing marketing services for a fee.

Costs.   The **flotation cost** to the issuing firm of selling securities includes the underwriting fee and all other expenses related to the offering. These other expenses include accounting and legal fees, a securities commission registration fee, and printing costs. Total flotation costs are the difference between what the securities are sold to investors for (the gross proceeds) and what the issuing firm actually receives (the net proceeds). Thus, if a $50 million par bond issue is sold to the public for $50.5 million and the issuing firm receives only $49.5 million, the flotation costs are $1 million, or slightly less than 2 percent ($1 million/$50.50 million = 0.0198 = 1.98 percent).

---

[4] The other provinces require only that a final prospectus be filed. However, when any of these four provinces is involved in a national issue, a preliminary prospectus is filed.

| Figure 10.2 |

Tombstone for Alliance Forest Products Common Stock Issue

Advertisements like this one appear in many financial sources, such as *The Globe and Mail* and *Financial Post*.

These securities having been sold publicly, this announcement appears as a matter of record only.

Initial Public Offering
and Secondary Offering

May 1994

ALLIANCE FOREST PRODUCTS INC.

$298,000,000

17,000,000 Common Share

Price: $17.00 per share

Burns Fry Limited

Lévesque Beaubien Geoffrion Inc.	Nesbitt Thomson Ltd.
RBC Dominion Securities Inc.	Salomon Brothers Canada Inc.
ScotiaMcLeod Inc. Wood Gundy Inc.	Richardson Greenshields of Canada Limited
McLean McCarthy Inc.	Toronto Dominion Securities Inc.

For common stock, flotation costs range from 3 to 10 percent for large, well-known firms to more than 20 percent for smaller firms. This high direct cost for small issues is a function of the risks involved and the higher actual distribution expenses, because more effort is required to sell small common stock issues. For bonds and preferred stocks, the costs to large issuers are often less than 2 percent. This is due to the lower degree of risk involved compared to common stocks. Their lower flotation costs are also due to the fact that bonds and preferred stock are usually sold in large blocks to institutional investors, whereas thousands of investors may purchase common stock.

PRIVATE PLACEMENTS

The private placement of securities has always been a means of financing. In recent years it has accounted for as much as 35 percent of total corporate financing in Canada. But even that is not as much as it may be in the future. This popularity is caused by some advantages that private issues have over public ones. For example, the issuing firm is spared the time, expense, and trouble of having to register the issue with any securities commission. By not going through the underwriting process, issue time may be reduced from at least a month to as little as a few hours. Moreover, the firm can maintain a lower profile because it does not have to disclose the financial and other data required in the registration process.

However, private issues also have some disadvantages. First, the lender may monitor the firm's activities more closely, either directly or through provisions in the loan agreement. If common stock financing is used, often the new investor is likely to gain substantial influence or even control of the firm. Also, investors cannot easily resell securities purchased through a private placement. Consequently, to compensate for this lack of liquidity, the cost of privately placed debt is generally *higher* than for public issues. Finally, the rising popularity of private placements is driving stock and bond investments away from the small investors and towards institutional investors, since investors must have $150,000 to be able to participate in a private placement.

BOUGHT DEALS

A bought deal occurs when one underwriter (or, less frequently, a small group of underwriters) buys an issue from a firm and sells the securities to investors. In this procedure, however, no banking group (syndicate) is formed, so that distribution may not be as wide or as quick as the traditional public offering. Therefore, the terms of a bought deal must be very attractive to the issuing firm. For example, this procedure is carried out without the benefit of an out clause; once the deal is signed the underwriter cannot terminate the agreement because of a substantial decrease in market price. In addition, the "spread" between the price at which the underwriter agrees to buy the securities from the issuing firm and the price at which he or she agrees to sell them to the investors is significantly below the usual underwriting spreads. For example, recently when Imperial Oil Ltd. wanted to issue $1 billion of equity, a bought deal was arranged with Gordon Capital that cost Imperial Oil 1.5 percent; if the issue had been underwritten it would have cost about 6 percent. To be successful with this procedure the underwriter usually has potential buyers lined up to purchase the issue through a private placement or a short-form prospectus before approaching the issuing firm. In fact, to use bought deals a corporation must be eligible for a short-form prospectus.

SHORT-FORM PROSPECTUS

In 1982 the provinces from Quebec westward modified their registration procedures for "certain reporting" issuers by adopting the Prompt Offering Prospectus (POP) system. This system allows qualified firms access to the capital markets without having to file a full prospectus. For example, to be eligible for the system in Ontario a firm must have publicly traded equity shares with a market value of more than $75 million and have filed with the Ontario Securities Commission (OSC) annual and interim financial statements for at least 36 months. For qualified firms, the POP system means that they can file a simplified document as an addendum to the comprehensive filing at the time of the issue.

The document is called a short-form prospectus because it omits much of the information found in a full prospectus; it is felt that for these reporting firms, the rest of the information is readily available from public sources—that is, filings with the exchange commission and annual reports. As a result of this system, the registration period has been reduced to five days from up to several weeks for the full prospectus.

The increased flexibility provided by a short-form prospectus has been welcomed by chief financial officers at large corporations. In recent years, more than half of all securities registered with the OSC were marketed through the POP system. The rapid acceptance of the short-form prospectus is due to its reduced cost and increased convenience—both of which are important when firms raise external capital. The reduced costs associated with the POP system primarily benefit firms that are considered less risky, as opposed to firms with more risk. Also, as a byproduct of the short-form prospectus procedure, more and more security issues—both bonds and stocks—take the form of private placements and bought deals, rather than general public offerings.

INVESTMENT DEALERS AND FINANCIAL ETHICS

Rarely are investment dealers accused of unethical or illegal activities. The reason is obvious—their continued business and profitability are tied directly to their reputation. Any word of any unethical or illegal activity can have serious short- and long-run consequences. However, exceptions do occur.

When auctioning United States government bonds, the U.S. Treasury awards them first to the highest bidder and then moves to the next-highest bidder. If the Treasury receives more than one bid at the price that exhausts the issue, it allocates the remaining bonds in proportion to the size of the bid. In 1990 Paul Mozer, the head of Salomon Brothers' government-bond trading desk, submitted bids for more than 100 percent of the four-year notes to be auctioned. He later followed this up with other similar bids, including a bid in December 1990 for a customer of Salomon Brothers, without the customer's consent. Mozer repeated this tactic in the spring of 1991, thereby attracting the attention of the Securities and Exchange Commission and the U.S. Justice Department. Finally, in August 1991, the U.S. Treasury Department announced that it had barred Salomon Brothers from bidding in government securities auctions for customer accounts. On August 19, 1991, *The Wall Street Journal* carried seven different articles about this event. Within days of the news release, Moody's Investors Service put Salomon on its credit "watch list," and subsequently downgraded its bond and commercial paper ratings.

The damage to Salomon's reputation not only impaired its ability to sell new securities but actually raised concerns about whether the firm would survive. In response to these actions, Paul Mozer and other employees implicated in the scandal were removed, while Salomon's chairman, president, vice-chairman, and general counsel were all asked to resign by the firm's board of directors. Warren Buffett, of Berkshire Hathaway Corporation, was appointed interim chairman; a new chief operating officer was appointed; the firm liquidated some assets to pay off bank loans and other borrowings and to forestall potentially serious liquidity problems; and it beefed up its internal controls.

Nine months later, on May 20, 1992, Salomon settled the suit with the U.S. government. The firm paid $122 million to the U.S. Treasury Department to settle charges that it had violated securities laws, and another $68 million to the U.S. Justice Department. It also established a $100 million restitution fund for payments of private damage claims that might arise from the 50 or so civil lawsuits it was facing. Though it has suffered both directly and indirectly from this scandal, since that time Salomon has reestablished itself as one of the leading investment dealers in the United States and the world.

Private markets, like the markets investment dealers trade in, provide strong incentives for ethical behaviour—by imposing substantial costs on the institutions and individuals who depart from ethical behaviour. Although private markets do not take care of all ethical concerns, in general, ethical behaviour is profitable. That is, firms that practise ethical behaviour tend to get business, while those that practise unethical behaviour suffer direct out-of-pocket costs and indirect costs in the form of lost opportunities. However, whereas vigorous private markets may contribute to ethical behaviour, they are not a substitute for it.

Concept Review Questions

- What is the primary source of financing for nonfinancial Canadian firms?
- What are the four basic alternatives available to firms for raising external funds?
- Describe the process firms employ for raising external funds. What role do investment dealers play?
- How has the POP system affected the issuance of securities?

COMMON STOCK: RIGHTS AND PRIVILEGES

Now that we understand some of the issues related to raising external funds, let us turn our attention to one of the sources of funds for firms—common stock. The common shareholders are both the owners of the firm and one of its suppliers of long-term capital. This capital may be in the form of funds invested in the firm directly in exchange for new shares of common stock, or it may occur through the action of the firm's board of directors by retaining funds rather than authorizing them to be paid out in the form of cash dividends.

INCOME

Common shareholders have a residual right to the income of the firm, in that the claims of creditors, lessors, the government, and preferred shareholders must be met before common shareholders receive cash dividends. Thus, if a firm has earnings before interest and taxes (EBIT) of $200,000, interest payments of $50,000, and taxes (at 35 percent) of $52,500, earnings after taxes (EAT) are $97,500. *Assuming that cash flows are sufficient*, firms typically pay out some proportion of their earnings in the form of cash dividends. They are not obligated to do so, and some firms, such as Mark's Work Wearhouse, Mitel, and White Rose, do not currently pay dividends.

The risk and potential returns are greater for common stock investors than for others with financial interests in the firm. To see why, consider our example: If EBIT drops to $50,000, with interest payments of $50,000, earnings after taxes are zero, and no funds are left for distribution to common shareholders. On the other hand, if EBIT increases to $600,000, with interest of $50,000 and taxes of $192,500, EAT is $357,500, and larger cash dividends may be paid out. The cash not paid out to common shareholders can be reinvested in the firm.

CONTROL

The firm's shareholders elect the members of the board of directors each year. Sometimes an outside or dissident group may challenge management by proposing its own slate of directors. These challenges, or **proxy fights**, represent one of the most effective means of attempting to turn around the fortunes of a firm. In the past, they have been rare; however, recently, more proxy fights have been initiated, including some involving major firms. Obviously, it is only in firms that are providing lacklustre performance (in terms of market price, dividends, and/or earnings) that successful proxy fights are possible.

Depending on the corporate charter or the law of the province in which the firm is incorporated, the board of directors is selected under a majority voting or a cumulative voting system. Under the **majority voting** system, each shareholder has one vote per director for each share of stock owned. Directors are elected if they secure 50 percent plus one of the votes cast. Instead of majority voting, the firm's charter or the province of incorporation may require **cumulative voting**, which permits multiple votes for a single director. Under cumulative voting, the total number of votes each shareholder can cast is determined first. If there are five directors to be elected, and a shareholder owns 100 shares of stock, he or she casts (5)(100) = 500 votes. However, under cumulative voting, the shareholder is allowed to cast all 500 votes for only one director. The purpose of cumulative voting is to allow minority groups representation on the board of directors—something that is precluded when majority voting is used.

In order to determine how many shares are needed to elect any given number of directors under cumulative voting, we can use the following formula:

$$\begin{matrix} \text{minimum number of shares} \\ \text{required to elect a} \\ \text{desired number of directors} \end{matrix} = \frac{\left(\begin{matrix} \text{total shares outstanding} \\ \text{and entitled to vote} \end{matrix} \right)\left(\begin{matrix} \text{number of} \\ \text{directors desired} \end{matrix} \right)}{\begin{matrix} \text{total number of directors} \\ \text{to be elected } + 1 \end{matrix}} + 1 \qquad (10.1)$$

For example, if a firm has 195,000 shares of stock authorized to vote and 12 directors are to be elected, a group wanting to elect 3 directors would have to control

$$\frac{(195,000)(3)}{12 + 1} + 1 = 45,001 \text{ shares}$$

On the other hand, if the minority group controls a given number of shares and wants to find out how many directors it can elect, Equation 10.1 can be modified to:

$$\text{number of directors that can} \atop \text{be elected with shares owned} = \frac{\left(\begin{array}{c}\text{number of shares} \\ \text{owned} - 1\end{array}\right)\left(\begin{array}{c}\text{total number of directors} \\ \text{to be elected} + 1\end{array}\right)}{\text{total shares outstanding and entitled to vote}} \quad (10.2)$$

To continue our example, suppose that the minority group controls 70,000 shares. How many directors can it elect? Employing Equation 10.2, the answer is

$$\frac{(70,000 - 1)(12 + 1)}{195,000} = 4.67, \text{ or } 4 \text{ directors}$$

Actually, the group may be able to do better than that if not all the shares outstanding are voted. For example, what happens if only 180,000 shares in total will be voted? In this case, the minority can elect

$$\frac{(70,000 - 1)(12 + 1)}{180,000} = 5.06, \text{ or } 5 \text{ directors}$$

A firm can partially thwart the intent of cumulative voting procedures by reducing the size of its board or by electing only a portion of the board each year. To see this, suppose the firm decides to elect only 6 instead of 12 directors each year, and they each hold office for two years. If our minority group still controls 70,000 shares, and assuming only 180,000 votes will be cast, then the number of directors the group can elect in any given year is

$$\frac{(70,000 - 1)(6 + 1)}{180,000} = 2.72, \text{ or } 2 \text{ directors}$$

By electing 2 directors this year and 2 directors next year, the minority group ends up with only 4 directors instead of the 5 they could have if all directors were elected each year.

In addition to electing the board of directors, shareholders are frequently asked to approve the selection of the firm's accounting auditor for the next year, and to vote on issues such as authorizing additional shares of common stock, approval of a merger financed by common stock, antitakeover amendments, and various other corporate governance issues.[5]

---

[5] For a summary of the impact of voting on antitakeover amendments and corporate governance items on the value of the firm see, for example, Gordon and Pound (1993).

CLAIM ON ASSETS

As in the case of income, common shareholders have a residual claim on the firm's assets in case of liquidation. Creditors, bondholders, and preferred shareholders all have a prior claim on assets and will be paid something before common shareholders receive anything in liquidation. This residual claim increases the risk to common shareholders.

LIMITED LIABILITY

Under our legal system shareholders have limited liability. Because corporations are distinct entities under the law, shareholders are not personally responsible for the firm's debts. The impact of limited versus unlimited liability on shareholders is illustrated in Figure 10.3. Say a firm has $1,000 in debt. With limited liability, if the value of the firm's assets falls below $1,000, shareholders can default and walk away from the firm. But if unlimited liability existed, when the value of the firm's assets fell below $1,000, shareholders would have to use their personal resources to pay off the bondholders.

With either limited or unlimited liability, shareholders may be disappointed if a firm's operating performance is poor. But the right to default and walk away from the firm is a valuable privilege that exists due to limited liability.[6]

Figure 10.3

Effect of Limited Versus Unlimited Liability on Shareholders

For a firm with $1,000 in debt, if the value of the firm at the maturity of the debt is below $1,000, with limited liability, as in (a), the shareholders default and bondholders own the firm. But with unlimited liability, as in (b), shareholders must reach into their own pockets to pay off the bondholders.

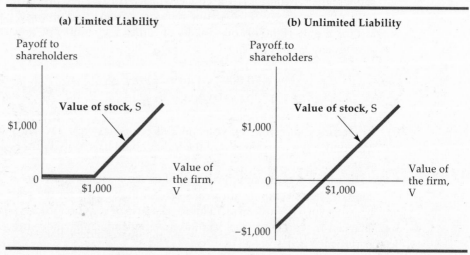

(a) Limited Liability   (b) Unlimited Liability

---

[6]This ability of shareholders to walk away from a firm in default is the same as a put option, which is discussed in Chapter 18.

PREEMPTIVE RIGHT

The **preemptive right** is a provision that grants shareholders the right to purchase new shares of common stock in the same proportion as their current ownership. Although this right used to be widespread, it is less so now because *many firms have amended their charters to eliminate the preemptive right.* One of the primary reasons for doing away with it is to provide the firm with more freedom to use common stock for mergers and acquisitions or other corporate purposes.

When the preemptive right exists, current shareholders have first claim on any new shares to be issued.[7] For example, if a firm had 100,000 shares of stock outstanding and decided to issue 25,000 new shares, a shareholder owning 1,000 shares would have the opportunity to purchase 250 new shares. By doing so, the shareholder would maintain his or her current percentage ownership of 1 percent of the firm's outstanding shares. (The use of preemptive rights to issue common stock is discussed in detail later in the chapter.)

RIGHT OF TRANSFER

Common shareholders generally have the right to transfer ownership to another investor. All that is required is for an investor to sell the stock to another person and sign the stock (endorse it on the back of the stock certificate) over to the buyer. If the stock is traded publicly, the shareholder may use the services of a securities broker to sell the stock. The purchaser of the stock (or the broker) sends the stock certificate to a transfer agent representing the firm. The transfer agent then issues a new certificate under the purchaser's name and records the transaction in the firm's records. At this point, the new owner is entitled to receive cash dividends and has any other rights or privileges associated with owning the common stock.

Concept Review Questions

- Define the terms *residual right, residual claim, preemptive right,* and *right of transfer* when applied to common shareholders.
- Describe the difference between majority voting and cumulative voting when electing a firm's board of directors.

FEATURES OF COMMON STOCK

AUTHORIZED AND OUTSTANDING SHARES

The firm's charter specifies the number of authorized shares—that is, the maximum number of shares that can be issued without amending the charter. Additional shares can be authorized by a vote of the common shareholders. For convenience, most firms have more authorized shares than they currently have issued. Under the Canada

---

[7] Rights are simply a call option, as discussed in Chapter 18.

Table 10.2

Common Shareholders' Accounts and Related Information for Andrés Wines Ltd. as of March 31, 1995

Remember that there is no cash in retained earnings and that book value is a meaningless figure.

Redeemable preferred stock, $10 stated value	
Unlimited number authorized, none outstanding	—
Common stock, unlimited number authorized	
Class A shares, nonvoting, 3,602,160 outstanding	$2,790,595
Class B shares, voting, 1,027,244 outstanding	411,747
	3,202,342
Retained earnings	39,212,552
Total shareholders' equity	$42,414,894

Earnings per share = net income/shares of common stock outstanding
= \$4,166,005/(3,602,160 + 1,027,244) = \$0.90

Dividends per share on common stock: Class A $0.598
  Class B $0.520

Book value per share = (total shareholders' equity − preferred stock)/shares outstanding
= (\$42,414,894 − \$0)/(\$3,602,160 + 1,027,244)
= \$9.16

Market price per share (range for year): Class A $11.50 − $10.00
  Class B $12.13 − $10.50

Source: Andrés wines Ltd. 1995 Annual Report.

Business Corporations Act (CBCA) and many provincial acts, there is no limit to the number of shares that can be issued; that is, firms incorporated under these acts have an unlimited number of authorized shares. For example, Table 10.2 shows that Andrés Wines Ltd. has an unlimited number of common shares authorized, but as of March 31, 1995, only about 4.6 million (the sum of outstanding Class A and B shares) have been issued. Outstanding shares are those held by the public. Firms can buy back outstanding shares from their investors; however, under the CBCA the repurchased shares must be cancelled. The number of shares of stock outstanding is employed when calculating per share figures, such as earnings per share or dividends per share.

PAR AND BOOK VALUE

Common stock can be issued with or without a par value. The **par value** of a share of common stock is stated in the firm's charter, but is of no financial significance. Firms with a specific par value for their common stock try to issue new stock at prices higher than par, because the shareholders are liable as creditors for the difference between the issuance price, if below par, and the par value of the stock. For this reason, most par values are very low. The difference between the issuance price and the par (or stated) value is recorded on the firm's balance sheet as additional paid-in capital.

Under the CBCA and most provincial acts, par value shares are not permitted. Thus, firms incorporated under any of these acts can no longer issue new shares with a par value. Consequently, no additional paid-in capital can currently arise from the sale of shares, although some Canadian balance sheets may still show additional paid-in capital from shares issued before the passage of the current federal and provincial acts. When no–par value shares are issued, the shares are reported in the common stock account at the full amount paid for the shares by the investors. For example, Table 10.2 shows that Andrés has no additional paid-in capital, with its common stock account representing the value of the shares at issuance. Finally, Andrés has retained earnings of more than $39 million. Retained earnings represent the total residual amount that has been transferred from the firm's income statements over the years—*it is not cash*. The total of the preferred stock, common stock, additional paid-in capital (if any), and retained earnings is equal to shareholders' equity. For Andrés, this is $42.4 million, as of March 31, 1995.

Book value per share of common stock reflects the "accounting-recorded" worth of the firm—*no economic meaning can be attached to book value per share.*[8] It is calculated by dividing the common shareholders' equity (or, equivalently, total assets minus total liabilities minus the book value of preferred stock) by the number of shares of common stock outstanding. Andrés had a book value of $9.16 per share at the end of the fiscal year 1995, but its stock traded between $12.13 and $10.50 during that year.

CLASSES OF COMMON STOCK

It is not uncommon for Canadian corporations to have more than one class of common stock. When two classes exist, one class has full voting privileges, whereas the other has no (or restricted) voting privileges. For example, Andrés Wines' Class B shares are voting, whereas their Class A shares are nonvoting. A second example is that of Molson Companies Ltd., whose charter allows for an unlimited number of Class A and B common shares. The company has more than 43 million Class A and more than 14 million Class B shares outstanding. The holders of Class B shares are entitled to one vote per share. However, the holders of the Class A shares are restricted in their voting power. Although they are entitled to one vote per share, they vote separately from the Class B shareholders and are restricted to the election of three members of the board of directors.

A more extreme example is that of Magna International, which has more than 60 million shares of Class A common stock outstanding and only 1.1 million shares of Class B common stock. Although the holders of Class A shares are entitled to one vote per share, they are subordinate to the Class B shares, which are entitled to 500 votes per share.

---

[8] An exception may occur for financial institutions or other similar firms in which the recorded book value may be a reasonable estimate of the current liquidation value of the firm.

In many instances the fully voting shares are retained by the founders of the corporation. Both classes of shares usually participate equally in dividends or liquidation and both are able to be listed on Canadian stock exchanges. In addition they both generally trade at similar price levels, as Table 10.2 shows for Andrés Wines.

A celebrated exception to this rule is the case of Canadian Tire. In April 1986, the voting and nonvoting stocks were trading for $19\frac{1}{8}$ and $16\frac{3}{8}$ respectively. In late 1986, the Canadian Tire dealers attempted to purchase 49 percent of the voting stock, 60 percent of which was owned by the Billes family. This action drove the voting stock prices to as high as $90 per share, whereas the price of nonvoting stock declined to the $11 range. This price gap narrowed when the Ontario Securities Commission blocked the takeover attempt. The commission ruled that the dealers and the Billes family had constructed the bid to allow the dealers to assume control of the firm while circumventing the clause in company bylaws that protects nonvoting investors' rights during a takeover attempt. By June 1987, the voting and nonvoting stocks were trading for approximately $50 and $15, respectively. Since then the stocks have been trading at a more normal differential. In mid-1996 the voting shares were trading at $18.50 and the nonvoting shares at $16.60.

The action of Canadian Tire and other firms induced the Alberta, Montreal, Toronto, and Vancouver exchanges to adopt identical measures, in November 1989, to stop the spread of nonvoting (or restricted) shares. Since then, firms have been prohibited from diluting the voting power of existing shareholders without their consent.

Concept Review Questions

- What does retained earnings represent? Is it cash?
- What is a company's book value? Does it have economic meaning?
- Explain why some companies have more than one class of common stock.

COMMON STOCK FINANCING

Although not the major external source of financing, common stock is often employed to raise external capital, especially for smaller, growing firms. Therefore it is important to understand more about the use of common stock as a means of raising long-term capital.

ISSUING EQUITY AND THE VALUE OF THE FIRM

In recent years a number of studies have examined the market impact of common stock issuance. The results, at first glance, have been surprising: When firms sell common stock publicly, their stock price declines. For industrial firms the decline amounts to 2 to 3 percent. Although that may not sound overwhelming, the fall in the market value represents a dollar amount equal to 10 to 20 percent of the money raised by the issue. Thus, the net increase in the value of the firm, ΔS, due to issuing new common stock for cash is equal to the net proceeds from the issue *minus* the decrease in the value of the outstanding stock. Stated another way, the cost of issuing common stock includes the direct flotation costs plus the indirect costs captured by the loss in value of the firm's outstanding stock.

How can we account for this result? In an efficient market, investor expectations are built into the share price. These expectations may change as the firm issues new common stock. Consider two reasons why the price of the firm's stock may fall:

1. INFORMATION ASYMMETRY.   Management always has some information about the firm that is not available to shareholders. What if this information allows management to determine when the firm is overvalued in the marketplace and when it is undervalued? Management will then attempt to issue new shares only when the firm is overvalued. This move benefits existing shareholders, but potential new shareholders are not stupid. They will anticipate this situation and discount it by offering to pay less for the stock at the new issue date. Dierkens (1991), for example, finds that firms in which there is more information asymmetry have larger losses in value when equity issues are sold.

2. INVESTMENT PROSPECTS.   Investment demands exist for most firms, sometimes due to growth options with high NPVs, other times for not-so-great projects. What if informed investors interpret the issuance of new common stock as a negative signal about the firm's investment projects? After all, if the new projects are really great, why should the firm let new shareholders in on them? In that case it could simply issue debt and let existing shareholders capture all the gain. Again, new investors are not stupid and will offer a lower price for the common stock on the new issue date. In a recent study Pilotte (1992) used the dividend status of the issuing firms as a proxy for growth opportunities. Nondividend-paying firms were considered to have more growth options, or opportunities, than firms that had either high and stable dividends or firms that had suspended their cash dividends. Pilotte found that firms that did not pay dividends suffered smaller losses in value when they issued securities than did those with either high/stable dividends or suspended dividends.

Although we do not know which, if either, of these explanations accounts for the decline in stock prices when common stock is sold, we do know the decline occurs. Instead of a public offering of stock, what about the private placement of common stock? Studies by Wruck (1989) and Hertzel and Smith (1993) show that when firms sell stock through a private placement they actually experience an *increase* in the value of the firm. How can these findings of an increase in value be accounted for? Firms that engage in private equity issues are typically smaller and sell a larger percentage of ownership (relative to the already outstanding shares) than firms that sell stock through a public offering. Cooney and Kalay (1993) argue that for such firms the uncertainty surrounding new capital investment projects is large, and by securing the private financing some of this uncertainty is resolved. Alternatively, Hertzel and Smith (1993) present results consistent with private equity placements providing more efficient transmission of information, so that firms with undervalued assets are encouraged to seek private capital.

When firms issue common stock publicly, they suffer a loss in value; when they do it privately, they enjoy a gain in value. What occurs when they issue other securities? As we discuss in Chapter 11, stock prices decline little, if at all, when the firm issues new debt. Effective managers must keep these findings in mind when contemplating how to raise long-term financing.

IPOs AND UNDERPRICING

When a firm first goes public with its common stock, the offering is referred to as an **initial public offering (IPO)**. This was the case for the Alliance Forest Products common stocks advertised with the tombstone, as shown in Figure 10.2. A number of studies have examined initial public offerings. By calculating the difference between the offering price and the price shortly after offering, these studies have examined the issue of **underpricing**. Underpricing is a real, but hidden, cost incurred by any firm when it first goes public. These studies have estimated that the magnitude of underpricing with IPOs is high—as much as 10 to 20 percent. As such, the cost of underpricing and the direct cash costs of financing must both be considered when raising equity capital.

Why does underpricing occur? Probably for at least two reasons. The first is that both the investment dealer and the issuing firm have some vested interest in seeing that the issue is fully sold. One way—but an expensive one—to ensure that the issue is sold is to underprice it. The second reason is that determining the market worth of a firm that has never been traded is more an art than a science.[9]

PRICING A NEW ISSUE

When a firm already has stock outstanding and is issuing additional shares, they are typically priced a few dollars below the closing price the day before the stock is sold. If the firm is making an initial public offering, however, the pricing decision is much more difficult.

One way to go about establishing the initial selling price is to determine what the total value of the firm should be after the issue, and then divide this value by the number of shares of common stock to be issued. For example, if we assume that NationWide Transport (NWT) is estimated to be worth $3.5 million and 350,000 shares of common stock will be issued, the estimated selling price is $3,500,000/350,000, or $10 per share. Note that we are interested in the total number of shares to be issued, including any privately held or founder's shares not issued to the public. If NWT decides to sell 150,000 shares, the offering would consist of 150,000 shares priced at $10 each, for gross proceeds (before flotation costs and other direct issuance expenses) of $1,500,000. To use this approach, however, we must answer the following question: How do we determine the firm's total value—in this case, $3,500,000?

One way to do this is to use the valuation approach described in Chapter 4. For the constant dividend growth situation, the value of the total firm can be estimated by[10]

$$S = \frac{D_1}{k_s - g} \tag{10.3}$$

---

[9] Another possibility is that underpricing is a signal of the quality of the issue. Garfinkel (1993) considered this proposition but did not find any support for it.

[10] It is assumed no debt exists.

where

  S = the value of an all-equity firm
  D_1 = total cash dividends expected to be paid to shareholders next year (at t = 1)
  k_s = the equity investors' required return
  g = the expected (compound) growth rate in cash dividends

Suppose that NWT expects earnings after taxes of $700,000 and plans to pay 50 percent out in the form of cash dividends, so that D_1 = $350,000. Also, the firm expects its earnings and dividends to grow at approximately 7 percent per year for the foreseeable future. We have estimated D_1 and g in Equation 10.3; all that is needed now is an estimate of k_s. Estimating k_s, however, is not easy, especially for a firm that has never been traded publicly. NWT's investment dealer can supply an estimate of k_s, we can use the k_s for some comparable publicly traded firm, or we can use some approach like adding a risk premium to the expected interest rate on long-term corporate bonds. If the rate on long-term bonds is expected to be 9 percent and the risk premium (of stocks over bonds) is determined to be 8 percent, then our estimate of k_s is 17 percent. With this we can estimate the value of NWT to be

$$S = \frac{\$350,000}{0.17 - 0.07} = \frac{\$350,000}{0.10} = \$3,500,000$$

In practice, an *ad hoc* approach based on comparative price/earnings ratios is often employed. The price/earnings (P/E) ratio is calculated by dividing the market price for a share of common stock by the earnings per share. To use this approach, NWT's investment dealer might examine P/E ratios for publicly traded firms in the same industry, as well as the P/E ratios of firms that have recently gone public. Other pertinent information—such as NWT's financial condition, growth prospects, quality and stability of management, and size—is also compared. Once a P/E ratio for the firm is estimated, the total market value is determined by

$$S = (\text{net income})(\text{estimated P/E of stock}) \tag{10.4}$$

Continuing with NWT, let us assume that NWT's investment dealer determines the stock's estimated P/E ratio is 5. The total value of NWT would be ($700,000)(5) = $3,500,000. Once the total value of the firm is determined, the pricing of the new shares to be issued proceeds as described previously. With either the dividend valuation or the comparative P/E approach, the pricing of new issues is an imperfect and subjective process.

RIGHTS OFFERING

The raising of funds through use of a preemptive right is called a **rights offering**. In rights offerings the firm's current shareholders have the first option of buying new shares of common stock. The importance of such offerings has tended to diminish over the years, as many firms have eliminated the preemptive right, with the increasing popularity of dividend reinvestment plans (Chapter 14) and the introduction of short-form prospectus procedures.

When a firm has a rights offering, each shareholder receives one right for each share of stock presently owned. To understand a rights offering, consider the example of Cross Prairie Air (CPA), which has decided to raise $5 million in additional funds by selling common stock at $10 per share. The $10 is the subscription price for the rights offering. CPA currently has 1 million shares of common stock outstanding with a market price of $11.50 per share. If the company elects to employ a rights offering, the firm is concerned about the following:

1. How many rights are required to purchase one additional share of stock?
2. What is the value of each right?
3. What effect does the rights offering have on the market price of each existing share of stock?

Number of Rights Needed to Purchase an Additional Share The number of additional shares to be issued, if CPA has not already determined it, is given by

$$\frac{\text{number of}}{\text{additional shares}} = \frac{\text{funds to be raised}}{\text{subscription price}} = \frac{\$5,000,000}{\$10} = 500,000 \text{ shares} \qquad (10.5)$$

The next step is to divide the number of additional shares into the number of existing shares to obtain the number of rights needed to subscribe to one additional share:

$$\frac{\text{number of rights}}{\text{to buy one}} = \frac{\text{existing shares}}{\text{additional shares}} = \frac{1,000,000}{500,000} = 2 \text{ rights} \qquad (10.6)$$

Therefore, shareholders of CPA have to surrender $10 plus two rights to purchase one additional share of stock during the rights offering.

Value of Stock and Rights When a firm undertakes a rights offering, a sequence of events takes place. First, the firm announces the proposed financing. For Cross Prairie Air, suppose this occurs on May 20. Shortly thereafter, trading begins for the rights on a when-issued basis. This simply means that a market exists for the new security, with delivery of the security (the rights in this case) to take place when it is received. Subsequently, on June 23, the record date occurs; all shareholders of CPA's common stock on the record date receive one right for each share of common stock held. As with cash dividends, stock splits, or stock dividends (discussed in Chapter 14), the ex day is set two business days before the record date. This is June 21 for CPA's rights offering.[11] All stocks traded before June 21 trade with the rights passing on to the purchaser (rights-on). However, purchasers on or after June 21 acquire the stock without the rights (or rights-off). On the record date, the rights are actually mailed to the firm's shareholders. On July 22 the rights will expire. This sequence of events is illustrated in Figure 10.4.

---

[11] If a weekend were included, the ex rights day would be June 19, not June 21. Prior to June 1995 the ex day was set four business days before the record date.

Figure 10.4

Timetable for Common Stock Rights Offering by Cross Prairie Air

The value of the stock drops by $0.50 on the ex rights day when the rights trade separately. The investor who does not exercise or sell his or her rights by July 22 (the expiration date) suffers a loss.

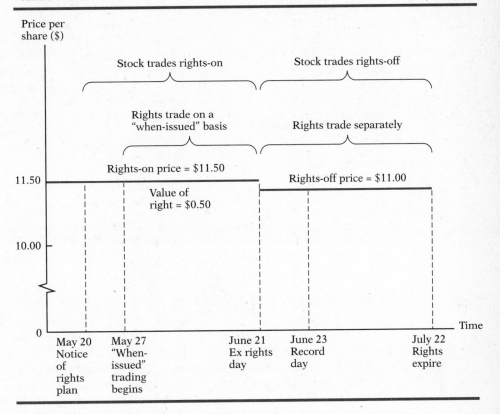

Rights-On.   It is clearly worth something to be able to purchase additional shares of a firm's common stock at a price below its existing market price per share. To determine the value of one right, the following formula can be used:

$$\frac{\text{value of}}{\text{one right}} = \frac{\text{market value of stock, rights on} - \text{subscription price}}{\text{number of rights needed to purchase one share} + 1}$$

$$v_r = \frac{P_o - P_s}{N + 1} \tag{10.7}$$

where

v_r = value of one right
P_o = rights-on market price per share
P_s = subscription price
N = number of rights needed to purchase an additional share of stock

Substituting the appropriate values for Cross Prairie Air, we have

$$v_r = \frac{\$11.50 - \$10}{2 + 1} = \frac{\$1.50}{3} = \$0.50$$

In Figure 10.4 we see that up to the ex rights day, the market price of the common stock is $11.50 per share. However, after the rights offering is announced, the price consists of two distinct elements—the value of the stock itself and the value of the right to purchase additional shares of the firm's common stock at a price below its current market value.

Ex Rights.   On the ex rights day, the stock and rights begin trading separately. The theoretical value of the right after the stock goes ex rights can be solved by

$$\frac{\text{value of}}{\text{one right}} = \frac{\text{market value of stock, ex rights} - \text{subscription price}}{\text{number of shares needed to purchase one share}}$$

(10.8)

$$v_r = \frac{P_x - P_s}{N} = \frac{\$11 - \$10}{2} = \$0.50$$

where P_x is the ex rights stock price per share and the other symbols are as defined previously. Other things being equal, the value of CPA's stock will drop by $0.50, the value of one right, to $11 on the ex rights day.[12]

Effect on the Position of shareholders   Shareholders have the choice of exercising their rights, selling them, or letting them expire. As long as they take some positive action, shareholders do not suffer any loss from a rights offering. However, if they take no action and let the rights expire, a loss is incurred. Consider a shareholder who owns 100 shares of CPA's common stock before the rights offering. Because of the rights offering, the investor can purchase 50 additional shares of common stock (remember it takes two rights for every share) at $10 each. The investor now owns 150 shares, which have a market value of $1,650 [(150 shares)($11)]. Subtracting the $500 paid for the 50 additional shares, the investor is back to his or her original value of $1,150. Thus, the investor is no better or worse off after exercising the rights.

Alternatively, the investor can sell the 100 rights for $0.50 each for a total of $50.[13] He or she now owns 100 shares of stock at $11 each, for a total of $1,100. The $1,100 market value of the stock plus the $50 received from the sale of the rights is exactly equal to the original value of the stock, $1,150. Finally, if the investor does not exercise or sell the rights, the investment is worth only $1,100; $50 was "thrown away" by not doing something with the rights. Clearly, investors should always take some positive action when they receive rights.

---

[12] The ex rights stock price may be calculated directly as:

$$P_x = \frac{P_o N + P_s}{N + 1} = \frac{\$11.50(2) + \$10}{3} = \$11$$

[13] This price assumes there is no brokerage, or selling, commission.

LISTING THE STOCK

In addition to selling stock to raise additional capital, publicly held firms must also decide whether the stock should be listed on an organized stock exchange. Small firms are typically traded in the over-the-counter market because there is simply not enough activity to justify listing. As a firm gets bigger, it may decide to apply for listing on one of the regional stock exchanges. A west coast firm might apply to the Vancouver Stock Exchange; one located in Edmonton might apply to the Alberta Stock Exchange. With continued growth, the firm may decide to apply for listing on the Montreal Stock Exchange, or if it is one of the nation's largest firms, it may apply to the Toronto Stock Exchange.

To apply for listing, the firm must meet certain conditions, a listing application must be filed with both the exchange and the appropriate provincial securities commission, and a fee must be paid. The minimum characteristics a firm must have if it wants a listing on the Toronto Stock Exchange are presented in Table 10.3. After a firm is listed, it must meet certain exchange requirements to continue its listing. The Ontario Securities Commission also requires that both quarterly and annual financial reports be published by listed firms.

Why do firms bother to apply for listing and comply with the additional financial reporting requirements placed on them? By listing, the firm is assured of a continuous secondary market for its common stock. This may make the stock more attractive to some investors and may even make it easier for the firm to issue more common stock in the future. In addition, listing gives firms a certain amount of free advertising and prestige.

Table 10.3

Toronto Stock Exchange Listing Requirements for Common Stock

Other considerations include the management of the applicant company and sponsorship of an applicant company by a member firm.

Profitability[a]

Cash flow before taxes (CFBT) for the most recent year must be at least $400,000. Earnings before taxes and extraordinary items for the most recent year must be at least $100,000.

Assets[a]

Net tangible assets of at least $5 million.

Market Value

The market value of the publicly held stock must be at least $2 million.

Public Ownership

At least 1 million shares must be publicly held, and there must be at least 300 shareholders who each own at least 100 shares.

---

[a] These requirements vary with the listing category, that is, industrial, mining, and oil and gas. Those shown here are for industrial firms.

REGULATION OF PUBLIC ISSUES

Securities regulation in Canada dates back to 1877 and the Canada Joint Stock Companies Act, which adopted provisions governing the disclosure of company contracts. Today, however, the regulation of the securities market is carried out by the provinces through provincial securities acts and similar legislation. In contrast, in the United States a federal body, the Securities and Exchange Commission (SEC), regulates the issuance and distribution of securities to the public.

The first modern Securities Act, emphasizing *full disclosure* of all pertinent information, was adopted by Ontario in 1945. There are two important objectives of this and all subsequent provincial securities acts. The first has been to regulate the new issues, or primary, market, where the proceeds from the sale of securities go to the issuing firm. Although the basic objective of all Canadian securities legislation is to provide full disclosure of all pertinent information, it does not attempt to prevent a firm from issuing highly questionable or risky securities. The second purpose of the various legislations has been to protect buyers and sellers of securities in the secondary market, where securities trade between individuals and/or institutions.

Regulation of the securities market has important consequences for managers. Because of this regulation, both the primary and the secondary markets are viewed as being orderly and efficient. Firms can issue securities with full confidence that the issue will be sold in a manner that secures the needed capital and provides investors a ready market for resale. Without the development of an extensive investment dealer community and efficient and orderly security markets, the costs and risks involved in issuing long-term securities would rise, increasing the firm's opportunity cost of capital, and through the capital budgeting process, influencing its investment decisions.

Concept Review Questions

■ Why does a company's stock price decline with a public common stock offering but increase with a private common stock offering?

■ Explain how investment dealers can estimate the stock price of a company that has never been traded publicly.

■ What factors are of concern to a firm that is about to use a rights offering?

■ Are existing shareholders made wealthier by a rights offering?

KEY POINTS

- Internally generated funds supply the majority of long-term financing needed by firms. However, about 40 percent is provided by new long-term issues, of which bonds play the largest part.
- Investment dealers provide marketing services, risk bearing, and monitoring to issuing firms.
- The use of a short-form prospectus, through the POP system, lowers the cost to large firms and increases the speed and flexibility of obtaining long-term financing. The POP system has also increased the use of bought deals.
- Par value (if it exists), book value, and market value are all quoted on a per share basis for common stock. Only market value has any financial meaning.

- Firms issue new common stock only infrequently; studies indicate they suffer a loss in market value when they do issue common stock publicly. Cash expenses average 15 percent and total costs average 25 percent of the total value of new public common stock issues.
- Rights offerings, while still used to issue common stock, are less frequent than underwritten issues.

QUESTIONS

10.1 Because large firms often have extensive and well-trained finance staffs, they appear to be incurring extra costs by employing the services of investment dealers. What reasons can you give for engaging the services of investment dealers?

10.2 Explain the difference between majority and cumulative voting. What are the advantages or disadvantages of the two plans from (a) the firm's standpoint, and (b) the viewpoint of minority shareholders?

10.3 Differentiate among par value, book value, and market value per share. Why is market value generally the only important figure? Under what limited circumstances may book value be of some importance? Explain.

10.4 The market price of a firm's common stock falls by 2 to 3 percent when it issues additional shares of common stock through a public offering. What possible reasons can we advance for this rather surprising finding? What happens when firms have a private placement of common stock? What possible reasons exist for this effect?

10.5 For underwritten common stock issues of $5 million in size, issuance costs average about 20 percent. Does this mean the cost of external common equity is roughly 20 percent higher than the cost of internally generated funds for these firms?

10.6 How might firms proceed when pricing a new issue of common stock? What makes this decision important?

10.7 The primary purpose of the preemptive right is to allow shareholders to maintain their proportionate ownership and control of a firm. How important do you believe this right is for the following:
a. The average shareholder of a firm listed on the Toronto Stock Exchange?
b. An institutional investor such as a mutual fund or a pension fund?
c. The shareholders of a closely held firm? Explain.

10.8 What advantages (real or imagined) exist when a firm decides to list its common stock? Which are real, and which imagined?

CONCEPT REVIEW PROBLEMS

See Appendix A for solutions.

CR10.1 Winnipeg Publishers is raising $500,000 in new equity. If direct flotation costs are estimated to be 15 percent of gross proceeds, how large does the offering need to be? How much will Winnipeg Publishers pay in flotation costs?

CR10.2 Cooper Corporation has a current stock price of $35 per share and needs to raise $10 million. The investment dealer underwriting Cooper's common stock offering stated that the offering price will have to be $32 per share because of indirect costs such as investors' concerns about information asymmetry and the firm's investment prospects. Direct flotation costs charged by the investment dealer are 5 percent of the issue price. How many shares must the firm sell to net $10 million after indirect and direct flotation costs?

CR10.3   ACI is going public and would like to issue 700,000 shares of common stock. Earnings for the year just completed were $700,000.

a.   Assume ACI has a growth rate of 8 percent and a required return on equity, k_s, of 12 percent, and it plans to have a dividend payout ratio of 70 percent. What should be ACI's initial offering price?

b.   Other firms similar to ACI have a P/E ratio of 18. If we apply this P/E ratio to ACI, what should be ACI's initial offering price?

CR10.4   Pantle Electronics is selling shares of common stock through a privileged subscription. Before the rights offering, the firm had 200,000 shares of common stock outstanding. Pantle plans to issue 20,000 shares at a subscription price of $12. After the stock went ex rights, the market price was $16. What was the price of Pantle Electronics common stock just before the rights offering?

PROBLEMS

10.1   Zhang Products recently sold a $30 million bond issue at par. The underwriting fees were 1.2 percent, and additional issuance costs were $125,000.

a.   How many dollars did Zhang net from the sale?

b.   What were the fees (including both underwriting and other issuance costs) as a percentage of the gross proceeds of the bond issue?

10.2   In an $80 million bond issue by Consumers Power, the bonds were purchased by the underwriting group at 99.125 percent of par and sold to the public at par, which was $1,000 per bond.

a.   What was the total amount Consumers Power received from the issue?

b.   What were the total underwriting costs? What were the underwriting costs as a percentage of the gross proceeds? What were the underwriting costs per $1,000 bond?

c.   If an underwriting dealer was also the seller, it received all the commission. Otherwise, members of the selling group could buy the bonds and sell them for a commission of $2.50 per bond. If a member of the selling group bought 50 bonds, how much in total did the selling group dealer make, and how much did the dealer pay to the underwriter for the bonds?

10.3   Precision Computers, a new and rather speculative firm, wishes to raise additional capital by selling stock and going public. The firm's investment dealer has suggested two alternatives. Plan I is a firm commitment offering of 1 million shares at $7.50 per share, with an underwriting fee of 8 percent of the gross proceeds. Plan II is a best efforts offering at $7.75 per share, subject to an underwriting commission of 3 percent of the expected gross proceeds sold, plus a $150,000 fee. The "best guess" is that 95 percent of the issue would be sold under plan II.

a.   Based on the net proceeds to the firm, which plan should Precision choose?

b.   Does your answer change if only 90 percent of the issue can be sold under the best efforts plan?

c.   All things considered, which plan would you recommend? Why?

10.4   Thomas Ltd. is planning a private placement of 60,000 new shares to an institutional investor at a 10 percent discount from the present market price of $40. There are presently 300,000 shares outstanding. If the current book value of the shareholders' equity is $6,000,000, calculate (a) book value per share both before and after the private placement, and (b) the market price per share after the private placement. Are existing shareholders better or worse off after the new shares are sold? Defend your answer, given your calculations.

10.5 Sylvie and her associates control 152,000 shares of Champion Ltd. and they desire representation on the firm's board. Champion has 500,000 shares outstanding, eight directors are to be elected, and cumulative voting is used. How many board members can Sylvie and her associates elect in each of the cases below?

a. All 500,000 shares vote.
b. Only 90 percent of the total shares vote.

10.6 Ken and George plan to pool their shares so they can both be elected to the board of directors. The firm has 1,000,000 shares of stock outstanding and plans to elect 10 directors. How many shares do Ken and George jointly need to control to obtain two seats on the board in each of the cases below?

a. Majority voting is employed.
b. Cumulative voting is employed.
c. The size of the board is reduced to five and cumulative voting is employed.

10.7 J. B. Eagen is a new firm that needs to raise $16,560,000 to begin operations. No debt will be used. Eagen's common stock is expected to pay a $4 cash dividend next year, and dividends and earnings are expected to grow at 9 percent per year for the foreseeable future. If k_s is 19 percent and the cost of issuing the stock is 8 percent of the gross proceeds from the sale, how many shares must be issued and sold?

10.8 Kletzin Enterprises is planning its first public offering of common stock. The CFO estimates that the equity investors' required return is between 11 and 14 percent. Earnings and cash dividends are expected to grow at 6 to 9 percent per year for the foreseeable future, and cash dividends to be paid next year, D_1, are $800,000.

a. What is the range of possible total current market values for the stock of Kletzin Enterprises?
b. If 500,000 shares of stock are issued, but 300,000 will be held by the founders, what are the maximum and minimum selling prices per share and the maximum and minimum total proceeds from the issue?

10.9 Gránd-B Enterprises is a new firm that needs to raise $6,412,500 through the issuance of 1 million shares of stock. No debt will be employed. Next year's cash dividends are expected to be $0.60 per share, and cash dividends and earnings are expected to grow at 8 percent per year for the foreseeable future. If k_s is 16 percent and the cost of issuing the stock is 10 percent of the gross proceeds, what percent of the issue must be sold in order for Grand-B to obtain the net amount of $6,412,500? (*Note:* Any unsold shares will be distributed among the firm's owners, so a total of 1 million shares will be outstanding.)

10.10 Spartan Energy is planning its first public offering. Its past growth in cash dividends and earnings has averaged 10 percent per year. Based on the number of shares Spartan is planning to issue, cash dividends and earnings per share for next year (t = 1) are expected to be $0.90 and $2, respectively. The firm's investment dealer, Lindsay & Sons, has recommended that the stock be issued at a price of $15 per share. (Ignore any flotation or issuance costs.)

a. What is the P/E ratio implied by the recommended market price?
b. Two firms similar to Spartan Energy have the following characteristics:

	Firm Y	Firm Z
Expected EPS	$ 1.50	$ 3.00
Expected DPS	0.80	1.25
Expected growth rate per year	7%	9%
Market price	$15.00	$45.00

For firm Y and firm Z, determine (1) their P/E ratios and (2) their implied k_s. Then calculate an estimated market price for Spartan Energy using, first, the separate P/Es and k_s's, and then an average of them. Based on these comparable firms, what range of prices is implied for Spartan?

c. What required return, or cost of equity capital, k_s, is implied by the price of $15 if investors' expectations of the future are consistent with the past?

d. You believe the rate calculated in (c) is high; it should be between 11.5 and 13 percent. The expected growth rate of 10 percent is okay. What issue price is implied, given these estimates?

e. Based on your analysis in (a) through (d), how would you respond to the Lindsay & Sons proposal?

10.11 Hawkeye Banks Ltd. has decided to use a rights offering to raise $5 million. Currently (before the rights offering) there are 500,000 shares of common stock outstanding, the market price per share is $68, and the subscription price has been set at $50 per share.
a. What is the approximate value of each right?
b. When, and by how much, will the stock drop in price?

10.12 A & M Industries is planning a rights offering of 50,000 shares at $40 each. The following timetable is planned:

Date	Action
August 4	Announcement
September 15	Ex rights
September 17	Record date
October 15	Rights expire

The market price on August 4 is $50 per share, and four rights are required for each additional share to be purchased. Assume there are no changes in market value except as a result of the rights offering.
a. What is the value of one right?
b. Can you infer how many shares of stock A & M had outstanding before the rights offering?
c. Trace the market price per share from August 4 to October 15.

10.13 Optics Ltd. has decided on a rights offering to raise $5.2 million for new equipment and working capital. The current market price per share before the offering was $84, the subscription price was set at $52, and seven rights are required to buy one more share.
a. Determine the value of the right and the ex rights price of the stock.
b. After announcing the offering, you receive a call from an irate shareholder who owns 700 shares of stock. The shareholder believes a personal loss will be suffered because Optics decided to issue additional stock at a price substantially below the current market value. To convince this shareholder otherwise, you promise to send a statement showing the effects of a rights offering on shareholder wealth, assuming (1) the shareholder exercises the rights, (2) the rights are sold (ignore brokerage costs), and (3) the rights expire. Prepare such a statement.

10.14 Mini Case Office Supplies, Ltd., is a fast-growing privately held firm. In order to continue expanding into new markets, it needs additional common stock financing.
a. What different methods are available for selling common stock? What are the advantages and disadvantages of each?

b. If Office Supplies decides to have the issue underwritten through a firm commitment offering, what sequence of events will occur?

c. If the current owners are concerned about giving up too much control of the firm in terms of voting rights, how might they proceed?

d. To determine the selling price of the new issue, Office Supplies has made the following estimates. The firm does not presently pay cash dividends, nor are there any plans to start paying them in the near future. Based on internal projections, the rate of growth is expected to be 40 percent per year for each of the next five years, after which it will be 10 percent per year to infinity. Because no dividends are paid, a variation of the dividend valuation model will be employed as one way to estimate the total value of Office Supplies. Under this approach the firm's free cash flow available after necessary expenses will be projected into the future, discounted at the opportunity cost of equity capital of 18 percent, and then the firm's liabilities will be subtracted. The free cash flow at time t = 0 is $3,000,000, and the liabilities are $25,000,000.

The second way that will be used to estimate the value of the firm is based on comparable P/E ratios. The firm's current earnings are $2,500,000 and, due to its high growth, a P/E ratio of 35 times earnings is believed to be appropriate.

1. Estimate Office Supplies' total equity value, S, using both the discounted cash flow approach and the comparable P/E approach.
2. Then average them together to determine the estimated equity value of Office Supplies.

e. Office Supplies will issue 5,000,000 shares of common stock. It will sell 2,000,000 to the public, 3,000,000 will be retained by the original owners, and the cash expenses of the sale will be 7 percent of the issue price.

1. What market price per share will the stock sell for? How much per share will Office Supplies receive after expenses? How much in total will it receive?
2. Why are issuance expenses higher with common stock, especially for a smaller firm, than for bonds?

f. In what market will Office Supplies stock trade? What are the advantages if in the future it decides to have its stock listed on one of the stock exchanges? What are the disadvantages?

REFERENCES

CARTER, RICHARD, and STEVEN MANASTER. "Initial Public Offerings and Underwriter Reputation." *Journal of Finance* 45 (September 1990): 1045–1067.

CLARKSON, PETER M., and JACK MERKLEY. "Ex Ante Uncertainty and the Underpricing of Initial Public Offerings: Further Canadian Evidence." *Canadian Journal of Administrative Sciences* 11 (March 1994): 54–67.

COONEY, JOHN W., JR., and AVNER KALAY. "Positive Information from Equity Issue Announcements." *Journal of Financial Economics* 33 (April 1993): 149–172.

DIERKENS, NATHALIE. "Information Asymmetry and Equity Issues." *Journal of Financial and Quantitative Analysis* 26 (June 1991): 181–199.

ECKBO, B. ESPEN, and RONALD W. MASULIS. "Adverse Selection and the Rights Offer Paradox." *Journal of Financial Economics* 32 (December 1992): 293–332.

GARFINKEL, JON A. "IPO Underpricing, Insider Selling and Subsequent Equity Offerings: Is Underpricing a Signal of Quality?" *Financial Management* 22 (Spring 1993): 74–83.

GORDON, LILLI A., and JOHN POUND. "Information, Ownership Structure, and Shareholder Voting: Evidence from Shareholder-Sponsored Corporate Governance Proposals." *Journal of Finance* 48 (June 1993): 697–718.

HANSEN, ROBERT S., and PAUL TORREGROSA. "Underwriting Compensation and Corporate Monitoring." *Journal of Finance* 47 (September 1992): 1537–1555.

HERTZEL, MICHAEL, and RICHARD L. SMITH. "Market Discounts and Shareholder Gains for Placing Equity Privately." *Journal of Finance* 47 (June 1993): 459–485.

MAYNES, ELIZABETH. "Evidence on the Value of a Stock Exchange Listing." *Canadian Journal of Administrative Sciences* 8 (September 1991): 179–191.

PILOTTE, EUGENE. "Growth Opportunities and the Stock Price Response to New Financing." *Journal of Business* 65 (July 1992): 371–394.

RITTER, JAY R. "The Long-Run Performance of Initial Public Offerings." *Journal of Finance* 46 (March 1991): 3–27.

ROBINSON, CHRIS, and ALAN WHITE. "Empirical Evidence on the Relative Valuation of Voting and Restricted Voting Shares." *Canadian Journal of Administrative Sciences* 7 (December 1990): 9–18.

SCHWARTZ, LAWRENCE P. "Bought Deals: The Devil that You Know." *Canadian Investment Review* 12 (Spring 1994): 21–27.

WRUCK, KAREN H. "Equity Ownership Concentration and Firm Value: Evidence from Private Equity Financing." *Journal of Financial Economics* 23 (June 1989): 3–28.

11 Liability Management

EXECUTIVE SUMMARY

Long-term debt and preferred stock are fixed-income-type securities, because both obligate the issuing firm to a series of payments over time. (The one exception is zero-coupon bonds, which obligate the firm to a lump-sum payment when the bond matures.) A primary measure of the riskiness of bonds is the bond rating. Other things being equal, the higher (lower) the rating, the lower (higher) the yield to maturity on the bond.

Zero-coupon bonds are sold at a discount and do not provide cash interest payments; rather, the interest provided is the difference between the original discounted selling price and the maturity value of the bond. As market interest rates fluctuate, the market price of zero-coupon bonds fluctuates more than the market price of similar coupon bonds.

Increasingly, firms have begun to practise long-term liability management with tactics such as bond refunding, buybacks, and interest rate swaps. With a "plain vanilla" swap, one firm raises fixed-rate financing while another raises floating-rate financing, and then they exchange interest payment streams. The advantage comes from each firm raising funds at its cheapest rate, and then switching from fixed to floating, or vice versa.

Another important aspect of long-term liability for firms is pension plan obligations. Pension plan obligations of firms represent claims by their employees that are similar to the claims of the firms' bondholders. Due to the significant size of pension plan obligations, financial managers require a basic understanding of how pension plans operate. In addition, preferred stock, due to its higher cost to the issuing firm, has been used less frequently. The creation of adjustable-rate preferred stock, however, has lowered the cost and broadened the appeal of preferred stock.

Conflicts of interest exist between bondholders and shareholders because what benefits one may cause the other to suffer a loss. These conflicts are intensified during periods of financial distress.

LONG-TERM DEBT

Long-term debt and preferred stock obligate the firm to pay a fixed annual return—interest on debt or cash dividends on preferred stock. To secure funds, managers choose from among the various kinds of long-term securities depending on world markets, what investors are currently interested in, and the firm's financial position. This chapter focuses primarily on the two main types of long-term securities—bonds and preferred stock.

BOND TERMS

When a firm borrows with bonds, it issues a long-term promissory note to a lender. The contract between the firm and the lender is called a bond **indenture**. For cash offerings, a copy of the indenture is included in the registration statement filed with the various provincial securities commissions. It is a legal document specifying all the provisions attached to the bond. One specific provision states that the lenders will receive regular interest payments, generally semiannually, during the term of the bond, and will receive the par or maturity value of the bond upon maturity. For example, if TransCanada PipeLines issues a 20-year, $100 million bond with a coupon rate of 10.3 percent, it will pay $10.3 million per year in interest each year until maturity. The interest will be paid in two semiannual instalments of $5.15 million each. On the maturity date in 20 years, TransCanada PipeLines would then repay the $100 million. Long-term corporate bonds typically have a 20- to 30-year maturity when issued, but recently Boeing, Ford Motor, and Texaco all issued bonds with a 50-year maturity, while Walt Disney and Coca Cola both issued 100-year bonds.

TRUSTEE

Bonds are not only long-term in nature, they are typically of substantial size. Issues of $50 to $500 million are not uncommon, and some are even larger. To ease communication between the issuing firm and the lenders, a trustee is appointed for all public issues of long-term debt. The primary responsibilities of the trustee (typically a trust company) are as follows:

1. To see that all the legal requirements for drawing up the bond indenture are met before issuance.
2. To monitor the action of the issuing firm to see that its performance is in agreement with the conditions specified by the indenture.
3. To take appropriate action on behalf of bondholders if the firm defaults on interest or principal payments.

SECURITY AND SENIORITY

Bonds come with many types of provisions. One primary distinction is between secured and unsecured bonds. We will discuss the provisions in order.

Forms of Secured Debt   The vast majority of secured debt consists of **mortgage bonds**, which may be *first mortgage bonds* if they have a primary claim on assets in the event of default, or *second mortgage bonds*, whose claim is subordinate to that of the first mortgage bondholders. Bonds come with many different types of restrictions, or protective convenants. Some mortgage bonds have a "closed-end provision" that prohibits the firm from issuing additional debt with equal priority against the pledged assets. With an "open-end provision," no specific limit on the amount of debt secured by the firm's assets exists. In between these two is a "limited open-end" mortgage, in which some limited amount of additional debt may be issued. To strengthen the position of the bondholder, the indenture also may contain an "after-acquired property" clause. This provision specifies that any property acquired by the firm in the future will also serve as collateral for the bonds.

A second form of secured debt is the **equipment trust certificate**, which frequently is used to finance railroad cars and airplanes. Here, the trustee acquires formal ownership of the asset in question. The issuing firm arranges to purchase the equipment and provides a down payment of 10 to 25 percent; the remainder is provided by the purchasers of the equipment trust certificates. The certificates are issued with varying maturities, often ranging from 1 to 15 years. After the entire issue is paid off, title to the equipment passes to the firm. Because the trustee holds title to the pledged equipment, equipment trust certificates provide good security to their purchasers.

Unsecured Debt   Unsecured bonds, called **debentures**, have no specific assets pledged as collateral. Instead, they are backed by the full faith and credit of the issuing corporation. Large firms with excellent credit ratings, such as Canadian Utilities, BCE Inc., and John Labatt, use debentures almost exclusively. Most debentures have a claim on assets in the event of default that comes after that held by bank loans, short-term debt, the government, and any mortgage bonds.

Although asset security is sometimes important, in the final analysis it is the firm's cash flow that determines the attractiveness of a bond issue. Debentures frequently contain a "negative pledge clause," which prohibits issuing new debt with a priority over the debentures' claim on assets. This provision generally applies to assets acquired in the future as well as to those already owned by the issuing firm.

Subordinated debentures, which have a claim on assets inferior to that of other debentures in the case of liquidation, are widely used in raising long-term debt capital. Subordinated debt allows the issuing firm to increase its borrowing without jeopardizing the security position of its other long-term debt.

One last form of unsecured bond is the **income bond**, which requires interest to be paid only to the extent that it is earned by the firm. Income bonds typically arise out of reorganizations. They are somewhat like preferred stock in that the firm is not required to pay interest if it is not earned. Income bonds have the advantage that any interest, if paid, is a tax-deductible expense, whereas cash dividends paid on preferred stock are not. The provisions attached to income bonds vary, but many are

cumulative; that is, if interest is not paid in a given period, it must be paid in the future if it is earned.

ADDITIONAL BOND PROVISIONS

Many different types of provisions and protective covenants occur in bonds.[1] Some of these were considered in the last section. There are four provisions that warrant additional consideration; these are the call provision, sinking funds, convertibility, and extendibility and retractability.

Call Provision   A **call provision** gives the issuing firm the option to call the bond for redemption before it matures. This provision states that if it calls the bond, the firm must pay an amount greater than the par or maturity value of the bond; the additional amount is the **call premium**. For most long-term bonds, the call premium starts out close to the coupon rate on the bond. Thus, if the firm wants to call the bonds soon after issuance, it pays a penalty of about one year's additional interest. This rate declines over time.

The call provision is valuable to the firm but potentially detrimental to investors. The problem for investors is that the call provision enables the issuing firm to substitute bonds with a lower coupon rate for bonds with a higher rate, or bonds with less protective covenants for ones with more stringent covenants.[2] To make them more attractive investments, many bonds now carry a 5-to 10-year "nonrefundable provision" if the coupon rate on the new bonds will be below the current coupon rate on the bond to be refunded.

Sinking Fund   A **sinking fund** provision requires the firm to retire a given number of bonds over a specified time period. The logic behind sinking funds is to encourage firms to adopt a systematic pattern for retiring the largest portion of the debt before the maturity date. Generally bonds are redeemed for the sinking fund at par. Although it is called a sinking fund, we should emphasize that a separate fund is *not* set up and accumulated over the life of the bonds. Rather, a given number of bonds *are actually retired each year.*

In most cases, the firm can decide how to meet the sinking fund provision. If market interest rates have increased, causing the price of the bonds to fall below the par or sinking fund price, the firm can buy sufficient bonds on the open market to meet the requirement. But if market interest rates are low (and therefore bond prices are high), the firm will call the bonds by lottery at par. This flexibility obviously benefits the issuing firm.

If the bonds are privately placed, the sinking fund provision is omitted because the bonds must be redeemed at par. In that case, instead of sinking funds, firms use **serial bonds**, which is a package of bonds that mature in different years. Serial bonds are similar to a bond with a sinking fund provision, because both provide for the periodic

---

[1] Protective covenants are discussed in detail in Chapter 13.

[2] Refunding a bond issue involves calling one issue and replacing it with another. Refunding is considered later in the chapter and in Appendix 11A.

repayment of the firm's debt. But the serial bond does not give the issuing firm an alternative—the bonds must be redeemed at par.

Convertibility Some bonds and preferred stock contain another feature—convertibility. **Convertible securities** are convertible bonds or convertible preferred stock, originally issued as debt or preferred stock, that can be exchanged for common stock of the issuing firm at the discretion of the investor. By combining elements of both debt and equity, convertible bonds assist in minimizing agency problems and conflicts between bondholders and shareholders. Convertibles are considered in Chapter 20.

Extendibility and Retractability Two other features that firms have used when issuing bonds are extendibility and retractability. These features offer the bondholder protection from a decline or rise in interest rates. An **extendible bond** is issued with a relatively short maturity, but the *bondholder* has the option to extend the maturity of the bond for an additional specified period of time, at the original interest rate. This extendibility feature would be exercised only if interest rates have fallen over the original life of the bond, thus allowing the investor to lock in the higher interest rate for a longer period of time.

A **retractable bond** is redeemable, at the option of the *investor*, on a specified date before the maturity date of the bond. If interest rates increase after the bond is issued, then, on the specified date, the investor would cash in the bond, at par value, and invest in another bond at the higher interest rate. Thus, a retractable bond is the reverse of an extendible bond; it protects investors from an increase in interest rates (and accompanying decrease in bond value) after the bond is issued. Both of these bonds are similar to callable bonds, *except that the option to redeem the bond belongs to the bondholder, not the issuer.*

Concept Review Questions

- What is the purpose of appointing a trustee for all long-term issuances?
- Give some examples of secured debentures and unsecured debentures.
- How do a callable bond and a convertible bond differ?

FINANCING WITH LONG-TERM DEBT

The frequency with which firms issue long-term debt varies considerably. At one extreme are large public utility firms, which may issue debt every few years. Other firms issue long-term debt only infrequently. But however often they employ it, managers must be aware of special considerations when they use long-term debt.

PRICING AND SELLING THE BOND ISSUE

Many large bond issues are underwritten through a firm commitment offering, although an increasing number are being offered through the POP system or short-form prospectus and private placement. The coupon interest rate is determined shortly before the bonds come to market, so that they may be sold at a price close to par. Most bonds are issued in denominations of $1,000 in **fully registered** form. This means that the registration agent for the issuing firm (often a trust company) will record the ownership of each bond, so that both interest and principal are paid directly to the owner of the bond. Until the last few decades, most bonds were issued in **bearer form**. When bearer bonds are employed, the certificate is the primary evidence of ownership. The owner must send in coupons for payment of interest, and the bond itself must be returned upon maturity for repayment of principal. Because of the risk of loss and the time and inconvenience involved in "clipping" coupons, most bonds are now issued in fully registered form.

The price of a bond is expressed as a percentage of its par value. Thus, a price of 99.5 means 99.5 percent of its $1,000 par value, or $995. When a bond is sold, the price is quoted net of accrued interest. This means the purchaser pays not only the purchase price, but also any interest that may have accrued between interest payment dates. Finally, the major secondary market for bonds is the over-the-counter (OTC) market.

BOND RATINGS

The most widely employed method for examining the relative quality of bonds is **bond ratings**, which reflect the probability of payment of both interest and principal. Two bonds with similar ratings and the same maturity have approximately the same yield to maturity.[3] The two major Canadian rating agencies are Dominion Bond Rating Service (DBRS) and Canadian Bond Rating Service (CBRS). Their ratings are described in Table 11.1.

The AAA/A++ and AA/A+ bonds are of high quality; A and BBB/B++ bonds are also viewed as being of "investment grade." Bonds with these four top grades may be held by banks and other institutional investors. BB/B+ and B bonds are more speculative with respect to payment of interest and principal; bonds rated below B are either in default or have other characteristics that make them highly speculative.

Many factors influence the determination of bond ratings, but some of the most important are these:

1. Accounting ratios such as the debt/equity ratio, times interest earned (i.e., EBIT/interest), and various profitability ratios (as discussed in Chapter 25), which provide some evidence of the strength and riskiness of the firm.
2. The current status of the firm in terms of its competitiveness and management. In addition, the industry or industries in which the firm is engaged is often a factor.
3. If the firm is in a regulated industry, such as public utilities, the attitude of the appropriate regulatory authorities.
4. Specific provisions or characteristics of the bonds. For example, first mortgage

---

[3] Exceptions occur when we compare bonds issued by industrial firms and those issued by public utilities. Because of different provisions and demand, the yields on utilities are typically higher than those of similarly rated corporate bonds.

Table 11.1

Bond Rating Classifications

Generally, both the Dominion Bond Rating Service and the Canadian Bond Rating Service rate a bond similarly, although differences in ratings can and do exist. Bonds in the top four classifications (AAA − BBB or A++ − B++, respectively) are considered "investment grade."

Dominion Bond Rating Service		Canadian Bond Rating Service	
AAA	Highest quality	A++	Highest quality
AA	Superior quality	A+	Very good quality
A	Medium grade securities	A	Good quality
BBB	Medium grade securities	B++	Medium grade securities
BB	Lower medium grade	B+	Lower medium grade
B	Medium speculative securities	B	Poor quality
		C	Speculative
CCC	Highly speculative securities	D	Default
CC	Securities in default (of interest or principal)		
C	Securities similar to CC		

Note: The ratings of both services may be modified by the addition of "high" or "low" to show relative standing within a classification.

bonds generally carry a rating one level higher than debentures for the same firm, and debentures are often rated one level higher than subordinated debentures.

When originally issued, most bonds are awarded a rating of B or above, with the highest-quality bonds carrying an AAA/A++ rating. Triple-A bonds are viewed by the rating agencies as having the lowest probability of default, so the issuing firms have to pay the least for debt financing. Table 11.2 indicates that between 1985 and 1994, the yield to maturity on AAA-rated bonds was, on average, about 1.31 percent below that for BBB bonds. The differences in yields to maturity, although for bonds already outstanding, illustrate the differences in coupon rates attached to bonds in different rating groups.

Notice in Table 11.2 that all bonds, even the long-term Government of Canada bonds, carry a risk premium above that of short-term Canadian treasury bills. Thus, we see that the average risk premium for long-term government bonds over this time period was 1.21 percent. As we move from long-term government bonds to corporate bonds, the yield to maturity increases due to default risk. Yield spreads between bonds also vary over time. In 1985, for example, long-term Government of Canada bonds had a yield to maturity of 11.17 percent, whereas corporate BBB bonds were yielding 12.09 percent, for a difference—a yield spread—of 0.92 percent (or 92 basis points). However, in 1994, the difference in yields between the same two bond categories was 2.96 percent (11.63 − 8.67). For firms entering the bond market, the going interest rate on standing issues of similar maturity and quality provides a good point of reference for estimating the coupon interest rate (and hence the before-tax cost) for a new bond issue.

Table 11.2

Yield to Maturity on Long-Term Canadian Government and Corporate Bonds

The differences in yields approximate the differences in coupon rates required from the issuing firm. Hence, other things being equal, firms strive for as high a rating as possible in order to reduce their interest costs.

Year	Government of Canada Bonds	Corporate Bonds			
		AAA	AA	A	BBB
1985	11.17	11.54	11.67	11.89	12.09
1986	9.58	10.01	10.16	10.34	11.13
1987	9.98	10.55	10.66	10.77	10.97
1988	10.18	10.65	10.81	11.00	11.26
1989	9.88	10.50	10.66	10.90	11.08
1990	10.82	11.62	11.76	11.95	12.42
1991	9.70	10.47	10.52	10.76	11.58
1992	8.75	9.59	9.59	9.87	11.37
1993	7.80	8.51	8.51	8.92	11.15
1994	8.67	8.76	9.28	9.52	11.63
Average yield	9.65	10.16	10.36	10.59	11.47
Average risk premium (yield − treasury bill yield)	1.21	1.72	1.92	2.15	3.03

Sources: ScotiaMcleod, *ScotiaMcleod's Handbook of Canadian Debt Market Indices* and Canadian Bond Rating Service, *Corporate Rating and Reports.*

What about the actual experience of bonds with respect to default? Do lower-quality bonds, with higher yields, actually have higher default rates? Canadian data to report on this issue are not readily available; however, studies in this area have been conducted in the United States. Table 11.3 presents cumulative default rates (for one year, three years, five years, seven years, and nine years after original issuance) for bonds issued by U.S. firms during the 1971–1991 period. As the table indicates, for bonds in the top three categories (the A's) default after nine years of issuance was 0.17 percent for AAA bonds, 1.79 percent for AA bonds, and 1.49 percent for A-rated bonds. The default experience has been low for these bonds. The default rate of BBB bonds is 4.09 percent after nine years. Moving to the noninvestment-grade bonds of BB, B, or C, we find that default rates for bonds issued in the 1971–1991 period are fairly high—from 14 percent after nine years for BB-rated bonds, to more than 35 percent of B-rated bonds. Finally, for C-rated bonds, we see that more than 35 percent of them defaulted within five years and almost 40 percent defaulted within seven years from the date they were issued. Based on this information we see that bond ratings at the time of original issue do a good job of differentiating low-risk from high-risk bonds.

Table 11.3

Mortality Rates for U.S. Firms by Original Bond Rating, 1971–1991

The default rates indicate the cumulative percentage of bonds that have defaulted one, three, five, seven and nine years after they were originally issued.

	Years After Original Issuance				
Original Rating	1	3	5	7	9
AAA	0.00%	0.00%	0.00%	0.17%	0.17%
AA	0.00	1.09	1.52	1.71	1.79
A	0.00	0.45	0.93	1.08	1.49
BBB	0.10	1.51	2.72	3.96	4.09
BB	0.00	4.53	8.97	14.02	14.02
B	1.72	14.90	25.00	30.09	35.54
C	1.55	26.01	35.40	38.85	na

Source: Adapted from Exhibit 10 in Edward I. Altman, "Revisiting the High-Yield Bond Market," *Financial Management* 21 (Summer 1992): 78–92

TERM LOANS

As an alternative to a bond issue, firms—especially smaller ones—also rely on bank borrowings. The mechanics of these borrowings often take the form of **term**, or amortized, **loans**. The purpose of the amortization is to see that principal and interest are paid off on some predetermined schedule. Firms that borrow from banks may be smaller than firms that raise funds through a public bond issue, and the maturity (or length) of financing is typically 5 to 10 years.

To illustrate, suppose Clark's Products borrowed $55,000 on a three-year loan to be repaid in three equal annual instalments. The nominal rate of interest is 12 percent on the declining principal balance of the loan. The annual payments, which include both principal and interest, are just an annuity. Thus, the size of each payment is

$$PV_0 = PMT(PVA_{k,n})$$
$$\$55,000 = PMT(PVA_{12\%,\,3yr})$$
$$PMT = \$55,000/2.402 = \$22,897.59$$

Hence, Clark's makes three equal annual payments of $22,897.59 to repay the loan.[4] The **amortization schedule**, which breaks down the payments between principal and interest, is presented in Table 11.4. Note that more of the payment goes to pay back the principal as the years go by. Also, the last payment, as shown in Table 11.4, is often slightly different from the earlier payments. Home mortgage or car loans typically employ exactly the same approach.

---

[4] Using a financial calculator, entering PV = $55,000, i = k = 12, n = 3, and selecting PMT results in a payment of $22,899.19. The difference of $1.60 (i.e., $22,899.19 − $22,897.59) is due to rounding. Most loans of this type are actually payable monthly or quarterly.

Table 11.4

Principal and Interest Amortized Over Three Annual Instalments at 12 Percent

As is typical of many term (or instalment) loans, the last payment differs from the earlier ones.

Year	Payment	Interest[a]	Principal Repayment	Remaining Balance
1	$22,897.59	$6,600.00	$16,297.59	$38,702.41
2	22,897.59	4,644.29	18,253.30	20,449.11
3	22,903.00[b]	2,453.89	20,449.11	0

[a] First-year interest is (0.12)($55,000); for year 2 it is (0.12)($38,702.41); and for year 3 it is (0.12)($20,449.11).
[b] This last payment is the sum of the remaining balance of $20,449.11 and the interest of $2,453.89.

DEBT FINANCING AND THE VALUE OF THE FIRM

In Chapter 10 we saw that firms issuing new equity experience a decrease in the value of their outstanding common stock. Does the same pattern hold for firms that issue bonds or take out bank loans? That is, does the value of a firm's common stock fall when it issues bonds or takes out a term loan? Table 11.5 indicates the valuation effect of various types of security sales and bank loans. Just as the value of a firm's common stock falls when it issues new equity offerings, likewise, as shown in Table 11.5, the issuance of convertible debt (which has characteristics of both debt and equity) results in a drop in value. Issuing straight (i.e., nonconvertible) debt, on the other hand, has little if any negative impact on the value of the firm.

Finally, we see from Table 11.5 that the bank loan review and renewal process plays an important role. Bank loan agreements in total have a positive impact on the value of the firm, but it is important to distinguish between new bank loan agreements and revisions of existing loan agreements. New loan agreements, as shown in Table 11.5, have no impact on the value of the firm. In revised loan agreements, the revision can be either favourable or unfavourable. A favourable loan revision involves lengthening the maturity of the loan, reducing the interest rate, increasing the size of the loan, or making the protective covenants less restrictive. Favourable revisions in bank loan agreements result in almost a 4 percent increase in the value of the firm's stock. On the other hand, an unfavourable revision is associated with a loss in value of almost 4 percent. Through their review process, banks provide access to information about the firm that is not otherwise available to the capital markets.

Concept Review Questions

- Are most bonds currently issued in bearer form or fully registered form? Why?
- What are some factors that influence a bond's rating?
- Describe the effects on a firm's stock price of issuing convertible debt, issuing straight debt, and obtaining a term loan.

Table 11.5

Impact of Securities Offerings and Bank Borrowing on the Value of the Firm's Common Stock

As firms sell securities or borrow from banks, shareholders revise their expectations, and common stock returns drop for unfavourable events and increase for favourable events.

	Two-Day Abnormal Return		
Type of Security Offering	**Smith**[a]	**James**[b]	**Lummer and McConnell**[c]
Common stock	−3.14%		
Convertible preferred stock	−1.44		
Preferred stock	−0.19		
Convertible bonds	−2.07		
Public straight bonds	−0.26	−0.11%	
Private placement of debt		−0.91	
Bank loan agreement		1.93	0.61%
New bank credit agreements			−0.01
Revised bank agreement—favourable			3.98
Revised bank agreement—unfavourable			−3.86

[a] Clifford Smith, "Investment Banking and the Capital Acquisition Process," *Journal of Financial Economics* 15 (January/February 1986): 3–29.
[b] Christopher James, "Some Evidence on the Uniqueness of Bank Loans," *Journal of Financial Economics* 19 (December 1987): 217–235.
[c] Scott L. Lummer and John J. McConnell, "Further Evidence on the Bank Lending Process and the Capital-Market Response to Bank Loan Agreements," *Journal of Financial Economics* 25 (November 1989): 99–122.

FINANCING IN THE 1990s

Because of dramatic shifts in inflation over time, innovations in the financial markets, and the development of world-wide capital markets, the degree of sophistication required for raising long-term capital has increased greatly. Firms now use many different forms of debt financing.

ZERO-COUPON BONDS

In the United States, in March 1981, Martin Marietta sold $175 million of 30-year bonds with a 7 percent coupon rate at 54 percent of par, for an effective yield to maturity of 13.25 percent. These securities were one of the first issues of **deep discount bonds**. Subsequently, many firms have issued **zero-coupon bonds**. The first Canadian issue of zero-coupon bonds was sold by Gulf Canada Ltd. in September 1981. The issue, which was divided into two maturities, 7 and 10 years, raised $48.8 million for Gulf. When the bonds are redeemed at par, the firm will have to pay a total of $234 million, thus providing bondholders with a yield to maturity of 18 percent.

These bonds, like Canadian treasury bills, are issued at a discount; that is, the interest is the difference between their original issue price and the maturity value. Why would any firm issue zero-coupon bonds? The answer is that these bonds have a yield (or cost) to maturity of approximately 1 percent less than similar-quality coupon bonds sold at par. The cost to the firm is lower primarily because these bonds are callable only at a substantial premium. From the purchaser's standpoint there are two advantages to a zero-coupon bond. First, because there are no periodic interest payments to be received, there is no reinvestment rate risk. That is, the purchaser can lock in the expected compound return irrespective of what happens to interest rates over the life of the bond.[5] Second, purchasers are much surer of not having the bond called by the issuing firm. Because of these characteristics, purchasers are willing to accept a lower return than on a coupon-paying bond.

Zero-coupon bonds have some unusual characteristics that differentiate them from the coupon-bearing bonds we valued in Chapter 4. To illustrate, assume that Anderson Products is planning a $100 million par value, 10-year, 12 percent zero-coupon issue. Assuming (for simplicity) that interest is compounded annually, the net proceeds, B_0, from the bond (ignoring flotation costs) are equal to

$$
\begin{aligned}
B_0(\text{zero-coupon}) &= \text{par}(PV_{k,n}) \\
&= \text{par}(PV_{12\%,10\text{yr}}) = \$100,000,000(0.322) \qquad (11.1) \\
&= \$32,200,000
\end{aligned}
$$

Anderson will receive approximately $32 million from the bond issue, and in 10 years it will repay $100 million to the purchasers of the bonds. Although annual cash interest payments are not made, Revenue Canada has ruled that *both the firm issuing the bonds and investors purchasing them* must impute and report interest (for tax purposes) just as if cash had changed hands. The actual amount of interest declared, as shown in Table 11.6, increases each year due to the compounding involved. Notice in the table that the total amount of interest (per $1,000 par value bond) of $678.03 is just equal to the difference between the par (or maturity) value of the bond and its original price of $321.97 per $1,000 bond. If market interest rates remain constant over the entire 10-year period, the values given in column 1 of Table 11.6 show the market value at time $t = 1$, $t = 2$, and so forth.

So far, so good. Zero-coupon bonds seem simple and straightforward. Now let us compare them with a similar coupon (or interest-bearing) bond. We will see that when market interest rates change, the *percentage* price change on a zero-coupon bond is greater than that on a coupon bond. This makes perfect sense: With the zero-coupon bond nothing is received (or paid) until maturity, whereas with a coupon bond the

---

[5] As discussed in Chapter 7, there is a reinvestment rate assumption built into any IRR (or yield to maturity) calculation. If you purchase a 15-year, 9.4 percent coupon bond at par that pays interest annually, your expected return is the bond's yield to maturity, which is 9.4 percent. However, *you will realize the 9.4 percent only if you can reinvest each of the nine annual interest payments* (received at time $t = 1$ through $t = 9$) *at 9.4 percent.*

Table 11.6

Present Value and Interest per Year for a 12 Percent, $1,000 Par, Zero-Coupon Bond

The interest on zero-coupon bonds is determined using the present value techniques discussed in Chapter 3.

Year	Present Value (12%) at End of Year[a] (1)	Present Value (12%) at Beginning of Year (2)	Interest (1) − (2) (3)
1	$ 360.61[b]	$321.97[c]	$ 38.64
2	403.88	360.61	43.27
3	452.35	403.88	48.47
4	506.63	452.35	54.28
5	567.43	506.63	60.80
6	635.52	567.43	68.09
7	711.78	635.52	76.26
8	797.19	711.78	85.41
9	892.86	797.19	95.67
10	1,000.00	892.86	107.14
			$678.03

[a] For more precision, a financial calculator was used instead of Table B.1.
[b] For year 1, $321.97(1.12) = $360.61; for year 2, $360.61(1.12) = $403.88. The rest were computed in a similar manner.
[c] The original selling price is simply the present value of $1,000 discounted at 12 percent for 10 years. Using a financial calculator, enter FV = 1,000, n = 10, and k = i = 12 and then select PV.

current market value is a function of both the periodic coupon interest payments and the bond's par value.

Consider Figure 11.1, which shows the percentage change from the original price for the Anderson Products 12 percent zero-coupon bond and a similar 12 percent interest-bearing 10-year bond. If the market interest rate on the bonds is 12 percent, then the coupon bond will sell at its par value of $1,000 (par bond), while the zero-coupon bond will sell at $322 per bond. Assume you are an investor who has an equal dollar amount to invest in either bond. For simplicity, assume this amount is $322,000. With that you can buy 1,000($322,000/$322) zero-coupon bonds or 322 ($322,000/$1,000) interest-bearing bonds. If market interest rates increase from 12 to 16 percent, which choice exposes you to more interest rate risk? To see, let us calculate the new market price for both bonds.

For the 322 12 percent coupon bonds, each with a par value of $1,000, their value is

$$B_0 = \$322,000(0.12)(PVA_{16\%,\,10yr}) + \$322,000\,(PV_{16\%,\,10yr})$$
$$= \$38,640(4.833) + \$322,000(0.227) = \$259,841.12$$

The 4 percent increase in interest rates led to a decrease in value of $62,158.88 (i.e.,$322,000 − $259,841.12), or a decrease of about 19.30 percent.

Figure 11.1

Percentage Price Fluctuations for Zero-Coupon Versus Coupon Bonds

This figure is based on 10-year, 12 percent bonds selling at their original price. However, the general relationships hold for all similar zero-coupon and coupon (interest-bearing) bonds.

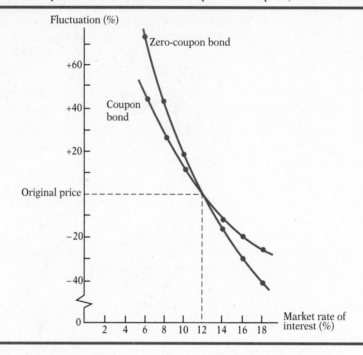

From Equation 11.1, for the 1,000 zero-coupon bonds with a total par value in 10 years of $1,000,000, we have

$$B_0(\text{zero-coupon}) = \$1,000,000(PV_{16\%,\,10yr}) = \$1,000,000(0.227) = \$227,000$$

Now the same 4 percent rise in interest rates leads to a decrease in value of $95,000 (i.e., $322,000 − $227,000), or a 29.50 percent decrease. These figures, when calculated for a number of other market interest rates and plotted (as in Figure 11.1), demonstrate the increased price volatility or interest rate risk that investors experience with zero-coupon as opposed to coupon bonds. By buying zero-coupon bonds, investors expose themselves to greater price fluctuations as market interest rates change.

So far we have considered a zero-coupon bond with 10 years to maturity. What happens to the interest rate risk (as evidenced by its price volatility) as the maturity is shortened? As Figure 11.2 shows, the shorter the maturity, the lower the interest rate risk. This is due to the reduced impact of discounting with short- versus long-maturity bonds. From the issuing firm's standpoint, the primary attraction of zeros is their reduced cost vis-à-vis similar coupon bonds. For investors, their primary advantage when compared to coupon-bearing bonds is that they lock in the return.

Figure 11.2

Relationship of a Zero-Coupon Bond's Price Fluctuation, the Current Market Rate of Interest, and Bond Maturity

This relationship for zero-coupon bonds is exactly the same as that shown in Figure 4.2 for coupon (interest-bearing) bonds.

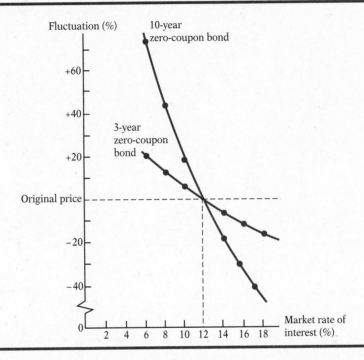

JUNK BONDS

Junk bonds, or high-yield bonds, are those rated BB/B+ and below. During the 1980s, Michael Milken, of the investment firm Drexel Burnham Lambert, helped create a massive new bond market centred around these bonds. Although there is no established junk-bond market in Canada, many Canadian firms go to the United States and issue junk bonds. Table 11.7 indicates that over the 1982–1991 period, junk bonds accounted for 15.6 percent of the total financing secured from publicly issued bonds in the United States. Because of their lower priority relative to other debt in the event of financial distress, junk bonds have elements of both debt and equity securities.

Junk bonds are issued by firms with low credit ratings that are willing to pay anywhere from 1.5 to 3 or 4 percent more than an AAA-rated firm to raise long-term debt. These are often growing firms that would rather borrow from the public than from banks or other financial institutions. In the mid-to late 1980s, junk bonds were widely used to finance mergers and in leveraged buyouts. The high levels of borrowing forced firms to be more competitive. But in late 1988, Michael Milken was forced to leave Drexel after he was indicted for securities fraud. Without Milken, confidence in the junk bond market fell. More important, some firms that had issued junk bonds,

Table 11.7

Total Publicly Issued Bonds and Junk (or High-Yield) Bonds in the United States, 1982–1991 (in $ millions)

Junk bond financing increased significantly in the 1980s before falling off. In 1991 and beyond, the amount of junk bond financing again increased.

Year	Total Straight Debt (1)	Total Junk Bonds (2)	Junk to Total (3) (2)/(1)
1982	$ 47,798	$ 2,798	5.8%
1983	46,903	7,417	15.8
1984	99,416	14,952	15.0
1985	101,098	14,670	14.5
1986	155,672	34,177	22.0
1987	126,541	30,680	24.2
1988	113,840	26,380	23.2
1989	152,145	27,661	18.2
1990	92,105	1,297	1.4
1991	156,663	9,901	6.3
Total	$1,092,181	$169,933	15.6

Source: Adapted from Exhibit 1 in Edward I. Altman, "Revisiting the High-Yield Bond Market," *Financial Management* 21 (Summer 1992): 78–92.

such as Integrated Resources, Hillsborough Holdings, and Campeau, got into severe financial difficulties. Finally, by February 1990 Drexel itself was in such severe financial difficulty that it filed for bankruptcy.

An era had come to an end. However, the junk bond market has since stabilized. Although we will not see the growth in junk bonds in the 1990s that existed in the 1980s, the junk bond market still has a role to play. Excesses occurred in the 1980s, but in many cases the firms using junk bonds were simply securing financing through a public cash offering instead of through private placements to institutional investors who traditionally supplied their long-term debt financing. Junk bonds will continue to fill an important role as a source of financing in the future, but a more traditional one.

VARIABLE RATES

The majority of loans made by chartered banks are now variable-rate loans. That is, the interest rate may vary over the 5- to 10-year life of the loan. Often the rate is expressed as some fixed percentage over the prime interest rate.[6] For example, the loan agreement may specify that the rate will be "2 percentage points over prime." This means that if the current **prime rate** charged by the bank to its best customers is 8 percent,

---

[6] As noted in Chapter 24, prime is an artificial (or administered) rate.

the interest rate on the loan will be 10 percent. Because the interest rate is typically changed every time the prime rate changes, the bank in effect varies the total payment required each period to pay the principal and interest on the loan. In addition to bank loans that carry adjustable rates, there are also floating-rate (or adjustable-rate) notes that are issued directly by firms via cash offerings to the public or through private placements.

OTHER INNOVATIONS

During the last 15 years the types of securities available for corporate use have expanded dramatically. Many of the new securities combine elements of debt, equity, variable interest rates, and the like into new securities. Although we have examined a few of the innovations, such as zero-coupon bonds and variable-rate loans and securities, many other innovations have been forthcoming. One of these is the increased use of asset-backed securities; this process is often referred to as *securitization*. Mortgage-backed securities, including collateralized mortgage obligations (CMOs), have been around for some time. But firms have also turned to other assets as collateral for financing. Thus, recently Citibank offered a $2.2 billion floating-rate note backed by credit card receivables. Likewise, GPA Group, an aircraft leasing firm based in Ireland, sold a $521 million Eurobond that was securitized by aircraft lease receivables. Developments in the next 15 years may not be as rapid as in the past 15, but innovative investment dealers will continue to come up with new ways to help firms raise capital.

Concept Review Questions

- Describe some different forms of debt financing firms have recently adopted.
- What are some advantages to a firm of issuing zero-coupon bonds?
- Why have junk bonds become a viable means of financing for some firms?

MANAGING LONG-TERM DEBT

Until recently, liability management consisted simply of deciding what securities to issue. Debt was left to mature, then was retired—perhaps with the proceeds from a new bond issue. High and volatile interest rates, the growth of international financial markets, and innovative investment dealers have changed all that, and the management of long-term liabilities has taken a dramatic turn. Let us consider some of the techniques now available.

REFUNDING

A few years ago, when interest rates were high, many firms issued long-term debt. What happened when market rates fell? Astute managers saw the fall in rates as an opportunity to replace (or refund) the older, high-interest-rate bond with a similar bond offering a lower coupon rate. In a bond **refunding**, the firm calls all the old bonds at a fixed price and simultaneously issues new, lower-coupon-rate bonds. The bond owners have no choice; when a bond is called it must be surrendered, for the firm stops paying interest on it. This process is discussed in Appendix 11A. The decision to refund depends on the net amount required to call the existing bond and the present value of the future incremental cash flows. It is thus just another use of the net present value (NPV) framework.

However, two complications can arise. First, how does the firm decide on the best time to refund? The answer depends primarily on the relationship of current market interest rates to forecasted interest rates next month, in three months, and so forth. The firm may benefit from a refunding today, but it must also consider whether it would be better off waiting, in the hope that interest rates will fall further.

To protect investors, many bonds now carry a provision that prohibits them from being called for refunding for a period of 5 to 10 years. This brings us to the second complexity: What can the firm do if it wants to refund a bond issue but is prohibited by some provision in the bond indenture?

ALTERNATIVES TO REFUNDING

Three alternatives are available when a firm is prohibited from refunding a bond issue.

1. One alternative is a public **tender offer**. This is an offer to the current bondholders to sell their bonds back to the firm at a predetermined price. This offer may not result in the retirement of the entire issue, but it can substantially reduce the size of the issue in question.
2. An alternative to the public tender offer is a **private market purchase**. Here the firm approaches one or several institutional investors who own a large amount of the firm's bonds and offers to buy them back. Another alternative sometimes employed is to swap debt for some of the firm's common stock.
3. The nonrefundable provision that has appeared in recent years appears to limit an issuing firm's flexibility to retire debt when interest rates fall. However, recently a strategy has been devised that enables firms to circumvent the nonrefundable provision. Firms have always been able to call bonds through a *cash call* with money raised by selling additional equity, selling assets, or from internally generated funds. But if interest rates have fallen and the issuing firm wants to retire debt without using a cash call, it might employ a "simultaneous tender and call" approach. The essence of this approach is to offer to buy back the bonds (through a tender offer) at a slight premium to the call price; at the same time the firm (or its investment dealer) threatens to call the bonds using a cash call.

Concept Review Question
- Describe three alternatives to refunding a bond issue.

INTEREST RATE SWAPS

Interest rate swaps are also used increasingly, especially with the widespread use of floating-rate (or variable-rate) financing. The idea is to separate the interest payments from the principal payments for long-term financing. The market for swaps is worldwide, especially because firms more and more are raising funds wherever they are cheapest, and then worrying about whether the financing is in the specific form or currency desired. In its simplest form, a swap is simply an agreement between two firms to exchange cash flows. In this section we consider interest rate swaps; in Chapter 17 currency swaps will be examined.

Our discussion will focus on "plain vanilla" interest rate swaps. In a plain vanilla swap, the currency is the same for both parties, and one party is looking to exchange fixed-rate debt financing for floating-rate financing, while the other party is looking to exchange floating-rate financing for fixed-rate financing.[7] Although there may be many reasons why firms want to switch from floating to fixed or vice versa, typically they are attempting to match their financing to their assets or to protect themselves from some type of interest rate risk. In a plain vanilla swap the principal amount, or "notational principal," is the same for both parties, and the floating rate employed is typically the six-month **London Interbank Offer Rate, LIBOR**.[8] (LIBOR is the rate that banks in different countries trade at.) Therefore, only the interest cash flows are of importance. Because the interest cash flows are actually netted against one another, only *the difference in the two interest streams* is sent from one party to the other party in a plain vanilla swap.

Suppose firm A needs $5,000,000 for five years and can borrow at a fixed rate of 10 percent, or it can borrow at a floating rate of LIBOR plus 1.5 percent. Firm B also needs $5,000,000 for five years, and it can borrow at a fixed rate of 12.50 percent or a floating rate of LIBOR plus 3.00 percent. The key to understanding why plain vanilla interest rate swaps exist is to focus on the comparative advantage that each of the firms has in terms of raising funds. This can be summarized as follows:

Party	Fixed Rate	Floating Rate
Firm B	12.50%	LIBOR + 3.00%
Firm A	10.00	LIBOR + 1.50
	Difference = 2.50%	1.50%

Note that firm A has an absolute advantage relative to firm B because it can borrow

---

[7] The parties involved in any swap are often referred to as the "counterparties."

[8] In the absence of barriers to capital flows, there would be no advantage to either party participating in plain vanilla interest rate swaps. A number of possible explanations have been advanced for why plain vanilla swaps are beneficial, including desires to change duration, underpriced credit risk, risk shifting, and information asymmetries. A swap contract can also be thought of and analyzed as a series of forward contracts. See Kapner and Marshall (1990) or Smith, Smithson, and Wilford (1990).

at a cheaper rate whether it employs fixed-rate or floating-rate financing. But, on a comparative basis, firm A can borrow more cheaply at the fixed rate, and firm B has an advantage over firm A in floating-rate borrowing. This can be seen by noting the 1.50 percent difference over LIBOR for floating-rate financing for firm B versus the 2.50 percent difference when fixed rate borrowing is employed. As long as the differences between the fixed- and floating-rate financing costs are not equal (i.e., both 2.50 percent or both 1.50 percent, in this example), the incentive exists for an interest rate swap. The spread differential of 2.50% − 1.50% = 1.00%, or 100 basis points, can be shared between the two parties and allows both of them to reduce their interest rate costs. Let us see how it is done.

First, firm A borrows from a lender or the financial markets at a fixed rate of 10 percent because that is where its comparative financing advantage exists. Likewise, firm B borrows at a floating rate of LIBOR + 3.00 percent because that is where its comparative financing advantage exists. Now the two firms will enter into a swap. For simplicity, we assume they will share the spread differential of 1.00 percent equally. To do so, firm B will agree to pay firm A a fixed rate of 12.50% − 0.50% = 12.00 percent on the $5,000,000 in financing. Firm A turns around and pays LIBOR + 3.00% to firm B to cover the floating-rate financing costs incurred by firm B. This sequence of cash flows is shown in Figure 11.3.

Firm A has achieved a 50-basis-point reduction in its borrowing rate as follows: It pays a fixed rate of 10 percent for its financing and also receives 12 percent fixed from firm B. This provides firm A with a 2 percent interest rate gain. Then firm A turns around and pays firm B LIBOR + 3.00 percent. Subtracting the 2.00 percent net gain, firm A's final cost is LIBOR + 1.00%, which is 50 basis points less than the cheapest floating-rate financing it could have obtained directly (which was LIBOR + 1.50%). Firm B also gains. It pays LIBOR + 3.00% for its financing, but it has received this same amount from firm A. Then firm B pays a fixed rate of 12.00 percent to firm A, which is 50 basis points less than the cheapest fixed-rate

Figure 11.3

Interest Cash Flows for a Plain Vanilla Interest Rate Swap

Only the net period-by-period difference between LIBOR + 3.00% and 12% will be sent from one firm to the other.

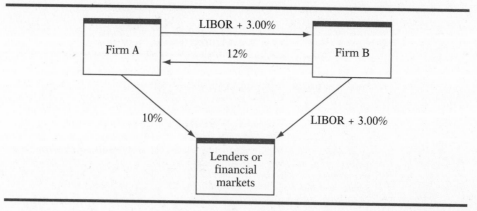

Table 11.8

Borrowing Costs With an Interest Rate Swap

In this plain vanilla swap the interest rate savings are shared equally between the two parties, and no transactions costs are considered. In practice, the financial institution arranging the swap typically claims some of the interest rate savings as its commission.

Firm	Transaction	Interest Rate
A	Pays fixed rate to third party	+ 10.00%
	Pays floating rate to firm B	+ LIBOR + 3.00
	Receives fixed rate from firm B	−12.00
	Net cost to firm A	LIBOR + 1.00%

Net savings = LIBOR + 1.50% − (LIBOR + 1.00%) = 0.50% = 50 basis points

Firm	Transaction	Interest Rate
B	Pays floating rate to third party	+ LIBOR + 3.00%
	Pays fixed rate to firm A	+ 12.00
	Receives floating rate from firm A	− (LIBOR + 3.00)
	Net cost to firm B	12.00%

Net savings = 12.50% − 12.00% = 0.50% = 50 basis points

financing of 12.50 percent it could have received directly. The final costs of borrowing for the two firms are summarized in Table 11.8. In this example, both firms were better off by exactly half of the spread differential of 1.00 percent. However, the gains do not have to be split equally between the parties.

Firms have a number of objectives when they enter into an interest rate swap. The primary ones are to reduce their financing costs and to hedge interest rate risks. Documentation of swaps is guided by standards which have been developed by the New York–based International Swap Dealer's Association and/or the British Bankers' Association. Swaps now come in many forms in addition to the plain vanilla interest rate swap. They include zero-coupon for floating-rate swaps, floating for floating (or basis) swaps, callable swaps, puttable swaps, extendible swaps, forward (or deferred) swaps, and delayed rate-setting swaps, among others.

To understand more about swaps, let us look at one that Hewlett-Packard entered into in 1992. The firm wanted to raise $100 million worth of Canadian dollars for three years and pay a floating interest rate. To accomplish this it entered into a swap with Société Générale Securities Corp. (SocGen), the New York investment banking arm of the big French bank. The swap, like many recent ones, is much different from the plain vanilla swap discussed previously. Hewlett-Packard ended up paying about a tenth of a point, or $100,000, less than it would have paid on a regular floating-rate issue. SocGen ended up marketing an equity-linked zero-coupon note, giving investors a return that depends on the future performance of Hewlett-Packard stock. At maturity, the investors who purchased the equity-linked zero-coupon note will receive between $90 and $143.60 for each $100 invested. Hewlett-Packard got the floating-rate financing desired in Canadian dollars. SocGen secured the agreement and also the opportunity to earn underwriting fees and generate commissions from trading in

Hewlett-Packard's stock and options. The interest rate swap provided benefits for all concerned.

Concept Review Questions

- Describe a plain vanilla interest rate swap.
- Why do firms use interest rate swaps?

PENSION PLAN LIABILITY

Most Canadian businesses have pension plans that commit them to retirement benefits for employees. The employees of these firms have claims against the assets of their respective pension funds that are similar to the claims bondholders have against the assets of the firms. As long as a firm's pension fund has an excess of assets over obligations the size of the plan's obligations is not a negative feature. However, if a firm's pension plan obligations exceed the plan's assets and the firm ceases operations for any reason, the firm is responsible for paying the difference. The size of a firm's pension plan obligation (liability) will therefore be of concern to any current or potential creditor of the firm. Furthermore, as financial managers we require a basic understanding of how pension plans operate since the accumulation of plan assets requires payments of cash that could be used alternatively.

TYPES OF PENSION PLANS

There are many different types of pension plans; however, they are all variants of either a defined benefit or defined contribution plan. A **defined benefit pension plan** specifies either the level of benefits to be received by employees during retirement or the method of calculating those benefits. For example, future pension payments may be specified as 65 percent of the average salary over the last five years of service. As a result, plan obligations can only be estimated, since they are based on the level of future salaries. However, to meet these obligations the firm must make contributions to the fund; the employees do not make any contribution. Any portion of the contributions not needed to pay current benefits is paid to a trust or insurance company and invested in a diversified portfolio. The return on the portfolio is used as a method of financing the firm's contribution. If the return on the portfolio is high, the firm will have to contribute less to the fund, and vice versa.

A **defined contribution pension plan** is one in which the firm promises to contribute a specific fixed amount to the pension fund on behalf of each individual employee. For example, the firm may agree to contribute an amount equal to 3 percent of each employee's salary to the fund. Because this is done on an individual basis, an employee may also contribute to his or her account as well. As with a defined benefit plan, total contributions are invested through a trust or insurance company. However, the income provided to an employee during retirement is based on the sum of accumulated contributions made on behalf of that specific employee and the investment return earned on his or her separate account.

In addition to those features of pension plans that have already been noted, a few other aspects are of interest. First, all contributions to a pension plan are tax-deductible expenses for the firms or individuals making them. Only when the employee retires and starts to receive pension income are taxes paid. Second, if an employee leaves a firm before retirement, that employee will qualify to receive retirement benefits from the firm provided that he or she remained with the firm for a prescribed number of years, say five. This is called **vesting** and may result in an individual receiving pension income from more than one firm. Third, it is becoming more and more common for retirement benefits to be portable. This means that an employee who has an interest in the pension plan of his or her current employer can transfer that interest to a new employer's plan or to a registered retirement savings plan (RRSP) when the employee changes jobs. Fourth, there is increasing pressure from unions and employee associations to move away from the fixed pension income to one that is indexed to inflation as reflected by the Consumer Price Index.

We have seen that the pension plan obligation of a firm using a defined contribution plan is relatively easy to calculate, since it is a percentage of current employee compensation, and that the obligation of a firm using a defined benefit plan can only be estimated, because it is based on future compensation. Accordingly, current and potential lenders have a more difficult time assessing the financial position of a firm that has a defined benefit plan. Because of this and the fact that they are the most commonly used pension plans, the following discussion is confined to defined benefit plans.

FUNDING

The amount of a firm's pension fund obligation is determined by an actuary. In essence the actuary must determine the amount of funds necessary for the firm to be able to honour its pension obligations. Abstracting from the many complications involved, the actuary must find the present value of the obligations (liabilities) to two distinct groups of employees: (1) those currently retired and (2) those currently employed, for both past and future services. To do so the actuary must make assumptions about average life expectancy, the rate of future salary increases, and the discount rate. A small change in any of these assumptions can have a very large impact on the expected plan obligation.

Once a value has been placed on the firm's obligations, the actuary would value the pension fund's assets. As with the valuation of the obligations, this value is the sum of two parts. The first is the present value of past contributions and is represented by the market value of the portfolio that these contributions have been invested in. The second is the present value of the expected future stream of contributions for future services. To make this calculation, the actuary must also make an assumption about what rate of return the portfolio is expected to have in the future.

REPORTING REQUIREMENTS

The results of this valuation process are reported in a note to the balance sheet. If the present value of expected retirement obligations is equal to the present value of the pension fund assets, the plan is said to be **fully funded**. However, this would usually not be the case. A firm may be in the situation in which pension fund assets are greater than its obligations. This was the case with Abitibi-Price, and the footnotes to its balance sheet revealed the following:

	1994	1993	1992
Pension fund assets	$763,000,000	$825,000,000	$726,400,000
Pension obligations	$697,000,000	$677,000,000	$619,000,000

In this case the pension fund was **overfunded** in each year because the value of plan assets exceeded its obligations for each year. On the other hand, a firm may be in the situation in which its pension plan obligations exceed plan assets. In such a case the plan is said to be **underfunded**. This was the situation with Ivaco in 1994, when its pension plan obligations were $283.2 million and plan assets were only $226.3 million. The difference of $56.9 million (i.e., $283.2 million − $226.3 million) is an **unfunded liability**. A firm is required to have its pension fund fully funded within 15 years from the date that the unfunded liability occurs. Consequently, if this were the first unfunded liability that Ivaco had incurred, it would have to have its pension fund fully funded by the end of the year 2009.

Firms must also show on an annual basis an estimate of the pension fund expense that would ensure full funding of the plan. For example, Ivaco showed an estimated pension fund expense of $18.1 million for 1994. This amount was less than the firm's actual contributions to its pension plan, so the difference between the two figures is shown as an accrued pension liability in the long-term debt section of its balance sheet. This item shows the cumulative liability that the firm has to its pension plan and for which it would be responsible if it ceased operations.

Concept Review Questions

- What are the two types of pension plans and how do they work?
- When is a pension plan fully funded, overfunded, or underfunded?

PREFERRED STOCK

Preferred stock is an intermediate form of financing between debt and equity. Like debt, preferred stock generally has a par value—typically $25, $50, or $100—and also pays a fixed return. But preferred stock legally is a form of ownership; cash dividends paid on preferred stock are similar to cash dividends on common stock in that they are not a tax-deductible expense for the issuing firm.

When preferred stock is issued, the selling price is set close to par. When a $100 par value, 13 percent preferred stock is issued, it will sell close to par and pay cash dividends of $13 [i.e., ($100)(0.13)] per year. The market price on preferred stock fluctuates; if the market yield (where yield = dividend per share/market price per share) on preferred stocks goes up, the market price of outstanding preferred stocks decreases. Because preferred stock is viewed by investors as being similar to bonds, the market yield on preferred stocks tends to move in much the same manner as the yield to maturity on bonds. As market interest rates on bonds rise, the market yield on preferred stocks also rises due to the declining price of the latter.

If the firm does not have sufficient cash flow to pay dividends on its preferred stock, it can omit the payment. Unpaid dividends on preferred stock are called **arrearages**. Most preferred dividends are *cumulative:* all past or present dividends must be paid before any further cash dividends are paid on the firm's common stock. Managers view dividends on preferred stock as they do any other fixed obligation, and they fully intend to pay the preferred dividends on time. However, preferred stock does provide a safety valve if the firm needs it.

Like common stock, preferred stock does not have any fixed maturity date. However, many recent issues of preferred stock make a provision for periodic repayment via a sinking fund. Virtually all preferred stock is callable at the option of the issuing firm. If a firm goes out of business, the claim of preferred shareholders is junior to that of any debt, but senior to that of common shareholders.

The use of preferred stock, like the issuance of long-term debt, may result in additional restrictions being placed on the firm in the form of limitations on the payment of cash dividends for common stock, maintenance of a minimum level of common equity, or a minimum requirement for the ratio of net working capital to the total debt and preferred stock of the firm. The primary function of these restrictions is to ensure that the firm can make cash dividend payments to its preferred shareholders. Although many preferred stocks have only limited voting rights, the tendency in recent years has been towards fuller voting rights.

From the firm's standpoint, preferred stock has certain advantages:

1. Because the returns to preferred shareholders are limited, financial leverage is possible, because any extraordinary cash flows accrue only to common shareholders.
2. Nonpayment of cash dividends on preferreds does not throw the firm into default.
3. Control of the firm generally remains with the common shareholders.

The primary disadvantage of preferred stock from the firm's standpoint is that cash dividends paid to service the preferred stock are not an allowable deduction for tax purposes. Unlike debt, which preferred stock approximates in many respects, dividends on preferred stock must be paid out of after-tax earnings. This treatment makes the cost of most preferred stock much higher than the cost of debt. Two industries that use preferred stock extensively are banking and public utilities. Banks have issued preferred stock in recent years in order to increase their capital base. They found that issuing preferred stock was preferable to issuing additional common stock in order to meet requirements for additional capital. Public utility firms, on the other hand, have used preferred stock for a long time. Due to their regulated nature, they can often pass the higher costs of preferred stock on to consumers through their customer rate base. Firms that have more than one issue of preferred stock outstanding include British Columbia Telephone, Canadian Utilities, National Bank, Québec-Téléphone, Royal Bank, and TransAlta Utilities.

In recent years, a new twist in preferred stock financing was introduced—**adjustable-rate preferred stock**. With this type of issue, there is no fixed cash dividend; instead, the dividend rate is tied to the prime rate and adjusted quarterly. The appeal of adjustable-rate preferred stock is twofold. First, it allows the issuing firm to issue preferred stock at a lower dividend rate than otherwise. Second, by doing so, the firm adds to its equity base (thereby improving the ratio of total debt to total assets) without issuing additional shares of common stock.

Concept Review Questions

- Describe the similarities of preferred stock to both debt and common equity.
- What are the advantages and disadvantages of preferred stock?

LONG-TERM FINANCING AND FINANCIAL DISTRESS

Differences and conflicts always exist between shareholders and bondholders. Shareholders want to maximize their return; as we know, higher returns and higher risks go hand-in-hand, so shareholders tend to favour higher risk. Bondholders, however, thought they purchased a much safer security; they become upset when the firm engages in activities that cause this safety to be eroded.

If the firm prospers, the common shareholders exercise their option to pay off the bondholders, and then claim everything else for themselves. Alternatively, if the firm fails, the shareholders (because of limited liability) walk away from the firm and turn it over to the bondholders. Although the shareholders may lose their initial investment, at least they are not liable for any further losses. We can summarize the effects as follows:

If the Firm Prospers	If the Firm Fails
Bondholders are paid off	Shareholders walk away
Shareholders claim the rest	Bondholders may receive something

Of course, there are many intermediate positions. We need to examine them briefly.

A firm facing financial distress has a number of alternatives open to it, depending on the severity of the situation. The fundamental decision is whether to modify the firm or to liquidate it. Within each alternative are out-of-court and in-court procedures. These are as follows:

OUT-OF-COURT ALTERNATIVES

1. An **extension** involves nothing more than the creditor's agreeing to delay the payments due from the firm; that is, it extends the payment schedule. The creditor and the firm both hope that with a little more time, the firm can right itself and proceed on its way.
2. A **composition** is more serious. It gives creditors only a pro rata settlement on their claims. Generally, creditors will agree to composition only when it appears

that they will receive more from accepting the settlement than from forcing the firm into bankruptcy, with its legal expenses and complications.
3. A "voluntary" liquidation is called an **assignment**. It is often more efficient, can be effected faster, and provides creditors with a higher settlement than an in-court liquidation. One problem, however, is getting all creditors to agree to the assignment.

IN-COURT ALTERNATIVES

The in-court alternatives are covered by the Bankruptcy and Insolvency Act of 1992. The basic alternatives for firms are as follows:

1. In a **liquidation**, the assets of the firm are sold under the direction of the courts, with the proceeds going to pay claimants in a general order of priority spelled out in the Act.
2. In a **reorganization**, the firm is actually put back on its feet, typically after extensive modifications both in terms of its businesses and in terms of the claims of creditors. Former shareholders usually end up with very little ownership in the reorganized firm.

    Although somewhat different in detail, the liquidation versus reorganization decision is no different conceptually than keeping or divesting assets, or divisions, of a firm, as discussed in Chapters 8 and 16. The issue is whether the parties (primarily the creditors) are better off (i.e., have a higher NPV) under liquidation or reorganization.

Concept Review Question

■ What are the out-of-court and in-court alternatives available to a firm experiencing financial distress?

KEY POINTS

- Bonds and preferred stock take many different forms. These alternatives assist firms in raising long-term funds as cheaply as possible while providing features that appeal to investors.
- AAA-rated bonds have the lowest cost, or yield to maturity, of any long-term corporate bonds; they also have the lowest failure rate. As the bond rating decreases, the cost to the firm goes, up as does the probability of failure.
- When firms issue straight debt or take out bank loans, the value of the firm is unaffected. However, when bank loan agreements are revised, common shareholders benefit if the revision is a favourable revision, and they lose if it is an unfavourable one.
- As interest rates fluctuate, zero-coupon bonds change in market price relatively more than similar coupon (or interest-bearing) bonds.
- Firms have increasingly begun to practise active liability management. Tactics include bond refundings (or buybacks) and interest rate swaps.
- In a plain vanilla interest rate swap, the parties retain their principal and simply swap interest payments.

- A firm's pension plan obligation (liability) is another form of debt and is, therefore, of concern to current and potential creditors.
- Preferred stock, while legally a form of equity, has many features that make it similar to debt.

QUESTIONS

11.1 You are a corporate treasurer. How would the following conditions influence your willingness to include a sinking fund provision and a call feature in a new bond issue?
a. Market interest rates are expected to fall.
b. Your firm anticipates heavy cash outflows in relation to its cash needs in the next 5 to 10 years.
c. Market interest rates are expected to fluctuate substantially, both above and below the coupon rate on the new issue.

11.2 "In a loan amortization schedule, the last payment will never be equal to the prior payments." Is this statement true or false? Why?

11.3 The percentage price fluctuation of zero-coupon bonds is greater than the percentage price fluctuation of similar coupon bonds as market interest rates fluctuate; it is also greater the longer the maturity of the zero. Explain.

11.4 In recent years, when interest rates were very high, a number of large firms issued medium-term (1- to 10-year) notes. These notes paid interest periodically, and the principal was repaid when the notes matured. Why do you think firms issued these notes instead of obtaining similar-maturity term loans?

11.5 Who are the parties in a plain vanilla interest rate swap? What condition has to exist for them to enter into a transaction? Why might each want to participate in the swap?

11.6 Who bears the risk and receives the rewards of the pension portfolio associated with a defined benefit and a defined contribution pension plan?

11.7 Preferred stock often is called a hybrid security. Why? It can be said that preferred stock combines the worst features of both common stock and bonds. Explain why this might be so.

11.8 If the corporate income tax were abolished, would we expect to see more, or less, debt? More, or less, preferred stock? Why?

CONCEPT REVIEW PROBLEMS

See Appendix A for solutions.

CR11.1 Desktop Industries has obtained a five-year, $100,000 term loan with an interest rate of 15 percent. Interest is paid annually. Prepare a loan amortization schedule for Desktop.

CR11.2 Assume Desktop Industries' term loan in CR11.1 required monthly payments. By developing an amortization schedule for the first five months of the loan, show how monthly payments will affect interest and principal repayments.

CR11.3 AT&E is considering issuing either a five-year zero-coupon bond or a five-year coupon-bearing bond with annual payments. Both bonds will pay a 10 percent interest rate. If AT&E needs $50 million from external debt financing, how many $1,000 maturity value zero-coupon bonds will have to be issued? How many $1,000 maturity value coupon-bearing bonds will have to be issued?

CR11.4 Katharine recently purchased a $1,000 maturity value, 10 percent, 20-year, zero-coupon bond and a 10 percent, 20-year, coupon-bearing bond at par. If, immediately after she purchased these bonds, overall bond rates increased by 2 percent, what was her percentage loss on each bond? (*Note*: Assume annual compounding.)

CR11.5   Bequet Electric can finance a $25 million expansion project for two years at a fixed rate of 12 percent or at a floating rate of LIBOR plus 2 percent. Reed Production also needs to borrow $25 million for two years and can finance the expansion at a fixed rate of 14 percent or a variable rate at LIBOR plus 5 percent. Establish an interest rate swap between the two, with each firm sharing equally in the benefits.

Problems

11.1   The Long Ltd. has no short-term debt, but it does have a $10 million, 10 percent coupon rate mortgage bond outstanding with a limited open-end provision. Additional 10 percent mortgage debt can be issued as long as all the following restrictions are met:
1.   Ratio of debt to equity (i.e., total debt/total shareholders' equity) remains below 0.4.
2.   Interest coverage (i.e., EBIT/interest) is at least 5.
3.   The depreciated value of the mortgaged assets is at least 2.5 times the mortgage debt.
The firm has a depreciated value of mortgage assets of $60 million, equity of $80 million, and earnings before interest and taxes (EBIT) of $12 million. Assuming that half the new bond issue would be used to add assets to the base of mortgaged assets, how much additional debt can Long issue?

11.2   Drummond Paper has a $50 million bond issue outstanding, with a 12 percent coupon rate. The current market interest rate on comparable-quality bonds is 11 percent. The bonds have 25 years to maturity but can be called with a premium equal to one year's interest.
a.   What is the market price of the bonds?
b.   How much is the call price on the bonds?
c.   Should Drummond Paper call these bonds or purchase them? In explaining your answer, remember to consider any other factors that might influence purchasing the bonds.

11.3   Huron Cement has just issued $30 million of 10-year, 10 percent coupon rate bonds. A sinking fund provision requires equal payments to be made at the end of each of the next 10 years, in order to retire one-tenth of the bonds each year. Huron's tax rate is 35 percent.
a.   How large must the annual sinking fund payments be to retire the bond in 10 equal instalments over the life of the bond? (*Note:* The bonds will be retired at their par value.)
b.   What is Huron's *annual* after-tax cash outlay to meet the interest and sinking fund obligations each year? [*Remember:* (1) Interest payments are tax-deductible, but sinking fund payments are not; and (2) no interest is paid on bonds once they are retired.]

11.4   Welker Products is taking out an eight-year, $44,000 term loan, with an interest rate of 16 percent per year. Interest is paid annually, and the firm's marginal corporate tax rate is 40 percent.
a.   What is the size of the yearly payment? (*Note:* Round all figures to the nearest dollar.)
b.   Determine the loan amortization schedule.
c.   Determine the net cash outflow per year to service both principal and interest after taking into account the tax deductibility of interest for tax purposes. (*Note:* Round to the nearest dollar.)

11.5   A four-year, 10 percent loan for $30,000 exists. Determine the amortization schedule if (a) annual discounting or (b) semiannual discounting is used. (*Note:* Round all figures to the nearest dollar.)

11.6   Brozik Products needs to raise approximately $10 million by issuing 20-year bonds. The following alternatives are available:

1. A public offering of $10 million of 8 percent coupon rate bonds at a price to net the firm $9,850,000.
2. A private placement of $10 million in bonds at par, with an 8.5 percent coupon rate and no flotation costs.
3. A public offering of a deep discount bond that will pay $400,000 in interest each year and have a maturity value of $25 million. The firm will net $9,800,000 from the bonds.
4. A private placement of zero-coupon bonds that will net the firm $9,900,000 and have a maturity value of $45 million.

   Interest payments are annual and the principal will not be repaid until maturity.

Which bond has the cheapest percentage cost to maturity? (*Note:* To solve this, calculate the IRR for each of the four options.)

11.7   Lloyd Industries has two alternative $10 million bonds it can issue. If the bond carries a fixed coupon rate, the interest rate will be 11 percent. If a variable rate bond is used, the rate will be pegged 1.5 percent above prevailing rates on one-year Canadian treasury bills and adjusted annually. In both cases interest is paid annually. A sinking fund of $1 million per year will begin at the end of year 1 for either bond. The firm's marginal tax rate is 40 percent.

a. Determine the year-by-year after-tax cash flows Lloyd will incur for each bond if one-year Canadian treasury bill rates turn out to be as follows:

Year	Prevailing One-Year Canadian Treasury Bill Rate
1	10.0%
2	9.5
3	9.0
4	10.0
5	10.5
6	12.0
7	13.0
8	12.0
9	11.5
10	11.0

b. Without discounting the cash flows, does it appear that one bond would be preferable if Lloyd knew what interest rates would be? Why?

11.8   Stephens needs $100 million in new debt financing. If the firm uses a coupon-bearing bond, the interest rate is 9.5 percent and the bond will be issued at par. If it uses a zero-coupon bond, the interest rate is 9.2 percent. Assume that interest is paid annually and either bond will have a maturity of 10 years.

a. If the coupon-bearing bond is employed, (1) what is the per year interest, and (2) what is the cash outflow (ignoring any taxes) in the tenth year?
b. If the zero-coupon bond is employed,
   1. What is the par value of the zero-coupon bond in order to raise the $100 million needed?
   2. What is the imputed interest in year 1? In year 2?
   3. What is the cash outflow in the tenth year?
c. What can we say about the cash flow demands that the two securities will place on Stephens?

11.9   Adkisson Railroad needs to raise $9.5 million for capital improvements. One possibility is a new preferred stock issue. The 8 percent dividend, $100 par value stock would be sold to investors to yield 9 percent. Flotation costs for an issue of this size amount to 5 percent of the gross proceeds. These costs will be deducted from the gross proceeds in determining the net proceeds of $9.5 million. Assume that the preferred stock will be outstanding for a long time (so it can be valued as a perpetuity).

a. At what price will the preferred be offered to investors? (Carry to three decimal places.)

b. How many shares must be issued to net $9.5 million?

11.10   Misra needs to raise $600,000. It has the following alternatives: (1) sell common stock at $50 per share; (2) sell 8 percent preferred stock at par ($100 par); or (3) sell 9 percent debentures at par ($1,000 par). Assume that there are no flotation costs. The firm expects EBIT to *increase* by 20 percent after the additional funds are secured and investments made. Partial balance and income statements are as follows:

Balance Sheet		Income Statement	
Current liabilities	$ 100,000	EBIT	$200,000
Common stock			
(100,000 outstanding)	300,000	Interest	20,000
Retained earnings	600,000	EBT	180,000
Total liabilities and		Taxes	63,000
shareholders' equity	$1,000,000	EAT	$117,000

a. What is the current EPS *before* the new financing is undertaken?

b. What is the estimated EPS under each of the financing plans, assuming that EBIT has increased?

11.11   Cooley Industries is a fast-growing conglomerate operating in the Atlantic provinces. Although it has used only short-term debt previously, Cooley is in the market for long-term financing. Based on its investment dealer's recommendation, two plans are being considered, as follows:

Plan I	Plan II
$20 million of straight debt issued at par (ignore flotation costs)	$20 million preferred stock issued at par (ignore flotation costs)
Par is $1,000 per bond	Par is $80 per share
12% coupon rate	11.5% dividend rate
Expected common stock P/E = 12 times	Expected common stock P/E = 13 times

EBIT is estimated to be $14 million; short-term interest (under either plan) is $1 million; the tax rate is 30 percent; and there are 3 million shares of common stock outstanding.

a. For plans I and II, determine the expected EPS.

b. If Cooley wants to maximize its market price per share, P_0, which plan should it choose?

11.12   **Mini Case**   Lennoxville Sports is in need of $25,000,000 of new long-term financing. Because it is not experienced in seeking new financing, it has employed you to provide it with advice.

a. If Lennoxville seeks long-term debt financing in the form of bonds or bank loans, what alternatives are available? What are the features of each?

b. If a bond issue is decided upon, what type of features might be included in the bond indenture? What is the impact of these provisions?

c. If the term structure of interest rates is upward-sloping, is a long-term bond issue necessarily best? What if the term structure is downward-sloping?

d. Two different bond issues are being considered: a 25-year coupon bond that will pay interest semiannually and carry a coupon interest rate of 12 percent, or a 25-year zero-coupon bond that has a yield to maturity of 11 percent (compounded semiannually).
   1. From the firm's standpoint, what are the advantages and disadvantages of a zero-coupon bond versus a coupon bond? What are the tax consequences?
   2. Ignoring flotation costs, what is the size of the zero-coupon bond issue?
   3. Assume that after either bond is issued, interest rates jump 2 percent. What is the new price of the two bonds? Which has the bigger percentage change in its value? Why?
   4. Independent of (3), assume it is now 10 years later. What are the cash flow consequences of the two different bonds on the firm? (*Note*: Assume the firm is profitable, and its marginal tax rate is 35 percent.) Compute the year-10 net cash flows associated with the two bonds.

e. Instead of issuing debt, Lennoxville could issue preferred stock. The preferred stock would carry a dividend of 11 percent.
   1. How is preferred stock similar to debt? To equity?
   2. What are the per year cash flows if everything is the same as in (d4) above?

REFERENCES

BLUME, MARSHALL E., DONALD B. KEIM, and SANDEEP A. PATEL. "Returns and Volatility of Low-Grade Bonds 1977–1989." *Journal of Finance* 46 (March 1991): 49–74.

FAMA, EUGENE. "What's Different about Banks?" *Journal of Monetary Economics* 15 (January 1985): 29–39.

FINNERTY, JOHN D. "An Overview of Corporate Securities Innovation." *Journal of Applied Corporate Finance* 4 (Winter 1992): 23–39.

GRANT, JOHN, MARY WEBB, and PETER HENDRICK. "Financing Corporate Canada in the 1990's." *Canadian Investment Review* 3 (Spring 1990): 9–16.

HAND, JOHN R. M., ROBERT W. HOLTHAUSEN, and RICHARD W. LEFTWICH. "The Effect of Bond Rating Agency Announcements on Bond and Stock Prices." *Journal of Finance* 47 (June 1992): 733–752.

KALOTAY, ANDREW, and BRUCE TUCKMAN. "Sinking Fund Prepurchases and the Designation Option." *Financial Management* 21 (Winter 1992): 110–118.

KAPNER, KENNETH R., and JOHN F. MARSHALL. *The Swaps Handbook: Swaps and Related Risk Management Instruments.* New York: New York Institute of Finance, 1990.

MITCHELL, KARLYN. "The Call, Sinking Fund, and Term-To-Maturity Features of Corporate Bonds: An Empirical Investigation." *Journal of Financial and Quantitative Analysis* 26 (June 1991): 201–222.

SMITH, CLIFFORD W., JR., CHARLES W. SMITHSON, and D. SYKES WILFORD. *Managing Financial Risk.* New York: Harper & Row, 1990.

WEISS, LAWRENCE A. "The Bankruptcy Code and Violations of Absolute Priority." *Journal of Applied Corporate Finance* 4 (Summer 1991): 71–78.

APPENDIX

11A
Refunding a Bond or Preferred Stock Issue

Refunding is the issuance of new securities to replace an existing bond or preferred stock issue. A firm occasionally refunds to get rid of overly restrictive provisions associated with the existing issue, but the primary motive is to replace existing financing with new financing whose cost is substantially less. This replacement is possible if the coupon rate on a new bond issue (or dividend rate on preferred stock) is substantially lower than the coupon (or dividend) rate on the existing issue. To refund an issue, firms exercise their option to call it.

The decision to refund can be approached in essentially the same manner as the replacement capital budgeting decision. To do this, the incremental (new minus old) after-tax cash flows must be calculated and then discounted to determine the net present value, NPV, of the proposed refunding. Thus,

$$NPV = \sum_{t=1}^{n} \frac{\Delta CF_t}{(1 + k_i)^t} - \Delta CF_0 \qquad (11A.1)$$

where

ΔCF_t = the incremental after-tax cash flows resulting from the refunding
k_i = the after-tax cost of the new bond issue
ΔCF_0 = the after-tax initial investment associated with the refunding

The decision rule is as follows:

1. If NPV is greater than zero—refund.
2. If NPV is less than zero—do not refund.
3. If NPV is equal to zero—you are indifferent.

In discounting the CFs, the current after-tax cost of the new issue is used as the discount rate because it represents the appropriate rate for the risk involved. Because one issue is simply replacing another and there is little risk involved, the use of a higher rate such as the firm's opportunity cost of capital is inappropriate.

To understand refundings, consider the example of St. John's Oil, which issued a 30-year, $50 million, 11.25 percent coupon rate bond five years ago at par, with flotation costs of $480,000. Canadian tax law mandates that the flotation cost associated with the issuance of debt be amortized over five years. Furthermore, if the bond is repaid before the end of the fifth year, any unamortized flotation cost is deducted in the year that the debt is repaid. Because five years have gone by, the flotation costs have been completely amortized. The bonds can be called at 106, so the call premium is 6 percent of $50 million. Because of a drop in long-term market interest rates, St. John's can now issue $50 million of 10 percent coupon rate bonds at par, with flotation costs of $875,000. To ensure that funds will be available when needed, the new bonds will be issued one month before the existing bonds are retired. The net proceeds from the new issue can be invested for one month at the treasury bill rate of 6 percent. St. John's marginal tax rate is 40 percent. The relevant data are as follows:

	Existing Issue	New Issue
Face value	$50 million	$50 million
Coupon interest rate	11.25%	10%
Original life	30 years	25 years
Remaining life	25 years	25 years
Flotation costs (remaining or total)	0	$875,000
Marginal tax rate	40%	
Interest overlap	1 month	
Call premium on existing bonds	6%	
Treasury bill rate	6%	

To determine the NPV, we use the following steps:

STEP 1: *Determine the Incremental Initial Investment Associated With Refunding.* This step involves the call premium, the flotation costs, writeoff for tax purposes of any unamortized flotation costs on the existing issue, and interest during the overlap period. First, we calculate the before-tax initial investment, as follows:

Before-Tax	
Call price on old bonds (106% of par)	$53,000,000
Additional interest paid during overlap period[a]	468,750
Less: Net proceeds of new issue[b]	49,125,000
Interest earned on new issue proceeds during overlap period[c]	245,625
Before-tax initial investment	$ 4,098,125

[a] One month's interest on old bonds = ($50,000,000)(0.1125)(1/12) = $468,750.
[b] Face value less flotation costs = $50,000,000 − $875,000 = $49,125,000.
[c] One month's interest on proceeds = ($49,125,000)(0.06)(1/12) = $245,625.

Next, the tax consequences must be taken into account. Even though the firm must pay a call premium of $3,000,000 ($53,000,000 − $50,000,000), this amount is not a tax-deductible expense. Accordingly, this calculation involves the following items: any unamortized flotation costs on the old bond that can be written off for tax purposes, the additional interest during the overlap period, and the present value of the annual amortization of the flotation costs on the new issue. The flotation costs on the new issue are $875,000. In compliance with the Income Tax Act this amount must be amortized over five years. Therefore, the firm will be able to deduct $175,000 ($875,000/5) at the end of years 1 through 5. The present value of these deductions is $175,000(PVA$_{10\%, 5yr}$) = $175,000(3.791) = $663,425. As a result, for St. John's Oil, the tax consequences affecting the initial investment are as follows:

Tax-Deductible Expenses

Unamortized flotation costs on old bond	$ 0
Additional interest paid during overlap period	468,750
Present value of new issue flotation costs amortization	663,425
Less: Additional interest earned on new issue proceeds	245,625
Total tax-deductible expenses	$ 886,550
Tax savings ($886,550)(0.40)	$ 354,620

Incremental Initial Investment

Before-tax outlay	$4,098,125
Less: Tax savings	354,620
Initial investment, ΔCF_0	$3,743,505

STEP 2: *Determine the Incremental Cash Savings Resulting From the Refunding.* This step involves the interest cash flows of the two issues, and the tax savings on them. For the old bonds, the following after-tax cash flow existed:

Interest on old bond ($50,000,000)(0.1125)	$5,625,000
Tax savings ($5,625,000)(0.40)	2,250,000
After-tax cash outflow on old bond	$3,375,000

For the new bonds St. John's proposes to issue, the after-tax cash outflow is as follows:

Interest on new bond ($50,000,000)(0.10)	$5,000,000
Tax savings ($5,000,000)(0.40)	2,000,000
After-tax cash outflow on new bond	$3,000,000

The incremental cash savings that will occur for each of the next 25 years is as follows:

Cash outflow on old bond	$3,375,000
Less: Cash outflow on new bond	3,000,000
Annual cash saving, ΔCF_t	$ 375,000

STEP 3: *Calculate the Net Present Value.* Now that the incremental initial investment and the annual cash savings are available, we can calculate the NPV of refunding, using the after-tax interest rate on the new bond issue as the discount rate. This after-tax rate is $0.10(1 - T)$, or 6 percent. With the after-tax cash flow stream as follows

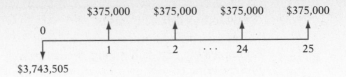

the net present value is

$$\text{NPV} = \$375,000(\text{PVA}_{6\%, \, 25\text{yr}}) - \$3,743,505$$
$$= \$375,000(12.783) - \$3,743,505$$
$$= \$4,793,625 - \$3,743,505 = \$1,418,625$$

Because the NPV is positive, the existing 11.25 percent bonds should be re-funded.[1] If the NPV were negative, St. John's would not want to refund the issue unless it wanted to remove some overly restrictive covenants imposed on the firm by the present bond issue. Refunding (or refinancing) a preferred stock issue uses the same concepts, except that the dividends on preferred stock are not tax-deductible.

PROBLEMS

11A.1 Johnson Management is considering whether to refund a $50 million, 20-year, 12 percent coupon rate bond issue that was sold five years ago. The flotation costs on the 12 per- cent bonds were $2 million. The $50 million in new 15-year bonds would carry an annual interest rate of 10 percent. A call premium of 7 percent would be required to retire the old bonds, and flotation costs of $1.75 million would apply to the new issue. The marginal tax rate is 30 percent, and there is a one-month overlap. The treasury bill rate is 8 percent. Should Johnson refund the bonds?

11A.2 Micro Computers currently has $150 million of 14 percent coupon rate bonds out-standing, with a remaining life of 25 years. They were issued five years ago with a flotation cost of $1.5 million. Right now, $150 million of 25-year, 12.5 percent coupon rate bonds could be issued at par to refund these bonds. Interest rates are not expected to decline further, flotation costs on the new bonds are $2.25 million, the call premium on the old bonds is 12 percent, there is a one-month overlap, and Micro's tax rate is 36 percent. The treasury bill rate is 9 percent. Should the firm refund the existing bonds?

---

[1] As presented, the refunding analysis keeps the firm's debt/equity ratio the same, but changes the cash flows to the firm. It can be argued that to neutralize risk, the cash flows (or the financial strain) on the firm should be kept the same. The present value of the cash savings, which is $4,793,625, represents the amount that could be borrowed (with principal and interest, at 10 percent, being paid over 25 years) with the same after-tax cash flow impact on the firm. If the size of this term loan, which neutralizes the cash flow risk differential, is larger than the initial investment required to refund the old bond, refunding should take place. The decision whether or not to refund remains the same if it is viewed in this manner, as opposed to the approach described in the text. This risk-neutralization approach is used for the lease versus purchase analysis considered in Chapter 15.

11A.3   Central P.E.I. Power & Light is considering refinancing $100 million of existing 13 percent dividend rate preferred stock. The preferred does not have a maturity date, but it can be called at 106.5 percent of par. The $100 million new preferred issue would carry a 12 percent dividend rate and require $2 million in flotation costs; there is a one-month overlap. The treasury bill rate is 8 percent. Central P.E.I.'s tax rate is 40 percent. Should Central P.E.I. refinance the preferred issue? (*Note:* Remember that dividends are an after-tax expense. This fact influences both the cash savings and the discount rate employed.)

12 Taxes and Capital Structure

EXECUTIVE SUMMARY

The firm's capital structure is the result of the interaction of many different factors. One factor is the business risk to which the firm is exposed. Other things being equal, the more business risk the firm has, the less financial risk it wants to incur.

In the absence of taxes and other imperfections, the firm's capital structure does not influence the value of the firm. The value of the firm is determined solely by its investment decisions, not by its financing decisions. However, once corporate taxes, personal taxes, and other tax issues are considered, the value of the firm is not completely independent of its capital structure. The amount of debt relative to the amount of equity employed may have an impact on the value of the firm.

We have available a number of tools for assessing the firm's capital structure. These include an analysis of the impact that changes in earnings before interest and taxes (EBIT) have on earnings per share (EPS); examination of coverage ratios; consideration of lender and bond rating standards; and an analysis of the firm's cash flow under different scenarios. Ultimately, the capital structure decision depends on the ability of the firm to take advantage of tax shields, the risk the firm is exposed to, and the necessity for financial slack.

RISK AND CAPITAL STRUCTURE

Until now we have not questioned the firm's debt/equity ratio, which signifies the amount of financial leverage being employed. We have taken it as a "given." For managers, however, it is not a given; it is one of the decisions firms have to make. The issue can be visualized as follows, where we have two different ways of slicing up the pie between shareholders and bondholders:

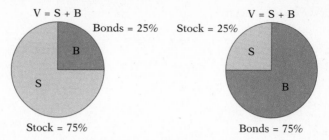

The question is this: Holding everything else constant, does the way we slice the pie affect its size? *By holding everything else constant, we are assuming that the firm's investments remain the same, as well as its underlying cash flows and everything else.* If everything remains the same, then should the value of the firm be affected by the way it is financed?

The answer to this simple question is not simple. In fact, a tremendous amount of controversy and discussion swirls around this question. In this chapter we examine capital structure theory, and the impact that corporate and personal taxes have on capital structure decisions. Then in Chapter 13 we examine the effects of various types of transaction costs on the choice of capital structure and discuss some empirical evidence that shows the evolving nature of capital structure decisions.

Determining a firm's financial structure means answering two basic questions: First, how should the firm's total sources of funds be divided between long-term and short-term financing? Second, what proportion of funds should be financed by debt and what proportion by equity? The first question, the maturity composition of the total sources of funds, requires focusing on the nature of the assets owned. We address short-term sources of funds in Chapter 21, where we see that the matching principle provides some guidance.

Now, however, we focus our attention on the long-term sources of funds—debt, leases, preferred stock, internally generated funds, and common stock. The proportions of these long-term sources describe the capital structure of the firm. Our focus is therefore on the second of the questions: What does theory say about the impact of the firm's capital structure on its value? For simplicity, we focus on the two main sources of capital—equity capital and debt capital.

BUSINESS RISK

One way to look at **business risk** is to quantify it as the relative dispersion (or variability) in the firm's earnings before interest and taxes (EBIT). Consider Table 12.1, which presents the expected sales and resulting EBIT in three different states of the economy for one firm, Consolidated National. The expected EBIT for Consolidated is $10,000, and the standard deviation is $3,098. The coefficient of variation (i.e., standard deviation/mean), which measures the relative variability of Consolidated's EBIT, is 0.31. If we were comparing it to another firm with an EBIT

Table 12.1

Probabilities, Sales, and EBIT for Consolidated National

Business risk is measured by the coefficient of variation of EBIT. The higher the coefficient of variation, the more business risk exists.

Probability	0.30	0.40	0.30
Sales	$24,000	$32,000	$40,000
Costs	18,000	22,000	26,000
Earnings before interest and taxes (EBIT)	$ 6,000	$10,000	$14,000

expected EBIT = 0.30($6,000) + 0.40($10,000)) + 0.30($14,000) = $10,000

$$\text{standard deviation} = [0.30(\$6,000 - \$10,000)^2 + 0.40(\$10,000 - \$10,000)^2$$
$$+ 0.30(\$14,000 - \$10,000)^2]^{0.5}$$
$$= (\$9,600,000)^{0.5} = \$3,098$$

coefficient of variation = standard deviation/expected EBIT
$$= \$3,098/\$10,000 \approx 0.31$$

coefficient of variation of 0.80, we would conclude that Consolidated National has less business risk.

Another way of thinking about the impact of business risk is presented in Figure 12.1. If two firms have the same expected EBIT, then the one with more business risk will experience much wider fluctuations in EBIT as its sales fluctuate. Both Consolidated National and the other firm might experience a 10 percent change in sales in a given year. But if the second firm has higher business risk, its EBIT might

Figure 12.1

Probability Distributions of EBIT for Low and High Business Risk Firms

For simplicity, the same expected EBIT is assumed. Other things being equal, low business risk firms will experience much smaller fluctuations in EBIT than will high business risk firms.

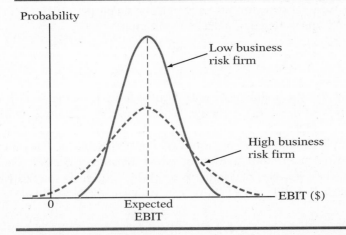

change by 25 percent from last year's, while Consolidated National's EBIT changes by only, say, 15 percent. This greater fluctuation in EBIT for the second firm is directly attributable to its greater business risk.

Business risk is caused primarily by the nature of the firm's operations. As a first approximation, we can think about business risk as a function of the industry in which the firm operates. But business risk is more complex than that. Other primary determinants of business risk are the following:

1. SENSITIVITY OF SALES TO GENERAL ECONOMIC FLUCTUATIONS   Firms whose sales fluctuate more when general economic conditions change have more business risk.
2. DEGREE OF COMPETITION AND SIZE   The smaller the firm and its share of the market, the greater its business risk.
3. OPERATING LEVERAGE[1]   The higher the proportion of fixed to variable operating costs, the more operating leverage exists and, hence, the more business risk. Firms in service industries often have low fixed operating costs and therefore a low amount of operating leverage. Steel firms, on the other hand, have high fixed operating costs and more operating leverage and business risk.
4. INPUT PRICE VARIABILITY   The more uncertain the input prices for the firm's products, the more business risk.
5. ABILITY TO ADJUST OUTPUT PRICES   Firms that are in a monopolistic or oligopolistic situation, or that face an inelastic demand curve for their products, may have greater ability to adjust output prices and so be exposed to less business risk.

Business risk is a direct function of the firm's accumulated investment (capital budgeting) decisions. As these decisions are made, they affect both the nature of the firm's business and the composition of its assets. Firms with low business risk often exist in such industries as food processing and grocery retailing. Cyclical manufacturing industries and steel, copper, or aluminum firms are generally regarded as having high business risk.

An old adage is that business risk and financial risk are interrelated, so that "The more business risk, the less financial risk." Although the adage is not always true in practice, it is important to remember that business risk appears to have a major impact on the amount of debt a firm is willing or able to undertake.

FINANCIAL RISK

Financial risk is a result of the firm's long-term financing decisions. **Financial risk** refers to (1) the increased variability of earnings available to the firm's common shareholders, and (2) the increased probability of financial distress borne by the firm's owners if financial leverage is employed by the firm. Financial leverage refers to the use of fixed-cost types of financing.[2] The primary sources are debt, leases, and preferred

---

[1] Operating leverage is considered in detail in Appendix 12A, as is its relation to financial leverage.
[2] Although some long-term bonds and leases have floating or variable rates, they are still a fixed-cost type of financing, because there are periodic payments required and they have a prior but limited claim before common shareholders receive anything. In addition, adjustable-rate preferred stock also exists; however, it still has the essential elements of a fixed-cost security.

stock. Although what we have to say applies equally to leases or preferred stock, we restrict our analysis to the major source of financial leverage—debt.

To see the impact of different amounts of debt on the firm, let us return to our example of Consolidated National. Assume it can employ three different capital structures, as follows:

Capital Structure A (zero debt)

Debt	$ 0
Common stock	30,000
Total liabilities and shareholders' equity	$30,000

Capital Structure B (30% debt at a 10% coupon rate)

Debt	$ 9,000
Common stock	21,000
Total liabilities and shareholders' equity	$30,000

Capital Structure C (60% debt at a 10% coupon rate)

Debt	$18,000
Common stock	12,000
Total liabilities and shareholders' equity	$30,000

Capital structure A has no debt. Capital structure B has 30 percent of the firm's capital structure in debt; capital structure C has 60 percent of the firm's capital structure in debt.

Table 12.2 shows the impact of the three different capital structures on Consolidated's earnings per share. (The three EBITs and associated probabilities are from Table 12.1.) For capital structure A, earnings per share range from $0.72 to $1.68. Under both B and C, the variation of the EPS is larger, ranging from $0.87 to $2.25 with 30 percent debt, and from $1.26 to $3.66 with 60 percent debt.

To determine the impact of financial risk, we can calculate the coefficient of variation of Consolidated's EPS for the three different capital structures. The expected EPS and standard deviation of EPS are calculated from the data in Table 12.2 (just as we calculated the expected EBIT and its standard deviation in Table 12.1). These are as follows:

	Expected EPS (1)	Standard Deviation of EPS (2)	Coefficient of Variation of EPS (2) ÷ (1) (3)
Capital structure A (zero debt)	$1.20	$0.37	0.31
Capital structure B (30% debt)	1.56	0.53	0.34
Capital structure C (60% debt)	2.46	0.93	0.38

Table 12.2

Earnings per Share for Three Capital Structures for Consolidated National

If there were preferred stock, those dividends would be subtracted from EAT to arrive at earnings available for common shareholders (EAC). Then EAC would be divided by the number of shares of common stock outstanding to arrive at the firm's EPS.

Probability	0.30	0.40	0.30
Capital Structure A (zero debt)			
EBIT	$6,000	$10,000	$14,000
Interest	0	0	0
EBT	6,000	10,000	14,000
Taxes (40%)	2,400	4,000	5,600
EAT	$3,600	$ 6,000	$ 8,400
EPS (based on 5,000 shares)	$ 0.72	$ 1.20	$ 1.68
Capital Structure B (30% debt)			
EBIT	$6,000	$10,000	$14,000
Interest	900	900	900
EBT	5,100	9,100	13,100
Taxes (40%)	2,040	3,640	5,240
EAT	$3,060	$ 5,460	$ 7,860
EPS (based on 3,500 shares)	$ 0.87	$ 1.56	$ 2.25
Capital Structure C (60% debt)			
EBIT	$6,000	$10,000	$14,000
Interest	1,800	1,800	1,800
EBT	4,200	8,200	12,200
Taxes (40%)	1,680	3,280	4,880
EAT	$2,520	$ 4,920	$ 7,320
EPS (based on 2,000 shares)	$ 1.26	$ 2.46	$ 3.66

Examining these data, we see that the EPS coefficient of variation when there is no debt (capital structure A) is 0.31, whereas it is 0.34 with 30 percent debt and 0.38 with 60 percent debt. Because an increase in the coefficient of variation signifies an increase in relative variability, we see that *financial risk increases as the firm adds more debt* to its capital structure. This increased riskiness is graphed in Figure 12.2. There we see that the dispersion of possible EPS outcomes increases substantially when 60 percent debt is employed, compared with no debt.

In Table 12.1 we calculated the coefficient of variation of Consolidated's EBIT to be 0.31. Note that the coefficient of variation of Consolidated's EPS under capital structure A is also 0.31. Is this just a coincidence? No. The reason these two are exactly the same is that they both represent the basic business risk of the firm. *Because capital structure A has no debt, it has no financial risk. Thus, the riskiness of the EPS under capital structure A reflects only business risk.* The coefficients of variation for capital

Figure 12.2

Probability Distributions of EPS for Different Capital Structures

Favourable financial leverage results in an increase in the expected EPS and also in the dispersion of the possible EPSs.

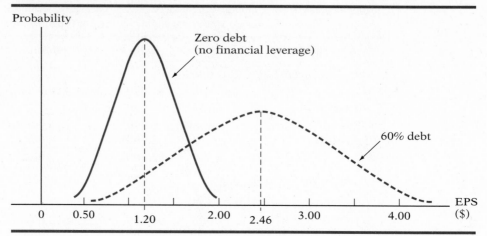

structures B and C, however, reflect the effects of *both* business and financial risk. That part *attributable only to financial risk* is measured by the difference between the coefficient of variation of 0.31 and either 0.34 for capital structure B or 0.38 for C.

This example confirms our earlier observation: Fluctuations in a firm's EPS are first and foremost a function of the firm's accumulated capital investment decisions. Once that is accounted for, the effects of the firm's capital structure on both the magnitude and fluctuations in earnings per share can be seen. In the Consolidated National example, note that a large part of the fluctuation in EPS was due to the impact of the past investment decisions. Then the impact of the mix of debt and equity employed can be seen.

IMPACT ON THE VALUE OF THE FIRM

We have just seen that financing decisions have two impacts on earnings. First, the financing decision can lead to higher (or lower) earnings per share when compared to the no-financial-leverage case. Second, as EBIT fluctuates, the use of financial leverage leads to larger movements in earnings per share when compared with the no-financial-leverage case. Although these impacts may be significant, we know from our previous discussion that it is not earnings per share that is important. Rather, it is the market value of the firm, V. Remember, the manager's ultimate success or failure is determined in the marketplace. The capital structure question must also be addressed from the standpoint of what impact different capital structures have on the market value of the firm—not just on the firm's earnings per share.

Concept Review Questions

■ What is the difference between business risk and financial risk?

- How is the coefficient of variation used to determine the impact of financial risk of different capital structures?
- Why can firms with low business risk have high financial risk, and vice versa?

CAPITAL STRUCTURE AND THE VALUE OF THE FIRM

The impact of changing capital structures on the value of the firm has been the subject of a tremendous amount of theoretical work. It all started with the argument that capital structure is a "mere detail." So to understand how firms should address the capital structure decision, it is important to have some idea of the major elements of capital structure theory.

THE DEVELOPMENT OF CAPITAL STRUCTURE THEORY

To highlight the issues involved, we start with a simplified example. The assumptions are as follows:

1. Only two types of securities are employed—long-term debt and common stock.
2. The firm is not expected to grow. Thus, the value of a share of stock can be determined by employing the basic no-growth dividend valuation approach (from Chapter 4) which capitalizes the perpetual cash dividend stream as follows:

$$P_0 = \frac{D_1}{k_s} \qquad (12.1)$$

where

P_0 = the current stock price
D_1 = the expected constant amount of cash dividends in perpetuity
k_s = the equity investor's required rate of return, or opportunity cost of equity capital

3. All earnings are assumed to be paid out in the form of cash dividends, so dividends equal earnings in each future time period. Accordingly, Equation 12.1 can be rewritten as

$$P_0 = \frac{EPS_1}{k_s} \qquad (12.2)$$

or for the firm as a whole

$$S = \frac{E}{k_s} \qquad (12.3)$$

where E is now the expected constant cash dividends (or earnings in perpetuity) and S is the total market value of the firm's stock.[3] In line with the discussion in Chapter 4, when there is no growth, the present value of growth opportunities (PVGO) is zero. Equation 12.3 is, therefore, a straightforward statement of the present value of the firm's assets in place when no growth is expected.

4.   There are no costs or penalties (such as legal fees or the disruption of operations resulting from default) if the firm does not pay interest on the debt, although the bondholders may take over the firm.

We are now in a position to investigate what impact, if any, the firm's capital structure can have on the value of the firm. We begin with the celebrated no-tax case presented by Modigliani and Miller (1958).

THE MODIGLIANI AND MILLER MODEL WITHOUT CORPORATE TAXES

In its simplest situation, a firm has only common stock and debt financing. For the moment, we also assume that *there are no corporate taxes.* Under these conditions, how does the firm's financing decision affect the value of the firm? To understand this question, consider True North Industries, which is an all-equity-financed firm. True North has an opportunity to receive $100,000 in cash flow from both its existing operations and a new investment. To receive the $100,000 in cash flow (or earnings before interest and taxes, EBIT), True North needs to make an additional $400,000 investment.[4] The equity investor's required rate of return is 10 percent.

If only common stock financing is used to raise the additional $400,000, the total market value of True North will be the present value of the dividends to the firm's shareholders. With EBIT of $100,000, no interest, and no corporate taxes, EBIT = earnings after tax, EAT; and, with all cash flows paid out as cash dividends, the dividends are a perpetual stream of $100,000. Using Equation 12.3, we find that the value of True North is

$$\text{value of True North's stock} = S = \frac{\$100,000}{0.10} = \$1 \text{ million}$$

When only common stock is employed, the total value of the firm, V, is equal to the value of the firm's common stock, S, which is $1 million.

What happens if True North decides to raise the $400,000 by issuing debt instead of common stock? The debt has an interest rate, k_b, of 6 percent, so that the earnings (and dividends) now available to True North's common shareholders are

---

[3] As we will see in Chapter 14, the impact of cash dividends on the value of the firm's common stock is also a subject of debate. To avoid complicating this discussion, it is easier to assume that all earnings are paid out in the form of cash dividends.

[4] The firm is not expected to grow; therefore, all cash flows are perpetuities. This implies that annual investment must equal the annual (economic) depreciation in order to maintain the assets in place. Accordingly, EBIT will equal cash flow.

EBIT	$100,000
Interest ($400,000)(0.06)	24,000
EBT	76,000
Taxes	zero for now
EAT	$ 76,000

If the earnings for common shareholders of $76,000 are *mistakenly divided by the previous all-equity required rate of return* of 10 percent, then the *apparent* value of True North's common stock (which is now the "levered" value of the equity, designated by the subscript L) is

$$\text{apparent value of True North's stock} = S_L = \frac{\$76,000}{0.10} = \$760,000$$

Finally, with the value of True North's debt equal to $400,000, the *apparent* total value of the levered firm, V_L, would be

$$\text{total firm value} = \text{apparent market value of levered common}$$
$$\text{stock} + \text{market value of debt}$$
$$V_L = S_L + B \qquad (12.4)$$
$$= \$760,000 + \$400,000 = \$1,160,000$$

If the equity investor's required return remains 10 percent, simply using debt instead of equity financing has apparently allowed True North to raise the value of the firm from $1 million to $1,160,000. At this point, Franco Modigliani and Merton Miller, both recent Nobel Prize winners in financial economics, raised an important question: "Is it reasonable for the required rate of return demanded by equity investors to be the same when debt, as opposed to common stock, is employed?" Their answer was no. *Equity risk has increased because the use of debt places a drain on the cash flow stream before anything goes to the common shareholders.* This risk is composed of (1) the possibility of not receiving any earnings or cash flow, and (2) increased variability in earnings and cash flows due to the increased amount of debt employed.

Modigliani and Miller (MM) developed their model given the following assumptions *in addition to those already mentioned*:

1. PERFECT CAPITAL MARKETS.   In perfect capital markets, buying and selling securities involves no brokerage fees. All investors have equal and costless access to information, and there are a large number of individual buyers and sellers, none of whom individually can affect market prices.
2. DEBT IS RISK-FREE.   Any debt issued by investors and firms is always riskless debt, no matter how much is issued. Therefore, the interest rate on all debt is the risk-free rate.

3. RISK CLASSES.   All firms can be grouped into risk classes based on the variance of their earnings before interest and taxes, EBIT.[5]

4. HOMOGENEOUS EXPECTATIONS.   Individual investors agree on the expected value of the future income of firms, that is, on each firm's earnings before interest and taxes, EBIT.

Using these assumptions, MM derived two propositions concerning the valuation of securities for firms with different capital structures: *The first says that the value of the firm is determined by its capital investment decisions, not by its financing decisions. The second says that as a firm adds more debt to its capital structure, its opportunity cost of equity capital increases.* Let us explore these two propositions more formally.

Proposition I   The equilibrium *market value of any firm when there are no corporate taxes is independent of its capital structure* and is found by capitalizing its expected EBIT by the appropriate cost of capital for an all-equity firm, k_s^U, in its risk class

$$V_L = S_L + B = \frac{\text{EBIT}}{k_s^U} = V_U \qquad (12.5)$$

where

V_L = the market value of a levered firm

S_L = the market value of stock for a levered firm

k_s^U = the equity investor's required rate of return for an all-equity-financed firm; the cost of equity capital for an all-equity-financed firm

V_U = the market value of an unlevered firm (Note that the unlevered value is denoted by the subscript U.)

Another way to state proposition I is this: The value of any firm when there are no taxes is determined by its capital investment decisions, not by its financing decisions. Other things being equal, various proportions of equity or debt may be employed, but the total market value of the firm is unaffected.

Proposition II   The cost of equity for a levered firm, k_s^L, is equal to the appropriate cost of capital for an all-equity firm, k_s^U, plus a risk premium equal to the debt/equity ratio times the spread between k_s^U and the cost of debt, k_b, as follows:

$$k_s^L = k_s^U + (k_s^U - k_b)(B/S_L) \qquad (12.6)$$

Thus, as the firm adds more debt to its capital structure, equity investors demand a higher return to compensate for the additional debt, and the opportunity cost of equity capital increases.

Taking the two propositions together, MM conclude in the no-tax case that there is no advantage or disadvantage to financing with common stock. *Any "savings" from debt financing are immediately offset by a higher return required by common sharehold-*

---

[5] At the time Modigliani and Miller developed their model, no complete model of risk and return (such as the capital asset pricing model, CAPM) existed. Risk classes were used by MM to allow for differences in risk among firms.

ers *(due to greater financial risk), leaving the firm and its shareholders in the same position as before.*

Now that we have presented the two propositions of MM, let us go back to the example of True North. According to MM, the total market value of True North must remain at $1 million (i.e., $V_L = V_U$), because nothing of value has been created. *In the no-tax case we can think of debt being a zero-NPV project;* that is why $V_L = V_U$. Subtracting the $400,000 in debt, we see that the value of the stock, S_L, in the MM no-tax case is $600,000. Because the earnings before taxes, EBT, going to True North's common shareholders are $76,000, Equation 12.3 can be rearranged and solved for the levered cost of equity capital:

$$\text{levered cost of equity capital} = k_s^L = \frac{\text{earnings available to shareholders}}{\text{market value of stock}}$$

$$= \frac{\$76,000}{\$600,000} = 0.1267 = 12.67\%$$

Alternately, we can use MM's proposition II (Equation 12.6) directly to determine the cost of equity funds to the firm and the return demanded by equity investors, once debt is added to the firm's financing mix. This is

$$k_s^L = k_s^U + (k_s^U - k_b)(B/S_L)$$
$$= 10\% + (10\% - 6\%)(\$400,000/\$600,000) = 12.67\%$$

MM concluded that common equity investors neither gained nor lost from the use of debt in the no-tax case. Thus, *the value of the firm does not change; rather, increased financial risk causes the shareholders' required rate of return to increase. Accordingly, the opportunity cost of equity capital increases so that any apparent gain from using cheaper debt financing is completely offset.*

Because the market value of the firm does not change with financial leverage, in the no-tax case the firm's opportunity cost of capital is also constant as financial leverage changes. When True North was all-equity-financed, its opportunity cost of capital was equal to its unlevered cost of equity capital, k_s^U, which was 10 percent. In the no-tax case its opportunity cost of capital must remain at 10 percent after it shifts to any amount of debt financing. Using Equation 12.7 (which is just Equation 6.1) to determine the firm's opportunity cost of capital, and with corporate taxes equal to zero, we have

$$\text{opportunity cost of capital} = k_b(1 - T)W_{\text{debt}} + k_s^L W_{\text{common equity}}$$

$$= k_b(1 - T)\left\{\frac{B}{B + S_L}\right\} + k_s^L\left\{\frac{S_L}{B + S_L}\right\}$$

$$= 6\% \ (1 - 0.00)\left(\frac{\$400,000}{\$1,000,000}\right) \quad\quad (12.7)$$

$$+ \ 12.67\%\left(\frac{\$600,000}{\$1,000,000}\right)$$

$$= 6.00\% \ (0.40) + 12.67\% \ (0.60) = 10.00\%$$

Figure 12.3

Value of the Firm and Opportunity Cost of Capital With No Taxes, According to Modigliani and Miller

As the firm moves to the right, it substitutes cheaper debt for more expensive equity capital. Because financial risk increases as you move to the right, the opportunity cost of equity capital increases, exactly offsetting any benefits from using more cheap debt financing.

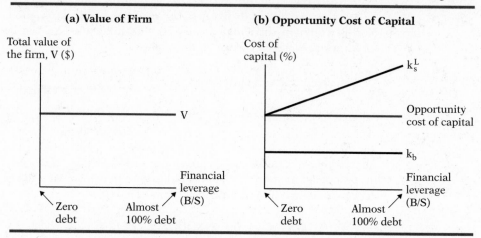

Modigliani and Miller's no-tax position is graphed in Figure 12.3. As the firm increases its financial leverage (by moving to the right), we see in Figure 12.3 (a) that the value of the firm remains constant. In Figure 12.3 (b) we see that the firm's opportunity cost of capital is constant regardless of the amount of financial leverage employed. Both the value of the firm and its cost of capital are independent of financial leverage in the absence of taxes.

WHERE TO LOOK FOR CAPITAL STRUCTURE IMPACTS ON FIRM VALUE

The importance of the Modigliani and Miller no-tax model is that (1) it presents a theoretical, rigorous statement of the value of the firm, where none existed before, and (2) it tells us where to look to determine whether the firm's capital structure affects the value of the firm. In effect, the MM no-tax case says:

If there are no taxes,

if there are no transactions costs, and

if the investment (or capital budgeting) policies of the firm are fixed,

then capital structure does not affect a firm's value.

To determine whether capital structure affects firm value, we will look at each one of these conditions separately. In the remainder of this chapter we will look at the impact of taxes, both corporate and personal. In Chapter 13 we will examine whether trans-action costs and capital investment policies of the firm cause its capital structure decisions to affect its value. Along the way we will see that a tremendous amount of attention has been devoted to answering the simple question, "Does the firm's capital structure affect its value?"

Concept Review Questions

- What assumptions did Modigliani and Miller make when they developed their corporate capital structure model?
- Describe Miller and Modigliani's proposition I and proposition II.
- Briefly explain Modigliani and Miller's capital structure model.

CORPORATE TAXES AND THE DEDUCTIBILITY OF INTEREST

Almost immediately after Modigliani and Miller published their no-tax article, they were reminded that corporate taxes are a fact of life for firms. Accordingly, they incorporated corporate taxes into their capital structure model.

THE MODIGLIANI AND MILLER MODEL WITH CORPORATE TAXES

Suppose we introduce corporate taxes into the True North example. We will assume that the marginal corporate tax rate, T, is 30 percent and that to obtain the $100,000 EBIT, True North still needs to raise the additional $400,000. Once corporate taxes are introduced, the earnings after taxes are

EBIT	$100,000
Interest	0
EBT	100,000
Taxes (30%)	30,000
EAT	$ 70,000

Because all earnings are paid out as cash dividends, the payment to *all* the investors of the unlevered firm is

$$\text{payments to all investors}^U = \text{EBIT}(1 - T) \qquad (12.8)$$

With only common stock being employed, the return demanded by investors is still 10 percent, that is, $k_s^U = 10$ percent, and the total value of True North, V_U, is equal to its unlevered stock value, which is

$$V_U = S_U = \frac{\text{EBIT}(1 - T)}{k_s^U}$$

$$= \frac{\$70,000}{0.10} = \$700,000 \qquad (12.9)$$

What happens when True North uses $400,000 of debt financing instead of equity financing? With $400,000 of debt at 6 percent, interest is $24,000. Therefore, with debt financing and corporate taxes, the earnings are

EBIT	$100,000
Interest ($k_b B$)	24,000
EBT	76,000
Taxes (30%)	22,800
EAT	$ 53,200

It is important to consider the impact that interest has on the taxes paid by the firm. *Because of interest, the firm actually pays less tax.* If no interest is present, the taxes are $100,000(0.30) = $30,000. With the interest of $24,000, the taxes drop to $22,800—a savings of $7,200 in taxes. The impact of interest on the amount of taxes actually paid by the firm is referred to as the *interest tax shield*. Other things being equal, the payment of interest by the firm shields (or reduces) the amount of corporate taxes paid by the firm.

Although earnings after-tax have declined due to the use of debt financing, the *debt financing has value because on an after-tax basis it costs the firm less than equity.* According to MM, the value of the levered firm, V_L, once corporate taxes are introduced, is equal to the unlevered value of the firm, V_U, plus the present value of the interest tax shield. The amount of interest per period is given by $k_b B$, and the interest tax shield is simply $Tk_b B$. Because debt is a perpetuity in the case being considered, the *present value of the interest tax shield* is given by capitalizing the interest tax shield at the appropriate discount rate, k_b, so that $Tk_b B/k_b = TB$. Once corporate taxes are introduced, while everything else remains as before, MM conclude that the value of the levered firm is[6]

$$V_L = V_U + TB \qquad (12.10)$$

Thus, the total value of True North once corporate taxes are introduced and the firm has $400,000 of debt outstanding is

$$V_L = \$700,000 + (0.30)(\$400,000) = \$820,000$$

Because the total value of the firm, V_L, is also equal to the sum of its levered stock, S_L, and bonds, B, the value of the stock of the levered firm is $S_L = V_L - B$. For True North, its stock will now be valued at $S_L = \$820,000 - \$400,000 = \$420,000$.

If the debt/equity ratio, B/S_L, is specified at ($400,000/$420,000), then proposition II (Equation 12.6) can be adjusted for taxes to determine the firm's levered cost

---

[6] Equation 12.10 is derived in Appendix 12B.

of equity capital. Thus,

$$k_s^L = k_s^U + (k_s^U - k_b)(1 - T)(B/S_L)$$
$$k_s^L = 10\% + (10\% - 6\%)(1 - 0.30)(\$400,000/\$420,000) \qquad (12.11)$$
$$= 10\% + 2.8\%(0.952) = 10\% + 2.67\% = 12.67\%$$

Note that the opportunity cost of equity capital of 12.67 percent is the same as it was in the no-tax case. Now that we know True North's levered cost of equity, k_s^L, we can use a modified version of Equation 12.9, which now reflects both corporate taxes and the interest paid on the debt financing, to solve directly for S_L:

$$S_L = \frac{(EBIT - k_b B)(1 - T)}{k_s^L} \qquad (12.12)$$

$$= \frac{\$53,200}{0.1267} \approx \$420,000$$

The numerator of Equation 12.12 is simply the EAT that we previously obtained for True North when it had $400,000 of debt outstanding.

Once the tax subsidy provided by the government is recognized, we see that by using debt, True North has increased the total value of the firm from $700,000 to $820,000. This is composed of the levered stock, S_L, valued at $420,000 and debt, B, valued at $400,000.

Let us now see what happens to True North's overall opportunity cost of capital. With all common stock financing, True North's opportunity cost of capital is still equal to its unlevered cost of equity capital, k_s^U, which is 10 percent. Once debt is introduced, we can use Equation 12.7 to determine True North's new opportunity cost of capital:

$$\text{opportunity cost of capital} = k_b(1 - T)\left\{\frac{B}{B + S_L}\right\} + k_s^L\left\{\frac{S_L}{B + S_L}\right\}$$

$$= 6\%(1 - 0.30)\left(\frac{\$400,000}{\$820,000}\right) + 12.67\%\left(\frac{\$420,000}{\$820,000}\right)$$

$$= 2.05\% + 6.49\% = 8.54\%$$

Figure 12.4 shows the MM results once corporate taxes are introduced. Note that *financial risk increases as debt is employed, as signified by the rising cost of common stock, k_s^L. Even with this increase in financial risk, the presence of corporate taxes has the effect of subsidizing the use of debt; the result is that increases in financial leverage lead to increases in the total value of the firm and decreases in the firm's overall opportunity cost of capital.* As long as firms are profitable, and the government provides an incentive for using debt through allowing interest to be tax-deductible, there is an advantage to using debt financing. This advantage leads to an increase in the value of the firm, providing that the investment decisions of the firm are unaffected.

Figure 12.4

Value of the Firm and Opportunity Cost of Capital With Corporate Taxes, According to Modigliani and Miller

When corporate taxes are introduced, the government, in effect, supplies a subsidy for the use of debt as long as firms are profitable. This happens because interest is a tax-deductible expense. By using debt, the firm can increase its total value and decrease its opportunity cost of capital.

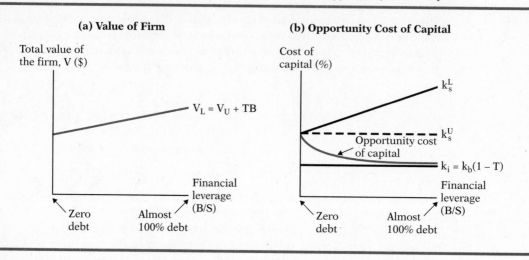

THE NO-TAX CASE VERSUS THE TAX CASE

The following table shows Modiglian and Miller's comparison of the all-stock to the stock-and-debt-financing plans for both the no-tax and the corporate tax case.

	No-Tax Case		Tax Case	
	All-Stock Financing	Combination Stock and Debt Financing	All-Stock Financing	Combination Stock and Debt Financing
Total stock value	$1,000,000	$600,000	$700,000	$420,000
Total debt value	0	$400,000	0	$400,000
Total value of firm	$1,000,000	$1,000,000	$700,000	$820,000
Cost of equity capital	10%	12.67%	10%	12.67%
After-tax cost of debt capital	6%	6%	4.2%	4.2%
Overall opportunity cost of capital	10%	10%	10%	8.54%

Thus, the overall conclusions are that (1) with no corporate taxes, the capital structure decision is irrelevant, and (2) once corporate taxes are considered, firms maximize their value and lower their opportunity cost of capital by employing debt. In fact, the more debt used, the greater the value of the firm.

Before going any further, let us stop and summarize the important conclusions and equations presented by the MM no-tax and tax cases. Table 12.3 summarizes this information. In part I for the no-tax case, the value of the firm, that is, $V_L = S_L + B$, is shown to be independent of the amount of financial leverage employed. Once corporate taxes are introduced, the value of the firm can be found via either $V_L = S_L + B$ or $V_L = V_U + TB$, and the value increases as the firm replaces equity with debt in its capital structure. Table 12.3, in parts II, III and IV, also summarizes the value of the unlevered equity, S_U, and the levered equity, S_L, for both the no-tax and the tax cases, along with the levered cost of equity capital, k_s^L, in both cases. From an applications standpoint, *always use the equations for the tax case; if no taxes exist, the equations employing taxes simply collapse into the no-tax equations.*

We used Equation 12.7 to determine the firm's opportunity cost of capital as follows:

$$\text{opportunity cost of capital} = k_b(1 - T)W_{\text{debt}} + k_s^L W_{\text{common equity}}$$

Two other approaches can also be employed to determine the firm's opportunity cost of capital when the MM tax case is being considered. The first says that the firm's opportunity cost of capital is equal to the unlevered cost of capital, which is just k_s^U, adjusted for taxes and the amount of debt employed, so that

$$\text{opportunity cost of capital} = k_s^U\left(1 - \left[T\left(\frac{B}{S_L + B}\right)\right]\right)$$

$$= 10\%\left(1 - \left[0.30\left(\frac{\$400,000}{\$820,000}\right)\right]\right) \qquad (12.13)$$

$$= 8.54\%$$

The second approach says that the opportunity cost of capital is equal to the after-tax operating cash flows to the firm if there is no debt, divided by the total market value of the firm, so

$$\text{opportunity cost of capital} = \frac{\text{EBIT}_{\text{at a zero debt level}}(1 - T)}{S_L + B}$$

$$= \frac{\$100,000(1 - 0.30)}{\$820,000} \qquad (12.14)$$

$$= 8.54\%$$

Table 12.3

Summary of the Fundamental Relationships for the MM No-Tax Case and the MM Corporate Tax Case

For simplicity, the tax-case equations should always be employed. If there are no corporate taxes, the tax-case equations collapse into the no-tax equations.

No-Tax Case	Tax Case

I. The Total Value of the Firm, V_L

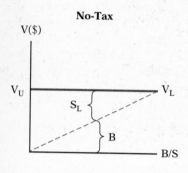
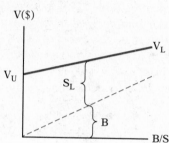
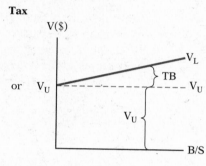

$$V_L = V_U$$
$$V_L = V_U = S_L + B$$

Note: The second equation is Equation 12.5.

$$V_L = S_L + B, \text{ or}$$
$$V_L = V_U + TB$$

Note: The second equation is Equation 12.10.

II. Value of the Equity If There Is No Debt, S_U

$$S_U = \frac{E}{k_s^U}$$

Note: This is Equation 12.3. Because there is no debt or taxes, EBIT = E.

$$S_U = \frac{EBIT\,(1 - T)}{k_s^U}$$

Note: This is Equation 12.9. Because there is no debt, EBIT = EBT.

III. Value of the Equity If There Is Debt, S_L

$$S_L = \frac{(EBIT - I)}{k_s^L}$$

Note: This is a modification of Equation 12.3. EBIT = E and $I = k_b B$.

$$S_L = \frac{(EBIT - I)(1 - T)}{k_s^L}$$

Note: This is Equation 12.12. $I = k_b B$.

IV. Levered Cost of Equity Capital, k_s^L

$$k_s^L = k_s^U + (k_s^U - k_b)(B/S_L)$$

Note: This is Equation 12.6.

$$k_s^L = k_s^U + (k_s^U - k_b)(1 - T)(B/S_L)$$

Note: This is Equation 12.11.

Equations 12.13 and 12.14 work just as well as Equation 12.7 when the MM tax case is considered. However, *remember that Equations 12.13 and 12.14 assume an MM corporate tax world; do not employ them to determine a firm's opportunity cost of capital unless the world you and the firm are operating in is the MM corporate tax world.*

REACTIONS TO THE MM CAPITAL STRUCTURE ARGUMENTS

When MM presented their capital structure theory in the late 1950s and early 1960s, many individuals, in both the business and the academic communities, immediately took issue with them. The arguments, in simple form, were: "Of course, capital structure is important. That is why we see firms purposefully select different capital structures—because they know capital structure is important and, accordingly, select the one most appropriate for their firm." An alternative reaction was: "If capital structure and the debt tax shield are important, why aren't all firms almost 100 percent debt financed, because that is the point at which the value of their firm would be maximized? All we have to do is examine a few firms and see that they are not 100 percent, or even close to 100 percent, debt financed. Therefore, MM, your theory is incorrect."

Do not fall into the trap of rejecting MM as irrelevant without considering the full meaning of their position. In the simplest terms, *MM's argument was that the value of the firm is determined solely by the capital investments it makes.* Thus, the underlying message delivered by MM was simply to restate that the primary means of creating value is to focus on the left-hand side of the balance sheet and make "good" capital investment decisions. According to MM, any other decisions, such as the capital structure decision (Chapters 12 and 13) or the dividend decision (Chapter 14), *are irrelevant as long as there are no transactions costs and these decisions do not affect the capital investment decisions made by the firm.*

Concept Review Questions

- Describe the effects of corporate taxes on Modigliani and Miller's model.
- Briefly summarize the difference in the conclusions and equations of the MM no-tax case and the MM tax case.

PERSONAL TAXES AND OTHER TAX-RELATED IMPACTS

Many more tax impacts on the value of the firm have been investigated in the last 30 years. First, we will examine the impact of personal taxes on the firm. Then we will consider other possible tax impacts on the firm's value.

PERSONAL TAXES AND THE VALUE OF THE FIRM

When MM developed their tax model, they included corporate taxes but not personal taxes on any income investors received from holding stocks or bonds. As a result, MM concluded, as shown in Equation 12.10, that the value of the levered firm is $V_L = V_U + TB$. Consequently, the gain from leverage, G_L, is simply the difference between the value of the levered and unlevered firms (which is the present value of the interest tax shield).

$$G_L = V_L - V_U = TB \qquad (12.15)$$

This gain from leverage, and consequently the value of the levered firm, increases as a firm uses more debt. Thus, the optimal capital structure employs almost 100 percent debt.

What happens to the gain from leverage and the value of a firm that uses debt when both corporate and personal taxes exist? *With the inclusion of personal taxes, the objective is to maximize income after all taxes (both corporate and personal).* Thus, the focus shifts from the firm's viewpoint to the viewpoint of investors and what they receive from investing in stocks and bonds after both corporate and personal taxes are paid. About 15 years after the original MM article, Merton Miller (1977) introduced personal taxes into the model and developed the following equation:[7]

$$V_L = V_U + \left[1 - \frac{(1 - T)(1 - T_{ps})}{(1 - T_{pb})}\right]B \qquad (12.16)$$

where

T = the corporate tax rate

T_{ps} = the personal tax rate on stock income (cash dividends and capital appreciation or loss)

T_{pb} = the personal tax rate on bond income (interest)

With this more complete and realistic tax structure, the gain from leverage is now[8]

$$G_L = \left[1 - \frac{(1 - T)(1 - T_{ps})}{(1 - T_{pb})}\right]B \qquad (12.17)$$

If the personal tax rates are zero ($T_{ps} = 0$ and $T_{pb} = 0$) *or if they are equal to one another for both stock income and bond income* ($T_{ps} = T_{pb}$), *the gain from leverage reduces to TB*. Thus, in either of these instances the benefits from the interest tax shield, once both corporate and personal taxes are considered, are the same as those provided by the MM corporate tax model.

What happens, however, if the effective personal tax rate on stock income is less than the effective tax rate on bond income? If T_{ps} is less than T_{pb}, then, other things being equal, the before-tax return on bonds must be high enough to compensate for the additional taxes that must be paid on bond income. If this were not true, investors

---

[7] Equation 12.16 is derived in Appendix 12B.

[8] The marginal personal tax rate on stock income, and on bond income, is assumed to be the same for all investors in Miller's model.

would never hold bonds. Although the firm receives a subsidy because of the tax-deductibility of the interest payment, this benefit may be offset because the interest payment has to be "grossed up" to compensate for the higher personal taxes that must be paid on the interest income. By grossing up, we mean that the interest paid by the firm is higher than it would be if personal taxes did not exist. Consequently, the gain from leverage diminishes and, in fact, will disappear completely if $(1 - T_{pb}) = (1 - T)(1 - T_{ps})$. If this happens, the results are the same as the MM model with no taxes: G_L will be zero, $V_U = V_L$, and, accordingly, the amount of debt used by a firm will not have any effect on its value. These relationships are illustrated in Figure 12.5.

Under the current Income Tax Act the corporate tax rate, T, is about 45 percent and the maximum personal tax rate is about 52 percent. If the *effective* personal tax rates on stock income and bond income are equal, then the gain from using debt is

$$G_L = \left[1 - \frac{(1 - 0.45)(1 - 0.52)}{(1 - 0.52)}\right]B = 0.45B$$

which is the same as that given by the MM model with only corporate taxes. We would conclude that there are substantial gains from using debt.

On the other hand, even with the stated marginal personal tax rate on stock income and bond income at 52 percent, there are two big tax advantages for investors who invest in stocks as opposed to bonds. First, as we will see in Chapter 14, T_{ps} is less than

Figure 12.5

Gains from Financial Leverage: MM Models (With and Without Taxes) and Miller's Model

Depending on the effective rate of personal taxes on stock versus bond income, Miller's model may indicate an intermediate value for the firm.

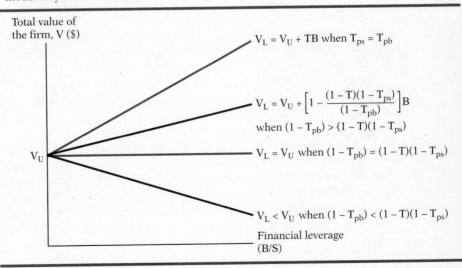

T_{pb} because of a dividend tax credit and, second, because more than 50 percent of the return from investing in stock comes from capital gains, and an investor does not have to realize the capital gain (and pay taxes on it) immediately.[9] These features of our tax laws mean that the effective tax rate on stock income is less than that for bond income. What if the effective tax rate on stock income, T_{ps}, is 30 percent? Then the gain from using debt is

$$G_L = \left[1 - \frac{(1 - 0.45)(1 - 0.30)}{(1 - 0.52)} \right] B = 0.198B$$

While still substantial, the subsidy is less than when the effective personal rates on stock and bond income are equal. Under the most likely scenario, the Miller model indicates that the value of the tax benefits to the firm is a compromise between the MM model with no taxes and the MM tax model. This effect is also illustrated in Figure 12.5.

OTHER TAX IMPACTS AND THE FIRM'S CAPITAL STRUCTURE DECISION

When arriving at his result, Miller traded off the corporate benefits of debt against the personal tax disadvantage of the resulting interest income; he did not consider any corporate disadvantages to debt, or the impact of different marginal tax rates between firms or individuals. As we will see, things become more complicated as we introduce more realistic aspects of the tax laws into the discussion.

Nondebt Tax Shields   *In the MM cases and in Miller's personal tax argument, interest is the only relevant deduction for tax purposes. However, firms also can, and do, shield themselves from paying taxes by using depreciation and depletion.* DeAngelo and Masulis (1980) recognized this and extended Miller's work by including the effects of these tax shields in addition to interest. DeAngelo and Masulis refer to tax shields arising from depreciation and depletion as "nondebt tax shields." *The existence of nondebt tax shields serves to decrease a firm's taxable income, thus causing a decline in the probability of being able to use all of the interest tax shield.* Consequently, as more debt is used, the expected value of the interest tax shield declines. The impact of nondebt tax shields reduces the incentive for the firm to use debt financing. Therefore, the firm is forced to balance the use of debt substitutes (such as depreciation and depletion) against the use of additional debt in order to be able to use all its tax deductions. Without considering any other factors, DeAngelo and Masulis demonstrated that this balancing procedure will lead to a capital structure that entails less than 100 percent debt (and more than zero debt).

Thus, the ability to utilize tax shields to the fullest extent possible is one factor that explains differences in the amount of debt employed. The ability to take full advantage of all the tax shields provided by the government is one of the primary factors affecting capital structure differences. Although the Income Tax Act allows operating losses to be carried back for three years and then forward for up to seven years, eventually firms may not be able to use the tax shields due to the lack of profitability. Thus, for a firm

---

[9] The tax rate on capital gains is 75 percent of the investor's marginal tax rate.

like American Ship Building, which has been unprofitable since 1987 and is not expected to recover soon (if ever), any additional tax shields quickly become meaningless. Likewise, XOMA, a biotech company, has been unprofitable since it went public in 1986. Tax shields are almost meaningless for firms such as these. Thus, it is not surprising that XOMA has a debt/equity ratio of about 0.01.

Bond Clienteles and Different Effective Marginal Tax Rates   In Miller's personal tax model all individual investors are assumed to have the same effective marginal tax rate. However, once uncertainty is introduced and the asymmetric nature of the tax laws for bond income is recognized, Park and Williams (1985) and Zechner (1990) both show how bondholder clienteles, based on differential personal marginal tax rates, exist for bonds that pay different effective rates of interest. The impact is that different firms will employ different amounts of debt depending on how risky the firms are and how much they have to pay at the margin for debt capital.

The Maturity Structure of Debt   Firms can also issue debt that matures at different times in the future. Thus, we could have two firms that are essentially the same except that they issue debt with different maturities. In practice, we see this happening all the time; firms that borrow from banks, for example, end up with shorter average maturities than similar firms which issue long-term bonds in the capital markets. In a multiperiod context, Lewis (1990) has shown that the firm's capital structure decision (that is, its debt/equity ratio) and its debt maturity structure (that is, the length of maturity of the debt) are intertwined. In such an environment, firms can have a variety of different mixes of capital structures and debt maturities that are consistent with maximizing the value of the firm. In addition, due to differences in the interest costs (if the term structure of interest rates is either upward- or downward-sloping), the tax implications for different debt financing strategies may not be equivalent.

With only corporate taxes we saw that the value of the firm should rise as firms substitute debt for equity financing. With personal taxes, firm value should still increase, but probably not as much, when debt is added to the capital structure. However, as more and more debt is added to the capital structure, the tax-deductibility of interest is less likely, due to the presence of depreciation, depletion, and other nondebt tax shields. In addition, different effective personal tax rates and different debt maturities lead firms to reach the point where the probability of the tax-deductibility of debt is low enough that there are no more benefits from adding extra debt. Thus, as shown in Figure 12.6, tax considerations by themselves suggest that firms will issue more than zero debt but less than 100 percent debt. The presence of taxes suggests there is some optimal level, or amount of debt, B^*, that leads to the maximization of the total market value of the firm.

Concept Review Questions

■ What is the difference between the Miller model and the Modigliani and Miller model?

■ Briefly describe how personal taxes affect the MM tax case and the MM no-tax case.

■ How does the use of tax shields and long-term debt affect corporate capital structure?

Figure 12.6

Gains from Financial Leverage: MM and Miller Models and the Impact of Nondebt Tax Shields

Once personal taxes and nondebt tax shields (such as depreciation and depletion) are considered, the gains from using financial leverage may be less than suggested by the MM tax case. An optimal capital structure, B^*/S, may exist at which the marginal benefits of additional debt are exactly offset by tax consequences of additional debt.

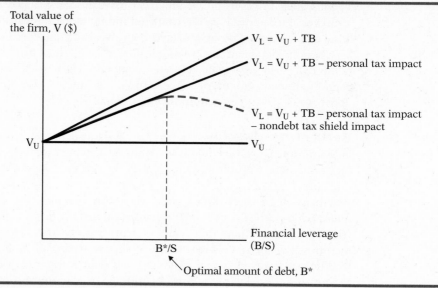

SETTING A FIRM'S DEBT/EQUITY RATIO

It should be clear by now that there is no single reason that we see different capital structures among industries and firms. We cannot make a blanket statement that firms should have a debt/equity ratio of 0.50 or 1.00, for example. But we can provide tools, guidelines, and some thoughts on planning ahead. The goal of the firm when determining its debt/equity ratio is to determine the firm's **debt capacity**. Knowing this will assist in maximizing the firm's value. By debt capacity, we mean the amount of debt, preferred stock, and leases a firm can effectively carry and service.

TOOLS FOR DIGGING

Some tools that can be employed to explore the capital structure issue include the following:

1. **EPS-EBIT ANALYSIS.** To employ **EPS-EBIT analysis**, we begin with the firm's estimated EBIT. Consider the example of Seaboard Industries, which currently has $2 million of 10 percent debt outstanding and 1 million shares of common stock with a market price of $20 each. Seaboard needs to raise

$10 million in new capital and has two alternatives. The first involves issuing 500,000 shares of additional common stock at $20 per share. The second would use debt financing to raise the $10 million. The debt would carry a coupon interest rate of 12 percent. After the new investment, Seaboard's EBIT is $6 million. As shown below, at the $6 million EBIT, Seaboard's EPS would be $2.32 with common stock financing or $2.76 with debt financing.

	Common Stock Financing (in millions)	Debt Financing (in millions)
EBIT	$6.00	$6.00
Interest	0.20	1.40[a]
EBT	5.80	4.60
Taxes (40%)	2.32	1.84
EAT	$3.48	$2.76
Number of shares of common stock (millions of shares)	1.50	1.00
EPS	$2.32	$2.76

[a] $200,000 on existing debt plus $1,200,000 interest on new debt.

Instead of simply calculating EPS, it is generally helpful to consider what happens to EPS at various EBIT levels. We can also calculate the crossover EBIT, EBIT*, which is the EBIT level that causes both financing alternatives to produce the same EPS, as follows:

$$\frac{(EBIT^* - I_1)(1 - T) - D_{ps1}}{N_1} = \frac{(EBIT^* - I_2)(1 - T) - D_{ps2}}{N_2} \qquad (12.18)$$

where

$EBIT^*$ = the unknown crossover point in EBIT

I_1, I_2 = the annual total interest charges under the two financing plans

T = the firm's marginal tax rate

N_1, N_2 = the number of shares of common stock outstanding under the two plans

D_{ps1}, D_{ps2} = the dollar amount of cash dividends on preferred stock under the two plans

EPS–EBIT analysis, although ignoring risk and the value of the firm, does provide some information on the impact of alternative financing plans on the firm's EPS.

2. COVERAGE RATIOS.   Most firms and analysts calculate various coverage ratios to ascertain how the firm's EBIT relates to the cash outflows resulting from the use of fixed-cost financing. These ratios range from the times interest earned and fixed charges coverage ratios discussed in Chapter 25 to more complicated ratios that take into account principal repayments, sinking fund payments, and/or cash dividends on preferred stock. The basic intent of all these ratios is to ascertain how safe the firm is in terms of meeting its fixed-cost financing charges.

3. LENDER STANDARDS.   Often a firm's lenders impose certain standards of financial performance. A bank loan or debt issue may contain financial performance standards that have to be met before assets can be sold, cash dividends paid, and so on. In addition, many larger firms tie their target capital structure decision to the bond rating the firm desires to maintain. For example, a firm may decide it always wants to be able to issue reasonable amounts of new debt with an A bond rating. Accordingly, the capital structure and other financial affairs are maintained at a level that achieves this result.

4. CASH FLOW ANALYSIS.   A final approach is to investigate what happens to the ability of the firm to survive a severe recession. This involves a scenario analysis, in which the firm focuses on the cash flow consequences under alternative, assumed future states of the economy.

All these tools assist managers in determining the firm's appropriate, or target, capital structure.

GUIDELINES FOR SETTING DEBT/EQUITY RATIOS

Although we have examined a wide variety of issues and factors related to a firm's capital structure decision, the primary results can be stated in a very straightforward way: *In making the capital structure decision, focus first and foremost on taxes, risk, and financial slack.*

1. TAXES.   For firms in a taxpaying position, an increase in the amount of debt reduces the taxes paid by the firm. Of course, it is not just whether the firm is in a taxpaying position that is important; it is also whether it is expected to remain in a taxpaying position. Firms with less assurance of being able to benefit from the various tax shields will use less debt.

2. RISK.   With or without bankruptcy, financial distress is costly. Although many factors affect risk, financial distress is most likely in firms that have high business risk. Business risk is often related to the type of assets employed. Where intangible assets play a major role, the value of the assets may erode quickly. Typically, firms that employ a lot of "brain power" or other intangible assets use less debt than do those whose assets have a ready secondary market. Also, competition and the nature of the industry often affect the firm's risk.

3. FINANCIAL SLACK.   In the long run, a firm's value depends first and foremost on the investment and operating decisions its managers make. These have the potential to add more value to the firm than its financing decisions. Therefore, firms want a certain amount of financial slack so they can react to new positive-NPV opportunities. This is one of the reasons that high-growth firms tend to use less debt.

PLANNING AHEAD

The firm's capital structure decisions cannot be made in a vacuum. They have to be part of the firm's complete financial plan, which takes into account its investment opportunities, operating strategy, dividend policy, and so forth.

In Chapter 26 we examine cash budgets and pro forma accounting statements. Although they do not tell you where to raise funds, they do provide insight into the anticipated amount and timing of the needs or surpluses. The use of sensitivity or scenario analysis is just as helpful when planning a firm's capital structure as it is for analyzing long-term investment decisions or the firm's cash budget. In addition, simulation is also useful because it allows the whole probability distribution of financial consequences to be examined. Remember that planning ahead, and having some financial slack, is important when considering how much debt the firm should have.

Concept Review Questions

- Briefly describe some methods used to determine a firm's debt capacity.
- What are three key variables that affect a firm's capital structure?

KEY POINTS

- Although the impact of capital structure changes on EPS is important, focus must be placed on the impact that different capital structures have on firm value.
- In the absence of taxes and other financial market imperfections, the choice of a capital structure is "a mere detail." The value of the firm is a function of the investment decisions it makes, not its financing decisions.
- Once corporate taxes are introduced, the firm can increase its total value and reduce its opportunity cost of capital by replacing equity financing with debt financing.
- If the effective personal tax rate on stock income is less than the effective personal tax rate on bond income, there is less advantage to the firm from using debt financing than implied by the MM tax case.
- The presence of nondebt tax shields, bond clienteles with different effective tax rates, and different maturity structures of debt suggests that firms will not employ as much debt as indicated by the MM tax case.
- The key variables that affect the capital structure choice are the ability to take advantage of tax shields, risk differences related to the assets employed by the firm and its competition, and the need to maintain financial slack due to growth opportunities.

QUESTIONS

12.1 Explain what causes business risk. What do you believe the relative business risk of the following would be: grocery stores, jewellers, farm equipment manufacturers, airlines? Why?

12.2 Financial leverage generally has two effects on earnings per share. Name these two effects and then explain why they occur.

12.3 In a world of no corporate taxes, the capital structure is a "mere detail." Explain why and under what conditions this is so.

12.4 "Investment decisions are all that are relevant; financing decisions have no significant impact on the value of the firm." Evaluate this statement.

12.5 Assume the MM no-tax model holds. A firm exists that has 20 percent of its capital structure in the form of debt which has a cost of 6 percent. Now the firm moves to 60 percent debt in its capital structure, again with a cost of 6 percent. What two effects occur as the firm moves from 20 percent debt to 60 percent debt? How do these effects counterbalance each other?

12.6   What happens when corporate taxes are introduced into the capital structure decision? Other things being equal, what should the firm do?

12.7   Compare the Modigliani and Miller no-tax case with the MM tax case. What similarities and differences are there between the two cases? What happens to the overall cost of capital under the no-tax case? Under the tax case? What limit does it approach in the tax case? What are the unlevered and levered costs of equity capital under the no-tax case? Under the tax case?

12.8   Taxes come in many shapes and forms. Explain how corporate taxes affect the capital structure decision. Then incorporate personal taxes into the discussion. What is the impact of nondebt tax shields on the interest tax shield? What other tax-based considerations also may come into play that affect a firm's capital structure decision?

12.9   Explain Miller's personal tax model. Under what circumstances does it lead to the same conclusion as MM without corporate taxes? With corporate taxes?

12.10   What key points should guide the firm when it plans its capital structure?

CONCEPT REVIEW PROBLEMS

See Appendix A for solutions.

CR12.1   Bristol Brush operates without debt and has EBIT of $4.5 million and an opportunity cost of capital of 15 percent.
a.   If the firm's earnings have a zero growth rate and all the MM assumptions are met, including no corporate taxes, what is the market value of the firm?
b.   Now assume Bristol issues $15 million in perpetual 10 percent bonds and uses the $15 million to retire equity in the firm. What are the cost of equity, the opportunity cost of capital, and the total value of the newly leveraged firm? Was Bristol's management able to increase the value of the firm by financing with cheaper debt?

CR12.2   Now assume that all the facts given in CR12.1 continue to hold, except Bristol Brush now has a corporate tax rate of 40 percent. What are the value of the firm, the cost of equity, and the opportunity cost of capital for the firm: **(a)** before issuing debt, and **(b)** after issuing debt under the MM tax case?

CR12.3   Sandra is analyzing two firms—Unleveraged Partners and Leveraged Partners. Unleveraged Partners is totally financed with equity, whereas Leveraged Partners believes the value of the firm can be increased with the use of debt and has $60 million of 8 percent bonds outstanding. The cost of equity for Unleveraged Partners is 12 percent. Both firms have EBIT of $30 million and a corporate tax rate of 40 percent. The marginal personal tax rate for all individuals is 48 percent on debt income and 35 percent on equity income.
a.   Employing the Miller model, what is the value of each firm? Is there a gain from the use of debt?
b.   Now assume Parliament passes a law instituting a flat tax rate of 30 percent for all corporate and individual income. What is the value of each firm? Is there a change in the gain from the use of debt?

CR12.4   Wafer Board Industries currently has $10 million of 8 percent debt outstanding and 500,000 shares of common stock. The firm needs $1 million to finance an expansion project and can raise the funds by issuing debt at 8 percent or selling stock at $25 per share. The tax rate is 36 percent, and after the expansion EBIT will be $3,750,000.

a. What is the EPS under each financing option?
b. What is the crossover EBIT at which the decision to finance with debt or equity will not affect the firm's EPS?

PROBLEMS

12.1 Two firms, A and B, have the following probability distributions of EBIT:

Probabilities	0.30	0.40	0.30
A's EBIT	$ 20,000	$ 40,000	$ 60,000
B's EBIT	$200,000	$280,000	$360,000

Which firm has more business risk? Why?

12.2 Provincial Systems is currently in the process of a substantial expansion programme. The $3.5 million programme will be financed by a stock issue (of 100,000 shares) or with a new 10 percent coupon rate bond issue. The firm's preexpansion income statement (in millions of dollars) is

Sales	$5.00
Operating costs	3.50
EBIT	1.50
Interest	0.25
EBT	1.25
Taxes (36%)	0.45
EAT	$0.80
EPS (200,000 shares)	$4.00 per share

After the expansion, the EBIT is expected to be $1.5, $2.5, or $3.5 million, with associated probabilities of 0.30, 0.40, and 0.30.
a. Determine the EPS for both plans with each different probability.
b. Calculate the expected EPS, the standard deviation, and the coefficient of variation of EPS for each plan.
c. Which plan has more risk? Explain.

12.3 Paul will invest $50,000 in a stock by borrowing (B) $30,000 and putting up $20,000 (S) himself. The cost of debt, k_b, is 8 percent, and there are no taxes. Paul expects a return, k_s^L, of 17 percent. What would Paul's return be without the use of financial leverage?

12.4 Scott Power is an electric utility that operates in a taxless world. It currently has $50 million in EBIT, $200 million in 5 percent coupon rate bonds outstanding, and $400 million in stock outstanding.
a. Determine the firm's yearly interest and earnings, and the firm's cost of equity capital, k_s^L. What is the opportunity cost of capital?

b. Scott has decided to issue $100 million in stock and use the proceeds to buy back $100 million in bonds. What must the new cost of equity capital be according to Modigliani and Miller? What is the firm's overall opportunity cost of capital?

12.5 Assume that the MM tax case holds. The market value of a firm that has $300,000 in debt is $1,200,000. The interest rate on debt is 12 percent, and the marginal corporate tax rate is 30 percent. If the firm were all-equity-financed, the required return (or cost of equity capital) would be 18 percent.
a. What is the firm's EBIT?
b. What would the market value be if the firm is all-equity-financed?

12.6 Rollins International is an all-equity firm that generates earnings before interest and taxes, EBIT, of $3 million per year. The cost of equity capital, k_s^U, is 16 percent, and its marginal tax rate, T, is 35 percent.
a. What is the market value of Rollins International?
b. If Rollins now issues $4 million of debt, what is the market value of the firm? The market value of the firm's stock?
c. What assumptions are you making in order to come up with your answers in (b)?

12.7 Assume that the MM tax case holds. A firm with EBIT of $2 million has a tax rate of 40 percent. Its cost of debt is 10 percent, it pays $500,000 per year in interest, and its unlevered cost of equity capital is 15 percent.
a. What is the market value of the firm?
b. What is its levered cost of equity?

12.8 Goering Brothers is an unlevered firm with an EBIT of $4 million. Its tax rate is 40 percent, and the opportunity cost of equity capital is 15 percent. Assume that the MM tax case holds and that Goering is fairly valued.
a. What is the market value of Goering?
b. Suppose that Goering now issues $10 million of 8 percent bonds. What is the new market value of Goering?
c. Assume that there are two firms, Y and Z, that are identical in all respects to the unlevered Goering and the levered Goering, respectively. Explain what will happen if the current market value of Y is $14 million, while that of Z is $23 million.

12.9 Laurentian Industries is presently an all-common-stock-financed firm, with 8,000 shares of common stock outstanding and a tax rate of 35 percent. Assume the MM tax case holds. The firm is evaluating two different financing plans, as follows:

Common Stock	Debt
2,000 additional shares	$60,000 at an 8% coupon rate
$k_s^U = 10\%$	$k_s^L = 10.2727\%$
EBIT = $50,000	EBIT = $50,000

a. If common stock is employed, what is (1) the total stock value, S, (2) earnings per share, EPS, (3) the market price per share, P_0, (4) total value of the firm, V, and (5) the firm's overall opportunity cost of capital?
b. Rework (a), assuming that debt financing is employed.
c. Explain why, under the given circumstances, the firm may be able to lower its opportunity cost of capital and raise the total value of the firm by employing debt financing.

12.10   Debt-Free Ltd. is an unlevered firm that has EBIT of $2 million and a required rate of return of 10 percent. The firm is contemplating issuing $4 million of 10 percent coupon bonds. The firm has a corporate tax rate of 50 percent and has estimated that the tax rates for its investors are 30 percent on stock income and 40 percent on bond income. Assume that Miller's personal tax case holds.

a. If only corporate taxes exist, what is the new total value of the firm and the gain from leverage?

b. With both corporate and personal taxes, what is the gain from leverage and the total value of the firm if it issues the debt?

c. Why is the gain from leverage and the total value of the firm less in (b) than in (a)?

12.11   A firm has long-term debt outstanding with a market value of $100,000. The corporate tax rate is 40 percent. Assume that Miller's personal tax case holds.

a. If there are no personal taxes, what is the value of the interest tax shield?

b. Now assume that personal taxes exist and the tax rate on bond income is twice the tax rate on stock income. At what personal tax rate on stock income does the advantage of debt financing vanish?

c. If the actual personal tax rate on stock income is 25 percent, and the relationship between personal taxes on stock and bond income from (b) still exists, what does this imply about the optimal level of debt for the firm?

12.12   Benefit Trust has $20 million of debt outstanding. The firm has a corporate tax rate of 45 percent. A survey by its investment banker has revealed that the marginal tax rate of the firm's common shareholders (average of dividends and capital gains) is 25 percent, whereas the marginal tax rate on bond income is 35 percent.

a. What is the firm's gain from using the $20 million of debt?

b. What would the gain to the firm be if all of its investors paid no taxes?

12.13   Harrison Appliances is considering raising $5 million by selling 200,000 shares of stock or by issuing 8 percent coupon rate bonds at par. There are presently 100,000 shares of common stock outstanding, the tax rate is 35 percent, and Harrison already pays $100,000 in interest before any new financing.

a. What is the crossover point where the EPS will be the same for either financing plan?

b. If you are told there is a 50 percent chance EBIT will be $600,000, and a 50 percent chance it will be $1,000,000, which plan would you recommend? Why?

12.14   Outboard Equipment is an all-equity-financed firm with the following financial statements:

Balance Sheet		Income Statement	
Total assets	$1,000,000	Sales	$2,500,000
		Operating costs	2,100,000
Common stock (50,000		EBIT=EBT (16%	
outstanding)	$ 250,000	of sales)	400,000
Retained earnings	750,000	Taxes (40%)	160,000
Total equity	$1,000,000	EAT	$ 240,000

Outboard Equipment is planning to raise $400,000 through the sale of common stock at $50 per share or through the issuance of debt with a 10 percent coupon rate. Once the expansion is completed, sales are expected to increase to $3,000,000; EBIT should be the same percentage of sales at this new level.

a. Determine Outboard Equipment's present EPS.
b. What is the crossover EBIT between the two financing plans?
c. Determine the EPS under the two plans.

12.15 A firm is considering two different financing plans. Under plan I the interest is $8,000 and there are 1,000 shares of common stock outstanding. Under plan II the interest is $2,000. If the crossover EBIT (i.e., EBIT*) is $20,000 and the tax rate is 30 percent, how many shares of common stock are outstanding for plan II?

12.16 Joy Regulator currently has 100,000 shares of common stock outstanding with a market price of $60 per share. It also has $2 million (par value) in 6 percent coupon rate bonds outstanding. The firm is considering a $3 million expansion programme that can be financed employing either (1) preferred stock sold at par with a 7 percent cash dividend, or (2) half common stock (sold at $60 per share) and half 8 percent coupon rate bonds (sold at par). The tax rate is 40 percent.

a. What is the indifferent EBIT between the two plans?
b. If EBIT is expected to be $1,000,000 after the financing, what is the EPS under the two plans?
c. If the marginal tax rate is 20 percent, what are your answers to (a) and (b)?

12.17 **Mini Case** Port Howard Products is presently an all-equity firm. It needs to raise $2,500,000 in additional funds. After raising the funds it expects EBIT to be $600,000. The firm's unlevered cost of equity capital, k_s^U, is 12 percent, and its before-tax cost of debt, k_b, is 8 percent.

a. If there are no corporate taxes, under MM what is the value of Port Howard Products if it employs common stock to raise the needed funds? Alternatively, what happens to k_s and the value of the firm if it employs debt to raise the needed funds? What happens to its opportunity cost of capital? What is the fundamental determinant of the value of the firm in the MM no-tax case?
b. Now assume that the corporate tax rate is 35 percent.
   1. What is the all-equity value of Port Howard Products?
   2. What is its value if $2,500,000 in debt is employed? What is the new k_s^l? The new opportunity cost of capital?
   3. What if everything is as in (2) except that now $4,000,000 in debt is employed?
c. So far the impact of personal tax has been ignored.
   1. What is Miller's argument concerning the impact of personal taxes?
   2. If the firm issues the $2,500,000 in debt, and the personal tax rates on debt and equity are both 40 percent, what is the value of Port Howard Products?
   3. What if everything is as in (c2) except now the personal tax rate on stock is 20 percent?
   4. Under what conditions, even after considering personal taxes, do we arrive at the same conclusion implied by the MM no-tax case? If T is 25 percent, and T_{pb} is 40 percent, what would the personal tax rate on stock, T_{ps}, have to be for the value of the firm to be independent of the firm's capital structure?

REFERENCES

BROUS, PETER A., and OMESH KINI. "The Valuation Effects of Equity Issues and the Level of Institutional Ownership: Evidence from Analysts' Earnings Forecasts." *Financial Management* 23 (Spring 1994): 33–46.

DAVIS, ALFRED H. R. "The Corporate Use of Debt Substitutes in Canada: A Test of Competing Versions of the Substitution Hypothesis." *Canadian Journal of Administrative Sciences* 11 (March 1994): 105–115.

———. "Effective Tax Rates as Determinants of Canadian Capital Structure." *Financial Management* 16 (Autumn 1987): 22–28.

DEANGELO, HARRY, and RONALD W. MASULIS. "Optimal Capital Structure Under Corporate and Personal Taxation." *Journal of Financial Economics* 8 (March 1980): 3–30.

EMERY, DOUGLAS R., and ADAM K. GEHR, JR. "Tax Options, Capital Structure, and Miller Equilibrium: A Numerical Illustration." *Financial Management* 17 (Summer 1988): 30–40.

HARRIS, MILTON, and ARTHUR RAVIV. "The Theory of Capital Structure." *Journal of Finance* 46 (March 1991): 297–355.

LEWIS, CRAIG M. "A Multiperiod Theory of Corporate Financial Policy under Taxation." *Journal of Financial and Quantitative Analysis* 25 (March 1990): 25–43.

MASULIS, RONALD W. *The Debt/Equity Choice.* Cambridge, Mass.: Ballinger, 1988.

MILLER, MERTON H. "Debt and Taxes." *Journal of Finance* 32 (May 1977): 261–275.

MODIGLIANI, FRANCO, and MERTON H. MILLER. "Corporate Income Taxes and the Cost of Capital: A Correction." *American Economic Review* 53 (June 1963): 433–443.

———. "The Cost of Capital, Corporation Finance, and the Theory of Investment." *American Economic Review* 48 (June 1958): 261–297.

MYERS, STEWART C. "Determinants of Corporate Borrowing." *Journal of Financial Economics* 5 (November 1977): 147–175.

PARK, SANG YONG, and JOSEPH WILLIAMS. "Taxes, Capital Structure, and Bondholder Clienteles." *Journal of Business* 58 (April 1985): 203–224.

PINEGAR, J. MICHAEL, and LISA WILBRICHT. "What Managers Think of Capital Structure Theory: A Survey." *Financial Management* 18 (Winter 1989): 82–91.

ZECHNER, JOSEF. "Tax Clienteles and Optimal Capital Structure under Uncertainty." *Journal of Business* 63 (October 1990): 465–491.

APPENDIX

12A

Operating, Financial, and Total Leverage

In Chapter 12 the topic of operating leverage was mentioned as one of the elements affecting business risk. Financial leverage was also discussed at length as we considered the firm's capital structure. The concepts of operating leverage and financial leverage can both be carried further.

OPERATING LEVERAGE

Operating leverage arises if a firm has fixed operating costs for such things as labour, rent, executive salaries, and the like. If a firm has only variable operating expenses, by definition it has no operating leverage. Operating leverage is the responsiveness of the firm's earnings before interest and taxes (EBIT) to fluctuations in sales. To understand operating leverage, let us continue with the example of Consolidated National from the chapter. In Table 12A.1, sales and other data are given for Consolidated. The present sales level is $32,000. This is the base level of sales at time period t = 0. Also shown are two possible sales levels for next year. Case 1 is an $8,000 decrease in sales; Case 2 represents an $8,000 increase. The question to be examined is this: How does EBIT respond to a 25 percent change in Consolidated's sales?

The 25 percent change in sales is determined as follows:

$$\text{percentage change in sales} = \frac{\$40,000 - \$32,000}{\$32,000} = \frac{\$8,000}{\$32,000} = 0.25 = 25\%$$

The percentage change in EBIT can be determined in a similar manner:

$$\text{percentage change in EBIT} = \frac{\$14,000 - \$10,000}{\$10,000} = \frac{\$4,000}{\$10,000} = 0.40 = 40\%$$

As Consolidated's sales change 25 percent, its EBIT changes by 40 percent. This magnification in the percentage change in EBIT because of a given percentage change in sales is called operating leverage. The **degree of operating leverage (DOL)** is defined as

$$\begin{aligned}\text{degree of operating leverage} \atop \text{from base level sales} = \text{DOL} &= \frac{\text{percentage change in EBIT}}{\text{percentage change in sales}} \\ &= \frac{\Delta\text{EBIT}/\text{EBIT}}{\Delta\text{sales}/\text{sales}}\end{aligned} \qquad (12A.1)$$

Table 12A.1

Base Level and Forecasted Sales and EBIT for Consolidated National

Operating leverage arises from the magnification of the fluctuation in sales, leading to a larger change in EBIT because of fixed operating costs.

	Case 1: Decrease	Case 2: Increase	
	Forecasted Sales, t + 1	Base Level Sales, t = 0	Forecasted Sales, t + 1
	−25%	+25%	
Sales	$24,000	$32,000	$40,000
Variable operating costs	12,000	16,000	20,000
Revenue before fixed operating costs	12,000	16,000	20,000
Fixed operating costs	6,000	6,000	6,000
EBIT	$6,000	$10,000	$14,000
	−40%	+40%	

Using Equation 12A.1, we find the degree of operating leverage for Consolidated:

$$DOL_{\$32,000} = \frac{40\%}{25\%} = 1.6 \text{ times}$$

Thus, from the base sales of $32,000, a given percentage change in sales leads to a percentage change in EBIT that is 1.6 times as large.

A second way to determine the degree of operating leverage at any base level of sales is

$$\frac{\text{degree of operating leverage}}{\text{from base level sales}} = DOL = \frac{\text{sales} - \text{variable cost}}{\text{EBIT}} \qquad (12A.2)$$

Using $32,000 as our base level of sales again, employing Equation 12A.2 and the data from Table 12A.1, DOL is

$$DOL_{\$32,000} = \frac{\$32,000 - \$16,000}{\$10,000} = \frac{\$16,000}{\$10,000} = 1.6 \text{ times}$$

Using either Equation 12A.1 or 12A.2, the degree of operating leverage is 1.6.

As the firm's sales increase, and assuming everything else stays constant, the degree of operating leverage declines, as shown:

Sales	Degree of Operating Leverage[a]
$12,000 or below	Undefined
18,000	3.00
24,000	2.00
32,000	1.60
40,000	1.43
46,000	1.35

[a] Calculated with Equation 12A.2.

Thus, as sales increase, there are lower percentage fluctuations in EBIT. However, as long as there are some fixed operating expenses, the concept of operating leverage indicates that percentage changes in EBIT will exceed percentage changes in sales.

FINANCIAL LEVERAGE

Financial leverage is the responsiveness of the firm's earnings per share to fluctuations in EBIT. Using data from Table 12.2, Table 12A.2 shows the impact of changes in Consolidated's EBIT on the reported EPS. When no debt is used, we see that a 40 percent change in EBIT leads to exactly a 40 percent change in EPS. However, with 20 percent of the capital structure in debt, a 40 percent change in EBIT leads to a 42.55 percent change in EPS. Finally, with 40 percent debt, a 40 percent change in EBIT leads to a 45.45 percent change in EPS. The magnification in EPS under capital structures B and C is caused by financial leverage.

Like the degree of operating leverage, the **degree of financial leverage** (DFL) can be calculated. Thus, DFL is

$$\text{degree of financial leverage from base level EBIT} = \text{DFL} = \frac{\text{percentage change in EPS}}{\text{percentage change in EBIT}} \qquad (12A.3)$$

$$= \frac{\Delta \text{EPS}/\text{EPS}}{\Delta \text{EBIT}/\text{EBIT}}$$

Using this equation and the information from Table 12A.2, the degree of financial leverage when EBIT is $10,000 and capital structure C (which has 40 percent debt) is employed is

$$\text{DEL}_{\$10,000} = \frac{45.45\%}{40\%} = 1.14 \text{ times}$$

From a base of $10,000 EBIT, a given percentage change in EBIT will bring about a percentage change in EPS that is 1.14 times as large. A second way to determine the degree of financial leverage is this:

$$\frac{\text{degree of financial leverage}}{\text{from base level EBIT}} = \text{DFL} = \frac{\text{EBIT}}{\text{EBIT} - \text{interest}} \qquad (12\text{A}.4)$$

For Consolidated, we can again calculate its degree of financial leverage

$$\text{DFL}_{\$10,000} = \frac{\$10,000}{\$10,000 - \$1,200} = \frac{\$10,000}{\$8,800} = 1.14 \text{ times}$$

which is the same as determined previously from Equation 12A.3.

Table 12A.2

Impact of Three Different Capital Structures on Consolidated National's Earnings per Share

The base case remains $32,000 in sales, which leads to EBIT of $10,000, as shown in Table 12A.1. All percentages are measured relative to this base.

	EBIT	Earnings per Share
Capital Structure A (zero debt)		
−40%	$ 6,000	$0.72	−40%
	10,000	1.20	
+40%	14,000	1.68	+40%
Capital Structure B (20% debt)		
−40%	$ 6,000	$0.81	−42.55%
	10,000	1.41	
+40%	14,000	2.01	+42.55%
Capital Structure C (40% debt)		
−40%	$ 6,000	$0.96	−45.45%
	10,000	1.76	
+40%	14,000	2.56	+45.45%

COMBINING OPERATING AND FINANCIAL LEVERAGE

We have seen that operating leverage causes a change in the volume of sales to have a magnified effect on the firm's EBIT. Likewise, financial leverage causes a change in the firm's EBIT to have a magnified effect on the firm's EPS. When operating and financial leverage are combined, even small changes in the level of sales can have a large impact on EPS, as shown in Table 12A.3. A 25 percent increase (decrease) in sales leads to a 45.45 percent increase (decrease) in EPS.

The **degree of combined leverage** (DCL) can be determined by using any one of the following equations:

$$\text{degree of combined leverage from base level sales} = \text{DCL} = \frac{\text{percentage change in EPS}}{\text{percentage change in sales}} \qquad (12A.5)$$

$$= \frac{\Delta \text{EPS}/\text{EPS}}{\Delta \text{sales}/\text{sales}}$$

Table 12A.3

Combined Leverage Effects for Consolidated National

Operating leverage arises from fixed costs of operation; financial leverage arises from fixed costs associated with financing. Combining both produces potentially wide swings in EPS as sales volume changes.

	Base Level Sales, t = 0	Forecasted Sales, t + 1		
	+25%			
Sales	$32,000	$40,000		
Less: Variable costs	16,000	20,000		
Revenues before fixed costs	16,000	20,000	DOL = $\frac{40\%}{25\%}$	
Less: Fixed costs	6,000	6,000		
EBIT	$10,000	$14,000	= 1.6 times	DCL = $\frac{45.5\%}{25\%}$
	+40%			= 1.82
Less: Interest	1,200	1,200		
EBT	8,800	12,800		
Less: Taxes (40%)	3,520	5,120	DFL = $\frac{45.45\%}{40\%}$	or
EAT	$ 5,280	$ 7,680		1.6 × 1.14
Earnings per share	$5,280/3,000 = $1.76	$7,680/3,000 = $2.56	= 1.14 times	= 1.82
	+45.45%			

or

$$DCL = \frac{sales - variable\ cost}{EBIT - interest} \qquad (12A.6)$$

or

$$DCL = (DOL)(DFL) \qquad (12A.7)$$

Using Equation 12A.6 at sales of $32,000 and capital structure C, we find the DCL to be

$$DCL_{\$32,000} = \frac{\$32,000 - \$16,000}{\$10,000 - \$1,200} = \frac{\$16,000}{\$8,800} = 1.82\ times$$

Similarly, using Equation 12A.7, we find the DCL to be

$$DCL = (1.6)(1.14) = 1.82\ times$$

This interrelationship between operating and financial leverage can be depicted as in Figure 12A.1. The triangle represents the magnification of sales fluctuations and the effect they have on both EBIT and EPS when there are both fixed operating costs and fixed financing costs.

Figure 12A.1

Graphic Depiction of the Relationship Between Operating and Financial Leverage

Firms like those in the airlines industry have both high operating and high financial leverage. As the sales, or load, factor changes, EPS fluctuates widely.

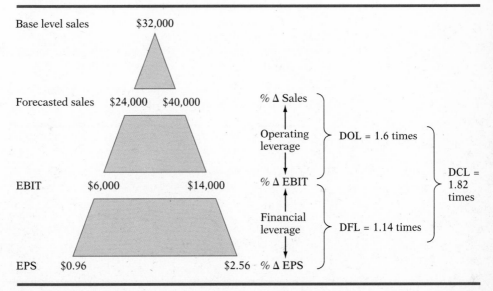

PROBLEMS

12A.1   Birch Industries produces various wood products. Its average selling price is $10 per unit. The variable cost is $6 per unit, and total fixed costs are $60,000.
a.   What would the firm's EBIT be if the number of units sold were 20,000, 30,000, or 40,000?
b.   Find the degree of operating leverage for each of the three production and sales levels given in (a).
c.   What conclusion can we draw about the degree of operating leverage as the sales increase?

12A.2   Toronto Press is a specialized publisher of high-quality books. Its EBIT is $3 million, interest is $500,000, the tax rate is 35 percent, and there are 1 million shares of common stock outstanding.
a.   What is Toronto's EPS?
b.   What is its degree of financial leverage?
c.   If EBIT increases by 50 percent, what are the absolute and percentage changes in EPS?
d.   Does the percentage change from (c) divided by the percentage change in EBIT of 50 percent (or 0.50) give you the answer as calculated in (b)? Explain why that outcome occurs.

12A.3   Tallman Brothers has the following income statement (in millions of dollars):

Sales	$50
Variable operating costs	24
Revenues before fixed operating costs	26
Fixed operating costs	13
EBIT	13
Interest	3
EBT	10
Taxes (30%)	3
EAT	$ 7

a.   At this level of sales, what is Tallman's degree of operating leverage?
b.   What is the degree of financial leverage?
c.   What is the degree of combined leverage?
d.   If sales should increase by 20 percent, by what percentage would earnings after tax increase?
e.   If sales increase by 20 percent, what is the new dollar level of EAT?

12A.4   British Replications Ltd. makes metal replicas of famous British buildings, people, and the like. Its current income statement (in millions of dollars) is

Sales	$20.0
Variable operating costs	8.0
Revenue before fixed operating costs	12.0
Fixed operating costs	4.0
EBIT	8.0
Interest	2.0
EBT	6.0
Taxes (40%)	2.4
EAT	$3.6

Earnings per share (1 million shares) are $3.60

a. Calculate the following: (1) Degree of operating leverage, (2) degree of financial leverage, (3) degree of combined leverage.

b. British Replications is considering changing to a new production process. Highly capital-intensive, the new process will double fixed costs to $8 million while lowering variable costs to $4 million at the current level of sales. If the investment required is financed by bonds, interest will increase by $600,000. If common stock is employed, 100,000 new shares will be issued. If sales remain constant, calculate the following for each financing method: (1) Earnings per share, (2) degree of combined leverage.

c. If we expected sales to increase substantially, which plan would we favour if we are interested in maximizing EPS?

APPENDIX 12B

Value of the Levered Firm with Corporate and Personal Taxes

In the chapter we saw how to value the levered firm: first, for the MM model where only corporate taxes are considered, and second for Miller's model where both corporate and personal taxes are included. In this appendix, we will see how two of the equations necessary for those calculations are derived.

VALUE OF THE LEVERED FIRM WITH CORPORATE TAXES

To understand how Equation 12.10 comes about, we return to the example of True North Industries. True North has a tax rate of 30 percent, EBIT of $100,000, and $400,000 of 6 percent coupon rate bonds outstanding. Its condensed income statement is

EBIT	$100,000
Interest ($k_b B$)	24,000
EBT	76,000
Taxes (30%)	22,800
EAT	$ 53,200

In this situation the payment to *all* investors of the levered firm is made up of two components: the \$53,200 paid to shareholders, which may be represented as $(\text{EBIT} - k_b B)(1 - T)$, and the \$24,000 [i.e., (\$400,000)(0.06)] in interest, $k_b B$, paid to bondholders. Therefore, the payment to all investors of the levered firm is

$$\text{payment to all investors}_L = (\text{EBIT} - k_b B)(1 - T) + k_b B$$

which may be rearranged to read

$$\text{payment to all investors}_L = \text{EBIT}(1 - T) + Tk_b B \qquad (12B.1)$$

To find the value of the levered firm, V_L, we determine the present value of Equation 12B.1. Note that the first term on the right-hand side of Equation 12B.1, $\text{EBIT}(1 - T)$, is identical to Equation 12.8. This is the payment made to the investors of the unlevered firm and, therefore, is discounted at the required return for the unlevered firm, k_s^U, as we did in Equation 12.9. The second term on the right-hand side of Equation 12B.1 represents the tax shield, or subsidy, provided by the interest payment on debt. Because all debt is assumed to be riskless in the Modigliani–Miller model, and assuming it is perpetual, the present value of the debt tax shield can be found by dividing it by k_b. The value of the levered firm is

$$V_L = \frac{\text{EBIT}(1 - T)}{k_s^U} + \frac{Tk_b B}{k_b} \qquad (12B.2)$$

Because the first term on the right-hand side is identical to Equation 12.9, which is the value of the unlevered firm, and the k_b's cancel in the second term, Equation 12B.2 can be rewritten as

$$V_L = V_U + TB \qquad (12B.3)$$

which is Equation 12.10, the value of the levered firm according to the MM corporate tax model.

VALUE OF THE LEVERED FIRM WITH CORPORATE AND PERSONAL TAXES

A similar approach can be used to find the value of the levered firm for Miller's model. In addition to a corporate tax rate, T, Miller's model also includes a personal tax rate on stock income, T_{ps}, which represents a weighted average of the personal tax rate on dividend and capital gains income and a personal tax rate on bond income, T_{pb}.

The payments to all investors in the levered firm are made up of two parts, and may be written as follows:

$\text{payment to all investors}_L$

$$= (\text{EBIT} - k_b B)(1 - T)(1 - T_{ps}) + k_b B(1 - T_{pb}) \qquad (12B.4)$$

where the first term is equal to the payment received by shareholders after both corporate and personal taxes have been deducted, and the second term is the after-personal-tax interest payment that the bondholders receive. Equation 12B.4 can be rearranged as follows:

payment to all investors$_L$

$$= \text{EBIT}(1 - T)(1 - T_{ps}) - k_b B(1 - T)(1 - T_{ps}) + k_b B(1 - T_{pb}) \qquad (12B.5)$$

The first term of Equation 12B.5 is identical to the after-tax payment that the shareholders of an unlevered firm would receive. The present value of this term is found by discounting it by k_s^U. The second term represents the payment that shareholders forgo by having debt outstanding, and the third term is the after-personal-tax payment received by bondholders. Because debt is assumed to be risk-free and perpetual, the present value of these two terms is obtained by dividing them by k_b. Therefore, combining the present value of these three terms, we obtain the following value of the levered firm:

$$V_L = \frac{\text{EBIT}(1 - T)(1 - T_{ps})}{k_s^U} - \frac{k_b B(1 - T)(1 - T_{ps})}{k_b} + \frac{k_b B(1 - T_{pb})}{k_b} \qquad (12B.6)$$

The first term in Equation 12B.6 represents the value of an unlevered firm, V_U; therefore, after we cancel k_b's in the second and third terms, Equation 12B.6 may be written as

$$V_L = V_U - B(1 - T)(1 - T_{ps}) + B(1 - T_{pb}) \qquad (12B.7)$$

which in turn, may be rearranged to

$$V_L = V_U + [(1 - T_{pb}) - (1 - T)(1 - T_{ps})]B$$

If we divide both terms in the squared bracket by $(1 - T_{pb})$, we obtain

$$V_L = V_U + \left[1 - \frac{(1 - T)(1 - T_{ps})}{(1 - T_{pb})}\right]B \qquad (12B.8)$$

which is Equation 12.16, the value of the levered firm for Miller's model.

It should be noted that the value of the unlevered firm that we obtain here is less than the value of the unlevered firm that we obtain from the MM corporate tax model. This becomes clear when we look at the first term of Equation 12B.6, which represents V_U, the value of the unlevered firm, and compare it to the first term of Equation 12B.2. The numerator for the value of the unlevered firm in Equation 12B.6 is less than that in Equation 12B.2 because of the inclusion of personal taxes on stock income. Therefore, the inclusion of this tax has lowered the value of the unlevered firm in comparison to the MM model, in which only corporate taxes are considered.

13

The Dynamics of the Capital Structure Decision

EXECUTIVE SUMMARY

Factors, in addition to tax issues, that can make the value of the firm less than completely independent of its capital structure are: financial distress costs, agency costs, signalling, and the impact of capital structure decisions on the firm's capital investment decisions.

In making the financing decision, the firm must consider two issues. First, does the firm's capital structure *directly* affect the value of the firm? The best answer finance can provide is that we think so, but the impact on firm value is much less than that provided by the investment decisions the firm makes. Second, do the firm's financing decisions preclude it from making value-enhancing investment decisions? The answer here is clear cut: If the financing decisions prevent a firm from undertaking positive-NPV investment projects, the total value of the firm is clearly diminished.

Firms do not employ almost 100 percent debt financing as suggested by the MM corporate tax model. The pecking order theory and observation of financing practice both suggest the capital structure decision is dynamic, sometimes involving equity and sometimes debt, as firms act as if they have a target capital structure.

Asset uniqueness is an important consideration in determining a firm's debt/equity ratio. The interests of shareholders and bondholders can be better aligned by using financing that has elements of both equity and debt. In addition, protective covenants are important in dealing with agency problems. Capital structure decisions and the future fortunes of the firm in terms of free cash flow may interact. Additional factors, such as growth options, product or input effects, economic conditions, and corporate control, also affect the amount of debt used by firms.

TRANSACTIONS COSTS AND CAPITAL STRUCTURE DECISIONS

In Chapter 12 we explored capital structure theory and the impact of tax laws on capital structure decisions. We started with the Modigliani and Miller model, which argues that *the value of the firm is solely a function of its investment decisions.* As long as financing decisions (including the cash dividend decision, as discussed in Chapter 14) do not affect the investment decisions, MM argue that in the absence of taxes and transactions costs the value of the firm is independent of its capital structure. We saw, once corporate taxes are introduced, that the government provides a subsidy to the firm in the form of an interest tax shield. That is, the direct costs of debt financing are tax-deductible, whereas the costs of equity financing are not. Smart firms would then employ almost 100 percent debt financing in order to take maximum advantage of the subsidy provided by the government. However, if Miller's personal tax argument is reasonable, the benefits of the interest tax shield are not as great as indicated by the MM corporate tax analysis.

In practice we do not see firms financing with virtually 100 percent debt. Why not? Capital structure theory suggests a number of reasons. One is that interest is not the only deduction that firms have for tax purposes; they also have nondebt tax shields in the form of depreciation and depletion. If firms are not likely to take full advantage of the interest tax subsidy, they are less likely to employ as much debt. In addition, there are other tax-related factors that suggest limits exist on the amount of debt employed.

Thus in Chapter 12 we explored the first of three places to look in order to determine if a firm's capital structure affected its total market value—taxes. In this chapter we begin by focusing on the second and third places. The second is transactions costs. The two primary transactions costs relate to financial distress and agency costs. In looking at the impact of transactions costs, we will ignore taxes, for the time being. The third is the firm's investment decision. The question is: Are the firm's investment and financing decisions independent decisions? To answer this question we will examine the signalling approach to capital structure decisions. Then we turn our attention to *the factors* firms take into consideration in making capital structure decisions.

FINANCIAL DISTRESS COSTS

Not all firms succeed; some experience periods of **financial distress**, when they do not have enough cash on hand or readily available to meet their current financial obligations; some may even fail. Think of owners of the firm (or its shareholders) as having an option to buy the bondholders' claim on the firm, as shown in Figure 13.1. If, at the maturity of the firm's debt, the value of the firm's assets is greater than the value of the debt, the shareholders exercise their option, pay off the bondholders, and claim the rest of the value of the firm for themselves. However, because of limited liability, in the event of a loss in value of the firm's assets, the shareholders exercise their alternative option and walk away from the firm, turning it over to the creditors.[1] Note

---

[1] The opportunity for shareholders to pay off the bondholders is the same as a call option on the firm, whereas the opportunity for shareholders to walk away from the firm is the same as a put option. Both of these options are discussed in Chapter 18.

Figure 13.1

The Payoff to Shareholders and Bondholders

If the value of the firm is greater than the bondholders' claim, shareholders pay off the bonds when they mature and claim the rest of the value of the firm. Otherwise, they exercise their option and walk away, turning the firm over to the bondholders.

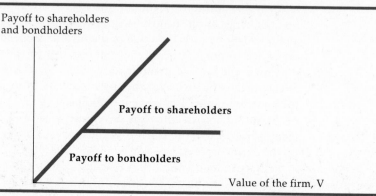

that the loss in value is what triggered exercising the option, i.e., turning the firm over to the bondholders. Many individuals think that bankruptcy leads to a loss in value. In fact it is just the reverse: *The loss in value is what leads to bankruptcy.*

Bankruptcy Costs   If shareholders walk away from the firm, there are direct costs associated with the transaction. These are **bankruptcy costs**, which include legal and other costs associated with the bankruptcy or reorganization proceedings. These are the "dead weight" costs of failing; only the accountants and lawyers benefit from them. How big are these costs? Studies of the direct costs of bankruptcy do not indicate they are large—they may be anything from less than 1 percent to a maximum of 4 or 5 percent of the firm's value. Although not trivial, bankruptcy costs per se are not large enough to make a material difference in the thrust of the Modigliani and Miller arguments.

In addition to the direct bankruptcy costs, there are other indirect costs associated with financial difficulties. These include risk shifting, failing to invest, and operational and managerial inefficiencies.

Risk Shifting   Firms maximize their value by accepting positive net present value projects and rejecting negative net present value projects. But, faced with severe financial difficulties, some perverse incentives may exist. Consider Waste Masters, whose current market-value-based balance sheet is:

Cash	$100	Debt	$115
Other assets	25	Equity	10

The debt matures in one year at $200, but because of the high risk of Waste Masters, its current market value is only $115.

Two investment projects are available for Waste Masters—a low-risk project and a high-risk one.

	Low-Risk			High-Risk	
Today	**Possible Payoffs Next Year**		**Today**	**Possible Payoffs Next Year**	

$160 (probability of 0.40) $400 (probability of 0.20)

$100 $100

$90 (probability of 0.60) $0 (probability of 0.80)

At a discount rate of 10 percent, the net present value of the low-risk project is $7.27, while the NPV of the high-risk project is −$27.27. Clearly, any ordinary firm would accept the low-risk project and reject the high-risk project.

But from the shareholders' standpoint there is no benefit from accepting the low-risk project, because it does not provide enough cash inflow even to pay off the debt, let alone benefit the shareholders. The shareholders conclude that the low-risk project should be rejected and the high-risk project accepted. If the high-risk project is accepted and succeeds, producing the payoff of $400, the bondholders can be paid off and the shareholders walk away with the rest. Financial managers who act solely in the interest of the firm's shareholders (and, therefore, not in the interests of *all* of the firm's providers of capital) would clearly favour the high-risk project. In fact, they may even invest in negative net present value projects. This type of problem is typically referred to as the **asset substitution problem**; it was originated by Jensen and Meckling (1976).

Failing to Invest   Conflicts of interest between shareholders and bondholders can also lead to firms' failing to raise additional equity capital. Say a firm has a "sure" winner that will produce an NPV of $25 in one year on a $50 investment. As in our Waste Masters example, the bondholders' claim is substantial, and bondholders do not want to invest any more in the firm. Unlike Waste Masters, this firm does not have enough cash on hand to fund the project; the only way to undertake this sure winner is to issue equity capital. Why would the shareholders (either the existing or new shareholders) ever make the investment? All, or virtually all, of the NPV will be claimed by the bondholders when the shareholders walk away from the firm in one year. The answer is, they would not make the investment.

The general point is this: Holding other things constant, any increase in the value of a firm making positive-NPV investments is shared between shareholders and bondholders. When the debt claims are substantial relative to the equity claims, virtually all of the gains from making positive-NPV investments are captured by the bondholders. Thus, it may not be in the shareholders' best interests to contribute additional capital even if "sure" NPV projects are forgone. This **underinvestment problem** was first examined by Myers (1977). In fact, faced with the previous situation, shareholders would favour distributing the assets of the firm to them in the form of a massive cash dividend. That way, they claim part of the assets. Of course, their gain comes at the expense of the bondholders.

Operational and Managerial Inefficiencies There are other possible consequences of impending financial distress. There may be increased inefficiency caused by key employees leaving or having their attention diverted from managing the firm as an ongoing entity. Customers may cancel orders if they are worried about the ability of the firm to deliver the product or service. There may be a tendency for the firm to skimp on employee training, product quality, and research and development, or even pay less attention to the safety of the work environment. Whatever form they take, increased inefficiencies do affect firms that are undergoing periods of high financial distress. In order to survive, the firm sacrifices some important activities that it normally undertakes, even though by doing so it may simply be buying a little more time.

The sum of the direct and indirect costs associated with bankruptcy and financial difficulties are called **financial distress costs**. Financial distress costs can affect the firm directly and also lead to increased returns being demanded by both bondholders and shareholders. As bondholders perceive the probability of financial distress increasing, they may require a higher expected return. Likewise, shareholders face the same concerns; accordingly, they will also require a higher expected return before investing additional capital.

How high are the total direct and indirect costs of financial distress? Direct costs, as we mentioned earlier, are not very large. But when indirect costs are included, some estimates place the financial distress costs at 10 to 20 percent of a firm's value. At that level, they are large enough to have an impact on the value of the firm. Although analysis of the costs of financial distress does not tell us what the firm's capital structure should be, it does suggest that firms with a greater probability of experiencing financial distress will borrow less.

AGENCY COSTS

Other transactions costs, as discussed originally in Chapter 1, may arise because of the presence of shareholders, managers, and bondholders. First, consider shareholders and managers. As long as the firm is owned and operated by a single entrepreneur, no complications arise because management and the owner are the same person. In this situation, the entrepreneur maximizes his or her wealth by balancing the combination of wages, perquisites (or "perks") such as a company car, company jet, luxurious office, and so on, and the market value of the firm's common stock.

As the firm grows, however, the entrepreneur may meet financing needs by raising external funds, either by sharing ownership with others (issuing common stock) or by incurring debt financing. Furthermore, as the firm grows, the providers of new capital (the principals) delegate decision-making authority to a separate management group (the agent). This delegation of decision-making authority may result in an agency problem if a conflict of interest arises between the agent and principal, or among the principals, that affects the firm's operations. Such conflicts can be resolved only by incurring agency costs.

As sole owner, the entrepreneur obtains part of his or her wealth through perks. In this situation, the owner not only receives all of the benefits of these perks but also bears all of their costs. However, if the entrepreneur sells part ownership of the firm to outsiders while retaining the management capacity, he or she has an incentive to increase perks. Now the entrepreneur will receive all of the benefits of these perks but will pay only his or her ownership fraction of their costs. If the new co-owners realize this agency problem before they buy into the firm, they will not be willing to pay as much for each share. The difference between the price of the share without and with the agency problem represents an agency cost that serves to reduce the value of the firm. On the other hand, the entrepreneur and the new co-owners may enter into a monitoring agreement to ensure that the entrepreneur acts in the best interest of *all* shareholders. In either case, agency costs are incurred.[2] As the firm uses less equity and more debt, the agency costs of equity decrease.

Another form of agency problem occurs between shareholders and bondholders. The fact that the bondholders' claims on the firm's income are fixed creates an incentive for shareholders to engage in riskier projects that transfer wealth from bondholders to shareholders, no matter what the possibility of financial distress. For example, assume that there are two projects, A and B, that the firm may undertake; both projects cost the same amount and have the same expected return and the same market value. However, the variance of the returns of project B is greater than that of project A. The shareholders of the firm may raise the needed funds through a bond issue by revealing only project A to potential lenders. If the firm has the ability to switch to project B after it has raised the funds, it will do so. Because both projects have the same market value, this switch will not affect the total market value of the firm. It does make the debt riskier, however, thus redistributing value from bondholders to shareholders. This is another form of asset substitution, which was discussed previously. To prevent such expropriation of their wealth, bondholders will demand various types of restrictive covenants and monitoring devices (as discussed later in this chapter). The cost of these instruments is another agency cost. As the use of debt increases, the agency costs of debt increase.

The impact of agency costs and their implication for the capital structure of the firm are shown in Figure 13.2. Note that the unlevered firm has agency costs—these are the agency costs of equity. For example, if the value of a firm with no debt and *in the absence of any agency costs* would be $500, and equity agency costs are $100 when the firm is unlevered (i.e., with no debt), then the observed value of the firm, V_U, is $500 − $100 = $400. As the firm adds debt, it reduces the agency costs of equity but increases the agency costs of debt. In the context of agency costs, the value of the firm is maximized at the point where total agency costs are minimized.

The analysis so far—which includes the tax subsidy associated with debt, personal taxes and other tax-related impacts, financial distress costs, and agency costs—is illustrated in Figure 13.3. In the MM tax model, once corporate taxes are considered, the value of the firm increases continuously as more debt is used. The value-maximizing firm would issue 100 percent debt. The introduction of personal taxes reduces the

---

[2] The impact of executive compensation plans, which serve to align the interests of managers and owners, has also been examined as they relate to capital structure decisions.

Figure 13.2

Agency Costs and Financial Leverage

While the agency costs of equity decrease with increasing financial leverage, the agency costs of debt increase. The optimal capital structure, in the absence of other considerations, minimizes total agency costs.

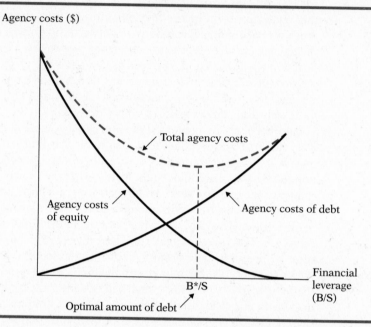

benefit of the interest tax shield somewhat, but firms still have an incentive to use more debt. However, once other tax-deductible items, such as depreciation and depletion, and the costs of financial distress and the agency costs are included, the total value of the firm becomes

$$V'_L = V_U + \begin{array}{c} \text{present value of} \\ \text{tax savings} \end{array} - \left(\begin{array}{c} \text{present value of} \\ \text{financial distress costs} \end{array} + \begin{array}{c} \text{present value} \\ \text{of agency costs} \end{array} \right) \quad (13.1)$$

where

$$V_U = \text{the unlevered value of the firm}$$
$$\text{tax savings} = TB - \text{nondebt tax shields}$$
$$\text{financial distress costs} = \text{costs that depend on the probability and costs associated} \\ \text{with financial distress}$$
$$\text{agency costs} = \text{agency costs of equity} + \text{agency costs of debt}$$

The tax impacts are shown in Figure 13.3 (a), and the additional impact of transactions costs, in the form of financial distress and agency costs, is shown in part (b) of Figure 13.3. Under this scenario there may be an optimal debt/equity ratio, B*/S, where the value of the firm is maximized. This optimum ratio, or more likely a range of alternative, almost equally desirable levels of financial leverage, would be such that

Figure 13.3

Gains from Leverage, Tax Aspects, and Transactions Costs

Part (a) indicates the gains from leverage considering taxes (as previously shown in Figure 12.6). Part (b) introduces the additional impact of transactions costs, in the form of financial distress and agency costs. Based on all of these factors, an optimal capital structure may exist.

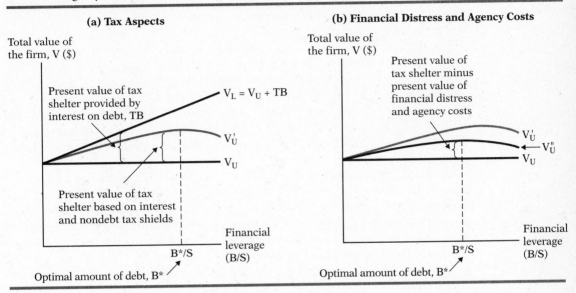

substituting one more dollar of debt for equity would raise the costs more than the benefits. Similarly, cutting back would lower the costs by less than the benefits are reduced.

Concept Review Questions

- Describe some types of bankruptcy costs.
- Give an example of why shareholders might prefer to accept a negative net present value project over a positive net present value project.
- Give some examples of financial distress costs.
- How is Miller and Modigliani's tax model affected by the presence of financial distress and agency costs?

IMPACT OF CAPITAL INVESTMENT DECISIONS

In the last section we examined transactions costs in the form of financial distress and agency issues. One topic that crept in was incentives either to overinvest or underinvest that exist under certain conditions. A related argument on the interrelations between the capital structure and capital investment decisions arises when we consider a signalling approach to capital structure decisions.

SIGNALLING

An alternative approach to examining the capital structure issue is based on the premise that managers as insiders have information—often called asymmetric information—that outside investors do not have access to. When financial markets react to the actions of firms as signs of insider information, **signalling** occurs. Thus, the choice of a capital structure can convey information about the firm to investors and cause a change in the value of the firm.

Ross (1977) developed a model in which the capital structure decision signals the firm's future prospects. Suppose there are two identical firms that investors see no difference between. Managers for both firms have information that has not been revealed to the financial markets. Suppose one firm has substantially better prospects than the other firm. By issuing debt, the firm with the better prospects signals this information to the financial markets. Under the Ross signalling model, increases in firm value (due to the previously unrevealed prospects) would be associated with increased debt issuance.

An alternative signalling model by Leland and Pyle (1977) is based on the idea that firms with "great" NPV projects will want to keep the proceeds of such projects to themselves, rather than share them with either new equity investors or debt investors. Under the Leland and Pyle model, the percentage of owner financing (as represented by the amount of the firm owned by insiders and the financing they provide) may be a credible signal of the future prospects of the firm.

These ideas have been further developed by Myers and Majluf (1984). They presented a model in which the current market value of the firm is considered along with new investment projects. Let us think first about the impact of the firm's current market value on its financing decisions. If the current shareholders of the firm perceive it as being overvalued at its present price, they would like some additional equity partners to share in the decline in the value of the firm. In that case, they would prefer to see additional common stock issued to finance any needs. On the other hand, if they consider the firm to be undervalued, existing common shareholders do not want additional equity partners to share in the expected increase in the market value of the firm.

What happens if we add new investment projects in our consideration of the current market value of the firm? Suppose a firm is undervalued by the market and the firm has a "good" investment project but can finance it only by issuing equity. The cost of the new financing may be so much that the new investors capture more than the NPV of the new project, resulting in a net loss to existing shareholders. Hence, the firm would bypass this "good" investment project. This underinvestment can be avoided if the firm finances the project with debt (i.e., debt that is not too risky) or internally generated funds.

Thus signalling arguments suggest that issuing equity sends a negative signal about the future prospects of the firm: If the prospects are so rosy, why share the anticipated benefits with new equity participants? In addition, there are indications that the firm's capital structure decision and its capital investment decisions are not always independent. In a dynamic context, capital structure becomes an ongoing, evolving decision. These relationships are incorporated in the **pecking order theory**, which was developed by Myers (1984). The pecking order theory suggests that:

1. Firms prefer internal (equity) financing first because: (a) the total costs of obtaining new external financing are substantial and can be minimized by avoiding going to the financial markets more often than is absolutely necessary; and (b) by not going to the financial markets, the firm does not draw specific attention to itself and its financial performance. (As discussed in Chapter 10, internal financing accounts for 50–75 percent of total financing for firms.) Poorly performing firms do not want to draw attention to themselves by having to sell a very expensive stock or bond issue which substantiates the lack of performance and/or weakness of the firm.

2. Firms prefer to pay cash dividends; hence some amount of cash flows out of the firm instead of funding capital investments. Under normal circumstances, reductions in the level of cash dividends are not viewed favourably by firms and their common shareholders. In fact, firms favour a "sticky" dividend policy: They increase cash dividends only when they think the higher level of dividends can be maintained and are reluctant to cut dividends when times get tough.

3. Given sticky cash dividend policies, uncertainty about future cash inflows from operations, and uncertainty concerning the cash outflow needs for capital investments, *firms want some financial flexibility in terms of a cash reserve*. When times are flush they will pay down debt, repurchase stock, or make acquisitions. When times are not so good, firms reduce the level of cash.

4. If external financing is needed, firms issue debt first. New equity financing is a last resort; both theoretical and empirical evidence indicates that by issuing equity the firm is signalling that its present and future prospects are not strong.

The pecking order theory attempts to pull together what we know from financial theory and what we observe in firms' actions. Firms appear to act much as described by the pecking order theory. They also act as if they have a target capital structure; that is, there is some target debt/equity ratio or range they attempt to stay close to over time.

Although many different models and conclusions have been suggested, the important point to remember is that *with a signalling approach, capital structure becomes more of a dynamic, ongoing, evolving decision. There is not a single optimal level of debt, because managers continually have access to information before it is available to outside investors.* And, depending on the nature of the information, managers may choose to issue debt or equity in amounts that at one time will push the firm towards an optimal debt/equity ratio or range but at another time may push the firm away from an optimal debt/equity ratio or range.

CAPITAL STRUCTURE IMPACTS ON FIRM VALUE

Earlier we indicated that the importance of the Modigliani and Miller no-tax model is that (1) it presented a theoretical, rigorous statement of the value of the firm, where none existed before, and (2) it tells us where to look to determine whether the firm's capital structure affects the value of the firm. The MM no-tax case says that:

If there are no taxes,

if there are no transactions costs, and

if the investment (or capital budgeting) policies of the firm are fixed,

then capital structure does not affect a firm's value.

We have examined each of these three possibilities and concluded that arguments can be and have been made about possible relationships between a firm's capital structure and its market value. Although neither managers nor academicians agree on all of the details, the bottom line on the impact of capital structure on the value of the firm is simple and straightforward: Due to tax impacts, transactions costs in the form of financial distress or agency costs, and interactions between capital structure and capital investment decisions, firms choose capital structures with more than zero debt and less than 100 percent debt. Our next task is to examine the *factors* that cause differences, and some of the items taken into consideration as firms make their capital structure decisions.

Concept Review Questions

- What is signalling and how is it related to corporate capital structure?
- What factors lead to capital structure having an impact on the market value of the firm?
- Explain the pecking order theory and how it affects corporate capital structure.

USING MODIGLIANI AND MILLER TO IDENTIFY FACTORS AFFECTING CAPITAL STRUCTURE DECISIONS

Thus far in our discussion of capital structures, we have used Modigliani and Miller as a means of guiding our search for factors that may lead firms to adopt one capital structure as opposed to another. In Chapter 12 we saw that the ability to utilize tax shields to the fullest extent possible is one factor that explains differences in the amount of debt employed. We will continue to use the same structure to assist in understanding differences in actual capital structures by first looking at financial distress and agency issues, and finally signalling and impacts on the firm's capital investment decisions.

FINANCIAL DISTRESS AND AGENCY CONSIDERATIONS

One of the continuing problems faced by firms is the divergent interests of shareholders, bondholders, and managers. These differences in orientation can lead to a variety of activities that reduce the value of the firm. In discussing these activities as they affect capital structure decisions, we examine asset uniqueness, the use of convertible and subordinated debt, and protective covenants.

Asset Uniqueness   Firms whose principal assets are intangible in nature, such as those that rely on brain power (or human capital), research and development, product quality, brand name and advertising, and the like, have higher costs of financial distress. If the firm gets into financial difficulty, these intangible assets can dissipate quickly, due to individuals leaving the firm or simply due to neglect. Such firms include those in the computer hardware, computer software, and drug industries. For this reason we see much less use of debt by firms such as Alias Research, Hewlett-Packard, Microsoft, Mitel Semiconductor, Biochem Pharma, and Merck.

On the other hand, firms that have substantial physical assets which have a ready secondary market can carry more debt. If you are in the hotel business and fail, there is a ready secondary market for hotel rooms. Likewise, there is a market for grocery stores (people have to eat), airplanes, and numerous other physical assets. Thus, we see higher debt usage by firms such as Canadian Tire, Marriott, Safeway, American Barrick, Canadian Airlines International, Federal Express, and Black & Decker.

The key issue is the potential loss in value if trouble comes. Some assets have a much better secondary market than others, which are likely to lose their value quickly. *It is not simply the probability of financial distress that is important; rather it is the potential loss in value of the assets.* Firms that would suffer a sizable loss in value of the assets tend to use less debt than those whose assets retain value.

Convertible and Subordinated Debt   One of the problems faced by firms is that the interests of shareholders and bondholders often diverge. Thus, as we discussed earlier, asset substitution or underinvestment problems may occur. One way to align the interests of the parties is to use financing that combines elements of both debt and equity. Convertible debt, which may be exchanged for common stock of the issuing firm, mitigates some of the divergent interests by combining elements of both debt and equity.[3] If the capital projects are a "success," the bondholders share in the upside benefits from investing in the capital projects. This is precisely why we often see smaller, younger firms, such as Andyne Computing, Soft Image, Shred-It Canada Corporation, and Neweast Wireless Technologies using convertible securities. Subordinated debt (i.e., debt that has a lower claim on assets in case of financial distress than other debt) has much the same effect, and it also tends to alleviate some of the divergent interests of bondholders and shareholders.

Protection   Another important means of dealing with some of the divergent interests of bondholders and shareholders is the incorporation of **protective covenants** as part of the bond (or loan agreement). These covenants are important because a violation of them can lead to the default of the issue. Four major sources of conflict between bondholders and shareholders are:

1. ASSET SUBSTITUTION   If firms sell bonds for a stated purpose and then use the funds from the bond offering to finance other, more risky projects, the value of the bondholders' claim is reduced. This is called asset substitution.
2. UNDERINVESTMENT   If all, or virtually all, of the benefits from a new capital investment accrue to the bondholders, firms (and the firm's shareholders) have an incentive to bypass positive net present value projects. This is referred to as the underinvestment problem.

---

[3] Convertible bonds are discussed in Chapter 20.

3. CLAIM DILUTION   If the firm sells bonds under the assumption that no additional bonds will be issued, the value of the existing bondholders' claim is reduced by the firm's issuing additional debt of the same or higher priority.
4. DIVIDEND PAYMENT   If the firm sells bonds with the assumption that the same level of dividends will be maintained, the value of the existing bondholders' claim is reduced by increasing the percentage of cash paid out as dividends.

In order to reduce these problems, all bonds and loan agreements have protective covenants written into them. Protective covenants cannot eliminate all sources of conflict between bondholders and shareholders, but they can reduce financial distress and agency costs. Table 13.1 lists typical bond covenants, divided into four categories.

Table 13.1

Some Typical Bond Covenants

Bond covenants are designed to address both financial distress and agency considerations.

I. Production/Investment Covenants

Restrictions on common stock investments, loans, extensions of credit, and advances

Restrictions on the disposition of assets

Secured debt that gives bondholders title to pledged assets until the bonds are paid in full

Restrictions on mergers

Requirements regarding the maintenance of assets

II. Covenants That Restrict Subsequent Financing Policy

Limitations on the issuance of any additional debt or on the priority of claim of new debt

Limitations on leases or sales-and-leasebacks

Inclusion of a sinking fund so the bondholders are paid off over time, rather than all at once at the maturity of the bond

Call provisions

III. Covenants That Restrict Payment of Dividends

Restrictions specifying the amount or source of funds that can be employed to pay dividends

Outright restrictions under certain circumstances

IV. Covenants That Reduce the Cost of Monitoring the Firm

Specification of required reports, such as annual and quarterly financial statements, having the reports audited, etc.

Specification of how certain restrictions will be computed

Certificates of compliance stating that the firm is fulfilling all of its obligations under the indenture

Required purchase of insurance

First are those that deal with the firm's production and investment policies. These are followed by financing covenants, dividend (or monitoring) covenants and, finally, bonding covenants. Smith and Warner (1979) examined 1974 and 1975 public issues of debt and found that 91 percent of them included covenants that restricted the issuance of additional debt, 23 percent restricted dividends, 39 percent restricted mergers, and 36 percent limited the sale of assets. Malitz (1986) studied senior nonconvertible debentures sold between 1960 and 1980 in terms of sinking fund provisions, limitations on future debt, and limitations on dividend payments. All of the bonds examined by Malitz had sinking fund provisions. Likewise, firms using more debt benefited to a greater extent than firms using less debt from provisions limiting additional debt and dividend payments. Also, smaller firms, for which information asymmetry is more likely, were more inclined to include restrictions of debt and dividends. These covenants appear less important for larger firms, due to the larger number of financing options available to them, the greater availability of public information about the firms, and the constant scrutiny they face from the financial markets, security regulators, underwriters, and bond-rating agencies.

Although financial distress and agency problems cannot be eliminated entirely, the amount and types of financing employed by firms make more sense once we consider asset uniqueness, the alignment benefits of convertible securities, and the role played by protective covenants in terms of controlling some of the financial distress and agency costs.

SIGNALLING, CAPITAL STRUCTURE, AND CASH FLOW

From a signalling standpoint, as well as from a financial distress/agency standpoint, we learned that there may be interactions between a firm's capital structure decisions and its capital investment decisions. Although our primary interest in this chapter is the firm's capital structure decision, our coverage would not be complete unless we consider some broader issues. First, we will look at the results of a number of studies that have examined how financial markets respond as firms take actions to either increase or decrease the amount of debt in their capital structure. Then we will examine how financial markets respond to actions that signal increased prospects for the firm (in the form of increased future cash flows) or diminished prospects (and reductions in expected cash flows).

Holding everything else constant, a firm could increase its reliance on debt either by issuing additional debt or by exchanging new debt for some of its outstanding common stock. Likewise, it could reduce its reliance on debt financing by issuing additional common stock or by exchanging new common stock for some of its outstanding debt. The first type of transaction is a leverage-increasing transaction, whereas the second is a leverage-reducing transaction. Table 13.2 summarizes the empirical results of a number of studies that examined leverage-increasing, leverage-neutral, and leverage-reducing transactions. The results presented in Table 13.2 (and other research on similar transactions) indicates the following: *(1) The stock market reacts positively to leverage-increasing transactions and negatively to leverage-reducing transactions, and (2) the larger the change in financial leverage, the greater the price reaction.*

Table 13.2

Impact of Capital Structure Changes on the Value of Common Stock

The two-day announcement period return indicates the increase (or decrease) in the stock price (or return) associated with the transaction. These transactions represent almost pure capital structure changes.

Type of Transaction	Security Issued	Security Retired	Average Sample Size	Two-Day Announcement Period Return
Transactions that Increase Leverage				
Stock repurchase	Debt	Common	45	21.9%
Exchange offer	Debt	Common	52	14.0
Exchange offer	Preferred	Common	9	8.3
Exchange offer	Debt	Preferred	24	2.2
Exchange offer	Income bonds	Preferred	24	2.2
Transactions with No Change in Leverage				
Exchange offer	Debt	Debt	36	1.6[a]
Security sale	Debt	Debt	83	0.2[a]
Transactions that Reduce Leverage				
Conversion-forcing call	Common	Convertible preferred	57	−0.4[a]
Conversion-forcing call	Common	Convertible bond	113	−2.1
Security sale	Convertible debt	Debt	15	−2.4
Exchange offer	Common	Preferred	30	−2.6
Exchange offer	Preferred	Debt	9	−7.7
Security sale	Common	Debt	12	−4.2
Exchange offer	Common	Debt	20	−9.9

[a] Not statistically different from zero.

Source: Adapted from Table 3 in Clifford W. Smith, Jr., "Investment Banking and the Capital Acquisition Process," *Journal of Financial Economics* 15 (January/February 1986): 3–29. Footnotes from the original table are omitted.

Because of asymmetric information (that is, differences in information available to the parties involved), we see that the impact on value is the most acute for transactions in which common stock is exchanged for debt, or debt for common stock. Because debt and preferred stock have claims that are senior to those held by common shareholders, their values are less sensitive to changes in capital structure when common stock is not involved. Also, the use of convertible debt results in smaller changes in value than when nonconvertible debt is used.

Up to now we have been concerned only with changes in capital structure. We now will widen the argument by considering Jensen's (1986) suggestion that agency conflicts over the payout of free cash flow (that is, cash flow above that needed to fund all positive net present value projects) also must be taken into consideration. The **free cash flow theory** predicts that for firms with positive cash flow, stock prices will

Table 13.3

Impact of Implied Changes in Corporate Cash Flow on the Value of Common Stock

As in Table 13.2, the two-day announcement period return indicates the increase (or decrease) in value. Changes in financing, investment policy, and cash dividend decisions are examined.

Type of Announcement	Average Sample Size	Two-Day Announcement Period Return
Implied Increase in Expected Corporate Cash Flow		
Common stock repurchases:		
intra-firm tender offer	148	16.2%
open market repurchase	182	3.6
targeted small holding	15	1.6
Calls of nonconvertible bonds	133	−0.1[a]
Dividend increases:		
dividend initiation	160	3.7
dividend increase	180	0.9
specially designated dividend	164	2.1
Investment increases	510	1.0
Implied Decrease in Expected Corporate Cash Flow		
Security sales:		
common stock	262	−1.6
preferred stock	102	0.1[a]
convertible preferred	30	−1.4
straight debt	221	−0.2[a]
convertible debt	80	−2.1
Dividend decreases	48	−3.6
Investment decreases	111	−1.1

[a] Not significantly different from zero.

Source: Adapted from Table 2 in Clifford W. Smith, Jr. "Investment Banking and the Capital Acquisition Process," *Journal of Financial Economics* 15 (January/February 1986): 3–29. Footnotes from the original table are omitted.

increase with unexpected increases in the payout to corporate claimholders and will decrease with unexpected increases in the demand for funds via new issues. In addition, the theory predicts that stock prices will increase with increasing tightness of the constraints binding the payout of future cash flow to claimants and will decrease with reductions in the tightness of these constraints. Table 13.3 summarizes the empirical results from a number of studies examining changes in financing, investment, and dividend policy that signify implied increases or decreases in corporate cash flow. In general, the results presented in the table agree with the predictions of the free cash flow theory.

Figure 13.4

Predicted Impact on Firm Value Associated With Various Capital Structure, Investment, and Dividend Decisions.

Capital structure decisions and their impact on the value of the firm may not be independent of the impact of implied changes in corporate cash flow on the value of the firm.

		Implied Cash Flow Change		
		Negative	**Zero**	**Positive**
	Decreasing financial leverage	Common sale Dividend decrease	Common sale to retire debt Convertible bond sale to retire debt Common/preferred exchange offer Preferred/bond exchange offer Common/bond exchange offer Call of convertible bonds Call of convertible preferred	Calls of nonconvertible bonds
Capital Structure Change	Zero	Convertible preferred sale Convertible bond sale Investment decrease	Bond/bond exchange offer Bond sale to retire debt	Investment increase
	Increasing financial leverage	Preferred sale Debt sale	Common repurchase financed with debt Bond/common exchange offer Preferred/common exchange offer Bond/preferred exchange offer Income bond/preferred exchange offer	Common repurchase Dividend increase Dividend initiations Specially designed dividends

Predicted negative abnormal returns

Predicted insignificant abnormal returns

Predicted positive abnormal returns

The joint impact of both capital structure decisions and changes in implied cash flow are summarized in Figure 13.4. Empirical results (from Tables 13.2, 13.3, and other studies) generally support the predictions summarized in Figure 13.4. Thus, whereas our concern is to assess the impact of capital structure on the value of the firm holding everything else constant, *in practice other things are not constant.* Many factors—some related directly to capital structure decisions, but others related to the firm's investment decisions or its cash dividend decisions—can have a positive, neutral, or negative impact on the value of the firm as the financial leverage of the firm changes. As shown in Figure 13.4, the predicted impact of actions undertaken by the firm may have two impacts—and these impacts may complement or contradict one another. For example, by issuing more common stock, the firm reduces the amount of financial leverage, indicating a decrease in value, and at the same time signals lower free cash flows in the future, also indicating a decrease in the value of the firm. Alternatively, by selling debt the firm increases its use of debt, which should lead to an increase in value, while it also signals lower free cash flows in the future. The predictions incorporated in Figure 13.4 suggest that the firm's capital structure decision is not independent of its investment and dividend decisions.

Concept Review Questions

- Explain why firms whose principal assets are intangible in nature would prefer lower debt levels than do firms with tangible assets.

- Give some examples of conflicts of interest between bondholders and shareholders that protective covenants may reduce.

- Describe the free cash flow theory and the relationship between a firm's cash flow and its capital structure.

OTHER FACTORS TO CONSIDER

In addition to the factors identified by the MM model, numerous others have been suggested as factors potentially affecting capital structure decisions. These include growth options, product or input market factors, economic conditions, and corporate control motives.[4]

GROWTH OPTIONS

One of the most important factors affecting capital structure decisions, and one we have not looked at yet, is the ability to take advantage of growth options. Where high future growth is possible (i.e., where there are many positive net present value projects that the competition will not immediately erode away), firms want financial slack. They do not want to be so loaded with debt that they hamper their flexibility

---

[4] When we look at firms domiciled in different countries, there are additional factors that we must consider. Some of these are discussed briefly in Chapter 17.

or future opportunity to secure additional capital as needed to make the necessary investments. Smith and Watts (1992), among others, find that firms that have more growth options have lower financial leverage. The existence of growth options is one reason that specialty retailers have a lower level of debt than general retailers; they have better growth prospects. Roots, Future Shop, and The Gap have much better growth prospects than Eaton's or Sears, for example; thus, they have less debt in their capital structures. Likewise, Corel Corp., Home Depot, and Philip Environmental all have high expected growth rates and many potential growth opportunities, and they use less debt.

PRODUCT OR INPUT MARKET FACTORS

In recent years a number of studies have identified possible relationships between product or input markets and the amount of financial leverage employed by the firm. Titman (1984) postulated that leverage increases to the extent to which a firm's products are not unique and do not require specialized service. Maksimovic and Zechner (1991) developed a model that suggests why firms within the same industry have different debt/equity ratios. They suggested that firms that adopt the technology chosen by the majority of the firms in the industry are partially hedged against shocks in production costs, since changes in production costs will be reflected in the price of the goods for all firms using the same technology. At the same time, firms that use the same technology are less levered than firms that adopt a technology chosen by fewer firms.

Kim and Maksimovic (1990) turn the analysis around and analyze the impact the firm's financial structure has on its production decisions. That is, they are concerned with whether using a large amount of debt, as evidenced by a high debt/equity ratio, affects a firm's production decisions. Using the passenger air transport industry (which has a high debt/equity ratio), they conclude that high debt levels are associated with suboptimal investment in capacity and inefficient combinations of variable production inputs. They also suggest that the air transport industry's high level of debt created a loss in efficiency which was large enough to dissipate a substantial fraction of the potential tax benefits of debt financing. These ideas suggest that factors not tradition-ally considered in finance may also affect a firm's capital structure decision.

ECONOMIC CONDITIONS

In a recent article, Berkovitch and Narayanan (1993) propose that the proportion of equity financing relative to debt financing is higher when economic conditions are improving. This follows because the average quality of the projects developed is lower in a time of economic expansion, and lower-quality projects are more likely to be financed with equity.

In a different vein, Shleifer and Vishny (1992) examine the ability of firms to sell assets in the face of financial distress. They argue that general economic conditions affect the ability of firms to employ more or less debt. Thus, when a firm in financial distress needs to sell assets, because of economic conditions its industry peers are likely to be experiencing financial difficulties themselves. This limits the potential buyers of the firm's assets; the result is to make assets cheap in times of weak economic condiitions. The overall impact is that asset liquidity is not constant over time, and therefore the amount of debt that can be effectively supported varies with economic conditions.

While our understanding of the impact of economic conditions on capital structure is in its infancy, these studies indicate possible relationships that may exist between overall economic conditions and a firm's capital structure.

CORPORATE CONTROL

Finally, let us consider another factor that affects a firm's capital structure decision. Assume a firm exists that is a tempting takeover candidate. What kind of capital structure action might it take to make it either less attractive to a potential acquiring firm or more expensive?[5] Harris and Raviv (1988), Israel (1991), and Stulz (1988) have developed models that predict potential takeover targets will increase their debt levels.[6] This increase in debt should be accompanied by a positive stock price reaction; at the same time, it should reduce the probability of being successfully taken over by another firm. We should stress that capital structure arguments based on corporate control motivations focus on short-run changes in capital structure taken in response to possible takeover threats. *Corporate control considerations say nothing about the long-run capital structure of firms.*

FACTORS TO LOOK FOR WHEN MAKING CAPITAL STRUCTURE DECISIONS

In Chapters 12 and 13 we have examined capital structure theory and considered numerous factors that may have an impact on a firm's capital structure decision. In order to summarize this material, it is helpful to consider the findings of a number of studies that have examined factors associated with different amounts of financial leverage. These findings are presented in Table 13.4. *These studies generally agree that leverage increases with nondebt tax shields, growth opportunities, fixed assets, and firm size, and that it decreases with volatility, advertising expenditures, research and development expenditures, bankruptcy probability, profitability, and uniqueness of the product.* It is safe to conclude that a firm's capital structure is affected by many factors. And, depending on the nature of the firm, the economy, and the competition, firms may at various points in time add to or reduce the amount of debt in their capital structure. Thus, available theory and empirical evidence support the notion that capital structure is a dynamic, ongoing, evolving decision.

Concept Review Questions

- Explain how a firm's growth potential and capital structure are interrelated.
- Several researchers have hypothesized that product/input considerations and economic conditions can affect a firm's capital structure. Briefly explain these theories and their conclusions.

---

[5] One question of importance is, "Whose interests are we trying to maximize by making the firm more difficult to take over?" We refer you to articles in the end-of-chapter references, as well as Chapter 16, where mergers and defensive tactics are discussed.

[6] As discussed in Chapter 16, there are a number of other actions firms undertake to make themselves less attractive merger candidates.

Table 13.4

Some Potential Determinants of Financial Leverage

Many studies have examined the relationship between firm-level capital structure and observable factors that may affect capital structure decisions.

Characteristic	Bradley, Jarrell, and Kim[a]	Chaplinsky and Niehaus[b]	Friend, Hasbrouch, and Long[c]	Gonedes, Long, and Chikaonda[d]	Long and Malitz[e]	Kester[f]	Kim and Sorensen[g]	March[h]	Titman and Wessels[i]
Volatility	−		−			−	+		−
Bankruptcy probability								−	
Fixed assets		+	+	+	+			+	+
Nondebt tax shields	+	+			−		−		
Advertising	−				−				
R&D expenditures	−		−		+	−			
Profitability					+				−
Growth opportunities		−				+			−
Size		−	+				−	+	−
Free cash flow		−							
Uniqueness		−							−

[a] Michael Bradley, Gregg Jarrell, and E. Han Kim, "On the Existence of an Optimal Capital Structure: Theory and Evidence," *Journal of Finance* 39 (July 1984): 857–878.

[b] Susan Chaplinsky and Greg Niehaus, "The Determinants of Inside Ownership and Leverage," working paper, University of Michigan, 1990.

[c] Irwin Friend and Joel Hasbrouch, "Determinants of Capital Structure," in Andy Chen, ed., *Research in Finance*, Volume 7 (New York: JAI Press, 1988), pp. 1–19; and Irwin Friend and Larry Long, "An Empirical Test of the Impact and Managerial Self-Interest on Corporate Capital Structure," *Journal of Finance* 43 (June 1988): 271–281.

[d] Nicholas J. Gonedes, Larry Long, and Mathias Chikaonda, "Empirical Results on Managerial Incentives and Capital Structure," working paper, University of Pennsylvania, 1988.

[e] Michael Long and Ileen Malitz, "The Investment-Financing Nexus: Some Empirical Evidence," *Midland Corporate Finance Journal* 3 (Fall 1985): 53–59.

[f] Carl W. Kester, "Capital and Ownership Structure: A Comparison of United States and Japanese Manufacturing Operations," *Financial Management* 15 (Spring 1986): 5–16.

[g] Wi Saeng Kim and Eric H. Sorensen, "Evidence on the Impact of the Agency Costs of Debt in Corporate Debt Policy," *Journal of Financial and Qualitative Analysis* 21 (June 1986): 131–44.

[h] Paul March, "The Choice Between Equity and Debt: An Empirical Study," *Journal of Finance* 37 (March 1982): 121–144.

[i] Sheridan Titman and Roberto Wessels, "The Determinants of Capital Structure Choices," *Journal of Finance* 43 (March 1988): 1–19.

Source: Adapted from Table IV in Milton Harris and Arthur Raviv, "The Theory of Capital Structure," *Journal of Finance* 46 (March 1991): 297–355. Footnotes from the original table are omitted.

KEY POINTS

- There are three places to look when examining the possible impact of capital structure decisions on the value of the firm: taxes, transactions costs, and interrelationships between the firm's financing decisions and its capital investment decisions.
- Transactions costs include financial distress costs and agency costs. The direct costs of bankruptcy are "small" (relatively speaking); however, once risk shifting, failure to invest, and other operational and managerial inefficiencies are considered, the costs of financial distress may be as high as 10 to 20 percent of firm value. At that level they may affect a firm's capital structure decisions. Agency costs can also lead to firms' using less than 100 percent debt.
- Both signalling and financial distress arguments indicate there may be interactions between a firm's financing decisions and its capital structure decisions.
- Because of taxes, transactions costs, and interactions between financing and investment decisions, firms choose capital structures that have more than zero debt and less than 100 percent debt.
- The pecking order theory and the observed behaviour of firms suggest that the capital structure decision is a dynamic, evolving process.
- Based on the MM model, taxes are one of the important determinants of capital structures. Asset uniqueness is another important factor because it is closely related to the potential loss in value if financial distress occurs.
- Convertible debt serves to combine the interests of both debt and equity, thereby lessening any conflicts of interest. Protective covenants are widely used in bonds and loan agreements in order to deal with possible conflicts of interest—especially between shareholders and bondholders.
- Capital structure decisions, investment decisions, and cash dividend decisions appear to be interrelated. One possible approach to considering the potential interactions is to combine the impact of leverage-changing decisions and the free cash flow theory.
- Other factors that need to be considered in making capital structure decisions are the presence of growth options, product or input effects, economic conditions, and implications provided by corporate control actions.
- The key variables that affect the capital structure choice are the ability to take advantage of tax shields, risk differences related to the assets employed by the firm and its competition, and the need to maintain financial slack due to growth opportunities.

QUESTIONS

13.1 What risk shifting, failure to invest, or other problems may arise when the probability of financial distress is high?

13.2 What are agency costs? What two types are evident? How do they affect the capital structure decision of the firm?

13.3 Firms may signal their intentions (or the state of the firm) to the investment community through their actions. What kinds of signals exist when capital structure decisions are considered?

13.4 Explain how investment decisions and capital structure decisions may be related to one another.

13.5 The Modigliani and Miller no-tax model tells us that (1) if there are no taxes, (2) if there are no transactions costs, and (3) if the investment (or capital budgeting) policies of the firm are fixed, then capital structure does not affect a firm's value. Provide a complete discussion of the theoretical aspects of capital structure and its possible impact on the value of the firm.

13.6 Explain the pecking order theory. How does it relate to what we observe in practice and to the idea of a target capital structure?

13.7 How would you go about explaining why we see so many different capital structures in practice, both between and within industries?

13.8 Why do we not see continually profitable firms financing with almost 100 percent debt in their capital structures?

13.9 Explain in detail how taxes and asset uniqueness assist in explaining some of the capital structures we see in practice.

13.10 The interests of shareholders and bondholders often diverge. What specific bond (or loan) covenants address each of the four sources of conflict between shareholders and bondholders discussed in the book?

13.11 How could changes in capital structure and changes in a firm's free cash flow interact? What types of actions indicate increases under both capital structure impacts and under the free cash flow theory? Which actions cause a positive/negative impact under one theory, but a negative/positive impact under the other?

13.12 Explain how other factors, in addition to those indicated by the MM model, may affect a firm's capital structure.

CONCEPT REVIEW PROBLEMS

See Appendix A for Solutions.

CR13.1 High Stakes Industries has had a long string of bad luck. All the firm's assets have been wiped out except for $100,000 in cash. On the liability side, the firm has debt of $150,000, due in one year. Two investment opportunities requiring an investment of $100,000 each and having a one-year payoff are available. The first project has a 20 percent probability of having a $200,000 cash flow and an 80 percent probability of having an $80,000 cash flow in one year. The second project has a 50 percent chance of receiving $130,000 and a 50 percent chance of receiving $110,000 in one year. The opportunity cost of capital is 15 percent.
a. What are the expected cash flows and standard deviation of the cash flows for each project?
b. What is the NPV of each project?
c. If you are a shareholder, which project would you prefer? If you are a bondholder, which project would you prefer?

CR13.2 Edgar Ltd. is an unlevered firm with a constant EBIT of $10 million per year. The corporate tax rate is 40 percent, and the cost of equity is 15 percent. Management is considering the use of debt that would cost the firm 10 percent regardless of the amount used. The firm's management asked a consulting firm to estimate the cost due to financial distress and the probability of these costs for each level of debt. The brokerage firm's analyst estimated present value of future financial distress is $10 million and the probability of financial distress would increase with leverage as follows:

Value of Debt (in millions)	Probability of Distress
$ 0	0%
20	5
25	10
30	15
35	30
40	60
$45	90

Using the pure MM model with corporate taxes, what is the optimal amount of debt for Edgar (without and with financial distress)?

CR13.3 Molin Industries has EBIT of $500,000, a tax rate of 30 percent, a market value of debt of $1,000,000, a cost of debt, k_b, of 8 percent, and a cost of equity, k_s^L, of 12 percent. The firm anticipates no future growth and a 100 percent dividend payout ratio.
a. What is the total market value of the firm?
b. What is the firm's opportunity cost of capital?
c. The firm is planning to increase its debt by $500,000 and use the proceeds to repurchase equity. The cost of all debt, k_b, will increase to 10 percent, and the cost of equity will increase to 14 percent. Should the firm proceed with the capital restructuring?

CR13.4 Logan Logging currently has no debt, an EBT of $400,000, a cost of equity of 15 percent, and 100,000 shares of common stock outstanding. The firm's tax rate is 40 percent. Logan is considering restructuring by selling debt and repurchasing equity. If the firm sells $800,000 in debt, the cost of debt, k_b, will be 10 percent and the cost of equity, k_s^L, will increase to 17 percent.
a. What effect will the increase in debt have on the value of the firm?
b. If the stock is repurchased at $16 per share, what is the per share price after the restructuring?
c. What is the per share price if stock is repurchased at $20 per share, instead of $16 as in part (b)?

PROBLEMS

13.1 Traynor Enterprises currently has $100 million of 13 percent (coupon rate) debt outstanding, its EBIT is $80 million, and its cost of equity capital, k_s^L, is 12 percent. Due to a decrease in interest rates, Traynor has decided to call the bond issue. (The bonds will be called at par.) Because Traynor is not at its target capital structure, it will issue either $150 million or $200 million of new debt at par. In either case, $100 million will be used to refund the existing bond issue. The remainder will be used to buy back outstanding shares of Traynor's common stock. If the $150 million bond issue is employed, then the coupon interest rate will be 10 percent and k_s^L will increase to 12.5 percent. If the $200 million issue is employed, then the coupon interest rate is 11 percent and k_s^L will be 14 percent. The corporate tax rate is 40 percent, and all earnings are paid out as cash dividends.
a. If the bonds are selling at 115 percent of par, what is the current total value, V, of the firm (before any refinancing)?
b. What is the total value, V, of the firm if the $150 million bond issue is sold? If the $200 million issue is sold? (Assume the market value of the bonds is equal to their par value.)
c. What action should Traynor take?

13.2 Howell Graphics is doing some capital structure planning. Its investment dealers have estimated after-tax costs of debt and equity at various levels of debt as follows:

Proportion of Debt	k_i	k_s
0.00	5.4%	12.0%
0.10	5.4	12.2
0.20	5.8	12.7
0.30	6.3	13.2

Proportion of Debt	k_i	k_s
0.40	6.9	14.1
0.50	7.9	15.6
0.60	9.0	17.4

Based on this information, at what ratio of total debt to total equity is Howell's target capital structure?

13.3 Big Three Enterprises is in the process of determining its target capital structure. The firm is currently all-equity-financed but is thinking about issuing debt and using the proceeds to retire some of its common stock. The risk-free rate is 6 percent, there is no growth, and all earnings are paid out as cash dividends. Based on a good deal of internal discussion and on some projections made by its investment dealers, Big Three has come up with the following schedule:

Proportion of Debt (1)	EPS (2)	Beta (3)	$k_s^L = k_{RF} + \beta(k_M - k_{RF})$ (4)	Market Price, P_0 (2)/(4) (5)
0.00	$2.00	0.80	10.8	$_____
0.10	2.20	____	11.4	19.30
0.20	2.38	1.00	____	19.83
0.30	2.55	1.10	____	____
0.40	2.68	____	13.5	____
0.50	2.80	1.40	____	____
0.60	2.90	____	____	17.90

a. Fill in the schedule above. At what proportion of debt is the market price maximized?
b. After you complete (a), your boss asks, "What will be the impact on the firm's overall opportunity cost of capital?" To provide an answer, you have begun preparing the following schedule:

Proportion of Debt (1)	After-Tax Cost of Debt (2)	Weighted Debt Cost (1) × (2) (3)	Proportion of Equity (4)	k_s^L [from (a)] (5)	Weighted Equity Cost (4) × (5) (6)	Opportunity Cost of Capital (3) + (6) (7)
0.00	4.8%	0	1.0	10.8%	10.8%	10.8%
0.10	4.8	____	____	____	____	____
0.20	5.1	____	____	____	____	____
0.30	5.4	____	____	____	____	____
0.40	6.0	____	____	____	____	____
0.50	6.9	____	____	____	____	____
0.60	7.8	____	____	____	____	____

Complete the schedule. Does the minimum opportunity cost of capital occur at the same proportion of debt to equity where the market price of Big Three's stock is maximized? Explain.

13.4 New Brunswick General is an all-equity firm. The firm has 200,000 shares of common stock outstanding, the EPS is $2, and all earnings are paid out to the shareholders as dividends. The current market value of the stock is $20 per share, and the opportunity cost of equity capital is 10 percent. General is considering two alternative plans to raise $3 million for a new and highly promising investment project, as follows:

Plan A: Issue 150,000 more shares of common stock at $20 per share.

Plan B: Issue $3 million of 9 percent coupon rate bonds.

After the new investment, General expects EBIT to be $1,400,000. The tax rate is 35 percent.
a. Calculate the EPS (and dividends per share) under each plan after the expansion.
b. If the opportunity cost of equity stays at 10 percent when common stock is employed, what is the new market price per share?
c. If bonds are used, the opportunity cost of equity capital increases to 12 percent. What is the new market price per share under that plan?
d. Explain why the market price calculated in (b) is higher than the beginning market price of $20. Then explain why the market price calculated in (c) is greater than that calculated in (b). How does this relate to the basic business of the firm, and the financing employed?
e. Which financing plan do you recommend? Why?

13.5 Armour Motors is undertaking a thorough cash flow analysis. At present the firm has no debt or preferred stock outstanding. Although Armour is profitable and expects substantial long-run positive cash flows, it is experiencing a temporary problem. The forecasted financial information for next year, before any financing, is as follows:

Cash inflows from sales	$6 million
Cash wages and salaries	$2.2 million
Cash payments for materials used in production process	$2.8 million
Other cash outflows *including taxes*	$700,000

Even though the year is expected to be a poor one, Armour is considering expanding through a $5 million bond issue with a 13 percent coupon interest rate. Armour's current cash position is $600,000. Under no circumstances does it want to lower its cash balance to less than $300,000. The tax rate is 30 percent.
a. Based on the forecasted information, what is the projected addition to Armour's cash level?
b. What is the amount of cash outflow for interest on the new bond issue before and after taxes?
c. Based on your analysis, should Armour issue the bond?

13.6 Mini Case You have just been hired as the Chief Financial Officer of Harrison Chemicals, a relatively young firm that has developed specialty chemical products to serve a number of "niche" markets. Until recently Harrison was a family-run business, but with the retirement of "Bull" Harrison, the founder of Harrison Chemicals, nonfamily professional management has been brought into the firm. Harrison has grown rapidly in recent years and expects to continue growing at a compound rate of 18 percent per year for the next four years. In planning for the future, you begin by examining Harrison's balance sheet:

Current assets	$150,000	Current liabilities	$275,000
Long-term assets	450,000	Long-term liabilities	25,000
Total assets	$600,000	Common stock	200,000
		Retained earnings	100,000
		Total liabilities and shareholder's equity	$600,000

Of the current liabilities, only $25,000 is bank debt; the rest are accounts payable and accrued liabilities. In visiting with others in the firm, you find out that in the past Harrison financed its expansion almost entirely with internally generated funds, and it has never paid any cash dividends.

a. What does the pecking order theory say about the capital structure decision? Based on what you know about Harrison Chemicals, does the pecking order theory appear to describe the firm?

b. Calculate Harrison Chemicals' debt/book equity ratio. If the debt/book equity ratio for the industry is 0.70 and the debt/market equity ratio for the industry is 0.46, how does Harrison's correspond with that of other firms in the chemical industry? What if you also find out that Harrison's earnings are $45,000 and its P/E ratio is about 7 times earnings, while the average P/E ratio for chemical firms is about 10 times earnings? (*Note:* Calculate debt/market equity and debt/industry-based market equity.) What conclusion do you reach about Harrison's capital structure?

c. The new President and CEO of Harrison wants to understand more about factors that affect capital structure decisions in practice. You need to provide that information by, first, discussing the factors suggested, using Modigliani and Miller to frame the discussion. Second, you need to provide a complete discussion of the impact of transaction costs and signalling on capital structure decisions. Third, discuss other possible factors that may affect a firm's capital structure decision. (Be sure to discuss in some detail the possible interrelationships between a firm's capital structure and its free cash flow.)

d. Harrison Chemical has employed very little debt relative to other chemical firms. Which of the factors discussed in (c) appear to be the most important ones that apply to Harrison? Why?

e. Based on the 18 percent growth expected for Harrison Chemicals, you have been estimating possible financing needs. Your conclusion is that Harrison will not be able to undertake all of the positive net present value capital investment projects necessary to achieve this level of growth without obtaining external financing. Harrison currently has 30,000 shares of common stock outstanding. You estimate the company will need $200,000 in additional capital immediately; this will last for one and a half to two years. The funds can be raised by selling 20,000 shares of common stock at $10 each; by selling 10,000 shares at $10 each and issuing $100,000 of 11 percent coupon rate bonds at their par value of $100,000; or by selling $200,000 of 11 percent bonds at their par value of $200,000. Harrison currently has $50,000 in total interest-bearing debt; the average interest rate on the existing debt is 10.5 percent. Earnings before interest and taxes (EBIT) for next year are estimated to be $80,000, and Harrison's tax rate is 40 percent. Determine the following:

1. The debt/equity ratio under the three alternatives.
2. Earnings after taxes and earnings per share under the three plans.
3. The interest coverage (times interest earned = EBIT/interest) under the three plans.
4. The crossover EBIT, EBIT*, between the all-common-stock financing plan and the all-debt financing plan.

f. In part (e) the emphasis was on the impact on the debt/equity ratio, earnings, and interest coverage for next year. What other factors need to be considered in determining the financing used and the resulting capital structure for Harrison? Given the data available, which financing plan do you want to recommend to the President and CEO of Harrison? Why is this plan superior to the other two?

REFERENCES

BERKOVITCH, ELAZAR, and M. P. NARAYANAN. "Timing of Investment and Financing Decisions in Imperfectly Competitive Financial Markets." *Journal of Business* 66 (April 1993): 219–248.

HARRIS, MILTON, and ARTHUR RAVIV. "Corporate Control Contests and Capital Structure." *Journal of Financial Economics* 20 (January/March 1988): 55–86.

ISRAEL, RONEN. "Capital Structure and the Market for Corporate Control: The Defensive Role of Debt Financing." *Journal of Finance* 46 (September 1991): 1391–1409.

JALILVAND, ABOLHASSAN, and TAE H. PARK. "Default Risk, Firm Characteristics, and the Valuation of Variable-Rate Debt Instruments." *Financial Management* 23 (Summer 1994): 58–68.

JENSEN, MICHAEL C. "Agency Costs of Free Cash Flow, Corporate Finance and Takeovers." *American Economic Review* 76 (May 1986): 323–339.

JENSEN, MICHAEL C., AND WILLIAM H. MECKLING. "Theory of the Firm: Managerial Behaviour, Agency Costs and Ownership Structure." *Journal of Financial Economics* 3 (October 1976): 305–360.

KIM, MOSHE, and VOJISLAV MAKSIMOVIC. "Technology, Debt and the Exploitation of Growth Options." *Journal of Banking and Finance* 14 (December 1990): 1113–1131.

LELAND, HAYNE, and DAVID PYLE. "Information Asymmetries, Financial Structure, and Financial Intermediation." *Journal of Finance* 32 (May 1977): 371–388.

MAKSIMOVIC, VOJISLAV, and JOSEF ZECHNER. "Debt, Agency Costs, and Industry Equilibrium." *Journal of Finance* 46 (December 1991): 1619–1643.

MALITZ, ILEEN. "On Financial Contracting: The Determinants of Bond Covenants." *Financial Management* 15 (Summer 1986): 18–25.

MEHRAN, HAMID. "Executive Incentive Plans, Corporate Control, and Capital Structure." *Journal of Financial and Quantitative Analysis* 27 (December 1992): 539–560.

MYERS, STEWART C. "Determinants of Corporate Borrowing." *Journal of Financial Economics* 5 (November 1977): 147–175.

MYERS, STEWART C. "The Capital Structure Puzzle." *Journal of Finance* 39 (July 1984): 575–592.

MYERS, STEWART C., and NICHOLAS S. MAJLUF. "Corporate Financing and Investment Decisions When Firms Have Information That Investors Do Not Have." *Journal of Financial Economics* 13 (June 1984): 187.

ROSS, STEPHEN. "The Determination of Financial Structure: The Incentive-Signalling Approach." *Bell Journal of Economics* 8 (Spring 1977)

SHLEIFER, ANDREI, and ROBERT W. VISHNY. "Liquidation Values and Debt Capacity: A Market Equilibrium Approach." *Journal of Finance* 47 (September 1992): 1343–66.

SMITH, CLIFFORD W., JR., and JEROLD B. WARNER. "On Financial Contracting: An Analysis of Bond Covenants." *Journal of Financial Economics* 7 (June 1979): 117–161.

SMITH, CLIFFORD W., JR., and ROSS L. WATTS. "The Investment Opportunity Set and Corporate Financing, Dividend, and Compensation Policies." *Journal of Financial Economics* 32 (December 1992): 263–292.

STULZ, RENE. "Managerial Control of Voting Rights: Financing Policies and the Market for

Corporate Control." *Journal of Financial Economics* 20 (January/February 1988): 25–54.

TITMAN, SHERIDAN. "The Effect of Capital Structure on a Firm's Liquidation Decision." *Journal of Financial Economics* 13 (March 1984): 137–151.

WEISS, LAWRENCE A. "Bankruptcy Dissolution: Direct Costs and Violation of Priority and Claims." *Journal of Financial Economics* 27 (October 1990): 285–314.

14

Dividend Policy

EXECUTIVE SUMMARY

The firm's cash dividend decision involves determining how much of internally generated funds to pay out in the form of dividends and how much to use for other corporate purposes. Under both the Miller and Modigliani and the residual dividend arguments, the value of the firm is independent of the firm's cash dividend policy. On the other hand, items related to taxes, cash flow and growth options, and signalling have been suggested as factors that influence dividend policy. Most firms follow a policy consistent with the smoothed residual dividend approach and the pecking order theory. They establish both a dollar amount per share they plan to maintain and a target dividend payout ratio around which they attempt to fluctuate. Then the firm finances its corporate needs with internally generated funds and debt while fluctuating around both its target payout ratio and its target capital structure.

Some firms elect to repurchase shares of their own outstanding common stock. The primary reasons are to use excess cash, provide additional returns to shareholders, and sometimes "leverage up" the firm. Both stock splits and stock dividends provide additional shares to the firm's current shareholders on a pro rata basis. The firm's cash dividend policy, along with repurchases and stock splits or stock dividends, appears to be used by firms to signal information about the firm's future cash flows.

DIVIDENDS AND FINANCING

In order to maximize the value of the firm, we need to understand a firm's cash dividend policy. The question is, does a high or a low (or no) cash dividend policy maximize the value of the firm? Or should the firm simply repurchase shares of its common stock—which can be an alternative approach for distributing cash flows back to the owners? We will see that the answers to these questions are somewhat messy, and we are not certain if a firm's dividend policy directly affects the value of the firm.

The decision to pay cash dividends is simultaneously a decision not to reinvest this same cash in the firm. To see this, consider the relationship between cash flow and possible uses, shown in Figure 14.1. A firm's available cash comes from two sources—

Figure 14.1

Relationship Between Cash Flow and Potential Uses of Cash

The more cash distributed to stockholders, the less available for maintaining ongoing operations and expansion, or the more new external financing that must be obtained.

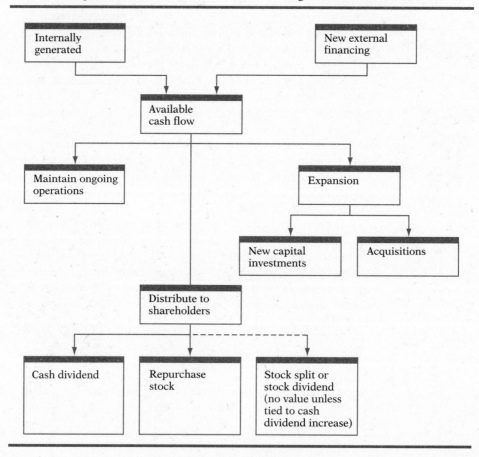

internally generated and new external financing. Once cash is on hand, it has three general uses. First, ongoing operations must be maintained. These include paying salaries, marketing expenses, taxes, and financing charges; repaying debts; buying materials; maintaining and updating equipment; and so forth. The remaining funds are then available for one of two purposes: expansion—through new capital investments or the acquisition of other firms—or distribution to the firm's shareholders. Other things being equal, the more cash distributed to shareholders, the less internally generated equity capital is available (which affects the firm's capital structure) and the smaller the firm's capital budget. Thus, the firm's cash dividend decision may simultaneously affect its capital structure and capital budgeting decisions. For analytical purposes we often separate the three decision areas—investment decisions, financing decisions, and dividend policy—but their interrelationships must be kept in mind.

Once the firm decides to make a distribution to investors, it has two primary means of doing so. These also appear in Figure 14.1. The first and most direct is through cash dividends. The second is through stock repurchases. Many firms also declare stock splits and stock dividends that they would like investors to consider valuable. As we shall see, however, in the absence of any signalling effects, neither a stock split nor a stock dividend by itself alters the value of the firm.

Before we discuss these topics, it is useful to understand the magnitude of cash dividends. Table 14.1 shows total earnings, taxes, and cash dividends for firms during

Table 14.1

Total Earnings, Taxes, and Cash Dividends for Nonfinancial Corporations, 1985–1994, (in millions)

Dividend payout ratios have increased due to continued increases in total cash dividends being paid, coupled with slow growth in earnings.

		Taxes			Dividends	
Year	Taxes (1)	Earnings Before Taxes (2)	Taxes as a Percentage of Before-Tax Earnings (1)/(2) (3)	Cash Dividends Declared (4)	Earnings After Taxes (5)	Dividend Payment Rates (4)/(5) (6)
1985	$17,731	$44,116	40%	$19,477	$26,385	74%
1986	14,194	34,833	41	17,802	20,639	86
1987	16,567	52,990	31	20,442	36,423	56
1988	17,587	60,435	29	24,781	42,848	58
1989	15,302	52,532	29	24,408	37,230	66
1990	10,424	27,754	38	24,781	17,330	143
1991	5,430	9,623	56	22,427	4,193	535
1992	3,513	6,190	57	21,024	2,677	785
1993	7,411	17,903	41	19,758	10,492	188
1994	13,010	39,293	33	22,281	26,683	84

Source: Quarterly Financial Statistics for Enterprises, Catalogue no. 61-008, Statistics Canada, various issues.

the 1985–1994 period. As we can see, taxes declined to 29 percent of earnings before rising in recent years. The total amount of cash dividends increased until 1990—from $19.5 billion in 1985 to $24.8 billion in 1990—and then declined to $19.8 billion in 1993 before increasing again in 1994. Until 1990 the percentage increase in cash dividends was substantially in excess of the increase in earnings (before or after taxes), and from 1991 through 1993 the decrease in dividends was substantially less than the decrease in earnings; this was accomplished by increasing the dividend payout ratio (cash dividends divided by earnings after taxes). It is easy to see that in both good times and bad, firms pay out a substantial portion of their earnings in the form of cash dividends.

Also, consider the following data, which show the percentage increase in both cash dividends and inflation:

Year	Total Cash Dividends (percentage change)	Consumer Price Index (percentage change)
1985	32.6	4.0
1986	−8.6	4.1
1987	14.8	4.4
1988	21.2	4.1
1989	−1.5	4.8
1990	1.5	4.8
1991	−9.5	5.6
1992	−6.3	1.5
1993	−6.0	1.8
1994	12.7	0.2
Mean	5.1	3.5

Source: *Quarterly Financial Statistics for Enterprises, catelogue no. 61–008* Statistics Canada; and *Bank of Canada Review*, various issues.

Many firms have expressly stated that one of their goals is to increase cash dividends at a rate at least equal to inflation. An examination of this data indicates that, although total cash dividends decreased in 5 of the years, over the entire 10 years they increased, on average, more than 1.5 times faster than inflation.

Although there are many differences among firms, in general they pay out a sizable portion of their cash flows in the form of cash dividends. This understanding is important given the many factors that influence dividend policy and the tremendous differences of opinion concerning the importance of dividend policy. We now turn to a discussion of these topics.

Concept Review Questions

- What are two primary means a firm can use to distribute excess cash to the firm's shareholders?

- Briefly describe the general change in dividends paid over the period 1984 to 1994.

DOES DIVIDEND POLICY MATTER? THE IRRELEVANCE ARGUMENTS

Next to the firm's appropriate capital structure and capital budgeting techniques, the dividend decision has probably generated the most discussion in financial management. The controversy centres around this question: Does the firm's cash dividend policy influence the value of its common stock? To address this question, we begin by discussing the arguments of those who say that cash dividends do not matter.

MILLER AND MODIGLIANI'S IRRELEVANCE ARGUMENT

As a follow-on to their capital structure irrelevance argument, which we encountered in Chapters 12 and 13, Miller and Modigliani (1961) also concluded that the firm's cash dividend policy does not affect the value of the firm. To understand this position it is important to note three items: First, they assumed that capital markets are perfect in that no taxes, brokerage fees, or flotation costs exist. Second, the firm's capital structure is fixed so that we do not mix dividend policy with the firm's capital structure policy. Third, the firm's investment policy is fixed in that the firm follows a value-maximizing policy of accepting all positive NPV projects.

To understand the reasoning behind the Miller and Modigliani argument, let us consider AMT Research. Its current market-value-based balance sheet is as follows:

Cash	$5,000	Debt	$20,000
Long-term assets	45,000	Equity	30,000 + NPV
Investment opportunity ($5,000 investment required)	NPV		
	$50,000 + NPV		$50,000 + NPV

The firm has $5,000 in cash that can be paid out to the firm's shareholders in the form of cash dividends or be invested in the new positive NPV investment opportunity. It seems that the firm has a dilemma: It can pay the cash dividend and return some of the firm to its owners, or it can take the investment opportunity and maximize its value. But it also has the ability to do both—that is, to pay the dividends and also make the wealth-maximizing investment. All it has to do is to raise more funds so that it has $5,000 to make the investment. The firm cannot issue debt, because that would change the capital structure proportions. Instead, the firm sells more stock. How much does it need to sell? That is easy—it needs to sell $5,000 worth of stock to replace the $5,000 paid out in dividends.

What happens to the value of the original shareholders' stock during the process of paying the cash dividend, selling more stock, and making the investment? Their original claim on the firm was for $30,000 + NPV. Because the investment and capital structure policies of AMT Research are unaffected, the total equity value of $30,000 + NPV must be unchanged. The value of the stock held by the original shareholders is now

$$\text{value of original shareholders' shares} = \text{equity value of firm} - \text{value of new shares}$$
$$= (\$30,000 + \text{NPV}) - \$5,000$$
$$= \$25,000 + \text{NPV}$$

But the original shareholders' have also received a cash dividend of $5,000. Hence, the value of their stock is unaffected, and we can conclude that dividend policy does not matter to the original shareholders, nor does it affect the value of the firm.

Providing that AMT Research takes all positive NPV investment opportunities, the value of the firm is maximized. All that has happened is that cash is being recycled. AMT Research pays it out with one hand to the original shareholders, while with the other hand it sells new stock to raise additional cash.[1]

Although the MM argument ignores taxes, flotation costs, and some other complications that exist in practice, it provides *the* frame of reference for considering what factors might cause cash dividends to affect the value of the firm. Before considering these issues, let us consider another version of the dividend irrelevance argument.

THE RESIDUAL THEORY OF DIVIDENDS

The basis of the **residual theory of dividends** is that investors are as well or better off if the firm retains and reinvests internally generated funds as they are if it pays them out, *provided* the investment opportunities facing the firm are at least as good as those facing investors. Under the residual theory, the firm's dividend policy would be the following:

1. Establish the optimum capital budget—that is, accept all projects with positive net present values.
2. Determine the amount of common equity needed to finance the new investments while maintaining the firm's target capital structure.
3. Use internally generated funds to supply this equity whenever possible.
4. Pay cash dividends only to the extent that internally generated funds remain after taking all appropriate capital investment opportunities.

The residual theory of dividends is concerned with the "leftover" internally generated funds. Under this theory, cash dividends should be paid only if there is cash left over after making the investment decision.

Consider Pacific Industries, which finances 40 percent of its investments via debt and the remaining 60 percent with common equity. The firm's internally generated funds are $12 million, which, in part or in total, can be distributed to the shareholders or reinvested in the firm. Pacific has the following independent investment opportunities to chose from[2]:

---

[1] Note that the original shareholders get the benefit of the positive NPV investment opportunity. All that the new shareholders receive is a fair return on their investment, provided that markets are efficient and the stock was sold at a fair price.

[2] For simplicity, the internal rate of return criterion is employed to measure project desirability. Since the projects are independent of each other, the ranking of project desirability is the same with internal rate of return as with net present value. The same results can be obtained using net present value, but the presentation is slightly more complex.

Project	Initial Investment (in millions)	IRR
A	$5	25%
B	3	21
C	6	18
D	6	16
E	4	13
F	5	10

These opportunities are graphed in Figure 14.2, along with the opportunity cost of capital of 14 percent. As indicated, projects A, B, C, and D, requiring a total initial investment of $20 million, should be undertaken. Out of this $20 million, $12 million [i.e., ($20 million) (0.60)] in equity financing would be used. Because the $12 million needed is exactly equal to the internally generated funds, Pacific would use these funds for capital investment and thus pay no cash dividends. The other $8 million required to finance the capital investments would be secured via debt financing.

If, on the other hand, Pacific's opportunity cost of capital had been higher, so that only projects A, B, and C had been undertaken, a total of $14 million would be needed for capital investment. Sixty percent of this, or $8.4 million [i.e., ($14 million) (0.60)], would be provided via internally generated funds. The remainder, $12 million minus $8.4 million, or $3.6 million, would be distributed to the firm's common shareholders as a cash dividend.

Figure 14.2

Investment Opportunities and Opportunity Cost of Capital Schedules for Pacific Industries

Pacific would accept all projects providing a return equal to or greater than its opportunity cost of capital of 14 percent. Thus, A, B, C, and D would be accepted, and E and F rejected.

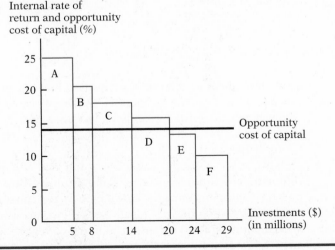

Under the residual dividend theory, cash dividends are paid only if funds are left over after accepting all profitable capital budgeting projects. *The value of the firm is a function of its investment decisions. Thus, like the MM argument, the residual theory suggests that dividend policy is a passive variable and has no influence on the value of the firm.*

We should pause here and clarify one point before going on. In Chapter 4, we said that cash dividends are the foundation for the valuation of common stock. Thus, the market value of a share of stock is equal to the present value of all future cash dividends. This is true, but the *timing* of the dividends can vary. When we say that dividend policy does not matter, we are simply saying that the present value of the future cash dividends remains unchanged even though dividend policy may influence their timing. Dividends, including liquidating dividends, can still be paid, but it is a matter of indifference when they are paid, as long as their present value remains unchanged.

Concept Review Questions

- Briefly describe the Miller and Modigliani dividend irrelevance argument.
- What is the firm's dividend payout policy under the residual theory of dividends?

WHY DO FIRMS PAY CASH DIVIDENDS?

Under the irrelevance argument, dividend policy does not affect the value of the firm. However, that is not all of the story. As we saw in Table 14.1, firms sometimes pay out more than 100 percent of total earnings in the form of cash dividends. In addition, firms appear to value some stability in terms of their dividend payout. To understand dividend policy better, we first examine taxes and their possible impact on the firm's dividend decision. Then we examine interrelationships among dividends, cash flow, and growth options. Third, we look at some signalling arguments related to the firm's cash dividend policy. Finally, we consider some other factors potentially related to the dividend decision.

TAXES AND THE FIRM'S CASH DIVIDEND POLICY

As we have discussed previously, taxes affect many financial decisions. They also come into play in the dividend decision. Firms that pay cash dividends do not get to deduct the dividends as an expense of doing business. Hence, cash dividends are paid out of the firm's after-tax cash flows. For the recipients of cash dividends, however, there are tax consequences.

As we saw in Chapter 8, the top (combined federal and provincial) tax rate for corporations is about 45 percent. For individuals there are three federal marginal tax rates on ordinary income, such as salaries, wages, and interest income. The amount of tax paid is based on the individual's taxable income, which is total income minus a set of exemptions and deductions. In addition, each province also levies a tax on personal income. Tables 14.2 and 14.3 show the federal and provincial rates applicable for

Table 14.2

1995 Individual Income Tax Rates

The provincial personal tax rates vary across Canada. The rates shown below are basic federal and provincial rates and do not include any federal or provincial surtaxes and flat taxes based on net or taxable income.

Federal			Provinces or Territories	Percentage of Federal Tax
Taxable Income	Basic Tax ($)	Marginal Rate (%)		
Up to $29,590	—	17	Alberta	45.5
$29,590 to $59,180	5,030	26	British Columbia	52.5
$59,180 and over	12,724	29	Manitoba	52.0
			New Brunswick	64.0
			Newfoundland	69.0
			Nova Scotia	59.5
			Ontario	58.0
			Prince Edward Island	59.5
			Saskatchewan	50.0
			Northwest Territories	45.0
			Yukon Territory	50.0

Source: Tax Facts and Figures 1995, Coopers & Lybrand (Canada).

Table 14.3

1995 Individual Income Tax Rates for Quebec Residents

Quebec administers its own tax system. Quebec residents receive a 16.5 percent abatement for their federal tax and then pay a provincial tax at the appropriate rate shown.

Taxable Income	Basic Tax ($)	Marginal Rate (%)
Up to $6,999	—	16
$ 7,000 to $13,999	1,120	19
$14,000 to $22,999	2,450	21
$23,000 to $49,999	4,340	23
$50,000 and over	10,550	24

Source: Tax Facts and Figures 1995, Coopers and Lybrand(Canada).

1995.[3] Furthermore, if financial assets such as common stock are held for investment purposes and then sold at a profit, a capital gains tax rate equal to 75 percent of the ordinary marginal tax rate applies.[4]

---

[3] The federal government collects all personal income taxes on behalf of the provinces and territories and then transfers them to the provincial treasuries. The only exception to this rule is the Province of Quebec, which administers its own tax system.

[4] There are also federal and provincial surtaxes and flat taxes. In our discussion we deal solely with the basic tax rates.

A person residing in any province or territory (except Quebec) on December 31 must pay provincial tax at the appropriate rate indicated in Table 14.2 based on his or her federal income tax. For example, a Manitoba resident with taxable income of $35,000 will pay a federal income tax of $6,436.60 [$5,030 + 0.26 ($35,000 − $29,590)] and a provincial tax of $3,347.03 (0.52 × $6,436.60). Thus (excluding surtax) this individual will have to pay a total income tax of $9,783.63 minus any nonrefundable tax credits.[5] For individuals residing in all provinces or territories other than Quebec, the **total marginal tax rate** is calculated by multiplying the federal marginal rate by 1 plus the provincial rate. Thus our Manitoba resident has a total marginal tax rate of 39.52 percent (0.26 × 1.52). Quebec residents receive an abatement of 16.5 percent of their basic federal tax but must pay Quebec income tax at the rates indicated in Table 14.3.

There are tax aspects for corporations and individuals receiving cash dividends. First let us look at firms which own shares of common stock in another firm. For Canadian corporations, 100 percent of the cash dividends received from the investment in another taxable Canadian firm are excluded from income. On the other hand, any capital gain realized from selling the stock is taxed at 75 percent of the firm's marginal tax rate. Thus, there is a significant tax advantage for corporations receiving cash dividends.

The argument is often made that because of different tax rates on ordinary income versus capital gains, individual investors would benefit from firms *not* paying cash dividends. To illustrate, assume a firm has a positive NPV project that requires an investment of $100. The firm also has free cash flow of $100. To make the investment, the firm has two alternatives. The first is to pay no cash dividends, and simply take the $100 in free cash flow and make the investment. The value of the firm will increase by $100, so current shareholders obtain the full benefit of the $100. The second alternative is to pay a cash dividend of $100, then turn around and sell $100 of new common equity to fund the positive NPV project. Considering the differential impact of taxes and that investors can decide when to pay the taxes if the return is in the form of capital gains, there is a tax deferral advantage to not paying cash dividends.

However, this advantage to receiving capital gains is offset by a dividend tax credit. As noted earlier, corporations pay dividends out of after-tax cash flows; therefore, the taxation of dividend income at the individual level constitutes double taxation. To alleviate part of this situation, the tax regulations employ a gross up and dividend tax credit system. This system requires that dividends received from taxable Canadian corporations be grossed up by 25 percent to arrive at taxable dividends. A dividend tax credit equal to 13.33 percent of taxable dividends is allowed to be deducted from federal income tax in arriving at the net federal tax payable. Table 14.4 is an illustration of this procedure for a person living in Ontario, with a federal marginal tax rate of 26 percent, who received $10,000 of dividends from a taxable Canadian corporation.

Table 14.4 shows that the gross-up and dividend tax credit method results in an effective tax rate on dividend income that is lower than the individual's total marginal

---

[5] Nonrefundable tax credits are found by taking the sum of, among other things, a basic personal amount for the person filing, an amount for his or her spouse, contributions to the Canada or Quebec Pension Plans, unemployment insurance premiums, and tuition fees. This sum is now multiplied by 17 percent to give nonrefundable tax credits. These credits are called nonrefundable because if they are more than an individual's federal income tax, the difference is *not* refunded to the individual.

Table 14.4

Calculation of After-Tax Dividends

The effective tax rate on dividend income is lower than the total marginal tax rate because of the gross-up and dividend tax credit.

Dividends received	$10,000
Add: Gross-up at 25%	2,500
Taxable dividends	12,500
Federal income tax (0.26 × $12,500)	3,250
Less: Dividend tax credit (0.1333 × $12,500)	1,667
Federal taxes payable	1,583
Add: Ontario tax (0.58 × $1,583)	918
₊Total tax	$ 2,501
Dividends after taxes ($10,000 − $2,501)	$ 7,499
Effective tax rate on dividends (total tax/dividends received)	25.01%
Total marginal tax rate for this Ontario resident (0.26 × 1.58)	41.08%

tax rate. It is also lower than the 30.81 percent (0.4108 × 0.75) that this individual would have to pay on capital gains. Thus individuals would have a slight preference for cash dividends. In effect, since the difference between these two rates is not large, the tax laws effectively wipe out the difference between the tax rate on ordinary income and that on capital gains for individuals. However, *common shareholders still have a choice of when to pay taxes if the returns came from capital gains instead of cash dividends.* Thus, it appears that (1) tax rate differences between income and capital gains for corporations and (2) deferral motives by individuals explain why firms pay cash dividends and, at the same time, continue to issue additional equity to replace the equity drained out through the dividend process.

In examining the tax impacts on dividend policy, Miller and Scholes (1978) argue that any tax disadvantage of dividends can be reduced by the investors' ability to offset dividend income by interest deductions on borrowing, combined with investment of the proceeds from borrowing in tax-sheltered investments such as insurance contracts and retirement funds. Whether this strategy has ever been employed widely is unknown. Numerous studies have attempted to determine whether taxes directly affect dividend policy; the results are mixed, and the answer is unclear.

Recently, Brennan and Thakor (1990) developed a model dealing with alternative procedures for distributing cash from corporations to shareholders. They show that even with the preferential tax treatment of capital gains, the majority of a firm's shareholders may support the receipt of cash dividends for small distributions. If the distribution is large, a repurchase of stock by the firm (which, others things being equal, drives up the value of the stock) is preferred. In another recent article, DeAngelo (1991) builds on logic similar to Miller's personal tax argument (see Chapter 12) and argues that, even with the tax differential and deferral implications, firms will pay cash dividends. His logic is as follows: (1) If all firms decided to adopt a low or zero payout policy, there would be less present consumption in the economy and an excess of future consumption; and (2) in equilibrium, adjustments must occur to override the tax benefits of deferral, so that firms *in aggregate* supply the appropriate mix of taxable cash dividends and capital gains. In conclusion, although the tax differential and deferral arguments may make intuitive sense, both theory and empirical evidence cast doubt on whether these factors affect dividend policy in any consistent manner.

DIVIDENDS, CASH FLOW, AND GROWTH OPTIONS

In Chapter 13 we examined the free cash flow theory developed by Jensen (1986); this theory also has relevance for interrelationships between a firm's investment decision and its dividend decision. The greater the amount of new investment undertaken by the firm, the smaller the cash dividend that can be paid, or the more new equity that needs to be issued. Firms with more growth opportunities channel cash to fund the growth options; accordingly, they have lower free cash flow and pay lower dividends. This cash flow argument by Jensen is also supported by two agency cost arguments.

From the standpoint of the firm's bondholders, any time the firm pays cash dividends without issuing new equity, the value of the bondholders' claim decreases. Smith and Warner (1979) and Kalay (1982), after evaluating dividend covenants contained in bonds, conclude that restrictions on dividend payout effectively impose a minimum investment requirement on the firm, thereby lowering the underinvestment problem. (The underinvestment problem was discussed in Chapters 12 and 13 when we examined the firm's capital structure decision.) Firms with more growth options can tolerate more restrictions on dividends; hence, firms with more growth options should pay out less in the form of cash dividends.

Finally, Rozeff (1982) and Easterbrook (1984) note that, other things being equal, paying dividends increases the frequency with which firms go to the equity markets to raise additional equity capital. By going to the equity markets, the firm is more frequently subjected to the intensive capital market monitoring and discipline that occurs at the time new funds are raised, thereby lowering agency costs. At the same time, establishing a dividend policy may also reduce agency costs. Firms will adopt policies that minimize total agency costs. Those firms with high growth rates and growth options and a high demand for capital have less reason to pay dividends, and they minimize agency costs by going periodically to the capital markets. Firms with lower growth options pay higher dividends, thus minimizing agency costs via their cash dividend policy. The important point is that firms that have more growth options are expected to pay lower cash dividends. From a free cash flow standpoint, we see that a firm's growth options and its dividend policy are linked together.

SIGNALLING

Another way to examine the cash dividend decision is from a signalling perspective. This perspective has been developed by Bhattacharya (1979), Miller and Rock (1985), Ambarish, John, and Williams (1987), and Ofer and Thakor (1987), among others. The underlying thrust of their arguments is that, in a risky world with heterogeneous expectations and less-than-perfect markets, the cash dividend policy communicates information—provides a signal—about the firm's future cash flows over and above any existing information. An increase in the payout ratio would be seen to indicate an increase in the future cash flows of the firm, and the market price of the firm's common stock would increase simply as a result of the increased cash dividends.

This viewpoint has been strengthened in recent years by empirical evidence.[6] Thus, the initiation of a dividend (that is, when a firm first starts to pay cash dividends) or an unexpected increase in cash dividends leads to an increase in the value of the firm's stock. Dividend initiations may also be associated with future increases in the firm's earnings (and hence its cash flow).[7] This line of theory and empirical support suggests that dividends may signal unique information about the future prospects of the firm.

SOME FURTHER ARGUMENTS FOR THE INFLUENCE OF DIVIDEND POLICY

In addition to the factors discussed previously, other less theoretical arguments have been made that either a high or a low dividend payout ratio may affect the value of the firm. Some of these arguments are as follows.

Resolution of Uncertainty   One argument presented in favour of a price effect is that by paying dividends, the firm resolves investor uncertainty. Because the retention of funds and promise of future dividends is uncertain, investors may prefer higher current dividends. Accordingly, they would bid up the market price for firms with higher payout ratios. Although the risk and return of the firm is not influenced, it is argued that investor *perception* of riskiness may decrease, thereby causing the market price to increase.

The basic valuation framework we have employed is $P_0 = D_1/(k_s - g)$, where P_0 is the current market price, D_1 is the cash dividend expected at time $t = 1$, k_s is the equity investors' required return, and g is the expected growth rate in cash dividends. If the investors' perception of risk decreases, their required return, k_s, will decrease. If the cash dividend, D_1, is \$3, k_s is 16 percent, and g is 8 percent, the initial price is

$$\text{price with no uncertainty resolution} = P_0 = \frac{\$3.00}{0.16 - 0.08} = \$37.50$$

If a higher payout ratio results in investors perceiving less uncertainty, and everything else remains the same, the required return might decrease to 15 percent. In that case, the market price would be

$$\text{price with uncertainity resolution} = P_0 = \frac{\$3.00}{0.15 - 0.08} = \$42.86$$

Thus, if a high payout ratio reduces investor perception of uncertainty, the market price of the firm's common stock increases.

Desire for Current Income   Another factor might be investor preferences for current income. In Chapter 4 (Figure 4.5), we examined the total returns on common stock investment between 1960 and 1994. Cash dividends provided 40 percent of the total returns from investing in common stock during this period. In addition, there is much less risk associated with cash dividends than with capital appreciation or loss, as

---

[6] Some of this evidence is summarized in Asquith and Mullins (1983) and Eades, Hess, and Kim (1985).
[7] See, for example, Healy and Palepu (1988).

evidenced by the much lower variability for the dividends. Investors with a preference for current income would favour a high-payout firm and thus might bid its price up.

Flotation Costs   As we discussed in Chapter 6, the presence of flotation costs makes the cost of internally generated common equity cheaper than the cost of issuing new common stock. If a firm's cost of internal common equity is 16 percent, then its cost of issuing new common stock may be 18 or 19 percent. This is due to the transaction costs and underpricing that occur when additional common stock is sold. Flotation costs may cause firms to favour retaining more funds, via a low dividend payout policy, because doing so reduces their cost of equity capital.

Brokerage Costs   In the absence of brokerage costs, investors could always buy or sell securities to create their own cash "dividend" stream if they did not like the policy followed by the firm. The presence of brokerage costs, however, means that investors receive less than 100 percent on the dollar when they buy or sell securities. Investors preferring high current income cannot sell stock without incurring additional costs. Likewise, those preferring a low level of current income also incur additional costs on reinvesting the cash dividends. The net effect may be to cut both ways—brokerage costs may create a preference for either a high or a low level of cash dividends.

Concept Review Questions

■ How is an individual's total marginal tax rate calculated?

■ Why would investors prefer a return in the form of capital gains rather than cash dividends?

■ How are a firm's growth options and its dividend policy related?

■ Describe how the dividend policy can "signal" a firm's financial position.

IS THERE AN OPTIMAL DIVIDEND POLICY?

We see that firms and individuals may have a preference for different kinds of dividend policies due to various factors and considerations. From the firm's standpoint, firms with substantial growth options may prefer a low-payout policy. Likewise, from an investor's standpoint, we see that certain investors might have a preference for high- or low-payout firms. Investors with low incomes and high current needs would favour high-payout firms. Investors in high income brackets would favour low-payout firms. This has often been called the **clientele effect**. That is, depending on the cash dividend policy that a firm establishes, it attracts a certain clientele of investors. Once that clientele is established, it may be that dividend policy does not directly influence the value of the firm's stock. A significant shift in the firm's cash dividend policy, however, would disrupt the firm's clientele, causing price effects until a new investor clientele owns the firm's common stock.

Despite extensive debate and substantial empirical testing, there is no consensus on the primary issue: whether or not the firm's cash dividend policy *by itself* influences the value of the common stock. Litzenberger and Ramaswamy (1982) concluded that higher dividend yields are associated with higher expected returns; this would imply that dividend policy does affect the value of the firm. However, Miller and Scholes

(1982) argue that Litzenberger and Ramaswamy introduced bias into the estimation procedure, which led to an overstatement of the effect of dividends. The best we can say right now is that the firm's cash dividend policy *may* influence the market value of the firm's stock—but then again, it may not. Our personal view is that Miller and Modigliani (1961), Black and Scholes (1974), Miller and Scholes (1978, 1982), and Miller (1986) are essentially correct: A firm's cash dividend policy does not affect the value of the firm, *providing* the policy does not affect its investment decisions. Most managers look at a number of other factors that come into play when the cash dividend decision is made.

OTHER FACTORS IN THE DIVIDEND DECISION

In addition to growth options and possible price effects, other factors appear to influence dividend policy in practice. These include liquidity and profitability, earnings stability, access to equity markets, and control.

Liquidity and Profitability   The cash position of the firm can influence cash dividends. Firms with a shortage of cash often restrict or discontinue cash dividends. Highly profitable firms with substantial cash positions often increase their cash dividends (or repurchase some of their outstanding common stock). One reason cash-rich firms pay more dividends is to provide greater protection against a possible takeover by another firm. By paying higher dividends, the cash-rich firm accomplishes two things: It makes its current shareholders happy, and it reduces its cash position, thus becoming a less tempting takeover target.

Earnings Stability   Another factor often considered in practice is the stability of the firm's earnings. Other things being equal, more stable firms are often in a better position to pay larger cash dividends than less stable firms. The reason is that they can plan for the future with much more certainty than can highly cyclical firms. Public utility firms, for example, pay high cash dividends. They can do this, in part, because of their relatively stable operating environment.

Access to Equity Markets   Smaller firms generally have much more difficulty or incur substantially higher costs when they attempt to raise external equity capital than do larger firms. Because their access to equity markets is limited, small firms pay lower cash dividends.

Control   For many small- and medium-sized firms, ownership control is an important issue. They may be reluctant to sell more common stock, opening ownership to "outsiders." They also will prefer to retain more internally generated funds to provide the equity capital needed for growth. By using internally generated common equity plus any borrowing required, they may be able simultaneously to maintain control *and* to meet the firm's capital needs.

CONSTRAINTS ON DIVIDENDS

Finally, certain constraints may inhibit the firm's ability to pay cash dividends. These involve contractual restrictions and legal restrictions.

Contractual Restrictions   Bond indentures, term loan agreements, and even preferred stock provisions may often impose restrictions on the payment of cash dividends. For example, a firm may be required to maintain a certain level of working capital or a minimum current ratio or times interest earned ratio (i.e., EBIT/interest). Another common restriction states that common shareholders may not be paid cash dividends until the preferred shareholders have received their dividends. Although these (and similar) restrictions typically do not inhibit the firm's ability to pay dividends, they may do so when a firm is experiencing financial difficulties. From the creditors' or preferred shareholders' points of view, that is exactly what restrictions of this type are intended to do.

Legal Restrictions   Federal and provincial acts governing incorporation of a firm provide statutory restrictions prohibiting the firm from paying cash dividends under certain conditions. For instance, the acts usually include a restriction on the firm's dividend-paying ability when the firm's liabilities exceed its assets, when the anticipated dividend exceeds the retained earnings, or when the dividend would be paid from the firm's invested capital.

Concept Review Questions

- Briefly describe the results of empirical studies on the relationship between dividend policy and the value of common stock.
- Describe how a firm's dividend policy is influenced by the firm's liquidity, profitability, earnings stability, access to equity markets, and control of the firm.

DIVIDEND POLICY IN PRACTICE

Neither theory nor empirical testing provides a complete answer to the question of whether dividend policy influences the market value of the firm's common stock. But, in practice, firms (and their boards of directors) act as though dividend policy *is* an important decision. They view it as being important both in and of itself and because of its signalling content. Stability of dividends is perceived as being important; firms prefer to maintain a steady and increasing level of cash dividends per share over time. Equally important, there is an extreme reluctance to reduce cash dividends. This reluctance to cut dividends is exhibited in Table 14.1. There we saw that after-tax earnings decreased significantly between 1990 and 1993 while cash dividends decreased only slightly. On the other hand, in 1994 when earnings after taxes increased by 120 percent, dividends increased by only 12.7 percent. Most firms in practice follow a **smoothed residual dividend policy**. After taking into account many of the items discussed previously, they set the cash dividend policy based on the following considerations:

1. The dividend is set at a constant dollar amount per share.
2. A target dividend payout ratio, which the firm plans to maintain over time, is established.
3. Dividends will be increased when and if it appears the increased dollar amount per share can be maintained.

4. The dollar amount of cash dividends paid per share will be decreased only with great reluctance.
5. Over the long run, the firm attempts to finance capital expenditures with internally generated funds and debt (supplemented only occasionally, if at all, by new common stock), while fluctuating around its target capital structure.

This smoothed residual dividend policy is consistent with some early work done by Lintner (1956). In addition, it is consistent with the pecking order theory suggested by Myers (as discussed in Chapter 13). A firm's dividend policy is determined simultaneously with its investment and financing decisions.

INTERFIRM DIFFERENCES

In assessing the firm's dividend policy in practice, it is useful to look at what firms actually do. In Table 14.5, the earnings per share, dividends per share, and dividend payout ratios are presented for Alcan Aluminium, British Columbia Telephone, and Canadian Pacific. Alcan Aluminium has had widely fluctuating dividends and payout ratios as its earnings fluctuated dramatically over the 1985–1994 period. B.C. Telephone has had a very stable dividend policy that involved paying out 60 to 80 percent of earnings in the form of cash dividends. Canadian Pacific had stable and increasing cash dividends in line with its increasing earnings per share between 1985 and 1990. From 1991 to 1993 dividends were cut significantly, but not eliminated, in response to negative earnings. In 1994 the firm maintained its dividend at the 1993 level, even though it showed a significant increase in earnings per share. These patterns are typical of some of the interfirm differences in cash dividends.

INDUSTRY DIFFERENCES

Dividend payout policies also vary, to an extent, depending on the primary industry in which the firm is involved. This variation results from different amounts of risk, profitability, growth opportunities, and regulation among industries. In the following list, we see a wide range of dividend payout ratios.

Industry	Payout Ratio
Wood and paper	27%
Chemicals, chemical products, and textiles	44
Electronic equipment and computer services	51
Petroleum and natural gas	57
Other fuels and electricity	95
Food	139
Machinery and equipment	25
Printing, publishing, and broadcasting	93
Iron, steel and related products	25

Source: Quarterly Financial Statistics for Enterprises, Statistics Canada, Catalogue no. 61–008.

Table 14.5

Dividend Payout for Three Firms

Alcan Aluminium's cash dividends and dividend payout ratio have fluctuated widely due to wide swings in earnings. British Columbia Telephone had more consistent payout ratios, while Canadian Pacific cut dividends in recent years.

	Alcan Aluminium Ltd.			British Columbia Telephone Company			Canadian Pacific Ltd.		
	Dividends per Share	EPS	Dividend Payout	Dividends per Share	EPS	Dividend Payout	Dividends per Share	EPS	Dividend Payout
1985	$0.49	$−0.81	*	$0.86	$1.10	78%	$0.48	$1.11	43%
1986	0.35	1.09	32%	0.86	1.23	70	0.48	0.50	96
1987	0.39	1.68	23	0.875	1.34	65	0.54	2.12	25
1988	0.59	3.85	15	0.91	1.45	63	0.64	2.50	26
1989	1.12	3.58	31	0.95	1.62	59	0.80	2.35	34
1990	1.12	2.33	48	1.02	1.72	59	0.92	1.11	83
1991	0.86	−0.25	*	1.10	1.78	62	0.63	−2.87	*
1992	0.45	−0.60	*	1.15	1.78	65	0.32	−1.50	*
1993	0.30	−0.54	*	1.19	1.81	66	0.32	−0.60	*
1994	0.30	0.34	88	1.23	1.88	65	0.32	1.16	28

*Not meaningful.

Source: Annual reports for each of the firms cited.

The wood and paper; machinery and equipment; and the iron, steel, and related products industries paid out less than 30 percent of their earnings in the form of cash dividends in 1994. On the other hand, the other fuels and electricity and the printing, publishing, and broadcasting industries paid out more than 90 percent of their earnings as cash dividends, while the food industry paid out more than 100 percent of its earnings in the form of cash dividends.

Not only do dividend payout ratios vary considerably among industries, they also vary among firms within a single industry. Consider the following data, which show the 1994 dividend payout ratios for firms in the wood and paper industry.

Firm	Dividends per Share	Payout Ratio
Abitibi-Price	$ 0	0%
Canfor	0.26	11.9
Cascades	0	0
Crestbrook Forest Industries	0.15	24.2
Domtar	0	0
Donohue	0.24	15.1
Fletcher Challenge	0.10	10.3
MacMillan Bloedel	0.60	44.0
Noranda Forest	0.40	39.6
Scott Paper	0.10	100.0

Source: Post Card Service, 1994 Financial Post Cards, Financial Post; and annual reports.

We see that Scott Paper paid out 100 percent of its earnings in 1994, while Abitibi-Price, Cascades, and Domtar paid no cash dividends. On the other hand, all of the other firms paid out between 10 and 44 percent of earnings in the form of cash dividends. These vastly different policies within an industry reflect the substantial differences among firms. Thus, although there do appear to be industry differences that influence cash dividend policies, we must not let these differences obscure the sizable interfirm differences that exist as well.

DIVIDEND CHANGES

We can also examine the actions taken by firms with respect to increasing or decreasing cash dividends. We have seen that firms prefer to maintain a constant dollar amount of dividends per share each year, increasing them only when they feel that the increase can be maintained and decreasing them only with great reluctance. During 1993 and 1994, 200 and 239 companies, respectively, increased their dividends, whereas 232 firms decreased them in 1993 and 88 in 1994.[8] The number of decreases is up dramatically from the 10 recorded in 1989 and is a reflection of the severe economic situation that faced many firms in the early 1990s.

---

[8] *Financial Post Dividend Record*, Financial Post.

One other aspect of dividend payment that deserves attention is the "extra" dividend. Many firms follow the practice of paying a regular cash dividend and then in good years declaring a **dividend extra**. This practice allows them to have a stated amount of cash dividends per share that can be supplemented, if desired, without raising the stated rate to a new higher level. In this way, the basic per share rate will not have to be cut in bad years. During 1993 and 1994, this practice was followed by 12 and 11 firms, respectively.

Concept Review Questions

- How is a firm's dividend policy established?
- Do dividend payout ratios vary among industries, among firms within an industry, or both?

DIVIDEND PAYMENT PROCEDURES

Cash dividends are normally paid quarterly. Assume that a firm has decided to pay a cash dividend of 75 cents each quarter. The relevant dates that shareholders would be concerned about if they owned or contemplated purchasing the stock, and the payment procedure, might be as follows:

Amount	Date Declared	Ex-Dividend Date	Date of Record	Date Payable
$0.75	January 21	February 12	February 14	March 12
0.75	April 15	May 8	May 10	June 11
0.75	July 15	August 6	August 10	September 9
0.75	October 14	November 6	November 10	December 10

1. DECLARATION (OR ANNOUNCEMENT) DATE   This is the date the board of directors meets and issues a statement declaring the next quarter's cash dividends. For our example, this is January 21 in the first quarter, April 15 in the second quarter, and so on. Once the dividends are declared, they become a legal liability of the firm. For example, the first announcement would indicate that a dividend of 75 cents a share will be paid on March 12 to shareholders of record as of February 14.

2. EX-DIVIDEND DATE   The **ex-dividend date** is an arbitrary date established for the convenience of the securities industry. The ex-dividend date is the second business day (i.e., Monday through Friday) preceding the record date as fixed by the firm. Establishing this date enables the firm (or its registrar, which is usually a trust company) to obtain an accurate determination of all shareholders by the record date. All shares owned before the ex-dividend date receive the cash dividend. Stock purchased on or after the ex day will not be entitled to the next cash dividend, because the new shareholder will not be listed as an owner of record on

the record date. For the firm in our example, the first quarter's record date was February 14; accordingly, the ex day is February 12.[9] If you purchased the stock on or before February 11, you would receive the dividend of 75 cents per share when it was paid on March 12. If you bought the stock on February 12, or any time thereafter, the former owner is entitled to the cash dividend paid on March 12.

3. RECORD DATE   The **record date** is the date the shareholder books are closed, to determine who the current shareholders are.

4. PAYMENT DATE   The **payment date** is the date when the firm actually mails the dividend cheque to its common shareholders.

The record date is important, but the ex-dividend date is actually more important in terms of deciding who is the owner of the stock for dividend purposes. Because of its importance for determining who is entitled to the next cash dividend, we would expect to see an adjustment in the firm's common stock market price on the ex-dividend date. If you owned the stock in our example on the day before the ex date, you would receive 75 cents on the next pay date. But because you will be 75 cents better off and the firm will be 75 cents worse off, what should happen to the market price of the firm's common stock on the ex day? Other things being equal, it should decrease by an amount approximately equal to the value of the cash dividend to be received.

DIVIDEND REINVESTMENT PLANS

In recent years, many firms have instituted **dividend reinvestment plans**. Under these plans, shareholders can reinvest their cash dividends in additional shares of common stock. The stock can be existing or newly issued shares. Under the first type of plan, a trust company acting as trustee accumulates funds from all shareholders electing this option and then purchases shares in the open market. Costs are borne on a pro rata basis but are generally small because of the volume of purchases.

In the second type of plan, the cash dividends go to buy newly issued shares of stock. In this plan, there may be a 3 to 5 percent reduction in the purchase price from the stock's current market price. Often no other fees are charged to the shareholders. A new-issue dividend reinvestment plan enables firms gradually to raise substantial amounts of new common stock capital. Dividend reinvestment plans are now a significant element in the issuance of new common stock, with some of Canada's largest companies, such as Alcan, Bank of Montreal, CanWest Global, Canadian Pacific, and Dominion Textile, having them.

Despite their growth in popularity, dividend reinvestment plans have one drawback from the shareholder's standpoint. Shareholders must pay taxes on the cash dividends each year, even though they never receive any cash. This factor has probably prevented more investors from signing up for dividend reinvestment plans.

---

[9] Note that in some cases a weekend will be involved, so the ex-dividend day is typically four calendar days preceding the record date. Prior to June 1995 the ex-dividend day was set at four business days before the record date.

REPURCHASING STOCK

In addition to paying cash dividends, firms sometimes repurchase their stock. However, unlike in the United States, where repurchased shares are either retired or held as treasury stock, in Canada, under the Canada Business Corporations Act, repurchased shares must be cancelled. Repurchasing may be accomplished by a tender offer to all the firm's shareholders, by purchasing stock in the secondary market, or by agreeing with one or a small group of the firm's major investors to buy their shares. Many repurchases are small in amount; others are very large. With fewer shares outstanding after a repurchase, other things being equal, the earnings per share of the remaining shares will increase. This increase should result in a higher per share market price.

For example, consider Northern Airlines, which has earnings after taxes of $10 million and plans to use 40 percent ($4 million) for cash dividends or for repurchasing some of the firm's common stock. Remember that neither usage affects the firm's reported net income or the total market value of the firm. There are 4 million shares outstanding, and the market price of the stock is $15 per share. Northern can use the $4 million to repurchase 250,000 shares of common stock at $16 per share,[10] or it can pay a cash dividend of $1 per share. The net effect of the repurchase would be as follows:

$$\text{current EPS} = \frac{\text{total earnings}}{\text{number of shares outstanding}} = \frac{\$10 \text{ million}}{4 \text{ million}} = \$2.50 \text{ per share}$$

$$\text{current P/E} = \frac{\text{market price per share}}{\text{earnings per share}} = \frac{\$15}{\$2.50} = 6 \text{ times}$$

$$\text{EPS after repurchasing 250,000 shares} = \frac{\$10 \text{ million}}{3.75 \text{ million}} = \$2.667 \text{ per share}$$

$$\text{expected market price after repurchasing} = (\text{P/E})(\text{EPS}) = (6)(\$2.667)$$
$$= \$16 \text{ per share}$$

From this example, we see that investors receive a $1 benefit either way. If cash dividends are paid, they receive the dollar directly; with the repurchase, the market price of the common stock increases by $1 to $16 per share. This occurs because we assumed that the shares would be repurchased at exactly $16 per share, and the P/E ratio remained constant. *If the firm pays less than $16, the remaining (or nonselling) investors are better off; if it pays more than $16, the remaining investors are worse off.*

Although this is a purely mechanical exercise so far, it serves to highlight some aspects of repurchasing. In fact, firms that repurchase their common stock *almost always repurchase shares while maintaining their current cash dividend policy.* With this background, it is now possible to consider some of the advantages and disadvantages of repurchasing.

---

[10] The $16 figure is chosen because it is the price at which nonselling investors are neither better nor worse off than selling investors.

Advantages of Stock Repurchases   From the firm's standpoint, there are a number of possible advantages to stock repurchases:

1. If a firm was generating a temporary excess of cash but did not want to adjust its stated cash dividend policy, it might decide to repurchase some of its stock. This provides nonselling shareholders with an alternative form of a dividend.
2. By repurchasing, a firm may reduce its future cash dividend requirements or, alternatively, may raise the dividends per share paid to its remaining shareholders without increasing the total cash flow drain on the firm.
3. Repurchases can be used to effect an immediate and often large-scale change in the firm's capital structure. For example, if a firm previously had no debt and decided its target capital structure should include 20 percent debt, it could issue a bond and use the proceeds to repurchase common stock, thereby effecting the capital structure realignment.
4. Repurchasing can also be used to signal information about the firm's future cash flows.

Disadvantages of Stock Repurchases   From the firm's standpoint, some disadvantages may result from repurchasing its own shares:

1. In the past, firms that repurchased substantial amounts of stock often had poorer growth and investment opportunities than firms that did not. Announcing a repurchase programme might signal to investors that good investment opportunities did not exist. This negative impact appears to have lessened in recent years as different types of firms started viewing repurchases as an alternative to increasing their dividend payout ratio.
2. From a legal standpoint, the provincial securities commissions may raise some questions if it appears the firm is using the repurchases to manipulate the price of its common stock.
3. Although a share repurchase may qualify the investor for a capital gain,[11] in most cases this is not what happens. Usually the shares are repurchased through a tender offer in which the investor knows that he or she is selling shares back to the company. In this more usual case, the firm is deemed to have paid a dividend "equal to the amount . . . by which the amount paid by the corporation . . . exceeds the paid-up capital.[12] The investor must then treat the deemed dividend as an ordinary dividend (the paid-up capital portion is not taxed). Consequently, the firm's common stock price might not react as favourably to the repurchase as expected.

On net, it appears that firms will continue to repurchase shares of their common stock. This is particularly true because repurchasing has gained favour as a means of

---

[11] Subsection 84(8) of the Income Tax Act also spells out very special conditions under which a repurchase qualifies as a capital gain. However, to date, these conditions have not been met, and this subsection is worded in such a way that it is unlikely that all of the conditions will ever be met.

[12] Income Tax Act, subsection 84(3).

attempting to fend off unwanted corporate suitors and as a means of "leveraging up" the firm's capital structure. Note, however, that reducing the proportion of cash or marketable securities in a firm's asset structure may increase the risk composition of the firm. This increased risk, if it occurs, must be balanced against the benefits expected to be derived from the repurchase.

Concept Review Questions

■ Describe the dividend payment procedures of a firm.

■ Explain what a dividend reinvestment plan is.

■ What are some advantages and disadvantages of a stock repurchase?

STOCK SPLITS AND DIVIDENDS

In addition to paying cash dividends, and sometimes repurchasing their own outstanding common stock, firms often issue more shares via a stock split or a stock dividend. Stock splits and stock dividends have exactly the same effect from a financial standpoint. For accounting purposes, however, there are differences between a stock split and a stock dividend.

STOCK SPLIT

The accounting treatment for a **stock split** is straightforward. For a 2-for-1 split, for example, the number of shares of common stock is doubled.[13] As shown in Table 14.6, Wilbur Industries had 1 million no–par value shares before the split. After the split, Wilbur had 2 million shares.

STOCK DIVIDEND

With a **stock dividend**, an accounting entry is made to transfer capital from the retained earnings account to the common stock account. The amount to be transferred is determined by the size of the stock dividend and the current market price of the firm's common stock. In our example, if Wilbur declares a 10 percent stock dividend, it will issue 100,000 (10 percent of 1,000,000 shares) more shares of stock. With a current market price of $10 per share, the transfer out of retained earnings will be $1,000,000. Finally, as also shown in Table 14.6, the common stock account will be increased by $1,000,000. Note that for both a stock split and a stock dividend, Wilbur's total shareholders' equity is $7 million both before and after the transaction.

---

[13] Under the Canada Business Corporations Act all shares are no–par value shares; therefore, there is no paid-in capital. Shares are recorded at their fair market value (issue price).

Table 14.6

Effect of Stock Split or Stock Dividend on Wilbur Industries Shareholders' Equity Accounts

In both cases, the total remains $7,000,000. However, a stock dividend involves capitalizing some of the firm's retained earnings by a transfer to the common stock account.

Before Stock Split or Stock Dividend	
Common stock (1 million shares outstanding, no par)	$2,550,000
Retained earnings	4,450,000
Total shareholders' equity	$7,000,000
After 2-for-1 Stock Split	
Common stock (2 million shares outstanding, no par)	$2,550,000
Retained earnings	4,450,000
Total shareholders' equity	$7,000,000
After 10 Percent Stock Dividend	
Common stock (1.1 million shares outstanding, no par)[a, b]	$3,550,000
Retained earnings[b]	3,450,000
Total shareholders' equity	$7,000,000

[a] 100,000 shares are issued.
[b] Based on a market price of $10, ($10)(100,000 shares) = $1,000,000 is added to the common stock. Retained earnings is reduced by $1,000,000.

BEWARE OF FALSE GIFTS

In the absence of any other simultaneous occurrence, the effects of a stock split or dividend can be summarized as follows:

1. There is no change in the firm's *total* assets, liabilities, shareholders' equity, earnings, cash dividends, or market value.
2. There is a drop in the *per share* earnings, cash dividends, and common stock market price, and a corresponding increase in the number of shares of common stock outstanding.

The consequence of a stock split or stock dividend is to increase the number of shares held by each investor. But each share is worth less, because nothing of value has been created. *The net effect would seem to be neither an increase nor a decrease* in the total market value of the firm. To see this, consider the example of Wilbur Industries again. In Table 14.7, we see that before the split Wilbur had total earnings of $1,150,000; total cash dividends of $460,000; and, with a stock price of $10 per share, a total market value of $10,000,000. After the 2-for-1 split, Wilbur still has earnings of $1,150,000, cash dividends of $460,000, and a total market value of $10,000,000.

Table 14.7

Effect of 2-for-1 Stock Split on Wilbur Industries and an Individual Investor

There can be no benefit from a stock split unless it causes the total market value of the firm to increase. Stock dividends are similar.

Wilbur Industries	Investor

Before Stock Split

Total earnings	$1,150,000	Owns 10,000 shares, which is
Total cash dividends	$460,000	equal to 1 percent of total
Total shares outstanding	1,000,000	shares outstanding

$$EPS = \frac{\$1,150,000}{1,000,000} = \$1.15$$

$$DPS = \frac{\$460,000}{1,000,000} = \$0.46$$

Cash dividends received
= (10,000 shares)($0.46) = $4,600

$$\text{Dividend payout ratio} = \frac{\$0.46}{\$1.15} = 40\%$$

Market value of stock
= (10,000 shares)($10) = $100,000

Market price per share = $10
Total market value, S = ($10)(1,000,000)
= $10 million

After Stock Split

Total earnings	$1,150,000	Owns 20,000 shares, which is
Total cash dividends	$460,000	equal to 1 percent of total
Total shares outstanding	$2,000,000	shares outstanding

$$EPS = \frac{\$1,150,000}{2,000,000} = \$0.575$$

$$DPS = \frac{\$460,000}{2,000,000} = \$0.23$$

Cash dividends received
= (20,000 shares)($0.23) = $4,600

$$\text{Dividend payout ratio} = \frac{\$0.23}{\$0.575} = 40\%$$

Market value of stock
= (20,000 shares)($5) = $100,000

Market price per share = $5
Total market value, S = ($5)(2,000,000)
= $10 million

Likewise, as also shown in Table 14.7, an investor owning 1 percent of Wilbur stock does not benefit directly from the stock split.[14]

---

[14] If a shareholder is entitled to a fractional share, then the firm will pay cash in lieu of the fractional share. For example, if an investor held 25 shares and a 10 percent stock dividend was declared, the shareholder would be entitled to 2.5 shares. If the market price of the stock was $30 per share, the shareholder would receive 2 full shares and $15 cash in lieu of the fractional share.

WHY DECLARE A STOCK SPLIT OR STOCK DIVIDEND?

In the absence of any value-creating activities, it would seem that not many companies would want to declare stock splits or stock dividends. However, some of Canada's largest firms, including Canfor, Cored, Imperial Oil, Ivaco, Newbridge Networks, and Stelco, have issued stock dividends in recent years. Why is this so? Some possible explanations are:

1. Some firms declare a stock split or stock dividend at the same time as a cash dividend. They view this action as an extension of the firm's cash dividend policy. If the firm actually increases its total cash dividend payout, then shareholders are receiving more total cash dividends. Note, however, that the firm's dividend payout ratio could be increased without simultaneously declaring a stock split or stock dividend.

2. Many firms apparently believe their stock has an optimal trading range. Perhaps this is between $20 and $50 per share. If the market price of the firm's common stock increases to, say, $70, the firm may declare a 2-for-1 split to drive the price down to about $35 per share. Implicit in this idea is that the total value of the firm will be more when it is in its "trading range" than when it is outside it.

3. A third possible reason for declaring stock splits or stock dividends involves the signalling idea discussed when we considered cash dividend policies. The essence of the argument is that firms declaring stock splits or dividends communicate information about the firm's future cash flows over and above any existing information. Theoretical and empirical evidence provided by Grinblatt, Masulis, and Titman (1984) and by McNichols and Dravid (1990), among others, lends support to this idea because the market value of a firm's stock tends, other things being equal, to increase when the firm declares a stock split.

4. A final possible reason sometimes given is "to conserve the firm's cash." Firms in financial difficulty fairly frequently say they will declare the dividend in the form of stock *rather* than cash. This allows the firms to conserve cash, but shareholders are worse off. Shareholders suffer the loss of the cash dividend, and, because the market value of each share of stock decreases proportionately as more shares are issued, the shareholders' total market value remains, at best, unchanged.

So why do firms continue to declare both stock dividends and stock splits? The answer appears to involve some elements of all the above reasons. Although issuing additional shares of stock is much more expensive than issuing cash dividends, firms often use both stock splits and stock dividends to supplement their cash dividend policy and to signal positive information about the future cash flows of the firm.

Concept Review Questions

- Describe the differences in accounting procedures for a stock split and a stock dividend.
- Why do firms declare stock splits or stock dividends?

KEY POINTS

- Firms pay out more than 60 percent of earnings as cash dividends. The rate of increase in cash dividend payouts exceeds the rate of inflation.
- Under both the Miller and Modigliani and residual dividend theories, the value of the firm is independent of the firm's cash dividend policy.
- The exclusion from income of 100 percent of cash dividends received by a Canadian corporation from another Canadian corporation serves as a significant incentive for firms to receive dividends.
- Tax impacts for individuals, in terms of differential tax rates on dividends versus capital gains, and the deferral option available with capital gains, do not appear to have much impact on a firm's dividend policy.
- Firms with substantial growth options appear to adopt lower dividend payout ratios. Also, firms appear to signal future cash flows via their dividend policy.
- In practice, firms act as if cash dividends are important. Most adopt a smoothed residual dividend policy. This policy includes maintaining a target payout ratio and a target capital structure.
- Other things being equal, stock repurchases increase the earnings per share and market price of the remaining shares.
- Neither stock splits nor stock dividends by themselves benefit shareholders. However, firms may signal future cash flow prospects with stock splits and stock dividends, as they do with cash dividends and stock repurchases.

QUESTIONS

14.1 Explain the tradeoff between paying cash dividends and retaining internally generated funds.

14.2 Discuss the Miller and Modigliani and the residual dividend theories and how they relate to the value of the firm.

14.3 Discuss factors related to taxes, growth options, and signalling that may affect a firm's cash dividend policy.

14.4 Describe what other factors and constraints may also influence the firm's cash dividend decision.

14.5 How do you think the following conditions would affect dividend payout ratios, in general? (*Note*: For some, the direction may not be clear.) Explain your answer.
a. Interest rates fall.
b. A reduction in the corporate tax rate is coupled with increased capital cost allowances.
c. Taxes decrease for individuals.
d. The firm is in a mature industry and faces intense foreign competition. It decides to meet the competition head-on.
e. The firm is repositioning itself into a new, young, growing industry.

14.6 Explain the smoothed residual dividend policy. How does this policy incorporate many of the observed practices of firms?

14.7 Discuss the relationship among the dividend declaration day, the ex-dividend date, the record day, and the payment date. What should the market price do on the ex-dividend date? Why?

14.8   When a firm repurchases shares of stock they must be cancelled. Therefore, the shares are not viewed as an asset, because they never show up on the left-hand (or asset) side of the firm's balance sheet. Why do firms pay money for them if they are not an asset? Are nonselling shareholders better or worse off after the firm repurchases shares? Explain.

14.9   Explain the main differences between a stock split and a stock dividend from **(a)** an accounting viewpoint and **(b)** an investor's standpoint.

14.10   Theoretically, investors should not benefit directly from a stock split or stock dividend.
a.   Explain fully why this is so.
b.   How would you react if an investor said her investment had a price of $50 before a 2-for-1 split, and a price of $28 after the split? Is the market still efficient?

CONCEPT REVIEW PROBLEMS _____

See Appendix A for solutions.

CR14.1   Lilly, a resident of Newfoundland, owns 4,000 shares of Rock Enterprises. During the year Rock pays a total dividend of $1.25 per share. Given that Lilly has a marginal tax rate of 26 percent, what is her after-tax dividend income?

CR14.2   Wise Holdings has the following market-value-based balance sheet (dollars in millions):

Current assets	$ 25		
Long-term assets	75		
Total assets	$100	Equity	$100

The company has 5 million shares of common stock outstanding and an EPS of $4, and it has declared a cash dividend of $1 per share. What are the firm's stock price and P/E ratio before the ex-dividend date? What are the stock price, P/E ratio, and total market value of equity after the ex-dividend date?

CR14.3   Assume Wise Holdings, in CR14.2, decides to repurchase $5 million of common stock (at $20 per share) rather than pay the $1 per share dividend. What would be the effect of the repurchase on the firm's market value of equity, stock price, and P/E ratio?

CR14.4   Andrew Entertainment Ltd. follows a residual dividend policy and has a debt/equity ratio of 2.
a.   If the firm has earnings of $900,000 and free cash flow and does not want to issue equity or change the firm's debt/equity ratio, what is the maximum amount of capital spending the firm can participate in?
b.   Assume Andrew is not concerned with small fluctuations in its debt/equity ratio, does not want to issue debt, and has $700,000 in investment opportunities. The firm has a cost of equity of 16 percent, a growth rate of 5 percent, and 100,000 shares of common stock outstanding. What is the firm's dividend per share and stock price?
c.   Andrew's management is concerned that the residual dividend policy causes too much fluctuation in the firm's dividends per share. The firm's management believes a dividend of [$1.75(1.05)] at time t = 1 will signal to the market the strength of Andrew's future earnings, thereby resulting in a lower cost of equity of 13 percent. What will Andrew's stock price be if management is correct?

PROBLEMS

14.1   Husky Manufacturing follows a residual cash dividend policy. For the next year, the firm expects to have internally generated funds of $1 million, profitable investment opportunities are $2 million, and the firm's target capital structure is 40 percent equity and 60 percent debt.
a.   How much should Husky pay out to its shareholders in cash dividends?
b.   What if profitable investment opportunities are $3 million? If they are $1.5 million?

14.2   Alexander International is considering seven average-risk capital expenditures as follows:

Capital Investment	CF_0	Internal Rate of Return
A	$200	25%
B	300	22
C	150	17
D	450	16
E	350	14
F	250	12
G	100	9

The firm's target capital structure is 30 percent debt and 70 percent equity. Alexander's opportunity cost of capital is 15 percent, and there is $1,200 available in internally generated funds that can be reinvested in the firm or paid out in the form of cash dividends.
a.   Which capital budgeting projects should be accepted? If the firm follows a residual dividend policy, how much is available to be paid out in the form of cash dividends?
b.   How does your answer change if Alexander's cost of capital is only 11 percent?

14.3   An investor in Nova Scotia purchases $11,825 of stock valued at $2.75 per share. During the year a dividend of $0.67 per share is paid. The federal marginal tax rate of the investor is 29 percent. Calculate the after-tax dividend income.

14.4   An individual in Ontario with taxable employment income of $64,500 derives additional income through investment. This investor has a choice between three equally risky and costly investments:
1.   663 shares of a corporation that will pay a dividend of $5.00 per share at the end of the year
2. $39,000 worth of bonds, bearing 8.5 percent interest for one year
3.   An investment that will result in $3,315 of capital gains

Calculate the after-tax income for each of the three alternatives. Which alternative provides the best return?

14.5   Kyle just invested the same amount of money in two stocks, A and B, which have returns as follows:

	Dividends Expected, D_1	Dividends Expected, D_2	Capital Gain Expected When Sold at End of Year 2 (after receiving any cash dividend)
Stock A	$100	$100	400
Stock B	0	0	600

Kyle's required return is 10 percent. His tax rate on this dividend income, after considering the dividend tax credit, is 23 percent, and his tax rate on capital gains is 33 percent.

a. Calculate the present value of his expected returns. Which stock provides higher returns? Why?

b. How much more would Kyle have to receive from stock B to be indifferent between the two stocks?

14.6 Viscione Industries is planning to liquidate in two years; that is, at time t = 2. At t = 0, the management was considering two alternative dividend policies. The first would be to pay a cash dividend of $2 at t = 1, followed by a liquidating dividend of $29.35 at t = 2. The second plan calls for a cash dividend of $10 at t = 1 and a liquidating dividend of $19.83 at t = 2.

a. If the cost of equity capital for Viscione Industries is 19 percent, which plan (if either) should *management* favour? (*Note*: Ignore any tax aspects and assume there is no uncertainty concerning whether the firm will actually have the cash to pay the dividends as indicated.)

b. Are there any practical considerations that need to be taken into account that might favour one over the other? Explain.

14.7 McCormick Steel has a current stock market value of $4 million. It has 1 million shares of stock outstanding and currently pays no cash dividends. Two dividend policies are under consideration. Plan I is to continue paying no cash dividends. Plan II involves selling $500,000 of new stock (with no flotation costs) and immediately paying the $500,000 to the existing (but not the new) shareholders. Because there are presently 1 million shares of common stock outstanding, every current shareholder would receive 50 cents per share in cash dividends. The new stock would have to be sold at $3.50 per share (the current market value of $4 million divided by the current 1 million shares, less the cash dividend of 50 cents).

a. How many shares will have to be issued to raise the $500,000? Compare the per share value of the current shareholders' holdings, taking into account both market price and dividends under plan I versus plan II. (*Note*: Ignore taxes.)

b. Now assume that McCormick also has to incur flotation costs of 20 cents per share, so the new stock will sell at $3.30 per share. How many shares will now have to be issued to raise the $500,000? Compare the total per share value of the current shareholders' holdings for both plans now.

c. Comparing your answers to (a) and (b), what can you say about the impact of flotation costs on the dividend (and valuation) decision?

14.8 A firm has adopted a smoothed residual dividend policy. This is supplemented by declaring a dividend extra as follows:

1. Regular dividends paid out are presently 30 percent of earnings. The firm wants to keep its regular dividend payout at 30 percent and will increase the regular payout only when net income increases for two consecutive years.

2. Once the regular dividend is increased, it remains at that level until it can be raised again (based on two consecutive years' increases in net income).

3. Each year the firm pays out a total of 40 percent of earnings by declaring an extra dividend. The size of the extra dividend is then the difference between the 30 percent payout policy and the 40 percent payout policy.

If the firm has earnings as follows, what are its regular and extra dividends per year?

t = 1	t = 2	t = 3	t = 4	t = 5	t = 6	t = 7	t = 8
$100	$100	$110	$140	$120	$160	$180	$220

14.9 On March 1 (a Thursday), the board of directors of Save-More Enterprises met and declared a cash dividend of 50 cents per share, payable on April 18 (a Wednesday) to shareholders of record as of March 22 (a Monday).

a. If you were going to purchase some stock in Save-More and wanted to receive this cash dividend, by what date would the purchase have to be made?

b. Approximately how much should the market price of Save-More drop on the ex-dividend day?

c. What happens to the cash dividend if you already own the stock and the firm declares bankruptcy on March 12?

14.10 A firm has 1,000,000 shares of common stock outstanding, selling at $90 per share. Its earnings after tax (EAT) are $6,000,000. Because it has excess cash, the firm has decided to buy back 200,000 shares of its common stock. However, because the excess cash has been invested in short-term marketable securities, the EAT will decrease to $5,000,000 once the repurchase is completed. If we assume the P/E ratio remains the same after the repurchase as it is now, what is the price per share that should be offered so that both selling and nonselling shareholders are indifferent to the repurchase?

14.11 Nelson Drug has 50,000 shares of stock outstanding, total earnings of $600,000, and a market price per share of $96. It pays a cash dividend of $4 per share.

a. Determine the (1) total market value, (2) EPS, (3) P/E ratio, and (4) dividend payout ratio.

b. Gary, who owns 2,000 shares, has expressed great displeasure with the management policies of Nelson Drug. Management has approached him with the idea of buying back his shares.

1. If the firm offers Gary $100 per share instead of paying a cash dividend of $4 per share, are the remaining shareholders better off, worse off, or the same? Assume that the P/E ratio remains the same.

2. If, after the repurchase, the firm elects to pay the same *total* dollar amount out in the form of cash dividends, what happens to the dividends per share? What, if anything, happens to the dividend payout ratio?

3. Discuss, but do not work out, what the general effect would be on the remaining shareholders if Nelson Drug had to pay $125 per share to repurchase the shares from Gary. (Assume that the firm spends more than $200,000, so it purchases all of Gary's shares.)

14.12 Markham Brothers has decided to go public. It has retained the services of an investment dealer who has indicated that a P/E ratio for Markham of about eight times earnings would be reasonable for a new offering of this type. In addition, the investment dealer figured an offering price of $40 per share would be appropriate. Markham Brothers has earnings after taxes (EAT) of $7.5 million and presently has 500,000 shares of common stock. How large a stock split would you recommend for Markham before the firm goes public?

14.13 Van Horn Distributors lists the following on its annual report (dollars in thousands):

Common stock, unlimited authorized, no–par value shares;	
issued 3,589,970 shares	$11,214
Retained earnings	49,496
Total	$60,710

a. What changes would occur if Van Horn declared a 2-for-1 stock split?

b. Independent of (a), what if Van Horn declared a 20 percent stock dividend and the market price was $25 per share?

14.14 Horizon Enterprises has 600,000 shares of common stock outstanding, and its EPS is $6. The firm has a dividend payout ratio of 20 percent and a current market price of $90 per share.

a. Before the split, what are Horizon's (1) total earnings; (2) total cash dividends; (3) cash dividends per share; (4) total market value; and (5) P/E ratio?

b. Jim owns 50 shares of Horizon. What are his (1) total cash dividends and (2) total market value?

c. Horizon declares a 3-for-1 stock split. What are the new (1) total earnings; (2) EPS; (3) total cash dividends; (4) dividends per share; (5) dividend payout ratio; (6) P/E ratio; and (7) total market value? [Note: Assume that there are no signalling effects in (c) or (d).]

d. After the split, what are Jim's total cash dividends and total market value?

e. Under what circumstances (if any) might an investor be better off after a stock split?

14.15 The SLP Corporation had a market price of $60 per share on September 1. On September 5, the firm announced a 20 percent stock dividend, payable October 20 to shareholders of record as of September 30. You own 90 shares of SLP.

a. What is the ex-dividend date?

b. If you sold your stock on September 20, what price would you receive? (Assume other things are equal and no brokerage costs.)

c. After the stock dividend, how many shares will you own?

d. What should be the market price per share, other things being equal, on September 28 if there are no signalling effects?

e. What is the total market value of your holdings both before and after the 20 percent stock dividend?

14.16 Mini Case Healthcare Plus is a six-year-old firm that serves the fast-growing need for quality physical fitness equipment for those older than 50. Its target debt to total value ratio is $33\frac{1}{3}$ percent. Up to this time, no cash dividends have been paid out. However, Healthcare Plus "went public" three years ago and now some investors are asking when the company will start paying cash dividends. There are 1 million shares of common stock outstanding.

a. What factors argue for the irrelevance of dividend policy? What factors argue for the relevance of dividend policy? In other words, explain why you believe cash dividends do or do not affect the market price for the firm's common stock.

b. Healthcare Plus estimates that the cash flow available to be paid out in the form of cash dividends, to pay down debt, or to fund new capital investments, is $2,000,000. It has the following set of independent capital investment opportunities available:

Project	Initial Investment	IRR
A	$ 100,000	50%
B	500,000	30
C	300,000	17
D	800,000	16
E	600,000	18
F	1,400,000	25
G	700,000	14
H	400,000	21

1. If the firms's opportunity cost of capital is 20 percent and it follows a residual dividend policy, what should the firm do?

2. What happens if everything is as in (1) except that Healthcare Plus initiates a policy of paying a cash dividend of $1.00 per share per year? (*Note:* Assume Healthcare Plus still takes all wealth-maximizing projects and that it will not increase its debt/total value ratio. Also, the capital projects are not divisible; that is, partial projects may not be undertaken.)

c. Assume now that the situation is as in (b2), except that the opportunity cost of capital is 15 percent and wealth-maximizing capital investments can be carried forward one year to time t = 1. If the cash flow at t = 1 is estimated to be $2,400,000, the cash dividends are still $1.00 per share (and will be paid in each year), and the following additional capital projects exist (in addition to those carried forward), what decisions should be made?

Project	Initial Investment	IRR
I	$ 500,000	18%
J	300,000	35
K	1,000,000	22
L	800,000	12

d. If Healthcare Plus starts the process of paying cash dividends, what sequence of events occurs? If investors are buying or selling the stock, how do they know whether they are entitled to receive a cash dividend or not?

e. What is a dividend reinvestment plan? What are the benefits to the firm? To shareholders? What tax consequences exist for shareholders?

f. One of the members of Healthcare Plus's board of directors recommends that the firm repurchase stock instead of paying cash dividends. Does this proposal make sense? Why or why not?

g. The same board member then suggests that instead of paying cash dividends, the firm pay the dividend in the form of additional shares of stock. Does this proposal make sense? Why or why not?

REFERENCES

ADJAOUD, FODIL. "The Information Content of Dividends: A Canadian Test." *Canadian Journal of Administrative Sciences* 1 (December 1984): 338–351.

AMBARISH, RAMASASTRY, KOSE JOHN, and JOSEPH WILLIAMS. "Efficient Signalling with Dividends and Investment." *Journal of Finance* 42 (June 1987): 321–344.

ASQUITH, PAUL, and DAVID W. MULLINS, JR. "The Impact of Initiating Dividend Payments on Shareholders' Wealth." *Journal of Business* 56 (January 1983): 77–96.

BHATTACHARYA, SUDIPTO. "Imperfect Information, Dividend Policy, and the 'Bird-in-the-Hand' Fallacy." *Bell Journal of Economics* 10 (Spring 1979): 259–270.

BLACK, FISCHER, and MYRON SCHOLES. "The Effects of Dividend Yield and Dividend Policy on Common Stock Prices and Returns." *Journal of Financial Economics* 1 (May 1974): 1–22.

BOOTH, L. D., and D. J. JOHNSTON. "The Ex-dividend Day Behavior of Canadian Stock Prices: Tax Changes and Clientele Effects." *Journal of Finance* 39 (June 1984): 457–476.

BRENNAN, MICHAEL J., and ANJAN V. THAKOR. "Shareholder Preferences and Dividend Policy." *Journal of Finance* 45 (September 1990): 993–1018.

DEANGELO, HARRY. "Payout Policy and Tax Deferral." *Journal of Finance* 46 (March 1991): 357–382.

DISHPANDE, SHREESH D., and VIJAY M. JOG . "Further Evidence on Dividend Resumption, Initiation and Information Asymmetry." *Canadian Journal of Administrative Sciences* 6 (June 1989): 25–36.

EADES, KENNETH M., PATRICK J. HESS, and E. HAN KIM. "Market Rationality and Dividend Announcements." *Journal of Financial Economics* 14 (December 1985): 581–604.

EASTERBROOK, FRANK H. "Two Agency-Cost Explanations of Dividends." *American Economic Review* 74 (September 1984): 650–659.

GRINBLATT, MARK S., RONALD W. MASULIS, and SHERIDAN TITMAN. "The Valuation Effects of Splits and Stock Dividends." *Journal of Financial Economics* 13 (December 1984): 461–490.

HANSEN, ROBERT S., RAMAN KUMAR, and DILIP K. SHOME. "Dividend Policy and Corporate Monitoring: Evidence From the Electric Utility Industry." *Financial Management* 23 (Spring 1994): 16–22.

HEALY, PAUL M., and KRISHNA G. PALEPU. "Earnings Information Conveyed by Dividend Initiations and Omissions." *Journal of Financial Economics* 21 (September 1988): 149–175.

KALAY, AVNER. "Stockholder–Bondholder Conflict and Dividend Constraints." *Journal of Financial Economics* 10 (June 1982): 211–233.

LANG, LARRY H. P., and ROBERT H. LITZENBERGER. "Dividend Announcement: Cash Flow Signalling vs. Free Cash Flow Hypotheses." *Journal of Financial Economics* 24 (September 1989): 181–192.

LINTNER, JOHN. "Distribution of Incomes of Corporations Among Dividends, Retained Earnings, and Taxes." *American Economic Review* 46 (May 1956): 97–113.

LITZENBERGER, ROBERT H., and KRISHNA RAMASWAMY. "The Effects of Dividends on Common Stock Prices: Tax Effects or Information Effects." *Journal of Finance* 37 (May 1982): 429–443.

MCNICHOLS, MAUREEN, and AJAY DRAVID. "Stock Dividends, Stock Splits, and Signalling." *Journal of Finance* 45 (July 1990): 857–880.

MILLER, MERTON H. "Behavioral Rationality in Finance: The Case of Dividends." *Journal of Business* 59 (October 1986): 451–468.

MILLER, MERTON H., and FRANCO MODIGLIANI. "Dividend Policy, Growth, and the Valuation of Shares." *Journal of Business* 34 (October 1961): 411–433.

MILLER, MERTON H., and KEVIN ROCH. "Dividend Policy and Asymmetric Information." *Journal of Finance* 40 (September 1985): 1031–1051.

MILLER, MERTON H., and MYRON S. SCHOLES. "Dividends and Taxes." *Journal of Financial Economics* 6 (December 1978): 333–364.

———. "Dividends and Taxes: Some Empirical Evidence." *Journal of Political Economy* 90 (December 1982): 1118–1141.

OFER, AHARON R., and ANJAN V. THAKOR. "A Theory of Stock Price Responses to Alternative Cash Disbursement Methods: Stock Repurchases and Dividends." *Journal of Finance* 42 (June 1987): 365–394.

ROZEFF, MICHAEL S. "Growth, Beta and Agency Costs as Determinants of Dividend Payout Ratios." *Journal of Financial Research* 5 (Fall 1982): 249–259.

RUMSEY, JOHN. "Testing for Tax Effects of Dividend Yields on Pre-Tax Returns." *Canadian Journal of Administrative Sciences* 9 (December 1992): 305–309.

SMITH, CLIFFORD W., JR., and JEROLD B. WARNER. "On Financial Contracting: An Analysis of Bond Covenants." *Journal of Financial Economics* 7 (June 1979): 117–161.

PART V

Financing, Investing, and the Global Environment

*L*et us go back to our basic objective—to maximize the value of the firm, or the size of the pie, which represents the market value of both equity and debt. Until now we have examined how managers make decisions in terms of acquiring long-term assets, raising long-term funds, and determining the firm's capital structure and dividend policy. The assets evaluated in the capital budgeting process have been individual assets such as new buildings or equipment. If these assets had a positive net present value they were obtained through acquisition, and financed by raising long-term funds. All of these decisions were made as if the firm operated in only one country and was not affected by international events. In this part we start by examining leasing (Chapter 15) as an alternative means of obtaining the services of an asset that has a positive net present value. Next, in Chapter 16, which discusses mergers and corporate restructuring, we extend the use of net present value to evaluate the acquisition or disposition of whole firms or divisions. Finally, in Chapter 17 we discuss international financial management and show the impact of globalization on financial decision making. Here, as in the past, our framework remains the same—to maximize the long-run market value of the firm.

15 *Leasing*

EXECUTIVE SUMMARY

Leases come in many sizes, shapes, and forms, but all require periodic lease payments from the lessee (the user) to the lessor (the owner). Unless the lease is cancellable, leasing obligates firms to make a series of legally enforceable payments similar to those required when debt financing is issued.

The decision to purchase or to lease an asset is a financing decision. The basis for comparison is the cash flows that occur if the asset is purchased versus those that arise if the asset is leased. This comparison is accomplished by performing an incremental analysis to determine the net present value of leasing versus purchasing. Risk is neutralized in terms of the cash flow demands on the firm by using the concept of an equivalent loan for the purchase alternative. However, instead of having to calculate the equivalent loan, we can use the firm's after-tax cost of borrowing as the discount rate to calculate the net present value of the lease. If the net present value of the lease is positive, the asset should be leased; otherwise (assuming that the capital budgeting NPV is positive), the asset should be purchased. As with other financial decisions, the analysis comes down to focusing on the proper incremental set of cash flows, their timing, and their riskiness.

LEASING AND THE FIRM

Firms often enter into rental agreements that are called **leases**. The owner of the property is the **lessor**, who leases it to the user, or the **lessee**. Virtually anything that is needed by the firm—machinery, buildings, warehouses, airplanes, computers, ships, and so forth—can be leased. We will look at leasing primarily from the standpoint of the lessee, but it is helpful to begin by understanding who provides lease financing. That is, who are the lessors?

Lease financing can be provided by manufacturers as part of their regular sales effort, or it can be provided by firms that specialize in lease financing. In the former category, GATX, a railroad car manufacturer, is the largest lessor of railcars and IBM is a major computer lessor. In the latter category, General Electric Capital, a subsidiary of General Electric, has acquired numerous small lessors to fit its specialized operations. With more than $7 billion invested in leased assets, General Electric Capital is the biggest lessor in North America. In addition, lease financing is increasingly being provided by chartered banks, subsidiaries of other firms, commercial finance companies, and independent leasing companies.

TYPES OF LEASES

Leases come in many sizes, shapes, and forms, but in all cases the lessee (who has acquired use of the asset) is required to make periodic payments to the lessor. These payments generally are made monthly, quarterly, or semiannually, with the first payment due when the lease agreement is signed.

Operating Lease An **operating lease** is a short-term lease that generally is cancellable. It is often used to finance office machines, cars, and similar relatively inexpensive assets that require periodic maintenance. These leases often are called "service" leases because the lessor generally is responsible for all service, as well as for any insurance or property taxes on the assets. The costs incurred by the lessor are built into the lease payments and thus passed along to the lessee. Large operating leases should be subjected to financial evaluation like that discussed later in the chapter; smaller ones, or leases of short duration, are typically not subjected to an extensive financial analysis.

Financial Lease The term **financial lease** is employed for tax purposes to identify a long-term, noncancellable contract between the lessor, who owns the asset, and the lessee, who agrees to lease the asset for some specified period of time. Financial leases are a form of long-term financing similar to borrowing. The lessee gains the use of the asset immediately but in return has entered into a binding obligation to make payments as specified in the lease contract. Entering into a lease is similar to borrowing in terms of the cash flow consequences to the lessee. For this reason, the financial analysis employed by lessees presented later in the chapter will compare the cash flow consequences of leasing versus borrowing. Most financial leases are *net* leases: The lessee agrees to provide maintenance and pay for insurance coverage and/or property taxes related to the leased asset.

Sale and Leaseback A **sale and leaseback** occurs when the owner of an asset decides to sell it to another party and then lease it back. This type of transaction occurs frequently when a firm wants to raise capital by selling a building or factory but also wants to maintain the use of the facility for some specified period of time. It is estimated that, on average, firms have 20 percent of their assets in real estate. An increasing number of firms are attempting to put these assets to more productive use through the use of sale and leaseback agreements. From the lessee's standpoint, the financial analysis of selling and leasing back versus borrowing is essentially the same as for other financial leases.

Leveraged Lease   A fourth major form of leasing, and one that has also become increasingly popular in recent years, is the **leveraged lease**. This arrangement involves three parties instead of two—the lender, who puts up much of the money; the lessor (or equity participant), who owns the asset; and the lessee. A leveraged lease is complicated from the standpoint of both lender and lessor, but it remains a financial lease from the standpoint of the lessee.

TAX CONSIDERATIONS

From the lessee's standpoint, the lease payments are an expense of doing business and are deductible for tax purposes. Because the lessor owns the asset, capital cost allowance (CCA) is allowed as a tax-deductible expense. However, if Revenue Canada considers that the lease agreement provides "payments on account of the purchase price of the property" instead of rent, the contract is treated as a sale for tax purposes.[1] In this case the lessee is deemed to have bought the asset from the lessor through an instalment loan repayable by the rent payments, and thus the lessee is required to take the CCA deductions. For example, Revenue Canada would consider the following lease-option agreements to be sales rather than leases.

1. Title to the leased asset automatically transfers to the lessee after a previously specified amount is paid in the form of rent.
2. The lessee is required to buy the asset from the lessor either during or at the end of the lease.
3. The lessee is required to guarantee that he or she or a third party will pay an option price to the lessor.
4. The lessee is able to acquire the asset at the end of the lease for a price substantially below its fair market price (say $5).

Revenue Canada will also consider a sale and leaseback agreement to be a secured loan agreement if the asset is sold for a price substantially different from its fair market value and if the lease-option agreement has one of the preceding conditions. In this situation the sale of the asset is considered not to have taken place; thus the lessee must take the CCA.

Except in the next section, when accounting issues are discussed, we assume the leases under discussion in the remainder of the chapter are financial leases for tax purposes.

ACCOUNTING FOR LEASES

Our primary concern is the evaluation of the financial consequences of leasing, but let us pause briefly to consider their accounting treatment. *There are vast differences in*

---

[1] See Revenue Canada, Taxation: Interpretation Bulletin, *Lease-Options Agreements: Sale-Leaseback Agreements,* No. IT 233R, February 11, 1983.

both terminology and treatment for accounting versus tax purposes. The main terminology difference is that accountants refer to long-term leases that have to be capitalized on the firm's financial statements as **capital leases**. Any other leases are called **operating leases**.

Until 1979, all leases provided "off-balance-sheet" financing. That is, the fact that the firm had the use of the assets, as well as contractual obligations to make periodic lease payments, showed up (if at all) only as a footnote. Because lease obligations are as binding as debt, however, the reported accounting statements tended to misrepresent a firm's position if it leased long-term assets. Under CICA 3065[2] a capital lease exists if one or more of the following conditions are met:

1. The lease transfers ownership of the property to the lessee by the end of the lease term or provides the lessee with an option to purchase the asset at a bargain price.
2. The lease term is equal to 75 percent or more of the estimated economic life of the property.
3. The present value of the lease payments is equal to 90 percent or more of the value of the leased property at the beginning of the lease.

If these requirements (which are a good deal different from the tax requirements) are met, the present value of the lease payments must be entered as a liability on the right-hand side of the balance sheet. A corresponding entry must also be made on the left-hand side to record the value of the asset. (This is typically lumped with other long-term assets of the firm.) This asset is then amortized over the lease term (or over the economic useful life of the asset if the lease allows for a transfer of ownership or a bargain purchase), resulting in a reduction in reported income. Any lease that does not meet the CICA criteria is considered an operating lease for accounting purposes.

The net effect of CICA 3065 has been for accounting statements to reflect somewhat more accurately the firm's debt-type obligations. To get around this reporting requirement, many firms are structuring long-term leases so they are technically *not* capital leases as specified by CICA 3065. These operating leases do not have to be shown on the firm's balance sheet and show up only in the footnotes accompanying the financial statements. Although many firms are keeping substantial lease obligations off their balance sheets, the benefits from doing so are questionable unless the lease is economically justified, as discussed subsequently, and unless we assume that analysts, investors, and bankers are naive and do not adjust for this continued off-balance-sheet financing.

Concept Review Questions

- What are some of the similarities and differences among an operating (service) lease, a financial lease, a sale and leaseback, and a leveraged lease?
- According to Revenue Canada, when will a lease agreement be considered to be a sale?
- Describe the differences between a capital lease and an operating lease.

---

[2] "Leases," Section 3065, *CICA Handbook, Accounting Regulations* (Toronto: Canadian Institute of Chartered Accountants, December 1978 and May 1988).

SETTING LEASE RATES

Although we are looking at leases primarily from the lessee's standpoint, it is helpful to understand what factors lessors consider in setting lease rates. If lessees understand this process, they will be in a better position to bargain knowledgeably with lessors.

For financial leases, the lessor wants to set a rate that provides a satisfactory return. This is done by focusing first on four items,[3] as follows:

1. The lessor's after-tax required rate of return on debt-type investments, k_i[4]
2. The lessor's marginal tax rate, T
3. The cost of the leased asset, CLA_0
4. The CCA class and prescribed CCA rate, d

When these items have been determined, the proper lease rate for the lessor to quote is determined using the following five-step procedure:

STEP 1:   Determine the ownership benefit. The tax benefit from owning the asset is the CCA tax shield.

STEP 2:   Calculate the present value of the ownership benefit. Employing the lessor's after-tax required rate of return on debt-type investments, we can determine the present value of the ownership benefit using Equation 15.1, as follows:[5]

$$\text{Present value of benefit} = \left[\frac{TdCLA_0}{k_i + d}\right]\left[\frac{1 + 0.5k_i}{1 + k_i}\right] \qquad (15.1)$$

STEP 3:   Calculate the amount to be recovered from lease payments. The net amount recoverable from lease payments is equal to the cost of the leased asset minus the present value of the benefit of ownership calculated in step 2, so that:

$$\text{net amount recoverable from lease payments} = CLA_0 - \text{present value of benefit} \qquad (15.2)$$

STEP 4:   Determine the after-tax lease payment, ATL. Because lease payments are made in advance (at the beginning of each period), the after-tax lease payments are determined by solving for ATL in the following formula:

$$\text{net amount recoverable from lease payments} = \left[\sum_{t=1}^{n} \frac{ATL}{(1 + k_i)^t}\right](1 + k_i) \qquad (15.3)$$

---

[3] Although resale values are important, for simplicity they are ignored. Resale values for lessors are examined in Problem 15.2.

[4] The logic behind using k_i as the lessor's minimum discount rate is similar to that discussed later in the chapter for lessees. If markets are perfect and the tax status and all other factors are similar between lessors and lessees, then the returns to lessors from leasing are exactly equal to the cost of leasing to lessees.

[5] As when we were evaluating capital projects in Chapter 8, this represents the present value of the tax shelter provided by the annual capital cost allowance, as shown by Equation 8.8, where the resale value is equal to zero.

In Equation 15.3, ATL is an annuity due. The term $(1 + k_i)$ converts ATL from an ordinary annuity to an annuity due.

STEP 5:   Determine the before-tax lease payment, L. To complete the process, the lessor adjusts the lease payment to its before-tax amount, as follows:

$$L = \frac{ATL}{(1 - T)} \qquad\qquad (15.4)$$

The lease rate L is what the lessor will quote to a prospective lessee. By doing so, the lessor will achieve the desired after-tax return on the leased asset. If any higher lease rate is quoted, the lessor's return increases accordingly.

To illustrate the setting of lease rates, assume that LeaseFirst Ltd. has been approached for a three-year lease on a $1 million piece of equipment. The equipment is in class 8, the CCA rate is 20 percent, and the equipment has a useful economic life of three years; LeaseFirst's marginal tax rate is 35 percent, its before-tax required return on debt-type investments is 13.85 percent, and no resale value is assumed. What lease rate will LeaseFirst quote if the yearly lease payments are made in advance?[6]

The specific steps employed by LeaseFirst are shown in Table 15.1. In the first two, the present value of the ownership benefit to LeaseFirst is found to be $231,410. Then in step 3 the amount to be recovered from lease payments is simply $1,000,000 − $231,410 or $768,590. In steps 4 and 5 the after- and before-tax lease payments are determined. By collecting three annual lease payments of $428,578, each payable at the beginning of the year, LeaseFirst will receive its 13.85 percent before-tax (or 9 percent after-tax) required rate of return.

Other things being equal, the following actions will serve to increase the lease rates quoted by lessors:

1. Using straight-line depreciation rather than the CCA methodology.
2. Raising the discount rate.
3. Increasing the number of payments by going to semiannual, quarterly, or monthly payments instead of yearly payments.

In practice, three other factors must be considered. The first is that the lessor still owns the asset, and there will be some resale value for most assets after the lease terminates. Resale values serve to lower the quoted lease rate. Second, it is important to realize that information asymmetries generally exist between lessors and lessees. Lessors often know more about the asset than the lessee, and they may have economies of scale not enjoyed by the lessee. Finally, lessors will adjust the quoted lease rates upward to account for the transaction costs of setting up the lease agreement, and they will also factor in the costs incurred in obtaining information about potential lessees and the lessee's risk of default. Thus, lease rates are actually set in a slightly more complex environment than the model outlined in Equations 15.1 through 15.4.

---

[6] The same basic procedure would be employed in determining semiannual, quarterly, or monthly lease payments.

Table 15.1

Setting a Lease Rate

Using this step by step procedure, we can determine the lease rates to quote for any leased asset.

Steps 1 and 2: Present value of ownership benefit

$$\begin{aligned}
\text{present value of benefit} &= \left[\frac{TdCLA_0}{k_i + d}\right]\left[\frac{1 + 0.5k_i}{1 + k_i}\right] \\
&= \left[\frac{(0.35)(0.20)(\$1,000,000)}{(0.09 + 0.20)}\right]\left[\frac{1 + 0.5(0.09)}{1.09}\right] \\
&= (\$241,379)(0.9587) = \$231,410
\end{aligned}$$

Step 3: The amount to be recovered from lease payments
$1,000,000 − $231,410 = $768,590

Step 4: Determine after-tax lease payments, ATL
$768,590 = $ATL(PVA_{9\%,\,3yrs})(1.09)$
$768,590 = $ATL(2.531)(1.09)$
   ATL = $768,590/2.759 = $278,576

Step 5: Calculate the before-tax lease payments, L
L = $278,576/(1 − 0.35) = $428,578

Concept Review Questions

- Describe the procedure a lessor should perform when setting lease rates.
- What are some factors that would affect the lease rates set by the lessor?

TO LEASE OR NOT TO LEASE?

If financial markets are perfect—that is, if there are no transaction costs, financial distress costs, taxes, information asymmetries, and so forth—then debt and lease obligations are valued exactly the same by lessors and lessees. In a perfect market, the cost of debt or lease financing would be the same, and the lessee would be indifferent between leasing and borrowing. Given less-than-perfect markets, however, it is important to consider reasons for leasing. Some valid reasons exist; others often advanced are dubious, at best.

GOOD REASONS FOR LEASING

Tax Benefits   One of the most important reasons for leasing is the tax benefits associated with leasing. Lessees often benefit from leasing if they have a lower marginal tax rate than lessors. Due to the difference in tax rates, the CCA tax benefit may be worth more to the lessor with a higher tax bracket, resulting in savings to the lessee.

Flexibility and Convenience   A second reason for leasing is that it may increase the flexibility of the firm. It is often preferable to lease certain types of assets rather than to purchase them. In addition, the convenience of having the lessor obtain, set up, and maintain assets may be a significant advantage at times, especially with highly technical pieces of equipment. By leasing, the firm has an easily exercisable option to expand on its asset base. This option is also valuable in today's rapidly changing economic environment.

Cancellation Option   Operating leases and even some longer-term financial leases, such as those on computers, often contain an option to cancel. That is, the user or lessee may have the option of cancelling the lease at its discretion. This option is valuable and enhances the desirability of leasing. However, the lessee must recognize that lessors charge a higher lease rate to compensate themselves for issuing this option. Some leases that initially appear to be expensive are fairly priced once this cancellation option is recognized and valued.

Other Factors   Three other factors also favour leasing. First, because many leases are set at a fixed rate (that is, the lease payments do not change), the lessee is not surprised by higher cash outflows as economic conditions or interest rates change. Second, lessors are increasingly providing value-added services such as maintenance, insurance, and so forth, which allow the lessees to focus their primary attention on their businesses, not on the maintenance of assets. Finally, for firms with international operations, leasing assets as opposed to buying them may provide some protection against having them expropriated by foreign governments. For all of these reasons, more and more firms are leasing instead of buying assets.

DUBIOUS REASONS FOR LEASING

Capital Conservation   One argument often advanced to justify leasing is the conservation of the firm's working capital. Those who offer this argument say that the lease provides "100 percent" financing. However, because virtually all lease agreements require the first payment in advance, even under the best of circumstances less than 100 percent financing is secured. For small firms there may be some validity in this argument, because they do not have the same access to the financial markets and therefore may have to finance the purchase with internally generated funds. Larger firms, however, can generally secure approximately the same amount of financing from the financial markets. For them, leasing does not appear to be a viable means of conserving working capital.

Increased Debt Capacity   Another argument often made is that the use of leases increases the firm's debt capacity. This is said to occur because the combination of leasing and borrowing results in more long-term financing (or debt capacity) than that achieved by borrowing alone. This argument assumes, however, that bankers, lenders, and the financial markets are naive and do not recognize that leasing places a financial obligation on the firm, just as borrowing does. If lease financing really increased borrowing capacity, lenders and the financial markets would be inefficiently assessing the risk and cash flow obligations of leases. This does not appear to be the case.

Avoidance of Restrictions   Bonds or term loans often impose restrictive covenants on the firm, potentially limiting its financial flexibility. By leasing the asset, the lessee may be able to avoid some of these restrictions. Although this argument often appears to have some justification in a technical sense, most of the time the actual restrictions on the firm due to bond or term loan covenants are substantially less than their perceived impact. This reason is not often of much importance as a reason for leasing instead of purchasing.

Concept Review Questions

- What are some good reasons and some not-so-good reasons to lease an asset?
- Comment on the statement: "By leasing I am able to increase my firm's debt capacity."

EVALUATION OF FINANCIAL LEASES

The evaluation of leases from the lessee's standpoint is straightforward as long as certain basic ideas are understood. These relate to (1) the interaction between the firm's capital budgeting decision and the decision to lease or purchase the asset, (2) why debt financing is the appropriate standard of comparison, and (3) the fact that an incremental analysis of the lease versus purchase cash flows is employed.

WHAT DECISION ARE WE CONCERNED WITH?

When a firm makes a capital budgeting decision concerning the possible acquisition of an asset, it calculates the net present value of the proposed project. If the capital budgeting NPV is positive, then the asset should be acquired because it assists in maximizing the value of the firm. *Capital budgeting implicitly assumes that assets to be acquired will be purchased.* If leasing is a strong possibility, however, then the basic capital budgeting decision must be supplemented by further analysis to determine whether the asset should be leased or purchased. To make this supplemental financing decision, we calculate the **net present value of leasing, NPV**$_{lease}$.[7] If the net present value from leasing is positive, then the asset should be acquired by leasing; otherwise, it should be purchased.

The basic capital budgeting decision and the lease evaluation decisions interact. If some specialized machinery needed by a firm has an NPV of $15,000, then the capital budgeting decision has been reached. If the machinery can be either leased or purchased, however, then a subsequent calculation (the net present value of leasing) must be made to determine the preferable means of financing. If this subsequent NPV$_{lease}$ is positive, then the use of the machinery should be secured by leasing. If the NPV$_{lease}$ is negative, then the machinery should be purchased.

---

[7] The net present value from leasing versus purchasing is sometimes called the net advantage of leasing (NAL). The internal rate of return (IRR) could also be employed to make the lease versus purchase decision, as shown later in the chapter.

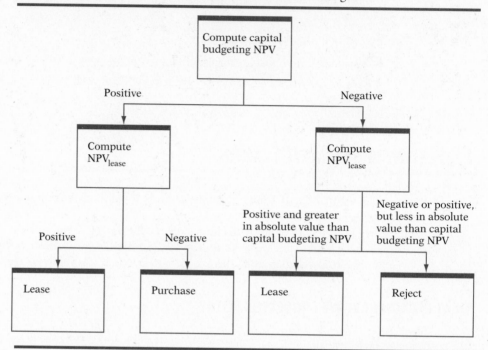

Figure 15.1

Interaction of Leasing and Capital Budgeting Decisions

If the capital budgeting NPV is positive, then the firm leases if NPV_{lease} (i.e., the net present value from leasing versus purchasing) is positive. Even if the capital budgeting NPV is negative, especially favourable lease terms can still lead to leasing.

One complication arises if the net present value in the original capital budgeting decision is negative. In this case, there may be instances in which the use of the assets still should be acquired if especially favourable lease terms are available. Consider a case in which the capital budgeting NPV is −$5,000, but the subsequent NPV_{lease} is $7,000. Because the net difference is a positive $2,000, the assets should be leased. If the NPV_{lease} were negative, however, or positive but less than $5,000, the assets would not be leased or purchased. All these conditions are summarized in Figure 15.1. For simplicity, we assume that the capital budgeting NPV is positive. Our concern is with the financing decision of whether the assets should be leased or purchased.

WHY COMPARE LEASING WITH BORROWING?

To evaluate whether leasing is preferable to purchasing, we need to make an assumption about the mode of financing used if the asset is purchased. Leasing imposes the same kind of financial commitment on the firm that borrowing does. Thus, the relevant standard of comparison to use when evaluating leasing is to compare it with purchasing the asset and financing the capital needs via borrowing. We are interested in neutralizing the risk between the two alternatives. The way to accomplish this is by establishing an equivalent borrowing amount that, in terms of the after-tax cash flows in each future period, is exactly the same as the after-tax lease cash flows. Doing this neutralizes the risk.

Although this step may sound complicated, it can be accomplished easily without ever calculating the implied loan. All that is required is that the discount rate employed be the after-tax borrowing rate of the firm. To neutralize risk differences in terms of the cash flow effects on the firm, we employ the lessee's after-tax borrowing rate, k_i, as the relevant discount rate. This after-tax borrowing rate is equal to $k_b(1 - T)$, where k_b is the lessee's before-tax borrowing rate, and T is the firm's marginal tax rate.

THE NET PRESENT VALUE OF LEASING VERSUS PURCHASING

A financial lease is evaluated in terms of the after-tax cash flows and opportunity costs incurred by leasing rather than purchasing the asset. The major elements of the decision are these:

1. The lease payments, L, made periodically by the lessee on an after-tax basis. In line with industry practice, we assume the first payment occurs at the time the lease is signed, time $t = 0$.
2. The capital cost allowance tax shield, calculated by multiplying the annual CCA by the lessee's marginal tax rate. By entering into a lease, the firm incurs an opportunity cost equal to the forgone CCA tax shield, which, as we saw in Chapter 8, goes on indefinitely.
3. The cost of the leased asset, CLA_0.

Employing these variables in an incremental framework, we calculate the net present value of leasing as follows:

$$\text{NPV}_{\text{lease}} = CLA_0 - \left\{ \left[\sum_{t=1}^{n} \frac{L_t (1 - T)}{(1 + k_i)^t} \right] (1 + k_i) + \left[\frac{TdCLA_0}{k_i + d} \right] \left[\frac{1 + 0.5k_i}{1 + k_i} \right] \right\} \quad (15.5)$$

Because the lease payments, L, are an annuity due, the term $(1 + k_i)$ converts them from an ordinary annuity to an annuity due. The $\text{NPV}_{\text{lease}}$ simply finds the cost of leasing the asset (the part of Equation 15.5 in braces, which includes both explicit and opportunity costs) versus the cost of the asset (represented by CLA_0). As long as the cost of leasing is less than the cost of the asset, Equation 15.5 will be positive and the asset should be leased.

To illustrate lease evaluation, let us consider the example of SolarSound, which is considering whether to lease or purchase some specialized equipment. The capital budgeting analysis indicating the equipment should be secured has already been completed. The remaining question is whether to lease or purchase the equipment. The equipment has a five-year useful economic life and is a class 10 asset, which has a CCA rate of 30 percent. The equipment's resale value is zero, the marginal tax rate is 40 percent, and the firm's before-tax cost of borrowing is 15 percent. The equipment costs $800,000 if purchased or can be leased for five years at $210,000 per year. The first lease payment is payable in advance.

To determine how to finance the equipment, the first step SolarSound undertakes is to calculate its after-tax cost of debt, k_i, which is the discount rate employed in Equation 15.5. Because k_b is 15 percent and the marginal tax rate is 40 percent, $k_i = k_b(1 - T) = 15\%(1 - 0.40) = 9$ percent. This is the discount rate that neutralizes the risk in terms of the after-tax cash flows under the two financing methods, and it should be used in the $\text{NPV}_{\text{lease}}$ analysis as follows:

$$\text{NPV}_{\text{lease}} = \begin{matrix} \text{cost of} \\ \text{asset} \end{matrix} - \left[\begin{matrix} \text{present value of} \\ \text{the lease payments} \end{matrix} + \begin{matrix} \text{present value of the forgone} \\ \text{CCA tax shield} \end{matrix} \right]$$

$$= \$800,000 - [\$210,000(1 - 0.40)(\text{PVA}_{9\%, 5\text{yr}})(1.09)$$
$$+ \text{ present value of the CCA tax shield}]$$

$$= \$800,000 [\$126,000(3.890)(1.09)$$
$$+ \text{ present value of the CCA tax shield}]$$

The present value of the CCA tax shield with Equation 15.1 is as follows:

$$\left[\frac{\text{TdCLA}_0}{k_1 + d} \right]\left[\frac{1 + 0.5k_i}{1 + k_i} \right] = \left[\frac{(0.40)(0.30)(\$800,000)}{0.09 + 0.30} \right]\left[\frac{1 + (0.5)(0.09)}{1 + 0.09} \right]$$
$$= \$235,992$$

Substituting this value of $\$235,992$ into the $\text{NPV}_{\text{lease}}$ equation, we have

$$\text{NPV}_{\text{lease}} = \$800,000 - (\$534,253 + \$235,992)$$
$$= \$800,000 - \$770,245 = \$29,755$$

Because the net present value of leasing versus purchasing is positive, SolarSound should lease the assets.

SOME COMPLICATIONS

This method for evaluating the leasing decision is straightforward. In addition, it is practical to employ and theoretically correct because it focuses attention on which means of financing is most consistent with the manager's goal. With this basic approach, the other complications often encountered can be readily incorporated into the analysis.

Two primary complications often occur—incremental operating costs, O_t, if an asset is purchased, and the estimated resale value, RV_n, if the asset is purchased. With these complications the $\text{NPV}_{\text{lease}}$ equation becomes

$$\text{NPV}_{\text{lease}} = \text{CLA}_0 - \left\{ \left[\sum_{t=1}^{n} \frac{L_t(1 - T)}{(1 + k_i)^t} \right](1 + k_i) + \left[\frac{\text{TdCLA}_0}{k_i + d} \right]\left[\frac{1 + 0.5k_i}{1 + k_i} \right] \right.$$
$$\left. - \left[\frac{1}{(1 + k_i)^n} \right]\left[\frac{\text{TdRV}_n}{k_i + d} \right] - \sum_{t=1}^{n} \frac{O_t(1 - T)}{(1 + k)^t} + \frac{RV_n}{(1 + k)^n} \right\} \qquad (15.6)$$

This equation, as in Chapter 8, assumes that if the asset is purchased, the asset class into which the asset is placed will continue after the asset is disposed of and that the asset is sold for less than its UCC so that there are no tax implications such as CCA recapture or capital gains associated with the project.[8] The appropriate opportunity cost of capital for the asset in question, k, is employed for discounting the incremental operating expenses and resale value, because risk neutralization does not extend to these items. If the asset's risk is equal to the average firm risk, then k is the firm's opportunity cost of capital.[9]

FINDING THE PERCENTAGE COST OF A LEASE

Instead of solving for the NPV_{lease} or equivalent loan, it is also possible to determine the percentage annual cost of the lease. This step involves solving for the internal rate of return, rather than the net present value. To solve for the cost of the lease, we can rearrange Equation 15.5 as follows:

$$CLA_0 - L_0(1 - T) = \sum_{t=1}^{n-1} \frac{L_t(1 - T)}{(1 + IRR)^t} + \left[\frac{TdCLA_0}{IRR + d}\right]\left[\frac{1 + 0.5IRR}{1 + IRR}\right] \quad (15.7)$$

Note that because the lease payments are payable in advance, the after-tax outlay associated with the initial payment, L_0, is subtracted from the cost of the leased asset, CLA_0. We then solve for the unknown percentage rate, IRR, by trial-and-error. This is the after-tax cost of the lease. The decision rule is as follows:

1. If cost of leasing, IRR, is less than cost of debt, k_i, accept.
2. If cost of leasing is greater than cost of debt, reject.
3. If cost of leasing is equal to cost of debt, you are indifferent.

Note that this relationship is exactly *opposite* that used in making capital budgeting decisions. The reason is that we are comparing cash outflows instead of cash inflows. Here, if the IRR is less than the specified rate, we accept; previously, it was just the reverse.

To illustrate this calculation, consider the lease for SolarSound. The left-hand side of Equation 15.7 is

$$CLA_0 - L_0(1 - T) = \$800,000 - \$126,000 = \$674,000$$

To find the IRR we must find the discount rate that equates the right-hand side of Equation 15.7 to $674,000. Solving for the internal rate of return, which is the effective after-tax percentage cost of the lease, we get 7.22 percent.[10] Because this cost is less than SolarSound's after-tax cost of debt of 9 percent, we make the same decision as before: lease the asset.

---

[8] See the discussion of Equation 8.8 in chapter 8 for the details of how RV_n is incorporated into the present value of the CCA tax shield.

[9] These topics are examined in Problems 15.9, 15.11, and 15.13.

[10] Because this is a lengthy and time-consuming trial-and-error calculation, it is best done by a computer.

Concept Review Questions

■ How is risk neutralization of cash flows between leasing and borrowing accomplished?

■ What complications can occur when evaluating an alternative to leasing, and how can they be incorporated into the analysis?

■ Describe how to calculate the annual percentage cost of a lease.

KEY POINTS

- Leasing is a major source of long-term financing. Tax implications and options to expand and cancel, along with value-added services, explain why leasing is increasingly popular.
- Leasing places a financial obligation similar to debt on the firm.
- Financial leases are evaluated by lessees based on the net present value of leasing versus purchasing the assets, using the after-tax cost of debt capital as the discount rate. This framework separates the capital budgeting (or investment) decision from the financing decision. Alternatively, the internal rate of return provides the same decision as the NPV_{lease} decision criterion.
- Incremental operating expenses for a purchased asset make leasing more attractive, whereas purchasing becomes more attractive if assets are expected to have some resale value at the end of the lease. A higher discount rate, which reflects the risk of the asset, should be employed when evaluating the effects of estimated resale values or incremental operating expenses.

QUESTIONS

15.1   How does CICA 3065, "Leases," reduce the ability of firms to employ off-balance-sheet financing? Will a firm benefit by this type financing?

15.2   What factors (both those discussed in the model covered by Equations 15.1 through 15.4 and others) affect the lease rates quoted by lessors? In which direction—an increase or a decrease in the quoted rate—does each affect lease rates?

15.3   Explain some of the valid and some of the dubious reasons for leasing.

15.4   How do capital budgeting and financing decisions, to lease or buy, interact? Be sure to discuss the case in which the capital budgeting NPV is negative while the NPV_{lease} is positive.

15.5   Explain why it is important to neutralize risk in terms of the cash flow obligations of the firm when conducting a lease or buy analysis. How does the after-tax cost of debt, k_i, relate to this issue?

15.6   The NPV_{lease} equation is

$$NPV_{lease} = CLA_0 - \left\{ \left[\sum_{t=1}^{n} \frac{L_t(1 - T)}{(1 + k_i)^t} \right](1 + k_i) + \left[\frac{TdCLA_0}{k_i + d} \right]\left[\frac{1 + 0.5k_i}{1 + k_i} \right] \right\}$$

Explain what each of the terms represents.

Concept Review Problems

See Appendix A for solutions.

CR15.1 Medical Equipment Rental is leasing ultrasound machines to physical therapy departments across the country. The firm has asked you to recommend an appropriate advance *monthly* rental fee. The cost of a machine is $32,000, and it has a useful life of five years. It is a class 8 asset with a CCA rate of 20 percent, and it has no expected resale value. If the tax rate is 40 percent and the before-tax cost of debt 9 percent, what is the monthly rental fee?

CR15.2 Employee Temp is considering purchasing or leasing laptop computers and portable printers for their employees. The computers and printers cost $50,000, have an economic life of five years, will be class 10 assets with a CCA rate of 30 percent, and have zero resale value. The firm's cost of debt is 12.31 percent, and its tax rate is 35 percent. If the lease payments are $11,000 per year in advance, what is the net present value of leasing the equipment? (*Note:* Round the after-tax cost of debt to the nearest whole percent.)

CR15.3 BCI Construction needs a crane that costs $100,000. The firm could borrow funds to purchase the crane at a before-tax cost of 14.29 percent or could rent the crane for $25,000 per year with the first payment made at time $t = 0$. The crane has an economic life of five years with a resale value of $15,000 at $t = 5$, and it will be a class 38 asset with a CCA rate of 30 percent. If the crane is purchased, annual maintenance costs of $4,000 will be incurred by BCI. The firm's opportunity cost of capital is 18 percent, and its tax rate is 30 percent. Should BCI lease the crane? (*Note:* Round the after-tax cost of debt to the nearest whole percent.)

Problems

15.1 Coyne Financial is setting lease rates for two pieces of equipment:

	Loader	Digger
CLA_0	$600,000	$900,000
Useful life	5 years	3 years
CCA rate	20 percent	30 percent

If the lease payments are made at the beginning of each period (i.e., $t = 0, t = 1, t = 2$, etc.), Coyne's marginal tax rate is 40 percent, and its before-tax return on debt-type investments is 18.34 percent, what lease rate, L, should be quoted on each piece of equipment?

15.2 TFX Leasing is assessing the impact of a number of different factors on the lease rates it quotes. Assume that the asset costs $350,000, has a five-year useful life, and is a class 8 asset (with a CCA rate of 20 percent). If TFX's marginal tax rate is 40 percent, determine the lease rate in each of the following cases. (*Note:* Assume that each part is independent of the other parts.)

a. TFX's required after-tax return on debt-type investments is 8 percent.

b. TFX's required after-tax return on debt-type investments is 10 percent.

c. TFX's required after-tax rate of return on debt-type investments is 8 percent, and the estimated resale value is $50,000. [*Note:* In calculating the present value of the resale value, use $RV_n(PV_{k,n})$ where $RV_n = $50,000$ and the opportunity cost of capital, k, is 14 percent.]

15.3 Hull Capital is setting lease rates for a $600,000 asset with a three-year useful life. The asset is a class 8 asset with a CCA rate of 20 percent. Hull's tax rate is 40 percent and its before-tax required rate of return on debt-type investments is 10 percent. Determine the lease rate under the following conditions:

a. The annual lease payments are payable in advance.

b. The lease payments are semiannual and made in advance. (*Note:* CCA is always a full-year deduction.)

15.4 Norton Industries needs three heavy-duty trucks that cost $100,000 in total. Saveway Leasing has offered to lease the trucks to Norton for a total of $25,000 per year for each of five years, with the lease payments payable in advance. The trucks are class 10 assets (CCA rate 30 percent) with a useful life of five years, the firm's marginal tax rate is 30 percent, and Norton's before-tax cost of debt is 10 percent. Should Norton lease or purchase the trucks? (Assume that the capital budgeting decision has already been made and the acquisition of the trucks is desirable.)

15.5 Central Trust Bank has just completed a capital budgeting analysis on some automatic teller units. The conclusion was that the bank should acquire the units. They cost $250,000, have a three-year economic life, and are class 9 assets (CCA rate 25 percent). Central Trust Bank has a 35 percent marginal tax rate, and its before-tax borrowing cost is 13.85 percent. Consider whether Central Trust Bank should purchase or lease the automatic tellers in each case:

a. The lease payment is $100,000 for each of three years, payable in advance.

b. The lease payment is $100,000 for each of three years, payable at the end of each year. (*Note:* The payments occur at $t = 1$, $t = 2$, and $t = 3$.)

c. The lease rate is $90,000 for each of three years, payable at the beginning of each year.

15.6 After completing a capital budgeting analysis, Great Pacific Railroad recently purchased some locomotives for $10 million. The locomotives will be in asset class 6 (CCA rate 10 percent) and have a 10-year useful life. Rebecca, one of the firm's directors, suggested that Great Pacific investigate a sale and leaseback agreement for the locomotives, as many other railroads are doing. Upon checking, you find that the locomotives can be sold for $10 million and then leased back for 10 years at $1.6 million per year, the lease payments being made in advance. Great Pacific's marginal tax rate is 40 percent and its before-tax cost of borrowing is 16.67 percent.

a. Should Great Pacific enter into the sale and leaseback agreement?

b. What is the maximum lease payment Great Pacific can pay?

15.7 A piece of equipment costs $300,000 and has a five-year useful life. For capital budgeting purposes the after-tax cash flows, CFs, are estimated to be $98,000 per year; the firm's marginal tax rate is 40 percent; and the opportunity cost of capital is 16 percent. The equipment is in class 38 (CCA rate, 30 percent); the lease rate, L, is $90,000 each year (at the beginning of the year) for five years; and the after-tax cost of borrowing, k_i, is 9 percent.

a. Should the use of the equipment be acquired?

b. After answering (a), determine if the equipment should be leased or purchased.

15.8 Fly-Hi Aviation is investigating whether new aircraft equipment is needed. The equipment, which requires an outlay of $550,000, has a three-year useful life and is in class 9 (CCA rate 25 percent). The net cash flows before taxes, CFBT, are $315,000 for each of three years. The expected resale value of the equipment is zero, the firm's tax rate is 40 percent, and the appropriate discount rate is 15 percent.

a. Should Fly-Hi acquire the new aircraft equipment?

b. After deciding the equipment should be acquired, Fly-Hi is now considering whether to lease or purchase. The lease would be $190,000 for each of three years, payable in advance.

Fly-Hi estimates its before-tax cost of borrowing is 15 percent. Should Fly-Hi lease or purchase the equipment?

c. What decision should Fly-Hi make in (b) if the net present value determined in (a) were −$15,000? Discuss the logic behind this decision.

15.9 Guaranteed Benefit Ltd. is evaluating leasing or purchasing an asset that has a positive NPV. The following basic conditions exist: CLA_0 is $210,000, n is 3, it is a class 8 asset with a 20 percent CCA rate, T is 35 percent, L is $82,000, k_i is 11 percent, lease payments are made annually in advance, and k is 15 percent.

a. Determine the base-case NPV_{lease}.

b. Determine the effect of the following conditions on the lease versus purchase decision for Guaranteed Benefit. (*Note:* Each part is independent of the other parts.)

1. If the asset is purchased, Guaranteed will incur incremental operating costs of $5,000 (before taxes) per year.

2. If the asset is purchased, Guaranteed estimates the resale value will be $45,000.

c. Independent of (a) and (b), suppose CLA_0 is $325,000, L is $90,000, n is 5, CCA rate is 20 percent, k_i is 13 percent, and k is 16 percent. If the asset is purchased, Guaranteed will incur incremental operating costs of $10,000 (before taxes) per year. Finally, Guaranteed estimates the before-tax resale value will be $75,000. Should Guaranteed now lease or purchase the asset?

15.10 Quality Leasing needs to set a lease rate on the following equipment: CLA is $200,000, n is 5 years, asset class is 7 (CCA rate 15 percent), T is 40 percent, k_b is 15 percent, and lease payments are made at the beginning of the year.

a. Determine the lease rate Quality will quote. (*Note:* Carry the lease rate to two decimal places.)

b. Parkland Resorts needs to lease the equipment. Determine the NPV_{lease} if everything is the same as for Quality and L is as determined in (a).

15.11 Marsh Distributors is considering a lease arrangement as a means of acquiring the use of some new equipment. The equipment costs $150,000, has a three-year useful life, and is a class 39 asset (CCA rate 25 percent). If purchased, the resale value is $10,000. The marginal tax rate is 30 percent, the appropriate opportunity cost of capital is 14 percent, and the before-tax cost of debt is 11.43 percent. If the three lease payments are made in advance, what is the maximum lease payment Marsh can make and still lease the asset? Assume that the NPV is positive.

15.12 LTI Ltd. has decided to acquire a new computer which the capital budgeting analysis indicates is economically justified. The cost of the computer is $500,000, and it can be leased at $120,000 per year with five annual payments made in advance. LTI's before-tax cost of debt is 10 percent, the marginal tax rate is 30 percent, and the computer is a CCA class 10 asset with a CCA rate of 30 percent.

a. By computing the NPV_{lease}, determine whether LTI should lease or purchase the computer.

b. Without calculating it, is the percentage cost of leasing higher or lower than the after-tax cost of debt? Why?

c. If the firm pays the maximum acceptable lease payment, what would be the percentage cost of leasing?

15.13 **Mini Case** Cantronics Systems is a medium-sized firm that specializes in energy- and cost-effective waste management systems. It has traditionally purchased equipment but is now considering leasing a new Systemease. Your job is to advise Cantronics on how to proceed.

a. The head of the accounting department is concerned about the impact of leasing on the firm's balance sheet. Briefly, how will the lease be treated? Explain why it is the tax treatment and not the accounting treatment that is important.

b. From the lessor's standpoint, what factors determine the lease rate quoted?

c. From the lessee's standpoint, why might Cantronics lease Systemease, instead of purchasing it?

d. The following information has been estimated for Systemease: The initial investment will be $1,400,000, and training costs of $150,000 are required. The equipment is a class 43 asset with a CCA rate of 30 percent and a seven-year useful life. The net cash flows before taxes are $500,000 each year, the firm's tax rate is 35 percent, and the appropriate opportunity cost of capital is 17 percent. Cantronics' before-tax cost of borrowing is 18.46 percent, and Systemease can be leased for $315,000 per year payable in advance.

   1. Should Cantronics acquire Systemease?
   2. Should it lease or purchase Systemease?

e. Assume everything is the same as in (d) except that now you find out there is a resale value at the end of the life of Systemease of $100,000, and additional maintenance charges of $30,000 per year before taxes will be required if Cantronics purchases Systemease. What decisions should now be made (in terms of acquiring or not acquiring the system, and leasing versus purchasing)?

REFERENCES

FINUCANE, THOMAS J. "Some Empirical Evidence on the Use of Financial Leases." *Journal of Financial Research* 11 (Winter 1988): 321–333.

FRANKS, JULIAN R., and STEWART D. HODGES. "Lease Valuation When Taxable Earnings Are a Scarce Resource." *Journal of Finance* 42 (September 1987): 987–1005.

LEASE, RONALD C., JOHN J. McCONNELL, and JAMES S. SCHALLHEIM. "Realized Returns and the Default and Prepayment Experience of Financial Leasing Contracts." *Financial Management* 19 (Summer 1990): 11–20.

LEWIS, CRAIG M., and JAMES S. SCHALLHEIM. "Are Debt and Leases Substitutes?" *Journal of Financial and Quantitative Analysis* 27 (December 1992): 497–511.

MUKHERJEE, TARUN K. "A Survey of Corporate Leasing Analysis." *Financial Management* 20 (Autumn 1991): 96–107.

SCHALLHEIM, JAMES S., RAMON E. JOHNSON, RONALD C. LEASE, and JOHN J. McCONNELL. "The Determinants of Yields on Financial Leasing Contracts." *Journal of Financial Economics* 19 (September 1987): 45–67.

SLOVIN, MYRON B., MARIE E. SUSHKA, and JOHN A. POLONCHEK. "Corporate Sale-and-Leasebacks and Shareholder Wealth." *Journal of Finance* 45 (March 1990): 289–299.

16

Mergers and Corporate Restructuring

EXECUTIVE SUMMARY

Firms both acquire and dispose of assets and take other actions that revolve around the control of assets. This area of activity is often referred to as the market for corporate control. Firms acquire assets internally through their capital investment decisions and externally via mergers and acquisitions. Although many reasons are advanced to justify a merger, there are two primary benefits to be derived. The first and most important is the expected economies, or synergism. A second is that in some cases there may be tax advantages that make merging desirable.

A merger is just another capital budgeting problem. To assess its economic desirability, managers must estimate the incremental expected cash inflows and outflows related to the merger. These projected net cash inflows are then discounted at the appropriate opportunity cost of capital and added to the current market value of the target firm. Then the cost, which differs depending on whether cash or stock is used, is determined. Once the costs are subtracted form the benefits, the NPV of the acquisition has been determined.

Numerous complexities exist in practice. Through it all, it is important to remember that mergers are simply one way, and not necessarily the most effective way, to contribute to the goal of maximizing the value of the firm.

Many defensive tactics can be employed by potential target firms. These consist of both preoffer and postoffer defenses. All have the goal of keeping the firm independent, or, if the firm is acquired, making sure the target's shareholders maximize their value.

Corporate restructurings are based on a two-pronged emphasis—recognition of corporate "fit" and maximizing NPV. Some typical restructuring activities involve leveraging up, using leveraged buyouts to go private, limited partnerships, voluntary restructuring, spinoffs, and divestitures. All focus on value creation and a better alignment of the interests of management with those of the firm's shareholders.

THE MARKET FOR CORPORATE CONTROL

Over time, firms can grow or shrink. Corporate restructuring is one of the most controversial and widely analyzed areas in financial management today. It includes the acquisition of other firms (or portions of firms), defensive tactics that are designed to maximize the value of the firm, and restructuring the assets or liabilities of the firm. In recent years, this area has become known as the **market for corporate control**, in which various management teams vie for the right to acquire and manage corporate assets and activities. The whole practice of financial management has undergone a dramatic shift in emphasis. Managers are more concerned now than ever before with maximizing the market value of the firm. Critics contend that all this emphasis on value creation has wasted management time and effort by drawing it away from the main operating activities of the firm. They also argue that it has eroded the competitive position (and research and development emphasis) of affected businesses. Supporters are quick to point out that the developments in the market for corporate control have increased the efficiency of the resource allocation process by reducing waste and the misuse of corporate free cash flows and assets.

To better understand the issues, we focus first on acquisitions by examining sources of potential gains and how to value them, along with some procedural issues. Our focus is from the standpoint of the **bidding firm**. The company it seeks to acquire is the **target firm**. Even though there are different legal means of accomplishing an

---

Table 16.1

Number of Mergers Involving Canadian Firms, 1984–1993

These figures show all acquisitions in industries subject to the Competition Act, previously the Combines Investigation Act.

Year	Foreign[a]	Domestic[b]	Total
1984	410	231	641
1985	466	246	712
1986	641	297	938
1987	622	460	1,082
1988	593	460	1,053
1989	691	400	1,091
1990	676	268	944
1991	544	195	739
1992	474	153	627
1993	399	201	600
Total	5,516	2,911	8,427

[a] Acquiring company is foreign-owned or foreign-controlled; the acquired company could have been foreign or Canadian.
[b] Acquiring company is Canadian-owned or -controlled; the acquired company could have been foreign or Canadian.

Source: Annual Report: Director of Investigation and Research, Competition Act, March 31, 1994.

acquisition, we will refer to any acquisition of another firm, or the division of another firm, as a **merger**. It is important to keep in mind, however, that many acquisitions are accomplished via *tender offers*. In a tender offer, cash is often offered by the bidding firm directly to the shareholders of the target firm. Often the management of the target firm is not consulted before the tender offer is made.

The level of corporate merger activity in Canada is not constant over time; instead, there are fluctuations in activity that are generally related to stock prices and economic activity. Table 16.1 shows the level of corporate merger activity for the 1984–1993 period. During this period, activity rose until 1989, after which it declined somewhat. The data indicate that foreign firms were very active in acquiring firms in Canada, accounting for 66 percent of all mergers over this period.

The diversity in the types of corporate restructuring that is taking place can be seen more directly by examining the largest mergers that occurred during 1994:

Bidding Firm	Target Firm	Value (in billions)
1. Rogers Communications Inc.	Maclean Hunter Ltd.	$3.1
2. American Barrick Resources Corp	Lac Minerals	2.2
3. Talisman Energy Inc.	Bow Valley Energy Inc. (unit of British Gas PLC)	1.8
4. IPL Energy (formerly Interprovincial Pipe Line System)	Consumers' Gas (unit of British Gas PLC)	1.2
5. Telus Corp.	Edmonton Telephone	0.7
6. Mouvement Desjardins Inc.	Laurentian Group Corp.	0.7
7. Shaw Communication Inc.	CUC Broadcasting Ltd.	0.6
8. Nike	Canstar Sports	0.5
9. Nesbitt Thomson	BurnsFry	0.4
10. Wal-Mart	Woolco	0.4

Two of the bidding firms (Nike and Wal-Mart) and two target firms (Bow Valley Energy and Consumers' Gas) were foreign firms or Canadian subsidiaries of foreign firms.

Source: The Globe and Mail, January 9, 1995, p. B1.

The transactions by eight of the bidding firms were mergers in which one firm acquired all of the assets of another firm. The other two transactions involved one firm acquiring part of the assets of another firm. These were Talisman Energy's purchase of 53 percent of Bow Valley Energy, and IPL Energy's purchase of Consumers' Gas from British Gas. In addition to these acquisitions, Horsham Corporation and Argo spent $1.2 billion in a restructuring takeover of Trizec Corporation by buying out Trizec's secured debenture holders, and Olympia & York's 61 percent stake in Abitibi-Price was sold to the public for $886 million by the bankers who had seized control of the stock after O & Y's reorganization in 1992. These examples from just a single year make clear that there are many diverse transactions in the market for corporate control. We will focus our attention first on mergers; then later in the chapter we will consider other parts of the market for corporate control.

Concept Review Questions

- What is meant by the term *market for corporate control*?
- Describe some tactics that management teams may use to acquire and manage other corporate activities or assets.

REASONS FOR MERGING

Attempting to grow by merging is an important part of corporate strategy for many firms. So it is important for managers to understand the potential benefits arising from a merger, as well as the danger signals in a deal. Let us look at some of the reasons, both sensible and dubious, for merging.

SENSIBLE REASONS

Any reasonable motive for merging has to include economic gains. These gains occur when the value of the combined bidder/target firm (BT) is more than the sum of the two separate firms (B, T) before the merger, so that

$$\text{value}_{BT} > \text{value}_B + \text{value}_T$$

Two sensible reasons relate to increased economies and tax considerations.

Increased Economies   A merger should improve economic performance. This improvement may come from economies of scale: The combined firm may be of sufficient size to be able to drive down production costs, distribution expenses, research and development costs, for example. The attempt to secure economies of scale is a primary reason why many mergers are undertaken. A separate but somewhat related motive is to seek economies by integrating vertically. *Vertical integration* refers to ensuring a continuous flow from acquisition of raw materials, through the various stages of production, to distribution and ultimate sale. A chemical firm that uses petroleum as a key raw material may decide to acquire an oil firm to achieve better vertical integration. By doing so, the chemical firm is attempting simultaneously to ensure adequate supplies of raw materials and to become more efficient by cutting the cost of raw materials acquisition.

Another possible economic benefit could come by merging two firms having overlapping expertise that may not be utilized when both are separate. For example, merging an electronics firm and a medical research firm may produce technology that neither firm operating independently could produce. Another benefit, market protection, may be achieved by acquiring competitors in order to increase market share, revenues, and profit margins. Although there may be some anti-combination considerations, increased international competition is resulting in less likelihood of the merger being challenged under the Competition Act. The higher profits resulting from such a merger will, however, tend to attract more competition in the future. Consequently, the market protection may be temporary.

Finally, a merger may create increased economies by removing inefficient management and taking a fresh (and unbiased) look at the utilization of the firm's cash flows and other resources. Bidding firms are often more open to an in-depth analysis of the economic consequences of alternative uses of the firm's assets, or even selling off part of the assets, than is a firm's current management.

All attempts to secure increased economies relate to **synergism**. Synergism, or the "2 + 2 = 5 effect," refers to the idea that the sum of two parts, or firms, is worth more than the two firms are worth apart. Synergistic benefits are the primary objective of sensible mergers. It is easy (and very tempting), however, to overestimate the anticipated benefits and to underestimate the costs and problems involved. For this reason, managers must take special care to ensure that the difficulties of integrating two firms into a smoothly flowing operation are recognized at the time the merger is considered. Also, it is important to ask whether the anticipated benefits of the acquisition accrue only to your firm, or to all firms. If they are expected to accrue only to your firm, be sure to ask why.

Tax Considerations   The other sensible reason for merging is to obtain tax benefits. If either the bidding or the target firm has incurred losses for tax purposes in the past, those losses can be carried back and then forward to offset the firm's tax liability. Sometimes, however, the losses are so severe that even after carrying them back or forward they are still not used up. The firm will lose these benefits unless it merges with another firm.

A second tax benefit may be due to the writeup of assets to a new tax basis; if this occurs, the combined firm will be allowed to write off more capital cost allowance, depreciation for tax purposes, thereby lowering its cash outflows for taxes.

A third, and controversial, tax effect relates to the possible increase in debt, due to the unused debt capacity of the target firm. If the target firm does not have too much debt, the bidding firm may be able to finance a large portion of the merger via issuing debt. Because interest is a tax-deductible expense, the combined firm can reduce taxes. An alternative, and nontax, benefit of using debt financing is that it provides additional incentives for management to create operating efficiencies so that the debt can be repaid.

DUBIOUS REASONS

In addition to the sensible reasons for merging, many dubious reasons are often given. Among the more commonly heard are these:

1. DIVERSIFICATION   It is often argued that the risk of the firm can be lowered by diversifying into two or more industries. Although such a move can reduce total risk, there is no evidence that the bidding firm gains. The reason is that in an efficient market, such as the financial markets in North America, Western Europe, and other developed countries, it is easier and cheaper for individual investors to obtain diversification directly, instead of having the firm do it. In effect, the combined firm performs a redundant service that is not valued by investors. In addition, any benefits secured by either the bidding or target firm's

bondholders through a coinsurance-type effect may be the result of a simple transfer of value from the firm's shareholders.

2. GROWTH FOR GROWTH'S SAKE   Firms often attempt to justify an acquisition by suggesting that it will enable the firm to keep growing in overall size (and presumably earnings), and that therefore the firm and its employees, managers, and shareholders will gain. But such growth does not produce anything of value unless it is accompanied by anticipated economies or tax benefits.

3. EARNINGS PER SHARE EFFECT   By acquiring another company, a firm often can achieve an immediate increase in EPS. This occurs because of the procedure accountants use to record the transaction—but it is, in fact, an illusion. This **EPS illusion**, unless it is accompanied by economic or tax benefits, does not serve the goal of maximizing the value of the firm. The accounting treatment of mergers is examined later.

Concept Review Questions

■ What are two viable reasons that would contribute to a financially sound merger between firms?

■ What are some dubious reasons for mergers—ones that will not result in a financially sound decision?

DECIDING WHETHER TO MERGE

In Chapter 7 we discussed the steps, or phases, in the capital budgeting process. The process for assessing whether to purchase assets via a merger is similar, but it has some additional considerations. The basic steps are:

1. Search and identification of growth opportunities
2. Estimation of the magnitude, timing, and riskiness of the incremental cash flows
3. Financial evaluation of the proposed merger
4. Negotiation
5. Implementation and integration

The first three steps are essentially identical to those discussed in Chapter 7 for any other capital investment decision. Where the merger evaluation process differs is in steps 4 and 5. Normally the bidder has to negotiate with the target; this process may require extensive time and effort. Finally, after an agreement has been reached, the merger has to be implemented, and over time the new operations have to be integrated into those of the successful bidding firm. Although all of the steps are important, we focus primarily on the financial aspects involved in evaluating whether the merger is worthwhile.

ANOTHER NPV PROBLEM

From the bidding firm's standpoint, a merger is another capital budgeting problem. To make the decision whether to merge, the bidding firm estimates the benefits in terms of the firm acquired and the incremental cash flows resulting from the acquisition, the costs in terms of the cash or securities to be offered, and the opportunity cost of capital that reflects the risk and forgone opportunities. Thus, the basic frame work is

$$NPV = \text{benefits} - \text{costs} \tag{16.1}$$

where

benefits = Δvalue + value$_T$
  costs = the price paid, in cash or stock

The Δvalue represents the present value of the incremental economic and/or tax benefits expected to arise due to the merger. Value$_T$ is the current (or preoffer) market value of the target firm. Note that in an efficient market and with no incremental benefits, the NPV would be zero because the bidding firm would not be willing to pay more than the current market value for the target firm. *For a positive NPV to exist, the bidding firm must be able to realize economic or tax benefits not available to the target firm.*

Benefits   For a publicly traded target, its current value (value$_T$) is simply the market price of its outstanding securities. The incremental benefits, Δ value, can be determined via

$$\Delta value = \sum_{t=1}^{n} \frac{\Delta CF_t}{(1 + k)^t} \tag{16.2}$$

where ΔCF_t is the incremental after-tax cash flows resulting from the acquisition of the target by the bidder, and k is the opportunity cost of capital appropriate for the incremental cash flows.[1]

The incremental after-tax cash flows, ΔCF_t, are made up of the following items:

1. Incremental cash operating inflows, incremental operating cash outflows, and the incremental depreciation. Therefore (as in Chapter 8 for a replacement capital budgeting decision), we have

Δafter-tax cash flows, $\Delta CF_t = \Delta CFBT_t(1 - T) + \Delta CCA_t(T)$

where

$\Delta CFBT_t$ = the incremental cash inflows in time period t
      T = the firm's marginal tax rate
ΔCCA_t = the incremental capital cost allowance in time period t

2. Any additional outlays for new equipment (including required increases in net working capital).
3. Finally, consideration of the sale of any of the target firm's assets, when the after-tax proceeds of the sale are anticipated to be greater or less than their going concern value (which is already reflected in the market value of the target firm).

---

[1] The approach presented here follows the net present value rule, based on using an opportunity cost, k, that incorporates the costs of both debt and equity. Alternatively, the adjusted present value approach discussed in Appendix 8A could also be used in making this decision.

The total ΔCF_t from the merger is the net incremental benefits, where for any year t,

$$\Delta CF_t = \Delta CFBT_t(1 - T) + \Delta CCA_t(T) - \begin{matrix} \Delta\text{investment in} \\ \text{long-term assets} \\ \text{and net} \\ \text{working capital} \end{matrix} \pm \begin{matrix} \text{after-tax gain or} \\ \text{loss on the} \\ \text{disposition of some of} \\ \text{the target firm's} \\ \text{assets (when above} \\ \text{or below their} \\ \text{going concern value)} \end{matrix} \qquad (16.3)$$

Most firms project incremental cash flows for 5 to 10 years and assume they revert to a no-growth situation thereafter. As with any other capital budgeting decision, sensitivity analysis can be used to assess the importance of the different input factors that go into determining the incremental value of the target.

Costs   The cost of the acquisition to the bidder is the value of the cash or securities (i.e., the offer price) the bidder will give to shareholders of the target firm. Cash is easier to consider than stock, so we will start by examining how the cost is determined when the bidder uses cash to effect the acquisition.

Cash.   If cash is employed, then the cost of the acquisition is simply the amount of cash itself. For example, assume that the bidder and target are both publicly traded all-equity firms that have market values of $250,000 and $150,000, respectively. To determine the incremental value, Δvalue, the bidder has estimated the incremental cash flows before tax, incremental CCA, and incremental investment (some of which occurs in the future) as shown in Table 16.2. (For simplicity, no incremental benefits are estimated beyond five years in this example.) Using the bidder's tax rate of 40 percent, and a discount rate of 15 percent, we find the incremental value of the target to be $61,012. The total benefits of the merger are the incremental value plus the present going concern value of the target, or

$$\text{benefits} = \Delta\text{value} + \text{value}_T = \$61,012 + \$150,000 = \$211,012$$

The bidder has to offer more than the current market value of the target, which is $150,000. With 10,000 shares of stock outstanding, the market price per share of the target before the merger is $15 (i.e., $150,000/10,000). Suppose that the bidder decides to offer $18.50 per share, or a total of $185,000, to the shareholders of the target firm. The net present value if the offer is financed with cash is

$$\text{NPV} = \text{benefits} - \text{costs} = \$211,012 - \$185,000 = \$26,012$$

The postmerger value of the combined firm will be the sum of the premerger value of the bidder of $250,000 plus the $26,012 NPV from the merger, or $276,012. Note that the bidder suffers an outflow of cash of $185,000 in order to effect the merger.

Suppose that there are 5,000 shares of stock of the bidding firm. Before the merger the stock was worth $50.00 (i.e., $250,000/5,000) per share. After the merger the per share value is approximately $55.20 (i.e., $276,012/5,000). Because cash was em-

Table 16.2

Estimated Incremental Value of Proposed Acquisition

In order to achieve all the benefits, the bidder estimates that it will have to invest an additional $30,000 in year 1 and $40,000 more in year 2.

Incremental Benefits and Investments

Year	ΔCFBT	ΔCCA[a]	ΔInvestment
1	$30,000	$10,000	$30,000
2	60,000	20,000	40,000
3	70,000	15,000	0
4	50,000	10,000	0
5	40,000	10,000	0

Calculation of Δvalue

Year	ΔCFBT(1 − T) +	ΔCCA(T) −	ΔInvestment =	ΔCF	× PV at 15%	Present Value
1	$18,000	$4,000	30,000	−$ 8,000	0.870	−$ 6,960
2	36,000	8,000	40,000	4,000	0.756	3,024
3	42,000	6,000	0	48,000	0.658	31,584
4	30,000	4,000	0	34,000	0.572	19,448
5	24,000	4,000	0	28,000	0.497	13,916

Δvalue = $61,012

[a] ΔCCA is for the investment in the column immediately to the right.

ployed, and the target's former shareholders sold their stock to the bidder for cash, all of the net benefits (i.e., the NPV) from the merger go to the bidder's shareholders.[2]

Stock.   What if common stock is used to finance the merger? In this case, the benefits of the merger are shared, because the target's shareholders end up owning part of the combined firm. Let us see what happens to the cost and the NPV when stock is employed.

Suppose that the same offer of $185,000 is made to the target's shareholders, but this time stock is employed. The premerger price of the bidding firm's stock is $50, so 3,700 (i.e., $185,000/$50) shares will be issued to acquire the target. With stock being employed, the shareholders of the target share in the fortunes (and costs) of the combined firm. The percent of the combined firm owned by the target's shareholders, as represented by W, is determined as follows:

$$W = \frac{\text{shares held by the target firm's former shareholders}}{\text{total shares outstanding after the merger}} \qquad (16.4)$$

$$= \frac{3,700}{5,000 + 3,700} = 0.425$$

---

[2] Sometimes mergers also involve the transfer of wealth from shareholders to bondholders, or vice versa. For example, if the cash employed to finance the deal was raised by issuing new debt, there is a transfer of wealth from bondholders to shareholders, along with the benefits of the merger itself.

In the combined firm, the target's former shareholders own 42.5 percent of the total firm.

To determine the cost of the merger when stock is employed, we use a slightly different procedure than before. The total value of the combined firm is given by

$$\begin{array}{ll}\text{total value of combined firm} \\ \text{when common stock is employed} \end{array} \begin{array}{l} = \text{value}_{BT} + \text{benefit} \\ = \$250,000 + \$211,012 \\ = \$461,012 \end{array} \qquad (16.5)$$

The cost when stock is employed is a function of the percent of the total value of the combined firm given up by the bidder's original shareholders, so

$$\text{cost with stock} = W(\text{value}_{BT}) \qquad (16.6)$$
$$= 0.425(\$461,012) = \$195,930$$

Note that this cost is higher than when cash was employed. The NPV, using Equation 16.1, is

$$\text{NPV} = \$211,012 - \$195,930 = \$15,082$$

Although the merger is still beneficial, the NPV is lower when stock is employed than when cash was used. This is always true if the same dollar value of cash or stock (the offer price of $185,000) is employed to finance the merger.

The use of cash or stock to finance the acquisition can be summarized as follows:

	Before Acquisition		After Acquisition	
	Bidder	**Target**	**Cash**	**Stock**
Market value	$250,000	$150,000	$276,012	$461,012
Number of shares	5,000	10,000	5,000	8,700
Price per share, P_0	$50	$15	$55.20	$52.99

When the same offer price is used for either cash or stock, we see that the total value of the combined firm is greater for the stock-financed acquisition. Due to sharing of the costs between the shareholders of the bidder and the target, the market value per share is $55.20 when cash is used versus $52.99 when stock is used. If all else is equal (i.e., if the offer price is the same in either case), then the bidder's existing shareholders are better off with a cash-financed acquisition.

This distinction between cash and stock financing is important. If cash is used, then the cost of the acquisition does not depend on the acquisition benefits. But if common stock is employed, the cost is a function of how the ownership is shared between the shareholders of the two firms. The use of either cash or stock tends to fluctuate over time. Until a few years ago, cash was being used more; however, recently stock has regained widespread use.

Often the term **exchange ratio** is used in discussing merger terms. It is:

$$\text{exchange ratio} = \frac{\substack{\text{market value of cash and/or securities} \\ \text{offered by bidding firm}}}{\text{market value of target firm's stock}} \qquad (16.7)$$

In our example the exchange ratio, with either cash or stock, is $185,000/$150,000 = 1.23. A higher exchange ratio is often required when cash is employed. This occurs because the target firm's shareholders give up ownership if cash is employed and because immediate income tax consequences (as discussed shortly) will result when cash, instead of stock, is employed.

TRYING TO AVOID MISTAKES

In any proposed merger numerous mistakes can be made. Perhaps this is why so many mergers that look good before completion turn out so poorly. Some of the ways to avoid mistakes are as follows:

1. RELY ON MARKET VALUES   It is often difficult to determine all of the value to be created using a present value approach. Although conceptually a merger is just a capital budgeting problem, and we could attempt to value the entire firm to be acquired, it is sounder to rely on the established market value for the target firm. In reasonably efficient markets the best estimate of the going concern value of any firm, given the current use of its cash flows and assets, is given by its present market value.

2. ESTIMATE INCREMENTAL CASH FLOWS   Only the incremental cash flows resulting from the proposed acquisition should be estimated. This simplifies the problem, but it is still easy to forget some of the incremental flows, or to overestimate inflows and underestimate outflows. Remember to ask, *"How will my use of the cash flows and assets be different from—and better than—their present use?"*

3. USE THE RIGHT OPPORTUNITY COST OF CAPITAL   The proper opportunity cost to employ relates to the incremental use of the cash flows and assets. If the incremental cash flows and assets are more risky than your firm's present cash flows and assets, then a higher opportunity cost of capital is necessary.

4. DO NOT FORGET TRANSACTIONS COSTS   The costs incurred for lawyers, accountants, and investment dealers often run into the millions of dollars. These costs cannot be ignored in the evaluation process.

5. BE CRITICAL   Often it is tempting to get carried away with a proposed acquisition. Surveys indicate a number of problems that firms run into when evaluating acquisitions. These include (1) underestimating the subsequent capital expenditures and additional investment in working capital required, (2) inability to reduce the target's ongoing cash outflows by as much as anticipated, after it is acquired, (3) longer transition periods and more transition-related cash outflows than anticipated, and (4) incorrect risk assessments. All of these problems serve to reduce the benefits of the merger from those anticipated.

Another time to be critical is when a bidding war breaks out in which more than one firm wants to acquire the target firm. In most bidding wars the bidder's shareholders will actually be better off if the bidding firm loses; the "winner's curse" of overpaying often accompanies the firm that is "successful" in making the winning bid.

6.   CONSIDER THE FORM OF THE FINANCING   The cash-versus-stock issue, and the amount of leverage the combined firm will have, are crucial decisions. Although this seems obvious, firms' managers often wake up a year or two later wondering whether they should have structured the deal differently. Numerous empirical and theoretical studies have examined the use of cash versus stock. These findings indicate that, other things being equal, both bidders and targets are better off if cash instead of stock is employed to finance an acquisition.

WHO BENEFITS FROM MERGERS?

Although there has been a lot of merger activity in recent years, it is doubtful that everyone has gained. Here is what we do know about mergers:

1.   Shareholders of the target companies almost always gain, because most mergers involve a premium being paid over the target firm's premerger market value. Premiums average 30 to 40 percent above the premerger market value, and some times go as high as 100 percent. Thus, substantial benefits accrue to the targets.

2.   Numerous studies concerning the postmerger value of the bidding firms indicate little or no increase in market value. Thus, studies have found no positive impact on the market value of bidding firms after a merger. In a recent study, Agrawal, Jaffe, and Mandelker (1992) examined the postmerger performance of successful bidding firms for five years after the merger completion date. Their findings indicate a loss in value of about 10 percent over this five-year period when stock was employed to finance the transaction; but if cash was employed there was no loss in value for the bidders. On the other hand, for 50 large mergers, Healy, Palepu, and Ruback (1992) find improved performance in terms of postmerger operating cash flow and asset productivity for successful bidding firms. Whether mergers lead to benefits from the standpoint of successful bidding firms is still a hotly debated issue—and one that will continue to be vigorously explored in the future.

3.   Investment dealers, lawyers, and accountants providing consulting and services to merger participants have benefited from the many mergers in recent years.

FREE CASH FLOW AND MERGERS

In 1986 Jensen presented the free cash flow hypothesis of mergers. He argued that managers with surplus, or free, cash flow over and above that needed for operating the firm will invest cash in negative net present value projects rather than pay it out to shareholders. The essence of the free cash flow hypothesis is that the presence of excess cash flow increases the agency costs of firms with poor investment opportunities. The hypothesis assumes that management values investments in operations more than investments in financial assets. This may come about because management perquisites increase with the investment in operations, even when these investments have a negative NPV. Therefore, once management has exhausted positive NPV projects, it proceeds to invest in negative NPV projects rather than pay these funds out to shareholders. In an empirical test of this hypothesis, Lang, Stulz, and Walking (1991) found that firms with high free cash flow and poor investment prospects actually decreased their shareholders' wealth by merging; however, firms with better investment prospects did not diminish the wealth of their shareholders when making an acquisition. They interpret these findings as providing support for the free cash flow hypothesis.

Concept Review Questions

■ What are the basic steps for evaluating a proposed merger?

■ For a positive NPV to exist, what must the bidding firm be able to realize?

■ Describe some mistakes that can be made in a merger and how the mistakes can be avoided.

■ Why would corporate managers of firms with excess free cash flow invest in negative net present value projects?

MECHANICS OF A MERGER

Buying another firm is much more complicated than most other business transactions. The details and the various options and factors affecting the merger can expand rapidly.

FORM OF THE ACQUISITION

Until now, we have used the term merger to refer to any acquisition or combination of companies. A merger, however, may take various forms:

1. In Canada, the essential features of a merger, or **statutory amalgamation**, are that the bidding firm acquires both the target's assets and liabilities by exchanging stock, cash, or other securities for the target firm's stock, and the target firm ceases to exist as a separate entity.
2. The term statutory amalgamation, or merger, is also used to cover the situation when two or more firms combine to form a completely new firm. A new legal entity is formed.
3. A merger can also be accomplished by acquiring just the assets of the target firm. If the target sells all its assets to the bidder, the proceeds from the sale (after paying off any liabilities) can be distributed to the target firm's shareholders, and the firm can be dissolved.
4. Forming a *holding company* is another way to acquire control over another firm, although complete ownership may not be held. A firm may acquire 40 to 50 percent ownership in another firm. Though it does not control all, or even a majority of, shares, it can exercise effective control over the other firm.

TAX IMPLICATIONS

An acquisition can be taxable or tax-free for the target firm's shareholders. If it is a taxable transaction, the target's shareholders must treat the transaction as a sale for tax purposes and report any capital gains or losses. For example, if you purchased stock originally for $10 per share and sold out through a merger at $50 per share, your capital gain is $40 per share. You would pay taxes during the current period on this $40 capital gain. If the merger is tax-free, you retain your original $10 cost in the shares of the new firm. Only when you subsequently sell the new stock at some later date will any capital gain or loss in value have to be reported.

To qualify as tax-free, the transaction must meet the following conditions:

1. In an amalgamation or merger four conditions must hold. First, each of the parties to the merger must be a "taxable Canadian corporation" as defined in Section 89(1) of the Income Tax Act. Second, all property of the target corporation immediately before the merger must become property of the bidding firm. Third, all liabilities of the target corporation immediately before the merger must become property of the bidding firm. Fourth, all shareholders of the target corporations must become shareholders of the bidding firm.

2. In an acquisition of stock, the requirements are that the bidding firm must be a taxable Canadian corporation, the target firm must receive only shares of the bidding firm, and after the exchange the bidding firm must own at least 10 percent of the voting shares of the target corporation. The firms must also be dealing "at arm's length," and immediately after the exchange the target must not control the bidding firm or own more than 50 percent of the bidding firm's shares.

3. To effect a tax-free acquisition of assets is more complicated. However, it is possible, and Section 85 of the Income Tax Act sets forth the criteria for such an acquisition.

ACCOUNTING TREATMENT

There are two basic accounting treatments for mergers: (1) **pooling of interests** and (2) **purchase**. Which method is employed can have a significant impact on the balance sheet and the profits reported for accounting purposes. However, the accounting criteria are such that pooling of interests is rarely used. If a merger is carried out through an exchange of voting shares, in accordance with the *CICA Handbook*, Section 1580.08, pooling of interests can be used *only if*, "none of the parties involved can be identified as the acquirer."[3]

---

[3] It has been suggested that when an acquirer cannot be identified, a new entity has been created, and therefore the assets and liabilities should be combined at their fair value (cost to the new entity). However, the CICA rejects this idea in favour of the pooling of interests method. See *CICA Handbook*, Section 1580, paragraphs 10, 11, and 20.

Balance Sheet Effects   In a pooling of interests, the consolidated balance sheet is constructed by simply adding together the two preexisting balance sheets. In a purchase, the assets acquired must be revalued to indicate the actual purchase price paid for the target firm. If a price greater than the book value of the assets is paid for the target company, the purchased assets must be revalued to reflect their fair market value. If the purchase price is more than the total fair *market value* of the assets acquired—due to trade names, marketing, or managerial expertise, and the like—then goodwill is created.

Income Statement Effects   The two different methods of accounting for a merger can also have an impact on the earnings reported by the combined firm. This occurs because under pooling of interests, assets are brought over at their current depreciated book value. Under the purchase method, assets are revalued to reflect the value of the merger. This means that more depreciation will be charged off in future years than under pooling of interests. Goodwill was also created, and it must be written off over a period not to exceed 40 years. The additional depreciation and goodwill amortization will result in a lower earnings per share under the purchase method than under the pooling of interest method. This accounting effect is part of the EPS illusion that mergers can have. So we see that earnings per share is subject to changes unrelated to the economic benefits of a merger.

Concept Review Questions

- What conditions must be met for an acquisition to be tax-free for the target firm's stareholders?
- What is the difference in a firm's balance sheet between the pooling of interests and purchase methods of accounting for mergers?

DEFENSIVE TACTICS

Firms have attempted to fend off unwanted takeovers through a number of actions. These basically fall into two main classifications—preoffer and postoffer defences.

PREOFFER DEFENCES

In the preoffer group, defences can be broken into three categories: general, shark-repellent charter amendments, and other repellents.

General Preoffer Defences

1. PRIVATE COMPANY   The best defence of all may be to be a privately owned company, such as McCain Foods.

2. BLOCKING STAKES   Companies with 50 percent or more of their stock owned by one individual or a tight-knit group can be all but invulnerable. This is why, for example, 77 percent of the voting control of Loblaw Companies Ltd. is in the hands of George Weston.

3. ESOP   In recent years many firms have instituted or enlarged employee stock ownership plans (ESOPs) in order to boost the percentage of the firm owned by employees. This is another approach to placing a sizable amount of stock in the hands of a group which should be less willing to sell the firm.

4. SIZE AND POLITICS   For a very few firms, such as IBM and Exxon, size alone may still be a valid defence. Likewise, certain companies, such as BCE or defence-oriented high-tech firms, may be immune to takeover due to potential political ramifications.

5. STRONG STOCK PRICE   One of the best defences is a strong stock price, which signifies that the investment community already believes in the firm, its management, and its growth prospects. Although this is no barrier to a determined bidder who wants the company at any cost, it will fend off many suitors.

Shark-Repellent Charter Amendments

6. STAGGERED BOARD   Under this tactic the board of directors is classified into three groups, with only one of the three groups elected every year. Though a bidder can acquire majority ownership via a tender offer, it cannot obtain complete control of the board and the firm immediately.

7. SUPERMAJORITY   Instead of needing only 50 percent of the votes plus one to approve a merger, many firms have asked their shareholders to change the bylaws and redefine the majority required to approve a merger. This **supermajority** is typically between two-thirds and 80 percent.

8. FAIR PRICE AMENDMENT   The supermajority provision may often be waived if the bidder pays all shareholders the same price. This amendment prevents "two-tiered bids" in which the first 80 percent of the shares tendered receive one price, and the last 20 percent receive a lower price for their stock.

Other Defences

9. DUAL CLASS RECAPITALIZATION   Many firms, such as Molson, have a class of supervoting stock that keeps control among the descendants of the founder or the builders of the business.

10. POISON PILLS   The term **poison pill** describes a family of shareholder rights agreements. When triggered by a tender offer or the accumulation of a certain percentage of the target's shares, it provides target shareholders with the right to purchase additional shares or to sell shares to the target at very attractive prices. Poison pills raise the potential cost of an acquisition to two or three times what it would otherwise be.

POSTOFFER DEFENCES

If all of the preoffer defences fail to work, then the target still has some postoffer defences it can call into play. These include the following:

1. LITIGATION   Many firms file suits to protect some of their defences that have been challenged by a bidder, or they accuse the bidding firm of violating anti-combination or securities laws.
2. ASSET RESTRUCTURING   Some firms purchase assets, or make another quick merger, to acquire assets the bidder does not want or that will create an anti-combination problem. An alternative is for the firm to sell its "crown jewels"—that is, the assets most desired by the bidder.
3. LIABILITY RESTRUCTURING   The targeted firm sells some shares to a friendly third party, called a **white squire**, or leverages up by issuing debt and/or buying back equity.
4. STANDSTILL AGREEMENT   Under a standstill agreement, the target gets the bidder to agree during the term of the agreement not to increase its stock holdings in the target firm above a specified percentage and, in many cases, to support the management of the target firm.

The above lists cover the majority of the defensive tactics used by firms fending off takeover bids, but new ones are always being devised. Two others should be mentioned: greenmail and golden parachutes. **Greenmail** (or targeted repurchases) occurs when an unfriendly bidder has purchased a significant stake in a target firm. Often, to get rid of the unwanted suitor, the target firm buys back the common stock at a premium over its current market value. As part of the deal, the suitor agrees not to purchase any new shares in the target for some specific period of time. A **golden parachute** is a supplemental compensation agreement for senior management that provides substantial additional compensation in case of a takeover and the resignation (forced or voluntary) of the covered executives.

Finally, if all else fails, target firms often try to find a "friendly" firm—a **white knight**—to merge with. This strategy also involves risk, however, because some white knights have turned out to be less chivalrous after the merger than the target anticipated.

THE TARGET'S RESPONSE AND AGENCY PROBLEMS

The management of the target firm has the responsibility of representing the interest of its owners, the shareholders. However, because of potential differences in orientation or focus, a serious agency problem might develop. Although selling out for cash or stock at a substantial premium might be in the best interests of the firm's shareholders, it might also result in the loss of jobs for many of the top management of the target firm. Because of differences in self-interests, what is best for one party may not always be best for the other. One argument made in favour of golden parachutes is to assist in overcoming agency problems of this kind. However, if the golden parachutes are too large, they may provide the wrong kind of incentive to management—which might result in their selling the firm on terms that do not provide shareholders as much benefit as possible.

Concept Review Questions

- Describe some tactics a firm may employ to fend off unwanted takeovers.
- What kind of agency problem may the target's management face?

CORPORATE RESTRUCTURING

Much of the recent merger activity in this country has involved mature firms. Because of limited growth opportunities in their core businesses, many firms are rethinking how they use the cash flows generated by the firm. Instead of simply plowing the funds back into the same kinds of activities, or diversifying into areas in which they have no expertise, the motivation now—more than ever—is towards maximizing the value of the firm. There are two main points behind this emphasis on creating value: First, there is the recognition that corporate "fit" is very important; that is, firms are streamlining their operations and refocusing more on their core business. Second, maximizing NPV, and therefore the market value of the firm, is more important than ever. This recognizes the increased attention that needs to be given to the questions *"When and how should I get into positive NPV projects where my unique strengths provide the best opportunity to create value?"* and *"When and how should I get out of certain projects that no longer offer unique value-creating NPV opportunities?"*

LEVERAGING UP

To increase efficiency and impose the discipline created by additional debt, as well as to make themselves less attractive takeover candidates, some firms in recent years "leveraged up." This trend reached its peak in the late 1980s and has since receded somewhat. In a **leveraging up** operation, the firm dramatically shrinks the number of shares of common stock outstanding (through stock repurchases) and increases the amount of debt financing employed. These moves often result in the company shifting from a 20 to 30 percent debt to total asset ratio up to 60 or even 70 percent. The two activities can be combined in a leveraged repurchase, in which the firm issues substantial amounts of debt and uses the proceeds to buy back some of its common stock. Leveraging up forces a firm to become even more conscious of its cash flows than it was previously, and it imposes a discipline on the ongoing operations of the firm that is often missing without the additional debt. Although debt has disadvantages, it is a way to impose market discipline and encourage firms to become more efficient and productive. At the same time, there is an additional benefit to the transaction: The firm becomes a less tempting takeover candidate because there is no "unused debt capacity" for a bidder to take advantage of.

GOING PRIVATE AND LEVERAGED BUYOUTS

Some firms in the 1980s ended up **going private**—that is, going from a publicly owned firm with common stock actively traded on a stock exchange or in the over-the-counter market to a privately held one controlled by a small group of owners. One of the reasons for going private is to avoid being acquired by another firm. Often the act of going private involves a management buyout. In a **management buyout**, the top management of the firm usually bands together, often with an outside partner, to take all or part of the business and turn it into a private company. Usually management buyouts are highly leveraged deals that are known as **leveraged buyouts (LBOs)**. In a leveraged buyout, a firm is acquired in a transaction that is financed largely by borrowing—often provided by institutional investors. The LBO debt can either be privately placed or be supplied by the use of junk (or high-yield) bonds. Other leveraged buyouts may not involve the management of the firm but may be triggered by outside investors. Although leveraged buyouts and management buyouts can be one and the same, it is possible for either one to occur separately.

The largest leveraged buyout of all time involved RJR Nabisco. In 1988, F. Ross Johnson, chief executive officer of RJR Nabisco, led a management-initiated proposal to take RJR private. That move touched off a bidding war that was ultimately won by the firm of Kohlberg Kravis Roberts & Co. (KKR). The final bid was a record $25 billion, which amounted to $109 per share of RJR's stock. Seventy-four percent, or $81 per share, was paid in cash; the rest was in new preferred stock and convertible debentures. These additional securities, often called *payment-in-kind* (or PIK), represented $28 per share of the package.

To finance the deal, KKR needed to raise $18.9 billion in cash. The money was raised as follows: Two billion dollars, the smallest part of the financing, came from KKR's equity investors and represented ownership in RJR Nabisco after the deal was completed. The second chunk, $11.9 billion in bank loans, came from 45 U.S., Japanese, European, and Canadian banks. Finally, the last chunk, $5 billion, was raised by selling notes to other investors.

Financing the deal was only part of the problem, because the bigger issue was how to manage RJR Nabisco effectively, sell off certain assets, and squeeze additional cash flow out of the existing operations. Efficient management of the firm was essential to pay the interest, pay down debt, and make sure the whole deal did not sink. By 1991 RJR Nabisco had made significant progress and even sold some of its stock to the public. But 1992 and 1993 were not as kind to RJR Nabisco. While the food portion of their business was doing fairly well, there was concern about the tobacco side. Continued liability suits from cancer victims, fear of a large tax increase in cigarettes, the Environmental Protection Agency report on the dangers of second-hand tobacco smoke, and the move by a major competitor (Philip Morris) to reduce the selling price of its main cigarette brand caused RJR Nabisco's stock price in 1993 to be 25 percent less than when it went public in 1991. In response, RJR Nabisco considered splitting into two separate arms—one food and the other tobacco, each having a separate class of common stock. The hope was that with two ownerships, the market value of the entire firm would not be brought down due to problems related to the tobacco arm of the firm. After much thought RJR Nabisco shelved the proposal to split into two separate firms.

LIMITED PARTNERSHIPS

Sometimes corporate restructuring involves a fundamental change in the legal structure of the business. Some firms, for example, have reorganized themselves as *limited partnerships*. In this case the shareholders are replaced by partners, and the firm's revenues and expenses are credited directly to the individual partners' accounts. These partnerships are generally known as master limited partnerships. A number of limited partnerships exist in the oil and gas industry, where producing properties have actually been spun off to partnerships. These partnership interests are then taken out of the firm itself and distributed to the firm's shareholders.

Typically, the management of a limited partnership is directly involved in how the firm is financed and where the cash flows go. This involvement creates additional incentives to make sound use of the cash flows generated. Finally, there is a tax advantage to a limited partnership. Shareholders really pay taxes twice—once at the corporate level when the corporation pays taxes, and again at the personal level. Under a limited partnership the proceeds are taxed only once, when they appear on the partners' personal income tax forms.

VOLUNTARY RESTRUCTURING

In the wake of subpar performance, or outright losses, firms often conclude that they need to restructure to become more competitive. This trend towards voluntary restructuring has gained momentum in recent years, as institutional investors have increased their ownership in firms and, more than ever, shareholders are demanding change and better performance from firms in which they own substantial stakes. Large institutional investors, such as pension funds, banks, insurance firms, and mutual funds, along with shareholder activist groups, are demanding change and better performance. This increased activity has been assisted by two changes by the Ontario Securities Commission (OSC) regulations. One is a requirement that firms provide fuller disclosure of executive compensation packages; this has put managers on the defensive. The other makes it easier for shareholders to communicate with each other and with managers. This new activism by shareholders is credited, in part, with leading to the removal of the chief executive officers of General Motors, IBM, American Express, and Westinghouse in the early 1990s.

In the face of needed change, firms take many actions. Some of them include selling assets and laying off employees.[4] Also, there is evidence that firms decrease the number of segments in which they operate and cut the costs of production. Other trends when firms undergo voluntary restructuring include cutting R & D, increasing capital investment, reducing the amount of debt, and also reducing cash dividends. With the increased emphasis on performance, firms will increasingly be involved in voluntary restructuring.

---

[4] See John, Lang, and Netter (1992).

SPINOFFS

One way for a firm to relinquish control of assets is to spin them off to shareholders. Sometimes this is done by simply distributing shares in the spinoff portion of the firm to the firm's present shareholders. Another approach is to sell part or all of the spinoff to new investors, thereby getting rid of assets and raising cash at the same time. This was the case with Sears in the early 1990s when it spun off 20 percent of Dean Witter Reynolds, using the proceeds to reduce debt, and made plans to divest itself of the remaining 80 percent shortly afterwards.

DIVESTITURES

Firms not only acquire businesses; they also continually have to ask "Should we continue to be in this business?" A negative response to this question leads to another form of corporate restructuring—divestiture. Too often in the past, divestitures carried negative connotations about how well the firm had done in managing the unit. But a **divestiture** should really be viewed as the product of good management, which is harvesting the fruits of past successful investments. The only question remaining should be "Can the firm create more value by holding on to the unit, because of some unique competitive advantage that a buyer does not have?"

The same basic ideas used when we considered the acquisition of assets are also of concern when a sale is contemplated. But instead of concerning ourselves with how much the firm can afford to pay to acquire assets, the issue now becomes how much the firm can sell the assets for. We are interested in whether the value of the firm is maximized by holding on to the assets or by selling them. The steps to be used in making the decision to keep or divest a division (or any group of assets) are as follows (see Figure 16.1):

STEP 1:   Estimate the operating after-tax cash flow stream associated with the division. Be sure to consider any impacts on the cash flows arising from complementary or substitute effects with other aspects of the firm's operations, as well as any future cash investments required in the division.

STEP 2:   Determine the opportunity cost of capital, k, that reflects the risk associated with the division.

STEP 3:   Calculate the present value of the CFs expected to accrue to the firm by keeping the division.

STEP 4:   Subtract the current market value of the division's associated liabilities.[5] This step produces the NPV of keeping the division, which is

$$NPV = \sum_{t=1}^{n} \frac{CF_t}{(1 + k)^t} - B \tag{16.8}$$

---

[5] Debt should be valued at today's market value, since that is the present value of the firm's future obligation, discounted at the appropriate rate.

Figure 16.1

Steps in Making the Divestiture Decision

These steps are similar to those employed when calculating the NPV of a proposed product, except now the market value of the liabilities supported by the division must be formally considered.

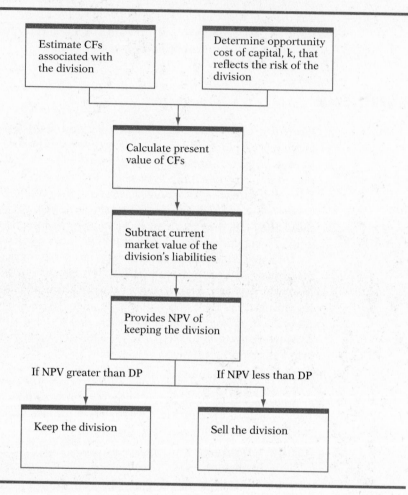

where

CF_t = the after-tax cash flows expected in year t from retention of the division

k = the opportunity cost of capital appropriate for the division

B = the current market value of the liabilities associated with the division

STEP 5: Compare the NPV of keeping the division with the net after-tax divestiture proceeds, DP, to be received if the division is sold. The decision rule is as follows:

1. If NPV is greater than DP, keep the division.
2. If NPV is less than DP, sell the division.
3. If NPV is equal to DP, you are indifferent.

In calculating the after-tax divestiture proceeds, two situations may exist. If the purchaser *acquires both the division's assets and associated liabilities*, the net after-tax amount received by the seller represents the divestiture proceeds, DP. But if the purchaser acquires only the division's assets, the seller retains the division's liabilities, which must—sooner or later—be paid off. To make a consistent comparison *when the seller retains the division's liabilities*, the net divestiture proceeds are calculated as follows:

$$\text{DP}\left(\begin{array}{c}\text{if seller retains}\\\text{division's liabilities}\end{array}\right) = \frac{\text{after-tax divestiture proceeds}}{\text{offered for the division}} - \text{B} \qquad (16.9)$$

To understand the divestiture decision, consider General Communications. General is evaluating whether it should keep or divest a small movie theatre operation. Cinevision Ltd. has offered to buy the theatre division for $7 million after taxes; it will not acquire any of the division's liabilities. To determine whether General should sell the division, it is necessary to estimate the after-tax cash flows (CFs) expected if it holds on to it. These cash flows should reflect (or be net of) any additional investments General will have to make in the future. The after-tax cash flows are shown in Table 16.3. Note that we have estimated year-by-year cash flows for the first five years and then assumed that they grow at a constant rate to infinity.

In addition, General has determined that the opportunity cost of capital is 12 percent and that the division's associated debt is $1 million. In years 2 and 3, additional investment is required if General keeps the theatre division. Based on its projected cash flows, the NPV of keeping the theatre division (after taking into account the division's debt) is $9.949 million, as shown in Table 16.3. Since this value far exceeds the after-tax divestiture proceeds of $6 million ($7 million from Cinevision, minus $1 million for the division's debt), General should retain the theatre division. By doing so, it maximizes the value of the firm.

In considering whether to keep or liquidate assets, the decision facing the firm is exactly the opposite of the capital budgeting or merger decision. It calculates the NPV of retaining the assets and continuing to operate them versus the after-tax cash proceeds from selling. If the benefits from keeping the assets are greater than the forgone opportunity cost arising from divesting, the assets are retained. Otherwise, they are disposed of.

This type of analysis can also be used to asses the financial desirability of voluntarily liquidating a firm. In the case of a voluntary liquidation, the NPV of continuing to operate is estimated with Equation 16.7. The liquidation proceeds represent the net after-tax proceeds available for distribution to the firm's shareholders, after all the firm's liabilities have been met.

Concept Review Questions

- Describe how a firm's leveraging up may increase its market value.
- What is a leveraged buyout, and how was one used in the purchase of RJR Nabisco?
- Describe how limited partnerships, voluntary restructuring, spinoffs, and divestitures may affect a firm's market value.
- What are the steps used in making divestiture decisions?

Table 16.3

Net Present Value of Theatre Division if Retained

Since the NPV of $9.949 million is greater than the divestiture proceeds of $6 million, General should retain its theatre division.

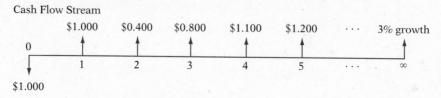

Cash Flow Stream

Present Value of Expected Cash Inflows

Year	Cash Flow (in millions)	Additional Investment (in millions)	CF (in millions)	PV at 12%	Present Value (in millions)
1	$1.000	0	$1.000	0.893	$0.893
2	1.000	0.600	0.400	0.797	0.319
3	1.000	0.200	0.800	0.712	0.570
4	1.100	0	1.100	0.636	0.700
5	1.200	0	1.200	0.567	0.680
Beyond 5	3% per year	0	13.733[a]	0.567	7.787

Present value of future cash inflows = 10.949

Less: Present market value of associated debt, B = 1.000

NPV = $9.949

$$^aV_5 = \frac{D_5(1 + g)}{k - g} = \frac{\$1.200(1.03)}{0.12 - 0.03} = \frac{\$1.236}{0.09} = \$13.733$$

KEY POINTS

- Mergers are only one part of the market for corporate control; related activities involve defences, leveraging up, going private and leveraged buyouts, limited partnerships, voluntary restructuring, spinoffs, and divestitures.
- Mergers should be undertaken only if they are expected to produce economic benefits in the form of increased economies or tax savings. Merger analysis is another net present value (NPV) problem. The costs differ depending on whether cash or stock is employed.
- To increase the reliability of the merger analysis, firms need to do the following:
  a. Rely on market values to the greatest extent possible.
  b. Consider the unique attributes of both the target and the bidder as the incremental cash flows are estimated.
  c. Focus on the risk and returns of the target in estimating the opportunity cost of capital.
  d. Include in their analysis the transaction costs to investment dealers, lawyers, accountants, and so forth.

e. Become very critical of all facets of the analysis, and avoid falling into the trap of overestimating the expected inflows or underestimating the magnitude of the additional outflows required and the time needed to reap the benefits of the acquisition.

f. Remember that cash financing benefits both the target and the bidder more than stock financing.

- Target shareholders benefit from acquisitions, but the evidence is that the bidder's shareholders either break even or lose value when firms merge.
- Defensive tactics can be broken into preoffer and postoffer.
- Corporate restructuring focuses on value creation and maximizing net present value. The firm's management must focus on these ideas and the options available to enhance the value of the firm when considering the acquisition or divestiture of assets, taking defensive measures, and considering the size, financing mix, or structure of the firm.

QUESTIONS

16.1 There are both sensible and dubious reasons for merging. What are they? What distinguishes them?

16.2 Two firms, X and Y, are in unrelated fields and are planning to merge. No synergy is expected, but the standard deviation of the combined companies' returns will be lower than the standard deviation of either firm's separate returns. Is this a valid reason for merging? Why or why not?

16.3 A merger is another NPV problem. Explain:

a. What Δvalue is, and what cash flows must be included.

b. Why we do not use a discounted cash flow analysis to estimate the total benefits from the proposed acquisition.

c. Why the costs are different if stock is employed instead of cash.

16.4 What are some of the typical mistakes made in evaluating proposed mergers?

16.5 Who benefits from a merger? Do you think anyone loses?

16.6 Identify the different legal forms for acquiring another firm.

16.7 A merger can be taxable or tax-free to the target firm's shareholders. Why is this important? How does a merger qualify to be tax-free?

16.8 Met Theatre acquired Victoria Pictures for $750 million, when Victoria's book value was only $185 million. From the standpoint of reported EPS, would Met rather report this merger as a purchase or as a pooling of interests? Why?

16.9 Identify the defensive tactics a firm may employ. Are greenmail and golden parachutes also defensive tactics in the same sense as the others?

16.10 What are the two prongs (or points) behind value creation via corporate restructuring? How do the various forms of restructuring relate to this two-pronged emphasis?

16.11 How should a firm go about deciding whether or not to divest one of its divisions? What role does the division's debt play in the decision?

CONCEPT REVIEW PROBLEMS

See Appendix A for solutions.

CR16.1 Marshall's is investigating the acquisition of Newman, an all-equity firm. Marshall's tax rate is 40 percent, and the appropriate opportunity cost of capital is 15 percent. Estimates of the incremental cash flows are:

Year	ΔCFBT	ΔCCA[a]	ΔInvestments
1	$250	—	$100
2	350	$20	120
3	400	40	—
4	450	40	—
5	500	40	—

[a] ΔCCA is for the Δinvestment in the column immediately to the right.

Newman's current price per share is $10, with 100 shares of stock outstanding. If Marshall's pays $12 in cash per share to obtain control of Newman, what is the NPV of the proposed takeover?

CR16.2   Goodtimes R Here is planning to purchase WaterWilly for $100 per share. Water-Willy's market value is $800,000, and it has 10,000 shares of common stock outstanding. Goodtimes' market value is $1,500,000, and it has 75,000 shares of common stock outstanding. Goodtimes estimates the incremental value after purchasing WaterWilly is $400,000.
a. If cash is used, what will be the price per share of Goodtimes both before and after the merger?
b. If stock is used, what will be the stock price of Goodtimes after the merger?

CR16.3   The following is premerger information on Barrett Partnerships and Exxon Corporation.

	Barrett	Exxon
Total earnings	$50,000	$75,000
Shares outstanding	10,000	20,000
Price per share	$40	$35

a. If Barrett exchanges one share of common stock for each share of Exxon, what will be the price of the new firm if the P/E ratio remains at Barrett's current P/E ratio?
b. What is the new price per share and P/E if the P/E ratio simply reflects the combined total market value and combined total earning value of the firms?

PROBLEMS

16.1   Dellva Printing is analyzing the possible acquisition of Big Sky Electric. Dellva's market value is $3,000,000, and its market price per share is $40. Big Sky's market value is $800,000; Dellva estimates the incremental value, Δvalue, is $250,000, and the total purchase price would be $1,000,000.
a. If cash is used, what is the NPV of the proposed acquisition?
b. What is the NPV if stock is employed?
c. Why is the NPV for a cash-financed merger greater than if stock is employed? How much more cash could be offered if the NPV for a cash-financed deal just equalled the NPV for the stock-financed deal?

16.2   Alberta Foods is investigating a possible acquisition financed with cash. It estimates the incremental benefits and investment as follows:

Year	ΔCFBT	ΔCCA^a	ΔInvestment
0	$ 0	$ 0	$300,000
1	40,000	60,000	—
2	50,000	96,000	—
3	60,000	57,000	—
4	100,000	45,000	—
5	100,000	42,000	—
6	70,000	0	—
7	20,000	0	—

^{a} ΔCCA is for the investment in the column immediately to the right.

Without the incremental investment, Alberta Foods estimates there will be very few benefits from the acquisition. Should it proceed with plans for the acquisition if the marginal tax rate is 35 percent and the appropriate opportunity cost of capital is 18 percent?

16.3   The estimated incremental benefits and investments for a proposed acquisition are:

Year	ΔCFBT	ΔCCA^a	ΔInvestment
0	$ 0	$ 0	$ 100,000
1	200,000	400,000	1,200,000
2	400,000	500,000	300,000
3	500,000	200,000	200,000
4 to ∞	800,000	50,000	200,000

^{a} ΔCCA is for the investment in the column immediately to the right.

The tax rate is 0.35, and the opportunity cost of capital is 20 percent. The present market value of the target is $1,000,000, and the bidder's market value is $4,500,000. What is the NPV if the target firm's shareholders will control 25 percent of the combined firm's shares after the acquisition? Should the proposed acquisition be completed?

16.4   Bill's Sporting Goods is examining the possible acquisition of Malatesta Industries. Bill's has estimated the following anticipated incremental benefits and investments:

Year	ΔCFBT	ΔCCA^a	ΔInvestment
0	$ 0	$ 0	$ 50,000
1	80,000	30,000	100,000
2	150,000	60,000	25,000
3	150,000	60,000	—
4	150,000	25,000	—
5	60,000	—	—

^{a} ΔCCA is for the investment in the column immediately to the right.

a. If Bill's tax rate is 0.30, calculate the incremental after-tax cash flows, ΔCF, expected from Malatesta.

b. The market value of Bill's before the merger is $900,000, and Malatesta Industries' pre-merger market value is $400,000. The market price per share of Bill's stock is $100, and the appropriate opportunity rate is 12 percent. Calculate the NPV for both a cash-financed and a stock-financed merger if Bill's pays a premium of 25 percent above Malatesta's current market value.

16.5 Longfellow has agreed to acquire Sherman Brothers. The following information is for the two firms prior to the merger:

	Longfellow	Sherman Brothers
Earnings	$600,000	$900,000
Shares of common stock outstanding	400,000	250,000
EPS	$1.50	$3.60
P/E ratio	21	21

The merger terms provide that two shares of Longfellow will be issued for every share of Sherman Brothers common stock.

a. Josh owns 100 shares of Longfellow stock. If the P/E of the combined firm is estimated to be 19, will he gain or lose from the transaction?

b. Are synergistic benefits evident?

c. How do you reconcile the answers to (a) and (b), which appear to conflict with each other?

16.6 Lamoureux Engine is evaluating four possible targets, which have the following financial data:

	P	Q	R	U
Benefits	$2,800,000	$3,900,000	$3,100,000	$4,500,000
Shares of common stock outstanding	200,000	300,000	100,000	400,000
Stock price per share	$10	$18	$30	$7
Expected earnings	$400,000	$600,000	$700,000	$600,000

Lamoureux presently has 800,000 shares of stock outstanding, its stock price is $14, and its expected earnings are $1.6 million without any merger. Assume that the target firms have no debt, no premium is paid, and cash is used to finance the mergers.

a. Calculate the NPV of the four proposed mergers. Are any of the mergers infeasible?

b. Calculate the postmerger EPS for the feasible merger candidates.

c. If only one merger can be undertaken, which one is it? Why?

16.7 The Jones Company is in the process of acquiring Imperial Valley Industries. Prior to the merger, the following information existed:

	Jones	Imperial Valley
Total earnings	$3,000,000	$1,000,000
Shares of common stock outstanding	1,000,000	500,000
P/E ratio	15 times	10 times

a. Find the premerger EPS, market price per share, and total market value for both firms.

b. If Jones exchanges one share of common stock for every two shares of Imperial Valley, how many shares of stock will be issued? What is the postmerger EPS for the combined firms? What percentage premium did Jones pay over Imperial Valley's premerger market value?

c. If the P/E stays at 15 times, what is the total value of the combined firm? At 14 times? Is any evidence of synergism indicated by the resulting market values?

16.8   Biller Textile is considering the acquisition of Omega Industries. Biller has estimated the following anticipated incremental benefits and investments:

Year	ΔCFBT	ΔCCA[a]	ΔInvestment	ΔNet Working Capital
0	$ 0	$ 0	$ 70,000	$ 0
1	200,000	30,000	200,000	30,000
2	200,000	90,000	100,000	10,000
3	300,000	90,000	—	10,000
4	300,000	90,000	—	10,000
5	200,000	70,000	—	—
6	100,000	0	—	—

[a] ΔCCA is for the investment in the column immediately to the right.

Omega's present market value is $600,000, and Biller's is $2,000,000. The marginal tax rate is 30 percent, the discount rate is 15 percent, and Biller has 80,000 shares of stock outstanding.

a. If the exchange ratio is 1.4, what is the NPV if cash is used? If stock is employed?

b. What is the NPV for both a cash-financed and a stock-financed merger if *all of the following conditions occur simultaneously* [while everything else remains as in (a)]?

   1. CFBT for years 7–10 becomes $100,000 each.
   2. Omega's present market value is $1,000,000.
   3. The marginal tax rate is 40 percent.
   4. The discount rate is 18 percent.
   5. The exchange ratio is 1.3.

16.9   Two firms, Ralston (R) and Sizemore (S), are going to merge. Ralston's market value is $11.75 million and its beta is 1.40; Sizemore has a market value of $25.50 million and a beta of 1.05. Both firms are all-equity-financed, no premium or synergism is involved, and the new firm will be all-equity financed. After merging, a new project with an NPV of $6.50 million and a beta of 1.50 will be undertaken. What will be the market value of firm RS, and what will be its beta? (*Note:* There are no transactions costs, and the new project is not reflected in the existing market values or betas.)

16.10   Philips Ltd. has just announced a tender offer for Mann Industries at a price of $100 per share. Six months ago Mann's market price per share was $50. During the last six months, the market portfolio, k_M, has risen from 1,000 to 1,200.

a. What is the *percentage increase* in the market portfolio during the last six months?

b. If the market is efficient and Mann's beta is 1.3, what is the dollar premium per share being offered for Mann?

c. If the actual market price of Mann's stock was $70 at the time of the offer, does this necessarily mean the market is inefficient?

16.11   Prince George Enterprises (PGE) has agreed to merge into Gerard. To accomplish the merger, two shares of Gerard will be exchanged for every share of PGE. Before the merger, the firms were as follows:

	Gerard	PGE
Earnings	$1,000,000	$1,000,000
Shares of common stock outstanding	500,000	500,000
EPS	$2	$3
P/E ratio	10	8

a. Calculate the postmerger EPS.
b. How much of the value of the combined firm can be attributed to synergistic effects?
c. Did the shareholders of PGE gain? How about Gerard's shareholders?

16.12   LEM is evaluating the possibility of divesting its African division. It estimates the division's after-tax flows for the next four years as follows: $CF_1 = \$200$, $CF_2 = \$215$, $CF_3 = \$230$, and $CF_4 = \$240$. After year 4, the cash flows are estimated to grow at 2 percent per year to infinity. The appropriate discount rate is 13 percent, the division's debt is $500, and the division can be divested for $2,200 (after taxes), but LEM retains the division's liabilities. Should LEM divest or keep the division?

16.13   Automation Industries has an offer of $8 million after taxes for its plastics machine division. The cash flows from the division presently are constant at $2 million per year and are expected to remain that way. The division's present debt is $11 million; it will be assumed by the buyer. However, Automation has been considering modernizing the division, with the following expected consequences:

Year	After-Tax Cash Flows Without Modernization (in millions)	− Additional Investment (in millions)	+ Additional After-Tax Cash Flows (in millions)	= Postmodernization CFs (in millions)
1	$2.0	$3.0	$ 0	_____
2	2.0	2.0	0	_____
3	2.0	1.0	1.0	_____
4	2.0	0	1.5	_____
5	2.0	0	2.0	_____
Beyond year 5	2.0	0	2.0	8% growth to infinity

If the modernization is done, then the division's debt will increase to $15 million. The appropriate opportunity cost of capital is 14 percent either way. The proposed purchaser will offer $24 million after-tax, contingent on the modernization being done and the purchaser assuming the $15 million in debt.

a. If Automation does not modernize, should it divest or keep the plastics machine division?
b. What if the division is modernized?
c. Based on your answers to (a) and (b), what course of action should Automation take?

16.14   Delores and Anita are trying to decide whether to liquidate their catering business or to continue with it. They can agree on the following estimated cash flows: $CF_1 = \$680$,

$CF_2 = \$680$, $CF_3 = \$740$, and $CF_4 = \$760$. They think growth will continue at 4 percent per year after year 4. The market value of the firm's debt is $1,500, and they estimate the firm's liquidation value is $5,200 after subtracting the $1,500. They cannot agree, however, on the proper discount rate to employ. Delores thinks 12 percent is relevant; Anita believes it should be 15 percent. Does the difference in discount rates have any impact on their decision? What course of action should they take?

16.15 Mini Case Sonny's is a rapidly growing firm that has just decided to have its stock listed on the Toronto Stock Exchange. To keep growing, it plans to make a few selected acquisitions during the next few years. At the same time, Sonny's has become more concerned about maximizing the value of the firm, and remaining independent.

a. Sonny's is concerned about issues that deal with the "market for corporate control." What is meant by that term?
b. What sensible reasons exist for merging? What dubious reasons?
c. Sonny's is considering acquiring Gilfords West. The following incremental benefits and investments have been estimated (in millions):

Year	ΔCFBT	ΔCCA[a]	ΔInvestment
1	$10	$3	$18
2	15	4	10
3	18	3	5
4	20	2	3
5	25	1	2
6	15		2
7	10		2

[a] ΔCCA is for the investment in the column immediately to the right.

If cash is employed, the current market value of Gilfords is $50 million, the opportunity cost of capital is 18 percent, and Sonny's marginal tax rate is 35 percent. What is the most Sonny's can pay for Gilfords and still proceed with the acquisition?
d. Now assume that stock will be employed. The market value of Sonny's is $400 million, and the number of shares of stock for Sonny's is 5 million. If Sonny's current shareholders will end up with at least 90 percent of the total number of shares outstanding in the combined firm, is a merger feasible? How many total shares will be outstanding after the merger?
e. Explain what the primary differences are to both the bidder and the target if cash is used instead of stock.
f. Many mistakes can occur that result in firms making inappropriate (i.e., nonwealth-maximizing) acquisitions. What are some of these mistakes?
g. If Sonny's wants to make itself a more difficult target, what kinds of steps can be taken? Which ones, in your opinion, are likely to be most effective? Can Sonny's completely protect itself from being taken over?
h. Discuss alternative corporate restructuring approaches.

References

AGRAWAL, ANUP, JEFFREY F. JAFFE, and GERSHON N. MANDELKER. "The Post-Merger Performance of Acquiring Firms: A Re-Examination of an Anomaly." *Journal of Finance* 47 (September 1992): 1605–1621.

AUERBACH, ALAN J., ed. *Corporate Takeovers: Causes and Consequences.* Chicago: University of Chicago Press, 1988.

COFFEE, JOHN C., JR., LOUIS LOWENSTEIN, and SUSAN ROSE-ACKERMAN, eds. *Knights, Raiders, and Targets: The Impact of the Hostile Takeover.* New York: Oxford University Press, 1988.

DATTA, DEEPAK K., GEORGE E. PINCHES, and V. K. NARAYANAN. "Factors Influencing Wealth Creation from Mergers and Acquisitions: A Meta-Analysis." *Strategic Management Journal* 13 (January 1992): 67–84.

DONALDSON, GORDON. "Voluntary Restructuring: The Case of General Mills." *Journal of Applied Corporate Finance* 4 (Fall 1991): 6–19.

HEALY, PAUL M., KRISHNA G. PALEPU, and RICHARD S. RUBACK. "Does Corporate Performance Improve After Mergers?" *Journal of Financial Economics* 31 (April 1992): 135–175.

INSELBAG, ISIK, and HOWARD KAUFOLD. "How to Value Recapitalizations and Leveraged Buyouts." *Journal of Applied Corporate Finance* 2 (Summer 1989): 87–96.

JENSEN, MICHAEL C. "Agency Costs of Free Cash Flow, Corporate Finance, and the Market for Takeovers." *American Economic Review* 76 (May 1986): 323–329.

JOHN, KOSE, LARRY H. P. LANG, and JEFFREY NETTER. "The Voluntary Restructuring of Large Firms in Response to Performance Decline." *Journal of Finance* 47 (July 1992): 891–917.

KAPLAN, STEVEN N. "The Staying Power of Leveraged Buyouts." *Journal of Financial Economics* 29 (October 1991): 287–313.

LANG, LARRY H. P., RENE STULZ, and RALPH A. WALKING. "A Test of the Free Cash Flow Hypothesis: The Case of Bidder Returns." *Journal of Financial Economics* 29 (October 1991): 315–335.

MICHEL, ALLEN, and ISRAEL SHAKED. "RJR Nabisco: A Case Study of a Complex Leveraged Buyout." *Financial Analysts Journal* 47 (September/October 1991): 15–27.

MOHAN, NANCY, M. FALL AININA, DANIEL KAUFMAN, and BERNARD J. WINGER. "Acquisition/ Divestiture Valuation Practices in Major U.S. Firms." *Financial Practice and Education* 1 (Spring 1991): 73–81.

STERN, JOEL M., G. BENNETT STEWART III, and DONALD H. CHEW, eds. *Corporate Restructuring and Executive Compensation.* Cambridge, Mass.: Ballinger, 1989.

17 *International Financial Management*

EXECUTIVE SUMMARY

In making investment decisions in a multinational context, the first step is to determine the appropriate opportunity cost of capital. It may be above or below the firm's domestic rate. However, since we are dealing with cash flows in a different currency, cash flows are typically converted into the currency of the parent company's country before the decisions are made. Capital structure and dividend decisions must also be made considering the overall objective of the multinational firm.

In financing foreign projects overseas, there are three choices of where to raise funds: in the firm's home country, in the host country, or in another country where costs are lower. The actual choice depends on the specifics of the situation. Raising funds, whether by borrowing or leasing, is truly international in scope.

Numerous specific considerations also come into play when accounting and tax aspects of multinational firms are examined. Throughout, the focus of financial management remains the same—that is, to maximize the market value of the firm—but additional complexities arise when the financial management of multinational firms is considered.

Virtually all firms, whether wholly domestic or multinational, face economic risks as foreign exchange rates change. As the world has moved from fixed to floating exchange rates, foreign exchange rates have become more volatile. And, increasingly, firms market and produce all over the world. Hedging some of a firm's foreign exchange exposure is now more important than ever.

Some hedging can be done by invoicing in the home currency, leading and lagging, establishing a reinvoicing centre, shifting production to countries where the sales will be made, or raising funds in the countries where they will be used. Although most firms use some or all of these approaches, increasingly they deal with much of their foreign exchange risk through the use of financial instruments.

Depending on the nature of the foreign exchange exposure, firms can purchase (go long in) forward contracts, futures, and swaps, or they can sell (go short in) the same financial instruments. Each has its own unique characteristics, costs, and benefits that must be considered as firms develop, monitor, and modify their foreign exchange risk exposure programmes.

FINANCIAL MANAGEMENT IN AN INTERNATIONAL CONTEXT

Until now we have focused on doing business in Canada, but, increasingly, firms make substantial portions of their sales outside of their home country. In recent years companies such as Bayer, Exxon, Philips Electronics, Nestlé, and Northern Telecom have made more than 75 percent of their total sales in foreign countries.

While many firms sell goods or services in foreign markets, they also actively work to place production and other operations internationally. Although many reasons exist for placing production facilities in various countries, there appear to be two primary reasons—and both of them relate to market imperfections. The first kinds of imperfection can be thought of as *structural imperfections*, which include natural ones (transportation costs, for example) and artificial ones. Examples of artificial structural imperfections include government restrictions on investment or imports, taxes, and subsidies. The second type of imperfection includes those that are inherent in the transactions or markets themselves. Some of these imperfections include uncertainty that a supplier will deliver an item, difficulties customers face in evaluating unfamiliar products, the cost of negotiating deals, economies of scale in production, purchasing or distribution that provides advantages to local firms and imposes barriers to newcomers, uncertainty about competitor actions, and the like. The challenge faced by firms in a multinational context is far broader than simply selling or producing goods or providing services outside of the home country.

When discussing international financial management, it is important to realize that although we might initially think about firms having a global orientation, in reality most of them attempt to implement their global strategy in narrower confines. Thus, firms in the European Union tend to invest primarily in Western Europe and now in Eastern Europe as well. The equivalent for Canadian firms is to invest principally in the United States, Mexico (through the North American Free Trade Agreement, NAFTA), and South America. For Japanese firms the equivalent is to invest primarily in South Korea, greater China, and Southeast Asia. After the home region is developed, firms often invest in other regions, especially in the United States, the European Common Market, or Japan. For example, we see automobile manufacturers from the United States, Japan, and Germany investing in plants in Canada. Multinational firms buy, produce, employ, distribute, and thus compete in many different countries at the same time. But the primary way of doing this is through regional clusters around their home country and, more weakly, in regional clusters elsewhere. However, one important aspect of international finance is not confined to any regional cluster—this is the raising of capital. Large firms, whether international or not, raise capital around the world wherever it is cheapest.

The essential goal of international financial management is exactly as we have discussed for Canadian-based firms: to maximize the value of the firm by focusing on the after-tax cash flows, the risks, and the opportunity costs. Thus, we come back to the basic concerns of financial management—this time by focusing attention on those activities outside of the home country.

One of the most important features of international financial management is that we need to deal with more than one currency. In Chapter 2 we looked at how foreign exchange markets operate and why exchange rates change. Therefore, here we begin by considering the topic of making investment decisions in an international context. That is, how do multinational companies make their capital budgeting decisions? Then we will examine international capital structure and dividend decisions, financing decisions, and accounting and tax issues. We will see that the basic concepts of financial management are still relevant, with some additional pitfalls to watch out for. We end the chapter by examining how multinational firms use forwards, futures, and swaps to hedge foreign exchange risk.

Concept Review Questions

- What are two primary reasons firms may place a production facility in a foreign country?
- How are domestic financial decisions and international financial decisions similar? How are they different?

CAPITAL BUDGETING IN AN INTERNATIONAL CONTEXT

We have examined how capital budgeting decisions are made for firms within a country. When investments are made outside the multinational firm's home country, the basic steps are the same; that is, we determine the opportunity cost of capital, identify the relevant incremental cash flows, and accept all projects with positive net present values. However, though the steps are the same, there are some additional complications to consider.

THE OPPORTUNITY COST OF CAPITAL

When discussing capital budgeting decisions for domestic firms we indicated the stand-alone principle should apply. That is, the project should stand alone in terms of cash flows, and the opportunity cost of capital applied to those cash flows should reflect the amount of risk related to the cash flows. An important question for multi-national firms is whether the opportunity cost of capital, k, for foreign projects should be different from that for similar-risk domestic projects. The answer to that question depends on two items: First, what is the systematic risk for multinational firms? Second, what are the expropriation and creditor risks?

Systematic Risk and Portfolio Concerns   Based on the capital asset pricing model, we know it is the nondiversifiable risk (measured by beta, β_j) that is important in determining the opportunity cost of equity capital. By operating in a number of countries, multinational firms expose themselves to economic cycles that are not perfectly in phase with one another. That is, while the world economy generally moves somewhat together, there are often important differences in demand among countries. For example, demand for a product in Canada will differ from demand for the same product in either Japan or Egypt. By having a significant portion of their operations and cash flows diversified over a number of countries, multinational firms may lessen the variability of their cash flows. This is true whether the nations they have diversified into are industrialized (such as the European Union and Japan), newly industrializing (such as Korea or Taiwan), or less developed (such as Honduras, Pakistan, or Zaire).

The important implication is that the nondiversifiable risk for a multinational firm may be less than if the firm had not diversified geographically. This means that the opportunity cost of equity capital will be lower and, other things being equal, the returns demanded will be lower.

Expropriation and Creditor Risks   The potential advantage from geographic diversification may be offset because of the increased possibility of expropriation of part or all of the firm's investment in a foreign subsidiary. We view expropriation broadly, to include not only pure nationalization but also lesser forms such as increased ownership by the host country.[1] In either case, the multinational loses part or all of its investment or claim on cash flows from its subsidiary. Expropriation may be gradual, with an increase in demand for participation by locals or the host government in the ownership of the business. Initially, it may take the form of a high tax or the right to buy the equity of the firm at some price. Often this price is extremely low relative to the market-determined worth of the subsidiary. A more dramatic form of expropriation was that suffered a number of years ago by some multinational firms with investments in Iran.

Multinational firms can use various strategies in attempting to minimize the risk of expropriation. Generally, these fall into two categories: The first involves positive approaches, such as joint ventures, local participation, prior agreements for sale, and the like. All are designed to foster a positive, long-term relationship. The second involves limiting the investment of the parent, or controlling the raw material, production, or sales process so the subsidiaries' success is fully dependent on the parent.

It should also be noted that default risk is often more serious in less-developed countries than in developed countries. Because bankruptcy laws similar to those in developed countries often do not exist, creditors have little recourse to recoup losses. This factor must also be considered when multinational firms make capital budgeting and marketing decisions.

If increased expropriation or creditor risk is present, it would offset, in part or total, any reduced opportunity cost from investing overseas. The net result is that the opportunity cost of capital may be the same, lower, or higher, for an international capital budgeting project. It all depends on the project itself and the country where the investment is made.

---

[1] Instances of "pure" expropriation by countries has decreased significantly over the last 15 to 20 years.

MAXIMIZE NET PRESENT VALUE

CanExport is a Canadian firm whose export business has risen to the point that it is worth establishing a subsidiary in Germany, Deutschco. Ignoring certain complications for a minute, there are two basic ways to calculate the net present value (NPV) of its German venture:

1. The project's NPV can be evaluated entirely in terms of the German mark. Then this figure can be converted into dollars at the current exchange rate.
2. The per year cash flows can be estimated in German marks and then converted into dollars at the expected exchange rate. These dollar cash flows can then be discounted at a dollar-based opportunity cost of capital to give the investment's NPV in dollars.

Under certain conditions these approaches both provide the same result; however, the second is most often employed in practice. We will use the second method in order to illustrate the primary issues involved in making capital budgeting decisions internationally. Assume the cash flows, CFs, in marks are as follows:

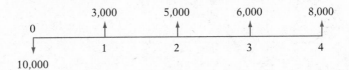

The appropriate Canadian opportunity cost of capital, k, is 18 percent and the risk-free rate, k_{RF}, is 7 percent. The 7 percent is obtained simply by looking in the newspaper for the rate on Canadian treasury bills. Likewise, assume the risk-free rate in Germany is 4 percent and that the spot rate is 1.5 marks to the dollar.

Before discounting, we must convert the cash flows in German marks into Canadian dollars. To do this we need to forecast what the exchange rates will be in the future. Rather than attempting to predict future exchange rates directly, it is preferable to recognize, as we have throughout, that markets are reasonably efficient. Therefore, based on the international Fisher effect (discussed in Chapter 2), we know that the current difference between Canadian and German interest rates provides the best estimate of the difference in future inflation rates. With the Canadian risk-free rate at 7 percent and the German risk-free rate at 4 percent, we see that there is a 3 percent difference in nominal interest rates. That means that *expected* inflation is approximately 7 percent in Canada, and it is approximately 4 percent in Germany.[2]

We said the current spot rate was 1.5 German marks to the dollar. But because expected inflation in Germany is somewhat lower than in Canada, interest rate parity

---

[2] Both nominal and real interest rates were discussed in Chapter 2. The nominal risk-free interest rate = real rate of interest + expected inflation. In this example, for simplicity, it is assumed that the real rate of interest is approximately zero.

tells us the mark is expected to appreciate against the dollar as follows:

$$\begin{pmatrix} \text{expected spot rate} \\ \text{at end of year} \end{pmatrix} = \begin{pmatrix} \text{spot rate at} \\ \text{start of year} \end{pmatrix}\begin{pmatrix} \text{inflation rate} \\ \text{differential} \end{pmatrix} \qquad (17.1)$$

$$= (1.50)\left(\frac{1.04}{1.07}\right) = 1.458 \text{ marks per dollar}$$

At the end of year 2 the expected rate of exchange would be:

$$\begin{pmatrix} \text{expected spot rate} \\ \text{at end of year 2} \end{pmatrix} = (1.50)\left(\frac{1.04^2}{1.07^2}\right) = 1.417$$

The expected rates of exchange for years 3 and 4 are calculated in a similar manner. The forecasted cash flows and expected exchange rates are then:

	Year				
	0	**1**	**2**	**3**	**4**
1. Cash flow in marks, CF	−10,000	3,000	5,000	6,000	8,000
2. Forecasted spot exchange rate	1.500	1.458	1.417	1.377	1.339
3. Cash flow in dollars, CF (row 1/row 2)	−6,667	2,058	3,529	4,357	5,975

Because we have converted these cash flows into dollars, we use the dollar-denominated opportunity cost of capital of 18 percent to calculate the net present value as follows:

$$\begin{aligned} \text{NPV} &= \$2,058(\text{PV}_{18\%,\,1\,\text{yr}}) + \$3,529(\text{PV}_{18\%,\,2\,\text{yr}}) \\ &\quad + \$4,357(\text{PV}_{18\%,\,3\,\text{yr}}) + \$5,975(\text{PV}_{18\%,\,4\,\text{yr}}) - \$6,667 \\ &= \$2,058(0.847) + \$3,529(0.718) + \$4,357(0.069) + \$5,975(0.516) \\ &\quad - \$6,667 = \$10,013 - \$6,667 = \$3,346 \end{aligned}$$

With a positive NPV, we would accept the project.

UNREMITTED FUNDS AND TAX CONSIDERATIONS

So far we have assumed all cash flows can be remitted (or brought) back to the parent company. Remitting funds is not as easy as we have assumed. A foreign subsidiary can remit funds to a parent in many ways, including the following: dividends, management fees, interest and principal payments on debt, and royalties on the use of trade names and patents. This topic quickly becomes messy, as many complexities occur in different countries. Multinational firms must pay special attention to remittance for two reasons: First, there may be current and/or future exchange controls. Many governments are sensitive to the charge of being exploited by foreign firms. They have therefore attempted to limit the ability of multinational firms to take funds out of the host country. The second reason is taxes. Not only do taxes have to be paid in the foreign country, the amount of taxes paid on funds remitted to Canada depends on the following:

1. Whether the payment is a dividend, a management fee, a royalty, or simply the payment of interest or principal.
2. Whether the foreign investment is a branch operation or a foreign affiliate.
3. Whether or not the foreign country has a tax treaty with Canada.

If CanExport sets up Deutschco as an unincorporated **foreign branch,** then not only are the cash flows taxed in Germany, but CanExport is taxed in Canada as if all cash flows of the branch are remitted each year. In addition a branch tax of 10–25 percent is imposed by host countries on branch profits earned in their jurisdiction. The Canadian firm is eligible for a foreign tax credit equal to the entire amount of the branch tax, provided that it has tax payable to deduct the credit from.

On the other hand, if Deutschco is set up as a corporation and CanExport owns at least 10 percent of its equity, the firm is a **foreign affiliate**. Any cash flows generated by Deutschco are subject only to German tax as long as no cash flows are repatriated to Canada. In this situation, when the cash flows are remitted to CanExport they are subject to a withholding tax. As long as the foreign country has a tax treaty with Canada (which Germany does), the cash flows can be treated like dividends from another taxable Canadian corporation. Consequently, as we saw in Chapter 8, no tax is paid by CanExport on these intercorporate dividends. However, since no tax is paid on the dividends, the withholding tax does not generate any foreign tax credit. Therefore, in this set of circumstances, the withholding tax is a deadweight loss to the Canadian parent corporation. If the host country does not have a tax treaty with Canada, the dividends are fully taxable in Canada in the year that they are remitted to the Canadian parent. All foreign taxes associated with the dividend are used as a tax credit against any Canadian corporate income tax payable on the dividend. Before CanExport calculates its tax payable on the remitted funds, they must be grossed up to their level before foreign tax. This is accomplished by dividing the sum of the amount remitted and the withholding tax by $(1 - \text{foreign tax rate})$. This grossed-up amount is multiplied by the Canadian tax rate to obtain tax payable, then a foreign tax credit equal to the foreign income tax and any withholding tax is deducted to arrive at the additional tax that CanExport must pay on the remitted funds.

If CanExport owns less than 10 percent of Deutschco's shares, any dividends paid to CanExport are treated the same way as ordinary income or interest income and are, therefore, taxed at CanExport's marginal rate. The same situation applies whether the host country is a treaty or nontreaty country. A tax credit equal to any withholding tax is allowed. In this case the dividends received by CanExport must be grossed up by $(1 - \text{withholding tax rate})$. CanExport calculates the tax that it must pay on the dividend by multiplying the grossed-up amount by the Canadian tax rate and then subtracting a foreign tax credit equal to the withholding tax.[3]

---

[3] The taxation of international income is a complex matter that cannot be dealt with adaquately here. For a detailed discussion of this matter see Thornton (1993), Chapter 11.

Table 17.1

After-Tax Cash Flows Remitted to Parent After German and Canadian Taxes

Because of taxes and restrictions on how funds are brought out of the host country, cash flows in the parent country's currency are required to make effective capital budgeting decisions.

	Year				
	0	**1**	**2**	**3**	**4**
1. Cash flow before taxes, in marks	−10,000	3,000	5,000	6,000	8,000
2. German corporate tax at 30% (1)(0.30)		−900	−1,500	−1,800	−2,400
3. Cash flow available for remittance to parent (1 − 2)		2,100	3,500	4,200	5,600
4. Tax withheld at 10% (3)(0.10)		−210	−350	−420	−560
5. Remittance after German taxes, in marks (3 − 4)		1,890	3,150	3,780	5,040
6. Forecasted spot exchange rate	1.500	1.458	1.417	1.377	1.339
7. Remittance received by parent, in dollars (5/6)	−6,667	1,296	2,223	2,745	3,764
8. Canadian corporate tax		0	0	0	0
9. Foreign tax credit, in dollars		0	0	0	0
10. Cash flow in dollars, CF (7 − 8 + 9)	−6,667	1,296	2,223	2,745	3,764

To illustrate some of the complexity, assume that Germany has a corporate tax rate of 30 percent and that it also withholds taxes at 10 percent on funds transferred out of the country. Assume as well that Deutschco is more than 10 percent owned by CanExport and that Deutschco will remit the cash flows annually in the form of dividends. In Table 17.1 we show the same initial cash flows in German marks as before, but *this time we assume they are before taxes*. Taking into account the German corporate taxes and the taxes withheld on remitted funds, row 5 provides the remitted cash flows in German marks. Row 7 shows how much the remitted funds are in Canadian dollars. In this situation, because Deutschco is a foreign affiliate in a treaty country, the dividends are tax-exempt and there are no foreign tax credits. This is reflected in rows 8 and 9. Finally, in row 10 the after-tax cash flows (CFs) in dollars are shown. The NPV is then

$$NPV = \$1,296(0.847) + \$2,223(0.718) + \$2,745(0.609) + \$3,764(0.516)$$
$$- \$6,667 = \$6,308 - \$6,667 = -\$359$$

Now the NPV is negative, and the project would be rejected.

This example illustrates some of the issues involved in determining the proper after-tax cash flows that multinationals must consider when making capital investment decisions. In practice, the issue becomes even more complex depending on taxes and how the funds can be brought out of the host country in order to channel them to the parent. These complications make the determination of the after-tax cash flow stream for international capital budgeting decisions even more challenging than for domestic capital budgeting projects.

EVALUATING ACQUISITIONS OUTSIDE THE BIDDER'S HOME COUNTRY

An acquisition of part or all of another firm is simply a big capital investment decision. The general procedures to employ in evaluating proposed acquisitions outside of the bidder's home country follow those discussed in Chapter 16. One complicating factor for merger evaluation of assets outside of the home country revolves around the impact of exchange rates on the process. The approach favoured by most firms is to do the analysis in the currency of the proposed target. Thus, if an acquisition is being contemplated in Mexico, the analysis would be done in terms of the Mexican peso. The one requirement of this approach is that there be a well-developed capital market in the country of the proposed target so that a good estimate of the opportunity cost of capital can be obtained. Once the net present value is determined in the foreign currency, it can be converted into units of the home country's currency at the present rate of exchange. If the capital market in the target's home country is not well-developed, firms generally convert the incremental year-by-year cash flows back to the currency of the home country and then proceed as discussed previously for any capital investment decision.

INTERNATIONAL INVESTMENT STRATEGY

Increasingly, the world is being viewed as one big market by the most aggressive and successful firms, whatever their home country. These firms are global firms that must compete effectively in many parts of the world to cover their enormous fixed investment, research and development costs, or both. The key is to develop the skills and corporate vision to capitalize on world-wide opportunities while dealing effectively with risks.

What does it take to develop an international investment strategy that will be effective in maximizing the value of the multinational firm? Some of the elements include:

1. An ability to understand and capitalize on those factors that have led to successful NPV projects and strategies for the domestic firm. Then the firm must transfer these opportunities to other countries while maintaining the competitive advantage that led to the firm's success in the first place. Advantages gained by patents that are about to run out or by trade restrictions, for instance, probably would not transfer into high NPV projects if implemented abroad.

2. An international approach requires a solid understanding of the best mechanisms for gaining successful and profitable entry into foreign countries. Must large capital investments for production facilities be made in the country, or can goods be imported effectively? What kinds of foreign ownership, licensing arrangements, and so forth, are required? These and other related questions must be addressed, and investment and expansion decisions made based on the answers. At the same time, successful multinational firms often simultaneously bring out products on a world-wide basis by using universal parts, no matter where the product is produced or sold. This is another of the keys to a successful global investment strategy.

3. The continual monitoring of the investment and its potential for the future is essential. Given the rapidly changing world, it is essential to assess whether to

increase the investment in a country, maintain it on a status quo level, or even reduce or abandon it. Successful multinational firms take advantage of changes in the investment and political climates to shift production, research and development, and other components of a global strategy from country to country based on the economic opportunities presented.

4. Finally, successful multinational firms have made a commitment to consider the international dimension of all investment decisions. One way to do so is to have a management structure that stresses local management while providing key executives with international experience. For example, Dow Chemical recently met this need by seeing to it that 20 of its top 25 executives had extensive international experience.

The multinational firm's primary objective remains the same as that of a domestic firm—to maximize the value of the firm by undertaking positive NPV projects. In doing so it builds upon the underlying financial management concepts presented throughout the book.

Concept Review Questions

- What are some major concerns when estimating the opportunity cost of capital for a multinational firm?
- Describe two different methods of calculating the net present value of a foreign project for a multinational firm.
- Why should firms be concerned about how foreign subsidiary profits are remitted back to the parent company?
- What are some of the elements of a successful international investment strategy?

CAPITAL STRUCTURE AND DIVIDEND ISSUES

When investments are made on an international basis, they are often accomplished through the use of subsidiaries set up in various countries. In these situations, the capital structure and dividend issues become more complex because of the numerous subsidiaries and the multiplicity of different laws, tax considerations, and government regulations. But the primary point to remember is that *the multinational firm's worldwide capital structure and dividend policy should not be just the residual* of the decisions made in individual country-based subsidiaries. Rather, world-wide issues need to be considered in order to maximize the value of the firm.

CAPITAL STRUCTURE CONSIDERATIONS

A number of considerations are important in determining the capital structure of a foreign subsidiary. First and foremost, it is important to recognize that unless the parent is willing to let the subsidiary fail and default on its debt, *there is no independent risk for the subsidiary's debt*. Rather, its debt is—explicitly or implicitly—guaranteed by the multinational parent. Given this, it is really the parent's overall capital structure, not the subsidiary's, that is of primary concern.

Once this point is understood, then the objective is to acquire funds in the most cost-effective manner at each subsidiary level. For example, a subsidiary that has low debt financing costs might have a capital structure of almost 100 percent debt. Yet another subsidiary with a much higher cost of debt could have a capital structure with much less debt. The objective of the multinational parent is to raise capital as cheaply as possible world-wide and make suitable adjustments at the overall firm level to achieve its target world-wide capital structure.

Finally, multinational firms often classify (and structure) their investment in a subsidiary as debt rather than equity. This is due to exchange controls and tax effects. From the standpoint of repatriating funds to the parent, a firm typically has wider latitude with interest and loan payments than with cash dividends or other reductions in equity. Also, by structuring the investment as debt, the parent generally can reduce its taxes.

Although some latitude exists, multinationals do not have complete freedom in choosing debt/equity ratios for foreign subsidiaries. If they have too little equity, they may run into restrictions placed on them by the host countries. But to the extent possible, the goal is to set up the foreign subsidiary's capital structure to minimize capital costs, subject to the requirement that the multinational parent be viewed as responsible by the host country. Then the multinational manages its capital structure on a global basis to maximize the value of the firm.

DIVIDEND POLICY

For firms with foreign subsidiaries, cash dividends are the most important means of transferring funds to the parent firm. Dividends often account for more than 50 percent of such remittances. In setting the dividend policy for subsidiaries, two important considerations are exchange controls and financing requirements.

Multinational firms often set the dividend requirements for subsidiaries at the same or a greater dividend payout ratio than that of the parent. Thus, if the parent firm has a 50 percent dividend payout ratio, then the foreign subsidiary is expected to contribute 50 percent of its earnings to the parent. By setting a dividend requirement, multinationals attempt to establish a world-wide cash dividend policy for their subsidiaries. This has two benefits: First, the subsidiaries are contributing their appropriate part to the parent's cash dividend policy. Second, and often more important, this world-wide policy provides the multinational firm with a rationale for dealing with the exchange or currency controls of different nations. Because many nations limit dividend remittances, either in absolute terms or as a percentage of either earnings or capital, multinational parents find it is important for subsidiaries to establish and meet a constant dividend requirement. Dividends are then paid each year to demonstrate a continuing policy to the local government where the subsidiary is located.

In addition to the need to remit funds in the form of dividends, subsidiaries have continuing financing needs. In high-growth situations, multinationals may need to reinvest more funds in the subsidiaries, while in low-growth areas the need for funds is lower. This difference in demand, other things being equal, suggests differing cash dividend policies between subsidiaries located in different countries. One way some multinationals deal with differing needs, while still establishing a stable dividend remittance policy, is to have high-need subsidiaries declare the dividend even though it is not remitted. By doing so, they establish the principle that dividends are a necessary cash flow associated with doing business. With a constant policy of paying (or at least declaring) dividends, multinational firms attempt to partially meet financing needs while maintaining the requirement for dividends to be remitted to the parent.

Concept Review Question

- What are the important links between a multinational's capital structure and dividend policies and the capital structure and dividend policies of its foreign subsidiaries?

INTERNATIONAL FINANCING ISSUES

Raising capital used to be restricted to what was available within the home country. But in today's international economy raising capital is an international activity. This is true for both domestic and multinational firms.

LONG-TERM INTERNATIONAL FINANCING

Both domestic Canadian and multinational firms, along with their foreign subsidiaries, raise funds in various international markets. For Canadian firms the most important foreign market from which to borrow funds is the United States. However, many Canadian firms raise funds throughout the world and are consequently faced with considerable differences in these markets as compared to those in North America. One of the biggest is the much broader role played by banks in the international market. Banks in Europe, the Middle East, and Asia have more flexibility than Canadian banks to combine banking, investment dealer functions, and direct investment. In addition, the banks often work closely with the country's government and may even be partially government-owned.

The Eurodollar system that operates in the international capital markets was developed in the 1950s as banks located outside the United States began to accept interest-bearing deposits in U.S. dollars. Although most of the early activity was centred in Europe, the system, often called the **Eurocurrency system**, is now world-wide and includes many different currencies. **Eurodollars** are simply dollars that are deposited in a foreign bank or foreign branches of Canadian banks. For example, a Canadian importer dealing with a British supplier may issue a cheque drawn on the Bank of Montreal in payment of goods received. The British company then deposits the cheque in its account at Barclay's Bank, thus creating a Canadian dollar deposit in Britain. Because the deposit is outside of Canada, it is a Eurodollar deposit. Barclay's in turn lends these funds to European, Asian, and African banks, corporations, and governments. Eurodollar loans are typically made in multiples of $1 million and have maturities lasting from a few days to 15 years or more. Generally these loans are unsecured, but they may contain certain restrictive provisions on the borrowing firm's activities. Large loans may be syndicated, with many banks participating; the lead bank coordinates the syndicate, structures the loan, and provides servicing when needed.

The interest rate for such loans is usually stated as some fixed percentage above the London Interbank Offered Rate (LIBOR), with adjustments at predetermined intervals. (LIBOR is the rate that banks in different countries trade with each other at.) Because LIBOR reflects the rate on liquid funds that move among the developed nations' money markets, it dampens borrowing based on interest rate speculation. Rates on Eurodollar loans typically are comparable to those in Canada, although sometimes Canadian firms have been able to obtain cheaper financing overseas.

When long-term debt is needed, both domestic and multinational firms borrow internationally. An **international bond** issue is one sold outside the country of the borrower; it can be a Eurobond or a foreign bond. A **Eurobond** is one underwritten by an international syndicate and sold primarily in countries other than the country in which the issue is denominated. Thus, a Eurobond could be denominated in the Canadian dollar, the German mark, or some other currency, but it would be sold mainly outside the country in which it was denominated. Although centred in Europe, the Eurobond market is truly international in scope and includes the Middle East and Asia. A **foreign bond** is one issued by a foreign borrower, but underwritten, sold, and denominated in one country. For example, a domestic Canadian firm might float a foreign bond in Switzerland, underwritten by a Swiss syndicate, and denominated in Swiss francs.

The Eurobond market has a number of distinguishing features:

1. Most bonds pay interest only once a year instead of semiannually.
2. Because of investor desire for anonymity, virtually all bonds are issued in bearer form, as opposed to the registered form prevalent in Canada.
3. Almost all Eurodollar issues are listed on one or more recognized securities exchanges—generally in London, Luxembourg, Frankfurt, or Switzerland.

In addition to the possibility of lower interest rates, another advantage to firms employing the Eurobond market is that they avoid registration with any securities commission in Canada. In recent years, many more Canadian-based firms have been turning to foreign capital markets to secure funds.

FINANCING DECISIONS

In raising capital and undertaking capital investment projects, multinational companies typically invest a relatively modest amount in equity capital and then raise the rest of the funds in some other manner. Three methods available for securing the majority of the funds are to raise them at home and export them, to raise cash by borrowing in a foreign country, or to borrow wherever interest rates are cheapest.

If a domestic firm raises cash by borrowing in its home country and then invests the funds in a subsidiary in a foreign country, it incurs an exchange rate risk. This risk has to be taken into account. An alternative is to borrow in the country where the foreign project is located. By doing so, the multinational receives a direct hedge against exchange rate fluctuations because they are borrowing in the same currency in which the investment has been made. The final alternative is to finance where interest rates are cheapest. Again, the firm has to look at exchange rate risk between where the financing is done and the home currency.

Each decision must take into account the specifics of the country, current and prospective international conditions, the length of financing needed, and the particular project. Experienced multinational firms find it is often best to use some combination of funds raised in the host country along with some provided from the domestic marketplace.

LEASING

Leasing can be employed domestically and, especially, internationally to gain flexibility, defer or avoid taxes, and safeguard assets. For these reasons, leasing is an important part of the financing strategy for many multinational firms.

Consider what happened in the airline industry a few years ago. With deregulation and greater opportunities for carriers to operate in many countries, airlines needed more planes suited to their specific requirements. But the back orders on aircraft were up to seven years in some cases. To gain the flexibility to take advantage of opportunities, many airlines leased planes from lessors who owned the planes through operating leases. Lessors had taken the standard operating lease and adapted it to the commercial airplane industry. Demand for operating leases was brisk because they gave airlines the flexibility to commit to new routes or increased service within a much shorter time frame.

Leasing in the international arena also may provide a substantial tax advantage through "double dipping." Through the different leasing rules of the lessor's and lessee's countries, a lease that is set up to double dip lets *both* parties be treated as the owner of the asset. Thus, both the lessor and the lessee are entitled to the capital cost allowance (depreciation) tax benefits. This results in higher returns for lessors and lower effective lease rates for lessees.

Double dipping is often achieved when the lessees are based in countries that examine the economic reality of the arrangement (such as Germany, Japan, Canada, and the United States) and the lessors are located in countries that simply look at the legal ownership of the lease (such as France, Great Britain, or Switzerland). The key difference is what is considered an operating lease versus what is considered a financial lease. By structuring the lease to take advantage of intercountry differences, savings result that benefit both the lessor and the lessee.

Leasing can also be used in order to limit the ownership of assets by subsidiaries in unstable countries. In the event of nationalization, the multinational parent often has more chance of recovering or receiving some compensation for assets taken over if they are not owned by the local subsidiary. Also, lease payments are sometimes treated differently from dividends, interest, or royalty payments. In these cases leasing also helps deal with the exchange controls that would make other means of bringing funds out of the host country unsatisfactory.

Concept Review Questions

■ Describe how a multinational firm may obtain debt in a foreign country.

■ What are Eurobonds and foreign bonds? How do they differ?

■ What are some advantages of leasing for a multinational firm?

INTERNATIONAL ACCOUNTING ISSUES

Accounting reporting requirements for foreign operations is another important issue that multinational firms must consider. When the results of foreign operations must be reported, multinational firms face additional problems beyond those faced by firms with only domestic operations. Under CICA 1650,[4] foreign operations must be classified as either integrated or self-sustaining. An integrated foreign subsidiary is one that is financially or operationally interdependent with the parent company. On the other hand, a self-sustaining foreign subsidiary is one that is financially and operationally independent of the parent firm. The classification of the subsidiary as integrated or self-sustaining is ultimately a matter of judgment on the part of the parent firm's management.

If a subsidiary is judged to be integrated, the parent will use the **temporal method** to translate the financial statements of the subsidiary to Canadian dollars. This means that monetary balance sheet items, such as cash and receivables or payables, and nonmonetary items reported at market value, are translated into Canadian dollars at the exchange rate prevailing on the final day of the subsidiary's fiscal year (i.e., current rate). Nonmonetary items carried at past prices, such as fixed assets and inventory carried at cost, are converted at the rate prevailing when the item was acquired (i.e., historical rate). In general the temporal method calls for revenue and expense items to be translated by using an average exchange rate for the year. However, revenues and expenses based on assets and liabilities translated at historical rates must also be translated by using the same historical rates (e.g., depreciation). On the other hand, all balance sheet items for self-sustaining foreign subsidiaries are translated at the current rate and all income statement items are translated at the average annual exchange rate.

The translation of any foreign subsidiary's financial statements can lead to "translation adjustments." For integrated subsidiaries these adjustments are considered to be "foreign currency exchange gains and losses" and usually flow through to the parent firm's income statement. In contrast, the translation adjustments for self-sustaining subsidiaries are not considered foreign currency exchange gains or losses. Consequently, they are deferred and reported as a separate equity account on the parent's balance sheet that adjusts each year to recognize fluctuations in the exchange rate during the year.

To see the impact of this procedure, consider a German self-sustaining subsidiary that purchases equipment for 100 marks (M) when 1M = \$0.50. The historical cost of the equipment is 100M. Assume that at a later date the exchange rate is 1M = \$0.80. The historical cost is still 100M, but the translated amount is now \$80. This \$80 will be reported on the parent's balance sheet as an asset and in a special equity account recording the foreign currency translation adjustment.

From the standpoint of analysis, if a subsidiary is judged to be integrated, the translation adjustments flow through to the parent's income statement, resulting in a roller-coaster effect on earnings. If the subsidiary is self-sustaining, the parent's assets

---

[4] The CICA 1650 stands for Canadian Institute of Chartered Accounts Section 1650, "Foreign Currency Translation" (*CICA Handbook*).

and equity change every year, depending on exchange rates. Furthermore, firms facing similar situations may report different results, depending on the parent's assessment of its relationship with the subsidiary. These and similar problems make the analysis of accounting statements for a multinational firm even more difficult and challenging than for a firm doing all its business within Canada.

Concept Review Questions

- What is the temporal method, and how does it affect a multinational firm's balance sheet?

FOREIGN EXCHANGE ISSUES

Since all firms face a variety of risks, risk is one of the fundamental items that financial managers must worry about. We have looked at some of these risks in other chapters. However, in our increasingly global business environment, firms face another risk that we have ignored—the change in the rate of exchange of one currency for another currency. Furthermore, since exchange rates change continuously—that is, day by day—financial mangers must deal with them directly. For example, assume that a Canadian exporter bills a customer in a foreign currency. The exporter has taken a risk, since the exchange rate may change before the bill can be paid. Most of this exchange risk, however, can be hedged. Although there are numerous ways of hedging, we will focus primarily on three: forward contracts, futures, and swaps.

Before we can deal with managing a firm's foreign exchange risk exposure, we need to understand what kind of exposure we should be concerned with.

WHAT DO WE MEAN BY "FOREIGN EXCHANGE EXPOSURE"?

Foreign exchange exposure can be broken down into three types: translation exposure, transaction exposure, and economic exposure. Figure 17.1 provides a convenient way to think about the three types of exposure.

Translation exposure is the easiest to deal with because it refers to the accounting treatment arising from fluctuations in exchange rates. Although not an inconsequential issue, translation exposure does not affect the economic value of the firm in the marketplace; consequently, we would like to ignore translation exposure completely. In practice, however, translation exposure is important since it affects the firm's GAAP income statement. Many of the protective covenants incorporated in debt securities or borrowings from banks contain provisions that are based on the firm's GAAP earnings. CFOs we have talked to indicate that the primary impact of changes in exchange rates is on the firm's cash flow; however, because of the way some financing agreements are structured, translation exposure occasionally enters the picture.

Transaction exposure refers to the impact of exchanging one currency for another when the rate of exchange between the currencies changes after the transaction occurs but before it is settled. Often transaction exposure is relatively short-term in nature. Many of the techniques discussed later in the chapter are designed to help firms protect themselves, at a cost, against adverse movements in exchange rates that would result in loss of value due to transaction exposure.

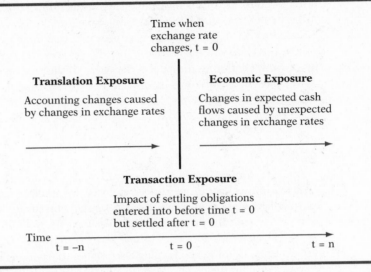

Figure 17.1

Translation, Transaction, and Economic Foreign Exchange Exposure

Translation exposure does not have a direct impact on the firm's cash flows; however, some exchange-induced changes in accounting reported figures, especially earnings, may trigger protective covenants in loan agreements. Firms hedge some, but generally not all, of their translation and economic exchange rate exposure.

Time when
exchange rate
changes, t = 0

Translation Exposure

Accounting changes caused
by changes in exchange rates

Economic Exposure

Changes in expected cash
flows caused by unexpected
changes in exchange rates

Transaction Exposure

Impact of settling obligations
entered into before time t = 0
but settled after t = 0

Time

t = –n   t = 0   t = n

Economic exposure refers to the impact of foreign exchange exposure that directly affects the cash flows and, thus, the long-run value of the firm. Whereas the effects of both translation and transaction exposure typically show up directly in a firm's GAAP accounting statements, the impact of economic exposure is not readily dealt with in the conventional accounting statements employed today.

Foreign exchange exposure is more important today than it was 30 years ago because of the increasing globalization of firms and the movement from fixed to floating exchange rates that has been accompanied by much greater volatility in exchange rates. At the same time, firms are more aware of how to hedge some or all of these risks.

Concept Review Question

■ Describe the three types of foreign exchange exposure discussed in this section.

OPERATING, INVESTMENT, AND FINANCING APPROACHES TO HEDGING EXCHANGE RATE RISK

Numerous approaches exist for hedging the firm's transaction or economic exposure. No one approach provides the best solution all of the time, and since the approaches are not mutually exclusive, firms normally employ a number of different approaches for dealing with part, or all, of their transaction or economic exchange rate risk exposure.

INVOICE IN THE HOME CURRENCY

Firms that sell products to foreign customers can mitigate any transaction-based foreign exchange problem by invoicing in the home currency. Thus, if a Mexican firm is exporting to Canada, it could require payment in pesos. Although this idea sounds great, the Canadian purchasers will recognize that they bear all of the foreign exchange risk in this transaction, and consequently will seek to negotiate a lower purchase price to account for the additional risk they bear. If the firm invoicing in the home currency is not careful, it will lower its cash flows by more than it would cost to go unhedged and bear any exchange rate losses, or, alternatively, to hedge the exchange rate exposure itself.

LEADING AND LAGGING

Transaction exposure can also be reduced by accelerating or delaying the timing of payments that are made or received in foreign currencies. To **lead** is to collect (or pay) early. A firm or subsidiary collecting a weak currency would like to collect early. To **lag** is to collect (or pay) later. Thus, a firm collecting a strong currency would like to collect later. Leading and lagging also applies to paying. Thus, a firm in a country with a weak currency which has debts to a firm in a strong-currency country will lead; that is, it will pay early. Likewise, a firm in a strong-currency country with debts to a firm in a weak-currency country will lag, or pay later.

Leading and lagging can be done with other independent firms or with subsidiaries. With other independent firms, constraints exist because it is impossible to force them to pay early or late in most cases. The best that can be done when dealing with independent firms is to time the cash outflows from the paying firm.

Between a parent firm and its subsidiaries, or between two subsidiaries, leading and lagging can be implemented on a much wider basis. Such items as receivables, payables, lease payments, royalties, management fees, interest or principal, dividends, and the like can all be led or lagged. Because leading and lagging have important implications for minimizing foreign exchange exposure, some countries have imposed restrictions on the practice. A sample of some of these restrictions is provided in Table 17.2.

REINVOICING CENTRE

Another means of dealing with transaction exposure is to set up a **reinvoicing centre**, which is a separate subsidiary responsible for all interfirm transfers. With a reinvoicing centre, the firm's various subsidiaries sell goods to other subsidiaries by going through the reinvoicing centre. Title passes to the centre and all transaction exposure (for transactions *within* the firm) lies with the centre. The centre then imposes a small charge for its services and resells the goods to another subsidiary or the parent. The

Table 17.2

Lead and Lag Restrictions for Selected Countries

These are some lead and lag guidelines established by various countries.

Country	Export Lead	Export Lag	Import Lead	Import Lag
Australia	Allowed—no limit	Allowed—no limit	Allowed—no limit	Allowed—no limit
Chile	90 days	90 days	Not allowed	120 days
Germany	Allowed—no limit	Allowed—no limit	Allowed—no limit	Allowed—no limit
Japan	360 days	360 days	360 days	360 days
Korea	Allowed—no limit	180 days	Not allowed	120 days
Spain	Allowed—no limit	30 days	90 days	90 days
United Kingdom	Allowed—no limit	Allowed—no limit	Allowed—no limit	Allowed—no limit
United States	Allowed—no limit	Allowed—no limit	Allowed—no limit	Allowed—no limit
Venezuela	Not allowed	Not allowed	Not allowed	Not allowed

benefits of a reinvoicing centre are that all transaction exposure for transfers within the firm is centrally located, expertise can be developed, and leading and lagging can be coordinated. The primary disadvantage is the cost associated with setting up and maintaining the centre.

LOCATE INVESTMENT WHERE SALES OCCUR

Another way to deal with some exchange rate risks is to locate subsidiaries in the countries where the final goods or services are to be sold. Thus, the decisions by two German auto makers, BMW and Mercedes-Benz, to build plants in the southeastern United States will insulate them from many exchange rate fluctuations between the German mark and the U.S. dollar, providing they sell the cars in the United States and they purchase all (or virtually all) of the component parts in the United States as well.

ACQUIRE FINANCING IN THE COUNTRY WHERE IT WILL BE USED

Another strategy to protect firms against some exchange rate risks is to acquire the financing where it will be employed. For example, if a firm needs financing in Thailand and has a plant there that will produce cash flows that can be used to pay the financing costs, the firm can insulate itself from certain exchange rate risks. In a coordinated policy, where investments, sales, financing, and repayment are all located within a county, firms can reduce some of their exchange rate exposure. Of course, when funds have to flow back to the parent, or to a subsidiary in another country, exchange rate risk still remains.

In addition to the operating, investing, and financing approaches for dealing with foreign exchange risk, over the last decade firms have made more and more use of forwards, futures, swaps, and options to hedge exchange rate risks. In the remainder of the chapter, we will consider the first three alternatives, leaving the last one to be discussed in the next chapter.

Concept Review Question

- Explain how a firm could decrease exchange rate risk by invoicing in the home currency, by leading or lagging, by using a reinvoicing centre, and by investing or obtaining financing in the foreign country.

HEDGING USING FORWARD CONTRACTS

A **foreign exchange forward contract** is an agreement drawn up for a given maturity or settlement day to deliver (or receive) units of one currency relative to the other currency based on the relationship of the then-existing spot price and the exercise price stated in the contract. Forwards are traded in many currencies for 1, 2, 3, 6, 9, and 12 months. For the major currencies—the dollar, sterling, yen, and mark—quotes are also available for 4 months, 5 months, and so forth. This over-the-counter market, through banks and investment dealers, can provide almost any kind of coverage using foreign exchange forward contracts.

To hedge an exchange rate exposure we need to take an offsetting position with a foreign exchange forward contract. For an illustration of this idea, consider Figure 17.2, where the change in firm value, ΔV, is depicted on the vertical axis, and the change in foreign exchange rates is on the horizontal axis. If, as in part A of Figure 17.2, we stand to lose (i.e., the value of the firm falls) as a foreign currency *weakens* relative to the home currency, we would *sell* a foreign exchange forward contract to offset the expected loss in value. Likewise, if we stand to lose as the foreign currency *strengthens* relative to the home currency, we would *buy* a foreign exchange forward contract, as indicated in part B of the figure. By taking such an offsetting position we are "covered" or "square" because no exchange rate risk exposure exists.

SELLING A FORWARD

Let us examine how a foreign exchange forward contract can be used to hedge against a possible loss as a foreign currency weakens. Assume we are selling goods to a Swiss firm with payment due in 90 days. The agreed-upon price is 2,000,000 Swiss francs, SF; the current spot rate of exchange is 1.15 SF/$; and the three-month forward rate of exchange is 1.25 SF/$. Because the forward rate is above the spot rate, the Swiss franc is expected to weaken against the dollar—that is, in the future it will take more francs to buy a dollar.

Figure 17.2

Use of Forward Contracts to Hedge Foreign Exchange Risk

The use of foreign exchange contracts is very widespread.

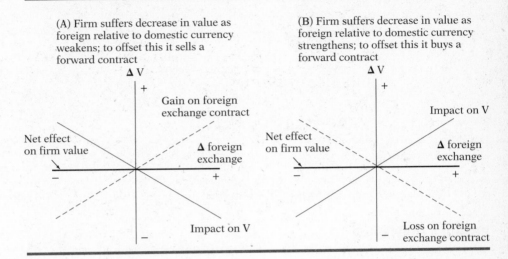

(A) Firm suffers decrease in value as foreign relative to domestic currency weakens; to offset this it sells a forward contract

(B) Firm suffers decrease in value as foreign relative to domestic currency strengthens; to offset this it buys a forward contract

First, let us see what might happen when we receive payment in three months under three different scenarios:

1. If in three months the then-existing spot rate of exchange is 1.25 SF/$, then the amount received, in dollars, is 2,000,000/1.25 = $1,600,000.
2. If in three months the Swiss franc weakens more quickly than now expected, and the spot rate then existing is 1.60 SF/$, then we receive 2,000,000/1.60 = $1,250,000, for a loss of $350,000 (i.e., $1,600,000 − $1,250,000).
3. If in three months the franc strengthens so the spot rate is 1.00 SF/$, then we receive 2,000,000/1.00 = $2,000,000, for a gain of $400,000 (i.e., $2,000,000 − $1,600,000).

Obviously, we are not indifferent among these outcomes.

To remove the uncertainty associated with what may happen with foreign exchange rates, we can hedge by *selling* a forward contract for 2,000,000 Swiss francs for delivery in 90 days with an exercise price at the existing three-month forward rate of 1.25 SF/$. This way we lock in $1,600,000. If the franc weakens faster than now expected, we gain by hedging; if the franc strengthens, then we incur an opportunity loss by hedging. That is, if we hedge and the spot rate in three months is 1.00 SF/$, we lose $400,000 because the 2,000,000 Swiss francs could have been converted to $2,000,000 when they were received. Thus, any gain or loss from the hedge exactly offsets the loss or gain from the foreign exchange exposure.

Ignoring the cost of the forward contract, we can depict what happens by selling (or going short) with the foreign exchange contract as follows:

Time Period	Event
t = 0	Sell 2 million Swiss francs forward for 90 days at an exercise price of 1.25 SF/$

t = 90

<------------------ 2 ------------------   <------------------ 1 ------------------

Deliver 2 million Swiss francs   Receive 2 million Swiss francs
as per the forward contract   from the Swiss purchaser

------------------ 3 ------------------>

Receive $1,600,000 from the
buyer of the forward contract

This is an example of taking a short position with a foreign exchange forward contract. Belief that the forward rate is an unbiased estimate of the expected future spot rate does not preclude hedging to protect against unexpected changes in the future spot rate.

BUYING A FORWARD

Firms may also need to take long positions with foreign exchange forward contracts. To understand this, assume that we are importing goods from Great Britain. The agreement is for the goods to cost 187,500 pounds. Payment will be made in four months in pounds. The current spot rate is 1.92 $/£. (Remember, with pounds the "normal" procedure is for the exchange rate to be quoted in dollars per pound.) The four-month forward rate is 1.84 $/£. In examining the forward and spot rates, we see that the pound is expected to weaken relative to the dollar. However, the Canadian purchaser is concerned that this trend may be reversed and wants to hedge against an increase in the pound. To do this, the importer takes a long position by *purchasing* a four-month foreign exchange forward contract with the exercise price set at the existing four-month forward rate of 1.84. By doing so, the importer is assured the cost will be (£187,500)(1.84) = $345,000. No matter what occurs, the price of $345,000 is locked in. Ignoring the cost of the forward contract, we can depict what happens by buying (or going long) with the foreign exchange forward contract:

Time Period	Event
t = 0	Purchase £187,500 forward for four months at an exercise price of 1.84 $/£

t = 4

<------------------ 1 ------------------

Pay seller of forward contract $345,000

------------------ 2 ------------------>   ------------------ 3 ------------------>

Receive £187,500 under the   Pay British firm £187,500
forward contract

OTHER CONSIDERATIONS WHEN USING FORWARD CONTRACTS

Now that we understand more about the use of forward contracts to hedge foreign exchange risk, a few other points should be mentioned. First, with any forward contract there is credit risk—one of the parties may default on the contract. Because of this possibility, the use of forwards is restricted to institutions, corporations, and governments with easy access to sufficient lines of credit to back them up. Second, the use of partial hedges is relevant for hedging part (instead of all) of the foreign exchange risk. Finally, in addition to the foreign exchange forwards discussed previously, there are also *forward* foreign exchange agreements. Whereas the traditional foreign exchange forward contract sets a rate in the future for the spot exchange of currencies, it is also possible to enter into forward contracts that at maturity fix the forward rate at that time. These and other developments are constantly occurring in the dynamic area of devising ways to assist firms in managing their foreign exchange risk.

Concept Review Questions

- When attempting to hedge exchange rate exposure, when should a multinational firm sell a foreign exchange forward contract, and when should it buy a foreign exchange forward contract?

- Describe what would happen to a short hedge if the spot rate of exchange is as expected, less than expected, and greater than expected.

HEGING USING FUTURES CONTRACTS

In addition to forward contracts, there are also **foreign exchange futures contracts**. The basic form of a futures contract is just like a forward contract; it obligates its owner to purchase a specified asset at the exercise price on the contract maturity date. But, unlike forward contracts, futures are of a fixed size and maturity date. Table 17.3 indicates the major foreign exchange futures listed in a recent issue of *The Wall Street Journal*. We see that futures were available for the yen, mark, Canadian dollar, pound, Swiss franc, Australian dollar, and the U.S. Dollar Index (USDX). The USDX is a measure of the U.S. dollar's composite value against several other currencies.

In examining the data for the yen, we see that the futures contract is traded on the International Monetary Market (IMM), which is located at the Chicago Mercantile Exchange. The contract size is 12.5 million yen, and the price is in dollars per thousand yen. Two contracts were available for the yen; and the open, high, low, settle, and change prices are given, along with the contract's lifetime high and low as well as the open interest. At the bottom of the quotes for the yen we see that the volume on the day's activity was 19,011 contracts, the previous day's volume was 21,742, and the open interest was 62,631 contracts—a decrease of 3,250.

In all cases except the USDX, delivery at the termination of the contract is physical; that is, a specific number of units of foreign currency have to be delivered, unless the contract is closed out first. Also, the minimum movement of a futures price is $12.50

Table 17.3

Major Foreign Exchange Futures Listed in a Recent Issue of *The Wall Street Journal*

There are other futures, futures options, and options listed.

	Open	High	Low	Settle	Change	Lifetime High	Lifetime Low	Open Interest
Japanese Yen (IMM)—12.5 million yen: $ per yen (.00)								
Mar	.6920	.6925	.6907	.6914	−.0025	.8357	.6780	59,352
June	.6942	.6942	.6927	.6932	−.0025	.7530	.6850	3,225
Est vol 19,011; vol Wed 21, 742; open int 62,631, −3,250.								
German Mark (IMM)—125,000 marks; $ per mark								
Mar	.5947	.5972	.5936	.5970	+.0031	.6012	.5000	58,357
June	.5949	.5967	.5937	.5968	+.0030	.6007	.5057	4,214
Sept	—	—	—	.5966	+.0030	.5980	.5410	241
Mr	—	—	—	.5968	+.0032	.5975	.5915	375
Est vol 36,349; vol Wed 49,872; open int 63,208, +61.								
Canadian Dollar (IMM)—$100,000 dlrs; $ per Can $								
Mar	.8381	.8390	.8357	.8376	—	.8595	.7890	25,204
June	.8325	.8315	.8294	.8304	—	.8522	.8107	3,419
Sept	.8245	.8250	.8240	.8242	—	.8468	.8100	225
Dec	.8225	.8225	.8225	.8210	+.0010	.8420	.8120	176
Est vol 2,580; vol Wed 5,045; open int 28,934, −384.								
British Pound (IMM)—62,500 pds; $ per pound								
Mar	1.6700	1.6734	1.6668	1.6704	+.0044	1.6734	1.4600	24,461
June	1,6440	1.6476	1.6416	1.6448	+.0042	1.6950	1.4400	2,183
Est vol 8,432; vol Wed 7,491; open int 26,473, +349.								
Swiss Franc (IMM)—125,000 francs; $ per franc								
Mar	.6670	.6697	.6641	.6695	+.0040	.6744	.5740	36,880
June	.6645	.6680	.6620	.6676	+.0040	.6725	.5850	1,320
Mr	—	—	—	.6670	+.0040	.6725	.6540	785
Est vol 20,472; vol Wed 27,463; open int 39,066, +325.								
Australian Dollar (IMM)—100,000 dlrs; $ per A $								
Mar	.7605	.7645	.7599	.7627	−.0001	.7854	.7055	3,256
Est vol 388; vol Wed 515; open int 3,313, +650.								
U.S. Dollar Index (FINEX)—500 times USDX								
Mar	92.75	92.95	92.45	92.464	−.36	105.65	92.25	4,770
June	93.42	93.42	93.25	93.10	−.37	100.43	92.80	273
Est vol 3,250; vol Wed 3,385; open int 5,045, +288.								
The Index: High 92.49; Low 92.16; Close 92.16, −.25.								

for the yen, mark, Canadian dollar, pound, and Swiss franc; it is $10 for the Australian dollar and $5 for the USDX.

SELLING A FUTURE

To understand the use of a futures contract (instead of a forward contract) to hedge foreign exchange risk, let us reconsider the two examples used previously. First, consider the Canadian firm selling to a Swiss firm with payment due in 90 days. The price was 2,000,000 Swiss francs, the current spot rate of exchange was 1.15 SF/$, and the three-month forward rate of exchange was 1.25 SF/$. *If the payment is due on the same date that the futures contract expires,* then a perfect hedge can be created to lock in the three-month forward rate of exchange of 1.25 by selling (or going short) 16 contracts. The 16 is determined by dividing the 2,000,000 francs by the number of francs per contract, which is 125,000 as shown in Table 17.3. In three months, on the delivery date, the Canadian firm receives 2,000,000 francs from the Swiss purchaser, delivers the 2,000,000 francs as promised when the 16 futures contracts were sold, and receives $1,600,000 (i.e., 2,000,000/1.25 = $1,600,000) under the futures contract. Again, the cost of the contract will have to be taken into consideration.

BUYING A FUTURE

The same basic ideas apply to the use of a futures hedge in the case of our other example, the Canadian firm importing goods from Britain that will cost £187,500. With a four-month forward rate of 1.84 $/£, and *assuming a futures contract exists that settles at the same time the payment is due,* the firm can lock in its cost of $345,000 [i.e., (£187,500)(1.84$/£) = $345,000] by purchasing (or going long in) the futures contract. The futures contract size is £62,500, as shown in Table 17.3, so the number of contracts needed is 187,500/62,500 = 3. When delivery occurs, the Canadian firm settles the futures contract by paying $345,000 and receiving £187,500, which it then uses to pay the British firm. In so doing the firm has reduced its risk exposure so that no matter what the actual rate of exchange is at settlement, the cost is $345,000 (plus the cost of the futures contracts).

OTHER CONSIDERATIONS WHEN USING FUTURES CONTRACTS

In practice, the size of the futures contract and its maturity rarely matches the firm's needs exactly. In that case perfect hedges are not possible. Also, it often happens that the currency needed to be hedged against does not have a traded futures contract. This is a case in which **cross-hedging** is required. A cross-hedge exists every time the underlying asset is of one form (or tied to one currency), but the futures contract is of another form (or tied to another currency). When a cross-hedge is needed, the typical approach is to find which futures contract most closely tracks the currency to be hedged. Suppose a Canadian firm sold some goods to an importer in Finland. There is no futures contract on the Finnish markka. The way to proceed is to determine the futures contract whose movements are most highly correlated with movements in the *spot* rate on the markka. To do that we might gather data on the spot rate for the markka, along with data on the futures prices of three different futures contracts—British pounds, Swiss francs, and German marks. Then we would calculate the *day-to-day changes* in all four series.

If the data for the spot rate on the markka and the German mark futures prices for 4 days are as follows, the first step is to determine the changes, or:

	Spot Rate		Futures	
Day	Markka/$	ΔMarkka/$	Mark/$	ΔMark/$
1	5.413		0.6301	
2	5.418	0.005	0.6303	0.0002
3	5.414	−0.004	0.6303	0.0000
4	5.407	−0.007	0.6294	−0.0009

Assuming we had sufficient data (in practice this means at least 50 observations)[5] then we run the following regression:

$$\Delta spot = \alpha + \beta \Delta futures$$

where

$\Delta spot$ is the change in the spot price, markka/$
$\Delta futures$ is the change in the futures price, mark/$

We would do the same for the other two futures contracts. Typically the one with the highest explanatory power, or R^2, would be chosen to hedge the exposure because that contract's futures price is most highly correlated with movements in the spot rate.

Concept Review Questions

■ How are foreign exchange futures contracts and foreign exchange forward contracts similar? How are they different?

■ Explain how to use a futures contract to offset exchange rate risk.

■ Define cross-hedging, and explain when it can be used to hedge exchange rate risk.

---

[5] Although we used "days" in the example, more often the data employed is weekly or monthly.

HEDGING USING SWAPS

In Chapter 11 we discussed interest rate swaps. Currency swaps also exist. In a plain vanilla currency swap, the transaction involves:

1. The exchange of principal denominated in one currency for principal denominated in another currency at the beginning of the swap, *and*

2a. Fixed interest payments in one currency into fixed interest payments in another currency, or

2b. Fixed interest payments in one currency into floating interest payments in another currency, or

2c. Floating interest payments in one currency into floating interest payments in another currency, *and*

3. Reexchange of the original principal at the end of the swap.

PARALLEL LOANS

To illustrate a currency swap, let us start with a **parallel** (or **back-to-back**) **loan**. A parallel loan involves two firms in separate countries arranging to borrow in each other's currency for a specific period of time, exchanging principal and interest payments, and at the agreed termination date returning the principal. For example, assume the current spot exchange rate between the Japanese yen and the Canadian dollar is 110 yen per dollar, ¥110/$1. A Canadian firm with a subsidiary in Japan wants to expand its operations in Japan and needs ¥550 million to do so. At the same time, a Japanese firm wants to expand its operations in Canada and needs to invest $5 million in its Canadian subsidiary. Both firms want to hedge any exchange rate risk exposure.

A straightforward way to accomplish this, which firms often used in the past, is a parallel loan. The structure of a typical parallel loan is shown in Figure 17.3. At the current rate of exchange of ¥110/$1, ¥550,000,000/110 = $5,000,000. To set up the parallel loan, the Canadian parent borrows in Canada and then lends the funds to the Japanese subsidiary in Canada, while the Japanese parent borrows in Japan and then lends the funds to the Canadian subsidiary in Japan. The two loans are for the same amount, at the current spot rate of exchange, and for a specified maturity of, say, six years. At the end of six years the loans are repaid to the original parent firm (and then the original lenders). Let us assume the fixed interest rate was 10 percent in Canada and 8 percent in Japan. During the life of the loan, the Canadian subsidiary would pay interest of (¥550,000,000)(0.08) = ¥44,000,000 per year to the Japanese parent. At the same time the Japanese subsidiary would pay the Canadian parent interest of ($5,000,000)(0.10) = $500,000 per year.

Default risk can be protected through a right of offset or through a third-party guarantee. A further agreement can provide for maintenance of the principal parity in case the spot rate of exchange between the two currencies changes. For example, if the

Figure 17.3

Structure of a Parallel, or Back-to-Back Loan

With a parallel loan firms can set the financing up so they loan/repay in the currency desired. Before swaps were introduced in 1981, parallel loans provided the same result; sometimes they are still employed to get around currency controls imposed in various countries.

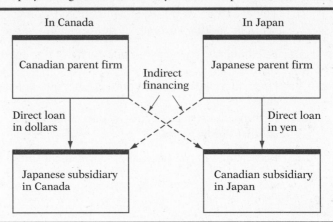

Canadian dollar weakened against the yen by 5 percent for a period of 30 days, the Canadian parent might have to advance additional dollars to the Japanese subsidiary to bring the principal value of the two loans back into agreement. A similar provision would apply if the yen weakened against the dollar.

CURRENCY SWAPS

Although the parallel loan is straightforward, in practice one of the big difficulties is to find the counter-firm that has exactly the offsetting need. To avoid this problem, currency swaps have been developed. In the above example, a currency swap would involve the Canadian parent raising the $5 million in Canada, while the Japanese firm raises ¥55 million in Japan. Then the firms agree to swap the initial principal, make interest payments on the swapped principal for six years, and then reswap the principal at the end of the six years. This sequence is depicted in Figure 17.4. Thus, the swap accomplishes everything the parallel loan does, much more easily.

Default risk has been reduced because now there is one combined agreement, the currency swap. In practice only the net amount, or difference, is transferred between the parties. Also, while both loans could be fixed-rate loans, it is more typical for at least one of the loans to be a floating-rate loan. Finally, with the growth of the swap market, intermediaries (such as Royal Bank, Bank of Montreal, and Nesbitt Burns) actually provide the services needed by a party (such as the Canadian parent), and then they seek to offset, or cover, their position. Hence, the role of the intermediary is *not* to bring the two parties together; rather, it is to provide the services needed, for a fee, and then hedge the resulting risk exposure. With the number of banks that have developed large swap operations, the cost to the firm is less now than it was in the early days of the swap market. Also, more sophisticated types of currency swaps can be

Figure 17.4

Structure of a Currency Swap

With this plain vanilla currency swap, the firms borrow where it is cheapest, swap principal and interest payments, and at the termination of the agreement reswap the initial principal. Many other variations of currency swaps also exist.

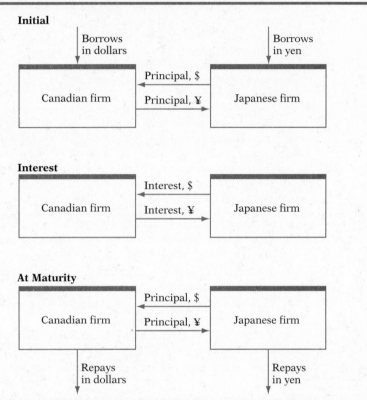

arranged; but the preceding discussion indicates the function of swaps as a means of dealing with exchange rate risk.

Concept Review Questions

- Describe how multinational firms use parallel loans to offset exchange rate risk exposure.
- What is one difficulty with a parallel loan and how does a currency swap correct for this difficulty?

KEY POINTS

- Key considerations when making international capital expenditure decisions include, in addition to items discussed for domestic decisions, forecasted exchange rates, taxes, and questions of how the funds are to be brought back to the home country.

- Capital structure, dividend policy, and other decisions must be made while keeping the view-point of the parent firm in mind.
- Although some differences exist, including some in areas of accounting and taxation, multinational firms apply all of the fundamental concepts and decision rules of financial management. The goal remains the same: to maximize the value of the firm by focusing on the magnitude and timing of cash flows, the risks incurred, and the opportunity costs.
- Virtually all firms, whether purely domestic or multinationals, may face economic exposure that makes them more or less vulnerable as exchange rates change.
- Types of exchange risk exposure include translation, transaction, and economic. Translation exposure is accounting-oriented; although it does not affect the firm's cash flows, it is sometimes important due to financial loan covenants. Transaction and economic exposure has direct cash flow implications. Firms employ a variety of approaches to hedge translation and economic exposure.
- Techniques employed to hedge some of the firm's translation and economic exposure include invoicing in the home currency, leading and lagging, using reinvoicing centres, locating investment where the sales occur, and raising financing where it will be used.
- Forward contracts, exchange rate futures, and currency swaps can be employed to lock in a specific rate of exchange; using one of them means the firm does not have to worry about whether exchange rates move for or against it.

Questions

17.1   What factors influence the opportunity cost of capital used when international capital budgeting decisions are made? What conclusions can be reached?

17.2   What two general methods are available for determining the NPV for an international capital budgeting project?

17.3   How can we estimate future exchange rates by using currently available data and assuming the market is efficient?

17.4   Explain how foreign exchange risk, repatriation of funds, expropriation risk, and credit risk all influence international capital budgeting decisions.

17.5   What are the main factors to consider when determining a multinational firm's capital structure?

17.6   Summarize the important aspects of a multinational firm's dividend policy.

17.7   What are the primary differences between the Eurobond market and the bond market in Canada?

17.8   Explain "double dipping" and other international aspects of leasing.

17.9   Distinguish among translation, transaction, and economic foreign exchange exposure. Why, with few exceptions, should firms not be concerned with translation risk?

17.10   "All firms have a foreign exchange problem." Do you agree or disagree with this statement? Why?

17.11   Operating, investment, and financing strategies exist for hedging foreign exchange risk. Although these seem very adequate, firms have increasingly moved to using financial instruments to assist them in hedging exchange rate risk. What deficiencies exist with operating, investing, or financing approaches to dealing with exchange rate risk?

17.12   What alternative methods are available for hedging exchange rate risk? How are they similar? How are they different?

17.13   Under what conditions would a Canadian firm go long in a forward or futures contract rather than go short?

17.14   Parallel loans existed long before currency swaps. Compare the advantages and disadvantages of currency swaps versus parallel loans.

CONCEPT REVIEW PROBLEMS

See Appendix A for solutions.

CR17.1 Your firm is evaluating a proposed expansion of its textile subsidiary in India. The cost of the expansion will be 900,000 rupees, with expected cash flows in year 1 of 300,000 rupees, in year 2 of 500,000 rupees, and in year 3 of 500,000 rupees. The current spot exchange rate is 30 rupees per Canadian dollar, the risk-free rate in India is 10 percent, and the risk-free rate in Canada is 5 percent. Ignoring taxes and remittance fees, what is the net present value of the project if the opportunity cost of capital is 15 percent?

CR17.2 The Canada Bottling Company is considering opening a wholly owned subsidiary in the United States. The cost of the subsidiary will be 720,000 U.S. dollars. Cash flows from the subsidiary will be 300,000 U.S. dollars in year 1, 500,000 U.S. dollars in year 2, 500,000 U.S. dollars in year 3, and 400,000 U.S. dollars in year 4. The U.S. subsidiary's corporate tax rate is 35 percent, while the Canadian corporate tax rate is 40 percent. The U.S. has a remittance fee of 3 percent for foreign companies. The current spot rate for a U.S. dollar per Canadian dollar is 0.80, the risk-free rate in Canada is 4 percent, and in the United States the risk-free rate is 6 percent. If the opportunity cost of capital is 10 percent, what is the net present value of the plant if the subsidiary remits funds each year?

CR17.3 A Canadian-based firm sold 200,000 bushels of grain to an Australian company for 500,000 Australian dollars. Payment for the grain will be received in six months. The current spot rate of exchange is A\$1.25 per Canadian dollar and the six-month forward rate of exchange is A\$1.15 per Canadian dollar.
a. Is the Australian dollar expected to strengthen or weaken relative to the Canadian dollar?
b. If the spot rate does not change, what amount in Canadian dollars will the Canadian firm receive for the grain? If the spot rate does drop, as predicted by the forward rate, what amount will the Canadian firm receive?
c. Establish a hedge using forward contracts to offset the exchange rate risk. Demonstrate the effectiveness of the hedge by showing the profit and loss if the spot price in six months is A\$1.35 per Canadian dollar.

CR17.4 Best Eastern has agreed to purchase equipment from an Italian firm in three months for 6,000,000 Italian lira. The current spot price is lira 1,200 per Canadian dollar, and the three-month forward rate is lira 1,150 per Canadian dollar.
a. If Best Eastern paid for the equipment today in Canadian dollars, what is the outlay?
b. What is the cost, in Canadian dollars, if Best Eastern waits and pays in three months and the spot rate at that time is equal to today's three-month forward rate?
c. Assuming futures contracts existed for the size and maturity needed, should Best Eastern buy or sell a futures contract to hedge the exchange rate exposure? What are the results if the spot rate in three months is lira 1,100 per Canadian dollar?

PROBLEMS

17.1 Douglas Communications is exploring whether to make an investment in Trinidad. The investment will cost 200,000 Trinidadian dollars and will generate expected cash flows of 100,000, 110,000, and 120,000 Trinidadian dollars in years 1, 2, and 3 respectively. The spot rate is 0.300 Trinidadian dollars per Canadian dollar, and the required rate of return, k, in Canadian dollars is 25 percent. The Canadian risk-free rate, k_{RF}, is 7 percent, and it is 12 percent in Trinidad. The real rate of interest in both countries is estimated to be 2 percent. Should the investment be made?

17.2   The expected cash flows, in pounds, from an investment in a foreign affiliate in Britain are as follows:

	Year				
	0	**1**	**2**	**3**	**4**
Cash flows	−300,000	100,000	125,000	150,000	150,000

Taxes in Britain have already been taken into account. The Canadian opportunity cost, k, is 16 percent, the Canadian corporate tax rate is 35 percent, and the current spot rate is 0.560 pounds to the dollar. The Canadian risk-free rate is 8 percent, whereas it is 11 percent in Britain, and the real rate of interest is 2 percent in both countries.

a.   Determine the expected spot rate of exchange for the next four years between the pound and the dollar.

b.   What are the after-tax cash flows in dollars? (*Note*: Ignore any foreign tax credits.)

c.   Should the project be undertaken?

17.3   Lytle Productions is evaluating whether to invest in a project in the Netherlands. The expected cash flows, in guilders, are as follows:

	Year					
	0	**1**	**2**	**3**	**4**	**5**
Cash flows	−100,000	20,000	30,000	40,000	40,000	40,000

The spot rate is 2.086 guilders per Canadian dollar. The discount rate, k, is 20 percent. The Canadian risk-free rate, k_{RF}, is 8 percent, while it is 6 percent in the Netherlands. Assuming that the real rate of return is zero, should the investment be made?

17.4   The before-tax cash flows in Austrian schillings and the forecasted spot exchange rates between the schilling and the dollar are as follows:

	Year		
	0	**1**	**2**	**3**
Cash flows before taxes	−40,000	20,000	40,000	50,000
Forecasted spot exchange rate	0.600	0.658	0.724	0.800

The corporate tax rate in Austria is 20 percent, and the tax rate for funds transferred out of Austria is 6 percent; the Canadian corporate tax rate is 35 percent.

a.   Calculate the after-tax cash flows in Canadian dollars if the Austrian firm is a foreign affiliate.

b.   If the opportunity cost of capital, k, in Canadian dollars is 15 percent, should the project be undertaken?

c.   Independent of (a) and (b), now assume that everything remains the same except that now the firm making the investment will own less than 10 percent of the shares of the Austrian firm. Should the project now be undertaken?

17.5 Calgary Petroleum is considering an investment in Jordan, a nontreaty country. The expected before-tax cash flows (CFBT) in the Jordanian dinar are as follows:

	Year						
	0	**1**	**2**	**3**	**4**	**5**	**6**
Cash flows before taxes	−80,000	30,000	30,000	40,000	40,000	50,000	50,00

The opportunity cost of capital, k, in Canadian dollars is 14 percent; the spot rate is JD 0.700 per Canadian dollar; the risk-free rate, k_{RF}, is 8 percent in Canada and 13 percent in Jordan; and the real rate of interest is 2 percent in both countries. Jordan's corporate tax rate is 25 percent, and it has a 5 percent withholding tax. The Canadian corporate tax rate is 40 percent.
a. Calculate the expected spot rates of exchange for years 1 through 6.
b. What are the expected after-tax cash flows in Canadian dollars?
c. Should the project be accepted?
d. Independent of (a) through (c), and everything remaining the same, Calgary fears the project may be expropriated after four years, resulting in little or no compensation. What is the project's NPV?

17.6 You are exporting goods to Mexico. The agreed-upon price is 8 billion pesos, the current spot rate is 2,750 pesos/$, and the three-month forward rate is 2,800 pesos/$.
a. How can you lock in your proceeds using a forward contract? What amount will you receive?
b. If in three months the actual spot rate of exchange is 2,900 pesos/$, did you benefit or lose by hedging? By how much?

17.7 Hunt Industries has just made a major sale to a Japanese firm. The payment will be ¥100 million. The payment will be made in 180 days, and the 180-day forward rate is ¥123.24/$.
a. How can Hunt lock in the dollar amount it will receive? What is the amount in dollars?
b. Assume Hunt does not hedge and the actual spot rate of exchange in 180 days is ¥125.80/$. How much would Hunt gain or lose by going unhedged? Now assume the spot rate of exchange in 180 days is ¥121.20/$. How much is Hunt's gain or loss by going unhedged?

17.8 Bergstrom's Systems has just agreed to sell some goods to a Malaysian firm. The agreed-upon price is 12 million ringgits, payment will be made in 90 days, and the current spot rate of exchange is 2.712 ringgits/$. Bergstrom's decides to hedge this against a possible weakening in the Malaysian ringgit by selling a 90-day forward contract with an exercise price of 2.900 ringgits/$.
a. What sequence of transactions takes place (both today and in 90 days)?
b. If the actual spot rate of exchange in 90 days is 3.150 ringgits/$, is Bergstrom's better or worse off by engaging in the forward contract? By how much?

17.9 We are importing goods from Spain, with the payment to be made in Spanish pesetas in two months. The agreed-upon price is 450 million pesetas, the spot rate of exchange is 109.95 pesetas/$, and the exercise price in the 60-day forward contract is 115.38.

a. What sequence of transactions takes place (both today and in 60 days)?

b. If the actual spot rate of exchange in 60 days is 118.35 pesetas/$, are we better or worse off by engaging in the forward contract? By how much?

17.10 LBG is selling to a British firm with the agreed-upon price at payment of £312,500. Payment is due on the same day the British pound futures contract expires, so a perfect hedge can be created. The current spot rate is $1.96/£, and the forward rate of exchange when the futures contract expires is currently $1.91/£.

a. If LBG wants to lock in its proceeds, what should it do? How many contracts are involved?

b. If at the receipt date (which is also the futures contract expiration date) the spot rate is $2.02/£, did LBG benefit or lose by hedging? By how much?

c. What if the agreed-upon price was £330,000? Could a perfect hedge have been formed?

d. What if the date the payment was to be received did not coincide with the date the futures contract expires? Could a perfect hedge have been formed?

17.11 You are a U.S. firm importing goods from Canada that will cost 875,000 Canadian dollars in three months. The payment is due on the last day of the month three months from now. The three-month Canadian futures contract expires one to two weeks before payment is due, and the three-month forward rate is C$1.221/US$.

a. Is a perfect hedge available? Why or why not?

b. In order to lock in your costs, what hedge (even if not perfect) should be placed?

c. If when you pay the bill the spot rate of exchange is C$1.150/US$, did you gain or lose on the transaction?

17.12 A Canadian-domiciled firm has a subsidiary in the Netherlands that needs a 45 million guilder loan; at the same time, a Netherlands-domiciled firm has a subsidiary in Canada that needs a $25 million loan. Assume the current exchange rate is 1.80 guilders/$. A four-year parallel loan is going to be set up; the interest rate is fixed for each loan, and it is 7 percent in the Netherlands and 10 percent in Canada.

a. Determine the structure of the parallel loan and the cash flows that are expected to be made from one firm to the other throughout the loan.

b. To protect against changes in exchange rates, the principal amount of the loan will be adjusted once each year. The firm whose home currency is weakening will have to increase its principal in the loan. Assume that the interest rate parity relationship (discussed in Chapter 2) holds and that the two interest rates are the risk-free rates for the respective countries. What are the expected spot rates at time $t = 1$, $t = 2$, and $t = 3$? (*Note:* Carry to three decimal places.) By how much will the Canadian- or Netherlands-domiciled firm have to increase the principal of the loan at times $t = 1, 2$, and 3? What will the new interest amount be for the three time periods for the new principal?

c. Instead of changing the principal, what other way could the change in interest rates be accomplished?

17.13 Mini Case CrossBarr Sports has just hired you to head up its international operations. Up until now the firm has not systematically considered how to evaluate investments in other countries or the financial price risk that its international operations exposes it to. However, with CrossBarr's rapid growth in foreign markets and its large amount of foreign transactions, more systematic attention to all aspects of its international operations is required.

To give you some direction, the president of the firm has posed the following questions:

a. What major factors need to be considered when determining the opportunity cost of capital for international projects?

b. We are currently evaluating two possible mutually exclusive investments. The information for both projects is as follows:

	Investment A		Investment B	
	Year	CF	Year	CF
Cash flows, in units	0	−50,000	0	−50,000
of the foreign currency	1	20,000	1	35,000
	2	40,000	2	55,000
	3	80,000	3	70,000
	4	60,000	4	80,000
	5	80,000	5	80,000
			6	60,000
Spot rate of exchange	2.00		5.00	
k_{RF} home currency	12%		12%	
k_{RF} foreign currency	15%		10%	

The real rate of return is 2 percent in all of the countries, and the opportunity cost is 16 percent for both projects. Which should be undertaken?

c. The remittance of funds causes problems when making international capital investment decisions. What are some of the key issues in terms of remitting funds?

d. What are important differences in making capital structure and dividend decisions for domestic firms versus multinational firms?

e. The president has been very impressed with your answers to his questions—so much so that he has taken them to the board of directors. Now they have asked to be briefed on the following issues:

1. Why, given that CrossBarr imports about as much as it exports, should CrossBarr consider hedging its foreign exchange risk? (As one director notes, "Over the long run exchange rates work things out, and therefore hedging is not needed.")

2. How can CrossBarr employ operating, investing, and financing strategies for dealing with exchange rate exposure? What are the strengths and weaknesses of each, and why may these strategies not "solve" all of CrossBarr's exchange rate risk problems?

Prepare your report.

f. Your report in (e) was so persuasive that the directors will meet again next week. They want a report on the use of financial instruments for dealing with exchange rate risk. In particular they need a clear, but simple, explanation of the techniques available, their strengths and weaknesses, and your recommendations about the strategy CrossBarr needs to employ in hedging exchange rate risk. You need to prepare this report also.

g. As part of your report in (f), the board of directors is concerned about how to go about hedging some of its exchange rate exposure in less-developed countries. As another board member notes, "For many of the countries there are no futures contracts traded." How are you going to respond to this concern?

h. CrossBarr has just placed an order for shoes manufactured in the Philippines. CrossBarr owes 8 million Philippine pesos in four months. The present spot rate is 26.20 pesos/$ and the current four-month forward rate is 26.75 pesos/$. CrossBarr is considering two alternatives: going unhedged, or hedging using a forward contract. The forward contract would be at the current forward rate and would cost $6,000.

1. Compare the alternative ways that CrossBarr can hedge. What do you recommend?

2. Assume four months have passed and the settlement day on the purchase has arrived. The actual spot rate is 27.15 pesos/$. Evaluate the results under the two alternatives.

3. Instead of an actual spot rate of 27.15 pesos/$ in (2), assume the actual spot rate turned out to be 26.00 pesos/$. Now evaluate the results of the two alternatives.

i. Because of the success of the CrossBarr name in Germany, a big order was just received from a German sporting goods chain. Payment of the 2.5 million marks will be in 90 days. The spot rate of exchange is 1.58M/$ (or $0.6320/M) while the 90-day forward rate is 1.60M/$ ($0.625/M). Three alternatives are being considered: going unhedged, hedging using a forward contract, and hedging using futures contracts. The forward contract would have an exercise price of 1.61M/$ and cost $23,000. The futures contracts are for 62,500 marks each, with an exercise price of 1.61M/$, and will cost $485 per contract.

1. Compare the alternative ways CrossBarr can hedge. What do you recommend?
2. Assume four months have passed and the settlement day on the sale has arrived. The actual spot rate is 1.63M/$. Evaluate the results under the three alternatives.
3. Instead of an actual spot rate of 1.63M/$ in (2), assume the actual spot rate turned out to be 1.58M/$. Now evaluate the results of the three alternatives.

REFERENCES

AHN, MARK J., and WILLIAM D. FALLOON. *Strategic Risk Management: How Global Corporations Manage Financial Risk for Competitive Advantage*. Chicago: Probus Publishing, 1991.

BESSEMBINDER, HENDRIK. "Forward Contracts and Firm Value: Investment Incentive and Contracting Effects." *Journal of Financial and Quantitative Analysis* 26 (December 1991): 519–532.

HODDER, JAMES E., and LEMMA W. SENBET. "International Capital Structure Equilibrium." *Journal of Finance* 45 (December 1990): 1495–1516.

JOHN, KOSE, LEMMA W. SENBET, and ANANT K. SUNDARAM. "Cross-Border Liability of Multinational Enterprises, Border Taxes, and Capital Structure." *Financial Management* 20 (Winter 1991): 54–67.

LESSARD, DONALD R. "Global Competition and Corporate Finance in the 1990s." *Journal of Applied Corporate Finance* 3 (Winter 1991): 59–72.

MAHAJAN, ARVIND. "Pricing Expropriation Risk." *Financial Management* 19 (Winter 1990): 77–86.

NANCE, DEANA R., CLIFFORD W. SMITH, JR., and CHARLES W. SMITHSON. "On the Determinants of Corporate Hedging." *Journal of Finance* 48 (March 1993): 267–284.

PORTER, MICHAEL E. "Capital Disadvantage: America's Failing Investment System." *Harvard Business Review* 70 (September/October 1992): 65–82.

SHAPIRO, ALAN C. *International Corporate Finance*, 2nd ed. Cambridge, Mass.: Ballinger, 1988.

SMITH, CLIFFORD W., JR., CHARLES W. SMITHSON, and D. SYKES WILFORD. *Managing Financial Risk*. New York: Harper & Row, 1990.

SMITH, CLIFFORD W., and RENE M. STULZ. "The Determinants of Firms' Hedging Policies." *Journal of Financial and Quantitative Analysis* 20 (December 1985): 391–405.

THORNTON, DANIEL B. *Managerial Tax Planning: A Canadian Perspective*. Toronto: John Wiley & Sons Canada Ltd., 1993.

Derivative Concepts in Financial Management

*T*he goal of maximizing the long-term value of the firm requires that economically sound investments be made and that those investments be financed by long-term sources of funds. A solid understanding of options will enhance the manager's ability to achieve this goal. An option provides the right, but not the obligation, to buy or sell an asset for a limited time at a specified price. Although the most familiar options are stock options—options to buy or sell shares of common stock—numerous corporate investment and financing decisions have options embedded in them. Consequently, only by understanding options will a manager be able to recognize and value the many embedded options incurred in financial problems. Therefore, in Chapter 18 we start by becoming familiar with the language of options and then with valuing them. In Chapter 19 we deal with recognizing and valuing embedded options in capital investment opportunities. Some of these relate to future investment opportunities or growth options that arise from current investments, while others relate to the option to abandon a capital investment at some time in the future. We also discuss how to use currency options as a hedge against foreign exchange risk. Finally, in Chapter 20 warrants and convertibles, two option-like sources of long-term funds, are discussed.

18

Options

EXECUTIVE SUMMARY

In recent years one of the biggest changes in finance, and in financial markets, has been the development and widespread use of options. An option provides the right, but not the obligation, to buy or sell a particular asset for a limited time at a specified price. Options on common stock were first traded on the Chicago Board Options Exchange in 1973. Since then, the importance of options has grown phenomenally. Option trading now takes place on a number of exchanges. In Canada, the Trans Canada Options Inc. (renamed Canadian Derivatives Clearing Corp. in Januaray 1996), was created in 1977 to control option trading on the Montreal, Toronto, and Vancouver stock exchanges.

The value of European options (which can be exercised only at maturity) on nondividend-paying stocks is determined by: (1) the price of the underlying asset, (2) the exercise price, (3) the time to expiration, (4) the risk-free rate, and (5) the variability of the underlying assets' returns. The binomial option pricing model deals with a world in which there are only two possible outcomes per period. The Black–Scholes option pricing model assumes there are many possible outcomes.

The value of a call option, which is an option to buy, is equal to the current market value of the underlying asset times the hedge ratio, minus the present value of the exercise price. The hedge ratio is simply the number of units of the underlying asset that are needed to replicate one option. The value of European call options can be determined readily using either the binomial option pricing model or the Black–Scholes option pricing model. Likewise, the value of an option to sell, called a put option, can be determined easily.

THE BASICS OF OPTIONS

Option trading is a specialized business, and its participants speak a language all their own. Why, then, should we be interested in options? The answer is that managers routinely come in contact with decisions or securities that have options embedded in them. Only by understanding options will we be in a position to recognize and value these often-hidden options. Our objective in this chapter is twofold: first, to develop an understanding of what options are all about and, second, to learn how to value options. In Chapter 19 we will apply this knowledge and see that owning equity in a firm is just like owning a call option on the assets of the firm. We will also see other uses of options and the concepts learned in this chapter.

An option provides its owner with the right, but not the obligation, to buy or sell a particular good for a limited time at a specified price. The most familiar options are stock options—options to buy or sell shares of common stock. The development of options has been a major financial success story. Since they were first developed and traded on the Chicago Board Options Exchange (CBOE) in 1973, options have become one of the biggest financial markets in the world. Option trading now takes place on a number of exchanges, both in North America and around the world. In addition to options on common stock, there are also options on stock indexes, bonds, commodities, futures, and foreign exchange rates.

Some of the major North American options exchanges and the options traded on them are the following:

Chicago Board Options Exchange
Individual stocks
General stock market indices
Treasury bonds

American Exchange
Individual stocks
General stock market indices
Oil and gas index
Transportation index
Treasury bills
Treasury notes

Philadelphia Exchange
Individual stocks
Foreign currencies
Gold and silver indices

Toronto Futures Exchange
Individual stocks
TSE 300 composite index
TSE 35 index
Toronto index participation units (TIPs)

Montreal Exchange

> Individual stocks
>
> Government of Canada bonds
>
> Bankers' acceptances

New options are introduced over time. At the same time, some options cease to exist if demand for them wanes. When options on stocks were first introduced, they were relatively short-term in nature. Thus, the longest maturity was less than six months. That market still exists, but in the last few years longer-term options, with maturities of up to three years, have begun being traded on major option exchanges.[1]

In order to discuss options we need to understand certain basic terms. These include:

1. CALL OPTION VERSUS PUT OPTION   A **call option** provides the owner of the option with the right, but not the obligation, to buy the underlying asset. Conversely, a **put option** provides the owner with the right, but not the obligation, to sell the asset.
2. EXERCISE PRICE (OR STRIKE PRICE)   The fixed price, stated in the option contract, at which the underlying asset may be purchased or sold is the **exercise (or strike) price**.
3. EXPIRATION DATE OR MATURITY   The maturity date is the date the option expires. After this date the option is worthless.
4. EXERCISING AN OPTION   The act of buying or selling the underlying asset via an option contract is called *exercising the option*.
5. AMERICAN OPTION VERSUS EUROPEAN OPTION   An **American option** may be exercised any time up to and including the expiration date. On the other hand, a **European option** can be exercised only at the expiration date.

A LOOK AT OPTIONS ON STOCKS

If you picked up *The Globe and Mail* and looked at the listed option quotations for Seagram Co. Ltd. in the Canadian Equity Options section, you might see something similar to:

Seagram Series	$44.50 Bid	Ask	Last	80 Vol	2532 Op Int
May96 $42½	2.60	2.85	3.00	10	65
$45	0.95	1.20	1.10	4	41
$45 p	1.15	1.40	1.25	50	60
Jul96 $47½	1.10	1.35	1.10	3	145
Oct96 $50	1.25	1.50	1.35	3	35
Jan97 $50	1.50	2.00	1.70	10	229

---

[1] These long-term options are referred to as "leaps" in *The Globe and Mail* and *The Wall Street Journal*.

At the top of the listing you will find (from left to right): the name of the underlying security, Seagram common stock, the closing price of the underlying asset on the previous day, $44.50, the total number of options on the underlying asset traded on the previous day, 80, and the total number of options outstanding on the underlying asseet on the previous day, 2532. Below this, the first column lists the exercise (or strike) prices available and the month in which the option expires. The letter "p" after the exercise price indicates the option is a put; those without a "p" are call options. These exercise prices are set fairly close to the prevailing market price of the stock. For volatile stocks, more exercise prices will be available; likewise, as the stock price changes, new exercise prices are opened for trading. Each contract is written for 100 shares, but the option prices are quoted per share. Upon purchase of an option, an investor would have the right, but not the obligation, to purchase (with a call option) or sell (with a put option) 100 shares of Seagram at the exercise (or strike) price.

The second column indicates the bid price (or the highest price offered to buy the option) at the close of markets on the previous day. The third column shows the ask price (or the lowest price demanded to sell the option) at the close of markets on the previous day. The fourth column shows the last price at which actual trades took place while the fifth column shows the number of contracts traded that day. The final column gives the total number of option outstanding.

If you purchased the May96 call option on Seagram with a strike price of $42.50, you would pay (100 shares)($3) = $300, plus any commission fee. Once you own the call option, you can exercise it by paying (100 shares)($42.50) = $4,250. The writer of the option is obligated to sell you 100 shares at $42.50 per share, providing you exercise the option.

Before proceeding, it is helpful to consider a few other terms often used when options are discussed. The buyer of an option contract has purchased the option and has a **long** position, or *holds the contract long*. On the other hand, the seller, or writer, of an option contract has a **short** position, or has sold the option. It should be noted that *investors* create, or "write," stock options. Thus, the options on Seagram common stock were created by investors, not by Seagram.

One often hears that an option is **in-the-money**. An option is in-the-money if it would produce a gain if exercised. A call option is in-the-money if the market price of the stock, P_0, is *greater* than the exercise price, X. Conversely, a put option is in-the-money if the market price of the stock, P_0, is *less* than the exercise price, X.

On the other hand, an option can be **out-of-the-money**. An option is out-of-the-money if it would produce a loss if exercised. A call option is out-of-the-money if the market price of the stock, P_0, is less than the exercise price, X. A put option is out-of-the-money if P_0 is greater than X.

VALUE OF A CALL OPTION AT EXPIRATION

The right to buy Seagram common stock at a specific exercise price as indicated in the call option is valuable. How valuable the option is depends on five specific factors to be discussed shortly. Before moving into the formal valuation of options, though, let us examine the value of a call option at one specific point in time: *at the date of expiration*.

For simplicity, we will restrict our discussion to European options—that is, options that can be exercised only at their maturity date.[2] The value of a call option on the expiration date can be summarized as follows:

Condition	Value of Call Option
Market price of stock is greater than the exercise price	market price − exercise price of the option
Market price is less than the exercise price	0

This relationship is shown graphically in Figure 18.1. We see that as long as the market price of the stock *at the expiration date* is below the exercise price, the call option is worthless. But if the market price of the common stock is greater than the exercise price, the value of the call option is equal to $P_0 - X$. The coloured line in Figure 18.1 indicates the lower limit on the call option's value. The value of a call option at

Figure 18.1

The Value of a Call Option at Expiration

If the market price of the stock, P_0, is greater than the exercise price, X, then at expiration the value of the option (as given by the 45° line) is $P_0 - X$. Otherwise, the call option at expiration is worthless.

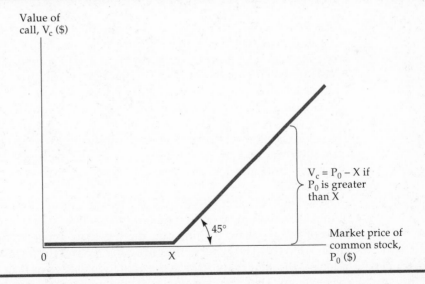

expiration is often written as

$$\text{value of call option at expiration, } V_c = \text{Max}(0, P_0 - X)$$

For example, assume you paid $300 [i.e., (100 shares)($3)] to purchase a May96 call option on 100 shares of Seagram with an exercise price of $42.50. The expiration date has now arrived. If the market price of Seagram common stock has increased and is now $47.50, while the exercise price is $42.50, you can exercise the option—purchase 100 shares at $42.50 per share—and immediately sell the shares at $47.50. The value of the option is (100 shares)($47.50 − $42.50) = $500. Your profit is equal to the value of the option of $500, less the $300 you paid for the option. Ignoring any commissions and taxes, your profit is $500 − $300 = $200. Alternatively, if the market price of Seagram common stock at the expiration date is $42.50 or below per share, you will throw the option away and incur a loss of $300.[3] The value of the call option on Seagram, V_c, at expiration is

$$100(P_0 - X) \quad \text{if } P_0 \text{ is greater than X}$$
$$0 \quad \text{if } P_0 \text{ is less than X}$$

Thus, we see that the relationship of the stock price to the exercise price determines whether an option has any value *at the expiration date of the option*. This condition is true for both call options and put options.

THE BUYER'S POSITION VERSUS THE SELLER'S POSITION

So far we have said that you can purchase an option, or, alternatively, you can write (sell) an option. There is a minor addition that needs to be made to what we said previously; this is to formally recognize the *option premium*. Although the potential benefit to the purchaser of a call option may be evident, why would anyone want to write or sell the option? (Remember, individuals write or sell options; the firm the option is on is *not* involved in creating the option.) The answer is that *on net* the seller expects to earn a profit. In the Seagram example above, the purchaser profits if at expiration the market price of Seagram is sufficiently above the exercise price to more than cover the cost of, or premium paid for, the option. This position is shown graphically in Figure 18.2 (a), where the price (or premium) paid per share for the option is $3.

How about the seller's position? For simplicity, assume the original writer, or seller, of the call option on Seagram common stock sold it for its current secondary market price of $3 per share. In this case the per share profit to the seller is shown in Figure 18.2 (b). The writer of the call option receives the premium and realizes a gain as long as the value of the stock at the expiration date is less than the exercise price *plus* the premium. Thus, the expiration date gain or loss to the buyer and to the writer are mirror images of each other. It is a zero-sum game, in which one can gain only at the expense of the other. Because only 10 to 15 percent of all stock options written end

---

[3] Thus, in order for the option holder to profit, the price of Seagram common stock has to be enough above the exercise price to cover the purchase price paid by the holder of the option; in this case, that price is $45.50.

Figure 18.2

Profit Opportunities for a Buyer and a Seller of a Seagram Call Option

With a premium of $3, the buyer profits if at expiration the price of Seagram common stock is above $45.50 otherwise the seller profits.

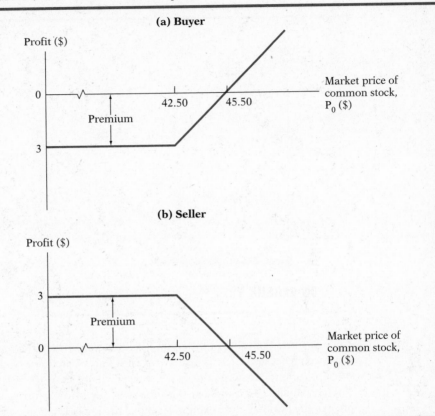

up being in-the-money at expiration, there are sufficient incentives for some individuals or investment dealers to write options.

Concept Review Questions

- Define an option.
- How do call options differ from put options?
- Define an in-the-money option and an out-of-the-money option.

VALUING EUROPEAN CALL OPTIONS

In the last section we discussed the value of the option on the expiration date. Now we need to determine how options are valued at times other than the expiration date.

Figure 18.3

The Value of a Call Option Before Expiration

The lower bound on the value is given by the solid coloured line. But, other things being equal, (a) the higher the price of the asset, P_0, (b) the longer the time to expiration, t, (c) the higher the risk-free rate, k_{RF}, or (d) the greater the variability, σ, the higher will be the value of the option, V_c, as indicated by the dashed line.

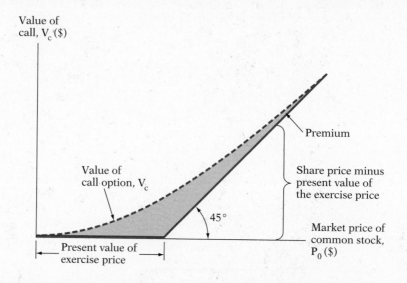

At these times the value of the option will be greater than the lower limit of its value. This occurs because there is risk: We do not know whether *at expiration* the value, or stock price in the case of options on stocks, will be above or below the exercise price. The probability of expiring in-the-money is one of the primary forces that keeps the price of the option before expiration above the lower limit of its value. Thus, the actual value of a call option *prior to the expiration date* will lie above the lower limit (given by $P_0 - X$, if P_0 is greater than X; or 0, if P_0 is less than X) shown previously in Figure 18.1. This is illustrated in Figure 18.3.

BASIC DETERMINANTS OF OPTION VALUES

The factors that determine an option's value can be broken down into two basic sets. The first relates to the option contract itself; the second relates to the underlying asset (or stock). The three factors related to the option contract that affect the option's value are the exercise price, the expiration date, and the level of interest rates, as indicated by the risk-free rate.

1. EXERCISE PRICE   Other things being equal, the higher the exercise price, the lower will be the value of a call option. This makes sense because the higher the

exercise price, the less likely it is that the market price of the underlying asset will be above the exercise price at the expiration date. As long as there is some probability that the price of the underlying asset will exceed the exercise price, however, the call option will have value.

2. EXPIRATION DATE   The longer the time until expiration, the higher the value of the call option. Thus, other things being equal, if you hold a six-month option and a one-year option, the one-year option is more valuable because there is more time for the market price of the underlying asset to fluctuate. This increase in time provides greater opportunity for the price of the underlying asset to move, and hence increases the value of the option.

3. RISK-FREE RATE   The level of interest rates also affects the value of call options. The reason is that the market price of the asset, P_0, is in today's dollars, while the exercise price is in future dollars. These must be stated at the same time, which is today, at time $t = 0$. Based on the time value of money, the present value of the exercise price is lower when the risk-free rate is high, and the present value of the exercise price is higher when the risk-free rate is low. Because the value of the call option is equal to at least the stock price, P_0, minus the *present value of the exercise price*, a call option is more valuable the higher the risk-free rate. Thus, the value of a call option is positively related to the level of interest rates, as measured by the risk-free rate.

In addition, two other factors related to the underlying asset also affect the value of call options. These are the price of the underlying asset and the variability (or riskiness) of the underlying asset.

1. ASSET PRICE   Other things being equal, the higher the price of the underlying asset, the more valuable the call option. This occurs because the higher the asset price is above the exercise price, the larger the return the owner of the option will reap at maturity.

2. VARIABILITY OF THE ASSET PRICE   Finally, the greater the variability of the underlying asset, the more valuable a call option will be. To see this, it is important to remember that a call option is valuable only when the market price of the underlying asset is greater than the exercise price. Call options on assets with greater price volatility will therefore be worth more, other things being equal. Consider two six-month call options, both with an exercise price, X, of $60, and a current market price, P_0, of $55. Let us assume the volatility of asset A is greater than that of asset B. The call option on asset A will be more valuable, because with more volatility there is more likelihood for A than for B that the value of the underlying asset will be above the exercise price. As a consequence, *no matter what the degree of risk aversion of an individual investor, we find high variability in the underlying asset desirable when valuing options.*

To summarize, the value of a call option is a function of five variables:

1. Price of the underlying asset, P_0
2. Exercise price, X
3. Time to expiration, t

4. Risk-free rate, k_{RF}
5. Variability[4] of the underlying asset, σ

Thus, the value of a call option, V_c, on a nondividend-paying stock, or asset, is

$$\text{value of call option, } V_c = f(P_0, X, t, k_{RF}, \sigma) \qquad (18.1)$$

where the plus (minus) sign by the variable indicates the effect of an increase in that variable on the price of the call option:

Variable	Effect of an Increase in Each Factor on V_c
Asset price, P_0	+
Exercise price, X	−
Time to expiration, t	+
Risk-free rate, k_{RF}	+
Variability of asset's return, σ	+

As long as it is before the expiration date, an increase in any of the following will cause the value of the call option to go up: the price of the asset, P_0; the time to expiration, t; the risk-free rate, k_{RF}; or the variability of the underlying asset, σ. Thus, increases in any of these four variables will cause the actual option value to be farther above the lower limit, as shown previously in Figure 18.3.

Likewise, decreases in the price of the underlying asset, the time to expiration, the risk-free rate, or the variability of the asset's return cause the dashed option value line in Figure 18.3 to snuggle closer to the solid lower-limit value line. For example, if a one-year option and a three-month option exist on the same asset and both have the same exercise price, their general relationship is shown in Figure 18.4.[5]

VALUING CALL OPTIONS THAT HAVE ONLY TWO POSSIBLE OUTCOMES

To understand how options are valued, we start with a situation in which there are only two possible outcomes. Then we will extend the discussion to value options that have many possible outcomes.

A Replicating Portfolio of Stock and Borrowing   Assume you want to value a call option that is good for one year to buy a share of stock of Xelab, Inc. The current price of Xelab is $50, the exercise price is $60, and the risk-free rate is 10 percent. To keep

---

[4] In the Black–Scholes model considered shortly, the variability is reflected by the standard deviation of the returns for the underlying asset, σ. For simplicity, we refer to the variability as the standard deviation, although in the binomial model considered in the next section the standard deviation is not *directly* calculated.

[5] The intercept of the diagonal 45° line in Figures 18.3 and 18.4 is equal to the present value of the exercise price. Not shown in either of these figures is that as time elapses and the option moves closer to its maturity, or expiration, date, the present value of the exercise price increases. Therefore, the diagonal 45° line actually shifts slightly to the right (while keeping the same slope).

Figure 18.4

The Value of a Call Option as the Time to Maturity Decreases

As the maturity date of the option draws nearer, the value of the option, other things being equal, snuggles closer and closer to the lower bound given by the solid coloured line.

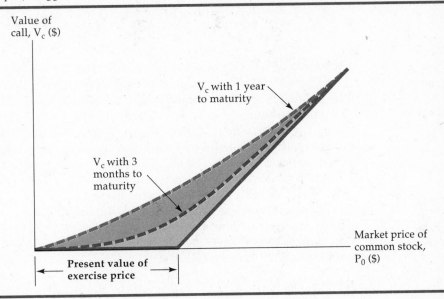

things simple, say there are only two possible outcomes—the price of Xelab will increase to $80 at the end of the year or it will decrease to $40—and the probability of each of the two outcomes is identical. If the price increases to $80, the call option is worth $80 − $60 = $20. On the other hand, if the price falls to $40, the call is worthless. Therefore, the possible payoffs are:

	Stock Price = $80	Stock Price = $40
One call is worth	$20	$0

Now consider what would have occurred if, instead of buying the option, you had purchased the stock directly and borrowed against it at 10 percent. *The amount of the borrowing is based on the lower stock price outcome*—in this case, $40. The size of the loan would have been $40/(1.10) = $36.36. Thus, you borrowed $36.36 (the principal) and will repay $40 (the principal plus interest) in one year. The possible payoffs from this strategy are:

	Stock Price = $80	Stock Price = $40
One share of stock is worth	$80	$40
Repay loan	−40	−40
Total payoff	$40	0

Note that when the stock price is $80 the payoff is $40 with the stock-and-loan transaction, but it is only $20 if the call is purchased. When the stock price is $40, the payoff is zero in both cases. The payoff of purchasing stock and taking out the loan is twice that of the payoff if the call is purchased. Therefore,

$$\text{value of two calls} = \text{original stock price} - \text{loan}$$
$$= \$50 - \$36.36 = \$13.64$$

If the value of two calls is equal to $13.64, then the value of a single call, V_c, is $13.64/2 = $6.82. For the case with only two outcomes, it is easy to value a call option. Along the way, we learned how to use the **binomial option pricing model**.

In order to value the call, we borrowed money and purchased stock in such a manner that we exactly replicated the payoff from the call option. This procedure creates a **replicating portfolio** whose payoff *exactly* matches the payoff from purchasing the call option directly. The number of shares of stock that are needed to replicate one option is called the **hedge ratio** (or **delta**). For Xelab, the hedge ratio is 1/2, because it took a half a share of stock to replicate the levered position indicated by the call option. If the total payoff with the stock-and-loan portfolio had been $60, instead of $40, the hedge ratio would then have been 1/3.

In this two-payoff case, the hedge ratio can be determined by comparing the possible spread of option prices with the possible spread of stock prices, so that

$$\text{hedge ratio} = \frac{\text{spread of option prices}}{\text{spread of stock prices}} = \frac{\$20 - \$0}{\$80 - \$40} = \frac{\$20}{\$40} = \frac{1}{2}$$

Let us stop for a minute and consider how we valued the call option on Xelab. Instead of valuing it directly, we saw that the value of the call option was equivalent to purchasing the underlying asset and borrowing against the asset. The only requirement in determining this replicating portfolio was that we employ the proper hedge ratio to make sure the position in the levered asset exactly matches the call option. This approach can be expressed as follows:

value of call option, V_c = (stock price)(hedge ratio) − present value of loan   (18.2)

where the present value of the loan in Equation 18.2 is the present value of the loan from before, adjusted by the hedge ratio. In the case of Xelab, the present value of the total loan is $36.36, and because we need only half a share of stock for the replicating portfolio, the appropriate value for the loan is ($36.36)(1/2) = $18.18. Using Equation 18.2, the value of the call option in this binomial, or two-outcome, world is

$$V_c = \$50(1/2) - \$18.18 = \$25 - \$18.18 = \$6.82$$

which is the same result we got before.

Likewise, if a call option does not exist on an asset, we now have the knowledge necessary to create a homemade call option. All you do is purchase the asset and borrow against it to replicate the position that would exist if a call option actually existed on the asset.

An Alternative Way to Value Options Consider one other aspect of our new-found knowledge about options. The value of the call option on Xelab is $6.82. What if the option did not sell for $6.82? Suppose, for example, it sold for $8? Then you can make a guaranteed profit with no risk by simply purchasing the stock, selling two call options, and borrowing $36.36. Likewise, if the call option sells for less than $6.82, you can make a guaranteed profit with no risk by selling the stock, buying two call options, and lending the balance of $36.36. This ability to profit is independent of your preference for risk. Remember the point we made earlier: No matter what your risk preferences, more volatility in the underlying asset is preferred because it leads to a higher option value. *The valuation of options does not depend on the risk preferences of individuals*; therefore, the simple assumption that all investors are risk neutral can be made.

This last insight leads to an alternative way to value call options; this is the **risk neutral** approach to option valuation. In our example, if the price of the option is either greater or less than $6.82, you can profit. The reason you profit is that if investors are risk neutral, the expected return from investing in Xelab stock is equal to the risk-free rate of interest, k_{RF}. Thus, the expected return from investing in Xelab is 10 percent. If we know the expected return is 10 percent, we can determine the probability of an upward or downward movement in the price of the stock. An increase to $80 is a 60 percent increase in value [i.e., ($80/$50) − 1 = 0.60 = 60 percent] from the current market price of $50; a fall in price to $40 is a decrease of 20 percent [i.e., ($40/$50) − 1 = −0.20 = −20 percent]. Therefore, the expected return from investing in Xelab is

$$\text{expected return} = \left(\begin{array}{c} \text{probability of} \\ \text{upward movement} \end{array} \right) \left(\begin{array}{c} \text{return from an} \\ \text{upward movement} \end{array} \right)$$
$$+ \left(\begin{array}{c} \text{probability of} \\ \text{downward movement} \end{array} \right) \left(\begin{array}{c} \text{return from a} \\ \text{downward movement} \end{array} \right)$$

$$10\% = (W)(60\%) + (1 - W)(-20\%)$$

Solving for W, the probability of an upward movement in the price of Xelab, we have

$$W = 30\%/80\% = 0.375$$

Thus, the probability of an upward movement in the price of Xelab to $80 is 0.375, while the probability of a downward movement to $40 is 1 − 0.375 = 0.625.[6]

---

[6] The general formula for determining the probability of an upward movement, W, is

$$\text{probability of upward movement, W,} = \frac{\text{interest rate} - \% \text{ downward change}}{\% \text{ upward change} - \% \text{ downward change}}$$

$$= \frac{0.10 - (-0.20)}{0.60 - (-0.20)} = 0.375$$

Now that we know the probability of an upward movement, W, in the stock price, we can calculate the expected value of the call option on Xelab in this risk neutral world. The expected value of the call option one year from now is

$$
\begin{aligned}
\text{expected value}_1 &= (\text{W})(\text{call value if stock price is \$80}) \\
&\quad + (1 - \text{W})(\text{call value if stock price is \$40}) \\
&= (0.375)(\$20) + (0.625)(\$0) = \$7.50
\end{aligned}
$$

This expected option value is one year hence. Therefore, it must be discounted back at 10 percent to determine the value of the call option today, which is

$$
\begin{aligned}
\text{value of call, } V_c &= \text{expected value}_1/(1 + k_{RF}) \\
&= \$7.50/(1.10) = \$6.82
\end{aligned}
$$

which is exactly the value we determined previously.

The previous discussion indicates there are two equivalent methods for valuing a call option. These are:

1. Determine the combination of the asset and borrowing that replicates the call option. Because the call option and the levered position in the asset must produce the same return, the call option and the replicating portfolio sell for the same price.
2. Determine the expected future value of the option and then discount it back to the present.

While this binomial, or two-possible-outcome, case appears simple, it contains virtually all of the underlying ideas needed in order to understand options and their valuation.[7]

VALUING OPTIONS THAT HAVE MANY POSSIBLE OUTCOMES

The previous example of Xelab assumed there were only two possible outcomes, or stock prices, and they occurred one year from now. What if we looked at six-month instead of one-year intervals? Then there would be more outcomes; those for the second six months would be contingent on what happened in the first six months. There is no reason to stop at six-month intervals—we could go to three-month intervals, one-month intervals, daily intervals, and even hourly intervals. Eventually we reach the place where prices change continuously and generate a continuous probability distribution of possible stock prices.

The Black–Scholes Option Pricing Model Although it seems like a major task to value options when prices change continuously, it really is straightforward. The **Black–**

---

[7] The binomial model can be extended to more possible outcomes, with those in successive periods being contingent on what occurs in the earlier periods. The basic approach is similar to what we have shown. See, for example, Cox and Rubinstein (1985) or Hull (1993).

Scholes option pricing model gives the correct expression for the value of European options on nondividend-paying stocks assuming continuous compounding. It consists of three equations. The primary one for valuing call options is

$$\text{value of call option, } V_c = P_0 N(d_1) - \frac{X}{e^{k_{RF}t}} N(d_2) \tag{18.3}$$

where

V_c = the value of the call option
P_0 = the current price of the stock
X = the exercise (or strike) price
t = time remaining before expiration of the option (expressed in decimal form as a portion of a year)
k_{RF} = continuously compounded risk-free rate of interest (in decimal form)
e = natural antilog of 1.00 or 2.71828
$N(d)$ = the probability that a standardized, normally distributed random variable will have a value less than or equal to d

The two subsidiary equations are

$$d_1 = \frac{\ln(P_0/X) + (k_{RF} + 0.5\sigma^2)t}{\sigma(t)^{0.5}} \tag{18.4}$$

$$d_2 = d_1 - \sigma(t)^{0.5} \tag{18.5}$$

where

$\ln(\ )$ = the natural logarithm of the number in parentheses[8]
σ = the standard deviation of the continuously compounded annual rate of return on the asset

Although Equation 18.3 looks complicated, it is simply a restated version of our replicating portfolio approach to valuing a two-outcome call option. Thus,

$$V_c = P_0 N(d_1) - \frac{X}{e^{k_{RF}t}} N(d_2)$$

stock   hedge   present value
price   ratio   of loan

Equation 18.3 employs exactly the same ideas we used to value a call option when only two outcomes existed. To determine the value of a call option, Black and Scholes simply employed the knowledge that the value of a call option has to be equal to an equivalent portfolio where $N(d_1)$ shares of stock are purchased and then borrowed

---

[8] When using your calculator to determine option values, be sure to note that ln means the LN key, as opposed to e, which means the e^x key.

against. As we saw previously in Equation 18.2, the value of the call option and the value of the equivalent replicating portfolio are one and the same.

Using the Black–Scholes Model To understand how to use the Black–Scholes model, it is best to start with an example. Assume the data are as follows:

P_0 = \$100 (current price of the stock)
X = \$90 (exercise price)
t = 6 months, or 0.50 of a year (maturity of the option)
k_{RF} = 10 percent, or 0.10 continuously compounded (annual risk-free rate)
e = 2.71828 (natural antilog of 1.00)
σ = 28 percent, or 0.28 (risk on a continuously compounded annual basis)

STEP 1: Calculate d_1 and d_2, rounding the answers to three decimal places:

$$d_1 = \frac{\ln(P_0/X) + (k_{RF} + 0.5\sigma^2)t}{\sigma(t)^{0.5}}$$

$$= \frac{\ln(100/90) + [0.10 + 0.5(0.28)^2]0.50}{(0.28)(0.50)^{0.5}}$$

$$= \frac{0.1054 + 0.0696}{0.1980} = \frac{0.1750}{0.1980} = 0.884$$

$$= d_2 = d_1 - \sigma(t)^{0.5} = 0.884 - 0.198 = 0.686$$

STEP 2: Compute $N(d_1)$ and $N(d_2)$ using a cumulative normal distribution function table (Table B.5, at the end of the book). To use this table, locate the number closest to the value of d in the appropriate d column. In our case d_1 = 0.884, and the closest tabled value is for 0.88, which gives a value for $N(d_1)$ of 0.811. Similarly, d_2 = 0.686, and the closest tabled $N(d_2)$ value (for 0.69) is 0.755.

STEP 3: Determine the value of the call option, V_c. This is done using the main equation (Equation 18.3) as follows:

$$V_c = P_0N(d_1) - \frac{X}{e^{k_{RF}t}}N(d_2) = \$100(0.811) - \frac{\$90}{e^{(0.10)(0.50)}}(0.755)$$

$$= \$81.10 - \$64.64 = \$16.46$$

The value of this call option with six months to maturity is approximately \$16.46.

In the Black–Scholes option pricing model, the value of an option on a nondividend-paying stock, or asset, is determined by the five variables discussed earlier: the current price of the asset, P_0; the stated exercise price, X; the current risk-free rate, k_{RF}; the time to expiration of the option, t; and the standard deviation of the asset, σ. When calculating options on stocks, we know the price, stated exercise price, and time to maturity. The current risk-free rate can be estimated based on the yield on Canadian treasury bills with the same time to maturity as the option. The only unknown is the standard deviation of the stock price, for which a starting value is typically estimated by determining the past variability in the stock's return.[9]

The most difficult part of the option pricing model to understand is given by Equations 18.4 and 18.5. Once these calculations are made, they are then used to estimate probabilities of occurrence. This is exactly the part of the Black–Scholes model that takes account of risk.

The Black–Scholes model indicates that

$$V_c = P_0 N(d_1) - \frac{X}{e^{k_{RF}t}} N(d_2)$$

The term $X/e^{k_{RF}t}$ is simply the present value of the exercise price when continuous discounting is employed. This means that the value of a call option is

$$V_c = P_0 N(d_1) - (\text{present value of } X)N(d_2)$$

The terms involving cumulative probabilities are the terms that take account of risk. If the stock had little or no risk (i.e., a very small standard deviation, σ), the calculated values for d_1 and d_2 would be large, and the probabilities would both approach the value of 1. If $N(d_1)$ and $N(d_2)$ both equal 1, then the option pricing model can be simplified to

$$V_c = P_0 - \text{present value of } X$$

which, as shown in Figures 18.3 and 18.4, is the lower bound on the value of a call option before the expiration date. (As always, if P_0 is less than the present value of X, then the option has a value of zero.) Thus, the expressions $N(d_1)$ and $N(d_2)$ capture the risk involved in the option. They are what cause the actual value of the option (as shown previously by the dashed lines in Figures 18.3 and 18.4) to be greater than the lower bound (i.e., the solid coloured line).

To derive their model, Black and Scholes made a number of assumptions:

1. There are no transactions costs or taxes.
2. The risk-free rate is constant over the life of the option.
3. The stock market operates continuously (both day and night).
4. The stock price is continuous; that is, there are no sudden jumps in price.
5. The stock pays no cash dividends.
6. The option can be exercised only at the expiration date (i.e., it is a European option).

---

[9] An alternative approach is to determine the *implied* standard deviation. If we take the actual market price on a call option, say yesterday's quoted price, and insert it into Equation 18.3, we know every variable except the standard deviation. The implied standard deviation necessary to produce the actual option price yesterday can then be determined. This procedure could be employed using data for some previous time period, or periods, to estimate the implied standard deviation. Then this implied standard deviation could be used to calculate today's market price for the call option.

7.   The underlying stock can be sold short without penalty.
8.   The distribution of returns on the underlying stock is lognormal.

Although some evidence exists that the Black–Scholes model tends to undervalue in-the-money options and overvalue out-of-the-money options, the model is still a good predictor of actual option prices. Upon first acquaintance with the Black–Scholes option pricing model, many think it is too complicated to be useful. Nothing could be farther from the truth. The Black-Scholes option pricing model, and the binomial option pricing model, have gained wide acceptance for valuing all kinds of options.[10]

Shortcuts for Valuing Call Options   The Black–Scholes formula is precise, but it requires considerable calculation, as shown in the three-step procedure discussed earlier. However, if our objective is to determine an *approximate* value of an option, it is simpler to use tables. Consider the same example used earlier in which

$$P_0 = \$100$$
$$X = \$90$$
$$t = 0.50$$
$$k_{RF} = 0.10$$
$$\sigma = 0.28$$

A simple procedure can be employed to find the approximate value of this call option:

STEP 1:   Calculate the standard deviation times the square root of time:

$$\sigma(t)^{0.5} = (0.28)(0.50)^{0.5} = 0.198$$

STEP 2:   Calculate the market price divided by the present value of the exercise price:

$$\frac{P_0}{x/e^{k_{RF}t}} = \frac{\$100}{\$90/e^{(0.10)\,(0.50)}} = 1.168$$

STEP 3:   Using the two values from steps 1 and 2, determine the tabled factor and multiply it by the share price.

Rounding to 0.20 for the standard deviation times the square root of time and to 1.16 for the market price divided by the present value of the exercise price, Table B.6 (in the back of the book) provides a value of 0.163. Multiplying the stock price of $100 by 0.163, we have the price of the call option, V_c, which is $16.30. This corresponds to the value of $16.46 determined earlier. Although use of these tables is not completely precise, it is close enough, because our emphasis is on understanding option pricing and valuation.

Concept Review Questions

■ Describe the three factors related to the option contract and the two factors related to the underlying asset that affect the value of an option.

---

[10] Other option pricing models exist. In practice, options that cannot be valued using the Black–Scholes model can often be valued by a more elaborate formulation of the binomial approach considered earlier.

- Describe how to use the binomial option pricing model to price a call option.
- How are the Black-Scholes option pricing model and the binomial option pricing model similar?
- Describe the three steps used when pricing an option using the Black-Scholes option pricing model.

Put Options

Up to now we have focused on call options, which are options to purchase. We also know that put options, which are the right, but not the obligation, to sell an underlying asset at a specific price for a predetermined period of time, also exist. The same five factors discussed previously for call options—the market price of the underlying asset, P_0; exercise (or strike) price, X; time to expiration, t; risk-free rate, k_{RF}; and standard deviation of the underlying asset's returns, σ—also affect the value of a put. The value of a put, V_P, *at maturity* is shown in Figure 18.5. As can be seen, the value of the put option at expiration is:

$$
\begin{array}{ll}
0 & \text{if } P_0 \text{ is greater than } X \\
X - P_0 & \text{if } P_0 \text{ is less than } X
\end{array}
$$

Figure 18.5

The Value of a Put Option at Expiration

If the market price of the asset, P_0, is less than the exercise price, X, then the value of the option at expiration (as given by the 45° line) is $X - P_0$. Otherwise, the put is worthless.

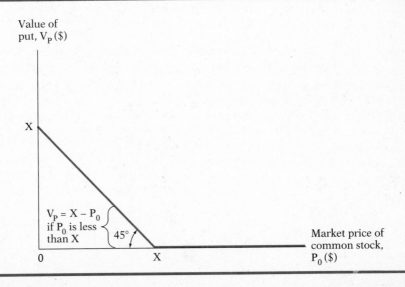

This is often written as

$$\text{value of put option at expiration, } V_p = \text{Max } (0, X - P_0)$$

Hence, for a put option the relationship is just the reverse of a call option. The put option has value only at its expiration date if the market price of the stock is *less* than the exercise price.

Although a put option is affected by the same five factors as a call option, the impact of an increase in each variable on the value of the put is somewhat different, as follows:

Variable	Effect of an Increase in Each Factor on V_p
Asset price, P_0	−
Exercise price, X	+
Time to expiration, t	either[11]
Risk-free rate, k_{RF}	−
Variability of asset's return, σ	+

As with a call option, the actual value of a put option, V_p, will be above the lower limit depicted in Figure 18.5, except at its expiration date.

VALUING EUROPEAN PUT OPTIONS

European put options, like European call options, can be exercised only at maturity. Once you know the value of a call option with a specific exercise price, determining the value of a put option is easy.[12] It is given by

$$\text{value of put option, } V_p = V_c + \frac{X}{e^{k_{RF}t}} - P_0 \tag{18.6}$$

where V_p is the value of the European put option, and the rest of the terms are as defined before. For our example, with a call option value of $16.46, the value of a put

---

[11] As t increases, normally V_p increases; but if the price of the underlying asset, P_0, is a good deal below the exercise price, X, then as t increases, V_p actually decreases.

[12] The principle of the put–call parity states that the value of a call option, plus the present value of the exercise price, equals the value of the put option plus the market price of the underlying asset, or

$$V_c + \frac{X}{e^{k_{RF}t}} = V_p + P_0$$

Therefore,

$$V_p = V_c + \frac{X}{e^{k_{RF}t}} - P_0$$

option (with everything else the same) is

$$V_p = V_c + \frac{X}{e^{k_{RF}t}} - P_0$$

$$= \$16.46 + \frac{\$90}{e^{(0.10)\,(0.50)}} - \$100 = \$16.46 + \$85.61 - \$100 = \$2.07$$

The reason for the relatively low value of the put option is the relationship of the market price of the stock to the exercise price. The call option can be exercised (i.e., has value) as long as the market price remains above the exercise price of $90. However, this put option becomes valuable only if the current market price drops by more than $10, so it is less than the exercise price of $90. In our example, the market price of the common stock is above the exercise price; consequently, the put option is not very valuable.

SHORTCUTS FOR VALUING PUT OPTIONS

Instead of employing Equation 18.6 to value the put option, we can use Table B.7 (in the back of the book). From our earlier calculations, $\sigma(t)^{0.5} = 0.198$ while $P_0/(X \div e^{k_{RF}t}) = 1.168$. Going to Table B.7, we find the tabled value is 0.025. Multiplying by the market price of $100 produces $2.50, which compares closely with the $2.07 calculated earlier.[13]

Throughout our discussion of options and their valuation, we have considered options that are written on the common stock of a firm. However, options exist in many forms; often the underlying asset is not common stock. Thus, the underlying asset could be crude oil, gold, the German mark, or one of many other assets. Hence, the ideas and application are general and are applied in many different settings. We will explore a number of these applications in the next chapter.

---

[13] We can also value European options on dividend-paying stocks. If only one known cash dividend is expected to be paid before the expiration of the option, the equations are

$$V_c^* = \left(P_0 - \frac{D}{e^{k_{RF}t^*}}\right)N(d_1) - \frac{X}{e^{k_{RF}t}}N(d_2)$$

and

$$V_P^* = V_c^* + \frac{X}{e^{k_{RF}t}} - P_0 + \frac{D}{e^{k_{RF}t^*}}$$

where

D = the cash dividend that will be paid before the expiration date
t^* = the time (in decimal form) in years until the dividend is expected to be paid

and the other terms are as defined before. If more than one cash dividend is expected before the expiration of the option, then the expression $D/e^{k_{RF}t^*}$ must be modified to reflect the present value of all known dividends to be paid before expiration of the option. Cash dividends tend to reduce the value of call options and to increase the value of put options.

Concept Review Questions

- What is a put option, and when is it valuable upon expiration?
- Describe how the value of a put option and the value of a call option are related.

KEY POINTS

- Options provide the right, but not the obligation, to buy (a call option) or sell (a put option) a particular asset for a limited time at a specified price.
- An in-the-money option has value if exercised at maturity; an out-of-the-money option has no value if exercised.
- Options are created, or sold, by investors, investment dealers, and the like. Other things being equal, the seller and the buyer are playing a zero-sum game; the profit (loss) to one party equals the loss (profit) to the other.
- The value of an option on a nondividend-paying stock, or asset, is a function of: (a) the price of the underlying asset, (b) the exercise price, (c) the time to expiration, (d) the risk-free rate, and (e) the variability of the underlying asset.
- Risk preferences are not important in valuing options. Any increase in the variability of the returns on the underlying asset leads to an increase in the price of the option.
- Both the binomial and the Black–Scholes models can be employed to value options. In either case the value of a call option = (the asset's price)(hedge ratio) − the present value of a loan (on the underlying asset).

QUESTIONS

18.1   What determines the lower limit on the value of a call option at expiration? Before expiration?

18.2   What incentives are there for buyers to purchase options and for writers to sell options? How does the premium enter into their decision process?

18.3   What five factors affect the value of a call option? How would a decrease in their level, other things being equal, affect the value of a call option?

18.4   Explain why risk is desirable when investing in options. How do the terms $N(d_1)$ and $N(d_2)$ capture this risk?

18.5   Discuss replicating portfolios and the hedge ratio. How do they enter into the valuation of call options when there are two possible outcomes? When there are many possible outcomes?

18.6   How do puts differ from calls? Why is a decrease in the market price of the underlying asset desirable if you hold a put option, but not desirable if you hold a call option?

18.7   Explain how an increase in any of the five factors determining a put option's value affects the value of the put option.

18.8   How do cash dividends affect the value of a call option? A put option?

CONCEPT REVIEW PROBLEMS

See Appendix A for solutions.

CR18.1   Attempting to make a quick profit, Jana paid $300 for a call option on 100 shares of TI stock with an exercise price of $55.00; she also paid $200 for a put option on 100 shares of ABM stock with an exercise price of $60.00 per share. What is Jana's total dollar profit if at the expiration date TI stock closed at $54 per share and ABM stock closed at $49 per share?

CR18.2 Tyco Company has a current stock price of $60 per share. Because of potentially profitable but risky capital budgeting decisions, the company's stock price will (with equal probability) either increase to $90 per share or drop to $50 per share at the end of one year. The cost of borrowing is 8 percent. Using the replicating portfolio approach, find the price of a call option for 100 shares of Tyco stock.

CR18.3 Using the risk neutral approach to option valuation, value the option in CR18.2.

CR18.4 Xerox's current stock price is $85 with a 0.30 instantaneous standard deviation of returns. The current nine-month risk-free rate is 6 percent. Using the Black–Scholes model, what is the value of a nine-month call option with an exercise price of $90?

CR18.5 Using the information in CR18.4, what is the price of a put option with an exercise price of $90 and nine months to expiration?

PROBLEMS

18.1 Prices for Cott common stock options listed by Canadian Derivatives Clearing Corp. appeared as follows in the Canadian Equity Options section of *The Globe and Mail*:

Cott Series	$11.00 Bid	Ask	Last	308 Volume
Jun96 $9 p	0.05	0.15	0.15	20
$10	1.45	1.65	1.45	60
$12	0.50	0.55	0.50	20
Jul96 $12	0.80	1.00	0.85	30
$13	0.60	0.75	0.70	20
Sep96 $12	1.25	1.45	1.35	30
$13	0.95	1.15	1.05	40
Jan97 $10 p	1.30	1.80	1.40	8
$14 p	3.60	4.10	3.65	20
Jan98 $8 p	1.15	1.60	1.60	20
$14 p	4.45	4.95	4.60	40

a. Which call options are in-the-money? Which put options?
b. For June 1996 calls, explain why the call price decreases as the exercise price increases. For January 1997 puts, why does the put price increase as the exercise price increases?
c. For both calls and puts, explain why the option price increases as the date of exercise increases.
d. What other factors influence an options value? In what direction?

18.2 A one-year option exists with an exercise price of $100. The current price of the stock is $80, and the two possible, equally likely, outcomes for the stock price at the end of the year are $120 or $60. The risk-free rate is 8 percent.
a. Using the replicating portfolio approach, determine the value of the option. What is the hedge ratio? What does the hedge ratio signify?
b. Now using the risk neutral approach, determine the probability that the stock will increase in price (or decrease in price). Now determine the value of the option using the risk neutral approach.

c. Why is the value of the option the same using either the replicating portfolio approach or the risk-neutral approach?

18.3 You just purchased a call option on a stock. The two possible equally likely outcomes in one year are $150 and $75, the exercise price is $100, and the current market price is $90. What is the value of the call option if the risk-free rate is

a. 12 percent?
b. 6 percent?

18.4 An option exists that has two equally likely outcomes in one year of $98 and $44. The current market price is $65, and the risk-free rate is 7 percent. What is the value of the call option, assuming everything else is equal, if the exercise price is

a. $70?
b. $60?

18.5 The current market price of Erie Trucking is $60, the exercise price is $65, the risk-free rate is 10 percent, and the two possible equally likely stock prices of Erie's common stock in one year are $95 and $35. What is the value of a call option on Erie's stock if

a. The prices are at time t = 1?
b. The prices are at t = 2?

18.6 The common stock of Martin is selling at $80.

a. If the exercise price is $70, k_{RF} = 0.12, and σ = 0.26, what is the value of (1) a three-month call option and (2) a six-month call option?
b. If the common stock price remains at $80, k_{RF} at 0.12, and σ at 0.26, what is the value of a *three-month* call option on Martin if the exercise price is (1) $60 or (2) $80?

18.7 The current market price of a share of stock is $50. A three-month call option exists on the stock with an exercise price of $55; the standard deviation is 0.40.

a. What is the value of the call option if the risk-free rate is (1) 0.15 or (2) 0.05? Why does the value of the call option decline as interest rates fall?
b. What is the value of the call if the risk-free rate is 0.15 and everything is the same as before except the standard deviation increases to 0.60?

18.8 The base case for Hercules Ground is as follows:

P_0 = $34	t = 0.60
X = $30	σ = 0.20
k_{RF} = 0.10	

a. Calculate the base-case value of a call option on Hercules Ground.
b. Calculate the value of a call option on Hercules Ground if the price increases by 50 percent. Do the same if each variable (i.e., X, k_{RF}, t, and σ) increases by 50 percent while the rest of the variables remain as in (a). In which variable is the call price of Hercules Ground most sensitive to a 50 percent increase? Least sensitive?
c. What is the value of the call option if all the variables in (a) *simultaneously* increase by 50 percent?

18.9 The common stock of Michelson Mutual is selling at $50.

a. What is the value of a three-month put option on Michelson if the risk-free rate is 0.08, a similar call option is valued at $2, and the exercise price is $60?
b. What is the value of the put option if everything remains the same as in (a), except the risk-free rate increases to 0.16, causing the call option's value to become $2.27?

c. What if everything is the same as in (a), except the current stock price is $45, causing the call option's value to become $0.86?

18.10   The following applies for a call option:

$P_0 = \$35$	$t = 0.65$
$X = \$40$	$\sigma = 0.20$
$k_{RF} = 0.11$	

a. Determine the value of a call option on the stock.
b. What is the value of a put option?
c. What is the value of the call option if the time to maturity drops to 0.30?

18.11   A stock sells for $70, the exercise price is $80, the time to maturity is 0.40, the risk-free rate is 0.09, and the standard deviation is 0.30.
a. What is the value of a call option on the stock?
b. What is the value of a put option?
c. If the market price of the stock increases to $85, what is the value of (1) the call option? (2) the put option?

18.12   Jordan Enterprises common stock has a current market value of $55. An option that will expire in 150 days exists. The risk-free rate is 8 percent, the exercise price is $75, and the standard deviation of Jordan's common stock returns is 0.90. (*Note*: Assume a 365-day year.)
a. What is the value of a call option on the stock?
b. What is the value of a put option?
c. The Bank of Canada just took action that unexpectedly increased interest rates to 15 percent. What is the new value of the call option? Of the put option?

18.13   In celebration of your birthday, your best friend gave you an option that expires in six months on 100 shares of Westerfield's common stock. Westerfield's, a very stable firm, is selling for $32, the exercise price is $25, the risk-free rate is 7 percent, and the standard deviation of Westerfield's stock returns is 0.25.
a. Do you have a strong preference whether the option is a call or a put? Why? What is the value of the call? The put?
b. Now assume that Westerfield's pays cash dividends. Without working it out, indicate why you are better off when cash dividends are paid in one case (the call or the put) whereas you are not better off in the other (i.e., the put or the call).

18.14   Hyper is a risky stock that just started paying cash dividends. The stock's price is $60, the exercise price is $55, the risk-free rate is 0.14, σ is 0.80, and the maturity of the option is 0.40 of a year. The next cash dividend will be $1 and will be paid in 0.20 of a year.
a. What is the value of a call option on Hyper (1) without cash dividends and (2) with cash dividends? (*Note*: See footnote 13 for the proper equations when cash dividends are present.)
b. What is the value of a put option on Hyper (1) without and (2) with cash dividends?

18.15   Mini Case   You have been hired by Century Resources to conduct a seminar on options and told to assume that the attendees know little or nothing about options. Therefore some combination of discussion and problems is appropriate.
a. Explain what options are. Be sure to differentiate between call and put options and between American and European options. Also, what do in-the-money and out-of-the-money mean with respect to call options and put options?

b. Discuss the factors that determine the value of any option. What specific effect do they have on the value of a call option? Of a put option? What about cash dividends on the stock if an option exists on that stock?

c. To introduce options you will employ the binomial option pricing model. Suppose a stock has a current market price of $40 and at the end of one year its price may with equal likelihood increase to $65 or decrease to $25. The exercise price is $45, and the risk-free rate of interest is 9 percent. Show how the value of the option can be determined, using first the replicating portfolio approach and then the risk neutral approach. Be sure to indicate to the seminar participants the hedge ratio and its importance in the replicating portfolio approach.

d. Explain how the Black–Scholes option pricing model is similar to the replicating portfolio approach employed to value the stock in (c). What variables are known, and what variables have to be estimated to employ the Black-Scholes model? What about an individual's attitude towards risk?

e. The following information has been gathered about a stock: The current market price is $65, the exercise price is $75, the time to maturity is six months (or 0.50 of a year), the risk-free rate is 9 percent, and the standard deviation is 0.55. What is the value of a call option on the stock? Of a put option?

f. What is the value of the call option from (e) if everything remains the same except:
1. The current market price is $55?
2. The exercise price is $65?
3. The maturity is three months?
4. The risk-free rate is 5 percent?
5. The standard deviation is 0.30?
   (*Note:* Consider each part separately.)

REFERENCES

BLACK, FISCHER, and MYRON SCHOLES. "The Pricing of Options and Corporate Liabilities." *Journal of Political Economy* 83 (May–June 1973): 637–654.

BUNCH, DAVID S., and HERB JOHNSON. "A Simple and Numerically Efficient Valuation Method for American Puts Using a Modified Geske–Johnson Approach." *Journal of Finance* 47 (June 1992): 809–816.

COX, JOHN, and MARK RUBINSTEIN. *Options Markets.* Englewood Cliffs, N.J.: Prentice-Hall, 1985.

GAGNON, LOUIS. "Empirical Evidence of the Canadian Government Bond Options Market." *Canadian Journal of Administrative Sciences* 11 (March 1994): 2–11.

HULL, JOHN C. *Options, Futures, and Other Derivative Securities,* 2nd ed. Englewood Cliffs, N. J.: Prentice-Hall, 1993.

JOHNSON, HERB, and DAVID SHANNO. "Option Pricing When the Variance Is Changing." *Journal of Financial and Quantitative Analysis* 22 (June 1987): 143–151.

PERRAKIS, STYLIANOS. "Option Pricing for Multinomial Stock Returns in Diffusion and Mixed Processes." *Canadian Journal of Administrative Sciences* 10 (March 1993): 68–82.

PERRAKIS, STYLIANOS, and PETER RYAN. "Options on Thinly Traded Stocks: Theory and Empirical Evidence." *Canadian Journal of Administrative Sciences* 11 (March 1994): 24–42.

19

Option Applications in Financial Management

EXECUTIVE SUMMARY

The joint claims of shareholders and bondholders on the firm can be analyzed in an option context. The shareholders' claim is simply a call option. In essence, shareholders have bought the firm's assets, borrowed the present value of the bondholders' claims on the firm, and bought a put (or default) option that allows them to walk away from the firm and give it to the bondholders. The default option arises from the limited liability aspect of stock ownership; that is, shareholders are liable for only what they invest directly.

Firms create value by making positive net present value investment decisions. The option pricing context shows that restructuring or simply reacting to changing economic conditions is likely to shift value from shareholders to bondhholders, or vice versa, but not create value.

Numerous options are hidden in all capital investments. The initial decision to proceed or not is an option. Likewise, the decision to continue with an ongoing project as opposed to terminating it is also an option. The contingent purchase of an asset, the ability to expand in the future, and the ability to delay making an investment are all call options that have value. Likewise, any abandonment opportunity, guarantee, loan, or insurance policy contains elements of put options. Knowing and understanding these options is an essential element in making value-enhancing investment decisions.

Options can also be used effectively to hedge against interest rate and foreign exchange risk while providing more flexibility than swaps, forward contracts or futures contracts. The added flexibility occurs because the options market provides the firm with the choice of exercising the option or letting it expire. Increasingly, financial managers are using a variety of products, loosely called "derivatives," to reduce costs and insulate the firm from some of the financing and operating risks to which it is exposed.

STOCK IS JUST A CALL OPTION

In Chapter 4 we considered how to value both bonds and stock based on the present value of their future cash flows. Although this approach is widely used, it has one major shortcoming: It fails to consider the simultaneous interaction between the value of a firm's stock and its bonds. Using the knowledge we just acquired about valuing options in Chapter 18, we can value the financial claims on a firm *and* take account of the interaction between the value of the firm's stock and its debt.

In a very informal way in Chapter 1 we employed option concepts to depict the value of the claims of both shareholders and bondholders on the firm. This representation is shown in Figure 19.1. The claim, or payoff, for the shareholders at the maturity of the debt is simply a call option, as shown in Figure 19.1 (a). The bondholders, on the other hand, provide long-term debt financing for the firm. Suppose the bondholders lend the firm money that *at its maturity date* is worth X dollars. As shown in Figure 19.1 (b), the bondholders have a fixed, but limited, claim on the assets and value of the firm. If the value of the firm, V, is greater than the bondholders' claim when the debt matures, the debt will be paid off and the shareholders gain control of the remaining assets of the firm. The dual claims of both shareholders and bondholders on the firm are shown in Figure 19.1 (c). The total value of the firm, V, is simply the sum of shareholders' claims, S, and bondholders' claims, B, or

total value of firm = shareholders' claims + bondholders' claims   (19.1)

$$V = S + B$$

Let us now develop these ideas in a more formal way, using the Black–Scholes option pricing model. To keep things clear, it helps to restate what calls, the current stock price, puts, and the exercise price are once we consider valuing the joint claims of shareholders and bondholders on the firm. Thus,

Value of calls and puts $\longrightarrow$	Value of equity and debt
V_c	S: the market value of the equity claims on the firm
P_0	V: value of the firm's assets
V_p	Default option: the value of the limited liability of shareholders; that is, the value of the shareholders' right to walk away from the debt of the firm and hand the firm over to the creditors.
$\dfrac{X}{e^{k_{RF}t}}$	B (riskless): the present value of the promised payments to zero-coupon bondholders, discounted at the risk-free rate; the value of the bonds if there is no risk of default.

When we are valuing the claims of both shareholders and bondholders, the shareholders' claim, S, is simply a call option on the value of the firm, V, so

shareholders' claim, S = call option on firm value

= total value of firm − bondholders' claim

= V − B

Figure 19.1

The Payoff to Shareholders and Bondholders

Shareholders have a call option on the assets of the firm. At maturity of the debt, if the value of the assets is greater than the bondholder claims, shareholders will pay off the bondholders and claim the remaining value of the firm.

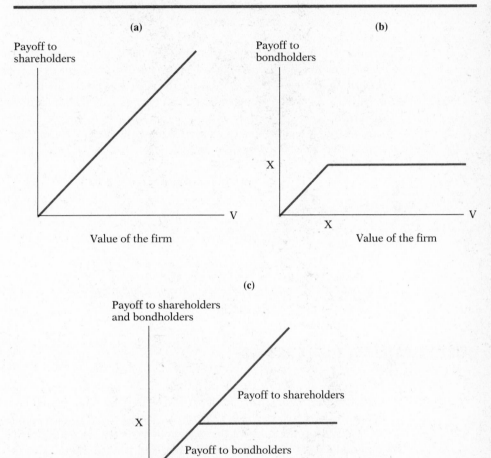

So far this is just a restatement of Equation 19.1. However, in an option pricing context, two separate items exist in place of the single risky claim of the bondholders, B. The first is equivalent to the risk-free present value of the exercise price. This value is what the bondholders' claim would be worth *if* there were no risk that the shareholders might default and turn the firm over to the bondholders. The second is the default, or put option, held by the shareholders. Due to limited liability, if the firm gets into serious financial difficulties, the shareholders have the option to walk away from the firm and turn it and all of its remaining assets and liabilities over to the creditors. Thus, the risky bondholders' claim, B, is equal to their riskless claim minus the default option which lowers the value of their riskless bonds, so that

bondholders' risky claim, B = bondholders' riskless claim
− default option

$$B = B(riskless) − default\ option \qquad (19.2)$$

Putting this all together, we see that the shareholders' claim is simply

$$shareholders'\ claim,\ S = V − B(riskless) + default\ option \qquad (19.3)$$

In effect, the shareholders have bought the firm's assets, borrowed the present value of the bondholders' riskless claims on the firm, and bought a put (or default) option that allows them to walk away from the firm and give it to the bondholders. The default option can be thought of as a loan guarantee that eliminates default risk for the shareholders.

Similarly, the market value of the risky bondholders' claim on the firm, B, may be determined by using either Equation 19.1:

$$bondholders'\ risky\ claim,\ B = V − S$$

or Equation 19.2:

$$bondholders'\ risky\ claim,\ B = B(riskless) − default\ option$$

From the bondholders' standpoint, the value of the put (default) option can be thought of as a *default risk discount* that bondholders apply to the current market value of the firm's riskless debt.

JOINT VALUATION OF EQUITY AND DEBT

An example might be helpful at this point. Zeffers, a well-known chemical firm, has a total market value, V, of $500; it has $400 face value of eight-year zero-coupon bonds; the risk-free rate is 0.12; and the annual standard deviation of Zeffers' assets is 0.40. What is the value of the shareholders' claim on Zeffers? What is the value of the bondholders' risky claim on Zeffers? And what is the value of the default option held by the shareholders?

To determine the value of the shareholders' claim we first need[1] d_1 and d_2. They are

$$d_1 = \frac{\ln(V/face\ value\ of\ bonds) + (k_{RF} + 0.05\sigma^2)t}{\sigma(t)^{.05}}$$

$$= \frac{\ln(500/400) + [0.12 + 0.5(0.40)^2]8}{0.40(8)^{.05}}$$

$$= \frac{0.2231 + 1.600}{1.1314} = \frac{1.8231}{1.1314} = 1.611$$

$$d_2 = d_1 − \sigma(t)^{.05} = 1.611 − 1.131 = 0.480$$

---

[1] Although Table B.6 could be employed, in this example we use Table B.5 for slightly greater precision.

From Table B.5, the cumulative distribution table, $N(d_1)$ is 0.946 and $N(d_2)$ is 0.684. The value of the stock is

$$S = VN(d_1) - \frac{\text{face value of debt}}{e^{k_{RF}t}} N(d_2)$$

$$= \$500(0.946) - \frac{\$400}{e^{(0.12)(8)}} (0.684)$$

$$= \$473.00 - \$104.76 = \$368.24$$

Because the total value of Zeffers is $500, the shareholders' claim of $368.24 is equal to about 74 percent of the total value of the firm.

Once we know the total value of the firm, which is $500, and the value of the shareholders' claim, which is $368.24, we can determine the value of Zeffers' bondholders' risky claim. This is

$$B = V - S = \$500 - \$368.24 = \$131.76$$

In order to determine the value of the default (or put) option, we need to determine the value of the riskless claim held by bondholders on the firm. Assuming continuous discounting, the present value of the zero-coupon bonds is equal to

$$B(\text{riskless}) = \frac{\$400}{e^{k_{RF}t}} = \frac{\$400}{e^{(0.12)(8)}} = \$153.16$$

Thus, if there were no risk of the shareholders defaulting and not paying off the bonds when they mature, the zero-coupon bonds would be worth $153.16. Using Equation 19.2, we find that the default option is

$$B = B(\text{riskless}) - \text{default option}$$
$$\$131.76 = \$153.16 - \text{default option}$$
$$\text{default option} = \$153.16 - \$131.76 = \$21.40$$

The default, or put, option held by Zeffers' shareholders has some value, but because the likelihood of severe financial difficulty (as shown by a large standard deviation) is not great, the option's value is limited.

Viewing the claims of shareholders and bondholders in an option context provides a number of important insights. Because stock is simply a call option on the firm's assets, we know that, other things being equal, the equity will become *more* valuable as:

1. The value of the firm's assets increases.
2. The size of the debt claim (i.e., the exercise price) decreases.
3. The maturity of the debt increases.
4. Interest rates increase.
5. The volatility of the firm's assets increases.

Similarly, viewing the value of a bond in an option-pricing framework indicates that, other things again being equal, the value of the bondholders' risky holding (i.e., B) will become *less* valuable when:

1. The value of the firm's assets decreases.
2. The promised payment (or size of the claim) decreases.[2]
3. The maturity of the debt grows longer.[3]
4. Interest rates increase.[4]
5. The volatility of the firm's assets increases.

To understand the effect on the claims of both shareholders and bondholders, consider a change in one of the variables that affects the value of call and put options—the volatility of the underlying asset.

WHAT IF RISK CHANGES?

With the sudden and unexpected death of Zeffers' founder, control has passed to the heirs, Sabestin and Dorothy. Being tired of the chemical business, they have just sold off more than half of the existing firm and acquired two biotech firms. Although the value of the firm's assets and the amount and maturity of its debt remain the same, the restructuring has resulted in more risk, as reflected in the more-than-doubling of the standard deviation of the firm's assets, from 0.40 to 0.85. Who wins and who loses with this restructuring?

Without making any calculations, we know that the stock of Zeffers is just a call option. As with any call option, more risk is desirable; that is, increases in risk result in a higher value for the owner of a call option. Thus, the shareholders should benefit from this restructuring. Who loses? Because the total value of the firm is unchanged (at least for the present), Zeffers' bondholders must lose. With no change in the value of the firm, the only way shareholders can benefit is if there is a transfer of value from Zeffers' bondholders to its shareholders.

To make sure our intuition is correct, let us determine the effect of the restructuring. Again, we need d_1 and d_2, which are now

$$d_1 = \frac{\ln(500/400) + [0.12 + 0.5(0.85)^2]8}{0.85(8)^{.05}}$$

$$= \frac{0.2231 + 3.8500}{2.4042} = \frac{4.0731}{2.4042} = 1.694$$

$$d_2 = 1.694 - 2.404 = -0.710$$

---

[2] If the promised payment (or exercise price) decreases, the present value of the zero-coupon bond, B(riskless), decreases. This effect has to be considered along with the change in the value of the put option when the value of the risky bond claim, B, is valued.

[3] Like reducing the exercise price, lengthening the maturity decreases the present value of the zero-coupon bond.

[4] Like reducing the exercise price and lengthening the maturity, raising the interest rate reduces the present value of the zero-coupon bond.

From Table B.5, $N(d_1)$ is 0.954 and $N(d_2)$ is 0.239. The value of Zeffers' stock is now

$$S = \$500(0.954) - \frac{\$400}{e^{(0.12)(8)}}(0.239)$$

$$= \$477.00 - \$36.60 = \$440.40$$

The new value of Zeffers bondholders' risky claim is

$$B = V - S = \$500 - \$440.40 = \$59.60$$

and the default option held by the shareholders is

$$\text{default option} = \$153.16 - \$59.60 = \$93.56$$

The effects are as follows:

Party/Claim	Value When $\sigma = 0.40$	$\sigma = 0.85$	Who Wins/Loses?
Shareholders	$368.24	$400.40	Gain of $72.16
Bondholders	131.76	59.60	Loss of $72.16
Default option	21.40	93.56	Gain of $72.16

The restructuring clearly benefited the shareholders, while the bondholders lost; value flowed away from the bondholders and towards the shareholders. The default, or put, option is also much more valuable. With the much higher level of risk, the likelihood of default has increased. If things take a turn for the worse, the limited liability feature of stock ownership is now more valuable than it was previously.

The message from viewing the shareholders' and bondholders' claims in an option framework is clear: *Unless additional value is created, the gains to one party (owners or creditors) come from losses incurred by the other party (creditors or owners).* A corollary to this conclusion is: *Value creation comes from making positive net present value investment decisions; restructuring or simply reacting to changing economic conditions is likely to shift value from one party to the other but not create value.*

ONE FINAL POINT

Those of you who have been reading very carefully might have noticed a possible inconsistency between our earlier discussion in Chapter 5 and the discussion in this chapter. In Chapter 5, when viewed in the context of the dividend valuation model and the capital asset pricing model (see the section entitled "Changes in Risk and Prices"), we said that, other things being equal, as risk increases, the market price of common stock decreases. Yet in the Zeffers example just discussed, when viewed in an option pricing context, *increases in risk increased the value of the shareholders' claim, and hence the price of common stock.* Which is correct?

In answering this question, it is important to keep two points in mind. First, the option pricing model simultaneously values both the stockholder and the bondholder claims, whereas the dividend valuation/CAPM approach focuses solely on the equity of the firm. Second, and more important to the current discussion, is the statement "other things being equal." Zeffers sold off half of its existing assets and used the proceeds to acquire two biotech firms. While risk (in the form of the standard deviation of the firm's assets) more than doubled, Zeffers' expected growth would also be expected to increase due to the nature of the biotech industry. To illustrate why there may be no inconsistency, assume the following conditions existed for Zeffers before the acquisition of the biotech firms:

$$
\begin{array}{ll}
k_{RF} = 8\% & g = 3\% \\
k_M = 15\% & D_1 = \$2 \\
\beta = 0.90 &
\end{array}
$$

Given this information, we can use the capital asset pricing model to estimate shareholders' required return, k_s, as

$$k_s = k_{RF} + \beta(k_M - k_{RF}) = 8\% + 0.90(15\% - 8\%) = 14.3\%$$

The price of Zeffers' stock before the acquisition of the biotech firms was

$$P_0 = \frac{D_1}{k_s - g} = \frac{\$2}{0.143 - 0.03} \approx \$17.70$$

What might have happened with the asset change? Suppose that β increased to 1.20 and the growth rate increased to 6 percent. Then the new required return would be

$$k_s(\text{new}) = 8\% + 1.20(15\% - 8\%) = 16.4\%$$

and the new market price would be

$$P_0 = \frac{\$2}{0.164 - 0.06} \approx \$19.23$$

Because *other things did not stay constant* (i.e., the growth rate, g, increased) there is no conflict between the prediction from the option pricing model and the dividend valuation/CAPM approach from Chapter 5. The lesson is simple: Use common sense, and make sure you do not miss something obvious by blindly applying financial models. The models we present throughout the book are just a convenient means of organizing our thought processes—and encouraging us to ask the right questions at the right time when making financial decisions. As such, financial models are a means to an end, rather than an end in themselves.

Concept Review Questions

- Using the concept of options, describe the pricing of a firm's stock and bonds.
- Using an option pricing context, describe what would happen to the value of shareholders' and bondholders' claims if the overall risk of a firm decreases.
- Comment on the following statement: The value of a firm can be increased by simply restructuring the firm.
- Does an inconsistency exist between the capital asset pricing model and the option pricing model when analyzing the relationship between a stock price and the risk of a firm?

CALL OPTIONS IN CAPITAL INVESTMENT DECISIONS

Options exist in many of the investment and financing decisions a firm makes. We will now examine some of the uses of option pricing theory in helping to make capital investment decisions; however, we do so in a simplified (i.e., Black–Scholes or simple binomial model) world. The same basic ideas, but with more complications than we illustrate, can be employed to more accurately determine the value of more complex options faced by firms. The main thrust is an understanding that *today's decision may depend on what options are available tomorrow.*

OPTIONS TO INVEST

An example of a call option is an option to buy another firm. Assume your firm is privately held and is embarking on some exciting new developments. If these developments are successful, you will need extensive marketing expertise you do not currently have. The outcome of the current developments should be known within a year. To protect yourself, you enter into an option to purchase Associated Wholesalers. The current market price of Associated is $56 per share, the risk-free rate is 0.11, the estimated standard deviation of Associated's stock is 0.20, and the exercise price (or contingent purchase price in one year) is $66. The first thing is to recognize that this option has all of the elements of any other option. In addition, it is a call option because you have the opportunity, but not the obligation, to buy Associated Wholesalers in one year.

What is the per share value of this call option? To find out, we can employ our three-step procedure from Chapter 18:

$$\sigma(t)^{0.5} = (0.20)(1)^{0.5} = 0.2000$$

$$\frac{P_0}{X/e^{k_{RF}t}} = \frac{\$56}{\$66/e^{(0.11)(1)}} = 0.9471$$

The tabled value from Table B.6 is 0.054, so the value of the option to invest is $56(0.054) = $3.02 per share. That is the price you should pay per share for the option to buy Associated Wholesalers in one year.

Figure 19.2

Option Value of Follow-On Opportunity

The ability in the future to accept or reject the follow-on investment is a call option. Ignoring this option understates the value creation potential of the original capital investment.

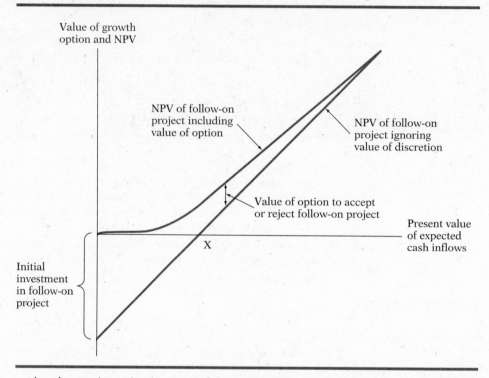

Another option exists in many of the traditional capital investments undertaken by a firm. These investments, as we saw in Chapters 7 and 8, can often be expanded upon, modernized, replaced, or abandoned. Decisions such as these are contingent on the present values of the future cash flows that result if the options are exercised. Thus, *if capital expenditures are made now, they often create opportunities to make additional capital expenditures in the future*. These future opportunities are, in effect, options that exist only if the current capital project is undertaken. As such, they are sometimes referred to as **growth options**. Previously we have discussed the idea of the present value of growth opportunities (PVGO). Figure 19.2 depicts the option-like aspects of these follow-on growth opportunities that exist in many capital investment projects, where the horizontal axis is the present value of the expected cash inflows and X is the initial investment in the follow-on opportunity.

To deal with these follow-on opportunities we need what many, especially in industry, refer to as the **strategic NPV**, which is

$$\text{strategic NPV} = \text{original NPV} + \text{value of follow–on opportunity} \quad (19.4)$$

For an option to make additional capital expenditures, the strategic NPV is

$$\text{strategic NPV} = \text{original NPV} + \text{follow-on call option}$$

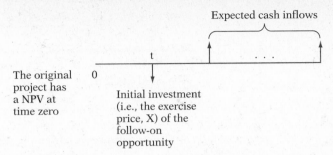

The original project has a NPV at time zero

0

Initial investment (i.e., the exercise price, X) of the follow-on opportunity

Expected cash inflows

By undertaking the original project, the firm gains the right, but not the obligation, to make a follow-on investment at time t in the future. The follow-on opportunity is simply a call option. The exercise price, X, for this follow-on option is the initial investment required at time t to undertake the follow-on project. The present market price, P_0, of the follow-on opportunity (needed in order to value the call option) is determined in a two-step procedure. First, the expected cash *inflows* from the follow-on project are discounted back to time t at the appropriate opportunity cost of capital. (Note that if we subtracted the follow-on project's initial investment at time t from the present value of the follow-on project's cash inflows, we would have the NPV of the follow-on project. *But the NPV of the follow-on project is not directly needed.*) Second, we then further discount the expected cash inflows back to time zero, to determine the current market value, P_0, of the expected cash inflows of the follow-on investment.

Consider Sanders Electronics, which is eyeing the rapid developments in automated receders. If it invests now, the NPV of a two-year project at the appropriate discount rate is −$45 million. Hence, Sanders's initial decision is to reject the move into automated receders. However, you point out that if Sanders does not make the present investment, expertise and opportunity may be lost due to competitors getting the jump on Sanders. You project that in two years a new generation of automated receders can go on-stream. The NPV of this additional, or contingent, project that could be undertaken in two years is $60 million, based on discounted cash inflows at time t = 2 of $800 million and an initial investment at time t = 2 of $740 million. In this light, the initial investment in the original negative NPV project creates a call option. If the results from the first two years are great, then Sanders exercises the follow-on investment option and proceeds; otherwise, it walks away from automated receders. If Sanders does not act now, however, the costs and time delays may be prohibitive in the future.

The key to the decision turns out to be the accuracy of the second NPV (in two years) of $60 million. Because automated receders may be risky, the actual NPV realized could be substantially more or less than $60 million. First, let us assume that the risk of automated receders is low, with a standard deviation of 0.10. Also, the risk-free rate is 0.09. The decision is then based on the following analysis.

First, we estimate the value of the call option. The time is two years; the value of the follow-on investment *today* (i.e., P_0) is the cash inflow of $800 million (expected in two years) discounted back to the present at the opportunity cost of capital of 0.20, or $800/e^{(0.20)(2)} = 536.26 million.[5] The exercise price is the investment required in

---

[5] For consistency we will use continuous discounting to move the cash inflows and cash outflows around when the Black–Scholes option pricing model is employed.

two years, which is $740 million. Thus, we see that

$P_0 = \$536.26$ million	$k_{RF} = 0.09$
$X = \$740$ million	$\sigma = 0.10$
$t = 2$ years	

Using the three-step option valuation procedure, the value today of this call option to invest two years from now is

$$\sigma(t)^{0.5} = (0.10)(2)^{0.5} = 0.1414$$

$$\frac{P_0}{X/e^{k_{RF}t}} = \frac{\$536.26}{\$740/e^{(0.09)(2)}} = 0.8676$$

From Table B.6, the tabled value is 0.013, and the value of the call option (to expand in two years) is $536.26 million(0.013) = $6.97 million.

The total value of the opportunity to invest in automated receders is its strategic NPV, which is equal to the sum of the first NPV that exists today plus the option to make the second investment in two years, or

$$\text{strategic NPV} = -\$45.00 \text{ million} + \$6.97 \text{ million} = -\$38.03 \text{ million}$$

If the variability of the returns from the second investment in automated receders is expected to be low, then Sanders should not enter this field.

Consider what happens, however, if the variability of expected returns from the second investment has a standard deviation of 0.32 (instead of 0.10 assumed previously). Using our three-step procedure, we have

$$\sigma(t)^{0.5} = (0.32)(2)^{0.5} = 0.4525$$

$$\frac{P_0}{X/e^{k_{RF}t}} = \frac{\$536.26}{\$740/e^{(0.09)(2)}} = 0.8676$$

From Table B.6, the tabled value is 0.122, and the value of the option to expand is ($536.26 million)(0.122) = $65.42 million. The strategic NPV = −$45 million + $65.42 million = $20.42 million. In this case, Sanders should proceed with the investment in automated receders.

What should you finally recommend? It all depends on how valuable the follow-on growth opportunities are expected to be. The key variable, and one that is hard to determine, is just how risky the follow-on opportunity is. Other things being equal, the more the variability in the follow-on opportunity's returns, the more valuable the call option becomes. Thus, as we noted in Chapter 9, risk may be beneficial in many capital budgeting decisions. Once an option pricing framework is employed, we see that greater risk (as shown by a larger standard deviation in the contingent project's returns) leads to a higher option value. Although there may be more risk, there is also the potential for substantially higher NPV projects.

OPTIONS TO DEFER

In addition to options to make follow-on investments, other situations exist in which the firm has the option of investing now or waiting until some time in the future to make the investment. Previously, our decision rule was simple: If the project has a positive NPV it should be accepted. However, life is more complicated, and often more information is gained by waiting (perhaps for additional test marketing, technological developments, changes in economic conditions, or to see what the competition does). In such cases the option to delay is valuable. The option-like aspects of this option to delay starting a project are shown in Figure 19.3.

Consider the example of Electroanalysis, which is investigating the launching of a new product. The product can be introduced today, or it can be delayed for one year. If it is introduced today, the initial investment is $90; the present value of the expected after-tax cash inflows of $10 per year in perpetuity at an opportunity cost of capital of 10 percent is $100. Hence, the product has a NPV of $10 as follows:

$$NPV = \frac{\$10}{0.10} - \$90 = \$100 - \$90 = \$10$$

Figure 19.3

Option Value of Delaying

Some capital investments are now-or-never projects. But those that can be delayed contain a call option, which has value.

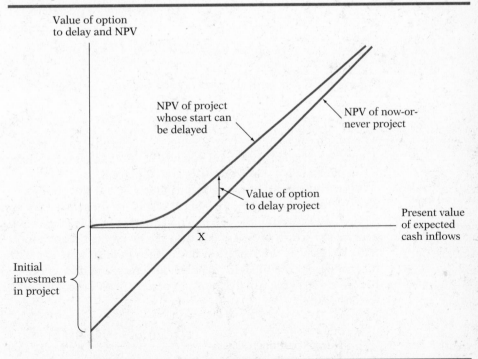

The value of the option to invest in the project today is simply $10. Thus, by investing $90 the firm immediately exercises the option to undertake the project today. But Electroanalysis knows there are major uncertainties about the product that should be resolved within the next year. To analyze this option to delay making the investment, we employ the binomial option pricing model from Chapter 18. The intermediate cash inflow is the after-tax cash inflow (or opportunity cost) from the project during the first year.

If the questions about the new product are resolved positively, the after-tax cash flow at time t = 1 will be $20 in perpetuity, and the present value of the project's after-tax cash inflows will be $20/0.10 = $200. The incremental return *above the total present value* of the cash flows of $100 if the investment is made right now is [($20 + $200)/$100] − 1 = 120 percent. Thus, if things turn out well, the incremental return is substantial.

But there is also a strong chance that the potential of the new product will not be realized. If things do not go well, the after-tax cash flow at time t = 1 will be $6, and the present value of the project's cash inflows will be $6/0.10 = $60. The incremental return in this case will be [($6 + $60)/$100] − 1 = −34 percent. So far we have not said anything about the probabilities associated with the two different possible outcomes. If the risk-free interest rate is 6 percent, assuming risk neutrality (as discussed in Chapter 18), the expected return from this investment is equal to the risk-free rate of 6 percent. So,

$$\text{Expected return} = \begin{pmatrix} \text{probability of} \\ \text{good outcome} \end{pmatrix} \begin{pmatrix} \text{return from} \\ \text{a good outcome} \end{pmatrix}$$
$$+ \begin{pmatrix} \text{probability of} \\ \text{bad outcome} \end{pmatrix} \begin{pmatrix} \text{return from} \\ \text{a bad outcome} \end{pmatrix}$$

$$6\% = (W)(120\%) + (1 - W)(-34\%)$$

Solving for W, the probability of a good outcome, we have

$$W = 40\%/154\% = 0.2597 \approx 0.26$$

Thus, the probability of a good outcome is about 26 percent, while the probability of a bad outcome is 1 − 0.26 = 0.74, or 74 percent.

What is the value of the option at time t = 1 if the good outcome occurs? The returns are $200 versus the investment of $90, so the value of the option is $110 (i.e., $200 − $90). What if the bad outcome occurs? In that case, the option has no value because the return of $60 is less than the investment required, or exercise price, of $90. To calculate the expected value of the option at time t = 0, we take the probability of occurrence times the possible outcomes, and discount them from time t = 1 back to t = 0 at the risk-free rate of 6 percent. Thus, the value of the option to defer for one year is

$$\text{Value of option to defer} = \frac{(\$110)(0.26) + (\$0)(0.74)}{1 + 0.06} = \$26.98 \approx \$27$$

If Electroanalysis defers investing in the product for one year, the value of the option to defer is $27. This is compared to the value of the option to invest right now, which is $100 − $90 = $10. What should Electroanalysis do? The decision is simple. The fact that the proposed product has a positive NPV today is not a sufficient reason for investing. The firm should wait one year and then either invest or exercise the option not to invest in the product.

Numerous other illustrations of call options exist in capital investments. Thus, an option to purchase land or any other asset is simply a call option. The opportunity cost of diverting excess capacity to some other use can be determined using option ideas. A series of operating decisions—to increase or reduce production, to expand the existing plant, to temporarily shut down a line or a plant—are all options that require managerial attention. Likewise, compound options exist—such as research and development projects—that may lead to new investment opportunities and affect the value of existing growth opportunities.

Viewed from an option standpoint, the greater the proportion of the firm's value that is dependent on the value of future discretional investments, the higher the risk of the firm's stock, other things being equal. Thus, a high-tech firm (such as one in the biotech industry) which has a large portion of its value accounted for by the present value of growth opportunities (PVGO), has higher stock risk than a mature firm whose value is largely dependent on the present value of the assets in place.

Concept Review Questions

- Describe some options available to management when making capital budgeting decisions.
- What is a strategic NPV, and how is it calculated?
- How would you proceed in analyzing an option to defer?

PUT OPTIONS IN CAPITAL INVESTMENT DECISIONS

In addition to call options, there are also put options in capital investments. We will consider two—options to abandon in the future and guarantees.

FUTURE ABANDONMENT DECISIONS

When a firm has the option to abandon a capital investment some time in the future, this is simply a put option. Assume your firm is making the investment in a new division (at time t = 0) that is expected to have a positive net present value of $1,000,000. But if cash inflows are low at the end of the first year, the firm plans to abandon (i.e., sell) the project for an after-tax cash inflow of $5 million. The present value at time t = 0 of the cash flows expected after year 1 is $6.5 million, the risk-free rate is 0.12, and the standard deviation of the project, assuming no abandonment, is 0.55. Thus,

$$P_0 = \$6.5 \text{ million} \qquad k_{RF} = 0.12$$
$$X = \$5 \text{ million} \qquad \sigma = 0.55$$
$$t = 1 \text{ year}$$

Using the three-step procedure, the value of the option to abandon (i.e., a put option) is

$$\sigma(t)^{0.5} = (0.55)(1)^{0.5} = 0.5500$$

$$\frac{P_0}{X/e^{k_{RF}}} = \frac{\$6.5}{\$5/e^{(0.12)(1)}} = 1.4657$$

From Table B.7, the tabled value is 0.067, and the value of the option to abandon is $6.5 million(0.067) = $435,500. The ability to get out of the proposed project has value. This has to be taken into consideration when calculating the project's net present value.[6] The strategic NPV including this option to abandon the project in the future is

$$\text{strategic NPV} = \$1,000,000 + \$435,500 = \$1,435,500$$

In Chapter 8 we discussed how to proceed when the issue was that of abandoning *today*, versus continuing to operate. In that case the value of the option to abandon today is simply the difference between the present value of the cash flows from continuing to operate and the after-tax proceeds from selling the assets. Now we can add to that calculation because we know how to proceed when abandonment in the future is also a possibility. In general, the option of abandoning is always available to firms. Too often this option is implicitly or explicitly ignored. Firms, however, should "cut and run" when the value of the firm is greater without the assets than it is with the assets.

Other examples of put options exist for firms. A common one is insurance coverage that is taken out on physical or human assets of the firm; this is simply a put option that can be exercised by the firm under certain conditions.

GUARANTEES

The final put option we will consider is more difficult, but the general issue involved is widespread because it deals with the topic of guarantees. A guarantee—whether granted by a firm, a financial institution, or a government—provides a floor, or exercise price, under which the cash flows cannot fall. There are many examples of guarantees that creep into financial transactions. Consider Megamarkets, which is

---

[6] In general, the valuation of abandonment options becomes more complicated because they may be exercised at the end of year 1, year 2, and so forth. This more general approach views the option to abandon as an American put on a dividend-paying stock, in which both the dividend payments and exercise price are uncertain. Numerical approximation techniques are required to value the general abandonment option.

planning to divest its textiles division to Modern Fabrics. To facilitate the sale, Megamarkets guarantees that the cash flows from the textiles division will not fall below $6 million for each of the next three years. The question is, how much extra should Megamarkets charge for this cash flow guarantee?

To determine the value of this guarantee, two items need to be considered. First, we need the actual forecasted cash flows and related information. Second, we need to recognize that the cash flow guarantees are simply a *series* of put options for which $6 million is the exercise price. If the forecasted cash flows are as follows, and the appropriate discount rate for the guarantees is 25 percent, then the present value, P_0, for each of the forecasted cash flows is

Year	Forecasted Cash Flow (in millions)	Present Value (at 25 percent) of Forecasted Cash Flows Employing Continuous Discounting (in millions)
1	$4.50	$4.50/e^{(0.25)(1)} = \$3.50$
2	5.50	$5.50/e^{(0.25)(2)} = 3.34$
3	8.00	$8.00/e^{(0.25)(3)} = 3.78$

If the standard deviation of the annual cash flow changes is 0.40 per year and the risk-free rate is 0.09, then

Year	Standard Deviation Times the Square Root of Time	Price (or Asset Value) Divided by the Present Value of the Exercise Price	Value of Guarantee (in millions)
1	$(0.40)(1)^{0.5} = 0.4000$	$\dfrac{\$3.50}{\$6/e^{(0.09)(1)}} = 0.6383$	$(0.691)(\$3.50) = \$2.42$
2	$(0.40)(2)^{0.5} = 0.5657$	$\dfrac{\$3.34}{\$6/e^{(0.09)(2)}} = 0.6665$	$(0.529)(3.34) = 1.77$
3	$(0.40)(3)^{0.5} = 0.6928$	$\dfrac{\$3.78}{\$6/e^{(0.09)(3)}} = 0.8253$	$(0.404)(3.78) = \underline{1.53}$
			Value of guarantee = $5.72

Using Table B.7 for valuing put options, the tabled values are entered in the last column to the right above and multiplied by the present value (or current market value) of the cash flow guarantees. In pricing the textile division, Megamarkets should add $5.72 million to the price quoted because of the cash flow guarantees provided to Modern Fabrics. Failure to do so results in an underpricing of the worth of the textiles division and associated guarantees.

Numerous other examples of guarantees exist for firms. Any loan made by firms to subsidiaries or other parties (other than the government, where there should be no risk) can be decomposed into a default-free loan and a loan guarantee, as follows:

$$\text{risky loan} = \text{default-free loan} - \text{loan guarantee}$$

Thus, any time a firm offers a loan, or guarantees debt issued by a subsidiary, an option exists. In addition, many firms employ swap contracts (as discussed in Chapters 11 and 17) to hedge some of the firm's risk. Guarantees exist in swap contracts. Thus, we see that many different guarantees exist that firms must understand. Keep looking, and you will find many more options, both in decisions that firms make and in everyday life.

Concept Review Questions

- What are some management capital investment decisions that can be modelled as put options?
- Explain what a guarantee is and how it can be valued.

USING OPTIONS TO MANAGE INTEREST RATE RISK

Options can also be employed to help firms deal with interest rate risk. Options on interest rates, which allow their owners to buy or sell bonds at a prearranged price, are available both on organized exchanges and over-the-counter from banks and other financial institutions. In addition, options on interest rate futures, called **futures options**, are widely available on some basic financial instruments such as government bonds, notes, and treasury bills, on Eurodollars, and on LIBOR.

Many uses are made of options or option-like features to reduce or manage interest rate risk. Consider a firm that is arranging long-term financing at a floating rate with a financial institution. The reason for doing so may be that floating interest rates are currently substantially lower than the firm could obtain if it employed fixed-rate financing. But the firm is concerned about its possible interest rate risk exposure if rates increase dramatically. One solution is to arrange with the financial institution to put an **interest rate cap** on the financing. An interest rate cap is nothing more than an option on the interest rate. It sets an upper bound on how high the floating interest rate can go. For example, the firm might arrange financing that will never go above 12 percent during the life of the agreement, no matter what happens to short-term interest rates.

Similarly, the firm may cut the cost of floating-rate financing by agreeing to put an **interest rate floor** on how low the interest rate may fall. This is just another option that can be incorporated into the financing agreement. Thus, the firm could agree that the interest rate on the loan would never fall below 7 percent, no matter how low short-term interest rates fall. If both a cap and a floor exist, the firm has entered into an **interest rate collar**, which constrains both how much and how little the floating-rate financing will cost the firm.

Other uses of options to hedge interest rate risk exist. A "participating cap" is structured for the user who needs a cap but is unwilling or unable to pay the up-front cost of the cap. Another is the "caption," which is simply a call option on a cap. Finally, there is the "swaption," which is an option on a swap. These and many other techniques have been developed in recent years as firms, and financial institutions serving them, figure out new ways to control some of the interest rate risk exposure.

As with any other type of hedge, the use of options to hedge interest rate risk is not costless. Firms have to continually evaluate their risk exposure, determine how much the value of the firm will be adversely affected as interest rates change, and determine whether the benefits of hedging outweigh the costs. In the last few years firms have become much more financially sophisticated in terms of planning for and hedging some of their interest rate risks.

Concept Review Question

- How can an option be used to reduce interest rate risk?

HEDGING USING CURRENCY OPTIONS

In Chapter 17 we discussed the use of the foreign exchange market to offset foreign exchange risk. Firms may also use currency options to hedge against foreign exchange risk. The currency options market operates in a manner similar to the foreign exchange futures market, except it allows the firm the choice of exercising the option or letting it expire. Table 19.1 presents some recent quotes on foreign exchange options listed on the Philadelphia Exchange for the British pound and the Swiss franc against the U.S. dollar.

Exchange-traded options are also available on the Philadelphia Exchange for the U.S. dollar versus the Australian dollar, the Canadian dollar, the German mark, and the Japanese yen. They are also available between the pound and the mark and between the mark and the yen. In addition to the Philadelphia Exchange, foreign exchange options are also available on the International Monetary Exchange (IMM), at the Chicago Mercantile Exchange, and on exchanges in London, the Netherlands and Singapore. Over-the-counter options can be obtained from banks or investment dealers against a number of other currencies, and for different amounts. Employing the basic ideas developed for valuing options using the Black–Scholes model, foreign currency options can be valued.[7] We will leave this issue to others and, instead, focus on using options to hedge a firm's foreign exchange risk exposure.

To illustrate options, let us use the British pound as an example. The contract is for £31,250. The last spot price of the pound, quoted in cents per pound, was 156.58, or $1.5658 per pound. The first column in Table 19.1 indicates the various exercise (or strike) prices available—they range from 155 (or $1.55) to 170 ($1.70). The second column lists the month in which the option expires. These range from May to September. The next two columns indicate the volume and last price for call options on the British pound. As we see, there are calls available for strike prices from 155 to

---

[7] The pricing of foreign exchange options is more complicated than discussed in Chapter 18. The share price, P_0, becomes the exchange rate. Then, instead of one interest rate, there are two—one for the domestic currency and one for the foreign currency. Finally, because the foreign interest rate is like a cash dividend, that complication also has to be taken into consideration. See, for example, Garman and Kohlhagen (1983).

Table 19.1

Some of the Foreign Exchange Options Listed in a Recent Issue of *The Wall Street Journal*

These options are listed on the Philadelphia Exchange. There are also options on the U.S. dollar versus the Australian dollar, the Canadian dollar, the French franc, the German mark, the Japanese yen, and the Swiss franc listed on the Philadelphia Exchange.

		Calls		Puts	
		Vol.	Last	Volume	Last
British Pound					156.58
31,250 Britsh Pounds—cents per unit					
155	May	21	2.12	110	0.60
155	Jun	2	3.55	4	2.00
155	Sep	8	5.20	—	—
$157\frac{1}{2}$	Jun	20	2.32	—	—
$157\frac{1}{2}$	Sep	80	3.97	—	—
160	May	10	0.40	—	—
160	Jun	2	1.35	—	—
165	Jun	10	0.42	—	—
$167\frac{1}{2}$	Jun	30	0.26	—	—
170	Jun	10	0.12	—	—
Swiss Franc					70.55
62,500 Swiss Francs—cents per unit					
68	Sep	—	—	5	1.27
$69\frac{1}{2}$	May	44	1.40	—	—
70	May	10	1.02	5	0.39
70	Jun	10	1.45	—	—
70	Sep	2	2.34	9	2.10
$70\frac{1}{2}$	May	—	—	3	0.52
71	May	107	0.42	100	0.74
71	Jun	13	1.01	—	—
72	Sep	10	1.50	—	—
73	Jun	38	0.42	—	—
75	Jun	2	0.14	—	—

170. For the June call with a strike price of $157\frac{1}{2}$, the volume was 20 and the price was 2.32 cents per pound. The last two columns provide the same information for puts.

BUYING A CALL

Assume we have a U.S. subsidiary of a Canadian firm that has purchased goods from a British manufacturer, with payment in the amount of £4,000,000 to be made in June. At the current spot rate of $1.5658 (from Table 19.1), the amount due *if settlement were today* is (4,000,000)(1.5658) = $6,263,200. What might happen when payment is made if the subsidiary does not hedge? Assume the spot rate at settlement is

---

1.53   The outflow is (4,000,000)(1.53) = $6,120,000. The subsidiary does not want to hedge.

1.59   The outflow is (4,000,000)(1.59) = $6,360,000. The subsidiary wants to hedge.

The subsidiary is concerned about the U.S. dollar weakening against the pound, which would make the actual spot price more than $1.5658 when payment is due. The size of the option is 31,250 British pounds per contract, so in order to hedge the subsidiary could purchase 4,000,000/31,250 = 128 June call options with a strike price of $157\frac{1}{2}$ (or $1.575). The cost of the option (from Table 19.1) is 2.32 cents per pound, so the cost per option is (31,250)($0.0232) = $725. With 128 options required, the total cost of the hedge is (128)($725) = $92,800. If the dollar weakens just a little against the pound, stays the same, or strengthens, the subsidiary will let the hedge expire; the cost to the subsidiary is simply the cost of the hedge, or $92,800.

What happens when payment is due if the U.S. dollar has weakened and is now trading at 1.64? The cash outflow to the subsidiary if they had not hedged would be (4,000,000)(1.64) = $6,560,000, which is $296,800 (i.e., $6,560,000 − $6,263,200) greater than indicated by the spot rate of exchange when the purchase was made. But, by buying the call, the subsidiary can lock in the cost of the £4,000,000 at $157\frac{1}{2}$, for an outlay of $6,300,000. The net cost to the subsidiary, compared with no change in the spot rate of exchange, is $6,300,000 − $6,263,200 = $36,800 plus the cost of the option of $92,800, for a total of $129,600. While the subsidiary did not fully offset the weakness in the dollar, at least it cut its loss from $296,800 if they had gone unhedged to $129,600. To obtain a "better" outcome, the subsidiary could have purchased a call with a lower strike price, but the cost of the call would have increased substantially.

BUYING A PUT

Instead of having to pay funds in another currency, our subsidiary might be selling goods to a British firm, with the payment to be made in pounds. Say the amount of the sale was £3,400,000. At the current spot rate of exchange of 1.5658, the dollar amount to be received is $5,323,720. What might happen when payment is received if the subsidiary does not hedge? Assume the spot rate at settlement is, again,

---

1.53   The inflow is (3,400,000)(1.53) = $5,202,000. The subsidiary wants to hedge.

1.59   The inflow is (3,400,000)(1.59) = $5,406,000. The subsidiary does not want to hedge.

To hedge, the subsidiary could purchase $3,400,000/31,250 = 108.8 \approx 109$ June put options with an exercise price of 155. Note that because the number of contracts does not come out to an even number, even under the best of circumstances a perfect hedge is not possible. The cost per option (from Table 19.1) is 2 cents per pound, so the total cost is $(31,250)(\$0.02)(109) = \$68,125$. If on settlement day the spot rate of exchange is 155.5, or 1.555 cents per pound, the subsidiary throws the option away; it is out the price of the option. However, if the dollar had weakened, the subsidiary would have benefited by being hedged.

OTHER CONSIDERATIONS WHEN USING CURRENCY OPTIONS

Currency options are similar to insurance against adverse movements in exchange rates. They can hedge part or all of the risk involved and at the same time allow the firm to benefit if exchange rates move in the firm's direction. Thus, one advantage currency options have over forward contracts, futures, or swaps is that the firm has not locked in a specific exchange rate irrespective of the movement in exchange rates. This is why firms sometimes prefer options over other forms of hedging instruments.

In addition to currency options, there are also *futures options*. The owner of a futures option, upon exercise, merely acquires a long or short futures position with the futures price equal to the exercise price of the option. All of these, and other, techniques are employed by firms to protect themselves against the effects of exchange rate risk.

Concept Review Questions

- What are some advantages of using currency options for hedging?
- Describe when and how a multinational firm will employ a currency call option to hedge exchange rate risk.
- When would a multinational firm use a put option to hedge against exchange rate risk?

GROWTH OF THE DERIVATIVES MARKET

Forwards, futures, swaps, caps, collars, options, and scores of related products are known collectively as **derivatives**. Their development in the last 15 years has revolutionized how firms and financial institutions manage their risks. There are at least three reasons for their growth: First, derivatives are cheaper to trade than the bonds, currencies, equities, and commodities from which they are derived. Second, they have become much more familiar both to financial institutions and to firms using them in recent years. Third, many countries have revised and eased the legal, fiscal, and regulatory restrictions on the use of derivatives.

A recent study by the Bank for International Settlements estimates that banks had outstanding exchange-traded derivatives of $3.5 trillion at the end of 1991, up from $583 billion five years earlier. The total swaps market is estimated to be in excess of

$5 trillion in contracts outstanding world-wide, which eclipses the value of all shares of stock listed on the New York and Tokyo stock exchanges combined. Another estimate is that the total derivatives market is as much as $10 trillion. Although the market has grown tremendously, there are also concerns that neither the banks, investment dealers, traders, or users of derivatives fully understand the risks well enough to price them properly. Some worry that a derivatives disaster could overwhelm the world's financial system.

In response to these concerns the Bank for International Settlements and the International Organization of Securities Commissions have both prepared new sets of international capital regulations that will apply to banks and investment dealers. Whereas derivatives were virtually unknown to financial managers 15 years ago, now financial managers have to understand derivatives and how they can be employed by the firm to reduce costs and insulate the firm from some of the financing and operating risks to which it is exposed.

Concept Review Question

- Why have derivative financial products become popular with firms in the past few years?

KEY POINTS

- The value of shareholder claims and bondholder claims on the firm may be considered simultaneously using option pricing techniques.
- According to option concepts, in effect, the shareholders have bought the firm's assets, borrowed the present value of the bondholders' claims on the firm, and also bought a put (or default) option that allows them to walk away from the firm and give it to the bondholders. This default option arises because shareholders have limited liability.
- Viewing the firm in an option pricing context indicates that unless actions are undertaken that create additional value for the firm, gains to one party (owners or creditors) come from losses incurred by the other party (creditors or owners).
- Firms create value by making positive net present value investment decisions; restructuring or simply reacting to changing economic conditions is likely to shift value from shareholders to bondholders, or vice versa, but not create value.
- Traditional capital budgeting analysis, based on discounted cash flows, ignores the value of flexibility and management's ongoing decision-making ability. Guarantees and options to make further investments in the future, to defer, or to abandon abound in capital investments; they must be recognized and valued.
- Abandonment in the future is an option that should always be recognized and built into capital budgeting decision making.
- Options can also be employed to hedge interest rate risk.
- Currency options provide the opportunity, but not the requirement, to lock in a specific rate of exchange.
- The derivatives market has expanded rapidly; many other features can be built into hedging instruments. Throughout, the emphasis must be on assessing the risk exposure of the firm, determining how much of its risk the firm wants to hedge, and examining the benefits and costs of hedging. If the firm does not hedge exchange rate risk, it can either ignore it, or price it—that is, pass the costs of not hedging on to others.

QUESTIONS

19.1 Jerome argues that options on stocks can and do exist but that stock cannot be viewed as an option. Set Jerome straight. Be sure to mention limited liability and its impact.

19.2 Strous Brothers has both common stock and zero-coupon debt outstanding. What impact will each of the following have on the market value of Strous' common stock and its debt? (Assume each part is independent of other parts and that "other things remain unchanged.")

a. Interest rates fall.

b. Strous retires its existing debt and issues an equal amount of longer-term debt.

c. Strous uses cash to acquire assets that are more risky than the firm's existing assets.

d. Strous issues more stock to retire some of its debt.

e. Unexpectedly, Strous received patent protection on two of its major products.

19.3 Why are capital budgeting projects and the opportunity to abandon a project closely related to call and put options?

19.4 The opportunity to expand or to delay is simply an option. What similarities and differences exist between these two options?

19.5 Compare the option to abandon today versus the option to abandon in the future. What major differences, if any, are there between these options?

19.6 Explain how to value guarantees and why guarantees—whether provided by firms or governments—are valuable.

19.7 Explain some of the ways in which options can be used to hedge, or limit, a firm's interest rate risk exposure.

19.8 In order to use an option to hedge foreign exchange risk, a premium must be paid to purchase the option. Assume the forward rate of exchange is 2.10 foreign to 1 domestic and you purchase a call with a strike price equal to the current forward rate. The premium paid reduces the *effective* strike price to 1.95 foreign/1 domestic. Taking into account the premium paid, there is substantially less than a 50 percent probability you will ever exercise the option. Why would you ever want to purchase an exchange rate option?

CONCEPT REVIEW PROBLEMS

See Appendix A for solutions.

CR19.1 The Fisher-Myron Corp. has a total market value of $20 million. The firm has $12 million in face value of zero-coupon debt with a maturity of 10 years. The annual standard deviation is 0.36. If the risk-free rate of return is 8 percent, what is:

a. The value of the shareholders' claim on Fisher-Myron?

b. The value of the bondholders' risky claim?

c. The value of the default option?

CR19.2 Fisher-Myron from CR19.1 is considering restructuring. The firm will issue $32 billion in 15-year zero-coupon bonds, buy back the $12 billion in 10-year bonds, and use the approximately $3 billion difference to repurchase stock. The standard deviation of the firm's assets is unchanged at 0.36, while the yield to maturity on the 10- and 15-year zero-coupon bonds is 10 percent. After this restructuring, what is the shareholders' value and what is the bondholders' value?

CR19.3   Waterhouse is considering expanding into the Russian market. Cost of a new production plant today will be $200 million, with expected after-tax cash flows of $35 million for each of 10 years. The firm's opportunity cost of capital is 15 percent.

a. Based on the project's NPV, should Waterhouse expand into the Russian market?

b. Rob, CFO, noted that one purpose of the new plant is to "get a jump on the competition." He commented that after a three-year period, if the Russian market is stronger than anticipated, the firm could make an investment of $50 million in a follow-up project that has a net present value of $40 million. The risk-free rate is 7 percent. If the standard deviation is 0.55, what is the strategic NPV of the project?

CR19.4   Sharon, assistant CFO of Waterhouse, noted that another option available is to abandon the project if cash flows are less than expected. Assume the present value (at $t = 0$) of the cash flows after three years is $60 million, the project can be sold for an after-tax cash inflow of $45 million, and σ and k_{RF} are the same as in CR19.3. Taking the results from CR19.3 and CR19.4 together, what is the project's strategic NPV?

CR19.5   Jim is considering purchasing a franchise licence from Hot Dog Haven and opening a hot dog stand on campus. For a franchising fee, Hot Dog Haven will supply management training, advertising, and specialty products. In addition, the Hot Dog Haven franchiser will guarantee a minimum after-tax cash flow of $10,000 each year for two years. Jim expects an after-tax cash flow of $15,000 in one year and $25,000 in two years. If the risk-free rate is 8 percent, Jim's required return is 18 percent, and the expected standard deviation of future cash flows is 0.45, what is the value of the guarantee?

CR19.6   Imports, Inc., the U.S. subsidiary of Canadian World-Wide Importers, has just purchased furniture worth 3,000,000 francs from a Swiss company. Payment for the shipment is due in May. Use the information in Table 19.1 to answer the following questions:

a. If the shipped furniture were paid for today in U.S. dollars, what would it cost?

b. Is Imports, Inc., concerned with the Swiss franc strengthening or weakening in relation to the U.S. dollar?

c. If Imports, Inc., attempts to use options to hedge its exposure, how many and what kind of options will the firm need to purchase?

d. What is the total cost of the hedge if options with a strike price of $0.70 and a maturity of May is used?

e. Assume the Swiss franc strengthens in relationship to the U.S. dollar to $0.80 per Swiss franc. What is the loss if Imports, Inc., had not purchased the options? If Imports, Inc., purchased the options, what is the total cash flow to the firm?

PROBLEMS

19.1   A firm has $40 million in outstanding zero-coupon debt that matures in four years. The market value of the firm's assets is $60 million, the standard deviation is 0.60, and the risk-free rate is 0.14.

a. What is the value of the firm's stock? Of its debt?

b. What is the value of the default option?

19.2   Bagamery has $1,000 in zero-coupon bonds outstanding that mature in five years. The market value of Bagamery's assets is $1,400, the standard deviation is 0.40, and the risk-free rate is 0.08.

a. What is the value of Bagamery's stock, debt, and the default option held by the share-holders?

b. Now assume that everything stays the same as in (a) except that unexpected inflation increases the risk-free rate to 0.13. What is the new value of Bagamery's stock, debt, and the default option? Explain your results.

c. Finally, assume that everything is the same as in (a) except that the standard deviation of the assets is reduced to 0.25 from 0.40. What is the new value of Bagamery's stock, debt, and the default option? Explain your results.

19.3 Silversheet has a market value of assets of $100. It has $90 in six-year zero-coupon bonds outstanding, the risk-free rate is 10 percent, and the standard deviation of the firm's assets is 0.45.

a. What is the value of the shareholders' claim? Of the bondholders' claim?

b. In order to finance a new project that will raise the market value of Silversheet's assets to $150, the firm plans to issue *an additional* $91.10 in six-year zero-coupon debt. What is the new value of the shareholders' claim? Of the bondholders' claim?

c. Comparing your answers to (a) and (b), how much of the total gain was claimed by the shareholders? By the bondholders? Explain.

19.4 Your firm is considering two new product lines. Product 1 is fairly certain and may result in a market value of the firm's assets as high as $80 million or as low as $60 million in two years. Product 2 is much more risky and may result in a market value for the firm of either $200 million or $0. Assume the outcomes for each product are equally likely and the firm's $40 million zero-coupon bonds mature in two years.

a. What are the possible outcomes for the shareholders from the two products?

b. What are the possible outcomes for the bondholders?

c. Which product would the shareholders favour? The bondholders? Explain.

19.5 Kleiner Designs is considering a number of acquisitions. On three of them, Kleiner wants to take out an option, pending further evaluation and developments. The three are as follows:

Firm	Current Market Price	Purchase (Exercise) Price	Terms of Option	Volatility of Stock
Green and Sons	$74	$72	30 days	0.15
Feldman	41	45	100	0.40
Longmore	67	80	182	0.85

If the risk-free rate is 0.12, what is the cost (or value) per share of each of the options? (*Note:* Use a 365-day year.)

19.6 Coopertronics must decide whether to purchase Megatron, a high-tech firm with a potential breakthrough in microsize motors. The funds required to complete testing and bring the motors to market can be as high as $100 million or as low as $50 million. The potential payoff is also uncertain because the present value of the cash inflows at time t = 0 could be as high as $175 million or as low as $60 million. The risk-free rate is 0.11, the standard deviation is 0.60, and the time period is two years.

a. How much should Coopertronics pay to purchase Megatron in a best-case scenario?

b. In a worst-case scenario?

19.7 A project has an NPV of $-\$80,000$. By accepting this project, however, in two more years you could make a subsequent investment of $250,000 and receive a present value (at time $t = 2$) of $300,000. The standard deviation of the subsequent project is 0.25, $k_{RF} = 0.08$, and the appropriate discount rate for bringing the cash inflows of $300,000 back to time $t = 0$ is 0.20.

a. Should you make the investment?

b. What would the standard deviation have to be so that you would be indifferent between accepting and rejecting the project?

19.8 NextSource is at the forefront of the developments in using lasers as a cost-effective alternative source of energy. To proceed farther requires an investment of $200 million today; the results will not be known until sometime in the future. NextSource estimates that under the most optimistic circumstances (with a probability of 0.20) the results will be known in two years. But a more realistic estimate (with a probability of 0.40) is that it will take three years for the results to be known. Finally, under the worst case (with a probability of 0.40) the results will not be known for four years. Their best estimates of the timing and cash flows are as follows:

Year	PV of Inflows (in millions)	Outlay – (in millions)	NPV = (in millions)	Standard Deviation
2	$1,500	$700	$800	0.50
3	1,200	800	400	0.50
4	800	900	−100	0.50

NextSource has determined that the appropriate opportunity cost of capital to discount the future inflows back to time $t = 0$ is 0.25. The risk-free rate is 0.10. Should NextSource proceed? (*Note:* All three outcomes are independent of one another. Also, do *not* take a weighted average of the input variables and then calculate a single option value. Instead, calculate one option value for each year and then weight them by the probability of occurrence.)

19.9 Wolfers had the opportunity to build a plant to produce snowgos. The investment required is $150, and the plant is expected to return $20 in perpetuity. The discount rate is 10 percent. It has just come to the attention of Wolfers management that they can delay building the plant for one year. The possible returns if building is delayed are $22 per year in perpetuity or $10 per year in perpetuity. The risk-free rate is 7 percent. Which should Wolfers do—invest now or delay making the decision for one year?

19.10 A firm has a capital investment that requires an expenditure of $500 and promises to return $52 per year in perpetuity. The discount rate is 10 percent. Alternatively, it can defer the investment for one year. The two possible outcomes are $56 per year in perpetuity or $44 in perpetuity. The risk-free rate is 4 percent.

a. Should the firm undertake the capital investment now, or should it delay making the decision for one year?

b. What decision should be made if the risk-free rate is 10 percent, instead of 4 percent? Does your answer make sense in terms of what happens to the value of a call option as the risk-free rate increases?

c. Finally, independent of (b), what decision should be made if everything is the same as in (a) except the two possible outcomes are $56 in perpetuity or $48 in perpetuity? Explain why this occurs.

19.11 A project can be abandoned at the end of one year; the proceeds would be $100,000. If the project continues, the present value (at $t = 0$) of the future proceeds past year 1 would equal $160,000. The risk-free rate is 0.10, and the volatility (standard deviation) of the project's cash flows, assuming no abandonment, is 1.30.

a. What is the value of the option to abandon?

b. If everything stays the same as in (a) except the standard deviation drops to 0.20, what is the value of the option to abandon? Why does this occur?

19.12 Without considering the opportunity to abandon, a project has an NPV of −$25. The project can be abandoned, however, at the end of *either* one or two years as follows:

Year Abandoned	Abandonment Value	Present Value (at time t = 0) of Future Cash Inflows if Project Is Not Abandoned
1	$150	$200
2	140	160

The risk-free rate is 0.09, and the volatility (standard deviation) of the project's cash flows is 0.70. Should the project be undertaken? Why or why not?

19.13 Ronaldson Ltd. is attempting to sell its electronics division to its current management in a leveraged buyout. To effect the sale, Ronaldson will guarantee that the free cash flows (i.e., cash flows over and above those required to meet normal outflows and make certain capital investments) of the electronics division will be a minimum of $6 million the first year, $7 million the second year, and $8 million the third year. Ronaldson estimates the free cash flow will actually be $5.5 million, $9.5 million, and $12 million, respectively, and that 25 percent is an appropriate discount rate for the estimated cash flows. If the standard deviation of the annual free cash flow changes is 0.32 per year, and the risk-free rate is 0.11, how much should Ronaldson ask over and above the "normal" price for the division due to the cash flow guarantees?

19.14 The government provides guarantees to certain groups, such as farmers, depositors in banks, and so forth. Assume that the forecasted cash flows are $100 for year 1 and $125 for year 2, while the guarantee is $115 each year. The appropriate discount rate for the forecasted cash flows is 0.25, the risk-free rate is 0.10, and the volatility of the cash flows is 0.35.

a. How much is this guarantee worth?

b. Who benefits from the guarantee? Who subsidizes the guarantee?

19.15 Your firm is buying the chemical division of Savewest Chemical. Two alternative four-year guarantees of the cash flows from the chemical division are being offered as follows:

Year	Guarantee One	Guarantee Two
1	$ 8.0	$ 4.50
2	9.0	7.00
3	9.0	11.00
4	10.0	13.00

The forecasted cash flows for the four years are as follows: year 1 = $10, year 2 = $13, year 3 = $15, and year 4 = $20. The appropriate discount rate for the cash flows is 0.20, the risk-free rate is 0.11, and the volatility of the cash flows is 0.50. If it does not affect the price you pay, which guarantee should you accept—one or two?

19.16 Wise Enterprises just purchased merchandise worth 1 million French francs, with payment due in francs in 90 days. The spot rate of exchange today is FF5.32/$. A three-month over-the-counter call option (from a bank) is available with the following characteristics:

Size of option	FF250,000
Strike price	FF5.30/$
Option premium, per option	$400

Assume Wise went ahead with purchasing the call options to hedge the exchange rate exposure. Today the options mature, and the current spot exchange rate is FF5.22/$.
a. Should Wise exercise the options?
b. At what spot exchange rate today would Wise be indifferent between exercising the options and letting them expire?

19.17 Toys-for-You just sold one of its subsidiaries to Kyoto Miniatures for 100 million yen, with payment to be received in yen in 40 days. The spot rate of exchange between the yen and the dollar is ¥110.25/$ or $0.009070/¥. Toys is concerned about changes in exchange rates, so it is considering hedging using put options. The options are for 6,250,000 yen each. The 88 option (that is, with an exercise exchange ratio of $0.0088/¥) costs 0.0036 cents per yen, the 89 option costs 0.0063 cents per yen, the $90\frac{1}{2}$ option costs 0.0116 cents per yen, and the 91 option costs 0.014 cents per yen.
a. What would it cost Toys if it uses the 88 option to hedge? The 89 option? The $90\frac{1}{2}$ option? The 91 option? (*Note:* The cost of the option on the yen is quoted in *fractions* of a cent; it is necessary to convert to dollars.)
b. Assume that Toys-for-You went ahead and purchased the 91 options. Today the options mature, and the current spot rate of exchange is $0.00915/¥. What should Toys do? What did the hedge cost Toys?
c. What should Toys do if the current spot rate of exchange is $0.00905/¥? What is the total cost to Toys?

19.18 Mini Case   Kelly just finished attending a seminar on advanced capital budgeting issues offered by the business school at the local university. During the seminar the option-like characteristics of many investment decisions were stressed repeatedly. The concept of "strategic NPV," which incorporates both the base-case NPV plus any option-like aspects, is particularly appealing to Kelly. Also, Kelly has heard some chief financial officers at competing companies discussing strategic NPVs. To implement this at Kirkwood International, Kelly decides to start applying these ideas when reviewing all capital budgeting proposals.
a. During the course of a conversation with some of the staff, Kelly is questioned: "What is a call option?" "What is a put option?" "What factors determine the value of call or put options?" "Why does any of this apply to the evaluation of proposed capital expenditures?" "What do you mean by strategic NPV?" How would you answer these questions?
b. At times in the past Kirkwood International has employed the sequential analysis approach discussed in Chapter 9. How, conceptually, could option techniques be employed instead of the sequential analysis approach?
c. To illustrate the use of option techniques, Kelly provides the following data on a proposed project:

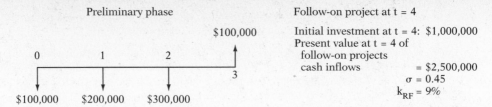

Preliminary phase

$100,000

Follow-on project at t = 4

Initial investment at t = 4: $1,000,000
Present value at t = 4 of
 follow-on projects
  cash inflows   = $2,500,000
             $\sigma = 0.45$
           $k_{RF} = 9\%$

What is the strategic NPV of the project if the discount rate is 18 percent? (*Note:* Use continuous discounting.)

d. Kelly notes that option ideas also apply to future abandonment decisions. One of Kirkwood International's divisions just brought forth the following proposed project:

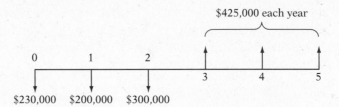

$425,000 each year

Due to the fact that the project is slightly more risky than Kirkwood's typical project, the discount rate is 20 percent.

1. What is the NPV of the project? Should it be accepted? (*Note:* Use continuous discounting.)

2. After questioning the division, Kelly finds that the cash outflows at times t = 0 and t = 1 have to be made no matter what. However, if all goes well, the project could be a real money winner. The problem is that the cash flows in years 3, 4, and 5 have a high degree of uncertainty. The standard deviation is 0.60, and the risk-free rate is 9 percent. No matter what occurs later on, the cash outflows at t = 0 and t = 1 have to be made. But the $300,000 outflow in year 2 is an option that will be exercised only if subsequent prospects look favourable. Given this new information, what is the project's strategic NPV? What decision should be made? (*Note:* As in part 1, use continuous discounting to determine the price, P_0, of the option at t = 0.)

3. In part 2, the option to abandon was not considered. Now Kelly finds out that not only can the project be expanded upon as in part 2, but if the project is abandoned at t = 2 the firm will receive $250,000 after-tax from the sale of assets invested in the project. What is the value of the option to abandon? (*Note:* As before use continuous discounting.) What is the final strategic NPV (which includes the NPV of the original project, the option to expand in part 2, and the option to abandon)? Should the firm proceed with the project?

e. To illustrate the use of options further, Kelly presents the following information, in which Kirkwood is proposing to sell a division for $10,000,000. In order to facilitate the sale, Kirkwood is preparing to guarantee the following net cash flows from the division for its first three years. The forecasted and guaranteed cash flows are projected to be equal as follows:

Year	Guaranteed Cash Flow	Forecasted Cash Flow
1	$2,000,000	$2,000,000
2	4,000,000	4,000,000
3	5,000,000	5,000,000

But there is uncertainty associated with the forecasted cash flows; hence their standard deviation is 0.35. The discount rate is 18 percent, and the risk-free rate is 9 percent. Kelly argues that the cash flow guarantees are valuable to the purchaser of the division. Why is this so? How much should be added to the $10,000,000 sale price to compensate Kirkwood for the guarantee it is providing?

REFERENCES

BIERMAN, HAROLD, JR. *Strategic Financial Planning.* New York: Free Press, 1980.

CLARKE, ROGER G., BRENT WILSON, ROBERT H. DAINES, and STEPHEN D. NADAULD. *Strategic Financial Management.* Homewood, Ill.: Irwin, 1988.

GARMAN, MARK B., and STEVEN W. KOHLHAGEN. "Foreign Currency Option Values." *Journal of International Money and Finance* 2 (March 1983): 231–237.

KESTER, W. CARL. "An Options Approach to Corporate Finance." In *Handbook of Corporate Finance,* edited by E. Altman. New York: Wiley, 1986.

MASON, SCOTT P., and ROBERT C. MERTON. "The Role of Contingent Claims in Corporate Finance." In *Recent Advances in Corporate Finance,* edited by Edward I. Altman and Marti G. Subrahmanyam. Homewood, Ill.: Richard D. Irwin, 1985.

MCDONALD, ROBERT, and DANIEL R. SIEGEL. "The Value of Waiting to Invest." *Quarterly Journal of Economics* 101 (November 1986): 707–728.

MCLAUGHLIN, ROBYN, and ROBERT A. TAGGART, JR. "The Opportunity Cost of Using Excess Capacity." *Financial Management* 21 (Summer 1992): 12–23.

MAJD, SAMAN, and ROBERT S. PINDYCK. "Time to Build, Option Value, and Investment Decision." *Journal of Financial Economics* 18 (March 1987): 7–27.

MERTON, ROBERT C., and ZVI BODIE. "On the Management of Financial Guarantees." *Financial Management* 21 (Winter 1992): 87–109.

MYERS, STEWART C. "Finance Theory and Financial Strategy." *Midland Corporate Finance Journal* 5 (Spring 1987): 6–13.

PINDYCK, ROBERT S. "Irreversible Investment, Capacity Choice, and the Value of the Firm." *American Economic Review* 78 (December 1988): 969–985.

SMITH, CLIFFORD W., JR. "Applications of Option Pricing Analysis." In *The Modern Theory of Corporate Finance,* 2nd ed., edited by Clifford W. Smith, Jr. New York: McGraw-Hill, 1990.

TRIGEORGIS, LENOS, and SCOTT P. MASON. "Valuing Managerial Flexibility." *Midland Corporate Finance Journal* 5 (Spring 1987): 14–21.

20 *Warrants and Convertibles*

EXECUTIVE SUMMARY

Warrants are long-term options issued by the firm, and their valuation follows the same procedures employed for valuing any other call option. However, there are complications that must be considered. First, due to the longer period before warrants expire, the effect of cash dividends, whose payment reduces the value of the underlying common stock, often has to be considered. Second, when warrants are exercised, the number of shares of common stock outstanding increases.

Convertible securities are, in effect, straight debt or preferred stock that also has an option attached. There are three values that are important when valuing convertibles—the straight debt or preferred stock value, the conversion value (i.e., its common stock value), and the value of the call option that can be exercised by the owner of the convertible. The most straightforward way to value convertibles is to value the straight debt or preferred stock and then value the call option. As with warrants, the presence of cash dividends, increases in the number of shares of common stock outstanding when the securities are converted, and changes in capital structure leading to changes in risk must be considered when valuing convertibles.

Because most convertibles contain a call provision, the firm can call the security for retirement. If the conversion value is above the call price, investors should convert; otherwise they should accept the call price. From the firm's standpoint, the optimal way to avoid wealth transfers is to call the convertible when its conversion value equals its call price. At the same time, the firm may not force conversion if the after-tax cash outflow is greater with conversion than without. Convertibles help firms and investors deal with risk, mitigate agency costs, and deal with asymmetric information and adverse financing costs.

WARRANTS

In Chapters 10 and 11 we considered the two main external sources of long-term financing for the firm—common stock and long-term debt. Now we examine two other securities employed by firms. These are warrants and convertibles, of which the most important are convertible bonds. Both of these types of securities have option-like characteristics. Hence, we employ our knowledge of options from Chapter 18 in order to understand and value warrants and convertibles.

THE DIFFERENCE BETWEEN WARRANTS AND CALL OPTIONS

Warrants are simply a long-term call option that allows the purchaser or holder to buy shares of stock in a firm at a specific price.[1] A significant amount of privately placed debt and a far smaller percentage of public offerings are packaged with warrants issued along with the debt. Warrants may also be given to investment dealers as compensation for underwriting services. Thus, a warrant is a long-term option that provides the investor with the right, but not the obligation, to buy a specific number of shares of common stock at a predetermined price for a certain period. Warrants are almost always detachable, which means that shortly after the package of securities is issued, the bonds and the warrants can be sold separately. Table 20.1 shows the characteristics of some warrants. The exercise price of these warrants ranges from $6.25 for Air Canada to $21 for the Laurentian Bank. All of these warrants have a low value, but if the price of the common stock into which they are convertible rises, so will the value of the warrant.

As you can tell from the preceding discussion, warrants are like call options. In fact, from the investor's standpoint, a warrant is almost exactly the same as a call option on the common stock of the issuing firm. One key difference is that options are created by investors themselves (i.e., the firm on which the option is written is *not* involved in creating options), whereas warrants are created by the firm. Hence, the firm is directly involved in determining the number of warrants issued, the term (or expiration date) of the warrants, and the exercise price at which the firm's common stock can be purchased. Because the firm creates the warrant, when warrants are exercised the number of shares of common stock outstanding increases.[2] In contrast, when a call option is exercised, the writer of the call is responsible for having the required shares, and the number of shares of stock that the firm has outstanding does not change. As we shall see subsequently, this increase in the number of shares outstanding when warrants are exercised influences their value.

---

[1] There are a few warrants outstanding that allow the purchase of the stock of another firm or the purchase of bonds.

[2] From an accounting standpoint, using the current number of shares of common stock outstanding to calculate earnings per share (EPS) produces basic EPS. Taking account of all the shares of common stock that will be outstanding after the warrants are exercised results in fully diluted EPS. The same accounting treatment exists for shares that may be issued when convertible securities are employed. See Chapter 25.

Table 20.1

Warrant Characteristics for Selected Firms

Most warrants can be exchanged for one share of common stock. Also, as the numbers indicate, many of the publicly traded warrants have a low price, as does the common stock for which the warrants can be exchanged.

Firm	Warrant Expiration Date	Warrant Exercise Price per Share	Warrant Number of Shares per Warrant	Common Stock Price per Share	Lower Limit of Warrant Value[a]	Actual Warrant Price	Premium Over Lower Limit[b]
Air Canada	12/6/95	$ 6.25	1	$ 7.500	$1.25	$1.78	$0.53
Cascades	8/31/97	10.00	1	6.250	0	1.55	1.55
Hollinger	9/30/98	20.00	1	12.375	0	2.40	2.40
Laurentian Bank of Canada	2/23/96	21.00	1	16.500	0	0.35	0.35
Numac Energy	4/15/95	10.50	1	7.375	0	0.005	0.005
Royal Oak Mines	5/30/96	8.75	1	4.550	0	0.55	0.55
Shaw Communication	4/16/96	16.00	1	8.750	0	0.20	0.20

[a] Maximum of (market price of common stock − exercise price)(number of shares purchased with one warrant) or zero, as given by Equation 20.1.
[b] Actual warrant price − lower limit of warrant price.

Source: Various financial publications as of March 10, 1995.

VALUING WARRANTS

Option Value   To understand the valuation of warrants, let us consider FirstGenetic, which has just issued some five-year warrants with an exercise price of $40. FirstGenetic's current stock market price is $31. Based on what we learned about call options from Chapter 18, the lower limit on the value of this warrant (or option to buy a share of FirstGenetic common stock) can be depicted as in Figure 20.1. Like any call option, however, the warrant will actually trade above the lower limit of its value. The height of the actual warrant price (given by the dashed line in Figure 20.1) above the lower limit will depend on the following:

Stock price, P_0

Exercise price, X

Time to maturity, t

Risk-free rate, k_{RF}

Variability of the underlying asset, σ

These are the same factors that determine the value of any call option.

Once a warrant is designed and issued, the exercise price is known. Also, for simplicity, let us hold the stock price, P_0, constant. In this situation, the height of the actual warrant price above the lower limit depends on three factors: the risk-free rate, k_{RF}; the time to maturity, t; and the standard deviation of the underlying asset's returns, σ. Of course, as time runs out, the actual price of the warrant snuggles closer and closer to the lower limit. On the final day of its life, its price hits the lower limit.

Figure 20.1

Relationship Between the Market Value of a Warrant and Its Lower Limit

Until expiration, the market value of a warrant (given by the dashed line) will be greater than the lower limit (given by the solid coloured line).

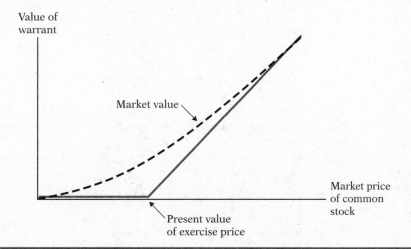

The lower limit on the value of a warrant is the maximum of (1) the market value of the common stock that it can be exercised for, minus the exercise price (for warrants that are in-the-money), or (2) zero (for warrants that are out-of-the-money). Thus,[3]

$$
\text{lower limit} = \text{MAX}\left[\left(\begin{array}{c} \text{market price of} \\ \text{common stock} \\ -\text{exercise price} \end{array} \right) \left(\begin{array}{c} \text{number of shares} \\ \text{purchased with} \\ \text{one warrant} \end{array} \right), 0 \right] \quad (20.1)
$$

If we ignore some complications for the present, determining the value of the FirstGenetic warrants is straightforward. As a young firm with extensive research and development needs, FirstGenetic does not pay any cash dividends on its common stock. The risk-free rate is 0.08, and the volatility of the returns on FirstGenetic's common stock is estimated to be 0.40. With a maturity of five years, an exercise price of $40, and a current market price of FirstGenetic's common stock of $31, we can treat warrants like any other call option and use Table B.6 to value the warrant as follows:

STEP 1:   Calculate the standard deviation times the square root of time:

$$
\sigma(t)^{0.5} = (0.40)\,(5)^{0.5} = 0.8944
$$

STEP 2:   Calculate the market price divided by the present value of the exercise price:

$$
\frac{P_0}{X/e^{k_{RF}t}} = \frac{\$31}{\$40/e^{(0.08)(5)}} = 1.1562
$$

STEP 3:   Multiply the tabled value by the stock price. From Table B.6, we find that the value is approximately 0.396, indicating a value of the FirstGenetic warrants of $31(0.396) = $12.28. Thus, even though FirstGenetic's current stock market price of $31 is less than the exercise price of $40, the warrant has considerable value due to the long time to maturity.

Some Complications   There are some complications that we have ignored thus far. The first is that the Black–Scholes option pricing model assumes no cash dividends are paid. Thus, it will not correctly value warrants issued by a dividend-paying firm. In fact, the warrantholder loses every time a cash dividend is paid, because the dividend reduces the stock price, P_0, and therefore the value of the warrant. To determine the warrant value when cash dividends are present, we can adjust the Black–Scholes model for any known cash dividends to be paid, or we can use the binomial method discussed in Chapter 18.

A second complication also exists. Remember from Chapter 18 that when a call option is exercised there is no change in either the firm's assets or the number of shares of common stock outstanding. But when warrants are exercised, the number of shares

---

[3] Later in the chapter, we use the adjusted market price, P_0^*, to account for the impact of dilution which occurs when warrants are exercised. When using Equation 20.1 in such a case, we would use the adjusted market price instead of the market price indicated in the equation.

of outstanding common stock increases. To illustrate the calculation of the warrant price in the presence of **dilution**—that is, an increase in the number of shares of common stock outstanding—assume that before the warrant was issued FirstGenetic was an all-equity firm that had 100,000 shares of common stock outstanding. At the current market price of $31 per share, the value of the firm, V, was ($31)(100,000) = $3,100,000. This was also the value of the equity of the firm, S. FirstGenetic sold 20,000 warrants at $10 per warrant, for a total of $200,000 [i.e., ($10)(20,000)]. Two points should be recognized here: First, the total value of FirstGenetic after the warrants are sold is $3,100,000 + $200,000 = $3,300,000. Second, the warrant purchasers appear to have received a good deal because they paid only $10 for warrants that we determined in the last section were worth $12.28. If the warrant purchasers got a good deal, then the firm did not because it sold the warrants for less than their worth. In fact, the warrant purchasers did not fare as well as it appears, nor did the firm fare as poorly, once we consider the impact of dilution.

To calculate the value of a warrant, allowing for dilution, we need to determine the value of the call option, or warrant, on the firm *after allowing for the immediate impact* of the financing proceeds secured from the warrant financing. To do this we determine an adjusted market price per share, P_0^*, and then calculate the value of the call option on the firm, V_c, given this adjusted market price. This adjusted market price takes account of the increase in the value of the firm due to the proceeds received from the warrant financing. The value of the warrant[4] after considering dilution is

$$\text{value of warrant with dilution} = \left(\frac{1}{1 + q}\right)(V_c) \qquad (20.2)$$

where q is the number of new shares that may be issued per share of existing common stock outstanding. After FirstGenetic sells the warrants, the total value of the firm is $3,300,000. Dividing $3,300,000 by the number of shares outstanding *before* any warrants are exercised (which is 100,000), we find that the adjusted current market price, P_0^*, of FirstGenetic is $33 per share. The number of original shares of common stock was 100,000, and the number of shares that can be issued due to the warrant financing is 20,000; hence q = 20,000/100,000 = 0.20.

The value of the warrant, or call option, V_c, using the adjusted market price, P_0^*, of $33, is determined as follows:

STEP 1: Calculate the standard deviation times the square root of time, which is just $(0.40)(5)^{0.5} = 0.8944$, as determined before.

STEP 2: Calculate the market price divided by the present value of the exercise price. Using the adjusted market price of $33, it is

$$\frac{P_0^*}{X/e^{k_{RF}t}} = \frac{\$33}{\$40/e^{(0.08)(5)}} = 1.2308$$

STEP 3: Multiply the tabled value by the stock price. From Table B.6, we find that the value is approximately 0.421, so the value of the warrant after considering the impact of the new financing is $33(0.421) = $13.89.

---

[4] Our discussion follows Galai and Schneller (1978).

Now, employing Equation 20.2, we can determine the value of the warrant after adjusting for dilution as follows :

$$\text{value of warrant with dilution} = [1/(1.20)](\$13.89) = \$11.58$$

Previously, before we considered the impact of any potential dilution on the value of the FirstGenetic warrant, its estimated value was $12.28. After allowing for dilution, we see that the value of the warrant is $11.58. Although the value of the warrant is less than previously estimated, the warrant purchasers still bought a warrant whose value was worth more than the $10 they paid for it. The firm received only $10 for a warrant with a theoretical value of $11.58.

Once warrants have been issued, they require little attention from the firm. Unlike that of convertibles (discussed next), the conversion of warrants cannot be forced. Thus the main control the firm has comes when the expiration date is set at the outset or if a step-up in the exercise price is specified. Other than that, the firm may attempt to purchase the warrants from investors and retire them if they desire to get rid of the warrants prior to their expiration date.

Concept Review Questions

- How are warrants and call options different?
- What complications are encountered when using the Black–Scholes option pricing model to price warrants?

CONVERTIBLES

Some bonds, and an even smaller percentage of preferred stock, contain another feature—convertibility. *Convertible securities* are bonds or preferred stock that contain a provision that allows them to be exchanged for common stock of the issuing firm at the discretion of the investor.[5] There is no charge for making this exchange, and the exchange can be made whenever the investor wishes. Thus, investors who own convertibles have an option-like security. Consider a $1,000 par convertible bond that has a stated **conversion** (or **exercise**) **price** of $50. The number of shares the bond can be converted into, called the **conversion ratio**, is the par value of the convertible security divided by the conversion price, or $1,000/$50 = 20 shares.

A few other characteristics of convertible bonds are as follows: First, convertible bonds are typically debentures, and they are generally subordinated. Thus, *most convertible bonds are convertible subordinated debentures.*[6] Second, when convertible bonds are designed and issued, their stated coupon interest rate is less than that required on nonconvertible bonds of similar quality and maturity, and their conversion price is set above the current market price of the firm's common stock. The lower

---

[5] There are a few convertibles outstanding that allow for the purchase of another firm's stock, or the purchase of bonds.

[6] Generally convertible subordinated debentures carry a bond rating that is one grade lower than the other long-term debt issued by the firm. Thus, if the firm's other bonds carry a rating of BBB, its convertible subordinated debentures would carry a bond rating of BB.

coupon interest rate is due to a feature of convertible debt that straight (nonconvertible) debt does not have—the option to convert the bond into common stock.

Table 20.2 presents some characteristics of convertible bonds for selected firms. The **conversion value** is simply the amount the bond is worth if it is immediately converted into common stock. The *dollar premium* is the difference between the actual price of the convertible bond and its conversion value. In examining Table 20.2, we see that the conversion value of all but two of the bonds (those issued by Cambridge Shopping Centres and Talisman Energy) is more than their par value of $1,000.

VALUING CONVERTIBLES

The owner of a convertible in essence owns a bond *and* a long-term call option on the firm's stock. This is very similar to owning a bond and a warrant. However, there is an important difference: To exercise the warrant, the investor keeps the bond and has to pay cash to the firm as determined by the exercise price in the warrant. To claim the shares with a convertible bond, the investor has to *surrender the bond* in order to exercise the call option.

In valuing convertibles there are three components that need to be considered: the straight bond value, the conversion value, and the call option value.

Straight Bond Value   The straight bond value, or price, is what the security would sell for if it were not convertible into common stock. This is nothing more than our familiar bond valuation model which, as first considered in Chapter 4, is

$$B_0 = \sum_{t=1}^{n} \frac{I}{(1 + k_b)^t} + \frac{M}{(1 + k_b)^n} = I(PVA_{k_b, n}) + M(PV_{k_b, n})$$

where B_0 is the current price, I is the interest per period, M is the maturity value of the bond, and k_b *is the market rate of interest on comparable quality and comparable maturity nonconvertible bonds.*

When firms issue convertible bonds they pay less in terms of the coupon interest rate than if the bond were not convertible. This makes sense, because the firm is also providing the investor with an option that has value. Suppose Shaws Discount Stores is issuing some $1,000 par value, 7 percent coupon rate convertible bonds. The market interest rate that Shaws would pay *if the bond were not convertible* is 11 percent, and the maturity of the convertible is 10 years. Assuming that interest is paid annually, the straight bond value (employing 11 percent as the discount rate) when the convertible is originally issued is

$$\text{straight bond value} = \$70(PVA_{11\%, 10yr}) + \$1,000(PV_{11\%, 10yr})$$
$$= \$70(5.889) + \$1,000(0.352) = \$764.23 \approx \$764$$

The straight bond value is a minimum value, or floor, below which the value of the convertible bond will not trade. Although the convertible bond is issued at a discount from its par, or maturity, value, *when it matures* its value solely as a bond will be

Table 20.2

Convertible Debt Characteristics for Selected Firms

Convertible bonds come in many shapes and sizes. Although not shown, most convertible bonds are callable and are also subordinated.

Firm	Bond or Note			Common Price per Share	Current Conversion Value[a]	Actual Convertible Price	Premium Over Conversion Value[b]
	Coupon Interest Rate	Maturity	Conversion Ratio				
Abitibi-Price	7.85	2003	66.670	19.375	1,291.73	1,365.00	73.27
Domtar	8.00	1998	153.846	11.750	1,807.69	1,880.00	72.30
Cambridge Shopping							
Centres	7.50	2004	28.161	12.000	337.93	775.00	437.07
Cascades	7.25	1998	153.846	7.750	1,192.31	1,335.00	142.69
Noranda Forest	7.25	2002	117.647	12.500	1,470.58	1,420.00	−50.58
Talisman Energy	8.50	2000	11.900	25.250	300.47	972.50	672.03

[a] (Market price of common stock)(conversion ratio).
[b] Actual convertible price − current conversion value.

Source: Various financial publications as of March 10, 1995.

Figure 20.2

Value of a Convertible Bond at Maturity

In (a), the conversion value is shown along with the straight bond value. If the value of the firm is low, the firm defaults on the bond; otherwise its straight bond value is the maturity value of the bond. In (b), the value of the convertible at maturity is shown to depend on the maximum of the curves in (a).

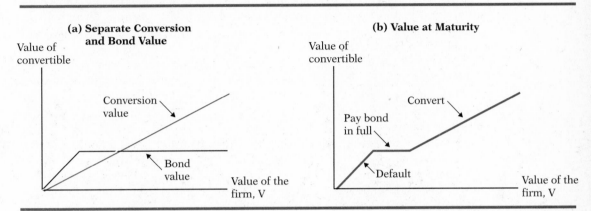

$1,000 per bond. This bond floor at the maturity of the bond is illustrated in Figure 20.2 (a). As long as the value of the firm at the maturity of the bond is sufficient, bondholders are protected by the straight bond value floor; otherwise the firm defaults on the bond, and the bondholders claim the firm's assets.

Conversion Value There is another floor that also limits the downward fluctuation in the market value of any convertible; this time it is provided by how much the convertible is worth solely in terms of its common stock value. Assume the conversion price for the Shaws Discount convertible bond is $50, and the market price of Shaws common stock when the convertible is first issued is $30 per share. The conversion ratio is $1,000/$50 = 20 shares of stock, and the original conversion value[7] is

$$\text{conversion value} = (\text{conversion ratio})(\text{common stock market price})$$

$$= (20)(\$30) = \$600 \tag{20.3}$$

At the instant in time when the convertible bond is sold, its conversion value—that is, how much the stock it can be converted into is worth—is $600. As the market price of the firm's stock increases or decreases, the conversion value of the convertible security will fluctuate accordingly. As also shown in Figure 20.2 (a), the conversion, or common stock, value is a straight upward-sloping line. At maturity, the value of a convertible is determined by the state of the firm and the value of its common stock. As shown in Figure 20.2 (b), at maturity the value of the convertible will depend on whether the firm is solvent or insolvent, and whether the conversion value is above or

---

[7] To be entirely correct, the price per share should be that which would exist if all available shares covered by warrants and convertible securities were already issued. If the number of additional shares of common stock potentially to be issued is not too great, the error caused by employing the current stock market price is minimal.

below the straight bond value (which at maturity is the bond's par value of $1,000 per bond).

Value Before Maturity So far we have considered the value of a convertible security at maturity. Before maturity, the straight bond value of the convertible will be less than at maturity; that is, it will be at a discount. The reason is that all convertibles have a coupon interest rate that is lower than the market rate of interest on comparable quality and maturity nonconvertible bonds when they are issued. Therefore, the straight bond value will be less than the par, or maturity, value. This is shown as a curved line in Figure 20.3 (a).

The straight bond value floor is not as solid as it looks; it will change as market interest rates fluctuate. Thus, if market interest rates go up, the straight bond value declines, and vice versa. Likewise, if the firm's financial condition deteriorates, the floor will also fall. The conversion value, which is the same as it is at maturity, is also shown in Figure 20.3 (a).

There is a third element that also needs to be taken into consideration when valuing convertible securities before maturity: the value of the option which exists. Before maturity, investors have the protection of the higher of the straight bond value floor or the conversion value floor, and they have also an option to convert the bond into common stock. Because this option is valuable, *the value of the convertible security before maturity will always be greater than the lower limit on its value.*

For example, assume the value of the option to convert is worth $15 per share of Shaws stock. The convertible debenture can be exchanged for 20 shares of Shaws common stock, and with the option on each share of stock worth $15, the conversion option is worth ($15)(20) = $300. Adding the option value to the straight bond

---

Figure 20.3

Value of a Convertible Bond Before Maturity

In (a), the conversion value is shown along with the bond value. As the value of the firm increases, the bond value first increases rapidly; then as the firm value increases further, the bond value approaches the maturity value of the bond. In (b), the higher of the bond or conversion value [from (a)] determines the lower limit on the value of the convertible. Due to the straight bond floor and the option to convert, the market value of the convertible is at a premium over the lower limit on the value of the convertible.

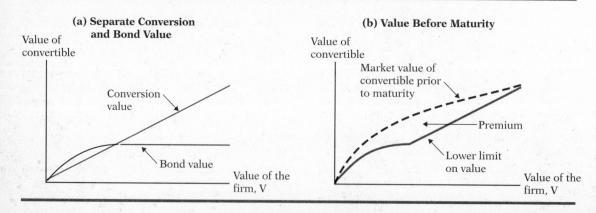

value of $764, we see that the value of the convertible before maturity is $300 + $764 = $1,064. The behaviour of the convertible security's price before maturity is shown in Figure 20.3 (b). The difference between the market price of the convertible and its lower limit is the premium, or value of the call option incorporated in the convertible bond. To determine the worth of a convertible before maturity, the most straightforward approach is to value the straight bond and then value the call option.

Valuing the call option is just like valuing warrants. In valuing the conversion option we must consider the same complications that affected the value of warrants. When the bonds convert, the firm no longer has to make interest payments or repay the face value of the bonds; however, dilution will occur since now there are more common shareholders to share the pie with. In addition, convertible bondholders of dividend-paying firms are missing out on any dividend payments. Consequently, if the dividend payment is higher than the interest received from holding the bonds, it may be in the bondholder's best interest to convert before the maturity date of the bonds in order to receive the dividend.

FORCING CONVERSION

Most convertibles contain a clause that allows the firm to call the security at a specific price. If the firm calls the convertible, the investor has a brief period, generally 30 days or less, to either convert the security or accept the call price. From the investor's standpoint the choice is obvious: If the conversion value is greater than the call price, convert; otherwise, accept the call price. Many firms call a convertible security only when the conversion value is greater than the call price; this situation is often referred to as a **forced conversion**. If the conversion value is less than the call price, the firm cannot force conversion; if the firm calls the issue, rational investors will accept the call price. This situation is often referred to as an **overhanging issue**.

From the firm's standpoint there are two straightforward reasons for calling a convertible. To understand these reasons, you need to know that the value of the firm, or size of the pie, is not affected when the convertible is called. However, *the relative position of shareholders and bondholders is affected by the timing of the call.*

The first reason for calling a convertible focuses on the relationship of the call price and the market value of the convertible. Consider what happens if the firm calls the security when the convertible's market value is below the call price. In that case the firm pays more for the bond than it is worth, thereby transferring wealth from shareholders to bondholders. Likewise, if the bond is not called when the conversion value is above the convertible's market value, bondholders are allowed to hold a valuable asset at the expense of shareholders. The optimal policy for the firm to follow based on the relationship of the call price and the market value of the convertible is to call the bonds *when their market value equals their call price.* Empirical evidence suggests that most firms do not follow this policy; they typically wait until the bond's market value is substantially above the call price.[8]

---

[8] See, for example, Ingersoll (1977), Mazzero and Moore (1992), or Singh, Cowan, and Nayar (1991).

Why do they do this? Because of the second reason for calling convertibles, which involves the cash outflows to the firm.[9] As long as the firm does not call the convertible, the after-tax cash outflow to service the convertible is a function of the interest rate on the convertible, the percent of the convertible outstanding, and the firm's effective tax rate. By forcing conversion, the new ongoing cash outflow to the firm equals the number of shares that will be issued by forcing conversion times the per share cash dividend rate, assuming the firm pays cash dividends. Interest is tax-deductible but the payment of cash dividends has to come out of after-tax cash flows. Thus, the firm's cash outflow generally increases after a conversion. From a cash flow standpoint, why should the firm force conversion if its after-tax cash outflow increases?[10]

HOW AND WHEN FIRMS EMPLOY CONVERTIBLES

One often hears the comment that convertibles are used on the one hand to provide cheap debt financing or on the other hand to allow the firm to sell common stock at a higher-than-market rate. The cheap debt financing argument rests on the premise that the coupon interest rate required with a convertible is less than the coupon rate that would have been required had the firm issued straight debt. However, you should be able to see that the logic behind this argument is faulty because the investor purchases *both* a bond and an option. The cheap debt financing argument ignores the option entirely.

Likewise, the argument that the firm can sell common stock at an "above-market price" rests on the assumption that the exercise price contained in the convertible is greater than the market price of the firm's common stock. The cheap equity argument, however, ignores both the bond and the option, and simply looks at the conversion value of the convertible versus the market price of the convertible. Given the nature of convertible securities, it is not surprising that the expected return required by investors falls between that required on straight bonds and on common stock. If investors require an expected return that falls between those of bonds and stocks, what does the cost to the firm have to be? You know enough finance not to be fooled by improper comparisons such as those incorporated in either the cheap debt or cheap equity financing arguments. Convertibles provide neither cheap debt nor cheap equity financing. Rather, they provide financing whose after-tax cost to the firm is between the costs of straight debt and common equity.

Firms employ convertibles when they provide benefits that are not generally available with other forms of financing. Let us briefly consider when and why firms use convertibles and warrants:

1. RISKY SITUATIONS Convertibles and bond/warrant combinations tend to be issued by smaller and more speculative firms, or sometimes by larger firms that

---

[9] This reason is supported by the results of Asquith and Mullins (1991).

[10] A number of other reasons have been suggested. Harris and Raviv (1985), for example, suggest that firms with favourable information will delay convertible calls to avoid depressing the firm's stock price. Other signalling or agency arguments have also been advanced. Some of the publications listed in the references at the end of the chapter review these other arguments.

have a high degree of risk. Suppose you are approached by a small firm that wants some debt financing to develop and manufacture the next generation of optical scanners. You know that if the project goes well you will get your money back. However, if the project does not do well, you will receive nothing. Although some information on the project exists, you know that the next generation of optical scanners rests on yet-to-be-proven advances the firm is still working on. Even if the technological advances do prove successful, the firm may be preempted by other firms that are also racing to develop the next generation of optical scanners. One way to compensate for the additional, hard-to-evaluate risk is to provide investors with a "piece of the action." This can be accomplished easily by granting investors an option that can be exercised if the firm is successful.

2. AGENCY COSTS Holders of the firm's straight debt are interested in the payment of principal and interest on the debt. To be more assured of receiving these payments, they favour low-risk investment projects. Shareholders, on the other hand, own a call option whose value increases when the firm undertakes high risk—high return projects. Therefore, shareholders want firms to issue debt as though it were going to be employed to finance low-risk projects, and then switch and undertake high-risk projects, thereby transferring wealth from bondholders to shareholders. To protect themselves from this possible expropriation of wealth, bondholders can require higher interest rates and more stringent bond covenants and restrictions. These actions are costly, however, and also restrict the flexibility of the firm. Using convertibles or warrants is a way to reduce these agency costs.

3. ASYMMETRIC INFORMATION AND ADVERSE FINANCING COSTS When firms issue new equity they suffer negative price reactions. Therefore, firms will issue equity only when the investment projects under consideration are not very good. Why share really good projects, and the expected increase in the value of the firm, with new equity holders? One possibility is that firms may issue convertible bonds to bridge the gap between the negative price consequences associated with an equity issue and the potential for costly financial distress associated with a debt issue. When coupled with a call provision that enables early forced conversion, convertibles provide an indirect way to issue equity that entails less adverse price impact than offering common stock.

4. INTERNATIONAL EXPOSURE Often when firms invest in international capital investment projects, or have substantial international exposure, they are exposed to additional risks. These include possible adverse actions by foreign host governments and exposure to fluctuating exchange rates. In such cases convertibles may tend to limit some of the firm's risk exposure due to the unusual risks faced by the firm, because they are debt instead of equity. A country might be tempted to simply expropriate an equity investment, but a debt claim may have more likelihood of being paid off—in part or in full.

5. TAX CONSEQUENCES When a firm issues debt that is convertible, or a debt/warrant package, the coupon interest rate is lower than it would have been if straight debt had been issued. Hence, the tax shield provided by the financing is reduced. This is a disadvantage if the firm is in a high tax-paying situation. Therefore, firms that have less use for the tax shields associated with interest tend to issue convertibles or bonds with warrants. Such firms generally have lower effective marginal tax rates.

Concept Review Questions

■ What are some of the characteristics of a convertible bond?

■ Define the three components that need to be considered when valuing convertible bonds.

■ Why do firms issue convertible securities?

KEY POINTS

- Warrants are simply long-term call options; hence the steps for determining their valuation proceed as do those for the valuation of any other option. Cash dividends and the increase in the number of shares of common stock outstanding when they are exercised (or converted) must be taken into consideration when valuing warrants.
- A convertible bond, in essence, is composed of a bond and a long-term option. The higher of the straight bond value and the conversion value of the security provides the floor, or minimum value, of the convertible. Due to the warrant, or long-term option part of the convertible, the convertible will trade before maturity at a premium to its minimum value.
- Cash dividends and the increase in the number of shares of common stock outstanding when the bond is converted must also be taken into account when valuing the warrant-like aspect of a convertible bond.
- Convertibles *do not provide* either cheap debt or cheap equity financing. Their cost to the firm, and the return required by investors, is between that of straight debt and common equity.
- Due to the call option contained in convertibles, the firm can force conversion if the market value of the convertible is greater than the call value. One rationale for forcing conversion, to minimize wealth transfers between bondholders and shareholders, applies when the market value equals the call price. However, most firms wait until the market value is substantially higher than the call price before calling convertibles. A second rationale focuses on the after-tax cash flow consequences to the firm; it shows that the firm should not force conversion if the after-tax cash outflows of the firm will increase as a result.
- Warrants and convertibles are generally employed when the firm's risk is high, to reduce agency costs, to deal with asymmetric information and adverse financing costs, to deal with international risks, and when the firm has little use for the tax shields associated with interest.

QUESTIONS

20.1   Warrants are very similar to any other call option. How should they be valued? What complications exist that are not present with short-term call options? How do the valuation procedures have to be modified to deal with these complications?

20.2   Under what circumstances, if ever, does it make sense to exercise a warrant prior to maturity?

20.3   Sometimes firms extend the lives of warrants that are about to expire unexercised. What is the cost of doing this?

20.4   Banks, insurance companies, and other lenders often require an "equity kicker" in the form of warrants to accompany a loan. When negotiating the loan, an alternative would have been to require a higher interest rate and/or additional loan restrictions. What are the advantages to the lender and to the borrower of the "equity kicker" arrangement?

20.5   How should convertibles be valued?

20.6   Consider three securities—common stock, straight bonds, and convertible bonds. In each case indicate how the security's value is affected. Which securities have their value affected the most/the least by the following?

a.   The price of the firm's common stock increases.
b.   Interest rates decline.
c.   The firm embarks on a risky new project.
d.   The firm increases its cash dividends on common stock.

20.7   One rationale for firms to follow is to call a convertible security when the conversion value equals the call price. Why is this so? In practice, firms tend to wait until the conversion value is substantially above the call price. What reasons can you suggest to explain this behaviour?

20.8   Under what circumstances, if any, does it make sense for an investor voluntarily to convert a convertible bond prior to maturity?

20.9   It has been argued that convertibles have substantial advantages to the firm as a means of financing. When compared to straight debt, the argument goes, firms get cheap debt financing because they pay less than the going market interest rate for the debt. Compared with selling common stock directly, firms are able to sell common stock at a price above the current market price of the firm's common stock. Thus, the firm is in a "heads I win, tails you lose" situation. Evaluate this argument.

20.10   What reasons exist for using convertibles or bonds with warrants?

20.11   Why, if everything else is equal, might an investor prefer a bond with a warrant attached instead of a convertible bond?

CONCEPT REVIEW PROBLEMS

See Appendix A for solutions.

CR20.1   Morris International has warrants outstanding with a three-year maturity and an exercise price of $35. The current market price for Morris's common stock is $28. If the risk-free rate is 6 percent and the volatility of Morris International's common stock is 0.30, what is the current price of the warrants? Assume the firm does not pay dividends and there are no dilution effects.

CR20.2   Bakers Supermarket recently issued 20-year, 12 percent, semiannual-interest-paying convertible debentures with a conversion price of $25 per share. Baker's common stock is trading at $10 per share.

a.   What is the straight bond value if other 20-year bonds of similar quality currently pay 14 percent semiannually?
b.   What is the conversion ratio and the conversion value of the bond?
c.   What is the value of the convertible before maturity if the value of an option on each share of stock the convertible can be exchanged for is $4.48?

PROBLEMS

20.1   Bryan Steel's common stock price is $34. A new warrant is being issued with an exercise price of $38, its life is 3.5 years, the risk-free rate is 0.10, and the volatility of Bryan's common stock is 0.45 per year. Ignoring any dilution that occurs when the warrants are exercised, what is the value of the warrant?

20.2 Warrants for Pleasure Industries allows its warrantholders to purchase 10 shares of common stock at the exercise price of $35. The market price of the common stock is $37.50, and the market price of a warrant is 15 percent greater than its lower limit value.

a. What is the market price of a warrant?

b. At what dollar premium over its lower limit value is the warrant selling?

20.3 Ross Systems, an all-equity firm that does not pay cash dividends on its common stock, wants to value some warrants it is considering issuing. The risk-free rate is 9 percent, the standard deviation of the firm's common stock is 0.50, the current price of the stock is $19, the warrants will have a four-year life, and the exercise price will be $30.

a. Ignoring possible dilution, what is the value of each warrant?

b. Taking into account the impact of dilution, Ross estimates the adjusted stock price, P_0^*, will be $20 and q will be 0.14. What is the value of each warrant? How much impact does dilution have on the warrant price?

c. What is the lower limit on the value of the warrant? How much of a premium over the lower limit is indicated by the value of the warrant in (b)?

d. Ross plans to sell 500,000 warrants. If it anticipates selling them at a 10 percent discount from their value, how much (ignoring any flotation or issuance costs) should Ross obtain from the financing?

20.4 Professional Developers, Ltd., pays cash dividends of $3 per share and has a dividend payout ratio of 75 percent and a P/E ratio of 10. To raise additional funds, Professional has decided to issue a $20,000,000, 25-year convertible debenture ($1,000 par) with a coupon rate of 11 percent and a conversion price of $50. Interest is paid yearly.

a. What is Professional's current EPS?

b. What is the market price per share of Professional's common stock?

c. What is the conversion value per bond?

d. If 60 percent of the convertible debentures are ultimately converted, how many additional shares of common stock will be issued?

e. If comparable quality nonconvertible bonds are yielding 12 percent, what is the initial straight bond value (per bond) of the convertible? What is its straight bond value in 10 years (assuming market interest rates remain constant)?

20.5 Ten years ago The Stayton Group issued 20-year, 11 percent, semiannual-interest-paying convertible debentures with a call provision of 10 percent above par allowed 10 years after issuance. The conversion price of the debentures is $50, and the current market price of Stayton common is $65.

a. What is the conversion value of the convertible debentures?

b. Straight debentures of similar risk and maturity to Stayton's convertible debentures have a semiannual return of 8 percent. If the value of an option on each share of stock the convertible can be exchanged for is $38.11, what is the value of the convertible before conversion?

c. Now assume Stayton calls the debentures at 10 percent above par. Is there a transfer of wealth? If so, from whom to whom?

20.6 A 30-year maturity, $1,000 par convertible bond will be issued at par; it has an 8 percent coupon rate. The market rate of interest on comparable quality and maturity straight bonds is 11 percent. Interest is paid yearly.

a. What is the straight bond value of the convertible?

b. What is the straight bond value if (1) the maturity is only 10 years, and (2) if it is only 4 years?

c. If the maturity is 30 years, what is the straight bond value if the market rate of interest is (1) 13 percent, (2) 9 percent, (3) 7 percent?

d. What general conclusions can you reach about the stability of the straight bond value, or floor, for convertibles?

20.7 NewPark Systems is an all-equity firm that is planning a $10,000,000 convertible bond issue. NewPark's investment dealers have suggested that the 10-year bonds carry an interest rate of 7.5 percent; comparable quality and maturity bonds are presently yielding 12 percent. The investment dealers have recommended that the conversion price be $24. NewPark does not pay cash dividends on its common stock, the current stock price is $20 per share, the adjusted market price, P_0^*, is $18 per share, the risk-free rate is 8.50 percent, the standard deviation of the firm's equity is 0.40, and q is 0.25. If the convertible bonds are expected to sell at their par value, should you accept the investment dealers' recommendations?

20.8 Jeff owns one convertible bond ($1,000 par) issued by Bellefonte Corp. He has gathered the following information:

Market price of the convertible bond	$1,280
Conversion price	20
Market price per share of common stock	25
Call price of the convertible bond	1,100

a. If Jeff converts right now, what is the value of the common stock received? Should he voluntarily convert?

b. Assume Bellefonte calls the convertible. At what common stock market price would Jeff be indifferent between converting and receiving the call price?

20.9 Microtonics needs to raise $35,000,000 in new financing. Due to the firm's fast growth, its investment dealer thinks subordinated debt is the best bet. Two alternative plans have been proposed.

Plan I	**Plan II**
Straight subordinated debt issued at par (ignore flotation costs)	Straight subordinated debt with warrants issued at par (ignore flotation costs)
20-year maturity	30 warrants per $1,000 par bond; each
10% coupon rate	warrant can be used to purchase one share
Expected common stock P/E = 8	of stock; the exercise price is $20
	20-year maturity
	9% coupon rate
	Expected common stock P/E = 8

The firm anticipates EBIT will be $16,000,000. Other interest charges are $2,000,000, the tax rate is 35 percent, and there are 2,000,000 shares of common stock outstanding.

a. Determine the straight bond value of the 9 percent subordinated debt issued in plan II. What is the implied value of the warrants?

b. Calculate the EPS and market value of the common stock for both plans. (*Note:* In calculating EPS do not worry about the common stock that would be issued if the warrants are exercised.) Which plan should be employed? Why?

c. Determine the EPS for plan II as in (b), but now assume that the warrants are exercised. If the P/E increases to 9 times after the warrants exercised, which plan should the firm choose? Does this agree with your conclusion in (b)? How much new cash will the firm receive when the warrants are exercised?

20.10   Wilmot Industries needs $10,000,000 for expansion. The company expects EBIT of $8,000,000 after the expansion, there is no other interest, the tax rate is 35 percent, and a common stock P/E of 9 times is estimated. There are currently 1,000,000 shares of common stock outstanding. Two financing plans being considered are as follows:

Plan I	Plan II
Straight debt at par (ignore flotation costs) with warrants	Convertible debt at par (ignore flotation costs)
20 warrants per $1,000 par bond; each for one share of common stock	Conversion price = $20
12% coupon rate	10% coupon rate
20-year maturity	20-year maturity
Expected common stock P/E = 9 times	Expected common stock P/E = 9 times

a. Determine the anticipated EPS under each plan and the market price per share. Which plan should Wilmot take? Why?

b. To further analyze the effects of the two plans, Wilmot estimates that in four years EBIT will be $13 million, and that (1) the warrants will all be exercised, because they expire in four years; or (2) it will have forced all the convertibles to be converted. Assuming full warrant exercise or full conversion, and a P/E of 10 under plan I and 11 under plan II, what is the new EPS and common stock market price? Which plan should be chosen? (*Note:* For plan II, assume no interest is paid in the fourth year.)

c. Why does the result in (b) conflict with your conclusion in (a)? Considering your answers to both (a) and (b), is it better to maximize value now (at time t = 0) or in four years?

20.11   **Mini Case**   Andrecomp is in the process of assessing its financing needs for the next year. Due to the high-risk but growing nature of its business, Andrecomp has a need for more financing. As CFO you are responsible for providing the financing plan. In evaluating the situation, you note that two years ago a large common stock financing was undertaken. Since then Andrecomp's stock price has fluctuated somewhat, but overall there has been little change in the stock price level. With that in mind, and knowing that substantial profits appear to be at least a year away, you have concluded that a direct stock offering is not desirable or feasible. At the same time, you are not sure a straight bond offering can provide the needed financing. Therefore, you are considering a bond/warrant issue or a convertible bond issue.

a. Summarize when a bond/warrant package and convertibles are desirable. Can they help Andrecomp and at the same time provide benefits to investors?

b. You are evaluating two different financing packages, both of which would raise $40,000,000. Andrecomp's value, V, is $100,000,000, of which $70,000,000 is equity and $30,000,000 is debt. The risk-free rate is 7 percent, comparable quality and comparable maturity debt costs 12 percent, there are 1,000,000 shares of common stock outstanding, and the standard deviation of the firm's equity is 0.60. The two plans are as follows:

Plan I	Plan II
Straight debt at par with warrants (ignore flotation costs)	Convertible debt at par (ignore flotation costs)
3 warrants per $1,000 par bond; each for one share of common stock; 3-year expiration	Conversion price = $125
Exercise price = $90	8% coupon rate
11% coupon rate	8-year maturity
20-year bond maturity	

1. Calculate the straight bond value of the bonds contained in the two plans.
2. Ignoring the impact of the financing on the stock price, calculate the approximate value of the warrant and the option contained in the convertible.
3. Assume that after considering dilution, the value of each warrant in plan I is $28.72, while the value of an option to convert each share of stock the convertible can be exchanged for in plan II is $32.67. What is the total value of each financing plan? What conclusion do you arrive at about the value of the two different plans? Does one appear to be superior in terms of the value to Andrecomp?

c. Andrecomp anticipates that EBIT will be $20,000,000, its interest on existing debt is $3,000,000 per year, and its marginal tax rate is 40 percent. Taking account of the additional interest with either financing plan, what will be the earnings per share, EPS, with each financing plan? (*Note:* Ignore any additional shares of common stock from exercise or conversion.) Now, what will EPS be in four years if EBIT is $30,000,000, interest on the total debt for the firm is $5,500,000, T is 40 percent, and (1) the warrants have all been exercised and the bond called for plan I, and (2) the convertible bond has been fully converted? What conclusions do you draw from the impact on EPS? Does this support or conflict with what you concluded in (b3)?

REFERENCES

ASQUITH, PAUL, and DAVID W. MULLINS, JR. "Convertible Debt: Corporate Call Policy and Voluntary Conversion." *Journal of Finance* 46 (September 1991): 1273–1289.

CROUHY, MICHEL, and DAN GALAI. "Common Errors in the Valuation of Warrants and Options on Firms with Warrants." *Financial Analysts Journal* 47 (September/October 1991): 89–90.

GALAI, DAN, and MIER A. SCHNELLER. "Pricing of Warrants and the Value of the Firm." *Journal of Finance* 33 (December 1978): 1333–1342.

HARRIS, MILTON, and ARTHUR RAVIV. "A Sequential Signalling Model of Convertible Debt Call Policy." *Journal of Finance* 40 (December 1985): 1263–1281.

HOWE, JOHN S., and PEIHWANG WEI. "The Valuation Effects of Warrant Extensions." *Journal of Finance* 48 (March 1993): 305–314.

INGERSOLL, JONATHAN. "An Examination of Corporate Call Policies on Convertible Securities." *Journal of Finance* 32 (May 1977): 463–478.

KIM, YONG CHEOL, and RENE M. STULZ. "Is There a Global Market for Convertible Bonds?" *Journal of Business* 65 (January 1992): 75–91.

MAZZERO, MICHAEL A., and WILLIAM T. MOORE. "Liquidity Costs and Stock Price Response to Convertible Security Calls." *Journal of Business* 65 (July 1992): 353–369.

MCCONNELL, JOHN J., and EDUARDO S. SCHWARTZ. "The Origin of LYONs: A Case Study in Financial Innovation." *Journal of Applied Corporate Finance* 4 (Winter 1992): 40–47.

ROSENGREN, ERIC S. "Defaults of Original Issue High-Yield Convertible Bonds." *Journal of Finance* 48 (March 1993): 345–362.

SINGH, AJAI, ARNOLD R. COWAN, and NANDKUMAR NAYAR. "Underwritten Calls of Convertible Bonds." *Journal of Financial Economics* 29 (March 1991): 173–196.

STEIN, JEREMY C. "Convertible Bonds as Backdoor Equity Financing." *Journal of Financial Economics* 32 (August 1992): 3–21.

PART VII

Short-Term Financial Management

*T*o maximize the value of the firm, or the size of the pie, the firm must concentrate on providing quality products and/or services in a timely manner. In addition, it must do an effective job in marketing, employee relations, and so forth. From a financial perspective, there are three crucial areas where decisions directly affect the value of the firm: its investment decisions, its financing decisions, and its short-term (or day-to-day) financial management decisions. To maximize the value of the firm we have:

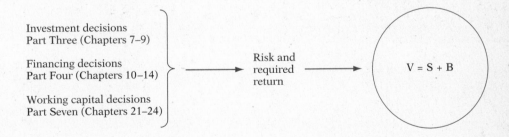

Investment decisions
Part Three (Chapters 7–9)

Financing decisions
Part Four (Chapters 10–14)

Working capital decisions
Part Seven (Chapters 21–24)

Risk and required return

$V = S + B$

Let us now examine the short-term financial management decisions of the firm. In Chapter 21 we examine the primary factors that are at play when a firm determines its short-term financial management policy. Then in Chapter 22 cash and marketable securities are examined, followed by accounts receivable and inventory in Chapter 23. In Chapter 24 we examine the sources of short-term financing. Throughout, the objective remains the same: to make decisions that maximize the long-run value of the firm.

21 Short-Term Financial Management Policy

EXECUTIVE SUMMARY

Effective management of current assets and current liabilities is at the core of financial management. Firms that are efficient devote much time and attention to short-term financial management. By doing so they are able to manage this portion of the firm's assets and liabilities in a manner that contributes to the overall goal of maximizing the value of the firm. Although there is much less theory to drive the firm's short-term financial management decisions than in the areas of capital budgeting, capital structure, and the like, the same forces of incremental cash flows, risks, and opportunity costs are at play when a firm's short-term financial management decisions are made.

To understand short-term financial management policy, it is important to understand the firm's cash cycle. Both the asset and the liability sides may be managed in an aggressive or a conservative manner. One guideline is the matching principle, whereby temporary assets are financed with temporary financing and permanent current and long-term assets are financed with permanent financing. Other things being equal, aggressive asset management lowers costs, whereas aggressive liability management lowers cash outflows related to interest. Both have the effect of increasing the returns, but they also increase the risk exposure of the firm.

Short-term financial management is not a one-time decision. The best strategy may vary, depending on the season of the year, the level of interest rates, or the stage of the business cycle. It is a dynamic area; the firm must be responsive to ongoing needs and goals, the state of the economy, trends in marketing and production, and the risks involved. As these factors change, the firm's short-term financial management policies must also change.

MANAGING SHORT-TERM ASSETS AND LIABILITIES

A firm's assets are normally classified as either current or long-term. Current assets are those expected to be converted into cash within one year. They are cash and marketable securities, accounts receivable, inventory, and other current assets such as prepaid expenses. Liabilities also are split between current and long-term, with current liabilities those expected to be paid within one year. Current liabilities include short-term debt, accounts payable, and other current liabilities such as accruals and the current portion of long-term debt. Sometimes the term **working capital** is used to refer to both current assets and current liabilities. Thus, short-term financial management, or working capital management, focuses on the coordinated control of the firm's current assets and current liabilities.

SHORT-TERM FINANCIAL MANAGEMENT DECISIONS

To gain some understanding of the types of decisions required in short-term financial management, consider Figure 21.1, which depicts the flow of cash through a firm. On the right-hand side of the figure are the long-term financial management areas, including capital investments, raising capital, and the related areas of determining the firm's opportunity cost of capital, capital structure, and dividend policy. The other aspect of financial management, which focuses on the short-term day-to-day activities of the firm, is depicted on the left-hand side of the figure. The basic short-term financial management decisions facing a firm include the following:

1. COLLECTIONS AND DISBURSEMENTS   One of the primary responsibilities of a firm is to manage the collection of funds from customers and to pay suppliers, employees, marketing costs, taxes, and so forth. This frequently includes the implementation of some type of cash and cheque collection system and the development of various systems for making cost-effective cash disbursements.
2. CASH CONCENTRATION   Managers also have the responsibility for designing and implementing a system to gather funds from the banks dealt with so the funds can be concentrated for effective management and investment purposes.
3. LIQUIDITY MANAGEMENT   The firm's liquidity—on both the asset side and the liability side—must also be managed. Liquidity management includes decisions regarding the synchronization of cash inflows and outflows, and determination of the expected surpluses or deficits of cash (via cash budgets as discussed in Chapter 26). Liquidity management also includes managing the firm's portfolio of short-term marketable securities and choosing the type and maturity structure of the firm's short-term borrowings.
4. BANK RELATIONS   Another responsibility is designing the firm's banking network and managing its banking relationships. This category includes determining which banks to deal with and the services that will be secured from each.
5. RECEIVABLES   Management of the firm's credit policy and the resulting collection procedures is also important. Although basic credit terms and customers must be determined in conjunction with marketing personnel, the ultimate

Figure 21.1

Flow of Cash Through a Firm

Both short-term and long-term financial management are important for achieving the goal of maximizing the value of the firm. Short-term financial management is more operationally focused and less theoretical than long-term financial management.

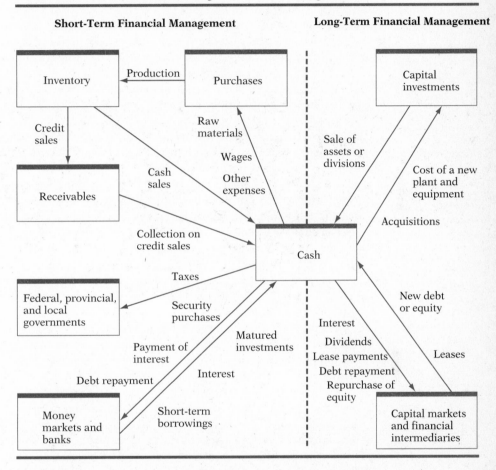

responsibility for implementation and maintenance falls in the short-term financial management area.

6.   INVENTORY   Inventory is the responsibility of many individuals within the firm. The major activities we are concerned with include determining how much investment in inventory is needed and how to finance it.

We will examine each of these areas in Chapters 21 to 24. Before doing so, it is important to understand more about short-term financial management in general, why it is needed, and how firms can proceed with estimating how much in the way of current assets and current liabilities they need.

WHY DO FIRMS HAVE SHORT-TERM ASSETS AND LIABILITIES?

In a world of perfect markets where there are no transactions costs, no time delays in the production, marketing, and cheque-clearing system, and no financial distress costs, the value of the firm would be independent of its current asset and current liability decisions. If that were true, there would be no need to study short-term financial management.

But markets are not perfect. Imperfect markets, and delays and/or costs, are what create the need for a firm to concern itself with short-term financial management. Let us briefly consider some of the reasons firms need current assets and current liabilities.

1. TRANSACTION COSTS   Transaction costs consist of (1) the service fees for buying and selling securities or (2) the potential loss in value when a "fire sale" must be made at a price below what could be received if more time were available. Because of transaction costs, firms hold cash or marketable securities with a major emphasis on liquidity—that is, the ability to be quickly and cheaply available as cash in order to meet short-term needs.

2. TIME DELAYS   Time delays arise in the production, marketing, and cash collection aspects of a firm's business. Because transactions do not happen instantaneously, many activities affect current asset and liability needs. These include (1) maintaining inventory (raw materials, work in process, or finished goods), (2) offering credit policies to help sell the product, (3) providing cash discounts for early payment, and (4) reducing the float when customers pay their bills. All these steps involve some costs that must be weighed against the benefits involved.

3. FINANCIAL DISTRESS COSTS   Financial distress costs include legal and other direct and indirect costs such as managerial time associated with reorganization, bankruptcy, or fending off financial difficulties. Because of the high cost most managers equate with financial distress, they tend to keep a significant amount of liquid balances, even though they generally earn less on these balances than on the firm's long-term asset investments. Alternatively, firms may incur costs to have access to credit markets, although they do not anticipate actually having to take advantage of this additional borrowing capacity.

Other items could be mentioned, but the point should be clear: In theory, short-term assets and liabilities are not needed; in practice, they become one of the most important topics managers must deal with. In this and the next three chapters, we will see the importance of effective short-term financial management decisions in maximizing the value of the firm.

THE IMPORTANCE OF SHORT-TERM ASSETS AND LIABILITIES

Short-term assets and liabilities typically make up a large part of a firm's total assets and liabilities. Consider the percentage breakdown of current assets and current liabilities (both compared to total assets) for nonfinancial firms for three recent years:[1]

---

[1] *Quarterly Financial Statistics for Enterprises* (Catalogue 61–008), Statistics Canada.

Current Assets			
Cash and marketable securities	6.6%	6.3%	7.3%
Accounts receivable	13.3	13.3	14.1
Inventory	12.4	14.1	15.6
Total current assets	32.3%	33.7%	37.0%
Current Liabilities			
Short-term debt	11.5%	10.2%	8.9%
Accounts payable and accrued liabilities	14.6	14.0	15.0
Total current liabilities	26.1%	24.2%	23.9%

Current assets account for about 35 percent of the total assets for nonfinancial firms, whereas current liabilities constitute about 25 percent. Among current assets, we see that there is approximately the same investment in inventory and receivables. For current liabilities, the largest percentages are in accounts payable and accrued liabilities. Comparing the three years (from right to left), we see that the investment in current assets decreased while the amount of current liabilities increased.

Some of the most significant reasons short-term financial management is important are as follows:

1. The size and volatility of current assets and current liabilities make them a major managerial concern. Managers spend much of their time on the day-to-day activities that revolve around short-term financial management.

2. The relationship between sales growth, or growth opportunities, and short-term assets and liabilities is both close and direct. As sales increase, firms must increase inventory and accounts payable. Increased sales generate a higher level of accounts receivable. So current assets and liabilities must be managed as firms increase or decrease their scale of operations and sales. At the same time, some of the current liabilities—especially accounts payable—tend to increase and decrease spontaneously as inventory and accounts receivable increase and decrease. This **spontaneous short-term financing** (due to the use of trade credit as discussed in Chapter 22) must be kept in mind as we consider both the current assets and their financing (by both current and long-term sources).

3. Financial problems show up first in a firm's current assets and liability accounts, especially its level of accounts receivable, inventory, and the flow of cash into and out of the firm. Firms that are doing well maintain control of their accounts receivable and inventory and ensure the continual flow of cash.

4. Current, or short-term, assets and liabilities are especially important for smaller firms, because these firms often carry a higher percentage of both than do larger firms. Their survival is much more dependent on effective short-term financial management than is that of larger firms.

Concept Review Questions

- Explain the terms *current assets, current liabilities, and working capital.*
- Why is short-term financial management important and necessary?
- Give some examples of short-term financial management decisions a firm must make.

Liquidity and the Cash Cycle

Liquidity is an important factor in determining a firm's short-term financial management policies. It is a function of the level and composition of current assets and current liabilities and the ability to raise cash when needed. The variability in current asset and current liability levels is also important; however, for many firms the ongoing level of current assets and liabilities is fairly steady. Accordingly, we focus our primary attention on the level, not the variability, of the firm's current assets and current liabilities. Marketable securities, which are short-term investments for excess cash, are highly liquid. Accounts receivable, which arise from the sale of the firm's goods or services, are less liquid than marketable securities. Inventory is a current asset but is often less liquid than accounts receivable.

Liquidity has two major aspects—ongoing liquidity and protective liquidity. **Ongoing liquidity** comprises the inflows and outflows of cash through the firm as the product acquisition, production, sales, payment, and collection process takes place over time. **Financial slack**, as discussed in Chapter 12, is the ability to adjust rapidly to unforeseen cash demands and to have backup means available to raise cash. We begin by addressing ongoing liquidity and defer a discussion of financial slack until later in the chapter.

The firm's ongoing liquidity is a function of its cash cycle. (The cash cycle is shown in the upper left part of Figure 21.1.) As raw materials are purchased, the firm's current liabilities increase through accounts payable. Subsequently, the firm pays for these purchases. During the same time, the raw materials are converted into finished goods through the production process. After reaching the finished goods inventory, they can be sold—for cash or on credit. In the latter case, accounts receivable are created. Finally, the accounts receivable are collected, resulting in cash. Ongoing liquidity is influenced by all aspects of the cash cycle, because increases in purchases, inventory, or receivables will decrease liquidity. A decrease in any of the three, other things being equal, will increase ongoing liquidity.

A helpful way to look at the cash flow for the firm is to analyze the firm's cash conversion cycle. A **cash conversion cycle** reflects the net time interval in days between actual cash expenditures of the firm on productive resources and the ultimate recovery of cash. As shown in Figure 21.2, once the purchase of the raw materials is made, the **days inventory** determines the average number of days it takes to produce and sell the product. The **days sales outstanding** determines the average number of days it takes to collect credit sales.[2] The **operating cycle**, which is

$$\text{operating cycle} = \text{days sales outstanding} + \text{days inventory} \qquad (21.1)$$

measures the total number of days from purchase to the time when cash is received. However, because the raw materials typically are not paid for immediately, we must also determine how long the firm defers its payments. The difference between the operating cycle and the **days payable** is the cash conversion cycle:

$$\text{cash conversion cycle} = \text{operating cycle} - \text{days payable} \qquad (21.2)$$

---

[2] Days sales outstanding is also referred to as average collection period.

Figure 21.2

Cash Conversion Cycle for a Typical Firm

By integrating both current assets and current liabilities, the cash conversion cycle emphasizes the firm's ongoing liquidity.

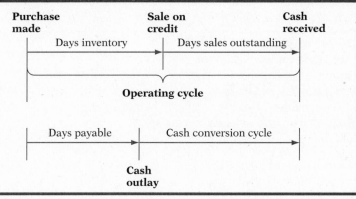

As the cash conversion cycle lengthens, the firm's ongoing liquidity worsens; as the cycle is shortened, the firm's ongoing liquidity improves.

To determine a cash conversion cycle, we employ the following steps:

STEP 1: Calculate the **receivables turnover**, which is:

$$\text{receivables turnover} = \frac{\text{sales}}{\text{accounts receivable}} \qquad (21.3)$$

STEP 2: Calculate the **inventory turnover:**

$$\text{inventory turnover} = \frac{\text{cost of goods sold}}{\text{inventory}} \qquad (21.4)$$

STEP 3: Determine the **payables turnover:**

$$\text{payables turnover} = \frac{\text{cost of goods sold} + \text{general, selling, and administrative expenses}}{\text{accounts payable} + \text{salaries, benefits, and payroll taxes payable}} \qquad (21.5)$$

STEP 4: Divide the three turnover ratios into 365 days to calculate the days sales outstanding, days inventory, and days payable, respectively.

$$\text{days sales outstanding} = 365/\text{receivables turnover} \qquad (21.6)$$

$$\text{days inventory} = 365/\text{inventory turnover} \qquad (21.7)$$

$$\text{days payable} = 365/\text{payables turnover} \qquad (21.8)$$

STEP 5: Using Equations 21.1 and 21.2, and the values determined in step 4 above, calculate the cash conversion cycle.

Table 21.1

Cash Conversion Cycle for Cancomp Ltd.

Although traditional liquidity measures indicate Cancomp's liquidity has deteriorated somewhat, its cash conversion cycle has actually improved during this period.

	1996	1995	1994
Liquidity Measures			
Current ratio (current assets/current liabilities)	1.21	1.17	1.36
Quick ratio [(assets − inventory) /current liabilities]	0.86	0.85	0.94
Net working capital (current assets − current liabilities; in millions of dollars)	$42.34	$34.96	$67.90
Turnover Ratios			
Receivables turnover	5.30	5.17	5.22
Inventory turnover	6.09	6.43	5.44
Payables turnover	6.08	7.77	6.12
Cash Conversion Cycle			
Days sales outstanding	68.83 days	70.59 days	69.84 days
Days inventory	59.93	56.76	67.10
Operating cycle	128.76	127.35	136.94
Less: Days payable	60.03	46.98	59.64
Cash conversion cycle	68.73 days	80.37 days	77.30 days

These steps are shown in Table 21.1 for Cancomp Ltd., for 1994, 1995, and 1996. An examination of various liquidity measures (current ratio, quick ratio, and net working capital) in Table 21.1 indicates that the firm's liquidity appears to have deteriorated somewhat over this period. By calculating the cash conversion cycle, however, we see that its ongoing liquidity has improved since 1994. The cash conversion cycle is a quick and convenient way to analyze the ongoing liquidity of the firm over time. Although it does not show how risky the cash flows are, it does focus on our main concern—cash flows.

Concept Review Questions

■ How is *ongoing liquidity* different from *protective liquidity*?

■ Explain how to calculate a firm's cash conversion cycle.

STRATEGY FOR CURRENT ASSET AND CURRENT LIABILITY MANAGEMENT

Essential elements that must be considered in establishing a firm's short-term financial management policies are cash flows, liquidity, risk, and the level of returns that are necessary to compensate for the risk. We begin by analyzing first the strategy for current asset management and then that for current liabilities.

CURRENT ASSETS

The major current assets are cash, marketable securities, accounts receivable, and inventory. We will examine these assets in some detail in Chapters 22 and 23. Here, it is helpful to consider the factors that influence a firm's investment in current assets.

Current Asset Levels   Many factors influence the general level of current assets. Four of the most important are:

1. NATURE OF THE FIRM'S BUSINESS   The specific activities pursued by the firm often have an important influence on the level of the firm's current assets. Retail firms have much larger inventories than manufacturing firms, leading to a larger percentage of current assets. On the other hand, fast-food chains, such as McDonald's and Wendy's, always have more current liabilities than current assets; due to the nature of the business, they operate—very successfully, we might add—with very few current assets.

2. THE SIZE OF THE FIRM   For large Canadian firms, current assets represent approximately 40 percent of total assets. In contrast, smaller firms may hold 65 to 70 percent of their total assets as current assets. The primary reasons for the differences are that (a) large firms can devote the necessary resources and attention to managing their current assets; (b) large firms may have some economies of scale in current asset or current liability management, or they may have more predictable cash flows; (c) large firms have more access to the capital market than smaller firms; and (d) as firms get larger they become more capital-intensive. By capital-intensive, we mean that they tend to use more machines and equipment in the production and distribution process.

3. RATE OF INCREASE (OR DECREASE) IN SALES   As sales increase, generally both accounts receivable and inventory also increase, along with a spontaneous increase in accounts payable. Consider Dominion Products, which has been analyzing its current assets and liabilities in relation to sales, as shown in Table 21.2. Current assets have averaged about 30 percent of sales, and current liabilities have been about 8 percent of sales. Note that as sales have increased, current assets have increased by roughly the same proportion. Likewise, current liabilities have tended to increase due to the spontaneous change in accounts payable as inventory expands.

4. STABILITY OF THE FIRM'S SALES   The more stable the sales, the lower the level of current assets. On the other hand, firms with highly volatile sales must have more current assets, particularly cash and inventory.

Aggressive Versus Conservative Management   In examining the firm's current asset policies, we will concentrate on the composition of the firm's balance sheet. We will examine the effect that changes in the firm's policies have on its asset composition, and thus on its cash conversion cycle, expense levels, and risk, and on the returns required by the firm. For the time being, we are not concerned with how the firm finances its current assets; *our concern is solely with the composition of these assets.* A firm can manage its current assets conservatively or aggressively. To see this, consider Figure 21.3, which illustrates both conservative (with higher current asset levels) and aggressive (with lower current asset levels) approaches.

Table 21.2

Working Capital for Dominion Products ($ in thousands)

Although there have been year-to-year fluctuations, the relationships among working capital components are stable enough for planning purposes.

Year	Current Assets	Current Liabilities	Net Working Capital	Sales	Current Assets/Sales	Current Liabilities/Sales	Net Working Capital/Sales
1	$ 74	$20	$54	$250	29.6%	8.0%	21.6%
2	77	21	56	284	27.1	7.4	19.7
3	90	26	64	275	32.7	9.5	23.3
4	92	25	67	298	30.9	8.4	22.5
5	98	23	75	315	31.1	7.3	23.8
6	110	30	80	375	29.3	8.0	21.3
Average					30.1%	8.1%	22.0%

Because current assets never drop to zero, we can think of the firm as having a need for some **permanent current assets** on an ongoing basis. At the same time, virtually all firms have a need for **seasonal** (or **temporary**) **current assets** that fluctuate over the year (or business cycle). The size of both the permanent and temporary current assets is determined, in part, by how aggressive a firm is regarding the level of current assets it maintains.

Other things being equal, an aggressive asset management policy leads to lower current assets, a shorter cash conversion cycle, lower expenses, and higher risk and higher returns required to compensate for the increased risk. Conservative asset management practices have just the opposite effects.

Level of Current Assets.   Aggressive asset management generally means lower levels of all current assets. The firm keeps only a minimal level of cash and marketable securities on hand and relies on effective management and the possibility of short-term borrowing to meet any unexpected cash needs. Likewise, aggressive management of accounts receivable and inventory will generally lead to lower levels of both.[3]

Cash Conversion Cycle.   More aggressive management shortens the cash conversion cycle. Remember from Equation 21.1 that the operating cycle is determined by adding the days inventory to the days sales outstanding. Aggressive asset management increases turnover, by lowering the average level of both receivables and inventory. Thus, an aggressive policy shortens the firm's operating cycle, which leads to a shorter cash conversion cycle. This shorter cash conversion cycle increases a firm's ongoing liquidity, because it does not have as large a proportion of its assets tied up in accounts receivable and inventory.

---

[3] In some circumstances, an aggressive policy regarding accounts receivable or inventory could result in a high level of one or both. This is an exception to the general idea that the more aggressive the current asset policy, the lower the level of current assets. As noted in Chapter 23, a net present value approach is employed to determine the proper level of accounts receivable and inventory to maintain.

Figure 21.3

Aggressive Versus Conservative Asset Management for Dominion Products

Aggressive management leads to higher risk and higher required returns; conservative management provides lower risk exposure and lower returns.

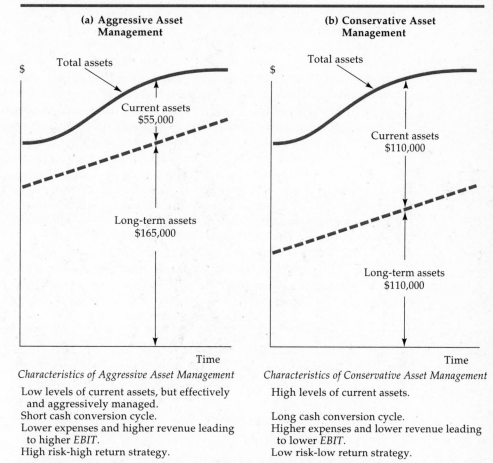

(a) Aggressive Asset Management

Total assets

Current assets $55,000

Long-term assets $165,000

Time

(b) Conservative Asset Management

Total assets

Current assets $110,000

Long-term assets $110,000

Time

Characteristics of Aggressive Asset Management

Low levels of current assets, but effectively and aggressively managed.
Short cash conversion cycle.
Lower expenses and higher revenue leading to higher *EBIT*.
High risk-high return strategy.

Characteristics of Conservative Asset Management

High levels of current assets.

Long cash conversion cycle.
Higher expenses and lower revenue leading to lower *EBIT*.
Low risk-low return strategy.

Expense and Revenue Levels.   Aggressive current asset management will have the effect of reducing expenses. Fewer accounts receivable will be carried, so there will be lower carrying costs. In addition, fewer receivables will have to be written off as uncollectible. Likewise, by keeping inventory to a minimum, the firm avoids the carrying cost associated with inventory, as well as the possibility for loss due to obsolescence, theft, and so forth. This, in turn, leads to higher earnings before interest and taxes (EBIT) and ultimately to higher cash flows, compared with the results of a conservative asset management policy.

A further effect of aggressive asset management may be to increase expected revenues, which could also lead to a higher EBIT level. This can occur in two ways: First, if returns from investing in long-term assets are higher than on short-term assets, which they typically are, then total cash inflows should increase. Second, the firm could attempt to increase total cash inflows by tailoring its credit-granting policy to encourage sales. These more lenient credit terms, however, would be granted only if they were expected to lead to a higher level of EBIT than without them.[4]

Risk and Return.   Finally, let us consider what happens to the risk and returns required by the firm. In Chapter 5 we developed the idea of the capital asset pricing model (CAPM) and nondiversifiable risk (beta) as a means of quantifying risk. Some of these ideas can be employed here, but it is easier to think of risk in terms of the variability in current assets, a scarcity of cash, or other adverse consequences. We can still maintain the conceptual framework that the higher the risk, the higher the return, and vice versa. Likewise, in Chapters 18 and 19 we introduced the idea of options, and we saw that the common stock of a firm is just a call option. Other things being equal, we know that more risk, as evidenced by an increase in the standard deviation of the firm's assets, benefits common shareholders at the expense of bondholders.

The risks associated with an aggressive asset position include the possibility of running out of cash or being otherwise so strapped for funds that effective management of the firm is impeded. Likewise, the firm might keep inventory so low that sales are lost when stockouts occur. The risk associated with an aggressive accounts receivable policy could also result in lost sales if too low a level is kept.

To see the effect of aggressive versus conservative asset management policies, while holding other risks constant, consider Dominion Products. It can adopt an aggressive or a conservative asset management position, with anticipated effects as follows:[5]

	Aggressive	Conservative
Sales	$375,000	$375,000
All expenses	325,000	335,000
EBIT	$ 50,000	$ 40,000

As shown previously in Figure 21.3, the aggressive approach results in only $55,000 in current assets, whereas the more conservative approach results in $110,000. The impact of fewer current assets and therefore lower expenses shows up in an anticipated EBIT of $50,000 for the aggressive plan, as opposed to only $40,000 with the conservative plan. Thus, by employing a more aggressive approach that exposes the firm to more risk, the firm has increased its anticipated EBIT, and ultimately its cash inflows.

---

[4] Based on accepting positive NPV projects, the tendency would be for higher, rather than lower, accounts receivable. They would still be aggressively and effectively managed, however, so that they do not get out of control.

[5] For simplicity, we assume total assets and revenues are constant.

CURRENT LIABILITIES

Now that we have considered current assets, let us consider the financing needed to support these assets. There are two fundamental decisions the firm must make with regard to financing: First, how much will it secure from short-term versus long-term debt (or liability) sources? Second, how much should the firm borrow in relation to what is put up by its owners? The first of these, the short-term versus the long-term question, is considered here. As we will see, the matching principle is widely employed to address this question. The second part, how much debt relative to equity should be employed, was discussed in Chapters 12 and 13. Here, we ignore this aspect of the problem and confine our attention to short-term financing.

Current Liability Levels   Retail firms carry more current assets than do manufacturing firms. This is primarily because retail firms have to carry more inventory. However, given that most merchandise for inventory is bought on credit, what would you expect the level of a typical retail firm's accounts payable to be, compared to that of a typical manufacturing firm? It will be larger, simply because larger inventories lead spontaneously to larger accounts payable. Thus, a major factor influencing the firm's level of current liabilities is its level of inventory and other current assets. Other things being equal, businesses that require high levels of current assets will tend to have fairly high levels of current liabilities.

A second element influencing the level of current liabilities is the amount of flexibility desired by the firm. If a firm has a low level of current liabilities, it has flexibility, because short-term borrowing can generally be easily employed. Also, accounts payable can be built up in an emergency without endangering the firm. If the firm already has a high level of current liabilities, however, then little flexibility is left. The more flexibility the firm wants, the less it will finance with current liabilities.

Aggressive Versus Conservative Management   Other things being equal, the lower the current liabilities, the more conservative the firm's liability management policies. As shown in Figure 21.4, the higher the level of current liabilities, the more aggressive the policy. This is exactly opposite the effects of an aggressive versus a conservative asset policy. In what follows in this section, *we focus on the liabilities, holding assets constant.* Then, in the next section, we will consider assets and liabilities together. An aggressive liability management policy results in higher current liabilities, a shorter cash conversion cycle, lower interest costs (if short-term rates are less than long-term rates), and higher risk and higher required returns. Conservative policies have just the opposite effect.

Level of Current Liabilities.   Current liabilities consist of accounts payable, short-term loans or notes payable, various accrued expenses, and the current principal portion of long-term debt due.[6] An aggressive management approach increases the firm's reliance on short-term liabilities. Accounts payable will be used to the greatest

---

[6] The management of current liabilities is discussed in Chapter 24.

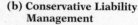

Figure 21.4

Aggressive Versus Conservative Liability Management for Dominion Products

Aggressive liability management is a high-risk–high-return strategy, whereas a conservative approach produces lower risks and lower returns.

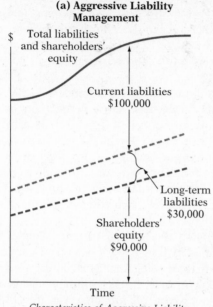

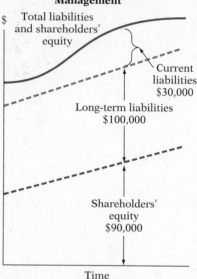

(a) Aggressive Liability Management

Total liabilities and shareholders' equity

Current liabilities $100,000

Long-term liabilities $30,000

Shareholders' equity $90,000

Time

Characteristics of Aggressive Liability Management

High levels of current liabilities.
Short cash conversion cycle.
Lower interest costs if short-term rates are lower than long-term rates.
High risk-high return strategy.

(b) Conservative Liability Management

Total liabilities and shareholders' equity

Current liabilities $30,000

Long-term liabilities $100,000

Shareholders' equity $90,000

Time

Characteristics of Conservative Liability Management

Low levels of current liabilities.
Long cash conversion cycle.
Higher interest costs if long-term rates are higher than short-term rates.
Low risk-low return strategy.

extent possible—and payments on them will be made as late as possible without incurring a bad credit reputation. Short-term borrowing will also be used extensively.

Cash Conversion Cycle.   By employing more accounts payable and accruals, aggressive liability management shortens the cash conversion cycle. Larger payables and accruals lead to a shorter payables turnover. This leads to a longer days payable and a shorter cash conversion cycle. Aggressive liability management tends to increase the ongoing liquidity of the firm by shortening the cash conversion cycle—but it also provides less future flexibility.

Interest Costs.   To understand fully the impact of aggressive versus conservative liability management on a firm's interest costs, we need to consider the term structure of interest rates discussed in Chapter 2. The yield curve plots the term to maturity versus the yield to maturity for borrowings that are equally risky but that differ in terms of length to maturity. Yield curves are generally upward-sloping—which means that long-term debt financing is more expensive than short-term debt financing. An expected benefit of an aggressive liability management programme is the ability to borrow funds at a cheaper rate, meaning lower cash outflows, than the firm would pay for long-term debt financing.

To see the expected benefits of an aggressive versus a conservative policy, consider again the example of Dominion Products. Figure 21.4 presented two different liability strategies. The aggressive one employs $100,000 in current liabilities and only $30,000 in long-term liabilities. The conservative policy employs $30,000 in current liabilities and $100,000 in long-term liabilities. If short-term interest rates are 10 percent and long-term rates are 14 percent, then the total before-tax interest cash outflow is $14,200 [i.e., (0.10)($100,000) + (0.14)($30,000)] for the aggressive policy, and $17,000 [i.e., (0.10)($30,000) + (0.14)($100,000)] for the conservative one. As long as long-term rates are higher than short-term rates, cash outflows associated with interest are reduced, leading to higher cash flows and earnings for the firm.

Risk and Return.   The main risk of an aggressive liability policy comes from general economic conditions and the continual need to refinance current liabilities. This is especially true if a firm is using extensive short-term financing through borrowing. Although the firm may be able to secure the financing, it is exposed to interest cost fluctuations. These fluctuating interest costs, and the continual need to refinance, increase the firm's risk exposure. An additional risk arises from reduced flexibility when the current liability level is high. Other things being equal, there are substantial risks associated with an aggressive liability policy that relies on large amounts of short-term debt. Greater returns are expected, however, by (1) reducing the cash conversion cycle, and (2) financing at interest rates that are generally (but not always) lower than long-term rates.

Concept Review Questions

- What factors affect a firm's level of current assets?
- Contrast an aggressive current asset management policy with a conservative current asset management policy.
- What are the effects on a firm of an aggressive current liability management policy and a conservative current liability management policy?

PUTTING IT ALL TOGETHER

We have considered separately both current assets and current liabilities. Now it is time to put them together and discuss the management of the firm's working capital in total. The three basic strategies a firm could follow, as illustrated in Figure 21.5, are aggressive, conservative, or matched. The matched strategy, which is often cited as a guideline employed for short-term financial management, is embodied in the matching principle, or the idea of self-liquidating debt.

Figure 21.5

Alternative Short-Term Financial Management Policies

By altering both its asset and its liability structure, the firm can vary its short-term financial management policies considerably.

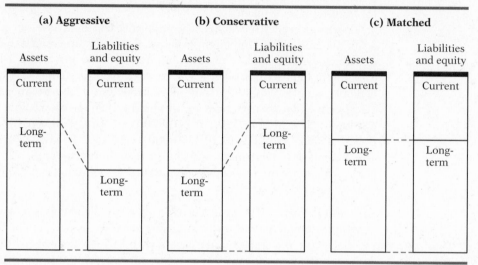

THE MATCHING PRINCIPLE

The **matching principle** can be stated as follows: Permanent investments in assets (both long-term and current) should be financed with permanent sources of financing, and temporary assets should be financed with temporary financing sources. The idea behind the matching principle is to match, or counterbalance, the cash-flow-generating characteristics of the assets with the maturity of the financing. A temporary buildup in current assets should be financed with current liabilities, which can be liquidated as the investment in current assets is reduced. A buildup in permanent current and long-term assets will take longer to convert to cash; thus, long-term financing will be needed.[7]

The matching principle can be applied to our previous discussion of aggressive versus conservative asset and liability policies. From Figure 21.5, we see that an aggressive asset policy calls for a low level of current assets, and a conservative policy calls for a high level. Likewise, an aggressive liability policy calls for a high level of current liabilities, and a conservative policy calls for a low level. To match them, the following rules apply:

1. If a firm has an aggressive current asset position (with a low level of current assets), then it should counterbalance its risks by employing a conservative liability position (with a low level of current liabilities).

---

[7] Matching can be done on the basis of maturity, cash flows, or duration. These topics are beyond our coverage.

Table 21.3

Impact of Alternative Current Asset and Liability Strategies on the Earnings of Dominion Products

A high-risk strategy employs low current assets and high current liabilities, whereas a low-risk strategy does just the opposite. The matching principle, which attempts to match temporary current assets and current liabilities, results in a tradeoff between risk and return.

	Asset and Liability Management Strategy				
	Aggressive Asset– Aggressive Liability	Aggressive Asset– Conservative Liability	Conservative Asset– Aggressive Liability	Conservative Asset– Conservative Liability	
Sales	$375,000	$375,000	$375,000	$375,000	Impact of asset
Expenses	325,000	325,000	335,000	335,000	← strategy
EBIT	50,000	50,000	40,000	40,000	
Interest	14,200	17,000	14,200	17,000	← Impact of
EBT	35,800	33,000	25,800	23,000	liability
Taxes (35%)	12,530	11,550	9,030	8,050	strategy
EAT	$ 23,270	$ 21,450	$ 16,770	$ 14,950	
	High-risk– high-return strategy	Intermediate positions more in line with matching principle		Low-risk– low-return strategy	

2. If a firm has a conservative current asset position (employing a high level of current assets), then it should counterbalance its risks by employing an aggressive liability position (with a low level of current liabilities).
3. If a firm has a moderate current asset position, then it should counterbalance its risks by employing a moderate liability position.

The implication of the matching principle is that the firm should establish some *target* for its net short-term financial management position that takes into account risks, the returns required, and the appropriate current asset and current liability positions.

To see this, let us reconsider Dominion Products. With an aggressive asset approach it employs fewer current assets, so expenses are reduced and anticipated EBIT and cash inflows increase, compared to a conservative approach. Likewise, an aggressive liability approach employs more current liabilities and results in lower total cash outflows for interest than a more conservative liability policy. As shown in Table 21.3, the following combinations exist for Dominion Products: (1) a high-risk–high-return policy employing both aggressive asset and aggressive liability strategies; (2) two intermediate matching strategies employing either an aggressive asset–conservative liability or a conservative asset–aggressive liability strategy;[8] and (3) a low-risk–low-return policy

---

[8] An alternative matching strategy would be a more moderate position in both current assets and current liabilities.

employing both conservative asset and conservative liability policies. Note that the two intermediate strategies embody the matching principle. In line with the risks involved, the aggressive strategy has anticipated earnings of $23,270, whereas the conservative strategy has anticipated earnings of only $14,950.

Which working capital strategy should Dominion select? As we know, it is not earnings that are important; it is the cash flows and market value of the firm. Assume that Dominion Products has 10,000 shares of stock outstanding. The anticipated earnings per share for the four strategies will be as follows:

	Anticipated EAT	÷	Number of Shares	=	Anticipated EPS
Aggressive asset–aggressive liability	$23,270		10,000		$2.327
Aggressive asset–conservative liability	21,450		10,000		2.145
Conservative asset–aggressive liability	16,770		10,000		1.677
Conservative asset–conservative liability	14,950		10,000		1.495

In determining the per share market value, we know that $P_0 = (EPS)(P/E)$, where P/E is the firm's price/earnings ratio. Because aggressive asset or liability policies are viewed by shareholders as being more risky, other things being equal, they should have a lower P/E ratio than more conservative policies. Dominion Products needs to estimate the potential impact of the various current asset and current liability strategies on its expected market value. One way is to forecast P/E's for various risk–return strategies. For our example, assume these estimates are as follows:

	Anticipated EPS	×	Anticipated P/E	=	Anticipated P_0
Aggressive asset–aggressive liability	$2.327		9		$20.94
Aggressive asset–conservative liability	2.145		10		21.45
Conservative asset–aggressive liability	1.677		11		18.45
Conservative asset-conservative liability	1.495		12		17.94

Based on these expected market values, Dominion should implement the matching strategy involving an aggressive asset–conservative liability policy, because it results in the highest anticipated market value.

RECOGNIZING AND DEALING WITH LIQUIDITY PROBLEMS

The firm's short-term financial management policies should consider many factors. No matter how much planning is done, however, the firm must be able to recognize signs of declining liquidity and know how to deal with the situation. Some of the most important signs of deteriorating liquidity are these:

1. An unexpected buildup in inventory (an increase in the days inventory).

2. An increase in the firm's level of outstanding accounts receivable (an increase in the days sales outstanding).
3. A decline in the firm's daily or weekly cash inflows.
4. Increased costs that the firm is unable to pass on to its customers.
5. A decline in the firm's net working capital, or an increase in its debt ratio.

These and similar occurrences indicate the firm has (or will have) a liquidity problem.

There are many different approaches for dealing with liquidity problems, depending on the source of the problem, its severity, and its expected length. Managers often take some of the following steps to deal with liquidity problems:

1. Control and reduce investment in inventory.
2. Reexamine and tighten up on credit and reduce the firm's level of accounts receivable.
3. Increase short-term or long-term debt, or issue equity.
4. Control overhead and increase awareness of the need for effective asset management.
5. Lay off employees.
6. Reduce planned long-term (capital) expenditures.
7. Reduce or eliminate cash dividends.

If these measures are not sufficient, more drastic steps will be necessary. The important point is that firms must plan for meeting ongoing liquidity problems as part of their short-term financial management policies.

FINANCIAL SLACK

Until now we have been talking about the firm's ongoing liquidity. There is, however, another aspect of liquidity, sometimes called financial slack, which is the ability to have liquid resources to meet unexpected cash demands. These demands may arise when, due to unforeseen circumstances, larger cash outflows (or smaller cash inflows) than expected occur. In some cases cash is needed to take advantage of unexpected opportunities. As we discussed earlier, firms with high growth opportunities, or growth options, have more desire for financial slack than do those with a low level of growth opportunities.

Planning the firm's short-term financial management policies and liquidity needs involves uncertainty. Some of this uncertainty can be eliminated by effective cash budgeting (discussed in Chapter 26), but uncertainty still remains. Effective managers, whether they follow a conservative, aggressive, or matched short-term financial management policy, always maintain some financial slack. This may be in the form of one or more **lines of credit**, which are short-term borrowing agreements the firm has negotiated with a bank. At the firm's discretion, it may borrow or pay back on the line of credit.

Another strategy is to maintain a fairly large marketable securities portfolio or to have a bond or stock issue ready. Other firms establish bank relations and keep the bank regularly informed about possible borrowing needs. An alternative approach, to be discussed in Chapter 24, is to factor (or sell) the firm's accounts receivable. Increasingly firms also hedge (as discussed in Chapter 11 for interest rate risk and in Chapter 17 for foreign exchange rates), to insulate themselves against severe adverse shifts in rates or prices. Effective short-term financial management involves a continual tradeoff between risk and return. To deal with the risk of running short on cash at a crucial point in time, firms establish various means of ensuring financial slack as they formulate their short-term financial management policies.

Concept Review Questions

- Explain the matching principle.
- What are some important signs of deteriorating liquidity?
- Describe some strategies of protective liquidity management.

KEY POINTS

- The goal of short-term financial management is to assist in maximizing the value of the firm. Short-term financial management focuses on the magnitude and timing of the cash flows and on the risks and returns involved. Although more operational in nature and based less on theory than is long-term financial management, effective short-term financial management is of vital importance to firms.
- The cash conversion cycle, by taking account of the turnover of receivables, inventory, and payables, provides information about ongoing liquidity.
- Both current assets and current liabilities may be managed conservatively or aggressively. A coordinated short-term financial management policy focuses on both asset and liability management.
- To finance current assets, many firms follow the matching principle: Temporary assets are financed with temporary funds, permanent assets with long-term sources of funds.
- Firms are also concerned about financial slack as they formulate their short-term financial management policies.

QUESTIONS

21.1   In a world of perfect markets, firms should not have current assets and current liabilities. What accounts for the sizable levels of current assets and current liabilities we observe in practice?

21.2   Determine the impact of the following actions on a firm's cash conversion cycle:
a. The firm loosens its credit terms, leading to increased sales and accounts receivable. Sales increase more than receivables, on a percentage basis.
b. Payments on accounts owed are stretched from a 20-day average to a 35-day average.
c. The firm borrows on a short-term note instead of stretching payables, as in (b).
d. By introducing new control procedures, the firm reduces its inventory.

21.3   Explain why the basic nature of the firm's business and its size influence the amount of current assets required. Do the same factors also influence current liabilities?

21.4   Consider how an aggressive (versus a conservative) asset management position influences (a) the level of current assets, (b) the cash conversion cycle, (c) expense levels, and (d) risk and returns required.

21.5 Consider how an aggressive (versus a conservative) liability management position influences (a) the level of current liabilities, (b) the cash conversion cycle, (c) interest costs, and (d) risk and returns required.

21.6 At certain times the term structure of interest rates may be such that short-term rates are higher than long-term rates. Does it follow that the firm should finance entirely with long-term debt during such periods? Explain.

21.7 The firm faces two primary decisions with respect to its financing: the percentage of short- or long-term financing to employ, and the amount of borrowing to use relative to the owners' contribution. Discuss both decisions and how they might affect each other.

21.8 What is the matching principle? How does its use relate to the firm's cash conversion cycle, and its risk and returns?

CONCEPT REVIEW PROBLEMS

See Appendix A for solutions.

CR21.1 Russell Corp. has a receivable turnover of 6.75, an inventory turnover of 9.54, and a payables turnover of 9.13.
a. What is Russell's operating cycle?
b. Its cash conversion cycle?

CR21.2 Two companies—MaxIncome and SafetyFirst—producing similar products have completely different short-term financial management policies. Income statements and balance sheets for each of the companies are:

Balance Sheet	MaxIncome	SafetyFirst
Cash and marketable securities	$ 6,598	$ 17,855
Accounts receivable	15,125	25,632
Inventory	18,365	46,123
Net long-term assets	48,306	48,306
Total assets	$88,394	$137,916
Short-term bank loans	$18,232	$ 5,362
Accounts payable	18,185	11,565
Long-term debt	4,930	77,816
Common stock	33,562	33,562
Retained earnings	13,485	9,611
Total liabilities and shareholders' equity	$88,394	$137,916
Income Statement		
Sales	$265,233	$302,555
Cost of goods sold	162,900	177,930
General, selling, and administrative expenses	87,716	118,617
Taxes	5,847	2,403
Net income, EAT	$ 8,770	$ 3,605

What are the current ratio (current assets/current liabilities), quick ratio [(current assets − inventory)/current liabilities, net working capital (current assets − current liabilities), and cash conversion cycle for each firm?

CR21.3   International Travel is considering adopting one of three short-term financial management policies: an aggressive policy, a matched policy, or a conservative policy. Ann, the CFO, projects sales for each policy under three different economic scenarios: a robust economy, a standard economy, and a poor economy.

Sales	Aggressive	Matched	Conservative
Robust	$900	$1,200	$1,400
Standard	$800	$1,000	$1,200
Poor	$500	$700	$900

In each case all expenses *except interest* are expected to be 50 percent of sales.

a.   Ann estimates interest costs will be $36 for the aggressive policy, $50 for the matched policy, and $66 for the conservative policy, no matter what the economic condition. If the firm's tax rate is 40 percent, the number of shares of common stock is 100, and there is an equal probability for each economic state, what are the expected earnings per share and the standard deviation of earnings per share for each policy?

b.   If investors assign a P/E ratio of 10 for the aggressive policy, 11 for the matched policy, and 12 for the conservative policy, which policy should International Travel adopt?

PROBLEMS

21.1   Malott Ltd. is planning to make a $10 million investment in long-term assets and is attempting to estimate how much additional net working capital will be needed to support this expansion. The long-term asset turnover ratio (sales/long-term assets) on the new investment is estimated to be 2. From past experience, Malott estimates its total asset turnover ratio (sales/total assets) is 1. Also, for every dollar increase in current assets the firm experiences, about 60 percent of the increase can be financed through spontaneous increases in current liabilities. Determine the increase in net working capital (current assets − current liabilities) that should accompany the anticipated increase in long-term assets.

21.2   Windsor Systems has the following turnover ratios: receivables turnover, 6.0; inventory turnover, 4.0; payables turnover, 3.75.

a.   Find Windsor Systems' cash conversion cycle.

b.   Now find its cash conversion cycle if receivables turnover improves to 7.0 and inventory turnover increases to 5.5.

c.   Now assume the inventory conversion period is as determined in (b) and the payables turnover increases to 5.3. If the firm then wants a cash conversion cycle of no more than 35 days, what must the receivables turnover be?

21.3   Wood Management Group is attempting to determine its optimal level of current assets. It is considering three alternative policies, as follows:

	Aggressive	Average	Conservative
Current assets	$ 500	$ 700	$ 900
Long-term assets	1,000	800	600
Total	$1,500	$1,500	$1,500

In any case, the firm will employ the following financing: current liabilities of $700, long-term debt of $200, and common equity of $600. Sales are expected to be $2,500. Because of lower costs with the more aggressive policies, the anticipated ratio of EBIT to sales is 13 percent with the aggressive policy; whereas it is 12 percent with the average risk policy and 11 percent with the conservative policy. Interest is $65, and the tax rate is 30 percent.

a. Determine anticipated net income under the three different plans.

b. In this problem we assumed that both total assets and sales are the same with any of the policies. Are these typically valid assumptions?

c. How, specifically, does the risk vary under the three plans? As part of your analysis, calculate the current ratio (current assets/current liabilities) and net working capital (current assets − current liabilities).

21.4 LeCompte Software keeps a large inventory, in order not to lose sales. Its new vice-president for finance has recommended that the firm's inventory be cut. Doing so would reduce the inventory level by $150,000 and allow the firm to forgo renewing a $150,000 note payable with a 12 percent interest rate that matures soon. An abbreviated income statement for LeCompte is as follows:

EBIT	$1,000,000
Interest	140,000
EBT	860,000
Taxes (35%)	301,000
Net income, EAT	$ 559,000

With 100,000 shares of stock outstanding and a P/E ratio of 10 times earnings, LeCompte's current stock price is $55.90.

a. Scenario 1: If the anticipated EBIT and P/E ratio are unaffected by the reduction in inventory and notes payable, what would the new market price be? (*Note:* Carry to three decimal places for EPS.)

b. Scenario 2: The marketing manager for LeCompte believes the inventory reduction will result in lower sales, and thus EBIT may decrease to $950,000. What would the anticipated market price be if this happens?

c. If there is a 60 percent chance that EBIT will stay at $1,000,000, and a 40 percent chance it will drop to $950,000, what action should LeCompte Software take?

d. What are your answers to (a) through (c) if the marginal tax rate is only 20 percent?

21.5 Three companies—Aggressive, Average, and Conservative—follow different working capital policies, as their names imply.

	Aggressive	Average	Conservative
Current assets	$ 300	$ 400	$ 600
Long-term assets	700	600	400
Total	$1,000	$1,000	$1,000
Current liabilities	$ 500	$ 350	$ 200
Long-term debt	100	250	400
Common equity	400	400	400
Total	$1,000	$1,000	$1,000

Selected income and balance sheet data are as follows:

	Aggressive	Average	Conservative
Sales	$1,800	$1,800	$1,800
Cost of goods sold	1,260	1,280	1,300
Cost of goods sold plus general, selling, and administrative expenses	1,560	1,580	1,600
Accounts receivable	120	160	240
Inventory	150	200	300
Accruals and accounts payable	250	200	100
Short-term borrowing	200	150	100

The interest rate on short-term debt is 10 percent, and on long-term debt it is 12 percent. The tax rate is 30 percent.

a. Determine the net income for each firm.
b. Calculate the cash conversion cycle for each firm.
c. What is the current ratio (current assets/current liabilities) and the net working capital (current assets − current liabilities) for each firm?
d. Are there other factors that would have to be taken into account in practice? What are the major ones?

21.6   Salomon & Morgan is considering whether to adopt plan I or plan II for its current assets and liabilities. Adopting one plan versus the other is expected to affect sales, expenses, and interest. As a result, taxes and anticipated earnings after tax (EAT) will also vary. Based on a 50 percent probability of a good or bad year, Salomon & Morgan's finance department has made the following projections:

	Plan I		Plan II	
	Good Year	Bad Year	Good Year	Bad Year
Probability	0.50	0.50	0.50	0.50
Sales	$900,000	$800,000	$850,000	$760,000
All expenses except interest and taxes	750,000	710,000	730,000	680,000
EBIT	150,000	90,000	120,000	80,000
Interest	20,000	17,000	18,000	15,000

(continued)

	Plan I		Plan II	
	Good Year	Bad Year	Good Year	Bad Year
EBT	130,000	73,000	102,000	65,000
Taxes (40%)	52,000	29,200	40,800	26,000
EAT	$ 78,000	$ 43,800	$ 61,200	$ 39,000

Salomon & Morgan has 10,000 shares of common stock outstanding. Risk will be measured by the coefficient of variation of earnings per share.

a. Calculate the mean EPS, standard deviation of EPS, and coefficient of variation of EPS for both plans.

b. If plan I carries an anticipated P/E ratio of 11 times earnings and plan II has an anticipated P/E of 10 times, which plan should Salomon & Morgan choose?

21.7 Williams has the following balance sheet and income statement:

Balance Sheet		Income Statement	
Cash and marketable securities	$ 50	Sales	$1,800
Accounts receivable	100	Cost of goods sold (70% of sales)	1,260
Inventory	100	General, selling, and administrative expenses	190
Long-term assets	600	EBIT	350
Total assets	$850	Interest	25
		EBT	325
Short-term debt	$ 50	Taxes (36%)	117
Accounts payable	70	Net income, EAT	$ 208
Salaries, benefits, and payroll			
taxes payable	40		
Other current liabilities	40		
Long-term debt	150		
Shareholders' equity			
(100 shares)	500		
Total liabilities and			
shareholders' equity	$850		

a. Determine Williams' current liquidity position by calculating its current ratio (current assets/current liabilities), net working capital (current assets − current liabilities), ratio of current assets to total assets, ratio of current liabilities to total assets, and cash conversion cycle.

b. If its current P/E ratio is 8 times earnings, what is Williams' present market price per share?

c. The marketing vice-president believes significant sales are being lost because of not offering enough credit to customers and lack of inventory. Working with the chief financial officer, she has prepared the following plan:

- $250 will be raised: $100 will be additional short-term debt with a 12 percent interest rate, and the other $150 will be additional long-term debt with a 14 percent interest rate.

- Cash will increase by a total of $50 (this includes the additional cash raised with the new financing), accounts receivable by $115, and inventory by $115. Because of the increase in inventory, accounts payable will increase $30. (*Note:* Current assets increase by $30 more than the $250, due to the $30 of spontaneous short-term financing provided by the increase in accounts payable.)
- Sales are expected to be $2,200, cost of goods sold will remain 70 percent of sales, and general, selling, and administrative expenses will increase by $30.
- All other accounts remain the same.

Because investors are expected to view the new plan as being more risky, the new P/E ratio is estimated to be 7 times earnings.

1. Calculating the same information as in (a), what is Williams' new liquidity position?
2. Calculate the new income statement. What is the new anticipated market price per share?
3. Should Williams proceed with the plan?

21.8 Jennings Distributors has the following balance sheet and income statement:

Balance Sheet		Income Statement	
Cash	$ 25,000	Sales	$900,000
Accounts receivable	60,000	Cost of goods sold	400,00
Inventory	65,000	General, selling, and	
Long-term assets	350,000	administrative expenses	100,00
Total assets	$500,000	All other expenses	250,000
		Net income, EAT	$150,000
Accounts payable, plus salaries, benefits, and payroll taxes payable	$ 80,000		
Other current liabilities	20,000		
Long-term debt	100,000		
Shareholders' equity (50,000 shares)	300,000		
Total liabilities and shareholders' equity	$500,000		

a. Determine Jennings' liquidity situation by calculating the current ratio (current assets/current liabilities), net working capital (current assets − current liabilities), the ratio of current assets to total assets, the ratio of current liabilities to total assets, and the cash conversion cycle.

b. What is the current market price per share of Jennings' stock if its P/E ratio is 8 times earnings?

c. David, Jennings' chief financial officer, is very conservative and believes that the current ratio needs to be raised to 2.0. To accomplish this, he proposes to sell 2,500 shares of common stock to net the firm $20 per share. The proceeds will be added to the firm's cash account. Assuming that everything else remains the same, determine the following:

1. Jennings' new liquidity position, as in (a).
2. Its new anticipated market price per share.
3. Whether or not Jennings should issue the stock.

21.9 Fredericton Manufacturing is preparing a two-year plan for its asset investments, as given in the following schedule. (For simplicity, long-term assets are assumed to be constant at $40 million, as is shareholders' equity. Thus, you have to concern yourself only with current assets, current liabilities, and long-term debt.)

	Date	Total Current Assets per Period (in millions)
Year 1	3/31	$30
	6/30	36
	9/30	42
	12/31	39
Year 2	3/31	33
	6/30	39
	9/30	45
	12/31	42

a. Current liabilities tend to equal one-third of Fredericton's current assets. If Fredericton has a total of $15 million in long-term debt every quarter, determine the amount of short-term borrowing required per quarter to complete the financing of the firm's current assets.

b. Instead of (a), assume that no long-term debt exists. How much short-term debt will be needed per quarter to match, or counterbalance, current assets?

c. If short-term interest rates are 9 percent and long-term rates are 11 percent, how much interest does Fredericton save over the two years by matching its current assets?

21.10 Mini Case DJ Fashions is an aggressive young firm that has grown dramatically during the last few years. Until now it has fared well, but lately it has been experiencing continuing working capital problems. You have been called in to evaluate DJ's operations and suggest changes in funding in order to meet the continuing working capital problems.

a. What do we mean by the term "short-term financial management"? What are the primary short-term financial management decisions faced by firms? How are they related to each other?

b. DJ Fashions' balance sheet and income statement are as follows:

Balance Sheet		Income Statement	
Cash and marketable securities	$ 125	Sales	$7,000
Accounts receivable	750	Cost of goods sold	3,150
Inventory	300	General, selling, and administrative	
Long-term assets	1,625	expenses	3,500
Total assets	$2,800	EBIT	350
		Interest	115
Short-term debt	$ 800	EBT	235
Accounts payable	800	Taxes (40%)	94
Salaries, benefits, and payroll		Net income, EAT	$ 141
taxes payable	400		
Other current liabilities	300		
Long-term debt	100		
Shareholders' equity	400		
Total liabilities and			
shareholders' equity	$2,800		

Determine DJ's current liability position by calculating its current ratio (current assets/current liabilities), ratio of current assets to total assets, ratio of current liabilities to total assets, and cash conversion cycle. In assessing DJ's liquidity position, focus on the figures calculated above and other information that can be gleaned from the balance sheet and income statement. What conclusions do you reach?

c. In order to improve its liquidity ratios, one alternative open to DJ is to increase the short-term debt by $1,000 and add the same amount to the cash position. Although this is just a cosmetic change, it does affect the figures calculated in (b). What are the new figures if everything else remains as in (b)?

d. Explain in detail what an aggressive versus a conservative liquidity management system entails. In addition to the levels of current assets and current liabilities, are there other factors that should be considered?

e. Does DJ have a liquidity problem? If so, what are the causes of the problem?

REFERENCES

COHN, RICHARD A., and JOHN J. PRINGLE. "Steps Toward an Integration of Corporate Financial Theory." In *Readings on the Management of Working Capital,* edited by Keith V. Smith. St. Paul, Minn.: West, 1980.

GENTRY, JAMES A., R. VAIDYANATHAN, and HEI WAI LEE. "A Weighted Cash Conversion Cycle." *Financial Management* 19 (Spring 1990): 90–99.

HILL, NED C., and WILLIAM L. SARTORIS. *Short-Term Financial Management.* New York: Macmillan, 1988.

KALLBERG, JARL G., and KENNETH L. PARKINSON. *Corporate Liquidity: Management and Measurement.* Homewood, Ill.: Irwin, 1993.

MORRIS, JAMES R. "The Role of Cash Balances in Firm Valuation." *Journal of Financial and Quantitative Analysis* 18 (December 1983): 533–545.

RICHARDS, VERLYN D., and EUGENE J. LAUGHLIN. "A Cash Conversion Cycle Approach to Liquidity Analysis." *Financial Management* 9 (Spring 1980): 32–38.

SCHERR, FREDERICK C. *Modern Working Capital Management.* Englewood Cliffs, N.J.: Prentice-Hall, 1989.

22 *Cash and Marketable Securities*

EXECUTIVE SUMMARY

Effective management of the firm's cash and marketable securities requires that we understand techniques for cash gathering and disbursing, how the firm's cash balance can be minimized, and the basic instruments and techniques of marketable securities portfolio management. Adequate cash is needed for ordinary operating purposes. However, because demand deposits do not provide interest, the firm wants to minimize its cash balance while maintaining sufficient liquid reserves.

Because of mail, processing, and transit floats, special techniques are employed to speed the gathering of cash coming into the firm. For managing disbursements, firms can benefit from using controlled disbursing systems and zero balance accounts. In evaluating the effectiveness of these systems, the incremental costs must be compared with the incremental benefits in a net present value framework. These same general considerations apply for the international aspects of a firm's cash management.

In determining the minimum cash balance to maintain, the firm can model or break down its expected cash inflows and outflows on a daily basis. By doing so, the firm can identify projected purchase or sale dates for marketable securities. The funds in the marketable securities portfolio must be invested for the highest possible return commensurate with the risk–return posture of the firm and the liquidity needs dictated by the projected inflows and outflows of cash.

THE CASH MANAGEMENT FUNCTION

Cash refers to currency on hand plus the demand deposits held in chequing accounts at various chartered banks. **Marketable securities** are the short-term investments the firm may hold temporarily that can be quickly converted into cash. Together, cash and marketable securities form the **liquid assets** of the firm. There are three main questions related to liquid asset management:

1. How should the firm design its cash-gathering and cash-disbursing systems?
2. How should the investment in liquid assets be split between cash and marketable securities?
3. How should the marketable securities portfolio be managed?

Before discussing these questions, however, we need to consider some general aspects of the cash management function. Because liquid assets generally provide lower returns than long-term assets, we need to understand why firms hold liquid assets. Then we will discuss the general risk–return aspects of liquid assets.

REASONS FOR HOLDING CASH

Firms hold cash for four basic reasons:

1. TRANSACTIONS PURPOSES   In the everyday course of business, firms need a certain minimum amount of cash on hand to meet cash outflow requirements. These include routine items such as paying the monthly bills, making payments to suppliers, and the like. In addition, cash is needed for major items such as tax payments, dividends, salaries, and paying interest and/or principal related to debt.
2. HEDGE AGAINST UNCERTAINTY   A second reason for holding liquid assets is as a hedge against uncertain future events. These funds often are held in the form of marketable securities. An alternative to holding liquid assets to hedge against uncertainty is to obtain a line of credit. With a line of credit from a bank, the firm can borrow up to a specified maximum amount over some period. Lines of credit generally require a commitment fee, whether they are used or not. Thus, financial slack is the second reason for holding cash.
3. FLEXIBILITY   Many firms hold substantial amounts of liquid assets in anticipation of taking advantage of unforeseen opportunities and having the capability to fund growth options, or opportunities, quickly and easily. Likewise, during periods of economic downturn, firms postpone capital expenditures and attempt to hoard liquid assets to weather the storm.
4. COMPENSATING BALANCE REQUIREMENT   Banks perform many services for firms, including the collection and disbursement of funds, handling interbank transfers, providing lines of credit, and making loans. The compensation received by the bank comes from two sources: direct fees and **compensating balances.** A compensating balance is a specified amount the firm agrees to leave on deposit in its chequing account. Typically this amount is set in relation to the size of the loan or the level of services provided.

RISK AND RETURN

The fundamental risk involved in holding too little cash is an inability to operate in the normal manner. If cash inflow is a problem, paying bills may have to be deferred, capital expenditures curtailed, short-term financing obtained, and assets sold. Growth options, or opportunities, that present themselves will have to be by-passed. In an extreme case, the firm may have to file for protection under the Bankruptcy Act or be forced into liquidation. The risk–return tradeoff for liquid assets involves the following:

1. Having enough cash and liquid reserves (or financial slack), in the form of marketable securities and/or lines of credit, to meet all the firm's obligations and take advantage of growth opportunities.
2. Not holding excess liquid reserves, because investment in long-term assets generally provides higher returns than short-term investments.
3. Maintaining a minimum cash balance while actively managing the firm's portfolio of marketable securities to ensure as high a return as possible commensurate with the risk involved.

These tradeoffs will guide our discussion as firms make liquid asset decisions consistent with maximizing the value of the firm.

Concept Review Questions

■ Why do firms hold cash?

■ What are some of the risks of holding too much cash? Of holding too little cash?

CASH MANAGEMENT TECHNIQUES

The flow of cash into and out of the firm is continual. Although the level of cash at any point in time is a function of many factors, certain cash management ideas are fundamental to any firm, whatever its size, industry, or the state of the economy. Two major aspects of cash management involve speeding the inflows through a cash-gathering system and controlling the outflows via a cash-disbursing system. Before discussing these, however, we need to understand payment systems.

PAPER-BASED VERSUS ELECTRONIC PAYMENT SYSTEMS

In Canada, the United States, and relatively few other countries, the major means of making noncash payments is through cheques. Although electronic payment is becoming more widespread, particularly for larger transactions between firms, we will start our discussion assuming a paper-based system. A paper-based system is in contrast to **giro systems,** which are employed in most European and many other countries for smaller transactions. These giro systems, often run by the postal service, operate on the basis of direct debits and credits. In a giro system, a seller sends an invoice to the buyer. The invoice includes a giro payment stub (called a giro acceptance) encoded with the seller's bank and account number. The buyer signs the stub, takes it to the local post office, transmits the information through the girobank, with the result being a debit to the buyer's account and a credit to seller's account.

We will discuss electronic payment systems for large transactions shortly; however, first we will consider cash-gathering and cash-disbursing in a paper-based system.

SPEEDING THE INFLOWS

The complexity of the cash-gathering system depends on the size of the firm and the scope of its operations. Small local firms have very simple systems; large national or multinational firms have very extensive systems. In the cash-gathering system, the concept of float is vital.

Float   **Float** is the length of time between when a cheque is written and when the recipient receives the funds and can draw upon them (when it has "good funds"). The **average collection float** is found by multiplying the number of days of float times the average daily dollar amount that is in the collection system. The sources of cash-gathering float, as shown in Figure 22.1, are:

1. MAIL FLOAT   The time that elapses between when a customer places the cheque in the mail and when the selling firm receives it and begins to process it is the **mail float.**
2. PROCESSING FLOAT   The time it takes the selling firm to deposit the cheque in its bank after receiving the cheque is the **processing float.**
3. TRANSIT FLOAT   The time required for the cheque to clear through the banking system until the recipient can draw upon it (i.e., has "good funds") is the **transit float**.

The Bank of Canada and the Canadian Payments Association are responsible for clearing cheques through the Canadian payments system. The 1980 revision of the Bank Act established the Canadian Payments Association, requiring all banks to join and providing near banks (such as trust companies and *caisses populaires*) with the option to join.

When a firm deposits a customer's cheque into its bank account, before the firm has access to these funds, the Canadian payments system must verify that the funds are in the customer's account, and then it transfers the funds to the firm's bank account via the Bank of Canada. To facilitate this process, the payments system has 10 settlement or clearing centres located in 10 major cities across Canada, connected to each other and the Bank of Canada by computer. This computerized network keeps transit float to a minimum by providing same-day settlement on cheques.

A firm should focus first on the processing float. That is, the firm must establish an efficient internal system to minimize the delay between receipt of the customer's cheque (if it comes directly to the firm) and when it is deposited in the bank. After this has been accomplished, other techniques for reducing float can be considered.

Decentralized Collections   Mail float can be minimized by having decentralized collection points located in parts of the country where the firm has many customers. Two basic devices used for this purpose are local offices and lockboxes.

Figure 22.1

Typical Payment System and Resulting Float

All three types of float are important and should be minimized as the firm strives to shorten its cash collection cycle.

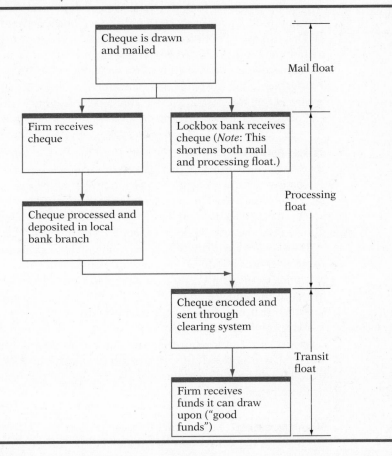

Local Offices.   If the firm has local offices in the major regions in which it operates, it can have collections directed to these offices. Once the cheques are received, they can be deposited in a local branch of the firm's bank.

Lockboxes.   If the firm does not have local offices, or if it wants to keep collections out of the local offices, a widely used alternative is to establish lockboxes. With a **lockbox,** the customer is directed to send the payment to a post office box in a specified city.[1] A bank picks up the mail several times a day and begins the clearing

---

[1] Lockboxes are often classified in two categories: wholesale lockboxes, which are designed for low-volume but high-dollar-value per item transactions, and retail lockboxes, which provide for efficient processing of high-volume, low-dollar-value cheques.

process while notifying the firm, via electronic means, that the cheques have been received. At the conclusion of the day, all cheque photocopies, invoices, deposit slips, and related materials are sent to the firm. To determine where to set up lockboxes, the firm can engage the services of banks or other cash management consulting services. Typically a national firm will establish lockboxes in various parts of the country, depending on its customer base and the regional efficiency of the postal service.

The purpose of both local office and lockbox collection points is to keep mail float to a minimum. Lockboxes also reduce the processing float. The benefits gained from the reduced float, however, must be compared to the cost involved. With a local office arrangement, the costs involve personnel, equipment, and space. With a lockbox arrangement, the cost is the fee charged by the bank either directly or through a compensating balance agreement.

Banking Network Large firms use a tiered banking arrangement by employing more than one bank for their gathering and disbursing systems. Using a local office system, customers mail their cheques to local offices that process and then forward them to local bank branches. The deposits are then transferred to the firm's head office account at its central concentration branch. The rationale for a tiered system is the reduction in mail float because the local offices are closer to the customers.

If lockboxes are used, they are generally set up in principal regions, and the number of local deposits is reduced. The regional bank branch maintains the lockbox, forwards the funds to the firm's central concentration branch, and sends the supporting documents to the firm. In addition, the lockbox should be close to the customers to be served so that mail float is kept to a minimum.

Once the funds are at the firm's central concentration bank, they can be used to meet the cash outflows of the firm, and any extra funds can be quickly invested in marketable securities. If the firm is short of cash, it can draw on its lines of credit. (The typical firm's banking network will also include various disbursement accounts at one or more banks.)

Other Approaches Some other approaches that could be employed to improve the efficiency of the collection process include the following:

1. SPECIAL HANDLING   To provide special handling of large amounts, a courier might be dispatched to collect a cheque directly, in order to reduce mail time.
2. PREAUTHORIZED CHEQUES   A **preauthorized cheque** system might be created when the firm receives a large volume of payments in fixed amounts from the same customers. With the preauthorized procedure, the customer authorizes the firm to draw cheques directly on the customer's demand deposit account. This method eliminates mail and processing float and increases the regularity and certainty of cash inflows to the firm.
3. RECEIPT OF PAYMENT REQUIRED   A third alternative is for the firm to demand that the payment be received (not just mailed) by a certain date. This system can be used if a customer is going to take advantage of a cash discount. The receipt of payment approach eliminates mail float.
4. PAYMENT BY ELECTRONIC TRANSFER   A fourth alternative would be for the firm to demand payment by an electronic transfer. This also eliminates float.

Because all these approaches have costs and benefits related to reducing the float, they must be considered when determining the most effective means of structuring the firm's cash-gathering system.

Analysis of Cash-Gathering Techniques   A basic model that can be employed to assess the cost effectiveness of various cash-gathering techniques compares the incremental costs with the incremental benefits:

$$\Delta C = \text{after-tax costs}$$
$$\Delta B = \text{after-tax benefits} = (\Delta t)(TS)(I_{daily})(1 - T) \qquad (22.1)$$

where

ΔC = the incremental after-tax costs of a new method compared to an existing method

ΔB = the incremental after-tax benefits associated with a new method compared to an existing method

Δt = the change in float time (in days)

TS = the size of the transaction

I_{daily} = the daily interest rate

T = the firm's marginal tax rate

With this method, the following decisions will be made:

1. If ΔC is greater than ΔB, stay with the present method.
2. If ΔC is less than ΔB, switch to the proposed method.
3. If ΔC is equal to ΔB, you are indifferent.

Note that $\Delta B - \Delta C$ is simply the net present value, NPV. The only difference from other NPVs is that discounting is not employed, due to the short periods involved.

This approach is extremely flexible. It can be conducted on a per unit or total basis, and on a daily or yearly basis. To illustrate its use, we first consider a lockbox example and then alternative transfer mechanisms.

Lockbox Example.   Suppose that your firm now has all collections sent to the home office. To increase efficiency and reduce float, a lockbox operation is being considered. You estimate that the reduction in float (both mail and processing) will be three days, the average cheque size is $440, the yearly rate of interest is 10 percent, and the firm's marginal tax rate is 30 percent. Employing Equation 22.1, we can find the approximate *per unit* benefits of the lockbox, as follows:

$$\Delta B = (\Delta t)(TS)(I_{daily})(1 - T) = (3)(\$440)(0.10/365 \text{ days})(0.70) = \$0.253$$

On a per unit basis, the benefits are $0.253 per cheque processed. If the after-tax costs charged for the lockbox are less than this amount, the lockbox operation should be established, because the incremental benefits will be greater than the incremental costs. In addition, any employee time freed would be another benefit that also should be taken into account.

Instead of determining the benefits on a per unit basis, we could calculate them on a daily basis. If there are 300 cheques per day, then the average daily volume of cheques processed through the lockbox is $132,000 [i.e., (300)($440)]. The incremental benefits *per day* are then

$$\Delta B = (3)(\$132{,}000)(0.10/365 \text{ days})(0.70) = \$75.95$$

Thus, if the bank charged less than $75.95 per day after tax (on a 365-day year), then the firm should implement the lockbox arrangement.

Finally, we can also use Equation 22.1 to determine the incremental benefits *per year*. To do this, *either the daily volume, TS, must be converted to a yearly basis, or the daily interest rate, I_{daily}, must be converted to a yearly interest rate.* The incremental after-tax benefits per year from the lockboxes are thus:

$$\Delta B = (3)[(365 \text{ days})(\$132{,}000)](0.10/365 \text{ days})(0.70) = \$27{,}720$$

or

$$\Delta B = (3)(\$132{,}000)(0.10)(0.70) = \$27{,}720$$

Again, we would make our decision by comparing the incremental costs to the incremental benefits. This time, however, we do it on a yearly basis, instead of on the per unit or per day basis determined previously.

Transfer Mechanism Example.   In the example above, we did not know the costs. We can also start out, however, by knowing what the incremental costs, ΔC, are, and then determine what the reduction in the float time, Δt, the average size, TS, or the yearly interest rate, I, would have to be for us to be indifferent between the two methods. Suppose that your firm has a 40 percent tax rate and is investigating whether one of two methods should be employed to move funds between two banks. The first method costs $5 per unit, and the alternative costs $1, so that $\Delta C = (\$5 - \$1)(1 - 0.40) = \$2.40$. The reduction in float time, Δt, is two days, and the yearly interest rate, I, is 10 percent. Setting ΔC equal to ΔB, we have

$$\Delta C = \Delta B$$

$$\$2.40 = (2)(TS)(0.10/365 \text{ days})(1 - 0.40)$$

$$TS = \frac{\$2.40}{(2)(0.10/365)(0.60)} = \$7{,}300 \text{ on a per unit basis}$$

If the average size of the cheque transferred between the two banks is at least $7,300, it pays to use the first method. If the reduction in float time were only one day, the size of the average transfer would have to be $14,600 for the first method to be justified.

In practice, the models become more complex, because there are additional considerations, such as having numerous locations and the service credits earned by having compensating balances at the banks. Nevertheless, the basic analytical concept of comparing the incremental costs versus the incremental benefits remains the same.

CONTROLLING THE OUTFLOWS

In the design of the firm's cash-disbursement system, the emphasis is on controlling and slowing down the outflow of cash as long as possible without incurring the ill will of the firm's suppliers. The place to begin is with payment procedures. They should be designed so that the firm pays *just before* the due date. Paying earlier simply reduces the time that cash is available to the firm for investment.

Controlled Disbursing   Unlike the system in the United States, where firms have devised complicated procedures to take advantage of the slow cheque-clearing procedures of the Federal Reserve System (transit float), Canada's branch banking system leaves little opportunity to extend the length of time a cheque takes to be cleared. However, Canadian firms can set up a **controlled disbursing** system to increase mail float by mailing cheques to suppliers from a distant location. For example, if a firm pays one of its Toronto-based suppliers with a cheque mailed from Toronto, the mail float may be one day. On the other hand, if the firm made its disbursement from Vancouver, the mail float would be increased substantially.

By maximizing mail float, the firm can increase its cash level and use the excess cash in other ways. However, the system does mean that suppliers will be without payment for an additional number of days. The ill will created among suppliers must be taken into account when a controlled disbursing system is being established. Furthermore, such a procedure is suited only to large nation-wide firms; smaller regional firms would be unable to carry out the procedure.

Zero Balance Accounts   When a large firm is organized on a divisional basis, invoices from suppliers often go to divisional finance offices for payment. If each division has its own disbursing bank, excess cash balances may build up, reducing the efficiency of the firm's cash-disbursing system. To prevent this buildup, the firm may establish a **zero balance account** system at its central concentration branch. Each division continues to write its own cheques, which are all drawn on individual disbursing accounts at the concentration branch. Although these accounts are like individual demand deposit accounts, they contain no funds. Thus their name, zero balance.

Each day the cheques written on the individual disbursing accounts presented for payment are paid by the concentration branch. As they are paid, a negative balance builds up in the individual accounts. At the end of the day, the negative balances are restored to zero by means of a credit from the firm's master account at the central concentration branch. Each day, the firm receives a report summarizing the activity of the various accounts, so that marketable securities can be bought or sold as needed, depending on the balance in the firm's master account. Zero balance accounts allow much more control, while maintaining divisional autonomy for payments. They are often an effective means of controlling the cash-disbursement system.

Other Approaches   Various other approaches for controlling cash disbursements include the following:

1.   CENTRALIZED PAYABLES   When a firm has many divisions, it could have the invoices received and verified at the divisional level but actually paid at the firm's headquarters. In this instance, all invoices must be forwarded to the central office

for payment. Control can be maintained, and the disbursement cycle may be slowed by this procedure.

2.   TIMING CHEQUE ISSUANCES   By issuing cheques at certain times during the week, the firm may increase its float. Thus, if average mail float is one and a half days, by issuing cheques on Wednesday or Thursday the firm may gain an extra two days (over the weekend) of float. Likewise, issuing a payroll on Friday afternoon also means that not all the cheques can clear the banking system before Monday of the next week.

The benefits and costs of all the cash-disbursing techniques must be analyzed. The basic framework to employ is the same as that presented earlier. In the disbursing situation, the benefit arises from the additional length of time the firm will have the funds available. This benefit has to be weighed against the additional costs incurred to gain better control of the disbursement of cash.

INTERACTIONS

Until now we have examined a number of techniques that could be used to improve the efficiency of the firm's cash-gathering system or to control the cash-disbursing system. In medium- to large-size firms, with various plants and offices, gathering and disbursing problems quickly become complex. In addition, there are obvious interactions between the two that must be taken into account. If the firm decides to employ lockboxes and/or have collections made by local offices, numerous bank branches and possibly more than one bank will be involved. Using controlled disbursing also will lead to creating accounts at still other bank branches. In the end the two decisions, gathering and disbursing, cannot be made in isolation. Rather, their joint effects, costs, and benefits must be considered in order to create an efficient cash management system that balances the risks and returns involved.

INTERNATIONAL CASH MANAGEMENT

In addition to managing domestic cash accounts, firms are paying increasing attention to the effective management of international cash flows.[2] Some of the major international money movement techniques are as follows:

1.   CONCENTRATION BANKING   To control the flow of funds internationally, firms concentrate their cash at a single bank within a country or on a regional level. Often European-wide systems are established at a bank in London or Amsterdam, whereas Asian systems are located at a bank in Hong Kong or Singapore. Once this is done, funds can be controlled and invested, and a zero balance type of procedure can be implemented.

---

[2] Canadian banks participate in SWIFT (Society for Worldwide Interbank Financial Telecommunications) a multinational bank transfer system. Canadian banks are also members of New York–based Clearing House Interbank Payment System (CHIPS), another international communications network that provides a one-day settlement procedure.

2. INTERNATIONAL TRANSFER   Using banks, firms can arrange for same-day settlement or other kinds of settlement procedures when funds move across international borders.

3. INTERNATIONAL LOCKBOX   This technique involves establishing one or more lockboxes in a country so that payments can be settled in the country where the currency is legal tender. With this system, cross-border cheque clearing is avoided, increasing the efficiency of the firm's cash system.

4. INTRACOMPANY NETTING   Many firms have large sums of money tied up in intracompany transactions. With these transactions, one subsidiary's payables are another subsidiary's receivables. To avoid the physical transfer of funds, many international companies "net" the funds flowing between subsidiaries once a month.

In addition, because of fluctuating foreign exchange rates, many firms follow a practice of leading or lagging. Thus, as discussed in Chapter 17, if a firm has a net asset position in a weak or potentially depreciating currency, it should expedite the disposal of the asset—it should lead. Alternatively, a firm with a net liability position in a weak currency should delay payment, or lag, hoping that the currency will weaken further. Faced with a strong currency, the firm would lead, or make payments as soon as possible. Similarly, it would lag, or delay, collection as long as possible in a strong currency. Although leading and lagging cannot eliminate the risk caused by exchange rate fluctuations, it is still an effective tool for international cash, accounts receivable, and short-term liability management.

Concept Review Questions

- Describe several approaches firms employ to decrease the cost of float.
- Describe how a zero balance account system can be used to control the cash-disbursing system of a firm.

Advances in Payment and Information Systems

Up to this point we have concentrated primarily on a paper-based cheque system. During the last 20 years or so there have been extensive discussions and projections about moving to a chequeless and paperless society. Substantial progress has been made during that time.

Electronic Payment Systems

Although cheques are still widely employed in Canada, there has been slow but steady movement towards the use of electronic payment systems, often referred to as **electronic funds transfer (EFT).** Electronic funds transfer involves the replacement of paper cheques with an electronic payment system and is being implemented by more firms to handle payments electronically. For example, **debit cards** are now available that allow retail customers to transfer funds directly from their bank account to a retailer's account. A debit card is very similar to a credit card; however, since funds are transferred immediately, the customer must have an account balance sufficient to cover the transaction. Firms using this system are able to eliminate accounts receivable and to have virtually immediate use of the cash. These developments in EFT interact with the Canadian payment system to essentially eliminate float.

ELECTRONIC DATA INTERCHANGE

At the same time that electronic payment systems have been growing, other advances in automation are affecting the whole ordering and payment system employed by firms. Increasingly, firms are using **electronic data interchange, (EDI),** which affects everything from the ordering and manufacturing cycle to the flow of documents related to shipment and payment. Electronic data interchange refers to the exchange of all transaction-related information between two firms in computer-readable form. Thus, its implications are important in all aspects of a firm—both financial and non-financial. Interfacing EDI with EFT enables firms to move from a paper-based system to a nonpaper-based system. Although there are obvious benefits to such a move, there are also costs. That is one of the reasons that moving to an integrated EDI/EFT system has been much slower than anticipated. At the same time, there is increasing evidence that progress has been and is still being made in implementing effective, cost-efficient EDI/EFT systems.

THE EDI EXPERIENCE AT NEWELL

Newell is a manufacturer of hardware, housewares, and office products that serves firms such as Kmart, Wal-Mart, Ace Hardware, and Canadian Tire. To streamline their whole operations, manage inventory, and reduce stockouts at their customers' sites, Newell has designed the following programme:

1. A retail store, such as Kmart, captures sales data at the point of sale when the UPC (universal price code) bars are scanned by laser at the checkout counter.
2. Sales data from various stores and warehouses are consolidated at the customer's headquarters daily and transmitted electronically to Newell.
3. When inventory falls to a predetermined level, a replenishment order is generated, and shipping documents are transmitted electronically to the appropriate Newell division.
4. Once an order has been shipped, the shipping data are transmitted electronically from the division to Newell headquarters.
5. An advance shipping notice and invoice are transmitted electronically to the customer's headquarters. The advanced shipping data are then retransmitted to individual stores by the customer's headquarters.
6. Newell is linked electronically to most of its common carriers, allowing it to monitor carrier performance and order progress from the time it is shipped until it arrives at the customer's warehouse or retail outlet.

Through EDI, Newell transmits the following items: point of sale data, forecasts, inventory data, purchase orders, advance shipping notices, invoices, electronic funds transfer, and information about shipping status. Although cheques are still used, more and more firms like Newell are turning to EDI/EFT.

Concept Review Questions

- Describe how the use of debit cards can benefit a firm.
- How does the system at Newell work?

Determining the Daily Cash Balance

Now that we have examined cash gathering and disbursing, the second question raised at the beginning of the chapter can be addressed: How should the investment in liquid assets be split between cash and marketable securities? The approach we examine is based on the idea that firms will attempt to keep as little cash in demand deposits as possible. We assume that the firm has a marketable securities portfolio of a sufficient size that funds can be transferred from it to the demand deposit account as needed. Because marketable securities typically earn higher returns than demand deposits held by firms (which typically earn no interest), there is an incentive to leave excess funds in the marketable securities portfolio.

GENERAL PROCEDURE

The following five-step procedure can be employed to determine the firm's daily cash balance. It involves estimating the major inflows and outflows and then modelling the routine cash flows.

STEP 1:   Prepare cash budgets on a monthly basis. Updates will be made as needed, often weekly,

STEP 2:   Break major cash inflows and outflows out of the cash budget. Major items would include such items as taxes, dividends, lease payments, debt service obligations, wages, and the like.

STEP 3:   Identify the timing of the major inflows and outflows expected to occur during the month. From this information, we can estimate approximate times when daily transfers into or out of the marketable securities portfolio may be needed.

STEP 4:   Model the remaining, or routine, cash inflows and outflows[3] to determine when (based on historical patterns) we would expect their inflow and outflow to occur during the month. In this process it is important to consider seasonal influences, day-of-the-month effects, day-of-the-week effects, vacations, and the like. The output of this modelling process provides an estimate of the net daily inflow or outflow from routine items. Based on this information, and the timing of the major inflows and outflows from step 3, the planned times for adding to or

---

[3] See references list at end of chapter.

selling marketable securities can be estimated. This step specifies the firm's estimated daily cash balance for each day of the month.

STEP 5: As the month progresses, compare the actual routine cash inflows and outflows with the projected ones. Also, the exact timing of major cash inflows and outflows is known, or can be more accurately estimated. Other developments can be added as they occur. The actual dates and amounts of marketable security purchases and sales will be adjusted from those estimated in step 4 as the month progresses.

This approach to estimating the intramonth (or daily) cash balance is shown in Figure 22.2. The goal is to maintain the actual cash balance at some predetermined level. Obviously, this level depends on the charges or credits the bank passes on to the firm. However, by breaking out the major items and then modelling the routine ones, the firm can easily breakdown its monthly cash budget into a day-by-day estimate of the necessary cash balance.

Transfers to and from the marketable securities portfolio use the same balancing of incremental costs and benefits discussed earlier. Therefore, it may not be profitable to switch funds to and from the marketable securities portfolio every day. If it costs $50 to move funds in or out of the marketable securities portfolio, the incremental interest,

Figure 22.2

Model for Estimating and Controlling the Firm's Cash Balance

In practice, other factors need to be addressed. These will cause the model to increase in complexity, but the basic concepts remain the same.

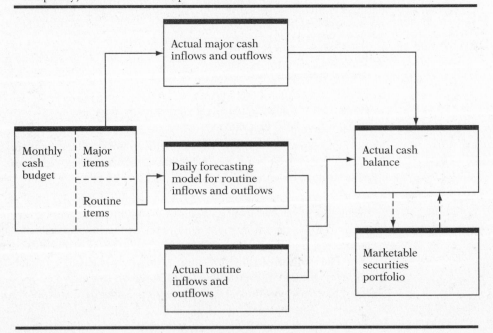

ΔI, from having funds in marketable securities is 4 percent, and the marginal tax rate is 40 percent, we can proceed as follows:

$$\Delta C = \Delta B$$
$$\Delta C = (\Delta t)(TS)(\Delta I_{daily})(1 - T)$$
$$\$50(1 - 0.40) = (1)(TS)(0.04/365 \text{ days})(1 - 0.40)$$

where Δt is specified as one day's gain in interest. Solving for TS, the amount of cash transferred, we have

$$TS = \frac{\$50(0.60)}{(0.04/365)\,(0.60)} = \$456{,}250$$

Therefore, there should be \$456,250 that can be left in marketable securities for at least one day before the transfer is made. If we estimate, based on our daily cash balance model, that funds can be transferred from cash to marketable securities and left for five days, then

$$\$30 = (5)(TS)(0.04/365 \text{ days})(0.60)$$
$$TS = \frac{\$30}{5(0.04/365)\,(0.60)} = \$91{,}250$$

In this case the transfer should be made if there is more than \$91,250 in excess funds in the firm's cash account. Similar calculations can be made if the differential interest rates change, or if the cost of the transaction increases or decreases. The point, however, is that the same basic benefit–cost framework can be used to determine when to transfer funds into and out of the marketable securities portfolio.

MODELS FOR DETERMINING THE TARGET CASH BALANCE

More formal models exist to help a firm determine its target cash balance, against which its actual cash balance can be compared. We will examine two: the Miller–Orr model and Stone's look-ahead model.

The Miller–Orr Model   The Miller–Orr model assumes cash inflows and outflows are uncertain and fluctuate randomly day-to-day. That is, the distribution of the daily net cash flow is described by a normal distribution. Figure 22.3 shows how the Miller–Orr model works. The model sets upper and lower control limits and a target cash balance. When the firm's cash balance reaches the upper control limit, H, the firm buys enough marketable securities to reduce its cash balance to the target cash balance, Z. Similarly, if the cash balance drops to the lower control limit, L, then the firm sells enough marketable securities to return its cash balance to the target again. The lower cash balance is set by management, depending on how much cash shortfall risk the firm is willing to accept.

Figure 22.3

The Miller–Orr Model for Cash Balance Management

With the Miller–Orr model, the firm sells marketable securities or transfers funds from the cash account to marketable securities as needed. Note that the average cash balance is greater than the target cash balance. If the lower control limit is set at zero, then the upper control limit and the target cash balance would shift down accordingly.

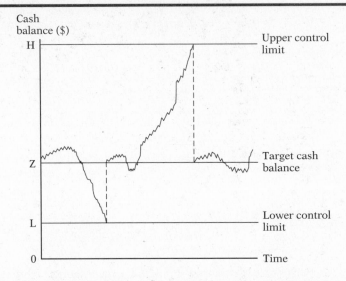

The Miller–Orr model depends on both opportunity and transactions costs.[4] The following variables are needed for the Miller–Orr model:

Z = the target cash balance
H = the upper control limit
L = the lower control limit
F = the fixed cost of buying or selling securities
k_{daily} = the opportunity cost of holding cash on a daily basis
σ^2 = the variance of the net daily cash flows

Then,

$$\text{target cash balance} = Z = \left[\frac{3F\sigma^2}{4k_{daily}}\right]^{1/3} + L \qquad (22.2)$$

and

$$\text{upper control limit} = H = 3Z - 2L \qquad (22.3)$$

---

[4] An earlier model developed by Baumol (1952) was based on the economic order quantity inventory model that is discussed in Appendix 23A.

The average daily cash balance is different from the target cash balance and equals

$$\text{average cash balance} = (4Z - L)/3$$

To illustrate the Miller–Orr model, suppose that L (the lower control limit) = zero, F = $300, k = 10% = 0.10 per year, and the standard deviation, σ, of the daily cash flows is $4,000. The daily compound opportunity cost is

$$(1 + k_{daily})^{365} - 1 = 0.10$$
$$(1 + k_{daily})^{365} = 1.10$$
$$1 + k_{daily} = (1.10)^{1/365}$$
$$1 + k_{daily} = 1.000261$$
$$k_{daily} = 0.000261$$

and the variance, σ^2, of the net daily cash flows is ($4,000)^2 = $16,000,000. Then the target cash balance, Z, is

$$Z = \left[\frac{3(\$300)\,(\$16,000,000)}{4(0.000261)}\right]^{1/3} + 0 \approx \$23,982 + 0 = \$23,982$$

The upper control limit, H, is

$$H = 3(\$23,982) - 2(0) = \$71,946$$

and the average cash balance is given by

$$\text{average cash balance} = [4(\$23,982) - 0]/3 = \$31,976$$

What occurs if everything is the same as before, except that the firm sets a lower control limit of $10,000? Then,

$$\text{target cash balance} = \$23,982 + \$10,000 = \$33,982$$
$$\text{upper control limit} = 3(\$33,982) - 2(\$10,000) = \$81,946$$
$$\text{average cash balance} = [4(\$33,982) - \$10,000]/3 = \$41,976$$

Thus, increasing or decreasing the lower control limit simply increases or decreases all of the levels by the amount of the change in the lower limit.

In examining the Miller–Orr model, note that the target cash balance is *not* midway between the upper and lower control limits. Therefore, the cash balance will, on average, hit the lower limit more often than the upper limit. This placement tends to limit the opportunity costs incurred.

The Miller–Orr model makes a number of assumptions, the most important of which are the following:

1. Daily cash flows are random and cannot be predicted. (Although this statement may apply for some companies, it does not for all.)
2. Transfers to and from marketable securities are instantaneous.
3. Seasonal and/or cyclical trends are not considered.
4. The cost of buying or selling securities is fixed regardless of the size of the transaction.
5. The term structure of interest rates is flat and the level of interest rates does not change.

When tested by firms, the Miller–Orr model does a reasonably good job if the distribution of net daily cash flows is approximately normal, the cash flows are random from day-to-day, and only one source of investment is available.

The Stone Model   The Stone model is similar in spirit to the Miller–Orr model, except that it places more attention on managing cash balances than on determining the optimal transaction size. Although upper and lower control limits are used, they do not automatically signal an investment or disinvestment decision. Rather, the action required depends upon the cash flows that are expected over the next few days. Figure 22.4 depicts the Stone model. The outer control limits function as do those in the Miller–Orr model. With the Stone model, however, once a firm hits or exceeds the outer control limits, it looks ahead a few days to determine whether within that time

---

Figure 22.4

The Stone Model for Cash Balance Management

With the Stone model, two upper and lower control limits are employed. When the firm hits (or exceeds) an outer control limit, it "looks ahead" a few days to determine if it will move back inside the inner control limit. If it will, then no action is taken. Otherwise, securities are bought or sold as needed.

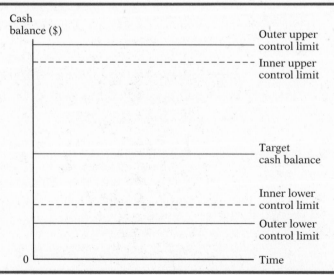

frame its anticipated cash balance will move to *within* the inner control limits. If the balance moves back inside the appropriate inner control limit *sometime* in the look-ahead period, no action is taken. If the cash balance is not expected to move within the inner control limit sometime in the look-ahead period, then a purchase or sale of marketable securities is triggered.

To illustrate Stone's model, assume that we have the following set of net cash flows (for simplicity we assume actual and expected cash flows are the same):

Day	Net Cash Flow
1	$20,000
2	−15,000
3	−45,000
4	15,000
5	10,000
6	20,000
7	−40,000
8	−10,000
9	−5,000
10	15,000

The initial cash balance is $60,000; the outer lower control limit is $25,000, and the inner lower limit is $35,000. As shown in Figure 22.5, on day 3 the outer lower control limit is breached (i.e., $60,000 + $20,000 − $15,000 − $45,000 = $20,000). Accordingly, the firm looks ahead a few days at anticipated net cash flows. Assume a three-day look-ahead policy is followed. We see that on days 4, 5, and 6 the cash balance increases and is at least as high as the inner lower control limit (as required by Stone's model). Thus, no transaction is made. On day 7, the outer lower control limit of $25,000 is again reached. The firm then looks ahead three days, as follows:

Day	Net Cash Balance
7	$25,000
8	25,000 − 10,000 = $15,000
9	15,000 − 5,000 = 10,000
10	10,000 + 15,000 = 25,000

Since at no time during the next three days will the cash balance return to the inner lower control limit of $35,000, a transaction is triggered. The firm sells $35,000 worth of securities on day 7 to bring its cash balance back up to the target of $60,000. This is also shown in Figure 22.5.

Unlike the Miller–Orr model, the Stone model does not provide an indication of how the outer upper and lower control limits are set. The Miller–Orr model, could be

Figure 22.5

The Stone Model in Action

At day 3 a possible sell signal is given. However, by looking ahead, the firm finds no action is required. On day 7 another sell signal is given. This time, by looking ahead, the firm finds that cash balances will not be sufficient without the sale of marketable securities.

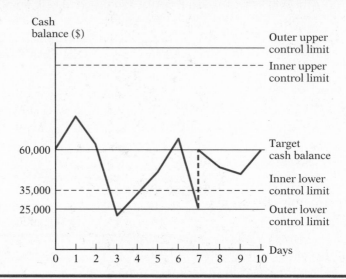

employed to determine both the target cash balance and the control limits, while the forecast (or look-ahead) period is set judgmentally. In contrast to the Miller–Orr model, the Stone model requires no assumptions except that transfers to/from marketable securities are instantaneous. This lack of assumptions means that the Stone model is an *ad hoc* model that relies solely on judgment and the firm's past experience. Although it is easy to adjust for seasonal or cyclical factors, there is no expectation that this model will lead to an optimal policy. Using the Stone model along with past experience and sensitivity analysis, however, provides an intuitive method for firms to set policies to control their cash balances.

Concept Review Questions

- Detail the five-step procedure employed to determine the firm's daily cash balance.
- Describe how to use the Miller–Orr model and the Stone model to determine target cash balances.

MANAGEMENT OF THE MARKETABLE SECURITIES PORTFOLIO

Excess cash above what is needed to meet the firm's cash balance requirement will be invested in marketable securities. Because of the need for liquidity and stability of principal, long-term bonds or common stock generally are not appropriate investments for temporary excess cash, unless some type of hedge is employed to counteract any potential loss of principal.[5]

INVESTMENT ALTERNATIVES

Managers have a choice of many different marketable securities for short-term investments. These are shown in Table 22.1. Treasury bills are direct obligations of the government. They are typically considered the safest marketable security. The yield on treasury bills is often used as a proxy for the risk-free rate, k_{RF}. All other marketable securities are viewed as being more risky, because they are not issued or backed directly by the government. Money market mutual funds are a pool of short-term marketable securities managed by an investment advisor.

In addition, in recent years numerous other investment alternatives have become available. Mortgage-backed and other asset-backed securities have become more popular. Other firms have invested heavily in Eurodollar- or LIBOR-denominated investments. Still others have bought long-term bonds and then entered into interest rate swaps (swaps are discussed in Chapter 11) to achieve a variable LIBOR rate return on their investment. Although these and many other innovations have occurred, we will focus on the basics of managing the marketable securities portfolio.

SELECTION CRITERIA

In assessing the selection of alternative marketable securities, we look at the risk, liquidity, maturity, and yield aspects of the alternative investments.

Risk   As general economic conditions change from boom to recession, market rates of interest change. In addition, monetary and fiscal policies can also influence market interest rates. As market interest rates go up, the market price of outstanding debt instruments decreases. As market interest rates go down, the market price of outstanding debt increases.

Figuring the Yield on Treasury Bills.   To examine the risks as economic conditions change, let us consider one specific money market security—treasury bills. Government of Canada treasury bills are noninterest-bearing discount securities that are sold through regular weekly and biweekly auctions, with 91- and 182-day maturity bills sold weekly and 365-day maturity bills sold every two weeks. Because they are redeemed at full face value at maturity, the interest earned is the difference between the face value (if held to maturity) and the discounted price.

To compare the yield on treasury bills with the yield on bonds, we must calculate the **bond equivalent yield, k_{BE},** of the treasury bill.[6]

---

[5] Because of the 100 percent dividend exclusion in calculating corporate taxable income, preferred stock may be employed also. A relatively recent development that has spurred this usage is adjustable rate preferred stock (discussed in Chapter 11).

[6] The bond equivalent yield is not calculated employing compound interest. Our presentation is in line with the use of bond equivalent yields in practice.

Table 22.1

Characteristics of Marketable Securities

Given the wide variety of securities, and maturities, firms can tailor a marketable securities portfolio to meet their needs.

Instrument	Description	Maturity	Interest	Marketability
Treasury bills	Short-term obligation of the federal government	91 days, 182 days, and 1 year	Discount	Excellent secondary market
Bankers' acceptances	Promissory note drawn for payment by a corporation on a certain date; payment guaranteed by a bank	30 to 90 days	Discount	Good secondary market
Commercial paper	Short-term promissory note issued under the general credit of the corporation	1 day to 1 year; usually 30, 60, and 90 days	Interest-bearing or discount	Limited secondary market, but dealer may arrange buy-back
Sales finance paper	Short-term secured, unsecured, or guaranteed paper issued by finance subsidiaries of corporations and finance companies	1 day to 1 year; usually 30, 60, and 90 days	Interest-bearing or discount	Good secondary market
Repurchase agreements (repurchase or buy-back contract)	Dealer sells government securities and simultaneously agrees to repurchase the securities on a certain date	1 day to 3 months	Repurchase price set higher than selling price, paid at maturity	Limited
Bank certificates of deposit	Promissory note from a bank or trust company to repay a deposit	Overnight to 7 years	Interest-bearing, paid at maturity	No secondary market
Negotiable certificates of deposit	Primissory note from a bank or trust company to repay a deposit	30 days to 1 year	Discount	Good secondary market
Eurodollar	Dollar-denominated time deposits at foreign (branches of) banks	1 day to 1 year	Interest-bearing, paid at maturity	Limited secondary market
Money market mutual funds	Pool of short-term money market instruments	Shares may be sold any time	Credited to account monthly	Good; provided by fund itself

$$k_{BE} = \left(\frac{P_M - P_0}{P_0}\right)\left(\frac{365}{n}\right) \qquad (22.4)$$

where

k_{BE} = the bond equivalent yield
P_M = the maturity value of the treasury bill
P_0 = the discounted price
n = the number of days until maturity

To illustrate, suppose that you purchase a 182-day treasury bill with a face value of $10,000 at a price of $9,500. What is your bond equivalent yield? Employing Equation 22.4, we have

$$k_{BE} = \left(\frac{\$10,000 - \$9,500}{\$10,000}\right)\left(\frac{365}{182}\right) = \frac{\$182,500}{\$1,729,000} = 10.56\%$$

Alternatively, if someone told you that the bond equivalent yield on a 182-day $10,000 treasury bill was 10.56 percent, and you wanted to find out how much you would pay for the security, we could rearrange Equation 22.4 and solve for P_0 as follows:

$$P_0 = \frac{P_M}{1 + (k_{BE})\left(\dfrac{n}{365}\right)} \qquad (22.5)$$

$$P_0 = \frac{\$10,000}{1 + (0.1056)\left(\dfrac{182}{365}\right)} = \$9,499.79 \approx \$9,500$$

To illustrate the risks that may exist with treasury bills, let us continue with our example. If we buy the 182-day treasury bill for $9,500 and hold it until maturity, then our bond equivalent yield is 10.56 percent. But what happens if we have to sell before it matures and interest rates on treasury bills have increased since we purchased the treasury bill? Suppose that we were forced to sell in 60 days, and the bond equivalent yield at that time was 11.00 percent.

To see the effect of having to sell when interest rates have moved higher, we first determine the price of the treasury bill with 122 (i.e., $182 - 60$) days to maturity as follows, using Equation 22.5:

$$P_0 \text{ selling price} = \frac{\$10,000}{1 + (0.11)\left(\dfrac{122}{365}\right)} = \$9,645.37$$

Then the actual bond equivalent yield over the 60 days the treasury bill was owned can be determined using Equation 22.6:

$$k_{BE} = \frac{(\text{selling price} - \text{purchase price})(365)}{(\text{purchase price})(\text{days owned})} \qquad (22.6)$$

$$= \frac{(\$9,645.37 - \$9,500)(365)}{(\$9,500)(60)} \approx 9.31\%$$

Because of changes in market rates of interest, which adversely affected the price of the treasury bill when we sold prematurely, our actual return was only 9.31 percent instead of our anticipated return of 10.56 percent.

Treasury bills are issued and backed by the government. Many other marketable securities are issued by individual firms or banks. **Commercial paper,** which is simply short-term unsecured borrowing, is issued by consumer finance companies or by industrial, retail, or even public utility firms. Likewise, many different banks issue negotiable **certificates of deposit,** which are short-term unsecured borrowings. The specific firm or issuer of the marketable security in these cases is responsible for payment. Managers must consider the ability of the firm issuing the marketable security to pay interest and principal on time.

Liquidity   Most marketable securities have excellent or good secondary markets. For commercial paper, however, it may be necessary to see if the issuing firm will redeem the security early if needed. Likewise, there is a limited secondary market for Eurodollars and **repurchase agreements.** Because firms use their marketable securities portfolio as a source of ready cash, the liquidity aspect of the investment also requires careful consideration.

Maturity   The maturity of the marketable securities is also of prime importance. Most large firms keep some cash invested overnight in repurchase agreements and other shorter-maturity securities. Then they follow a layered approach of matching longer cash availability with investments in longer-term marketable securities.

Yield   The final selection criterion is the yield on the marketable securities. Table 22.2 presents the yields on three securities during the 1988–1994 period. We see that yields went up and then fell significantly between 1991 and 1993 before increasing slightly in 1994. Also notice that treasury bills, because they are backed by the government of Canada, are the least risky of the securities and consequently always have the lowest yield. Other securities have higher returns, depending on their risk and liquidity. For example, the yield on bankers' acceptances is slightly higher than the yield on treasury

Table 22.2

Yields on Three-Month Money Market Instruments

Treasury bills, being the least risky instrument, provide the lowest returns. Other more risky and less liquid securities provide higher returns.

	Year						
Instrument	1988	1989	1990	1991	1992	1993	1994
Treasury bills	9.46%	12.0%	12.8%	8.76%	6.56%	4.84%	5.51%
Bankers' acceptances	9.60	12.2	13.0	8.83	6.62	4.90	5.62
Commercial paper	9.65	12.2	13.0	8.89	6.73	4.97	5.68

Source: "Selected Canadian Bond Yields & Other Interest Rates," *Bank of Canada Review,* March 1995.

bills with the same maturity, whereas the return on commercial paper is higher than that on bankers' acceptances of comparable maturity.

THE MARKETABLE SECURITIES PORTFOLIO

The interaction of risk, liquidity, and maturity determines the returns. The firm's risk–return posture then determines the specific composition of the marketable securities portfolio. Very risk averse firms might have a marketable securities portfolio composed almost entirely of treasury bills. More aggressive firms will opt for a large portion in higher-yielding Eurodollars or certificates of deposit issued by overseas branches of Canadian-based banks. The impact of the returns on a big marketable securities portfolio, particularly when short-term interest rates are high, can be significant.

Concept Review Questions

■ What are some marketable securities used by firms for short-term investments?

■ How do risk, liquidity, maturity, and yield affect the composition of a firm's marketable securities portfolio?

KEY POINTS

- Management of the firm's liquid assets focuses on cash inflows and outflows, the tradeoff between holding cash versus investing in marketable securities, and how to structure the marketable securities portfolio.
- Because of float, firms attempt to speed the cash-gathering process while controlling (or slowing) disbursements. The primary means for speeding collections are lockboxes and an efficient banking arrangement. Disbursements are managed by using controlled disbursing, zero balance accounts, and similar arrangements.
- When comparing cash management alternatives, the incremental costs and benefits are analyzed in a NPV framework.
- Determining the amount to hold in a firm's demand deposit account versus the amount to invest in marketable securities depends on forecasting and the incremental interest to be earned in marketable securities. The Miller–Orr and Stone models provide insight on how firms control their cash balances.
- Risk, liquidity, maturity, and yield (or return) concerns determine how the firm's marketable securities portfolio is structured.

QUESTIONS

22.1 The objective of the firm is to maximize the value of the firm. Given that the return on real assets typically exceeds the return on marketable securities, explain why firms generally keep 5 to 10 percent of their assets in cash and marketable securities.

22.2 Explain the different types of float and how they affect the firm's cash-gathering system. Do these same types of float apply to the firm's cash-disbursing system?

22.3   How can the firm speed up the cash-gathering process? Which float does each attempt to shorten?

22.4   Identify procedures the firm can employ to control the disbursement of cash. How does each serve to (a) increase float or (b) lower the firm's cash balance needs?

22.5   What impact would the following have on the firm's average cash balance?
a.   Interest rates on marketable securities decrease.
b.   Cost of trading marketable securities increases.
c.   The firm agrees to raise its compensating balance.
d.   A zero balance account procedure is implemented.
e.   New billing procedures allow a better correspondence between cash inflows and cash outflows.

22.6   Analyze the specific assumptions incorporated in the Miller–Orr and Stone models for determining the firm's target cash balance. What similarities and differences exist between the models?

22.7   Discuss the criteria that influence the firm's marketable securities selection procedure.

22.8   Treasury bills are widely employed by firms as an investment for temporary excess cash. Given that they have the lowest yield of any marketable security, why are treasury bills chosen?

22.9   During the last 25 years or so, many retail firms and others that issue credit cards have shifted from billing all customers on the last day of the month to "cycle billing." With cycle billing, customers are billed (often in alphabetical order) throughout the month. From the standpoint of the credit card issuer, what effect does cycle billing have on cash flows and average cash balances? Does it also have an impact on accounts receivable? Explain.

CONCEPT REVIEW PROBLEMS

See Appendix A for solutions.

CR22.1   It takes Casablanca Company six days to receive and deposit cheques from customers. Management of Casablanca is considering a lockbox system to decrease float time to four days. Average daily collections are $20,000 and the cost of funds is 6 percent.
a.   What will be the reduction in outstanding cash balances as a result of implementing the lockbox system?
b.   If the firm's tax rate is 36 percent, what is the maximum daily charge that Casablanca can afford to pay for the lockbox system?

CR22.2   Kathy, assistant controller of KT Gear, is analyzing the firm's management of cash and marketable securities. Brokerage fees are $100 per transfer, the firm's tax rate is 40 percent, and incremental interest from having funds in marketable securities is 5 percent. If fund transfers occur every seven days, what is the minimum amount that should be transferred? (*Note:* Assume a 365-day year.)

CR22.3   Kathy, from CR22.2, would like to use the Miller–Orr model to analyze KT Gear's cash balance policy. The standard deviation of the net daily cash flow is $10,000. To meet compensating balance agreements, the firm keeps a minimum of $500,000 in the bank. What are KT Gear's recommended target cash balance, upper control limit, and average cash balance?

CR22.4   Tony, cash manager for KJI Inc., is considering the purchase of a treasury bill for $9,900 that will mature in 50 days for $10,000.
a.   What is the bond equivalent yield on the treasury bill?
b.   After 10 days, the bond equivalent yield on 40-day treasury bills increased to 7.5%, and at that time Tony was forced to sell the treasury bill and move funds into the firm's cash account. What was the bond equivalent return on the treasury bill?

PROBLEMS

22.1 Melton & Sons projects that its sales will be $120 million next year. All sales are for credit, but the credit policies are in good shape because there are very few bad debts and payments are mailed on time. Melton is concerned, however, about the cost of float time. Its marginal tax rate is 30 percent.
a. If funds could be invested to earn 7 percent, what is the incremental daily benefit of a 1-day reduction in float time using a 365-day year?
b. What is the daily benefit of a 1.5-day reduction in float if the funds could earn 8 percent?

22.2 Beta Ltd. currently has all incoming cheques sent directly to its headquarters. The average mail time is 4 days, processing time is 2.5 days, and transit time is 1 day. The average cash inflow is $2 million per calendar day.
a. What is the average collection float in dollars?
b. Although internal processing time is 2.5 days, Beta is actually able to record the incoming cheques for accounting purposes on its accounting records in 1 day. How much in dollars does Beta have recorded on its accounting records that are not actually "good funds" in its bank account?
c. By modifying its system, Beta can reduce total float time by 2.25 days. The proposed system will cost $350,000 before taxes per year to operate, the interest rate is 12 percent, a 365-day year is assumed, and the marginal tax rate is 40 percent. Should Beta implement the modified cash collection system?

22.3 Mead-Naylor currently has a centralized cash receiving system located in Vancouver. Its average float time on collections is 5.7 days. A bank has approached Mead-Naylor, offering to establish a lockbox system that should reduce the float time to 2.9 days. (Thus the net reduction is 5.7 − 2.9, or 2.8 days.) Mead-Naylor's daily collections are $600,000, and excess funds can be invested at 10 percent. If there are 800 cheques per day, how much is the maximum Mead-Naylor can afford to pay *per cheque* for the lockbox operation? Assume a 365-day year and a tax rate of 30 percent.

22.4 Harcourt Supply presently uses a two-lockbox system that has a total average daily transaction balance of $1 million (based on a 365-day year). The banks do not charge a direct fee, but Harcourt has agreed to keep a total of $2 million in compensating balances on which no interest is paid.

Fred, a recent graduate, has recommended that Harcourt switch to a new lockbox system. The savings in float time would be 1.2 days, the average cheque size is $500, the interest rate is 9 percent, and the firm's marginal tax rate is 34 percent. Through a new agreement with its banks, Harcourt would have its compensating balance reduced to $1.8 million (still no interest paid), pay $0.05 per cheque processed, and pay additional fixed fees of $50,000 to the banks each year. Based on the yearly incremental costs and benefits, should Harcourt make the switch recommended by Fred?

22.5 Presently, Reuss Industries is using a lockbox arrangement. Reuss believes, however, that it can save money by eliminating the lockbox system and handling the process internally. The lockbox costs $5 per day and $0.50 per cheque processed. Currently, 400 cheques per day are being processed. If Reuss eliminates the lockbox, total costs will be $40,000 per year before taxes, and float time will increase by 2 days. Assume the average transaction size is $500 per cheque, the yearly interest rate is 11 percent, a 365-day year is employed, and the tax rate is 40 percent.
a. Should Reuss eliminate the lockbox system? (*Note:* Compute the yearly incremental costs and benefits.)
b. At what incremental float time would Reuss be indifferent between the two approaches?

22.6 ElectroSystems has been growing so fast it has not examined its cash-gathering system.

Presently, all cash comes into its corporate office. A downturn in the economy, however, has affected both sales and profitability. Now appears to be an appropriate time to review the cash-gathering system.

A consulting firm, for a fee of $100,000, has just presented the following information to ElectroSystems:

Present	**Proposed**
Home office collection system costing $75,000 per year.	Five lockboxes; the cost per cheque processed is $0.30.
Average daily volume is $900,000, with an average cheque size of $1,500, based on receipts for 270 days per year.	Twice-daily transfer of funds from *each* lockbox via electronic transfer at a cost of $8 each.
	Reduction in float time of 2.6 days.
	Home office expenses of $50,000 per year.

a. If ElectroSystems can earn 9 percent on the excess funds and it has a marginal tax rate of 40 percent, what are the yearly incremental after-tax costs and benefits of moving to the new system (ignoring the consultant's one-time fee of $100,000)? Should the switch be made? (*Note:* When calculating ΔC, assume that cheques are processed only 270 days a year. When calculating ΔB, assume the $900,000 is available for all 365 days.)

b. Was the consultant's report worthwhile?

22.7 Andy of Hudson Bay Tire needs to know how much money would be saved by a controlled disbursing system. The average daily payables are $200,000, the controlled disbursing will add 1.5 days to the float, and the excess funds can be invested at 13 percent. Based on a 365-day year and a marginal tax rate of 30 percent, what are the yearly incremental benefits associated with the controlled disbursing system?

22.8 St. Lawrence Marine Supplies has set up a controlled disbursing system with two banks. The net benefit ($\Delta B - \Delta C$) of the system to St. Lawrence is $28,700 per year. If St. Lawrence writes 200 cheques per day with an average amount of $400, how many days of additional float will St. Lawrence obtain if the interest rate is 7 percent and the banks charge $0.10 per cheque cleared? Assume a 365-day year and that St. Lawrence is operating at a loss so that taxes are not relevant.

22.9 Southeast Imports has determined that its daily standard deviation of cash flows is $50,000. The opportunity cost of holding cash is 9.5 percent per year, the cost of buying or selling marketable securities is $150, and the firm has established a minimum cash level of $150,000. What is Southeast Imports' target cash balance, its upper and lower control limits, and its average cash balance? (*Note:* Assume a 365-day year.)

22.10 The variance of the daily cash flow for a firm is $9,000,000, the opportunity cost of holding cash is 11 percent per year, and the cost of buying or selling marketable securities is $200 per transaction.

a. What is the target cash balance, the upper control limit, and the average cash balance? (*Note:* Assume a 365-day year.)

b. What happens to your answers in (a) if the cost of holding funds drops by 25 percent, to 8.25 percent per year?

c. Independent of (b), what happens to your answers in (a) if the cost of buying or selling marketable securities increases by 25 percent, to $250 per transaction?

22.11 After trying the Miller–Orr model, Tracy Production has decided to employ the Stone model. It has established a target cash balance and control limits as follows:

Outer upper control limit	$100,000
Inner upper control limit	90,000
Target cash balance	50,000
Inner lower control limit	30,000
Outer lower control limit	20,000

Tracy's present cash balance is $70,000. If its cash flows (actual and expected) are as follows and it employs a two-day look-ahead period, what action is required? (*Note:* If it has to buy or sell securities, buy or sell enough to bring it back to its target cash balance.)

Day	Net Cash Flow
1	$40,000
2	5,000
3	−10,000
4	−30,000
5	− 5,000
6	25,000
7	−15,000
8	−10,000
9	5,000
10	−10,000

22.12   A 91-day treasury bill with a $10,000 maturity value was purchased at 97.40 (as a percent of its maturity value).
a.   What is the bond equivalent yield on the treasury bill?
c.   If the treasury bill must be sold with 35 days left to maturity when the bond equivalent yield is 11.5 percent, what bond equivalent yield was earned while the T-bill was owned?

22.13   Sam's Supers had excess cash that it used to purchase a $1 million (maturity value), 182-day treasury bill when the bond equivalent yield was 7.9 percent.
a.   What market price (ignoring transactions costs) did Sam's pay? (*Note:* Round all answers to the nearest dollar.)
b.   After 80 days, Sam's had to sell the treasury bill. Due to heavy government financing, the bond equivalent yield had climbed to 8.40 percent when Sam's sold the bill. What was the actual bond equivalent yield on the treasury bill over the time when Sam's owned it?
c.   If Sam's sells the treasury bill after 120 days, how do the answers in (a) and (b) change?

22.14   Spivey Energy has the following schedule of excess cash available and cash needs over the next six months:

Time	Cash Availability/Needs
Now	$2 million excess cash
In 2 months	An additional $2 million excess cash
In 4 months	$2 million cash needed
In 6 months	An additional $2 million cash needed

The structure of short-term interest rates is as follows:

Now		Expected in 2 Months	
Maturity Period	**Yield (Annual)**	**Maturity Period**	**Yield (Annual)**
2 months	7.3%	2 months	8.0%
4 months	7.4	4 months	8.1
6 months	7.5		

Assume that once marketable securities are purchased, they are held to maturity. If it costs $100 every time marketable securities are purchased, which securities should be purchased to maximize the before-tax income from the added investment? [*Hint:* Remember the yields are on an annual basis. To convert to monthly, just divide the yearly figure by 12. For simplicity, (1) do *not* compound your results, and (2) take the transactions costs at the end of the period.]

22.15 Mini Case You have just been hired by Worldwide Toys as their cash manager. On your first day on the job you find that the cash management system is in disarray. Consequently, it must be overhauled, and in the process you must educate your employees and the firm's management.

a. As a first step you find that the three basic issues relating to cash (or liquid asset) management are not clearly understood. Explain these issues.

b. There has been a lot of confusion concerning the issue of float. Explain what float is, how it exists for both cash inflows and cash outflows, what parts can be controlled (and how), and how the issue of "good funds" relates to float. The firm's accounting manager has typically provided estimates of "good funds" by examining the firm's day-by-day cash account as recorded by the firm's accounting system. Is this a good policy? Explain.

c. Two alternatives to the present cash flow system have been presented to you. What decisions should be made in each case?

  1. Lockbox: Average collection float is presently 6.3 days. By going to a lockbox system, the firm can reduce the float to 2.8 days. The daily collections are $1,500,000, excess funds can be invested at an incremental rate of 8 percent, and there are 2,500 cheques per day. The bank will charge $200 per day plus 20 cents per cheque processed. Worldwide's effective tax rate is 40 percent. (*Note:* Assume a 365-day year throughout, and calculate the daily benefits and costs.)

  2. Controlled disbursing: The firm's average daily payables are $800,000, consisting of 1,000 cheques, and the present payable float is 1.5 days. The new payables float will be 3.4 days. The charge for the new system will be $400 per day plus 8 cents per cheque. The tax rate is still 40 percent, and the interest rate is 8 percent.

d. To determine the firm's target cash balance, you decide to implement the Miller–Orr model. Based on sampling over the last year, the daily standard deviation of the cash flows has been estimated to be $800,000. Given the uncertainty involved, the minimum cash level has been set at $1,000,000. The opportunity cost of holding cash is 8 percent per year, and the cost of buying or selling marketable securities is $300. Assuming a 365-day year, what are the target cash balance, the upper and lower control limits, and the average cash balance?

e. Excess funds will be invested in marketable securities. Summarize the different types of marketable securities available. Also, indicate what risks must be considered when constructing the firm's marketable securities portfolio.

f. Two different treasury bills exist as follows:

$10,000 maturity value, 90-day bill with P_0 of $9,780

$10,000 maturity value, 245-day bill with P_0 of $9,390

  1. Which treasury bill has the higher bond equivalent yield?

2. Now assume that the treasury bill has to be sold by Worldwide Toys in 70 days. The bond equivalent yield on the shorter maturity bill is 8.70 percent, whereas it is 8.90 percent on the longer-maturity bill. What would the actual yield on the two treasury bills be over this period?

REFERENCES

BAUMOL, WILLIAM J. "The Transactions Demand for Cash: An Inventory Theoretic Approach." *Quarterly Journal of Economics* 66 (November 1952): 545–556.

CUDJOE, JAMES, and GREG FLIGHT. "Implementing an International EDI/EFT Program— General Electric's Experience." *Journal of Cash Management* 12 (May/June 1992): 19–22.

FIX, JOHN N., and JOHN R. RANDELLI. "Treasury Management in 1992: The Shape of the Industry." *Journal of Cash Management* 12 (November/December 1992): 18–22.

HOSSFIELD, T. "The Interbank Deposit Market in Canada." *Bank of Canada Review*, February 1986, pp. 3–12.

HUNTER, W. T. *Canadian Financial Markets*. Peterborough, N.H.: Broadview Press, 1986.

KAHN, RANDY, and ROBERT ROSDORFF. "Practical Applications of Financial EDI." *Journal of Cash Management* 12 (January/February 1992): 20–23.

MAIER, STEVEN F., and JAMES H. VANDER WEIDE. "What Lockbox and Disbursement Models Really Do." *Journal of Finance* 38 (May 1983): 361–371.

MILLER, MERTON H., and DANIEL ORR. "A Model of the Demand for Money by Firms." *Quarterly Journal of Economics* 80 (August 1966): 413–435.

SARPKAYA, S. *The Money Market in Canada*, 2nd ed. Toronto: Butterworths, 1980.

STONE, BERNELL K. "The Use of Forecasts and Smoothing in Control-Limit Models for Cash Management." *Financial Management* 1 (Spring 1972): 72–84.

STONE, BERNELL K., and TOM W. MILLER. "Daily Cash Forecasting and Seasonal Resolution: Alternative Models and Techniques for Using the Distribution Approach." *Journal of Financial and Quantitative Analysis* 20 (September 1985): 335–351.

23

Accounts Receivable and Inventory

EXECUTIVE SUMMARY

Accounts receivable represents a sizable percentage of most firms' assets. The primary determinants of the receivables level are the industry, the level of total sales, and the firm's credit and collection policies. Firms cannot discriminate on price; however, they may offer different conditions of sale. Therefore, the most important credit-granting decisions are (1) who will receive credit and (2) what the conditions of the sale will be.

The actual credit decision involves an analysis of the size and timing of the cash flows involved and of the risks in a present value framework. Those credit opportunities with positive NPVs should be accepted, and those with negative NPVs should be rejected. The receivables pattern approach to managing collections focuses on the payment and receivables pattern relative to the month the sale occurred. As such, it is not influenced by the level of sales.

Like accounts receivable, inventory also represents a sizable percentage of most firms' assets. The basic costs associated with inventory are carrying costs, ordering costs, and costs associated with running short. The ABC method, the economic order quantity model, material requirements planning, and just-in-time are all models employed to manage a firm's inventory. NPV techniques are employed to make inventory decisions because, as with accounts receivable, the decisions are similar to those necessary for any other investment the firm makes.

RECEIVABLES, INVENTORY, AND THE FIRM

To complete our analysis of the firm's current assets, we turn our attention to accounts receivable and inventory. Firms typically sell goods and services on both a cash and a credit basis. In the former, cash is received immediately; in the latter, the extension of

trade credit leads to the establishment of accounts receivable. Receivables represent credit sales that have not been collected. Over time, as the customers pay these accounts, the firm receives the cash associated with the original sale. If the customer does not pay an account, a **bad debt** loss is incurred. To make sales, most firms carry various types of inventory. Firms carry inventory to ensure a smooth production cycle and to assist in the marketing effort. Without both receivables and inventory, most firms would cease to operate or would be much less efficient.

The investment in accounts receivable and inventory is similar to the long-term, or capital budgeting, decision discussed in Chapters 7–9, so many of the techniques used in this chapter are similar to those used in making capital budgeting decisions. Throughout, the emphasis is on the magnitude, timing, and riskiness of the cash flows, and the opportunity costs associated with a firm's investment in receivables and inventory. The goal in managing these is still to maximize the overall value, V, of the firm.

IMPORTANCE OF RECEIVABLES AND INVENTORY

The financial goals of the firm must be coordinated with its marketing and production efforts. There is always a tradeoff between risk and return, and different departments often want different policies. Nowhere is this more evident than in determining and maintaining proper levels of receivables and inventory. The marketing department may want lenient credit terms and collection policies in order to increase sales; the marketing effort also benefits from high inventory levels. With high inventory levels, the firm can promise immediate delivery, knowing that it will not lose sales because of stock outages. Higher inventory levels help the production department as well, enabling it to purchase in larger quantities, use longer production runs, and suffer less down time or unanticipated adjustments in the production schedule. These varying desires often conflict, however, with the objectives of the chief financial officer. Other things being equal, the CFO wants to minimize the firm's accounts receivable and inventory levels. Lower levels have two important financial benefits: First, less financing has to be secured, because the firm has less investment in receivables and inventory. Second, profits should be higher relative to sales or assets, because long-term investments are expected to generate higher returns than short-term assets.

The result must be a tradeoff between risk and return. On the one hand, there is the risk of not granting enough credit or having enough inventory, thereby suffering sales losses. On the other hand, too high a level of receivables and inventory has a cost that may offset any sales or production benefits. A coordinated effort, involving marketing, production, and finance, is required to balance the risks and the returns. Most firms have substantial investments in receivables and inventory. Large manufacturing firms may have "only" 30 percent of total assets invested in receivables and inventory. But more than 50 percent of the total assets of most retail and smaller manufacturing firms is invested in receivables and inventory, and that figure increases to more than 60 percent for wholesale firms.

The investment in both receivables and inventory is influenced by many factors. One primary determinant is the industry in which the firm operates. The industry effect is caused by competition, the characteristics of the product, the production process, and so forth. Recent surveys of credit policies have indicated that the actions of competitors are the major factor governing the credit terms granted. At the same time, trade credit is more likely to be extended if the seller has a cost advantage over competing suppliers or lenders or has (or can achieve) greater market power.[1] Likewise, a firm's investment in inventory is largely influenced by production processes and the requirements imposed by competition. The importance of the industry effect cannot be minimized when examining a firm's investment in both receivables and inventory. Inventory management techniques are examined later in the chapter. For now, let us concentrate on receivables.

SIZE OF ACCOUNTS RECEIVABLE

The size of the investment in accounts receivable is influenced by factors in addition to industry effect, cost advantage, and market power effect. First, as shown in Figure 23.1, is total sales. Certain credit policies, such as liberal payment periods, encourage more sales. The state of the economy, the aggressiveness of the firm's marketing efforts, and other like factors also influence sales. As total sales increase, the level of credit sales and the investment in receivables usually increases. Second, the firm's

---

Figure 23.1

Factors Affecting the Investment in Accounts Receivable

The level of sales, percentage of credit sales, and credit and collection policies determine the level of the firm's accounts receivable. Likewise, the credit management operation directly influences the flow of funds to the firm's cash account.

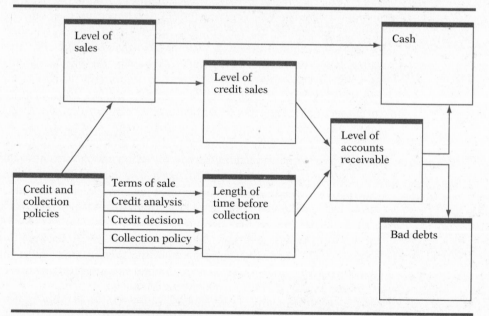

---

[1] For a discussion of these and other accounts receivable issues, see Mian and Smith (1992).

credit and collection policies also influence the size of the investment in receivables. These policies can be broken down into four distinct areas:

1. Terms and conditions of credit sales
2. Credit analysis
3. Credit decision
4. Collection policy

The decisions in these areas largely determine the length of time between the granting of credit and the receipt of cash. As the length of time before collection increases, the firm's investment in receivables increases. Shortening the days sales outstanding reduces the firm's investment in receivables. The level of investment in accounts receivable is a function of the firm's industry, its total sales, and its credit and collection policies.

Concept Review Questions

- What are the benefits and the risks of minimizing the firm's accounts receivable and inventory levels?
- Describe factors that affect the size of a firm's accounts receivable.

CREDIT AND COLLECTION MANAGEMENT

In this section, we will explore in more detail the four main aspects of credit and collection policies. In doing so, we want to see how they are established and the effect they can have on the value of the firm.

TERMS AND CONDITIONS OF SALE

Although most firms and industries grant trade credit, there are substantial variations. If the goods are produced to the customer's specifications, the selling firm may ask for cash before delivery. If the deliveries are irregular or if some risk is involved, the seller may require **cash on delivery (COD)**. If ordinary trade credit is granted, goods are on an open account, with payment due in some prespecified length of time, such as 30 or 60 days. As an inducement to encourage early payment, firms often offer a cash discount. If a firm sells on a 2/10, net 30 basis, customers who pay within 10 days receive a 2 percent discount; in any case, full payment is due within 30 days. In an open account agreement, the seller delivers the goods and provides an invoice, which constitutes the customer's bill and contains the terms of the arrangement. Likewise, in some industries **seasonal dating** is employed, with payment being timed to coincide with the buyer's anticipated cash inflows.

If the goods are large in size, or if the seller is unsure about the payment ability of the customer, other devices may be employed. The most common is a draft, which is just a written order to pay a specified amount of money at a specified point in time to a given person (or to the bearer). The selling firm might agree to sell the goods only if the sale is made through a draft. If a **sight draft** is employed, before receiving title to the goods, the customer would have to pay when the draft is presented. Alternatively, the draft could be a **time draft**, which states that payment will be made a certain number of days after presentation to the customer. A time draft can be accepted by the customer or the customer's bank. If the customer accepts the draft, he or she acknowledges acceptance in writing on the back of the draft. This then becomes a **trade acceptance**. If the draft is accepted by the customer's bank, it becomes a **banker's acceptance**. The bank substitutes its creditworthiness for the customer's. As noted in Chapter 22, banker's acceptances are a major short-term marketable security; most of them arise from international trade.

The wide variety of terms and conditions have some logic to them, but tradition within an industry also plays a part. Sellers will demand early payment if the customers are in a high-risk class, if the accounts are small, or if the goods are perishable.

INTERNATIONAL PURCHASES AND SALES

Although most domestic trade is on an open-account basis, this is not true for firms involved in international purchases or sales. Due to the lack of credit knowledge, communications difficulties, and the like, the process becomes more complex. Most international trade requires three main documents: (1) an order to pay, or draft; (2) a bill of lading; and (3) a letter of credit. We know about the draft, but let us briefly consider the other two documents.

A **bill of lading** is a shipping document that has a number of functions. Primary among these are to serve as a contract to order the shipment of goods from one party (the seller) to another (the customer) and provide title to the goods. The bill of lading and the draft proceed together. Their use is recognized in international law, and banks or other financial institutions in virtually all countries handle these documents. By using the draft and bill of lading, a seller can sell the goods and still obtain protection because title is not released until the draft has been accepted.

The letter of credit is the third document. A **letter of credit** is a written statement made by the customer's bank that it will pay out money (or honour a draft drawn on it), providing the bill of lading and other details are in order. Before the seller ships the goods, a letter of credit must be supplied. This letter is often irrevocable and confirmed by a bank in the seller's country. By obtaining the letter of credit, the seller ascertains before shipping the goods the creditworthiness of the customer and the certainty of payment. Once the goods are shipped, they are covered by the bill of lading and accompanied by a draft (typically a time draft) that must be accepted by the customer's bank. All this may seem complicated, but it is routine in international trade.

CREDIT ANALYSIS

To conduct a credit analysis, information is needed about the creditworthiness and paying potential of the customer. Among the numerous sources that exist for securing this information are these:

1. ACCOUNTING STATEMENTS   Based on accounting statements provided by the potential customer, a credit-granting firm may judge the stability and cash-generating ability of the customer.

2. CREDIT RATINGS AND REPORTS   Dun & Bradstreet is probably the best known and most comprehensive credit agency. Its regular *Reference Book* provides credit ratings of about 2 million firms, both domestic and foreign. A typical credit report includes the following information:

    a. Summary of recent accounting statement(s).
    b. Key ratios and trends over time.
    c. Information from the firm's suppliers indicating the firm's payment pattern.
    d. Description of the firm's physical condition and unusual circumstances related to the firm or its owners.
    e. A credit rating indicating the agency's assessment of the creditworthiness of the potential customer.

3. BANKS   Most banks maintain credit departments and may provide credit information on behalf of their customers.

4. TRADE ASSOCIATIONS   Many trade associations provide reliable means of obtaining credit information.

5. COMPANY'S OWN EXPERIENCES   Past experiences of the firm may have led to some formal guidelines to look for when gathering credit information and sizing up the creditworthiness of a potential customer.

CREDIT DECISION

Once the information is collected, a credit decision has to be made. That is, should credit be granted (and under what terms of sale) or not? To do this, many firms employ an approach based on classifying potential customers into risk classes. With such a system, a firm might form a number of risk classes, as follows:

Risk Class	Estimated Percentage of Uncollectible Sales	Percentage of Customers in This Class
1	0–1%	35%
2	$1–2\frac{1}{2}$	30
3	$2\frac{1}{2}–4$	20
4	4–6	10
5	More than 6	5

Customers in class 1 might be extended credit automatically and their status reviewed only once a year. Those in class 2 might receive credit within specific limits, with their status checked semiannually. Similar decisions could be made for the other categories. To protect against the possibility of loss, customers in class 5 might have to accept goods on a COD basis. This requirement for group 5 is perfectly legal, because it is the terms of the sale, *not* the sale price or cash discount (if any), that are affected. Some objective basis must exist, however, for placing a customer in one risk class as opposed to another.

To make the risk class judgment, many firms use **credit scoring models**. A typical model is as follows:

Variable	Weight	Credit Score[a]	Risk Class
Fixed charges coverage	4	Greater than 47	1
Quick ratio	11	40–47	2
Years in business		32–39	3
(maximum of 15)	1	24–31	4
		Less than 24	5

[a] Credit score = 4(fixed charges coverage) + 11(quick ratio) + 1(years in business).

Based on either statistical or some other method of analysis, firms determine the relevant variables that are reliable indicators of their customers' creditworthiness. In this example three variables and their weights have been determined. The three variables are fixed charges coverage [(EBIT + lease expenses)/(interest + lease expenses)]; quick ratio [(current assets − inventory)/current liabilities]; and years in business. Suppose that a new customer with the following conditions applies for credit:

Fixed charges coverage	3.5
Quick ratio	0.8
Years in business	11.0

The customer's credit score would be 4(3.5) + 11(0.8) + 1(11) = 33.8, which would place it in risk category 3.

In larger firms, this type of approach to limiting risk exposure to credit losses is being supplemented by computer-based information systems. Smaller firms often employ time-sharing computer facilities to achieve many of the same benefits. For example, through Dun & Bradstreet a firm could designate a set of accounts to be monitored periodically for significant changes in the information in the D&B data base. If and when changes occur, that information can be electronically transmitted to the firm granting trade credit so that it can take action by reducing or eliminating credit granting to the firm in question.

Many complexities can be introduced in making credit decisions, but let us start out with the basics. To make the decision, firms compare the costs of granting credit with the benefits to be derived from granting credit, taking into account risk and the magnitude and timing of the cash flows.

The Basic Model   To make the credit decision, the firm needs the following information:

cash inflows = the cash benefits expected to arise from the sale of goods on credit
cash outflows = the cash outflows associated with the goods to be sold. (Note that any fixed costs are not relevant, because they will be incurred by the firm whether or not credit is granted.)
T = the firm's marginal tax rate

The after-tax cash flow, CF_t, received by a firm from a credit sale can be summarized by[2]

$$CF_t = (CFBT_t)(1 - T) \qquad (23.1)$$

where $CFBT_t$ (cash flow before taxes) equals cash inflows minus cash outflows in time period t.

To determine whether to grant credit, we compare the present value of the benefits with the cost of granting credit, given the risks involved. The net present value, NPV, for the credit-granting decision is

$$NPV = \frac{CF_t}{k} - CF_0 \qquad (23.2)$$

where[3]

CF_t = the after-tax cash flows in each time period
  k = the after-tax opportunity cost of capital reflecting the risk class of the potential customer
CF_0 = the investment the firm makes in its accounts receivable

The decision rule for the net present value when making the credit-granting decision is as follows:

1.   If NPV is greater than zero, grant credit.
2.   If NPV is less than zero, do not grant credit.
3.   If NPV is equal to zero, be indifferent.

Making the Credit Decision   To use Equation 23.2, the granting firm's investment in accounts receivable, CF_0, and the net cash flows expected from granting credit,[4] CF_t, must be determined. These are:

$$CF_0 = (VC)(S)(DSO/365 \text{ days}) \qquad (23.3)$$

and

$$CF_t = [S(1 - VC) - S(BD) - CD](1 - T) \qquad (23.4)$$

where

 VC = the variable cash outflow of producing and selling the goods as a percentage of cash inflows
  S = the cash inflows (sales) expected each period

---

[2] This is the same as Equation 8.6, except no capital cost allowance (CCA) is shown. The focus is on the variable cash flows associated with production and selling, assuming that the firm already has the necessary long-term assets in place. CCA is not relevant. If the credit decision requires a sizable investment in new equipment, CCA must be included.

[3] Equation 23.2 is the perpetuity form for the net present value. If the benefits are not expected to continue until infinity, then NPV techniques for limited-life projects should be employed.

[4] For simplicity, we ignore cash discounts in Equation 23.4.

DSO = days sales outstanding

BD = bad debts as a percentage of cash inflows from sales

CD = the dollar amount of additional credit department cash outflow for administering or collecting the accounts receivable

T = the firm's marginal tax rate

To illustrate this approach to the credit-granting decision, consider Empire Electronics, which groups firms into risk categories. Two of these risk classes, X and Y, are shown below:

Risk Class	Opportunity Cost of Capital (k)	Days Sales Outstanding (DSO)	Sales (S)	Bad Debts as a Percentage of Sales (BD)	Additional Collection Department Cash Outflows (CD)
X	18%	55 days	$200,000	9%	$10,000
Y	22	60	250,000	11	13,000

At present Empire does not grant credit to firms in either class. The question is, should Empire modify its terms and now extend credit to firms in either or both risk classes? In addition to the data given above, Empire's variable cash outflows are 82 percent of sales, and its tax rate is 35 percent.

To make the decision, let us first consider class X. We can find the additional initial investment (at cost) in accounts receivable using Equation 23.3, as follows:

$$CF_0 = (VC)(S)(DSO/365 \text{ days})$$
$$= (0.82)(\$200,000)(55/365) = \$24,712$$

The additional expected cash inflows, CF_t, are found using Equation 23.4, as follows:

$$CF_t = [S(1 - VC) - S(BD) - CD](1 - T)$$
$$= [\$200,000(1 - 0.82) - \$200,000(0.09) - \$10,000](1 - 0.35)$$
$$= (\$36,000 - \$18,000 - \$10,000)(0.65) = (\$8,000)(0.65) = \$5,200$$

Thus, if Empire grants credit to firms in risk class X, it benefits by receiving incremental expected after-tax cash inflows of $5,200 per period. To obtain these additional CFs, Empire must make an additional investment of $24,712 in accounts receivable. Employing a time line, the cash flows are as follows:

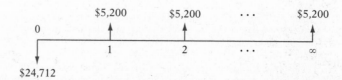

The net present value, which is the benefit to the firm from granting credit to firms in risk class X, employing Equation 23.2, is

$$\text{NPV} = \frac{CF_t}{k} - CF_0 = \frac{\$5,200}{0.18} - \$24,712 = \$28,889 - \$24,712 = \$4,177$$

Because the net present value is positive, Empire should grant credit to potential customers in risk class X. By doing so, it is making a decision that increases the value of the firm.

The same calculations can be carried out for firms in risk class Y:

$$CF_0 = (0.82)(\$250,000)(60/365) = \$33,699$$

and

$$CF_t = [\$250,000(1 - 0.82) - \$250,000(0.11) - \$13,000](1 - 0.35)$$
$$= (\$45,000 - \$27,500 - \$13,000)(0.65) = (\$4,500)(0.65) = \$2,925$$

The net present value is then

$$\text{NPV} = \frac{\$2,925}{0.22} - \$33,699 = \$13,295 - \$33,699 = -\$20,404$$

Because the net present value is negative, Empire would not grant credit to firms in risk class Y.

In the first case, the additional investment in accounts receivable was less than the present value of the expected cash inflows arising from granting credit[5]. In the second case, the investment was greater. Thus, credit should be granted to customers in risk class X, but not to those in risk class Y.

COLLECTION POLICY

Once the granting decision has been made, we cannot ignore the final step—namely, following up to ensure the collection of these receivables. The rate at which receivables are converted into cash measures the efficiency of the collection policy. To ensure collections, we establish a collections department that is responsible for monitoring and following up on receivables. We first consider some techniques for monitoring accounts receivable; then we consider how to analyze changes in collection policies.

Managing Collections   Two basic techniques for monitoring the receivables investment are the days sales outstanding and the receivables pattern approach.

---

[5] In addition to the standard credit decision just discussed, the same basic approach can be employed to analyze the size of the cash discount offered or the terms of sale. Although these are also important issues, both the cash discount offered and the terms of sale are influenced by competition and are subject to infrequent change.

Days Sales Outstanding.   The days sales outstanding is calculated by dividing the firm's accounts receivable by average daily sales:

$$\text{days sales outstanding} = \frac{\text{accounts receivable}}{\text{sales}/365\text{days}} \qquad (23.5)$$

If a firm's receivables are $1,800,000 and its sales for the year are $14,600,000, its days sales outstanding, DSO, is

$$\text{DSO} = \frac{\$1,800,000}{\$14,600,000/365} = \frac{\$1,800,000}{\$40,000} = 45 \text{ days}$$

The DSO is easy to calculate, but it is not very effective for internal use in monitoring a firm's collections. It is an aggregate measure and tends to hide many individual differences among customers. In addition, the DSO is influenced by changes in the level of receivables or changes in the level of sales outside of the month the sales are made. If receivables increase to $2,000,000, the days sales outstanding goes to 50 days in our example [$2,000,000 ÷ ($14,600,000/365)]. If receivables stay at the original level of $1,800,000, the DSO can also increase to 50 days if sales drop to $13,140,000 [$1,800,000 ÷ ($13,140,000/365)]. From a control standpoint, the increase in the level of receivables to $2,000,000 might require different actions by the collection department from those needed if sales decreased to $13,140,000.

A Receivables Pattern Approach.   Instead of using the days sales outstanding or some other aggregate measure of accounts receivable, it is better to take a management-by-exception approach, using receivables pattern data for the firm's receivables. The **receivables pattern** is that percentage of credit sales remaining unpaid in the month of the sale and in subsequent months. The key to understanding receivables patterns is to remember that each month's credit sales are kept separate, as are the collections received on these credit sales. Consider a firm that has credit sales of $100,000 in January. Collections on the $100,000 are as follows:

Month	Collections from January Sales	Payment Pattern	Receivables from January Sales Outstanding at End of Month	Receivables Pattern
January	$10,000	10%	$90,000	90%
February	30,000	30	60,000	60
March	30,000	30	30,000	30
April	30,000	30	0	0

In January, 10 percent of the credit sales are paid, followed by 30 percent each in February, March, and April.[6] The receivables pattern, which is simply 100 percent minus the cumulative percentage payments, declines from 90 percent in January to zero in April. This information is graphed in Figure 23.2.

---

[6] For simplicity, we ignore bad debts.

Figure 23.2

Graph of Payment and Receivables Pattern for January Credit Sales

The receivables pattern in (b) is derived from the payment pattern in (a). By focusing on the receivables pattern, the firm can easily determine whether payments are being made in the manner expected.

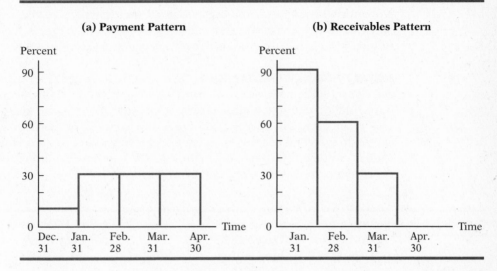

(a) Payment Pattern

(b) Receivables Pattern

Because the receivables pattern approach relates uncollected accounts receivable to the months in which they arise, it has two significant advantages from a management standpoint: First, it disaggregates the receivables into their collection pattern relative to the month in which they occur. Second, because accounts receivable are related to sales in the month of origin, they are sales-dependent only in the month of origin. No matter what the sales pattern, any changes in payment behaviour can be recognized immediately.

Table 23.1

Budgeted Versus Actual Accounts Receivable Patterns

Looking across the bottom two rows, we see that since November, the actual receivables still outstanding both one and two months after the sales have been greater than the budgeted receivables. The slow collection is not unique to the January credit sales.

	October	November	December	January	February	March
Budgeted						
Percent of same month sales	90%	91%	93%	91%	91%	90%
Percent of 1 month before	65	64	62	61	61	62
Percent of 2 months before	36	26	24	22	20	20
Actual						
Percent of same month sales	91%	93%	96%	90%	88%	89%
Percent of 1 month before	70	68	69	66	65	65
Percent of 2 months before	34	32	30	30	28	30

To see how we might exercise control, consider Table 23.1, which provides both budgeted and actual receivables patterns over a six-month period. Note that the budgeted receivables pattern was 91, 61, and 20 percent for January sales, whereas the actual receivables are 90, 65, and 30, respectively. In both the first and second months after the credit sales, the collections came in more slowly than expected. Further examination of Table 23.1 indicates this same pattern has been occurring since November. Focusing on the exceptions, or the deviations of the actual from the projected pattern, puts management in a good position to change the collection policy or modify the classes of customers who are eligible to receive credit.

Analysis of Changes in Collection Policy   Now that we have some idea of how to analyze and control collections, we can evaluate other important questions. Should we change our existing credit-granting or collection policies? To evaluate whether to change policies and, possibly, curtail credit previously granted, we simply employ the NPV approach. A second decision is to tighten or loosen collection procedures related to existing customers. Consider the following, which shows the existing collection experience and proposed effects of improving the firm's collection procedures:

Situation	Opportunity Cost of of Capital (k)	Days Sales Outstanding (DSO)	Sales (S)	Bad Debts as a Percentage of Sales (BD)	Collection Department Cash Outflows (CD)
Old	15%	60 days	$1,000,000	10%	$50,000
New	15	55	1,000,000	7	90,000

Under the existing procedures, the days sales outstanding is 60 days, sales are $1,000,000, bad debts are 10 percent of sales, and collection department cash outflows are $50,000. By expanding our collections department, we would be able to reduce the days sales outstanding to 55 days, and bad debts would drop to only 7 percent. Our collection department cash outflows, however, would increase from $50,000 to $90,000. The question is this: Will the firm benefit from increasing its collection efforts?

To answer, we begin by calculating the incremental initial investment and incremental cash flows after taxes that are associated with the revised procedures. Then we can employ Equation 23.2 to determine whether the change adds to the profitability of the firm. The incremental investment, ΔCF_0, is equal to

$$\text{incremental investment} = \text{investment, new (N)}$$
$$- \text{investment, old (O)}$$
$$\Delta CF_0 = (VC_N)(S_N)(DSO_N/365)$$
$$- (VC_O)(S_O)(DSO_O/365)$$

(23.6)

If the variable cash outflows are 80 percent of sales in either case, then using the data given above, the incremental investment is

$$\Delta CF_0 = (0.80)(\$1,000,000)(55/365) - (0.80)(\$1,000,000)(60/365)$$
$$= \$120,548 - \$131,507 = -\$10,959$$

By reducing the days sales outstanding from 60 to 55 days, the new collection plan frees \$10,959 that can be used elsewhere in the firm.

The incremental cash flow after-tax, ΔCF_t, due to the change in the collection policy is

$$\text{incremental after-tax} \atop \text{cash flow} = {\text{after-tax cash} \atop \text{flow, new (N)}} - {\text{after-tax cash} \atop \text{flow, old(O)}}$$

$$\Delta CF_t = [S_N(1 - VC_N) - S_N(BD_N) - CD_N](1 - T) \atop -[S_O(1 - VC_O) - S_O(BD_O) - CD_O](1 - T)} \tag{23.7}$$

If the tax rate is 40 percent, then the incremental after-tax cash flow due to implementing the new collection policy is

$$CF_t = [\$1,000,000(1 - 0.80) - \$1,000,000(0.07) - \$90,000](1 - 0.40)$$
$$-[\$1,000,000(1 - 0.80) - \$1,000,000(0.10) - \$50,000](1 - 0.40)$$
$$= (\$200,000 - \$70,000 - \$90,000)(0.60) - (\$200,000 - \$100,000$$
$$- \$50,000)(0.60)$$
$$= (\$40,000)(0.60) - (\$50,000)(0.60) = \$24,000 - \$30,000 = -\$6,000$$

Implementing the tighter policy reduces cash inflows by \$6,000 per period. To determine whether the firm should implement the proposed change, we calculate the NPV as follows:

$$\text{net present value} = \frac{-\$6,000}{0.15} - (-\$10,959)$$
$$= -\$40,000 + \$10,959 = -\$29,041$$

Because the net present value is negative, the firm is worse off with the new policy.

To carry this idea a little further, consider what would happen if everything were the same as in the preceding example, except that the days sales outstanding decreases to 40 days if we undertake the new collection policy. The incremental after-tax cash flows are still −\$6,000 as before, but the firm is able to reduce its investment in receivables even more than before. With a 40-day average DSO, the incremental investment is

$$\Delta CF_0 = (0.80)(\$1,000,000)(40/365) - (0.80)(\$1,000,000)(60/365)$$
$$= \$87,671 - \$131,507 = -\$43,836$$

The NPV if the days sales outstanding drops to 40 days is

$$\text{NPV} = \frac{-\$6,000}{0.15} - (-\$43,836) = -\$40,000 + \$43,836 = \$3,836$$

Because the NPV is positive, the firm would now proceed to implement the proposed change in collection policy.

Still other things might happen if the firm implements a new collection policy. One possibility is that the tighter collection policy might reduce sales. Any changes of this type can be investigated employing the approach just described. By focusing on the cash flows, risks, and opportunity costs, we can determine whether a change in the firm's credit-granting or collection policies will benefit the firm (those with positive NPVs) or not (those with negative NPVs). By making credit and collection management decisions that increase the value of the firm, we can assist in achieving our goal of maximizing the value of the firm. Policies should be based on maximizing net cash inflows, spending time on large or risky accounts, and looking beyond the immediate future. Then, the maximum benefits can be secured at the least possible cost.

Concept Review Questions

- What does a typical credit report contain?
- Describe how a credit scoring model can help a firm assign customers to risk classes.
- Describe two basic techniques for monitoring a firm's accounts receivable.

INVENTORY MANAGEMENT

Inventory, like receivables, represents a sizable investment and must be managed effectively. Although the formal responsibility for the control of inventory lies with operating divisions, financial managers are also concerned about it. The more efficiently the firm manages its inventory, the lower the investment required—which, other things being equal, will increase the value of the firm.

TYPES OF INVENTORY

Firms have different types of inventories. The three most common are raw materials, work-in-process, and finished goods. *Raw materials* consist of goods that are used to manufacture a product. *Work-in-process inventory* consists of partially completed goods requiring additional work before they become finished goods. *Finished goods* are those goods on which production has been completed and that are ready for sale.

For manufacturing firms, the purpose of holding inventory is to uncouple the acquisition of the goods, the stages of production, and selling activities. Without inventory, particularly work-in-process inventory, each stage of production would be dependent on the preceding stage's finishing its operation. As a result, there would be delays and considerable idle time at certain stages of production. Likewise, the raw materials and finished goods inventory uncouple the purchasing and selling functions from the production function. Manufacturing firms hold all three types of inventory. Wholesale and retail firms typically hold only a finished goods inventory. Service firms may have no inventory except for a few supplies related to their activities.

BENEFITS FROM INVENTORY INVESTMENT

In addition to uncoupling the firm's operations, a number of other benefits may be associated with the investment a firm makes in its inventory:

1. TAKING ADVANTAGE OF QUANTITY DISCOUNTS   Often suppliers will offer customers quantity discounts if they purchase a certain number of items at the same time. To take advantage of such discounts, firms need to hold inventory.
2. AVOIDING STOCK OUTAGES   When a firm runs out of inventory, it has a stock outage. If this occurs in the production process, it may disrupt the production cycle and even cause it to stop. If finished goods are not on hand, sales may be lost and the firm's reliability as a supplier comes into question.
3. MARKETING BENEFITS   Often there are distinct marketing benefits in terms of increased sales associated with having a full and complete line of merchandise. Also, developing the reputation for always being able to supply the needed items may be part of the firm's marketing strategy.
4. INVENTORY SPECULATION   In times of inflation, or if other factors are causing prices to increase, firms can benefit by increasing inventory. Other things being equal, this will increase the profitability of the firm.

COSTS OF INVENTORY INVESTMENT

The cost of a firm's investment in inventory consists of three main elements—ordering costs, carrying costs, and costs of running short.

1. ORDERING COSTS   The primary costs associated with ordering inventory include the clerical costs of placing the order, plus transportation and shipping costs.
2. CARRYING COSTS   Carrying costs include the direct investment the firm has in its inventory, including storage, insurance, property tax, and spoilage and deterioration. In addition, there is an opportunity cost associated with having funds tied up in nonproductive or excess inventory. Thus, if the firm keeps $5 million in inventory when only $2 million is needed, it has $3 million tied up that could be used elsewhere.
3. COSTS OF RUNNING SHORT   The main costs associated with running short (stock outages) include lost sales, loss of customer goodwill, and disruption of the firm's production process.

To avoid these costs, firms attempt to control their inventory levels.

ALTERNATIVE APPROACHES FOR MANAGING INVENTORY

Many different approaches exist for managing inventory. Four important ones are the ABC method, the economic order quantity approach, material requirements planning, and the just-in-time method.

The ABC Method   A simple approach to inventory management is the **ABC method**. To illustrate, consider a firm that has thousands of inventory items, ranging from very expensive to very inexpensive. The A items require a high investment. For example, 10 percent of the items may account for 50 percent of the dollar inventory investment. Category B items might constitute 30 percent of the items and 35 percent of the dollar value, while the C items contribute 60 percent of the items but only 15 percent of the dollar investment. By separating the inventory into different groups, firms can concentrate on items for which effective inventory control is most important. A formal system involving extensive and frequent monitoring is likely for category A items. Items in group B will be reviewed and adjusted less frequently—perhaps quarterly—and C items may be reviewed only annually. The ABC method has two advantages: It focuses attention where it will do the most good, and it makes the financial management of inventory paramount. That is, other considerations (marketing, production, purchasing) are met, and then financial considerations are employed to control the firm's inventory investment.

The EOQ Model   A slightly more complex model for managing inventory is the **economic order quantity (EOQ)** model. The primary purpose of the economic order quantity model is to determine how often and what quantity to order, and the average inventory to have on hand. The traditional EOQ model assumes constant demand, constant carrying costs, and constant ordering costs. However, adding safety stocks to the model and modifying the basic EOQ model can make the EOQ approach to inventory management more realistic. The basic elements of the EOQ model are presented in Appendix 23A.

MRP and Just-in-Time   Under **material requirements planning (MRP)**, computers are used to schedule the deliveries of material and parts close to the time they are needed. MRP is a top-down system that starts with an annual sales forecast.

A more sophisticated and complete method of inventory management is the **just-in-time** approach. With this system the firm contracts with suppliers for both the goods *and* the time they will be received. Because the firm wants to maintain almost zero inventory, the suppliers must be located nearby in order to make delivery on a daily or even hourly basis. From the firm's standpoint, the method requires a totally different approach to the production and management process. That is why it often takes new or completely redesigned plants and labour contracts to achieve the anticipated benefits of the just-in-time approach to controlling investment in inventory.

Effective management of the firm's inventory involves a balancing of the costs and benefits associated with the investment in inventory. Investment in inventory is really just like any other investment a firm makes. Thus the NPV framework can also be employed to assist the firm in deciding whether to increase or decrease inventory investment.

ANALYSIS OF INVESTMENT IN INVENTORY

Often when a firm is considering an investment in some new long-term assets, such as building a new plant, streamlining storage facilities, and the like, part of that problem involves investment in current assets. As we saw in Chapter 8, any changes in net working capital (current assets minus current liabilities) must be analyzed as part of this larger problem.

However, some investments in inventory may not relate to the acquisition of long-term assets by the firm. Consider, for example, Thrifty Stores. After an extensive study by its marketing and finance departments, the firm concluded that it could increase its sales significantly by increasing its level of finished goods inventory. The increased sales would result from carrying a more complete line, resulting in multiple sales and increased customer traffic. In support of this plan, it has data from a pilot study in its Halifax store. The firm's inventory would have to be increased by $4 million, and the increased after-tax cash flows, CF_t, are estimated to be $600,000 per year. Assuming the cash flows are expected to last for a long time, the timeline for the cash flows is as follows:

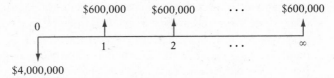

The question is this: Should the additional investment in the inventory be made?

After further evaluation, the firm has concluded that a 12 percent discount rate is appropriate. Employing Equation 23.2, we find that the net present value of this inventory buildup is

$$\text{NPV} = \frac{\$600,000}{0.12} - \$4,000,000 = \$5,000,000 - \$4,000,000 = \$1,000,000$$

Because the net present value is positive, the increased inventory investment should be made.

However, what happens if Thrifty estimates that there will be increased expenses (storage, losses, and so forth) resulting from the increased inventory level carried? These expenses are expected to reduce cash inflows by $70,000 per year. In addition, the senior vice-president believes that $80,000 of the estimated cash flows are extremely unlikely to come in. The additional investment is still $4 million, but the expected cash inflows are now $450,000 (i.e., $600,000 − $70,000 − $80,000) per year, which produces the following projected cash flow stream:

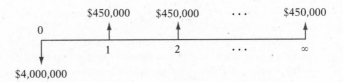

The net present value is now

$$\text{NPV} = \frac{\$450,000}{0.12} - \$4,000,000 = \$3,750,000 - \$4,000,000 = -\$250,000$$

Obviously, based on this set of expected cash flows and the 12 percent opportunity cost of capital, Thrifty should not increase its inventory investment.

Three points must be stressed about making inventory decisions: First, the emphasis has to be on cash flows. Second, because various types of inventory are held by firms, close attention should be devoted to the most important items. Management by exception can be used to control investment in all other items. Finally, the risks and returns must be considered. For many firms, inventory is the most important single investment.

INTERACTION OF ACCOUNTS RECEIVABLE AND INVENTORY DECISIONS

Until now we have considered separately the management of receivables and the management of inventory. In practice, there are interactions between the firm's accounts receivable and its inventory. This interaction is often hard to see or to achieve, however, because the functions of inventory management and receivables management are typically separate areas of responsibility within the firm. To the extent possible, inventory and receivables policies should be developed and evaluated on a joint basis, because there are tradeoffs between them. The investment includes those cash outflows required for the incremental investment in receivables given by Equation 23.3 plus the incremental investment in inventory. Likewise, the benefits are the incremental cash inflows from the joint receivables/inventory decision. Combinations of tighter inventory control with relaxed credit, looser inventory policy and tighter credit, and varying mixes between these two can be evaluated in terms of the cash flow consequences to the firm. Viewing the investment in these two current assets in an integrated manner puts the firm in a better position to maximize its value.

Concept Review Questions

- Describe the costs and benefits of holding inventory.
- Describe different approaches a firm may employ to manage its inventory.
- How does the material requirements planning method differ from the just-in-time approach?

KEY POINTS

- Accounts receivable and inventory represent a significant investment. Funds tied up in these uses are as costly as those employed elsewhere in the firm.
- Management of accounts receivable involves the following areas: terms and conditions of credit sales, credit analysis, credit decision, and collection policy.
- Decisions on granting credit, changing credit or collection policies, and the investment in inventory involve an analysis of the magnitude and timing of the cash flows, risks, returns, and opportunity costs. This analysis is accomplished by calculating the net present value, NPV, of the proposed change in the firm's credit, collection, or inventory policies. For simplicity, the perpetuity form of the net present value decision criteria is employed.

- Days sales outstanding is always influenced by changes in the level of sales; however, the receivables pattern approach is affected only by changes in sales in the month of origin.
- The primary costs to consider in making inventory decisions are ordering costs, carrying costs, and the costs of running short.

QUESTIONS

23.1   Explain how the four parts of the firm's credit and collection policies interact.

23.2   What would be the effect of changes in the following on the level of accounts receivable?
a.   The economy improves, and interest rates decline.
b.   The credit manager tightens up on past due accounts.
c.   The credit terms are changed from 3/10, net 30, to 2/10, net 30.
d.   The firm's selling and production expenses decline relative to those of other firms.

23.3   Gail, the credit manager, is being criticized for the deterioration in her performance because the days sales outstanding has increased, as have bad debts. Under what circumstances is this criticism unjustified?

23.4   Why is the receivables pattern approach superior to the days sales outstanding in monitoring collections?

23.5   What would be the effect of the following on the level of inventory held by the firm?
a.   Inflation increases.
b.   The firm's suppliers switch from truck to air freight delivery.
c.   Competition increases in the firm's sales market.
d.   The firm's production cycle becomes shorter.

CONCEPT REVIEW PROBLEMS

See Appendix A for solutions.

CR23.1   Markus & Associates uses the following model to determine customer trade credit:
credit score = 5(current ratio) + 7(times interest earned) − 9(debt to tangible net worth)

Three of Markus & Associates' customers have the following ratios:

	A	B	C
Current ratio	2.2	2	2.5
Times interest earned	6	5	4
Debt to tangible net worth	2	4	3

What is each customer's credit score?

CR23.2   Brad is unhappy with his firm's collection of accounts. The firm currently has annual sales of $20 million, 15 percent bad debt, and days sales outstanding of 65. Brad wants to decrease both the percentage of bad debts and the days sales outstanding by doubling the size of the firm's collection department budget from $250,000 to $500,000. It is estimated that bad debts would decline to 12 percent and days sales outstanding would decrease to 55. However, Hillary, the marketing director, pointed out that sales would also decrease, to an estimated $17 million. If variable costs are 70 percent of sales, the tax rate is 35 percent, and the opportunity cost of capital is 14 percent, should the collection department budget be increased?

CR23.3 Specht Enterprises believes the firm's after-tax cash flows could be increased by $200,000 per year if it increased its inventory by $1.5 million. If the firm's opportunity cost of capital is 15 percent, what is the net present value of increasing the firm's inventory?

PROBLEMS

23.1 Deschamps Industries offers credit terms of 3/10, net 45. Twenty percent of its customers pay on the discount date, 40 percent pay on the net date, and the other 40 percent pay in 60 days. If Deschamps's average investment in accounts receivable is $500,000 and variable costs are 80 percent of sales, what is Deschamps's annual sales? Assume a 365-day year. (*Note*: Carry to five decimal places.)

23.2 River City Recreation has decided to offer credit during its fall bicycle sale. Sales are expected to be 500 units at $450 each, and River City's cost is $315 per bike. The firm estimates that 94 percent of the customers will make their payments, and the others will have to be written off as bad debts. To eliminate the bad debts, NeverFail Credit will supply customer credit reports for a one-time fee of $1,500, plus $7.50 per report. Should River City obtain the credit information? (*Note*: Do not worry about taxes.)

23.3 Hamilton Iron Works is in the process of evaluating its credit standards. Two potential classes of new customers exist, as follows:

Risk Class	Opportunity Cost of Capital (k)	Days Sales Outstanding (DSO)	Sales (S)	Bad Debts as a Percentage of Sales (BD)	Collection Department Cash Outflows (CD)
4	16%	45 days	$511,999	8%	$15,000
5	20	55	438,000	12	25,000

The variable cash outflows as a percentage of sales are 80 percent, and the tax rate is 30 percent. Should Hamilton extend credit to potential customers in risk class 4? In risk class 5? (Assume a 365-day year.)

23.4 Mark's is evaluating whether to grant credit to a risky class of potential customers. Variable cash outflows are 82 percent of sales, the days sales outstanding is 65 days, sales per year (based on a 365-day year) are $10,950,000, bad debts are 12 percent of sales, additional collection department cash outflows are $300,000 per year, and the opportunity cost of capital is 12 percent. At what marginal tax rate is Mark's indifferent between granting and not granting credit to this new class of customers?

23.5 Butcher Products is a new firm. All sales are on credit, and the sales and payments for the first six months are as follows:

	March	April	May	June	July	August
Credit sales	$1,500	$2,000	$2,400	$2,800	$3,700	$4,900
Payments—same month	200	400	500	600	700	800
Payments—1 month later		600	800	1,000	1,250	1,500
Payments—2 months later			500	700	800	850

After two months the uncollected sales are written off as bad debts. Calculate the receivables pattern for Butcher. Is it becoming more or less effective? What is happening to its bad debts? Are there any indications of change occurring in July and August?

23.6 Mutual Worldwide employs the days sales outstanding (based on a 365-day year) to monitor its receivables. The sales and receivables pattern for the four months of February through May are as follows:

	February	March	April	May	June	July
Credit sales	$150,000	$200,000	$300,000	$300,000		
Receivables—same month sales	120,000	160,000	237,000	234,000		
Receivables—1 month before		60,000	80,000	114,000	108,000	
Receivables—2 months before		0	0	0	0	0

Total sales for the year are $2,555,000.

a. Calculate the days sales outstanding (using the total yearly sales) for each of three months— March, April, and May.

b. What do your results from (a) suggest about the effectiveness of Mutual's collection policies?

c. Now calculate the receivables pattern for Mutual. Is its collection policy less effective in May than in March or April?

d. Explain why you got conflicting results from the days sales outstanding versus the receivables pattern approach.

23.7 Perry Air Conditioning has annual credit sales of $1.6 million. Current collection department cash outflows are $35,000, bad debts are 1.5 percent of sales, and the days sales outstanding is 30 days. Perry is considering easing its collection efforts so that collection department outflows will be reduced to $22,000 per year. The change is expected to increase bad debts to 2.5 percent of sales and to increase the days sales outstanding to 45 days. In addition, sales are expected to increase to $1.75 million. If the discount rate is 16 percent, variable cash outflows are 75 percent of sales, and the marginal tax rate is 35 percent, should Perry make the change?

23.8 Big Rock Data believes its collection policy may be out of hand. Currently, the firm has sales of $6 million and days sales outstanding of 55 days, bad debts are 6 percent of sales, and yearly collection department cash outflows are $100,000. Its existing variable cash outflows are 80 percent of sales. If it tightens the collection policy significantly, it anticipates that sales will drop to $5 million, the days sales outstanding will become 25 days, bad debts will be 3 percent of sales, and collection department cash outflows will be $75,000 per year. At this level of sales, variable cash outflows will be 83 percent of sales. Assume the corporate tax rate is 30 percent, and use a 365-day year.

a. If the opportunity cost of capital is 14 percent, should Big Rock tighten its collection policy?

b. What if the opportunity cost is 20 percent?

23.9 Gupta Sales has $500,000 in overdue receivables that it is considering writing off as worthless. It has been approached by a collection agency. The agency will charge $75,000 plus 50 percent of the first $200,000 collected by the agency and 25 percent of the rest collected. Gupta estimates there is a 60 percent probability that a total of $150,000 will be collected, a 30 percent probability that a total of $300,000 will be collected, and a 10 percent probability that a total of $450,000 will be collected.

a. Should Gupta employ the collection agency?

b. If the collection agency's fixed charge is $125,000, instead of $75,000, should Gupta employ the agency?

23.10 La Salle Street Stores is considering three different mutually exclusive proposals for increasing its inventory level. The initial investments and after-tax cash flows are as follows:

Inventory Level	Initial Investment (CF_0)	Opportunity Cost of Capital (k)	After-Tax Cash Flow (CF_t)
A	$300,000	12%	$ 50,000
B	600,000	15	110,000
C	900,000	18	175,000

Which, if any, of the new inventory levels should La Salle Street Stores adopt?

23.11 The Mukherjee Group presently carries an average inventory valued at $5 million. New management has proposed to reduce the inventory to $3.5 million. The expected loss in after-tax cash flows due to increased stock outages will be $200,000 per year if inventory is reduced, but losses due to theft and spoilage should decrease by $20,000 (after taxes). If the appropriate cost of capital is 16 percent, should the inventory be reduced?

23.12 Gordon Showrooms sells to its customers on a credit basis. It is considering loosening its credit-granting standards to two additional risk classes, P and Q.

Risk Class	Opportunity Cost of Capital (k)	Days Sales Outstanding (DSO)	Sales (S)	Bad Debt as a Percentage of Sales (BD)	Collection Department Cash Outflows (CD)
P	15%	50 days	$ 800,000	6%	$200,000
Q	20	60	1,300,000	10	60,000

Variable costs are 75 percent of sales, a 365-day year is used, and Gordon's tax rate is 40 percent. In addition, granting credit to customers in risk class P would require an investment of an additional $60,000 in inventory. Extending credit to risk class Q would require an additional $150,000 investment in inventory beyond that required for class P.

a. Should Gordon grant credit to customers in risk class P?

b. Assuming Gordon has already decided to grant credit to class P, should it also grant credit to customers in risk class Q?

23.13 Mini Case Aerovac Industries has grown so rapidly that it has not had time to examine carefully its accounts receivable and inventory policies. Now, during the present slowdown in economic activity, the decision has been made to undertake a careful analysis of these important functions. As the senior analyst in the finance department, you have been assigned the responsibility for undertaking this analysis and for making sure Aerovac's policies are appropriate.

a. Your boss keeps saying that the investment in receivables and inventory is just as important as the investment in long-term assets, and that the analysis of this investment must take the same approach as any other investment made by the firm. Why is this so?

b. Explain, in some detail, what the major credit and collections policies are.

c. Aerovac is investigating changing its credit-scoring model in order to tighten up its credit-granting policy. The present model is 5(interest coverage) + 6(current ratio), + 0.9(years in business). The proposed model is 4(interest coverage) + 4(quick ratio) + 1.5(years in business). [*Note:* Interest coverage = EBIT/interest; current ratio = current assets/

current liabilities; and quick ratio = (current assets − inventory)/current liabilities.] Two firms have data as follows:

	Firm A	Firm B
EBIT	$600,000	$800,000
Interest	100,000	90,000
Current assets	100,000	80,000
Inventory	30,000	45,000
Current liabilities	50,000	60,000
Years in business	8	12

What are the credit scores under the existing and the proposed models?

d. Aerovac believes that instead of changing the credit-scoring model, it needs to employ a higher opportunity cost of capital and also increase its collection department expenditures to enable it to follow up more promptly. The existing and proposed policies for two classes of customers are as follows:

Risk Class	Opportunity Cost of Capital (k)	Days Sales Outstanding (DSO)	Sales (S)	Bad Debts as a Percentage of Sales (BD)	Collection Department Cash Outflows (CD)
Existing					
1	14%	40 days	$15,000,000	4%	$250,000
2	16	60	30,000,000	8	600,000
Proposed					
1	16%	30 days	$13,000,000	1%	$300,000
2	17	35	25,000,000	2	700,000

Variable costs remain at 70 percent of sales in either case, and the firm's marginal tax rate is 35 percent. For which risk class, if either, should the proposed change be made? [*Note:* Calculate the NPV for risk class 1 under the existing policy, and then under the proposed policy. Then use the difference in the two NPVs to determine whether to stay with the existing policy (i.e., if NPV_{old} is greater than NPV_{new}) or switch to the new policy (i.e., if NPV_{new} is greater than NPV_{old}). Do the same for risk class 2.]

e. Aerovac uses days sales outstanding to measure the performance of its collections manager. Is this appropriate? Why or why not?

f. Briefly explain the interrelationship between a firm's receivables and inventory decisions.

REFERENCES

BERANEK, WILLIAM, and FREDERICK C. SCHERR. "On the Significance of Trade Credit Limits." *Financial Practice and Education* 1 (Fall/Winter 1991): 39–44.

EMERY, GARY W. "A Pure Financial Explanation for Trade Credit." *Journal of Financial and Quantitative Analysis* 19 (September 1984): 271–285.

GALLINGER, GEORGE W., and P. BASIL HEALEY. *Liquidity Analysis and Management.* Reading, Mass.: Addison-Wesley, 1987.

KALLBERG, JARL G., and KENNETH L. PARKINSON. *Corporate Liquidity: Management and Measurement.* Homewood, Ill.: Irwin, 1993.

MIAN, SHEHZAD, and CLIFFORD W. SMITH, JR. "Accounts Receivable Management and Policy: Theory and Evidence." *Journal of Finance* 47 (March 1992): 169–200.

SMITH, JANET K. "Trade Credit and Information Asymmetry." *Journal of Finance* 42 (September 1987): 863–872.

WALIA, T. S. "How Much Cash Is Tied Up in Your Accounts Receivable?" *Journal of Cash Management* 10 (July/August 1990): 48–50.

APPENDIX

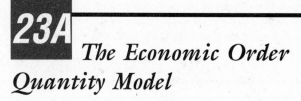

23A
The Economic Order Quantity Model

Effective management of inventory is a complex and constant problem for all organizations. In this appendix we highlight some of the main elements of inventory management by examining the basic decision, the economic order quantity model, the assumptions involved, quantity discounts, and safety stocks. The primary purpose of the economic order quantity model is to determine how often and what quantity to order and the average inventory to have on hand.

THE BASIC INVENTORY DECISION

Although inventories differ substantially, all inventory has three costs—ordering, carrying, and shortage. Initially we focus on ordering and carrying costs; the costs of running short will be considered when we add safety stocks to the inventory model. To consider the inventory problem, the following symbols and terms are used:

C = carrying costs expressed in dollars per unit of inventory, $20
O = ordering costs expressed in dollars per order placed, $250
Q = order quantity expressed in units
S = sales per year expressed in units, 3,600

Consider an example: Reynolds Ltd. sells 3,600 units per year of a given item and is trying to determine the number of times per year and the quantity, Q, to order. If inventory usage is constant over time and no safety stocks are kept, Reynolds's inventory will go to zero just before an order is received. With an order size of Q, the average inventory on hand is simply Q divided by 2, or Q/2. The total carrying costs

Table 23A.1

Carrying, Ordering, and Total Costs for Reynolds Ltd.

An order of 300 units appears to minimize total costs. If either 310 or 290 units are ordered, for example, total costs increase to $6,003.

Size of Order (Q) (1)	Average Inventory (Q/2) (2)	Carrying Cost (Q/2)(C) (3)	Number of Orders per Year (S/Q) (4)	Ordering Cost (S/Q)(O) (5)	Total Cost (3 + 5) (6)
100	50	$1,000	36.0	$9,000	$10,000
200	100	2,000	18.0	4,500	6,500
300	150	3,000	12.0	3,000	6,000
400	200	4,000	9.0	2,250	6,250
500	250	5,000	7.2	1,800	6,800
600	300	6,000	6.0	1,500	7,500

are then the average inventory times the carrying cost per unit, C, or

$$\text{Carrying costs} = \left(\frac{Q}{2}\right)(C) = \frac{QC}{2} \qquad (23A.1)$$

We can determine the total ordering costs similarly. With sales of S units per year, the number of orders placed per year is simply S divided by Q (the order size), or S/Q. Because each order costs an amount O to place, the total ordering costs are[1]

$$\text{Ordering costs} = \left(\frac{S}{Q}\right)(O) = \frac{SO}{Q} \qquad (23A.2)$$

Thus, Reynolds's total costs are equal to the carrying costs plus the ordering costs, so

$$\text{Total costs} = \text{carrying costs} + \text{ordering costs}$$
$$= \frac{QC}{2} + \frac{SO}{Q} \qquad (23A.3)$$

To maximize its market price, Reynolds must minimize the total cost of ordering and carrying inventory. How can we determine when Reynolds should order inventory and what size, Q, the order should be? One way would be to employ a trial-and-error approach. As shown in Table 23A.1, if the order quantity is assumed to be 100 units, both the carrying costs of $1,000 and the ordering costs of $9,000 can be determined, leading to total costs of $10,000.

---

[1] Some portion of the ordering costs may be fixed while the rest vary, depending on the number of units ordered. This modification can easily be included, but for simplicity the ordering costs are assumed to be $250 regardless of the number of units per order.

Figure 23A.1

Determination of the Minimum Total Cost and Economic Order Quantity

In the absence of safety stock, the minimum total cost occurs when the total ordering cost just equals the total carrying cost. This then determines the optimum size of the order, or EOQ.

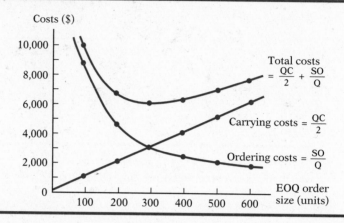

Similarly, by increasing the order quantity to 200, 300, and so forth, the other total costs in Table 23A.1 can be calculated. By inspection, it appears that the total costs are minimized at $6,000, which occurs when the order quantity is 300 units and orders are placed 12 times a year. Plotting these data in Figure 23A.1 also suggests that total costs are minimized when the order quantity is 300 units.

THE EOQ MODEL

There is a more direct way to determine the optimal order quantity, which is called the economic order quantity, or EOQ. This is done by differentiating Equation 23A.3 with respect to Q and setting the result equal to zero.[2] The optimum value of Q is

$$EOQ = \left(\frac{2SO}{C}\right)^{0.5} \tag{23A.4}$$

---

[2] The first derivative with respect to Q defines the slope of the total cost curve. Setting this equal to zero specifies the minimum (zero slope) point. Thus

$$\frac{dTC}{dQ} = \frac{C}{2} - \frac{SO}{Q^2} = 0; \text{ therefore, } \frac{C}{2} = \frac{SO}{Q^2} \text{ or } Q^2 = \frac{2SO}{C}. \text{ Consequently, } Q = \left(\frac{2SO}{C}\right)^{0.5}.$$

To verify that this is a minimum instead of a maximum value, the second derivative must be positive—which it is.

Figure 23A.2

Inventory Position and Order Point Without Safety Stock

With a lead time of seven days, Reynolds places an order when the inventory level drops to 70 units.

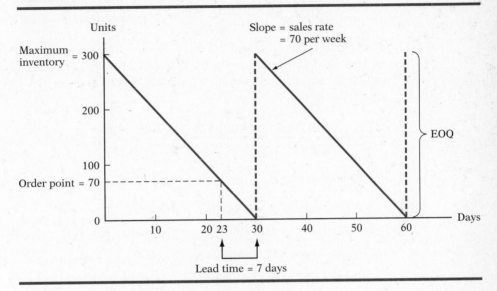

Using the EOQ formula for Reynolds, we have

$$\text{EOQ} = \left(\frac{2(3,600)(\$250)}{\$20}\right)^{0.5} = (90,000)^{0.5} = 300 \text{ units}$$

which is the same as obtained by the trial-and-error approach in Table 23A.1.

Once the EOQ quantity is determined, we can see how the inventory for Reynolds varies over time. As shown in Figure 23A.2, the inventory varies from a high of 300 units to a low of zero. The average number of units on hand at any time will be 150 units. Because 12 (3,600 divided by the EOQ of 300) orders will be placed a year, the firm will place an order approximately every 30 days. The slope of the line in Figure 23A.2 indicates the rate of sales per week. As it becomes steeper, sales are increasing per unit of time. A gentler slope signifies fewer sales per unit of time. For Reynolds, the slope indicates that 70 units are sold per week. Because the delivery time is seven days, Reynolds will order additional inventory every time its stock on hand falls to 70 units. Doing this should cause the inventory to reach zero on the same day the next delivery is received.

QUANTITY DISCOUNTS

Often the firm can take advantage of quantity discounts when it orders. Suppose Reynolds does not receive a quantity discount when it orders 300 units at a time. If Reynolds increases the order to 400 units, the supplier will reduce the purchase price by $0.35 per unit. To determine whether it should take advantage of this discount, Reynolds must examine the incremental benefits in relation to the incremental costs. The savings to Reynolds because of the lower purchase price is

$$\text{savings from quantity discount} = (\text{discount per unit})(\text{number of units})$$
$$= (\$0.35)(3,600) = \$1,260$$

The cost is the additional carrying cost minus the savings in ordering costs due to cutting the number of orders per year from 12 to nine. The additional carrying costs can be calculated by employing a modification of Equation 23A.1 (where Q' is the new order size):

$$\frac{Q'C}{2} - \frac{(EOQ)/(C)}{2} = \frac{(400)(\$20)}{2} - \frac{(300)(\$20)}{2} = \$4,000 - \$3,000 = \$1,000$$

The savings in ordering costs, using a modification of Equation 23A.2, is

$$\frac{SO}{EOQ} - \frac{(SO)}{Q'} = \frac{(3,600)(\$250)}{300} - \frac{(3,600)(\$250)}{400} = \$3,000 - \$2,250 = \$750$$

The net increase in costs to Reynolds is $\$1,000 - \$750$, or $\$250$.[3] Because the incremental costs are $250, whereas the incremental benefits are $1,260, Reynolds should increase the order size to 400 units. Thus, the EOQ approach serves as a point of departure to determine the benefits of quantity discounts and other changes in costs to the firm.

EOQ ASSUMPTIONS

The three major assumptions of the EOQ model are these:

1. Constant or uniform demand
2. Constant carrying costs
3. Constant ordering costs

To make the EOQ approach useful when there is uncertainty and demand is not constant, safety stocks must be added. Carrying costs are often not constant per unit but may vary because of the size of the inventory carried. This situation may be handled through a modification of the original total cost model. Finally, ordering costs may vary because of economies achieved if larger instead of smaller shipments are made. Again, this problem can be dealt with by modifying the original model. Even though the EOQ model is simple and assumes both certainty and constant costs, it can easily be modified to accommodate more realistic conditions.

---

[3] This increase in costs of $250 can be seen in Table 23A.1, where the total costs are $6,000 when the order size is 300 units, whereas they are $6,250 at an order size of 400 units.

Figure 23A.3

Inventory Position and Order Point With Uncertainty and Safety Stock

Uncertain demand and delivery times are cushioned by the safety stock. Without it, Reynolds would have experienced three stock outages.

(a) Expected Demand and Lead Time

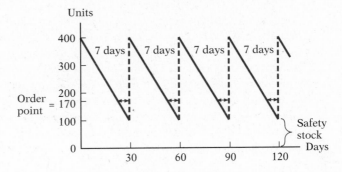

(b) Actual Demand and Lead Time

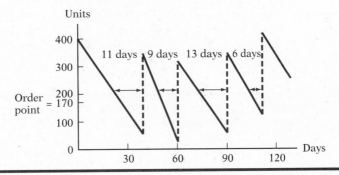

SAFETY STOCKS

Until now we have not allowed for uncertainty—in demand or in delivery time. To deal with uncertainty, most firms employ a safety stock. Let us assume that Reynolds decides that a safety stock of 100 units is needed to meet these uncertainties. Although the inclusion of this safety stock does not change the EOQ of 300 units, it does increase the level of inventory held. This idea is illustrated in Figure 23A.3(a). Note that with a safety stock of 100 units, the order point is set at 170 units instead of the previous 70.

In Figure 23A.3(b) the actual experience of Reynolds is shown. In the first segment, we see that the sales rate is somewhat less than expected. [The slope of the line is less than in Figure 23A.3(a).] At the order point of 170, an order is placed for 300 more units. However, instead of taking seven days, delivery actually takes eleven days. The inventory has been depleted to 70 units before the order is received. In the second segment, sales are higher than expected. [This is represented by steeper slope than in Figure 23A.3(a).] With the time from placing the order until its receipt being nine days, the stock falls to 30 units before the next order of 300 is received. As a result of the heavy demand and slow delivery, the safety stock has virtually been depleted. During the third and fourth segments, both demand and delivery times continue to fluctuate. However, by the receipt of the fourth shipment, the inventory has been built back up. This example emphasizes the role of the safety stock in absorbing random fluctuations in both demand and delivery times.

Determining the amount of the safety stock is not always easy, but some points should be mentioned. First, the greater the uncertainty in either demand or delivery times, the larger the safety stock should be. Second, how critical is it if a firm runs out of inventory? Will the firm incur substantial lost sales, lose goodwill, or have to shut down the production line? Finally, how much does it incur in additional carrying costs by increasing safety stock? Ultimately, the amount of safety stock carried involves a balancing of the costs incurred if stock runs out versus those arising from carrying more inventory. To maximize the market value of the firm, we should not add safety stock beyond the point where the additional carrying costs equal the benefits derived from avoiding a stock outage.

PROBLEMS

23A.1   A firm has a demand for 5,600 units per year, the carrying cost per unit is $10, and the ordering cost is $70 per order.
a.   Fill in the blanks in the following table.

Size of Order (Q) (1)	Average Inventory (Q/2) (2)	Carrying Cost (Q/2)(C) (3)	Number of Orders per Year (S/Q) (4)	Ordering Cost (S/Q)(O) (5)	Total Cost (3 + 5) (6)
80	_____	_____	_____	_____	_____
160	_____	_____	_____	_____	_____
280	_____	_____	_____	_____	_____
400	_____	_____	_____	_____	_____
700	_____	_____	_____	_____	_____

b.   What is the EOQ?

23A.2   King's Drug Stores sells 225,000 rolls of camera film a year. Its carrying costs are $0.10 per roll, and ordering costs are $200 per order.
a.   What is the economic order quantity?
b.   Its supplier now offers King's a quantity discount of $0.01 per roll if the order is increased to 90,000 rolls. Should King's take advantage of the quantity discount?
c.   What other factors might also influence the decision to take or not to take the quantity discount?

23A.3   City Tool Company needs 122,500 units per year. The carrying costs per unit are $5, ordering costs are $1,000 per order, and the safety stock (already on hand) is 4,000 units. The expected delivery time is five days.
a.   What is the economic order quantity?
b.   What is the optimal number of orders to place per year?
c.   Assuming a 365-day year, at what inventory level should a reorder be placed?

23A.4   Dewitt Lawn and Garden Centre sells 50,000 bags of potting soil annually. The firm keeps a safety stock of 1,000 bags on hand, carrying costs are $0.10 per bag, and ordering costs are $25 per order. The lead time is nine days. Assume a 365-day year and carry all calculations to two decimal places.
a.   What is Dewitt's EOQ?
b.   How often is an order for more potting soil placed?
c.   What is the reorder point?
d.   What is Dewitt's average potting soil inventory?

24

Short-Term Financing

EXECUTIVE SUMMARY

Firms make extensive use of short-term financing. For some, it provides the major source of financing. The use of short-term financing is a function of both the nature of the firm's business and how aggressive it wants to become in matching (or financing) its temporary assets with temporary liabilities. Firms that are aggressive in their use of short-term financing employ substantially larger amounts of such financing than firms that adopt a conservative position.

Trade credit financing is readily available in most industries. It is costless if cash discounts are taken. Bank loans can be obtained through single transaction loans, a line of credit, or secured financing involving either receivables or inventory. Many finance companies also provide short-term loans to firms, especially when accounts receivable or inventory are involved. Larger firms have access to commercial paper. The direct costs of all these sources are available, but this is only one item that requires attention. For this reason, effective managers assess both the risks and the returns associated with alternative sources of short-term financing as they make decisions that they hope will maximize the value of the firm.

SOURCES AND IMPORTANCE OF SHORT-TERM FINANCING

Among numerous sources of short-term financing are trade credit and short-term borrowing by the firm. Trade credit arises when one firm purchases goods from another firm and does not pay cash immediately. This creates an account payable for the purchasing firm. Trade credit often is called *spontaneous short-term financing* because it tends to expand automatically as firms purchase more goods and build up inventory. There are also **negotiated short-term financing** sources. To secure short-term borrowed funds from these sources, the firm must enter into negotiations with chartered banks, finance companies, and the like.

Aside from the matching principle discussed in Chapter 21, firms use short-term financing for two other reasons. The first is to meet seasonal needs. As firms enter into that part of the year when accounts receivable and inventory expand, they employ short-term financing. Later, when cash inflows increase, they pay down the short-term financing. The second reason is to "roll" it into longer-term financing. Many firms use short-term financing until the total amount of financing needed becomes large enough to justify long-term debt (or equity) financing.

SIZE OF SHORT-TERM FINANCING

To see the importance of short-term financing, consider that small manufacturing firms (with assets of less than $10 million), retail firms, and wholesale firms usually have current liabilities that are 35 percent or more of total assets. For larger manufacturing firms, the current liabilities drop to about 25 percent. The large size of current liabilities for small manufacturing firms, retail firms, and wholesale firms is due to the fact that these firms have large amounts of current assets. Under the matching principle, we expect such firms to have large amounts of current liabilities, which they do. The majority of these current liabilities are in the form of accounts payable and short-term borrowings—the focus of this chapter. The other short-term liabilities include various accrued items, such as wages and taxes, and current maturities of long-term debt or lease obligations. The amount of current liabilities varies both among industries and among firms in the same industry.

Short-term financing is more important than ever because of a firm's size, the varying nature of a firm's needs over the course of the year, changes in business conditions and interest rates, and changes in the money market and financing alternatives. Securing funds at the most cost-effective rate is vitally important. At the same time, the firm must ensure the availability of funds, no matter what the time of year or economic conditions. In this chapter we focus on the nature of short-term financing available, how to determine its effective annual interest cost, and the typical conditions surrounding alternative sources of short-term financing.

COST OF SHORT-TERM FINANCING

In determining the cost of alternative sources of short-term financing, three important ideas must be kept in mind:

1. For the purpose of comparison, we express the costs in the same units over the same period of time. If one source costs $800 for a month's financing, and another charges a monthly rate of interest of 1.5 percent for the same amount of funds, it is not immediately obvious which is more expensive. To deal with this difference, all costs are expressed in the same units over the same time period.

Because of simplicity and tradition, we convert all costs to an effective annual rate (or cost) stated in percentage terms.

2. The ultimate cost to the firm is influenced by the tax rate of the firm. The after-tax cost to the firm is

$$\text{after-tax cost} = (\text{before-tax cost})(1 - \text{the tax rate})$$

$$k_i = k_b(1 - T) \tag{24.1}$$

where k_i is the after-tax cost, k_b is the before-tax annual cost, and T is the firm's marginal tax rate. Although a firm can employ either the before- or after-tax cost for decision-making purposes, its ultimate cost is the after-tax cost given by Equation 24.1.

3. The basic equation to calculate the before-tax effective annual interest rate, or $k_{\text{effective annual}}$, for any short-term financing is:

$$k_{\text{effective annual}} = \left(1 + \frac{\text{costs} - \text{benefits}}{\text{net amount of financing}}\right)^m - 1 \tag{24.2}$$

where m is the number of compounding periods per year.

To see these ideas in practice, consider the cost of a $100,000 loan on which the bank will charge interest of $3,500, which will be paid in 90 days when the loan is repaid. The before-tax annual effective cost of this loan, employing Equation 24.2 and a 365-day year, is

$$k_{\text{effective annual}} = \left(1 + \frac{\$3,500}{\$100,000}\right)^{365/90} - 1 = \left(1 + \frac{\$3,500}{\$100,000}\right)^{4.055556} - 1$$

$$= 1.1497 - 14.97\%$$

The after-tax cost, if the firm has a 35 percent tax rate, is

$$k_i = (14.97\%)(1 - 0.35) = 9.73\%$$

Thus, the firm's after-tax annual cost is 9.73 percent.

Consider what would happen to the same firm if its tax rate were either 20 percent or 0 percent. With a 20 percent tax rate, the after-tax cost is

$$k_i \text{ with 20 percent tax rate} = (14.97\%)(1 - 0.20) = 11.98\%$$

If the firm's tax rate is zero, then the after-tax cost is the same as the before-tax cost, so

$$k_i \text{ with zero tax rate} = (14.97\%)(1 - 0) = 14.97\%$$

This example shows the importance of the firm's tax rate for the cost of borrowing.

As the tax rate increases, other things being equal, the firm's after-tax cost of borrowing decreases.[1]

Throughout most of this chapter, we will employ Equation 24.2 and assume either a 365-day year (or occasionally 12 equal months). But there is another complication that arises when determining the effective annual rate. It involves nominal versus effective annual rates. Before examining how to determine the effective interest rate for a number of different types of short-term financing, let us pause and examine this issue.

Effective Annual Versus Nominal Interest Rate   The annual rate at which many loans and financial instruments are quoted is the stated or nominal interest rate. Thus, you may make an investment that pays interest at a nominal annual rate of 8 percent. The effective annual interest rate adjusts the nominal rate based on the frequency of compounding employed and the number of days assumed in a year. When a nominal rate is given, the effective annual rate can be determined as follows:

$$k_{\text{effective annual}} = \left(1 + \frac{k_{\text{nominal}}}{m}\right)^m - 1 \tag{24.3}$$

where

$k_{\text{effective annual}}$ = the effective annual rate of interest
k_{nominal} = the nominal annual rate of interest
m = the number of compounding intervals per year

As long as there is only one compounding interval per year ($m = 1$), the effective annual rate is equal to the nominal rate. But as the compounding interval decreases, the effective annual rate increases. To see this relationship, consider the impact of the compounding period on a 12 percent annual nominal rate:

Compounding Interval	Effective Annual Rate $k_{\text{effective annual}} = \left(1 + \frac{0.12}{m}\right)^m - 1$
Annually ($m = 1$)	12.000%
Semiannually ($m = 2$)	12.360
Quarterly ($m = 4$)	12.551
Monthly ($m = 12$)	12.683
Daily ($m = 365$)	12.747
Continuously[2]	12.750

[1] If compounding is not employed, the simple interest cost is given by

$$k_{\text{effective annual}} = \left(\frac{\text{cost} - \text{benefits}}{\text{net amount of financing}}\right)\left(\frac{365 \text{ days}}{\text{total number of days funds borrowed}}\right)$$

$$= \left(\frac{\$3,500}{\$100,000}\right)\left(\frac{365}{90}\right) = 14.19\%$$

Simple interest always understates the annual effective interest rate.
[2] For the continuous case, the effective annual rate is $k_{\text{effective annual}} = e^{k_{\text{nominal}}} - 1 = e^{0.12} - 1 = 12.750\%$.

Often, the interest rates that banks and other lenders quote are effective annual rates. But for most other instruments—including bonds, mortgage loans, and commercial loans—only the nominal rate may be stated.[3]

Assume, for example, that your firm wants to borrow money for a period of one year. Bromont National Bank quotes a nominal annual rate of 12.5 percent compounded quarterly. Eastern Bank quotes a nominal annual rate of 12.2 percent compounded daily. Which alternative will give your firm a lower before-tax cost?

Employing Equation 24.3, from Bromont National Bank the effective annual cost is

$$k_{\text{effective annual}} = \left(1 + \frac{0.125}{4}\right)^4 - 1 = 13.098\%$$

From Eastern, the effective annual cost is

$$k_{\text{effective annual}} = \left(1 + \frac{0.122}{365}\right)^{365} - 1 = 12.973\%$$

After adjusting for the difference in the compounding intervals, we see that the before-tax cost of the loan from Eastern Bank is 12.97 percent, whereas it is 13.10 percent from Bromont National. Other things being equal, we want the cheapest financing available. Therefore, you would recommend that the loan be obtained from Eastern Bank.

Concept Review Questions

- Describe some alternative sources of short-term financing.
- What important ideas must be considered when determining the effective annual cost of alternative sources of short-term financing?

Accounts Payable, or Trade Credit

Most firms make purchases from other firms on credit. This transaction shows up on the purchaser's accounting records as an account payable. Trade credit is a spontaneous source of financing. If a firm typically makes purchases of $3,000 per day and pays its bills in 30 days, then the average accounts payable outstanding are $90,000. What happens, however, if as the busy season of the year draws near, purchases increase to $5,000 per day? While the firm still pays in 30 days, the accounts payable have increased to $150,000. This difference of $60,000 ($150,000 − $90,000) in accounts payable occurred spontaneously as the firm geared up for its busy season. The firm generated $60,000 in additional financing just by increasing its purchases and taking advantage of the trade credit offered by its suppliers.

---

[3] The Bank Act specifies that, for virtually all consumer loans, the annual percentage rate, APR, of the loan must be stated. Although many might think the APR is the effective annual rate stated in percent terms, the way it is employed is as a nominal annual rate per year, but compounded monthly. Thus, it is not an effective annual rate. See Chapter 3 for a discussion of this point.

COST OF TRADE CREDIT

Instead of being concerned about granting credit, as in Chapter 23, let us assume that you are now the recipient of trade credit. Trade credit terms typically are expressed, as, for example, 1/10, net 30, which means that a 1 percent **cash discount** applies if the account is paid within 10 days. If not, the account should be paid in full within 30 days. If the firm takes advantage of the 1 percent discount, there is no cost associated with the trade credit. That is, 10 days of credit is available at no cost to the purchaser. If the firm does not take the cash discount, there is a direct cost to the firm. This annual cost is

$$k_{\text{effective annual}} = \left(1 + \frac{\text{discount percent}}{100\% - \text{discount percent}}\right)^{365/(\text{date paid} - \text{discount date})} - 1 \qquad (24.4)$$

The direct before-tax annual cost of not taking a 1 percent discount by paying in 10 days is

$$k_{\text{effective annual}} = \left(1 + \frac{1}{100 - 1}\right)^{365/(30 - 10)} - 1 = 20.13\%$$

Note in Equation 24.4 that the discount not taken is related to the number of additional days for which credit is obtained. With terms of 1/10, net 30, the 1 percent cash discount is the interest cost for an additional 20 days of credit. This assumes the purchaser pays on the 30th day if the cash discount is not taken. Often firms stretch their payables by not paying on the net date. What happens to the direct annual cost if the firm stretches its payables by paying them later—say, 50 days after the invoice date? The cost is

$$k_{\text{effective annual}} = \left(1 + \frac{1}{100 - 1}\right)^{365/(50 - 10)} - 1 = 9.60\%$$

This is lower than before, because 40 (instead of 20) days of credit were obtained. The effect of **stretching payables** is to reduce the direct cost of trade credit.

Firms that pass up cash discounts can reduce the direct cost by stretching their payables. The effect of this practice, however, is to incur an opportunity cost. This cost is the loss of supplier goodwill, resulting in possible curtailment of trade credit. Equally important, a firm that continually stretches its payables will suffer lower credit ratings, thereby raising the future cost of funds. Firms should always take advantage of the free credit period (10 days in our example). Nevertheless, in assessing the desirability of stretching payables (if the cash discount is not taken), both direct and opportunity costs must be considered.

ADVANTAGES OF TRADE CREDIT

Trade credit has a number of advantages as a source of short-term financing. First, it is readily available and can be conveniently obtained as a normal part of the firm's everyday activities. Second, it is free (and actually results in a reduction in the purchase price) if the discount is taken. Third, it is flexible and can expand or contract as purchases expand or contract. Finally, there are no restrictive terms (or formal agreements). For these reasons, all efficiently managed firms take advantage of trade credit. Not to do so would increase the financial burden on the firm, resulting in lower returns.

Concept Review Questions

- Explain what a spontaneous source of financing is and give an example of such a source.
- What are the advantages and costs to a firm offering trade credit?

UNSECURED LOANS

Unsecured loans[4] occur in two forms: bank loans and commercial paper. Bank loans are short-term borrowings obtained from banks or finance companies; commercial paper is a short-term security sold in the money market to investors. Firms must negotiate a bank loan or issue commercial paper—as opposed to obtaining trade credit, which occurs spontaneously.

BANK LOANS

Most bank loans have maturities of one year or less and often have a variable interest rate—that is, one that fluctuates over the life of the loan as interest rates change. The basic interest rate charged by banks is called the prime rate.[5] It is defined as the rate at which their best customers can borrow.[6] Rates on loans are generally tied to prime, so the borrower pays prime plus half a percent, prime plus 1 percent, and so on. With a prime rate loan, as the bank's prime rate changes, so will the interest rate charged the borrowing firm.

Types of Bank Loans   A bank loan may be a single (transaction) loan or a line of credit. A **transaction loan** is made by the bank for a specific purpose. To obtain a transaction loan, the parties sign a promissory note. The note specifies the amount borrowed, the

---

[4] Some of these loans and even commercial paper may actually be backed by specific assets of the firm. This type of credit enhancement has gained popularity in recent years, as firms have moved to provide collateral to reduce the cost of financing. For simplicity we refer to all loans in this section as unsecured loans.

[5] Each bank sets its own prime rate, but competition forces them to be similar. Generally, the major banks set prime a certain number of percentage points (typically 1 to 2 percent) above the rate on negotiable certificates of deposit issued by banks. Other banks typically follow suit; however, prime may vary slightly. Some banks also use other rates, such as the treasury bill rate or the London Interbank Offered Rate (LIBOR), in addition to prime.

[6] Although prime is the rate banks supposedly charge their best customers, they also loan below prime to very important and financially strong firms. These firms have the option of issuing commercial paper, which typically has a yield below the prime rate. Because of this competitive factor, banks may occasionally split the difference between the prime rate and the commercial paper rate for loans to very sound major firms. From the firm's standpoint bank loans may provide more flexibility than issuing commercial paper. Also, with relationship banking, firms may occasionally pay a little more interest simply to maintain and strengthen relationships with their (main) bank.

interest rate on the loan, the maturity date and repayment schedule, collateral (if any) involved, and any other conditions agreed upon by the two parties. When the note is signed, the borrower receives the loan.

A line of credit is another type of agreement between a bank and a firm. A line of credit agreement means the firm can borrow up to some maximum amount over a specified period. For example, the agreement may be that the firm can borrow, or draw down, a $500,000 line of credit over the next year. This amount, or any portion of it, may be borrowed during this period. Repayment can be made as desired, but by the end of the agreement all borrowings must be paid off.[7] Although lines of credit can be informal agreements in which the lender has no legal obligation to make the loan, often they are formal agreements for which the firm pays a **commitment fee** to the bank, whether or not it draws on the line of credit.[8]

The Monitoring Role of Banks Firms can obtain funds from the money and capital markets or from banks (and other financial institutions). Because of their role as an "inside" provider of funds, banks have access to information about the firm and its actions that is not available to the public. Thus, there is less information asymmetry (and less of a moral hazard problem) between the firm and the provider of funds when the firm borrows from a bank instead of going directly to the money or capital markets. The direct benefits to the firm are twofold: First, the increased monitoring improves the likelihood of the firm fulfilling its payment obligation to the bank, and therefore reduces the cost of financial distress. Second, the increased monitoring reduces the direct cost to the firm of obtaining financing. This reduced cost to the firm of obtaining financing still results in the bank obtaining a higher return than from its other investment alternatives. The unique role of banks has received substantial empirical and theoretical attention in recent years. These advances provide far greater understanding of the important role played by banks as providers of funds to firms.[9]

Cost of Bank Loans The cost of bank loans depends on the conditions attached to the agreement. We illustrate three different types—regular interest, discount interest, and instalment interest. The effects of variable interest rates, compensating balance agreements, and interest for lines of credit are also considered.

Regular Interest. The cost of a loan with regular interest can be solved employing Equation 24.2. Assume that there is a $10,000 loan, the bank will charge prime plus 1 percent, prime is 9 percent per year, and the loan is for 73 days. The two-step process to solve for the annual before-tax cost is as follows:

STEP 1: Determine the interest paid:

$$\text{interest paid} = \left(\begin{array}{c}\text{amount} \\ \text{borrowed}\end{array}\right)\left(\begin{array}{c}\text{annual} \\ \text{interest rate}\end{array}\right)\left(\begin{array}{c}\text{portion of year} \\ \text{borrowed for}\end{array}\right)$$

$$= (\$10,000)(0.10)(73/365) = \$200$$

---

[7] Many lines of credit have a provision that sometime during the period the line is in effect, perhaps for a minimum of 30 days, the firm has to have zero borrowings from the line.

[8] The commitment fee may be $\frac{1}{4}$ to $\frac{3}{4}$ of 1 percent per year. Thus, on a $5 million line of credit, the commitment fee could be $12,500 to $37,500 annually, whether or not the line was used.

[9] See the references at the end of the chapter.

STEP 2: Employing Equation 24.2, determine $k_{\text{effective annual}}$, which is

$$k_{\text{effective annual}} = \left(1 + \frac{\$200}{\$10,000}\right)^{365/73} - 1 = 10.41\%$$

Note that even though the stated rate is 10 percent, the effective annual rate is 10.41 percent.

Discount Interest. Under **discount interest**, the bank deducts the interest at the beginning of the loan. In such a case, the borrower in our example receives $9,800 ($10,000 − $200). From step 1 above, the interest is still $200. In step 2, $9,800 (the amount actually secured) replaces the $10,000 previously employed. The effective annual cost of a discounted loan employing Equation 24.2 is

$$k_{\text{effective annual}} = \left(1 + \frac{\$200}{\$9,800}\right)^{365/73} - 1 = 10.63\%$$

Because the bank does not lend the full amount, the cost of a discounted loan is higher than that of a loan with regular interest.

Instalment Interest. Instead of paying the loan off in a lump sum, banks and many other financial institutions charge **instalment interest**, with payments made monthly. In this case the total amount of interest is calculated and added to the original face value of the note. Then the monthly instalment represents a payment of both principal and interest. Let us assume that we borrow $10,000 for 1 year, that we agree to pay interest at a 13 percent annual stated rate, and that 12 monthly payments will be made. The note will be for the principal of $10,000 plus the interest of $1,300 [i.e., ($10,000)(0.13)] for a total of $11,300. The monthly payment is $941.67 ($11,300/12).

To solve for the cost of an instalment loan, we employ present value techniques for an annuity. Thus,

$$PV_0 = PMT(PV_{k_{\text{effective annual}},n})$$

where PV is the present value, PMT is the per period payment, $k_{\text{effective annual}}$ is the effective before-tax cost per period, and n is the number of periods. Thus,

$$\$10,000 = \$941.67 \, (PVA_{k_{\text{effective annual}},n})$$

$$PVA_{?\%, 12 \text{ yr}} = \$10,000/\$941.67 = 10.169$$

From Table B.2, this is slightly less than 2 percent per month, or 24 percent per year. The cost of an instalment loan is always slightly less than twice the stated rate.[10]

Variable-Rate Loans. Now that we know how interest is calculated, we can con-

---

[10] With a financial calculator, we enter PV = 10,000, PMT = 941.67, and n = 12 and then select the $k_{\text{effective annual}}$ = i button to solve for the exact rate of 1.932 percent per month. Multiplying by 12 to convert to a yearly rate, we find the before-tax cost to be 23.18 percent.

sider some additional complications. The first is a **variable-rate** loan. What if a firm needed to borrow $10,000 for 150 days and was going to pay prime plus 1 percent? Interest would be calculated employing the regular method. If prime were 12 percent annually for the first 73 days, $13\frac{3}{4}$ percent for the next 30 days, and $14\frac{1}{2}$ percent for the remaining 47 days, what would be the cost to the firm? To solve this problem, the two-step procedure described above can be used.

STEP 1: Determine the interest paid:

Prime Rate	Prime Plus 1 Percent	Number of Days	Interest Cost in Dollars	
12%	13%	73	($10,000)(0.13)(73/365)	= $260.00
$13\frac{3}{4}$	$14\frac{3}{4}$	30	($10,000)(0.1475)(30/365)	= 121.23
$14\frac{1}{2}$	$15\frac{1}{2}$	47	($10,000)(0.1550)(47/365)	= 199.59
			Total interest	= $580.82

STEP 2: Employing Equation 24.2, determine the before-tax effective annual cost, which is

$$k_{\text{effective annual}} = \left(1 + \frac{\$580.82}{\$10,000}\right)^{365/150} - 1 = 14.73\%$$

Compensating Balance. A compensating balance is an amount many corporate customers consent to maintain in their demand deposit account if a loan is taken out. The compensating balance may be an average over some period, such as a month, or a minimum figure below which the account cannot drop. Average compensating balances are typical for firms. Two situations can be identified: The first is one in which the compensating balance agreed upon is less than the amount the firm typically keeps in the bank. In this case, the agreement does not change the cost to the firm. The second case is one in which the agreed-on compensating balance is more than the amount the firm keeps in its demand deposit account. To illustrate this, let us use the same $10,000, 10 percent loan for 73 days that we used when computing the cost of both regular and discount interest.

Assume that the firm agrees to a $2,000 compensating balance, when the firm typically does not keep any money on deposit at the bank. The effect of the agreement is to reduce the proceeds of the loan by $2,000. If the loan is not discounted, the before-tax cost is

$$k_{\text{effective annual}} = \left(1 + \frac{\$200}{\$10,000 - \$2,000}\right)^{365/73} - 1 = 13.14\%$$

If the loan is discounted and a $2,000 compensating balance is required, then the before-tax effective annual cost becomes:

$$k_{\text{effective annual}} = \left(1 + \frac{\$200}{\$10,000 - \$2,000 - \$200}\right)^{365/73} - 1 = 13.50\%$$

Line of Credit. Finally, let us consider a more complicated situation, in which a line of credit is involved. Suppose a firm negotiates a 91-day, $1,000,000 bank line of credit that has a 0.5 percent annual commitment fee on the unused portion of the line, and an interest rate of prime plus 1 percent. Assume, for simplicity, that there is no compensating balance and that during the entire 91-day period the prime rate is 10 percent. For the first 30 days the firm borrows $100,000 on the line of credit. For the remaining 61 days, an additional $300,000 is borrowed, so that $400,000 in total short-term financing is obtained. What is the cost of the loan? To answer this, we can still use our two-step procedure. There are, however, a few other complications.

STEP 1: Determine the commitment fee and interest per period.

commitment fee = (unused portion)(annual commitment fee)(portion of year)

Using the equation, we obtain

first 30 days	($1,000,000 − $100,000)(0.005)(30/365) = $369.86
next 61 days	($1,000,000 − $400,000)(0.005)(61/365) = 501.37

Then the interest is determined as follows:

first 30 days	($100,000)(0.11)(30/365) = $ 904.11
next 61 days	($400,000)(0.11)(61/365) = 7,353.42

STEP 2: Employing a modification of Equation 24.2, we can determine the effective annual cost of the line of credit. This modification is necessary because the total costs and the average amount borrowed must be calculated and then annualized as follows:

$$k_{\text{effective annual}} = \left(1 + \frac{\text{total commitment fee} + \text{interest}}{\text{average net amount of financing}}\right)^{365/\text{total number of days}} - 1 \qquad (24.5)$$

The total of the commitment fees and interest is $369.86 + $501.37 + $904.11 + $7,353.42 = $9,128.76. The average net amount of financing is determined as follows:

$$\text{average net amount of financing} = (\$100,000)\left(\frac{30}{91}\right) + (\$400,000)\left(\frac{61}{91}\right)$$

$$= \$32,967.03 + \$268,131.87$$

$$= \$301,098.90$$

The before-tax percentage cost of the credit line is

$$k_{\text{effective annual}} = \left(1 + \frac{\$9,128.76}{\$301,098.90}\right)^{365/91} - 1 = 12.73\%$$

If the firm agrees to a 5 percent compensating balance on the total line of credit, the calculations will have to be redone if this change reduces the net amount of financing obtained. Suppose that the firm presently keeps no compensating balance in the bank. The effect of the 5 percent agreement is to reduce the net funds obtained by $50,000 [i.e., ($1,000,000)(0.05)]. Therefore, with the compensating balance agreement, the before-tax cost increases as follows:

$$k_{\text{effective annual}} = \left(1 + \frac{\$9,128.76}{\$301,098.90 - \$50,000}\right)^{365/91} - 1 = 15.40\%$$

COMMERCIAL PAPER

Another important source of short-term borrowing is commercial paper, a short-term promissory note sold by large firms to obtain financing. In recent years the market for commercial paper has grown rapidly. Because it is an alternative to short-term bank loans, the presence of a large commercial paper market tends to exert a downward pressure on borrowing costs for larger firms.

Nature and Use of Commercial Paper   The principal issuers of commercial paper include finance companies, banks, and large industrial firms. The issue size is commonly in multiples of $100,000. Commercial paper has a maturity of a few days to one year or more, but the most popular maturities are 30, 60, and 90 days.[11] The paper is sold through dealers or via direct placement. Dealers, who generally charge 0.125 percent commission, typically are used by firms that infrequently issue commercial paper. Larger firms, such as consumer finance companies, which obtain part of their permanent financing from commercial paper, generally market commercial paper directly.

Commercial paper is rated as to its quality. For example, the Dominion Bond Rating Service rates commercial paper as follows:

R-1: Prime investment quality
R-2: Medium grade securities
R-3: Speculative securities

A high, medium, or low is added to each rating to show the relative riskiness within a class. The purpose of the ratings is to provide the commercial paper buyer some indication of the riskiness of the investment. From the issuing firm's standpoint, ratings are important because they influence the cost of financing. Other things being equal, the higher the rating, the lower the cost to the firm.

Cost of Commercial Paper   The rate (or yield) on commercial paper tends to be 1 to 2 percentage points below the prime rate. This differential fluctuates as both general economic conditions and the level of interest rates change. Like treasury bills, commercial paper is sold at a discount from its par value. At maturity, the difference between the selling price and the par value is the interest earned by the investor. Consider a $100,000, 180-day issue of commercial paper sold at $95,000. When it

---

[11] With these maturities, the firm avoids having to file a prospectus.

matures in 180 days, the firm will pay the holder $100,000. Employing Equation 24.2, we find that the before-tax annual cost to the firm is

$$k_{\text{effective annual}} = \left(1 + \frac{\$5,000}{\$100,000 - \$5,000}\right)^{365/180} - 1 = 10.96\%$$

This rate typically will be lower than the cost of a bank loan, due to the lower yield on commercial paper than the prime rate charged by banks.

Other costs also enter into the picture. In most cases, issuers must back their commercial paper 100 percent with lines of credit from chartered banks. This line of credit may cost the firm from 0.25 to 0.75 percent annual interest. Another common procedure is for the commercial paper issuer to have a compensating balance at a bank. In addition, there is a relatively small fee ($10,000 to $25,000) to have the commercial paper rated. Because of these additional costs, the savings from issuing commercial paper may not be as great as a firm originally thought. Suppose that the commercial paper issue just analyzed was backed by a line of credit that had a commitment fee of 0.5 percent a year. The total fee would be

$$(\$100,000)(0.005)(180/365) = \$246.58$$

Adding this fee to the interest of $5,000 results in a total cost of $5,246.58. Employing Equation 24.2, we find that the before-tax effective annual cost of the commercial paper is now[12]

$$K_{\text{effective annual}} = \left(1 + \frac{\$5,246.58}{\$95,000}\right)^{365/180} - 1 = 11.52\%$$

Although commercial paper may be an attractive form of short-term financing, it is available only to relatively large firms. Also, the commercial paper market may dry up occasionally, forcing firms to use bank loans. Firms that make extensive use of commercial paper also keep their lines of communication open with banks and typically borrow from banks in addition to using the commercial paper market.

Concept Review Questions

- Describe different types of short-term bank loans.
- What is a compensating balance?
- If commercial paper is typically a cheaper source of financing than borrowing from financial institutions, explain why all firms do not finance their short-term borrowings using commercial paper.

---

[12] Note that the commitmemnt fee is *not* deducted from the financing received in the denominator. This approach treats the commitment fee as an ongoing cost that is paid over time and is *not* a lump-sum deduction at the outset. If the comittment fee is deducted at the outset, the net proceeds are $94,753.42 (i.e., $95,000 − $246.68), and the before-tax cost is

$$k_{\text{effective annual}} = \left(1 + \frac{\$5,246.58}{\$94,753.42}\right)^{365/180} - 1 = 11.55\%$$

This approach is also employed for the processing costs, factoring commissions, and warehousing fees discussed subsequently.

SECURED LOANS

Because the lender requires it, or to obtain cheaper financing, firms often use receivables or inventory to obtain short-term financing. Procedures for short-term financing are described below.

FINANCING WITH ACCOUNTS RECEIVABLE

Financing with accounts receivable involves pledging receivables or factoring them. The **pledging** of receivables involves the specific use of receivables as collateral for the loan. If the borrower defaults on the loan, the funds provided when the receivables are collected will go to repay the loan. **Factoring** involves the sale of accounts receivable. The factoring firm is responsible both for credit checking and for collection of the receivables. Many banks engage in making accounts receivable loans or in purchasing receivables. Commercial finance companies and other specialized factoring firms also provide accounts receivable financing to firms. In addition, in recent years many firms have issued securities in the money or capital markets that are secured with accounts receivable. This security ranges from short-term receivables to longer-term receivables such as home mortgages and automobile loans.

Pledging Accounts Receivable   Under a pledging agreement, the borrower uses the accounts receivable as collateral for the loan. The specific agreement between the borrower and the lending institution spells out the details of the transaction. The amount of the loan is stated as a percentage of the receivables pledged. In addition, the borrower typically pays a processing fee, which often is 1 percent of the total receivables pledged. This processing fee compensates the lending institution for the time involved in reviewing the pledged receivables.

If the loan agreement is based on all the firm's receivables, then the lender has no control over the quality of the receivables pledged. An alternative procedure is for the lender to review specific invoices to decide which ones it will lend against. This method is somewhat more expensive to the lender, because the lender must review each invoice and the creditworthiness of the customer, before deciding whether to lend against the invoice. If the lender accepts all receivables, it may be willing to grant a loan for only 60 to 70 percent of the face value of the receivables. When it "screens" invoices, the loan agreement typically increases to 85 to 90 percent of the face value of the receivables.

The cost of accounts receivable financing is a function of both the processing fee and the annual interest rate charged. Because of the basic creditworthiness of the borrower, loans secured by receivables often have a stated interest rate of 2 to 4 percent above prime. To illustrate the cost, consider Hammond Associates, which sells merchandise on a net 45 days basis. Its average credit sales are $9,000 per day, and the days sales outstanding is 60 days, resulting in accounts receivable averaging $540,000. All the receivables are pledged to the bank, which will lend 75 percent of the amount pledged at 2.5 percent over prime. The loan will be for $405,000 [i.e., ($540,000)(0.75)] for 60 days. There also is a 0.75 percent processing fee on all receivables pledged. If prime currently is 7.8 percent per year, the cost of this loan can be found by employing the same two-step approach described earlier.

STEP 1:   Determine the interest paid and other costs:

$$
\begin{aligned}
\text{processing fee} &= (0.0075)(\$9,000)(60 \text{ days}) = \$\ 4,050 \\
\text{interest} &= (0.103)(\$405,000)(60/365) \quad = \ \underline{\ \ 6,857} \\
\text{total processing fee and interest} &\qquad\qquad\qquad = \$10,907
\end{aligned}
$$

STEP 2:   Employing Equation 24.2, we find that the effective annual before-tax cost is

$$
k_{\text{effective annual}} = \left(1 + \frac{\$10,907}{\$405,000}\right)^{365/60} - 1 = 17.55\%
$$

The processing fee increases the cost of the loan substantially above the nominal interest charge of 10.3 percent the bank levies for the loan.[13]

Factoring Accounts Receivable   Instead of pledging its receivables, an alternative procedure employed in industries such as finished apparel, textiles, and home furnishings is to sell (or factor) them. Through factoring, a firm sells its accounts receivable to a bank or other firm engaged in factoring. The receivables may be sold without recourse; in such a case the factor makes the credit-granting decision and incurs any losses from nonpayment by the firm's customers. Alternatively, recourse factoring can be employed. Under recourse factoring, the granting firm typically makes the credit-granting decision and, therefore, bears the consequences of any nonpayment by the customers.

Factoring operates in two basic ways. The first is **maturity factoring**, in which the factor purchases all receivables and remits the proceeds to the seller as they are collected. The typical maturity factoring procedure is shown in Figure 24.1. Firms that employ maturity factoring are primarily interested in avoiding credit analysis and collection expenses, and in the regularity of the cash flow. The charge for maturity factoring is the commission, which is between 0.75 percent and 2 percent of the total receivables factored.

To illustrate this type of factoring, consider Gandy Wholesale. To avoid setting up a credit and collection department, it factors all its receivables. If the average month has $200,000 in receivables and the factoring commission is 1.5 percent per month, then Gandy pays $3,000 per month [i.e., ($200,000)(0.015)], or $36,000 per year [($3,000)(12)], to the factor. For this amount, the factor assumes all bookkeeping and collection expenses. If this procedure allows Gandy to reduce these expenses by $1,400 per month, then the net additional cost is $1,600 per month. The effective annual cost is then

$$
k_{\text{effective annual}} = \left(1 + \frac{\$1,600}{\$200,000}\right)^{12/1} - 1 = 10.03\%
$$

---

[13] Instead of using accounts receivable as collateral, some firms set up "captive finance companies" to provide ongoing accounts receivable financing. Mian and Smith (1992) argue that secured debt, in the form of accounts receivable financing, and captive finance companies serve as a means of segregating the accounts receivable cash flows from the firm's operating cash flows. By doing so they assist in controlling underinvestment problems. Mian and Smith observe that larger, more creditworthy firms establish captive finance companies, whereas smaller, more risky firms employ debt secured by accounts receivable.

Figure 24.1

Maturity Factoring Procedure

Under maturity factoring, the firm turns almost all of its credit and receivables management functions over to the factor.

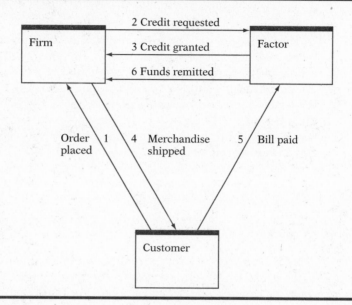

The second factoring method is **advance factoring**, in which the factor provides a loan against the receivables. Thus, on the first of the month, a firm could borrow against the receivables it is selling. If the average due date is the 20th of the month, the factor will charge interest from the 1st to the 20th. This interest typically is 2 to 4 percent more than the annual prime rate. In addition, the factor still charges a factoring commission.

With advance factoring, the cost consists of both the factoring commission and the interest. To illustrate, Gandy Wholesale is now considering advance instead of maturity factoring. The receivables to be sold total $400,000, and they have an average due date of 1 month. The factoring commission is 0.5 percent, the annual prime rate is 9 percent, and the loan is for 1 month at 2 percent over prime. The factor will loan an amount equal to 70 percent of the face value of the receivables, or $280,000 [i.e., ($400,000)(0.70)], and the savings to Gandy will be $1,000 per month. Employing the two-step procedure, we proceed as follows:

STEP 1: Determine the interest paid and all other costs:

$$
\begin{aligned}
\text{factoring commission} &= (0.005)(\$400,000) = \$2,000 \\
\text{interest} &= (0.11)(\$280,000)(1/12) = \underline{2,567} \\
\text{total commission and interest} &= \underline{4,567} \\
\text{Less: Reduced cash outflows} &= \underline{1,000} \\
&\ \ \$3,567
\end{aligned}
$$

STEP 2:   Using Equation 24.2, the before-tax effective annual cost is

$$k_{\text{effective annual}} = \left(1 + \frac{\$3,567}{\$280,000}\right)^{12/1} - 1 = 16.41\%$$

As we saw with selling receivables, the cost increases when a fee is charged in addition to the basic interest rate.

The advantages of factoring from the firm's standpoint can be fourfold: First, the entire credit and collection operation can be shifted to the factor. This can result in a sizable savings to the selling firm. Second, more effective and timely cash management can be obtained. Third, if advance factoring is employed, then firms also may secure accelerated short-term financing from the factoring procedures. Finally, factors will often be willing to borrow money from the firm during periods when the firm has excess cash. For these reasons, factoring is becoming more common as an ongoing part of many firms' short-term financing strategy. Factoring is often a continuous process. Once the cycle is established, the firm automatically sends the receivables to the factor. Under continuous factoring, accounts receivable financing becomes a spontaneous source of short-term financing.

FINANCING WITH INVENTORY

A firm's inventory provides a second source of security for short-term loans. Because of the large size of the inventory for many firms and the associated carrying costs, firms often use part or all of their inventory to obtain short-term financing. The procedures are much like those discussed when receivables are employed. That is, the bank determines the percentage of the inventory value for which it will provide a loan. There are alternative methods, however, by which inventory can be secured.

The borrower can pledge all of its inventory under a blanket lien. This is simple, but because the borrower is free to sell the inventory, the bank has the least protection. Because of this weakness, some types of inventory are secured through the use of a trust receipt. This type of lending agreement, also known as *floor planning*, is used by automobile dealers, equipment dealers, and others who deal in costly items. With a trust receipt, an automobile dealer might reach an agreement with a bank to finance the inventory. When cars are shipped to the dealer, they are paid for in large part with funds borrowed from the bank. The trust receipt specifies that the goods are held in trust for the lender. When the cars are sold, the dealer obtains a release from the bank and then applies the proceeds to pay the loan. Under a trust receipt agreement, the bank periodically inspects the automobile dealer's inventory of cars to ensure that the pledged security is still on hand.

Another method is warehouse financing. Under a public (or terminal) warehouse agreement, the inventory is stored on the premises of a third party. The third party releases the inventory to the borrower only when authorized to do so by the lender. The lender can then maintain strict control over the collateral. Sometimes the warehouse is set up as a field warehouse. This is accomplished by establishing a separate building or area directly on the borrower's premises. To provide inventory control, the bank employs a third party to run the field warehouse. A warehouse receipt is issued by the warehouse company when it receives additional inventory. This receipt goes to the bank, and inventory cannot be released without the bank's permission.

The basic cost of inventory loans typically consists of two parts. The first is the processing fee if a blanket lien is employed, or the cost of storing the inventory if a public or field warehouse agreement is employed. Second, there is the interest cost, which is typically 2 to 4 percentage points above the prime rate. Consider a firm that employs a field warehouse agreement. The inventory loan is for 90 days, the amount of the inventory is $500,000, and the bank will lend 70 percent of the value of the collateral. The amount of the loan is $350,000 [i.e., ($500,000)(0.70)]. The field warehouse fee is $40 per day, the interest rate is 2 percent over prime, and prime is 11 percent. The annual before-tax cost is computed as follows:

STEP 1:   Determine the interest paid and all other costs:

$$
\begin{aligned}
\text{field warehousing fee} &= (\$40)(90) &&= \$\ 3,600 \\
\text{interest} &= (0.13)(\$350,000)(90/365) &&= \underline{11,219} \\
\text{total warehousing fee and interest} &&&= \$14,819
\end{aligned}
$$

STEP 2:   The effective annual before-tax cost is determined using Equation 24.2, so that:

$$
k_{\text{effective annual}} = \left(1 + \frac{\$14,819}{\$350,000}\right)^{365/90} - 1 = 18.31\%
$$

Firms often enter into continuous agreements to finance their inventory through the use of field or terminal warehouse procedures. Like the use of factoring with accounts receivable, the continual use of these forms of inventory financing creates a spontaneous form of short-term financing.

Concept Review Questions

- Describe the difference between pledging receivables and factoring receivables when securing short-term financing.
- What are the advantages of factoring accounts receivable?
- Differentiate between a *blanket lien*, a *trust receipt*, and *warehouse financing*.

CHOOSING AMONG SHORT-TERM FINANCING SOURCES

In this chapter we have stressed the cost of alternative sources of short-term financing. Some of these sources, such as trade credit and factoring or field warehouse loans, are spontaneous. That is, they tend to expand or contract automatically as the firm's accounts receivable and inventory expand or contract. Other sources of short-term financing are negotiated between the borrower and the lender.

To determine what sources of short-term financing to employ, firms should consider four specific items: matching, cost, availability, and flexibility. By matching, we mean the firm must decide how much risk it is willing to incur in financing temporary assets with temporary liabilities. As discussed in Chapter 21, a more aggressive posture will require the firm to employ more sources and amounts of short-term financing than a conservative posture.

The second important item that influences the short-term financing selection is its cost. Employing the concepts developed in this chapter, we can determine the direct cost of alternative short-term financing sources. This is an important consideration, but there is more than the direct cost of the sources. Opportunity costs must also be considered. If firms anticipate the continued need to borrow from banks, good banking relations need to be maintained even if the bank charges a higher direct cost than some other source. Trade credit (if stretched) may be less costly than an inventory loan, but if stretching occurs continually, the firm may suffer from reduced credit ratings in the future. Thus, opportunity costs must be considered along with the direct costs when determining the total cost of alternative sources of short-term financing.

The availability of credit is the third item to be considered when evaluating financing sources. If a firm cannot borrow through an unsecured loan or commercial paper offering, then some type of secured means will have to be employed. Also, over the course of the business cycle, certain sources of funds may be more or less available. Availability refers to both the amount of and the conditions attached to the short-term financing. Only by examining both features will managers be in a position to consider the firm's short-term financing sources over time.

Finally, there is the issue of flexibility. Flexibility refers to the ability of the firm to pay off a loan and still retain the ability to renew or increase it. With factoring, bank loans, and lines of credit, the firm can pay off the loan when it has surplus funds. Flexibility also refers to how easily the firm can secure or increase the financing on short notice. A line of credit can be increased quickly and easily, but a negotiated short-term loan may take longer to secure. Trade credit, factoring of receivables, and field warehousing provide spontaneous sources of short-term financing that increase the firm's flexibility.

All of these items must be considered when a firm looks at its sources of short-term financing. Although the direct cost is a key element, it does not always provide the final answer, because there are also opportunity costs relating to matching, availability, and flexibility. Because of the difficulty of quantifying opportunity costs, a practical approach is to rank sources according to their direct costs, and then consider these other factors. If the opportunity costs are significant, the ranking of the desirability of one source of short-term financing compared with another will change. Finally, because the firm's financing needs change over time, multiple sources of short-term financing must be considered, even if some of them are not being employed currently.

Concept Review Question

- What are four specific items that should be considered when determining the source of short-term financing?

KEY POINTS

- In order to compare the cost of alternative short-term financing arrangements, an effective annual rate, or cost, is determined. The procedure involves finding the nominal yearly cost and then converting it to an effective yearly rate of interest.

- The effective annual interest rate provides the before-tax cost of alternative financing sources. Other dollar costs in addition to interest (or sometimes benefits) often need to be considered in order to find the cost of financing.
- Trade credit, continuous factoring of accounts receivable, and field warehousing provide spontaneous short-term financing. Bank loans and commercial paper are negotiated short-term financing sources.
- Although some short-term financing is unsecured, in recent years credit enhancement has become very popular. Thus, secured short-term financing has become more common. Accounts receivable may be used to secure bank loans or to obtain direct financing from the money and capital markets; an alternative is to factor accounts receivable. Inventory financing is also widely employed.
- The specific short-term financing a firm employs depends on matching considerations, cost, availability, and flexibility.

QUESTIONS

24.1 The equation for calculating the before-tax effective annual interest rate, or cost of short-term financing, is

$$k_{\text{effective annual}} = \left(1 + \frac{\text{costs} - \text{benefits}}{\text{net amount of financing}}\right)^m - 1$$

Discuss why this approach must be employed.

24.2 The effective annual rate is a function of the compounding interval. Explain how this influences the effective rate.

24.3 Other things being equal, how would changes in the following conditions affect a firm's after-tax cost of funds?
a. The prime rate increases.
b. The bank changes from discount interest to regular interest.
c. The bank's compensating balance request decreases.
d. Tax rates increase (assume the firm is profitable).

24.4 With discount interest, the interest is deducted at the beginning of the loan, thereby reducing the net amount of financing obtained.
a. Discuss the effect of discount interest on the effective annual cost of the loan.
b. What if a compensating balance agreement exists? Or what if commitment fees or loan processing (origination) fees are deducted at the start of the loan? Is the effect on the cost of the loan the same as with discount interest?

24.5 For many of the short-term financing sources, the direct cost is made up of the interest plus some other charge (or requirement). Explain this other charge for the following:
a. Line of credit.
b. Discount interest.
c. Instalment interest.
d. Compensating balance.
e. Commercial paper.
f. Pledging accounts receivable.
g. Advance factoring.
h. Inventory loans.

CONCEPT REVIEW PROBLEMS

See Appendix A for solutions.

CR24.1   Ricardo's TV & Appliance is evaluating the cost of trade credit with terms of 1/15, net 30.
a.   What is the effective annual cost of the trade credit?
b.   What is the cost if Ricardo's can stretch its payables from 30 days to 60 days?

CR24.2   National Book Company needs a short-term loan of $500,000 for 275 days. Frontier Bank has offered three different types of loans: a regular-interest loan with a stated rate of 12 percent, an 8 percent discount loan, and a 7 percent instalment loan with nine equal monthly payments. What is the effective annual cost for each type of loan? (*Note:* Use a 365-day year.)

CR24.3   Regale borrowed $20,000 for a 60-day period to finance the increased sales and activities around the Christmas holidays. The rate on the bank loan remained at 10 percent for 20 days, then increased to 12 percent for 20 days, and then dropped to 8 percent for the remainder of the lending period. What was the effective annual cost to Regale? (*Note:* Use a 365-day year.)

CR24.4   Margo Industries has obtained a line of credit of $500,000 for the next 180 days with a commitment fee of 1 percent on the unused portion and an interest rate of 15 percent. In the first 60 days the firm borrowed $200,000 on the line of credit, then increased the borrowing to $400,000 for another 100 days. The firm then paid off the line of credit and maintained a balance of zero for the remaining 20 days. Based on a 365-day year, what was the effective annual cost of the line of credit?

CR24.5   South Shore Imports is issuing $1 million in commercial paper with a maturity of 60 days. A line of credit for 100 percent of the face value of the commercial paper was established with a financial institution; the commitment fee is 0.5 percent of the line of credit and the firm has agreed to a compensating balance of 1 percent of the line of credit. Assume South Shore does not currently keep any funds at the financial institution, and use a 365-day year. What is the effective annual cost of the commercial paper if it is sold to investors for $985,000?

CR24.6   Minnow Industries has decided to borrow against its receivables, which average $80,000 per month. The firm's bank will lend against 80 percent of the receivables at 12 percent with a processing fee of 0.5 percent of the amount borrowed. The receivables can also be factored: The factor will accept 80 percent of the monthly receivables for a factoring fee of 2 percent per month. If factoring is selected, collection expenses will decrease by $200 per month. What is the effective annual cost of each financing option (assuming 12 equal months)?

PROBLEMS

24.1   What is the effective annual rate on an account paying 7 percent compounded continuously? What if it is compounded quarterly? Yearly?

24.2   A financial institution uses continuous compounding and claims that a dollar deposited today will be worth $2.7183 after 20 years. What is the nominal rate of interest?

24.3   A firm receives trade credit terms of 2/15, net 45. Based on a 365-day year, what is the before-tax effective annual cost if payment is made (**a**) by the 15th day, (**b**) on the 45th day, (**c**) by stretching to 60 days past the invoice date, (**d**) 90 days past the invoice date? What other costs or considerations should be considered in addition to this direct cost?

24.4 DeVito Industries has four choices for a $50,000, one-year loan from a bank. Which one of the following has the lowest before-tax effective annual interest rate?
1. A 14 percent annual interest rate with no compensating balance agreement. Interest is paid at the end of the year.
2. A 13 percent annual interest rate discounted, with no compensating balance agreement.
3. A 9 percent annual stated interest rate with instalment interest, paid in 12 equal instalments.
4. An 11 percent annual interest rate discounted, with a 10 percent compensating balance agreement. DeVito does not typically keep any funds in this bank.

24.5 Key Computers has just received a *net* amount (after interest and any compensating balance agreement) of financing of $450,000 for 146 days. Its bank loaned the money at a 15 percent annual rate, employing discount interest. The firm agreed to a $50,000 compensating balance, and Key keeps an average of $30,000 on deposit in the bank. If the tax rate is 40 percent, what is the after-tax effective annual interest rate on the loan? Assume a 365-day year.

24.6 Sewards has negotiated a line of credit as follows: a 120-day, $2,000,000 line that has a 0.6 percent annual rate commitment fee on the unused portion of the line and an interest rate of prime plus 2 percent. Sewards anticipates borrowing $750,000 during the first 75 days, and an additional $900,000 (for a total of $1,650,000) over the last 45 days.
a. If prime is expected to be 11 percent, what is the expected before-tax annual interest rate, or cost, to Sewards? (Assume a 365-day year.)
b. What is the expected before-tax interest rate if Sewards borrows the maximum on each of the 120 days?
c. How do you explain the difference in the answers between (a) and (b)?

24.7 Burnaby Wholesalers has a six-month, $1 million line of credit agreement with the Third National Bank. There is a 0.5 percent per year commitment fee charged on the unused portion of the line. The prime rate is 14 percent per year, and the interest rate on the line of credit is 1 percent over prime. Over the next six months, Burnaby Wholesalers anticipates drawing on the line of credit as follows:

Month	Additional Borrowed (Repaid) per Month	Total Borrowed per Month
April	$100,000	$ 100,000
May	300,000	400,000
June	400,000	800,000
July	200,000	1,000,000
August	−300,000	700,000
September	−400,000	300,000

By October 1, the line is paid off in full.
a. What is the expected before-tax effective annual interest rate to Burnaby Wholesalers? (*Note:* Do not worry about a 365-day year; simply treat each month as one-twelfth of the total.)
b. If Burnaby Wholesalers decides to borrow its full line of credit every month ($1,000,000 per month), what would its expected before-tax annual interest rate be? What if Burnaby borrows nothing during the 6 months?
c. Now suppose that the prime rate decreased to 12 percent. What is the expected before-tax effective annual interest rate if the borrowing is as in (a)?

24.8 Datatech is planning a $2 million issue of 270-day commercial paper. The interest rate is 11.5 percent per year, and Datatech will incur $15,000 in other issue-related expenses.

Interest is to be discounted, and a 365-day year is to be used.

a. What is the before-tax effective annual interest rate for the commercial paper issue?

b. What is the after-tax cost if Datatech's marginal tax rate is 35 percent? If it is 25 percent?

c. What are some other factors Datatech would need to consider in addition to the direct cost?

24.9 Barnes & Field presently uses maturity factoring at a before-tax effective annual cost of 18 percent. Under advance factoring, which is being considered, Barnes & Field would sell $1,200,000 of receivables with an average due date of 20 days. The factoring commission is 0.25 percent, the prime rate is 8 percent, and the factor will make the loan for 20 days at 3 percent over prime. The factor will loan 50 percent of the face value of the receivables. (Assume a 365-day year.)

a. By calculating the before-tax effective annual interest rate, determine whether Barnes & Field should switch to advance factoring.

b. What decision would be made if everything is the same as in (a) except the loan is at 2 percent over prime and the factor will loan (or advance) $1,000,000?

24.10 Delta Industries has employed factoring for a number of years. Its sales average $1 million dollars every 30 days, with 80 percent being credit sales. The days sales outstanding, DSO, is 30 days, so the length of the loan is 30 days. The factor charges a 1 percent factoring commission on the total receivables. In addition, any loan, which may be up to 75 percent of credit sales, carries an interest rate of 11 percent per year. The factor employs a 365-day year. Delta Industries estimates that the factoring agreement results in two savings: (1) a $1,000 reduction in credit and collection expenses for every 30-day period, and (2) a reduction in bad debts equal to 0.5 percent of the credit sales.

Recently, a finance company approached Delta about a loan involving the pledging of receivables. The loan could be up to 75 percent of receivables. The costs would be interest at 9 percent per year plus a 0.75 percent processing fee on the size of the loan.

a. By computing the effective annual interest rate, determine which plan is preferable.

b. If Delta Industries borrows only $200,000 per 30 days on average, which plan is preferable? (*Note:* If Delta factors the receivables, it still receives the $1,000 reduction in credit and collection expenses, plus the benefit of the 0.5 percent reduction in bad debts on the total receivables of $800,000, because it continues selling all the remaining receivables to the factor on a maturity factor basis.)

24.11 Charter United has to build up its inventory for a 4-month period each year to meet future sales demands. It is considering a bank loan with a field warehouse security agreement. The inventory during this 4-month period averages $500,000 per month. The bank will loan a maximum of 70 percent of the average inventory at prime plus 1 percent. Prime is 9 percent per year. The field warehousing agreement costs $2,400 per month. (*Note:* Use 12 months, not 365 days.)

a. If Charter United borrows $250,000, what is the before-tax effective annual interest rate on the loan?

b. If Charter United borrows the maximum, what is the rate on the loan?

24.12 Medicine Hat Press has experienced a severe cash squeeze and needs $300,000 for the next 75 days. The most likely source is to borrow against its inventory. Determine the better financing alternative of the two that are available. Use a 365-day year and calculate the before-tax effective annual interest rate.

a. The Rocky Mountain Bank will lend the $300,000 at a rate of 12 percent per year. It requires, however, that a field warehouse security agreement be employed. The field warehousing costs are $30 per day. Finally, Medicine Hat Press believes that because of lower efficiency, before-tax cash flows will be reduced by $2,500 during this 75-day period.

b. Bishop Finance will loan Medicine Hat Press the $300,000 at a rate of 18 percent per year under a blanket lien agreement. There are no other charges associated with this loan.

24.13   Green's Wholesalers presently uses a 90-day public warehouse agreement to finance most of its inventory. The average amount of inventory is $2,000,000, the bank lends Green's 75 percent of the value of the inventory, and the public warehousing fee is $200 per day. Total transportation costs for the 90-day period make up 1 percent of the average value of the inventory, the prime rate is 8 percent, and the bank will loan at 2 percent over prime. Green's is considering establishing a field warehouse on its premises, which would eliminate transportation costs but would cost $450 per day. The interest rate is 1 percent over prime, and the loan amount remains the same. (*Note:* Assume a 365-day year.)

a.   What is the before-tax effective annual interest rate for the public warehouse financing agreement?

b.   Does the effective annual rate on the loan increase or decrease under the field warehousing agreement? By how much?

24.14   The Clark Corporation has a need for $300,000 in short-term financing for the next 30 days. Based on the following four options, which source should Clark select to minimize its costs? (Calculate the before-tax effective annual interest rate.)

1.   A 91-day line of credit with a bank in the amount of $500,000. There is a 1 percent per year commitment fee on the unused portion, and the rate of interest on borrowed funds is 14 percent per year.
2.   Forgo cash discounts on $300,000 of payables. The terms are 2/10, net 40.
3.   Issue commercial paper with a 30-day maturity. If the entire $300,000 is borrowed, the maturity value of the issue will be $305,000. The firm incurs $1,000 in additional expenses.
4.   Obtain a 30-day loan against $400,000 worth of receivables. The factor will loan an amount equal to 75 percent of the receivables. The factoring commission is 0.5 percent, and the interest rate is 15 percent per year.

24.15   **Mini Case**   Mielke Products, a Edmonton-based firm, manufactures and distributes legal and financial services and products directly to consumers. The firm has grown rapidly, causing a need for short-term financing. Part of its sales are for cash, but a majority are for credit. The credit sales are financed with short-term borrowings. As the CFO, you have decided that the whole short-term financing strategy needs to be reevaluated.

a.   What is the difference between spontaneous and negotiated short-term financing? Would you expect Mielke to be more likely to use spontaneous or negotiated short-term financing?

b.   How does the size of the firm, in general, influence its use of short-term financing? Its industry? Its aggressiveness versus conservatism?

c.   Previously, the firm has not costed out various short-term financing alternatives. Explain how, by using the effective annual interest rate, the firm can capture the relevant costs and benefits of alternative financing alternatives.

d.   Mielke can borrow from a bank at a nominal rate of 16.85 percent with interest compounded monthly. What is the effective annual interest rate of the loan?

e.   Presently Mielke has two bank loans. The first is a six-month loan for $1,000,000 based on discount interest that carries an interest rate of 16 percent. The firm has agreed to a compensating balance of $100,000; typically Mielke would have only $15,000 in the bank. The second is a 180-day, $2,500,000 line of credit that has an annual commitment fee of 2 percent on the unused portion of the line. Over the last 180 days the interest rates and usage have been as follows:

	First 75 Days	Second 75 Days	Last 30 Days
Interest rate	14.50%	15.75%	16%
Total borrowing	$1,250,000	$1,000,000	$1,900,000

What is the effective annual interest rate on both? (*Note*: Use a 365-day year for the line of credit.)

f. Mielke presently pays all of its accounts payable as soon as they are received. Why is this a good (or bad) policy? What about adopting a policy of paying all accounts 30 days past the due date?

g. Instead of the bank loans, Mielke is investigating pledging and/or factoring its receivables. Two alternatives are as follows:

Pledging Receivables	Factoring Receivables
The loan is for 6 months.	The agreement is for 6 months.
Total receivables are $3,000,000; of which the loan is for 70 percent.	The loan is for 70 percent of the receivables, which are $3,000,000
The processing fee is 1 percent of the receivables pledged every 6 months.	The factoring commission is 0.8 percent of the total receivables, per every 6 months.
The interest rate is 15 percent.	The interest rate is 16 percent.

What is the effective annual interest rate, or cost, for both? Should either of these be employed instead of the present bank loan and/or line of credit?

h. What other factors need to be considered in deciding between alternative short-term sources of financing?

REFERENCES

BESANKO, DAVID, and GEORGE KANATAS. "Credit Market Equilibrium with Bank Monitoring and Moral Hazard." *Review of Financial Studies* 6 (No. 1, 1993): 213–232.

FARRAGHER, EDWARD J. "Factoring Accounts Receivable." *Journal of Cash Management* 6 (March–April 1986): 38–42.

HAWKINS, GREGORY. "An Analysis of Revolving Credit Agreements." *Journal of Financial Economics* 10 (March 1982): 59–81.

HILL, NED C., WILLIAM L. SARTORIS, and SUE L. VISSCHER. "The Components of Credit Line Borrowing Costs." *Journal of Cash Management* 3 (October–November 1983): 47–56.

JAMES, CHRISTOPHER. "Some Evidence on the Uniqueness of Bank Loans." *Journal of Financial Economics* 19 (December 1987): 217–235.

LUMMER, SCOTT L., and JOHN J. MCCONNELL. "Further Evidence on the Bank Lending Process and the Capital-Market Response to Bank Loan Agreements." *Journal of Financial Economics* 25 (November 1989): 99–122.

MACPHEE, WILLIAM A. *Short-Term Business Borrowing: Sources, Terms and Techniques.* Homewood, Ill.: Dow Jones-Irwin, 1984.

MIAN, SHEHZAD, and CLIFFORD W. SMITH, JR. "Accounts Receivable Management and Policy: Theory and Evidence." *Journal of Finance* 47 (March 1992): 169–200.

MOSKOWITZ, L. A. *Modern Factoring and Commercial Finance.* New York: Thomas Y. Crowell, 1977.

RAJAN, RAGHURAM G. "Insiders and Outsiders: The Choice Between Informed and Arm's-Length Debt." *Journal of Finance* 47 (September 1992): 1367–1400.

ROSENTHAL, JAMES A., and JUAN M. OCAMPO. "Analyzing the Economic Benefits of Securitized Credit." *Journal of Applied Corporate Finance* 1 (Fall 1988): 32–44.

Financial Planning and Small Business Finance

*T*hroughout this book, we have used the pie concept to visualize what is important in financial management. We found that the ingredients going into the pie are only part of the process; what is ultimately important is to maximize the size of the pie, or to maximize the long-run value of the firm, V, in the financial marketplace. Accounting numbers are one measure of the size of the pie; unfortunately, they are not the correct measure of the economic worth of the firm. In trying to maximize the size of the pie, too often managers focus on accounting figures of sales, assets, liabilities, shareholders' equity, and net income. Although it is important to understand accounting ideas, we must be careful not to confuse maximizing accounting numbers with maximizing the market value of the firm. Thus,

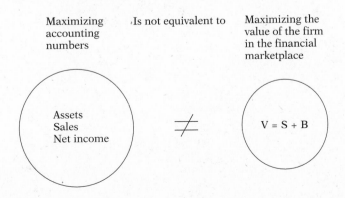

Maximizing accounting numbers	Is not equivalent to	Maximizing the value of the firm in the financial marketplace
Assets Sales Net income	$\neq$	$V = S + B$

Chapter 25 focuses on accounting-based ideas, while Chapter 26 emphasizes the primary importance that cash flow, *not* net income, plays in financial forecasting and planning. In Chapter 27 we discuss small business finance and apply the topics examined throughout the previous chapters to the operation of small businesses.

25

Analyzing Accounting Statements

EXECUTIVE SUMMARY

Accounting statements are derived from a historical, cost-based accrual system employing generally accepted accounting principles. The two primary accounting statements are the income statement and the balance sheet. By converting these statements to common-size statements and employing ratios, we can perform an accounting analysis of a firm. It is important to remember that the analysis should be done over a number of years, that industry data should be employed, and that the analysis may raise additional questions that require further probing.

The primary point to remember about analysis of accounting statements is that its purpose is to provide clues to the magnitude, timing, and riskiness of expected cash flows. Analysis of accounting statements is useful only if it provides additional information regarding these variables, which largely determine the expected future value and riskiness of the firm.

DIFFERENT STATEMENTS FOR DIFFERENT PURPOSES

Different types of accounting statements focus on different financial activities of the firm. The three types of statements used by most firms are:

1. Financial accounting statements prepared according to generally accepted accounting principles (GAAP). These data are presented in various publications and reported to the firm's shareholders in the **annual report.**
2. Tax reporting statements. Because of differences between what is allowed for tax reporting (Revenue Canada Taxation regulations) and what is required for GAAP

purposes, separate tax statements are prepared. Tax consequences are of vital concern because the payment of taxes is a direct cash outflow for the firm.

3.   Reports for internal management. Firms often develop their own internal reporting requirements, which are based on divisions, cost centres, or some other unit. Included are such items as direct costing, contribution margin analysis, standard costs and variances, and transfer pricing.

Our interest in this chapter is in analyzing accounting statements, but we must specify *which* statements. The statements we focus on are those in category 1—the financial accounting statements prepared for external use and based on generally accepted accounting principles. (For purposes of our discussion, we will call them simply accounting statements, although more specifically they are *financial* accounting statements.) The objective of the generally accepted accounting principles on which accounting statements are based is to provide a consistent and objective account of the firm's status based on historical costs, where revenues and expenses are matched over the appropriate time periods. There are two reasons for focusing on GAAP statements: First, because these are prepared for the public, it is by analyzing GAAP statements that investors, creditors, and others gauge the performance of the firm. Second, unless we are employed by the firm, the GAAP statements are all we have; neither tax nor internal management statements are made public.

Concept Review Question

■ Describe the different types of accounting statements prepared by a firm.

THE BASIC ACCOUNTING STATEMENTS

The annual report that a firm issues to shareholders contains important information. The primary accounting statements it contains are the income statement and the balance sheet. The income statement records the flow of revenue and related expenses through the firm over some period of time, typically a year. The balance sheet is a snapshot of the firm's assets, liabilities, and owner's claims as of a specific point in time—the end of its fiscal year. These two statements, along with the statement of changes in financial position (discussed in the next chapter) and the discussion accompanying the statements, provide an accounting picture of the firm. Typically, an annual report provides statements for two or three years, along with summary information for several more years.

Accounting statements report what happened to the firm in terms of sales, assets, liabilities, earnings, dividends, and so forth, over time. This information is one of the inputs investors and the general investment community use to form expectations about the required returns and riskiness of the firm. As investors form or revise their expectations about the magnitude, timing, or riskiness of the firm's returns, the market value of the firm will be affected. Understanding accounting statements is therefore important for investors, creditors, and the firm's management.

Table 25.1

Income Statement for Loblaw Companies Ltd. (in millions)

The format of this statement differs from that reported in Loblaw's annual report, primarily because of the inclusion of preferred stock dividends.

	1994	1993	1992
Net sales	$9,999.9	$9,356.1	$9,261.6
Cost of goods sold, selling and administrative expenses[a]	9,592.9	9,155.7	9,068.5
Operating profit	272.3	200.4	193.1
Adjustment: Special provision			10.0
Earnings before interest and taxes, EBIT	272.3	200.4	183.1
Interest	62.1	51.3	58.2
Earnings before taxes, EBT	210.2	149.1	124.9
Income taxes	83.5	55.7	45.1
Net income, EAT	126.7	93.4	79.8
Preferred stock dividend	6.7	8.9	10.7
Earnings available to common shareholders, EAC	120.0	$ 84.5	$ 69.1

[a] Includes $134.7, $122.4, and $115.7 in GAAP depreciation expense in 1994, 1993, and 1992, respectively; and $105.1, $93.3, and $86 in lease expense, respectively.

The analysis we will make here is based on Loblaw Companies Ltd. The company sells food and general merchandise in Canada as well as in the St. Louis and New Orleans areas of the United States.[1]

INCOME STATEMENT

The income statement presents a summary of revenues and expenses for the firm during the last year. Table 25.1 presents the last three years' income statements for Loblaw. Here are some highlights of the income statement:

1. As is common in the retail food industry, Loblaw does not show its cost of goods sold as a separate item. Consequently, we cannot calculate the firm's **gross margin**—that is, sales minus cost of goods sold. For most firms, gross margin can be calculated, and it indicates what the firm sells goods for in relation to the cost of the goods.
2. **Operating profit** measures the earnings of the firm after all expenses except interest and taxes and before any adjustments.

---

[1] The information on Loblaw came from its 1994 annual report. Some minor adjustments have been made to simplify the presentation and to improve consistency. The report noted the firm's intention to sell its U.S. retail business. In early 1995 the firm announced that it had sold its retail subsidiaries in the United States.

3. Adjustments for Loblaw reflect a special provision to anticipate losses on the company's investment in, and guarantees for, its U.S. subsidiary, P.J. Schmitt.
4. The net operating income, or earnings before interest and taxes (EBIT) reflects the firm's earnings before the costs of financing and income taxes.
5. Subtracting interest expenses results in earnings before taxes (EBT). We then subtract income taxes to arrive at net income, or earnings after tax (EAT). Note that since the firm has preferred stock outstanding, cash dividends on it have been subtracted from net income to arrive at the **earnings available for common shareholders (EAC)**.
6. Because GAAP statements are prepared on an accrual, not a cash, basis, the $126.7 million in net income in 1994 does not mean that Loblaw earned $126.7 million in cash. In Table 25.1, we see that Loblaw's net sales and net income increased over these three years.

One item of interest is the earnings per share (EPS). By putting earnings on a per share basis, the effects of changes in the number of shares of common stock outstanding can be held constant. Earnings per share is calculated as follows:

$$\text{EPS} = \frac{\text{earnings available for common shareholders}}{\text{number of shares of common stock}} = \frac{\text{net income} - \text{cash dividends on preferred stock (if any)}}{\text{number of shares of common stock outstanding}} \quad (25.1)$$

For Loblaw in 1994, EPS was $120/79.8 = $1.51.[2] During 1993 it was $1.07, and in 1992 it was $0.88. After adjusting for differences in the number of shares of common stock outstanding, Loblaw's earnings per share increased significantly over the three-year period.

There are actually two EPS figures that could be reported, depending on whether any complex securities, such as convertible securities, warrants, or stock options, are employed by a firm:

1. BASIC EPS   The first is basic EPS as calculated using Equation 25.1.
2. FULLY DILUTED EPS   The second is fully diluted EPS, in which the earnings available for common shareholders are divided by the total number of shares of common stock that would be outstanding after total conversion of the issue. Because our interest is in financial management, not accounting, we focus primarily on basic EPS, or just EPS.

BALANCE SHEET

The balance sheet provides a record of the firm—its assets, liabilities, and resulting shareholders' equity—as of the end of its fiscal year. In looking at a balance sheet (Table 25.2), it is important to recognize that the figures are presented in terms of

---

[2] There were 79.8 million shares of stock outstanding at the end of 1994, 79.4 million at the end of 1993, and 78.9 million at the end of 1992.

Table 25.2

Balance Sheet for Loblaw Companies Ltd. (in millions)

The balance sheet lists assets, liabilities, and resulting shareholders' equity, or net worth, of the firm at a specific time. Because it is based on historical cost, it is not indicative of the market value of the firm.

	1994	1993	1992
Assets			
Current assets			
Cash and short-term investments	$ 215.5	$ 271.9	$ 208.0
Accounts receivable	170.1	160.9	183.9
Inventories	700.7	653.1	642.9
Prepaid expenses and other assets	32.4	30.9	17.1
Total current assets	1,118.7	1,116.8	1,051.9
Long-term assets			
Gross property and equipment	2,596.8	2,308.2	2,028.1
Less: Accumulated depreciation	993.4	894.5	796.7
Net property and equipment	1,603.4	1,413.7	1,231.4
Investments	94.3	84.1	94.1
Goodwill	44.0	48.7	52.0
Other	86.8	79.4	44.7
Total long-term assets	1,828.5	1,625.9	1,422.2
Total assets	$2,947.2	$2,742.7	$2,474.1
Liabilities and Shareholders' Equity			
Current liabilities			
Notes payable[a]	$ 56.9	$ 37.8	$ 5.6
Accounts payable and accruals	1,016.3	931.0	862.8
Income taxes payable	15.9	0.0	0.0
Total current liabilities	1,089.1	968.8	868.4
Long-term liabilities			
Long-term debt	600.8	653.0	497.8
Lease obligations	65.6	69.3	74.2
Deferred taxes	39.7	29.8	42.1
Other	30.1	19.0	19.4
Total long-term liabilities	736.2	771.1	633.5
Shareholders' equity			
Preferred stock	90.9	91.3	129.7
Common stock	232.8	228.1	222.8
Contributed surplus	8.3	8.5	8.6
Retained earnings	782.8	683.5	618.0
Foreign currency translation adjustment	7.1	(8.6)	(6.9)
Total shareholders' equity	1,121.9	1,002.8	972.2
Total liabilities and shareholders' equity	$2,947.2	$2,742.7	$2,474.1

[a] Contains current maturities of long-term debt.

historical costs; they do not reflect market values, the effects of inflation, or other current information. A balance sheet thus provides, at best, only a very rough idea of the value of the firm.[3] Some key aspects of the balance sheet are:

1. The assets are divided into current (less than or equal to one year) and long-term (more than one year). Note that property and equipment is presented on both a gross basis and a net basis. The net basis reflects accumulated GAAP depreciation charged over the years as an expense in order to match expenses with associated revenues.

2. Liabilities are also divided into current and long-term. Although not shown directly on the balance sheet, lease obligations for Loblaw are recorded as part of its long-term debt. The present value of long-term capital lease commitments is recorded as a long-term liability, and a corresponding dollar amount is included in the property and equipment account to show the use of assets acquired by long-term capital leases. **Deferred taxes** represent the difference in the taxes actually paid to Revenue Canada (discussed in Chapter 8) and those reported for GAAP purposes.

3. Both preferred and common stock are shown in the shareholders' equity section. As we saw in Chapter 10, the Canada Business Corporations Act (CBCA) allows firms to issue only no–par value common stock; therefore, the amount shown as common stock should represent the value that the firm actually realized when the stock was issued. The fact that Loblaw has "contributed surplus" shows that some of its shares were issued before the CBCA was passed. Note that Loblaw, like most firms that are international in nature, has an equity account that reflects foreign currency adjustments.

4. Retained earnings is an account that reflects the sum of the firm's net income over its life, less all cash dividends paid and any other adjustments. In a sense, it is a balancing account that (a) ties together the income statement and the balance sheet, and (b) allows assets to equal liabilities and shareholders' equity. It is important to recognize that *retained earnings is a claim on assets,* not an asset account. The retained earnings account *does not contain any cash;* the only cash is in the current asset account entitled "cash and short-term investments."

   Table 25.2 shows that Loblaw has increased both its current and long-term assets over the three-year period. On the other side, the current liabilities and shareholders' equity have also increased over this same period; however, long-term liabilities increased in 1993 but decreased slightly in 1994.

---

[3] A figure often reported is book value per share, which is calculated as:

$$\text{book value per share} = \frac{\text{shareholders' equity}}{\text{number of shares of common stock outstanding}}$$

For Loblaw in 1994, this was $1,121.9/79.8 = $14.06. In 1993, it was $12.63; in 1992, it was $12.32. Book value per share is not a meaningful figure because it does not represent the market value, the replacement value, or the liquidation value of the firm.

Table 25.3

Statement of Retained Earnings for Loblaw Companies Ltd. (in millions)

The retained earnings statement ties together the income statement and the balance sheet by reconciling net income, less any cash dividends paid and any other adjustments made, with the changes in the retained earnings account.

	1994	1993	1992
Retained earnings at beginning of year	$683.5	$618.0	$567.8
Net income	126.7	93.4	79.8
Cash dividends			
Preferred stock	(6.7)	(8.9)	(10.7)
Common stock	(20.7)	(19.0)	(18.9)
Retained earnings at end of year	$782.8	$683.5	$618.0)

STATEMENT OF RETAINED EARNINGS

Because the firm is owned by shareholders, some of its earnings are generally distributed to them in the form of cash dividends. The **statement of retained earnings** (Table 25.3) shows the disposition of the earnings reported from the firm's income statement. This disposition allows us to determine what affected the retained earnings account from year to year. The statement is not significant for financial analysis purposes; but it is important to recognize that retained earnings is a claim on assets, not an asset account. This is why there is no cash in the retained earnings account to pay dividends, purchase property and equipment, or do anything else.

Using the common stock cash dividend figure presented in Table 25.3, and knowing the number of shares of common stock outstanding, we can calculate the dividends per share—the dollar amount of cash dividends paid to common shareholders during the year:

$$\text{dividend per share} = \frac{\text{total cash dividends paid to common shareholders}}{\text{number of shares of common stock outstanding}} \qquad (25.2)$$

For 1994, the dividend per share figure was $20.7/79.8 = $0.26 per share. This compares with $0.24 in 1993 and 1992. Loblaw thus had a relatively constant cash dividend over the period.

Concept Review Questions

- Describe the items that are presented in an income statement.
- What are the two kinds of earnings per share?
- Describe the key aspects of the balance sheet.

ANALYSIS OF ACCOUNTING STATEMENTS

A firm's balance sheet reports its assets, liabilities, and shareholders' equity at a point in time; the income statement reports operations over the period of a year. Careful analysis of these statements can provide some clues about future cash flows. The point of this analysis is to help diagnose trends that indicate the magnitude, timing, or riskiness of the firm's future cash flows.

When conducting an analysis, we need to keep four ideas in mind:

1. It is necessary to look at trends; generally three to five years' worth of data are necessary to ascertain how the firm's performance is changing over time.
2. It is helpful to compare the firm's performance to that of the industry (or industries) in which it operates.[4] Although industry averages may not indicate where a firm wants to be, because of different markets, management philosophy, or whatever, the comparison is helpful in analyzing trends.
3. *The importance of carefully reading and analyzing the annual report—including the discussion accompanying the statements—cannot be overemphasized.* Often these will point to other factors—such as contractual obligations, past and future financing policies, plans for further expansion or restructuring, or the sale of part of the firm's assets—that significantly affect the entire analysis.
4. The analysis may raise further questions for which additional information is needed. The important point is not to view the analysis as an end in itself.

COMMON-SIZE STATEMENTS

Income Statement   One of the simplest and most direct ways to analyze changes over time is to calculate a **common-size statement.** A common-size income statement is constructed by dividing the various components of the income statement by *net sales.* Thus, net sales equals 100 percent, and everything else is presented as a percentage of net sales. Loblaw's common-size income statement is presented in Table 25.4. Note that since the cost of goods sold is not shown as a separate item, we cannot show **gross profit margin** (gross margin divided by sales); only **net profit margin** is shown. Comparing Loblaw and the retail food industry, we see that Loblaw has about the same relative cost of goods sold and expenses over the period, with the consequence that the firm's net income has been close to that of the industry.

Balance Sheet   A common-size balance sheet can be calculated in the same manner, except that all the statement components are divided by *total assets* to put them on a common percentage basis. Loblaw's common-size balance sheet is presented in Table 25.5. An analysis of this statement indicates that Loblaw's current assets declined over the period. Compared to others in the retail food industry, Loblaw carries a substantially lower amount in accounts receivable but about the same amount of

---

[4] It is often difficult to find comparabvle industry data. If good industry data are unavailable, it is generally best to use one or more similar firms for comparison. We used The Oshawa Group and Metro-Richelieu to generate "industry" data.

Table 25.4

Common-Size Income Statement for Loblaw Companies Ltd. and the Retail Food Industry

A common-size income statement is calculated by dividing the various components by net sales; thus net sales equal 100 percent.

	Loblaw Companies Ltd.			Industry		
	1994	1993	1992	1994	1993	1992
Net Sales	100.0%	100.0%	100.0%	100.0%	100.0%	100.0%
Cost of goods sold, selling and administration expenses	97.3	97.9	98.0	98.2	98.3	98.6
Earnings before interest and taxes, EBIT	2.7	2.1	2.0	1.8	1.7	1.4
Interest	0.6	0.5	0.6	0.2	0.3	0.2
Earnings before taxes, EBT	2.1	1.6	1.4	1.6	1.4	1.2
Income taxes	0.8	0.6	0.5	0.6	0.5	0.4
Net income (net profit margin)	1.3	1.0%	0.9%	1.0%	0.9%	0.8%

inventory. Examining the investment in long-term assets, we see that Loblaw is well above the industry in property and equipment but has less in "other" assets.

An analysis of the liabilities indicates that Loblaw has more in accounts payable but less in notes payable than the industry. In recent years, Loblaw has increased its reliance on long-term debt. Deferred taxes are lower for Loblaw than for the retail food industry. Overall, Loblaw exhibits some substantial differences from the industry in terms of the composition of its assets, liabilities and shareholders' equity.

RATIO ANALYSIS

Another useful approach is to compute ratios. These ratios compare accounting variables and draw from both the income statement and the balance sheet. Although many different ratios can be calculated, we will focus on a basic set. The ratios are grouped into five categories, as follows:[5]

1. Liquidity ratios, which indicate the firm's ability to meet its short-run obligations.
2. Asset management ratios, which indicate how efficiently the firm is using its assets.
3. Debt management ratios, which deal with the amount of debt in the firm's capital structure and its ability to service (or meet) its legal obligations.

---

[5] These five groups are convenience groupings which indicate that analysts might use them in combination to examine some aspect of the firm's operations. The ratios presented are general-purpose ratios applicable to most manufacturing and retail firms. However, some are not very useful or relevant in the financial, public utility, transportation, and service industries.

Table 25.5

Common-Size Balance Sheet for Loblaw Companies Ltd. and the Industry

All assets, liabilities, and shareholders' equity accounts are expressed as a percentage of total assets. The use of a common-size statement highlights relative percentages in accounts receivable, inventory, long-term assets, and short-term liabilities.

	Loblaw Companies Ltd.			Industry		
	1994	1993	1992	1993	1992	1991
Assets						
Current assets						
Cash and short-term investments	7.3%	9.9%	8.4%	2.9%	2.1%	0.4%
Accounts receivable	5.8	5.9	7.4	19.4	19.6	20.1
Inventories	23.8	23.8	26.0	24.1	23.6	24.0
Prepaid expenses	1.1	1.1	0.7	1.8	1.8	0.9
Total current assets	38.0	40.7	42.5	48.2	47.1	45.4
Long-term assets						
Net property and equipment	54.4	51.6	49.8	32.4	33.6	35.5
Other	7.6	7.7	7.7	19.4	19.3	19.1
Total long-term assets	62.0	59.3	57.5	51.8	52.9	54.6
Total assets	100.0%	100.0%	100.0%	100.0%	100.0%	100.0%
Liabilities and Shareholders' Equity						
Current liabilities						
Notes payable[a]	1.9%	1.4%	0.2%	3.4%	2.7%	4.6%
Accounts payable and accruals	34.6	33.9	34.9	29.3	30.3	31.5
Income taxes payable	0.5	0.0	0.0	0.8	0.7	0.3
Total current liabilities	37.0	35.3	35.1	33.5	33.7	36.4
Long-term liabilities						
Long-term debt and leases	23.6	27.0	23.9	10.0	12.4	13.0
Deferred taxes	1.3	1.1	1.7	2.8	2.5	2.3
Shareholders' equity	38.1	36.6	39.3	53.7	51.4	48.3
Total liabilities and shareholders' equity	100.0%	100.0%	100.0%	100.0%	100.0%	100.0%

[a] Contains current maturities of long-term debt.

4. Profitability ratios, which relate net income to sales, assets, or shareholders' equity.

5. Market ratios, which indicate what is happening to the firm's relative market price, earnings, and cash dividends.

Liquidity Ratios   Liquidity ratios measure the firm's ability to fulfil its short-term commitments out of current or liquid assets. These ratios focus on current assets and liabilities and are often of lesser importance than other ratios when considering the long-run viability and profitability of the firm. The two primary liquidity ratios are the current ratio and the quick ratio.

The **current ratio** measures the ability of the firm to meet obligations due within one year with short-term assets in the form of cash, marketable securities, accounts receivable, and inventory. It is calculated as follows (for Loblaw in 1994):

$$\text{Current ratio} = \frac{\text{current assets}}{\text{current liabilities}} = \frac{\$1,118.7}{\$1,089.1} = 1.0 \qquad (25.3)$$

The current ratio assumes a regular cash flow and that both accounts receivable and inventory can be readily converted into cash. A current ratio of 2.0 is sometimes employed as a standard of comparison. Current ratios of 1.0 and less are sometimes considered low and indicative of financial difficulties. However, this is only a rule of thumb; the specific industry that the firm is in will be the determining factor in what is considered high or low. As we will see, this rule of thumb does not hold for firms in the retail food industry. Very high ratios suggest excess current assets that probably are having an adverse effect on the long-run profitability of the firm because excess current assets imply higher carrying costs.[6]

By subtracting out inventory, which often is not highly liquid, we can calculate the **quick ratio,** which measures the firm's ability to meet its short-term obligations with cash, marketable securities, and accounts receivable:

$$\text{Quick ratio} = \frac{\text{current assets} - \text{inventory}}{\text{current liabilities}} = \frac{\$1,118.7 - \$700.7}{\$1,089.1} = 0.4 \qquad (25.4)$$

Also called the *acid test ratio,* this ratio measures the near-term ability of the firm to meet its current liabilities without using its inventory. Quick ratios of less than 1.0 are not alarming in and of themselves. Very high quick ratios suggest excess cash, a credit policy that needs revamping, or a change needed in the composition of current versus long-term assets.

Asset Management Ratios   Asset management ratios are sometimes called activity ratios. They look at the amount of various types of assets and attempt to determine whether they are too high or too low with regard to current operating levels. If too many funds are tied up in certain types of assets that could be more productively employed elsewhere, the firm is not as profitable as it should be. Four basic asset management ratios are the days sales outstanding,[7] inventory turnover, long-term asset turnover, and total asset turnover.

The days sales outstanding ratio estimates how many days it takes on average to collect the sales of the firm. By dividing sales (in the denominator) by 365, we

---

[6] Any interpretation of ratios is relative—either to the firm itself over time, or to the industry in which the firm operates. Also, knowledge of management's intent may be necessary. Consequently, what is "high" or "low," or "satisfactory" or "unsatisfactory," can be determined only in the context of a specific detailed analysis. Notice that too high a ratio may be just as indicative of a problem as too low a ratio. However, the action required is often far different.

[7] Days sales outstanding is sometimes called the average collection period.

determine average sales per day. Then, when receivables are divided by average sales, we can determine how many days it will take to collect the receivables:

$$\text{Days sales outstanding} = \frac{\text{accounts receivable}}{\text{sales}/365} = \frac{170.1}{\$9,999.9/365} = 6.2 \text{ days} \qquad (25.5)$$

This ratio provides an indication of how effective the credit-granting and management activities of the firm are. It can also be calculated using average accounts receivable for the year. If credit sales are available, then it would be preferable to employ that figure rather than total sales. A very high days sales outstanding probably indicates many uncollectible receivables and, consequently, increased carrying costs and lower earnings. A low ratio may indicate that credit-granting policies are overly restrictive, thus hurting sales.

The second asset management ratio is the inventory turnover ratio:

$$\text{Inventory turnover} = \frac{\text{cost of goods sold}}{\text{inventory}} = \frac{\$9,592.9}{\$700.7} = 13.7 \qquad (25.6)$$

This ratio can also be calculated using an average of the year's beginning and ending inventories. The higher the inventory turnover ratio, the more times a year the firm is moving, or turning over, its inventory. Other things being equal, and assuming that sales are progressing smoothly, a higher inventory turnover ratio suggests efficient inventory management. Low inventory turnover figures often indicate obsolete inventory or lack of effective inventory management, which may also result in lower earnings.

The **long-term asset turnover** ratio provides an indication of the firm's ability to generate sales based on its long-term asset base. For some industries, this figure is important; in others, like banking and many service industries, it is of questionable value. It is calculated as follows:

$$\text{Long-term asset turnover} = \frac{\text{sales}}{\text{long-term assets}} = \frac{\$9,999.9}{\$1,828.9} = 5.5 \qquad (25.7)$$

By comparing long-term assets (primarily property and equipment) to sales, this ratio provides an indication of how effective the firm is in using these assets. The higher the ratio, other things being equal, the more effective the utilization. A low ratio may indicate that the firm's marketing effort or basic area of business requires attention.

Total asset turnover provides an indication of the firm's ability to generate sales in relation to its total asset base. For Loblaw, it is

$$\text{Total asset turnover} = \frac{\text{sales}}{\text{total assets}} = \frac{\$9,999.9}{\$2,947.2} = 3.4 \qquad (25.8)$$

A high total asset turnover normally reflects good management, whereas a low ratio suggests the need to reassess the firm's overall strategy, marketing effort, and capital expenditure programme. For example, excess accounts receivable and/or inventory would cause total assets to increase, which in turn causes the total asset turnover ratio to decline.

Debt Management Ratios   Debt management ratios focus on the liabilities and share-holders' equity from the balance sheet and on the income statement.[8] Three primary ratios in this category are total debt to total assets, times interest earned, and fixed charges coverage.

The **total debt to total assets** ratio is calculated as follows:

$$\frac{\text{Total debt to}}{\text{total assets}} = \frac{\text{total debt}}{\text{total assets}} = \frac{\$1,089.1 + \$736.2}{\$2,947.2} = 0.62 \qquad (25.9)$$

This ratio attempts to measure how much of the total funds are being supplied by creditors. Total debt includes all current debt plus long-term debt, lease obligations, and so forth. A high ratio indicates the use of financial leverage to magnify earnings, whereas a low ratio indicates relatively low use of creditor funds. Loblaw has 62 percent of its *book-value-based* capital structure in debt-type instruments.

The second debt management ratio, **times interest earned,** is

$$\text{Times interest earned} = \frac{\text{earnings before interest}}{\text{interest}} = \frac{\$272.3}{\$62.1} = 4.4 \qquad (25.10)$$

The ability of the firm to meet its interest payments (on both short- and long-term debt) is measured by this ratio. It shows how far EBIT can decline before the firm probably will have trouble servicing its interest obligations. A high ratio indicates a safe situation, but that perhaps not enough financial leverage is being used. A low ratio may call for immediate action.

The **fixed charges coverage** ratio provides a more comprehensive picture of the firm's ability to meet its legal financing requirements. While variations of this ratio exist, the one we calculate is

$$\frac{\text{Fixed charges}}{\text{coverage}} = \frac{\text{EBIT} + \text{lease expenses}}{\text{interest} + \text{lease expense}} = \frac{\$272.3 + \$105.1}{\$62.1 + \$105.1} = 2.3 \qquad (25.11)$$

This is a more comprehensive ratio than times interest earned and includes lease expenses,[9] which are also a fixed legal obligation. Leasing is essentially like debt in that

---

[8] An important ratio for creditors is **days purchases outstanding**:

$$\text{days purchases outstanding} = \frac{\text{accounts payable}}{\text{credit purchases}/365}$$

which provides an idea of how promptly the firm pays its bills. Accounts payable can be obtained for virtually all firms. (For some firms, it is necessary to refer to the discussion in the annual report to separate accounts payable from accruals.) The problem comes with credit purchases, which are virtually never reported in accounting statements. If total purchases are available, they are often used instead. Otherwise, some annual reports provide sufficient information so that a percentage of the cost of goods sold, such as 60 percent, may be employed as an estimate of purchases. For Loblaw, a thorough analysis of its annual report fails to provide any information on accruals or purchases—credit or otherwise.

[9] *Lease expenses is an income statement account that is often found only in the discussion accompanying a firm's accounting statements.* Do not confuse it with "lease obligations" or "capitalized lease obligations" accounts that are reported either on the balance sheet or in the discussion accompanying the accounting statements.

it results in a fixed cost to the firm[10] and uses up some of the firm's debt capacity. By debt capacity, we mean the amount of fixed-cost financing the firm can effectively employ in order to maximize its value. To be even more complete, the denominator may also include sinking fund payments on long-term debt, and/or preferred dividends multiplied by $[1/(1 - \text{tax rate})]$.[11] A high fixed charges ratio is more desirable than a low one, other things being equal. However, the question of financial leverage still needs to be considered.

Profitability Ratios   Three profitability ratios, which focus on the profit-generating ability of the firm, are net profit margin, return on total assets, and return on equity. The net profit margin, as discussed when we calculated a common-size income statement, is

$$\text{Net profit margin} = \frac{\text{net income}}{\text{sales}} = \frac{\$126.7}{\$9,999.9} = 1.3\% \qquad (25.12)$$

A low net profit margin indicates that (1) the firm is not generating enough sales relative to its expenses, (2) expenses are out of control, or (3) both. It is a widely used ratio of the efficiency of management. Net profit margins vary considerably by industry, with, for example, jewellery stores having much higher profit margins than grocery stores.

The second profitability ratio, **return on total assets**, indicates the ability of the firm to earn a satisfactory return on all the assets it employs. It is calculated as follows:

$$\text{Return on total assets} = \frac{\text{net income}}{\text{total assets}} = \frac{\$126.7}{\$2,947.2} = 4.3\% \qquad (25.13)$$

Also known as *return on investment,* (ROI), this ratio tells us how effective the firm is in terms of generating income, given its asset base. It is an important measure of the efficiency of management. The higher the ratio the better, because this provides some indication of future growth prospects.

The last profitability ratio is **return on equity,** (ROE), which is

$$\text{Return on equity} = \frac{\text{net income}}{\text{shareholders' equity}} = \frac{\$126.7}{\$1,121.9} = 11.3\% \qquad (25.14)$$

This ratio provides an accounting-based indication of the effectiveness of the firm and its management. It is directly affected by the return on total assets and the amount of financial leverage employed. However, this ratio, although helpful, does not focus on

---

[10] Many leases have a required payment and then a contingent payment based on sales. In addition, much of the debt being issued by firms is not strictly fixed but may float as general interest rates change. However, both of these are still fixed-cost types of financing because they have a legal claim on income and do not share in the final distribution of earnings, as do common shareholders.

[11] Equation 25.11 is calculated on a before-tax basis. Because sinking fund payments and preferred dividends are both after-tax payments, dividing them by $(1 - \text{tax rate})$ gives the amount of before-tax funds necessary to make the after-tax payment.

the actual returns to the firms' owners in terms of cash dividends and/or market appreciation. For this reason, *return on equity is not a reliable measure of returns*.

Market Ratios   The last set of ratios is somewhat different, because they focus more on the investors' viewpoint. These ratios are the price/earnings ratio, dividend yield, and dividend payout. The price/earnings (P/E) ratio indicates how much investors are willing to pay for the firm's current earnings. It is

$$\text{Price/earnings} = \frac{\text{market price per share}}{\text{earnings per share}} = \frac{\$22.75}{\$1.51} = 15.1 \text{ times} \qquad (25.15)$$

In Chapter 4 we discussed two possible causes of high P/E ratios—little or no earnings or high expected growth. For Loblaw it looks as if we can rule out the possibility of little or no expected earnings. Thus, the P/E ratio indicates how investors view the future prospects of Loblaw. Because P/E ratios fluctuate over time, it is helpful to look at trends for both the company and the stock market in general.

The second market ratio is the dividend yield. For Loblaw it is

$$\text{Dividend yield} = \frac{\text{dividends per share}}{\text{market price per share}} = \frac{\$0.26}{\$22.75} = 1.1\% \qquad (25.16)$$

Because returns from investing in stocks come from cash dividends and from appreciation or loss in market price, these sources of return are part of the total return expected by investors. Generally, firms with high growth prospects have relatively low cash dividends and a relatively high market price, meaning they have a low dividend yield. Conversely, firms with low growth prospects typically have higher dividend yields.

Finally, the dividend payout ratio provides an indication of how the firm is splitting its earnings between returning them to common shareholders and reinvesting them in the firm. It is calculated as follows:

$$\text{Dividend payout} = \frac{\text{dividends per share}}{\text{earnings per share}} = \frac{\$0.26}{\$1.51} = 17.2\% \qquad (25.17)$$

High-growth firms typically reinvest most of their earnings instead of paying them out, resulting in low payout ratios. Slow-growth firms in stable industries typically pay out a much higher percentage of their earnings. Dividend payout ratios are an important part of the cash dividend policy decision.

The ratios for Loblaw and for the retail foods industry are presented in Table 25.6.

The du Pont System   In an attempt to improve its financial analysis, du Pont introduced an information system that highlights relationships which might otherwise be missed. The **du Pont system** ties together three ratios: net profit margin, total asset turnover, and total debt to total assets. The return on total assets is thus seen to be

$$\begin{array}{l} \text{Return on} \\ \text{total assets} \end{array} = \left(\begin{array}{l} \text{net profit} \\ \text{margin} \end{array} \right) \left(\begin{array}{l} \text{total} \\ \text{asset} \\ \text{turnover} \end{array} \right) = (1.26\%)(3.4) = 4.3\% \qquad (25.18)$$

Table 25.6

Ratios for Loblaw Companies Ltd. and the Retail Food Industry

By comparing Loblaw and the industry over time, we can spot trends that may not be evident when only a single year is examined.

Ratio	Calculation	Loblaw Companies Ltd.			Industry		
		1994	1993	1992	1994	1993	1992
Liquidity							
Current	current assets / current liabilities	1.0	1.2	1.2	1.4	1.4	1.2
Quick	current assets − inventory / current liabilities	0.4	0.5	0.5	0.7	0.7	0.6
Asset Management							
Days sales outstanding	accounts receivable / sales/365	6.2 days	6.3 days	7.3 days	15.1 days	15.5 days	17.7 days
Inventory turnover	cost of goods sold / inventory	13.7	14.0	14.1	19.2	19.1	17.1
Long-term asset turnover	sales / long-term assets	5.5	5.8	6.5	9.1	8.7	7.6
Total asset turnover	sales / total assets	3.4	3.4	3.7	4.7	4.6	4.1

(continued)

Table 25.6 *continued*

Ratio	Calculation	Loblaw Companies Ltd.			Industry		
		1994	1993	1992	1994	1993	1992
Debt Management							
Total debt to total assets	$\dfrac{\text{total debt}}{\text{total assets}}$	0.62	0.63	0.61	0.46	0.49	0.52
Times interest earned	$\dfrac{\text{EBIT}}{\text{interest}}$	4.4	3.9	3.2	8.9	6.6	6.1
Fixed charges coverage	$\dfrac{\text{EBIT + lease expenses}}{\text{interest + lease expenses}}$	2.3	2.0	1.9	2.4	2.1	2.0
Profitability							
Net profit margin	$\dfrac{\text{net income}}{\text{sales}}$	1.3%	1.0%	0.9%	1.0%	0.9%	0.7%
Return on total assets	$\dfrac{\text{net income}}{\text{total assets}}$	4.3%	3.4%	3.2%	4.7%	4.1%	3.1%
Return on equity	$\dfrac{\text{net income}}{\text{shareholders' equity}}$	11.3%	9.3%	8.2%	8.8%	8.1%	6.4%
Market							
Price/earnings	$\dfrac{\text{market price per share}}{\text{earnings per share}}$	15.1 times	19.9 times	21.0 times	12.3 times	14.0 times	15.8 times
Dividend yield	$\dfrac{\text{dividends per share}}{\text{market price per share}}$	1.1%	1.1%	1.3%	2.4%	2.1%	2.2%
Dividend payout	$\dfrac{\text{dividends per share}}{\text{earnings per share}}$	17.2%	22.4%	27.3%	43.4%	35.2%	40.4%

The importance of breaking out the net profit margin and total asset turnover as components of the return on total assets, instead of calculating return on total assets directly, is that it focuses attention on the separate ideas of profitability and asset utilization. Loblaw's profitability as measured by net profit margin is better than that of the retail food industry; its asset utilization is lower than that of the industry, leading to a lower return on total assets.

The second part of the du Pont system focuses on the capital structure, or financial leverage, employed by the firm. Loblaw is using 62 percent debt (in book value terms) in its capital structure. Instead of calculating return on equity directly, as we did earlier, we can also calculate it as:

$$\text{return on equity} = \text{return on total assets} \bigg/ \left(1 - \frac{\text{total debt}}{\text{total assets}}\right) \qquad (25.19)$$

$$= 4.3\%/(1 - 0.62) = 11.3\%$$

Using this approach, we see that return on equity is influenced by (1) net profit margin and total asset turnover, which jointly affect the return on total assets; and (2) the financial leverage employed. In order to improve return on equity, a firm has three choices: increase the profit margin, increase total asset turnover, or use more debt. Correspondingly, reducing the net profit margin, total asset turnover, or using less debt will lower the firm's return on equity.

CONCLUSIONS FROM THE LOBLAW ANALYSIS

Based on the common-size statements, the ratios, and the du Pont system, we can make the following observations:

1. Loblaw's liquidity remained constant over the period, but it is slightly lower than that of the retail food industry as a whole. This suggests that Loblaw has adopted a more aggressive short-term financial management policy position than the industry.
2. Its receivables are significantly below the industry average and are collected more than twice as fast as the industry's. The firm holds about the same amount of inventory as the industry and turns it over a little more slowly than the industry. However, overall the firm manages receivables and inventory very well compared to the industry.
3. Loblaw's long-term and total asset turnovers have both remained fairly steady in recent years. In comparison to the retail food industry, however, Loblaw is generating more sales from its total assets.
4. Although Loblaw's debt is higher than that of the industry, its coverage ratios are virtually the same as those of the industry.
5. Comparing Loblaw's net profit margin with that of the industry, we see that it is slightly higher than the industry average. However, because it uses more debt than the industry, its return on equity is much higher than that of the industry.

6. Finally, Loblaw's P/E ratio is higher than that of the industry, suggesting that the firm is regarded as having brighter growth prospects. Consistent with this belief, Loblaw is paying out a significantly smaller percentage of its earnings in the form of cash dividends.

Our analysis suggests that Loblaw has a slightly higher profit margin, but a significantly higher return on equity than the industry. Although Loblaw has a lower total asset turnover than the industry, it achieves its higher return on equity by using more debt. Loblaw has significantly lower receivables than the industry and inventory about equal to that of the industry, and it is generating lower revenue per dollar of assets, but it appears very capable of servicing its debt.

LIMITATIONS

Our in-depth analysis of Loblaw provided many insights into the firm's financial condition. But any analysis of accounting statements is subject to the following limitations:

1. The basic data arise from the accounting process and are therefore based on historical costs. Because one of the main purposes of financial accounting is to match revenues and expenses in the appropriate period, there may be little or no *direct* relationship to the firm's cash flows, especially in the short run.
2. The accounting process allows for alternative treatment of numerous transactions. Thus, two identical firms may report substantially different accounting data by employing alternative GAAP treatments.
3. "Window dressing" may appear in accounting statements. For example, by taking out a long-term loan before the end of its fiscal year and holding the proceeds as cash, a firm could significantly improve its current and quick ratios. Once the fiscal year has ended, the firm could turn around and pay back the loan—but the transaction has already served its purpose.
4. For the many firms that are multidivisional, sufficient data are generally not reported to enable outsiders to examine the performance of the various divisions. Also, it is often difficult to find comparable industry data for multidivisional firms.
5. Inflation can have material effects on the firm that are not fully reflected in accounting statements. This is especially true for inventory and long-term assets, which may be seriously understated when inflation is present. The comparability of data within a firm over time, and also between firms, is therefore limited.
6. For firms with substantial international operations, other reporting problems exist in addition to those faced by domestic firms.
7. Industry averages are generally *not* where the successful firm wants to operate; rather, it wants to be at the top end of the performance ladder. Also, finding an appropriate industry for comparison is often not as simple as it sounds.

In addition to the data contained in accounting statements, many other sources of financial data exist. Some of these are listed in Table 25.7.

Table 25.7

Sources of Financial Data

There are a great many sources of financial data. When in doubt about the availability of these or other sources, check with the reference librarian at your library.

Publication	Type of Information
Canadian Sources	
Annual reports of companies	Individual company data
Bank of Canada, *Review*	Monetary and other financial statistics
Consumer and Corporate Affairs, *Canada Corporations Bulletin*	Statistical data on Canadian corporations
Dun & Bradstreet's *Canadian Key Directory*	Business profile of top 3 percent of Canadian companies
Dun & Bradstreet's *Key Business Ratios*	Ratio analysis of top 3 percent of Canadian companies
Financial Post's *Corporation Service*	Individual companies' financial statements
Financial Post's *Dividend Record*	Record of stock dividends
Insurance Canada, *List of Securities*	Market value of all securities owned by Canadian companies
Moody's *Handbook of Common Stock*	Canadian companies on NYSE, dividend and stock performance
Moody's *Bond Record*	Performance of corporate, convertible, government, and municipal bonds
Moody's *Dividend Record*	List of dividends
Toronto Stock Exchange, *TSE Review*	Stock market activity of the TSE
U.S. Sources	
Bank and Quotation Record	Prices and yields of securities
Barron's	Security markets, individual securities, and analysis of individual companies
Cash Flow	General coverage of cash and working capital trends
Dun's Business Month	General coverage, current trends
Federal Reserve Bulletin	Aggregate financial data
Moody's Bank & Finance, Industrial, OTC Industrial, OTC Unlisted, International, and *Transportation* Manuals	Individual company data
Robert Morris Associates, *Annual Statement Studies*	Industry financial ratios
Standard & Poor's *Corporation Records*	Individual company data
Standard & Poor's *Industry Surveys*	Industry data
Statistical Bulletin of the Securities and Exchange Commission	Stock market activity and corporate security issues
Value Line Investment Survey	Individual company data

Concept Review Questions

- What four key ideas should be considered when conducting an analysis of the balance sheet and income statement?
- On what basis is a common-size income statement prepared? A common-size balance sheet?
- How is a firm's return on equity related to the firm's return on assets? To net profit margin? To total asset turnover?
- Describe some of the problems and limitations of any analysis using accounting statements.

KEY POINTS

- It is very important not to become overly enamoured with analyzing and/or maximizing accounting numbers. Accounting numbers are only a means to an end; the purpose of the firm is to produce and sell quality products or services and make financial decisions that lead to the maximization of the value of the firm.
- An income statement is presented over a period of time (typically a year), whereas a balance sheet is presented as of an instant in time.
- Ratios can be grouped into categories; five common groupings are liquidity, asset management, debt management, profitability, and market.
- Common-size accounting statements and ratios should be analyzed over time and compared to the industry. They should also form the basis for asking further questions about the firm.
- Limitations of accounting statements include their use of historical cost basis, alternative generally accepted treatments available, window dressing at the end of the year, sometimes incomplete divisional data, lack of inflation adjustment, and difficulties in reflecting the financial consequences of international operations.

QUESTIONS

25.1 Accounting statements may be prepared under generally accepted accounting principles, for tax purposes, or for internal management purposes. Explain why we focus on those prepared under GAAP, and what the strengths and/or weaknesses of GAAP statements are.

25.2 If preferred stock is outstanding, the numerator of the earnings per share calculation is earnings available to common shareholders (net income − cash dividends on preferred stock), whereas it is simply net income if there is no preferred stock outstanding. Explain why this adjustment is necessary.

25.3 Book value per share, which is often referred to when someone is "touting" a common stock investment, is calculated by dividing shareholders' equity by the number of shares of common stock outstanding.
a. Based on your knowledge of the accounting process, why do you think that book value per share is generally not indicative of the value of the common stock?
b. Can you think of some specific situations in which book value may provide a reasonable estimate of value?

25.4 Explain in detail why:
a. net income does not reflect cash.
b. retained earnings do not include any cash.

25.5 Anna has been asked to conduct a complete analysis of the ability of Westbrook Enterprises to service its long-term financing obligations. In doing so, she determined that the firm has the following fixed-charge obligations over the next few years:

1. Interest of $2 million per year for each of the next three years.
2. Sinking fund payments of $1 million per year for each of the next three years. (A sinking fund is a required obligation often present when bonds are issued in order to retire some of the bonds before maturity.)
3. Lease payments of $1.5 million per year for each of the next three years.
4. Cash dividends on preferred stock of $1 million per year for each of the next three years. (The tax rate is 40 percent.)

How would you advise Anna to proceed with the analysis? Should any new ratios be calculated?

25.6 Financial leverage arises from the use of financing sources that require a fixed-cost type of financing. By employing financial leverage, the firm may be able to magnify gains (and losses) to common shareholders. Which one of these situations has the most (least) financial leverage? Why?

	A	B	C	D	E	F
Short-term debt	$ 0	$ 0	$ 0	$ 20	$ 20	$ 0
Long-term debt	0	0	50	0	30	20
Leases	0	0	0	20	0	30
Preferred stock	0	50	0	10	0	0
Common stock	$150	100	100	100	100	100

CONCEPT REVIEW PROBLEMS

See Appendix A for solutions.

CR25.1 Walk-EZ Shoes has operating profit, or EBIT, of $700,000. Interest expense for the year was $100,000, preferred dividends paid were $50,000, common dividends were $200,000, and taxes were $70,000. The firm has 30,000 shares of common stock outstanding and 10,000 warrants with a conversion privilege of one warrant for one share of stock. The probability of the warrants' conversion is 50 percent; therefore, there is likelihood of 5,000 warrants being converted.

a. Calculate the basic earnings per share, and the fully diluted earnings per share.
b. What was the increase in retained earnings?

CR25.2 MTM has a net profit margin of 5 percent, total asset turnover of 2.5, and a total debt to total asset ratio of 0.40. What is the firm's return on equity?

CR25.3 The following information concerns two competitors, Jarvus and Barkell.

Balance Sheet

	Jarvus	Barkell
Assets		
Cash and marketable securities	$ 72,345	$138,722
Accounts receivable	41,343	73,848
Inventory	193,827	43,024
Net long-term assets	12,290	22,290
Total assets	$319,805	$277,884

Balance Sheet

	Jarvus	Barkell
Liabilities and Shareholders' Equity		
Short-term bank loans	$ 54,678	$ 20,400
Accounts payable	55,705	22,556
Accruals	35,480	18,776
Long-term debt	22,116	43,555
Common stock	93,076	95,408
Retained earnings	58,750	77,189
Total liabilities and equity	$319,805	$277,884
Income Statement		
Sales	$701,092	$757,098
Cost of goods sold	564,504	622,020
Gross margin	136,588	135,078
Selling and administrative expenses	51,160	61,380
Depreciation	6,376	6,632
Miscellaneous expenses	8,108	14,228
EBIT	70,944	52,838
Interest on short-term debt	5,468	2,040
Interest on long-term debt	2,677	4,016
EBT	62,799	46,782
Taxes	25,119	18,632
Net income	$ 37,680	$ 28,150

Calculate the accounting ratios for both firms.

a. To which firm would you as a credit manager or short-term lender be most likely to approve the extension of short-term trade credit or grant a short-term loan?

b. To which one would you as a banker be most likely to extend long-term credit?

c. In which firm would you as an investor be most likely to buy stock?

PROBLEMS

25.1 Complete the balance sheet, sales, and net income information below, given the following data:

Long-term asset turnover	4.0
Total asset turnover	2.4
Total debt to total assets	0.6
Current ratio	2.0
Quick ratio	1.0
Net profit margin	5.0%
Days sales outstanding (365-day year)	15.208

Cash	$____	Current liabilities	$____
Accounts receivable	____	Long-term debt	____
Inventory	____	Common stock	100

(continued)

Net plant and equipment	600	Retained earnings	_____
Total assets	$ ___	Total liabilities and shareholders' equity	$ ___
Sales	$ ___	Net income	$ ___

25.2 Hibbard & Associates has the following data:

> long-term asset turnover = 3.5
> total asset turnover = 2.0

What percentage of total assets are current assets?

25.3 Wiebe Industries has a gross profit margin (gross margin/sales) of 25 percent on sales of $500,000 (all credit). Cash and marketable securities are $10,000, accounts receivable are $40,000, inventory is $50,000, and the current ratio is 2.0.

a. What are Wiebe's days sales outstanding (use a 365-day year), inventory turnover, and quick ratio?

b. How much should inventory be if management wants the inventory turnover to increase to 10 times a year?

c. What would the accounts receivable be if management wants the days sales outstanding to be 21.9 days?

25.4 Wallace Systems is applying for a bank loan. It has given the bank the following data:

Balance Sheet

Cash	$ 40,000	Accounts payable	$ 5,000
Accounts receivable	40,000	Notes payable	20,000
Inventory	70,000	Long-term debt	75,000
Net plant and equipment	225,000	6% preferred stock	25,000
Total assets	$375,000	Common stock (30,000 shares outstanding)	150,000
		Retained earnings	100,000
		Total liabilities and shareholders'equity	$375,000
Sales	$390,000		
Net income	$ 61,500		
Dividends per share on common stock	$0.80		
Market price per share of common stock	$60		

As part of your analysis of the firm's request for a loan, you have decided to calculate the following items: (1) earnings per share of common stock, (2) dividend payout, (3) return on total assets, (4) return on equity, (5) current ratio, and (6) quick ratio.

a. What are the calculated amounts for the six items?

b. What can you conclude about the past profitability of Wallace Systems based on this data? Lacking any other information, would you recommend approving or disapproving the loan request?

25.5   Hickory Mills has applied to your firm for credit for future purchases it wants to make. As a first step, you calculated the following information:

	Year −1	Year 0
Current ratio	2.00	2.00
Quick ratio	1.25	1.34
Cash/total assets	10.00%	15.45%
Accounts receivable/total assets	15.00%	15.00%
Inventory/total assets	15.00%	15.00%

a.   *Based on just this information,* do you believe credit should be granted to Hickory Mills? Why or why not?

b.   Upon further analysis, you gather the relevant data for the two years, which is

	Year −1	Year 0
Cash	$ 100	$ 170
Accounts receivable	150	165
Inventory	150	165
Total assets	1,000	1,100
Accounts payable	100	200
Notes payable	100	50
Sales	3,000	2,000
Cost of goods sold	1,800	1,500
Credit purchases	1,300	1,200

Calculate the following: (1) days sales outstanding, (2) inventory turnover, and (3) days purchases outstanding. [*Note:* As given in footnote 8, days purchases outstanding equals accounts payable/(credit purchases/365).] Based on this further analysis, what conclusion do you reach now?

25.6   Indicate the impact of the following transactions on the current ratio, total debt to total assets, and return on total assets. Use a plus sign (+) to indicate an increase, a minus sign (−) to indicate a decrease, and a zero (0) to indicate either no effect or an indeterminate effect. Assume that the initial current ratio was greater than 1.0.

	Current Ratio	Total Debt to Total Assets	Return on Assets
a. Cash acquired through a short-term bank loan	_____	_____	_____
b. Accounts receivable are collected	_____	_____	_____
c. Payment made to creditors for previous purchases	_____	_____	_____
d. Cash acquired through issuance of additional common stock	_____	_____	_____
e. Cash dividend declared and paid (the dividend has not been shown as an accrual)	_____	_____	_____

25.7 The following are the balance sheet and income statement for Decca Components:

Balance Sheet

Cash and marketable securities	$ 100,000	Accounts payable	$ 50,000
Accounts receivable	650,000	Notes payable	350,000
Inventory	1,050,000	Long-term debt	2,000,000
Property, plant, and equipment	6,000,000	Common stock	1,000,000
Less: Accumulated depreciation	(2,000,000)	Retained earnings	2,400,000
Total assets	$5,800,000	Total liabilities and	
		shareholders' equity	$5,800,000

Income Statement

Sales	$16,000,000
Cost of goods sold	10,000,000
Gross margin	6,000,000
Other expenses	3,000,000
EBIT	3,000,000
Interest	300,000
EBT	2,700,000
Income taxes	1,080,000
Net income	$ 1,620,000

a. Calculate the following ratios: (1) current, (2) quick, (3) total debt to total assets, (4) net profit margin, and (5) total asset turnover.
b. Using the du Pont formula, calculate return on equity.
c. Now suppose that Decca Components has decided to reduce its risk of running out of cash. To accomplish this, it will issue $1,000,000 in long-term debt and add the same amount to its cash and marketable securities account. This debt will be financed at a 10 percent yearly rate. What is the impact of this transaction on the ratios calculated in (a) and (b) above?

25.8 The following data apply to Stern Products:

Sales	$1,000,000
Cost of goods sold	800,000
Net income	50,000
Total debt	250,000
Preferred stock	100,000
Common stock	100,000
Retained earnings	50,000
Days sales outstanding (365-day year)	36.5 days
Inventory turnover	5

a. Determine (1) total asset turnover, (2) net profit margin, (3) return on total assets, and (4) return on equity.

b. If sales and cost of goods sold are constant and all the following events occur *simultaneously,* what are the new net income, total debt, and return on equity?
1. Inventory turnover increases to 10.
2. Days sales outstanding decreases to 18.25 days.
3. Return on assets increases to 15 percent.
4. There are no changes in long-term assets; any reduction in assets causes an equal dollar-for-dollar reduction in the firm's debt.

25.9 An abbreviated balance sheet is shown below:

Total assets	$800
Current liabilities	$ 50
Long-term debt	150
Common stock (100 shares outstanding)	100
Retained earnings	500
Total liabilities and shareholders' equity	$800

a. If return on equity equals 10 percent, find net income and return on total assets.
b. What is the firm's earnings per share?
c. If it pays out one-quarter of its current earnings as cash dividends, what are the dividends per share?
d. If the market price of the firm's common stock is $9 per share, what is the price/earnings ratio and the dividend yield?

25.10 Drake Motors has the following balance sheet and income statement:

Balance Sheet

Total assets	$2,500,000	Total debt	$1,000,000
		Shareholders' equity	1,500,000
		Total liabilities and shareholders' equity	$2,500,000

Income Statement

Sales	$5,000,000
Cost of goods sold	3,500,000
Gross margin	1,500,000
Operating expenses	900,000
EBIT	600,000
Interest	100,000
EBT	500,000
Income taxes (40%)	200,000
Net income	$ 300,000

a. If Drake has 50,000 shares of common stock outstanding, determine its present (1) total debt to total assets, (2) return on total assets, (3) return on equity, and (4) earnings per share.

b. Drake Motors is considering whether to renovate one of its existing plants by making an additional $1 million investment in total assets. The renovation will reduce the cost of goods sold by $300,000 per year, whichever plan is adopted. Two possible plans have been considered for financing the renovation. Plan I keeps the existing ratio of total debt to total assets and requires 20,000 additional shares of common stock to be issued; the new level of *total* interest paid is $150,000 per year. Plan II employs all-debt financing, no common stock is issued, and the new level of *total* interest is $225,000 per year.

1. Determine total debt to total assets, return on total assets, return on equity, and earnings per share under plans I and II.
2. Based on your analysis, do you think Drake Motors should renovate the plant? If yes, should plan I or plan II be used?

25.11 Mini Case Accounting information for Corning Inc. for 3 recent years is as follows:

Income Statement (in millions)

	For Fiscal Year		
	−2	−1	0
Sales	$2,301.5	$2,575.9	$3,049.6
Cost of goods sold	1,405.2	1,600.9	1,925.7
Selling, general, and administrative expenses	438.6	491.8	581.8
Research and development	95.2	109.6	124.5
Other expense (−) or income (+)	−7.6	+48.8	+64.5
Interest	41.0	44.5	54.0
Taxes	103.2	116.9	136.1
Net income	$ 210.7	$ 261.0	$ 292. 0

Balance Sheet (in millions)

	−2	−1	0
Assets			
Current assets			
Cash and marketable securities	$ 156.5	$ 352.8	$ 133.0
Accounts receivable	397.5	452.4	527.2
Inventory	254.0	238.5	314.5
Other	121.8	125.6	123.2
Total current assets	929.8	1,169.3	1,097.9
Long-term assets			
Net property, plant, and equipment	991.5	1,160.6	1,351.8
Investments	818.3	826.0	804.5
Other	158.3	204.8	257.8
Total long-term assets	1,968.1	2,191.4	2,414.1
Total assets	$2,897.9	$3,360.7	$3,512.0
Liabilities and Shareholders' Equity			
Current liabilities			
Accounts payable	$ 125.1	$ 158.6	$ 191.5
Short-term debt	18.5	40.4	52.8
Other	365.1	483.0	395.2
Total current liabilities	508.7	682.0	639.5

Liabilities and Shareholders' Equity, Continued

Long-term liabilities

Long-term debt	499.0	624.5	611.2
Deferred taxes	71.0	53.1	72.8
Other	258.5	258.3	307.5
Total long-term liabilities	828.5	935.9	991.5

Shareholders' equity

Convertible preferred stock	0	31.6	30.7
Common stock	233.8	255.5	139.6
Retained earnings	1,275.5	1,436.4	1,640.6
Currency translation adjustment	51.4	19.3	70.1
Total shareholders' equity	1,560.7	1,742.8	1,881.0
Total liabilities and shareholders' equity	$2,897.9	$3,360.7	$3,512.0

Other information

Shares of common stock (in millions)	88.86	94.22	91.85
Dividends paid on common stock (in millions)	$86.0	$99.7	$85.3
Common stock price range	$34\frac{7}{8}$–$22\frac{1}{2}$	$49\frac{3}{8}$–$32	$51\frac{3}{4}$–$34\frac{7}{8}$

a. Accounting statements are prepared based on a set of generally accepted accounting principles, GAAP. What are some of the key ideas underlying GAAP that influence all accounting statements? What is the significance of these assumptions for an analyst examining a firm's accounting statements?

b. Prepare common-size income statements and balance sheets for Corning for the last three years.

c. Now calculate ratios for the firm. (*Note:* Because lease expenses are not available, do not calculate fixed charges coverage. Also, for the market ratios, take an average of the high and low stock prices for the per share market price.)

d. What trends are evident from the analysis?

e. What additional information would be helpful in completing the analysis?

f. What limitations exist with any analysis of this type?

REFERENCES

BALL, BEN C., JR. "The Mysterious Disappearance of Retained Earnings." *Harvard Business Review* 65 (July–August 1987): 56–63.

DEBERG, CURTIS L., and BROCK MURDOCH. "The Immateriality of Primary EPS: What the Data Reveal." *Financial Analysts Journal* 47 (September/October 1991): 91–95.

FOSTER, GEORGE. *Financial Statement Analysis,* 2nd ed. Englewood Cliffs, N.J.: Prentice-Hall, 1986.

GOMBOLA, MICHAEL J., and J. EDWARD KETZ. "Financial Ratio Patterns in Retail and Manufacturing Organizations." *Financial Management* 12 (Summer 1983): 45–56.

HELFERT, ERICH A. *Techniques of Financial Analysis,* 7th ed. Homewood, Ill.: Irwin, 1991.

KAPLAN, ROBERT S., and DAVID P. NORTON. "The Balanced Scorecard—Measures that Drive Performance." *Harvard Business Review* 70 (January–February 1992): 71–79.

PINCHES, GEORGE E., KENT A. MINGO, and J. KENT CARUTHERS. "The Stability of Financial Patterns in Industrial Organizations." *Journal of Finance* 28 (May 1973): 389–96.

WARFIELD, TERRY D., and JOHN J. WILD. "Accounting Recognition and the Relevance of Earnings as an Explanatory Variable for Return." *Accounting Review* 67 (October 1992): 821–42.

26
Financial Planning and Forecasting

EXECUTIVE SUMMARY

The primary means of forecasting cash flows relies on the cash budget, which includes all operating, investment, and financing cash inflows and outflows. The cash budget may be supplemented by pro forma statements. The usefulness of cash forecasts depends on accurate sales forecasts. Yet the future is inherently uncertain. Cash forecasting must therefore include the ability to ask alternative questions. Accurate, yet flexible, forecasts are a valuable tool in financial management.

There is no model or theory that leads directly to the optimum financial and strategic plan. Consequently, the process involves trial and error. In the short run, the emphasis is primarily on the acquisition or investment of short-term funds. In the longer run the emphasis is on the long-term investment, financing, and strategy of the firm. Inherent in the financial planning process is the consideration and evaluation of various options (to expand, shut down, secure different kinds of financing, and so forth) that are available to the firm.

CASH FLOW ANALYSIS

Although accounting statements, as examined in Chapter 25, are prepared at least yearly for all firms, they do not directly tell us about the firm's past or expected cash flows, or about what actions should be taken to maximize the market value of the firm. Figure 26.1 shows that a firm's cash inflows arise from its operations (sales and collection of receivables), its investments in securities or subsidiaries, and its financing through bonds and stock or taking out loans. The firm's outflows, also shown in Figure 26.1, go to its operations (materials, wages and salaries, rent, taxes, etc.), to meeting its short-term financial management and long-term investment needs, and to

Figure 26.1

Sources of Cash Inflows and Outflows

Inflows will not equal outflows over any period of time except by chance. The excess of inflows (outflows) over outflows (inflows) results in an increase (decrease) in the firm's cash account.

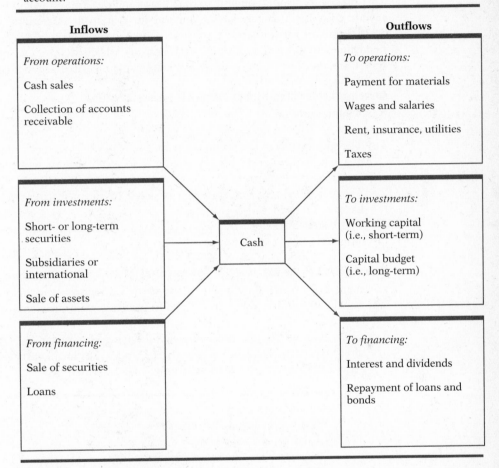

Inflows		Outflows

From operations:

Cash sales

Collection of accounts receivable

From investments:

Short- or long-term securities

Subsidiaries or international

Sale of assets

From financing:

Sale of securities

Loans

Cash

To operations:

Payment for materials

Wages and salaries

Rent, insurance, utilities

Taxes

To investments:

Working capital (i.e., short-term)

Capital budget (i.e., long-term)

To financing:

Interest and dividends

Repayment of loans and bonds

its financing needs through the payment of interest and dividends, and the repayment of loans and bonds.

STATEMENT OF CHANGES IN FINANCIAL POSITION

In recognition of the importance of cash flows, a **statement of changes in financial position**[1] must be reported along with a firm's balance sheet and income statement. The purpose of the statement of changes in financial position (SCFP) is to explain

---

[1] CICA *Handbook*, Section 1540, "Statement of Changes in Financial Position," October 1, 1985.

changes in a firm's liquid assets or cash equivalents (i.e., cash and marketable securities net of bank loans) over a year. The statement of changes for Loblaw is shown in Table 26.1.[2] Note two items: (1) The statement is broken into three basic categories—operating activities, investing activities, and financing activities; and (2) due to the way most firms present their SCFP, the specific accounts shown in Table 26.1 do not correspond directly to the inflows and outflows shown in Figure 26.1. We see that Loblaw generated $329 million in cash from operations in 1994, used $325.3 million for investment activities, had a net outflow of $32.7 million in its financing activities, and paid $27.4 million in cash dividends. The net result was a $56.4 million decrease in the cash and marketable securities account during the year.

Advantages of the Statement of Changes in Financial Position   The SCFP is helpful for the following reasons:

1. The specific focus on the three separate activities of operations, investments, and financing is beneficial. This is especially so given that these are the three main functions of all firms.
2. The statement removes the effect of accruals, and it restates such items as collectibles or salaries on a cash basis.
3. The statement breaks out gross, as opposed to net, figures for such items as long-term debt transactions.

Disadvantages of the Statement of Changes in Financial Position   At the same time, the statement does not fully convert all items to cash flows, and it introduces some additional confusion in other areas. The statement's main problems are:

1. The operating activities part of the SCFP can be presented in one of two ways: the direct approach or the indirect approach. Under the direct approach the operating activities portion of the statement might be presented as:

Operating activities	
Collections from customers	$ 600,000
Payments to suppliers	(300,000)
Payments to employees for salaries	(180,000)
Payments to creditors for interest	(15,000)
Miscellaneous payments	(10,000)
Payments for taxes	(20,000)
Net cash flow provided by operating activities	$ 75,000

The indirect approach starts from the firm's net income and then makes adjustments as needed. Comparing the direct approach (above) for determining the cash flow from operating activities with the indirect approach used by Loblaw and

---

[2] Additional data, not reflected explicitly in a firm's published income statement and balance sheet, are required to reproduce a firm's published SCFP. This topic is covered in financial accounting books, such as Horngren, Sundem, Elliott, and Thornton (1995).

Table 26.1

Statement of Changes in Financial Position for Loblaw Companies Ltd. (in millions)

Loblaw uses the indirect method for presenting its SCFP. Many other firms also use this method, even though the direct method provides more useful cash flow information.

	1994	1993	1992
Operations			
Net earnings	$126.7	$ 93.4	$ 79.8
Depreciation	134.7	122.4	115.7
Gain on sale of fixed assets	(1.7)	(0.9)	(0.7)
Deferred income taxes	11.6	11.6	(4.0)
Other	2.3	3.4	14.4
	273.6	229.9	205.2
Provided from working capital	55.4	51.9	68.1
Cash flow from operations	329.0	281.8	273.3
Investment			
Purchase of fixed assets	338.7	(314.6)	(198.1)
Acquisitions	—	—	(48.9)
Proceeds from sale of fixed assets	17.3	4.5	10.2
Net (increase) decrease in other items	(3.9)	(29.5)	22.4
	(325.3)	(339.6)	(214.4)
Net cash (out) in before financing dividends	3.7	(57.8)	58.9
Financing			
Long-term debt: Borrowings	3.0	205.2	16.5
Repayments	(40.0)	(28.2)	(34.9)
Capital Stock: Issued	4.7	5.3	4.6
Retired	(0.4)	(38.4)	(56.2)
Other	—	5.7	—
	(32.7)	149.6	(70.0)
Dividends	(27.4)	(27.9)	(34.3)
INCREASE (DECREASE) IN CASH	(56.4)	63.9	(45.4)
Cash at beginning of period	271.9	208.0	253.4
CASH AT THE END OF PERIOD[a]	$215.5	$271.9	$208.0

[a] Cash is defined as cash and short-term investments net of bank advances and notes payable.

shown in Table 26.1, we see that the direct approach provides much more useful information in terms of determining the sources and uses of cash from operations. Although the CICA allows either method, most firms have adopted the indirect method. This choice reduces the usability of the SCFP.

2. The statement does not reconcile the differences between taxes as reported on the firm's income statement with what was actually paid.

3. The statement permits but does not require separate disclosure of the cash flows associated with discontinued operations and extraordinary items.
4. Noncash investing and financing activities (such as capital leases, debt/equity swaps, and asset exchanges) are not included on the statement. They are simply reported in a supplemental statement or in narrative form.
5. Interest or dividends received by the firm, as well as interest paid, are treated as operating activities; however, dividends paid by the firm are treated as a financing activity. This inconsistency in treatment is, at best, misleading.

The SCFP is a step in the right direction, but it has one other disadvantage—it only reports what has happened in the past. Although firms can only react to whatever cash flows occur, most plan for the future by estimating inflows and outflows. To do this, firms use cash budgets and pro forma statements.

CASH BUDGETS

An important part of the forecasting process is the development of the firm's **cash budget**, which is just a detailed statement of the expected inflows and outflows. Cash budgets can be estimated for any period of time—often a month, a quarter, or a year. These budgets serve two purposes: First, they alert the firm to future cash needs or surpluses. Second, they provide a standard against which subsequent performance can be judged.

In preparing a cash budget, it is necessary to include all inflows and outflows expected by the firm. Thus, a detailed analysis of past cash flows is needed. Although the future cannot be expected to be exactly like the past, a thorough examination of past cash flow trends is the first step in effective cash flow forecasting by means of cash budgets.

The major items to be considered when estimating a cash budget are the following:

Cash Inflows	Cash Outflows
Cash sales	Cash purchases
Collection of accounts receivable	Payment of accounts payable
Income from investments	Wages and salaries
Income from subsidiaries	Rent, insurance, and utilities
Dividends from international ventures	Advertising, selling, and other related cash expenses
Sale of assets	Taxes (local, provincial, federal, and international)
Sale of securities	Capital investments
Loans	Interest and dividends
	Repayment of loans

A six-step procedure can be used to develop a cash budget:

1. Develop a scenario with an explicit set of assumptions.
2. Estimate sales.

3. Determine the cash inflows expected from operations.
4. Calculate the cash outflows expected to arise from operations.
5. Estimate any other expected cash inflows and outflows.
6. Determine the expected financing needed or surplus available.

Developing Different Scenarios The first step in developing a cash budget is to determine the assumed conditions, or the scenario the cash budget is to cover. Because we are dealing with the future, which is uncertain, this is an important step. Assumptions concerning the state of the economy, competitors' actions, conditions in the financial markets, and similar factors need to be spelled out in detail to set the stage for the rest of the analysis. Then another set of assumptions can be specified and the analysis redone to see the impact on the firm's cash flow position. This process is often called *scenario analysis*. Its purpose is to see how sensitive cash flows are to changes in the input data (or assumptions).

It is far better to allow for a range of outcomes than to rely on a single estimate. A firm that develops only a single estimate is likely to be caught short if there is a large deviation from the expected outcome. Likewise, managers can determine which estimates have the most impact on the firm's expected cash flows; then they can spend more time and money, if necessary, trying to improve these estimates. Finally, the longer the planning period, the more important the analysis of a number of sets of assumptions becomes. By doing these analyses, managers can gain an understanding of the possible consequences different events could have on the firm's cash inflows and outflows.

Forecasting Sales The key element in developing an accurate cash budget is the sales forecast, which provides the basis for determining the size and timing of many of the forecasted cash inflows and outflows. The sales forecast can be based on an internal or an external analysis. The following are some forecasting techniques and their strengths and weaknesses:

Method	Time Period (Short, Medium, Long)	Accuracy	Reflects Changing Conditions?
Internal			
Linear regression	S, M	Depends	No
Sales force composite	S, M	Depends	Yes
Time series	S, M, L	Often highly accurate	Yes, but often slow
External			
Market survey	M, L	Depends	Yes
Multivariate regression	S, M, L	Depends	Yes, if built in

Three popular internal methods are linear regression, sales force composite, and time series analysis. Linear regression takes past sales and projects them into the future without any adjustment. The sales force composite method bases expected sales on estimates provided by sales personnel and the firm's marketing department.

Consistency of forecasts is a major concern when the sales force composite method is employed. Forecasted sales might be the sum of separate forecasts made by managers of many of the firm's units. Left to their own devices, these managers will make different assumptions about inflation, growth in the economy, growth in market share, and so forth. Therefore, some method of maintaining consistent assumptions is crucial for the accuracy of the sales force composite method. Finally, time series models are available for forecasting expected sales based on past sales. These methods require more statistical expertise, but they are often best for generating accurate forecasts based on past data.

An external sales forecast, on the other hand, starts with factors outside the firm. This could be done by contracting with a firm to do a market research study or contacting other firms like Data Resources or Chase Econometrics, which specialize in preparing macroeconomic and industry forecasts. A statistical model that relates the firm's past sales to the projected level of gross domestic product, automobile sales, or whatever is most relevant might also be developed. Most firms use a variety of methods for forecasting sales. Whatever method is used, firms often start the forecast on a divisional basis in order to obtain better accuracy. Once the divisional forecasts are made, they are combined into an overall forecast of expected sales.

Linear Regression and Forecasting   Assume that in order to forecast sales we use linear regression plus information obtained from a sales force composite approach. Bartley Instruments, a robot components firm, begins with an analysis of its past sales (see Figure 26.2). Simple linear regression techniques can be used to forecast sales naively simply by extrapolating the past trend in sales. Sales is the dependent variable (indicated by Y), and time is the independent variable (designated by X). The regression model to be estimated, ignoring the residual error term, is

$$Y_t = \alpha + \beta X_t \tag{26.1}$$

where

Y_t = the forecasted sales in time period t
α = alpha, the intercept of the fitted regression equation
β = beta, the slope of the fitted regression equation
X_t = the time period

This method is easy to employ. Let us use the data from Figure 26.2 and forecast Bartley's 19X9 sales. The historical sales are as follows:

Year	Sales (Y_t) (in millions)	Period (X_t)
19X3	$2.10	1
19X4	1.85	2
19X5	3.00	3
19X6	2.90	4
19X7	4.05	5
19X8	4.15	6

Figure 26.2

Projected Sales for Bartley Instruments

Bartley has experienced slow but reasonably steady growth since 19X4. The 19X9 projection assumes an "average" rate of growth—slightly higher than last year, but lower than the year before that.

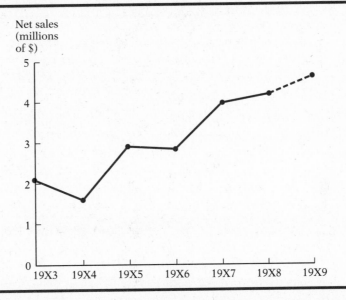

The time periods are converted to 1 for the first year through 6 for 19X8. The exact procedure, the formulas employed, and the calculations are shown in Table 26.2. Based on this, the estimated regression equation is

$$Y_t = \$1.332 + \$0.479X_t$$

Because we want to forecast sales for 19X9, which is period 7, we substitute as follows:

$$19X9 \text{ forecasted sales} = \$1.332 + \$0.479(7)$$
$$= \$1.332 + \$3.353 = \$4.685 \text{ million}$$

If we wanted to forecast the subsequent year's sales, the same procedure would be employed, except the time period would be 8, resulting in forecasted sales of $5.164 million.

This approach is simple and inexpensive to implement. For a firm (or divisions of a firm) in a stable environment, it may provide a reasonable degree of accuracy. Because it ignores any factor *not* captured by a simple linear extrapolation of past sales, however, it can be misleading. Thus, influences of changes in the business cycle on the sales of the firm are ignored. This is why other forecasting techniques and management expertise are needed when forecasting sales.

Based on simple linear regression, Bartley's 19X9 estimated sales are $4.685 million. This information is supplemented by the sales force composite forecast, along

Table 26.2

Estimated Regression Equation to Forecast Sales of Bartley Instruments

Linear regression provides a simple means of projecting sales; however, because it is based solely on past sales, it ignores any other factors (such as the state of the economy) that may influence actual sales.

	Sales (Y_t) (1)	Period (X_t) (2)	$Y_t X_t$ (1)(2) (3)	X_t^2 (2)^2 (4)
	2.10	1	2.10	1
	1.85	2	3.70	4
	3.00	3	9.00	9
	2.90	4	11.60	16
	4.05	5	20.25	25
	4.15	6	24.90	36
Totals	18.05	21	71.55	91

Means

$$\bar{Y} = \Sigma Y_t/n = 18.05/6 = 3.008$$
$$\bar{X} = \Sigma X_t/n = 21/6 = 3.50$$

Calculation of β (slope)

$$\beta = \frac{\Sigma Y_t X_t - (n)(\bar{Y})(\bar{X})}{\Sigma X_t^2 - n(\bar{X}^2)}$$

$$= \frac{71.550 - (6)(3.008)(3.50)}{91 - (6)(3.50^2)} = \frac{71.550 - 63.168}{91 - 73.500} = 0.479$$

Calculation of α (intercept)

$$\alpha = \bar{Y} - \beta\bar{X} = 3.008 - (0.479)(3.50) = 1.332$$
$$Y_t = \$1.332 + \$0.479X_t$$

with what Bartley knows about the actions of the competition and the estimated performance of the economy in the next year. Based on this analysis, Bartley arrives at an estimate of sales of $4.5 million.

Bartley is interested in both the expected level and the potential variability of sales. If the expected variability is small, then Bartley will have more confidence in its forecast. In that event, its operating plans can be relatively simple. If the sales forecasts are not so solid, then Bartley will want to build a lot of flexibility into its plans and to monitor trends closely.

Cash Inflow From Operations   Once sales have been estimated, we can determine expected cash inflows. Because most firms sell (at least in part) on credit, the pattern of

Table 26.3

Estimated Cash Inflows From Operations for Bartley Instruments (in thousands)

With a lag in the collection of accounts receivable, the cash inflow from sales ends up being less volatile than the sales pattern.

	February	March	April	May	June	July	August
1. Total sales	$200.00	$300.00	$430.00	$500.00	$440.00	$400.00	$300.00
2. Collections—1-month lag (42% of total sales)		84.00	126.00	180.60	210.00	184.80	168.00
3. Collections—2-month lag (28% of total sales)			56.00	84.00	120.40	140.00	123.20
4. Total collections (row 2 + row 3)			182.00	264.60	330.40	324.80	291.20
5. Cash sales (30% of total sales)			129.00	150.00	132.00	120.00	90.00
6. Total operating cash inflows			$311.00	$414.60	$462.40	$444.80	$381.20

collections must be examined. First, Bartley "distributes" its estimated sales over the months of the year. This may be done by using a historical percentage of the sales that occur each month. For example, assume that February has historically accounted for 4.4 percent of total yearly sales. The estimated February sales are then $(0.044)(\$4.5 \text{ million}) \approx \$200,000$. The estimated monthly sales for February through August are shown in Table 26.3.

Bartley knows that 30 percent of its sales are cash sales, and the remaining are credit sales. The collection of sales made on credit is estimated to occur as follows: 42 percent of total sales are credit sales that will be collected in the month following the sale; the remaining 28 percent are credit sales that will be collected two months after the sales are made. For simplicity, we assume that there are no bad debts. In April, Bartley's sales are $430,000, of which $129,000 are for cash. In addition, Bartley expects to collect 28 percent of the sales made two months ago ($56,000), and 42 percent of last month's sales, for another $126,000. The operating cash inflows are estimated to be $311,000, which is substantially less than April's expected sales of $430,000. This difference is due to the delayed receipt of cash because of credit sales.

Cash Outflow From Operations   Next comes the forecast of expected cash outflows from operations. This begins with an estimate of the materials and related supplies needed in the production process. For Bartley, this figure is estimated to be 40 percent of expected sales, with the purchases made two months ahead of the anticipated sale. Of these purchases, Bartley pays cash for 20 percent, and the other 80 percent becomes an account payable. Bartley has a policy of paying all accounts payable in the month after they arise. In April, Bartley has total purchases of $176,000 (0.40 times June's expected sales of $440,000), of which $35,200 are for cash (see Table 26.4). In addition, $160,000 in accounts payable from the preceding month must be paid.

Table 26.4

Estimated Cash Outflows From Operations for Bartley Instruments (in thousands)

Many different classifications of cash outflows from operations can be employed. Which specific ones are most appropriate depends on the firm making the cash forecast.

	March	April	May	June	July	August
1. Total purchases (40% of expected sales; purchased 2 months ahead)	$200.00	$176.00	$160.00	$120.00	$100.00	$ 80.00
2. Credit purchases (80% of total purchases)	160.00	140.80	128.00	96.00	80.00	64.00
3. Payment of credit purchases (1-month lag)		160.00	140.80	128.00	96.00	80.00
4. Cash purchases (20% of current month's total purchases)		35.20	32.00	24.00	20.00	16.00
5. Wages, rent, selling, and other cash expenses[a]		146.30	186.00	188.80	168.00	145.50
6. Interest[a]		8.00	32.00	8.00	8.00	32.00
7. Taxes[a]		40.00	5.00	30.00	5.00	5.00
8. Total operating cash outflow (row 3 + row 4 + row 5 + row 6 + row 7)		$389.50	$395.80	$378.80	$297.00	$278.50

[a] As estimated by the firm based on past and expected trends.

Bartley also has other cash outflows related to operations. For simplicity, these can be broken into three categories: The first is wages, rent, selling, and other cash outflows. The other two are interest and taxes. The reason for breaking out the last two separately is that they may vary from month to month. Total expected cash outflows related to operations are $389,500 in April.

Other Cash Inflows or Outflows Once all cash flows from operations are determined, we can turn our attention to other possible inflows or outflows. Bartley has two other expected inflows and three other expected outflows. The inflows are from the sale of assets and cash dividends received from a small foreign subsidiary. The outflows arise from the payment of cash dividends, repayment of a loan, and from capital investments. After all these other inflows and outflows are estimated, they are netted to produce the following monthly figures (in thousands):

	April	May	June	July	August
Net other inflow (+) or outflow (−)	−$45.00	−$98.00	−$55.00	−$95.00	$52.00

Table 26.5

Net Cash Flow and Financing Needed or Surplus Available for Bartley Instruments (in thousands)

Note that row 1 in the bottom part of the table—cash and marketable securities at start of period—is carried over as the previous month's end-of-period cash figure from row 3.

	April	May	June	July	August
Calculating Net Cash Inflow or Outflow					
1. Total operating cash inflow	$311.00	$414.60	$462.40	$444.80	$381.20
2. Total operating cash outflow	− 389.50	− 395.80	− 378.80	− 297.00	− 278.50
3. Other net inflow (+) or outflow (−)	− 45.00	− 98.00	− 55.00	− 95.00	+ 52.00
4. Net cash inflow (+) or outflow (−) (row 1 + row 2 + row 3)	−$123.50	−$ 79.20	$ 28.60	$ 52.80	$154.70
Calculating Short-Term Financing Needed					
1. Cash and marketable securities at start of period	$ 70.00	−$ 53.50	−$132.70	−$104.10	−$ 51.30
2. Change in cash balance (net cash inflow or outflow)	− 123.50	− 79.20	28.60	52.80	154.70
3. Cash at end of period (row 1 + row 2)	− 53.50	− 132.70	− 104.10	− 51.30	103.40
4. Minimum cash balance required	− 20.00	− 20.00	− 20.00	− 20.00	− 20.00
5. Cumulative short-term financing needed (−) or surplus (+) (row 3 + row 4)	−$ 73.50	−$152.70	−$124.10	−$ 71.30	$ 83.40

THE CASH BUDGET

Once we know all anticipated cash inflows and outflows, we can determine the expected net cash inflow or outflow each month to see if additional financing will be needed. As shown in the top part of Table 26.5, Bartley is projecting that total cash outflows will exceed total cash inflows by $123,500 in April. The bottom part of the table shows that Bartley has $70,000 cash on hand on April 1 and a minimum cash balance of $20,000 that it needs to maintain. This results in an estimated final cash position of −$73,500 at the end of April.

In Table 26.5, we see that Bartley has a negative cumulative expected cash position for the months of April, May, June, and July. In August the expected cash position is positive. The worst month is May, when the cash position is estimated to be −$152,700. Obviously, Bartley must do something—cut production, reduce other expenses, increase collections, or secure short- or long-term financing to cover the expected shortfall. Armed with the information obtained from the cash budget, Bartley can plan for the future. If borrowing is planned, the lender can be notified and appropriate plans made. When excess cash is available, its investment can be planned. But the basis for borrowing or investment decisions is the firm's expected cash position as estimated by its cash budget.

Concept Review Questions

- Explain why the statement of changes in financial position is broken down into three basic categories.
- Discuss the procedures used to develop a firm's cash budget.
- Describe and explain different methods a firm may employ to forecast sales.

FORECASTING IN PRACTICE

SCENARIO ANALYSIS

Although forecasting techniques can be implemented by hand, most firms, large and small, are turning to computerized approaches, often employing spreadsheets like Lotus 1–2–3® or Excel. This forecasting process might involve the firm, and its divisions, preparing three different forecasts, or scenarios—a best case, a most likely (or normal) case, and a worst case.

Assume that the forecast and cash budget for Bartley Instruments that we developed in the last two sections was for the normal case. Then we need to develop a best-case scenario, along with a worst-case scenario. In forecasting the best-case scenario, we need to be aware of the problems caused by high growth. As firms grow, their sales increase. Because most firms sell on credit, at least in part, the firm will need to finance a larger amount of accounts receivable. Likewise, larger inventory levels will be necessary. As growth continues, the firm will need to expand its plant and facilities, requiring additional investment in long-term assets. The funding for some of these increased needs can be provided by increased accounts payable, which will also grow with the firm. The rest, however, has to come from two main sources—internally generated funds that are not paid out to the shareholders, and new external financing.

High rates of growth may put a firm in a cash bind. This occurs because it cannot finance the rapid cash needs with internally generated funds. As one step, most high-growth firms have low or zero cash dividend payouts. In addition, they build financial slack into the planning process. The ultimate solution to the cash needs of a growing firm is to acquire additional financing in the form of long-term debt, or additional common stock financing. However, many firms follow a "pecking order" approach to financing (see Chapters 13 and 14) and have a strong aversion to issuing additional common stock. In such a case, the growth of the firm may be constrained, or the firm may have to adopt a higher than desired debt/equity ratio. Thus, although growth is generally desirable, it places a strain on the cash needs of the firm that must be planned for. Failure to do this planning is one of the primary shortcomings of many growing firms.

Likewise, problems may arise if the worst-case scenario occurs. In the worst case, both sales and cash inflows fall, but often cash outflows do not fall as fast. This is especially true if the firm has many fixed cash outflows (as opposed to variable cash outflows) that do not fall as sales and cash inflows fall. The net result may be that in the very short run problems are not too bad, but they get worse and worse unless the firm takes drastic actions to cut fixed cash outflows. Realistic forecasting of both the best- and worst-case scenarios may expose potential cash flow problems, but the causes and remedies are very different in the two cases.

SEASONALITY

One problem that often arises in practice is how to forecast for periods shorter than a year, during which the firm experiences seasonal patterns in its cash flows. Let us assume we have 12 quarters of past sales data as follows:

	1	2	3	4
Year −3	$X_1 = 193$	228	237	234
Year −2	245	229	324	309
Year −1	301	358	373	$X_{12} = 356$

(Note that the sales figure for the first quarter of year −3 is labelled X_1, and so on.) Our task is to use the data from the three years to forecast the next eight quarterly sales figures. We begin by plotting the data as in Figure 26.3. In looking at it, we see a definite upward trend in the sales data, and it appears there is some seasonality also.

Figure 26.3

Quarterly Sales for 12 Quarters

Visual examination of quarterly sales indicates an upward trend in sales and also suggests a seasonal pattern.

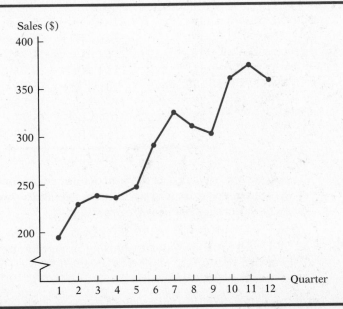

First we employ linear regression to forecast sales for each of the next eight quarters. The data are as follows:

Sales (Y_t)	Period, (X_t)
$193	1
228	2
237	3
234	4
245	5
289	6
324	7
309	8
301	9
358	10
373	11
356	12

Employing the same approach discussed previously, we find that the resulting linear regression equation is

$$\text{sales} = \alpha + \beta X_t = \$184.816 + \$15.759 X_t$$

Because we have 12 periods of data for estimating the regression equation, the forecasted sales, quarter-by-quarter for the next 8 periods (or two years), are:

Period	Forecasted Sales
13	$184.816 + $15.759(13) = $390
14	184.816 + 15.759(14) = 405
15	184.816 + 15.759(15) = 421
16	184.816 + 15.759(16) = 437
17	184.816 + 15.759(17) = 453
18	184.816 + 15.759(18) = 468
19	184.816 + 15.759(19) = 484
20	184.816 + 15.759(20) = 500

Now we have obtained an estimate of future sales, but we have ignored seasonality. If we assume that past seasonal patterns are likely to continue, we can determine quarterly seasonal adjustment factors as follows:

STEP 1:   Determine a 4-quarter moving average for the first four actual observations. Note that because the number of observations is even, the average is for 2.5 quarters (halfway between quarter 2 and quarter 3).

STEP 2: Move down one observation and determine a second 4-quarter moving average. That is, drop the first observation and pick up the fifth observation. This second 4-quarter moving average is centred halfway between quarters 3 and 4.

STEP 3: Average the two consecutive 4-quarter moving averages from steps 1 and 2. This centred moving average is now correctly positioned at quarter 3.

STEP 4: Repeat steps 1 through 3, moving down one observation at a time.

The resulting calculations for the 12 quarters are as follows:

Period	Actual Value (1)	4-Quarter Moving Average (2)	Centred 4-Quarter Moving Average (3)	Ratio of Actual to Centred 4-Quarter Moving Average (1)/(3) (4)
1	$193			
2	228			
		223.00		
3	237		229.500	1.033
		236.00		
4	234		243.625	0.960
		251.25		
5	245		262.125	0.935
		273.00		
6	289		282.375	1.023
		291.75		
7	324		298.750	1.085
		305.75		
8	309		314.375	0.983
		323.00		
9	301		329.125	0.915
		335.25		
10	358		341.125	1.049
		347.00		
11	373			
12	356			

Note that because we are using a 4-quarter moving average, it is impossible to calculate any seasonal indices (i.e., column 4 above) for the first two or the last two quarters.

The next step is to assign the seasonal indices to their respective quarters:

	Quarter				
	1	2	3	4	Total
Year −3			1.033	0.960	
Year −2	0.935	1.023	1.085	0.983	
Year −1	0.915	1.049	—	—	
Total	1.850	2.072	2.118	1.943	
Average	0.925	1.036	1.059	0.972	3.992

If we had more observations—at least five for each quarter—it would be helpful to drop the high and the low values (per quarter) at this point. Because we have only two, however, we will keep all the data. The sum of the average seasonal coefficients should total 4.000 because there are 4 quarters; instead, in this example it sums to only 3.992. To determine an adjusted quarterly seasonal index we proceed as follows:

Adjusted Seasonal Index	
Quarter 1:	$(0.925)(4.000/3.992) = 0.927$
Quarter 2:	$(1.036)(4.000/3.992) = 1.038$
Quarter 3:	$(1.059)(4.000/3.992) = 1.061$
Quarter 4:	$(0.972)(4.000/3.992) = 0.974$
Total	4.000

Using the adjusted seasonal indices is easy: All we do is multiply the adjusted seasonal indices times the previously estimated forecasts. The original and seasonally adjusted forecasted sales are as follows:

Period	Forecasted Sales Based on Linear Regression (1)	Seasonal Adjustment Factor (2)	Seasonally Adjusted Forecasted Sales (1)(2) (3)
13	$390	0.927	$362
14	405	1.038	420
15	421	1.061	447
16	437	0.974	426
17	453	0.927	420
18	468	1.038	486
19	484	1.061	514
20	500	0.974	487

Because sales are seasonally higher in the second and third quarters, seasonally adjusting the simple linear regression forecasts results in substantially higher forecasted sales in those quarters, with lower forecasted sales in the first and fourth quarters. Both the unadjusted and seasonally adjusted forecasts are shown in Figure 26.4. Seasonal adjusting is very important in practice and improves many forecasts, provided there is some fairly consistent seasonal pattern to the firm's sales.[3]

---

[3] The same basic procedures would be employed with monthly data, except that 12-month moving averages would be employed.

Figure 26.4

Fitted Regression Equation and Forecasted Quarterly Sales, With and Without Seasonal Adjustment

Adjusting for seasonality can materially increase or decrease per quarter sales as compared to a forecast based on simple linear regression.

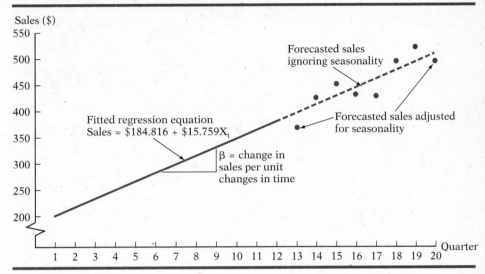

INFLATION

Inflation can have a profound impact on the cash flows of the firm. The whole forecasting process must be reexamined in times of rapid changes in the inflation rate. Very different strategies may be necessary during periods of rapid inflation, because the firm may not be able (or want) to pass on the effects of inflation to its customers. The presence of inflation also causes suppliers of funds to change strategies to protect themselves from its effect. They may provide only variable-rate financing, in which the interest rate charged on a bond or loan is adjusted over time. Many banks lend primarily on a variable-rate basis. All these factors, and many more, make the cash flow estimation process more difficult. The consequence is to reduce the reliability of the forecast, which makes close monitoring and evaluation of various scenarios even more important.

Effective management is enhanced by the development of cash budgets, which help managers plan and control. Once the cash budget is determined, many firms employ a **rolling forecast** that is updated every week, month, or quarter. But some care is in order. First, cash budgets are based on a set of specific assumptions—from the sales forecast on. Because events will differ in the future, the ability to do scenario analysis is essential. Second, cash needs may fluctuate *within* the budgeting period. Even though there may be plenty of cash on hand by the end of the period, different inflow and outflow patterns may leave the firm short of cash within the period.

Concept Review Questions

■ Describe how to incorporate seasonal patterns in a firm's forecasted sales.

■ What is the impact of inflation on a firm's forecasted sales?

PRO FORMA ACCOUNTING STATEMENTS

Pro forma statements project the firm's expected revenues, expenses, and position at the end of a forecast period.[4] Although less detailed than cash budgets, these forecasts are often required by current and prospective lenders. There are two basic approaches to developing pro forma statements:

1. One approach takes as its input the projections arising from the cash budget. These projections are then modified to account for differences between the firm's cash flows and its GAAP accounting data.
2. The second is the **percentage of sales method**, which starts with the historical relationship of sales to various income statement and balance sheet items. Pro forma statements and financing needs or surpluses are then estimated. This procedure may be naive if it assumes that all the firm's costs are variable and vary directly with sales. In practice, some costs are fixed; therefore, judgment is employed when estimating how some expenses are expected to change.

We use the percentage of sales method to estimate financing needs based on pro forma statements. Note that because pro forma statements start with accounting data, this method may not be as precise as a cash budgeting approach to projecting cash flows and financing needs. However, its simplicity and its focus on the impact on reported accounting statements may make it a supplement to the more elaborate cash budgeting process. Also, banks often require pro forma statements as part of a loan agreement. We will use Smith Products, a manufacturer of specialty tools, to illustrate the use of proforma statements. Smith begins by making its best estimate of next year's sales, which is $22 million. If sales are substantially higher or lower than the estimate, the pro forma statements will be off.

PRO FORMA INCOME STATEMENT

The next step is to estimate the historical relationship of expenses to sales for Smith. This is done by dividing Smith's income statement categories—cost of goods sold; selling, general, and administrative expenses; interest expenses; taxes; and cash dividends—by sales. If we use this information directly in a naive manner, Smith Products' estimated, or pro forma, income statement is as shown in Table 26.6. Based on this approach, Smith Products would expect net income to be $924,000; with projected cash dividends of $330,000, $594,000 would be shown as a transfer from the income

---

[4] Pro forma statements can also be constructed for some past period. Comparison with actual past performance may best show the effect of some planned major event, such as a proposed merger or restructuring.

Table 26.6

Present and Pro Forma Income Statement for Smith Products If Expenses Are Projected Naively Using a Strict Percentage of Sales Approach (in thousands)

This naive approach ignores fixed costs and often produces an estimate of net income that is biased low.

	Actual for Last Year	Basis of Projection	Pro Forma for Next Year
Sales	$20,000		$22,000
Cost of goods sold	13,500	Percentage of sales	14,850[a]
Gross margin	6,500		7,150
Selling, general, and administrative expenses	4,500	Percentage of sales	4,950
EBIT	2,000		2,200
Interest	600	Percentage of sales	660
EBT	1,400		1,540
Taxes (40%)	560	Historical tax rate	616
Net income	840		924
Cash dividends	300	Percentage of sales	330
Transferred to retained earnings	$ 540		$ 594

[a] $14,850 = ($22,000/$20,000)($13,500). The other percentage of sales estimates were calculated in the same manner.

statement to retained earnings on the firm's balance sheet.[5] The new retained earnings amount is equal to the previous years' retained earnings plus the amount transferred from the pro forma income statement.

After further analysis, Smith Products decides that all expenses and outflows will *not* vary directly with sales. Specifically, the firm estimates that the cost of goods sold will be 66 percent of sales, that selling, general, and administrative expenses will be 23 percent of sales, and that cash dividends will be $350,000. The same interest of $660,000 and the same 40 percent tax rate will be assumed. Smith Products' revised pro forma income statement is shown in Table 26.7. This analysis shows that net income is expected to be $1.056 million, and the estimated amount transferred to retained earnings will be $706,000. With these estimates, we can now proceed to estimate the balance sheet and obtain a rough approximation of the financing needed to support this expected increase in sales.

PRO FORMA BALANCE SHEET AND FINANCING NEEDED

Smith's present balance sheet is given in Table 26.8, along with the projected asset and liability accounts, assuming most of them maintain their historical relationship to sales. Net long-term assets are projected based on the firm's current capital investment plan. Note that three items are not projected: Notes payable, long-term debt and lease

---

[5] Since the naive approach assumes that all costs are variable, it generally produces as estimate of net income that is *biased low*. This results from ignoring the presence of fixed operating costs that are spread over more sales dollars as sales increase. However, if sales are decreasing and fixed operating costs are actually present, then the naive percentage of sales method produces an estimate of net income that is too high.

Table 26.7

Revised Pro Forma Income Statement for Smith Products Based on a Modified Percentage of Sales Method and Judgment (in thousands)

By taking account of fixed costs, Smith Products obtains a more realistic estimate of its expected net income.

	Basis of Projection	Pro Forma for Next Year
Sales		$22,000
Cost of goods sold	Judgment: 66% of sales	14,520
Gross margin		7,480
Selling, general, and administrative expenses	Judgment: 23% of sales	5,060
EBIT		2,420
Interest	Percentage of sales	660
EBT		1,760
Taxes (40%)	Historical tax rate	704
Net income		1,056
Cash dividends	Management forecast	350
Transferred to retained earnings		$ 706

obligations, and common stock are negotiated items that do not change as sales fluctuate. All other balance sheet items, except for net long-term assets and retained earnings, are assumed to change proportionally as sales change. Based on this procedure, Smith Products can obtain a rough estimate of its financing needs of $984,000. This is calculated as follows:

Total assets	$16,000,000
Less: Total liabilities and shareholders' equity	15,016,000
Additional financing needed (or surplus available)	$ 984,000

This figure, of course, assumes that the estimated increase in retained earnings is exactly equal to Smith's internally generated funds. In addition, it is based on maintaining the cash account at its forecasted level of $440,000.

A slight modification can be made if a firm plans to draw down its cash account to meet part of its needs. To illustrate, assume that Smith plans to draw its cash account down by $240,000. In that case, the financing needed is

Total assets	$16,000,000
Less: Total liabilities and shareholders' equity	15,016,000
Additional financing needed	984,000
Less: Cash drawn down	240,000
External financing needed	$ 744,000

Table 26.8

Forecast of Changes in Balance Sheet Items for Smith Products (in thousands)

In this example, judgment was used to estimate the long-term assets, and the naive percentage of sales method was used to forecast the other items.

	Actual for Last Year	Basis of Projection	Pro Forma for Next Year
Assets			
Cash	$ 400	Percentage of sales	$ 440[a]
Accounts receivable	2,100	Percentage of sales	2,310
Inventory	3,000	Percentage of sales	3,300
Total current	5,500		6,050
Net long-term assets	8,500	Judgment	9,950
Total assets	$14,000		$16,000
Liabilities and Shareholders' Equity			
Accounts payable	$ 1,300	Percentage of sales	$ 1,430
Notes payable	900	n.a.[b]	900
Accrued wages and taxes	1,200	Percentage of sales	1,320
Total current	3,400		3,650
Long-term debt and lease obligations	3,800	n.a.	3,800
Deferred taxes	600	Percentage of sales	660
Total long-term liabilities	4,400		4,460
Common stock	3,000	n.a.	3,000
Retained earnings	3,200	Pro forma income statement	3,906[c]
Total shareholders' equity	6,200	Total	6,906
			15,016
		Additional needed	984
Total liabilities and shareholders' equity	$14,000	Total to balance	$16,000

[a] $440 = ($400/$20,000)($22,000). The other percentage of sales estimates were calculated in the same manner.
[b] Not applicable.
[c] $3,200 from last year plus transfer to retained earnings of $706 from Table 26.7.

Table 26.9

Revised Pro Forma Balance Sheet for Smith Products (in thousands)

By increasing its ratio of total debt to total assets from 55.7 percent (Table 26.8) to 56.9 percent, Smith can meet the proposed increase without additional common equity financing.

Assets		Liabilities and Shareholders' Equity	
Cash	$ 456	Accounts payable	$ 1,430
Accounts receivable	2,310	Notes payable	900
Inventory	3,300	Accrued wages and taxes	1,320
Total current	6,066	Total current	3,650
Net long-term assets	9,950	Long-term debt and lease obligations	4,800
Total assets	$16,016	Deferred taxes	660
		Total long-term liabilities	5,460
		Common stock	3,000
		Retained earnings	3,906
		Total shareholders' equity	6,906
		Total liabilities and shareholders' equity	$16,016

Now, of course, Smith Products must decide how to finance the needed expansion. To illustrate the basic elements, assume that Smith decides to finance the total $984,000 by issuing $1 million in additional long-term debt.[6] As shown in the revised balanced sheet in Table 26.9, this results in Smith's long-term debt and lease obligations account increasing by $1 million to $4.8 million, and the difference between the $984,000 needed and the $1 million obtained (i.e., $16,000) is added to the firm's cash account.[7] Obviously, all prospective projects and many other factors have to be considered when firms plan for the future.

Concept Review Questions

- What are two basic approaches to developing pro forma statements?
- Describe how to develop a pro forma income statement and balance sheet using the percentage of sales method.

FINANCIAL AND STRATEGIC PLANNING

The essence of planning is to ensure that the firm is following a dynamic policy that emphasizes the creation of value and avoids options that destroy value. Financial and strategic planning processes and models come in many sizes and shapes. In any model,

---

[6] It issues $1 million instead of $984,000 due simply to rounding the financing off to the nearest million dollars.

[7] Actually, the income statement should be reestimated to take into account additional interest above the existing $660,000 due to Smith's increasing its debt by $1 million. This would affect the size of the transfer to retained earnings. For simplicity, these secondary effects are ignored.

Figure 26.5

Relationship Between Short- and Long-Term Financial and Strategic Planning

In the short term, the emphasis is on quarterly cash flows. In the longer term, the emphasis is on the cumulative cash inflows or outflows and the financial and strategic aspects.

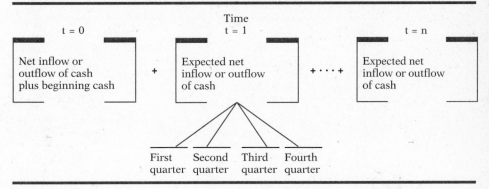

however, there is an important relationship between the short- and long-run aspects. Consider Figure 26.5, which shows the relationships between a firm's short- and long-term cash flows. The firm is experiencing cash inflows and outflows during the current period. At the end of this period, the net inflow or outflow, plus the beginning cash balance, determines how much cash is available at the start of period 1. To emphasize the longer-term aspects, firms may start with short-term cash budgets (e.g., monthly or quarterly) and then move to yearly cash budgets.

Long-term planning, in a sense, is just a continuation of the ideas discussed earlier for short-term planning. But there are some differences in emphasis. Consider Figure 26.6, which depicts the firm's long-term needs. Note that the long-term requirements depend on the amount of spontaneous short-term financing secured, along with the amount of short-term borrowing employed. Firms that adopt an aggressive short-term financial management strategy (as discussed in Chapter 21) will, other things being equal, need less long-term financing. Also, in the long run the firm's strategic plan, its ability to forecast accurately, and the need for flexibility all become more important than in the short run, although the basic emphasis remains the same.

The long-term approach begins by continuing what was done in the short term. Obviously, the farther in the future, the less detail in the cash budget. Likewise, the farther in the future, the more uncertainty concerning the projected cash flows. The longer-term cash budget should reflect any anticipated expansion, replacement, or restructuring of the firm's assets. Then the sources of financing need to be evaluated. During the planning process the firm should consider various alternative plans and their possible consequences. An important part of the planning process involves consideration of the various options (to expand, delay or defer, abandon, and so forth) faced by the firm. Whatever the final plan adopted, the important point to remember is that financial planning forces the firm to consider its goals and needs in advance. By doing so, firms can consider all of the options available to them, ensure their flexibility, and keep attention focused on the goal of maximizing the market value of the firm.

Figure 26.6

How Short- and Long-Term Financing Meet a Firm's Needs

Spontaneous short-term financing (through accounts payable, factoring of receivables, and continuous inventory loans) meets part of the firm's cumulative financing needs (as represented by the solid wavy line). The rest are met by short-term borrowings and long-term financing.

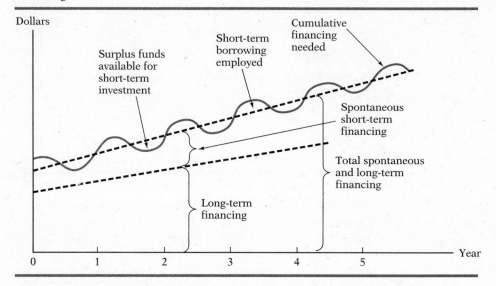

Concept Review Questions

■ How are short-term and long-term financial planning models related?

■ What is the main goal of establishing a financial and strategic planning model?

KEY POINTS

- The statement of changes in financial position (SCFP), which is required to be presented along with an income statement and balance sheet, records the firm's past flow of cash. Because most firms employ the indirect approach to presenting the SCFP, the information is not as useful as it could be.
- Cash budgeting, perhaps supplemented by pro forma analysis, is the main method of forecasting cash flows and financing needs or excesses. Accurate forecasting of sales is most important when making any kind of financial projections.
- In practice, firms employ scenario analysis, find ways to deal with seasonality, and deal with inflation when making cash forecasts.
- Financial and strategic planning is a trial-and-error activity that does not attempt to minimize risk. Rather, it is the process of deciding which risks to take and which are not worth taking. Throughout the planning process all of the options available to the firm must be

continually considered, or employed as the frame of reference, so that effective financial management decisions can be made.

QUESTIONS

26.1   Explain both the advantages and disadvantages of the statement of changes in financial position in terms of providing useful cash flow information.

26.2   Explain the various components of a firm's cash budget. How can sales be estimated? Why may a cash budget not be sufficient for planning *within* a given period?

26.3   What are the strengths and weaknesses of and the differences between the cash budget and the percentage of sales method of forecasting future cash flows?

26.4   Gates Electronics is considering making the following policy changes. In each case, indicate whether *in the next period* the move will provide more cash inflows and/or reduce outflows ($+$), provide more outflows and/or reduce inflows ($-$), or have an indeterminate or no effect (0).

a.   The firm becomes more socially responsible.   _____

b.   Increased competition is leading to price cutting and increased promotional expenses.   _____

c.   The firm decides to sell only for cash; previously some sales had been on credit.   _____

d.   By shifting to more debt, the firm expects its return on equity to increase.   _____

e.   The firm decides to change its inventory method from one GAAP method to another GAAP method.   _____

f.   The firm's dividend payout ratio is reduced.   _____

g.   Parliament changes the tax laws, resulting in lower CCA rates.   _____

26.5   How would you go about distinguishing *after the fact* between good and bad financial and strategic planning versus good or bad luck?

CONCEPT REVIEW PROBLEMS

See Appendix A for solutions.

CR26.1   Samson is attempting to predict sales for the next three years using linear regression. What are the expected sales in the next three years?

Year	Sales (Y_t) (millions)
-4	$10.0
-3	10.0
-2	10.5
-1	11.5
0	13.0

CR26.2   After reviewing your predicted sales for the next three years, from CR26.1, the CFO decided it is important to incorporate seasonality effects into the sales estimates. Quarterly sales for Samson for the past three years are given below. Based on these years of data, estimate quarterly sales for the next eight quarters.

	Quarterly Sales (in millions)			
Year	1	2	3	4
−2	$2.35	$2.50	$2.90	$2.75
−1	2.60	2.75	3.15	3.00
0	2.85	3.15	3.65	3.35

CR26.3 Bluestar Electronics has sales for November and December of $165,000 and $175,000, respectively. Estimated sales are:

January	$220,000	May	$200,000
February	275,000	June	175,000
March	250,000	July	150,000
April	230,000	August	150,000

The firm makes 20 percent of its sales for cash, 50 percent are on credit and collected one month after the sale, and 30 percent are on credit and collected two months after the sale (assume there are no bad debts). Material costs are 20 percent of projected sales two months hence, and labour is 50 percent of next month's estimated sales. Bluestar typically pays for 25 percent of the materials two months prior to the sale and for 75 percent of the materials one month prior to the sale. The estimated administrative expenses are $25,000 per month. The firm anticipates paying $50,000 in taxes in both January and April. It will have a $150,000 cash outflow in May for new equipment. The minimum desired cash balance is $70,000; that is the beginning balance in January. Prepare a cash budget for the months of January through June and indicate the per month cumulative short-term financing needed (−) or surplus (+).

CR26.4 Dartmouth Manufacturing has the following balance sheet and income statement. The firm estimates sales will increase by 10 percent next year. All income statement and balance sheet items are assumed to be a function of sales except long-term assets, short- and long-term debt, common stock, and dividends paid. These entries will remain constant, except for long-term assets, which will increase to $40, and taxes, which will be $8. Using the percent of sales method, develop a pro forma income statement and balance sheet for Dartmouth Manufacturing. Will the firm need outside financing to support the 10 percent growth?

Balance Sheet (in millions)

Assets

Cash and marketable securities	$ 5
Accounts receivable	20
Inventory	18
Long-term assets	$27
Total assets	$70

Liabilities and Shareholders' Equity

Short-term bank loan	$ 9
Accounts payable	11

Liabilities and Shareholders' Equity (*continued*)

Accruals	10
Long-term debt	15
Common stock	10
Retained earnings	15
Total liabilities and shareholders' equity	$70

Income Statement (in millions)

Net sales	$40
Cost of goods sold	10
Gross margin	30
Selling and administrative expenses	10
EBIT	20
Interest	2
EBT	18
Taxes	7
Net income	11
Cash dividends	3
Transferred to retained earnings	$ 8

PROBLEMS

26.1 The SCFP for Varity Corporation for three recent years was as follows (in millions):

	0	−1	−2
Cash Provided by Operations			
Net income	$92.1	$81.7	$ 4.5
Add (deduct) items not affecting working capital:			
Deferred income taxes	7.6	6.4	1.8
Depreciation and amortization	89.2	75.2	68.0
Provision for loss on liquidation of an associate company	—	—	59.7
Gain on sale of assets	(25.2)	(25.8)	(64.4)
Excess (deficiency) of dividends received over equity in earnings of finance subsidiaries	(7.4)	21.8	(4.1)
Payment of pension obligation	(14.0)	—	—
Exchange adjustments and other	(3.5)	(3.8)	11.2
	138.8	155.5	76.7

Working Capital Provided by Operations

Net change in noncash working capital balances:

Increase in receivables	(32.2)	(1.1)	(9.8)
Increase in inventories	(4.2)	(27.3)	(4.7)
Decrease (increase) in prepaid expenses	10.8	(3.6)	(6.0)
Increase (decrease) in accounts payable and accruals	(55.6)	73.5	90.4
Foreign currency translation adjustment to net current assets excluding cash	(2.3)	13.8	9.9
Cash provided by operations	55.3	210.8	156.5

Cash Provided by (Used for) Investment Activities

Acquisition of K-H Corporation

Net noncash assets acquired	$433.2			
Kelsey-Hayes notes issued	(420.2)			
Varity common shares issued	(88.8)			
Cash acquired, net of $44.3 million expended		75.8	—	—
Additions to fixed assets		(75.6)	(45.3)	(46.4)
Proceeds from sale of fixed assets		36.0	36.3	78.9
Additions to investments		(13.2)	(7.2)	(7.5)
Proceeds from disposal of investments		33.6	—	12.0
Disposition of business		12.6	35.8	—
Additions to other assets and intangibles		(3.5)	(14.7)	(4.5)
		65.7	4.9	32.5

Cash Provided by (Used for) Financing Activities

Increase (decrease) in bank borrowing	15.5	3.5	(14.8)
Increase in long-term debt	60.7	7.5	84.6
Reduction in long-term debt	(92.6)	(151.3)	(204.8)
Issue of class I preferred shares, net	—	—	69.7
Dividends paid on preferred shares	(18.2)	(15.9)	(13.6)
Other	(2.3)	(0.3)	(5.9)
	(36.9)	(156.5)	(84.8)

Effect of foreign currency translation on cash

Increase in cash during the year	(0.5)	(1.0)	—
Cash and bank term deposits at beginning of year	83.6	58.2	104.2
Cash and bank term deposits at end of year	218.6	160.4	56.2
	$302.2	$218.6	$160.4

---

a. Analyze the firm's financial performance for the three years and comment on the primary sources of cash, the primary uses of cash, and any apparent trends. How else (in terms of a general approach) could the operating section of the statement be constructed?

b. What else would you like to know that is not reflected or apparent on Varity's SCFP?

26.2 Fraser Ltd. has sales data for the last seven years as follows:

Year	Sales	Year	Sales
1	$ 470	5	$ 1,535
2	800	6	1,705
3	1,080	7	1,831
4	1,350		

a. Use linear regression to predict sales for years 8, 9, and 10.

b. Plot (using graph paper) your estimated regression equation and the forecasted values for years 8, 9, and 10. Then plot the actual sales data for years 1 through 7. What conclusions can you draw about the growth in past sales and the estimated sales for years 8, 9, and 10?

26.3   MFD Ltd.'s revenue (in millions) for five recent years is shown below:

1	$11,353	4	$12,078
2	11,860	5	13,451
3	11,414		

a. Based on linear regression, forecast revenue for year 6.

b. How close is this to actual year 6 revenue of $14,146?

c. Based on actual revenue for years 1 through 6, plus actual revenue for years 7, 8, and 9 of $15,151, $15,747, and $15,296, respectively, forecast year 10 revenue.

d. How close is this to actual year 10 revenue of $16,405? What does this suggest about the use of linear regression for forecasting MFD's revenue for this time period?

26.4   Richlund Products has forecast its cash flows for the next two months as follows:

	First Month	**Second Month**
Total operating cash inflow	$210 million	$150 million
Total operating cash outflow	−140 million	−135 million
Other net inflow (+) or outflow (−)	−30 million	−90 million

Richlund's beginning cash balance is $15 million, and its minimum cash balance is $10 million. Determine Richlund's cumulative financing needed (−) or surplus (+) for both months.

26.5   Sydney & Sons is in the process of developing its cash budget for the months of January, February, March, and April. Twenty percent of sales are for cash; 50 percent of total sales are for credit and collected the next month. The remaining 30 percent are for credit and collected in two months. There are no bad debts.

Purchases of raw materials are made in the month prior to the expected sale and average 45 percent of expected sales. They are paid for in the month following their purchase. Wages, rent, and selling expenses are $300,000 in January and will increase by $50,000 per month. Interest of $25,000 is payable every month. Taxes of $55,000 are payable in each month. Cash dividends of $100,000 are payable in February. Finally, capital expenditures of $200,000 are forecast for January, and another $50,000 are expected in April.

Actual sales for November and December and forecasted sales for the next five months are as follows:

November	$1,000,000	March	$1,800,000
December	900,000	April	2,300,000
January	1,000,000	May	2,500,000
February	1,400,000		

Cash on hand on January 1 is $100,000, and a $50,000 minimum cash balance is required each month.

a. Prepare a cash budget for January, February, March, and April.
b. What is the maximum level of short-term financing required?
c. Suppose that sales receipts come in uniformly over the month, but all outflows are paid by the 10th of the month. Discuss the effect this would have on the cash budget. Would the cash budget just completed be valid? If not, what could be done to adjust the budget?
d. Now suppose Sydney & Sons reestimates its forecasted sales as follows:

January	$ 800,000	April	$1,900,000
February	1,100,000	May	2,200,000
March	1,500,000		

What is the effect of this on Sydney & Sons' cash budget in (a)? What is the maximum level of short-term financing now required?

26.6 Columbia Precision Products has forecast its cash flows for the next year as follows:

| | Quarter | | | |
	First	Second	Third	Fourth
Total operating cash inflow	$175	$195	$220	$200
Total operating cash outflow	−120	−140	−180	−120
Other net inflow or outflow	−50	−90	−60	−30

a. Determine Columbia's net cash inflow or outflow per quarter and its cumulative short-term financing needs by quarter, if its beginning cash balance is $25 and its minimum cash balance is $15.
b. What is the maximum amount of short-term financing needed? In what quarter does it occur?
c. Ignoring any costs of short-term financing, is Columbia as well off at the end of the year as at the beginning?
d. The effective annual before-tax costs of alternative short-term financing sources are given below. Which one should be chosen? Is there any reason why the cheapest source might not be chosen?

Bank line of credit	16%	Accounts receivable loan	13%
Inventory loan	15	Factoring receivables	18
Stretching payables	20	Commercial paper (six months)	12

26.7 North Bay Limited has quarterly sales data for the past three years as follows:

| | Quarter | | | |
	1	2	3	4
Year −3	300	275	295	370
Year −2	325	285	320	405
Year −1	365	325	360	440

a. Estimate a regression equation based on these 12 quarters of data.
b. Using the regression estimates calculated in (a), forecast the next 8 quarters (ignoring any potential seasonality).
c. Based on the 4-quarter moving average approach, determine adjusted quarterly seasonal indices.
d. Using the forecasted sales from (b) and the adjusted seasonal indices from (c), determine the seasonally adjusted forecasted sales for the next 8 quarters. How much, on average, does adjusting for seasonality increase or decrease sales for the first quarter, second quarter, third quarter, and fourth quarter?

26.8 MJD Ltd.'s condensed income statement as of December 31 is:

	(in millions)
Sales	$4,841.4
Operating expenses	4,333.5
Income from operations	507.9
+ Other income	37.9
EBIT	545.8
Interest	180.7
EBT	365.1
Taxes	83.5
Net income	$ 281.6

a. If we had perfect foresight and knew next year's sales were going to be $5,432.2 million, estimate next year's income statement employing the percentage of sales method.
b. What differences exist between your pro forma income statement and MJD's actual income statement for the year, listed below?

	(in millions)
Sales	$5,432.2
Operating expenses	4,823.7
Income from operations	608.5
+ Other income	70.0
EBIT	678.5
Interest	185.9
EBT	492.6
Taxes	124.9
Net income	$ 367.7

c. Do you believe some of these differences could be anticipated to obtain a more accurate pro forma income statement? Why or why not?

26.9 Laurier Ltd.'s estimated sales for next year are $30 million. The percentage of sales for items that vary directly with sales for Laurier is given below:

Cash	5%	Accounts payable	15%
Accounts receivable	25	Accruals	10
Inventory	30	Net profit margin	5

Its net long-term assets are $6 million, notes payable are $2 million, long-term debt is $2 million, and common stock is $5 million. Laurier's present retained earnings are $5.1 million, and its dividend payout ratio is 40 percent.

a. Prepare a pro forma balance sheet and indicate the estimated amount of additional financing needed. Assume that long-term debt will be used to finance any shortfall.

b. What happens if Laurier's sales are $40 million and its long-term assets increase to $8 million? If long-term debt is used, how does the ratio of total debt to total assets in (b) compare with the same ratio for (a)?

26.10 MacDonald-Cartier has decided to embark on a rapid expansion. Its most recent income statement and balance sheet are as follows:

Income Statement (in millions)

Sales	$30.0
Cost of goods sold	15.0
Selling, general, and administrative expenses	6.0
EBIT	9.0
Interest	1.0
EBT	8.0
Taxes (40%)	3.2
Net income	4.8
Cash dividends	3.0
Transferred to retained earnings	$ 1.8

Balance Sheet (in millions)

Current assets	$ 6.0	Accounts payable	$ 2.0
Long-term assets	14.0	Notes payable	2.0
Total assets	$20.0	Long-term debt	6.0
		Common stock	3.0
		Retained earnings	7.0
		Total liabilities and shareholders' equity	$20.1

In attempting to determine its financial condition and needs, MacDonald-Cartier believes the following will happen:

Sales	$40.0
Cost of goods sold	Same percent of sales as current year
Selling, general, and administrative expenses	$ 9.0
Interest	$ 1.0 (initially, before additional financing)
Taxes	Same percent of EBT as current year
Cash dividends	$ 3.0 (initially)
Current assets	$ 7.0
Long-term assets	$23.0
Accounts payable	$ 3.0
Notes payable	$ 2.0
Long-term debt	$ 6.0 (initially)
Common stock	$ 3.0

a. Based on these estimates, prepare a pro forma income statement and balance sheet for MacDonald-Cartier. How much additional financing (regardless of where it comes from) do you estimate the firm needs?

b. What happens if MacDonald-Cartier acquires sufficient additional long-term debt financing to keep its ratio of total debt to total assets at its original level? Assume interest expenses increase by $500,000.

c. By cutting its cash dividends in addition to the step taken in (b), can MacDonald-Cartier finance all its cash needs? What do you think will happen to the market price of MacDonald-Cartier's common stock if it cuts cash dividends? Do you see any alternative means of raising the needed funds?

26.11 St. Vincent Minerals is planning to meet its long-term needs. To arrive at its needs, it has come up with the following estimates:

	Year				
	1	2	3	4	5
Net cash inflow (+) or outflow (−) before short-term financing cash flows	$20	−$15	−$30	−$60	−$10
Short-term financing cash flows	− 3	− 4	− 4	− 6	− 2
Total cash inflow (+) or outflow (−)	$17	−$19	−$34	−$66	−$12

St. Vincent's beginning cash balance is $30. The minimum cash balance is $15 in years 1 and 2, $20 in year 3, and $25 in years 4 and 5. Prepare a year-by-year statement to show the maximum amount of long-term financing St. Vincent will need.

26.12 Tate Systems is completing its long-run planning process. As a part of this, it has estimated the following needs for long-term funds and the amount it expects to provide out of internally generated equity funds:

	Year				
	1	2	3	4	5
Long-term financing needed per period	$5	$20	$15	$30	$43
To be provided by internally generated equity funds per period	− 6	− 7	− 7	− 8	− 10
To be raised externally (+) or surplus (−) per period	−$1	$13	$ 8	$22	$33

Tate's present capital structure contains $40 in debt and $60 in common equity. A primary goal when raising long-term capital is to remain as close as possible to this percentage target capital structure. Either long-term debt or common stock can be issued in amounts of $15 each. (*Note:* It is okay if Tate raises too much long-term capital in any period and those funds are carried forward to the next year, but it cannot have a shortfall. That is, Tate cannot borrow on a short-term basis to cover any shortfall in long-term capital.)

a. Determine in which years Tate needs to secure additional long-term financing.

b. Indicate, by year, whether long-term debt or common stock should be issued. (Remember that the additional internally generated funds each year are added to the firm's equity base.)

c. What is the resulting capital structure at the end of year 5 and the ratio of total debt to total assets?

26.13 Mini Case You have been on the job for a month as an analyst in the finance department of Playmore Enterprises. Every three months the firm plans for the next year and also assesses the firm's long-run financial strategy. The current planning process has been assigned to you to complete, after which it will be reviewed, and modified as needed, by the divisional vice president and other senior management.

a. As a first step you have gathered the last three years' statements of changes in financial position. In brief, they are as follows:

	Year		
	−2	**−1**	**0**
Operating Activities			
Net income	$200	$245	$240
Depreciation	45	65	75
Other	(100)	50	180
	145	360	495
Investing Activities	(90)	(175)	(160)
Financing Activities			
Net change in debt	150	(200)	(50)
Dividends paid	(50)	(60)	(70)
	100	(260)	(120)
Net increase (decrease) in cash and marketable securities	155	(75)	215
Cash and marketable securities at beginning of the year	80	235	160
Cash and marketable securities at the end of the year	$235	$160	$375

What is the purpose of the statement of changes in financial position? In what format does Playmore Enterprises present its statement? What can we determine about Playmore from its statement of changes in financial position?

b. In order to develop a 4-quarter cash budget, you decide to estimate sales based on linear regression. Sales for the past eight quarters are as follows:

Quarter	Sales
−7	$500
−6	525
−5	520
−4	580
−3	580
−2	560
−1	590
0	610

Based on linear regression, what are estimated sales for the next four quarters? Are there other factors that need to be taken into consideration when forecasting sales? Also, without actually doing it, how would you adjust for seasonality?

c. In order to develop its cash budget, Playmore has made the following estimates: Forty percent of sales are for cash, 40 percent are credit and collected in the following quarter, and 20 percent are credit and collected in two quarters. There are no bad debts. Purchases are made in the quarter prior to the expected sales and average 35 percent of expected sales. They are paid in the quarter following their purchase. The other estimates have been made as follows:

| | Year | | | |
	1	2	3	4
Salaries	$100	$105	$105	$115
Selling, general, and administrative expenses	125	130	125	130
Interest	60	40	40	30
Taxes	20	20	20	20
Capital expenditures	50	130	80	70
Repay debt	100	—	100	20
Dividends	30	30	35	35

The present level of cash on hand should be taken from part (a), above, and past and projected sales are given in (b). The minimum cash balance is $80. Develop the firm's cash budget for the next four quarters. What does your analysis indicate?

d. In addition to the projected cash budget, you are considering preparing pro forma financial statements. What is the basic procedure employed in preparing pro forma statements? What are their strengths? Their weaknesses?

e. In preparing your report, what still remains?

REFERENCES

BERNSTEIN, PETER L., and THEODORE H. SILBERT. "Are Economic Forecasters Worth Listening To?" *Harvard Business Review* 62 (September–October 1984): 32–40.

COOPER, KERRY, and R. MALCOLM RICHARDS. "Investing the Alaskan Project Cash Flows: The Sohio Experience." *Financial Management* 17 (Summer 1988): 58–70.

CORNELL, BRADFORD, and ALAN C. SHAPIRO. "Financing Corporate Growth." *Journal of Applied Corporate Finance* 1 (Summer 1988): 6–22.

DONALDSON, GORDON. "Financial Goals and Strategic Consequences." *Harvard Business Review* 63 (May–June 1985): 56–66.

DRTINA, RALPH E., and JAMES A. LARGAY. "Pitfalls in Calculating Cash Flow from Operations." *Accounting Review* 60 (April 1985): 314–326.

GENTRY, JAMES A., PAUL NEWBOLD, and DAVID T. WHITFORD. "Profiles of Cash Flow Components." *Financial Analysts Journal* 46 (July–August 1990): 41–48.

GEORGOFF, DAVID M., and ROBERT G. MURDICK. "Manager's Guide to Forecasting." *Harvard Business Review* 64 (January–February 1986): 110–120.

HORNGREN, CHARLES T., GARY L. SUNDEM, JOHN A. ELLIOTT, and DANIEL B. THORNTON. *Introduction to Financial Accounting,* 1st Canadian ed. Scarborough, Ont.: Prentice Hall, 1995.

MALLOUK, BRENDA. "Statements of Changes in Financial Position: Switching from Working Capital to Cash Base." *CGA Magazine* 22 (January 1988): 44–49.

MICHEL, ALLEN, and ISRAEL SHAKED. "Airline Performance Under Deregulation: The Shareholders' Perspective." *Financial Management* 13 (Summer 1984): 5–14.

SKINNER, ROSS. *Accounting Standard in Evolution.* Toronto: Holt, Rinehart & Winston, 1987.

27

Small Business Finance

EXECUTIVE SUMMARY

Financing is the single most difficult problem faced by entrepreneurs and owner-managers of small businesses. Although there are many reasons for this, an important one is that they are generally more intent on capitalizing on an opportunity they believe exists for a particular product or service rather than on the means of either obtaining the necessary funding or learning how to handle the financial aspects of the business. Successful small business owners take steps to ensure that every advantage available works in their favour.

Starting with a business plan that clearly outlines the entrepreneur's goals and objectives and the means of achieving them leads to private and public sources of financial assistance, namely the banks, credit institutions, venture capitalists, and government programmes. The business plan, therefore, is the key document, providing the road map for the other potential "team" members, as well as forcing entrepreneurs to come to grips with detailed parameters for the business.

Governments, at all levels, are taking an ever-increasing interest in the role that small businesses are playing in the growth and development of their respective economies. In the future, small businesses will have to stay abreast of technological advances in order to remain competitive. Successful small businesses will find their specialized niches and possibly enter into joint ventures to exploit them fully.

ECONOMIC SIGNIFICANCE OF SMALL BUSINESS

Before we can describe the significance of small business to the Canadian economy, we must first answer this question: What is a small business? Unfortunately, there is no clear cut definition. Rather, the definition changes depending on the needs of the user, but it usually contains a statement about the number of employees, sales, or asset size. In government statistics, firms with fewer than 100 employees in the manufacturing sector, fewer than 50 employees in the service sector, or less than $5 million in sales are classified as small businesses.

Although each entrepreneur often feels as if he or she is operating alone without making a significant contribution to the overall economy, the following information on small business performance shows quite the opposite.[1]

1. There were 934,650 registered businesses in Canada during 1990, of which 97.2 percent (908,480) had fewer than 50 employees.
2. Businesses with fewer than 100 employees accounted for 52 percent of all Canadians employed in the private sector, and 45 percent of Canadians are employed in businesses with less than 50 employees.
3. Between 1980 and 1990 the number of new businesses grew by 40 percent; almost all of this growth was accounted for by small businesses.
4. Small businesses account for more than 80 percent of new jobs created in Canada and make up 50 percent of all private sector firms performing research and development.

Although these four points demonstrate the importance of small business to the Canadian economy, they do not reveal the level of risk associated with small business, especially during the first few years—approximately 50 percent of new businesses fail by the end of the third year. Although this failure rate is not as high as conventional wisdom might suggest, it does point out the significant risk that entrepreneurs take and the need for good planning and adequate financing.

Concept Review Question
- Why are small businesses important to the Canadian economy?

THE ISSUE OF SMALL BUSINESS FINANCE

Because of the essential contribution that the small business sector makes to our economy, every effort is made by the federal and provincial governments to help small businesses maximize their opportunities to compete both domestically and internationally. Tangible evidence of both federal and provincial governments' interest is the increased number of programmes now available to small businesses in a wide range of fields and activities. However, these programmes are usually viewed as a "supplementary" source of funding for small businesses, which are expected to obtain their financing from the private sector. One way for entrepreneurs to enhance their chances of obtaining financing from either the private or the public sector is to prepare a comprehensive business plan.

---

[1] See *Taking Care of Business: Report of the Standing Committee on Industry* (House of Commons, October 1994).

THE BUSINESS PLAN

The business plan is vital to the startup and growth of the business, both as a management tool and a vehicle for raising the necessary financing. The plan is your, the entrepreneur's, blueprint for success. It defines your objectives, and it provides a yardstick for keeping the business on target as it grows. For investors, the plan provides a framework to tell them who you are and why you need the requested funding. Consequently, the business plan must demonstrate the viability and the risks, as you see them, of your proposed (or expanding) business, plus your knowledge and understanding of the various components necessary for successfully attaining your objectives. Based on this information, the prospective investors can evaluate you, the individuals who will manage the business, and the potential return on their investment.

Because your business plan will be the first showpiece for your project and will reveal to financiers your capabilities, it is vital that it be carefully prepared. Although the body of a business plan is usually 10 to 15 pages in length, most have many appendices. Consequently, it is not uncommon to have a business plan of 50 or more pages. Thus the planning process itself will be a valuable exercise in consolidating your thinking, placing components in perspective, and generally increasing your chances of success. Every business plan, then, should contain the following elements:

1. SUMMARY   Every financier has more business plans and related material to read than he or she can possibly digest. Therefore, the summary should not exceed two pages and should clearly address the pertinent reasons why somebody should invest in your business, covering such topics as the product, service, or technology you are offering; the market potential; a description of yourself and other management personnel, if any; abbreviated financial forecasts; and the desired financing, including what the funds will be used for, and repayment plans.

2. THE BUSINESS   A detailed description of the proposed business should include the product, service, or technology; the location and potential market—target customer, competition, market research, marketing strategy—and risks; the legal form of the business (proprietorship, partnership, corporation); and key management personnel and employees. If the business is to be set up as a corporation, the composition and function of the board of directors should be stated. Appendices should be used to provide the résumés of key employees; detailed information on competition; and any market research that has been done for your product, preferably by an independent source.

3. THE FINANCIAL SECTION   A key component of every business plan is the financial section. It should include projected income statements, cash flows, and balance sheets. The projections should cover a period of three years, which is a realistic time frame to make assumptions without projecting too far into the future. The cash flow forecasts, in particular, should be done on a monthly basis, at least until a position of positive cash flow has been attained. Because of the length of these statements, it is not uncommon to place them in an appendix and simply refer to them in the financial section of the plan. Since the fewer questions that are left unanswered the better received the business plan will be, the appendix should also contain all assumptions used in constructing the financial data. For

example, any assumptions used in constructing the sales and cost of goods sold figures on the income statement should be disclosed, and since salaries are a major expense for most small businesses, a detailed breakdown of all salaries and fringe benefits is essential. It is also imperative that anyone looking at the projected cash flows knows the assumed terms on which accounts receivable will be collected and accounts payable paid.

The financial component of the business plan integrates all of the other elements of the plan, expressed in dollars, and is a means of considering whether the business is an attainable project. Developing the proper financial forecasts is, therefore, a critical factor in obtaining funding for your business. Accordingly, it is important that the forecasts clearly establish the need for funds in the amount requested, demonstrate your ability to repay the loan, and indicate your understanding of the financial implications of your planned business growth.

Many small businesses underestimate their needs, particularly in the startup period. By the time their shortfall is finally identified, expenditures have reached the point of no return. If the company gets into a bind, the cost of funds can be very high. Great care should be taken not to underestimate the amount of money you think will be required; it is much more prudent to overestimate, as opposed to underestimate, your needs.

FUNDING

The most common source of startup financing is from personal funds—through savings, a home mortgage, or relatives. Once beyond the startup stage, the financing of a small business, like a large firm, comes basically in two forms—debt or equity financing. Although relatively few new businesses grow to become large ones, those that want to expand find it difficult to raise funds, especially equity investment. For example, in 1992 growing small and medium-sized businesses raised 52 percent of their financing from external sources; however, less than 1 percent was raised through the public equity markets.[2]

TAXES

Individuals who own an unincorporated business share in the profits of the business based on a formal, or informal, agreement. Each owner's share of the business's profits is then taxed at his or her personal tax rate, even if the profits are retained in the business. As we saw in Chapter 14, for individuals residing in all provinces other than Quebec the total marginal tax rate is calculated by multiplying the federal marginal rate by 1 plus the provincial rate. Table 14.2 shows that the maximum federal personal tax rate is 29 percent and the maximum provincial personal tax rate is 69 percent. Therefore, the maximum personal marginal tax rate, for individuals outside of Quebec, is about 49 percent (0.29×1.69). On the other hand, from our discussion of

---

[2] See *Strategies for Success: A Profile of Growing Small and Medium-sized Enterprise.* Statistics Canada, Catalogue No. 61-523R, 1994.

corporate tax rates in Chapter 8 we saw that the maximum marginal corporate tax rate is 45 percent (0.28 + 0.17).

If taxes were our only concern, it would seem as if taxation does not provide a significant incentive to incorporate. However, as was also noted in Chapter 8, for firms that earn less than $200,000 the maximum small business tax rate is about 22 percent (0.12 + 0.10). Since most small businesses earn less than $200,000, the correct comparison is between personal and small business total tax rates. With this comparison we see that there may be a significant tax advantage to incorporation. If the owner's personal tax rate is higher than the small business corporate tax rate on the same amount of income, then the business should be incorporated. If not, it would benefit the owner to operate an unincorporated business, i.e., a sole proprietorship or a partnership.

Another incentive for a small business to incorporate is that all capital gains earned on the stock of small businesses are eligible for a $500,000 lifetime exemption. That is to say that the common shareholders of a small firm pay no taxes on their first $500,000 of capital gains.

Concept Review Questions

- What is the purpose of a business plan?
- What are the key elements of a business plan?
- How are most small businesses financed initially?
- How will taxes influence whether a small business is incorporated or not?

OBTAINING DEBT FINANCING

Debt financing can be obtained from two principal sources, private and public. Under the former are personal loans, bank loans, and to some extent loans by venture capitalists. Public sources include federal and provincial government programmes and agencies, and the Federal Business Development Bank (FBDB).

Because small businesses are generally precluded from the financial markets, bank loans are the most common form of outside financial aid and, generally speaking, the least expensive. However, in a new venture, the bank or lending institution will generally require a personal guarantee for the loan. This could mean an assignment against your home and other personal assets as well as having your spouse or partner cosign the loan. A company that cannot get a loan from a bank must turn to other sources of short-term capital such as commercial finance companies. Therefore, good bank relations are a must for a small business.

Bankers are in a position to give advice on financing your business and other related matters. When you meet your banker, if you are prepared with a well-developed business plan, you will be in a better position to be able to receive this advice and other relevant information about the business you are about to enter into. Although your banker cannot be expected to be an expert on your business, a helpful banker can be an entrepreneur's best friend and an auxiliary member of the management team. Consequently, it is wise to keep your banker informed. He or she does not like surprises any more than you do and, if made aware, should be able to help you anticipate situations.

PRIVATE SOURCES

Because funds are needed for different purposes, the methods used to obtain them are different.

Banks   Banks provide various types of loans and services to facilitate small business operations. Four of these are:

1. OPERATING LOANS   **Operating loans** may include lines of credit and are provided by chartered banks for day-to-day operations. As discussed in Chapter 24, the amount and conditions are negotiated with the bank, which in turn will demand adherence to the terms under which the operating loans are granted.
2. TERM LOANS   These are loans made by chartered banks for plant expansion or renovation, machinery and equipment, land and buildings, and what they classify as "other worthwhile purposes." Generally for a period of up to five years, they require repayment on an amortized basis, at regular intervals, at the negotiated rate of interest. Because interest on any loan is a tax-deductible expense, an amortization schedule, like the ones discussed in Chapter 11, can be constructed to partition each payment between principal and interest. If, for example, payment is made monthly, the 12 interest portions of the schedule are summed and recorded as part of interest expense on the business's tax return.
3. EQUIPMENT FINANCING   **Equipment financing** includes loans made by chartered banks to a company wishing to purchase machinery or equipment, which in turn is used as collateral.
4. LETTERS OF CREDIT   Letters of credit are particularly valuable to small businesses involved in international trade. As we saw in Chapter 23, they are issued by the bank on behalf of its clients and guarantee payment for merchandise, in accordance with specified terms and conditions.

Venture Capital   Certainly one of the major problems facing small business is finding **venture capital** (that is, new high-risk capital). One way to look at the initial financing stages is to break them into phases, as follows:

1. SEED MONEY FINANCING   A small amount of financing is needed to prove a concept or develop a product.
2. STARTUP AND FIRST-LEVEL FINANCING   Financing for firms that need money for research and development, initial production, marketing, and the like.
3. SECOND-LEVEL FINANCING   Financing for firms that are producing and selling a product but are not breaking even yet.
4. THIRD-LEVEL OR MEZZANINE FINANCING   Financing for a firm that is producing a product, breaking even, and considering an expansion.
5. FOURTH-LEVEL OR BRIDGE FINANCING   Financing provided for firms that are likely to go public within the next year.

Seed money almost always comes from personal savings or loans and from investments by family and friends. Startup and first-level financing is needed to get the firm up and running and to help it meet production quality and quantity standards so that it may begin to break even. Although some firms provide startup and first-level financing, many venture capital firms avoid this type of financing. Second-level financing is designed to help firms reach an economic breakeven point. Third-level, or mezzanine, financing is often provided by venture capital firms. Some large industrial or financial firms (such as the Royal Bank) have venture capital operations, but most of this type of financing is provided by smaller firms specializing in providing venture capital. Some of these same firms also provide fourth-level, or bridge, financing. Other venture capital financing is provided by pension funds, foreign investors, insurance companies, individual investors and families, and endowments and foundations.

For every ten first-level venture capital investments, only five may make it beyond a few years. Consequently, because of the very high risk in first- and second-level financing, and the long time before the firm is successful (if it ever is), we see why venture capital firms are reluctant to invest in these stages. They believe, probably rightly so, that the risk/reward prospects are better for later-level investments.

Working Capital   As was noted in Chapter 21, short-term financial management or working capital management is especially important for the day-to-day operations of any firm. However, it is even more important for small businesses since they carry a higher percentage of both current assets and current liabilities than larger firms do. Consequently, using accounts receivable and inventories is an integral part of short-term financing for small businesses. The same techniques available to large firms—pledging or factoring of accounts receivable, floor planning or warehouse financing of inventories, and trade credit—that we discussed in Chapter 24 are also available to, and widely used by, small businesses.

Leasing   Leasing is another type of private financing. As discussed in Chapter 15, it allows the company the use of machines, vehicles, office equipment, and buildings on a rental basis. It is an ideal form of financing for a small company either in a startup position or with limited capital since (1) it permits the company the use of the facilities without an investment of capital; (2) the company from which the facilities are leased is generally responsible for maintenance and upkeep; and (3) the small company can be protected against rapid changes in technology, such as computers and software.

PUBLIC SOURCES

The main source of public funds is government guaranteed loans for business improvement and project financing.

Business Improvement Loans   Business improvement loans are term loans guaranteed by the federal government for specific purposes and limits, available through all chartered banks and other approved lenders. These loans are offered under the federal government's Small Business Loans Act (SBLA) to finance up to 90 percent of all eligible assets such as land, premises, and equipment.

Project Financing   Project financing is in the form of term loans provided by the Federal Business Development Bank (FBDB) to new and existing businesses, particularly small businesses, that cannot obtain funds on reasonable terms and conditions from private sector institutions. As the name suggests, **project financing** makes funds available for the financing of a specific undertaking, such as feasibility studies, the purchase of equipment and/or machinery, or working capital in conjunction with the project.

It is beyond the scope of this chapter to outline all government programmes. Necessary information can be obtained from the regional offices of Industry Canada, the Federal Business Development Bank, and provincial development agencies. These agencies are generally listed prominently in telephone directories, or information about them may be obtained through the many outlets of various financial institutions. Also, it is always a good idea for an entrepreneur seeking assistance from government programmes to first discuss them with his or her bank manager, who should be familiar with what is available. After these discussions the bank manager will be in a position to advise the entrepreneur as to whether he or she would be better off applying for a loan under the Small Business Loans Act or through the Federal Business Development Bank.

Small Business Loans Act   The Small Business Loans Act (SBLA) came into effect in January 1961 and is designed to help new and existing small business enterprises obtain term loans from chartered banks and other designated lenders to help finance specified long-term assets—*not* inventory, working capital, or the refinancing of existing debt. SBLA loans are made to small businesses engaged in communications, construction, fishing, manufacturing, retail trade, service business (including insurance and real estate agencies), transportation, and wholesale trade. For a firm to qualify for an SBLA loan, its gross revenue must not exceed $5 million during the year in which the application is made. Under the programme, the federal government guarantees to repay approved lenders 85 percent of any losses incurred because of the failure of a qualified borrower. This guarantee covers a maximum of $250,000 of loans per eligible business. In return, the lender agrees to charge a maximum interest rate of 3 percent over the prime rate for loans used to purchase, instal, improve, and modernize machinery, equipment, buildings, and land. In addition, to move the programme to full cost recovery and to provide an incentive to financial institutions to use conventional financing wherever possible, the government has imposed an annual fee of 1.25 percent on the lender's average outstanding balance on SBLA loans. All loans granted under the Act are secured by the assets financed and must be repaid within 10 years.

From 1961, when the act went into effect, to March 31, 1993, approved lenders took out 316,144 business improvement loans worth more than $9 billion, for an average loan of $28,164. During this time the government reimbursed lenders $396.4 million based on 17,613 claims they made under the loan guarantee provision of the Act.[3]

---

[3] Small Business Loans Act, *Annual Report on Operations,* March 31, 1993.

FEDERAL BUSINESS DEVELOPMENT BANK

The Federal Business Development Bank is the main federal agency involved in small business financing. Established in 1975 as a Crown corporation, it has the specific objective of promoting and assisting small and medium-sized businesses in Canada at the start up stage or some other stage in their development. FBDB financing is available through loans, loan guarantees, equity participation, or any combination of these that best meets the needs of the small business. The majority of the financial assistance, however, is in the form of term loans for the purchase of long-term assets (including other businesses). In addition, unlike loans received under the SBLA, these loans may be used for the refinancing of existing debt and for working capital purposes. To be eligible for an FBDB loan a firm must show that it is unable to obtain financing from private-sector institutions at reasonable rates and conditions. Thus the FBDB is a supplementary source of funds to small and medium-sized businesses and, therefore, is not in competition with private sector institutions.

The FBDB has offices across Canada and makes loans in all regions of the country. For the year ending March 31, 1993, the Bank's loan volume increased 9 percent to $640.6 million. During the same period the number of loans and guarantees authorized also rose 11 percent to 4,241; more than one-half of the loans were for $100,000 or less. The interest rate charged by the FBDB is normally 2 to 3 percent higher than the prime rate charged by the chartered banks. The length of the loan depends on the circumstances; it is usually for a five-year period, but longer terms may be negotiated. An important feature is that if the applicant should be in a position to justify the need, arrangements can be made to pay only interest to the bank, with the payment of the principal deferred until the business is firmly established.

The FBDB has a requirement that the borrower supplement any funds it provides with additional funds from other sources. As the following information shows, the FBDB helped to finance projects of a variety of types worth more than $913.9 million in 1993.[4]

Project Financing (in millions)

	1989	1990	1991	1992	1993
FBDB	$ 926.7	$ 903.9	$518.8	$585.7	$640.6
Other sources	445.0	399.2	254.5	319.7	273.3
Total	$1,371.7	$1,303.1	$773.3	$905.4	$913.9
Nature of Projects					
Land, building, machinery, and equipment	$ 903.9	$ 821.1	$511.6	$531.0	$520.4
Working capital and refinancing	298.4	291.8	170.0	270.6	259.1
Change of ownership	137.4	162.0	59.8	68.6	86.7
Other purposes	32.0	28.2	31.9	35.2	47.7
Total	$1,371.7	$1,303.1	$773.3	$905.4	$913.9

---

[4] See Federal Business Development Bank, *Annual Report 1993*.

These data show that in 1993, as in the other years, more than 40 percent of the financing for these projects came from other sources and that the vast majority of the funds were used to purchase land, buildings, and machinery and equipment.

Management Services In addition to providing financial services, the FBDB also administers the Counselling Assistance for Small Enterprises (CASE) programme, which provides individual counselling by experienced business people to numerous entrepreneurs every year. Through its Management Services Division it also provides business management seminars and workshops to cater to local business needs in small centres across Canada. The following data from the FBDB's 1993 annual report shows the extent of its involvement in this area in recent years.

	1989	1990	1991	1992	1993
CASE: assignments completed	8,937	10,219	11,413	9,759	8,052
Management training seminars: participants	19,519	20,748	25,221	21,221	16,458
Management workshops: participants	27,190	33,346	41,814	49,120	54,367

OTHER GOVERNMENT PROGRAMMES

Because small businesses tend to be distributed across Canada in proportion to the population, they play an important role in the regional development of the country. In response, regional agencies have been set up to focus on specific regional concerns. The most important of these agencies are the Atlantic Canada Opportunities Agency (ACOA), the Federal Office of Regional Development—Quebec (FORD—Q), the Federal Office of Economic Development for Northern Ontario (FedNor), and Western Economic Diversification Canada (WD). These agencies aid small business by targeting their funds at gaps in public financial markets and key growth industries. In particular, they provide funds for business startups and expansions requiring longer time horizons to recoup investments, and they take greater risks than the chartered banks will.

Concept Review Questions

- What is the most common source of debt financing for small businesses?
- What are the five phases of initial financing a small firm typically experiences?
- What are the private sources of debt financing available to small businesses?
- What types of loans are available from public sources? What agencies provide these loans?

OBTAINING EQUITY FINANCING

Small businesses rarely have the opportunity to obtain equity funding by going public. Investment dealers have to be convinced of the marketability of a proposed public offering. Furthermore, the cost of placing a small issue for a small company is usually disproportionately large. So the small company that wants to become bigger by increasing its share capitalization will probably first seek private sources of equity capital or, second, look to an external source, such as the venture capital market. Although there are reportedly more than 500 private venture capital companies nationwide, a lot of venture capital firms would rather not invest small amounts of funds as start up capital. They usually are committing amounts in excess of $500,000, with varying conditions in their agreements.[5] Also, most venture capital firms prefer to enter the financial picture at or beyond the third level of a firm's development, when the business has a track record, is showing some growth potential, and needs an infusion of cash to support growth.

To address the problems that small businesses encounter in raising equity capital, the FBDB formed its Venture Capital Division in 1983. However, when the FBDB provides equity capital it takes only a minority position and holds its investments for an average of from four to seven years, thereby encouraging the firm to obtain investments from the private sector at the same time. The FBDB's 1993 annual report states that "the $102.5 million that it has invested in firms across the country has been complemented by an additional $341.4 million . . . ." Table 27.1 shows a sample of the many and varied sources of venture capital across Canada.

Table 27.1

A Sample of Venture Capital Sources

Venture capital is available from a variety of sources. To ensure its position, the venture capitalist usually receives significant voting stock in the firm.

Alberta	British Columbia	Nova Scotia
Aeonian Capital Corp., Calgary *Prime targets:* forest products, film, energy, and industrial manufacturing companies *Minimum funding:* not specified *Tradeoffs:* directorships, 25 to 50 percent interest	**Bawlf Management and Assoc.,** Vancouver *Prime targets:* equity or debt investments in young companies or turnaround situations *Minimum funding:* $500,000 *Tradeoffs:* minimum 50 percent interest, directorships	**Scotia Capital Corp, Ltd.,** Halifax *Prime targets:* equity and debt investments in wide range of Nova Scotia companies *Minimum funding:* none *Tradeoffs:* up to 40 percent equity positions, directorships

(continued)

---

[5] See *FOCUS 2000: Report of the Task Force on Making Investment Capital Available* (Ottawa: The Canadian Chamber of Commerce, August 1988).

Table 27.1 Continued

Ontario	Quebec	Others sources: Associations/Clubs
Canadian Industrial Innovation Centre/Waterloo, Waterloo *Prime targets:* inventors, entrepreneurs with new products *Minimum funding:* none *Tradeoffs:* varying percentages of product royalties	**Innocan, Inc.,** Montreal *Prime targets:* manufacturing and service companies *Minimum funding:* $1,000,000 *Tradeoffs:* directorships, control desired	**Association of Canadian Venture Capital Companies,** Toronto Member profile listings are available free of charge **Department of Business Development and Tourism,** Winnipeg *Prime targets:* manufacturing, processing, high-technology research and development, computer software, heavy equipment repair and maintenance, commercial air and water transportation companies, tourism, and selected farm-service businesses *Minimum funding:* $35,000 *Tradeoffs:* up to 49 percent of voting shares
Northern Telecom Ltd., Mississauga *Prime targets:* convertible debt and equity investment in fast-growing, high-technology firms *Minimum funding:* $250,000 *Tradeoffs:* minority positions, directorships	**Société de Developpement de l'Entreprise Québécois (Sodeq),** St. George, Beauce *Prime targets:* rapid-growth Quebec companies, some startups *Minimum funding:* $50,000 *Tradeoffs:* minority equity positions, directorships	
Royal Bank Venture Capital Ltd., Toronto *Prime targets:* a wide range, including forestry, chemical, transportation, and publication companies *Minimum funding:* $200,000 *Tradeoffs:* 5 to 30 percent equity	**Corporation Financière du Centre du Quebéc, Inc.,** Trois-Rivierès *Prime targets:* equity and debt investments in Quebec firms involved in real estate, distribution, consulting, and industrial manufacturing *Minimum funding:* $500,000 *Tradeoffs:* 34 to 100 percent voting shares	

*Source: Canadian Business, Vol. 59, No. 10 (October 1986), 108.

Only a small number of businesses ever grow into large ones, but small firms in high-tech industries, especially electronics, computers, and communications, are likely candidates to grow into large firms. Such firms are in a position to raise capital by going public with a stock issue. However, an initial public offering (IPO) is not without costs, both explicit and implicit. For example, the explicit costs of an IPO consist of not only the flotation costs associated with the underwriter's fees, but also underpricing of the issue. As we noted in Chapter 10, underpricing is a real, but hidden, cost of issuing stock for the first time. It derives from the uncertainty associated with pricing a stock that has no previous public market price. At the time of the initial offering, the price may be as much as 15–20 percent below the price that prevails in the market *after* the offering. On the other hand, IPOs usually trade on the over-the-counter market, not on an organized exchange, and as a consequence the entrepreneur is subject to only limited disclosure requirements. However, if the firm continues to grow to the point where it can be listed on an organized exchange, it will have to comply with more requirements. For example, the entrepreneur will now have to comply with the stock exchange's listing requirements and divulge more information about the firm's financial position on a quarterly basis. This requirement to file quarterly financial statements potentially carries an implicit cost if the firm sacrifices its long-term objectives due to a greater need for short-term earnings. The emphasis on short-term earnings may cause the firm to undertake projects with the shortest payback period instead of the highest net present value and thus cause the value of the firm to decline in the long run. The implication of this is that there are significant costs associated with going public. Firms must be constantly on the lookout for projects with the highest NPV and not emphasize short-term earnings, but underpricing is a one-time occurrence since with subsequent issues there will be an existing market price.

Concept Review Question

■ Where do most small businesses obtain their equity financing?

FINANCIAL CONTROL AND PLANNING

A small business generally has a limited supply of funds, and short-term borrowing from chartered banks can fill only day-to-day needs. Liquidity is, therefore, crucial for the small business operator. Thus a very basic need of the small business operator is the ability to prepare a monthly cash flow statement, which includes a projection of cash requirements. The cash budget, as we saw in Chapter 26, is critical in assessing the company's needs for short-term funds. It is simply a forecast of cash receipts and disbursements against which actual cash experience is measured and is, consequently, the most important single tool of small business control.

In addition, the control of cash calls for a replanning process, because if changes are needed they must be carried out quickly to ensure that the correct policy is properly executed. Then a revised cash budget is prepared, and a cash report is drawn up to determine whether the cash control plan is working. Today, there are many electronic spreadsheet programmes that simplify this cash budgeting process immeasurably.

CONTROLLING CREDIT, COLLECTIONS, AND INVENTORY

The most difficult task in the control process, whether one is dealing with credit, collections, or inventory, is the establishment of a policy that states the standards or yardsticks against which to assess the performance of the company in these aspects of the operation. The difficulty also arises because, in most cases, the personal interests of the entrepreneur have been the motivating force for getting the business started, rather than the apparent need for control and the rigidity of details related to operational procedures. Nevertheless, to ensure any measure of success, a policy must be outlined and its conditions implemented and adhered to. The result of unsound policies is, of course, excessive losses in accounts receivable that could eventually become worthless and tie up capital that may be badly needed—a very common occurrence for the small business. Sound credit policies for a small business, like those discussed for large firms in Chapter 23, begin with a thorough knowledge of the customer's financial position to determine the terms and conditions of sale and the collection policy.

On the other side of the ledger, inventory control is of equal concern. Even the smallest operation will tend to find itself in difficulty without adequate, written, well-organized, readily available records of the various categories of its inventory. Thus two important strategies, particularly for the small manufacturer, are to order in economical quantities and to establish optimal reordering points, details of which have been discussed previously in Appendix 23A.

FINANCIAL PERFORMANCE ANALYSIS

The methods discussed in Chapter 25 for analyzing the performance of large firms are equally applicable to the accounting analysis of small businesses. Once again, we use common-size statements and ratio analysis to assess the performance of the business. However, of the many ratios discussed in Chapter 25, the following are probably the most significant for analyzing the performance of a small business.

1. Current ratio
2. Quick ratio
3. Days sales outstanding
4. Inventory turnover
5. Total asset turnover
6. Total debt to total assets
7. Times interest earned
8. Net profit margin
9. Return on total assets
10. Return on equity

The purpose of any ratio analysis is to be able to observe trends and changes that may provide clues about future cash flows rather than simply obtaining a single number from each ratio. A minimum of three years' data, if that much is available, should at least provide a feel for what is going on in the small business.

Because of the significance of current assets for small businesses, special attention must be paid to the current and quick ratios as well as the days sales outstanding and inventory turnover. As a firm grows, the growth in receivables, inventories, and long-term assets will most likely outpace the growth in cash generated from the firm's operations. Although the firm is growing, it is still a small business and consequently faces a restricted source of external financing. Accordingly, the financing of this growth in assets will usually take the form of term loans directly from chartered banks or through government programmes. These loans will cause the firm's debt management ratios to deteriorate and eventually to prompt questions from lenders. If this happens, the firm would be forced to obtain more equity financing or to curtail its growth. Thus it is important for a small business, especially a growing one, to use ratio analysis as an integral part of its overall financial control and planning process to achieve balanced growth and to ensure survival.

PLANNING THE FINANCIAL FUTURE

Typically, entrepreneurs spend much of their time on the operational aspects and too little on planning in general. Often, they have gone into business in the first place because of interest and presumably expertise in a product or service. Once in business, entrepreneurs tend to concentrate their efforts on what they know and like doing the best, and financial planning does not usually fit into that category. Nevertheless, it is as important as the product or service, for without financing, no business can exist. A major reason for financial planning is to force entrepreneurs to think about the future of their small business in very real terms, thereby developing solutions to potential problems before a crisis occurs.

Before it is possible for entrepreneurs to make an estimate of the growth and future direction of their company, they must decide what their major goals and objectives are and what strategy they will use to achieve them. Once these have been formulated in broad terms, the entrepreneurs can then focus specifically on sales, production, and employees. The emphasis required for each will, of course, depend on the type of business. The basic components of financial planning are the income statement, balance sheet, cash flow statement, and capital budget. Again, the relative emphasis on these four components will depend on the type of business; for example, a service industry may require little or no capital budget. Because of the very limited financial expertise of most small business management, more emphasis is often placed on accounting-generated financial statements than on financial planning and forecasting, as discussed in Chapter 26.

A financial plan is an indication of what the entrepreneur perceives will occur in a future period of time, usually the next one to three years. Many large companies look at periods of five years or more in their financial planning, but it is much more realistic for small business people to think in terms of three years. It is, of course, not enough that entrepreneurs anticipate the growth and development of their small business and the avenues for achieving their goals and objectives; they must also have a system for providing continuous feedback about the progress being made in reaching the objectives. So although details on the operational aspects of the small business explain actions to be taken during the planning stages in an effort to reach the firm's goals, it is the financial plan that reflects the ultimate returns expected to result from the operations. With today's access to computers, the management information system can readily supply progress reports that will enable entrepreneurs to assess the results on an ongoing basis.

Concept Review Questions

■ Why is a cash budget important to a small business?

- Why are short-term ratios important for small businesses?
- Why may the personal interests of the entrepreneur be an impediment to sound financial planning?

SMALL BUSINESS IN THE FUTURE

During the next decade, small businesses will face many new challenges and opportunities emerging from an information economy, in which the ability to compile, transform, and apply knowledge has become a key element in business success. Recent developments in computer and telecommunication technologies have increased office efficiency and business capability to such an extent that economies of scale are no longer a crucial advantage. As a result, even a small firm can be competitive. In this new competition, small businesses, like businesses in general, must take a broader look at their competition and markets. Technology has overcome distances, and various trade agreements, such as the North American Free Trade Agreement, are dismantling trade barriers. Consequently, in the future small businesses must look beyond local markets. They can no longer rely on the safety of isolation to build size and experience in a local market before moving beyond it. Now, right from startup, a small business may be in competition with large, international firms. In such an environment small firms will have to be more aggressive and enter export markets to protect their domestic market.

Increasingly, technology will determine competitiveness. In the future, as technological innovation accelerates, small businesses will have to make timely use of technology to remain competitive or else risk losing to a competitor who adopts it first. To be in the forefront of technology, firms will have to be alert for innovations from all over the world; in today's information economy technology knows no borders. Findings from one part of the world quickly form the basis for products in another.

Given the time and resources necessary, how can a small business enter broader markets and obtain up-to-date technology? One way is for a small business to enter into a joint venture with a large, established or international firm. The large firm can provide capital, expertise, technology, and entry into new markets. This will serve as a counterbalance to the shortening product life cycles and increased customer demand for semicustomized products brought about by the rapid pace of technological change, while at the same time allowing the small firm to retain its flexibility and independence. Furthermore, the small firm should use its flexibility to its advantage by responding to customer demands in a particular niche overlooked by or impractical for large firms, and not by servicing very wide product lines. The access to new markets, particularly international ones, will help the small firm exploit its specialized niche to the fullest.

Concept Review Question

- What implications does the new competition have for small business?

KEY POINTS

- Small businesses are a vital component of the Canadian economy, accounting for more than 97 percent of all enterprises and creating more than 80 percent of new jobs.
- The business plan is the single most important document for a small business. The suppliers of funds look for a well-thought-out business plan which includes a financial section that clearly establishes the need for the requested funds and a realistic repayment schedule.
- Small businesses are precluded from capital markets; therefore, banks are their major source of private debt financing. Government guaranteed loans are also available to small businesses under the Small Business Loans Act, through the Federal Business Development Bank, or from regional agencies.
- Very few small businesses grow into large ones. Those that do find it difficult to raise equity financing in the capital markets. As a result small firms rely on venture capitalists for equity financing.
- The proper management policies and standards regarding liquid assets are crucial for success of a small business.
- Now and in the future small businesses will face a new competition which is placing more emphasis on technology and management skills, flexibility, and exploiting niche products in international markets.

QUESTIONS

27.1 How frequently should the business plan be prepared?

27.2 You would like to purchase a small manufacturing company for $50,000 but you can raise only $10,000. A rich uncle might be able to help you but only after you have answered the following questions: What is your business? Why do you need the money? How do you plan to repay the money? At what rate of interest and over what period of time? How can he be certain you can pay him back? Did you try anywhere else? If you did not, why not? If you did, why were you turned down? Indicate how you would respond to his questions.

27.3 What are some of the more significant features of the Small Business Loans Act? Is it available for all types of business? In all provinces?

27.4 What is the Federal Business Development Bank? How do its functions differ from those of the chartered banks?

27.5 "If a new business cannot raise cash in the marketplace, the worst thing the government can do is to make it rely on government programmes." Do you agree with this statement? Why or why not?

27.6 With the numerous federal programmes available, as well as the services of the Federal Business Development Bank, why do provinces have their own programmes?

27.7 "Venture capital firms cannot take ownership of more than 25 percent of any small business, and, like banks, they are lenders, not investors." Do you agree with this statement? Why or why not?

27.8 Should venture capital firms invest in a service as opposed to a manufacturing business? If yes, under what conditions might they be interested? If no, why not?

CONCEPT REVIEW PROBLEMS

See Appendix A for solutions.

CR27.1   Start-Up Distributors borrowed $36,050 on a term loan with an annual interest rate of 13 percent. The length of the loan is five years and it must be repaid with annual payments. What is the principal repayment in the third year?

CR27.2   CRF Enterprises is a medium-sized firm whose CFO, Debbie, is in the midst of preparing a cash budget for next year. Under the most likely case, sales (cash inflows) are estimated to be $100,000, $120,000, $140,000, and $100,000, respectively, for the four quarters. Cost of goods sold is $40,000 plus 20 percent of sales per quarter; selling, general, and administrative expenses are $10,000 plus 5 percent of sales per quarter; and interest expenses are $5,000 per quarter. Taxes (at a 40 percent rate) are paid quarterly on the inflows and outflows. Other net cash inflows (+) or outflows (−) per quarter are +$10,000, −$50,000, −$60,000, and +$20,000, respectively. Cash on hand at the beginning of quarter 1 is $20,000, and a minimum cash balance of $15,000 must be maintained. Under its loan agreement, CRF can borrow funds during the year but must be out of debt by the end of quarter 4.

a.   Help Debbie prepare a cash budget for the next four quarters for CRF. Will CRF violate its loan agreement?

b.   With a pessimistic forecast, sales will be $20,000 less *each* quarter, and other net cash outflows will be cut to −$40,000 in quarter 2 and −$50,000 in quarter 3. Will CRF violate its loan agreement?

c.   With an optimistic forecast, sales will increase by $20,000 *each* quarter. Can CRF increase its other net cash outflows to a total of $70,000 in quarter 2 and −$75,000 in quarter 3 and still meet its loan agreement?

PROBLEMS

27.1   Alex Industries has annual purchases of $730,000 and average accounts payable of $60,000. Credit terms granted to Alex Industries are 1/10, net 30. Is the firm paying all of its bills in time to take advantage of the 1 percent discount? Assume a 365-day year.

27.2   Harbour Import needs $400,000 for the next 91 days. Two alternative sources are available:

a.   A loan secured by accounts receivable. The firm's bank has agreed to lend Harbour 70 percent of the value of its pledged receivables (which are just large enough to provide the $400,000 loan). The interest rate is 11 percent per year. In addition, there is a processing fee of 1 percent (for the 91-day period) of the value of the *total* receivables pledged.

b.   An insurance company has agreed to loan the $400,000 at a rate of 9 percent per year, using a loan secured by Harbour's inventory. A field warehousing agreement will be used; it costs $2,100 per 30 days.

By calculating the before-tax effective annual rate, determine which financing source should be employed.

27.3   You have been looking for an opportunity to get started in a small business and have heard about Spencer Distribution. Only now, however, have you received their financial statements. Before looking any further into Spencer's operations, you need to calculate a number of ratios to give you a better idea of what its performance has been. The financial data are as follows:

Balance Sheet as of January 31

Cash	$ 100	Accounts payable	$ 85,700
Accounts receivable	89,200	Bank loan	53,200
Inventory	82,900	Accrued expenses	5,900
Other current assets	5,400	Mortgage at 9.5%	64,300
Land	18,900	Owner's equity	88,100
Long-term assets net of		Total	$297,200
depreciation	100,700		
Total	$297,200		

Income Statement for the Year Ended January 31

Sales		$766,500
Cost of goods sold		549,700
Gross margin		216,800
Trucking expenses	$34,400	
Sales commissions	34,600	
Wages and salaries	79,200	
Depreciation	9,000	
Bank charges and interest	6,400	
All other expenses	39,200	202,800
Net income		$ 14,000

a. Calculate the following ratios: (1) current ratio, (2) quick ratio, (3) days sales outstanding (use a 365-day year), (4) inventory turnover, (5) total debt to total assets, (6) net profit margin, and (7) return on equity.

b. Using the information calculated in (a), interpret your results in light of the following:
   1. A current ratio of at least 2.50 to 1 is normal in the industry.
   2. A quick ratio of at least 1.50 to 1 is normal in the industry.
   3. Spencer Distribution offers net 30-day credit terms.
   4. The industry inventory turnover is 12 times.
   5. A normal total debt to total asset ratio is 0.55.
   6. Net profit margin for the industry is 2.5 percent.
   7. Return on equity for the industry is 16 percent.

c. What other information would you like to have before making a decision on whether this is the opportunity you have been waiting for?

27.4 The Beaton Company has a sales level that varies considerably throughout the year. Mr. Beaton has managed to keep the business going, but not without a struggle. Concerned that this condition might continue indefinitely, he decided to prepare a plan for the next six months. He has already calculated his expected sales for the first six months and has compiled the following additional data.
   1. Sixty percent of sales are for cash; estimated sales for January through June are $3,000, $5,000, $7,000, $12,000, $8,000, and $7,000 respectively. They were $3,000 for December.
   2. All accounts receivable are received the month following the sale; there are no bad debts.
   3. Purchases, which equal 55 percent of sales, must be made one month in advance of the expected sale and paid for in the month of the expected sale.

4. Wages are $1,250 per month; when sales go higher than $8,000 per month, an additional employee must be hired at $500 per month.
5. Rent is $500 per month but will increase by 10 percent in March.
6. All other operating expenses total $250 a month.
7. An insurance premium of $750 must be paid May 15.
8. Building repairs must be carried out and paid for in February, at an estimated cost of $500.
9. Taxes of $250 are due in January and April; in the other months they are $50.
10. The firm has an initial cash balance of $2,000 on January 1; its minimum cash balance is $1,500.
11. The firm can borrow on a line of credit at 12 percent per year (1 percent per month). Interest is paid the month following the loan. Beaton's tax rate is 20 percent.
12. No loans are outstanding at January 1.
a. Prepare a cash budget for Beaton.
b. Based on the cash budget, how much will Beaton borrow or repay in each month?

27.5 Mini Case A friend is about to start a small business and has come to you for advice. He has been trying to raise funds but cannot. Everyone he approaches for funds asks to see his business plan. Not only does he not have a business plan, he does not know what one is.

a. He asks you what a business plan is. In your opinion, why should any small business owner-manager need such a plan?
b. He has come to realize that banks are very important for small businesses. He asks you to discuss each of the following statements relative to dealing with bankers.
   1. Your relationship with them is important.
   2. Bankers are more likely to give you a loan if they know about your business.
   3. Your banker probably would not be of much help in avoiding business surprises.
   4. Bankers are not interested in lending to brand-new firms if there is little or no collateral.
   5. Never ask a banker for money without also asking for advice and information.
c. Your friend listened carefully to your advice. He prepared a sound business plan and was well prepared to talk to his banker. As a result his bank has approved his request for a four-year term loan. The loan will be for $50,000 beginning July 1. The loan agreement calls for a 12 percent annual interest rate compounded monthly, with payments to be made monthly. He now asks you the following:
   1. Construct a loan amortization schedule for the first six months and determine the total interest expense associated with the loan for the year ending December 31.
   2. Using the information in (c.1) and the following information from the cash budget in his business plan for the year ended December 31, determine his business' income taxes payable: sales revenue = $300,000; cost of goods sold = $250,000 (including CCA of $25,000); administrative expenses = $35,000; corporate tax rate = 25 percent.
   3. If all of the conditions described in (c.2) hold except that the amount of CCA increases to $40,000, causing the cost of goods sold to increase accordingly, determine the taxes payable. What would happen with the interest expense in this situation?
d. Your friend now asks your advice about the choice between buying or leasing a piece of used equipment. The equipment is still in good shape and can be used for another five years. It is in asset class 8 (CCA rate, 20 percent), the firm's tax rate is 25 percent, and the before-tax cost of borrowing is 13.34 percent. The equipment will cost $200,000, but it can be leased for $54,000 per year, payable at the beginning of each of the five years.
   1. If the NPV is positive, should the equipment be leased or purchased?
   2. What decision should be made if 10 semiannual lease payments of $27,000 each (payable at the beginning of each six-month period) are made? (*Note:* CCA can be calculated only on an annual basis.)

REFERENCES

Association of Canadian Venture Capital Companies. *Venture Capital in Canada: A Guide and Sources*. Prepared by Mary Macdonald and Associates, 1992.

BEAMISH, P. W., and H. MUNRO. "The Export Performance of Small and Medium-Size Canadian Manufacturers." *Canadian Journal of Administrative Sciences* 3 (June 1986): 29–40.

BUERGER, JAMES E., and THOMAS A. ULRICH. "What's Important to Small Business in Selecting a Financial Institution." *Journal of Commercial Bank Lending* 69 (October 1986): 3–9.

FLETCHER, JAMES M. "Venture Capital in Canada." *Canadian Investment Review* 5 (Spring 1992): 99–103.

GRAY, DOUGLAS A., and BRIAN F. NATTRAS. *Raising Money: The Canadian Guide to Successful Business Financing*. Toronto: McGraw-Hill Ryerson, 1993.

KORKIE, BOB. "Market Line Deviations and Market Anomalies with Reference to Small and Large Firms." *Journal of Financial and Quantitative Analysis* 21 (June 1986): 161–180.

KRYZANOWSKI, L., and M. C. To. "Small-Business Debt Financing: An Empirical Investigation of Default Risk." *Canadian Journal of Administrative Sciences* 2 (June 1985): 24–42.

LEVIN, RICHARD I., and VIRGINIA R. TRAVIS. "Small Company Finance: What the Books Don't Say." *Harvard Business Review* 57 (November–December 1987): 30–32.

WILLIAMSON, IAIN. *Financing Start-up Companies in Canada*. Toronto: Productive Publications, 1988a.

———. *Successful Small Business Financing in Canada*. Toronto: Productive Publications, 1988b.

Solutions to Concept Review Problems

Chapter 1

CR1.1

Sales	$700,000
Cost of goods sold	100,000
Administrative expenses	300,000
Depreciation	50,000
Earnings before interest and taxes, EBIT	250,000
Interest	60,000
Earnings before taxes, EBT	190,000
Taxes (40%)	76,000
Earnings after tax, EAT (Net income)	$114,000

CR1.2

a.

Cash inflow	
Sales	$700,000
Cash outflows	
Cost of goods sold	100,000
Administrative expenses	300,000
Interest	60,000
Taxes	76,000
Dividends paid	100,000
Total cash outflows	$636,000

Net cash flow from operations $700,000 − $636,000 = $64,000

b. Cash from sales = $420,000, so the net cash flow from operations = $420,000 − $636,000 = −$216,000.

CR1.3

	Cash Inflows		Cash Outflows	
Sales for cash	$26,000	Cash expenses	$12,000
Cash on hand	500	Interest	6,000
Total	$26,500	Taxes	3,200
		Cash dividend	500
		Short-term debt	1,500
		Total	$23,200

Net cash flow = $26,500 − $23,200 = $3,300

CR1.4   a.
$$\text{projected return} = \frac{\$11,000}{\$10,000} - 1 = 10\%$$

b.
$$\text{NPV} = \frac{\$11,000}{1.15} - \$10,000 = -\$435$$

CR1.5   **Projected Income Statement**

Sales	$80,000
Cost of goods sold	60,000
Depreciation	15,000
Earnings before interest and taxes, EBIT	5,000
Interest	10,000
Earnings before taxes, EBT	−5,000
Taxes (40%)	0
Earnings after tax, EAT (net income)	−$5,000

Projected Cash Flow

Total cash inflows	$64,000
Cash outflow	
Expenses	$48,000
Interest expense	10,000
Total cash outflow	$58,000

Cash surplus = $64,000 − $58,000 = $6,000
Their calculations were correct, and yes, it is possible to have a negative net income and a positive net cash flow.

Chapter 2

CR2.1   a. $20,000(74.9625) = ¥1,499,250
b.   M47,356(0.9408) = $44,552.52
c. $15,000(0.4752) = £7,128

CR2.2 $E(S_{2/1}) = [3.7037(1.06)]/1.03 = $ FF 3.8116

Chapter 3

CR3.1 $FV_3 = \$25,000(FV_{8\%, 3yr}) = \$25,000(1.260) = \$31,500$

$FV_7 = \$31,500(FV_{10\%/2, 2\times4yr}) = \$31,500(1.477) = \$46,525.50$

CR3.2

a. $PV_0 = \dfrac{\$5,000}{\left(1 + \dfrac{0.10}{12}\right)^{3(12)}} = \$3,709$

b. $k_{\text{effective annual}} = \left(1 + \dfrac{0.10}{12}\right)^{12} - 1 = 10.47\%$

CR3.3

a. $\$1,000,000/20 = \$50,000$ per year

$PV_0 = \$50,000(PVA_{8\%,20yr}) = \$50,000(9.818) = \$490,900$

b. $PV_0 = \$490,900(1.08) = \$530,172$

CR3.4

a. $NPV = \$140,000(PV_{12\%,\,1yr}) + \$200,000(PV_{12\%,\,2yr}) + \$250,000(PV_{12\%,\,3yr})$
$- \$500,000$

$= \$140,000(0.893) + \$200,000(0.797) + \$250,000(0.712) - \$500,000$

$= -\$37,580$

b. $\dfrac{\$140,000}{(1 + IRR)^1} + \dfrac{\$200,000}{(1 + IRR)^2} + \dfrac{\$250,000}{(1 + IRR)^3} = \$500,000$

By trial-and-error, using 8 percent, the present value of the cash inflows is $499,540, which is slightly less than the $500,000 initial cash outflow. Therefore, the IRR is slightly less than 8 percent. By financial calculator the IRR is 7.96 percent.

CR3.5

If the 2.9 percent financing is taken, the payment is:

$\$20,000 = PMT\left[\dfrac{1 - [1/(1 + 0.029/12)^{2 \times 12}]}{0.029/12}\right]$

$PMT = \$858.74$

If the rebate is taken and the remainder financed at 8 percent by the bank, the payment is:

$\$18,000 = PMT\left[\dfrac{1 - [1/(1 + 0.08/12)^{2 \times 12}]}{0.08/12}\right]$

$PMT = \$814.09$; take the rebate

CR3.6

a. Equation 3.26 can be used because the payment period coincides with the compounding period.

$PV_0 = PMT\left\{\dfrac{1 - \left[1 \middle/ \left(1 + \dfrac{k_{\text{nominal}}}{m}\right)^{mn}\right]}{\dfrac{k_{\text{nominal}}}{m}}\right\}$

Solving for PMT:

$\$150,000 = PMT\left\{\dfrac{1 - [1/(1 + 0.1075/12)^{12 \times 25}]}{0.1075/12}\right\}$

$PMT = \$150,000/103.94008 = \$1,443.14$ per month

The balance remaining on the principal after the first payment is

$PV_1 = \$1,443.14\left\{\dfrac{1 - [1/(1 + 0.1075/12)^{299}]}{0.1075/12}\right\} = \$149,900.70$

b. The method of calculation is the same except that the beginning balance becomes the remaining principal at the end of the first month ($149,900.70) and the amortization period has gone down by one month to 299.

$$\$149,900.70 = PMT\left\{\frac{1 - [1/(1 + 0.1125/12)^{299}]}{0.1125/12}\right\}$$

$$PMT = \$149,900.70/100.11551 = \$1,497.28$$

Calculating the balance at the end of the second month:

$$PV_2 = \$1,497.28\left\{\frac{1 - [1/(1 + 0.1125/12)^{298}]}{0.1125/12}\right\} = \$149,808.99$$

c. $k_{EM} = k_{nominal}/m = 0.009375 = 0.9375\%$

Interest paid $= (PV_1)(k_{EM}) = (\$149,900.70)(0.009375) = \$1,405.32$

Principal paid $=$ payment $-$ interest paid $= \$1,497.28 - \$1,405.32 = \$91.96$

Alternatively;

Principal paid $= PV_1 - PV_2 = \$149,900.70 - \$149,808.99 = 91.71$

The different answers from the two methods are due to rounding differences.

Chapter 4

CR4.1

a. $B_0 = \$50(PVA_{4\%,\,30yr}) + \$1,000(PV_{4\%,\,30yr})$

$\qquad = \$50(17.292) + \$1,000(0.308)$

$\qquad = \$864.60 + \$308.00 = \$1,172.60$

b. $B_0 = \$1,149.15$

CR4.2

The interest per semiannual period is $(0.06)(\$1,000)/2 = \$30$, and the number of periods is $(2)(20) = 40$. Since the bond is selling at a discount, the YTM will be more than 3 percent for half a year. Trying 4 percent.

$$B_0 = \$30(PVA_{4\%,\,40yr}) + \$1,000(PV_{4\%,\,40yr})$$

$$\qquad = \$30(19.793) + \$1,000(0.208) = \$801.79$$

Therefore, the semiannual YTM must be between 3 and 4 percent. By financial calculator, the semiannual YTM is 3.25 percent, so the YTM on an annual basis is 6.50 percent.

CR4.3

You would be willing to pay

$$P_0 = \frac{\$6.50}{0.10} = \$65 \text{ per share}$$

The NPV $= P_0 -$ market price $= \$65 - \$70 = -\$5$.
Or, the expected return is:

$$k_x = \frac{\$6.50}{\$70} = 9.29\%$$

which is less than the required rate of return of 10 percent; therefore, you should not buy the preferred stock.

CR4.4

$$P_0 = \frac{\$1.65(1.06)}{0.14 - 0.06} = \frac{\$1.749}{0.08} = \$21.86$$

CR4.5

Dividend (or Price)		× PV at 14%	= Present Value
$D_1 = \$1.65(1.20)$	$= \$1.98$	0.877	$ 1.74
$D_2 = 1.65(1.20)^2$	$= 2.38$	0.769	1.83
$D_3 = 1.65(1.20)^3$	$= 2.85$	0.675	1.92
$D_4 = 1.65(1.20)^4$	$= 3.42$	0.592	2.02
$D_5 = 3.42(1.06)$	$= 3.62$		
$P_4 = \dfrac{3.62}{0.14 - 0.06} = \dfrac{3.62}{0.08}$	$= 45.25$	0.592	26.79
			$\$34.30 = P_0$

CR4.6

$$P_0 = \frac{\$2.00(1 - 0.15)}{0.20 - (-0.15)} = \frac{\$1.70}{0.35} = \$4.86$$

CR4.7

$$\text{return} = \frac{\$2.50(1.06) + [\$35(1.06) - \$35]}{\$35} = 13.57\%$$

Chapter 5

CR5.1

$$\bar{k}_{IBM} = 0.2(-15) + 0.6(10) + 0.2(35) = 10\%$$

$$\bar{k}_{DC} = 0.2(42) + 0.6(12) + 0.2(-30) = 9.6\%$$

$$\bar{k}_{market} = 0.2(-8) + 0.6(10) + 0.2(25) = 9.4\%$$

CR5.2

$$\sigma_{IBM} = [0.2(-15 - 10)^2 + 0.6(10 - 10)^2 + 0.2(35 - 10)^2]^{0.5} = (250)^{0.5} = 15.81\%$$

$$\sigma_{DC} = [0.2(42 - 9.6)^2 + 0.6(12 - 9.6)^2 + 0.2(-30 - 9.6)^2]^{0.5} = 22.96\%$$

$$\sigma_{market} = [0.2(-8 - 9.4)^2 + 0.6(10 - 9.4)^2 + 0.2(25 - 9.4)^2]^{0.5} = 10.46\%$$

$$CV_{IBM} = \frac{15.81\%}{10\%} = 1.58$$

$$CV_{DC} = \frac{22.96\%}{9.6\%} = 2.39$$

CR5.3

$$\bar{K}_{p+IBM} = 0.8(9.4) + 0.2(10) = 9.52\%$$

$$\bar{K}_{p+DC} = 0.8(9.4) + 0.2(9.6) = 9.44\%$$

CR5.4

$$\beta_{Bram} = \frac{10.56\%(0.45)}{8.67\%} = 0.55$$

$$\beta_{Itel} = \frac{12.15\%(0.85)}{8.67\%} = 1.19$$

CR5.5

$$k_{Bram} = 6.0\% + 0.55(11.0\% - 6.0\%) = 8.75\%$$

$$k_{Itel} = 6.0\% + 1.19(11.0\% - 6.0\%) = 11.95\%$$

CR5.6

$$k_{Bram} = 8.0\% + 0.55(13.0\% - 8.0\%) = 10.75\%$$

$$k_{Itel} = 8.0\% + 1.19(13.0\% - 8.0\%) = 13.95\%$$

CR5.7

a. $P_{0_{Bram}} = \dfrac{\$2.00(1.03)}{0.0875 - 0.03} = \$35.83$

$P_{0_{Itel}} = \dfrac{\$4.00(1.06)}{0.1195 - 0.06} = \$71.26$

b. $P_{0_{Bram}} = \dfrac{\$2.00(1.03)}{0.1075 - 0.03} = \$26.58$

$P_{0_{Itel}} = \dfrac{\$4.00(1.06)}{0.1395 - 0.06} = \$53.33$

Chapter 6

CR6.1

$$\$1,198 = \sum_{t=1}^{40} \frac{\$50}{(1 + k_b/2)^t} + \frac{\$1,000}{(1 + k_b/2)^{40}}$$

$k_b = 4\%$ semiannually, or 8 percent annually

$k_i = 8\%(1 - 0.35) = 5.20\%$

CR6.2 $k_{ps} = \$8.50/\$93 = 9.14\%$

CR6.3 $k_{s(\text{dividend valuation approach})} = \dfrac{\$7.20(1 - 0.50)}{\$40} + 0.04 = 13\%$

$k_{s(\text{capital asset pricing model})} = 6\% + 1.5(12\% - 6\%) = 15\%$

$k_{s(\text{bond yield + risk premium})} = 8\% + 6\% = 14\%$

The average cost of equity capital is $(13\% + 15\% + 14\%)/3 = 14\%$.

CR6.4

Component	Cost	Weight	Cost of Capital
Debt	5.20%	0.20	1.04%
Preferred stock	9.14	0.10	0.91
Common equity	14.00	0.70	9.80
Opportunity cost of capital			11.75%

CR6.5 Short-term debt: $10,000,000

Long-term debt:

$$B_0 = \sum_{t=1}^{40} \frac{\$60}{(t + 0.045)^t} + \frac{\$1,000}{(1 + 0.045)^{40}} = \$1,276$$

market value of long-term debt $= \left(\dfrac{\$30,000,000}{\$1,000}\right)(\$1,276) = \$38,280,000$

Preferred stock:

$$k_{ps} = \frac{\$12}{0.10} = \$120$$

market value of preferred stock $= \left(\dfrac{\$10,000,000}{\$100}\right)(\$120) = \$12,000,000$

Equity:

market value of equity $= (2,000,000)(\$37.50) = \$75,000,000$

Market value weights:

Component		Weight
Short-term debt	$10,000,000	0.074
Long-term debt	38,280,000	0.283
Preferred stock	12,000,000	0.089
Equity	75,000,000	0.554
Total market value	$135,280,000	1.000

CR6.6

$$k_{\text{short-term}} = 6\%(1 - 0.35) = 3.90\%$$

$$k_{\text{long-term}} = 9\%(1 - 0.35) = 5.85\%$$

$$k_{ps} = 10\%$$

Common equity:

$$k_s = (\$4/\$37.50) + 0.06 = 16.67\%$$

$$k_s = 6\% + 1.2(15\% - 6\%) = 16.80\%$$

$$k_s = 9\% + (15\% - 9\%) = 15\%$$

The average $k_s = (16.67\% + 16.80\% + 15\%)/3 = 16.16\%$.

CR6.7

Component	Cost	Weight	Cost of Capital
Short-term debt	3.90%	0.074	0.29%
Long-term debt	5.85	0.283	1.66
Preferred stock	10.00	0.089	0.89
Common equity	16.16	0.554	8.95
Opportunity cost of capital			11.79%

CR6.8

$$\text{New } k_s = [\$4/(\$37.50 - \$3.50)] + 0.06 = 17.76\%$$

Component	Cost	Weight	Cost of Capital
Short-term debt	3.90%	0.074	0.29%
Long-term debt	5.85	0.283	1.66
Preferred stock	10.00	0.089	0.89
Common equity	17.76	0.554	9.84
Opportunity cost of capital			12.68%

CR6.9

$$\beta_U = \frac{1.5}{1 + (1 - 0.40)(0.50)} = 1.15$$

$$\beta_{\text{levered division}} = (1.15)[1 + (1 - 0.35)(20\%/80\%)] = 1.34$$

$$k_{\text{division}} = 6\% + 1.34(15\% - 6\%) = 18.06\%$$

Component	Cost	Weight	Cost of Capital
Long-term debt	5.85%	0.20	1.17%
Common equity	18.06	0.80	14.45
Divisional opportunity cost of capital			15.62%

Chapter 7

CR7.1   Using the simulated annuity approach

($350,000 + $250,000 + 80,000)/3 = $226,667

$500,000/226,667 = 2.206

$PVA_{?\%, 3yr} \approx 17\%$

$NPV = 350,000(PV_{17\%, 1yr}) + 250,000(PV_{17\%, 2yr}) + 80,000(PV_{17\%, 3yr}) - 500,000$

$= 350,000(0.855) + 250,000(0.731) + 80,000(0.624) - 500,000$

$= 299,250 + 182,750 + 49,920 - 500,000$

$= \$31,920$

Since NPV is greater than zero using an IRR of 17 percent, a higher discount rate is required to make NPV = 0; trying 22 percent

$NPV = 350,000(PV_{22\%, 1yr}) + 250,000(PV_{22\%, 2yr}) + 80,000(PV_{22\%, 3yr}) - 500,000$

$= 350,000(0.820) + 250,000(0.672) + 80,000(0.551) - 500,000$

$= 287,000 + 168,000 + 44,080 - 500,000$

$= -\$920$

By financial calculator, $IRR_A = 21.82\%$

$$IRR_B = \left(\frac{\$800,000}{\$500,000}\right)^{1/3} - 1 = 16.96\%$$

CR7.2

$NPV_A = \$350,000(PV_{10\%, 1yr}) + \$250,000(PV_{10\%, 2yr})$
$\quad\quad + \$80,000(PV_{10\%, 3yr}) - \$500,000$

$\quad = \$84,730$

$NPV_B = \$800,000(PV_{10\%, 3yr}) - \$500,000 = \$100,800$

CR7.3 $\$500,000 = \dfrac{\$8,000,000}{(1 + IRR)^1} + \dfrac{\$8,000,000}{(1 + IRR)^2} + \dfrac{-\$20,00,000}{(1 + IRR)^3}$

By trial-and-error, $IRR \approx 19\%$ and $\approx 1581\%$.

$NPV = \$8,000,000(PVA_{10\%, 2yr}) + (-\$20,000,000)(PV_{10\%, 3yr}) - \$500,000$
$\quad = -\$1,632,000$

Do not accept C.

CR7.4   PROJECT A:

$FV_3 = \$350,000(FV_{10\%, 2yr}) + \$250,000(FV_{10\%, 1yr}) + \$80,000 = \$778,500$

$MIRR_A = \left(\dfrac{FV_n}{CF_0}\right)^{1/n} - 1 = \left(\dfrac{\$778,500}{\$500,000}\right)^{1/3} - 1 = 15.90\%$

PROJECT B:

$FV_3 = \$800,000$

$MIRR_B = \left(\dfrac{\$800,000}{\$500,000}\right)^{1/3} - 1 = 16.96\%$

B, as accepted by NPV, would also be accepted by MIRR.

CR7.5   *Select Seed*
NVP:

$$NPV = \$3,000(PV_{12\%,1yr}) + \$2,000(PV_{12\%,2yr}) + \$1,000(PV_{12\%,3yr}) - \$4,000 = \$985$$

IRR:
Using the simulated annuity approach

$$(\$3,000 + \$2,000 + \$1,000)/3 = \$2,000$$

$$\$4,000/\$2,000 = 2.00$$

$$PV_{?\%,3yr} \approx 23\%$$

$$NPV = \$3,000(PV_{23\%,1yr}) + \$2,000(PV_{23\%,2yr}) + \$1,000(PV_{23\%,3yr}) - \$4,000 = \$298$$

The NPV is greater than zero using an IRR of 23 percent, so a higher discount rate is required.
Trying 29%

$$NPV = \$3,000(PV_{29\%,1yr}) + \$2,000(PV_{29\%,2yr}) + \$1,000(PV_{29\%,3yr}) - 4,000 = -\$7$$

By financial calculator, IRR = 28.86%

MIRR:

$$FV_3 = \$3,000(FV_{12\%,2yr}) + \$2,000(FV_{12\%,1yr}) + \$1,000 = \$7,002$$

$$MIRR = \left(\frac{FV_3}{CF_0}\right)^{1/n} - 1 = \left(\frac{\$7,002}{\$4,000}\right)^{1/3} - 1 = 20.52\%$$

Cheap Seed
NPV:

$$NPV = \$630(PV_{12\%,1yr}) + \$630(PV_{12\%,2yr}) + \$420(PV_{12\%,3yr}) - \$840 = \$523.74$$

IRR:

$$\$840 = \frac{\$630}{(1 + IRR)^1} + \frac{\$630}{(1 + IRR)^2} + \frac{\$420}{(1 + IRR)^3}$$

$$IRR = 48.30\%$$

MIRR:

$$FV_3 = \$630(FV_{12\%,2yr}) + \$630(FV_{12\%,1yr}) + \$420 = \$1,915.62$$

$$MIRR = \left(\frac{\$1,915.62}{\$840}\right)^{1/3} - 1 = 31.63\%$$

Plant the select seed; it has the higher NPV.

CR7.6

Year	0	1	2	3
Challenger (select seed)	−$4,000	$3,000	$2,000	$1,000
Defender (cheap seed)	+840	−630	−630	−420
Incremental cash flows	−$3,160	$2,370	$1,370	$ 580

Using the simulated annuity approach

$$(\$2,370 + \$1,370 + \$580)/3 = \$1,440$$

$$\$3,160/\$1,440 = 2.194$$

$$PVA_{?\%,3yr} \approx 18\%$$

$$NPV = \$2,370(PV_{18\%,1yr}) + \$1,370(PV_{18\%,2yr}) + \$580(PV_{18\%,3yr}) - \$3,160 = \$184.27$$

The NPV is greater than zero using an IRR of 18%, so a higher discount rate is required. Trying 23%

$$NPV = \$2,370(PV_{23\%, 1yr}) + \$1,370(PV_{23\%, 2yr}) + \$580(PV_{23\%, 3yr}) - \$3,160 = -\$16.16$$

By financial calculator, $\Delta IRR = 22.58\%$

Because ΔIRR is greater than the opportunity cost of capital of 12 percent, choose the challenger—plant the select seed.

CR7.7

$$NPV_{A \text{ over 3 years}} = \$25,000(PVA_{15\%, 3yr}) - \$40,000 = \$17,075$$

$$NPV_{A \text{ over 9 years}} = \$17,075 + \$17,075(PV_{15\%, 3yr}) + \$17,075(PV_{15\%, 6yr}) = \$35,686.75$$

$$NPV_B = \$13,200(PVA_{15\%, 9yr}) - \$40,000 = \$22,990.40$$

Accept A.

CR7.8

$$\text{equivalent annual } NPV_A = \frac{\$17,075}{(PVA_{15\%, 3yr})} = \frac{17,075}{2.283} = \$7,479.19$$

$$\text{equivalent annual } NPV_B = \frac{\$22,990.40}{(PVA_{15\%, 9yr})} = \frac{\$22,990.40}{4.772} = \$4,817.17$$

Accept A.

CR7.9

Project	NPV
A	$21
B	41
C	0
D	27
E	36
F	18

Take A, D, E, and F, with a total NPV of $102.

Chapter 8

CR8.1

a. Capital cost = $200,000 + $5,000 = $205,000

1996

1/2 Capital cost	$102,500
CCA = $102,500 × 0.30	(30,750)
UCC end of 1996	$ 71,750

1997

Add: 1/2 Capital cost	$102,500
UCC beginning of 1997	174,250
CCA = $174,250 × 0.30	(52,275)
UCC end of 1997	$121,975

1998

UCC beginning of 1998	$121,975
CCA = $121,975 × 0.30	(36,593)
UCC end of 1998	$ 85,382

b. No, Revenue Canada assumes all assets are purchased halfway through the year.

CR8.2   a.   Capital Cost = $18,400 × 5 = $92,000

1996

1/2 Capital cost	$46,000
CCA = $46,000(0.4)	(18,400)
UCC end of 1996	$27,600

1997

Add: 1/2 Capital cost	$46,000
UCC beginning of 1997	73,600
CCA = $73,600 × 0.40	(29,440)
UCC end of 1997	$44,160

1998

CCA = $44,160 × 0.40	$(17,664)
UCC end of 1998	$ 26,496

or UCC formula method (Equation 8.1)

$$UCC_4 = \$92,000\left(1 - \frac{0.40}{2}\right)(1 - 0.40)^2 = \$26,496$$

b.   Proceeds from sale = 0.50($92,000) = $46,000

Addition to pool = 0.50 (net aquisitions)

= 0.50 (cost of new cars − proceeds from sale of old cars)

= 0.50 ($87,000 − $46,000) = $20,500

CR8.3

	Class 7	Class 9
CCA rate	15%	25%
UCC before	$82,500.00	$97,800.00
Net acquisitions	31,500.00	(14,000.00)
Addition to UCC	15,750.00	(14,000.00)
New UCC balance	98,250.00	83,800.00
CCA	14,737.50	20,950.00
UCC after	$83,512.50	$62,850.00

For class 7, purchases are greater than the lower of cost or proceeds from the disposed asset, so the 50% Rule applies. Therefore, one-half of net acquisitions ($43,500 − $12,000) is added to the beginning UCC, giving the new balance. The CCA for the year is obtained by multiplying the new UCC balance ($98,250) by the CCA rate (0.15).

For class 9, the lower of cost or proceeds from the disposition is greater than purchases, so the 50% Rule is not in effect. In this case net acquisitions turns out to be negative $14,000 ($32,000 − $46,000). Therefore, the new UCC balance is obtained by subtracting this amount from the beginning UCC. The CCA for the year is obtained by multiplying the new UCC balance by the CCA rate of 0.25.

CR8.4

Initial investment:	
Machine cost	$200,000
+ shipping and installation	100,000
Capital cost, C_0	$300,000
+ increase in net working capital	40,000
Initial investment, CF_0	$340,000

The $500,000 is a sunk cost.

Operating cash flows:

Cash inflows	$650,000
− cash outflows	400,000
CFBT$_t$	$250,000

$$\text{Operating } CF_t = CFBT_t(1 - T) + CCA(T)$$

$$= \$250,000(1 - 0.35) + CCA(T)$$

$$= \$162,500 + CCA(T)$$

Ending cash flows:

Estimated resale value, RV	$10,000
+ Release of net working capital	40,000
ECF	$50,000

$$NPV = \sum_{t=1}^{6} \frac{CFBT_t(1 - T)}{(1 + k)^t} + \left\{ \left[\frac{TdC_0}{k + d} \right]\left[\frac{1 + 0.5k}{1 + k} \right] - \left[\frac{1}{(1 + k)^6} \right]\left[\frac{Td(RV)}{k + d} \right] \right\}$$

$$+ \frac{ECF}{(1 + k)^6} - CF_0$$

$$= \$162,500(PVA_{14\%, 6yr}) + \left\{ \left[\frac{(0.35)(0.30)\$300,000}{0.14 + 0.30} \right]\left[\frac{1 + 0.5(0.14)}{1.14} \right] \right.$$

$$\left. - (PV_{14\%, 6yr})\left[\frac{(0.35)(0.30)(\$10,000)}{0.14 + 0.30} \right] \right\} + (PV_{14\%, 6yr})(\$50,000) - \$340,000$$

$$= \$378,925$$

NPV is positive; therefore, they should expand.

CR8.5   The only thing that changes is the CFBT$_t$. It must be decreased by $125,000 to reflect the lost sales of the premium wine.

The new CFBT$_t$ = $250,000 − $125,000 = $125,000

CFBT$_t$(1 − T) = $125,000(0.65) = $81,250

NPV = $81,250(3.889) + {$67,195 − $1,088} + $22,800 − $340,000 = $65,701

Therefore, still expand.

CR 8.6

Incremental initial investment:	
Capital cost (new refrigerators)	$335,000
− Proceeds from sale (old refrigerators)	100,000
Incremental capital cost, ΔC_0, and incremental initial investment, ΔCF_0	$235,000

Incremental operating cash flows, ΔCFBT

	Year			
	1	2	3	4
New				
1. Unit price	$10.00	$10.00	$10.00	$10.00
2. Unit sales	81,600	83,232	84,897	86,595
3. New revenues [(1) × (2)]	$816,000	$832,320	$848,970	$865,950

	Year			
	1	2	3	4
Old				
4. Unit price	$10.00	$10.00	$10.00	$10.00
5. Unit sales	75,750	76,508	77,273	78,045
6. Old revenues [(4) × (5)]	$757,500	$765,080	$772,730	$780,450
7. Δrevenues [(3) − (6)]	$58,500	$67,240	$76,240	$85,500
Operating costs				
8. New [(3) × (0.75)]	$612,000	$624,240	$636,728	$649,462
9. Old [(6) × (0.80)]	$606,000	$612,064	$618,184	$624,360
10. Δcosts [(8) − (9)]	$6,000	$12,176	$18,544	$25,102
11. ΔCFBT [(7) − (10)]	$52,500	$55,064	$57,696	$60,398
12. ΔCFBT(1 − T)[(11) × (0.60)]	$31,500	$33,038	$34,618	$36,239

Incremental ending cash flow

Net resale value of new refrigerators	$50,000
− Net resale value of old refrigerators	20,000
Incremental net resale value, ΔRV and Incremental ending cash flow, ΔECF	$30,000

$$NPV = \sum_{t=1}^{4} \frac{\Delta CFBT(1 - T)}{(1 + k)^t} + \left\{ \left[\frac{Td(\Delta C_0)}{k + d} \right] \left[\frac{1 + 0.5k}{1 + k} \right] - \left[\frac{1}{(1 + k)^4} \right] \left[\frac{Td(\Delta RV)}{k + d} \right] \right\}$$

$$+ \frac{\Delta ECF}{(1 + k)^4} - \Delta CF_0$$

$$NPV = (PV_{12\%,\ 1yr})\$31,500 + (PV_{12\%,\ 2yr})\$33,038 + (PV_{12\%,\ 3yr})\$34,618$$

$$+ (PV_{12\%,\ 4yr})\$36,239 + \left\{ \left[\frac{(0.40)(0.20)(\$235,000)}{0.12 + 0.20} \right] \left[\frac{1.06}{1.12} \right] \right.$$

$$- (PV_{12\%,\ 4yr}) \left[\frac{(0.40)(0.20)(\$30,000)}{0.12 + 0.20} \right] \right\}$$

$$+ (PV_{12\%,\ 4yr})(\$30,000) - \$235,000$$

$$= -\$62,930.51$$

Therefore, since NPV is negative, do not replace.

Chapter 9

CR9.1

$$NPV\ (5\ year) = \$2,000,000(PVA_{15\%,\ 5yr}) - \$8,000,000 = -1,296,000$$

$$NPPV\ (10\ year) = \$2,000,000(PVA_{15\%,\ 10yr}) - \$8,000,000 = \$2,038,000$$

The expected net present value $= -\$1,296,000(0.50) + \$2,038,000(0.50) = \$371,000$.

CR9.2

a. The estimated inflows are $(600)(\$100) = \$60,000$, while the estimated outflows are $30,000$; therefore, the after-tax operating cash flows $= (\$60,000 - \$30,000)(1 - 0.28) = \$21,600$ per year.

$$NPV = \$21,600(PVA_{10\%,\ 4yr}) - \$60,000 = \$8,472$$

b.

Percent Change	Arrangements Sold per Year	NPV
−30%	420	−$12,070
−20	480	− 5,222
−10	540	1,625
0	600	8,472
+10	660	15,319
+20	720	22,166
+30	780	29,014

CR9.3

The breakeven point in dollars is

$$CF_t(PVA_{10\%, 4yr}) - \$60,000 = 0$$

$$CF_t(3.170) - \$60,000 = 0$$

$$CF_t = \$18,927$$

In units the breakeven point is

$$[(units)(\$100)(1 - 0.50)](1 - 0.28) = \$18,927$$

$$units = \$18,927/\$36 \approx 526$$

CR9.4

a. The operating cash flows per year are $14,400 for a downturn and $30,240 for an improved economy.

$$NPV_{downturn} = \$14,400(PVA_{10\%,4yr}) - \$60,000 = -\$14,352$$

$$NPV_{improved} = \$30,240(PVA_{10\%,4yr}) - \$60,000 = \$35,861$$

b. expected NPV $= -14,352(0.30) + \$8,472(0.40) + \$35,861(0.30) = \$9,842$

$$\sigma = [0.30(-\$14,352 - \$9,842)^2 + 0.40(\$8,472 - \$9,842)^2$$

$$+ 0.30(\$35,861 - \$9,842)^2]^{0.50}$$

$$= \$19,480$$

Chapter 10

CR10.1

The gross offering is $= \$500,000/(1 - 0.15) = \$588,235$, so the flotation costs are $88,235.

CR10.2

net proceeds per share $= \$32(1 - 0.05) = \$30.40$
number of shares $= \$10,000,000/\$30.40 = 328,947$

CR10.3

a. EPS $= \$700,000/700,000 = \$1$ per share

dividend $= (\$1)(0.70) = \$0.70$

$$P_0 = \frac{D_1}{k_s - g} = \frac{\$0.70(1.08)}{0.12 - 0.08} = \$18.90$$

b. $P_0 = (18)(\$1) = \$18$

CR10.4

N, the number of rights to buy one additional share, is given by

$$N = \frac{existing\ shares}{additional\ shares} = \frac{200,000}{20,000} = 10$$

Setting Equation 10.7 equal to Equation 10.8, we have

$$\frac{P_0 - P_s}{N + 1} = \frac{P_x - P_s}{N}$$

$$\frac{P_0 - \$12}{10 + 1} = \frac{\$16 - \$12}{10}$$

$$10(P_0 - \$12) = 11(\$4)$$

$$10P_0 = \$44 + 120$$

$$P_0 = \$164/10 = \$16.40$$

The rights-on stock price is $16.40.

Chapter 11

CR11.1

Year	Payment	Interest	Principal Repayment	Remaining Balance
1	$29,833	$15,000	$14,833	$85,167
2	29,833	12,775	17,058	68,109
3	29,833	10,216	19,617	48,492
4	29,833	7,274	22,559	25,933
5	29,823	3,890	25,933	0

CR11.2 Using Equation 3.9 adjusted for monthly compounding to calculate PMT:

Month	Payment	Interest	Principal Repayment	Remaining Balance
1	$2,379	$1,250	$1,129	$98,871
2	2,379	1,236	1,143	97,728
3	2,379	1,222	1,157	96,571
4	2,379	1,207	1,172	95,399
5	2,379	1,192	1,187	94,212

CR11.3

$B_0(\text{zero-coupon}) = \$1,000(PV_{10\%, 5yr}) = \$621$

number of zero-coupon bonds $= \$50,000,000/\$621 = 80,515$

number of coupon-bearing bonds $= \$50,000,000/\$1,000 = 50,000$

CR11.4 The bond prices before the increase were: zero-coupon bond $= \$1,000(PV_{10\%, 20yr}) = \$149$, and coupon-bearing bond $= \$1,000$. After the increase, $B_0(\text{zero-coupon}) = \$1,000(PV_{12\%, 20yr}) = \$104$ and $B_0(\text{coupon-bearing}) = \$100(PV_{12\%, 20yr}) + \$1,000(PV_{12\%, yr}) = 850.90$. The percentage loss was $(\$104 - \$149)/\$149 = -30.20\%$ for the zero-coupon bond and $(\$850.90 - \$1,000)/\$1,000 = -14.91\%$ for the coupon-bearing bond.

CR11.5 Bequet should borrow at the floating rate, while Reed borrows at the fixed rate.

Bequet	Pays floating rate to third party	LIBOR + 2.00%
	Pays fixed rate to Reed	11.50
	Receives floating rate from Reed	−(LIBOR + 2.00)
	Net cost to Bequet	11.50%
Reed	Pays fixed rate to third party	14.00%
	Pays floating rate to Bequet	LIBOR + 2.00
	Receives fixed rate from Bequet	−11.50
	Net cost to Reed	LIBOR + 4.50%

Chapter 12

CR12.1   a. $V_U = \dfrac{\$4.5 \text{ million}}{0.15} = \$30 \text{ million}$

b. $k_S^l = 0.15 + (0.15 - 0.10)(\$15/\$15) = 20\%$

opportunity cost of capital $= (0.10)(\$15/\$30) + (0.20)(\$15/\$30) = 15\%$

$V_L = S_L + B = \$30 \text{ million}$
No.

CR12.2   a. $V_U = \dfrac{\$4.5 \text{ million } (1 - 0.40)}{0.15} = \$18 \text{ million}$

$k_S^U = 0.15 + (0.15 - 0.10)(1 - 0.40)(0/\$18) = 15\%$

opportunity cost of capital $= 15\%$

b. $V_L = \$18 \text{ million} + 0.40(\$15 \text{ million}) = \$24 \text{ million}$

$k_S^l = 0.15 + (0.15 - 0.10)(1 - 0.40)(\$15/\$9) = 20\%$

opportunity cost of capital $= (10\%)(\$15/\$24)(1 - 0.40) + (20\%)(\$9/\$24) = 11.25\%$

CR12.3   a. $V_U = \dfrac{\$30 \text{ million } (1 - 0.40)}{0.12} = \$150 \text{ million}$

$V_L = \$150 \text{ million} + \left[1 - \dfrac{(1 - 0.40)(1 - 0.35)}{(1 - 0.48)}\right]\$60 \text{ million} = \$165 \text{ million}$

The gain from leverage is $15 million.

b. $V_U = \dfrac{\$30 \text{ million}(1 - 0.30)}{0.12} = \$175 \text{ million}$

$V_L = \$175 \text{ million} + \left[1 - \dfrac{(1 - 0.30)(1 - 0.30)}{(1 - 0.30)}\right]\$60 \text{ million} = \$193 \text{ million}$

With $T_{PS} = T_{PB}$, the gain from leverage is $TB = \$18$ million.

CR12.4   a.

	Equity Financing	Debt Financing
EBIT	$3,750,000	$3,750,000
Interest	800,000	880,000
EBT	2,950,000	2,870,000
Taxes (36%)	1,062,000	1,033,200
EAT	$1,888,000	$1,836,800
Shares	500,000 + ($1,000,000/$25)	500,000
	= 540,000	
EPS	$3.50	$3.67

b. $\dfrac{(\text{EBIT}^\star - \$800,000)(1 - 0.36)}{\$540,000} = \dfrac{(\text{EBIT}^\star - \$880,000)(1 - 0.36)}{500,000}$

$\text{EBIT}^\star = \$1,880,000$

Chapter 13

CR13.1

a. PROJECT I:

expected CF = 0.20($200,000) + 0.80($80,000) = $104,000

σ = [0.2($200,000 − $104,000)^2 + 0.8($80,000 − $104,000)^2]$^{0.5}$ = $48,000

PROJECT II:

expected CF = 0.50($130,000) + 0.50($110,000) = $120,000

σ = [0.5($130,000 − $120,000)^2 + 0.5($110,000 − $120,000)^2]$^{0.5}$ = $10,000

b. $\text{NPV}_\text{I} = \dfrac{\$104,000}{1.15} - \$100,000 = -\$9,565$

$\text{NPV}_\text{II} = \dfrac{\$120,000}{1.15} - \$100,000 = \$4,348$

c. A shareholder would prefer project I because if the $200,000 cash flow occurs, the firm can pay off the debt and the shareholders take the rest; a bondholder would prefer project II.

CR13.2

$$V_\text{U} = \frac{\$10 \text{ million}(1 - 0.40)}{0.15} = \$40 \text{ million}$$

	Without Financial Distress	**With Financial Distress Costs**
Debt	$V_\text{L} = V_\text{U} + \text{TB}$	$V_\text{L} = V_\text{U} + \text{TB} - \text{financial distress}$
$ 0	$40	$40.0
20	48	47.5
25	50	49.0
30	52	50.5
35	54	51.0
40	56	50.0
45	58	49.0

With no financial distress, use $45 million debt. When financial distress is considered, employ $35 million of debt.

CR13.3

a. $S_\text{L} = \dfrac{[\$500,000 - (0.08)(\$1,000,000)](1 - 0.30)}{0.12} = \$2,450,000$

$V = S_\text{L} + B = \$2,450,000 + \$1,000,000 = \$3,450,000$

b. $\begin{matrix} \text{opportunity cost} \\ \text{of capital} \end{matrix} = 8\%(1 - 0.30)\left(\dfrac{\$1,000,000}{\$3,450,000}\right) + 12\%\left(\dfrac{\$2,450,000}{\$3,450,000}\right) = 10.15\%$

c. $S_\text{L} = \dfrac{[\$500,000 - (0.10)(\$1,500,000)](1 - 0.30)}{0.14} = \$1,750,000$

$V = S_\text{L} + B = \$1,750,000 + \$1,500,000 = \$3,250,000$

Do not restructure.

CR13.4

a. $S = V_U = \dfrac{\$400,000(1 - 0.40)}{0.15} = \$1,600,000$

$S_L = \dfrac{[\$400,000 - (0.10)(\$800,000)](1 - 0.40)}{0.17} = \$1,129,412$

$V_L = S_L + B = \$1,129,412 + \$800,000 = \$1,929,412$; the value of the firm increased by $329,412.

b. $800,000/$16 = 50,000 shares of common stock will be retired; 50,000 shares will be outstanding. $P_0 = \$1,129,412/50,000 = \$22.59$.

c. $800,000/$20 = 40,000 shares; 60,000 shares will be outstanding. $P_0 = \$1,129,412/60,000 = \$18.82$.

Chapter 14

CR14.1

Dividends received (4,000 × $1.25)	$5,000
Add: Gross-up at 25%	1,250
Taxable dividends	6,250
Federal income tax (0.26 × $6,250)	1,625
Less: Dividend tax credit (0.1333 × $6,250)	833
Federal taxes payable	792
Add: Newfoundland tax (0.69 × $792)	546
Total tax	$1,338
Dividends after taxes ($5,000 − $1,338)	$3,662

CR14.2   Before the ex-dividend date $P_0 = \$100,000,000/5,000,000 = \$20$ and P/E = $20/$4 = 5 times. The dividends paid are (5,000,000)($1) = $5,000,000, so after the ex-dividend date the market value of equity is $100,000,000 − $5,000,000 = $95,000,000, $P_0 = \$95,000,000/5,000,000 = \$19$, and P/E = $19/$4 = 4.75 times.

CR14.3   The shares repurchased = $5,000,000/$20 = 250,000; number of common shares outstanding = 5,000,000 − 250,000 = 4,750,000; so the market value of equity = $95,000,000, $P_0 = \$95,000,000/4,750,000 = \$20$, the new EPS is [($4)(5,000,000)]/4,750,000 = $4.21, and P/E = $20/$4.21 = 4.75 times.

CR14.4

a. New debt = $900,000(2/1) = $1,800,000, so total capital expenditures = $2,700,000.

b. dividends = $900,000 − $700,000 = $200,000

DPS = $200,000/$100,000 = $2

$P_0 = \dfrac{\$2(1.05)}{0.16 - 0.05} = \$19.09$

c. $P_0 = \dfrac{\$1.75(1.05)}{0.13 - 0.05} = \$22.97$

Chapter 15

CR15.1

$$\begin{array}{l} \text{present value of} \\ \text{ownership benefits} \end{array} = \left[\dfrac{(0.40)(0.20)(\$32,000)}{(0.054 + 0.20)} \right]\left[\dfrac{1.027}{1.054} \right] = \$9,821$$

$$\text{amount recovered from the lease} = \$32,000 - \$9,821 = \$22,179$$

$$\$22,179 = \text{ATL}\left[\frac{1 - [1/(1.0045)^{60}]}{0.0045}\right](1.0045)$$

$$\text{ATL} = \$421 \text{ and } L = \$701$$

CR15.2

$$\text{NPV}_{\text{lease}} = \$50,000 - \left\{\$11,000(1 - 0.35)(\text{PVA}_{8\%,\,5\text{yr}})(1.08) + \left[\frac{(0.35)(0.30)\$50,000}{0.08 + 0.30}\right]\left[\frac{1.04}{1.08}\right]\right\}$$

$$= \$50,000 - (\$30,834 + \$13,304) = \$5,858$$

CR15.3

$$\text{NPV}_{\text{lease}} = \$100,000 - \left\{\$25,000(1 - 0.30)(3.791)(1.10) + \left[\frac{(0.30)(0.30)\$15,000}{0.10 + 0.30}\right]\left[\frac{1.05}{1.10}\right]\right.$$

$$- (0.621)\left[\frac{(0.30)(0.30)\$15,000}{0.10 + 0.30}\right] - \$4,000(1 - 0.30)(3.127)$$

$$\left. + \$15,000(0.437)\right\}$$

$$= \$100,000 - (\$72,977 + \$21,477 - \$2,096 - \$8,756 + \$6,555) = \$9,843$$

BCI should lease the crane.

Chapter 16

CR16.1

$$\Delta\text{value} = \$50(\text{PV}_{15\%,\,1\text{yr}}) + \$98(\text{PV}_{15\%,\,2\text{yr}}) + \$256(\text{PV}_{15\%,\,3\text{yr}}) + \$286(\text{PV}_{15\%,\,4\text{yr}}) + \$316(\text{PV}_{15\%,\,5\text{yr}})$$

$$= \$607$$

$$\text{benefit} = \$607 + \$10(100) = \$1,607; \text{cost} = \$12(100) = \$1,200; \text{NPV} = \$1,607 - \$1,200 = \$407$$

CR16.2

a. benefit = \$400,000 + \$800,000 = \$1,200,000
    NPV = \$1,200,000 − \$1,000,000 = \$200,000

$$P_{0\,\text{before}} = \frac{\$1,500,000}{75,000} = \$20$$

$$P_{0\,\text{after}} = \frac{\$1,500,000 + \$200,000}{75,000} = \$22.67$$

b. stock issued = \$1,000,000/\$20 = 50,000 shares
    value of combined firm = \$1,500,000 + \$1,200,000 = \$2,700,000
    W = [50,000/(75,000 + 50,000)] = 0.4
    cost = 0.4(\$2,700,000) = \$1,080,000

$$\text{NPV} = \$1,200,000 - \$1,080,000 = \$120,000$$

$$P_{0\,\text{after}} = \frac{\$1,500,000 + \$1,200,000}{125,000} = \$21.60$$

CR16.3

a. Barrette's premerger EPS = \$50,000/10,000 = \$5, while its premerger P/E = \$40/5 = 8.

$$EPS_{new} = \frac{\$50,000 + \$75,000}{10,000 + 20,000} = \$4.17$$

$$P_{o\,new} = (\$4.17)(8) = \$33.16$$

b.

$$V = (\$40)(10,000) + (\$35)(20,000) = \$1,100,000$$

$$P_{0\,new} = \frac{\$1,100,000}{30,000} = \$36.67$$

$$P/E_{new} = \frac{\$36.67}{\$4.17} = 8.79 \text{ times}$$

Chapter 17

CR17.1

	0	1	2	3
Cash flow in rupees	−900,000	300,000	500,000	500,000
Forecasted spot exchange rate	30	31.43	32.93	34.49
Cash flow in dollars	−30,000	9,545	15,184	14,497

$$NPV = \$9,545(PV_{15\%,1yr}) + \$15,184(PV_{15\%,2yr}) + \$14,497(PV_{15\%,3yr}) - \$30,000$$
$$= -\$678$$

CR17.2

	0	1	2	3	4
Cash flow before taxes, in U.S. dollars	−720,000	300,000	500,000	500,000	400,000
U.S. corporate tax at 35%		105,000	175,000	175,000	140,000
Cash flow available for remittance to parent		195,000	325,000	325,000	260,000
Tax withheld at 3%		5,850	9,750	9,750	7,800
Remittance after U.S. taxes, in U.S. dollars		189,150	315,250	315,250	152,200
Forecasted spot exchange rate	0.80	0.82	0.83	0.85	0.86
Remittance received by parent, in Canadian dollars	−900,000	230,671	379,819	370,882	176,977
Canadian corporate tax		0	0	0	0
Foreign tax credit		0	0	0	0
Cash flow in Canadian dollars, CF	−900,000	230,671	379,819	370,882	176,977

$$NPV = \$230,671(PV_{10\%,\ 1yr}) + \$379,819\ (PV_{10\%,\ 2yr}) + \$370,882\ (PV_{10\%,\ 3yr})$$
$$+ \$176,977(PV_{10\%,\ 4yr}) - \$900,000 = \$22,817$$

CR17.3

a. Strengthen.

b. A\$500,000/1.25 = \$400,000 and A\$500,000/1.15 = \$434,783.

c. In six months receive A\$500,000; at A\$1.35/\$1 this is \$370,370. The loss of \$64,413 (i.e., \$434,783 − \$370,370) is made up by the gain on the forward contract. The Canadian firm receives \$434,783.

CR17.4   **a.** Lira 600,000,000/1,200 = \$500,000

b. Lira 600,000,000/1,150 = \$521,739

c. Buy, and lock in the price of \$521,739.

Chapter 18

CR18.1 V_c = Max(0, \$54 − \$55)(100) = \$0

V_p = Max(0, \$60 − \$49)(100) = \$1,100

profit = \$0 + \$1,100 − \$300 − \$200 = \$600

CR18.2   If the call is purchased, the payoff is:

	Stock Price = \$90	Stock Price = \$50
Buy a call	100 (\$90 − \$60) = \$3,000	0

If a loan for \$5,000/1.08 = \$4,629.63 is taken out and stock is purchased, the payoff is:

	Stock Price = \$90	Stock Price = \$50
Buy stock	\$ 9,000	\$5,000
Repay loan	−5,000	−5,000
Total payoff	\$ 4,000	\$ 0

The payoff from buying stock with the loan is \$4,000/\$3,000 = $1\frac{1}{3}$ as much as from buying the option. Therefore, the value of $1\frac{1}{3}$ calls = \$6,000 − \$4,629.63 = \$1,370.37, and the value of 1 call for 100 shares = (\$1,370.37)(3/4) = \$1,028.

CR18.3   return from upward movement = $\dfrac{\$90}{\$60} - 1 = 50\%$

return from downward movement = $\dfrac{\$50}{\$60} - 1 = -16.67\%$

The probability of an upward movement is:

8% = (W)(50%) + (1 − W)(−16.67%); so W = 0.37

expected value$_1$ = (0.37)(\$3,000) + (0.63)(0) = \$1,100

$V_c = \dfrac{\$1,110}{1.08} = \$1,028$

CR18.4 $d_1 = \dfrac{\ln(85/90) + [0.06 + 0.5(0.30)^2]0.75}{(0.30)(0.75)^{0.5}} = 0.083$

$d_2 = 0.083 - (0.30)(0.75)^{0.5} = -0.177$

From Table B.5, $N(d_1) \approx 0.532$, while $N(d_2) \approx 0.429$.

$V_c = \$85(0.532) - \dfrac{\$90}{e^{(.06)(0.75)}}(0.429) = \$8.31$

CR18.5 $V_p = \$8.31 + \dfrac{\$90}{e^{(0.06)(0.75)}} - \$85 = \$9.35$

Chapter 19

CR19.1

a. $d_1 = \dfrac{\ln(20/12) + [0.08 + 0.5(0.36)^2]10}{(0.36)(10)^{0.5}} = 1.721$

$d_2 = 1.721 - (0.36)(10)^{0.5} = 0.583$

From Table B.5, $N(d_1) \approx 0.957$ and $N(d_2) \approx 0.719$.

$S = \$20(0.957) - \dfrac{\$12}{e^{(0.08)(10)}}(0.719) = \$15.263$ million

b. $B = \$20 - \$15.263 = \$4.737$ million

c. default option $= \dfrac{\$12}{e^{(0.08)(10)}} - \$4.737 = \$0.655$ million

CR19.2

The proceeds from the new issue is $\$32,000,000/(1.10)^{15} \approx \$7.661$ million, while it costs $\$12,000,000/(1.10)^{10} \approx \$4.627$ million to retire the existing bonds. The approximately $3 million remaining after refinancing is employed to retire stock, so the total value of the firm remains at $20 million.

$d_1 = \dfrac{\ln(20/32) + [0.08 + 0.5(0.36)^2]15}{(0.36)(15)^{0.5}} = 1.221$

$d_2 = 1.221 - (0.36)(15)^{0.5} = -0.173$

From Table B.5, $N(d_1)$ is ≈ 0.889 and $N(d_2)$ is ≈ 0.433.

$S = \$20(0.889) - \dfrac{\$32}{e^{(0.08)(15)}}(0.433) = \$13.607$ million

$B = \$20 - \$13.607 = \$6.393$ million

CR19.3

a. NPV $= \$35,000,000(PVA_{15\%,\,10yr}) - \$200,000,000 = -\$24,335,000$

Do not expand.

b. The present value of the inflows at $t = 3$ is $50 million + $40 million = $90 million.

$P_0 = \$90$ million$/e^{(0.15)(3)} = \$57.387$

$\sigma(t)^{0.5} = (0.55)(3)^{0.5} = 0.953$

$\dfrac{P_0}{x/e^{k_{RF}t}} = \dfrac{\$57.387}{\$50/e^{(0.07)(3)}} = 1.416$

From Table B.6, the value is ≈ 0.474, so the value of the option to expand is ($57.387 million)(0.474) = $27,201,438. The strategic NPV is $-\$24,335,000 + \$27,201,438 = \$2,866,438$.

CR19.4

$\sigma(t)^{0.5} = 0.953$

$\dfrac{P_0}{x/e^{k_{RF}t}} = \dfrac{\$60}{\$45/e^{(0.07)(3)}} = 1.645$

From Table B.7, the factor is ≈ 0.116, so the option to abandon = ($60 million)(0.116) = $6,960,000. The strategic NPV = $2,866,438 + $6,960,000 = $9,826,438.

CR19.5

present value of forecasted cash flow$_1 = \$15,000/e^{(0.18)(1)} = \$12,529$

present value of forecasted cash flow$_2 = \$25,000/e^{(0.18)(2)} = \$17,442$

Year 1:

$\sigma(t)^{0.5} = (0.45)(1)^{0.5} = 0.450$

$$\frac{P_0}{x/e^{k_{RF}t}} = \frac{\$12,529}{\$10,000/e^{(0.08)(1)}} = 1.357$$

Year 2:

$$\sigma(t)^{0.5} = (0.45)(2)^{0.5} = 0.636$$

$$\frac{P_0}{x/e^{k_{RF}t}} = \frac{\$17,442}{\$10,000/e^{(0.08)(2)}} = 2.047$$

The two tabled values from Table B.7 are ≈ 0.058 and 0.033; the value of the guarantee is $(\$12,529)(0.058) + (\$17,442)(0.033) = \$1,302$.

CR19.6   a. $\$3,000,000(0.7055) = \$2,116,500$

b.   Strengthening.

c. $\$3,000,000/\$62,500 = 48$ call options

d. $(48)(62,500)(\$0.0102) = \$30,600$

e.   cost $= \$3,000,000(0.80) = \$2,400,000$; loss $= \$2,400,000 - \$2,116,500 = \$283,500$.

With the option, the firm locked in a price of $\$3,000,000(0.70) = \$2,100,000$, plus the cost of the option of $\$30,600$, for a total cash flow of $\$2,130,600$; the savings was $\$2,400,000 - \$2,130,600 = \$269,400$.

Chapter 20

CR20.1 $(0.30)(3)^{0.5} = 0.5196$

$$\frac{\$28}{\$35/e^{(0.06)(3)}} = 0.9578$$

price $= \$28(0.181) = \$5.07$

CR20.2   a. $B_0 = \$60(PVA_{7\%, 40yr}) + \$1,000(PV_{7\%, 40yr}) = \$867$

b.   conversion ratio $= \$1,000/\$25 = 40$ and conversion value $= (40)(\$10) = \$40$

c.   value of the conversion option $= 40(\$4.48) = \$179$

value of convertible $= \$867 + \$179 = \$1,046$

Chapter 21

CR21.1   a.   days sales outstanding $= 365/6.75 = 54.07$

days inventory $= 365/9.54 = 38.26$

operating cycle $= 54.07 + 38.26 = 92.33$

b.   days payable $= 365/9.13 = 39.88$

cash conversion cycle $= 92.33 - 39.88 = 52.35$

CR21.2

Ratio	MaxIncome	Safety First
current ratio	1.10	5.29
quick ratio	0.60	2.57
net working capital	$3,671	$72,683
receivables turnover	17.54	11.80
inventory turnover	8.87	3.86
payables turnover	13.78	25.64
cash conversion cycle	35.47	111.26

CR21.3

a.

	Aggressive	Matched	Conservative
Earnings per share			
Robust economy	$2.48	$3.30	$3.80
Standard economy	2.18	2.70	3.20
Poor economy	1.28	1.80	2.30
Expected EPS	$1.98	$2.60	$3.10
Standard deviation	$0.51	$0.62	$0.61

b.

$P_{0_{aggressive}} = 10(\$1.98) = \$19.80$

$P_{0_{matched}} = 11(\$2.60) = \$28.60$

$P_{0_{conservative}} = 12(\$3.10) = \$37.20$

Adopt the conservative policy.

Chapter 22

CR22.1

a. $(6 - 4)(\$20,000) = \$40,000$

b. $\Delta B = (\$40,000)(2)(0.06/365)(1 - 0.36) = \$8.42$

CR22.2

$\$100(1 - 0.40) = (7)(TS)(0.05/365)(1 - 0.40)$

$TS = \$104,286$

CR22.3

The daily compounded opportunity cost is:

$(1 + k_{daily})^{365} - 1 = 0.05$

$k = 0.000134$

$Z = \left[\dfrac{3(\$100)(\$10,000)^2}{4(0.000134)}\right]^{1/3} + \$500,000 = \$538,252$

The upper control limit is $3(\$538,252) - 2(\$500,000) = \$614,756$, and the average cash balance is $[4(\$538,252) - \$500,000]/3 = \$551,003$.

CR22.4

a. $k_{BE} = \left(\dfrac{\$10,000 - \$9,900}{\$9,900}\right)\left(\dfrac{365}{50}\right) = 7.37\%$

b. $P_0 = \dfrac{\$10,000}{1 + 0.075\left(\dfrac{40}{365}\right)} = \$9,918.48$

$k_{BE} = \left(\dfrac{(\$9,918.48 - \$9,900)}{\$9,900}\right)\left(\dfrac{365}{10}\right) = 6.81\%$

Chapter 23

CR23.1

$$\text{credit score}_A = 5(2.2) + 7(6) - 9(2) = 35$$
$$\text{credit score}_B = 5(2) + 7(5) - 9(4) = 9$$
$$\text{credit score}_C = 5(2.5) + 7(4) - 9(3) = 13.5$$

CR23.2

$$\Delta CF_0 = (0.70)(\$17{,}000{,}000)(55/365) - (0.70)(\$20{,}000{,}000)(65/365) = -\$700{,}000$$
$$\Delta CF_t = [\$17{,}000{,}000(1 - 0.70) - \$17{,}000{,}000(0.12) - \$500{,}000](1 - 0.35)$$
$$- [\$20{,}000{,}000(1 - 0.70) - \$20{,}000{,}000(0.15) - \$250{,}000](1 - 0.35)$$
$$= -\$123{,}500$$
$$NPV = \frac{-\$123{,}500}{0.14} - (-\$700{,}000) = -\$182{,}143$$

No.

CR23.3

$$NPV = \frac{\$200{,}000}{0.15} - \$1{,}500{,}000 = -\$166{,}667$$

Chapter 24

CR24.1

a.

$$k_{\text{effective annual}} = \left(1 + \frac{0.01}{1 - 0.01}\right)^{365/(30-15)} - 1 = 27.71\%$$

b.

$$k_{\text{effective annual}} = \left(1 + \frac{0.01}{1 - 0.01}\right)^{365/(60-15)} - 1 = 8.49\%$$

CR24.2

Interest with regular interest $= (\$500{,}000)(0.12)(275/365) = \$45{,}205$

$$k_{\text{effective annual}} = \left(1 + \frac{\$45{,}205}{\$500{,}000}\right)^{365/275} - 1 = 12.17\%$$

Interest with discount interest $= (\$500{,}000)(0.08)(275/365) = \$30{,}167$

$$k_{\text{effective annual}} = \left(1 + \frac{\$30{,}137}{\$469{,}863}\right)^{365/275} - 1 = 8.60\%$$

Interest with instalment interest $= (\$500{,}000)(0.07)(275/365) = \$26{,}370$

$$\text{monthly payment} = \frac{\$500{,}000 + \$26{,}370}{9} = \$58{,}486$$

$(PVA_{?\%,9}) = \$500{,}000/\$58{,}486 = 8.549$. From Table B.2, $k \approx 1\%$ per month, or 12% per year. By financial calculator, we get 12.49% per year.

CR24.3

$$\text{Interest} = (\$20,000)(0.10)(20/365) + (\$20,000)(0.12)(20/365)$$
$$+ (\$20,000)(0.08)(20/365) = \$109.59 + \$131.51 + \$87.67 = \$328.77$$

$$k_{\text{effective annual}} = \left(1 + \frac{\$328.77}{\$20,000}\right)^{365/60} - 1 = 10.43\%$$

CR24.4

Commitment fee = $(\$500,000 - \$200,000)(0.01)(60/365) + (\$500,000 - \$400,000)(0.01)(100/365) + (\$500,000 - 0)(0.01)(20/365) = \$493.15 + \$273.97 + \$273.97 = \$1,041.09$. Interest = $(\$200,000)(0.15)(60/365) + (\$400,000)(0.15)(100/365) = \$4,931.51 + \$16,438.36 = \$21,369.87$. Average financing = $(\$200,000)(60/180) + (\$400,000)(100/180) = \$288,888.89$.

$$k_{\text{effective annual}} = \left(1 + \frac{\$1,041.09 + \$21,369.87}{\$288,888.89}\right)^{365/180} - 1 = 16.36\%$$

CR24.5

Interest is $15,000, while the commitment fee is $(\$1,000,000)(0.005)(60/365) = \$821.92$.

$$k_{\text{effective annual}} = \left(1 + \frac{\$15,000 + \$821.92}{\$985,000 - \$10,000}\right)^{365/60} - 1 = 10.29\%$$

CR24.6

The loan amount is $(\$80,000)(0.80) = \$64,000$ in either case. With the bank the processing fee is $(\$64,000)(0.005) = \$320$ and the interest is $(\$64,000)(0.12)(1/12) = \$640$.

$$k_{\text{effective annual}} = \left(1 + \frac{\$320 + \$640}{\$64,000}\right)^{12/1} - 1 = 19.56\%$$

The factoring fee is $(\$64,000)(0.02) = \$1,280$.

$$k_{\text{effective annual}} = \left(1 + \frac{\$1,280 - \$200}{\$64,000}\right)^{12/1} - 1 = 22.24\%$$

Chapter 25

CR25.1

a.

EBIT	$700,000
Interest	100,000
EBT	600,000
Taxes	70,000
EAT, or net income	530,000
Dividends on preferred stock	50,000
Earnings available for common shareholders	$480,000

$$\text{basic EPS} = \frac{\$480,000}{30,000} = \$16.00$$

$$\text{fully diluted EPS} = \frac{\$480,000}{40,000} = \$12.00$$

b. $480,000 - $200,000 = $280,000

CR25.2

return on equity = $12.5\%/(1 - 0.40) = 20.8\%$

CR25.3

	Jarvus	Barkell
current ratio	2.1	4.1
quick ratio	0.8	3.4
days sales outstanding	21.5	35.6

	Jarvus	Barkell
inventory turnover	2.9	14.5
long-term asset turnover	57.0	34.0
total asset turnover	2.2	2.7
total debt to total assets	0.5	0.4
times interest earned	8.7	8.7
net profit margin	5.4%	3.7%
return on total assets	11.8%	10.1%
return on equity	24.8%	16.3%

a. Both suppliers and short-term lenders are concerned with liquidity ratios; they would favour Barkell.

b. Jarvus has more debt but the same times interest earned as Barkell. Jarvus is more profitable; a slight nod to Jarvus.

c. Shareholders are particularly concerned with profitability ratios; another slight nod to Jarvus.

Chapter 26

CR26.1

Sales (Y_t)	Period (X_t)	$Y_t X_t$	X_t^2
10.0	1	10.0	1
10.0	2	20.0	4
10.5	3	31.5	9
11.5	4	46.0	16
13.0	5	65.0	25
Totals 55.0	15	172.5	55

$\bar{Y} = \Sigma Y_t/n = 55/5 = 11$

$\bar{X} = \Sigma X_t/n = 15/5 = 3$

$\beta = [172.5 - (5)(11)(3)]/[55 - 5(3^2)] = 0.75$

$\alpha = 11 - 0.75(3) = 8.75$

$Y_t = \$8.75 + \$0.75X_t$

The predicted sales for the next three years are \$13.25 million, \$14.00 million, and \$14.75 million.

CR26.2

Sales (Y_t)	Period (X_t)	$Y_t X_t$	X_t^2
2.35	1	2.35	1
2.50	2	5.00	4
2.90	3	8.70	9
2.75	4	11.00	16
2.60	5	13.00	25
2.75	6	16.50	36
3.15	7	22.05	49
3.00	8	24.00	64
2.85	9	25.65	81
3.15	10	31.50	100
3.65	11	40.15	121
3.35	12	40.20	144
Totals 35.00	78	240.10	650

$$\bar{Y} = \Sigma Y_t / n = 35/12 = 2.91667$$

$$\bar{X} = \Sigma X_t / n = 78/12 = 6.50$$

$$\beta = [240.10 - (12)(2.91667)(6.50)]/[650 - 12(6.50^2)] = 0.08811$$

$$\alpha = 2.91667 - 0.08811(6.50) = 2.344$$

$$Y_t = \$2.344 + \$0.088X_t$$

Adjusted seasonal indices are 0.928, 0.975, 1.089, and 1.008 for quarters 1, 2, 3, and 4, respectively.

	Predicted Without Adjustment	**Predicted With Adjustment**
Year 1		
Quarter 1	3.49	3.24
Quarter 2	3.58	3.49
Quarter 3	3.66	3.99
Quarter 4	3.75	3.78
Year 2		
Quarter 1	3.84	3.56
Quarter 2	3.93	3.83
Quarter 3	4.02	4.38
Quarter 4	4.10	4.13

CR26.3

Cumulative short-term financing needed $(-)$ or surplus $(+)$ per month is $-\$65,250$, $-\$46,750$, $-\$27,750$, $+\$32,250$, $-\$34,000$, and $-\$10,000$.

CR26.4

	Actual for Last Year	**Pro Forma**
Net sales	$40	$44
Cost of goods sold	10	11
Gross margin	30	33
Selling and administrative expenses	10	11
EBIT	20	22
Interest	2	2
EBT	18	20
Taxes	7	8
Net income	11	12
Cash dividends	3	3
Transferred to retained earnings	$ 8	$ 9

	Actual for Last Year	**Pro Forma**
Cash and marketable securities	$ 5	$5.50
Accounts receivable	20	22.00
Inventory	18	19.80
Long-term assets	27	40.00
Total assets	$70	$87.30
Short-term bank loan	$9	$9.00
Accounts payable	11	12.10

	Actual for Last Year	**Pro Forma**
Accruals	10	11.00
Long-term debt	15	15.00
Common stock	10	10.00
Retained earnings	15	24.00
Total liabilities and shareholders' equity	$70	81.10
	Additional needed	6.20
	Total to balance	$87.30

The firm needs $6.2 million in outside financing.

Chapter 27

CR27.1

Total payment per year: $PMT = PV_0/(PVA_{13\%,\ 5yr}) = \$36{,}050/3.605 = \$10{,}000$

Year	Payment	Interest	Principal Repayment	Remaining Balance
1	$10,000	$4,686.50	$5,313.50	$30,736.50
2	10,000	3,995.75	6,004.25	24,732.25
3	10,000	3,215.19	6,784.81	17,974.44

CR27.2

a. For quarter 1:

Cost of goods sold = $40,000 + sales (0.20)

= $40,000 + $100,000(0.20) = $60,000

Selling, general, and
administrative expenses = $10,000 + $100,000(0.05) = $15,000

Taxes = (cash inflows − cash outflows)(0.40)

= ($100,000 − $60,000 − $15,000 − $5,000)(0.40) = $8,000

Total operating inflows are $100,000, whereas total operating outflows are $88,000 ($60,000 + $15,000 + $5,000 + $8,000). After calculating the same information for the other three quarters, the net cash inflow or outflow per quarter is:

	Quarter			
	1	**2**	**3**	**4**
1. Total operating cash inflow	$100,000	$120,000	$140,000	$100,000
2. Total operating cash outflow	−88,000	−99,000	−110,000	−88,000
3. Other net inflow (+) or outflow (−)	+10,000	−50,000	− 60,000	+20,000
4. Net cash inflow (+) or outflow (−) (1 + 2 + 3)	+$ 22,000	−$ 29,000	−$ 30,000	+$ 32,000

The short-term financing needed is calculated as follows:

	Quarter			
	1	2	3	4
1. Cash at start of period	$20,000	$42,000	$13,000	−$17,000
2. Change in cash balance	+22,000	−29,000	−30,000	+32,000
3. Cash at end of period (1 + 2)	42,000	13,000	−17,000	15,000
4. Minimum cash balance required	−15,000	15,000	−15,000	−15,000
5. Cumulative short-term financing needed (−) or surplus (+) (3 + 4)	+$27,000	−$2,000	−$32,000	$ 0

Under the most likely scenario, CRF has to borrow in quarters 2 and 3 and will just break even in quarter 4. It will not violate the loan agreement.

b. Under the pessimistic sales forecast, the final figures (you calculate them!) are as follows:

	Quarter			
	1	2	3	4
Net cash inflow (+) or outflow (−)	+$13,000	−$28,000	−$29,000	+$23,000
Cumulative short-term financing needed (−) or surplus (+)	+$18,000	−$10,000	−$39,000	−$16,000

Because it will still be borrowing to meet the negative cumulative outflow in quarter 4, CRF would violate the loan agreement (unless some cash inflows other than borrowing are found).

c. For the optimistic forecast, we have

	Quarter			
	1	2	3	4
Net cash inflow (+) or outflow (−)	+$31,000	−$40,000	−$36,000	+$41,000
Cumulative short-term financing needed (−) or surplus (+)	+$36,000	−$4,000	−$40,000	+$1,000

Yes, CRF can increase the other net cash outflows as planned.

Financial Tables

Table B.1

Present Value Factors for $1 Discounted at k Percent for n Periods:

$$PV_{k,n} = \frac{1}{(1 + k)^n}$$

Discount Rate, k

Period, n	1%	2%	3%	4%	5%	6%	7%	8%	9%	10%	11%	12%	13%	14%	15%	16%	17%	18%	19%	20%
1	0.990	0.980	0.971	0.962	0.952	0.943	0.935	0.926	0.917	0.909	0.901	0.893	0.885	0.877	0.870	0.862	0.855	0.847	0.840	0.833
2	0.980	0.961	0.943	0.925	0.907	0.890	0.873	0.857	0.842	0.826	0.812	0.797	0.783	0.769	0.756	0.743	0.731	0.718	0.706	0.694
3	0.971	0.942	0.915	0.889	0.864	0.840	0.816	0.794	0.772	0.751	0.731	0.712	0.693	0.675	0.658	0.641	0.624	0.609	0.593	0.579
4	0.961	0.924	0.888	0.855	0.823	0.792	0.763	0.735	0.708	0.683	0.659	0.636	0.613	0.592	0.572	0.552	0.534	0.516	0.499	0.482
5	0.951	0.906	0.863	0.822	0.784	0.747	0.713	0.681	0.650	0.621	0.593	0.567	0.543	0.519	0.497	0.476	0.456	0.437	0.419	0.402
6	0.942	0.888	0.837	0.790	0.746	0.705	0.666	0.630	0.596	0.564	0.535	0.507	0.480	0.456	0.432	0.410	0.390	0.370	0.352	0.335
7	0.933	0.871	0.813	0.760	0.711	0.665	0.623	0.583	0.547	0.513	0.482	0.452	0.425	0.400	0.376	0.354	0.333	0.314	0.296	0.279
8	0.923	0.853	0.789	0.731	0.677	0.627	0.582	0.540	0.502	0.467	0.434	0.404	0.376	0.351	0.327	0.305	0.285	0.266	0.249	0.233
9	0.914	0.837	0.766	0.703	0.645	0.592	0.544	0.500	0.460	0.424	0.391	0.361	0.333	0.308	0.284	0.263	0.243	0.225	0.209	0.194
10	0.905	0.820	0.744	0.676	0.614	0.558	0.508	0.463	0.422	0.386	0.352	0.322	0.295	0.270	0.247	0.227	0.208	0.191	0.176	0.162
11	0.896	0.804	0.722	0.650	0.585	0.527	0.475	0.429	0.388	0.350	0.317	0.287	0.261	0.237	0.215	0.195	0.178	0.162	0.148	0.135
12	0.887	0.788	0.701	0.625	0.557	0.497	0.444	0.397	0.356	0.319	0.286	0.257	0.231	0.208	0.187	0.168	0.152	0.137	0.124	0.112
13	0.879	0.773	0.681	0.601	0.530	0.469	0.415	0.368	0.326	0.290	0.258	0.229	0.204	0.182	0.163	0.145	0.130	0.116	0.104	0.093
14	0.870	0.758	0.661	0.577	0.505	0.442	0.388	0.340	0.299	0.263	0.232	0.205	0.181	0.160	0.141	0.125	0.111	0.099	0.088	0.078
15	0.861	0.743	0.642	0.555	0.481	0.417	0.362	0.315	0.275	0.239	0.209	0.183	0.160	0.140	0.123	0.108	0.095	0.084	0.074	0.065
16	0.853	0.728	0.623	0.534	0.458	0.394	0.339	0.292	0.252	0.218	0.188	0.163	0.141	0.123	0.107	0.093	0.081	0.071	0.062	0.054
17	0.844	0.714	0.605	0.513	0.436	0.371	0.317	0.270	0.231	0.198	0.170	0.146	0.125	0.108	0.093	0.080	0.069	0.060	0.052	0.045
18	0.836	0.700	0.587	0.494	0.416	0.350	0.296	0.250	0.212	0.180	0.153	0.130	0.111	0.095	0.081	0.069	0.059	0.051	0.044	0.038
19	0.828	0.686	0.570	0.475	0.396	0.331	0.277	0.232	0.194	0.164	0.138	0.116	0.098	0.083	0.070	0.060	0.051	0.043	0.037	0.031
20	0.820	0.673	0.554	0.456	0.377	0.312	0.258	0.215	0.178	0.149	0.124	0.104	0.087	0.073	0.061	0.051	0.043	0.037	0.031	0.026
21	0.811	0.660	0.538	0.439	0.359	0.294	0.242	0.199	0.164	0.135	0.112	0.093	0.077	0.064	0.053	0.044	0.037	0.031	0.026	0.022
22	0.803	0.647	0.522	0.422	0.342	0.278	0.226	0.184	0.150	0.123	0.101	0.083	0.068	0.056	0.046	0.038	0.032	0.026	0.022	0.018
23	0.795	0.634	0.507	0.406	0.326	0.262	0.211	0.170	0.138	0.112	0.091	0.074	0.060	0.049	0.040	0.033	0.027	0.022	0.018	0.015
24	0.788	0.622	0.492	0.390	0.310	0.247	0.197	0.158	0.126	0.102	0.082	0.066	0.053	0.043	0.035	0.028	0.023	0.019	0.015	0.013
25	0.780	0.610	0.478	0.375	0.295	0.233	0.184	0.146	0.116	0.092	0.074	0.059	0.047	0.038	0.030	0.024	0.020	0.016	0.013	0.010
26	0.772	0.598	0.464	0.361	0.281	0.220	0.172	0.135	0.106	0.084	0.066	0.053	0.042	0.033	0.026	0.021	0.017	0.014	0.011	0.009
27	0.764	0.586	0.450	0.347	0.268	0.207	0.161	0.125	0.098	0.076	0.060	0.047	0.037	0.029	0.023	0.018	0.014	0.011	0.009	0.007
28	0.757	0.574	0.437	0.333	0.255	0.196	0.150	0.116	0.090	0.069	0.054	0.042	0.033	0.026	0.020	0.016	0.012	0.010	0.008	0.006
29	0.749	0.563	0.424	0.321	0.243	0.185	0.141	0.107	0.082	0.063	0.048	0.037	0.029	0.022	0.017	0.014	0.011	0.008	0.006	0.005
30	0.742	0.552	0.412	0.308	0.231	0.174	0.131	0.099	0.075	0.057	0.044	0.033	0.026	0.020	0.015	0.012	0.009	0.007	0.005	0.004
35	0.706	0.500	0.355	0.253	0.181	0.130	0.094	0.068	0.049	0.036	0.026	0.019	0.014	0.010	0.008	0.006	0.004	0.003	0.002	0.002
40	0.672	0.453	0.307	0.208	0.142	0.097	0.067	0.046	0.032	0.022	0.015	0.011	0.008	0.005	0.004	0.003	0.002	0.001	0.001	0.001
45	0.639	0.410	0.264	0.171	0.111	0.073	0.048	0.031	0.021	0.014	0.009	0.006	0.004	0.003	0.002	0.001	0.001	0.001	*	*
50	0.608	0.372	0.228	0.141	0.087	0.054	0.034	0.021	0.013	0.009	0.005	0.003	0.002	0.001	0.001	0.001	*	*	*	*

*PV is zero to three decimal places.

Table B.1 (Continued)

$PV_{k,n}$

Discount Rate, k

Period, n	21%	22%	23%	24%	25%	26%	27%	28%	29%	30%	31%	32%	33%	34%	35%	40%	45%	50%	55%	60%
1	0.826	0.820	0.813	0.806	0.800	0.794	0.787	0.781	0.775	0.769	0.763	0.758	0.752	0.746	0.741	0.714	0.690	0.667	0.645	0.625
2	0.683	0.672	0.661	0.650	0.640	0.630	0.620	0.610	0.601	0.592	0.583	0.574	0.565	0.557	0.549	0.510	0.476	0.444	0.416	0.391
3	0.564	0.551	0.537	0.524	0.512	0.500	0.488	0.477	0.466	0.455	0.445	0.435	0.425	0.416	0.406	0.364	0.328	0.296	0.269	0.244
4	0.467	0.451	0.437	0.423	0.410	0.397	0.384	0.373	0.361	0.350	0.340	0.329	0.320	0.310	0.301	0.260	0.226	0.198	0.173	0.153
5	0.386	0.370	0.355	0.341	0.328	0.315	0.303	0.291	0.280	0.269	0.259	0.250	0.240	0.231	0.223	0.186	0.156	0.132	0.112	0.095
6	0.319	0.303	0.289	0.275	0.262	0.250	0.238	0.227	0.217	0.207	0.198	0.189	0.181	0.173	0.165	0.133	0.108	0.088	0.072	0.060
7	0.263	0.249	0.235	0.222	0.210	0.198	0.188	0.178	0.168	0.159	0.151	0.143	0.136	0.129	0.122	0.095	0.074	0.059	0.047	0.037
8	0.218	0.204	0.191	0.179	0.168	0.157	0.148	0.139	0.130	0.123	0.115	0.108	0.102	0.096	0.091	0.068	0.051	0.039	0.030	0.023
9	0.180	0.167	0.155	0.144	0.134	0.125	0.116	0.108	0.101	0.094	0.088	0.082	0.077	0.072	0.067	0.048	0.035	0.026	0.019	0.015
10	0.149	0.137	0.126	0.116	0.107	0.099	0.092	0.085	0.078	0.073	0.067	0.062	0.058	0.054	0.050	0.035	0.024	0.017	0.012	0.009
11	0.123	0.112	0.103	0.094	0.086	0.079	0.072	0.066	0.061	0.056	0.051	0.047	0.043	0.040	0.037	0.025	0.017	0.012	0.008	0.006
12	0.102	0.092	0.083	0.076	0.069	0.062	0.057	0.052	0.047	0.043	0.039	0.036	0.033	0.030	0.027	0.018	0.012	0.008	0.005	0.004
13	0.084	0.075	0.068	0.061	0.055	0.050	0.045	0.040	0.037	0.033	0.030	0.027	0.025	0.022	0.020	0.013	0.008	0.005	0.003	0.002
14	0.069	0.062	0.055	0.049	0.044	0.039	0.035	0.032	0.028	0.025	0.023	0.021	0.018	0.017	0.015	0.009	0.006	0.003	0.002	0.001
15	0.057	0.051	0.045	0.040	0.035	0.031	0.028	0.025	0.022	0.020	0.017	0.016	0.014	0.012	0.011	0.006	0.004	0.002	0.001	0.001
16	0.047	0.042	0.036	0.032	0.028	0.025	0.022	0.019	0.017	0.015	0.013	0.012	0.010	0.009	0.008	0.005	0.003	0.001	0.001	0.001
17	0.039	0.034	0.030	0.026	0.023	0.020	0.017	0.015	0.013	0.012	0.010	0.009	0.008	0.007	0.006	0.003	0.002	0.001	0.001	*
18	0.032	0.028	0.024	0.021	0.018	0.016	0.014	0.012	0.010	0.009	0.008	0.007	0.006	0.005	0.005	0.002	0.001	0.001	*	*
19	0.027	0.023	0.020	0.017	0.014	0.012	0.011	0.009	0.008	0.007	0.006	0.005	0.004	0.004	0.003	0.002	0.001	*	*	*
20	0.022	0.019	0.016	0.014	0.012	0.010	0.008	0.007	0.006	0.005	0.005	0.004	0.003	0.003	0.002	0.001	0.001	*	*	*
21	0.018	0.015	0.013	0.011	0.009	0.008	0.007	0.006	0.005	0.004	0.004	0.003	0.003	0.002	0.002	0.001	*	*	*	*
22	0.015	0.013	0.011	0.009	0.007	0.005	0.005	0.004	0.004	0.003	0.003	0.002	0.002	0.002	0.001	0.001	*	*	*	*
23	0.012	0.010	0.009	0.007	0.006	0.005	0.004	0.003	0.003	0.002	0.002	0.002	0.001	0.001	0.001	*	*	*	*	*
24	0.010	0.008	0.007	0.006	0.005	0.004	0.003	0.003	0.002	0.002	0.002	0.001	0.001	0.001	0.001	*	*	*	*	*
25	0.009	0.007	0.006	0.005	0.004	0.003	0.003	0.002	0.001	0.001	0.001	0.001	0.001	0.001	0.001	*	*	*	*	*
26	0.007	0.006	0.005	0.004	0.003	0.002	0.002	0.002	0.001	0.001	0.001	0.001	0.001	*	*	*	*	*	*	*
27	0.006	0.005	0.004	0.003	0.002	0.002	0.002	0.001	0.001	0.001	0.001	0.001	*	*	*	*	*	*	*	*
28	0.005	0.004	0.003	0.002	0.002	0.002	0.001	0.001	0.001	0.001	0.001	*	*	*	*	*	*	*	*	*
29	0.004	0.003	0.002	0.002	0.002	0.001	0.001	0.001	0.001	*	*	*	*	*	*	*	*	*	*	*
30	0.003	0.003	0.002	0.002	0.001	0.001	0.001	0.001	*	*	*	*	*	*	*	*	*	*	*	*
35	0.001	0.001	0.001	0.001	*	*	*	*	*	*	*	*	*	*	*	*	*	*	*	*
40	*	*	*	*	*	*	*	*	*	*	*	*	*	*	*	*	*	*	*	*
45	*	*	*	*	*	*	*	*	*	*	*	*	*	*	*	*	*	*	*	*
50	*	*	*	*	*	*	*	*	*	*	*	*	*	*	*	*	*	*	*	*

*PV is zero to three decimal places.

Table B.2

Present Value Factors for an Annuity of $1 Discounted at k Percent for n Periods:

$$PVA_{k,n} = \sum_{t=1}^{n} \frac{1}{(1+k)^t} = \frac{1 - [1/(1+k)^n]}{k}$$

Period, n	Discount Rate, k																			
	1%	2%	3%	4%	5%	6%	7%	8%	9%	10%	11%	12%	13%	14%	15%	16%	17%	18%	19%	20%
1	0.990	0.980	0.971	0.962	0.952	0.943	0.935	0.926	0.917	0.909	0.901	0.893	0.885	0.877	0.870	0.862	0.855	0.847	0.840	0.833
2	1.970	1.942	1.913	1.886	1.859	1.833	1.808	1.783	1.759	1.736	1.713	1.690	1.668	1.647	1.626	1.605	1.585	1.566	1.547	1.528
3	2.941	2.884	2.829	2.775	2.723	2.673	2.624	2.577	2.531	2.487	2.444	2.402	2.361	2.322	2.283	2.246	2.210	2.174	2.140	2.106
4	3.902	3.808	3.717	3.630	3.546	3.465	3.387	3.312	3.240	3.170	3.102	3.037	2.974	2.914	2.855	2.798	2.743	2.690	2.639	2.589
5	4.853	4.713	4.580	4.452	4.329	4.212	4.100	3.993	3.890	3.791	3.696	3.605	3.517	3.433	3.352	3.274	3.199	3.127	3.058	2.991
6	5.795	5.601	5.417	5.242	5.076	4.917	4.767	4.623	4.486	4.355	4.231	4.111	3.998	3.889	3.784	3.685	3.589	3.498	3.410	3.326
7	6.728	6.472	6.230	6.002	5.786	5.582	5.389	5.206	5.033	4.868	4.712	4.564	4.423	4.288	4.160	4.039	3.922	3.812	3.706	3.605
8	7.652	7.325	7.020	6.733	6.463	6.210	5.971	5.747	5.535	5.335	5.146	4.968	4.799	4.639	4.487	4.344	4.207	4.078	3.954	3.837
9	8.566	8.162	7.786	7.435	7.108	6.802	6.515	6.247	5.995	5.759	5.537	5.328	5.132	4.946	4.772	4.607	4.451	4.303	4.163	4.031
10	9.471	8.983	8.530	8.111	7.722	7.360	7.024	6.710	6.418	6.145	5.889	5.650	5.426	5.216	5.019	4.833	4.659	4.494	4.339	4.192
11	10.368	9.787	9.253	8.760	8.306	7.887	7.499	7.139	6.805	6.495	6.207	5.938	5.687	5.453	5.234	5.029	4.836	4.656	4.486	4.327
12	11.255	10.575	9.954	9.385	8.863	8.384	7.943	7.536	7.161	6.814	6.492	6.194	5.918	5.660	5.421	5.197	4.988	4.793	4.611	4.439
13	12.134	11.348	10.635	9.986	9.394	8.853	8.358	7.904	7.487	7.103	6.750	6.424	6.122	5.842	5.583	5.342	5.118	4.910	4.715	4.533
14	13.004	12.106	11.296	10.563	9.899	9.295	8.745	8.244	7.786	7.367	6.982	6.628	6.302	6.002	5.724	5.468	5.229	5.008	4.802	4.611
15	13.865	12.849	11.938	11.118	10.380	9.712	9.108	8.559	8.061	7.606	7.191	6.811	6.462	6.142	5.847	5.575	5.324	5.092	4.876	4.675
16	14.718	13.578	12.561	11.652	10.838	10.106	9.447	8.851	8.313	7.824	7.379	6.974	6.604	6.265	5.954	5.668	5.405	5.162	4.938	4.730
17	15.562	14.292	13.166	12.166	11.274	10.477	9.763	9.122	8.544	8.022	7.549	7.120	6.729	6.373	6.047	5.749	5.475	5.222	4.990	4.775
18	16.398	14.992	13.754	12.659	11.690	10.828	10.059	9.372	8.756	8.201	7.702	7.250	6.840	6.467	6.128	5.818	5.534	5.273	5.033	4.812
19	17.226	15.678	14.324	13.134	12.085	11.158	10.336	9.604	8.950	8.365	7.839	7.366	6.938	6.550	6.198	5.877	5.584	5.316	5.070	4.843
20	18.046	16.351	14.877	13.590	12.462	11.470	10.594	9.818	9.129	8.514	7.963	7.469	7.025	6.623	6.259	5.929	5.628	5.353	5.101	4.870
21	18.857	17.011	15.415	14.029	12.821	11.764	10.836	10.017	9.292	8.649	8.075	7.562	7.102	6.687	6.312	5.973	5.665	5.384	5.127	4.891
22	19.660	17.658	15.937	14.451	13.163	12.042	11.061	10.201	9.442	8.772	8.176	7.645	7.170	6.743	6.359	6.011	5.696	5.410	5.149	4.909
23	20.456	18.292	16.444	14.857	13.489	12.303	11.272	10.371	9.580	8.883	8.266	7.718	7.230	6.792	6.399	6.044	5.723	5.432	5.167	4.925
24	21.243	18.914	16.936	15.247	13.799	12.550	11.469	10.529	9.707	8.985	8.348	7.784	7.283	6.835	6.434	6.073	5.746	5.451	5.182	4.937
25	22.023	19.523	17.413	15.622	14.094	12.783	11.654	10.675	9.823	9.077	8.422	7.843	7.330	6.873	6.464	6.097	5.766	5.467	5.195	4.948
26	22.795	20.121	17.877	15.983	14.375	13.003	11.826	10.810	9.929	9.161	8.488	7.896	7.372	6.906	6.491	6.118	5.783	5.480	5.206	4.956
27	23.560	20.707	18.327	16.330	14.643	13.211	11.987	10.935	10.027	9.237	8.548	7.943	7.409	6.935	6.514	6.136	5.798	5.492	5.215	4.964
28	24.316	21.281	18.764	16.663	14.898	13.406	12.137	11.051	10.116	9.307	8.602	7.984	7.441	6.961	6.534	6.152	5.810	5.502	5.223	4.970
29	25.066	21.844	19.188	16.984	15.141	13.591	12.278	11.158	10.198	9.370	8.650	8.022	7.470	6.983	6.551	6.166	5.820	5.510	5.229	4.975
30	25.808	22.396	19.600	17.292	15.372	13.765	12.409	11.258	10.274	9.427	8.694	8.055	7.496	7.003	6.566	6.177	5.829	5.517	5.235	4.979
35	29.409	24.999	21.487	18.665	16.374	14.498	12.948	11.655	10.567	9.644	8.855	8.176	7.586	7.070	6.617	6.215	5.858	5.539	5.251	4.992
40	32.835	27.335	23.115	19.793	17.159	15.046	13.332	11.925	10.757	9.779	8.951	8.244	7.634	7.105	6.642	6.233	5.871	5.548	5.258	4.997
45	36.095	29.490	24.519	20.720	17.774	15.456	13.606	12.108	10.881	9.863	9.008	8.283	7.661	7.123	6.654	6.242	5.877	5.552	5.261	4.999
50	39.196	31.424	25.730	21.482	18.256	15.762	13.801	12.233	10.962	9.915	9.042	8.304	7.675	7.133	6.661	6.246	5.880	5.554	5.262	4.999

Table B.2

PVA$_{k,n}$ (Continued)

Period, n	\multicolumn{20}{c}{Discount Rate, k}																		
	21%	22%	23%	24%	25%	26%	27%	28%	29%	30%	31%	32%	33%	34%	35%	40%	45%	50%	55%	60%
1	0.826	0.820	0.813	0.806	0.800	0.794	0.787	0.781	0.775	0.769	0.763	0.758	0.752	0.746	0.741	0.714	0.690	0.667	0.645	0.625
2	1.509	1.492	1.474	1.457	1.440	1.424	1.407	1.392	1.376	1.361	1.346	1.331	1.317	1.303	1.289	1.224	1.165	1.111	1.061	1.016
3	2.074	2.042	2.011	1.981	1.952	1.923	1.896	1.868	1.842	1.816	1.791	1.766	1.742	1.719	1.696	1.589	1.493	1.407	1.330	1.260
4	2.540	2.494	2.448	2.404	2.362	2.320	2.280	2.241	2.203	2.166	2.130	2.096	2.062	2.029	1.997	1.849	1.720	1.605	1.503	1.412
5	2.926	2.864	2.803	2.745	2.689	2.635	2.583	2.532	2.483	2.436	2.390	2.345	2.302	2.260	2.220	2.035	1.876	1.737	1.615	1.508
6	3.245	3.167	3.092	3.020	2.951	2.885	2.821	2.759	2.700	2.643	2.588	2.534	2.483	2.433	2.385	2.168	1.983	1.824	1.687	1.597
7	3.508	3.416	3.327	3.242	3.161	3.083	3.009	2.937	2.868	2.802	2.739	2.677	2.619	2.562	2.508	2.263	2.057	1.883	1.734	1.605
8	3.726	3.619	3.518	3.421	3.329	3.241	3.156	3.076	2.999	2.925	2.854	2.786	2.721	2.658	2.598	2.331	2.109	1.922	1.764	1.628
9	3.905	3.786	3.673	3.566	3.463	3.366	3.273	3.184	3.100	3.019	2.942	2.868	2.798	2.730	2.665	2.379	2.144	1.948	1.783	1.642
10	4.054	3.923	3.799	3.682	3.571	3.465	3.364	3.269	3.178	3.092	3.009	2.930	2.855	2.784	2.715	2.414	2.168	1.965	1.795	1.652
11	4.177	4.035	3.902	3.776	3.656	3.543	3.437	3.335	3.239	3.147	3.060	2.978	2.899	2.824	2.752	2.438	2.185	1.977	1.804	1.657
12	4.278	4.127	3.985	3.851	3.725	3.606	3.493	3.387	3.286	3.190	3.100	3.013	2.931	2.853	2.779	2.456	2.196	1.985	1.809	1.661
13	4.362	4.203	4.053	3.912	3.780	3.656	3.538	3.427	3.322	3.223	3.129	3.040	2.956	2.876	2.799	2.469	2.204	1.990	1.812	1.663
14	4.432	4.265	4.108	3.962	3.824	3.695	3.573	3.459	3.351	3.249	3.152	3.061	2.974	2.892	2.814	2.478	2.210	1.993	1.814	1.664
15	4.489	4.315	4.153	4.001	3.859	3.726	3.601	3.483	3.373	3.268	3.170	3.076	2.988	2.905	2.825	2.484	2.214	1.995	1.816	1.665
16	4.536	4.357	4.189	4.033	3.887	3.751	3.623	3.503	3.390	3.283	3.183	3.088	2.999	2.914	2.834	2.489	2.216	1.997	1.817	1.666
17	4.576	4.391	4.219	4.059	3.910	3.771	3.640	3.518	3.403	3.295	3.193	3.097	3.007	2.921	2.840	2.492	2.218	1.998	1.817	1.666
18	4.608	4.419	4.243	4.080	3.928	3.786	3.654	3.529	3.413	3.304	3.201	3.104	3.012	2.926	2.844	2.494	2.219	1.999	1.818	1.666
19	4.635	4.442	4.263	4.097	3.942	3.799	3.664	3.539	3.421	3.311	3.207	3.109	3.017	2.930	2.848	2.496	2.220	1.999	1.818	1.666
20	4.657	4.460	4.279	4.110	3.954	3.808	3.673	3.546	3.427	3.316	3.211	3.113	3.020	2.933	2.850	2.497	2.221	1.999	1.818	1.667
21	4.675	4.476	4.292	4.121	3.963	3.816	3.679	3.551	3.432	3.320	3.215	3.116	3.023	2.935	2.852	2.498	2.221	2.000	1.818	1.667
22	4.690	4.488	4.302	4.130	3.970	3.822	3.684	3.556	3.436	3.323	3.217	3.118	3.025	2.936	2.853	2.498	2.222	2.000	1.818	1.667
23	4.703	4.499	4.311	4.137	3.976	3.827	3.689	3.559	3.438	3.325	3.219	3.120	3.026	2.938	2.854	2.499	2.222	2.000	1.818	1.667
24	4.713	4.507	4.318	4.143	3.981	3.831	3.692	3.562	3.441	3.327	3.221	3.121	3.027	2.939	2.855	2.499	2.222	2.000	1.818	1.667
25	4.721	4.514	4.323	4.147	3.985	3.834	3.694	3.564	3.442	3.329	3.222	3.122	3.028	2.939	2.856	2.499	2.222	2.000	1.818	1.667
26	4.728	4.520	4.328	4.151	3.988	3.837	3.696	3.566	3.444	3.330	3.223	3.123	3.028	2.940	2.856	2.500	2.222	2.000	1.818	1.667
27	4.734	4.524	4.332	4.154	3.990	3.839	3.698	3.567	3.445	3.331	3.224	3.123	3.029	2.940	2.856	2.500	2.222	2.000	1.818	1.667
28	4.739	4.528	4.335	4.157	3.992	3.840	3.699	3.568	3.446	3.331	3.224	3.124	3.029	2.940	2.857	2.500	2.222	2.000	1.818	1.667
29	4.743	4.531	4.337	4.159	3.994	3.841	3.700	3.569	3.446	3.332	3.225	3.124	3.030	2.941	2.857	2.500	2.222	2.000	1.818	1.667
30	4.746	4.534	4.339	4.160	3.995	3.842	3.701	3.569	3.447	3.332	3.225	3.124	3.030	2.941	2.857	2.500	2.222	2.000	1.818	1.667
35	4.756	4.541	4.345	4.164	3.998	3.845	3.703	3.571	3.448	3.333	3.226	3.125	3.030	2.941	2.857	2.500	2.222	2.000	1.818	1.667
40	4.760	4.544	4.347	4.166	3.999	3.846	3.703	3.571	3.448	3.333	3.226	3.125	3.030	2.941	2.857	2.500	2.222	2.000	1.818	1.667
45	4.761	4.545	4.347	4.166	4.000	3.846	3.704	3.571	3.448	3.333	3.226	3.125	3.030	2.941	2.857	2.500	2.222	2.000	1.818	1.667
50	4.762	4.545	4.348	4.167	4.000	3.846	3.704	3.571	3.448	3.333	3.226	3.125	3.030	2.941	2.857	2.500	2.222	2.000	1.818	1.667

Table B.3

Future Value Factors for $1 Compounded at k Percent for n Periods:

$$FV_{k,n} = (1 + k)^n$$

Compound Rate, k

Period, n	1%	2%	3%	4%	5%	6%	7%	8%	9%	10%	11%	12%	13%	14%	15%	16%	17%	18%	19%	20%
1	1.010	1.020	1.030	1.040	1.050	1.060	1.070	1.080	1.090	1.100	1.110	1.120	1.130	1.140	1.150	1.160	1.170	1.180	1.190	1.200
2	1.020	1.040	1.061	1.082	1.102	1.124	1.145	1.166	1.188	1.210	1.232	1.254	1.277	1.300	1.323	1.346	1.369	1.392	1.416	1.440
3	1.030	1.061	1.093	1.125	1.158	1.191	1.225	1.260	1.295	1.331	1.368	1.405	1.443	1.482	1.521	1.561	1.602	1.643	1.685	1.728
4	1.041	1.082	1.126	1.170	1.216	1.262	1.311	1.360	1.412	1.464	1.518	1.574	1.630	1.689	1.749	1.811	1.874	1.939	2.005	2.074
5	1.051	1.104	1.159	1.217	1.276	1.338	1.403	1.469	1.539	1.611	1.685	1.762	1.842	1.925	2.011	2.100	2.192	2.288	2.386	2.488
6	1.062	1.126	1.194	1.265	1.340	1.419	1.501	1.587	1.677	1.772	1.870	1.974	2.082	2.195	2.313	2.436	2.565	2.700	2.840	2.986
7	1.072	1.149	1.230	1.316	1.407	1.504	1.606	1.714	1.828	1.949	2.076	2.211	2.353	2.502	2.660	2.826	3.001	3.185	3.379	3.583
8	1.083	1.172	1.267	1.369	1.477	1.594	1.718	1.851	1.993	2.144	2.305	2.476	2.658	2.853	3.059	3.278	3.511	3.759	4.021	4.300
9	1.094	1.195	1.305	1.423	1.551	1.689	1.838	1.999	2.172	2.358	2.558	2.773	3.004	3.252	3.518	3.803	4.108	4.435	4.785	5.160
10	1.105	1.219	1.344	1.480	1.629	1.791	1.967	2.159	2.367	2.594	2.839	3.106	3.395	3.707	4.046	4.411	4.807	5.234	5.695	6.192
11	1.116	1.243	1.384	1.539	1.710	1.898	2.105	2.332	2.580	2.853	3.152	3.479	3.836	4.226	4.652	5.117	5.624	6.176	6.777	7.430
12	1.127	1.268	1.426	1.601	1.796	2.012	2.252	2.518	2.813	3.138	3.498	3.896	4.335	4.818	5.350	5.936	6.580	7.288	8.064	8.916
13	1.138	1.294	1.469	1.665	1.886	2.133	2.410	2.720	3.066	3.452	3.883	4.363	4.898	5.492	6.153	6.886	7.699	8.599	9.596	10.699
14	1.149	1.319	1.513	1.732	1.980	2.261	2.579	2.937	3.342	3.797	4.310	4.887	5.535	6.261	7.076	7.988	9.007	10.147	11.420	12.839
15	1.161	1.346	1.558	1.801	2.079	2.397	2.759	3.172	3.642	4.177	4.785	5.474	6.254	7.138	8.137	9.266	10.539	11.974	13.590	15.407
16	1.173	1.373	1.605	1.873	2.183	2.540	2.952	3.426	3.970	4.595	5.311	6.130	7.067	8.137	9.358	10.748	12.330	14.129	16.172	18.488
17	1.184	1.400	1.653	1.948	2.292	2.693	3.159	3.700	4.328	5.054	5.895	6.866	7.986	9.276	10.761	12.468	14.426	16.672	19.244	22.186
18	1.196	1.428	1.702	2.026	2.407	2.854	3.380	3.996	4.717	5.560	6.544	7.690	9.024	10.575	12.375	14.463	16.879	19.673	22.901	26.623
19	1.208	1.457	1.754	2.107	2.527	3.026	3.617	4.316	5.142	6.116	7.263	8.613	10.197	12.056	14.232	16.777	19.748	23.214	27.252	31.948
20	1.220	1.486	1.806	2.191	2.653	3.207	3.870	4.661	5.604	6.727	8.062	9.646	11.523	13.743	16.367	19.461	23.106	27.393	32.429	38.338
21	1.232	1.516	1.860	2.279	2.786	3.400	4.141	5.034	6.109	7.400	8.949	10.804	13.021	15.668	18.822	22.574	27.034	32.324	38.591	46.005
22	1.245	1.546	1.916	2.370	2.925	3.604	4.430	5.437	6.659	8.140	9.934	12.100	14.714	17.861	21.645	26.186	31.629	38.142	45.923	55.206
23	1.257	1.577	1.974	2.465	3.072	3.820	4.741	5.871	7.258	8.954	11.026	13.552	16.627	20.362	24.891	30.376	37.006	45.008	54.649	66.247
24	1.270	1.608	2.033	2.563	3.225	4.049	5.072	6.341	7.911	9.850	12.239	15.179	18.788	23.212	28.625	35.236	43.297	53.109	65.032	79.497
25	1.282	1.641	2.094	2.666	3.386	4.272	5.427	6.848	8.623	10.835	13.585	17.000	21.231	26.462	32.919	40.874	50.658	62.669	77.338	95.396
26	1.295	1.673	2.157	2.772	3.556	4.549	5.807	7.396	9.399	11.918	15.080	19.040	23.991	30.167	37.857	47.414	59.270	73.949	92.092	114.48
27	1.308	1.707	2.221	2.883	3.733	4.822	6.214	7.988	10.245	13.110	16.739	21.325	27.109	34.390	43.535	55.000	69.345	87.260	109.59	137.37
28	1.321	1.741	2.288	2.999	3.920	5.112	6.649	8.627	11.167	14.421	18.580	23.884	30.633	39.204	50.066	63.800	81.134	102.97	130.41	164.84
29	1.335	1.776	2.357	3.119	4.116	5.418	7.114	9.317	12.172	15.863	20.624	26.750	34.616	44.693	57.575	74.009	94.927	121.50	155.19	197.81
30	1.348	1.811	2.427	3.243	4.322	5.743	7.612	10.063	13.268	17.449	22.892	29.960	39.116	50.950	66.212	85.850	111.06	143.37	184.68	237.38
35	1.417	2.000	2.814	3.946	5.516	7.686	10.677	14.785	20.414	28.102	38.575	52.800	72.068	98.100	133.18	180.31	243.50	328.00	440.70	590.67
40	1.489	2.208	3.262	4.801	7.040	10.286	14.974	21.725	31.409	45.259	65.001	93.051	132.78	188.88	267.86	378.72	533.87	750.38	1051.7	1469.8
45	1.565	2.438	3.782	5.841	8.985	13.765	21.002	31.920	48.327	72.890	109.53	163.99	244.64	363.68	538.77	795.44	1170.5	1716.7	2509.7	3657.3
50	1.645	2.692	4.384	7.107	11.467	18.420	29.457	46.902	74.358	117.39	184.56	289.00	450.74	700.23	1083.7	1670.7	2566.2	3927.4	5788.9	9100.4

Table B.3 (Continued)

$FV_{k,n}$

Period, n	Compound Rate, k																			
	21%	22%	23%	24%	25%	26%	27%	28%	29%	30%	31%	32%	33%	34%	35%	40%	45%	50%	55%	60%
1	1.210	1.220	1.230	1.240	1.250	1.260	1.270	1.280	1.290	1.300	1.310	1.320	1.330	1.340	1.350	1.400	1.450	1.500	1.550	1.600
2	1.464	1.488	1.513	1.538	1.563	1.588	1.613	1.638	1.664	1.690	1.716	1.742	1.769	1.796	1.823	1.960	2.103	2.250	2.403	2.560
3	1.772	1.816	1.861	1.907	1.953	2.000	2.048	2.097	2.147	2.197	2.248	2.300	2.353	2.406	2.460	2.744	3.049	3.375	3.724	4.096
4	2.144	2.215	2.289	2.364	2.441	2.520	2.601	2.684	2.769	2.856	2.945	3.036	3.129	3.224	3.322	3.842	4.421	5.063	5.772	6.554
5	2.594	2.703	2.815	2.932	3.052	3.176	3.304	3.436	3.572	3.713	3.858	4.007	4.162	4.320	4.484	5.378	6.410	7.594	8.947	10.486
6	3.138	3.297	3.463	3.635	3.815	4.002	4.196	4.398	4.608	4.827	5.054	5.290	5.535	5.789	6.053	7.530	9.294	11.391	13.867	16.777
7	3.797	4.023	4.259	4.508	4.768	5.042	5.329	5.629	5.945	6.275	6.621	6.983	7.361	7.758	8.172	10.541	13.476	17.086	21.494	26.844
8	4.595	4.908	5.239	5.590	5.960	6.353	6.768	7.206	7.669	8.157	8.673	9.217	9.791	10.395	11.032	14.758	19.541	25.629	33.316	42.950
9	5.560	5.987	6.444	6.931	7.451	8.005	8.595	9.223	9.893	10.604	11.362	12.166	13.022	13.930	14.894	20.661	28.334	38.443	51.640	68.719
10	6.728	7.305	7.926	8.594	9.313	10.086	10.915	11.806	12.761	13.786	14.884	16.060	17.319	18.666	20.107	28.925	41.085	57.665	80.042	109.95
11	8.140	8.912	9.749	10.657	11.642	12.708	13.862	15.112	16.462	17.922	19.498	21.199	23.034	25.012	27.144	40.496	59.573	86.498	124.06	175.92
12	9.850	10.872	11.991	13.215	14.552	16.012	17.605	19.343	21.236	23.298	25.542	27.983	30.635	33.516	36.644	56.694	86.381	129.75	192.30	281.47
13	11.918	13.264	14.749	16.386	18.190	20.175	22.359	24.759	27.395	30.288	33.460	36.937	40.745	44.912	49.470	79.371	125.25	194.62	298.07	450.36
14	14.421	16.182	18.141	20.319	22.737	25.421	28.396	31.691	35.339	39.374	43.833	48.757	54.190	60.182	66.784	111.12	181.62	291.93	462.00	720.58
15	17.449	19.742	22.314	25.196	28.422	32.030	36.062	40.565	45.587	51.186	57.421	64.359	72.073	80.644	90.158	155.57	263.34	437.89	716.10	1152.9
16	21.114	24.086	27.446	31.243	35.527	40.358	45.799	51.923	58.808	66.542	75.221	84.954	95.858	108.06	121.71	217.80	381.85	656.84	1110.0	1844.7
17	25.548	29.384	33.759	38.741	44.409	50.851	58.165	66.461	75.862	86.504	98.540	112.14	127.49	144.80	164.31	304.91	553.68	985.26	1720.4	2951.5
18	30.913	35.849	41.523	48.039	55.511	64.072	73.870	85.071	97.862	112.46	129.09	148.02	169.56	194.04	221.82	426.88	802.83	1477.9	2666.7	4722.4
19	37.404	43.736	51.074	59.568	69.389	80.731	93.815	108.89	126.24	146.19	169.10	195.39	225.52	260.01	299.46	597.63	1164.1	2216.8	4133.4	7555.8
20	45.259	53.358	62.821	73.864	86.736	101.72	119.14	139.38	162.85	190.05	221.53	257.92	299.94	348.41	404.27	836.68	1688.0	3325.3	6406.7	12089
21	54.764	65.096	77.269	91.592	108.42	128.17	151.31	178.41	210.08	247.06	290.20	340.45	398.92	466.88	545.77	1171.4	2447.5	4987.9	9930.4	19342
22	66.264	79.418	95.041	113.57	135.53	161.49	192.17	228.36	271.00	321.18	380.16	449.39	530.56	625.61	736.79	1639.9	3548.9	7481.8	15392	30948
23	80.180	96.889	116.90	140.83	169.41	203.48	244.05	292.30	349.59	417.54	498.01	593.20	705.65	838.32	994.66	2295.9	5145.9	11222	23857	49517
24	97.017	118.21	143.79	174.63	211.76	256.39	309.95	374.14	450.98	542.80	652.40	783.02	938.51	1123.4	1342.8	3214.2	7461.6	16834	36979	79228
25	117.39	144.21	176.86	216.54	264.70	323.05	393.63	478.90	581.76	705.64	854.64	1033.6	1248.2	1505.3	1812.8	4499.9	10819	25251	57318	126765
26	142.04	175.94	217.54	268.51	330.87	407.04	499.92	613.00	750.47	917.33	1119.6	1364.3	1660.1	2017.1	2447.2	6299.8	15688	37876	88843	202824
27	171.87	214.64	267.57	332.95	413.59	512.87	634.89	784.64	968.10	1192.5	1466.6	1800.9	2208.0	2702.9	3303.8	8819.8	22747	56815	137706	324518
28	207.97	261.86	329.11	412.86	516.99	646.21	806.31	1004.3	1248.9	1550.3	1921.3	2377.2	2936.6	3621.9	4460.1	12347	32984	85222	213445	519229
29	251.64	319.47	404.81	511.95	646.23	814.23	1024.0	1285.6	1611.0	2015.4	2516.9	3137.9	3905.7	4853.3	6021.1	17286	47826	127834	330840	830767
30	304.48	389.76	497.91	634.82	807.79	1025.9	1300.5	1645.5	2078.2	2620.0	3297.2	4142.1	5194.6	6503.5	8128.6	24201	69348	191751	512803	*
35	789.75	1053.4	1401.8	1861.1	2465.2	3258.1	4296.7	5653.9	7424.0	9727.9	12720	16599	21617	28097	36448	130161	444508	*	*	*
40	2048.4	2847.0	3946.4	5455.9	7523.2	10347	14195	19426	26520	36118	49074	66520	89963	121392	163437	700037	*	*	*	*
45	5313.0	7694.7	11110	15994	22958	32860	46899	66749	94740	134106	189325	266579	374389	524464	732857	*	*	*	*	*
50	13780	20796	31279	46890	70064	104358	154948	229349	338443	497929	730406	*	*	*	*	*	*	*	*	*

*FV is greater than 999999.

Table B.4

Future Value Factors for an Annuity of $1 Compounded at k Percent for n Periods:

$$FVA_{k,n} = \sum_{t=0}^{n-1} (1+k)^t = \frac{(1+k)^n - 1}{k}$$

Period, n	1%	2%	3%	4%	5%	6%	7%	8%	9%	10%	11%	12%	13%	14%	15%	16%	17%	18%	19%	20%
1	1.000	1.000	1.000	1.000	1.000	1.000	1.000	1.000	1.000	1.000	1.000	1.000	1.000	1.000	1.000	1.000	1.000	1.000	1.000	1.000
2	2.010	2.020	2.030	2.040	2.050	2.060	2.070	2.080	2.090	2.100	2.110	2.120	2.130	2.140	2.150	2.160	2.170	2.180	2.190	2.200
3	3.030	3.060	3.091	3.122	3.152	3.184	3.215	3.246	3.278	3.310	3.342	3.374	3.407	3.440	3.473	3.506	3.539	3.572	3.606	3.640
4	4.060	4.122	4.184	4.246	4.310	4.375	4.440	4.506	4.573	4.641	4.710	4.779	4.850	4.921	4.993	5.066	5.141	5.215	5.291	5.368
5	5.101	5.204	5.309	5.416	5.526	5.637	5.751	5.867	5.985	6.105	6.228	6.353	6.480	6.610	6.742	6.877	7.014	7.154	7.297	7.442
6	6.152	6.308	6.468	6.633	6.802	6.975	7.153	7.336	7.523	7.716	7.913	8.115	8.323	8.536	8.754	8.977	9.207	9.442	9.683	9.930
7	7.214	7.434	7.662	7.898	8.142	8.394	8.654	8.923	9.200	9.487	9.783	10.089	10.405	10.730	11.067	11.414	11.772	12.142	12.523	12.916
8	8.286	8.583	8.892	9.214	9.549	9.897	10.260	10.637	11.028	11.436	11.859	12.300	12.757	13.233	13.727	14.240	14.773	15.327	15.902	16.499
9	9.369	9.755	10.159	10.583	11.027	11.491	11.978	12.488	13.021	13.579	14.164	14.776	15.416	16.085	16.786	17.519	18.285	19.086	19.923	20.799
10	10.462	10.950	11.464	12.006	12.578	13.181	13.816	14.487	15.193	15.937	16.722	17.549	18.420	19.337	20.304	21.321	22.393	23.521	24.709	25.959
11	11.567	12.169	12.808	13.486	14.207	14.972	15.784	16.645	17.560	18.531	19.561	20.655	21.814	23.045	24.349	25.733	27.200	28.755	30.404	32.150
12	12.683	13.412	14.192	15.026	15.917	16.870	17.888	18.977	20.141	21.384	22.713	24.133	25.650	27.271	29.002	30.850	32.824	34.931	37.180	39.581
13	13.809	14.680	15.618	16.627	17.713	18.882	20.141	21.495	22.953	24.523	26.212	28.029	29.985	32.089	34.352	36.786	39.404	42.219	45.244	48.497
14	14.947	15.974	17.086	18.292	19.599	21.015	22.550	24.215	26.019	27.975	30.095	32.393	34.883	37.581	40.505	43.672	47.103	50.818	54.841	59.196
15	16.097	17.293	18.599	20.024	21.579	23.276	25.129	27.152	29.361	31.772	34.405	37.280	40.417	43.842	47.580	51.660	56.110	60.965	66.261	72.035
16	17.258	18.639	20.157	21.825	23.657	25.673	27.888	30.324	33.003	35.950	39.190	42.753	46.672	50.980	55.717	60.925	66.649	72.939	79.850	87.442
17	18.430	20.012	21.762	23.698	25.840	28.213	30.840	33.750	36.974	40.545	44.501	48.884	53.739	59.118	65.075	71.673	78.979	87.068	96.022	105.93
18	19.615	21.412	23.414	25.645	28.132	30.906	33.999	37.450	41.301	45.599	50.396	55.750	61.725	68.394	75.836	84.141	93.406	103.74	115.27	128.12
19	20.811	22.841	25.117	27.671	30.539	33.760	37.379	41.446	46.018	51.159	56.939	63.440	70.749	78.969	88.212	98.603	110.28	123.41	138.17	154.74
20	22.019	24.297	26.870	29.778	33.066	36.786	40.996	45.762	51.160	57.275	64.203	72.052	80.947	91.025	102.44	115.38	130.03	146.63	165.42	186.69
21	23.239	25.783	28.676	31.969	35.719	39.993	44.865	50.423	56.765	64.002	72.265	81.699	92.470	104.77	118.81	134.84	153.14	174.02	197.85	225.03
22	24.472	27.299	30.537	34.248	38.505	43.392	49.006	55.457	62.873	71.403	81.214	92.503	105.49	120.44	137.63	157.41	180.17	206.34	236.44	271.03
23	25.716	28.845	32.453	36.618	41.430	46.996	53.436	60.893	69.532	79.543	91.148	104.60	120.20	138.30	159.28	183.60	211.80	244.49	282.36	326.24
24	26.973	30.422	34.426	39.083	44.502	50.816	58.177	66.765	76.790	88.497	102.17	118.16	136.83	158.66	184.17	213.98	248.81	289.49	337.01	392.48
25	28.243	32.030	36.459	41.646	47.727	54.865	63.249	73.106	84.701	98.347	114.41	133.33	155.62	181.87	212.79	249.21	292.10	342.60	402.04	471.98
26	29.526	33.671	38.553	44.312	51.113	59.156	68.676	79.954	93.324	109.18	128.00	150.33	176.85	208.33	245.71	290.09	342.76	405.27	479.43	567.38
27	30.821	35.344	40.710	47.084	54.669	63.706	74.484	87.351	102.72	121.10	143.08	169.37	200.84	238.50	283.57	337.50	402.03	479.22	571.52	681.85
28	32.129	37.051	42.931	49.968	58.403	68.528	80.698	95.339	112.97	134.21	159.82	190.70	227.95	272.89	327.10	392.50	471.38	566.48	681.11	819.22
29	33.450	38.792	45.219	52.966	62.323	73.640	87.347	103.97	124.14	148.63	178.40	214.58	258.58	312.09	377.17	456.30	552.51	669.45	811.52	984.07
30	34.785	40.568	47.575	56.085	66.439	79.058	94.461	113.28	136.31	164.49	199.02	241.33	293.20	356.79	434.75	530.31	647.44	790.95	966.71	1181.9
35	41.660	49.994	60.462	73.652	90.320	111.43	138.24	172.32	215.71	271.02	341.59	431.66	546.68	693.57	881.17	1120.7	1426.5	1816.7	2314.2	2948.3
40	48.886	60.402	75.401	95.026	120.80	154.76	199.64	259.06	337.88	442.59	581.83	767.09	1013.7	1342.0	1779.1	2360.8	3134.5	4163.2	5529.8	7349.9
45	56.481	71.893	92.720	121.03	159.70	212.74	285.75	386.51	525.86	718.90	986.64	1358.2	1874.2	2590.6	3585.1	4965.3	6879.3	9531.6	13203	18281
50	64.463	84.579	112.80	152.67	209.35	290.34	406.53	573.77	815.08	1163.9	1668.8	2400.0	3459.5	4994.5	7217.7	10435	15089	21813	31515	45497

Compound Rate, k

Table B.4 (Continued)

$FVA_{k,n}$

Period, n

Compound Rate, k

n	21%	22%	23%	24%	25%	26%	27%	28%	29%	30%	31%	32%	33%	34%	35%	40%	45%	50%	55%	60%
1	1.000	1.000	1.000	1.000	1.000	1.000	1.000	1.000	1.000	1.000	1.000	1.000	1.000	1.000	1.000	1.000	1.000	1.000	1.000	1.000
2	2.210	2.220	2.230	2.240	2.250	2.260	2.270	2.280	2.290	2.300	2.310	2.320	2.330	2.340	2.350	2.400	2.450	2.500	2.550	2.600
3	3.674	3.708	3.743	3.778	3.813	3.848	3.883	3.918	3.954	3.990	4.026	4.062	4.099	4.136	4.173	4.360	4.553	4.750	4.952	5.160
4	5.446	5.524	5.604	5.684	5.766	5.848	5.931	6.016	6.101	6.187	6.274	6.362	6.452	6.542	6.633	7.104	7.601	8.125	8.676	9.256
5	7.589	7.740	7.893	8.048	8.207	8.368	8.533	8.700	8.870	9.043	9.219	9.398	9.581	9.766	9.954	10.946	12.022	13.188	14.448	15.810
6	10.183	10.442	10.708	10.980	11.259	11.544	11.837	12.136	12.442	12.756	13.077	13.406	13.742	14.086	14.438	16.324	18.431	20.781	23.395	26.295
7	13.321	13.740	14.171	14.615	15.073	15.546	16.032	16.534	17.051	17.583	18.131	18.696	19.277	19.876	20.492	23.853	27.725	32.172	37.262	43.073
8	17.119	17.762	18.430	19.123	19.842	20.588	21.361	22.163	22.995	23.858	24.752	25.678	26.638	27.633	28.664	34.395	41.202	49.258	58.756	69.916
9	21.714	22.670	23.669	24.712	25.802	26.940	28.129	29.369	30.664	32.015	33.425	34.895	36.429	38.029	39.696	49.153	60.743	74.887	92.073	112.87
10	27.274	28.657	30.113	31.643	33.253	34.945	36.723	38.593	40.556	42.619	44.786	47.062	49.451	51.958	54.590	69.814	89.077	113.33	143.71	181.59
11	34.001	35.962	38.039	40.238	42.566	45.031	47.639	50.398	53.318	56.405	59.670	63.122	66.769	70.624	74.697	98.739	130.16	171.00	223.75	291.54
12	42.142	44.874	47.788	50.895	54.208	57.739	61.501	65.510	69.780	74.327	79.168	84.320	89.803	95.637	101.84	139.23	189.73	257.49	347.82	467.46
13	51.991	55.746	59.779	64.110	68.760	73.751	79.107	84.853	91.016	97.625	104.71	112.30	120.44	129.15	138.48	195.93	276.12	387.24	540.12	748.93
14	63.909	69.010	74.528	80.496	86.949	93.926	101.46	109.61	118.41	127.91	138.17	149.24	161.18	174.06	187.95	275.30	401.37	581.86	838.19	1199.3
15	78.330	85.192	92.669	100.82	109.69	119.35	129.86	141.30	153.75	167.29	182.00	198.00	215.37	234.25	254.74	386.42	582.98	873.79	1300.2	1919.9
16	95.780	104.93	114.98	126.01	138.11	151.38	165.92	181.87	199.34	218.47	239.42	262.36	287.45	314.89	344.90	541.99	846.32	1311.7	2016.3	3072.8
17	116.89	129.02	142.43	157.25	173.64	191.73	211.72	233.79	258.15	285.01	314.64	347.31	383.30	422.95	466.61	759.78	1228.2	1968.5	3126.2	4917.5
18	142.44	158.40	176.19	195.99	218.04	242.59	269.89	300.25	334.01	371.52	413.18	459.45	510.80	567.76	630.92	1064.7	1781.8	2953.8	4846.7	7868.9
19	173.35	194.25	217.71	244.03	273.56	306.66	343.76	385.32	431.87	483.97	542.27	607.47	680.36	761.80	852.75	1491.6	2584.7	4431.7	7513.4	12591
20	210.76	237.99	268.79	303.60	342.94	387.39	437.57	494.21	558.11	630.17	711.38	802.86	905.88	1021.8	1152.2	2089.2	3748.8	6648.5	11646	20147
21	256.02	291.35	331.61	377.46	429.68	489.11	556.72	633.59	720.96	820.22	932.90	1060.8	1205.8	1370.2	1556.5	2925.9	5436.7	9973.8	18053	32236
22	310.78	356.44	408.88	469.06	538.10	617.28	708.03	812.00	931.04	1067.3	1223.1	1401.2	1604.7	1837.1	2102.3	4097.2	7884.3	14961	27983	51579
23	377.05	435.86	503.92	582.63	673.63	778.77	900.20	1040.4	1202.0	1388.5	1603.3	1850.6	2135.3	2462.7	2839.0	5737.1	11433	22443	43375	82527
24	457.22	532.75	620.82	723.46	843.03	982.25	1144.3	1332.7	1551.6	1806.0	2101.3	2443.8	2840.9	3301.0	3833.7	8033.0	16579	33666	67233	132045
25	554.24	650.96	764.61	898.09	1054.8	1238.6	1454.2	1706.8	2002.6	2348.8	2753.7	3226.8	3779.5	4424.4	5176.5	11247	24040	50500	104213	211273
26	671.63	795.17	941.46	1114.6	1319.5	1561.7	1847.9	2185.7	2584.4	3054.4	3608.3	4260.4	5027.7	5929.7	6989.7	15747	34860	75751	161531	338038
27	813.68	971.10	1159.0	1383.1	1650.4	1968.7	2347.8	2798.7	3334.8	3971.8	4727.9	5624.8	6687.8	7946.8	9436.5	22046	50548	113628	250374	540862
28	985.55	1185.7	1426.6	1716.1	2064.0	2481.6	2982.6	3583.3	4302.9	5164.3	6194.5	7425.7	8895.8	10649	12740	30866	73295	170443	388081	865381
29	1193.5	1447.6	1755.7	2129.0	2580.9	3127.8	3789.0	4587.7	5551.8	6714.6	8115.8	9802.9	11832	14271	17200	43214	106279	255666	601527	*
30	1445.2	1767.1	2160.5	2640.9	3227.2	3942.0	4813.0	5873.2	7162.8	8730.0	10632	12940	15738	19124	23221	60501	154106	383500	932368	*
35	3755.9	4783.6	6090.3	7750.2	9856.8	12527	15909	20188	25596	32422	41029	51869	65504	82636	104136	325400	987794	*	*	*
40	9749.5	12936	17154	22728	30088	39792	52571	69377	91447	120392	158300	207874	272613	357033	466960	*	*	*	*	*
45	25295	34971	48301	66640	91831	126382	173697	238387	326688	447019	610723	833058	*	*	*	*	*	*	*	*
50	65617	94525	135992	195372	280255	401374	573877	819103	*	*	*	*	*	*	*	*	*	*	*	*

* FVA is greater than 999999.

Table B.5

Cumulative Distribution Function

d	0.00	0.01	0.02	0.03	0.04	0.05	0.06	0.07	0.08	0.09
−3.00	0.001	0.001	0.001	0.001	0.001	0.001	0.001	0.001	0.001	0.001
−2.90	0.002	0.002	0.002	0.002	0.002	0.002	0.002	0.001	0.001	0.001
−2.80	0.003	0.002	0.002	0.002	0.002	0.002	0.002	0.002	0.002	0.002
−2.70	0.003	0.003	0.003	0.003	0.003	0.003	0.003	0.003	0.003	0.003
−2.60	0.005	0.005	0.004	0.004	0.004	0.004	0.004	0.004	0.004	0.004
−2.50	0.006	0.006	0.006	0.006	0.006	0.005	0.005	0.005	0.005	0.005
−2.40	0.008	0.008	0.008	0.008	0.007	0.007	0.007	0.007	0.007	0.006
−2.30	0.011	0.010	0.010	0.010	0.010	0.009	0.009	0.009	0.009	0.008
−2.20	0.014	0.014	0.013	0.013	0.013	0.012	0.012	0.012	0.011	0.011
−2.10	0.018	0.017	0.017	0.017	0.016	0.016	0.015	0.015	0.015	0.014
−2.00	0.023	0.022	0.022	0.021	0.021	0.020	0.020	0.019	0.019	0.018
−1.90	0.029	0.028	0.027	0.027	0.026	0.026	0.025	0.024	0.024	0.023
−1.80	0.036	0.035	0.034	0.034	0.033	0.032	0.031	0.031	0.030	0.029
−1.70	0.045	0.044	0.043	0.042	0.041	0.040	0.039	0.038	0.038	0.037
−1.60	0.055	0.054	0.053	0.052	0.051	0.049	0.048	0.047	0.046	0.046
−1.50	0.067	0.066	0.064	0.063	0.062	0.061	0.059	0.058	0.057	0.056
−1.40	0.081	0.079	0.078	0.076	0.075	0.074	0.072	0.071	0.069	0.068
−1.30	0.097	0.095	0.093	0.092	0.090	0.089	0.087	0.085	0.084	0.082
−1.20	0.115	0.113	0.111	0.109	0.107	0.106	0.104	0.102	0.100	0.099
−1.10	0.136	0.134	0.131	0.129	0.127	0.125	0.123	0.121	0.119	0.117
−1.00	0.159	0.156	0.154	0.152	0.149	0.147	0.145	0.142	0.140	0.138
−0.90	0.184	0.181	0.179	0.176	0.174	0.171	0.169	0.166	0.164	0.161
−0.80	0.212	0.209	0.206	0.203	0.200	0.198	0.195	0.192	0.189	0.187
−0.70	0.242	0.239	0.236	0.233	0.230	0.227	0.224	0.221	0.218	0.215
−0.60	0.274	0.271	0.268	0.264	0.261	0.258	0.255	0.251	0.248	0.245
−0.50	0.309	0.305	0.302	0.298	0.295	0.291	0.288	0.284	0.281	0.278
−0.40	0.345	0.341	0.337	0.334	0.330	0.326	0.323	0.319	0.316	0.312
−0.30	0.382	0.378	0.374	0.371	0.367	0.363	0.359	0.356	0.352	0.348
−0.20	0.421	0.417	0.413	0.409	0.405	0.401	0.397	0.394	0.390	0.386
−0.10	0.460	0.456	0.452	0.448	0.444	0.440	0.436	0.433	0.429	0.425
−0.00	0.500	0.496	0.492	0.488	0.484	0.480	0.476	0.472	0.468	0.464

Table B.5

Cumulative Distribution Function (*Continued*)

d	0.00	0.01	0.02	0.03	0.04	0.05	0.06	0.07	0.08	0.09
0.00	0.500	0.504	0.508	0.512	0.516	0.520	0.524	0.528	0.532	0.536
0.10	0.540	0.544	0.548	0.552	0.556	0.560	0.564	0.567	0.571	0.575
0.20	0.579	0.583	0.587	0.591	0.595	0.599	0.603	0.606	0.610	0.614
0.30	0.618	0.622	0.626	0.629	0.633	0.637	0.641	0.644	0.648	0.652
0.40	0.655	0.659	0.663	0.666	0.670	0.674	0.677	0.681	0.684	0.688
0.50	0.691	0.695	0.698	0.702	0.705	0.709	0.712	0.716	0.719	0.722
0.60	0.726	0.729	0.732	0.736	0.739	0.742	0.745	0.749	0.752	0.755
0.70	0.758	0.761	0.764	0.767	0.770	0.773	0.776	0.779	0.782	0.785
0.80	0.788	0.791	0.794	0.797	0.800	0.802	0.805	0.808	0.811	0.813
0.90	0.816	0.819	0.821	0.824	0.826	0.829	0.831	0.834	0.836	0.839
1.00	0.841	0.844	0.846	0.849	0.851	0.853	0.855	0.858	0.860	0.862
1.10	0.864	0.867	0.869	0.871	0.873	0.875	0.877	0.879	0.881	0.883
1.20	0.885	0.887	0.889	0.891	0.893	0.894	0.896	0.898	0.900	0.901
1.30	0.903	0.905	0.907	0.908	0.910	0.911	0.913	0.915	0.916	0.918
1.40	0.919	0.921	0.922	0.924	0.925	0.926	0.928	0.929	0.931	0.932
1.50	0.933	0.934	0.936	0.937	0.938	0.939	0.941	0.942	0.943	0.944
1.60	0.945	0.946	0.947	0.948	0.950	0.951	0.952	0.953	0.954	0.954
1.70	0.955	0.956	0.957	0.958	0.959	0.960	0.961	0.962	0.962	0.963
1.80	0.964	0.965	0.966	0.966	0.967	0.968	0.969	0.969	0.970	0.971
1.90	0.971	0.972	0.973	0.973	0.974	0.974	0.975	0.976	0.976	0.977
2.00	0.977	0.978	0.978	0.979	0.979	0.980	0.980	0.981	0.981	0.982
2.10	0.982	0.983	0.983	0.983	0.984	0.984	0.985	0.985	0.985	0.986
2.20	0.986	0.986	0.987	0.987	0.987	0.988	0.988	0.988	0.989	0.989
2.30	0.989	0.990	0.990	0.990	0.990	0.991	0.991	0.991	0.991	0.992
2.40	0.992	0.992	0.992	0.992	0.993	0.993	0.993	0.993	0.993	0.994
2.50	0.994	0.994	0.994	0.994	0.994	0.995	0.995	0.995	0.995	0.995
2.60	0.995	0.995	0.996	0.996	0.996	0.996	0.996	0.996	0.996	0.996
2.70	0.997	0.997	0.997	0.997	0.997	0.997	0.997	0.997	0.997	0.997
2.80	0.997	0.998	0.998	0.998	0.998	0.998	0.998	0.998	0.998	0.998
2.90	0.998	0.998	0.998	0.998	0.998	0.998	0.998	0.999	0.999	0.999
3.00	0.999	0.999	0.999	0.999	0.999	0.999	0.999	0.999	0.999	0.999

Table B.6

Call Option Value for Nondividend-Paying Stocks (in decimal form) Relative to Share Price

Standard Deviation Times the Square Root of Time

Share Price ÷ PV of Exercise Price	0.05	0.10	0.15	0.20	0.25	0.30	0.35	0.40	0.45	0.50	0.55	0.60	0.65	0.70	0.75	0.80	0.85	0.90	0.95	1.00	1.05	1.10
0.40	*	*	*	*	*	*	*	0.002	0.005	0.010	0.017	0.025	0.036	0.047	0.061	0.075	0.091	0.107	0.125	0.143	0.161	0.180
0.45	*	*	*	*	*	*	0.002	0.005	0.010	0.017	0.026	0.037	0.049	0.063	0.079	0.095	0.112	0.130	0.148	0.167	0.186	0.206
0.50	*	*	*	*	*	0.001	0.004	0.009	0.017	0.026	0.038	0.051	0.065	0.081	0.098	0.115	0.133	0.152	0.171	0.191	0.210	0.230
0.55	*	*	*	*	*	0.003	0.008	0.016	0.026	0.037	0.051	0.066	0.082	0.099	0.117	0.136	0.155	0.174	0.194	0.214	0.233	0.253
0.60	*	*	*	*	0.002	0.007	0.014	0.024	0.037	0.051	0.066	0.083	0.100	0.119	0.137	0.157	0.176	0.196	0.216	0.236	0.256	0.275
0.65	*	*	*	0.001	0.005	0.012	0.023	0.035	0.050	0.066	0.083	0.101	0.119	0.138	0.158	0.177	0.197	0.217	0.237	0.257	0.277	0.296
0.70	*	*	0.002	0.004	0.010	0.020	0.033	0.048	0.065	0.082	0.100	0.119	0.138	0.158	0.178	0.198	0.218	0.238	0.257	0.277	0.297	0.316
0.75	*	*	0.002	0.008	0.018	0.031	0.046	0.063	0.081	0.100	0.119	0.138	0.158	0.178	0.198	0.218	0.238	0.258	0.277	0.297	0.316	0.335
0.80	*	*	0.005	0.015	0.028	0.044	0.062	0.080	0.099	0.118	0.138	0.158	0.178	0.198	0.218	0.237	0.257	0.277	0.296	0.316	0.335	0.354
0.82	*	*	0.007	0.019	0.033	0.050	0.068	0.087	0.106	0.126	0.146	0.166	0.186	0.206	0.225	0.245	0.265	0.284	0.304	0.323	0.342	0.361
0.84	*	0.002	0.010	0.023	0.039	0.057	0.075	0.094	0.114	0.134	0.154	0.174	0.193	0.213	0.233	0.253	0.272	0.292	0.311	0.330	0.349	0.367
0.86	*	0.003	0.013	0.028	0.045	0.063	0.082	0.102	0.122	0.142	0.161	0.181	0.201	0.221	0.241	0.260	0.280	0.299	0.318	0.337	0.356	0.374
0.88	*	0.005	0.017	0.034	0.052	0.070	0.090	0.110	0.129	0.149	0.169	0.189	0.209	0.229	0.248	0.268	0.287	0.306	0.325	0.344	0.362	0.381
0.90	*	0.008	0.022	0.040	0.059	0.078	0.098	0.117	0.137	0.157	0.177	0.197	0.217	0.236	0.256	0.275	0.294	0.313	0.332	0.351	0.369	0.387
0.92	0.001	0.012	0.028	0.047	0.066	0.086	0.106	0.125	0.145	0.165	0.185	0.205	0.225	0.244	0.263	0.283	0.302	0.320	0.339	0.357	0.376	0.393
0.94	0.003	0.017	0.035	0.054	0.074	0.094	0.114	0.134	0.153	0.173	0.193	0.213	0.232	0.252	0.271	0.290	0.309	0.327	0.346	0.364	0.382	0.400
0.96	0.006	0.023	0.042	0.062	0.082	0.102	0.122	0.142	0.162	0.181	0.201	0.220	0.240	0.259	0.278	0.297	0.316	0.334	0.352	0.370	0.388	0.406
0.98	0.012	0.031	0.051	0.071	0.091	0.111	0.130	0.150	0.170	0.189	0.209	0.228	0.247	0.266	0.285	0.304	0.322	0.341	0.359	0.377	0.394	0.412
1.00	0.020	0.040	0.060	0.080	0.099	0.119	0.139	0.159	0.178	0.197	0.217	0.236	0.255	0.274	0.292	0.311	0.329	0.347	0.365	0.383	0.400	0.418
1.02	0.031	0.050	0.070	0.089	0.109	0.128	0.148	0.167	0.186	0.205	0.224	0.243	0.262	0.281	0.299	0.318	0.336	0.354	0.372	0.389	0.406	0.423
1.04	0.045	0.061	0.080	0.099	0.118	0.137	0.156	0.175	0.194	0.213	0.232	0.251	0.270	0.288	0.306	0.324	0.342	0.360	0.378	0.395	0.412	0.429
1.06	0.060	0.073	0.091	0.109	0.128	0.146	0.165	0.184	0.203	0.221	0.240	0.258	0.277	0.295	0.313	0.331	0.349	0.366	0.384	0.401	0.418	0.435
1.08	0.075	0.086	0.102	0.119	0.137	0.156	0.174	0.192	0.211	0.229	0.248	0.266	0.284	0.302	0.320	0.338	0.355	0.373	0.390	0.407	0.424	0.440
1.10	0.091	0.100	0.114	0.130	0.147	0.165	0.183	0.201	0.219	0.237	0.255	0.273	0.291	0.309	0.327	0.344	0.362	0.379	0.396	0.412	0.429	0.445
1.12	0.107	0.113	0.126	0.141	0.157	0.174	0.192	0.209	0.227	0.245	0.263	0.281	0.298	0.316	0.333	0.351	0.368	0.385	0.401	0.418	0.435	0.451
1.14	0.123	0.127	0.138	0.152	0.167	0.184	0.201	0.218	0.235	0.253	0.270	0.288	0.305	0.323	0.340	0.357	0.374	0.391	0.407	0.424	0.440	0.456
1.16	0.138	0.141	0.150	0.163	0.177	0.193	0.210	0.226	0.243	0.261	0.278	0.295	0.312	0.329	0.346	0.363	0.380	0.396	0.413	0.429	0.445	0.461
1.18	0.153	0.154	0.162	0.174	0.187	0.203	0.219	0.235	0.251	0.268	0.285	0.302	0.319	0.336	0.353	0.369	0.386	0.402	0.418	0.434	0.450	0.466
1.20	0.167	0.168	0.174	0.185	0.198	0.212	0.227	0.243	0.259	0.276	0.292	0.309	0.326	0.342	0.359	0.375	0.392	0.408	0.424	0.440	0.455	0.471
1.25	0.200	0.200	0.204	0.212	0.223	0.235	0.249	0.264	0.279	0.295	0.310	0.326	0.342	0.358	0.374	0.390	0.406	0.421	0.437	0.452	0.468	0.483
1.30	0.231	0.231	0.233	0.239	0.247	0.258	0.271	0.284	0.298	0.313	0.328	0.343	0.358	0.373	0.389	0.404	0.419	0.435	0.450	0.465	0.480	0.494
1.35	0.259	0.259	0.260	0.264	0.271	0.281	0.292	0.304	0.317	0.331	0.345	0.359	0.374	0.388	0.403	0.418	0.433	0.447	0.462	0.476	0.491	0.505
1.40	0.286	0.286	0.286	0.289	0.294	0.302	0.312	0.323	0.335	0.348	0.361	0.375	0.389	0.403	0.417	0.431	0.445	0.460	0.474	0.488	0.502	0.516
1.45	0.310	0.310	0.311	0.312	0.317	0.323	0.332	0.342	0.353	0.364	0.377	0.390	0.403	0.416	0.430	0.444	0.458	0.471	0.485	0.499	0.512	0.526
1.50	0.333	0.333	0.333	0.335	0.338	0.343	0.351	0.360	0.370	0.381	0.392	0.404	0.417	0.430	0.443	0.456	0.469	0.483	0.496	0.509	0.522	0.535
1.75	0.429	0.429	0.429	0.429	0.429	0.431	0.435	0.440	0.446	0.453	0.461	0.470	0.480	0.490	0.500	0.511	0.522	0.533	0.545	0.556	0.567	0.579
2.00	0.500	0.500	0.500	0.500	0.500	0.501	0.502	0.505	0.508	0.513	0.519	0.525	0.533	0.540	0.549	0.558	0.567	0.576	0.586	0.595	0.605	0.615
2.25	0.556	0.556	0.556	0.556	0.556	0.556	0.556	0.558	0.560	0.563	0.567	0.571	0.577	0.583	0.590	0.597	0.604	0.612	0.620	0.629	0.637	0.646
2.50	0.600	0.600	0.600	0.600	0.600	0.600	0.600	0.601	0.602	0.604	0.607	0.610	0.614	0.619	0.624	0.630	0.636	0.643	0.650	0.657	0.665	0.672
2.75	0.636	0.636	0.636	0.636	0.636	0.636	0.636	0.637	0.637	0.639	0.641	0.643	0.646	0.650	0.654	0.659	0.664	0.670	0.676	0.682	0.688	0.695
3.00	0.667	0.667	0.667	0.667	0.667	0.667	0.667	0.667	0.667	0.668	0.669	0.671	0.673	0.676	0.680	0.684	0.688	0.693	0.698	0.703	0.709	0.715
3.50	0.714	0.714	0.714	0.714	0.714	0.714	0.714	0.714	0.714	0.715	0.715	0.716	0.718	0.720	0.722	0.724	0.728	0.731	0.735	0.739	0.743	0.748
4.00	0.750	0.750	0.750	0.750	0.750	0.750	0.750	0.750	0.750	0.750	0.751	0.751	0.752	0.753	0.754	0.756	0.759	0.761	0.764	0.767	0.771	0.775
4.50	0.778	0.778	0.778	0.778	0.778	0.778	0.778	0.778	0.778	0.778	0.778	0.778	0.779	0.780	0.781	0.782	0.784	0.785	0.788	0.790	0.793	0.796

Share Price Divided by the Present Value of the Exercise Price

*Value is zero to three decimal places.

Table B.6

Call Option Value (Continued)

Share Price Divided by the Present Value of the Exercise Price (rows) × Standard Deviation Times the Square Root of Time (columns)

	1.15	1.20	1.25	1.30	1.35	1.40	1.45	1.50	1.55	1.60	1.65	1.70	1.75	2.00	2.25	2.50	2.75	3.00	3.50	4.00	4.50	5.00
0.40	0.200	0.219	0.239	0.259	0.279	0.299	0.319	0.338	0.358	0.378	0.397	0.416	0.435	0.525	0.607	0.679	0.742	0.795	0.876	0.929	0.962	0.981
0.45	0.225	0.245	0.265	0.285	0.305	0.325	0.345	0.364	0.384	0.403	0.422	0.440	0.459	0.546	0.625	0.694	0.754	0.805	0.883	0.933	0.964	0.982
0.50	0.250	0.270	0.290	0.310	0.330	0.349	0.369	0.388	0.407	0.426	0.444	0.462	0.480	0.565	0.641	0.708	0.766	0.814	0.888	0.936	0.966	0.983
0.55	0.273	0.293	0.313	0.333	0.352	0.371	0.391	0.409	0.428	0.446	0.464	0.482	0.500	0.582	0.656	0.720	0.775	0.822	0.893	0.939	0.967	0.983
0.60	0.295	0.315	0.335	0.354	0.373	0.392	0.411	0.429	0.448	0.465	0.483	0.500	0.517	0.597	0.668	0.731	0.784	0.829	0.897	0.942	0.969	0.984
0.65	0.316	0.336	0.355	0.374	0.393	0.411	0.430	0.448	0.466	0.483	0.500	0.517	0.534	0.611	0.680	0.740	0.792	0.835	0.901	0.944	0.970	0.985
0.70	0.336	0.355	0.374	0.393	0.411	0.429	0.447	0.465	0.482	0.499	0.516	0.532	0.548	0.624	0.691	0.749	0.799	0.841	0.905	0.946	0.971	0.985
0.75	0.354	0.373	0.392	0.410	0.428	0.446	0.464	0.481	0.498	0.514	0.531	0.547	0.562	0.636	0.700	0.757	0.805	0.846	0.908	0.948	0.972	0.986
0.80	0.372	0.391	0.409	0.427	0.444	0.462	0.479	0.496	0.512	0.528	0.544	0.560	0.575	0.646	0.709	0.764	0.811	0.851	0.911	0.949	0.973	0.986
0.82	0.379	0.397	0.415	0.433	0.451	0.468	0.485	0.501	0.518	0.534	0.549	0.565	0.580	0.650	0.713	0.767	0.814	0.853	0.912	0.950	0.973	0.986
0.84	0.386	0.404	0.422	0.439	0.457	0.474	0.490	0.507	0.523	0.539	0.554	0.570	0.585	0.654	0.716	0.770	0.816	0.854	0.913	0.950	0.973	0.986
0.86	0.392	0.410	0.428	0.445	0.463	0.479	0.496	0.512	0.528	0.544	0.559	0.575	0.589	0.658	0.719	0.772	0.818	0.856	0.914	0.951	0.974	0.987
0.88	0.399	0.417	0.434	0.451	0.468	0.485	0.501	0.518	0.533	0.549	0.564	0.579	0.594	0.662	0.722	0.775	0.820	0.858	0.915	0.652	0.975	0.987
0.90	0.405	0.423	0.440	0.457	0.474	0.490	0.507	0.523	0.538	0.554	0.569	0.584	0.598	0.666	0.725	0.777	0.822	0.859	0.916	0.952	0.974	0.987
0.92	0.411	0.429	0.446	0.463	0.479	0.496	0.512	0.528	0.543	0.559	0.573	0.588	0.602	0.669	0.728	0.780	0.824	0.861	0.916	0.953	0.975	0.987
0.94	0.417	0.435	0.452	0.468	0.485	0.501	0.517	0.533	0.548	0.563	0.578	0.592	0.607	0.673	0.731	0.782	0.826	0.862	0.917	0.953	0.975	0.987
0.96	0.423	0.440	0.457	0.474	0.490	0.506	0.522	0.537	0.553	0.568	0.582	0.597	0.611	0.676	0.734	0.784	0.827	0.865	0.918	0.954	0.975	0.987
0.98	0.429	0.446	0.463	0.479	0.495	0.511	0.527	0.542	0.557	0.572	0.586	0.601	0.615	0.679	0.737	0.787	0.829	0.865	0.919	0.954	0.975	0.987
1.00	0.435	0.451	0.468	0.484	0.500	0.516	0.532	0.547	0.562	0.576	0.591	0.605	0.618	0.683	0.739	0.789	0.831	0.866	0.920	0.954	0.976	0.988
1.02	0.440	0.457	0.473	0.489	0.505	0.521	0.536	0.551	0.566	0.580	0.595	0.609	0.622	0.686	0.742	0.791	0.833	0.868	0.921	0.955	0.976	0.988
1.04	0.446	0.462	0.478	0.494	0.510	0.526	0.541	0.556	0.570	0.585	0.599	0.612	0.626	0.689	0.744	0.793	0.834	0.869	0.921	0.955	0.976	0.988
1.06	0.451	0.467	0.484	0.499	0.515	0.530	0.545	0.560	0.574	0.589	0.602	0.616	0.629	0.692	0.747	0.795	0.836	0.870	0.922	0.956	0.976	0.988
1.08	0.456	0.473	0.488	0.504	0.520	0.535	0.550	0.564	0.578	0.592	0.606	0.620	0.633	0.695	0.749	0.797	0.837	0.871	0.923	0.956	0.976	0.988
1.10	0.462	0.478	0.493	0.509	0.524	0.539	0.554	0.568	0.582	0.596	0.610	0.623	0.636	0.698	0.752	0.799	0.839	0.873	0.924	0.957	0.977	0.988
1.12	0.467	0.483	0.498	0.513	0.529	0.543	0.558	0.572	0.586	0.600	0.614	0.627	0.640	0.700	0.754	0.800	0.840	0.874	0.924	0.957	0.977	0.988
1.14	0.472	0.487	0.503	0.518	0.533	0.548	0.562	0.576	0.590	0.604	0.617	0.630	0.643	0.703	0.756	0.802	0.842	0.875	0.925	0.957	0.977	0.988
1.16	0.477	0.492	0.507	0.522	0.537	0.552	0.566	0.580	0.594	0.607	0.621	0.634	0.646	0.706	0.758	0.804	0.843	0.876	0.926	0.958	0.978	0.989
1.18	0.482	0.497	0.512	0.527	0.541	0.556	0.570	0.584	0.597	0.611	0.624	0.637	0.649	0.708	0.760	0.806	0.844	0.877	0.926	0.958	0.978	0.989
1.20	0.486	0.501	0.516	0.531	0.546	0.560	0.574	0.588	0.601	0.614	0.627	0.640	0.653	0.711	0.763	0.807	0.846	0.877	0.927	0.958	0.978	0.989
1.25	0.498	0.513	0.527	0.541	0.556	0.569	0.583	0.597	0.610	0.623	0.635	0.648	0.660	0.717	0.768	0.811	0.849	0.881	0.928	0.959	0.978	0.989
1.30	0.509	0.523	0.537	0.551	0.565	0.579	0.592	0.605	0.618	0.631	0.643	0.655	0.667	0.723	0.772	0.815	0.852	0.883	0.930	0.960	0.979	0.989
1.35	0.519	0.533	0.547	0.561	0.574	0.587	0.600	0.613	0.626	0.638	0.650	0.662	0.674	0.729	0.777	0.819	0.855	0.885	0.931	0.961	0.979	0.989
1.40	0.529	0.543	0.557	0.570	0.583	0.596	0.609	0.621	0.633	0.645	0.657	0.669	0.680	0.734	0.781	0.822	0.858	0.888	0.933	0.962	0.979	0.990
1.45	0.539	0.552	0.566	0.579	0.591	0.604	0.616	0.629	0.641	0.652	0.664	0.675	0.687	0.739	0.785	0.826	0.860	0.890	0.934	0.962	0.980	0.990
1.50	0.549	0.561	0.574	0.587	0.599	0.612	0.624	0.636	0.647	0.659	0.670	0.682	0.692	0.744	0.789	0.829	0.863	0.892	0.935	0.963	0.980	0.990
1.75	0.590	0.602	0.613	0.624	0.635	0.646	0.657	0.668	0.678	0.688	0.699	0.709	0.719	0.765	0.806	0.843	0.874	0.900	0.940	0.966	0.982	0.991
2.00	0.625	0.635	0.645	0.655	0.665	0.675	0.684	0.694	0.703	0.713	0.722	0.731	0.740	0.783	0.821	0.854	0.883	0.908	0.944	0.968	0.983	0.992
2.25	0.655	0.663	0.672	0.681	0.690	0.699	0.708	0.716	0.725	0.733	0.742	0.750	0.758	0.797	0.833	0.863	0.890	0.913	0.948	0.970	0.984	0.992
2.50	0.680	0.688	0.696	0.704	0.711	0.719	0.727	0.735	0.743	0.751	0.759	0.766	0.774	0.810	0.843	0.872	0.897	0.918	0.951	0.972	0.985	0.992
2.75	0.702	0.709	0.716	0.723	0.730	0.737	0.745	0.752	0.759	0.766	0.773	0.781	0.788	0.821	0.852	0.879	0.902	0.922	0.953	0.973	0.986	0.993
3.00	0.721	0.727	0.734	0.740	0.747	0.753	0.760	0.767	0.773	0.780	0.786	0.793	0.799	0.831	0.859	0.885	0.907	0.926	0.955	0.974	0.986	0.993
3.50	0.753	0.758	0.763	0.769	0.774	0.780	0.785	0.791	0.797	0.802	0.808	0.814	0.819	0.847	0.872	0.895	0.915	0.933	0.959	0.977	0.987	0.994
4.00	0.779	0.783	0.787	0.792	0.796	0.801	0.806	0.811	0.816	0.821	0.826	0.831	0.836	0.860	0.883	0.904	0.922	0.938	0.962	0.978	0.988	0.994
4.50	0.799	0.803	0.807	0.810	0.814	0.818	0.823	0.827	0.831	0.836	0.840	0.844	0.849	0.871	0.892	0.911	0.927	0.942	0.965	0.980	0.989	0.994

Table B.7

Put Option Value for Nondividend-Paying Stocks (in decimal form) Relative to Share Price

Row label: **Share Price Divided by the Present Value of the Exercise Price** · Column group: **Standard Deviation Times the Square Root of Time**

S/PV(X)	0.05	0.10	0.15	0.20	0.25	0.30	0.35	0.40	0.45	0.50	0.55	0.60	0.65	0.70	0.75	0.80	0.85	0.90	0.95	1.00	1.05	1.10
0.40	1.500	1.500	1.500	1.500	1.500	1.500	1.501	1.502	1.505	1.510	1.517	1.525	1.536	1.547	1.561	1.575	1.591	1.607	1.625	1.643	1.661	1.680
0.45	1.222	1.222	1.222	1.222	1.222	1.223	1.224	1.227	1.232	1.239	1.248	1.259	1.272	1.286	1.301	1.317	1.334	1.352	1.370	1.389	1.408	1.428
0.50	1.000	1.000	1.000	1.000	1.000	1.001	1.004	1.009	1.017	1.026	1.038	1.051	1.065	1.081	1.098	1.115	1.133	1.152	1.171	1.191	1.210	1.230
0.55	0.818	0.818	0.818	0.818	0.819	0.822	0.827	0.834	0.844	0.856	0.869	0.884	0.900	0.918	0.935	0.954	0.973	0.992	1.012	1.032	1.052	1.072
0.60	0.667	0.667	0.667	0.667	0.669	0.674	0.681	0.691	0.703	0.717	0.733	0.749	0.767	0.785	0.804	0.823	0.843	0.862	0.882	0.902	0.922	0.942
0.65	0.538	0.538	0.539	0.540	0.544	0.551	0.561	0.574	0.588	0.604	0.621	0.639	0.658	0.677	0.696	0.716	0.736	0.755	0.775	0.795	0.815	0.835
0.70	0.429	0.429	0.429	0.432	0.439	0.449	0.461	0.477	0.493	0.511	0.529	0.548	0.567	0.587	0.606	0.626	0.646	0.666	0.686	0.706	0.726	0.745
0.75	0.333	0.333	0.335	0.341	0.351	0.364	0.380	0.396	0.414	0.433	0.452	0.472	0.491	0.511	0.531	0.551	0.571	0.591	0.611	0.630	0.650	0.669
0.80	0.250	0.250	0.255	0.265	0.278	0.294	0.312	0.330	0.349	0.368	0.388	0.408	0.428	0.448	0.468	0.487	0.507	0.527	0.546	0.566	0.585	0.604
0.82	0.220	0.220	0.227	0.238	0.253	0.270	0.288	0.307	0.326	0.345	0.365	0.385	0.405	0.425	0.445	0.465	0.484	0.504	0.523	0.542	0.561	0.580
0.84	0.190	0.192	0.200	0.213	0.229	0.247	0.266	0.285	0.304	0.324	0.344	0.364	0.384	0.404	0.424	0.443	0.463	0.482	0.501	0.520	0.539	0.558
0.86	0.163	0.166	0.176	0.191	0.208	0.226	0.245	0.265	0.284	0.304	0.324	0.344	0.364	0.384	0.404	0.423	0.443	0.462	0.481	0.500	0.518	0.537
0.88	0.136	0.141	0.154	0.170	0.188	0.207	0.226	0.246	0.266	0.286	0.306	0.326	0.345	0.365	0.385	0.404	0.424	0.443	0.462	0.480	0.499	0.517
0.90	0.111	0.119	0.134	0.151	0.170	0.189	0.209	0.229	0.249	0.268	0.288	0.308	0.328	0.348	0.367	0.386	0.406	0.424	0.443	0.462	0.480	0.498
0.92	0.088	0.099	0.115	0.134	0.153	0.173	0.192	0.212	0.232	0.252	0.272	0.292	0.311	0.331	0.350	0.370	0.389	0.407	0.426	0.444	0.463	0.480
0.94	0.067	0.081	0.099	0.118	0.138	0.158	0.177	0.197	0.217	0.237	0.257	0.277	0.296	0.315	0.335	0.354	0.372	0.391	0.410	0.428	0.446	0.464
0.96	0.048	0.065	0.084	0.104	0.124	0.144	0.164	0.183	0.203	0.223	0.243	0.262	0.281	0.301	0.320	0.339	0.357	0.376	0.394	0.412	0.430	0.447
0.98	0.032	0.051	0.071	0.091	0.111	0.131	0.151	0.171	0.190	0.210	0.229	0.249	0.268	0.287	0.306	0.324	0.343	0.361	0.379	0.397	0.415	0.432
1.00	0.020	0.040	0.060	0.080	0.100	0.119	0.139	0.159	0.178	0.197	0.217	0.236	0.255	0.274	0.292	0.311	0.329	0.347	0.365	0.383	0.400	0.418
1.02	0.011	0.030	0.050	0.069	0.089	0.109	0.128	0.147	0.167	0.186	0.205	0.224	0.243	0.261	0.280	0.298	0.316	0.334	0.352	0.369	0.387	0.404
1.04	0.006	0.023	0.041	0.060	0.080	0.099	0.118	0.137	0.156	0.175	0.194	0.213	0.232	0.250	0.268	0.286	0.304	0.322	0.339	0.357	0.374	0.391
1.06	0.003	0.017	0.034	0.052	0.071	0.090	0.109	0.127	0.146	0.165	0.183	0.202	0.220	0.238	0.257	0.275	0.292	0.310	0.327	0.344	0.361	0.378
1.08	0.001	0.012	0.028	0.045	0.063	0.082	0.100	0.118	0.137	0.155	0.174	0.192	0.210	0.228	0.246	0.264	0.281	0.299	0.316	0.333	0.349	0.366
1.10	*	0.009	0.023	0.039	0.056	0.074	0.092	0.110	0.128	0.146	0.164	0.182	0.200	0.218	0.236	0.253	0.271	0.288	0.305	0.322	0.338	0.355
1.12	*	0.006	0.018	0.034	0.050	0.067	0.085	0.102	0.120	0.138	0.156	0.173	0.191	0.209	0.226	0.243	0.261	0.278	0.294	0.311	0.327	0.344
1.14	*	0.004	0.015	0.029	0.044	0.061	0.078	0.095	0.113	0.130	0.148	0.165	0.182	0.200	0.217	0.234	0.251	0.268	0.284	0.301	0.317	0.333
1.16	*	0.003	0.012	0.025	0.039	0.055	0.072	0.089	0.106	0.123	0.140	0.157	0.174	0.191	0.208	0.225	0.242	0.258	0.275	0.291	0.307	0.323
1.18	*	0.002	0.009	0.021	0.035	0.050	0.066	0.082	0.099	0.116	0.133	0.150	0.166	0.183	0.200	0.217	0.233	0.250	0.266	0.282	0.298	0.313
1.20	*	0.001	0.007	0.018	0.031	0.045	0.061	0.077	0.093	0.109	0.126	0.142	0.159	0.176	0.192	0.209	0.225	0.241	0.257	0.273	0.289	0.304
1.25	*	*	0.004	0.012	0.023	0.035	0.049	0.064	0.079	0.095	0.110	0.126	0.142	0.158	0.174	0.190	0.206	0.221	0.237	0.252	0.268	0.283
1.30	*	*	0.002	0.008	0.017	0.027	0.040	0.053	0.068	0.082	0.097	0.112	0.127	0.143	0.158	0.173	0.189	0.204	0.219	0.234	0.249	0.263
1.35	*	*	0.001	0.005	0.012	0.021	0.032	0.045	0.058	0.071	0.085	0.100	0.114	0.129	0.144	0.159	0.173	0.188	0.203	0.217	0.232	0.246
1.40	*	*	*	0.003	0.009	0.017	0.026	0.037	0.049	0.062	0.075	0.089	0.103	0.117	0.131	0.145	0.160	0.174	0.188	0.202	0.216	0.230
1.45	*	*	*	0.002	0.006	0.013	0.021	0.031	0.042	0.054	0.067	0.079	0.093	0.106	0.120	0.133	0.147	0.161	0.175	0.188	0.202	0.215
1.50	*	*	*	0.001	0.004	0.010	0.017	0.026	0.036	0.047	0.059	0.071	0.084	0.097	0.110	0.123	0.136	0.149	0.163	0.176	0.189	0.202
1.75	*	*	*	*	0.001	0.003	0.006	0.011	0.017	0.024	0.033	0.042	0.051	0.061	0.072	0.083	0.094	0.105	0.116	0.127	0.139	0.150
2.00	*	*	*	*	*	0.001	0.002	0.005	0.008	0.013	0.019	0.025	0.033	0.042	0.049	0.058	0.067	0.076	0.086	0.095	0.105	0.115
2.25	*	*	*	*	*	*	0.001	0.002	0.004	0.007	0.011	0.016	0.021	0.027	0.034	0.041	0.049	0.057	0.065	0.073	0.082	0.090
2.50	*	*	*	*	*	*	*	0.001	0.002	0.004	0.007	0.010	0.014	0.019	0.024	0.030	0.036	0.043	0.050	0.057	0.065	0.072
2.75	*	*	*	*	*	*	*	*	*	0.002	0.004	0.007	0.010	0.013	0.018	0.022	0.028	0.033	0.039	0.045	0.052	0.059
3.00	*	*	*	*	*	*	*	*	*	0.001	0.003	0.004	0.007	0.010	0.013	0.017	0.021	0.026	0.031	0.037	0.042	0.048
3.50	*	*	*	*	*	*	*	*	*	*	0.001	0.002	0.003	0.005	0.007	0.010	0.013	0.017	0.021	0.025	0.029	0.034
4.00	*	*	*	*	*	*	*	*	*	*	*	0.001	0.002	0.003	0.004	0.006	0.009	0.011	0.014	0.017	0.021	0.025
4.50	*	*	*	*	*	*	*	*	*	*	*	*	0.001	0.002	0.003	0.004	0.006	0.008	0.010	0.013	0.015	0.018

*Value is zero to three decimal places.

Put Option Value (*Continued*)

Standard Deviation Times the Square Root of Time

Row label column: **Share Price Divided by the Present Value of the Exercise Price**

	1.15	1.20	1.25	1.30	1.35	1.40	1.45	1.50	1.55	1.60	1.65	1.70	1.75	2.00	2.25	2.50	2.75	3.00	3.50	4.00	4.50	5.00
0.40	1.700	1.719	1.739	1.759	1.779	1.799	1.819	1.838	1.858	1.878	1.897	1.916	1.935	2.025	2.107	2.179	2.242	2.295	2.376	2.429	2.462	2.481
0.45	1.448	1.468	1.487	1.507	1.527	1.547	1.567	1.586	1.606	1.625	1.644	1.663	1.681	1.769	1.847	1.917	1.977	2.028	2.105	2.155	2.186	2.204
0.50	1.250	1.270	1.290	1.310	1.330	1.349	1.369	1.388	1.407	1.426	1.444	1.462	1.480	1.565	1.641	1.708	1.766	1.814	1.888	1.936	1.966	1.983
0.55	1.091	1.111	1.131	1.151	1.170	1.190	1.209	1.228	1.246	1.265	1.283	1.300	1.318	1.400	1.474	1.538	1.593	1.640	1.711	1.757	1.785	1.802
0.60	0.962	0.982	1.001	1.021	1.040	1.059	1.078	1.096	1.114	1.132	1.150	1.167	1.184	1.264	1.335	1.397	1.451	1.496	1.564	1.608	1.635	1.651
0.65	0.875	0.884	0.893	0.912	0.931	0.950	0.968	0.986	1.004	1.021	1.039	1.055	1.072	1.150	1.219	1.279	1.330	1.374	1.440	1.482	1.508	1.523
0.70	0.764	0.784	0.802	0.821	0.840	0.858	0.876	0.893	0.911	0.928	0.945	0.961	0.977	1.052	1.119	1.178	1.227	1.270	1.333	1.374	1.399	1.414
0.75	0.688	0.707	0.725	0.742	0.762	0.779	0.797	0.814	0.831	0.848	0.864	0.880	0.896	0.969	1.034	1.090	1.139	1.180	1.241	1.281	1.305	1.319
0.80	0.622	0.641	0.659	0.677	0.694	0.712	0.729	0.746	0.762	0.778	0.794	0.810	0.825	0.896	0.959	1.014	1.061	1.101	1.161	1.199	1.223	1.236
0.82	0.599	0.617	0.635	0.653	0.670	0.687	0.704	0.721	0.737	0.753	0.769	0.784	0.799	0.870	0.932	0.987	1.033	1.072	1.131	1.169	1.193	1.206
0.84	0.576	0.594	0.612	0.630	0.647	0.664	0.681	0.697	0.714	0.729	0.745	0.760	0.775	0.845	0.907	0.960	1.006	1.045	1.103	1.141	1.164	1.177
0.86	0.555	0.573	0.591	0.608	0.625	0.642	0.659	0.675	0.691	0.707	0.722	0.737	0.752	0.821	0.882	0.935	0.981	1.019	1.076	1.114	1.136	1.149
0.88	0.535	0.553	0.570	0.588	0.605	0.621	0.638	0.654	0.670	0.685	0.701	0.716	0.730	0.798	0.859	0.911	0.956	0.994	1.051	1.088	1.110	1.123
0.90	0.516	0.534	0.551	0.568	0.585	0.602	0.618	0.634	0.650	0.665	0.680	0.695	0.709	0.777	0.837	0.889	0.933	0.970	1.027	1.063	1.085	1.098
0.92	0.498	0.516	0.533	0.550	0.566	0.583	0.599	0.615	0.630	0.645	0.660	0.675	0.689	0.756	0.815	0.867	0.911	0.948	1.003	1.040	1.061	1.074
0.94	0.481	0.498	0.515	0.532	0.549	0.565	0.581	0.597	0.612	0.627	0.642	0.656	0.670	0.737	0.795	0.847	0.889	0.926	0.981	1.017	1.039	1.051
0.96	0.465	0.482	0.499	0.515	0.532	0.548	0.564	0.579	0.594	0.609	0.624	0.638	0.652	0.718	0.776	0.826	0.869	0.905	0.960	0.995	1.017	1.029
0.98	0.449	0.466	0.483	0.500	0.516	0.532	0.547	0.563	0.578	0.592	0.607	0.621	0.635	0.700	0.757	0.807	0.850	0.885	0.939	0.974	0.996	1.008
1.00	0.435	0.451	0.468	0.484	0.500	0.516	0.532	0.547	0.562	0.576	0.591	0.605	0.618	0.683	0.739	0.789	0.831	0.866	0.920	0.954	0.976	0.988
1.02	0.421	0.437	0.454	0.470	0.486	0.501	0.517	0.532	0.546	0.561	0.575	0.589	0.603	0.666	0.722	0.771	0.813	0.848	0.901	0.935	0.956	0.968
1.04	0.407	0.424	0.440	0.456	0.472	0.487	0.502	0.517	0.532	0.546	0.560	0.574	0.587	0.650	0.706	0.754	0.796	0.831	0.883	0.917	0.938	0.949
1.06	0.395	0.411	0.427	0.443	0.458	0.474	0.489	0.503	0.518	0.532	0.546	0.560	0.573	0.635	0.690	0.738	0.779	0.814	0.866	0.899	0.920	0.931
1.08	0.382	0.399	0.414	0.430	0.445	0.461	0.475	0.490	0.504	0.518	0.532	0.546	0.559	0.621	0.675	0.723	0.763	0.797	0.849	0.882	0.902	0.914
1.10	0.371	0.387	0.402	0.418	0.433	0.448	0.463	0.477	0.492	0.505	0.519	0.532	0.546	0.607	0.661	0.708	0.748	0.782	0.833	0.866	0.882	0.897
1.12	0.360	0.375	0.391	0.406	0.421	0.436	0.451	0.465	0.479	0.493	0.506	0.520	0.533	0.593	0.647	0.693	0.733	0.767	0.817	0.850	0.870	0.881
1.14	0.349	0.365	0.380	0.395	0.410	0.425	0.439	0.453	0.467	0.481	0.494	0.507	0.520	0.580	0.633	0.679	0.719	0.752	0.802	0.835	0.854	0.866
1.16	0.339	0.354	0.369	0.384	0.399	0.414	0.428	0.442	0.456	0.469	0.483	0.496	0.508	0.568	0.620	0.666	0.705	0.738	0.788	0.820	0.839	0.851
1.18	0.329	0.344	0.359	0.374	0.389	0.403	0.417	0.431	0.445	0.458	0.471	0.484	0.497	0.556	0.608	0.653	0.692	0.725	0.774	0.806	0.825	0.836
1.20	0.320	0.335	0.350	0.364	0.379	0.393	0.407	0.421	0.434	0.448	0.461	0.473	0.486	0.544	0.596	0.641	0.679	0.712	0.760	0.792	0.811	0.822
1.25	0.298	0.313	0.327	0.341	0.356	0.369	0.383	0.397	0.410	0.423	0.435	0.448	0.460	0.517	0.568	0.611	0.649	0.681	0.728	0.759	0.778	0.789
1.30	0.278	0.292	0.307	0.321	0.334	0.348	0.361	0.374	0.387	0.400	0.412	0.424	0.436	0.492	0.542	0.585	0.621	0.652	0.699	0.729	0.748	0.758
1.35	0.260	0.274	0.288	0.302	0.315	0.328	0.341	0.354	0.367	0.379	0.391	0.403	0.415	0.469	0.518	0.560	0.596	0.626	0.672	0.702	0.720	0.730
1.40	0.244	0.257	0.271	0.284	0.297	0.310	0.323	0.335	0.348	0.360	0.372	0.383	0.395	0.448	0.495	0.537	0.572	0.602	0.647	0.676	0.694	0.704
1.45	0.229	0.242	0.255	0.268	0.281	0.294	0.306	0.318	0.330	0.342	0.354	0.365	0.376	0.429	0.475	0.515	0.550	0.579	0.623	0.652	0.669	0.679
1.50	0.215	0.228	0.241	0.254	0.266	0.278	0.290	0.302	0.314	0.326	0.337	0.348	0.359	0.410	0.456	0.495	0.530	0.558	0.602	0.630	0.647	0.657
1.75	0.162	0.173	0.184	0.195	0.206	0.217	0.228	0.239	0.250	0.260	0.270	0.280	0.290	0.336	0.378	0.414	0.445	0.472	0.511	0.537	0.553	0.562
2.00	0.125	0.135	0.145	0.155	0.165	0.175	0.184	0.194	0.203	0.213	0.222	0.231	0.240	0.283	0.321	0.354	0.383	0.407	0.444	0.468	0.483	0.491
2.25	0.099	0.108	0.117	0.125	0.134	0.143	0.152	0.161	0.169	0.178	0.186	0.195	0.203	0.242	0.277	0.308	0.335	0.357	0.392	0.415	0.428	0.436
2.50	0.080	0.088	0.096	0.104	0.111	0.119	0.127	0.135	0.143	0.151	0.159	0.166	0.174	0.210	0.243	0.272	0.297	0.318	0.351	0.372	0.385	0.392
2.75	0.065	0.072	0.079	0.087	0.094	0.101	0.108	0.116	0.123	0.130	0.137	0.144	0.151	0.185	0.215	0.242	0.266	0.286	0.317	0.337	0.349	0.356
3.00	0.054	0.061	0.067	0.073	0.080	0.086	0.093	0.100	0.107	0.113	0.120	0.126	0.133	0.164	0.193	0.218	0.240	0.260	0.289	0.308	0.320	0.326
3.50	0.039	0.044	0.049	0.054	0.060	0.065	0.071	0.077	0.082	0.088	0.094	0.099	0.105	0.133	0.158	0.181	0.201	0.218	0.245	0.262	0.273	0.279
4.00	0.029	0.033	0.037	0.042	0.046	0.051	0.056	0.061	0.066	0.071	0.076	0.081	0.086	0.110	0.133	0.154	0.172	0.188	0.212	0.228	0.238	0.244
4.50	0.022	0.025	0.029	0.033	0.037	0.041	0.045	0.049	0.053	0.058	0.062	0.067	0.071	0.093	0.114	0.133	0.150	0.164	0.187	0.202	0.211	0.217

C

Answers to Selected Problems

All answers are based on using the financial tables or a financial calculator for present and future values and the Black–Scholes formulas for option values.

Chapter 1

1.2	$24,900

Chapter 2

2.2	a.	8.78%; 9.58%
2.3	a.	6.95%; 6.91%; 7.13%; 7.30%
	b.	5.62%; 3.95%; 3.91%; 4.13%; 4.30%
2.5	a.	9%; 10%; 10.66%; 10.99%; 11.19%; 11.60%; 11.73%; 11.80%
	b.	9%; 10.12%; 10.91%; 11.37%; 11.69%; 12.34%; 12.56%; 12.67%
2.7		3.256M/£ or 0.307£/M
2.9		1,298,544 lira/$
2.10		0.165; 0.178; 0.199

Chapter 3

3.1	a.	$511.55
	b.	$1,097.85
	c.	$1,157.40
	d.	$1,698.72
3.2		Company plan is $219,318; your plan is $228,820
3.3	a.	$1,496.25
	b.	$1,630.91
	c.	$1,880.75

3.4		$8,415.38
3.10	a.	7.23%
	b.	6.04%
	c.	Approximately 10%
	d.	7.27%
3.13	a.	6.19%
	c.	−$49.96
3.14	a.	$11,525.47
	b.	$1,525.47
3.15	a.	$1,082.04
	b.	14.69%
3.16	a.	$30,000
	b.	$37,500
	c.	$24,780; $32,137.50
3.17	a.	17%
	b.	40%
	c.	25%
3.20	a.	$3,130.81
	b.	$31.77
	c.	$1,049.58
	d.	$1,730.46
	e.	$1,454.54
3.22	a.	$928.18
	b.	$29.11
	c.	$947.15
	d.	$1,147.15
3.24		7.25%; 7.19%; 7%
3.25	a.	$557.00; $59,735.84
	b.	$59,745.54

c.

Interest	Principal
$500.00	$45.22
512.11	43.70
524.22	42.24
536.33	40.82
548.42	39.47
523.15	43.36

Principal at end of month 6 is $59,745.19

3.26
    a. $423.60; $485.02

    b. $365.74

    c. $1,460.40; $1,606.44

    d. $2,007,821

    e. $1,250; $801

    f. $784.40; $966.38; $58.40

    g. 15.91%

    h. $13,660.27; $13,472.50; $13,428.64; $13,407.13; $13,406.40

    i. Virtually identical

3A.1
    a. $73,000

    b. $133,500

3A.3
    a. 20%

    b. $30

    c. $45

    d. $15

    e. $54

    f. 80%

    g. $35; $78

    h. $10

    i. $95; $114

    j. $72

Chapter 4

4.3
    a. 7%

    b. 12%

4.5
    a. 10%

    b. Approximately 9%

4.6
    a. $4,636.36

    b. $3,764.72

4.8
    a. $33.33

    b. $108

    c. $36.55

4.9
    $26.12

4.10
    a. $208,000

    b. $173,526.58

4.11
    $11.70

4.12
    a. $83.96

b. $92.61

c. $83.96

Chapter 5

5.2   **b.** AB: $\bar{k}$ = 35%; σ = 15.49%
          AC: $\bar{k}$ = 45%; σ = 7.75%

5.4   **a.** 12.5%

          b. 9%; 7.81%; 4.58%

5.5   **a.** 11.25%; 13.14%

5.6   **a.** $\bar{k}_N$ = 2%; σ_N = 4.10%; $\bar{k}_O$ = 8%; σ_O = 10.84%

          b.

$\bar{K}_p$	σ_p
2.0%	4.10%
3.5	3.18
5.0	4.97
6.5	7.78
8.0	10.84

5.10   **a.** 17%

          b. 14.5%

5.11   13.49%

5.12 k_{RF} = 7%; k_M = 12.60%

5.14   28.44%

5.15   **a.** $\bar{k}_A$ = 18%; σ_A = 19.39%; $\bar{k}_B$ = 21%; σ_B = 31.37%

          b. +0.31

5.18   **a.** 9.90%

          b. 0.99%

          c. 0.20; 0.55; 0.25

5.20   **a.** $22.50

          b. $26.25

          c. $35.00

          d. $34.67

5.21   **a.** 10%; $50.00

          b. 12%; $37.50

          c. 14%; $30.00

          d. 8%; $75.00

5A.1   **a.** $\bar{k}_A$ = 18%; σ_A = 11.23%; $\bar{k}_B$ = 34%; σ_B = 23.32%

          b. 188.0; +0.72

5A.2   **a.** $\bar{k}_H$ = 6%; σ_H = 12.31%; $\bar{k}_T$ = 9%; σ_T = 7.65%

          b. −3; −0.03

5A.3   a. 10.5%; 10%

            b. 26.31%; 14.84%

            c. 10.375%; 23.08%

Chapter 6

6.5   a. 9%

            b. 11.37%; 19%; 17%

            d. 15.79%

            e. 13.66%

6.6   13%

6.7   a. 14.18%

            b. 16.58%

6.8   a. 11%

            b. 5.85%

            c. 5.20%

            d. 9.78%

6.9   15.08%

6.12   9.50%; 9.80%; 10.20%

6.13   a. 13%

            c. 11%; 17.4%

6.15   a. 0.987; 1.119

            b. 16.25%; 17.40%

Chapter 7

7.1   a. A: 1.75 years; B: 3.14 years

            b. $NPV_A = \$97.05$; $NPV_B = \$320.90$

7.3   15.69%

7.4 $NPV_X = 10,002.03$; $NPV_Y = 13,500$; $IRR_X = 15.78\%$; $IRR_Y = 14.19\%$

7.6   a. $NPV_A = \$2,122$; $NPV_B = \$1,259$

            b. $IRR_A = 17.80\%$; $IRR_B = 14.96\%$

7.8   a. $NPV_C = \$11,160$; $NPV_D = \$13,254$

            b. $IRR_C = 20.82\%$; $IRR_D = 17.04\%$

7.9   a. 19%; 15%

            b. $3,001.95; $4,992.45

            c. 13.98%

            d. 16.21%; 14.09%

7.11 $NPV_{apartment} = \$824,000$; $NPV_{recreation} = -\$70,400$; $NPV_{both} = \$1,275,200$

7.13	$225.30; $199
7.15	**a.** 23.38% and $435; 21.27% and $599
	b. $200; $192
7.16	**a.** $NPV_A = \$13,646$; $NPV_B = -\$3,332$; $NPV_C = \$10,558$; $NPV_D = \$4,320$; $NPV_E = \$10,825$; $NPV_F = \$7,225$
	b. Projects A, D, and E
	c. $NPV = \$28,791$; loss $= \$17,783$
7.17	Opportunity cost of capital $= 13\%$; $NPV = \$11,226$

Chapter 8

8.1	$6,126.66
8.2	$2,800; $7,385; $7,794.50
8.3	$146,176.50 or $98,176.50
8.6	$26,179
8.8	$NPV = -\$49,383.93$
8.10	$2,950.50; $5,015.70; $3,510.99; $2,457.69; $1,720.39
8.12	$NPV = \$15,816.33$
8.14	$NPV = -\$205,844$
8.16	$-\$21,000$
8.17	$NPV_{abandon} = \$995$; $NPV_{modernize} = -\$908$
8.18	$NPV_{abandon} = \$300$; $NPV_{overhaul} = \$836$; $NPV_{replace} = -\$53.94$
8A.2	**a.** 8%
	b. 6%
	c. Opportunity cost of capital $= 6.56\%$; $NPV = \$47,381$
8A.4	**a.** $-\$375$
	b. $-\$32,290$
	c. $46,732; $31,123; $32,536
8A.5	**a.** $-\$1,285,000$
	b. $329,160
	c. $2,036,552
	d. $1,080,712
	e. $-\$215,230$

Chapter 9

9.1	**a.** $1,983
9.2	$\beta_{project} = 1.5$
	b. $NPV = \$5,070$

9.3	a.	$CV_A = 0.21$; $CV_B = 0.28$
	b.	$NPV_A = -\$6,057$; $NPV_B = \$17,227$
9.5		$579,328
9.6		-$101,689
9.7	a.	$1,769; -$88; $492; $926
9.10		$1,400,000; $2,800,217

Chapter 10

10.1	a.	$29,515,000
	b.	1.62%
10.4	a.	$20; $22.67
	b.	$39.33
10.5	a.	2
	b.	3
10.8	a.	$10 to $40 million
	b.	Selling price: $80; $20; proceeds: $16 million; $4 million
10.9		95%
10.10	a.	7.5
	b.	$39.13 to $50
	c.	16%
	d.	$60; $30

Chapter 11

11.1		$14,000,000
11.9	a.	$88.889
	b.	112,500
11.10	a.	$1.17
	b.	$1.28; $0.95; $1.08
11.11	a.	$2.47; $2.27
11A.1	a.	NPV = $1,386,297
11A.2		NPV = -$4,711,988
11A.3		NPV = -$281,200

Chapter 12

12.1		$CV_A = 0.39$; $CV_B = 0.22$
12.2	a.	Stock: $2.67; $4.80; $6.93; debt: $2.88; $6.08; $9.28
	b.	Stock: $4.80; $1.65; 0.34; debt: $6.08; $2.48; 0.41

12.5	a.	$285,428.57
	b.	$1,110,000
12.8	a.	$16,000,000
	b.	$20,000,000
12.9	a.	$325,000; $3.25; $32.50; $325,000; 10%
	b.	$286,000; $3.67; $35.75; $346,000; 9.39%
12.11	a.	$40,000
	b.	28.57%
	c.	$10,000
12.16	a.	$1,390,000
	b.	$3.18; $3.65
	c.	$9,525,000; $4.94; $4.86
12A.3	a.	2.00
	b.	1.30
	c.	2.60
	d.	52%
	e.	$10.64
12A.4	a.	1.50; 1.33; 2.00
	b.	$3.27 and $3.24; 2.67 and 2.96

Chapter 13

13.1	a.	$450,000,000
	b.	$462,000,000; $448,600,000
13.4	a.	$2.60; $3.67
	b.	$26
	c.	$30.60

Chapter 14

14.1	a.	$200,000
	b.	−$200,000; $400,000
14.3		$1,980.93
14.7	a.	$142,857; $4; $4
	b.	$151,515; $4; $3.97
14.10		$93.75
14.12		3 for 1
14.14	a.	$3,600,000; $720,000; $1.20; $54,000,000; 15 times
	b.	$60; $4,500

c. $3,600,000; $2; $720,000; $0.40; 20%; 15 times; $54,000,000

d. $60; $4,500

Chapter 15

15.1	$183,944; $399,089
15.2	a. $98,062
	b. $104,280
	c. $91,792
15.5	a. $8,997
	b. $23,803
	c. $26,929
15.7	a. $20,852
	b. −$17,462
15.8	a. $10,020
	b. $80,412
15.9	a. $21,638
	b. $29,058; −$544
	c. $21,755
15.10	a. $59,772.27
	b. 0
15.12	a. $13,844

Chapter 16

16.1	a. $50,000
	b. $37,500
16.4	a. −$50,000; −$35,000; $98,000; $123,000; $112,500; $42,000
	b. $79,791; $51,506
16.8	a. $52,089; $36,609
	b. −$41,688; −$25,267
16.9	$43.75 million; 1.21
16.10	a. 20%
	b. $37

Chapter 17

17.1	−$19,821
17.3	$729

17.8	b.	$328,407
17.10	a.	5 contracts
	b.	Lost $34,375
17.11	b.	9 contracts
	c.	Gain $23,769

Chapter 18

18.3	a.	$15.36
	b.	$12.83
18.5	a.	$14.09
	b.	$15.54
18.6	a.	$12.58; $15.06
	b.	$21.82; $5.42
18.9	a.	$10.81
	b.	$9.92
	c.	$14.67
18.10	a.	$1.49
	b.	$3.73
	c.	$0.40
18.11	a.	$2.68
	b.	$9.85
	c.	$10.85; $3.02
18.14	a.	$15.67; $14.98
	b.	$7.67; $7.95

Chapter 19

19.1	a.	$41.91 million; $18.09 million
	b.	$4.76 million
19.5		$2.98; $2.44; $12.90
19.6	a.	$136 million
	b.	$14 million
19.9		$54
19.11	a.	$30,672
	b.	$0
19.12		$8
19.15		$6.38; $6.46

19.16   a. Yes

b. 5.30 FF/$

Chapter 20

20.1 $13.88

20.8   b. $22

20.10   a. $39.78; $40.95

b. 63.92; 61.96

Chapter 21

21.2   a. 54.75 days

b. 21.17 days

c. 9.73

21.3   a. $182; $164.5; $147

c. 0.71; 1.00; 1.29; −$200; $0; $200

21.4   a. $57.07

b. $53.82

c. $55.77

d. $68.80; $70.24; $66.24; $68.64

21.5   a. $145.6; $122.5; $99.4

b. 9.29; 43.27; 110.16

c. 0.60; 1.14; 3.00; −$200; $50; $400

21.6   a. $6.09; $1.71; 0.28; $5.01; $1.11; 0.22

b. $66.99; $50.10

21.7   a. 1.25; $50; 0.29; 0.24; 21.56 days

b. $16.64

c. 1.61; $200; 0.47; 0.29; 57.62 days; $17.11

21.9   a. $5; $9; $13; $11; $7; $11; $15; $13

b. $20; $24; $28; $26; $22; $26; $30; $28

c. $600,000

Chapter 22

22.1   a. $44.14

b. $75.66

22.4 $\Delta C = \$45,210; \Delta B = \$71,280$

22.5	**a.**	$\Delta C = \$20,895$; $\Delta B = \$26,400$
	b.	1.58 days
22.6	**a.**	$\Delta C = \$27,120$; $\Delta B = \$126,360$
22.8	6.43 days	
22.12	**a.**	10.71%
	b.	10.1%

Chapter 23

23.3	$152,250; −$17,660	
23.4	46.25%	
23.7	$61,740	
23.8	**a.**	−$135,959
	b.	$36,541
23.11	$375,000	
23.12	**a.**	$385,808
	b.	$34,726
23A.3	**a.**	7,000
	b.	17.5
	c.	5,678

Chapter 24

24.3	**a.**	No cost
	b.	27.86%
	c.	17.81%
	d.	10.33%
24.5	10.51%	
24.7	**a.**	16.00%
	b.	15.56%; $2,500
	c.	13.86%
24.9	**a.**	22.16%
	b.	16.66%
24.11	**a.**	23.10%
	b.	19.36%
24.12	**a.**	21.31%
	b.	19.33%
24.14	19.63%; 27.86%; 27.24%; 25;73%	

25.2		42.9%
25.3	**a.**	29.2 days; 7.5 times; 1.0
	b.	$37,500
	c.	$30,000
25.7	**a.**	4.50; 1.88; 0.41; 10.12%; 2.76
	b.	47.65%
25.8	**a.**	2.0; 5.0%; 10.0%; 20.0%
	b.	$55,000; $120,000; 22.2%

Chapter 26

26.2	**a.**	$2,159.80; $2,386.50; $2,613.20
26.3	**a.**	$13,355.4 million
	b.	$790.6 million less
	c.	$16,469.9 million
	d.	$64.9 million greater
26.4		$45 million; $30 million
26.6	**a.**	$15; −$20; −$40; $10
26.7	**a.**	$Y_t = \$275.89 + \$9.67X_t$
	b.	$402; $411; $421; $431; $440; $450; $460; $469
	c.	1.015; 0.875; 0.945; 1.165
	d.	$408; $360; $398; $502; $447; $394; $435; $546
26.9	**a.**	1.5 million
	b.	6.7 million; 64.7%
26.11		$32; $13; −$26; −$97; −$109

Chapter 27

27.2	**a.**	17.81%
	b.	16.30%
27.3	**a.**	1.23; 0.65; 42.48 days; 6.63; 0.70; 1.8%; 15.9%

Glossary

abandonment decision Capital budgeting decision in which the net present value of continuing to operate is compared with the after-tax proceeds if the project is discontinued.

ABC method Inventory control procedure in which items are grouped in categories by their value. Group A items require high investment and the most control.

adjustable-rate preferred stock Preferred stock where the cash dividend rate is tied to a bank's prime rate and is adjusted quarterly.

adjusted present value Base-case net present value of a project if financed solely with equity plus the present value of any financing side effects.

advance factoring Short-term financing in which a lender (factor) provides a loan against a firm's receivables.

agency costs The sum of financial contracting costs, costs of monitoring, and loss of wealth when agents pursue their own interests.

agency relationship Results when a principal delegates decision-making authority to an agent. Agency relationships involve management, shareholders, creditors, and/or other stakeholders.

American option A call or put option that can be exercised at any time up to and including its expiration date.

amortization schedule Schedule that shows how a term loan will be paid off by specifying both the principal and interest payments made per payment.

annual percentage rate (APR) Legally specified nominal interest rate determined by multiplying the per period rate by the number of periods in the year.

annual report Report issued by a corporation to shareholders that contains basic accounting statements as well as management's opinion of the past year's operations and prospects for the future.

annuity A series of equal cash flows for a specified number of periods.

annuity due A series of equal cash flows for a specified number of periods, with each cash flow occurring at the beginning of the period.

arbitrage pricing theory (APT) The Theory that the required return on any asset is a function of a number of factors, not just the risk-free rate and the expected return on the market portfolio as given by the capital asset pricing model.

arrearage An overdue payment; used to describe cash dividends on cumulative preferred stock that have not been paid.

ask price The lowest price demanded (asked) by a seller to sell a security.

asset beta Unlevered beta that indicates

the riskiness of the firm's assets, without regard for how the firm is financed. Beta for an all-equity firm or unlevered set of assets.

asset substitution Occurs when a firm invests in more risky assets than those expected by the firm's bondholders (or other creditors).

assignment An out-of-court procedure for liquidating a firm.

asymmetric information Information is known to some, but not all, of the concerned parties.

average collection float The number of days of float times the average daily dollar amount in the collection system.

bad debt Occurs when a seller extends credit to a buyer, and the buyer fails to pay the account.

balance sheet Accounting statement that records the assets of the firm and claims against them (liabilities and equities), as of a specific moment in time.

Bank of Canada Canada's central bank.

banker's acceptance A draft drawn on a specific bank by a seller to obtain payment for goods that have been shipped (sold) to a customer. The bank, by accepting (or endorsing) the draft, assumes the obligation of payment at the due date.

banking group See *syndicate*.

bankruptcy costs Includes legal and other direct costs associated with bankruptcy or reorganization procedures.

bearer form Bonds that are not registered (or recorded) by the firm (or its agent). No owner's name appears on the bond certificate, so whoever holds it is the owner.

best efforts Procedure for selling a security issue in which an investment dealer agrees to market the issue, but it is not underwritten and there is no guarantee the full amount of the issue will be sold.

beta, β_j A measure of an asset's non-diversifiable, or systematic, risk. Calculated by (1) regressing the returns for an asset against the returns for the market portfolio or (2) dividing the covariance between the returns on an asset and the market portfolio by the variance of the market's return.

bid price The highest price that has been offered (bid) to buy a security.

bidding firm The firm that is buying another firm in a merger or acquisition.

bill of lading Shipping document that authorizes the shipment of goods from one party (the seller) to another (the customer).

binomial option pricing model Option pricing model in which the underlying asset can take on only two possible (discrete) values in the next time period for each possible value in the present time period.

Black–Scholes option pricing model A model for valuing European call or put options which assumes the distribution for the instantaneous rate of return on the underlying asset is normal and constant over time.

bond A long-term (typically 10 years or more) promissory note issued by the borrower promising to pay a specified interest per year and/or maturity value.

bond equivalent yield Means of converting the discount yield on treasury bills to an approximate 365-day annualized yield.

bond rating Estimates supplied of the probability of repayment of principal and interest on a bond.

book value Assets minus liabilities, or shareholders' equity.

book value per share Common shareholders' equity divided by the number of shares of common stock outstanding.

bought deal One underwriter buys securities from an issuing firm and sells them directly to a small number of investors.

breakeven analysis Analysis of the level of sales at which a project's NPV is just equal to zero.

business improvement loans Loans made under the Small Business Loans Act by chartered banks for new, or additions to, fixed equipment, buildings, or leasehold improvements.

business risk Risk caused by the basic nature of the industry in which the firm operates.

call option The right, but not the obligation, to purchase an asset at a stated price within a specified time period.

call premium The difference between a bond's or preferred stock's par value and what the firm has to pay to call it for retirement.

call provision Stipulation in a bond or preferred stock issue allowing the firm to retire the securities before maturity.

capital asset pricing model (CAPM) A model of required rates of return for financial assets. The required rate of return is equal to the risk-free rate plus a risk premium based on the expected return on the market portfolio and the asset's non-diversifiable risk as measured by beta.

capital budget A statement of the firm's planned long-term investment projects, usually done annually.

capital budgeting The process by which long-term investments are generated, analyzed, and placed in the capital budget.

capital budgeting process The four capital budgeting steps are: search for and identification of growth opportunities; estimating the magnitude, timing, and riskiness of cash flows; selection or rejection; and control and postcompletion audit.

capital cost Total cost of putting an asset into productive use, including acquisition and installation costs.

capital cost allowance (CCA) Represents the portion of the total cost of a depreciable asset that a business is allowed to charge against its income in a given year when filing its tax return.

capital gain The difference between the selling price of an asset and its original cost, provided the selling price is greater than the original cost.

capital lease A lease that meets certain GAAP requirements and accordingly must be capitalized and shown as both an asset and a liability on the firm's balance sheet.

capital market Financial market where long-term (longer than one-year) financial assets such as bonds, preferred stock, or common stock are bought or sold.

capital market line Set of all efficient portfolios, consisting of various combinations of the risk-free asset and the market portfolio.

capital rationing A situation where a constraint is placed on the funds available such that some wealth-maximizing capital budgeting projects cannot be accepted.

capital structure The long-term financing of the firm, typically represented by bonds, leases, preferred stock, and common stock.

cash Currency on hand and demand deposits.

cash budget A detailed forecast of all expected cash inflows and outflows by the firm for some period of time.

cash conversion cycle The net time interval in days between actual cash expenditure by the firm on its productive resources and the ultimate recovery of cash.

cash discount A provision often included in a firm's credit terms. Payment within the discount period allows the customer to reduce the cost of the purchase.

cash dividend The distribution of some of the firm's cash to investors who own common or preferred stock.

cash flow The actual cash coming into a firm (cash inflow) or paid out by a firm (cash outflow).

cash flow after tax (CF) Equals cash flow before tax minus taxes (CFBT − taxes); or cash flow before tax, times 1 minus the marginal tax rate, plus capital cost allowance times the marginal tax rate [CFBT(1 − T) + CCA(T)].

cash flow before tax (CFBT) Equals cash inflows minus cash outflows.

cash offering Primary market transaction in which a firm sells securities to the general public for cash.

cash on delivery (COD) Term of sale where payment is required at the time the goods are delivered to the buyer.

CCA rate The rate designated by the Income Tax Act for each asset class as the maximum rate that can be applied to the undepreciated capital cost (UCC) in arriving at capital cost allowance (CCA) for a year.

CCA recapture The negative undepreciated capital cost (UCC) balance resulting from transactions occurring during the year.

certificate of deposit (CD) A short-term time deposit issued by a bank.

characteristic line A line indicating the relationship between the rates of return on an asset or portfolio and the corresponding rates of return on the market portfolio.

chief financial officer (CFO) The individual ultimately responsible for making and implementing financial decisions in a firm.

clientele effect The tendency of firms to

attract a certain kind of shareholder, depending on the cash dividend policy maintained by the firm.

coefficient of variation (CV) A measure of relative riskiness calculated by dividing the standard deviation by the mean (or expected value) of the distribution.

commercial paper Short-term nonsecured promissory note issued by commercial finance and industrial firms.

commitment fee A fee charged by the lender on a line of credit; generally charged on the unused portion of the line.

common-size statement Accounting statement expressed in percentage terms.

common stock A document that represents (residual) ownership in a corporation. The common shareholder is the last to receive any distribution of earnings or assets.

compensating balance Money on deposit with a bank to compensate the bank for services rendered.

complementary projects Two or more capital budgeting projects that interact positively so that the total cash flows, if all are undertaken, are more than the simple sum of their individual cash flows.

composition Out-of-court agreement between a firm and its creditors whereby the creditors receive less than the total amount due them in full settlement of their claim.

compound rate Rate applicable when interest is earned not only on the initial principal, but also on the accumulated interest from previous periods.

compounding The process of finding the future value of a series of cash flows; the inverse of discounting.

consol Perpetual coupon rate bond.

constant-growth model Form of the dividend valuation model in which cash dividends are expected to grow at a constant percentage rate, g, until infinity. The price of the stock is $P_0 = D_1/(k_s - g)$.

controlled disbursing System in which the firm directs cheques to be mailed from a distant city to maximize the amount of mail float before the cheque is received by the supplier.

controller The individual in a firm who normally is responsible for preparing financial statements, for cost accounting, for in-

ternal auditing, for budgeting, and for the tax department.

conversion price The effective price paid for common stock by converting a convertible security into common stock.

conversion ratio The number of shares of common stock received for converting a convertible security; equals the par value of the convertible divided by the conversion price.

conversion value The value of a convertible security in terms of the common stock into which it can be converted. It equals the conversion ratio times the market price per share of common stock.

convertible security Bond or preferred stock that, at the option of the owner, may be exchanged for a predetermined number of shares of common stock.

corporation A legal entity formed to conduct business and given the power to act as an individual.

correlation A statistical measure of the degree of linear relationship between two random variables. It can vary from +1.0 (perfect positive correlation), to 0.0 (no relationship), to −1.0 (perfect negative correlation).

coupon interest rate The stated percentage rate of interest on a bond relative to its par value.

covariance A statistical measure of the degree of linear relationship between two random variables. Similar to correlation, except that the covariance is not bounded by +1.0 and −1.0.

credit-scoring model Point-based system used to determine the creditworthiness of customers based on key financial and credit characteristics.

creditors Persons to whom or firms to which money is owed. The firm's creditors include those that have fixed-type financial claims on the firm arising from short- or long-term debt.

cross-hedge Hedge required where no futures contract exists in the underlying asset or commodity being hedged.

cumulative Provision in many preferred stocks and income bonds which requires that all past cash dividends or interest be paid in full before any additional dividend or interest is paid.

cumulative voting System of electing the board of directors whereby each share is entitled to one vote. Because shareholders can vote more than once for a single director, cumulative voting encourages minority representation on the board of directors.

current ratio Current assets divided by current liabilities.

days inventory The number of days in the year, 365, divided by inventory turnover.

days payable The number of days in the year, 365, divided by payable turnover.

days purchases outstanding Accounts payable divided by credit purchases per day.

days sales outstanding Accounts receivable divided by the average sales per day (sales/365 days).

debenture Unsecured long-term borrowing by a firm backed only by its full faith and credit.

debit card A card that allows retail customers to transfer funds directly from their bank account to a retailer's account.

debt capacity The amount of debt or debt-type securities (such as leases and preferred stock) a firm can service.

deep discount bond Bond whose coupon interest rate is set substantially below the prevailing market interest rate at the time of issue. Accordingly, the bond must be sold at a discount from its par (maturity) value.

default premium Additional return required to compensate an investor for the risk that the bond issuer will not be able to make interest payments or repay the principal amount on schedule, or that the firm issuing stock will fail.

deferred taxes A liability account on the balance sheet that represents the additional income tax due in the future arising because the firm has claimed larger expenses (primarily depreciation) for tax purposes than for GAAP accounting purposes.

defined benefit pension plan Retirement plan in which the recipient will receive a fixed and predefined set of benefits upon retirement.

defined contribution pension plan Retirement plan in which there is an amount contributed by the firm on behalf of all plan participants. The benefits to be received depend on the size of the contributions and how much they have earned.

degree of combined leverage (DCL) Measure of the responsiveness of percentage changes in earnings per share (EPS) to percentage changes in sales. Caused by both operating leverage and financial leverage. Calculated as follows: $(\Delta EPS/EPS) \div (\Delta sales/sales)$, or (sales − variable costs)/(EBIT − interest), or (degree operating leverage)(degree of financial leverage).

degree of financial leverage (DFL) Measure of the responsiveness of percentage changes in earnings per share (EPS) to percentage change in EBIT. Calculated as follows: $(\Delta EPS/EPS) \div (\Delta EBIT/EBIT)$, or EBIT/(EBIT − interest).

degree of operating leverage (DOL) A measure of the responsiveness of percentage changes in EBIT to percentage changes in sales. Calculated as follows: $(\Delta EBIT/EBIT) \div (\Delta sales/sales)$, or (sales − variable costs)/EBIT.

derivatives Futures, options, swaps, and other custom-tailored financial instruments whose value is tied to fluctuations in other securities or markets.

dilution Reduction in the percentage ownership and income to which each share of common stock is entitled.

direct placement Sale of securities from the firm to the ultimate purchaser, without the services of an investment dealer.

discount (on a bond) Difference between the current market price on a bond selling below its par value and its par value.

discount interest Process whereby a lender deducts the interest at the start of the loan.

discount rate The rate used to calculate the present value of future cash flows.

discounting The process of finding the present value of a series of future cash flows; the inverse of compounding.

disinflation A slowing down in the rate of inflation. Although there may still be inflation, it is at a lower rate than before.

diversifiable risk That part of an asset's total risk that can be eliminated in a diversified portfolio. Also called company-specific or unsystematic risk.

diversifying Investing in more than one asset when the assets do not move proportionally in the same direction at the same time.

divestiture Decision by a firm to sell off some of its assets.

dividend extra Practice of paying an extra or special cash dividend in addition to the regular dividend.

dividend payout ratio Dividends per share divided by earnings per share, or total cash dividends divided by net income.

dividend per share Calculated by dividing total cash dividends to common shareholders by the number of shares of common stock outstanding. Reflects how much in cash dividends the investor will receive for owning one share of stock.

dividend reinvestment plan Plan in which shareholders can elect to have their cash dividends reinvested in order to purchase additional shares of common stock.

dividend valuation model Model that says the current market price of common stock is equal to the present value of all expected cash dividends discounted at the investor's required rate of return.

dividend yield Dividend per share divided by market price per share.

divisional opportunity cost of capital Cost of capital for a specific division of a firm, or for a set of projects that have been grouped together; the minimum required return for projects as risky as those faced by the division.

du Pont system An accounting-based system of analysis that focuses on profitability, asset utilization, and financial leverage.

earnings after tax (EAT) Calculated by subtracting cost of goods sold; general, selling, and administrative expenses; depreciation; interest; and taxes from sales. Also called net income.

earnings available for common shareholders (EAC) Equals net income minus cash dividends on preferred stock.

earnings before interest and taxes (EBIT) Earnings before interest on debt and income taxes are deducted; also called net operating income.

earnings before tax (EBT) Earnings before income taxes are deducted.

earnings per share (EPS) Calculated by taking net income minus any cash dividends on preferred stock, and then dividing by the number of shares of common stock outstanding.

economic exposure Extent to which the value of a firm will change due to an adjustment in exchange rates.

economic life The length of time an asset will be economically useful.

economic order quantity (EOQ) The optimal inventory order size that minimizes total cost, which is the sum of the ordering plus the carrying costs.

effective annual interest rate Actual interest rate earned (paid) after adjusting the nominal or stated interest rate for the frequency of compounding employed.

effective interest rate The per period rate of interest, taking account of both the frequency of compounding and the nominal rate of interest.

efficient frontier Set of portfolios that have the highest expected return at each level of risk, and the lowest risk at each level of expected return.

efficient market Market in which security prices adjust rapidly to the announcement of new information so that current market prices fully reflect all available information, including risk.

efficient market hypothesis The proposition that in an efficient market prices react quickly and unambiguously to new information.

efficient portfolio A portfolio that provides the highest expected return for a given amount of risk, and the lowest risk for a given expected return.

electronic data interchange (EDI) Electronic transmission of virtually all of a firm's business correspondence.

electronic funds transfer Payment made electronically instead of using a paper-based cheque.

ending cash flow The net after-tax cash inflow or outflow that occurs when a capital budgeting project is terminated.

EPS–EBIT analysis A technique used

when examining the effect of alternative capital structures on a firm's earnings per share.

EPS illusion The increase in earnings per share that can result solely from a merger.

equilibrium When the expected return equals the required rate of return, assets are neither overpriced nor underpriced.

equipment financing Bank loans to buy equipment; the equipment is used as collateral.

equipment trust certificate Form of security in which the trustee holds title to the assets until the security is paid off in full by the firm employing the financing.

equivalent annual cost The present value of the cash outflows of a capital budgeting project divided by the present value of an annuity over the project's life. Used when a project only has cash outflows.

equivalent annual NPV The net present value of a capital budgeting project divided by the present value of an annuity over the project's life. This produces a yearly equivalent NPV that allows mutually exclusive projects with unequal lives to be compared.

Eurobond Bond underwritten by an international syndicate and sold primarily in countries other than the country in which the issue is denominated.

Eurocurrency system The world-wide system in which one country's currency is on deposit in another country.

Eurodollars U.S. dollars deposited in a U.S. branch bank located outside the United States or in a foreign bank.

European option A call or put option that can be exercised only at its expiration date.

event risk Risk caused by a drastic, unanticipated increase in a firm's debt or circumstances that causes the market price of its outstanding bonds to fall.

ex ante **(expected or required) rate of return** The return required or expected before the fact from investing in stocks, bonds, or real assets.

ex-dividend date The date set by the securities industry to determine who is entitled to receive a cash dividend, stock dividend, or stock split; two business days (Monday through Friday) before the record date.

ex post **(realized) rate of return** The return realized after the fact from investing in stocks, bonds, or real assets.

exchange ratio The relationship of the market value of the cash and securities offered by the bidding firm divided by the market value of the target firm in a proposed merger.

exercise (strike) price Price at which the owner of an option can buy (a call option) or sell (a put option) the underlying asset.

expansion project Capital budgeting project designed to improve the firm's ability to produce or market its goods by expanding its scale of operations.

expectations theory Theory that (implied) forward interest rates are unbiased estimates of expected future interest rates.

expectations theory of forward exchange rates Theory that the expected future spot rate of exchange at time t equals the current t-period forward exchange rate.

expected NPV The mean or average net present value obtained from a probability distribution of possible NPVs.

expected return on a portfolio, $\overline{K}_p$ The average of the expected returns for a group of assets weighted by the proportion of the portfolio devoted to each asset.

extendible bond A short-term bond on which the bondholder has the option to extend the maturity for an additional specified period, at the original interest rate.

extension An out-of-court procedure by which creditors grant a debtor additional time to pay the full amount of past-due obligations.

factoring The sale of a firm's accounts receivable as a means of speeding up the inflow of funds, or to obtain a loan.

feasible set The set of all possible portfolios.

50% Rule One-half of net acquisitions is added to the asset class in the taxation year; the remaining one-half is added in the following year.

finance The money resources available to governments, firms, or individuals, and the management of these monies.

financial distress Situation in which a firm

is having difficulty meeting its financial obligations.

financial distress costs   The sum of the direct and indirect costs associated with bankruptcy and financial difficulties.

financial intermediaries   Financial institutions such as banks, trust companies, *caisses populaires,* insurance companies, pension funds, and investment companies that assist in the transfer of funds from suppliers to demanders of funds.

financial lease   Long-term lease that meets certain criteria as set by Revenue Canada.

financial leverage   The use of securities bearing a fixed charge to finance a portion of the firm's capital needs. Arises from using bonds, preferred stock, or leases.

financial management   The acquisition, management, and financing of resources for firms by means of money, with due regard for prices in external economic markets.

financial manager   Anyone directly engaged in making or implementing financial decisions.

financial markets   Markets which deal with cash flows over time and that facilitate bringing together the suppliers of funds and the demanders of funds.

financial risk   A source of risk arising if the firm uses financing sources that have a fixed but prior claim relative to common stock.

financial slack   Ability of a firm to adjust rapidly to unforeseen cash demands by having backup means available to raise cash.

firm commitment offering   Primary market transaction where an investment dealer guarantees the issuing firm a fixed price for the securities sold.

Fisher effect   The nominal, or observed, risk-free interest rate is approximately equal to the real rate of interest plus expected inflation.

fixed charges coverage   Earnings before interest and taxes plus lease expenses, divided by the sum of interest charges plus lease expenses.

float   The length of time between when a cheque is written and when the recipient receives the funds and can draw upon them (has "good funds").

flotation cost   Cost of issuing new stock or bonds. The difference between what the securities are sold to the public for and what the firm receives, plus any other costs such as accounting and legal fees.

forced conversion   Situation that can arise if the conversion value of a convertible security is greater than the call price; the issuer can force investors to convert by calling the security.

foreign affiliate   A foreign incorporated subsidiary that has at least 10 percent of its equity owned by the Canadian parent firm.

foreign bond   Bond issued by a foreign borrower, but underwritten, sold, and denominated in one country.

foreign branch   An unincorporated subsidiary.

foreign exchange rate   The price of a unit of a country's currency relative to the price of a unit of another country's currency.

forward contract   An arrangement to buy or sell a specified amount of a given asset on a specified future date, at a price set when the contract is entered into.

forward interest rate   The rate of interest sometime in the future.

forward rate of exchange   The rate of exchange between two currencies as set today, but with the transaction to occur at some specified future date.

free cash flow theory   Free cash flow is the cash flow above that needed to fund all positive NPV projects. The free cash flow theory states that a firm's stock price will increase with unexpected increases in payout to claimholders and decrease with unexpected decreases in the demand for funds via new issues.

fully funded   The present value of expected retirement obligations is equal to the present value of the pension fund assets.

fully registered   Process whereby bonds are registered with respect to principal and interest. The registration agent keeps a list and mails out interest cheques to the bondholders.

future value   The amount to which a lump sum, or series of cash flows, will grow by a given future date when compounded at a given interest rate.

future value factor, $FV_{k,n}$ Set of factors that for different rates, k, and periods, n, converts a present value into a larger future value.

future value factor for an annuity, FVA$_{k,n}$ Set of factors that for different rates, k, and periods, n, converts an annuity into a single future value.

futures contract Standardized contract to buy or sell a specified amount of a given asset on a specified future date.

futures options An option on a futures contract.

generally accepted accounting principles (GAAP) Reporting requirements established by the Canadian Institute of Chartered Accountants (CICA) that determine the rules by which firms produce accounting statements.

giro system Electronic payment system employed in many countries (often run through the postal system). Provides direct transfer from the payor to the payee.

going private Process by which a publicly owned firm whose common stock is actively traded becomes a privately held firm.

golden parachute Special employment contract granted to key executives in case of termination due to a merger.

greenmail Practice whereby a stake in a target firm is purchased, then sold back to the firm at some price above its current market value.

gross margin Net sales minus cost of goods sold.

gross profit margin Gross margin divided by net sales.

growth option An option to make an additional capital investment in the future that can only exist if some proposed or current project is funded.

growth rate, g Compound percentage growth rate (often, but not always, in cash dividends).

hard capital rationing Situation where positive net present value cannot be accepted due to the inability to raise external funds.

hedge ratio (delta) The number of units of an asset that are needed to hedge one unit of a liability.

hurdle rate The minimum acceptable return. It is the rate against which a project's internal rate of return is compared.

in-the-money Option that has value and is worth converting at the asset's current market price. A call option is in-the-money when the market price is above the exercise price; a put option is in-the-money when the current market price is less than the exercise price.

income bond Bond that will pay interest only if the firm has the earnings to do so.

income statement Accounting statement that records the results of the firm's operations over some period of time, typically a year; shows revenues, expenses, and resulting net income (or loss).

incremental cash flows The cash flows from a new project or venture minus the cash flows on an existing project or venture.

incremental IRR approach Method used to evaluate mutually exclusive projects to ensure the same ranking is obtained using the internal rate of return (IRR) as with net present value (NPV).

indenture Legal agreement between the issuing firm and the bondholders. Provides the specific terms of the bond.

independent projects Capital budgeting projects whose cash flows are unrelated. Acceptance of one has no bearing on whether another project is accepted or rejected.

inflation A condition in which the price level increases; reflects changes in purchasing power.

inflation premium Additional return for expected inflation that investors require in addition to the real rate of interest.

initial investment The net after-tax cash outflow needed to get a capital budgeting project started. This outflow typically occurs immediately (at time t = 0), but for large projects it may be spread out over a number of time periods.

initial public offering (IPO) The original sale of a firm's securities to the public. A primary market transaction.

instalment interest Interest is computed on the total principal for the total life of the loan; then, using annuities, a fixed payment per period is made, with part of it going to principal and part to interest.

interest The rate paid on money that is borrowed, or received on money lent; usually stated as a percentage rate per year.

interest rate cap Option, or contract, that places an upper limit on the interest rate in a floating-rate financing instrument.

interest rate collar Option, or contract, that places both an upper and lower limit on the interest rate in a floating-rate financing instrument.

interest rate floor Option, or contract, that places a lower limit on the interest rate in a floating-rate financing instrument.

interest rate line Line that shows the relationship between dollars today and dollars in the next period. The slope is the per period rate of interest.

interest rate parity Theory that the interest rate differential between two countries is equal to the difference between the forward exchange rate and the spot exchange rate.

interest rate risk Change in market price of a bond as general interest rates change. Long-term bonds have more interest rate risk than short-term bonds, thereby leading to a maturity premium on long-term bonds.

interest rate swap Agreement between two parties to swap interest, but not principal, payments.

internal rate of return (IRR) The discount rate that equates the present value of a series of cash inflows with the initial investment at time t = 0.

internally generated funds Those cash flows generated by the firm's operations that can be paid out to shareholders or reinvested in the business.

international bond A bond sold outside the country of the borrower.

international Fisher effect Theory that differential rates of inflation between two countries are reflected by differences in their respective risk-free rates.

interrelated projects Capital budgeting projects in which the cash flows are intertwined so they cannot be examined separately.

inventory turnover Cost of goods sold divided by inventory.

investment dealer A firm that serves as a middle party between the financial markets and the demanders of capital. The investment dealer specializes in underwriting and selling new securities, and advising corporate clients.

investment opportunities line Line or schedule that shows possible capital investments ranked in order by their internal rate of return.

issue-specific premium Compensation for risk that arises from the characteristics of the securities and the provisions attached to them.

junk bond Bond rated BB/B+ or below.

just-in-time Inventory (and production) system in which inventory is minimized by contracting with suppliers so deliveries are made, often daily or hourly, as needed for production.

lag To collect (pay) late due to a strong (weak) domestic currency relative to a foreign currency.

lead To collect (pay) early to take advantage of a weak (strong) domestic currency relative to a foreign currency.

lease A rental agreement whereby the lessee obtains the use of an asset in exchange for an agreement to make payments to the lessor.

lessee The user of a leased asset.

lessor The owner of an asset that is leased to someone else.

letter of credit An agreement sent by one party (generally a bank) to another, concerning funds that will be made available. Usually a buyer supplies a letter of credit to the seller when they are unknown to each other.

leveraged buyout (LBO) Transaction in which a publicly owned firm is acquired by someone else (or a group), financed largely by borrowing.

leveraged lease A lease in which the lessor generally supplies 20 to 30 percent of the funds and borrows the rest from a lender.

leveraging up When a firm dramatically increases its amount of debt and at the same time shrinks the number of shares of common stock outstanding.

limited liability Under the law, shareholders can lose no more than they have invested in a firm; they are not personally liable for the firm's debts.

line of credit Agreement between a firm and a bank whereby the firm can borrow up to a maximum amount.

liquid assets A firm's cash and marketable securities.

liquidation The process of dissolving the firm by selling its assets.

liquidity preference theory Theory that interest rates reflect both expectations about future interest rates and a maturity premium that compensates longer-term investors for greater interest rate risk.

liquidity premium Additional return to compensate investors for additional transactions costs that arise due to investing in less liquid stocks or bonds.

lockbox An arrangement whereby a firm has its customers make payments to a post office box. A local bank branch makes collections from the box, processes the cheques, and forwards the money to the firm's central bank.

London Interbank Offered Rate (LIBOR) Interest rate at which banks in different countries trade.

long Taking an ownership position in a financial or real asset.

long-term asset turnover Sales divided by long-term (fixed) assets.

mail float The length of time between when a customer places a cheque in the mail and when the selling firm receives it and begins to process it.

majority voting A system of electing the board of directors whereby a simple majority is required to elect each director.

management buyout Top management, usually with the assistance of an outside partner, takes all or part of a firm and turns it into a private firm.

market for corporate control Market where various management teams vie for the right to acquire and manage corporate activities and assets.

market portfolio The portfolio of all risky assets. For the stock market, the Toronto Stock Exchange (TSE) 300 index is often used as a proxy for the market portfolio.

market price of risk The slope of the capital market line; the equilibrium expected reward per unit of risk.

market rate of interest Current interest rate, or yield to maturity, on bonds based on the current market prices of bonds.

market segmentation theory Theory that interest rates reflect different supply and demand conditions for bonds of various maturities.

marketable security Short-term debt security that can be quickly converted into cash with little or no loss of principal.

matching principle A guideline for working capital management that holds that temporary assets should be financed by temporary financing and permanent assets should be financed by permanent sources of financing.

material requirements planning Centralized inventory and production system to coordinate orders and inventory with production needs.

maturity The length (or term) to redemption of a bond expressed in years. At maturity, the borrower must redeem the bond at its par value.

maturity factoring Short-term financing in which the factor purchases all a firm's receivables and forwards the proceeds to the seller as they are collected.

maturity premium Additional return required on longer-term bonds to compensate the investor for the greater price fluctuation as market interest rates change.

mean (expected value) The weighted average of all possible outcomes, where the weights are the probabilities assigned to the expected outcomes.

merger The acquisition of a firm, a division of a firm, or part or all of its assets by another firm. Also known as statutory amalgamation.

modified internal rate of return (MIRR) The discount rate that equates the initial investment at time $t = 0$ with a project's terminal value, where the terminal value is the future value of the cash inflows, compounded at some required rate of return, k.

money market   Financial market in which funds are borrowed or lent for short periods of time (up to one year).

moral hazard   When asymmetric information exists so that information available to the firm's managers is superior to that available to outside investors. Managers can take unobservable self-interested actions that are detrimental to the principles (shareholders or bondholders).

mortgage bond   Bond secured by a lien on real property of the firm, such as buildings or equipment.

multiple internal rates of return   Condition that may arise when calculating the internal rate of return (IRR) if there are non-simple cash flows.

mutually exclusive projects   Capital budgeting alternatives of which only one can be selected.

negotiated short-term financing   Short-term financing such as bank loans or loans secured by accounts receivable or inventory that are negotiated and have a specific length.

net acquisitions   The capital cost of new assets minus the lesser of the capital cost or net proceeds from the sale of assets in the same class. The new assets must be put in use in the same year as the other assets are sold.

net present value (NPV)   The present value of the future cash flows, discounted at the opportunity cost of capital, or required rate of return, minus the initial investment.

net present value of leasing (NPV$_{lease}$)   Method to decide whether an asset should be leased or purchased. The NPV equals the cost of the asset minus the present value of the after-tax lease payments and the forgone capital cost allowance (CCA) tax shield, where the after-tax cost of borrowing is used as the discount rate.

net profit margin   Net income divided by sales.

net resale value   The amount that a firm expects to resell an asset for, net of any disposal costs, at the end of the asset's useful life.

net working capital   Current assets minus current liabilities.

no-growth model   Form of the dividend valuation model in which no growth in future cash dividends is expected. Therefore, $P_0 = D_1/k_s$.

nominal interest rate   Stated or observed interest rate per year.

nominal risk-free interest rate   Stated or observed interest rate; equal to the real rate of interest plus an inflation premium.

noncapital loss   See *operating loss*.

nondiversifiable risk   That part of an asset's total risk that cannot be eliminated in a diversified portfolio, also called systematic or market risk. Measured by beta.

nonsimple cash flow   A set of cash flows whose sign changes from positive to negative (or vice versa) more than once. For every change in sign, there may be one internal rate of return.

ongoing liquidity   A function of the expected inflows and outflows of cash through the firm over time.

operating cash flows   Cash flows after tax, that are expected to occur over the economic life of a capital investment project.

operating cycle   Part of the cash conversion cycle; equal to the days inventory plus the days sales outstanding.

operating lease   Term used in accounting to describe any lease that does not meet the criteria established for capital leases.

operating leverage   The use of assets which require fixed operating costs no matter what the level of sales.

operating loans   Loans negotiated with banks, usually by small businesses, for day-to-day operations.

operating loss   An operating loss occurs when a firm's allowable expenses and deductions exceed its revenues.

operating profit   Net sales minus all expenses except interest and taxes, but before any adjustments. If there are no adjustments, operating profit equals earnings before interest and tax.

opportunity cost   The cost associated with an alternative or forgone opportunity bypassed.

opportunity cost of capital   Required return that is forgone by investing in real assets rather than in a similar-risk investment, such as securities.

option The right, but not the obligation, to buy or sell an underlying asset at a fixed price during a specified time period.

ordinary annuity A series of equal cash flows for a specified number of periods, with each cash flow occurring at the end of the period.

organized security exchange Formal organizations that have a physical location and exist to bring together buyers and sellers of securities in the secondary market.

out clause A clause in an underwriting agreement that would cause the contract to be voided if the security's market price falls below a predetermined level.

out-of-the-money Option that does not have value at the asset's current market price. A call option is out-of-the-money when the market price is below the exercise price; a put option is out-of-the-money when the current market price is higher than the exercise price.

over-the-counter (OTC) market A market for securities based on telecommunications facilities that bring together buyers and sellers of securities. Many stocks and most bonds trade in the OTC market.

overfunded When the present value of pension plan assets exceeds its obligations for each year.

overhanging issue Convertible security whose conversion value is less than its call price, so that conversion cannot be forced.

overpriced The expected return on an investment is less than the required rate of return.

par (maturity) value The stated or face value of a bond, typically $1,000 per bond.

par value (of common stock) An arbitrary value employed for accounting purposes; rarely has any economic significance.

parallel (back-to-back) loans Parent domestic firm loans to the domestic subsidiary of a foreign parent firm, while the foreign parent firm loans to the foreign subsidiary of the parent domestic firm. Accomplishes the same result as a swap of currencies.

partnership An unincorporated business owned by two or more individuals.

payable turnover (Cost of goods sold +

general, selling, and administrative expenses)/(accounts payable + salaries, benefits, and payroll taxes payable).

payback period The amount of time τ (in years) it will take for the expected cash inflows from a capital budgeting project to just equal the initial investment at time $t = 0$.

payment date The date set by a firm when a cash dividend, stock split, or stock dividend will be paid.

pecking order theory Capital structure and financing theory which suggests that firms value the flexibility associated with financial slack; internally generated funds will be used first, then debt, and finally new common stock.

percentage of sales method Method of developing pro forma statements where historical percentages of items to sales or assets are used for projection purposes.

permanent current assets The minimum current assets the firm always needs to have on hand to maintain its operations.

perpetuity A stream of equal cash flows expected to continue forever; an infinite annuity.

pledging Short-term borrowing in which the loan is secured by the borrower's accounts receivable.

poison pill Tactic used to make a merger more difficult. If a tender offer or the accumulation of a certain percent of ownership occurs, target shareholders have the right to purchase additional shares, or to sell shares to the target at very attractive prices.

pooling of interests An accounting method employed when firms merge. The assets of the two firms are added together on an account-by-account basis to form the combined firm's postmerger balance sheet.

portfolio A combination of various assets, or securities, owned for investment.

portfolio beta A weighted average of the betas for the assets in the portfolio, where the weights are determined by the proportion devoted to each asset.

preauthorized cheque A cheque that does not require the signature of the person on whose account it is drawn.

preemptive right A provision that allows current common shareholders to purchase additional shares offered by the firm before the shares are offered to outsiders.

preferred stock   Stock that has a prior but limited claim on assets and income before common stock, but after debt.

premium (on a bond)   Difference between the current market price of a bond selling above its par value and its par value.

present value   The value today of a given future lump sum, or series of cash flows, when discounted at a given rate.

present value factor, $PV_{k,n}$ Set of factors that for different rates, k, and periods, n, converts a future value into a smaller present value.

present value factor for an annuity, $PVA_{k,n}$ Set of factors that for different rates, k, and periods, n, converts an annuity into its present value.

present value of growth opportunities (PVGO)   Value created by the presence of profitable future investment opportunities that are expected to return more than the required rate of return.

present value profile   A graph that plots the relationship between a project's net present value and the discount rate employed.

price/earnings ratio (P/E)   Market price per share of common stock divided by earnings per share.

primary market   Market in which financial assets are originally sold, with the proceeds going to the issuing firm (or government).

prime rate   An administered interest rate the bank's best customers are supposedly charged. Most customers will pay more than prime, such as "prime plus 2 percent."

principal   The amount of money that must be repaid by a borrower. Interest is figured on the principal. Alternatively, the amount lent by a lender. The lender will receive the principal and interest upon maturity.

private market purchase   Purchase by a firm of its own bonds (or stock) directly from an institutional investor.

private placement   Financing directly between a demander of funds and a supplier of funds that bypasses the public.

pro forma statements   Forecasted accounting statements; typically an income statement and a balance sheet.

probability   The chance of a single event's occurrence. A probability distribution is a listing of all possible outcomes and their chances of occurrence.

probability of success   Likelihood that the net present value will be positive when simulation is employed.

processing float   The length of time it takes a firm to process and deposit a customer's cheque after receiving it.

profitability index   The present value of future cash flows, discounted at the required rate of return divided by the initial investment for the project.

project debt capacity   Incremental contribution that a capital investment makes to the firm's ability to borrow. As firms add more profitable opportunities, they generate more future cash inflows, leading to the ability to service more debt.

project financing   Loans made under government programmes to finance specific projects.

proprietorship   An unincorporated business owned by one individual.

prospectus   See *registration statement*.

protective covenants   Provisions written into bonds or loan agreements.

protective liquidity   The ability to adjust rapidly to unforeseen cash demands, and to have backup sources of cash available.

proxy fight   An attempt by an outside group to obtain control of the firm's board of directors. This is done by soliciting proxies, which are authorizations given by a shareholder that let someone else exercise the shareholder's voting rights at a shareholder meeting.

public offering   Sale of securities to the general public by a firm; can be either a general cash offer or a rights offering.

purchase   An accounting method employed when firms merge. The assets of the target firm are revalued to their fair market value, and any remaining difference between the purchase price and the revalued assets is recorded as goodwill.

purchasing power parity   Theory that the expected differential rate of inflation for two countries is equal to the expected spot rate of exchange t periods in the future divided by the current spot rate of exchange.

pure play firm Firm in the same line of business with the same operating risk as a division of a firm.

put option The right, but not the obligation, to sell an asset at a stated price within a specified time period.

quick ratio Current assets minus inventory divided by current liabilities.

real rate of interest Interest rates in the absence of inflation; i.e., nominal risk-free interest rate adjusted for inflation.

receivables pattern Method for analyzing a firm's receivables calculated by determining the percentage of credit sales still outstanding in the month of the sale and in subsequent months.

receivables turnover Sales divided by accounts receivable.

record date The date determined by a firm when the shareholder books are closed to determine who the current shareholders are.

red herring Preliminary prospectus that can be distributed when a proposed security offering is being reviewed by a Provincial Securities Commission.

refunding Process of replacing an old bond issue with a new one; often done if market interest rates have dropped so that the firm can save on interest costs.

registration statement Statement filed with a Provincial Securities Commission when a firm plans to issue securities to the public.

regulatory project Capital budgeting project that is required for which no measurable cash inflows are expected to occur.

reinvestment rate risk Risk that arises when a bond is called or matures and investors have to reinvest in a bond with a lower coupon interest rate.

reinvoicing centre Centre set up through which all intrafirm transfers involving more than one currency flow. Allows firms to net out transfers, thereby helping to deal with exchange rate exposure.

reorganization An in-court procedure under the Bankruptcy Act during which the firm is revitalized.

replacement chain Means of handling unequal lives for mutually exclusive capital budgeting projects. The projects are replicated over and over again until they have the same life.

replacement project Capital budgeting project that replaces existing assets that are physically or economically obsolete.

replicating portfolio Process of valuing an option by taking a levered position in the underlying asset.

repurchase agreement Sale of government securities by a bank or a government securities dealer with a simultaneous agreement to repurchase them in a certain number of days at a specified price.

required (rate of) return The minimum return necessary to attract a firm or investor to make an investment.

residual theory of dividends A theory which specifies that firms should first make all their capital budgeting decisions. After the necessary financing has been secured, any remaining internally generated funds would be paid out as cash dividends.

retained earnings An equity account on the balance sheet that reflects the sum of the firm's net income (losses) over its life, less all cash dividends paid.

retractable bond A bond that is redeemable, at the option of the investor, on a specified date before the bond's maturity.

return For any period, the sum of cash dividends, interest, and so forth, and any capital appreciation or loss (the difference between the beginning and ending market values).

return on equity Net income divided by shareholders' equity; or return on total assets divided by 1 minus the total debt to total asset ratio.

return on total assets Net income divided by total assets; or net profit margin times total asset turnover.

rights offering Means of selling common stock whereby current shareholders have the first opportunity of buying the issue.

risk The degree of uncertainty associated with something happening, or a situation in which there is exposure to possible loss. In finance, the terms risk and uncertainty are frequently used interchangeably.

risk-free rate, k_{RF} The interest rate on assets that are viewed as being free of any risk premium. In nominal terms, the risk-free rate equals the real rate of interest plus an inflation premium.

risk-neutral Approach employed for valuing options; in a risk-free world the return on the option is equal to the risk-free rate.

risk premium The difference between the required rate of return on an asset and the risk-free rate.

rolling forecast Process in which cash budgets are updated by dropping the most recent period and adding another period in the future.

sale and leaseback An arrangement arising when one firm sells an asset to another and simultaneously agrees to lease the property back for a specified period of time.

scenario analysis The process of simultaneously changing a number of input variables to see what the effect is on the outcome.

seasonal (temporary) current assets The difference between the firm's total current assets and its permanent current assets.

secondary market Market for financial assets that have already been issued. This market includes both the organized security exchanges and the over-the-counter market.

security market line (SML) Graphic representation of the capital asset pricing model (CAPM). Shows the relationship between nondiversifiable risk (beta) and required rates of return for individual assets or portfolios of assets.

selling group A group of investment dealers formed to assist the syndicate in the selling of a large issue of securities.

sensitivity analysis An analysis of the effect of changing one of the input variables (or assumptions) at a time to ascertain how much the result is affected.

separation theorem The choice of investments is independent of consumption preferences. All investors accept or reject the same projects based on net present value.

sequential analysis Method of analyzing capital budgeting projects when risk, and therefore the opportunity cost, varies over the life of the project.

serial bonds Bonds issued at the same time, but with different years to maturity.

Typically, the coupon interest rate may vary depending on the maturity.

shareholder wealth maximization An objective of the firm is to maximize the total market value of the firm by maximizing the per share price, P_0.

short Selling, or promising to deliver an asset in the future. The mirror image of owning, or being long in an asset.

short-form prospectus An abbreviated registration statement that can be used by well-known, financially stable firms. General company information is omitted, and the registration period is reduced to five days.

sight draft An order to pay on sight.

signalling Process of conveying information through a firm's actions.

simple cash flow A sequence of cash flows where there is only one change in sign (from positive to negative, or vice versa). There will be no more than one internal rate of return.

simulation Method of calculating the probability distribution of possible outcomes from a project.

sinking fund Required payments to retire part of a bond or preferred stock issue before maturity.

smoothed residual dividend policy Cash dividend policy whereby the firm sets a long-run target dividend payout ratio and ties it to a specific dividend per share, while fluctuating around its target capital structure.

soft capital rationing Situation where positive net present value projects are not accepted due to internal constraints imposed by management.

spontaneous short-term financing Short-term financing that tends to expand (contract) as the firm's current assets expand (contract).

spot interest rate Interest rate today.

spot rate of exchange The current rate of exchange between two currencies for immediate delivery.

spreadsheet programme Computer programme that allows data to be manipulated.

stakeholder Parties in addition to shareholders, management, and creditors that have an interest in the firm. Includes employees, customers, suppliers, and the community at large.

stand-alone principle A capital budgeting

project should be evaluated by comparing it with the return that could be secured by investing in a similar-risk project.

standard deviation, σ A statistical measure of the spread of a distribution from its mean or expected value. The square root of the variance.

statement of changes in financial position Accounting statement that attempts to trace the flow of cash into and out of the firm during the year.

statement of retained earnings Accounting statement that shows the disposition of earnings from the firm's income statement.

statutory amalgamation The acquisition of a firm where the acquiring firm acquires both the target firm's assets and liabilities, and the target firm ceases to exist as a separate entity. Also known as a merger.

stock dividend A means of issuing additional shares of common stock. From an accounting standpoint, it involves a transfer from retained earnings to the common stock account.

stock split An action to increase the number of shares of common stock outstanding.

strategic NPV Value of the original NPV plus the follow-on call or put option.

stretching payable Practice of not paying an account by its net date, but taking longer to pay the bill.

subordinated debenture Unsecured long-term borrowing of the firm that has a lower claim than other unsecured claims.

substitute projects A situation in which the acceptance of two or more capital budgeting projects results in total cash flows less than the sum of the individual cash flows.

sunk cost Cost that has already occurred and cannot be altered; accordingly, it does not influence subsequent decisions.

supermajority Provision requiring more than 50 percent (often two-thirds or even 80 percent) approval for a merger.

syndicate A group of investment dealers who have agreed to cooperate in purchasing and then reselling a security issue.

synergism The idea that the value of two firms is greater than the sum of their separate values; the "2 + 2 = 5 effect."

system-wide project A group of capital budgeting projects which must all be accepted or rejected as a package, because they are 100 percent complementary.

target capital structure The planned-for capital structure, or the debt/market value of equity ratio, around which the firm attempts to fluctuate.

target firm A firm that is being pursued or is bought out in a merger.

taxes A fee levied on individuals or firms by a federal, provincial, or local government unit.

temporal method The accounting method used to translate the financial statements of a foreign subsidiary into Canadian dollars.

tender offer An offer by a firm or group directly to share- or bondholders to purchase their stock or bonds at a certain price.

term loan Loans with maturities of 1 to 10 years that are paid off by periodic payments over the life of the loan. The payment is fixed at a given dollar amount per period, with more going to pay interest in the early payments and more to pay principal in the later payments.

term structure The relationship between the yield to maturity and the length to maturity for bonds that are equally risky.

terminal loss The positive undepreciated capital cost (UCC) remaining in an asset class after all of the assets have been disposed of.

time draft A draft that must be paid at a stated future date.

times interest earned Earnings before interest and taxes divided by interest charges.

total asset turnover Sales divided by total assets.

total debt to total assets A ratio that indicates how much of the firm's funds are being supplied by its creditors.

total marginal tax rate The marginal tax rate resulting when a provincial tax rate is added to the federal tax rate.

total risk For a security or portfolio, total risk is measured by its standard deviation.

trade acceptance Time draft drawn upon and accepted by a firm.

trade credit Interfirm credit that arises when one firm sells to another through a credit sale. It appears as an account receivable on the seller's books and as an account payable on the buyer's records.

transaction costs Any explicit or implicit cost connected with making a transaction. It could be a commission associated with buying or selling assets (explicit), or the time spent reading and interpreting information (implicit).

transaction exposure Extent to which a given exchange rate change will affect the value of foreign exchange transactions into which the firm has already entered.

transaction loan Bank loan made for a specific purpose for a predetermined length of time.

transit float The length of time it takes for a cheque to clear through the banking system until the recipient can draw upon it (have "good funds").

translation exposure The accounting exposure when exchange rates change.

treasurer The individual in a firm who is normally responsible for seeing that funds are obtained as needed, for making sure cash is collected and invested, for maintaining relations with banks and other financial institutions, and for seeing that bills are paid on time.

treasury bill Short-term security issued by the Canadian government. Issued weekly, T-bills mature in one year or less and are often used as a proxy for the risk-free rate.

uncertainty A situation in which the probabilities can be ascertained only subjectively. In finance, the terms risk and uncertainty are often used interchangeably.

undepreciated capital cost (UCC) Total cost of all assets in a class minus the accumulated capital cost allowance (CCA) for that class.

underfunded A firm's pension plan obligations exceed plan assets.

underinvestment Occurs when a firm fails to take all growth opportunities (i.e., all positive net present value opportunities) because they primarily benefit the firm's bondholders (or other creditors), not the firm's shareholders.

underpriced The expected return on an investment is greater than the required rate of return.

underpricing Issuance of securities below their fair market value.

underwriting The process whereby an investment dealer purchases securities from an issuing firm and then immediately resells them.

unfunded liability The difference between pension plan obligations and plan assets.

variable-rate loan Loan on which the interest rate is not fixed, but fluctuates based on the prime rate, LIBOR, or some other rate.

variance, σ^2 A statistical measure of the spread of a distribution from its mean or expected value.

venture capital Early stage financing for smaller startup firms.

vesting The entitlement of employees to part or all of their pension when leaving an employer before retirement.

warrant A long-lived call option to purchase a fixed number of shares of common stock at a predetermined price during some specified time period.

weighted average cost of capital The cost of the last dollar of additional funds secured; the firm's opportunity cost of capital or required return for projects of average risk.

white knight The friendly third firm in a situation in which one firm (the potential bidding firm) is attempting to take over a target firm.

white squire Friendly firm where a large percentage of another firm's common stock is placed to ward off any potential takeover by a third firm.

working capital The firm's current assets and current liabilities.

yield curve A plot of the relationship between yield to maturity and length (or term) to maturity for equally risky bonds.

yield to call (YTC) The compound return earned on a bond purchased at a given price and held until it is called.

yield to maturity (YTM)   The compound return earned on a bond if it is purchased at a given price and held to maturity. The rate of return that equates the present value of the anticipated interest payments and principal to the bond's current market value.

zero balance account   System whereby the bank and the firm create a demand deposit account that contains no funds. Each day the bank transfers enough funds into the account to meet all cheques presented for payment.

zero-coupon bond   Long-term bond issued at a discount from its par value, for which interest each period is simply the difference in the market value at the beginning and end of the period.

Index

VALUATION (4)

Bond (with annual interest)

$$B_0 = \sum_{t=1}^{n} \frac{I}{(1 + k_b)^t} + \frac{M}{(1 + k_b)^n}$$

Common stock (when held for n periods)

$$P_0 = \sum_{t=1}^{n} \frac{D_t}{(1 + k_s)^t} + \frac{P_n}{(1 + k_s)^n}$$

Nongrowing stock

$$P_0 = D/k_s$$

The *value of a common stock (constant growth)*

$$P_0 = D_1/(k_s - g)$$

Expected rate of return from a common stock

$$k_x = (D_1/P_0) + g$$

Common stock with growth opportunities

$$P_0 = (EPS_1/k_s) + PVGO$$

One period *return on a common stock*

$$k = \frac{D_1 + (P_0 - P_0)}{P_0}$$

RISK AND RETURN (5)

Expected (or mean) return

$$\bar{k} = \sum_{i=1}^{n} k_i P_i$$

Standard deviation,

$$\sigma = \left[\sum_{i=1}^{n} (k_i - \bar{k})^2 P_i \right]^{0.5}$$

Expected return on a portfolio of Z stocks

$$\bar{K}_p = W_A \bar{k}_A + W_B \bar{k}_B + \cdots + W_Z \bar{k}_Z$$

Total risk for a two asset portfolio

$$\sigma_p = (W_A^2 \sigma_A^2 + W_B^2 \sigma_B^2 + 2W_A W_B \sigma_A \sigma_B Corr_{AB})^{0.5}$$

Security market line equation for security j

$$k_j = k_{RF} + \beta_j(k_M - k_{RF})$$

Beta for asset j

$$\beta_j = Cov_{jM}/\sigma_M^2$$

OPPORTUNITY COST OF CAPITAL (6)

Opportunity cost of capital

$$k = k_i W_{debt} + k_{ps} W_{preferred\ stock} + k_s W_{common\ equity}$$

After-tax cost of debt

$$k_i = k_b(1 - T)$$

After-tax cost of preferred stock

$$k_{ps} = D_{ps}/P_{np}$$

Cost of internal equity—constant growth model

$$k_s = (D_1/P_0) + g$$

Cost of internal equity—CAPM

$$k_s = k_{RF} + \beta_j(k_M - k_{RF})$$

(continued)

Cost of external equity (dividend valuation model)

$$k_e = (D_1/P_{np}) + g$$

Unlevered, or asset, beta

$$\beta_{asset} = \beta_U = \frac{\beta_{levered\ firm}}{1 + (1 - T)(B/S)}$$

CAPITAL BUDGETING (7–9)

Modified internal rate of return

$$MIRR = \left[\frac{FV_n}{CF_0}\right]^{1/n} - 1$$

Equivalent annual NPV

$$equivalent\ annual\ NPV = NPV_n/PVA_{k,n}$$

After-tax operating cash flow

$$CF_t = CFBT_t - taxes_t = CFBT_t(1 - T) + CCA_t(T)$$

Net present value (expansion project)

$$NPV = \sum_{t=1}^{n} \frac{CFBT_t(1 - T)}{(1 + k)^t} + \left\{\left[\frac{TdC_0}{k + d}\right]\left[\frac{1 + 0.5k}{1 + k}\right] - \left[\frac{1}{(1 + k)^n}\right]\left[\frac{Td(RV)}{k + d}\right]\right\}$$
$$+ \frac{ECF}{(1 + k)^n} - CF_0$$

Net present value (replacement project)

$$NPV = \sum_{t=1}^{n} \left[\frac{\Delta CFBT_t(1 - T)}{(1 + k)^t}\right] + \left\{\left[\frac{Td(\Delta C_0)}{k + d}\right]\left[\frac{1 + 0.5k}{1 + k}\right] - \left[\frac{1}{(1 + k)^n}\right]\left[\frac{Td(\Delta RV)}{k + d}\right]\right\}$$
$$+ \frac{\Delta ECF}{(1 + k)^n} - CF_0$$

RAISING LONG-TERM FUNDS (10)

Rights-on value of one right

$$v_r = (P_0 - P_s)/(N + 1)$$

Ex-rights value of one right

$$v_r = (P_x - P_s)/N$$

TAXES AND CAPITAL STRUCTURE (12)

Modigliani-Miller's Proposition I (no taxes)

$$V_L = S_L + B = EBIT/k_s^U = V_U$$

Modigliani-Miller's Proposition II (no taxes)

$$k_s^L = k_s^U + (k_s^U - k_b)(B/S_L)$$

Modigliani-Miller value of an unlevered firm with corporate taxes is

$$V_U = S_U = \frac{EBIT(1 - T)}{k_s^U}$$

Modigliani-Miller value of a levered firm with corporate taxes

$$V_L = V_U + TB$$

Modigliani-Miller's Proposition II (with corporate taxes)

$$k_s^L = k_s^U + (k_s^U - k_b)(1 - T)(B/S_L)$$

Modigliani-Miller's Proposition I (with corporate taxes)

$$S_L = \frac{(EBIT - k_b B)(1 - T)}{k_s^L}$$